➜ Marketing: An Introduction
8/e

Marketing: An Introduction
8/e

Gary Armstrong
University of North Carolina

Philip Kotler
Northwestern University

Upper Saddle River, New Jersey 07458

Library of Congress Cataloging-in-Publication Data
Armstrong, Gary.
    Marketing : an introduction / Gary Armstrong, Philip Kotler.--8th ed.
        p.   cm.
    Kotler's name appears first on the earlier ed.
    Includes bibliographical references and index.
    ISBN 0-13-186591-9 (alk. paper)
1. Marketing.   I. Kotler, Philip.   II. Title.
HF5415.K625 2006
658.8--dc22

                                                          2005027193

Acquisitions Editor: Katie Stevens
VP/Editorial Director: Jeff Shelstad
Product Development Manager: Ashley Santora
Editorial Assistant: Christine Ietto
Media Project Manager: Peter Snell
Marketing Manager: Ashaki Charles
Marketing Assistant: Joanna Sabella
Associate Director, Production Editorial: Judy Leale
Managing Editor, Production: Renata Butera
Production Editor: Theresa Festa
Permissions Coordinator: Charles Morris
Manufacturing Buyer: Diane Peirano
Design/Composition Manager: Christy Mahon
Composition Liaison: Nancy Thompson
Designer: Steve Frim
Interior Design: Jill Little
Cover Design: Anthony Gemmellaro
Cover Illustration/Photo: Shayle Keating
Director, Image Resource Center: Melinda Reo
Manager, Rights and Permissions: Zina Arabia
Manager: Visual Research: Beth Brenzel
Manager, Cover Visual Research & Permissions: Karen Sanatar
Image Permission Coordinator: Richard Rodrigues
Photo Researcher: Teri Stratford
Composition: Carlisle Publishing Services
Full-Service Project Management: Lynn Steines, Carlisle Editorial Services
Printer/Binder: Courier–Kendallville/Coral Graphics
Typeface: 10/12 Times

Pearson Education Ltd.   Pearson Education Australia PTY, Limited
Pearson Education Singapore, Pte. Ltd.   Pearson Education North Asia Ltd.
Pearson Education Canada, Ltd.   Pearson Educación de Mexico, S.A. de C.V.
Pearson Education—Japan   Pearson Education Malaysia, Pte. Ltd.

ISBN: 0-13-186591-9

To Kathy, Betty, Mandy, Matt, K.C., Keri, Delaney, Molly, and Macy; Nancy, Amy, Melissa, and Jessica

About the Authors

As a team, Gary Armstrong and Philip Kotler provide a blend of skills uniquely suited to writing an introductory marketing text. Professor Armstrong is an award-winning teacher of undergraduate business students. Professor Kotler is one of the world's leading authorities on marketing. Together they make the complex world of marketing practical, approachable, and enjoyable.

Gary Armstrong is Crist W. Blackwell Distinguished Professor of Undergraduate Education in the Kenan-Flagler Business School at the University of North Carolina at Chapel Hill. He holds undergraduate and masters degrees in business from Wayne State University in Detroit, and he received his Ph.D. in marketing from Northwestern University. Dr. Armstrong has contributed numerous articles to leading business journals. As a consultant and researcher, he has worked with many companies on marketing research, sales management, and marketing strategy. But Professor Armstrong's first love is teaching. His Blackwell Distinguished Professorship is the only permanent endowed professorship for distinguished undergraduate teaching at the University of North Carolina at Chapel Hill. He has been very active in the teaching and administration of Kenan-Flagler's undergraduate program. His recent administrative posts include Chair of the Marketing Faculty, Associate Director of the Undergraduate Business Program, Director of the Business Honors Program, and others. He works closely with business student groups and has received several campus-wide and business school teaching awards. He is the only repeat recipient of the school's highly regarded Award for Excellence in Undergraduate Teaching, which he won three times. In 2004, Professor Armstrong received the UNC Board of Governors Award for Excellence in Teaching, the highest teaching honor bestowed at the University of North Carolina at Chapel Hill.

Philip Kotler is one of the world's leading authorities on marketing. He is the S. C. Johnson & Son Distinguished Professor of International Marketing at the Kellogg School of Management, Northwestern University. He received his master's degree at the University of Chicago and his Ph.D. at MIT, both in economics. Dr. Kotler is author of *Marketing Management,* now in its twelfth edition and the most widely used marketing textbook in graduate schools of business. He has authored more than 20 other successful books and more than one hundred articles in leading journals. He is the only three-time winner of the coveted Alpha Kappa Psi award for the best annual article published in the *Journal of Marketing.* He was named the first recipient of two major awards: the *Distinguished Marketing Educator of the Year Award* given by theAmerican Marketing Association and the *Philip Kotler Award for Excellence in Health Care Marketing* presented by the Academy for Health Care Services Marketing. Other major honors include the 1978 Paul Converse Award of the AMA, honoring his original contribution to marketing, the European Association of Marketing Consultants and Sales Trainers Prize for Marketing Excellence, the 1995 Sales and Marketing Executives International (SMEI) Marketer of the Year award, the 2002 Academy of Marketing Science Distinguished Educator Award, and honorary doctoral degrees from Stockholm University, the University of Zurich, Athens University of Economics and Business, DePaul University, the Cracow School of Business and Economics, Groupe H.E.C. in Paris, the Budapest School of Economic Science and Public Administration, and the University of Economics and Business Administration in Vienna. Professor Kotler has been a consultant to many major U.S. and foreign companies in the areas of marketing strategy and planning, marketing organization, and international marketing. He has been Chairman of the College of Marketing of the Institute of Management Sciences, a Director of the American Marketing Association, a Trustee of the Marketing Science Institute, a Director of the MAC Group, a member of the Yankelovich Advisory Board, a member of the Copernicus Advisory Board, and a member of the Advisory Board of the Drucker Foundation. He has traveled extensively throughout Europe, Asia, and South America, advising and lecturing to many companies about global marketing opportunities.

Brief Contents

Contents

Welcome to the Eighth Edition!

Our goal with the eighth edition of *Marketing: An Introduction* is to create an even more effective text from which to learn about and teach marketing. Most students learning marketing want a broad, complete picture of basic marketing principles and practices. However, they don't want to drown in a sea of details, or to be overwhelmed by marketing's complexities. Instead, they want a text that's complete yet easy to manage and master.

The eighth edition of *Marketing: An Introduction* serves all of these important needs for marketing students. It strikes a careful balance between depth of coverage and ease of learning. Unlike more abbreviated texts, *Marketing: An Introduction* provides a complete overview of marketing. Unlike longer, more complex texts, however, its moderate length makes it easy to cover in a given quarter or semester.

More than ever before, the eighth edition of *Marketing: An Introduction* makes learning and teaching marketing more effective, easier, and more enjoyable. The text's approachable style and design are well suited to the beginning marketing student. "Road to Marketing" aids help students to learn, link, and apply important concepts. The text takes a practical approach—concepts are applied through countless examples of situations in which well-known and little-known companies assess and solve their marketing problems.

Finally, the eighth edition presents the latest marketing thinking. It builds on an innovative and integrative marketing framework, one that positions marketing simply as the art and science of creating value *for* customers in order to capture value *from* customers in return.

In all, the eighth edition of *Marketing: An Introduction* is the best edition yet. So buckle up and let's get rolling down the road to learning marketing!

Gary Armstrong
University of North Carolina at Chapel Hill

Philip Kotler
Northwestern University

Preface

The Road to Marketing: Creating Customer Value and Relationships

Today's marketing is all about building profitable customer relationships. It starts with understanding consumer needs and wants, deciding which target markets the organization can serve best, and developing a compelling value proposition by which the organization can attract, keep, and grow targeted consumers. If the organization does these things well, it will reap the rewards in terms of market share, profits, and customer equity. From beginning to end, the eighth edition of *Marketing: An Introduction* presents and develops this integrative customer-value/customer-equity framework.

Marketing is much more than just an isolated business function—it is a philosophy that guides the entire organization. The marketing department cannot build profitable customer relationships by itself. Marketing is a company-wide undertaking. It must drive the company's vision, mission, and strategic planning. It involves broad decisions about who the company wants as its customers, which needs to satisfy, what products and services to offer, what prices to set, what communications to send and receive, and what partnerships to develop. Thus, marketing must work closely with other departments in the company and with other organizations throughout its entire value-delivery system to create superior customer value and satisfaction.

How Do We Get You Moving?

The eighth edition of *Marketing: An Introduction* builds on five major themes:

1. **Creating Value for Customers in Order to Capture Value from Customers in Return** Today's marketers must be good at *creating customer value* and *managing customer relationships*. They must attract targeted customers with strong value propositions. Then, they must keep and grow customers by delivering superior customer value and effectively managing the company-customer interface. Today's outstanding marketing companies understand the marketplace and customer needs, design value-creating marketing strategies, develop marketing programs that deliver value and satisfaction, and build strong customer relationships. In return, they capture value from customers in the form of sales, profits, and customer equity.

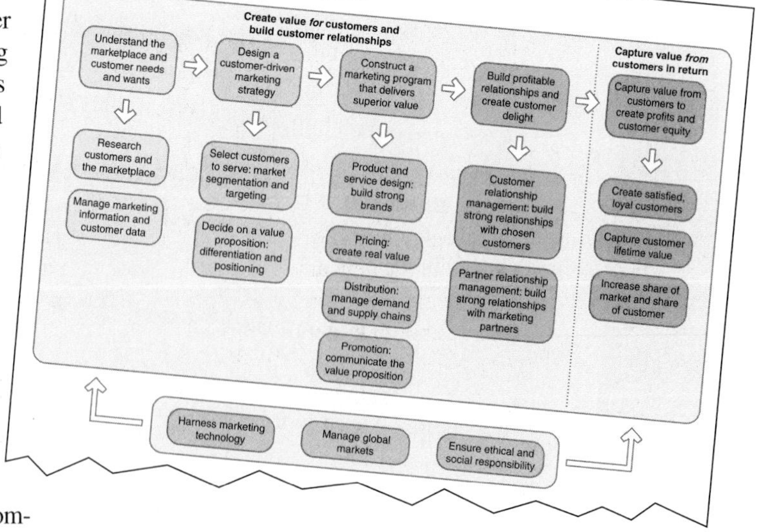

   Marketers must also be good at *partner relationship management*. They must work closely with partners inside and outside the company to jointly build profitable customer relationships. Successful marketers are now partnering effectively with other company departments to build strong company value chains. And they are joining with outside partners to build effective demand and supply chains and effective customer-focused alliances.

FIGURE 1.6 An Expanded Model of the Marketing Process

2. **Building and Managing Strong Brands to Create Brand Equity** Well-positioned brands with strong brand equity provide the basis upon which to build profitable customer relationships. Today's marketers must be good at positioning their brands powerfully and managing them well.

3. **Measuring and Managing Return on Marketing** Marketing managers must ensure that their marketing dollars are being well spent. In the past, many marketers spent freely on big, expensive marketing programs, often without thinking carefully about the financial returns on their spending. But all that is changing rapidly. Measuring and managing return on marketing investments has become an important part of strategic marketing decision making.

4. **Harnessing New Marketing Technologies in this Digital Age** New digital and other high-tech marketing developments are dramatically changing both buyers and the marketers who serve them. Today's marketers must know how to leverage new computer, information, communication, and transportation technologies to connect more effectively with customers and marketing partners in this new digital age.

5. **Marketing in a Socially Responsible Way Around the Globe** As technological developments make the world an increasingly smaller place, marketers must be good at marketing their brands globally and in socially responsible ways.

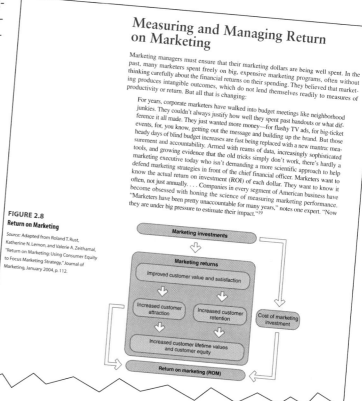

FIGURE 2.8
Return on Marketing
Source: Adapted from Roland T. Rust, Katherine N. Lemon, and Valerie A. Zeithamal, "Return on Marketing: Using Consumer Equity to Focus Marketing Strategy," *Journal of Marketing*, January 2004, p. 112.

Important Improvements and Additions

The eighth edition of *Marketing: An Introduction* has been thoroughly revised to reflect the major trends and forces that are impacting marketing in this age of customer value and relationships. This new edition **strengthens and extends the customer value framework** built in previous editions. The **revised marketing communications chapter** details major shifts in the ways that marketers now communicate customer value through a wide array of new, more targeted, more personalized media. The completely **restructured pricing chapter** focuses on understanding and capturing customer value as the basis for setting sound prices. And new sections in several chapters highlight the topics of marketing accountability and **measuring return on marketing investment**.

The eighth edition includes new and expanded material on a wide range of other topics, including managing customer relationships, brand strategy and positioning, supplier satisfaction and partnering, supply chain management, data mining and data networks, buzz marketing and experiential marketing, "Madison & Vine" communications approaches, value-based pricing, dynamic pricing, marketing channel developments, environmental sustainability, cause-related marketing, marketing and diversity, socially responsible marketing, new marketing technologies, global marketing strategies, and much, much more.

The eighth edition contains other important changes. Many new chapter-opening examples and "Marketing at Work" exhibits illustrate important new concepts with actual business applications. Countless new examples have been added within the running text. All tables, figures, examples, and references throughout the text have been thoroughly updated. The eighth edition of *Marketing: An Introduction* contains mostly new photos and advertisements that illustrate key points and make the text more effective and appealing. The new video cases located in the video appendix bring the real world directly into the classroom. We don't think you'll find a fresher, more current, or more approachable text anywhere.

Marketing: An Introduction— A Learning Approach

Marketing: An Introduction, eighth edition, guides new marketing students down the intriguing, discovery-laden road to learning marketing. Its goal is to help students master the basic concepts and practices of modern marketing in an enjoyable and practical way. Achieving this goal involves a constant search for the best balance among the "three pillars" that support the text—theories and concepts, practices and applications, and pedagogy. *Marketing: An Introduction* provides complete and up-to-date coverage of marketing concepts, brings the concepts to life with real examples of marketing practices, and presents both theory and practice in a way that makes them easy and enjoyable to learn.

In the eighth edition, we continue to focus on pedagogy as an effective teaching and learning tool. To help students learn, link, and apply important marketing concepts more effectively, *Marketing: An Introduction* is filled with "Road Map" learning tools throughout each chapter. These pedagogical guides help students by challenging them to stop and think at important junctures in their journey, previewing chapter material, reviewing and linking key chapter concepts, and providing practical marketing-application exercises through which students apply newly-learned marketing concepts in realistic situations.

The following innovative chapter-opening, within-chapter, and end-of-chapter "Road to Marketing" learning devices help students to learn, link, and apply major concepts as they progress along their journey toward learning marketing:

- *Road Map: Previewing the Concepts* A section at the beginning of each chapter briefly previews chapter concepts, links them with previous chapter concepts, outlines chapter learning objectives, and introduces the chapter-opening vignette.
- *Linking the Concepts* "Concept Checks" inserted at key points in each chapter serve as "speed bumps" to slow students down and ensure that they are grasping and applying key concepts.
- *Rest Stop: Reviewing the Concepts* A summary of key concepts at the end of each chapter.
- *Navigating the Key Terms* A list of the chapter's key terms.
- *Travel Log* "Discussing the Issues" and "Applications Questions" help students to keep track of and apply chapter concepts.
- *Under the Hood: Focus on Technology* Application exercises provide discussion on important and emerging marketing technologies in this digital age.
- *Focus on Ethics* Situation descriptions and questions highlight important issues in marketing ethics.

> **Linking the Concepts**
>
> Stop here for a moment and stretch your legs. What have you learned so far about marketing? For the moment, set aside the more formal definitions we've examined and try to develop your own understanding of marketing.
>
> - In your own words, what *is* marketing? Write down your definition. Does your definition include such key concepts as customer value and relationships?
> - What does marketing *mean* to you?
> - What brand of athletic shoes did you purchase last? How does it affect your life on a daily basis? Describe your relationship with Nike, New Balance, Reebok, Adidas, or whatever company made the shoes you purchased.

> **Focus on Ethics**
>
> The marketing concept focuses on satisfying customer's needs and wants, but what if doing so places the consumer at risk? Although marketed and sold legally, the health impacts of tobacco and alcohol are well known. In addition, the impact of poor nutrition has recently come into the national spotlight. More specifically, the Food and Drug Administration (FDA) has issued warnings about the level of trans-fatty acids present in some food products. In response, companies including McDonald's, Kraft Foods, and Frito-lay, have recently been re-evaluating their products and making changes. For example, McDonald's now offers either french fries or a bag of sliced fruit with each Happy Meal.
>
> 1. What ethical responsibilities do companies producing products that have potentially adverse health effects have to consumers?
> 2. Can a company truly consider the long-term welfare of the consumer and of society while also maximizing profits?
> 3. Break into small groups. Divide into teams within each group and debate whether or not marketing potentially unhealthy products is ethical.

Marketing: An Introduction takes a practical marketing-management approach, providing countless real-life examples that bring life to the marketing journey. Carefully constructed chapter-opening vignettes and "Marketing at Work" highlight stories that reveal the drama of modern marketing, showing how:

- **NASCAR** creates avidly loyal fans by selling not just stock car racing but a high-octane, totally involving experience.
- **Best Buy** builds the right relationships with the right customers by targeting profitable "angel" customers while exorcizing unprofitable "demon" customers.

- **Nike's** "Just do it!" strategy has matured as this venerable market leader has moved from maverick to mainstream.
- How tiny nicher **Jones Soda** has learned that small can be beautiful-and very profitable.
- **Toyota's Scion** brand targets Gen Y without shouting "Buy This Car."
- **Lexus** leads the luxury car market with the philosophy that if you "delight the customer, and continue to delight the customer, you will have a customer for life."
- **FIJI Water** brings you more than just a liquid you drink to wash down a sandwich—it gives you "The Taste of Paradise!"
- **Apple** Computer founder Steve Jobs used dazzling customer-driven innovation to first start the company and then to remake it again 20 years later.
- **Toys "R" Us** taught the toy industry a low-pricing lesson, then got a bitter dose of its own medicine in return.
- Little **Whole Foods Market** thrives by carving out its own turf in colossus Wal-Mart's shadow.
- Award-winning ad agency **CP+B** has become the agency of the moment by preaching that "anything and everything is an ad."
- **Google** succeeds despite the dot-com meltdown by focusing on simplifying users' Web experiences.

MARKETING AT WORK 2.2

Jones Soda: Staying True to Your Niche

Every great product has a secret formula. Coca-Cola's legendary recipe is locked deep within the vaults beneath its Atlanta headquarters. KFC mixes different parts of its 11 herbs and spices at three separate facilities to safeguard the Colonel's secret blend. And McDonald's hunted down its original special-sauce mix for Big Macs last year as part of its turnaround effort.

Jones Soda, the small Seattle soft drink maker, has its own secret ingredient—one that has created buzz, produced 30 percent yearly revenue growth in a flat beverage market, drawn major distribution partners such as Starbucks and Target, and brought in $30 million in annual revenue. That ingredient: a small but growing following of devout customers. These are not just any customers—Jones Soda knows its niche. It targets young buyers—12- to 24-year-olds—who appreciate the brand's wacky, irreverent attitude. By focusing in on these customers, listening to them, and giving them what they want, Jones Soda is thriving in the shadows of the soft drink giants.

Virtually everything about a Jones Soda, from labels to flavors, comes from its carefully targeted customers. That's important because "the reality is that consumers don't need our s___," founder and CEO Peter van Stolk says unapologetically. The world isn't necessarily clamoring for another soda, even if it tastes like the bubbl___ So how ___ unnec___

quotes found on the Web site and underneath bottle caps ("It's not broken, it just needs duct tape")—come straight from Jones enthusiasts.

Van Stolk also encouraged customers to submit photos, and the eccentric and strangely captivating images on Jones's stark black-and-white bottle labels have come largely from fans. And as the site became flooded with hundreds of thousands of cute, but useless, baby snapshots, he launched myJones to offer customers 12-packs of soda with custom-made labels for $34.95. myJones has since blossomed into one of the cornerstones of the Jones Soda brand.

Jones also stays close to its 12- to 24-year-old customers with a pair of roving RVs. The two flame-festooned vehicles spend nine months out of the year visiting Jones-friendly sites, from small skate parks in the middle of nowhere to major extreme-games competitions such as the X ___ The R___ ___ in place___

■ Jones Soda sticks closely to its niche—virtually everything about a Jones Soda, from labels to flavors, comes directly from its carefully targeted customers.

up to being in sync with target customers. "It's the difference between being real and saying you're real," van Stolk says, taking a not-so-subtle sw___ at a certai___ "Real Th___

ADDITIONAL LEARNING AIDS

Video cases Every chapter is supplemented with a written case and accompanying video to bring chapter material to life. Video cases are located in Appendix 1.

Marketing Plan A sample marketing plan located in Appendix 2 helps students apply and understand important marketing planning concepts.

Glossary and Indexes At the end of the book, an extensive glossary provides quick reference to the key terms found in the book. Subject, company, and author indexes reference all information and examples in the book.

More than ever before, the eighth edition of *Marketing: An Introduction* makes teaching and learning marketing easier, more effective, more practical, and more enjoyable.

Appendix 2 Marketing Plan

The Marketing Plan: An Introduction

As a marketer, you'll need a good marketing plan to provide direction and focus for your brand, product, or company. With a detailed plan, any business will be better prepared to launch a new product or build sales for existing products. Nonprofit organizations also use marketing plans to guide their fundraising and outreach efforts. Even government agencies put together marketing plans for initiatives such as building public awareness of proper nutrition and stimulating area tourism.

THE PURPOSE AND CONTENT OF A MARKETING PLAN

Unlike a business plan, which offers a broad overview of the entire organization's mission, objectives, strategy, and resource allocation, a marketing plan has a more limited scope. It serves to document how the organization's strategic objectives will be achieved through specific marketing strategies and tactics, with the customer as the starting point. It is also linked to the plans of other departments within the organization. Suppose a marketing plan calls for selling 200,000 units annually. The production department must gear up to make that many units, the finance department must have funding available to cover the expenses, the human resources department must be ready to hire and train staff, and so on. Without the appropriate level of organizational support and resources, no marketing plan can succeed.

Although the exact length and layout will vary from company to company, a marketing plan usually contains the sections described in Chapter 2. Smaller businesses may create shorter or less formal marketing plans, whereas corporations frequently require highly structured marketing plans. To guide implementation effec___ly, every ___ of the plan m___ described ___

helps marketers learn more about their customers' requirements, expectations, perceptions, and satisfaction levels. This deeper understanding provides a foundation for building competitive advantage through well-informed segmenting, targeting, and positioning decisions. Thus, the marketing plan should outline what marketing research will be conducted and how the findings will be applied.

THE ROLE OF RELATIONSHIPS

The marketing plan shows how the company will establish and maintain profitable customer relationships. In the process, however, it also shapes a number of internal and external relationships. First, it affects how marketing personnel work with each other and with other departments to deliver value and satisfy customers. Second, it affects how the company works with suppliers, distributors, and strategic alliance partners to achieve the objectives listed in the plan. Third, it influences the company's dealings with other stakeholders, including government regulators, the media, and the community at large. All of these relationships are important to the organization's success, so they should be considered when a marketing plan is being developed.

FROM MARKETING PLAN TO MARKETING ACTION

Companies generally create yearly marketing plans, although some plans cover a longer period. Marketers start planning well in advance of the implementation date to allow time for marketing research, thorough analysis, management review, and coordination between departments. Then, after each action program begins, ___rketers monitor ongoing results, com___

A Total Teaching and Learning Package

A successful marketing course requires more than a well-written book. Today's classroom requires a dedicated teacher and a fully-integrated teaching system. A total package of teaching and learning supplements extends this edition's emphasis on effective teaching and learning. The following aids support *Marketing: An Introduction*.

SUPPLEMENTS FOR INSTRUCTORS

The following supplements are available to adopting instructors.

Annotated Instructor's Edition (ISBN: 0-13-168715-8)

The new *Annotated Instructor's Edition* includes an insert at the front of each chapter, which serves as a quick reference for the entire supplements package. Suggestions for using materials from the Instructor's Manual, PowerPoint slides, Test Item File, Video Library, and online material are offered for each section within every chapter. This edition also includes Video Teaching Notes.

Instructor's Manual in Print with Video Guide (ISBN: 0-13-186595-1)

The instructor's handbook for this text provides suggestions for using features and elements of the text. This *Instructor's Manual with Video Case Notes* includes a chapter overview, objectives, outlines, detailed lecture outline (incorporating key terms, text art, chapter objectives and references), review questions with answers, and support for end-of-chapter material. Also included is a **new** "Great Ideas" section that has student projects/assignments, classroom management strategies, and more, to provide a springboard for innovative learning experiences in the classroom. The Instructor's Manual also features the following elements:

■ Support for end-of-chapter material, along with additional student projects and "Outside Examples" assignments, offering instructors additional lecture material. The examples may be a further development of a concept or company briefly mentioned in the chapter, or perhaps new material that helps to further develop a concept in the text.

■ "Professors on the Go!" serves to bring key material upfront in the manual, where an instructor who is short on time can take a quick look and find key points and assignments to incorporate into the lecture, without having to page through all the material provided for each chapter.

Test Item File (ISBN: 0-13-186596-X)

Featuring more than two thousand new questions, 100+ questions per chapter, this Test Item File has been written specifically for the eighth edition. Questions range from multiple choice and true/false to essay and application. All essay questions are organized by level of difficulty and include page references.

Instructor's Resource Center

Register. Redeem. Login.

www.prenhall.com/irc is where instructors can access a variety of print, media, and presentation resources available with this text in downloadable, digital format. For most texts, resources are also available for course management platforms such as Blackboard, WebCT, and Course Compass.

It gets better. Once you register, you will not have additional forms to fill out, or multiple usernames and passwords to remember to access new titles and/or editions. As a registered faculty member, you can login directly to download resource files, and receive immediate access and instructions for installing Course Management content to your campus server.

Need help? Our dedicated technical support team is ready to assist instructors with questions about the media supplements that accompany this text. Visit: http://247.prenhall.com/ for answers to frequently asked questions and toll-free user support phone numbers.

All instructor resources in one place. It's your choice. Available via a password-protected site at www.prenhall.com/armstrong or on CD-ROM (0-13-186797-8). Resources include:

■ *Instructor's Manual:* chapter-by-chapter or download the entire manual as a .zip file.
■ *Test Item File:* View chapter-by-chapter or download the entire test item file as a .zip file.
■ *TestGen EQ for PC/Mac:* Download this easy-to-use software; it's preloaded with the eighth edition test questions and a user's manual.

- *Image bank (on CD only):* Access many of the images, ads, and illustrations featured in the text. Ideal for PowerPoint customization.
- *PowerPoints:* When it comes to PowerPoints, Prentice Hall knows one size does not fit all. That's why we offer instructors more than one option.

    PowerPoint BASIC: This simple presentation includes only basic outlines and key points from each chapter. No animation or forms of rich media are integrated, which makes the total file size manageable and easier to share online or via e-mail. BASIC was also designed for instructors who prefer to customize PowerPoints and want to be spared from having to strip out animation, embedded files, or other media rich features.

    PowerPoint MEDIA RICH (on CD only): This media rich alternative includes basic outlines and key points from each chapter, plus advertisements and art from the text, images not included in the text, discussion questions, Web links, and embedded video snippets from the accompanying video library. This is the best option for a complete presentation solution. Instructors can further customize this presentation using the image library featured on the Instructor's Resource Center on CD-ROM.

    PowerPoints for Classroom Response Systems (CRS): These Q&A style slides are designed for classrooms using "clickers" or classroom response systems. Instructors who are interested in making CRS a part of their course should contact their Prentice Hall representative for details and a demonstration. CRS is a fun and easy way to make your classroom more interactive.

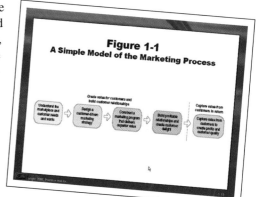

Figure 1-1
A Simple Model of the Marketing Process

- *Online Courses:* See OneKey below. Compatible with BlackBoard and WebCT.

TestGen Test Generating Software

Prentice Hall's test-generating software is available from the *IRC Online* (www.prenhall.com/armstrong) or from the *IRC on CD-ROM*.

- PC/Mac compatible; preloaded with all of the Test Item File questions.
- Manually or randomly view test bank questions and drag-and-drop to create a test.
- Add or modify test bank questions using the built-in Question Editor.
- Print up to 25 variations of a single test and deliver the test on a local area network using the built-in QuizMaster feature.
- Free customer support is available at media.support@pearsoned.com or call 1-800-6-PROFESSOR between 8:00 A.M. and 5:00 P.M. CST.

Custom Videos

The video library features 16 exciting segments, *all new* to this edition. All segments are available online (www.prenhall.com/armstrongvideo), on VHS (ISBN: 0-13-186599-4), and on DVD (ISBN: 0-13-186600-1). Here are just a few of the videos filmed in 2004 and 2005:

- Harley-Davidson and how brand image is managed through global marketing strategies
- American Express and the modern marketing environment
- The NFL and the importance of social responsibility
- Song Airlines and pricing strategies
- Eaton's approach to B2B issues, including buyer behavior
- Hasbro's views on distribution channels and logistics management
- Reebok's retailing and wholesaling policies
- Wild Planet's strategies in the consumer markets

Transparencies (ISBN: 0-13-186598-6)

Features 15 to 20 color acetates per chapter selected from the media rich set of PowerPoints, which includes images from text.

AdCritic.com

Prentice Hall and AdAge are bringing the most current ads and commentary from advertising experts into your classrooms. Only Prentice Hall can offer students 16 weeks of access to a special AdCritic.com site that includes AdAge's encyclopedia of articles at a deeply discounted rate. An access code is available only when shrink-wrapped with a Prentice Hall text, so be sure and specify the appropriate package with your local bookstore in advance. Please visit www.prenhall.com/marketing for a tour of the AdCritic site.

WebSurveyor

WebSurveyor Corporation is the leading provider of online survey software that empowers people with real-time feedback to drive their business decisions. Through its Academic Grant Program, WebSurveyor provides students with the practical experience of conducting online surveys. WebSurveyor can be used for hands-on market research projects, social and political studies, or any other information gathering assignments deemed appropriate by the instructor. Through the grant program, students are getting the same software that is used by industry practitioners worldwide to collect and analyze vital data.

Instructors at universities, colleges, community colleges, business and trade schools applying for the grant are requested to fill out a brief online form at: www.websurveyor.com/prenhall. WebSurveyor's evaluation committee will make a decision within five business days.

SUPPLEMENTS FOR STUDENTS

OneKey

Available through Course Compass, Blackboard, and WebCT, classroom resources for students are available in one spot. Resources include:

- Additional quizzing for review
- Case Pilot to aid in analyzing cases
- Marketing Toolkit: Interactive Modules to aid in review of understanding key concepts
- Marketing Updates: Bringing current articles to the classroom
- Much more

OneKey requires an access code, which professors can ask to be shrink-wrapped free with new copies of this text. Please contact your local sales representative for the correct ISBN. Codes may also be purchased separately at www.prenhall.com/marketing.

Study Guide (ISBN: 0-13-238052-8)

Armstrong and Kotler's study guide with flashcards provides students on the go with a valuable resource. The study guide is delivered in one compact binder and can be packaged at no additional cost with new copies of this text. The study guide can also be purchased separately at www.prenhall.com/marketing.

www.prenhall.com/armstrong

This site contains two student quizzes per chapter. The Concept Check Quiz is to be administered prior to reviewing the chapter, in order to assess the student's initial understanding. The Concept Challenge Quiz is to be administered after reviewing the chapter.

MORE STAND-OUT RESOURCES

Announcing SafariX Textbooks Online—*Where the Web meets textbooks for student savings!*

Marketing: An Introduction, eighth edition, is also available as a WebBook! SafariX WebBooks offer study advantages no print textbook can match. With an Internet-enhanced SafariX WebBook, students can search the entire text for key concepts; navigate easily to a page number, reading assignment, or chapter; or bookmark important pages or sections for quick review at a later date. Some key features:

- Digital textbook delivery that saves students as much as 50 percent off the print edition's suggested list price.
- Internet-based service making textbook content available anytime, anywhere there is a Web connection.

- Easy navigation, which makes finding pages and completing assignments easy and efficient.
- Search, bookmark, and note-taking tools that save study time and reduce frustration by making critical information immediately accessible. Organizing study notes has never been easier!
- Ability to print pages on the fly making critical content available for offline study and review.

Prentice Hall is pleased to be the first publisher to offer students a new choice in how they purchase and access required or recommended course textbooks. For details and a demonstration, visit www.prenhall.com/safarix.

Classroom Response Systems (CRS)

This exciting new wireless polling technology makes classrooms, no matter how large or small, even more interactive because it enables instructors to pose questions to their students, record results, and display those results instantly. Students answer questions using compact remote control style transmitters. Prentice Hall has partnerships with leading classroom response systems providers and can show you everything you need to know about setting up and using a CRS system. We'll provide the classroom hardware, software, and support and show you how your students can save.

- Enhance interactivity
- Capture attention
- Get instant feedback
- Access comprehension

Learn more at www.prenhall.com/crs.

Coming Fall 2006

Study on the go with VangoNotes—chapter reviews from yout text in downloadable mp3 format. Now wherever you are—whatever you're doing—you can study by listening to the following for each chapter of your textbook:

- *Big Ideas:* Your "need to know" for each chapter
- *Practice Test:* A gut check for the Big Ideas—tells you if you need to keep studying
- *Key Terms:* Audio "flashcards" to help you review key concepts and terms
- *Rapid Review:* A quick drill session—use if right before your test

VangoNotes are **flexible**; download all the material directly to your player, or only the chapters you need. And they're **efficient**. Use them in your car, at the gym, walking to class, or wherever. So get yours today. And get studying.

VangoNotes.com.

Acknowledgments

No book is the work only of its authors. We owe much to the pioneers of marketing who first identified its major issues and developed its concepts and techniques. Our thanks also go to our colleagues at the Kenan-Flagler Business School, University of North Carolina at Chapel Hill, and at the J. L. Kellogg Graduate School of Management, Northwestern University, for ideas and suggestions. We owe very special thanks to Keri Miksza for her constant and invaluable advice, assistance, and involvement throughout every phase of the project. We thank Andrea Meyer for her able assistance in developing high-quality video cases, Marian Wood for help in creating the marketing plan, and Mandy Roylance for her skillful development of end-of-chapter material. Thanks also go to Lew Brown of the University of North Carolina at Greensboro for his help in developing selected marketing stories for the text.

Many reviewers at other colleges and universities provided valuable comments and suggestions for this and previous editions. We are indebted to the following colleagues for their thoughtful input into this and previous editions:

Eighth Edition Reviewers

Sana Akili, Iowa State University
Turina R. Bakken, Madison Area Tech College
Richard (Rich) Brown, Freed–Hardeman
  University
Patrick J. Demerath, Troy
  University–Montgomery Campus
Peter T. Doukas, Westchester Community College
Paul Dowling, University of Utah
P. Renee Foster, Delta State University
Melissa Moore, Mississippi State University
Andrew T. Norman, Drake University

Deborah Owens, University of Akron
Rick Polio, University of Bridgeport
Paul R. Redig, Milwaukee Area Tech
  College–Mequon Campus
Robert C. Reese, Illinois Valley Community
  College
Jeffery B. Schmidt, University of Oklahoma
Rodger Singley, Illinois State University
Steve Vitucci, Tarleton State University–Central
  Texas

Former Reviewers

Rajshri Agarwal, Iowa State University
Gemmy Allen, Mountain View College
Abi Almeer, Nova University
Arvid Anderson, University of North
  Carolina–Wilmington
Mernoush Banton, University of Miami
Arnold Bornfriend, Worcester State College
Donald Boyer, Jefferson College
Alan Brokaw, Michigan Technological University
S. Allen Broyles, University of Tennessee
Alejandro Camacho, University of Georgia
William Carner, University of Texas–Austin
Gerald Cavallo, Fairfield University
Mee-Shew Cheung, University of Tennessee
Lucette Comer, Florida International University
Michael Conard, Teikyo Post University

Ron Cooley, South Suburban College
June Cotte, University of Connecticut
Ronald Cutter, Southwest Missouri State
  University
John de Young, Cumberland County College
Lee Dickson, Florida International University
Mike Dotson, Appalachian State University
Peter Doukas, Westchester Community College
Thomas Drake, University of Miami
Renee Florsheim, Loyola Marymount University
David Forlani, University of North Florida
Jack Forrest, Middle Tennessee State University
John Gauthier, Gateway Technical Institute
Eugene Gilbert, California State
  University–Sacramento
Charles Goeldner, University of Colorado–Boulder

Diana Grewel, University of Miami
Carol Gwin, Baylor University
Richard Hansen, Ferris State University
Esther Headley, Wichita State University
Sandra Heusinkveld, Normandale Community
  College
Steve Hoeffler, University of North Carolina at
  Chapel Hill
Kathy Illing, Greenville Technical College
James Jeck, North Carolina State University
Robert Jones, California State
  University–Fullerton
Eileen Keller, Kent State University
James Kennedy, Navarro College
Eric Kulp, Middlesex Community College
Ann Kuzma, Minnesota State
  University–Mankato
Ed Laube, Macomb Community College
Martha Leham, Diablo Valley College
Ron Lennon, Barry University
Gregory Lincoln, Westchester Community College
John Lloyd, Monroe Community College
Dorothy Maas, Delaware County Community
  College
Ajay Manrai, University of Delaware
Lalita Manrai, University of Delaware
James McAlexander, Oregon State University
Donald McBane, Clemson University
Debbora Meflin, Bullock–California State
  Polytechnic University
Randall Mertz, Mesa Community College
Herbert Miller, University of Texas–Austin
Veronica Miller, Mount Saint Mary's College
Mark Mitchell, University of South
  Carolina–Spartanburg
Joan Mizis, St. Louis Community College
Melissa Moore, University of Connecticut
Robert Moore, University of Connecticut
William Morgenroth, University of South
  Carolina–Columbia
Linda Moroble, Dallas County Community College
Sandra Moulton, Technical College of Alamance
Jim Muney, Valdosta State
Lee Neuman, Bucks County Community College
Dave Olsen, North Hennepin Community College
Thomas Paczkowski, Cayuga Community College

George Paltz, Erie Community College
Tammy Pappas, Eastern Michigan University
Alison Pittman, Brevard Community College
Lana Podolak, Community College of Beaver
  County
Joel Porrish, Springfield College
Robert L. Powell, Gloucester County College
Eric Pratt, New Mexico State University
Rebecca Ratner, University of North Carolina at
  Chapel Hill
William Rodgers, St. Cloud State University
Robert Ross, Wichita State University
Andre San Augustine, University of Arizona
Dwight Scherban, Central Connecticut College
Eberhard Scheuing, St. John's University
Pamela Schindler, Wittenburg University
Jeff Schmidt, University of
  Illinois–Champaign–Urbana
Roberta Schultz, Western Michigan University
Raymond Schwartz, Montclair State University
Donald Self, Auburn University–Montgomery
Raj Sethuraman, University of Iowa
Reshima H. Shah, University of Pittsburgh
Jack Sheeks, Broward Community College
Herbert Sherman, Long Island
  University–Southhampton
Dee Smith, Lansing Community College
Gordon Snider, California Polytechnic School of
  San Luis Obispo
Jim Spiers, Arizona State University
Karen Stone, Southern New Hampshire
  University
Peter Stone, Spartanburg Technical College
Steve Taylor, Illinois State University
Ira Teich, Long Island University
Jerry L. Thomas, San Jose State University
Donna Tillman, California State Polytechnic
  University
Andrea Weeks, Fashion Institute of Design and
  Merchandising
Summer White, Massachusetts Bay Community
  College
Bill Worley, Allan Hancock College
Merv Yeagle, University of Maryland
Ron Young, Kalamazoo Valley Community
  College

We also owe a great deal to the people at Prentice Hall who helped develop this book. Our editor, Katie Stevens, provided caring and valuable support, advice, and assistance and ably managed the many facets of this complex revision project. We appreciate the professional support and positive attitude of Prentice Hall's marketing manager, Ashaki Charles. We also would like to acknowledge our production editors, Mary Ellen Morrell and Theresa Festa, and our designer, Steve Frim. We are proud to be associated with the professionals at Prentice Hall.

Finally, we owe many thanks to our families for all of their support and encouragement—Kathy, Betty, Mandy, Matt, KC, Keri, Delaney, Molly, and Macy from the Armstrong family and Nancy, Amy, Melissa, and Jessica from the Kotler family. To them, we dedicate this book.

Gary Armstrong
Philip Kotler

→ Marketing: An Introduction
8/e

Chapter 1

→ AFTER STUDYING THIS CHAPTER, YOU SHOULD BE ABLE TO

1. define *marketing* and outline the steps in the marketing process

2. explain the importance of understanding customers and the marketplace, and identify the five core marketplace concepts

3. identify the key elements of a customer-driven marketing strategy and discuss the marketing management orientations that guide marketing strategy

4. discuss customer relationship management, and identify strategies for creating value *for* customers and capturing value *from* customers in return

5. describe the major trends and forces that are changing the marketing landscape in this age of relationships

Marketing: Managing Profitable Customer Relationships

Road Map Previewing the Concepts

Fasten your seat belt! You're about to begin an exciting journey toward learning about marketing. In this chapter, to start you off in the right direction, we will first introduce you to the basic concepts. We'll start with a simple question: What *is* marketing? Simply put, marketing is managing profitable customer relationships. The aim of marketing is to create value for customers and to capture value in return. Chapter 1 is organized around five steps in the marketing process—from understanding customer needs, to designing customer-driven marketing strategies and programs, to building customer relationships and capturing value for the firm. Understanding these basic concepts, and forming your own ideas about what they really mean to you, will give you a solid foundation for all that follows.

Our first stop: NASCAR. In only a few years, NASCAR has swiftly evolved from a pastime for beer-guzzling Bubbas into a national marketing phenomenon. How? By creating high-octane value for its millions of fans. In return, NASCAR captures value from these fans, both for itself and for its many sponsors. Read on and see how NASCAR does it.

When you think of NASCAR, do you think of tobacco-spitting rednecks and run-down race tracks? Think again! These days, NASCAR (the National Association for Stock Car Auto Racing) is much, much more. In fact, it's one great marketing organization. And for fans, NASCAR is a lot more than stock car races. It's a high-octane, totally involving experience.

As for the stereotypes, throw them away. NASCAR is now the second-highest rated regular-season sport on TV—only the NFL draws more viewers—and races are seen in 150 countries in 23 languages. NASCAR fans are young, affluent, and decidedly family-oriented—40 percent are women. What's more, they are 75 million strong—according to one survey, one in three Americans follows NASCAR. Most important, fans are passionate about NASCAR. A hardcore NASCAR fan spends nearly $700 a year on NASCAR-related clothing, collectibles, and other items. NASCAR has even become a cultural force, as politicians scramble to gain the favor of a powerful demographic dubbed "NASCAR dads."

What's NASCAR's secret? Its incredible success results from a single-minded focus: creating lasting customer relationships. For fans, the NASCAR relationship develops through a careful blend of live racing events, abundant media coverage, and compelling Web sites.

Each year, fans experience the adrenalin-charged, heart-stopping excitement of NASCAR racing firsthand by attending national tours to some two dozen tracks around the country. NASCAR races attract the largest crowds of any U.S. sporting event. About 168,000 people attended the recent Daytona 500, far more than attended the Super Bowl, and the Allstate Brickyard 400 sells out its more than 300,000 seats each year.

At these events, fans hold tailgate parties, camp and cook out, watch the cars roar around the track, meet the drivers, and swap stories with other NASCAR enthusiasts. Track facilities even include RV parks next to and right inside the racing oval. Marvels one sponsor, "[In] what other sport can you drive your beat-up RV or camper into the stadium and sit on it to watch the race?" NASCAR really cares about its customers and goes out of its way to show them a good time. For example, rather than fleecing fans with over-priced food and beer, NASCAR tracks encourage fans to bring their own. Such actions mean that NASCAR might lose a sale today, but it will keep the customer tomorrow.

To further the customer relationship, NASCAR makes the sport a wholesome family affair. The environment is safe for kids—uniformed security guards patrol the track to keep things in line. The family atmosphere extends to the drivers, too. Unlike the aloof and often distant athletes in other sports, NASCAR drivers seem like regular guys. They are friendly and readily available to mingle with fans and sign autographs. Fans view drivers as good role models, and the long NASCAR tradition of family involvement creates the next generation of loyal fans.

Can't make it to the track? No problem. NASCAR TV coverage reaches 20 million viewers weekly. Well-orchestrated coverage and in-car cameras put fans in the middle of the action, giving them vicarious thrills that keep them glued to the screen. "When the network gets it right, my surround-sound bothers my neighbors but makes my ears happy," says Angela Kotula, a 35-year old human resources professional.

NASCAR also delivers the NASCAR experience through its engaging Web sites. NASCAR.com serves up a glut of information and entertainment—in-depth news, driver bios, background information, online games, community discussions, and merchandise. True die-hard fans can subscribe to TrackPass to get up-to-the-minute standings, race video, streaming audio from the cars, and access to a host of archived audio and video highlights. TrackPass with PitCommand even delivers a real-time data feed, complete with the GPS locations of cars and data from drivers' dashboards.

But a big part of the NASCAR experience is the feeling that the sport, itself, is personally accessible. Anyone who knows how to drive feels that he or she, too, could be a champion NASCAR driver. As 48-year-old police officer Ed Sweat puts it: "Genetics did not bless me with the height of a basketball player, nor was I born to have the bulk of a lineman in the NFL. But . . . on any given Sunday, with a rich sponsor, the right car, and some practice, I could be draftin' and passin', zooming to the finish line, trading paint with Tony Stewart. . . . Yup, despite my advancing age and waistline, taking Zocor, and driving by a gym . . . I could be Dale Jarrett!"

Ultimately, such fan enthusiasm translates into financial success for NASCAR, and for its sponsors. Television networks pay on average $470 million per year for the rights to broadcast NASCAR events. The sport is third in licensed merchandise sales, behind only the NFL and the NCAA. And marketing studies show that NASCAR's fans are more loyal to the sport's sponsors than fans of any other sport. They are three times more likely to seek out and buy sponsors' products and services than nonfans, and 72 percent of NASCAR fans consciously purchase sponsors products because of the NASCAR connection.

Just ask Ted Wuebben, a big fan of NASCAR driver Rusty Wallace, whose car is sponsored by Miller beer. "I only drink Miller Lite," he says, "not because it tastes great or it's less filling, but because of Rusty." Or talk to dental hygienist Jenny German, an ardent fan of driver Jeff Gordon. According to one account: "She actively seeks out any product he endorses. She drinks Pepsi instead of Coke, eats Edy's ice cream for dessert, and owns a pair of Ray-Ban sunglasses. 'If they sold underwear with the number 24 on it, I'd have it on', German says."

Because of such loyal fan relationships, NASCAR has attracted more than 250 big-name sponsors, from Wal-Mart, Home Depot, and Target, to Procter & Gamble, FedEx, Coca-Cola, and the U.S. Army. In all, corporations spend more than $1 billion a year for NASCAR sponsorships and promotions. Sprint Nextel is shelling out $750 million over the next 10 years to be a NASCAR sponsor and to put its name on the Nextel Cup series. "I could pay you $1 million to try and not run into our name at a NASCAR race and you would lose," says a Nextel spokesperson. Other sponsors eagerly pay up to $20 million per year to sponsor a top car and to get their corporate colors and logos emblazoned on team uniforms and on the hoods or side panels of team cars. Or they pay $3 million to $5 million a year to become the "official" (fill-in-the-blank) of NASCAR racing. Is it worth the price? Office Depot certainly thinks so. It began sponsoring a car when its surveys showed that 44 percent of rival Staples' customers would switch office supply retailers if Office Depot hooked up with NASCAR.

So if you're still thinking of NASCAR as rednecks and moonshine, you'd better think again. NASCAR is a premier marketing organization that knows how to create customer value that translates into deep and lasting customer relationships. "Better than any other sport," says a leading sports marketing executive, "NASCAR listens to its fans and gives them what they want." In turn, fans reward NASCAR and its sponsors with deep loyalty and the promise of lasting profits.[1]

Today's successful companies have one thing in common: Like NASCAR, they are strongly customer focused and heavily committed to marketing. These companies share a passion for satisfying customer needs in well-defined target markets. They motivate everyone in the organization to help build lasting customer relationships through superior customer value and satisfaction. As Wal-Mart founder Sam Walton asserted: "There is only one boss. The customer. And he can fire everybody in the company from the chairman on down, simply by spending his money somewhere else."

What Is Marketing?

Marketing, more than any other business function, deals with customers. Although we will soon explore more detailed definitions of marketing, perhaps the simplest definition is this one: Marketing is managing profitable customer relationships. The twofold goal of marketing is to attract new customers by promising superior value and to keep and grow current customers by delivering satisfaction.

Wal-Mart has become the world's largest retailer, and the world's largest company, by delivering on its promise, "Always low prices. Always!" At Disney theme parks, "imagineers" work wonders in their quest to "make a dream come true today." Dell leads the personal computer industry by consistently making good on its promise to "be direct." Dell makes it easy for customers to custom-design their own computers and have them delivered quickly to their doorsteps or desktops. These and other highly successful companies know that if they take care of their customers, market share and profits will follow.

Sound marketing is critical to the success of every organization. Large for-profit firms such as Procter & Gamble, Toyota, Wal-Mart, IBM, and Marriott use marketing. But so do not-for-profit organizations such as colleges, hospitals, museums, symphony orchestras, and even churches.

You already know a lot about marketing—it's all around you. You see the results of marketing in the abundance of products in your nearby shopping mall. You see marketing in the advertisements that fill your TV screen, spice up your magazines, stuff your mailbox, or enliven your Web pages. At home, at school, where you work, and where you play, you see marketing in almost everything you do. Yet, there is much more to marketing than meets the consumer's casual eye. Behind it all is a massive network of people and activities competing for your attention and purchases.

This book will give you a complete and formal introduction to the basic concepts and practices of today's marketing. In this chapter, we begin by defining *marketing* and the marketing process.

MARKETING DEFINED

What *is* marketing? Many people think of marketing only as selling and advertising. And no wonder—every day we are bombarded with television commercials, direct-mail offers, sales calls, and Internet pitches. However, selling and advertising are only the tip of the marketing iceberg.

Today, marketing must be understood not in the old sense of making a sale—"telling and selling"—but in the new sense of *satisfying customer needs.* If the marketer does a good job of understanding consumer needs; develops products and services that provide superior customer value; and prices, distributes, and promotes them effectively, these products will sell very easily. Thus, selling and advertising are only part of a larger "marketing mix"—a set of marketing tools that work together to satisfy customer needs and build customer relationships.

Broadly defined, marketing is a social and managerial process by which individuals and organizations obtain what they need and want through creating and exchanging value with others. In a narrower business context, marketing involves building profitable,

FIGURE 1.1 A Simple Model of the Marketing Process

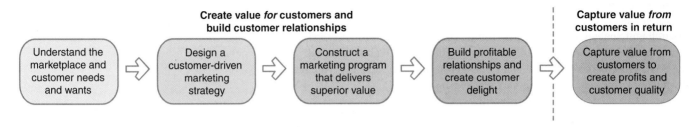

Create value *for* customers and
build customer relationships

Capture value *from*
customers in return

Understand the
marketplace and
customer needs
and wants

Design a
customer-driven
marketing
strategy

Construct a
marketing program
that delivers
superior value

Build profitable
relationships and
create customer
delight

Capture value from
customers to
create profits and
customer quality

Marketing
The process by which companies create value for customers and build strong customer relationships in order to capture value from customers in return.

value-laden exchange relationships with customers. Hence, we define **marketing** as the process by which companies create value for customers and build strong customer relationships in order to capture value from customers in return.[2]

THE MARKETING PROCESS

Figure 1.1 presents a simple five-step model of the marketing process. In the first four steps, companies work to understand consumers, create customer value, and build strong customer relationships. In the final step, companies reap the rewards of creating superior customer value. By creating value *for* consumers, they in turn capture value *from* consumers in the form of sales, profits, and long-term customer equity.

In this and the next chapter, we will examine the steps of this simple model of marketing. In this chapter, we will review each step but focus more on the customer relationship steps—understanding customers, building customer relationships, and capturing value from customers. In Chapter 2, we'll look more deeply into the second and third steps—designing marketing strategies and constructing marketing programs.

Understanding the Marketplace and Customer Needs

As a first step, marketers need to understand customer needs and wants and the marketplace within which they operate. We now examine five core customer and marketplace concepts: (1) *needs, wants, and demands*; (2) *marketing offers (products, services, and experiences)*; (3) *value and satisfaction*; (4) *exchanges and relationships*; and (5) *markets*.

CUSTOMER NEEDS, WANTS, AND DEMANDS

Needs
States of felt deprivation.

The most basic concept underlying marketing is that of human needs. Human **needs** are states of felt deprivation. They include basic *physical* needs for food, clothing, warmth, and safety; *social* needs for belonging and affection; and *individual* needs for knowledge and self-expression. These needs were not created by marketers; they are a basic part of the human makeup.

Wants
The form human needs take as shaped by culture and individual personality.

Wants are the form human needs take as they are shaped by culture and individual personality. An American *needs* food but *wants* a Big Mac, french fries, and a soft drink. A person in Mauritius *needs* food but *wants* a mango, rice, lentils, and beans. Wants are shaped by one's society and are described in terms of objects that will satisfy needs. When backed by buying power, wants become **demands**. Given their wants and resources, people demand products with benefits that add up to the most value and satisfaction.

Demands
Human wants that are backed by buying power.

Outstanding marketing companies go to great lengths to learn about and understand their customers' needs, wants, and demands. They conduct consumer research and analyze mountains of customer data. Their people at all levels—including top management—stay close to customers. For example, at Southwest Airlines, all senior executives handle bags, check in passengers, and serve as flight attendants once every quarter. Harley-Davidson's chairman regularly mounts his Harley and rides with customers to get feedback and ideas. And at Panera Bread, CEO and Chairman Ron Shaich, regularly visits one or another of the company's more than 800 bakery-cafés to interact with customers. Introducing himself as an employee who "works for Panera Bread," he speaks with customers to see what is on their minds.[3]

■ Learning about and understanding customers: Panera Bread chief executive Ron Shaich regularly visits one or another of the company's more than 800 bakery-cafés to interact with customers.

MARKET OFFERINGS—PRODUCTS, SERVICES, AND EXPERIENCES

Consumers' needs and wants are fulfilled through a **market offering**—some combination of products, services, information, or experiences offered to a market to satisfy a need or want. Market offerings are not limited to physical *products*. They also include *services,* activities or benefits offered for sale that are essentially intangible and do not result in the ownership of anything. Examples include banking, airline, hotel, tax preparation, and home repair services. More broadly, market offerings also include other entities, such as *persons, places, organizations, information,* and *ideas.* For example, for EarthShare, a nationwide network of America's leading environmental organizations, the "marketing offer" is environmental education and charitable workplace giving.

Market offering
Some combination of products, services, information, or experiences offered to a market to satisfy a need or want.

Many sellers make the mistake of paying more attention to the specific products they offer than to the benefits and experiences produced by these products. These sellers suffer from **marketing myopia.** They are so taken with their products that they focus only on existing wants and lose sight of underlying customer needs.[4] They forget that a product is only a tool to solve a consumer problem. A manufacturer of quarter-inch drill bits may think that the customer needs a drill bit. But what the customer *really* needs is a quarter-inch hole. These sellers will have trouble if a new product comes along that serves the customer's need better or less expensively. The customer will have the same *need* but will *want* the new product.

Marketing myopia
The mistake of paying more attention to the specific products a company offers than to the benefits and experiences produced by these products.

Smart marketers look beyond the attributes of the products and services they sell. By orchestrating several services and products, they create *brand experiences* for consumers. For example, Walt Disney World is an experience; so is a ride on a Harley-Davidson motorcycle. Your Nike's are more than just shoes; they are an empowering experience that makes you "faster than you think." And you don't just watch a NASCAR race; you immerse yourself in the NASCAR experience. "What consumers really want [are offers] that dazzle their senses, touch their hearts, and stimulate their minds," declares one expert. "They want [offers] that deliver an experience."[5]

CUSTOMER VALUE AND SATISFACTION

Consumers usually face a broad array of products and services that might satisfy a given need. How do they choose among these many market offerings? Customers form expectations about the value and satisfaction that various market offerings will deliver and buy accordingly. Satisfied customers buy again and tell others about their good

How can you help protect the prairie and the penguin?

Simple. Visit www.earthshare.org and learn how the world's leading environmental groups are working together under one name. And how easy it is for you to help protect the prairies and the penguins and the planet.

www.earthshare.org

One environment. One simple way to care for it. Earth Share

■ Products do not have to be physical objects: Here, the "product" is an idea: "how easy it is for you to help protect the prairies and the penguins and the planet."

Exchange
The act of obtaining a desired object from someone by offering something in return.

Market
The set of all actual and potential buyers of a product or service.

experiences. Dissatisfied customers often switch to competitors and disparage the product to others.

Marketers must be careful to set the right level of expectations. If they set expectations too low, they may satisfy those who buy but fail to attract enough buyers. If they raise expectations too high, buyers will be disappointed. Customer value and customer satisfaction are key building blocks for developing and managing customer relationships. We will revisit these core concepts later in the chapter.

EXCHANGES AND RELATIONSHIPS

Marketing occurs when people decide to satisfy needs and wants through exchange relationships. **Exchange** is the act of obtaining a desired object from someone by offering something in return. In the broadest sense, the marketer tries to bring about a response to some market offering. The response may be more than simply buying or trading products and services. For instance, a political candidate wants votes, a church wants membership, an orchestra wants an audience, and a social action group wants idea acceptance.

Marketing consists of actions taken to build and maintain desirable exchange *rela-tionships* with target audiences involving a product, service, idea, or other object. Beyond simply attracting new customers and creating transactions, the goal is to retain customers and grow their business with the company. Marketers want to build strong relationships by consistently delivering superior customer value. We will expand on the important concept of managing customer relationships later in the chapter.

MARKETS

The concepts of exchange and relationships lead to the concept of a market. A **market** is the set of actual and potential buyers of a product. These buyers share a particular need or want that can be satisfied through exchange relationships.

Marketing means managing markets to bring about profitable customer relationships. However, creating these relationships takes work. Sellers must search for buyers, identify their needs, design good market offerings, set prices for them, promote them, and store and deliver them. Activities such as product development, research, communication, distribution, pricing, and service are core marketing activities.

Although we normally think of marketing as being carried on by sellers, buyers also carry on marketing. Consumers do marketing when they search for the goods they need at prices they can afford. Company purchasing agents do marketing when they track down sellers and bargain for good terms.

Figure 1.2 shows the main elements in a modern marketing system. In the usual situation, marketing involves serving a market of final consumers in the face of competitors. The company and the competitors send their respective offers and messages to consumers, either directly or through marketing intermediaries. All the actors in the system are affected by major environmental forces (demographic, economic, physical, technological, political/legal, social/cultural).

Each party in the system adds value for the next level. All the arrows represent relationships that must be developed and managed. Thus, a company's success at building profitable relationships depends not only on its own actions but also on how well the entire system serves the needs of final consumers. Wal-Mart cannot fulfill its promise of low prices unless its suppliers provide merchandise at low costs. And Ford cannot deliver high quality to car buyers unless its dealers provide outstanding sales and service.

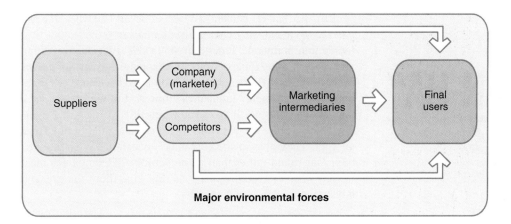

FIGURE 1.2
**Elements of a Modern
Marketing System**

Designing a Customer-Driven Marketing Strategy

Once it fully understands consumers and the marketplace, marketing management can design a customer-driven marketing strategy. We define **marketing management** as the art and science of choosing target markets and building profitable relationships with them. The marketing manager's aim is to find, attract, keep, and grow target customers by creating, delivering, and communicating superior customer value.

To design a winning marketing strategy, the marketing manager must answer two important questions: *What customers will we serve (what's our target market)?* and *How can we serve these customers best (what's our value proposition)?* We will discuss these marketing strategy concepts briefly here, and then look at them in more detail in the next chapter.

Marketing management
The art and science of choosing target markets and building profitable relationships with them.

SELECTING CUSTOMERS TO SERVE

The company must first decide *who* it will serve. It does this by dividing the market into segments of customers (*market segmentation*) and selecting which segments it will go after (*target marketing*). Some people think of marketing management as finding as many customers as possible and increasing demand. But marketing managers know that they cannot serve all customers in every way. By trying to serve all customers, they may not serve any customers well. Instead, the company wants to select only customers that it can serve well and profitably. For example, Nordstrom stores profitably target affluent professionals; Family Dollar stores profitably target families with more modest means.

Some marketers may even seek *fewer* customers and reduced demand. For example, many power companies have trouble meeting demand during peak usage periods. In these and other cases of excess demand, companies may practice *demarketing* to reduce the number of customers or to shift their demand temporarily or permanently. For instance, to reduce demand for space on congested expressways in Washington, D.C., the Metropolitan Washington Council of Governments has set up a Web site encouraging commuters to carpool and use mass transit (www.commuterconnections.org).

Thus, marketing managers must decide which customers they want to target, and on the level, timing, and nature of their demand. Simply put, marketing management is *customer management* and *demand management*.

CHOOSING A VALUE PROPOSITION

The company must also decide how it will serve targeted customers—how it will *differentiate and position* itself in the marketplace. A company's *value proposition* is the set of benefits or values it promises to deliver to consumers to satisfy their needs. Porsche promises driving

Red Bull Energy Drink is a unique combination of Taurine, Glucuronolactone, B-vitamins and other important nutrients. It improves performance, increases endurance and concentration, improves reaction speed and stimulates the metabolism. In short, Red Bull vitalizes both body and mind.

RED BULL GIVES YOU WIIINGS.

■ Value propositions: Red Bull Energy Drink "vitalizes both body and mind. It Gives You Wiiings."

Production concept
The idea that consumers will favor products that are available and highly affordable and that the organization should therefore focus on improving production and distribution efficiency.

Product concept
The idea that consumers will favor products that offer the most quality, performance, and features and that the organization should devote its energy to making continuous product improvements.

Selling concept
The idea that consumers will not buy enough of the firm's products unless it undertakes a large-scale selling and promotion effort.

performance and excitement: "What a dog feels like when its leash breaks." By contrast, Toyota's Sienna minivan provides practical family transportation: "It has everything kids want and everything you need." Propel Fitness Water by Gatorade is "made for bodies in motion." Red Bull energy drink, on the other hand, "vitalizes both body and mind." It captures 70 percent of the energy drink market by promising "It gives you wiiings!"

Such value propositions differentiate one brand from another. They answer the customer's question "Why should I buy your brand rather than a competitor's?" Companies must design strong value propositions that give them the greatest advantage in their target markets.

MARKETING MANAGEMENT ORIENTATIONS

Marketing management wants to design strategies that will build profitable relationships with target consumers. But what *philosophy* should guide these marketing strategies? What weight should be given to the interests of customers, the organization, and society? Very often, these interests conflict.

There are five alternative concepts under which organizations design and carry out their marketing strategies: the *production, product, selling, marketing,* and *societal marketing concepts.*

The Production Concept   The **production concept** holds that consumers will favor products that are available and highly affordable. Therefore, management should focus on improving production and distribution efficiency. This concept is one of the oldest orientations that guides sellers.

The production concept is still a useful philosophy in some situations. For example, Asian computer maker Legend dominates the highly competitive, price-sensitive Chinese PC market through low labor costs, high production efficiency, and mass distribution. However, although useful in some situations, the production concept can lead to marketing myopia. Companies adopting this orientation run a major risk of focusing too narrowly on their own operations and losing sight of the real objective—satisfying customer needs and building customer relationships.

The Product Concept   The **product concept** holds that consumers will favor products that offer the most in quality, performance, and innovative features. Under this concept, marketing strategy focuses on making continuous product improvements.

Product quality and improvement are important parts of most marketing strategies. However, focusing *only* on the company's products can also lead to marketing myopia. For example, some manufacturers believe that if they can "build a better mousetrap, the world will beat a path to their door." But they are often rudely shocked. Buyers may well be looking for a better solution to a mouse problem but not necessarily for a better mousetrap. The better solution might be a chemical spray, an exterminating service, or something that works better than a mousetrap. Furthermore, a better mousetrap will not sell unless the manufacturer designs, packages, and prices it attractively; places it in convenient distribution channels; brings it to the attention of people who need it; and convinces buyers that it is a better product.

The Selling Concept   Many companies follow the **selling concept**, which holds that consumers will not buy enough of the firm's products unless it undertakes a large-scale

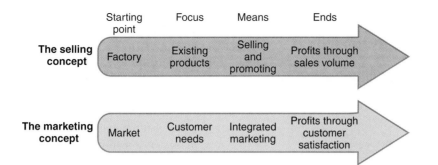

FIGURE 1.3
The Selling and Marketing Concepts Contrasted

selling and promotion effort. The concept is typically practiced with unsought goods—those that buyers do not normally think of buying, such as insurance or blood donations. These industries must be good at tracking down prospects and selling them on product benefits.

Such aggressive selling, however, carries high risks. It focuses on creating sales transactions rather than on building long-term, profitable customer relationships. The aim often is to sell what the company makes rather than making what the market wants. It assumes that customers who are coaxed into buying the product will like it. Or, if they don't like it, they will possibly forget their disappointment and buy it again later. These are usually poor assumptions.

The Marketing Concept The **marketing concept** holds that achieving organizational goals depends on knowing the needs and wants of target markets and delivering the desired satisfactions better than competitors do. Under the marketing concept, customer focus and value are the *paths* to sales and profits. Instead of a product-centered "make and sell" philosophy, the marketing concept is a customer-centered "sense and respond" philosophy. It views marketing not as "hunting," but as "gardening." The job is not to find the right customers for your product, but to find the right products for your customers.

Figure 1.3 contrasts the selling concept and the marketing concept. The selling concept takes an *inside-out* perspective. It starts with the factory, focuses on the company's existing products, and calls for heavy selling and promotion to obtain profitable sales. It focuses primarily on customer conquest—getting short-term sales with little concern about who buys or why.

In contrast, the marketing concept takes an *outside-in* perspective. As Herb Kelleher, Southwest Airlines' colorful CEO, puts it, "We don't have a marketing department; we have a customer department." And in the words of one Ford executive, "If we're not customer driven, our cars won't be either."[6] The marketing concept starts with a well-defined market, focuses on customer needs, and integrates all the marketing activities that affect customers. In turn, it yields profits by creating lasting relationships with the right customers based on customer value and satisfaction.

Implementing the marketing concept often means more than simply responding to customers' stated desires and obvious needs. *Customer-driven* companies research current customers deeply to learn about their desires, gather new product and service ideas, and test proposed product improvements. Such customer-driven marketing usually works well when a clear need exists and when customers know what they want.

In many cases, however, customers *don't* know what they want or even what is possible. For example, even 20 years ago, how many consumers would have thought to ask for now-commonplace products such as cell phones, PDAs, notebook computers, digital still and video cameras, 24-hour online buying, and satellite navigation systems in their cars? Such situations call for *customer-driving* marketing—understanding customer needs even better than customers themselves do and creating products and services that meet existing and latent needs, now and in the future. As an executive at 3M puts it: "Our goal is to lead customers where they want to go before *they* know where they want to go."

Marketing concept
The marketing management philosophy that holds that achieving organizational goals depends on knowing the needs and wants of target markets and delivering the desired satisfactions better than competitors do.

■ Customer-driving marketing: Even 20 years ago, how many consumers would have thought to ask for now-commonplace products such as cell phones, personal digital assistants, notebook computers, and digital still and video cameras: Marketers must often understand customer needs even better than customers themselves do.

Societal marketing concept
A principle of enlightened marketing that holds that a company should make good marketing decisions by considering consumers' wants, the company's requirements, consumers' long-run interests, and society's long run interests.

The Societal Marketing Concept The **societal marketing concept** questions whether the pure marketing concept overlooks possible conflicts between consumer *short-run wants* and consumer *long-run welfare*. Is a firm that satisfies the immediate needs and wants of target markets always doing what's best for consumers in the long run? The societal marketing concept holds that marketing strategy should deliver value to customers in a way that maintains or improves both the consumer's *and the society's* well-being.

Consider the fast-food industry. You may view today's giant fast-food chains as offering tasty and convenient food at reasonable prices. Yet many consumer nutritionists and environmental groups have voiced concerns. They point to fast feeders like Hardee's, who are promoting a new wave of monster meals like the Monster Thickburger—two 1/3-pound slabs of Angus beef, four strips of bacon, three slices of American cheese, and mayonnaise on a buttered bun, delivering 1,420 calories and 102 grams of fat. Such unhealthy fare, they claim, is leading consumers to overeat, contributing to a national obesity epidemic. What's more, the products are wrapped in convenient packaging, but this leads to waste and pollution. Thus, in satisfying short-term consumer wants, the highly successful fast-food chains may be harming consumer health and causing environmental problems in the long run.[7]

As Figure 1.4 shows, companies should balance three considerations in setting their marketing strategies: company profits, consumer wants, *and* society's interests. Johnson & Johnson does this well. Its concern for societal interests is summarized in a company document called *Our Credo*, which stresses honesty, integrity, and putting people before profits. Under this credo, Johnson & Johnson would rather take a big loss than ship a bad batch of one of its products.

Consider the tragic tampering case in which eight people died in 1982 from swallowing cyanide-laced capsules of Tylenol, a Johnson & Johnson brand. Although Johnson & Johnson believed that the pills had been altered in only a few stores, not in the factory, it quickly recalled all of its product and launched an information campaign to instruct and reassure consumers. The recall cost the company $100 million in earnings. In the long run, however, the company's swift recall of Tylenol strengthened consumer confidence and loyalty, and today Tylenol remains one of the nation's leading brands of pain reliever.

FIGURE 1.4

Three Considerations Underlying the Societal Marketing Concept

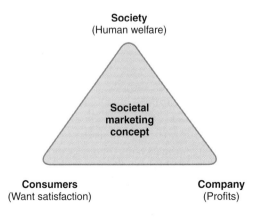

Society
(Human welfare)

Societal marketing concept

Consumers
(Want satisfaction)

Company
(Profits)

Johnson & Johnson management has learned that doing what's right benefits both consumers and the company. Says former CEO, Ralph Larsen, "The Credo should not be viewed as some kind of social welfare program . . . it's just plain good business. If we keep trying to do what's right, at the end of the day we believe the marketplace will reward us." Thus, over the years, Johnson & Johnson's dedication to consumers and community service has made it one of America's most-admired companies *and* one of the most profitable.[8]

Preparing a Marketing Plan and Program

The company's marketing strategy outlines which customers the company will serve and how it will create value for these customers. Next, the marketer develops a marketing program that will actually deliver the intended value to target customers. The marketing program builds customer relationships by transforming the marketing strategy into action. It consists of the firm's *marketing mix*, the set of marketing tools the firm uses to implement its marketing strategy.

The major marketing mix tools are classified into four broad groups, called the *four Ps* of marketing: product, price, place, and promotion. To deliver on its value proposition, the firm must first create a need-satisfying market offering (product). It must decide how much it will charge for the offer (price) and how it will make the offer available to target consumers (place). Finally, it must communicate with target customers about the offer and persuade them of its merits (promotion). We will explore marketing programs and the marketing mix in much more detail in later chapters.

■ The societal marketing concept: Johnson & Johnson's Credo stresses putting people before profits. Johnson & Johnson's quick product recall following a tragic Tylenol tampering incident some years ago cost the company $100 million in earnings but strengthened consumer confidence and loyalty.

 Linking the Concepts

Stop here for a moment and stretch your legs. What have you learned so far about marketing? For the moment, set aside the more formal definitions we've examined and try to develop your own understanding of marketing.

■ In *your own words*, what *is* marketing? Write down *your* definition. Does your definition include such key concepts as customer value and relationships?
■ What does marketing *mean* to you? How does it affect your life on a daily basis?
■ What brand of athletic shoes did you purchase last? Describe your relationship with Nike, New Balance, Reebok, Adidas, or whatever company made the shoes you purchased.

Building Customer Relationships

The first three steps in the marketing process—understanding the marketplace and customer needs, designing a customer-driven marketing strategy, and constructing marketing programs—all lead up to the fourth and most important step: building profitable customer relationships.

CUSTOMER RELATIONSHIP MANAGEMENT

Customer relationship management (CRM) is perhaps the most important concept of modern marketing. Until recently, CRM has been defined narrowly as a customer data management activity. By this definition, it involves managing detailed information about individual customers and carefully managing customer "touchpoints" in order to maximize customer loyalty. We will discuss this narrower CRM activity in a later chapter dealing with marketing information.

More recently, however, customer relationship management has taken on a broader meaning. In this broader sense, **customer relationship management** is the overall process of building and maintaining profitable customer relationships by delivering superior customer value and satisfaction. It deals with all aspects of acquiring, keeping, and growing customers.

Customer relationship management

The overall process of building and maintaining profitable customer relationships by delivering superior customer value and satisfaction.

Customer perceived value

The customer's evaluation of the difference between all the benefits and all the costs of a marketing offer relative to those of competing offers.

Relationship Building Blocks: Customer Value and Satisfaction   The key to building lasting customer relationships is to create superior customer value and satisfaction. Satisfied customers are more likely to be loyal customers and to give the company a larger share of their business.

Lifetime supply of fresh air with every purchase.

The next generation gas/electric
Prius with Hybrid Synergy Drive.®
Best emission rating for a gas-powered
production vehicle. Best estimated

The power to move forward.

fuel economy in a mid-size car.® All
with the best interests of the earth
in mind. Take a deep breath everyone.
The Prius is here. *toyota.com*

PRIUS START NOW.

GET THE FEELING   ⊕ TOYOTA

■ Perceived customer value: When deciding whether to purchase a Prius, customers will weigh its benefits against the benefits of owning another hybrid or non-hybrid brand.

Customer Value.   Attracting and retaining customers can be a difficult task. Customers often face a bewildering array of products and services from which to choose. A customer buys from the firm that offers the highest **customer perceived value**—the customer's evaluation of the difference between all the benefits and all the costs of a market offering relative to those of competing offers.

For example, Toyota Prius hybrid automobile owners gain a number of benefits. The most obvious benefit is fuel efficiency. However, by purchasing a Prius, the owners also may receive some status and image values. Driving a Prius makes owners feel and appear more environmentally responsible. When deciding whether to purchase a Prius, customers will weigh these and other perceived values of owning the car against the money, effort, and psychic costs of acquiring it. Moreover, they will compare the value of owning a Prius against that of owning another hybrid or non-hybrid brand. They will select the brand that gives them the greatest perceived value.

Customers often do not judge product values and costs accurately or objectively. They act on *perceived* value. For example, is the Prius really the most economical choice? In reality, it might take years to save enough in reduced fuel costs to offset the car's higher sticker price. However, Prius buyers perceive that they are getting real value. A recent survey of the ownership experiences of 69,000 new car buyers showed that Prius owners perceived more overall value for their money than buyers of any other new car.[9]

Customer Satisfaction.   **Customer satisfaction** depends on the product's perceived performance relative to a buyer's expectations. If the product's performance falls short of expectations, the customer is dissatisfied. If performance matches expectations, the customer is satisfied. If performance exceeds expectations, the customer is highly satisfied or delighted.

Customer satisfaction

The extent to which a product's perceived performance matches a buyer's expectations.

Outstanding marketing companies go out of their way to keep important customers satisfied. Highly satisfied customers make repeat purchases and tell others about their good experiences with the product. Most studies show that higher levels of customer satisfaction lead to greater customer loyalty, which in turn results in better company performance.[10] The key is to match customer expectations with company performance. Smart companies aim to *delight* customers by promising only what they can deliver, then delivering *more* than they promise (see Marketing at Work 1.1).

However, although the customer-centered firm seeks to deliver high customer satisfaction relative to competitors, it does not attempt to *maximize* customer satisfaction. A company can always increase customer satisfaction by lowering its price or increasing its services. But this may result in lower profits. Thus, the purpose of marketing is to generate customer value profitably. This requires a very delicate balance: The marketer must continue to generate more customer value and satisfaction but not "give away the house."

Customer Relationship Levels and Tools   Companies can build customer relationships at many levels, depending on the nature of the target market. At one extreme, a company with many low-margin customers may seek to develop *basic relationships* with them. For example, Procter & Gamble (P&G) does not phone or call on all of its Tide customers to get to know them personally. Instead, P&G creates relationships through brand-building advertising, sales promotions, a 1-800 customer response number, and its Tide FabricCare Network Web site (www.Tide.com). At the other extreme, in markets with few customers and high margins, sellers want to create *full partnerships* with key customers. For example, P&G customer teams work closely with Wal-Mart, Safeway, and other large retailers. In between these two extreme situations, other levels of customer relationships are appropriate.

Today, most leading companies are developing customer loyalty and retention programs. Beyond offering consistently high value and satisfaction, marketers can use specific marketing tools to develop stronger bonds with consumers. For example, many companies now offer *frequency marketing programs* that reward customers who buy frequently or in large amounts. Airlines offer frequent-flyer programs, hotels give room upgrades to their frequent guests, and supermarkets give patronage discounts to "very important customers."

Other companies sponsor *club marketing programs* that offer members special discounts and create member communities. For example:[11]

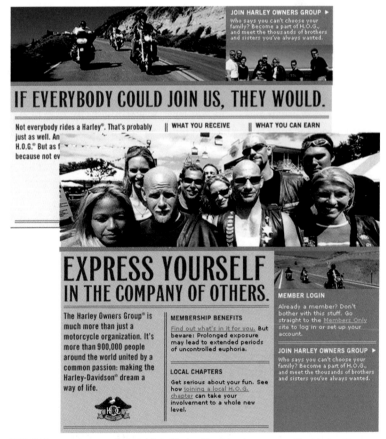

> Harley-Davidson sponsors the Harley Owners Group (H.O.G.), which gives Harley riders "an organized way to share their passion and show their pride." H.O.G membership benefits include two magazines (Hog Tales and Enthusiast), a H.O.G. Touring Handbook, a roadside assistance program, a specially designed insurance program, theft reward service, a travel center, and a "Fly & Ride" program enabling members to rent Harleys while on vacation. The company also maintains an extensive H.O.G. Web site, which offers information on H.O.G. chapters, rallies, events, and benefits. The worldwide club now numbers more than 1,300 local chapters and 900,000 members.

To build customer relationships, companies can add structural ties as well as financial and social benefits. A business marketer might supply customers with special equipment or online linkages that help them manage their orders, payroll, or inventory. For example, McKesson

■ Building customer relationships: Harley-Davidson sponsors the Harley Owners Group (H.O.G.), which gives Harley owners "an organized way to share their passion and show their pride." The worldwide club now numbers more than 1,300 local chapters and 900,000 members.

MARKETING AT WORK   1.1

Customer Relationships: Delighting Customers

Top-notch marketing companies know that delighting customers involves more than simply opening a complaint department, smiling a lot, and being nice. These companies set very high standards for customer satisfaction and often make seemingly outlandish efforts to achieve them. Consider the following example:

A man bought his first new Lexus—$45,000 piece of machinery. He could afford a Mercedes, a BMW, or a Cadillac, but he bought the Lexus. He took delivery of his new honey and started to drive it home, luxuriating in the smell of the leather interior and the glorious handling. On the interstate, he put the pedal to the metal and felt the Gs in the pit of his stomach. The lights, the windshield washer, the gizmo cup holder that popped out of the center console, the seat heater that warmed his bottom on a cold winter morning—he tried all of these with mounting pleasure. On a whim, he turned on the radio. His favorite classical music station came on in splendid quadraphonic sound that ricocheted around the interior. He pushed the second button; it was his favorite news station. The third button brought his favorite talk station that kept him awake on long trips. The fourth button was set to his daughter's favorite rock station. In fact, every button was set to his specific tastes. The customer knew the car was smart, but was it psychic? No. The mechanic at Lexus had noted the radio settings on his trade-in and duplicated them on the new Lexus. The customer was delighted. This was his car now—through and through! No one told the mechanic to do it. It's just part of the Lexus philosophy: Delight a customer and continue to delight that customer, and you will have a customer for life. What the mechanic did cost Lexus nothing. Not one red cent. Yet it solidified the relationship that could be worth high six figures to Lexus in customer lifetime value. Such relationship-building passions in dealerships around the country have made Lexus the nation's top-selling luxury vehicle.

Studies show that going to extremes to keep customers happy, although sometimes costly, goes hand in hand with good financial performance. Delighted customers come back again and again. Thus, in today's highly competitive marketplace, companies can well afford to lose money on one transaction if it helps to cement a profitable long-term customer relationship.

For companies interested in delighting customers, exceptional value and service are more than a set of policies or actions—they are a companywide attitude, an important part of the overall company culture. Employees at the Café Un Deux Trois in Minneapolis learn about customer service from the restaurant's owner Michael Morse. Morse once overheard a customer raving about the egg rolls at the Chinese restaurant across the street. The next time the customer visited the café, Morse served him those very egg rolls.

Southwest Airlines is well known for its low fares and prompt arrivals. But its friendly and often funny flight staff goes to great lengths to delight customers. In one instance, after pushing away from the departure gate, a Southwest pilot spied an anguished passenger, sweat streaming from her face, racing down the jetway only to find that she'd arrived too late. He returned to the gate to pick her up. Says Southwest's President, "It broke every rule in the book, but we congratulated the pilot on a job well done."

Corporation, a leading pharmaceutical wholesaler, has set up a Supply Management Online system that helps retail pharmacy customers manage their inventories, order entry, and shelf space. The system also helps McKesson's medical-surgical supply and equipment customers optimize their supply purchasing and materials management operations.[12]

THE CHANGING NATURE OF CUSTOMER RELATIONSHIPS

Dramatic changes are occurring in the ways in which companies are relating to their customers. Yesterday's companies focused on mass marketing to all customers at arm's length. Today's companies are building more direct and lasting relationships with more carefully selected customers. Here are some important trends in the way companies are relating to their customers.

Relating with More Carefully Selected Customers   Few firms today still practice true mass marketing—selling in a standardized way to any customer who comes along. Today, most marketers realize that they don't want relationships with every customer. Instead, companies now are targeting fewer, more profitable customers. Called *selective relationship management*, many companies now use customer profitability analysis to weed out losing customers and to target winning ones for pampering. Once they identify profitable

■ *Delighting customers: Southwest Airlines's friendly and often funny flight staff goes to great lengths to delight customers.*

Four Seasons Hotels, long known for its outstanding service, tells its employees the story of Ron Dyment, a doorman in Toronto, who forgot to load a departing guest's briefcase into his taxi. The doorman called the guest, a lawyer in Washington, D.C., and learned that he desperately needed the briefcase for a meeting the following morning. Without first asking for approval from management, Dyment hopped on a plane and returned the briefcase. The company named Dyment Employee of the Year.

Similarly, the Nordstrom department store chain thrives on stories about its service heroics, such as employees dropping off orders at customers' homes or warming up cars while customers spend a little more time shopping. In one case, a salesclerk reportedly gave a customer a refund on a tire—Nordstrom doesn't carry tires, but the store prides itself on a no-questions-asked return policy. There's even a story about a man whose wife, a loyal Nordstrom customer, died with her Nordstrom account $1,000 in arrears. Not only did Nordstrom settle the account, it also sent flowers to the funeral.

There's no simple formula for taking care of customers, but neither is it a mystery. According to the CEO of L.L.Bean, "A lot of people have fancy things to say about customer service ... but it's just a day-in, day-out, ongoing, never-ending, unremitting, persevering, compassionate kind of activity." For the companies that do it well, it's also very rewarding.

Sources: Examples and quotes are from Denny Hatch and Ernie Schell,"Delight Your Customers,"Target Marketing, April 2002, pp. 32–39; Dana James,"Lighting the Way," *Marketing News,* April 1, 2002, pp. 1, 11; Patricia Sellers, "Companies That Serve You Best," *FORTUNE,* May 31, 1993, pp. 74–88; Chip R. Bell and Ron Zemke,"Service Magic," Executive Excellence, May 2003, p. 13; and Fiona Haley, "Fast Talk," *Fast Company,* December 2003, p. 57. Also see "Lexus Retains Best-Selling Luxury Brand Title for Fifth Year in a Row," January 5, 2005, accessed at www.lexus. com/about/press_releases/index.html; and Mark J. Arnold, et. al.,"Customer Delight in a Retail Context: Investigating Delightful and Terrible Shopping Experiences," *Journal of Business Research,* August 2005, p. 1132.

customers, firms can create attractive offers and special handling to capture these customers and earn their loyalty.

But what should the company do with unprofitable customers? If it can't turn them into profitable ones, it may even want to "fire" customers that are too unreasonable or that cost more to serve than they are worth. For example, banks now routinely assess customer profitability based on such factors as an account's average balances, account activity, services usage, branch visits, and other variables. For most banks, profitable customers with large balances are pampered with premium services, whereas unprofitable, low-balance ones get the cold shoulder. ING Direct, however, selects accounts differently. It seeks relationships with customers who don't need or want expensive pampering while firing those who do.[13]

ING Direct is the fast-food chain of financial services. With a handful of offerings including savings accounts, CDs, and home equity loans, the bank is about as no-frills as it gets. Yet its profits are downright gaudy, soaring 45 percent just last year. ING's secret? Selective relationship management. The bank lures low-maintenance customers with high interest rates. Then, to offset that generosity, the bank does 75 percent of its transactions online, avoids amenities like checking, and offers bare-bones service. In fact, ING routinely "fires" overly demanding customers. By ditching clients who are too time-consuming,

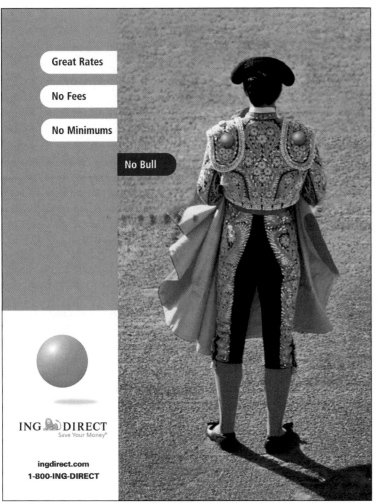

Great Rates

No Fees

No Minimums

No Bull

ING DIRECT
Save Your Money®

ingdirect.com
1-800-ING-DIRECT

■ Selective relationship management: ING Direct seeks relationships with customers who don't need or want expensive pampering, routinely "firing" overly demanding customers. The bank lures low-maintenance customers with high interest rates and no fees or minimums. "No bull!"

the company has driven its cost per account to a third of the industry average.

CEO Arkadi Kuhlmann explains: "We need to keep expenses down, which doesn't work when customers want a lot of [hand-holding]. If the average customer phone call costs us $5.25 and the average account revenue is $12 per month, all it takes is 100,000 misbehaving customers for costs to go through the roof. So when a customer calls too many times or wants too many exceptions to the rule, our sales associate can basically say: Look, this doesn't fit you. You need to go back to your community bank and get the kind of contact you're comfortable with. . . . It's all about finding customers who are comfortable with a self-serve business; we try to get you in and out fast. . . . Even though our touch is light and short, it's all about how you feel in the end. The smile at a take-out window can be just as satisfying as good service at a sit-down restaurant. While this makes for some unhappy customers, [those are the] ones you want out the door anyway."

Relating for the Long Term   Just as companies are being more selective about which customers they choose to serve, they are serving chosen customers in a deeper, more lasting way. Today's companies are going beyond designing strategies to *attract* new customers and create *transactions* with them. They are using customer relationship management to *retain* current customers and build profitable, long-term *relationships* with them. The new view is that marketing is the science and art of finding, retaining, *and* growing profitable customers.

Why the new emphasis on retaining and growing customers? In the past, growing markets and an upbeat economy meant a plentiful supply of new customers. However, companies today face some new marketing realities. Changing demographics, more sophisticated competitors, and overcapacity in many industries mean that there are fewer customers to go around. Many companies are now fighting for shares of flat or fading markets.

As a result, the costs of attracting new consumers are rising. In fact, on average, it can cost 5 to 10 times as much to attract a new customer as it does to keep a current customer satisfied. Sears found that it costs 12 times more to attract a customer than to keep an existing one. Given these new realities, companies now go all out to keep profitable customers.[14]

Relating Directly   Beyond connecting more deeply with their customers, many companies are also connecting more *directly*. In fact, direct marketing is booming. Consumers can now buy virtually any product without going to a store—by telephone, mail-order catalogs, kiosks, and online. Business purchasing agents routinely shop on the Web for items ranging from standard office supplies to high-priced, high-tech computer equipment.

Some companies sell *only* via direct channels—firms such as Dell, Expedia, and Amazon.com, to name only a few. Other companies use direct connections to supplement their other communications and distribution channels. For example, Sony sells PlayStation consoles and game cartridges through retailers, supported by millions of dollars of mass-media advertising. However, Sony uses its Web site (www.PlayStation.com) to build relationships with game players of all ages. The site offers information about the latest games, news about events and promotions, game guides and support, and even online forums in which game players can swap tips and stories.

Some marketers have hailed direct marketing as the "marketing model of the next century." They envision a day when all buying and selling will involve direct connections between companies and their customers. Others, although agreeing that direct marketing will play a growing and important role, see it as just one more way to approach the marketplace. We will take a closer look at the world of direct marketing in Chapters 13 and 14.

PARTNER RELATIONSHIP MANAGEMENT

When it comes to creating customer value and building strong customer relationships, today's marketers know that they can't go it alone. They must work closely with a variety of marketing partners. In addition to being good at *customer relationship management*, marketers must also be good at **partner relationship management**. Major changes are occurring in how marketers partner with others inside and outside the company to jointly bring more value to customers.

Partner relationship management
Working closely with partners in other company departments and outside the company to jointly bring greater value to customers.

Partners Inside the Company   Traditionally, marketers have been charged with understanding customers and representing customer needs to different company departments. The old thinking was that marketing is done only by marketing, sales, and customer support people. However, in today's more connected world, marketing no longer has sole ownership of customer interactions. Every functional area can interact with customers, especially electronically. The new thinking is that every employee must be customer focused. David Packard, late cofounder of Hewlett-Packard, wisely said, "Marketing is far too important to be left only to the marketing department."[15]

Today, rather than letting each department go its own way, firms are linking all departments in the cause of creating customer value. Rather than assigning only sales and marketing people to customers, they are forming cross-functional customer teams. For example, P&G assigns "customer development teams" to each of its major retailer accounts. These teams—consisting of sales and marketing people, operations specialists, market and financial analysts, and others—coordinate the efforts of many P&G departments toward helping the retailer be more successful.

Marketing Partners Outside the Firm   Changes are also occurring in how marketers connect with their suppliers, channel partners, and even competitors. Most companies today are networked companies, relying heavily on partnerships with other firms.

Marketing channels consist of distributors, retailers, and others who connect the company to its buyers. The *supply chain* describes a longer channel, stretching from raw materials to components to final products that are carried to final buyers. For example, the supply chain for personal computers consists of suppliers of computer chips and other components; the computer manufacturer; and the distributors, retailers, and others who sell the computers.

Through *supply chain management*, many companies today are strengthening their connections with partners all along the supply chain. They know that their fortunes rest not just on how well they perform. Success at building customer relationships also rests on how well their entire supply chain performs against competitors' supply chains. These companies don't just treat suppliers as vendors and distributors as customers. They treat both as partners in delivering customer value. On the one hand, for example, Lexus works closely with carefully selected suppliers to improve quality and operations efficiency. On the other hand, it works with its franchise dealers to provide top-grade sales and service support that will bring customers in the door and keep them coming back.

Beyond managing the supply chain, today's companies are also discovering that they need *strategic* partners if they hope to be effective. In the new, more competitive global environment, going it alone is going out of style. *Strategic alliances* are booming across almost all industries and services. For example, Dell joins forces with software creators such as Oracle and Microsoft to help boost business sales of its servers and their software. And Volkswagen is working jointly with agricultural processing firm Archer Daniels Midland to further develop and utilize biodiesel fuel.

Sometimes, even competitors work together for mutual benefit. For example, oral-care competitors Procter & Gamble and Philips joined forces to create the innovative

■ Partnership relationship management: Both Netflix and Wal-Mart benefit from their DVD-rental partnership. Wal-Mart promotes Netflix's service. In return, Netflix provides links advertising DVD sales on Wal-Mart.com.

IntelliClean system, a combination power toothbrush and toothpaste dispensing system. And Wal-Mart and Netflix partnered to their mutual benefit:

> Wal-Mart initially developed its own online and mail-order DVD-rental service business, competing with industry pioneer Netflix and late-comers Blockbuster and Amazon.com. However, after achieving lackluster results, the giant retailer recently turned its DVD rental service over to Netflix. Both Wal-Mart and Netflix gain from this partnership. Wal-Mart will promote the Netflix service. In return, Netflix will provide links advertising DVD sales on Wal-Mart.com. Thus, the agreement bolsters both Netflix's leadership in DVD movie rentals and Wal-Mart's strong movie sales business, while also providing customers even more choices and convenience.[16]

As Jim Kelly, former CEO at UPS, puts it, "The old adage 'If you can't beat 'em, join 'em', is being replaced by 'Join 'em and you can't be beat.' "[17]

Capturing Value from Customers

The first four steps in the marketing process involve building customer relationships by creating and delivering superior customer value. The final step involves capturing value in return, in the form of current and future sales, market share, and profits. By creating superior customer value, the firm creates highly satisfied customers who stay loyal and buy more. This, in turn, means greater long-run returns for the firm. Here, we discuss the outcomes of creating customer value: customer loyalty and retention, share of market and share of customer, and customer equity.

CREATING CUSTOMER LOYALTY AND RETENTION

Good customer relationship management creates customer delight. In turn, delighted customers remain loyal and talk favorably to others about the company and its products. Studies show big differences in the loyalty of customers who are less satisfied, somewhat satisfied, and completely satisfied. Even a slight drop from complete satisfaction can create an enormous drop in loyalty. Thus, the aim of customer relationship management is to create not just customer satisfaction, but customer delight.[18]

Companies are realizing that losing a customer means losing more than a single sale. It means losing the entire stream of purchases that the customer would make over a lifetime of patronage. For example, here is a dramatic illustration of **customer lifetime value**:

> Stew Leonard, who operates a highly profitable four-store supermarket in Connecticut and New York, says that he sees $50,000 flying out of his store every time he sees a sulking customer. Why? Because his average customer spends about $100 a week, shops 50 weeks a year, and remains in the area for about 10 years. If this customer has an unhappy experience and switches to another supermarket, Stew Leonard's has lost $50,000 in revenue. The loss can be much greater if the disappointed customer shares the bad experience with other customers and causes them to defect. To keep customers coming back, Stew Leonard's has created what the *New York Times* has dubbed the "Disneyland of Dairy Stores," complete with costumed characters, scheduled entertainment, a petting zoo, and animatronics throughout the store. From its humble beginnings as a small dairy store in 1969, Stew Leonard's has grown at an amazing pace. It's built 29 additions onto the original store, which now

Customer lifetime value
The value of the entire stream of purchases that the customer would make over a lifetime of patronage.

serves more than 250,000 customers each week. This legion of loyal shoppers is largely a result of the store's passionate approach to customer service. Rule #1 at Stew Leonard's—The customer is always right. Rule #2—If the customer is ever wrong, reread rule #1![19]

Stew Leonard is not alone in assessing customer lifetime value. Lexus estimates that a single satisfied and loyal customer is worth $600,000 in lifetime sales. The customer lifetime value of a Taco Bell customer exceeds $12,000.[20] Thus, working to retain and grow customers makes good economic sense. In fact, a company can lose money on a specific transaction but still benefit greatly from a long-term relationship.

This means that companies must aim high in building customer relationships. Customer delight creates an emotional relationship with a product or service, not just a rational preference. L.L.Bean, long known for its outstanding customer service and high customer loyalty, preaches the following "golden rule": Sell good merchandise, treat your customers like human beings, and they'll always come back for more." Hanging on to customers is "so basic, it's scary," claims one marketing executive. "We find out what our customers' needs and wants are, and then we overdeliver."[21]

■ Customer lifetime value: To keep customers coming back, Stew Leonard's has created the "Disneyland of dairy stores." Rule #1—The customer is always right. Rule #2—If the customer is ever wrong, reread Rule #1.

GROWING SHARE OF CUSTOMER

Beyond simply retaining good customers to capture customer lifetime value, good customer relationship management can help marketers to increase their **share of customer**—the share they get of the customer's purchasing in their product categories. Thus, banks want to increase "share of wallet." Supermarkets and restaurants want to get more "share of stomach." Car companies want to increase "share of garage" and airlines want greater "share of travel."

To increase share of customer, firms can offer greater variety to current customers. Or they can train employees to cross-sell and up-sell in order to market more products and services to existing customers. For example, Amazon.com is highly skilled at leveraging relationships with its 45 million customers to increase its share of each customer's purchases. Originally an online bookseller, Amazon.com now offers customers music, videos, gifts, toys, consumer electronics, office products, home improvement items, lawn and garden products, apparel and accessories, jewelry, and an online auction. In addition, based on each customer's purchase history, the company recommends related products that might be of interest. In this way, Amazon.com captures a greater share of each customer's spending budget.

Share of customer
The portion of the customer's purchasing that a company gets in its product categories.

BUILDING CUSTOMER EQUITY

We can now see the importance of not just acquiring customers, but of keeping and growing them as well. One marketing consultant puts it this way: "The only value your company will ever create is the value that comes from customers—the ones you have now and the ones you will have in the future. Without customers, you don't have a business."[22] Customer relationship management takes a long-term view. Companies want not only to create profitable customers, but to "own" them for life, capture their customer lifetime value, and earn a greater share of their purchases.

What Is Customer Equity? The ultimate aim of customer relationship management is to produce high *customer equity*.[23] **Customer equity** is the combined discounted customer lifetime values of all of the company's current and potential customers. Clearly, the more loyal the firm's profitable customers, the higher the firm's customer equity. Customer equity may

Customer equity
The total combined customer lifetime values of all of the company's customers.

be a better measure of a firm's performance than current sales or market share. Whereas sales and market share reflect the past, customer equity suggests the future. Consider Cadillac:

> In the 1970s and 1980s, Cadillac had some of the most loyal customers in the industry. To an entire generation of car buyers, the name "Cadillac" defined American luxury. Cadillac's share of the luxury car market reached a whopping 51 percent in 1976. Based on market share and sales, the brand's future looked rosy. However, measures of customer equity would have painted a bleaker picture. Cadillac customers were getting older (average age 60) and average customer lifetime value was falling. Many Cadillac buyers were on their last car. Thus, although Cadillac's market share was good, its customer equity was not.
>
> Compare this with BMW. Its more youthful and vigorous image didn't win BMW the early market share war. However, it did win BMW younger customers with higher customer lifetime values. The result: In the years that followed, BMW's market share and profits soared while Cadillac's fortunes eroded badly. Thus, market share is not the answer. We should care not just about current sales but also about future sales. Customer lifetime value and customer equity are the name of the game. Recognizing this, Cadillac has become cool again by targeting a younger generation of consumers with new high-performance models and its highly successful Break Through advertising campaign.[24]

Building the Right Relationships with the Right Customers   Companies should manage customer equity carefully. They should view customers as assets that need to be managed and maximized. But not all customers, not even all loyal customers, are good investments. Surprisingly, some loyal customers can be unprofitable, and some disloyal customers can be profitable. Which customers should the company acquire and retain? "Up to a point, the choice is obvious: Keep the consistent big spenders and lose the erratic small spenders," says one expert. "But what about the erratic big spenders and the consistent small spenders? It's often unclear whether they should be acquired or retained, and at what cost."[25]

The company can classify customers according to their potential profitability and manage its relationships with them accordingly. Figure 1.5 classifies customers into one of four relationship groups, according to their profitability and projected loyalty.[26] Each group requires a different relationship management strategy. "Strangers" show low profitability and little projected loyalty. There is little fit between the company's offerings and their needs. The relationship management strategy for these customers is simple: Don't invest anything in them.

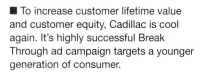
■ To increase customer lifetime value and customer equity, Cadillac is cool again. It's highly successful Break Through ad campaign targets a younger generation of consumer.

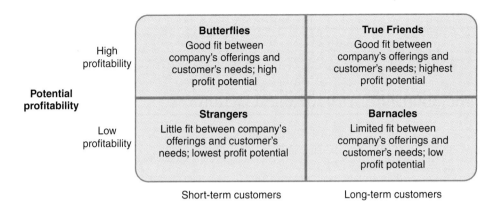

FIGURE 1.5
Customer Relationship Groups

Source: Reprinted by permission of *Harvard Business Review.* Adapted from "The Mismanagement of Customer Loyalty" by Werner Relnartz and V. Kumar, July 2002, p. 93. Copyright © by the president and fellows of Harvard College; all rights reserved.

"Butterflies" are profitable but not loyal. There is a good fit between the company's offerings and their needs. However, like real butterflies, we can enjoy them for only a short while and then they're gone. An example is stock market investors who trade shares often and in large amounts, but who enjoy hunting out the best deals without building a regular relationship with any single brokerage company. Efforts to convert butterflies into loyal customers are rarely successful. Instead, the company should enjoy the butterflies for the moment. It should use promotional blitzes to attract them, create satisfying and profitable transactions with them, and then cease investing in them until the next time around.

"True friends" are both profitable and loyal. There is a strong fit between their needs and the company's offerings. The firm wants to make continuous relationship investments to delight these customers and nurture, retain, and grow them. It wants to turn true friends into "true believers," who come back regularly and tell others about their good experiences with the company.

"Barnacles" are highly loyal but not very profitable. There is a limited fit between their needs and the company's offerings. An example is smaller bank customers who bank regularly but do not generate enough returns to cover the costs of maintaining their accounts. Like barnacles on the hull of a ship, they create drag. Barnacles are perhaps the most problematic customers. The company might be able to improve their profitability by selling them more, raising their fees, or reducing service to them. However, if they cannot be made profitable, they should be "fired" (see Marketing at Work 1.2).

The point here is an important one: Different types of customer require different relationship management strategies. The goal is to build the *right relationships* with the *right customers.*

 Linking the Concepts

We've covered a lot of territory. Again, slow down for a moment and develop *your own* thoughts about marketing.

- In *your own words*, what *is* marketing and what does it seek to accomplish?
- How well does Lexus manage its relationships with its customers? What customer relationship management strategy does it use? What relationship management strategy does Wal-Mart use?
- Think of a company for which you are a "true friend." What strategy does this company use to manage its relationship with you?

The New Marketing Landscape

As the world spins on, dramatic changes are occurring in the marketplace. Richard Love of Hewlett-Packard observes, "The pace of change is so rapid that the ability to change has now become a competitive advantage." Yogi Berra, the legendary New York Yankees catcher, summed it up more simply when he said, "The future ain't what it used to be." As the marketplace changes, so must those who serve it.

MARKETING AT WORK 1.2

Best Buy: Building the Right Relationships with the Right Customers

"The customer is always right." Right? After all, that slogan has become the guiding principle of most successful marketing firms. But these days, more and more marketers are discovering a new truth: Some customers can be way, way wrong—as in unprofitable. Increasingly, these companies are taking special care of their profitable customers while shunning those they lose money on.

Consider Best Buy, the nation's leading consumer electronics retailer. Since its humble beginnings in 1966 as a small Minnesota home and car stereo chain, Best Buy has transformed itself into a profitable 825-store, $25-billion mega-retailer. Today's Best Buy stores are huge, warehouse-like emporiums featuring a treasure trove of goods—from consumer electronics, home office equipment, and appliances, to software, CDs, and DVDs—all at low discount prices.

Despite the company's success, however, Best Buy now faces storm clouds on the horizon. Wal-Mart, the world's largest retailer, and Dell, the largest computer maker, are rapidly encroaching on Best Buy's profitable consumer electronics turf. In 1997, neither of these competitors even appeared on the list of top consumer electronics retailers. By 2003, however, Wal-Mart had shot up to the number-two position, with $15.7 billion in consumer electronics sales versus Best Buy's $19.5 billion. Dell was in fourth place with $6.3 billion. Best Buy CEO Brad Anderson fears that Best Buy could end up in what retailers call the "unprofitable middle," unable to compete against Wal-Mart's massive buying power for price-sensitive store

shoppers or against Dell's direct model for more affluent online customers.

To better differentiate itself in this more crowded marketplace, Best Buy has rolled out a new strategy designed to better identify and serve its best customers. The strategy draws on the research of consultant Larry Selden, a Columbia University business professor. Selden argues that a company should see itself as a portfolio of *customers*, not product lines. His research has identified two basic types of customers: angels and demons. Angel cus-

tomers are profitable, whereas demon customers may actually cost a company more to serve than it makes from them. In fact, Selden claims, serving the demons often wipes out the profits earned by serving the angels.

Following this logic, Best Buy assigned a task force to analyze its customers' purchasing habits. Sure enough, the analysts found a host of angels—some 20 percent of Best Buy's customers who produced the bulk of its profits. According to the *Wall Street Journal:* "Best Buy's angels are customers who boost profits at the

■ Best Buy's customer-centricity strategy: Serve the angel customers while exorcizing the demons. Stores targeting upper-income "Barrys" steer them into comfy areas that mimic media rooms popular with home-theater fans.

In this section, we examine the major trends and forces that are changing the marketing landscape and challenging marketing strategy. We look at four major developments: the new digital age, rapid globalization, the call for more ethics and social responsibility, and the growth in not-for-profit marketing.

THE NEW DIGITAL AGE

The recent technology boom has created a new digital age. The explosive growth in computer, telecommunications, information, transportation, and other technologies has had a major impact on the ways companies bring value to their customers.

consumer-electronics giant by snapping up high-definition televisions, portable electronics, and newly released DVDs without waiting for markdowns or rebates."

The task force also found demons: "The [demons are Best Buy's] worst customers . . . the underground of bargain-hungry shoppers intent on wringing every nickel of savings out of the big retailer. They buy products, apply for rebates, return the purchases, then buy them back at returned-merchandise discounts. They load up on 'loss leaders', severely discounted merchandise designed to boost store traffic, then flip the goods at a profit on eBay. They slap down rock-bottom price quotes from Web sites and demand that Best Buy make good on its lowest-price pledge." CEO Anderson learned that these demon customers could account for up to 100 million of Best Buy's 500 million customer visits each year. "They can wreak enormous economic havoc," he says.

So, after deciding that the customer was *not* always right, Anderson set out to ditch the demon customers. In 2004, Best Buy started testing a "Customer Centricity" strategy in 100 of its stores. It began by combing through these stores' sales records and customer databases to distinguish between good and bad customers. To attract the angels, the stores began stocking more merchandise and offering better service to them. For example, the stores set up digital photo centers and a "Geek Squad," which offers one-on-one in-store or at-home computer assistance to high-value buyers. It established a Reward Zone loyalty program, in which regular customers can earn points toward discounts on future purchases. To discourage the demons, it removed them from its marketing lists, reduced the promotions and other sales tactics that tended to attract them, and installed a 15-percent restocking fee.

However, Best Buy didn't stop there. Customer analysis revealed that its best customers fell into five groups: "Barrys," high-income men; "Jills," suburban moms; "Buzzes," male technology enthusiasts; "Rays," young family men on a budget; and small business owners. The company instructed each Customer Centricity store to analyze the customers in its market area and to align its product and service mix to reflect the make-up of these customers. Further, it trained store clerks in the art of serving the angels and exorcising the demons.

Store clerks receive hours of training in identifying desirable customers according to their shopping preferences and behavior. [At one store targeting upper-income Barrys] . . . blue-shirted sales clerks prowl the DVD aisles looking for promising candidates. The goal is to steer them into a back room that showcases $12,000 high-definition home-theater systems. Unlike the television sections at most Best Buy stores, the room has easy chairs, a leather couch, and a basket of popcorn to mimic the media rooms popular with home-theater fans. At stores popular with young Buzzes, Best Buy is setting up videogame areas with leather chairs and game players hooked to mammoth, plasma-screen televisions. The games are conveniently stacked outside the playing area, the glitzy new TVs a short stroll away.

Will Best Buy's new strategy work? Anderson realizes that his unconventional strategy is risky and that Best Buy must be careful. For one thing, tailoring store formats to fit local customers is expensive—the costs in the test stores have been about one percent to two percent higher. Moreover, shunning customers—good or bad—can be very risky. "The most dangerous image I can think of is a retailer that wants to fire customers," he notes—before letting them go, Best Buy first tries to turn its bad customers into profitable ones. "The trickiest challenge may be to deter bad customers without turning off good ones," observes an industry analyst. However, early results show the Customer Centricity test stores have "clobbered" the traditional Best Buy stores—posting sales gains more than triple those of stores with conventional formats. The company is now converting additional stores to the new format.

So, is the customer always right? Not necessarily. While this might hold true for a company's best customers, it simply doesn't apply to others. As one marketer put it, "The customer is always right, but they aren't all the right customers." Best Buy knows that the goal is to develop the best customer portfolio, one built on the right relationships with the right customers.

Sources: Quotes and extracts from Gary McWilliams, "Analyzing Customers, Best Buy Decides Not All Are Welcome," *Wall Street Journal*, November 8, 2004, p. A1. Additional information from Laura Heller, "At Crossroads, Best Buy Charges Ahead with Customer Centricity," *DSN Retailing Today*, January 10, 2005, p.13; Larry Selden and Geoffrey Colvin, *Angel Customers and Demon Customers: Discover Which Is Which and Turbo-Charge Your Stock* (New York: Penguin Group, 2003); Joshua Freed, "The Customer Is Always Right? Not Anymore," July 5, 2004, accessed at www.sfgate.com; Laura Heller, "Doing to Demographics What's Never Been Done Before," *DSN Retailing Today*, September 6, 2004, p. 44; "Best Buy Co., Inc.," Hoovers Company Records, April 15, 2005, p. 10209; and Gary McWilliams and Steven Gray, "Slimming Down Stores," *Wall Street Journal*, April 29, 2005, p. B1.

Now, more than ever before, we are all connected to each other and to things near and far in the world around us. Where it once took weeks or months to travel across the United States, we can now travel around the globe in only hours or days. Where it once took days or weeks to receive news about important world events, we now see them as they are occurring through live satellite broadcasts. Where it once took weeks to correspond with others in distant places, they are now only moments away by phone or the Internet.

The technology boom has created exciting new ways to learn about and track customers and to create products and services tailored to individual customer needs. Technology is also helping companies to distribute products more efficiently and effectively. And it's helping

■ The new digital age: The recent technology boom has had a major impact on the ways marketers connect and bring value to their customers.

Internet
A vast public web of computer networks, which connects users of all types all around the world to each other and to an amazingly large information repository.

them to communicate with customers in large groups or one-to-one.

Through videoconferencing, marketing researchers at a company's headquarters in New York can look in on focus groups in Chicago or Paris without ever stepping onto a plane. With only a few clicks of a mouse button, a direct marketer can tap into online data services to learn anything from what car you drive to what you read to what flavor of ice cream you prefer. Or, using today's powerful computers, marketers can create their own detailed customer databases and use them to target individual customers with offers designed to meet their specific needs.

Technology has also brought a new wave of communication and advertising tools—ranging from cell phones, fax machines, CDs, and interactive TVs to video kiosks at airports and shopping malls. Marketers can use these tools to zero in on selected customers with carefully targeted messages. Through e-commerce, customers can learn about, design, order, and pay for products and services, without ever leaving home. Then, through the marvels of express delivery, they can receive their purchases in less than 24 hours. From virtual reality displays that test new products to online virtual stores that sell them, the technology boom is affecting every aspect of marketing.

The Internet   Perhaps the most dramatic new technology is the **Internet**. Today, the Internet links individuals and businesses of all types to each other and to information all around the world. It allows anytime, anywhere connections to information, entertainment, and communication. Companies are using the Internet to build closer relationships with customers and marketing partners. Beyond competing in traditional market*places*, they now have access to exciting new market*spaces*.

The Internet has now become a truly global phenomenon. The number of Internet users worldwide is expected to reach almost 1.4 billion by 2007.[27] This growing and diverse Internet population means that all kinds of people are now going to the Web for information and to buy products and services.

These days, it's hard to find a company that doesn't use the Web in a significant way. Most traditional "brick-and-mortar" companies have now become "click-and-mortar" companies. They have ventured online to attract new customers and build stronger relationships with existing ones. The Internet also spawned an entirely new breed of "click-only" companies—the so-called "dot-coms." During the Web frenzy of the late 1990s, dot-coms popped up everywhere, selling anything from books, toys, and CDs, to furniture, home mortgages, and 100-pound bags of dog food via the Internet. The frenzy cooled during the "dot-com meltdown" of 2000, when many poorly conceived e-tailers and other Web start-ups went out of business. Today, despite its turbulent start, online consumer buying is growing at a healthy rate.

If consumer e-commerce looks promising, business-to-business e-commerce is just plain booming. Business-to-business (B2B) transactions were projected to reach $4.3 trillion this year, compared with only $107 billion in consumer purchases. It seems that almost every business has set up shop on the Web. Giants such as GE, IBM, Siemens, Microsoft, Dell, and many others have moved quickly to exploit the B2B power of the Internet.[28]

Thus, the technology boom is providing exciting new opportunities for marketers. We will explore the impact of the new digital age in more detail in Chapter 14.

RAPID GLOBALIZATION

As they are redefining their relationships with customers and partners, marketers are also taking a fresh look at the ways in which they connect with the broader world around them. In an increasingly smaller world, many marketers are now connected *globally* with their customers and marketing partners.

■ Many U.S. companies have developed truly global operations. Coca-Cola offers more than 400 different brands in more than 200 countries including BPM Energy drink in Ireland, Bitter Mare Rosso in Spain, Sprite Ice Cube in Belgium, Fanta in Chile, and NaturAqua in Hungary.

Today, almost every company, large or small, is touched in some way by global competition. A neighborhood florist buys its flowers from Mexican nurseries, while a large U.S. electronics manufacturer competes in its home markets with giant Japanese rivals. A fledgling Internet retailer finds itself receiving orders from all over the world at the same time that an American consumer-goods producer introduces new products into emerging markets abroad.

American firms have been challenged at home by the skillful marketing of European and Asian multinationals. Companies such as Toyota, Siemens, Nestlé, Sony, and Samsung have often outperformed their U.S. competitors in American markets. Similarly, U.S. companies in a wide range of industries have developed truly global operations, making and selling their products worldwide. Coca-Cola offers a mind-boggling 400 different brands in more than 200 countries. Even MTV has joined the elite of global brands, delivering localized versions of its pulse-thumping fare to teens in 164 countries around the globe.[29]

Today, companies are not only trying to sell more of their locally produced goods in international markets, they also are buying more supplies and components abroad. For example, Isaac Mizrahi, one of America's top fashion designers, may choose cloth woven from Australian wool with designs printed in Italy. He will design a dress and e-mail the drawing to a Hong Kong agent, who will place the order with a Chinese factory. Finished dresses will be air freighted to New York, where they will be redistributed to department and specialty stores around the country.

Thus, managers in countries around the world are increasingly taking a global, not just local, view of the company's industry, competitors, and opportunities. They are asking: What is global marketing? How does it differ from domestic marketing? How do global competitors and forces affect our business? To what extent should we "go global"? We will discuss the global marketplace in more detail in Chapter 15.

THE CALL FOR MORE ETHICS AND SOCIAL RESPONSIBILITY

Marketers are reexamining their relationships with social values and responsibilities and with the very Earth that sustains us. As the worldwide consumerism and environmentalism movements mature, today's marketers are being called on to take greater responsibility for the social and environmental impact of their actions. Corporate ethics and social responsibility have become hot topics for almost every business. And few companies can ignore the renewed and very demanding environmental movement.

The social-responsibility and environmental movements will place even stricter demands on companies in the future. Some companies resist these movements, budging only when forced by legislation or organized consumer outcries. More forward-looking companies, however, readily accept their responsibilities to the world around them. They view socially responsible actions as an opportunity to do well by doing good. They seek ways to profit by serving the best long-run interests of their customers and communities.

Some companies—such as Patagonia, Ben & Jerry's, Honest Tea, and others—are practicing "caring capitalism," setting themselves apart by being civic-minded and responsible. They are building social responsibility and action into their company value and mission statements. For example, when it comes to environmental responsibility, outdoor gear marketer Patagonia is "committed to the core." "Those of us who work here share a strong commitment to protecting undomesticated lands and waters," says the company's Web site. "We believe in using business to inspire solutions to the environmental crisis." Patagonia backs these words with actions. Each year it pledges at least 1 percent of its sales or 10 percent of its profits, whichever is greater, to the protection of the natural environment.[30] We will revisit the relationship between marketing and social responsibility in greater detail in Chapter 16.

THE GROWTH OF NOT-FOR-PROFIT MARKETING

In the past, marketing has been most widely applied in the for-profit business sector. In recent years, however, marketing also has become a major part of the strategies of many not-for-profit organizations, such as colleges, hospitals, museums, symphony orchestras, and even churches. Consider the following example:

"Want to feed your soul?" implores a subway ad for Marble Collegiate Church in New York City. "We've got a great menu." Indeed, Marble Collegiate has something on its plate for almost every type of spiritual consumer. It has ministries targeting senior citizens; young singles; older singles; gays and lesbians; entrepreneurs; artists, actors, and writers; men; women; children; and people who love singing gospel music, to name a few. Like many other religious institutions working to

■ Broadening connections: Marble Collegiate Church's advertising agency has produced ads with hip, youth-oriented messages.

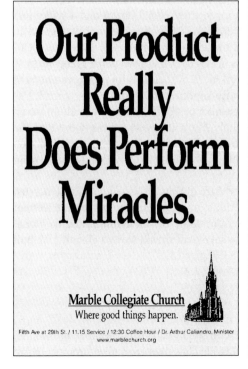

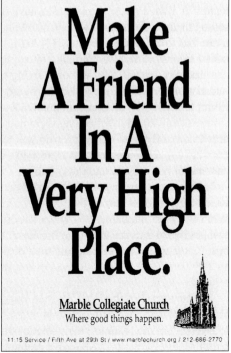

maintain their shrinking flocks, Marble Collegiate is borrowing marketing tools and tactics from companies selling more worldly goods. It is tailoring its "brand" and "core product"—religion itself—to the needs of spiritually minded people who may be wary of conventional religious organizations. To get its message out, it anointed a Madison Avenue advertising agency as its missionary. The agency produced a slick marketing campaign with hip, youth-oriented messages. One ad urges potential parishioners to "Make a friend in a very high place." Exhorts another: "Our product really does perform miracles." All the marketing seems to be working. Marble Collegiate's Web site traffic has increased by 30 percent since its ad campaign launched, and the church has had its highest attendance in more than 30 years.[31]

Similarly, private colleges, facing declining enrollments and rising costs, are using marketing to compete for students and funds. Many performing arts groups—even the Lyric Opera Company of Chicago, which has seasonal sellouts—face huge operating deficits that they must cover by more aggressive donor marketing. Finally, many long-standing not-for-profit organizations—the YMCA, the Salvation Army, the Girl Scouts—have lost members and are now modernizing their missions and "products" to attract more members and donors.[32]

Government agencies have also shown an increased interest in marketing. For example, the U.S. military has a marketing plan to attract recruits to its different services, and various government agencies are now designing *social marketing campaigns* to encourage energy conservation and concern for the environment or to discourage smoking, excessive drinking, and drug use. Even the once-stodgy U.S. Postal Service has developed innovative marketing to sell commemorative stamps, promote its priority mail services against those of its competitors, and lift its image. In all, the U.S. Government is the nation's twenty-eighth largest advertiser, with an annual advertising budget of more than $1 billion.[33]

So, What Is Marketing? Pulling It All Together

At the start of this chapter, Figure 1.1 presented a simple model of the marketing process. Now that we've discussed all of the steps in the process, Figure 1.6 presents an expanded model that will help you pull it all together. What is marketing? Simply put, marketing is the process of building profitable customer relationships by creating value for customers and capturing value in return.

The first four steps of the marketing process focus on creating value for customers. The company first gains a full understanding of the marketplace by researching customer needs and managing marketing information. It then designs a customer-driven marketing strategy based on the answers to two simple questions. The first question is "What consumers will we serve?" (market segmentation and targeting). Good marketing companies know that they cannot serve all customers in every way. Instead, they need to focus their resources on the customers they can serve best and most profitably. The second marketing strategy question is "How can we best serve targeted customers?" (differentiation and positioning). Here, the marketer outlines a value proposition that spells out what values the company will deliver in order to win target customers.

With its marketing strategy decided, the company now constructs a marketing program—consisting of the four marketing mix elements, or the four Ps—that transforms the marketing strategy into real value for customers. The company develops product offers and creates strong brand identities for them. It prices these offers to create real customer value and distributes the offers to make them available to target consumers. Finally, the company designs promotion programs that communicate the value proposition to target consumers and persuades them to act on the market offering.

Perhaps the most important step in the marketing process involves building value-laden, profitable relationships with target customers. Throughout the process, marketers practice customer relationship management to create customer satisfaction and delight. In creating customer value and relationships, however, the company cannot go it alone. It

FIGURE 1.6   An Expanded Model of the Marketing Process

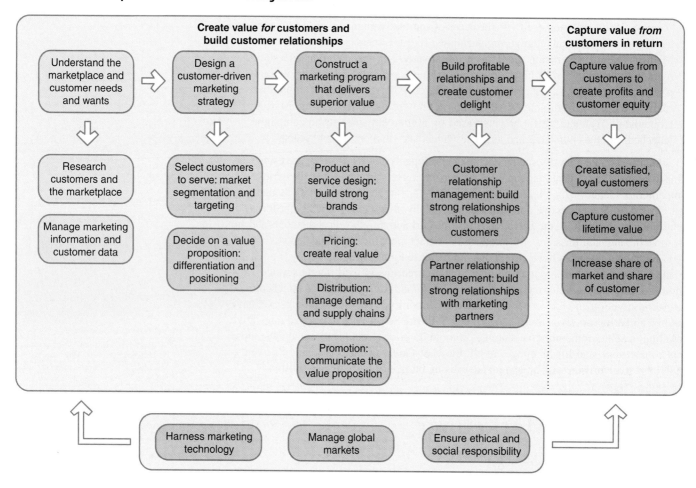

must work closely with marketing partners both inside the company and throughout the marketing system. Thus, beyond practicing good customer relationship management, firms must also practice good partner relationship management.

The first four steps in the marketing process create value *for* customers. In the final step, the company reaps the rewards of its strong customer relationships by capturing value *from* customers. Delivering superior customer value creates highly satisfied customers who will buy more and will buy again. This helps the company to capture customer lifetime value and greater share of customer. The result is increased long-term customer equity for the firm.

Finally, in the face of today's changing marketing landscape, companies must take into account three additional factors. In building customer and partner relationships, they must harness marketing technology, take advantage of global opportunities, and ensure that they act in an ethical and socially responsible way.

Figure 1.6 provides a good roadmap to future chapters of the text. Chapters 1 and 2 introduce the marketing process, with a focus on building customer relationships and capturing value from customers. Chapters 3, 4, and 5 address the first step of the marketing process—understanding the marketing environment, managing marketing information, and understanding consumer behavior. In Chapter 6, we look more deeply into the two major marketing strategy decisions: selecting which customers to serve (segmentation and targeting) and deciding on a value proposition (differentiation and positioning). Chapters 7 through 13 discuss the marketing mix variables, one by one. Then, the final three chapters examine the special marketing factors: marketing technology in the digital age, global marketing, and marketing ethics and social responsibility.

So, here we go, down the road to learning marketing. We hope you'll enjoy the journey!

REST STOP → REVIEWING THE CONCEPTS

Today's successful companies—whether large or small, for-profit or not-for-profit, domestic or global—share a strong customer focus and a heavy commitment to marketing. The goal of marketing is to build and manage profitable customer relationships. Marketing seeks to attract new customers by promising superior value and to keep and grow current customers by delivering satisfaction. Marketing operates within a dynamic global environment, which can quickly make yesterday's winning strategies obsolete. To be successful, companies will have to be strongly market focused.

1. Define *marketing* and outline the steps in the marketing process.

Marketing is the process by which companies create value for customers and build strong customer relationships in order to capture value from customers in return.

The marketing process involves five steps. The first four steps create value for customers. First, marketers need to understand the marketplace and customer needs and wants. Next, marketers design a customer-driven marketing strategy with the goal of getting, keeping, and growing target customers. In the third step, marketers construct a marketing program that actually delivers superior value. All of these steps form the basis for the fourth step, building profitable customer relationships and creating customer delight. In the final step, the company reaps the rewards of strong customer relationships by capturing value from customers.

2. Explain the importance of understanding customers and the marketplace, and identify the five core marketplace concepts.

Outstanding marketing companies go to great lengths to learn about and understand their customers' needs, wants, and demands. This understanding helps them to design want-satisfying market offerings and build value-laden customer relationships by which they can capture customer lifetime value and greater share of customer. The result is increased long-term customer equity for the firm.

The core marketplace concepts are needs, wants, and demands; market offerings (products, services, and experiences); value and satisfaction; exchange and relationships; and markets. Wants are the form taken by human needs when shaped by culture and individual personality. When backed by buying power, wants become demands. Companies address needs by putting forth a value proposition, a set of benefits that they promise to consumers to satisfy their needs. The value proposition is fulfilled through a market offering, which delivers customer value and satisfaction, resulting in long-term exchange relationships with customers.

3. Identify the key elements of a customer-driven marketing strategy and discuss marketing management orientations that guide marketing strategy.

To design a winning marketing strategy, the company must first decide *who* it will serve. It does this by dividing the market into segments of customers (*market segmentation*) and selecting which segments it will cultivate (*target marketing*). Next, the company must decide *how* it will serve targeted customers (how it will *differentiate and position* itself in the marketplace).

Marketing management can adopt one of five competing market orientations. The *production concept* holds that management's task is to improve production efficiency and bring down prices. The *product concept* holds that consumers favor products that offer the most in quality, performance, and innovative features; thus, little promotional effort is required. The *selling concept* holds that consumers will not buy enough of the organization's products unless it undertakes a large-scale selling and promotion effort. The *marketing concept* holds that achieving organizational goals depends on determining the needs and wants of target markets and delivering the desired satisfactions more effectively and efficiently than competitors do. The *societal marketing concept* holds that generating customer satisfaction *and* long-run societal well-being are the keys to both achieving the company's goals and fulfilling its responsibilities.

4. Discuss customer relationship management, and identify strategies for creating value for customers and capturing value from customers in return.

Broadly defined, *customer relationship management* is the process of building and maintaining profitable customer relationships by delivering superior customer value and satisfaction. The aim of customer relationship management is to produce high *customer equity*, the total combined customer lifetime values of all of the company's customers. The key to building lasting relationships is the creation of superior *customer value* and *satisfaction*.

Companies want not only to acquire profitable customers, but to build relationships that will keep then and grow "share of customer." Different types of customer require different customer relationship management strategies. The marketer's aim is to build the *right relationships* with the *right customers*. In return for creating value *for* targeted customers, the company captures value *from* customers in the form of profits and customer equity.

In building customer relationships, good marketers realize that they cannot go it alone. They must work closely with marketing partners inside and outside the company. In addition to being good at customer relationship management, they must also be good at *partner relationship management*.

5. Describe the major trends and forces that are changing the marketing landscape in this new age of relationships.

As the world spins on, dramatic changes are occurring in the marketing arena. The boom in computer, telecommunications, information, transportation, and other technologies has created exciting new ways to learn about and track customers, and to create products and services tailored to individual customer needs.

In an increasingly smaller world, many marketers are now connected *globally* with their customers and marketing partners. Today, almost every company, large or small, is touched in some way by global competition. Today's marketers are also reexamining their ethical and societal responsibilities. Marketers are being called upon to take greater responsibility for the social and environmental impact of their actions. Finally, in the past, marketing has been most widely applied in the for-profit business sector. In recent years, however, marketing also has become a major part of the strategies of many not-for-profit organizations, such as colleges, hospitals, museums, symphony orchestras, and even churches.

Pulling it all together, as discussed throughout the chapter, the major new developments in marketing can be summed up in a single word: *relationships*. Today, marketers of all kinds are taking advantage of new opportunities for building relationships with their customers, their marketing partners, and the world around them.

Navigating the Key Terms

Customer equity (21)
Customer lifetime value (20)
Customer perceived value (14)
Customer relationship management (14)
Customer satisfaction (14)
Demands (6)
Exchange (8)
Internet (26)

Market (8)
Marketing (6)
Marketing concept (11)
Marketing management (9)
Marketing myopia (7)
Market offering (7)
Needs (6)

Partner relationship management (19)
Product concept (10)
Production concept (10)
Selling concept (10)
Share of customer (21)
Societal marketing concept (12)
Wants (6)

Travel Log

Discussing the Issues

1. Review the definitions of marketing discussed at the beginning of the chapter. Which definition most closely aligned with your own definition of marketing before you read the chapter? Why?

2. Why is understanding customer wants so critical for marketers? How are the concepts of value and satisfaction related to each other? Explain the difference between transactions and relationships.

3. Why is target market selection important for a customer-driven marketing strategy? How might target market selection impact customer satisfaction?

4. Compare and contrast the marketing concept and the societal marketing concept. Do you agree that marketers have an obligation to consider society's long-run well-being when creating marketing offers?

5. How does a company benefit from building relationships with its customers and partners? What are some ways in which a company can build more profitable customer relationships?

6. What recent changes in the marketing landscape do you think have had the most significant impact on creating customer value and building marketing relationships?

Application Questions

1. Consumers usually choose from a tremendous variety of products and services to satisfy a given need or want. Consider your need for nourishment. How does that need translate into different wants? What marketing offers are available to satisfy your needs that also appeal to your wants? How might other consumers in different market segments meet the same need for nourishment?

2. Companies measuring customer lifetime value determine the potential profit from the stream of purchases a customer makes throughout a lifetime of patronage. When banks began tracking the profitability of individual customers, some found that a subset of their customers actually cost them money, rather than generating profits. Should banks "fire" their unprofitable customers? What are the consequences

of such an action? How might considering the lifetime value of a customer impact a bank's perspective on these customers? How might eliminating unprofitable customers affect a bank's customer equity both positively and negatively?

3. Think of a company in your town with which you have a relationship. Review Figure 1.5. Which relationship group do you fall into? What value do you get from the relationship, and how does that company capture value from you in return?

Under the Hood: Focus on Technology

Building customer relationships that lead to customer satisfaction is the key to good marketing. For many companies, customer relationship management depends not only on the employees who interact with customers but also on software. CRM software tracks each customer's interaction with the company across a variety of business lines in multiple locations. By combining bits of information from all customer "touchpoints," companies try to maximize the value delivered by the next customer interaction. In addition, by using CRM software, marketers can make educated guesses about a customer's lifetime value and the company's customer equity.

1. Visit www.crm2day.com to learn more about how marketers rely on software to build relationships with customers. What are some of the potential downsides to managing relationships using databases?

2. Can software really help marketers manage customer relationships?

3. How might marketers use CRM software to help grow share of customer?

Focus on Ethics

The marketing concept focuses on satisfying customer's needs and wants, but what if doing so places the consumer at risk? Although marketed and sold legally, the health impacts of tobacco and alcohol are well known. In addition, the impact of poor nutrition has recently come into the national spotlight. More specifically, the Food and Drug Administration (FDA) has issued warnings about the level of trans-fatty acids present in some food products. In response, companies including McDonald's, Kraft Foods, and Frito-lay, have recently been re-evaluating their products and making changes. For example, McDonald's now offers either french fries or a bag of sliced fruit with each Happy Meal.

1. What ethical responsibilities do companies producing products that have potentially adverse health effects have to consumers?

2. Can a company truly consider the long-term welfare of the consumer and of society while also maximizing profits?

3. Break into small groups. Divide into teams within each group and debate whether or not marketing potentially unhealthy products is ethical.

Videos

The Harley-Davidson video case that accompanies this chapter is located in Appendix 1 at the back of the book.

➡️ **AFTER STUDYING THIS CHAPTER, YOU SHOULD BE ABLE TO**

1. explain companywide strategic planning and its four steps
2. discuss how to design business portfolios and develop growth strategies
3. explain marketing's role in strategic planning and how marketing works with its partners to create and deliver customer value
4. describe the elements of a customer-driven marketing strategy and mix, and the forces that influence it
5. list the marketing management functions, including the elements of a marketing plan, and discuss the importance of measuring and managing return on marketing

Company and Marketing Strategy: Partnering to Build Customer Relationships

Road Map Previewing the Concepts

Ready to travel on? In the first chapter, we explored the marketing process by which companies create value for consumers in order to capture value in return. On this leg of our journey, we dig deeper into steps two and three of the marketing process—designing customer-driven marketing strategies and constructing marketing programs. To begin, we look at the organization's overall strategic planning. Next, we discuss how marketers, guided by the strategic plan, work closely with others inside and outside the firm to serve customers. We then examine marketing strategy and planning—how marketers choose target markets, position their market offerings, develop a marketing mix, and manage their marketing programs. Finally, we look at the important step of measuring and managing return on marketing investment.

First stop: Nike. During the past several decades, Nike has forever changed the rules of sports marketing strategy. In the process, it has built the Nike swoosh into one of the world's best-known brand symbols. But the Nike we know today is far, far different from the brash young start-up company of 40 years ago. As Nike has grown and matured—moving from maverick to mainstream—its marketing strategy has matured as well. To stay on top in the intensely competitive sports apparel business, Nike will have to keep finding fresh ways to bring value to its customers.

The Nike "swoosh"—it's everywhere! Just for fun, try counting the swooshes whenever you pick up the sports pages or watch a pickup basketball game or tune into a televised golf match. Through innovative marketing, Nike has built the ever-present swoosh into one of the best-known brand symbols on the planet. But 40-some years ago, when young CPA Phil Knight and college track coach Bill Bowerman cofounded the company, Nike was just a brash, young upstart in the athletic footwear industry.

In those early days, Knight and Bowerman ran Nike by the seat of their pants. In 1964, the pair chipped in $500 apiece to start Blue Ribbon Sports. In 1970, Bowerman dreamed up a new sneaker tread by stuffing a piece of rubber into his wife's waffle iron. The Waffle Trainer quickly became the nation's best-selling training shoe. In 1972, the company became Nike, named after the Greek goddess of victory. The swoosh was designed by a graduate student for a fee of $35. By 1979, Nike owned 50 percent of the U.S. running shoe market. It all seemed easy then. Running was in, sneakers were hot, and Nike had the right stuff.

During the 1980s, under Phil Knight's leadership, Nike revolutionized sports marketing. To build its brand image and market share, Nike spent lavishly on big-name endorsements, splashy promotional events, and in-your-face "Just Do It" ads. At Nike, however, good marketing meant more than just promotional hype and promises—it meant consistently building strong relationships with customers based on real value. Nike's initial success resulted from the technical superiority of its running and basketball shoes. To this day, Nike leads the industry in research-and-development spending.

But Nike gave customers much more than good athletic gear. Customers didn't just wear their Nikes, they *experienced* them. As the company stated on its Web page (www.nike.com), "Nike has always known the truth—it's not so much the shoes, but where they take you." Beyond shoes, apparel, and equipment, Nike marketed a way of life, a sports culture, a just-do-it attitude. As Phil Knight said at the time: "Basically, our culture and our style is to be a rebel." The company was built on a genuine passion for sports, a maverick disregard for convention, and a belief in hard work and serious sports performance.

Throughout the 1980s and 1990s, still playing the role of the upstart underdog, Nike sprinted ahead of its competition. Between 1988 and 1997, Nike's revenues grew at an annual rate of 21 percent; annual return to investors averaged an eye-popping 47 percent. Nike leveraged its brand strength, moving aggressively into new product categories, sports, and regions of the world. The company slapped its familiar swoosh logo on everything from sunglasses and soccer balls to batting gloves and hockey sticks. Nike invaded a dozen new sports, including baseball, golf, ice and street hockey, skateboarding, wall climbing, and hiking. It seemed that things couldn't be going any better.

In the late 1990s, however, Nike stumbled and its sales slipped. The whole industry suffered a setback, as a "brown shoe" craze for hiking and outdoor shoe styles ate into the athletic sneaker business. Moreover, Nike's creative juices seemed to run dry. Ho-hum new sneaker designs collected dust on retailer shelves as buyers seeking a new look switched to competing brands. To make matters worse, Nike was fighting off allegations that it was overcommercializing sports and exploiting child labor in Asian sweatshops.

But Nike's biggest obstacle may have been its own incredible success. The brand appeared to suffer from big-brand backlash, and the swoosh may have become too common to be cool. As sales moved past the $10 billion mark, Nike moved from maverick to mainstream. Rooting for Nike was like rooting for Microsoft. Instead of antiestablishment, Nike *was* the establishment. Once the brat of sports marketing, Nike now had to grow up and act its age.

And grow up it has. In recent years, Nike's marketing strategy has matured. The company still spends hundreds of millions of dollars each year on very creative advertising, innovative brand-building promotions, and big-name endorsers. For example, Nike signed basketball phenom LeBron James to a $90 million endorsement contract a few years back, and in the Athens Olympics, Nike athletes brought home 50 gold medals plus dozens more silver and bronze. But Nike has toned down its antiestablishment attitude—its marketing is a bit less edgy. And the company is now devoting much more attention to mundane marketing details. "Gone are the days when Nike execs, working on little more than hunches, would do just about anything and spend just about any amount in the quest for publicity and market share," says one Nike observer. "More and more, Nike is searching for the right balance between its creative and its business sides, relying on a newfound financial and managerial discipline to drive growth."

The new Nike has returned to the basics—focusing on innovation, methodically assessing new market opportunities, developing new product lines, and reworking its information and distribution systems. According to the industry observer:

> In the old days, Nike operated pretty much on [marketing] instinct. It took a guess as to how many pairs of shoes to churn out and hoped it could cram them all onto retailers' shelves. Not anymore. Nike has overhauled its computer systems to get the right number of sneakers to more places in the world more quickly. [It] also overhauled its supply-chain system, which often left retailers either desperately awaiting delivery of hot shoes or struggling to get rid of the duds. The old jerry-built compilation strung together 27 different computer systems worldwide, most of which couldn't talk with the others. . . . Nike has spent $500 million to build a new system. [Now, according to Nike] the percentage of shoes it makes without a firm order from a retailer has fallen from 30 percent to 3 percent, while the lead time for getting new sneaker styles to market has been cut to six months from nine.

The old seat-of-the-pants Nike had difficulty going global; at the new Nike, more than 50 percent of sales now come from international markets, and these markets are growing rapidly. The old Nike also stumbled with its acquisitions, trying to force its own super-heated marketing culture onto them. The new Nike has learned to give its acquired brands some independence. As a result, acquisitions such as Cole Haan dress shoes, Converse retro-style sneakers, Hurley International skateboard gear, Bauer in-line and hockey skates, and Starter Official affordable sneakers now account for more than 10 percent of Nike's revenues and a quarter of its sales growth.

The new, more mature Nike is once again achieving stunning results. In the past four years, Nike's sales have grown 50 percent to more than $14 billion. The company captures a 40 percent share of the U.S. branded athletic footwear market; the next-biggest competitor is Reebok at 13 percent. A relative newcomer to soccer, Nike recently became the top soccer shoe marketer in Europe, with a 35 percent market share, edging out long-time leader Adidas, at 31 percent. Nike's evolving marketing prowess over the years has also been good for investors. An investment of $1,000 in Nike in 1980 would be worth more than $64,000 today.

And founder Phil Knight's 27 percent stake in Nike is worth $6.2 billion, making him one of the world's richest people.

To stay on top, however, Nike will have to keep its marketing strategy fresh, finding new ways deliver the kind of innovation and value that built the brand so powerfully in the past. No longer the rebellious, antiestablishment upstart, Nike must continually reassess and rekindle its meaning to customers. Says Knight, "Now that we've [grown so large], there's a fine line between being a rebel and being a bully. [To our customers] we have to be beautiful as well as big."[1]

Marketing strategies and programs are guided by broader, companywide strategic plans. Thus, to understand the role of marketing, we must first understand the organization's overall strategic planning process. Like Nike, all companies must look ahead and develop long-term strategies to meet the changing conditions in their industries and ensure long-term survival.

Companywide Strategic Planning: Defining Marketing's Role

Each company must find the game plan for long-run survival and growth that makes the most sense given its specific situation, opportunities, objectives, and resources. This is the focus of **strategic planning**—the process of developing and maintaining a strategic fit between the organization's goals and capabilities and its changing marketing opportunities.

Strategic planning sets the stage for the rest of the planning in the firm. Companies usually prepare annual plans, long-range plans, and strategic plans. The annual and long-range plans deal with the company's current businesses and how to keep them going. In contrast, the strategic plan involves adapting the firm to take advantage of opportunities in its constantly changing environment.

At the corporate level, the company starts the strategic planning process by defining its overall purpose and mission (see Figure 2.1). This mission then is turned into detailed supporting objectives that guide the whole company. Next, headquarters decides what portfolio of businesses and products is best for the company and how much support to give each one. In turn, each business and product develops detailed marketing and other departmental plans that support the companywide plan. Thus, marketing planning occurs at the business-unit, product, and market levels. It supports company strategic planning with more detailed plans for specific marketing opportunities.[2]

Strategic planning
The process of developing and maintaining a strategic fit between the organization's goals and capabilities and its changing marketing opportunities. It involves defining a clear company mission, setting supporting objectives, designing a sound business portfolio, and coordinating functional strategies.

FIGURE 2.1 Steps in Strategic Planning

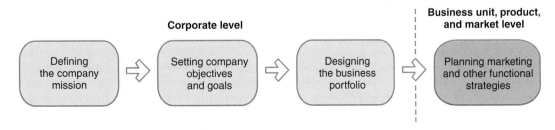

37

DEFINING A MARKET-ORIENTED MISSION

An organization exists to accomplish something. At first, it has a clear purpose or mission, but over time its mission may become unclear as the organization grows, adds new products and markets, or faces new conditions in the environment. When management senses that the organization is drifting, it must renew its search for purpose. It is time to ask: What is our business? Who is the customer? What do consumers value? What *should* our business be? These simple-sounding questions are among the most difficult the company will ever have to answer. Successful companies continuously raise these questions and answer them carefully and completely.

Many organizations develop formal mission statements that answer these questions. A **mission statement** is a statement of the organization's purpose—what it wants to accomplish in the larger environment. A clear mission statement acts as an "invisible hand" that guides people in the organization. Studies have shown that firms with well-crafted mission statements have better organizational and financial performance.[3]

Some companies define their missions myopically in product or technology terms ("We make and sell furniture" or "We are a chemical-processing firm"). But mission statements should be *market oriented* and defined in terms of customer needs. Products and technologies eventually become outdated, but basic market needs may last forever.

A market-oriented mission statement defines the business in terms of satisfying basic customer needs. For example, Charles Schwab isn't just a brokerage firm—it sees itself as the "guardian of our customers' financial dreams." Likewise, eBay's mission isn't simply to hold online auctions and trading. Instead, it connects individual buyers and sellers in "the world's online marketplace." Its mission is to be a unique Web community in which people can shop around, have fun, and get to know each other, for example, by chatting at the eBay Café. Table 2.1 provides several other examples of product-oriented versus market-oriented business definitions.

Management should avoid making its mission too narrow or too broad. A pencil manufacturer that says it is in the communication equipment business is stating its mission too

Mission statement
A statement of the organization's purpose—what it wants to accomplish in the larger environment.

TABLE 2.1
Market-Oriented Business Definitions

Company	Product-Oriented Definition	Market-Oriented Definition
Amazon.com	We sell books, videos, CDs, toys, consumer electronics, hardware, housewares, and other products.	We make the Internet buying experience fast, easy, and enjoyable—we're the place where you can find and discover anything you want to buy online.
America Online	We provide online services.	We create customer connectivity, anytime, anywhere.
Disney	We run theme parks.	We create fantasies—a place where America still works the way it's supposed to.
eBay	We hold online auctions.	We connect individual buyers and sellers in the world's online marketplace, a unique Web community in which they can shop around, have fun, and get to know each other.
Home Depot	We sell tools and home repair and improvement items.	We empower consumers to achieve the homes of their dreams.
Nike	We sell shoes.	We help people experience the emotion of competition, winning, and crushing competitors.
Revlon	We make cosmetics.	We sell lifestyle and self-expression; success and status; memories, hopes, and dreams.
Ritz-Carlton Hotels	We rent rooms.	We create the Ritz-Carlton experience—one that enlivens the senses, instills well-being, and fulfills even the unexpressed wishes and needs of our guests.
Wal-Mart	We run discount stores.	We deliver low prices, every day, and give ordinary folks the chance to buy the same things as rich people.

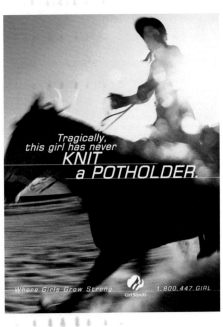

■ Mission statements: The Girl Scouts' mission is to be a place "Where Girls Grow Strong."

broadly. Missions should be *realistic*. Singapore Airlines would be deluding itself if it adopted the mission to become the world's largest airline. Missions should also be *specific*. Many mission statements are written for public relations purposes and lack specific, workable guidelines. Such generic statements sound good but provide little real guidance or inspiration.

Missions should fit the *market environment*. The Girl Scouts of America would not recruit successfully in today's environment with its former mission: "to prepare young girls for motherhood and wifely duties." Today, its mission is to be the place "where girls grow strong." The organization should also base its mission on its *distinctive competencies*. Finally, mission statements should be *motivating*. A company's mission should not be stated as making more sales or profits—profits are only a reward for undertaking a useful activity. A company's employees need to feel that their work is significant and that it contributes to people's lives. For example, Microsoft's aim is to help people to "realize their potential"—"your potential, our passion" says the company. Wal-Mart's mission is to "Give ordinary folks the chance to buy the same things as rich people."

SETTING COMPANY OBJECTIVES AND GOALS

The company needs to turn its mission into detailed supporting objectives for each level of management. Each manager should have objectives and be responsible for reaching them. For example, Monsanto operates in the agricultural biotechnology business. It defines its mission as "improving the future of farming . . . improving the future of food . . . abundantly and safely." It seeks to help feed the world's exploding population while at the same time sustaining the environment. Monsanto ads ask us to "Imagine innovative agriculture that creates incredible things today."

This mission leads to a hierarchy of objectives, including business objectives and marketing objectives. Monsanto's overall objective is to build profitable customer relationships by developing better agricultural products and getting them to market faster at lower costs. It does this by researching products that safely help crops produce more nutritious, higher yields, while reducing chemical spraying. But research is expensive and requires improved profits to plow back into research programs. So improving profits becomes another major Monsanto objective. Profits can be improved by increasing sales or reducing costs. Sales can be increased by improving the company's share of the U.S. market, by

■ Monsanto defines its mission as "improving the future of farming . . . improving the future of food . . . abundantly and safely." Its ads ask us to "Imagine innovative agriculture that creates incredible things today." This mission leads to specific business and marketing objectives.

Business portfolio
The collection of businesses and products that make up the company.

Portfolio analysis
The process by which management evaluates the products and businesses making up the company.

Growth-share matrix
A portfolio-planning method that evaluates a company's strategic business units in terms of their market growth rate and relative market share. SBUs are classified as stars, cash cows, question marks, or dogs.

entering new foreign markets, or both. These goals then become the company's current marketing objectives.[4]

Marketing strategies and programs must be developed to support these marketing objectives. To increase its U.S. market share, Monsanto might increase its products' availability and promotion. To enter new foreign markets, the company may cut prices and target large farms abroad. These are its broad marketing strategies. Each broad marketing strategy must then be defined in greater detail. For example, increasing the product's promotion may require more salespeople and more advertising; if so, both requirements will have to be spelled out. In this way, the firm's mission is translated into a set of objectives for the current period.

DESIGNING THE BUSINESS PORTFOLIO

Guided by the company's mission statement and objectives, management now must plan its **business portfolio**—the collection of businesses and products that make up the company. The best business portfolio is the one that best fits the company's strengths and weaknesses to opportunities in the environment. Business portfolio planning involves two steps. First, the company must analyze its *current* business portfolio and decide which businesses should receive more, less, or no investment. Second, it must shape the *future* portfolio by developing strategies for growth and downsizing.

Analyzing the Current Business Portfolio The major activity in strategic planning is business **portfolio analysis**, whereby management evaluates the products and businesses making up the company. The company will want to put strong resources into its more profitable businesses and phase down or drop its weaker ones.

Management's first step is to identify the key businesses making up the company. These can be called the strategic business units. A *strategic business unit* (SBU) is a unit of the company that has a separate mission and objectives and that can be planned independently from other company businesses. An SBU can be a company division, a product line within a division, or sometimes a single product or brand.

The next step in business portfolio analysis calls for management to assess the attractiveness of its various SBUs and decide how much support each deserves. Most companies are well advised to "stick to their knitting" when designing their business portfolios. It's usually a good idea to focus on adding products and businesses that fit closely with the firm's core philosophy and competencies.

The purpose of strategic planning is to find ways in which the company can best use its strengths to take advantage of attractive opportunities in the environment. So most standard portfolio-analysis methods evaluate SBUs on two important dimensions—the attractiveness of the SBU's market or industry and the strength of the SBU's position in that market or industry. The best-known portfolio-planning method was developed by the Boston Consulting Group, a leading management consulting firm.[5]

The Boston Consulting Group Approach. Using the Boston Consulting Group (BCG) approach, a company classifies all its SBUs according to the **growth-share matrix** shown in Figure 2.2. On the vertical axis, *market growth rate* provides a measure of market attractiveness. On the horizontal axis, *relative market share* serves as a measure of company strength in the market. The growth-share matrix defines four types of SBUs:

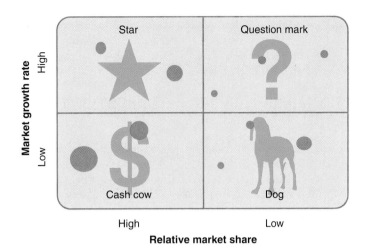

FIGURE 2.2
The BCG Growth-Share Matrix

Stars. Stars are high-growth, high-share businesses or products. They often need heavy investment to finance their rapid growth. Eventually their growth will slow down, and they will turn into cash cows.

Cash cows. Cash cows are low-growth, high-share businesses or products. These established and successful SBUs need less investment to hold their market share. Thus, they produce a lot of cash that the company uses to pay its bills and to support other SBUs that need investment.

Question marks. Question marks are low-share business units in high-growth markets. They require a lot of cash to hold their share, let alone increase it. Management has to think hard about which question marks it should try to build into stars, and which should be phased out.

Dogs. Dogs are low-growth, low-share businesses and products. They may generate enough cash to maintain themselves but do not promise to be large sources of cash.

The ten circles in the growth-share matrix represent a company's ten current SBUs. The company has two stars, two cash cows, three question marks, and three dogs. The areas of the circles are proportional to the SBU's dollar sales. This company is in fair shape, although not in good shape. It wants to invest in the more promising question marks to make them stars and to maintain the stars so that they will become cash cows as their markets mature. Fortunately, it has two good-sized cash cows. Income from these cash cows will help finance the company's question marks, stars, and dogs. The company should take some decisive action concerning its dogs and its question marks. The picture would be worse if the company had no stars, if it had too many dogs, or if it had only one weak cash cow.

Once it has classified its SBUs, the company must determine what role each will play in the future. One of four strategies can be pursued for each SBU. The company can invest more in the business unit in order to *build* its share. Or it can invest just enough to *hold* the SBU's share at the current level. It can *harvest* the SBU, milking its short-term cash flow regardless of the long-term effect. Finally, the company can *divest* the SBU by selling it or phasing it out and using the resources elsewhere.

As time passes, SBUs change their positions in the growth-share matrix. Each SBU has a life cycle. Many SBUs start out as question marks and move into the star category if they succeed. They later become cash cows as market growth falls, then finally die off or turn into dogs toward the end of their life cycle. The company needs to add new products and units continuously so that some of them will become stars and, eventually, cash cows that will help finance other SBUs.

Problems with Matrix Approaches. The BCG and other formal methods revolutionized strategic planning. However, such centralized approaches have limitations. They can be difficult, time-consuming, and costly to implement. Management may find it difficult to define SBUs and measure market share and growth. In addition, these approaches focus on classifying *current* businesses but provide little advice for *future* planning.

MARKETING AT WORK   2.1

The Walt Disney Company: Strategic Planning for a Happy-Ever-After Ending

When you think of The Walt Disney Company, you probably think first of theme parks and animated films. And no wonder. Since the release of its first Mickey Mouse cartoon more than 75 years ago, Disney has grown to become the undisputed master of family entertainment. It perfected the art of movie animation. From pioneering films such as *Snow White and the Seven Dwarfs*, *Fantasia*, and *Pinocchio* to more recent features such as *Monsters, Inc., Finding Nemo, The Incredibles, Valiant*, and *Cars*, Disney has brought pure magic to the theaters, living rooms, and hearts and minds of audiences around the world.

But perhaps nowhere is the Disney magic more apparent than at the company's premier theme parks. Each year, more than 40 million people flock to The Walt Disney World Resort alone—13 times more than visit Yellowstone National Park—making it the world's number one tourist attraction. What brings so many people to The Walt Disney World Resort? Part of the answer lies in its many attractions. The resort's four major theme parks—Magic Kingdom, Epcot, Disney-MGM Studios, and Disney's Animal Kingdom—brim with such attractions as the Twilight Zone Tower of Terror, Soarin' Over California, the Kilimanjaro Safaris, and Big Thunder Mountain Railroad.

But the real "Disney Magic" lies in the company's obsessive dedication to its mission to "make people happy" and to "make a dream come true." Disney goes to extremes to fulfill guests' expectations and dreams. Its theme parks are so highly regarded for outstanding customer service that many of America's leading corporations send managers to Disney University to learn how Disney does it.

You might be surprised to learn, however, that theme parks and movies are only part of a much bigger Disney story. Parks and resorts account for only about 25 percent of today's Disney empire; movies and entertainment make up another 28 percent. The rest comes from a diverse portfolio of businesses that have been acquired by Disney over the past two decades.

In fact, The Walt Disney Company has become a real study in strategic planning. In 1985, Disney's then-new chief officer, Michael Eisner, set up a high-powered, centralized strategic planning unit, charged with seeking out and nurturing new growth opportunities and setting the company's strategic path. Throughout the late 1980s and the 1990s, seeking growth, the strategic planning group engineered a series of major acquisitions, including the mid-1990s purchase of

■ *For more than 75 years, The Walt Disney Company has been the undisputed master of family entertainment. But it will take masterful strategic planning—along with some big doses of the famed "Disney Magic"—to give the modern Disney a happy-ever-after ending.*

Formal planning approaches can also place too much emphasis on market-share growth or growth through entry into attractive new markets. Using these approaches, many companies plunged into unrelated and new high-growth businesses that they did not know how to manage—with very bad results. At the same time, these companies were often too quick to abandon, sell, or milk to death their healthy mature businesses. As a result, many companies that diversified too broadly in the past now are narrowing their focus and getting back to the basics of serving one or a few industries that they know best.

Because of such problems, many companies have dropped formal matrix methods in favor of more customized approaches that are better suited to their specific situations. Moreover, unlike former strategic-planning efforts, which rested mostly in the hands of senior managers at company headquarters, today's strategic planning has been

Capital Cities/ABC, which almost doubled Disney's size.

By the early 2000s, the group had transformed The Walt Disney Company into a $30 billion international media and entertainment colossus. The company now owns all or part of hundreds of companies and divisions, organized into four major business groups:

- *Studio Entertainment.* Four television production companies, eight movie and theatrical production companies, and a distribution company (including Walt Disney Pictures, Touchstone Pictures, Hollywood Pictures, Miramax Films, Dimension Films, and Buena Vista Theatrical Productions); and four music labels (Walt Disney Records, Hollywood Records, Buena Vista Records, and Lyric Street Records).
- *Media Networks.* A major broadcast television network (ABC, plus ten company-owned television stations); a dozen cable television networks (including the Disney Channel, Toon Disney, SOAPnet, ESPN, A&E, the History Channel, Lifetime Television, E! Entertainment, and ABC Family); three radio networks (ESPN Radio, ABC Radio, and Disney Radio, plus seventy-one radio stations); and the Walt Disney Internet Group (nineteen Internet sites including Disney Online, Disney's Daily Blast, ABC.com, ESPN.com, Family.com, NASCAR.com, and NBA.com).
- *Parks and Resorts.* Eleven parks and thirty-five resort hotels on three continents (including Disneyland Resort Paris, Tokyo Disney Resort, and Hong Kong Disneyland); Disney Cruise Line; Disney Vacation Club; and ESPN Zone.

- *Consumer Products.* Three Disney Merchandise Licensing divisions; four Disney Publishing divisions (including Hyperion Books, Disney Press, and *Disney Adventures*, the number-one children's magazine in the United States); the Baby Einstein Company (developmental media for infants); four Disney Retail groups (including Disney Stores Worldwide and Disney Direct Marketing); and Buena Vista Games Disney content for the interactive gaming community).

Whew! That's an impressive list. However, for Disney, managing this diverse portfolio of businesses has become a real *Monsters, Inc.* During the last half of the 1980s, the smaller, more focused Disney experienced soaring sales and profits. Revenues grew at an average rate of 23 percent annually; net income grew at 50 percent a year. In contrast, at least until recently, the larger, more complex Disney has struggled for consistent profitability and growth.

Disney's centralized strategic planning group frequently bore the blame for the transformed company's uneven performance. Operating from on high, the group reached for the stars—overreached, according to some. Many critics assert that the company has grown too large, too diverse, and too distant from the core strengths that made it so successful in earlier years. At the same time, the strategic planning group reviewed and often rejected the strategies proposed by the company's business unit managers. The group was criticized for "having too much power and quashing ideas that weren't its own," notes one analyst. It even came to be called by some "the business prevention department."

In 2004, disagreements over Disney's long-term strategic direction erupted into high-level boardroom brawls, resulting in Eisner's ouster as chairman and resignation as CEO. Tellingly, less than two weeks after assuming the reins at The Walt Disney Company, new Chief Executive Robert Iger set a priority of decentralizing the company's strategic planning. In a move popular with most Disney executives, Iger broke up the centralized strategic planning group, returning most of the group's functions to Disney's division managers. He is betting that the individual business units, which are closer to their markets, can do a better job of planning growth strategies than the centralized unit did. As part of an expected corporate overhaul, Iger will no doubt take a fresh look at Disney's disparate portfolio of businesses.

Thus, for Disney, bigger isn't necessarily better. And more decentralized, strategic planning seems to make better sense than on-high planning. One thing seems certain—creating just the right blend of businesses to make up the new Magic Kingdom won't be easy. It will take masterful strategic planning—along with some big doses of the famed "Disney magic"—to give the modern Disney story a happy-ever-after ending.

Sources: Merissa Marr, "Disney Cuts Strategic-Planning Unit," *Wall Street Journal,* March 28, 2005, p. A3; "No Wonder Theme Parks Seem More Crowded—They Are," December 20, 2004, accessed at http://themeparks.about.com; "The Walt Disney Company," *Hoover's Company Records,* May 15, 2005, p. 11603; Jacqueline Doherty, "Better Days for Disney," *Barron's,* March 21, 2005, p. 14; Laura M. Holson, "Disney Intends to Overhaul Planning Unit," *New York Times,* March 26, 2005, p. C2; and information from www.disney.go.com, June 2005.

decentralized. Increasingly, companies are placing responsibility for strategic planning in the hands of cross-functional teams of divisional managers who are close to their markets.

For example, consider The Walt Disney Company. Most people think of Disney as theme parks and wholesome family entertainment. But in the mid-1980s, Disney set up a powerful, centralized strategic planning group to guide the company's direction and growth. Over the next two decades, the strategic planning group turned The Walt Disney Company into a huge but diverse collection of media and entertainment businesses. The newly transformed company proved hard to manage and performed unevenly. Recently, Disney's new chief executive disbanded the centralized strategic planning unit, decentralizing its functions to divisional managers (see Marketing at Work 2.1).

Developing Strategies for Growth and Downsizing Beyond evaluating current businesses, designing the business portfolio involves finding businesses and products the company should consider in the future. Companies need growth if they are to compete more effectively, satisfy their stakeholders, and attract top talent. "Growth is pure oxygen," states one executive. "It creates a vital, enthusiastic corporation where people see genuine opportunity." At the same time, a firm must be careful not to make growth itself an objective. The company's objective must be "profitable growth."

Marketing has the main responsibility for achieving profitable growth for the company. Marketing must identify, evaluate, and select market opportunities and lay down strategies for capturing them. One useful device for identifying growth opportunities is the **product/market expansion grid**, shown in Figure 2.3.[6] We apply it here to Starbucks:

> More than 20 years ago, Howard Schultz hit on the idea of bringing a European-style coffeehouse to America. People needed to slow down, he believed—to "smell the coffee" and enjoy life a little more. The result was Starbucks. This coffeehouse doesn't sell just coffee, it sells *The Starbucks Experience.* "There's the Starbucks ambience," notes an analyst, "The music. The comfy velvety chairs. The smells. The hissing steam." Says Starbucks Chairman Schultz, "We aren't in the coffee business, serving people. We are in the people business, serving coffee." People around the globe now flock to Starbucks, making it a powerhouse premium brand. Some 30 million customers now visit the company's more than 9,200 stores worldwide each week.
>
> Growth is the engine that keeps Starbucks perking—the company targets (and regularly achieves) jaw-dropping revenue growth exceeding 20 percent each year. Starbucks' success, however, has drawn a full litter of copycats, ranging from direct competitors such as Caribou Coffee to fast-food merchants (such as McDonald's McCafé) and even discounters (Wal-Mart's Kicks Coffee). To maintain its phenomenal growth in an increasingly overcaffeinated marketplace, Starbucks must brew up an ambitious, multipronged growth strategy.[7]

First, Starbucks management might consider whether the company can achieve deeper **market penetration**—making more sales to current customers without changing its products. It might add new stores in current market areas to make it easier for more customers to visit. In fact, Starbucks is adding an average of 28 stores a week, 52 weeks a year—its ultimate goal is 30,000 stores worldwide. Improvements in advertising, prices, service, menu selection, or store design might encourage customers to stop by more often, stay longer, or to buy more during each visit. For example, Starbucks has added drive-through windows to many of its stores. A company debit card lets customers prepay for coffee and snacks or give the gift of Starbucks to family and friends. And to get customers to hang around longer, Starbucks now offers T-Mobile HotSpot wireless Internet access in many of its stores.

Second, Starbucks management might consider possibilities for **market development**—identifying and developing new markets for its current products. For instance, managers could review new *demographic markets.* Perhaps new groups—such as seniors or ethnic groups—could be encouraged to visit Starbucks coffee shops for the first time or to buy more from them. Managers also could review new *geographical markets.* Starbucks is now expanding swiftly into new U.S. markets, especially smaller cities. And it's expanding rapidly in new global markets. In 1996, Starbucks had only 11 coffeehouses outside North America. It now has more than 2,650, with plenty of room to grow. "We're just scratching the

Product/market expansion grid
A portfolio-planning tool for identifying company growth opportunities through market penetration, market development, product development, or diversification.

Market penetration
A strategy for company growth by increasing sales of current products to current market segments without changing the product.

Market development
A strategy for company growth by identifying and developing new market segments for current company products.

FIGURE 2.3
The Product/Market Expansion Grid

	Existing products	New products
Existing markets	Market penetration	Product development
New markets	Market development	Diversification

surface in China," says Starbucks' CEO. We have 150 stores and the potential for more than 2,000 there."

Third, management could consider **product development**—offering modified or new products to current markets. For example, Starbucks has introduced new reduced-calorie options, such as Frappuccino Light Blended Beverages. It recently added Chantico, an indulgent, chocolate beverage to its menu to draw in more non-coffee drinkers. To capture consumers who brew their coffee at home, Starbucks has also pushed into America's supermarket aisles. It has a cobranding deal with Kraft, under which Starbucks roasts and packages its coffee while Kraft markets and distributes it. And the company is forging ahead into new consumer categories. For example, it's bringing out a line of Starbucks coffee liqueurs.

Fourth, Starbucks might consider **diversification**—starting up or buying businesses outside of its current products and markets. For example, in 1999, Starbucks purchased Hear Music, which was so successful that it

■ Strategies for growth: To maintain its phenomenal growth in an increasingly overcaffeinated marketplace, Starbucks has brewed up an ambitious, multipronged growth strategy.

spurred the creation of the new Starbucks entertainment division. Beginning with just selling and playing compilation CDs, Hear Music now has its own XM Satellite Radio station. It is also installing kiosks (called Media Bars) in select Starbucks stores that let customers download music and burn their own CDs while sipping their lattes. As a next step, Starbucks is investing in Hear Music retail outlets, which will be music stores first and coffee shops second.

In a more extreme diversification, Starbucks might consider leveraging its strong brand name by making and marketing a line of branded casual clothing consistent with the "Starbucks Experience." However, this would probably be unwise. Companies that diversify too broadly into unfamiliar products or industries can lose their market focus, something that some critics are already concerned about with Starbucks.

Companies must not only develop strategies for *growing* their business portfolios but also strategies for **downsizing** them. There are many reasons that a firm might want to abandon products or markets. The market environment might change, making some of the company's products or markets less profitable. The firm may have grown too fast or entered areas where it lacks experience. This can occur when a firm enters too many foreign markets without the proper research or when a company introduces new products that do not offer superior customer value. Finally, some products or business units simply age and die. One marketing expert summarizes the problem this way:

> Companies spend vast amounts of money and time launching new brands, leveraging existing ones, and acquiring rivals. They create line extensions and brand extensions, not to mention channel extensions and subbrands, to cater to the growing number of niche segments in every market. . . . Surprisingly, most businesses do not examine their brand portfolios from time to time to check if they might be selling too many brands, identify weak ones, and kill unprofitable ones. They tend to ignore loss-making brands rather than merge them with healthy brands, sell them off, or drop them. Consequently, most portfolios have become [jammed] with loss-making and marginally profitable brands. Moreover, the surprising truth is that most brands don't make money for companies. Many corporations generate fewer than 80 to 90 percent of their profits from fewer than 20 percent of the brands they sell, while they lose money or barely break even on many of the other brands in their portfolios.[8]

When a firm finds brands or businesses that are unprofitable or that no longer fit its overall strategy, it must carefully prune, harvest, or divest them. Weak businesses usually require a disproportionate amount of management attention. Managers should focus on promising growth opportunities, not fritter away energy trying to salvage fading ones.

Product development
A strategy for company growth by offering modified or new products to current market segments.

Diversification
A strategy for company growth through starting up or acquiring businesses outside the company's current products and markets.

Downsizing
Reducing the business portfolio by eliminating products or business units that are not profitable or that no longer fit the company's overall strategy.

Planning Marketing: Partnering to Build Customer Relationships

The company's strategic plan establishes what kinds of businesses the company will operate in and its objectives for each. Then, within each business unit, more detailed planning takes place. The major functional departments in each unit—marketing, finance, accounting, purchasing, operations, information systems, human resources, and others—must work together to accomplish strategic objectives.

Marketing plays a key role in the company's strategic planning in several ways. First, marketing provides a guiding *philosophy*—the marketing concept—that suggests that company strategy should revolve around building profitable relationships with important consumer groups. Second, marketing provides *inputs* to strategic planners by helping to identify attractive market opportunities and by assessing the firm's potential to take advantage of them. Finally, within individual business units, marketing designs *strategies* for reaching the unit's objectives. Once the unit's objectives are set, marketing's task is to help carry them out profitably.

Customer value and satisfaction are important ingredients in the marketer's formula for success. However, as we noted in Chapter 1, marketers alone cannot produce superior value for customers. Although it plays a leading role, marketing can be only a partner in attracting, keeping, and growing customers. In addition to *customer relationship management*, marketers must also practice *partner relationship management*. They must work closely with partners in other company departments to form an effective *value chain* that serves the customer. Moreover, they must partner effectively with other companies in the marketing system to form a competitively superior *value-delivery network*. We now take a closer look at the concepts of a company value chain and value-delivery network.

PARTNERING WITH OTHER COMPANY DEPARTMENTS

Value chain

The series of departments that carry out value-creating activities to design, produce, market, deliver, and support a firm's products.

Each company department can be thought of as a link in the company's **value chain**.[9] That is, each department carries out value-creating activities to design, produce, market, deliver, and support the firm's products. The firm's success depends not only on how well each department performs its work but also on how well the activities of various departments are coordinated.

For example, Wal-Mart's goal is to create customer value and satisfaction by providing shoppers with the products they want at the lowest possible prices. Marketers at Wal-Mart play an important role. They learn what customers need and stock the store's shelves with the desired products at unbeatable low prices. They prepare advertising and merchandising programs and assist shoppers with customer service. Through these and other activities, Wal-Mart's marketers help deliver value to customers.

However, the marketing department needs help from the company's other departments. Wal-Mart's ability to offer the right products at low prices depends on the purchasing department's skill in developing the needed suppliers and buying from them at low cost. Wal-Mart's information technology department must provide fast and accurate information about which products are selling in each store. And its operations people must provide effective, low-cost merchandise handling.

A company's value chain is only as strong as its weakest link. Success depends on how well each department performs its work of adding customer value and on how well the activities of various departments are coordinated. At Wal-Mart, if purchasing can't wring the lowest prices from suppliers, or if operations can't distribute merchandise at the lowest costs, then marketing can't deliver on its promise of lowest prices.

Ideally, then, a company's different functions should work in harmony to produce value for consumers. But, in practice, departmental relations are full of conflicts and misunderstandings. The marketing department takes the consumer's point of view. But when marketing tries to develop customer satisfaction, it can cause other departments to do a poorer job *in their terms*. Marketing department actions can increase purchasing costs, dis-

■ The value chain: Wal-Mart's ability to offer the right products at low prices depends on the contributors of people in all of the company's departments—marketing, purchasing, information systems, and operations.

rupt production schedules, increase inventories, and create budget headaches. Thus, the other departments may resist the marketing department's efforts.

Yet marketers must find ways to get all departments to "think consumer" and to develop a smoothly functioning value chain. Marketing management can best gain support for its goal of customer satisfaction by working to understand the company's other departments. Marketing managers need to work closely with managers of other functions to develop a system of functional plans under which the different departments can work together to accomplish the company's overall strategic objectives.

Jack Welch, General Electric's highly regarded former CEO, told his employees: "Companies can't give job security. Only customers can!" He emphasized that all General Electric people, regardless of their department, have an impact on customer satisfaction and retention. His message: "If you are not thinking customer, you are not thinking."[10]

PARTNERING WITH OTHERS IN THE MARKETING SYSTEM

In its quest to create customer value, the firm needs to look beyond its own value chain and into the value chains of its suppliers, distributors, and, ultimately, customers. Consider McDonald's. McDonald's 31,500 restaurants worldwide serve more than 50 million customers daily, capturing more than a 40 percent share of the burger market.[11] People do not swarm to McDonald's only because they love the chain's hamburgers. In fact, consumers typically rank McDonald's behind Burger King and Wendy's in taste. Consumers flock to the McDonald's *system*, not just to its food products. Throughout the world, McDonald's finely-tuned system delivers a high standard of what the company calls QSCV—quality, service, cleanliness, and value. McDonald's is effective only to the extent that it successfully partners with its franchisees, suppliers, and others to jointly deliver exceptionally high customer value.

More companies today are partnering with the other members of the supply chain to improve the performance of the customer **value-delivery network**. For example, Toyota knows the importance of building close relationships with its suppliers. In fact, it even includes the phrase "achieve supplier satisfaction" in its mission statement.

Value-delivery network
The network made up of the company, suppliers, distributors, and ultimately customers who "partner" with each other to improve the performance of the entire system.

Achieving satisfying supplier relationships has been a cornerstone of Toyota's stunning success. U.S. competitors often alienate their suppliers through self-serving, heavy-handed dealings. "The [U.S. automakers] set annual cost-reduction targets [for the parts they buy]," says one supplier. "To realize those targets, they'll do anything. [They've unleashed] a reign of terror, and it gets

■ Toyota partners with its suppliers and helps them meet its very high expectations. Creating satisfied suppliers helps Toyota produce lower-cost, higher-quality cars, which in turn results in more satisfied customers.

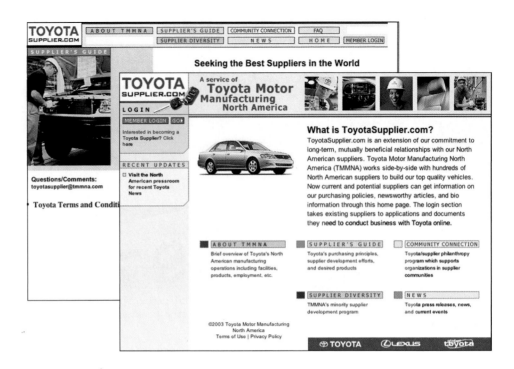

worse every year." Says another, "[Ford] seems to send its people to "hate school" so that they learn how to hate suppliers." By contrast, in survey after survey, auto suppliers rate Toyota as their most preferred customer. Rather than bullying suppliers, Toyota partners with them and helps them to meet its very high expectations. It learns about their businesses, conducts joint improvement activities, helps train their employees, gives daily performance feedback, and actively seeks out supplier concerns. Says one delighted Toyota supplier, "Toyota helped us dramatically improve our production system. We started by making one component, and as we improved, [Toyota] rewarded us with orders for more components. Toyota is our best customer."

Such high supplier satisfaction means that Toyota can rely on suppliers to help it improve its own quality, reduce costs, and develop new products quickly. For example, when Toyota recently launched a program to reduce prices by 30 percent on 170 parts that it would buy for its next generation of cars, suppliers didn't complain. Instead, they pitched in, trusting that Toyota would help them achieve the targeted reductions, in turn making them more competitive and profitable in the future. In all, creating satisfied suppliers helps Toyota to produce lower-cost, higher-quality cars, which in turn results in more satisfied customers.[12]

Increasingly in today's marketplace, competition no longer takes place between individual competitors. Rather, it takes place between the entire value-delivery networks created by these competitors. Thus, Toyota's performance against Ford depends on the quality of Toyota's overall value-delivery network versus Ford's. Even if Toyota makes the best cars, it might lose in the marketplace if Ford's dealer network provides more customer-satisfying sales and service.

Linking the Concepts

Here's a good place to pause for a moment to think about and apply what you've read in the first part of this chapter.

■ Why are we talking about companywide strategic planning in a marketing text? What *does* strategic planning have to do with marketing?

■ What are Starbucks' mission and strategy? What role does marketing play in helping Starbucks to accomplish its mission and strategy?

■ What roles do other Starbucks departments play, and how can Starbucks' marketers partner with these departments to maximize overall customer value?

Marketing Strategy and the Marketing Mix

The strategic plan defines the company's overall mission and objectives. Marketing's role and activities are shown in Figure 2.4, which summarizes the major activities involved in managing marketing strategy and the marketing mix.

Consumers stand in the center. The goal is to build strong and profitable customer relationships. Next comes **marketing strategy**—the marketing logic by which the company hopes to achieve these profitable relationships. Through market segmentation, targeting, and positioning, the company decides which customers it will serve and how. It identifies the total market, then divides it into smaller segments, selects the most promising segments, and focuses on serving and satisfying customers in these segments.

Guided by marketing strategy, the company designs a *marketing mix* made up of factors under its control—product, price, place, and promotion (the four Ps). To find the best marketing strategy and mix, the company engages in marketing analysis, planning, implementation, and control. Through these activities, the company watches and adapts to the actors and forces in the marketing environment. We will now look briefly at each activity. Then, in later chapters, we will discuss each one in more depth.

Marketing strategy
The marketing logic by which the business unit hopes to achieve its marketing objectives.

CUSTOMER-CENTERED MARKETING STRATEGY

As we emphasized throughout Chapter 1, to succeed in today's competitive marketplace, companies need to be customer centered. They must win customers from competitors, then keep and grow them by delivering greater value. But before it can satisfy consumers, a company must first understand their needs and wants. Thus, sound marketing requires a careful customer analysis.

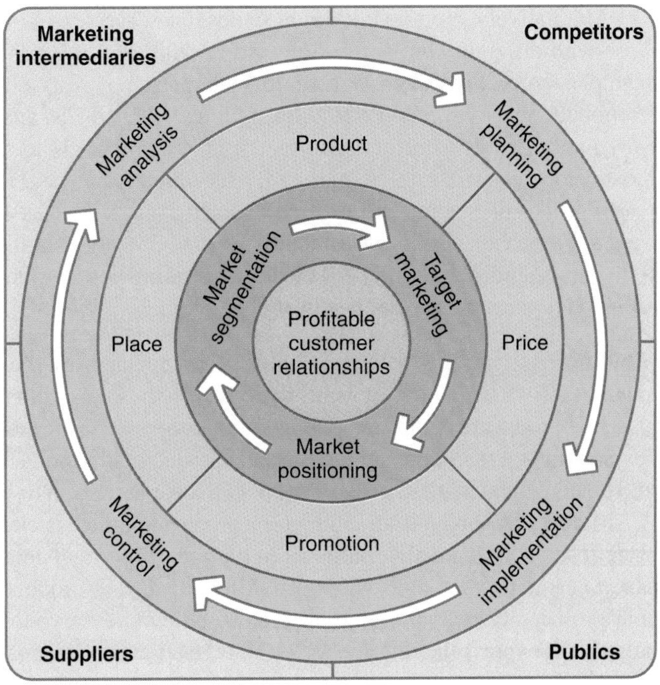

FIGURE 2.4
Managing Marketing Strategy and the Marketing Mix

Companies know that they cannot profitably serve all consumers in a given market—at least not all consumers in the same way. There are too many different kinds of consumers with too many different kinds of needs. And most companies are in a position to serve some segments better than others. Thus, each company must divide up the total market, choose the best segments, and design strategies for profitably serving chosen segments. This process involves three steps: *market segmentation*, *target marketing*, and *market positioning*.

Market Segmentation   The market consists of many types of customers, products, and needs. The marketer has to determine which segments offer the best opportunities. Consumers can be grouped and served in various ways based on geographic, demographic, psychographic, and behavioral factors. The process of dividing a market into distinct groups of buyers who have different needs, characteristics, or behaviors and who might require separate products or marketing programs is called **market segmentation**.

Every market has segments, but not all ways of segmenting a market are equally useful. For example, Tylenol would gain little by distinguishing between low-income and high-income pain reliever users if both respond the same way to marketing efforts. A **market segment** consists of consumers who respond in a similar way to a given set of marketing efforts. In the car market, for example, consumers who want the biggest, most comfortable car regardless of price make up one market segment. Customers who care mainly about price and operating economy make up another segment. It would be difficult to make one car model that was the first choice of consumers in both segments. Companies are wise to focus their efforts on meeting the distinct needs of individual market segments.

Target Marketing   After a company has defined market segments, it can enter one or many of these segments. **Target marketing** involves evaluating each market segment's attractiveness and selecting one or more segments to enter. A company should target segments in which it can profitably generate the greatest customer value and sustain it over time.

A company with limited resources might decide to serve only one or a few special segments or "market niches." Such "nichers" specialize in serving customer segments that major competitors overlook or ignore. For example, Arm & Hammer has a lock on the baking soda corner of most consumer goods categories, including toothpaste, deodorizers, and others. White Wave, maker of Silk Soymilk, has found its niche as the nation's largest soymilk producer. And by operating in the shadows of soft drink giants like Coca-Cola and Pepsi, nicher Jones Soda has learned that small can be beautiful—and very profitable (see Marketing at Work 2.2).

Alternatively, a company might choose to serve several related segments—perhaps those with different kinds of customers but with the same basic wants. Pottery Barn, for example, targets kids, teens, and adults with the same lifestyle-themed merchandise in different outlets: the original Pottery Barn, Pottery Barn Kids, and PB Teen. Or a large company might decide to offer a complete range of products to serve all market segments. Most companies enter a new market by serving a single segment, and if this proves successful, they add segments. Large companies eventually seek full market coverage. They want to be the General Motors of their industry. GM says that it makes a car for every "person, purse, and personality." The leading company normally has different products designed to meet the special needs of each segment.

Market Positioning   After a company has decided which market segments to enter, it must decide what positions it wants to occupy in those segments. A product's *position* is the place the product occupies relative to competitors in consumers' minds. Marketers want to develop unique market positions for their products. If a product is perceived to be exactly like others on the market, consumers would have no reason to buy it.

Market positioning is arranging for a product to occupy a clear, distinctive, and desirable place relative to competing products in the minds of target consumers. As one positioning expert puts it, positioning is "how you differentiate your product or company in the mind of your prospect. It's why a shopper will pay a little more for your brand. The trick is to figure out how to express the difference."[13] Thus, marketers plan positions that distinguish their

---

Market segmentation
Dividing a market into distinct groups of buyers who have distinct needs, characteristics, or behaviors and who might require separate products or marketing programs.

Market segment
A group of consumers who respond in a similar way to a given set of marketing efforts.

Target marketing
The process of evaluating each market segment's attractiveness and selecting one or more segments to enter.

Market positioning
Arranging for a product to occupy a clear, distinctive, and desirable place relative to competing products in the minds of target consumers.

MARKETING AT WORK   2.2

Jones Soda: Staying True to Your Niche

Every great product has a secret formula. Coca-Cola's legendary recipe is locked deep within the vaults beneath its Atlanta headquarters. KFC mixes different parts of its 11 herbs and spices at three separate facilities to safeguard the Colonel's secret blend. And McDonald's hunted down its original special-sauce mix for Big Macs last year as part of its turnaround effort.

Jones Soda, the small Seattle soft drink maker, has its own secret ingredient—one that has created buzz, produced 30 percent yearly revenue growth in a flat beverage market, drawn major distribution partners such as Starbucks and Target, and brought in $30 million in annual revenue. That ingredient: a small but growing following of devout customers. These are not just any customers—Jones Soda knows its niche. It targets young buyers—12- to 24-year-olds—who appreciate the brand's wacky, irreverent attitude. By focusing in on these customers, listening to them, and giving them what they want, Jones Soda is thriving in the shadows of the soft drink giants.

Virtually everything about a Jones Soda, from labels to flavors, comes from its carefully targeted customers. That's important because "the reality is that consumers don't need our s___," founder and CEO Peter van Stolk says unapologetically. The world isn't necessarily clamoring for another soda, even if it tastes like blue bubble gum. So how do you sell an unnecessary product? If you're van Stolk, a 41-year-old former ski instructor who started Jones 10 years ago, you hand the product over to customers. Strategy gurus might call that a good example of how to "cocreate unique value." Van Stolk has a more down-to-earth but no less profound way to describe it: "People get fired up about Jones because it's theirs."

It all started with the Web site Jones Soda launched in 1997. Hundreds of comments poured in from customers, and van Stolk quickly took up their suggestions and online votes for neon colors, wacky names (like Fufu Berry, Whoop Ass, MF Grape, and Bada Bing!), and offbeat flavors (including blue bubblegum, crushed melon, and twisted lime—or even strange seasonal flavors like fruitcake or turkey and gravy). Even the "Deep Thoughts"—like quotes found on the Web site and underneath bottle caps ("It's not broken, it just needs duct tape")—come straight from Jones enthusiasts.

Van Stolk also encouraged customers to submit photos, and the eccentric and strangely captivating images on Jones's stark black-and-white bottle labels have come largely from fans. And as the site became flooded with hundreds of thousands of cute, but useless, baby snapshots, he launched myJones to offer customers 12-packs of soda with custom-made labels for $34.95. myJones has since blossomed into one of the cornerstones of the Jones Soda brand.

Jones also stays close to its 12- to 24-year-old customers with a pair of roving RVs. The two flame-festooned vehicles spend nine months out of the year visiting Jones-friendly sites, from small skate parks in the middle of nowhere to major extreme-games competitions such as the X Games. The RVs also turn up in places where they're less welcome, such as high schools to which they weren't invited. "The more deviant you can be, the better," says RV driver Chris King, 32, on a crackling cell phone. "Kids love to see you get kicked out of places. I, personally, am banned from Nassau County in New York." The idea is simple. Kids come in and grab a bunch of Jones Soda stuff—buttons, stickers, key chains—while King studies them for a mental inventory of what's hot and what's not.

Whereas its mainstream competitors work at making something for everyone, Jones Soda understands the importance of sticking to its niche. As only van Stolk can put it, "The customer's not always right. [Bleep] that. If you're always trying to cater to everyone, you have no soul." To van Stolk, the Web site, the labels, the RVs, and the various stunts just add

■ *Jones Soda sticks closely to its niche—virtually everything about a Jones Soda, from labels to flavors, comes directly from its carefully targeted customers.*

up to being in sync with target customers. "It's the difference between being real and saying you're real," van Stolk says, taking a not-so-subtle swipe at a certain "Real Thing" mega-rival. "If you're able to listen to customers from their perspective," he says, "not everything they say will make sense. Not everything they do will be right. But you'll know more about what you have to do because of it."

Staying so close to customers will become more of a challenge as Jones grows and its customers start buying its soda at the likes of Panera Bread, Target, and Starbucks instead of the local skate shop. But so far, Jones Soda has learned that small can be beautiful—and very profitable. Sales last year jumped 37 percent. Profits more than quadrupled.

Sources: Adapted from "Cracking Jones Soda's Secret Formula," by Ryan Underwood. *Fast Company*, March 2005, pp. 74–75. © 2005 Gruner & Jahr USA Publishing. Adapted with permission. Also see Christopher Steiner, "Soda Jerk," *Forbes*, April 11, 2005, p. 74.

MAN'S BEST FRIEND
Another reason to pay bills automatically with your Visa card.

A lot can happen to your mail, so why not use your Visa® check card or credit card to pay important bills automatically? Simply schedule payments for monthly bills like phone, cable/satellite and gym membership dues. Bills are securely paid on time every month, while the need for writing checks, finding stamps, addressing envelopes and scolding your pet is virtually eliminated. To get started, go to **visa.com/billpay**.

VISA
it's everywhere you want to be.

■ Market positioning: Visa is everywhere you want to be.

Marketing mix
The set of controllable tactical marketing tools—product, price, place, and promotion—that the firm blends to produce the response it wants in the target market.

products from competing brands and give them the greatest advantage in their target markets.

BMW makes "the ultimate driving machine"; Ford is "built for the road ahead"; and Kia promises "the power to surprise." MasterCard gives you "priceless experiences"; Visa is "everywhere you want to be." Target says "expect more, pay less." And at Caesar's Palace in Las Vegas, you can "live famously." Such deceptively simple statements form the backbone of a product's marketing strategy.

In positioning its product, the company first identifies possible competitive advantages upon which to build the position. The company can offer greater customer value either by charging lower prices than competitors do or by offering more benefits to justify higher prices. But if the company *promises* greater value, it must then *deliver* that greater value. Thus, effective positioning begins with actually *differentiating* the company's market offering so that it gives consumers more value. Once the company has chosen a desired position, it must take strong steps to deliver and communicate that position to target consumers. The company's entire marketing program should support the chosen positioning strategy.

DEVELOPING THE MARKETING MIX

After deciding on its overall marketing strategy, the company is ready to begin planning the details of the marketing mix, one of the major concepts in modern marketing. The **marketing mix** is the set of controllable, tactical marketing tools that the firm blends to produce the response it wants in the target market. The marketing mix consists of everything the firm can do to influence the demand for its product. The many possibilities can be collected into four groups of variables known as the "four Ps": *product, price, place,* and *promotion.* Figure 2.5 shows the marketing tools under each *P.*

Product means the goods-and-services combination the company offers to the target market. Thus, a Ford Escape product consists of nuts and bolts, spark plugs, pistons, headlights, and thousands of other parts. Ford offers several Escape models and dozens of optional features. The car comes fully serviced and with a comprehensive warranty that is as much a part of the product as the tailpipe.

Price is the amount of money customers have to pay to obtain the product. Ford calculates suggested retail prices that its dealers might charge for each Escape. But Ford dealers rarely charge the full sticker price. Instead, they negotiate the price with each customer, offering discounts, trade-in allowances, and credit terms. These actions adjust prices for the current competitive situation and bring them into line with the buyer's perception of the car's value.

Place includes company activities that make the product available to target consumers. Ford partners with a large body of independently owned dealerships that sell the company's many different models. Ford selects its dealers carefully and supports them strongly. The dealers keep an inventory of Ford automobiles, demonstrate them to potential buyers, negotiate prices, close sales, and service the cars after the sale.

Promotion means activities that communicate the merits of the product and persuade target customers to buy it. Ford spends more than $2.4 billion each year on advertising, about $353 per vehicle, to tell consumers about the company and its many products.[14] Dealership salespeople assist potential buyers and persuade them that Ford is the best car for them. Ford and its dealers offer special promotions—sales, cash rebates, low financing rates—as added purchase incentives.

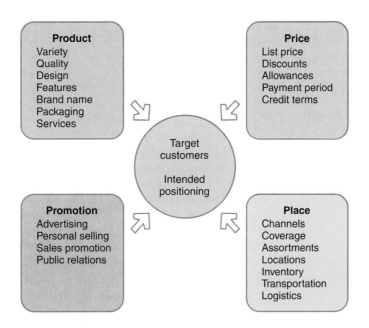

FIGURE 2.5
The Four *P*s of the Marketing Mix

An effective marketing program blends all of the marketing mix elements into a coordinated program designed to achieve the company's marketing objectives by delivering value to consumers. The marketing mix constitutes the company's tactical tool kit for establishing strong positioning in target markets.

Some critics think that the four Ps may omit or underemphasize certain important activities. For example, they ask, "Where are services?" Just because they don't start with a *P* doesn't justify omitting them. The answer is that services, such as banking, airline, and retailing services, are products too. We might call them *service products*. "Where is packaging?" the critics might ask. Marketers would answer that they include packaging as just one of many product decisions. All said, as Figure 2.5 suggests, many marketing activities that might appear to be left out of the marketing mix are subsumed under one of the four Ps. The issue is not whether there should be four, six, or ten Ps so much as what framework is most helpful in designing marketing programs.

There is another concern, however, that is valid. It holds that the four Ps concept takes the seller's view of the market, not the buyer's view. From the buyer's viewpoint, in this age of customer relationships, the four Ps might be better described as the four Cs:[15]

Four Ps	Four Cs
Product	Customer solution
Price	Customer cost
Place	Convenience
Promotion	Communication

Thus, while marketers see themselves as selling products, customers see themselves as buying value or solutions to their problems. And customers are interested in more than just the price; they are interested in the total costs of obtaining, using, and disposing of a product. Customers want the product and service to be as conveniently available as possible. Finally, they want two-way communication. Marketers would do well to think through the four Cs first and then build the four Ps on that platform.

Managing the Marketing Effort

In addition to being good at the *marketing* in marketing management, companies also need to pay attention to the *management*. Managing the marketing process requires the four marketing management functions shown in Figure 2.6—*analysis*, *planning*, *implementation*, and *control*.

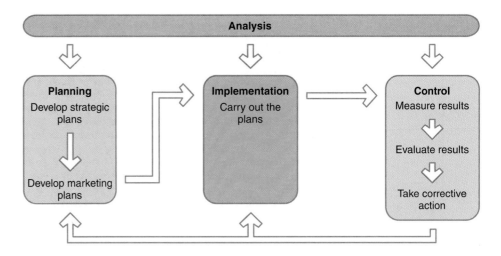

The company first develops companywide strategic plans, and then translates them into marketing and other plans for each division, product, and brand. Through implementation, the company turns the plans into actions. Control consists of measuring and evaluating the results of marketing activities and taking corrective action where needed. Finally, marketing analysis provides information and evaluations needed for all of the other marketing activities.

MARKETING ANALYSIS

SWOT analysis

An overall evaluation of the company's strengths (S), weaknesses (W), opportunities (O), and threats (T).

Managing the marketing function begins with a complete analysis of the company's situation. The marketer should conduct a **SWOT analysis**, by which it evaluates the company's overall strengths (S), weaknesses (W), opportunities (O), and threats (T) (see Figure 2.7). Strengths include internal capabilities, resources, and positive situational factors that may help the company to serve its customers and achieve its objectives. Weaknesses include internal limitations and negative situational factors that may interfere with the company's performance. Opportunities are favorable factors or trends in the external environment that the company may be able to exploit to its advantage. And threats are unfavorable external factors or trends that may present challenges to performance.

The company must analyze its markets and marketing environment to find attractive opportunities and identify environmental threats. It must analyze company strengths and weaknesses as well as current and possible marketing actions to determine which opportunities it can best pursue. The goal is to match the company's strengths to attractive opportunities in the environment, while eliminating or overcoming the weaknesses and minimizing the threats. Marketing analysis provides inputs to each of the other marketing management functions. We discuss marketing analysis more fully in Chapter 3.

MARKETING PLANNING

Through strategic planning, the company decides what it wants to do with each business unit. Marketing planning involves deciding on marketing strategies that will help the company attain its overall strategic objectives. A detailed marketing plan is needed for each business, product,

FIGURE 2.7

SWOT Analysis

	Positive	Negative
Internal	**Strengths** Internal capabilities that may help a company reach its objectives	**Weaknesses** Internal limitations that may interfere with a company's ability to achieve its objectives
External	**Opportunities** External factors that the company may be able to exploit to its advantage	**Threats** Current and emerging external factors that may challenge the company's performance

or brand. What does a marketing plan look like? Our discussion focuses on product or brand marketing plans.

Table 2.2 outlines the major sections of a typical product or brand marketing plan. (See Appendix 2 for a sample marketing plan.) The plan begins with an executive summary, which quickly overviews major assessments, goals, and recommendations. The main section of the plan presents a detailed analysis of the current marketing situation as well as potential threats and opportunities. It next states major objectives for the brand and outlines the specifics of a marketing strategy for achieving them.

A *marketing strategy* consists of specific strategies for target markets, positioning, the marketing mix, and marketing expenditure levels. In this section, the planner explains how each strategy responds to the threats, opportunities, and critical issues spelled out earlier in the plan. Additional sections of the marketing plan lay out an action program for implementing the marketing strategy along with the details of a supporting *marketing budget*. The last section outlines the controls that will be used to monitor progress and take corrective action.

MARKETING IMPLEMENTATION

Planning good strategies is only a start toward successful marketing. A brilliant marketing strategy counts for little if the company fails to implement it properly. **Marketing implementation** is the process that turns marketing *plans* into marketing *actions* in order to accomplish strategic marketing objectives. Whereas marketing planning addresses the *what* and *why* of marketing activities, implementation addresses the *who*, *where*, *when*, and *how*.

Many managers think that "doing things right" (implementation) is as important as, or even more important than, "doing the right things" (strategy). The fact is that both are critical to success, and companies can gain competitive advantages through effective implementation. One firm can have essentially the same strategy as another, yet win in the

Marketing implementation
The process that turns marketing strategies and plans into marketing actions in order to accomplish strategic marketing objectives.

TABLE 2.2   Contents of a Marketing Plan

Section	Purpose
Executive summary	Presents a brief summary of the main goals and recommendations of the plan for management review, helping top management to find the plan's major points quickly. A table of contents should follow the executive summary.
Current marketing situation	Describes the target market and company's position in it, including information about the market, product performance, competition, and distribution. This section includes: • A *market description* that defines the market and major segments, then reviews customer needs and factors in the marketing environment that may affect customer purchasing. • A *product review* that shows sales, prices, and gross margins of the major products in the product line. • A review of *competition,* which identifies major competitors and assesses their market positions and strategies for product quality, pricing, distribution, and promotion. • A review of *distribution,* which evaluates recent sales trends and other developments in major distribution channels.
Threats and opportunities analysis	Assesses major threats and opportunities that the product might face, helping management to anticipate important positive or negative developments that might have an impact on the firm and its strategies.
Objectives and issues	States the marketing objectives that the company would like to attain during the plan's term and discusses key issues that will affect their attainment. For example, if the goal is to achieve a 15 percent market share, this section looks at how this goal might be achieved.
Marketing strategy	Outlines the broad marketing logic by which the business unit hopes to achieve its marketing objectives and the specifics of target markets, positioning, and marketing expenditure levels. It outlines specific strategies for each marketing-mix element and explains how each responds to the threats, opportunities, and critical issues spelled out earlier in the plan.
Action programs	Spells out how marketing strategies will be turned into specific action programs that answer the following questions: *What* will be done? *When* will it be done? *Who* is responsible for doing it? *How* much will it cost?
Budgets	Details a supporting marketing budget that is essentially a projected profit-and-loss statement. It shows expected revenues (forecasted number of units sold and the average net price) and expected costs (of production, distribution, and marketing). The difference is the projected profit. Once approved by higher management, the budget becomes the basis for materials buying, production scheduling, personnel planning, and marketing operations.
Controls	Outlines the control that will be used to monitor progress and allow higher management to review implementation results and spot products that are not meeting their goals.

■ Marketers must continually plan their analysis, implementation, and control activities.

marketplace through faster or better execution. Still, implementation is difficult—it is often easier to think up good marketing strategies than it is to carry them out.

In an increasingly connected world, people at all levels of the marketing system must work together to implement marketing strategies and plans. At Black & Decker, for example, marketing implementation for the company's power tools, outdoor equipment, and other products requires day-to-day decisions and actions by thousands of people both inside and outside the organization. Marketing managers make decisions about target segments, branding, packaging, pricing, promoting, and distributing. They talk with engineering about product design, with manufacturing about production and inventory levels, and with finance about funding and cash flows. They also connect with outside people, such as advertising agencies to plan ad campaigns and the news media to obtain publicity support. The sales force urges Home Depot, Lowe's, Wal-Mart, and other retailers to advertise Black & Decker products, provide ample shelf space, and use company displays.

Successful marketing implementation depends on how well the company blends its people, organizational structure, decision and reward systems, and company culture into a cohesive action program that supports its strategies. At all levels, the company must be staffed by people who have the needed skills, motivation, and personal characteristics. The company's formal organization structure plays an important role in implementing marketing strategy; so do its decision and reward systems. For example, if a company's compensation system rewards managers for short-run profit results, they will have little incentive to work toward long-run market-building objectives.

Finally, to be successfully implemented, the firm's marketing strategies must fit with its company culture, the system of values and beliefs shared by people in the organization. A study of America's most successful companies found that these companies have almost cult-like cultures built around strong, market-oriented missions. At companies such as Dell, Nordstrom, Citicorp, and P&G, "employees share such a strong vision that they know in their hearts what's right for their company."[16]

MARKETING DEPARTMENT ORGANIZATION

The company must design a marketing organization that can carry out marketing strategies and plans. If the company is very small, one person might do all of the research, selling, advertising, customer service, and other marketing work. As the company expands, a marketing department emerges to plan and carry out marketing activities. In large companies, this department contains many specialists. Thus, General Electric and Microsoft have product and market managers, sales managers and salespeople, market researchers, advertising experts, and many other specialists. To head up such large marketing organizations, many companies have now created a *chief marketing officer* (or CMO) position.

Modern marketing departments can be arranged in several ways. The most common form of marketing organization is the *functional organization*. Under this organization, different marketing activities are headed by a functional specialist—a sales manager, advertising manager, marketing research manager, customer service manager, or new-product manager. A company that sells across the country or internationally often uses a *geographic organization*. Its sales and marketing people are assigned to specific countries, regions, and districts. Geographic organization allows salespeople to settle into a territory, get to know their customers, and work with a minimum of travel time and cost.

Companies with many very different products or brands often create a *product management organization*. Using this approach, a product manager develops and implements a complete strategy and marketing program for a specific product or brand. Product management first appeared at P&G in 1929. A new company soap, Camay, was not doing well, and a young P&G executive was assigned to give his exclusive attention to developing and promoting this product. He was successful, and the company soon added other product managers.[17] Since then, many firms, especially consumer products companies, have set up product management organizations.

For companies that sell one product line to many different types of markets and customers that have different needs and preferences, a *market* or *customer management organization* might be best. A market management organization is similar to the product management organization. Market managers are responsible for developing marketing strategies and plans for their specific markets or customers. This system's main advantage is that the company is organized around the needs of specific customer segments.

Large companies that produce many different products flowing into many different geographic and customer markets usually employ some *combination* of the functional, geographic, product, and market organization forms. This ensures that each function, product, and market receives its share of management attention. However, it can also add costly layers of management and reduce organizational flexibility. Still, the benefits of organizational specialization usually outweigh the drawbacks.

Marketing organization has become an increasingly important issue in recent years. As we discussed in Chapter 1, many companies are finding that today's marketing environment calls for less focus on products, brands, and territories and more focus on customers and customer relationships. More and more companies are shifting their brand management focus toward *customer management*—moving away from managing just product or brand profitability and toward managing customer profitability and customer equity. And many companies now organize their marketing operations around major customers. For example, companies such as P&G and Black & Decker have large teams, or even whole divisions, set up to serve large customers like Wal-Mart, Target, or Home Depot.

MARKETING CONTROL

Because many surprises occur during the implementation of marketing plans, the marketing department must practice constant marketing control. **Marketing control** involves evaluating the results of marketing strategies and plans and taking corrective action to ensure that objectives are attained. Marketing control involves four steps. Management first sets specific marketing goals. It then measures its performance in the marketplace and evaluates the causes of any differences between expected and actual performance. Finally, management takes corrective action to close the gaps between its goals and its performance. This may require changing the action programs or even changing the goals.

Operating control involves checking ongoing performance against the annual plan and taking corrective action when necessary. Its purpose is to ensure that the company achieves the sales, profits, and other goals set out in its annual plan. It also involves determining the profitability of different products, territories, markets, and channels.

Strategic control involves looking at whether the company's basic strategies are well matched to its opportunities. Marketing strategies and programs can quickly become outdated, and each company should periodically reassess its overall approach to the marketplace. A major tool for such strategic control is a **marketing audit**. The marketing audit is a comprehensive, systematic, independent, and periodic examination of a company's environment, objectives, strategies, and activities to determine problem areas and opportunities. The audit provides good input for a plan of action to improve the company's marketing performance.[18]

The marketing audit covers *all* major marketing areas of a business, not just a few trouble spots. It assesses the marketing environment, marketing strategy, marketing organization, marketing systems, marketing mix, and marketing productivity and profitability. The audit is normally conducted by an objective and experienced outside party. The findings may come as a surprise—and sometimes as a shock—to management. Management then decides which actions make sense and how and when to implement them.

Marketing control
The process of measuring and evaluating the results of marketing strategies and plans, and taking corrective action to ensure that objectives are achieved.

Marketing audit
A comprehensive, systematic, independent, and periodic examination of a company's environment, objectives, strategies, and activities to determine problem areas and opportunities and to recommend a plan of action to improve the company's marketing performance.

Measuring and Managing Return on Marketing

Marketing managers must ensure that their marketing dollars are being well spent. In the past, many marketers spent freely on big, expensive marketing programs, often without thinking carefully about the financial returns on their spending. They believed that marketing produces intangible outcomes, which do not lend themselves readily to measures of productivity or return. But all that is changing:

> For years, corporate marketers have walked into budget meetings like neighborhood junkies. They couldn't always justify how well they spent past handouts or what difference it all made. They just wanted more money—for flashy TV ads, for big-ticket events, for, you know, getting out the message and building up the brand. But those heady days of blind budget increases are fast being replaced with a new mantra: measurement and accountability. Armed with reams of data, increasingly sophisticated tools, and growing evidence that the old tricks simply don't work, there's hardly a marketing executive today who isn't demanding a more scientific approach to help defend marketing strategies in front of the chief financial officer. Marketers want to know the actual return on investment (ROI) of each dollar. They want to know it often, not just annually. . . . Companies in every segment of American business have become obsessed with honing the science of measuring marketing performance. "Marketers have been pretty unaccountable for many years," notes one expert. "Now they are under big pressure to estimate their impact."[19]

Return on marketing (or marketing ROI)
The net return from a marketing investment divided by the costs of the marketing investment.

■ Return on marketing: Companies can assess return on marketing in terms of standard marketing performance measures. Such analysis showed that Campbell's recent "Soup at Hand" advertising campaign nearly doubled both the product's trial rate and repeat use.

In response, marketers are developing better measures of *return on marketing*. **Return on marketing** (or *marketing ROI*) is the net return from a marketing investment divided by the costs of the marketing investment. It measures the profits generated by investments in marketing activities.

It's true that marketing returns can be difficult to measure. In measuring financial ROI, both the *R* and the *I* are uniformly measured in dollars. But there is as yet no consistent definition of marketing ROI. "It's tough to measure, more so than for other business expenses," says one analyst. "You can imagine buying a piece of equipment, . . . and then measuring the productivity gains that result from the purchase," he says. "But in marketing, benefits like advertising impact aren't easily put into dollar returns. It takes a leap of faith to come up with a number."[20]

A company can assess return on marketing in terms of standard marketing performance measures, such as brand awareness, sales, or market share. Campbell's Soup uses sales and share data to evaluate specific advertising campaigns. For example, analysis revealed that its recent Soup at Hand advertising campaign, which depicted real-life scenarios of consumers using the portable soup, nearly doubled both the product's trial rate and repeat use rate after the first year. The Soup at Hand campaign received a Gold Effie, an advertising industry award based on marketing effectiveness.[21]

Increasingly, however, marketers are using customer-centered measures of marketing impact, such as customer acquisition, customer retention, and customer lifetime value. Figure 2.8 views marketing expenditures as investments that produce returns in the form of more profitable customer relationships.[22] Marketing investments result in

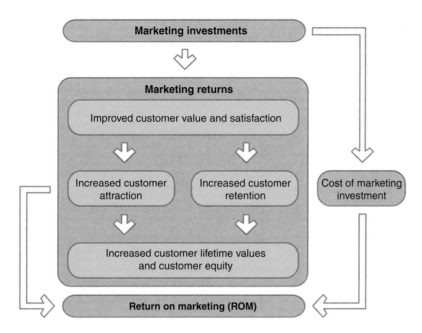

FIGURE 2.8
Return on Marketing

Source: Adapted from Roland T. Rust, Katherine N. Lemon, and Valerie A. Zeithamal, "Return on Marketing: Using Consumer Equity to Focus Marketing Strategy," *Journal of Marketing,* January 2004, p. 112.

improved customer value and satisfaction, which in turn increases customer attraction and retention. This increases individual customer lifetime values and the firm's overall customer equity. Increased customer equity, in relation to the cost of the marketing investments, determines return on marketing.

Regardless of how it's defined or measured, the return on marketing concept is here to stay. "All good marketers live and die by measurements of their results," states the marketing productivity consultant. "Projections are made, marketing is delivered, results are measured, and the knowledge is applied to guide future marketing. . . . The return on marketing investments is integral to strategic decisions at [all levels] of the business."[23]

REST STOP → REVIEWING THE CONCEPTS

In Chapter 1, we defined *marketing* and outlined the steps in the marketing process. In this chapter, we examined companywide strategic planning and marketing's role in the organization. Then, we looked more deeply into marketing strategy and the marketing mix, and reviewed the major marketing management functions. So you've now had a pretty good overview of the fundamentals of modern marketing. In future chapters, we'll expand on these fundamentals.

1. Explain companywide strategic planning and its four steps.

Strategic planning sets the stage for the rest of the company's planning. Marketing contributes to strategic planning, and the overall plan defines marketing's role in the company. Although formal planning offers a variety of benefits to companies, not all companies use it or use it well.

Strategic planning involves developing a strategy for long-run survival and growth. It consists of four steps: defining the company's mission, setting objectives and goals, designing a business portfolio, and developing functional plans. *Defining a clear company mission* begins with drafting a formal mission statement, which should be market oriented, realistic, specific, motivating, and consistent with the market

environment. The mission is then transformed into detailed *supporting goals and objectives* to guide the entire company. Based on those goals and objectives, headquarters designs a *business portfolio,* deciding which businesses and products should receive more or fewer resources. In turn, each business and product unit must develop *detailed marketing plans* in line with the companywide plan.

2. Discuss how to design business portfolios and develop strategies for growth and downsizing.

Guided by the company's mission statement and objectives, management plans its *business portfolio,* or the collection of businesses and products that make up the company. The firm wants to produce a business portfolio that best fits its strengths and weaknesses to opportunities in the environment. To do this, it must analyze and adjust its *current* business portfolio and develop growth and downsizing strategies for adjusting the *future* portfolio. The company might use a formal portfolio-planning method. But many companies are now designing more customized portfolio-planning approaches that better suit their unique situations. The *product/market expansion grid* suggests four possible growth paths: market penetration, market development, product development, and diversification.

3. Assess marketing's role in strategic planning and explain how marketers partner with others inside and outside the firm to build profitable customer relationships.

Under the strategic plan, the major functional departments—marketing, finance, accounting, purchasing, operations, information systems, human resources, and others—must work together to accomplish strategic objectives. Marketing plays a key role in the company's strategic planning by providing a *marketing-concept philosophy* and *inputs* regarding attractive market opportunities. Within individual business units, marketing designs *strategies* for reaching the unit's objectives and helps to carry them out profitably.

Marketers alone cannot produce superior value for customers. A company's success depends on how well each department performs its customer value-adding activities and how well the departments work together to serve the customer. Thus, marketers must practice *partner relationship management*. They must work closely with partners in other company departments to form an effective *value chain* that serves the customer. And they must partner effectively with other companies in the marketing system to form a competitively superior *value-delivery network*.

4. Describe the elements of a customer-driven marketing strategy and mix, and the forces that influence it.

Consumer relationships are at the center of marketing strategy and programs. Through market segmentation, target marketing, and market positioning, the company divides the total market into smaller segments, selects segments it can best serve, and decides how it wants to bring value to target consumers. It then designs a *marketing mix* to produce the response it wants in the target market. The marketing mix consists of product, price, place, and promotion decisions.

5. List the marketing management functions, including the elements of a marketing plan, and discuss the importance of measuring and managing return on marketing.

To find the best strategy and mix and to put them into action, the company engages in marketing analysis, planning, implementation, and control. The main components of a *marketing plan* are the executive summary, current marketing situation, threats and opportunities, objectives and issues, marketing strategies, action programs, budgets, and controls. To plan good strategies is often easier than to carry them out. To be successful, companies must also be effective at *implementation*—turning marketing strategies into marketing actions.

Much of the responsibility for implementation goes to the company's marketing department. Marketing departments can be organized in one or a combination of ways: *functional marketing organization, geographic organization, product management organization*, or *market management organization*. In this age of customer relationships, more and more companies are now changing their organizational focus from product or territory management to customer relationship management. Marketing organizations carry out *marketing control*, both operating control and strategic control. They use *marketing audits* to determine marketing opportunities and problems and to recommend short-run and long-run actions to improve overall marketing performance.

Marketing managers must ensure that their marketing dollars are being well spent. Today's marketers face growing pressures to show that they are adding value in line with their costs. In response, marketers are developing better measures of *return on marketing*. Increasingly, they are using customer-centered measures of marketing impact as a key input into their strategic decision making.

Navigating the Key Terms

Travel Log

Discussing the Issues

1. Define strategic planning. List and briefly describe the four steps that lead managers and the firm through the strategic planning process. What role does marketing play in strategic planning?

2. Review the Boston Consulting Group's growth-share matrix. Which one of the cells provides the primary revenues for the organization's growth? How can the BCG growth-share matrix be used to assess both the current product portfolio and plan for the future?

3. Do you agree that the value chain is only as strong as its weakest link? How can partnering with other organizations to form a value delivery network further strengthen a firm's performance?

4. Discuss the differences between market segmentation, target marketing, and market positioning.

5. Define each of the four Ps. What insight might a firm gain by considering the four Cs rather than the four Ps?

6. What role do analysis, planning, implementation, and control play in the marketing process? How are these four marketing management functions related to one another?

Application Questions

1. In a small group, discuss whether the following statement from Burton Snowboards North America, manufacturers and marketers of a leading snowboard brand, meets the five criteria of a good mission statement: "Burton Snowboards is a rider-driven company solely dedicated to creating the best snowboarding equipment on the planet."

2. The product/market expansion grid can be useful in identifying growth opportunities for companies through market penetration, product development, market development, and diversification. Consider a food retailer like Subway, which makes sandwiches and offers chips and drinks. Think creatively to describe one growth opportunity for Subway for each of the four product/market expansion grid cells.

3. In recent years, shoe endorsements that once belonged exclusively to pro athletes have branched out to include entertainers. For example, rapper 50 Cent signed an endorsement contract with Reebok and is now promoting a collection of Reebok shoes. Says 50 Cent, "athletes are seasonal. Our presence is year round." Does this shift in endorsements signal a change in Reebok's segmentation, targeting, and positioning strategies? What are the benefits and drawbacks of such a change in endorsers?*

*For more information, see Michael McCarthy, "Rappers Sample Athletes' Turf," *USA TODAY*, July 4, 2005.

Under the Hood: Focus on Technology

In order to improve 911 emergency services, the FCC required cell phone carriers to be able to establish subscribers' locations within 100 meters by the end of 2005. To do so, service providers are relying on two different approaches. One uses phones with built-in GPS chips, while the other triangulates between three or more cell towers to pinpoint a caller's location. This technology, already in use in Hong Kong, Tokyo, and Helsinki for some time, has drawn the interest of marketers who envision other uses such as sending promotional offers to customers as they walk past their store.

1. In a small group, brainstorm potential marketing uses for this technology other than those discussed above.

2. Assume you are a member of a cell phone carrier's marketing team selling this technology to retailers. Develop both a product-oriented and a market-oriented mission statement for the company.

3. What limitations does the product-oriented mission statement have that the market-oriented statement overcomes?

Focus on Ethics

Ever since trailblazers like The Body Shop entered the market, companies have been blurring the traditional lines between corporate America and nonprofit organizations. Ben & Jerry's, for example, has not one but three mission statements—a product mission, an economic mission, and a social mission. Other companies associate themselves with causes as a part of their community outreach efforts. Avon supports breast cancer awareness. Wal-Mart offers rewards to good teachers.

1. Ben & Jerry's details its three mission statements on its Web site at www.benjerry.com/our_company/our_mission.

Visit the site and learn more about the company's efforts to be socially responsible. Do Ben & Jerry's mission statements truly reflect the company's goals and activities? As a consumer, were your impressions of the company changed after reading the mission statement?

2. Is it ethical for companies to use social causes to sell products and services?

3. Discuss the role that a company's mission statement can have in encouraging ethical and socially responsible corporate behavior.

Videos

The Mayo video case that accompanies this chapter is located in Appendix 1 at the back of the book.

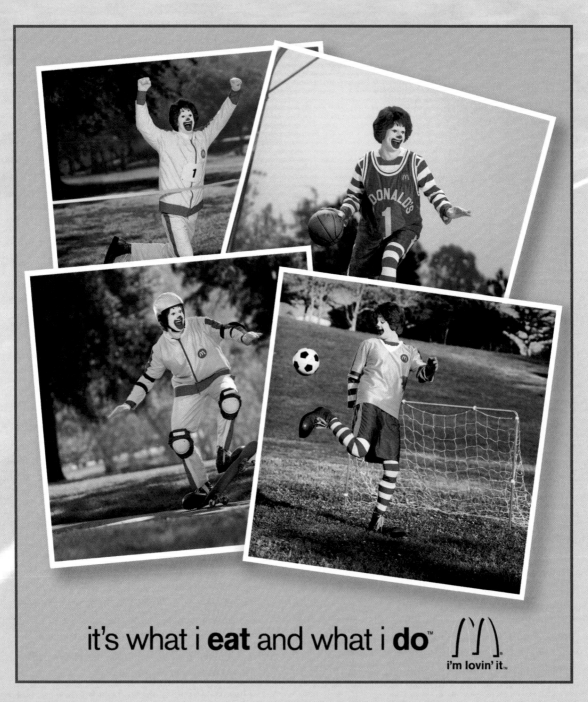

it's what i **eat** and what i **do**™ i'm lovin' it™

→ **AFTER STUDYING THIS CHAPTER, YOU SHOULD BE ABLE TO**

1. describe the environmental forces that affect the company's ability to serve its customers

2. explain how changes in the demographic and economic environments affect marketing decisions

3. identify the major trends in the firm's natural and technological environments

4. explain the key changes in the political and cultural environments

5. discuss how companies can react to the marketing environment

The Marketing Environment

Road Map Previewing the Concepts

In Part 1 (Chapters 1 and 2), you learned about the basic concepts of marketing and the steps in the marketing process for building profitable relationships with targeted consumers. In Part 2, as you continue your journey toward learning about marketing, we'll look deeper into the first step of the marketing process—understanding the marketplace and customer needs and wants. In this chapter, you'll discover that marketing does not operate in a vacuum but rather in a complex and changing environment. Other *actors* in this environment—suppliers, intermediaries, customers, competitors, publics, and others—may work with or against the company. Major environmental *forces*—demographic, economic, natural, technological, political, and cultural—shape marketing opportunities, pose threats, and affect the company's ability to serve customers and develop lasting relationships with them. To understand marketing, and to develop effective marketing strategies, you must first understand the context in which marketing operates.

At our first stop, we'll look at an American icon, McDonald's. More than half a century ago, Ray Kroc spotted an important shift in U.S. consumer lifestyles and bought a small chain of restaurants. He built that chain into the vast McDonald's fast-food empire. But while the shifting marketing environment brought opportunities for McDonald's, it has also created challenges.

In 1955, Ray Kroc, a 52-year-old salesman of milk-shake mixing machines, discovered a string of seven restaurants owned by Richard and Maurice McDonald. Kroc saw the McDonald brothers' fast-food concept as a perfect fit for America's increasingly on-the-go, time-squeezed, family-oriented lifestyles. Kroc bought the small chain for $2.7 million, and the rest is history.

McDonald's grew quickly to become the world's largest fast-feeder. Its more than 30,000 restaurants worldwide now serve nearly 50 million customers each day, racking up system-wide sales of more than $56 billion annually. The Golden Arches are one of the world's most familiar icons, and other than Santa Claus, no character in the world is more recognizable than Ronald McDonald. "By making fast food respectable for middle-class families," says an industry analyst, "the Golden Arches did for greasy spoons what Holiday Inn did for roadside motels in the 1950s and what Sam Walton later did for the discount retail store."

But just as the changing marketplace has provided opportunities for McDonald's, it has also presented challenges. In fact, by early in this decade, the once-shiny Golden Arches had lost some of their luster, as the company struggled to address shifting consumer lifestyles. While McDonald's remained the nation's most-visited fast-food chain, its sales growth slumped, and its market share fell by more than 3 percent between 1997 and 2003. In 2002, the company posted its first-ever quarterly loss.

What happened? In this age of obesity lawsuits and $5 lattes, McDonald's seemed a bit out of step with the times. Consumers were looking for fresher, better tasting food and more upscale atmospheres. As a result, McDonald's was losing share to what the industry calls "fast-casual" restaurants. New competitors such as Panera Bread, Baja Fresh, Pret a Manger, and Cosi were offering more imaginative meals in more fashionable surroundings. And for busy consumers who'd rather "eat-out-in," even the local supermarket offered a full selection of pre-prepared, ready-to-serve gourmet meals to go.

Americans were also seeking healthier eating options. Fast-food patrons complained about too few healthy menu choices. Worried about their health, many customers were eating less at fast-food restaurants. As the market leader, McDonald's bore the brunt of much of this criticism. In one lawsuit, recently reopened by a New York appeals court, the parents of two teenage girls even charged that McDonald's was responsible for their children's obesity and related health problems, including diabetes.

Reacting to these challenges, in early 2003, McDonald's announced a turnaround plan—the "Plan to Win"—to better align the company with the new marketplace realities. The plan included the following initiatives:

Back to Basics—McDonald's began refocusing on what made it successful: consistent products and reliable service. It began pouring money back into existing stores, speeding up service, training employees, and monitoring restaurants to make sure they stay bright and clean.

If You Can't Lick 'Em, Join 'Em—To find new ways to compete better with the new breed of fast-casual competitors, and to expand its customer base, McDonald's has experimented with new restaurant concepts. For example, it has tested upscale *McCafé* coffee shops, which offer leather seating, a knowledgeable staff, and espresso in porcelain cups, along with made-to-order drinks, gourmet sandwiches, and Internet access. It is also testing a *Bistro Gourmet* concept in a handful of restaurants in the United States, which offers high-back leather chairs, a made-to-order omelet breakfast bar, and food served on real china.

Kids can still get their Happy Meals, but parents can feast on more sophisticated fare, such as panini sandwiches, gourmet burgers, and crème brûlée cheesecake.

"It's what i **eat** and what i **do** . . . i'm lovin' it"—McDonald's recently unveiled a major multi-faceted education campaign to help consumers better understand the keys to living balanced, active lifestyles. The "it's what i **eat** and what i **do** . . . i'm lovin' it" theme underscores the important interplay between eating right and staying active. The company assembled a Global Advisory Council of outside experts in the areas of nutrition, wellness, and activity to provide input on its menu choice and variety, education outreach, and promoting physical fitness. McDonald's has introduced a trimmer, fitter Ronald McDonald. He has expanded his role as Chief Happiness Officer to be global ambassador of fun, fitness, and children's well-being, inspiring and encouraging kids and families around the world to eat well and stay active. McDonald's has also refreshed its GoActive.com Web site, which offers tips on how to lead a balanced active lifestyle as well as a Family Fitness Tool Kit. And the McDonald's Passport to Play in-school program, motivates children in 31,000 schools around the country to be more active in unique and fun ways during grade school physical education classes. Even the harshest McDonald's critics, although still skeptical, applaud these actions.

Improving the Fare—McDonald's has worked to provide more choice and variety on its menu. For example, it introduced a "Go Active! Happy Meal for adults featuring a Premium Salad, a bottle of Dasani water, and a "Stepometer," which measures physical activity by tracking daily steps. It now offers Chicken McNuggets made with white meat, Chicken Selects wholebreast strips, low-fat "milk jugs," and a line of Premium Salads, such as its Fruit & Walnut Premium Salad, consisting of apple slices and seedless grapes with a side of low-fat vanilla yogurt and candied walnuts. Within only a year of introducing its Premium Salads, McDonald's became the world's largest salad seller—it has sold more than 400 million salads to date.

McDonald's efforts to realign itself with the changing marketing environment appear to be paying off. By almost any measure, the fast-food giant is now back in shape. The company is posting steady, even startling, sales and profit increases, and customers and stockholders alike are humming the chain's catchy jingle, "i'm lovin' it." A former McDonald's CEO summed it up this way: "Ray Kroc used to say he didn't know what we would be selling in the year 2000, but whatever it was we would be selling the most of it. He recognized early on that consumer needs change and we want to change with them."[1]

Marketers need to be good at building relationships with customers, others in the company, and external partners. To do this effectively, they must understand the major environmental forces that surround all of these relationships. A company's **marketing environment** consists of the actors and forces outside marketing that affect marketing management's ability to build and maintain successful relationships with target customers. Successful companies know the vital importance of constantly watching and adapting to the changing environment.

The environment continues to change rapidly, and both consumers and marketers wonder what the future will bring. More than any other group in the company, marketers must be the trend trackers and opportunity seekers. Although every manager in an organization needs to observe the outside environment, marketers have two special aptitudes. They have disciplined methods—marketing research and marketing intelligence—for collecting information about the marketing environment. They also spend more time in the customer and competitor environments. By carefully studying the environment, marketers can adapt their strategies to meet new marketplace challenges and opportunities.

The marketing environment is made up of a *microenvironment* and a *macroenvironment*. The **microenvironment** consists of the actors close to the company that affect its ability to serve its customers—the company, suppliers, marketing intermediaries, customer markets, competitors, and publics. The **macroenvironment** consists of the larger societal forces that affect the microenvironment—demographic, economic, natural, technological, political, and cultural forces. We look first at the company's microenvironment.

The Company's Microenvironment

Marketing management's job is to build relationships with customers by creating customer value and satisfaction. However, marketing managers cannot do this alone. Figure 3.1 shows the major actors in the marketer's microenvironment. Marketing success will require building relationships with other company departments, suppliers, marketing intermediaries, customers, competitors, and various publics, which combine to make up the company's value delivery network.

THE COMPANY

In designing marketing plans, marketing management takes other company groups into account—groups such as top management, finance, research and development (R&D), purchasing, operations, and accounting. All these interrelated groups form the internal environment. Top management sets the company's mission, objectives, broad strategies, and policies. Marketing managers make decisions within the strategies and plans made by top management.

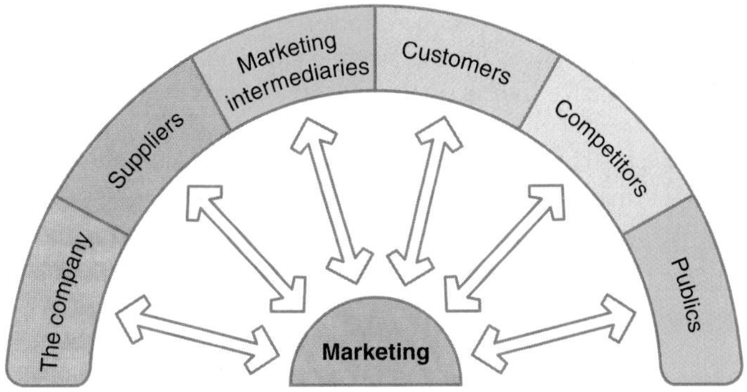

Marketing environment
The actors and forces outside marketing that affect marketing management's ability to build and maintain successful relationships with target customers.

Microenvironment
The actors close to the company that affect its ability to serve its customers—the company, suppliers, marketing intermediaries, customer markets, competitors, and publics.

Macroenvironment
The larger societal forces that affect the microenvironment—demographic, economic, natural, technological, political, and cultural forces.

FIGURE 3.1
Actors in the Microenvironment

Marketing managers must also work closely with other company departments. Finance is concerned with finding and using funds to carry out the marketing plan. The R&D department focuses on designing safe and attractive products. Purchasing worries about getting supplies and materials, whereas operations is responsible for producing and distributing the desired quality and quantity of products. Accounting has to measure revenues and costs to help marketing know how well it is achieving its objectives. Together, all of these departments have an impact on the marketing department's plans and actions. Under the marketing concept, all of these functions must "think consumer." They should work in harmony to provide superior customer value and satisfaction.

SUPPLIERS

Suppliers form an important link in the company's overall customer value delivery system. They provide the resources needed by the company to produce its goods and services. Supplier problems can seriously affect marketing. Marketing managers must watch supply availability—supply shortages or delays, labor strikes, and other events can cost sales in the short run and damage customer satisfaction in the long run. Marketing managers also monitor the price trends of their key inputs. Rising supply costs may force price increases that can harm the company's sales volume.

Most marketers today treat their suppliers as partners in creating and delivering customer value. Wal-Mart goes to great lengths to work with its suppliers. For example, it helps them to test new products in its stores. And its Supplier Development Department publishes a *Supplier Proposal Guide* and maintains a supplier Web site, both of which help suppliers to navigate the complex Wal-Mart buying process. It knows that good partnership relationship management results in success for Wal-Mart, suppliers, and, ultimately, its customers.

Marketing intermediaries
Firms that help the company to promote, sell, and distribute its goods to final buyers; they include resellers, physical distribution firms, marketing service agencies, and financial intermediaries.

MARKETING INTERMEDIARIES

Marketing intermediaries help the company to promote, sell, and distribute its goods to final buyers. They include resellers, physical distribution firms, marketing services agencies, and financial intermediaries. *Resellers* are distribution channel firms that help the company find customers or make sales to them. These include wholesalers and retailers, who buy and resell merchandise. Selecting and partnering with resellers is not easy. No longer do manufacturers have many small, independent resellers from which to choose. They now face large and growing reseller organizations such as Wal-Mart, Target, Home Depot, Costco, and Best Buy. These organizations frequently have enough power to dictate terms or even shut the manufacturer out of large markets.

Physical distribution firms help the company to stock and move goods from their points of origin to their destinations. Working with warehouse and transportation firms, a company must determine the best ways to store and ship goods, balancing factors such as cost, delivery, speed, and safety. *Marketing services agencies* are the marketing research firms, advertising agencies, media firms, and marketing consulting firms that help the company target and promote its products to the right markets. *Financial intermediaries* include banks, credit companies, insurance companies, and other businesses that help finance transactions or insure against the risks associated with the buying and selling of goods.

Like suppliers, marketing intermediaries form an important component of the company's overall value delivery system. In its quest to create satisfying customer relationships, the company must do more than just optimize its own performance. It must partner effectively with marketing intermediaries to optimize the performance of the entire system.

Thus, today's marketers recognize the importance of working with their intermediaries as partners rather than simply as channels through which they sell

■ Partnering with marketing intermediaries: Coca-Cola provides Wendy's with much more than just soft drinks. It also pledges powerful marketing support.

their products. For example, when Coca-Cola signs on as the exclusive beverage provider for a fast-food chain, such as McDonald's, Wendy's, or Subway, it provides much more than just soft drinks. It also pledges powerful marketing support.

> Coke assigns cross-functional teams dedicated to understanding the finer points of each retail partner's business. It conducts a staggering amount of research on beverage consumers and shares these insights with its partners. It analyzes the demographics of U.S. zip code areas and helps partners to determine which Coke brands are preferred in their areas. Coca-Cola has even studied the design of drive-through menu boards to better understand which layouts, fonts, letter sizes, colors, and visuals induce consumers to order more food and drink. Such intense partnering efforts have earned Coca-Cola a 68 percent share of the U.S. fountain soft drink market, compared with a 22 percent share for Pepsi.[2]

CUSTOMERS

The company needs to study five types of customer markets closely. *Consumer markets* consist of individuals and households that buy goods and services for personal consumption. *Business markets* buy goods and services for further processing or for use in their production process, whereas *reseller markets* buy goods and services to resell at a profit. *Government markets* are made up of government agencies that buy goods and services to produce public services or transfer the goods and services to others who need them. Finally, *international markets* consist of these buyers in other countries, including consumers, producers, resellers, and governments. Each market type has special characteristics that call for careful study by the seller.

Public

Any group that has an actual or potential interest in, or impact on, an organization's ability to achieve its objectives.

COMPETITORS

The marketing concept states that to be successful, a company must provide greater customer value and satisfaction than its competitors do. Thus, marketers must do more than simply adapt to the needs of target consumers. They also must gain strategic advantage by positioning their offerings strongly against competitors' offerings in the minds of consumers.

No single competitive marketing strategy is best for all companies. Each firm should consider its own size and industry position compared to those of its competitors. Large firms with dominant positions in an industry can use certain strategies that smaller firms cannot afford. But being large is not enough. There are winning strategies for large firms, but there are also losing ones. And small firms can develop strategies that give them better rates of return than large firms enjoy.

PUBLICS

The company's marketing environment also includes various publics. A **public** is any group that has an actual or potential interest in, or impact on, an organization's ability to achieve its objectives. We can identify seven types of publics.

1. *Financial publics.* These influence the company's ability to obtain funds. Banks, investment houses, and stockholders are the major financial publics.
2. *Media publics.* These carry news, features, and editorial opinion. They include newspapers, magazines, and radio and television stations.

■ Publics: Wal-Mart Good.WORKS efforts, such as the Wal-Mart Teacher of the Year program, recognize the importance of community publics. "Supporting our communities is good for everyone," says this ad.

3. *Government publics.* Management must take government developments into account. Marketers must often consult the company's lawyers on issues of product safety, truth in advertising, and other matters.
4. *Citizen-action publics.* A company's marketing decisions may be questioned by consumer organizations, environmental groups, minority groups, and others. Its public relations department can help it stay in touch with consumer and citizen groups.
5. *Local publics.* These include neighborhood residents and community organizations. Large companies usually appoint a community-relations officer to deal with the community, attend meetings, answer questions, and contribute to worthwhile causes.
6. *General public.* A company needs to be concerned about the general public's attitude toward its products and activities. The public's image of the company affects its buying.
7. *Internal publics.* These include workers, managers, volunteers, and the board of directors. Large companies use newsletters and other means to inform and motivate their internal publics. When employees feel good about their company, this positive attitude spills over to external publics.

A company can prepare marketing plans for these major publics as well as for its customer markets. Suppose the company wants a specific response from a particular public, such as goodwill, favorable word of mouth, or donations of time or money. The company would have to design an offer to this public that is attractive enough to produce the desired response.

The Company's Macroenvironment

The company and all of the other actors operate in a larger macroenvironment of forces that shape opportunities and pose threats to the company. Figure 3.2 shows the six major forces in the company's macroenvironment. In the remaining sections of this chapter, we examine these forces and show how they affect marketing plans.

DEMOGRAPHIC ENVIRONMENT

Demography
The study of human populations in terms of size, density, location, age, gender, race, occupation, and other statistics.

Demography is the study of human populations in terms of size, density, location, age, gender, race, occupation, and other statistics. The demographic environment is of major interest to marketers because it involves people, and people make up markets. The world population is growing at an explosive rate. It now totals more than 6.4 billion and will exceed 8.1 billion by the year 2030.[3] The world's large and highly diverse population poses both opportunities and challenges.

Changes in the world demographic environment have major implications for business. For example, consider China. More than a quarter century ago, to curb its skyrocketing population, the Chinese government passed regulations limiting families to one child each. As a result, Chinese children—known as "little emperors and empresses"—are being showered with attention and luxuries under what's known as the "six-pocket syndrome." As many as six adults—two parents and four doting grandparents—may be indulging the

FIGURE 3.2
Major Forces in the Company's Macroenvironment

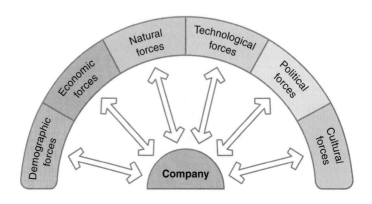

whims of each "only child." Parents in the average Beijing household now spend about 40 percent of their income on their cherished only child. Among other things, this trend has created huge market opportunities for children's educational products.

In China's increasingly competitive society, parents these days are desperate to give Junior an early edge. That's creating opportunities for companies peddling educational offerings aimed at kids. Disney, for example, is moving full speed into educational products. Magic English, a $225 Disney package that includes workbooks, flash cards, and 26 videodisks, has been phenomenally successful. Disney has also launched interactive educational CD-ROMs featuring the likes of Winnie the Pooh and 101 Dalmations' Cruella DeVille. Disney isn't alone in catering to lucrative Chinese coddled-kiddies market. For example, Time Warner is testing the waters in Shanghai with an interactive language course called English Time. The 200-lesson, 40-CD set takes as long as four years for a child to complete. Time Warner is expecting strong sales, despite the $3,300 price tag.[4]

■ Demographics and business: Chinese regulations limiting families to one child have resulted in what's known as the "six-pocket syndrome." Chinese children are being showered with attention and luxuries creating opportunities for marketers.

Interestingly, the one-child policy is creating another major Chinese demographic development—a rapidly aging population. In what some deem a potential "demographic earthquake," by 2004, an estimated 58 percent of the Chinese population will be over age 40. And because of the one-child policy, close to 75 percent of all Chinese households will be childless, either because they chose to have no children or because their only child has left the nest. The result is an aging society that will need to be more self-reliant, which, in turn, will cause a large growth in service markets such as senior education, leisure clubs, and nursing homes.[5]

Thus, marketers keep close track of demographic trends and developments in their markets, both at home and abroad. They track changing age and family structures, geographic population shifts, educational characteristics, and population diversity. Here, we discuss the most important demographic trends in the United States.

Changing Age Structure of the Population   The U.S. population stood at almost 298 million in 2005 and may reach almost 364 million by the year 2030.[6] The single most important demographic trend in the United States is the changing age structure of the population. The U.S. population contains several generational groups. Here, we discuss the three largest groups—the baby boomers, Generation X, and Generation Y—and their impact on today's marketing strategies.

The Baby Boomers.   The post-World War II baby boom produced 78 million **baby boomers**, born between 1946 and 1964. Since then, the baby boomers have become one of the most powerful forces shaping the marketing environment. Today's baby boomers account for about 28 percent of the population, earn about $1 trillion in disposable income annually, and hold three-quarters of the nation's financial assets.[7]

Marketers typically have paid the most attention to the smaller upper crust of the boomer generation—its more educated, mobile, and wealthy segments. These segments have gone by many names. In the 1980s, they were called "yuppies" (young urban professionals), "bumpies" (black upwardly mobile professionals), and "DINKs" (dual-income, no-kids couples). In the 1990s, yuppies and DINKs gave way to a new breed, with names such as "DEWKs" (dual-earners with kids) and "MOBYs" (mother older, baby younger). Now, to the chagrin of many in this generation, they are acquiring such titles as "WOOFs" (well-off older folks) or even "GRUMPIES" (just what the name suggests).

Baby boomers
The 78 million people born during the baby boom following World War II and lasting until the early 1960s.

As a group, the baby boomers are the most affluent Americans. However, although the more affluent boomers have grabbed most of the headlines, baby boomers cut across all walks of life, creating a diverse set of target segments for businesses. There are wealthy boomers but also boomers with more modest means. And almost 25 percent of the 78 million boomers belong to a racial or ethnic minority.

The youngest boomers are now in their early forties; the oldest are entering their sixties. Thus, the boomers have evolved from the "youthquake generation" to the "backache generation." The maturing boomers are rethinking the purpose and value of their work, responsibilities, and relationships. They are approaching life with a new stability and reasonableness in the way they live, think, eat, and spend. As they reach their peak earning and spending years, the boomers constitute a lucrative market for new housing and home remodeling, financial services, travel and entertainment, eating out, health and fitness products, and high-priced cars and other luxuries.

It would be a mistake to think of the boomers as aging, staid retirees. In fact, the boomers are spending $30 billion a year on *anti*-aging products and services. And unlike previous generations, boomers are likely to postpone retirement. Many boomers are rediscovering the excitement of life and have the means to play it out. For example, one-half of all U.S. adults took adventure vacations within the past five years. Some 56 percent of these travelers were boomers. And thanks to the baby boomers, the RV market is exploding.[8]

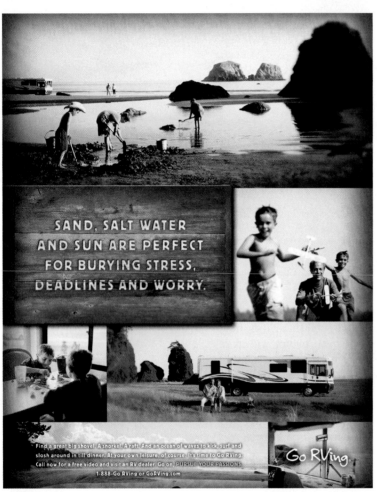

It seems that every younger boomer family needs an RV to take the classic American family vacation before the kids grow up and leave home. The older boomers, now empty-nesters, use an RV to visit their grandchildren or to see America at their own pace. RVs come in all sizes and price ranges, but most of today's RVs are a far cry from the good old "travel trailer." With prices ranging up to $1 million or more, the latest luxury RVs offer everything even the most affluent boomer craves. With amenities ranging from plasma TVs, convection ovens, and washer-dryer combinations to slide-out rooms, Internet service, home theaters, and even working fireplaces, RVs can be crafted into a true home away from home. "RVs are selling like hotcakes," says an RV industry association executive. "And baby boomers are in their prime RV years."

■ It would be a mistake to think of the boomers as aging and staid. Many are rediscovering the excitement of life and have the means to play it out. "Baby boomers are in their prime RV years."

Generation X. The baby boom was followed by a "birth dearth," creating another generation of 49 million people born between 1965 and 1976. Author Douglas Coupland calls them **Generation X**, because they lie in the shadow of the boomers and lack obvious distinguishing characteristics. Others call them the "baby busters," the "yiffies"—young, individualistic, freedom-minded few, or the "generation caught in the middle" (between the larger baby boomers and later Generation Yers).

The Generation Xers are defined as much by their shared experiences as by their age. Increasing divorce rates and higher employment for their mothers made them the first generation of latchkey kids. Having grown up during times of recession and corporate downsizing, they developed a more cautious economic outlook. They care about the environment and respond favorably to socially responsible companies. Although they seek success, they are less materialistic; they prize experience, not acquisition. They are cau-

Generation X
The 49 million people born between 1965 and 1976 in the "birth dearth" following the baby boom.

tious romantics who want a better quality of life and are more interested in job satisfaction than in sacrificing personal happiness and growth for promotion. Often, family comes first, career second.

As a result, the Gen Xers are a more skeptical bunch. "Marketing to Gen Xers is difficult," says one marketer, "and it's all about word of mouth. You can't tell them you're good, and they have zero interest in a slick brochure that says so. You have to rely on somebody they know and trust to give you instant credibility. They have a lot of 'filters' in place."[9]

Once labeled as "the MTV generation" and viewed as body-piercing slackers who whined about "McJobs," the Gen Xers have now grown up and are beginning to take over. The Gen Xers are displacing the lifestyles, culture, and materialistic values of the baby boomers. They represent close to $1.4 trillion in annual purchasing power. By the year 2010, they will have overtaken the baby boomers as a primary market for almost every product category.[10]

With so much potential, many companies are focusing on Gen Xers as an important target segment. For example, consider the banking industry:[11]

As the Gen Xers progress in their careers, start families, and settle into home ownership, banks are responding with programs to help them manage their finances. For example, home financing is a major issue. To help out, Washington Mutual (WaMu to its customers) ran a marketing campaign showing young home buyers how they can simplify the home buying process. The "Buying a Home" page on WaMu's Web site is an "all-you-ever-wanted-to-know" resource for new-home financing. Generation Xers also worry about saving money for their children's college educations—one study showed that 26 percent of Gen Xers felt that education costs would be out of reach by the time their children were ready for college. To meet this need, the Life Stages section of WaMu's Web site offers "College Savings 101," and other educational planning tools. But marketing to Gen X consumers requires fresh approaches. So rather than bombarding them with brash marketing pitches, WaMu combines softer marketing approaches with community-oriented programs. For example, to gain favor with Gen Xers who have young families with small children, WaMu developed WaMoola for Schools. This program sets aside $1 for every new checking account opened during the year and then distributes the funds to local schools. Or customers can earn WaMoola points for their schools by making purchases with their Washington Mutual Visa Check Cards.

Generation Y. Both the baby boomers and Gen Xers will one day be passing the reins to **Generation Y** (also called echo boomers). Born between 1977 and 1994, these children of the baby boomers now number 72 million, dwarfing the Gen Xers and almost equal in size to the baby boomer segment. The echo boom has created a large teen and young adult market. With an average disposable income of $91 a week, the nation's teens spend $169 billion a year and influence another $30 billion in family spending. After years of bust, markets for teen and young-adult games, clothes, furniture, and food have enjoyed a boom.[12]

Generation Y oldsters have now graduated from college and are moving up in their careers. Like the trailing edge of the Gen Xers ahead of them, one distinguishing characteristic of Generation Y is their utter fluency and comfort with computer, digital, and Internet technology. Some 9 out of 10 teens have a home computer, 73 percent of teens surf the Internet every day, and over 80 percent of 15 to 19 year olds own a mobile phone. In all, they are an impatient, now-oriented bunch. "Blame it on the relentless and dizzying pace of the Internet, 24-hour cable news cycles, cell phones, and TiVo for creating the on-demand, gotta-get-it-now universe in which we live," says one observer. "Perhaps nowhere is the trend more pronounced than among the Gen Y set."[13]

Generation Y represents an attractive target for marketers. However, reaching this message-saturated segment effectively requires creative marketing approaches. For example, the popularity of action sports with Gen Yers has provided creative marketing opportunities for products ranging from clothes to video games, movies, and even beverages. Mountain Dew's edgy and irreverent positioning makes it a natural for the action-sport crowd. But more than just showing snowboarders, skateboarders, and surfers in its ads, Mountain Dew has become a true action-sports supporter. It sponsors the ESPN XGames,

Generation Y
The 72 million children of the baby boomers, born between 1977 and 1994.

MARKETING AT WORK 3.1

Toyota's Scion: Targeting Gen Y Without Shouting "Buy This Car"

In the late 1990s, as Toyota's management team peered through the corporate windshield, it took great pride in the company's accomplishments in the U.S. market. Riding a wave of loyal baby boomers who had grown up with its Toyota and Lexus models, the company had become one of the nation's most powerful automobile brands.

Yet when the team looked down at the corporate dashboard, they saw the "check engine" light flashing. As the baby boomers had aged, the age of the average Toyota customer had risen as well. The median Toyota buyer was 49; the median Lexus buyer was 54. Too few younger customers were lining up to buy Toyotas. Some 63 million Gen Yers would be reaching driving age by 2010, and Toyota wasn't speaking their language. In fact, Toyota's strong reputation among the baby boomers for quality, efficiency, and value had translated to more youthful consumers as, well, "stodgy."

Other auto manufacturers were facing this same Gen Y problem. Honda's durable, easy-to-customize Civic had met with some success with younger buyers, but that brand's appeal was fading. Honda followed with the boxy Element, which one observer described as a "Swiss Army knife on wheels," and which Honda promoted as "a dorm room on wheels." The Element sold well but often attracted the wrong market—boomers and Gen Xers (average age 41) looking for something to transport their flowers and power tools. Toyota had also tried before with three vehicles in its Genesis Project: the frumpy Echo, an edgy Celica, and a pricey but impractical MR2 Spider. Each had failed to score with young people.

So, in the early 2000s, Toyota went back to the drawing board. The challenge was to keep Gen Y from seeing Toyota as "old people trying to make a young person's car." Success depended on understanding this new generation of buyers, a segment of strangers to most car marketers. "They demand authenticity, respect for their time, and products built just for them," observed a senior Toyota executive. "They are in their early 20s, new to us, and have changed every category they have touched so far. It's the most diverse generation ever seen."

The search for a new, more youthful model began in Toyota's own driveway. Following orders to "loosen up," Toyota engineers in Japan had designed and successfully introduced a boxy new microvan, the bB, and a five-door hatchback, the "ist" (pronounced "east"). The company decided to rename these vehicles and introduce them in the United States. Thus was born Toyota's new Gen Y brand, the Scion (Sigh-un). In the Scion, Toyota created not just a new car brand, but new marketing approaches as well.

Accelerate to Memorial Day weekend in late May 2003. Twenty-something Toyota reps sporting goatees and sunglasses have set up shop near a major intersection in San Francisco's Haight-Ashbury district. Standing under banners heralding the new Scion brand, with hip-hop music blaring in the background, the reps encourage young passersby to test drive two new models, the Scion xA hatchback and the Scion xB van.

■ To target Gen Yers, with their "built-just-for-them" preferences, Toyota positioned the Scion on personalization. "Personalization begins here—what moves you?"

the Vans Triple Crown, and numerous action-sport athletes. It even started its own grassroots skate park tour, the Mountain Dew Free Flow Tour. As a result of these and other actions, Mountain Dew has become the beverage of choice for men ages 18 to 24.[14]

The automobile industry is aggressively targeting this future generation of car buyers. By 2010, Generation Y will buy one of every four new cars sold in the United States. Toyota even created a completely new brand—the Scion—targeted to Gen Yers (see Marketing at Work 3.1). Other automakers are using a variety of programs and pitches to lure Generation Y as they approach their key car-buying years. For example, BMW offers a motor sports training program for young drivers, some of whom are too young to have licenses. As a part of its "Ultimate Driving Experience" tour, BMW offers go-kart drivers between the ages of 15 and 23 an array of scholarships, training, and race experience to help develop their racing careers. "We are courting teenagers," says a BMW marketing executive. "BMW is the premier brand for youth, so we have a reason to work harder with the next generation."[15]

This was not your typical Toyota sales event—it was the opening round in a campaign to solve, finally, the Gen Y riddle. And it signaled the most unorthodox new-car campaign in the company's 70-year history—a campaign that was edgy, urban, and underground. To speak to Gen Y, Toyota shunned traditional marketing approaches and employed guerilla tactics. Its young marketing team put up posters with slogans like "No Clone Zone" and "Ban Normality," even projecting those slogans onto buildings at night. It held "ride-and-drive" events, like the one in San Francisco, to generate spontaneous test drives by taking its cars to potential customers instead of waiting for them to find their way to showrooms. It put brochures in alternative publications such as *Urb* and *Tokion,* and it sponsored events at venues ranging from hip-hop nightclubs and urban pubs to library lawns.

Toyota assigned Dawn Ahmed and Brian Bolain, two young members of its product development staff, to head the U.S. promotional campaign. Understanding the "built-just-for-them" preferences of the Gen Y target market, Ahmed and Bolain decided to position the Scion on *personalization.* They appealed to the new youth-culture club of "tuners," young fans of tricked-out vehicles (such as BMW's wildly successful MINI Cooper) who wanted to customize their cars from bumper to bumper. "We saw that the tuner phenomenon was really spreading, and took that idea of customization to a totally different level," Ahmed notes. "It comes back to that thing of rational versus emotional," observes Bolain. "Scion buy-

ers have all the rational demands of a Toyota buyer, but they also want more fun, personality, and character."

So, along with all of the traditional Toyota features—like lots of airbags, a power moon roof, and a 160-watt Pioneer stereo with MP3 capability—the Scion offers lots of room for individual self-expression. The staff worked with after-market auto-parts suppliers to develop specially-designed Scion add-ons. To create their own one-of-a-kind cars, customers can select from 40 different accessory products, such as neon interior lighting and illuminated cup holders, wake-the-dead stereo systems, and stiffer shocks. As Bolain points out, "[We wanted the Scion to be a] blank canvas on which the consumer can make the car what they would like it to be."

Toyota dealers who have agreed to sell Scions provide special areas in their showrooms where customers can relax, check out the cars, and create their own customized Scions on computers linked to Scion's Web site. And Scion buyers do, indeed, customize their cars. The Scion xA and Scion xB start at "no haggle" prices below $13,000 and $14,000, respectively. But 48 percent of Scion buyers spend another $1,000 to $3,000 to customize their cars. Two-thirds of buyers labor at the Scion Web site, configuring just the car they want before ever walking into the dealership.

How is Toyota's Scion strategy working? The California launch was so successful that Toyota quickly rolled out the Scion nationally, finishing the process in June 2004. Scion blew past its first-year, 60,000-unit sales target by

mid-2004, selling 100,000 units for the year. Toyota set a 150,000-unit goal for 2005. And it introduced a third model, the Scion tC coupe, which adds more power and driving pleasure to the Scion equation. Most importantly, the Scion is bringing a new generation of buyers into the Toyota family. Ninety percent of Scion buyers have never before owned a Toyota. And the average age of a Scion buyer is 36, a figure that overstates the average age of a Scion driver, given that many parents are buying the car for their kids.

All this success, however, brings new challenges. For example, according to an industry analyst, Gen Y consumers "disdain commercialism and don't really want 'their brand' to be discovered." To maintain its appeal to these young buyers, as the brand becomes more mainstream, Scion will have to keep its models and messages fresh and honest. Says VP Jim Farley, "We want to [reach out to youthful buyers] without shouting 'Buy This Car.' "

Sources: Quotes from Lillie Guyer, "Scion Connects in Out-of-Way Places," *Advertising Age,* February 21, 2005, p. 38. Also see Brett Corbin, "Toyota's Scion Line Banks on Tech-savvy Younger Drivers," *Business First,* June 18, 2004, p. 11; Norihiko Shirouzu, "This Is Not Your Father's Toyota," *Wall Street Journal,* March 26, 2002; Christopher Palmeri, Ben Elgin, and Kathleen Kerwin, "Toyota's Scion: Dude, Here's Your Car," *Business Week,* June 9, 2003, p. 44; Nick Kurczewski, "Who's Your Daddy? Staid Toyota Gets a Hip Implant," *New York Times,*" July 25, 2004, p. 12; Patrick Paternie, "Driven by Personality," *Los Angeles Times,* January 6, 2005, p. E34; Karl Greenberg, "Dawn Ahmed," *Brandweek,* April 11, 2005, p. 33; and Chris Woodyard, "Outside-the-Box Scion Scores Big with Young Drivers," May 3, 2005, accessed at www.detnews.com/2005/autoinsider/0505/03/1auto-170121.htm.

Generational Marketing. Do marketers have to create separate products and marketing programs for each generation? Some experts warn that marketers have to be careful about turning off one generation each time they craft a product or message that appeals effectively to another. Others caution that each generation spans decades of time and many socioeconomic levels. For example, marketers often split the baby boomers into three smaller groups—leading boomers, core boomers, and trailing boomers—each with its own beliefs and behaviors. Similarly, they split Generation Y into Gen Y adults and Gen Y teens. Thus, marketers need to form more precise age-specific segments within each group. More important, defining people by their birth date may be less effective than segmenting them by their lifestyle or life stage.

The Changing American Family The "traditional household" consists of a husband, wife, and children (and sometimes grandparents). Yet, the once American ideal of the two-child, two-car suburban family has lately been losing some of its luster.

In the United States today, married couples with children now make up only about 34 percent of the nation's 111 million households, and this percentage is falling. Married couples with children make up 23 percent; married couples without children make up 28 percent; and single parents comprise another 16 percent. A full 32 percent are non-family households—single live-alones or adult live-togethers of one or both sexes.[16]

More people are divorcing or separating, choosing not to marry, marrying later, or marrying without intending to have children. Marketers must increasingly consider the special needs of nontraditional households, because they are now growing more rapidly than traditional households. Each group has distinctive needs and buying habits.

The number of working women has also increased greatly, growing from under 30 percent of the U.S. workforce in 1950 to just over 60 percent today.[17] However, that trend may be slowing. After increasing steadily since 1976, the percentage of women with children under age one in the workforce has fallen during the past few years. Meanwhile, more men are staying home with their children, managing the household while their wives go to work. According to the census, the number of stay-at-home dads has risen 18 percent since 1994.[18]

The significant number of women in the workforce has spawned the child day-care business and increased consumption of career-oriented women's clothing, financial services, and convenience foods and services. An example is Dream Dinners, Inc., a national franchise chain created by a busy working mom who invited fellow busy moms to her catering kitchen to prepare make-ahead meals. People visiting a Dream Dinners store can prepare up to a dozen family meals in under two hours, with clean up handled by the store's staff. Using workstations, they prepare healthy meals ranging from Kung Pao Chicken to New England Pot Roast, take them home in coolers, and store them in the freezer until needed. A dozen meals, each serving four to six people, cost under $200. With over 150 locations, Dream Dinners gives precious family time back to harried working parents.[19]

With Dream Dinners you'll enjoy...

◯ **Giving your family healthy, wholesome meals**
Home-cooked without the hassle!

◯ **Saving money and time with less grocery shopping and fewer fast-food stops**
No after work/school panic about what to make!

◯ **Quick and easy clean up**
Simple because there's no mess from preparing the meal

◯ **Dinner around the table**
With your family!

◯ **12 family-sized entrees**
Averaging under $200

DREAM DINNERS
...Life just got easier

■ Businesses like Dream Dinners have arisen to serve the growing number of working women. The chain was created by a busy working mom who invited fellow busy mothers to her catering kitchen to prepare make-ahead meals. With Dream Dinners, "Life just got easier."

Geographic Shifts in Population   This is a period of great migratory movements between and within countries. Americans, for example, are a mobile people with about 14 percent of all U.S. residents moving each year. Over the past two decades, the U.S. population has shifted toward the Sunbelt states. The West and South have grown, while the Midwest and Northeast states have lost population.[20] Such population shifts interest marketers because people in different regions buy differently. For example, research shows that people in Seattle buy more toothbrushes per capita than people in any other U.S. city; people in Salt Lake City eat more candy bars; people from New Orleans use more ketchup; and people in Miami drink more prune juice.

Also, for more than a century, Americans have been moving from rural to metropolitan areas. In the 1950s, they made a massive exit from the cities to the suburbs. Today, the migration to the suburbs continues. And more and more Americans are moving to "micropolitan areas," small cities located beyond congested metropolitan areas. Drawing refugees from rural and suburban America, these smaller micros offer many of the advantages of metro areas—jobs, restaurants, diversions, community organizations—but without the population crush, traffic jams, high crime rates, and high property taxes often associated with heavily urbanized areas.[21]

The shift in where people live has also caused a shift in where they work. For example, the migration toward micropolitan and suburban areas has resulted in a rapid increase in the number of people who "telecommute"—work at home or in a remote office and conduct their business by phone, fax, modem, or the Internet. This trend, in turn, has created a booming SOHO (small office/home office) market. One in every five Americans is now working out of the home with the help of electronic conveniences such as personal computers, cell phones, fax machines, and handheld organizers.

Many marketers are actively courting the home office segment of this lucrative SOHO market. One example is FedEx Kinko's Office and Print Centers:

Founded in the 1970s as a campus photocopying business, Kinko's was bought by FedEx in 2004. Its locations were renamed FedEx Kinko's Office and Print Centers. As the new name suggests, FedEx Kinko's is now much more than a self-service copy shop. Serving primarily small office/home office customers, it has reinvented itself as the well-appointed office outside the home. New ads proclaim, "Our office is your office." Where once there were only copy machines, FedEx Kinko's 1,200 centers now offer a full range of business services, including binding and finishing, color copying and printing, document management, shipping services, computer rental, T-Mobile HotSpot wireless Internet connections, and much more. People can come to a FedEx Kinko's store to do all their office jobs: They can copy, send and receive faxes, use various programs on the computer, go on the Internet, order stationery and other printed supplies, ship packages, and even rent a conference room or conduct a teleconference. As more and more people join the work-at-home trend, FedEx Kinko's offers an escape from the isolation of the home office.[22]

■ Geographic shifts. To serve the burgeoning small office/home office market, FedEx Kinko's has reinvented itself as the well-appointed office outside the home. "Our office is your office," says the company.

A Better-Educated, More White-Collar, More Professional Population   The U.S. population is becoming better educated. For example, in 2003, 85 percent of the U.S. population over age 25 had completed high school and 27 percent had completed college, compared with 69 percent and 17 percent in 1980. Moreover, nearly two-thirds of high school graduates now enroll in college within 12 months of graduating.[23] The rising number of educated people will increase the demand for quality products, books, magazines, travel, personal computers, and Internet services.

The workforce also is becoming more white collar. Between 1950 and 1985, the proportion of white-collar workers rose from 41 percent to 54 percent, that of blue-collar workers declined from 47 percent to 33 percent, and that of service workers increased from 12 percent to 14 percent. Between 1983 and 1999, the proportion of managers and professionals in the workforce increased from 23 percent to more than 30 percent. Job growth is now strongest for professional workers and weakest for manufacturers. Between 2002 and 2012 the number of professional workers is expected to increase 25 percent and manufacturing 3 percent.[24]

Increasing Diversity   Countries vary in their ethnic and racial makeup. At one extreme is Japan, where almost everyone is Japanese. At the other extreme is the United States, with people from virtually all nations. The United States has often been called a melting pot—diverse groups from many nations and cultures have melted into a single, more homogenous whole. Instead, the United States seems to have become more of a "salad bowl" in which various groups have mixed together but have maintained their diversity by retaining and valuing important ethnic and cultural differences.

Marketers are facing increasingly diverse markets, both at home and abroad as their operations become more international in scope. The U.S. population is 68 percent white, with Hispanics at almost 14 percent and African Americans at about 13 percent. The U.S. Asian American population now totals about 4 percent of the population, with the remaining 1 percent made up of American Indian, Eskimo, and Aleut. Moreover, more than 34 million people living in the United States—more than 12 percent of the population—were born in another country. The nation's ethnic populations are expected to explode in coming decades. By 2050, Hispanics will comprise 24 percent of the U.S. population, with African Americans at 13 percent and Asians at 9 percent.[25]

Most large companies, from Procter & Gamble, Sears, Wal-Mart, and Bank of America to Levi Strauss and General Mills, now target specially designed products, ads, and promotions to one or more of these groups. For example, Allstate worked with Kang & Lee Advertising, a leading multicultural marketing agency, to create an award-winning marketing campaign aimed at the single largest Asian group in the country—Chinese Americans. Creating culturally significant messages for this market was no easy matter. Perhaps the most daunting task was translating Allstate's iconic "You're In Good Hands With Allstate®" slogan into Chinese.[26]

■ Multicultural marketing: Allstate created an award-winning marketing campaign aimed at the single largest Asian group in the country—Chinese Americans. The most daunting task: translating Allstate's iconic "You're In Good Hands With Allstate®" slogan into Chinese.

There's nary a U.S.-born citizen who doesn't know that, when it comes to insurance, you are in good hands with Allstate. But to Chinese Americans, Allstate was not the first insurance company that came to mind. So Allstate asked Kang & Lee Advertising to help it translate the "good hands" concept into the Chinese market. The trick was to somehow make the company's longtime brand identity relevant to this group. Problem was, the English slogan just doesn't make sense in any Chinese dialect. After months of qualitative consumer research and discussion with Chinese American Allstate agents, Kang & Lee came up with a Chinese-language version of the tag line, which, roughly translated, says "turn it over to our hands, relax, and be free of worry." The campaign started in Seattle and New York, and has since expanded to California. Studies in the first two cities show that awareness of Allstate in the Chinese American community had doubled within six months of the start of the campaign.

Diversity goes beyond ethnic heritage. For example, many major companies have recently begun to explicitly target gay and lesbian consumers. A Simmons Research study of readers of the National Gay Newspaper Guild's 12 publications found that, compared to the average American, respondents are 12 times more likely to be in professional jobs, almost twice as likely to own a vacation home, 8 times more likely to own a notebook computer, and twice as likely to own individual stocks. They are twice as likely as the general population to have a household income between $60,000 and $250,000. More than two-thirds have graduated from college and 21 percent hold a master's degree.[27]

In addition, gays and lesbians tend to be early adopters of trends that eventually are adopted by mainstream America. For example, according to one expert, "in the weeks following an episode of the Bravo hit show *Queer Eye for the Straight Guy*—in which five gay men, known as the Fab 5, make over a low-maintenance straight man—many businesses whose products are featured have seen a significant sales boost." Lucky Brand jeans saw a 17 percent sales jump for the two months following a mention on *Queer Eye.* And since an episode in which Thomasville Furniture was plugged as a shopping hot spot, sales of its Patchwork leather upholstery have jumped 50 percent.[28]

Companies in several industries are now waking up to the needs and potential of the gay and lesbian segment, a $485 billion market. For example, Gay.com, a Web site that attracts more than two million unique visitors each month from more than 100 countries, has also attracted a diverse set of well-known advertisers, from IBM, eBay, Quicken Mortgage, Saturn, Absolut, and AT&T to American Airlines and Neiman Marcus. Here are examples of gay and lesbian marketing efforts:[29]

American Express Financial Advisors launched print ads that depict same-sex couples planning their financial futures. The ads ran in *Out* and *The Advocate,* the two highest-circulation national gay publications. The company's director of segment marketing, Margaret Vergeyle, said: "We're targeting gay audiences with ads and promotions that are relevant to them and say that we understand their specific needs. Often, gay couples are very concerned about issues like Social Security benefits and estate planning, since same-sex marriages often are not recognized under the law."

IBM fields a paid, full-time sales team dedicated to bringing GLBT (Gay Lesbian Bisexual Transgender) decision makers in contact with IBM. The company recently targeted the gay small-business community with an ad that ran in *The Advocate, Out,* and about 40 other gay-themed publications. The ad pictures a diverse group of men and women and links IBM's Armonk, N.Y., headquarters with well-known gay communities: "Chelsea/Provincetown/The Castro/Armonk." The six people shown in the ad are among the 1,100 IBM employees who make up the company's GLBT Network. IBM launched the GLBT group three years ago when research showed that gay business owners are more likely to buy from gay salespeople.

Last year, Avis, the rental car company, devoted about 5 percent of its ad-vertising and marketing budget to the gay community. Its ad campaign highlights its policy for domestic partners to automatically be included as additional drivers. "It's a loyal group and an affluent group, and one that our research shows will respond to marketing that speaks to their consumer needs," says an Avis spokesperson. Avis' strategy also includes sponsorship of gay pride festivals and the placement of coupons noting that for every rental, Avis will donate a dollar to the nonprofit Gay and Lesbian Alliance Against Defamation.

Another attractive segment is the more than 54 million people with disabilities in the United States—a market larger than African Americans or Hispanics—representing almost $1 trillion in annual spending power. People with mobility challenges, for example, represent a growing market for travel, sports, and other leisure-oriented products and services. Consider the following example:[30]

In the past, Volkswagen has targeted people with disabilities who want to travel. For example, one marketing campaign for its EuroVan touted the vehicle's extra-wide doors, high ceilings, and overall roominess, features that accommodate

■ Volkswagen targets people with disabilities by teaming each year with non-profit VSA arts to sponsor its "Driving Force" competition, designed to identify promising young artists with physical, cognitive, or mental disabilities.

most wheelchair lifts and make driving more fun for people with disabilities. Volkswagen even modified its catchy tag line "Drivers Wanted" to appeal to motorists with disabilities, coining the new slogan "All Drivers Wanted." Volkswagen also teams each year with nonprofit VSA arts to sponsor its "Driving Force" competition, designed to identify promising young artists with physical, cognitive, or mental disabilities. "America's love affair with the automobile extends beyond the visual cues of engines and sheet metal," proclaims a VW spokesperson. "Volkswagen believes that the 'heartware' is equally as important as the 'hardware.' For people with disabilities, the automobile provides both freedom of mobility and self-expression."

As the population in the United States grows more diverse, successful marketers will continue to diversify their marketing programs to take advantage of opportunities in fast-growing segments.

 Linking the Concepts

Pull over here for a moment and think about how deeply these demographic factors impact all of us and, as a result, marketers' strategies.

■ Apply these demographic developments to your own life. Think of some specific examples of how the changing demographic factors affect you and your buying behavior.
■ Identify a specific company that has done a good job of reacting to the shifting demographic environment—generational segments (baby boomers, Gen Xers, or Generation Y), the changing American family, and increased diversity. Compare this company to one that's done a poor job.

ECONOMIC ENVIRONMENT

Economic environment
Factors that affect consumer buying power and spending patterns.

Markets require buying power as well as people. The **economic environment** consists of factors that affect consumer purchasing power and spending patterns. Nations vary greatly in their levels and distribution of income. Some countries have *subsistence economies*—they consume most of their own agricultural and industrial output. These countries offer few market opportunities. At the other extreme are *industrial economies,* which constitute rich markets for many different kinds of goods. Marketers must pay close attention to major trends and consumer spending patterns both across and within their world markets. Following are some of the major economic trends in the United States.

Changes in Income   Throughout the 1990s, American consumers fell into a consumption frenzy, fueled by income growth, a boom in the stock market, rapid increases in housing values, and other economic good fortune. They bought and bought, seemingly without caution, amassing record levels of debt. However, the free spending and high expectations of those days were dashed by the recent recession. In fact, we are now facing the age of the "squeezed consumer." Along with rising incomes in some segments have come increased financial burdens. Consumers now face repaying debts acquired during earlier spending splurges, increased household and family expenses, and saving ahead for college tuition payments and retirement.

These financially squeezed consumers have adjusted to their changing financial situations and are spending more carefully. *Value marketing* has become the watchword for many marketers. Rather than offering high quality at a high price, or lesser quality at very low prices, marketers are looking for ways to offer today's more financially cautious buyers greater value—just the right combination of product quality and good service at a fair price.

Marketers should pay attention to *income distribution* as well as average income. Income distribution in the United States is still very skewed. At the top are *upper-class* consumers, whose spending patterns are not affected by current economic events and who are a major market for luxury goods. There is a comfortable *middle class* that is somewhat careful about its spending but can still afford the good life some of the time. The *working class* must stick close to the basics of food, clothing, and shelter and must try hard to save. Finally, the *underclass* (persons on welfare and many retirees) must count their pennies when making even the most basic purchases.

Over the past three decades, the rich have grown richer, the middle class has shrunk, and the poor have remained poor. In 2003, 12 percent of American households had an annual income of $100,000 or more, compared to just 4 percent in the early 1990s. Meanwhile, the share of income captured by the bottom 20 percent of income-earning households decreased from 4 percent to 3.6 percent.[31]

This distribution of income has created a tiered market. Many companies—such as Nordstrom and Neiman-Marcus department stores—aggressively target the affluent. Others—such as Dollar General and Family Dollar stores—target those with more modest means. In fact, such dollar stores are now the fastest growing retailers in the nation. Still other companies tailor their marketing offers across a range of markets, from the affluent to the less affluent. For example, Levi-Strauss currently markets four different jeans lines. The Signature line of low-priced Levi's are found on the shelves of low-end retailers such as Wal-Mart and Target. Levi's moderately priced Red Tab line sells at retailers such as Kohl's and JCPenney. The Premium and Vintage lines sell at high-end retailers such as Nordstrom and Urban Outfitters. You can buy Levi 501 jeans at any of three different price levels. The Red Tab 501s sell for around $35, the Premium 501s for about $100, and the Vintage 501s for $300 or more.[32]

Changing Consumer Spending Patterns Table 3.1 shows the proportion of total expenditures made by U.S. households at different income levels for major categories of goods and services. Food, housing, and transportation use up the most household income. However, consumers at different income levels have different spending patterns. Some of these differences were noted over a century ago by Ernst Engel, who studied how people shifted their spending as their income rose (see Table 3.1). He found that as family income rises, the percentage spent on food declines, the percentage spent on housing remains about constant (except for such utilities as gas, electricity, and public services, which decrease), and both the percentage spent on most other categories and that devoted to savings increase. **Engel's laws** generally have been supported by later studies.

Changes in major economic variables such as income, cost of living, interest rates, and savings and borrowing patterns have a large impact on the marketplace. Companies watch these variables by using economic forecasting. Businesses do not have to be wiped out by an economic downturn or caught short in a boom. With adequate warning, they can take advantage of changes in the economic environment.

Engel's laws
Differences noted over a century ago by Ernst Engel in how people shift their spending across food, housing, transportation, health care, and other goods and services categories as family income rises.

TABLE 3.1
Consumer Spending at Different Income Levels

| Expenditure | Percent of Spending at Different Income Levels | | | |
	$10–20,000	$20–30,000	$30–40,000	$70,000 and Over
Food	15.3	15.1	13.9	11.6
Housing	34.0	33.3	32.0	30.9
Utilities	8.6	8.0	7.2	4.9
Clothing	4.6	4.1	4.3	4.5
Transportation	18.9	18.3	20.1	17.6
Health care	8.7	7.9	6.8	4.2
Entertainment	4.1	4.1	4.4	5.8
Contributions	2.8	3.4	3.1	3.5
Insurance	3.9	6.5	8.3	14.8

Source: *Consumer Expenditure Survey, 2002*, U.S. Department of Labor, Bureau of Labor Statistics, April 2004, accessed at www.bls.gov/cex/2002/Standard/income.pdf.

NATURAL ENVIRONMENT

The **natural environment** involves the natural resources that are needed as inputs by marketers or that are affected by marketing activities. Environmental concerns have grown steadily during the past three decades. In many cities around the world, air and water pollution have reached dangerous levels. World concern continues to mount about the possibilities of global warming, and many environmentalists fear that we soon will be buried in our own trash.

Marketers should be aware of several trends in the natural environment. The first involves growing *shortages of raw materials*. Air and water may seem to be infinite resources, but some groups see long-run dangers. Air pollution chokes many of the world's large cities, and water shortages are already a big problem in some parts of the United States and the world. Renewable resources, such as forests and food, also have to be used wisely. Nonrenewable resources, such as oil, coal, and various minerals, pose a serious problem. Firms making products that require these scarce resources face large cost increases, even if the materials do remain available.

A second environmental trend is *increased pollution*. Industry will almost always damage the quality of the natural environment. Consider the disposal of chemical and nuclear wastes; the dangerous mercury levels in the ocean; the quantity of chemical pollutants in the soil and food supply; and the littering of the environment with nonbiodegradable bottles, plastics, and other packaging materials.

A third trend is *increased government intervention* in natural resource management. The governments of different countries vary in their concern and efforts to promote a clean environment. Some, like the German government, vigorously pursue environmental quality. Others, especially many poorer nations, do little about pollution, largely because they lack the needed funds or political will. Even the richer nations lack the vast funds and political accord needed to mount a worldwide environmental effort. The general hope is that companies around the world will accept more social responsibility, and that less expensive devices can be found to control and reduce pollution.

In the United States, the Environmental Protection Agency (EPA) was created in 1970 to set and enforce pollution standards and to conduct pollution research. In the future, companies doing business in the United States can expect continued strong controls from government and pressure groups. Instead of opposing regulation, marketers should help develop solutions to the material and energy problems facing the world.

Concern for the natural environment has spawned the so-called green movement. Today, enlightened companies go beyond what government regulations dictate. They are developing *environmentally sustainable* strategies and practices in an effort to create a world economy that the planet can support indefinitely. They are responding to consumer demands with more environmentally responsible products. For example, General Electric is using its "ecomagination" to create products for a better world—cleaner aircraft engines, cleaner locomotives, cleaner fuel technologies.

Other companies are developing recyclable or biodegradable packaging, recycled materials and components, better pollution controls, and more energy-efficient operations. 3M runs a Pollution Prevention Pays program that helps prevent pollution at the source—in products and manufacturing processes. Over the past 30 years, the program has prevented 2.2 billion pounds of pollutants and saved nearly $1 billion. McDonald's has a long-standing rainforest policy and a commitment to purchasing recycled products and to energy-efficient restaurant construction techniques. And UPS's fleet of 70,000 boxy brown trucks now includes some 1,800 alternative-fuel vehicles, 2,500 low-emissions vehicles, and a growing number of electric vehicles.

These companies are looking to do more than just good deeds. More and more, companies are recognizing the link between a healthy ecology and a healthy economy. They are learning that environmentally responsible actions can also be good business (see Marketing at Work 3.2).[33]

TECHNOLOGICAL ENVIRONMENT

The **technological environment** is perhaps the most dramatic force now shaping our destiny. Technology has released such wonders as antibiotics, organ transplants, miniaturized

■ Responding to consumer demands for more environmentally responsible products, General Electric is using its "ecomagination" to create products for a better world.

electronics, laptop computers, and the Internet. It also has released such horrors as nuclear missiles, chemical weapons, and assault rifles. It has released such mixed blessings as the automobile, television, and credit cards.

Our attitude toward technology depends on whether we are more impressed with its wonders or its blunders. For example, what would you think about having a tiny little transmitters implanted in all of the products you buy that would allow tracking products from their point of production through use and disposal? On the one hand, it would provide many advantages to both buyers and sellers. On the other hand, it could be a bit scary. Either way, it's already happening:[34]

Envision a world in which every product contains a tiny transmitter, loaded with information. As you stroll through the supermarket aisles, shelf sensors detect your selections and beam ads to your shopping cart screen, offering special deals on related products. As your cart fills, scanners detect that you might be buying for a dinner party; the screen suggests a wine to go with the meal you've planned. When you leave the store, exit scanners total up your purchases and automatically charge them to your credit card. At home, readers track what goes into and out of your pantry, updating your shopping list when stocks run low. For Sunday dinner, you pop a Butterball turkey into your "smart oven," which follows instructions from an embedded chip and cooks the bird to perfection.

Seem far-fetched? Not really. In fact, it might soon become a reality, thanks to tiny radio-frequency identification (RFID) transmitters—or "smart chips"—that can be embedded in the products you buy. Beyond benefits to consumers, the RFID chips also give producers and retailers an amazing new way to track their products electronically—anywhere in the world, anytime, automatically—from factories, to warehouses, to retail shelves, to recycling centers. RFID technology is already in use. Every time consumers flash an ExxonMobil Speed-Pass card to purchase gas at the pump or breeze through an automated toll booth, they're using an RFID chip. Many large firms are adding fuel to the RFID fire. Procter & Gamble plans to have the chips on products in broad distribution as soon as 2008. And mega-retailers such as Wal-Mart, Best Buy, and Albertson's have ordered their top suppliers to be RFID-capable as early as next year.

MARKETING AT WORK ┃ 3.2

Gibson: Making Money *and* Leaving the World a Better Place

If a tree falls in the rain forest and no one is there to trumpet its eco-friendliness, does it still make a sound? It might—if that wood is destined for an electric guitar. Gibson Guitar, the iconic guitar maker, has worked since the late 1980s to make its wood supply environmentally sustainable. Gibson's electric-guitar division recently switched to 100 percent fair-trade-certified wood. Other Gibson divisions, including Baldwin Piano, plan to follow suit.

Yet unlike Starbucks, The Body Shop, and other businesses that eagerly brandish their green deeds, Gibson CEO Henry Juszkiewicz doesn't much care to flaunt his environmental credentials (the guy drives a Hummer, after all). What matters to him is ensuring that Gibson has enough exotic wood, mostly mahogany, to keep making guitars for generations.

"We're mercenaries. We're a company. We're for-profit," Juszkiewicz says in his Nashville office, packed with so many music-industry mementos it looks like his own private Hard Rock Cafe. "I'm not a conservationist." High-end guitar enthusiasts, after all, demand that their instruments be made of exotic woods. But prices for exotics can swing wildly, governed by an unsteady supply and the threat that some species may be placed on an extinction watch list.

Juszkiewicz wanted to eliminate the guesswork by building a network of growers rather than relying on brokers scouring world markets for the best prices. He approached the

Rainforest Alliance, a nonprofit conservation group, to discuss buying wood from Mexican suppliers certified as sustainable. (Such growers are graded against environmental, labor, and community standards—and for responsible harvesting.)

But that hardly made a dent in Gibson's sourcing problems. So the company hired away two Rainforest Alliance employees to source wood in Costa Rica and Brazil. "Within the first year of hiring these guys, they were able to develop significant sources," Juszkiewicz says. "We went from less than 1 percent usage of certified product to something like 80 percent." Since then, Gibson has forged a direct relationship with growers in Guatemala. That provides both stability of supply and quality, since Gibson is able to instruct farmers on its exacting specifications.

Initially, Juszkiewicz says, Gibson paid a premium for purchasing wood this way. Now buying direct creates modest savings—and the relationships help curb traditional slash-and-burn harvesting, which threatens supplies of precious woods. "In the short run, a slight price increase won't necessarily hurt them because a guitar is a higher-value product," says an industry expert. "In the long run, it helps ensure that they can tap this supply not just in 5 years but in 50 years."

Tensie Whelan, executive director of the Rainforest Alliance, says she's seeing a critical mass of CEOs discovering that environmentally friendly practices can be good business. But she still teases Juszkiewicz, one of the first: "He'll say he's a businessman, that he's just out to make money. But believe me, he's passionate about wanting to leave the world a better place."

Source: Adapted with permission from Ryan Underwood, "In Tune with the Environment," *Fast Company,* February 2005, p. 26.

■ *Gibson Guitar works to make its exotic hardwood supply environmentally sustainable. The company has learned that environmentally friendly practices can also be good business.*

The technological environment changes rapidly. Think of all of today's common products that were not available 100 years ago, or even 30 years ago. Abraham Lincoln did not know about automobiles, airplanes, radios, or the electric light. Woodrow Wilson did not know about television, aerosol cans, automatic dishwashers, air conditioners, antibiotics, or computers. Franklin Delano Roosevelt did not know about xerography, synthetic detergents, tape recorders, birth control pills, or earth satellites. John F. Kennedy did not know about personal computers, cell phones, DVD players, or the Internet.

New technologies create new markets and opportunities. However, every new technology replaces an older technology. Transistors hurt the vacuum-tube industry, xerography hurt the carbon-paper business, the automobile hurt the railroads, and CDs hurt phonograph records. When old industries fought or ignored new technologies, their businesses declined. Thus, marketers should watch the technological environment closely. Companies that do not keep up will soon find their products outdated. And they will miss new product and market opportunities.

The United States leads the world in research and development spending. Total U.S. R&D spending reached an estimated $312 billion in 2005. The federal government was the largest R&D spender at about $98 billion.[35] Scientists today are researching a wide range of promising new products and services, ranging from practical solar energy, electric cars, and cancer cures to voice-controlled computers and genetically engineered food crops.

Today's research usually is carried out by research teams rather than by lone inventors such as Thomas Edison, Samuel Morse, or Alexander Graham Bell. Many companies are adding marketing people to R&D teams to try to obtain a stronger marketing orientation. Scientists also speculate on fantasy products, such as flying cars, three-dimensional televisions, and space colonies. The challenge in each case is not only technical but also commercial—to make *practical, affordable* versions of these products.

■ Technological environment: Technology is perhaps the most dramatic force shaping the marketing environment. Here, a herder makes a call on his cell phone.

As products and technology become more complex, the public needs to know that these are safe. Thus, government agencies investigate and ban potentially unsafe products. In the United States, the Food and Drug Administration (FDA) has set up complex regulations for testing new drugs. The Consumer Product Safety Commission sets safety standards for consumer products and penalizes companies that fail to meet them. Such regulations have resulted in much higher research costs and in longer times between new-product ideas and their introduction. Marketers should be aware of these regulations when applying new technologies and developing new products.

POLITICAL ENVIRONMENT

Marketing decisions are strongly affected by developments in the political environment. The **political environment** consists of laws, government agencies, and pressure groups that influence or limit various organizations and individuals in a given society.

Political environment
Laws, government agencies, and pressure groups that influence and limit various organizations and individuals in a given society.

Legislation Regulating Business Even the most liberal advocates of free-market economies agree that the system works best with at least some regulation. Well-conceived regulation can encourage competition and ensure fair markets for goods and services. Thus, governments develop *public policy* to guide commerce—sets of laws and regulations that limit business for the good of society as a whole. Almost every marketing activity is subject to a wide range of laws and regulations.

Increasing Legislation. Legislation affecting business around the world has increased steadily over the years. The United States has many laws covering issues such as competition, fair trade practices, environmental protection, product safety, truth in advertising, consumer privacy, packaging and labeling, pricing, and other important areas (see Table 3.2). The European Commission has been active in establishing a new framework of laws covering competitive behavior, product standards, product liability, and commercial transactions for the nations of the European Union.

Several countries have gone further than the United States in passing strong consumerism legislation. For example, Norway bans several forms of sales promotion—trading stamps, contests, premiums—as being inappropriate or unfair ways of promoting products. Thailand requires food processors selling national brands to market low-price brands also, so that low-income consumers can find economy brands on the shelves. In India, food companies must obtain special approval to launch brands that duplicate those already existing on the market, such as additional cola drinks or new brands of rice.

Understanding the public policy implications of a particular marketing activity is not a simple matter. For example, in the United States, there are many laws created at the

TABLE 3.2 Major U.S. Legislation Affecting Marketing

Legislation	Purpose
Sherman Antitrust Act (1890)	Prohibits monopolies and activities (price fixing, predatory pricing) that restrain trade or competition in interstate commerce.
Federal Food and Drug Act (1906)	Forbids the manufacture or sale of adulterated or fraudulently labeled foods and drugs. Created the Food and Drug Administration.
Clayton Act (1914)	Supplements the Sherman Act by prohibiting certain types of price discrimination, exclusive dealing, and tying clauses (which require a dealer to take additional products in a seller's line).
Federal Trade Commission Act (1914)	Establishes a commission to monitor and remedy unfair trade methods.
Robinson-Patman Act (1936)	Amends Clayton Act to define price discrimination as unlawful. Empowers FTC to establish limits on quantity discounts, forbid some brokerage allowances, and prohibit promotional allowances except when made available on proportionately equal terms.
Wheeler-Lea Act (1938)	Makes deceptive, misleading, and unfair practices illegal regardless of injury to competition. Places advertising of food and drugs under FTC jurisdiction.
Lanham Trademark Act (1946)	Protects and regulates distinctive brand names and trademarks.
National Traffic and Safety Act (1958)	Provides for the creation of compulsory safety standards for automobiles and tires.
Fair Packaging and Labeling Act (1966)	Provides for the regulation of packaging and labeling of consumer goods. Requires that manufacturers state what the package contains, who made it, and how much it contains.
Child Protection Act (1966)	Bans sale of hazardous toys and articles. Sets standards for child-resistant packaging.
Federal Cigarette Labeling and Advertising Act (1967)	Requires that cigarette packages contain the following statement: "Warning: The Surgeon General Has Determined That Cigarette Smoking Is Dangerous to Your Health."
National Environmental Policy Act (1969)	Establishes a national policy on the environment. The 1970 Reorganization Plan established the Environmental Protection Agency.
Consumer Product Safety Act (1972)	Establishes the Consumer Product Safety Commission and authorizes it to set safety standards for consumer products as well as exact penalties for failure to uphold those standards.
Magnuson-Moss Warranty Act (1975)	Authorizes the FTC to determine rules and regulations for consumer warranties and provides consumer access to redress, such as the class action suit.
Children's Television Act (1990)	Limits number of commercials aired during children's programs.
Nutrition Labeling and Education Act (1990)	Requires that food product labels provide detailed nutritional information.
Telephone Consumer Protection Act (1991)	Establishes procedures to avoid unwanted telephone solicitations. Limits marketers' use of automatic telephone dialing systems and artificial or prerecorded voices.
Americans with Disabilities Act (1991)	Makes discrimination against people with disabilities illegal in public accommodations, transportation, and telecommunications.
Children's Online Privacy Protection Act (2000)	Prohibits Web sites or online services operators from collecting personal information from children without obtaining consent from a parent and allowing parents to review information collected from their children.
Do-Not-Call Implementation Act (2003)	Authorized the FTC to collect fees from sellers and telemarketers for the implementation and enforcement of a National Do-Not-Call Registry.

national, state, and local levels, and these regulations often overlap. Aspirins sold in Dallas are governed both by federal labeling laws and by Texas state advertising laws. Moreover, regulations are constantly changing—what was allowed last year may now be prohibited, and what was prohibited may now be allowed. Marketers must work hard to keep up with changes in regulations and their interpretations.

Business legislation has been enacted for a number of reasons. The first is to *protect companies* from each other. Although business executives may praise competition, they sometimes try to neutralize it when it threatens them. So laws are passed to define and prevent unfair competition. In the United States, such laws are enforced by the Federal Trade Commission and the Antitrust Division of the Attorney General's office.

The second purpose of government regulation is to *protect consumers* from unfair business practices. Some firms, if left alone, would make shoddy products, tell lies in their advertising, and deceive consumers through their packaging and pricing. Unfair business practices have been defined and are enforced by various agencies.

The third purpose of government regulation is to *protect the interests of society* against unrestrained business behavior. Profitable business activity does not always create a better quality of life. Regulation arises to ensure that firms take responsibility for the social costs of their production or products.

Changing Government Agency Enforcement. International marketers will encounter dozens, or even hundreds, of agencies set up to enforce trade policies and regulations. In the United States, Congress has established federal regulatory agencies, such as the Federal Trade Commission, the Food and Drug Administration, the Federal Communications Commission, the Federal Energy Regulatory Commission, the Civil Aeronautics Board, the Consumer Product Safety Commission, and the Environmental Protection Agency.

Because such government agencies have some discretion in enforcing the laws, they can have a major impact on a company's marketing performance. At times, the staffs of these agencies have appeared to be overly eager and unpredictable. Some of the agencies have been dominated by lawyers and economists who lacked a practical sense of how business and marketing work. In recent years, the Federal Trade Commission has added staff marketing experts, who can better understand complex business issues.

New laws and their enforcement will continue to increase. Business executives must watch these developments when planning their products and marketing programs. Marketers need to know about the major laws protecting competition, consumers, and society. They need to understand these laws at the local, state, national, and international levels.

Increased Emphasis on Ethics and Socially Responsible Actions

Written regulations cannot possibly cover all potential marketing abuses, and existing laws are often difficult to enforce. However, beyond written laws and regulations, business is also governed by social codes and rules of professional ethics.

Socially Responsible Behavior. Enlightened companies encourage their managers to look beyond what the regulatory system allows and simply "do the right thing." These socially responsible firms actively seek out ways to protect the long-run interests of their consumers and the environment.

The recent rash of business scandals and increased concerns about the environment have created fresh interest in the issues of ethics and social responsibility. Almost every aspect of marketing involves such issues. Unfortunately, because these issues usually involve conflicting interests, well-meaning people can honestly disagree about the right course of action in a given situation. Thus, many industrial and professional trade associations have suggested codes of ethics. And more companies are now developing policies, guidelines, and other responses to complex social responsibility issues.

The boom in e-commerce and Internet marketing has created a new set of social and ethical issues. Online privacy issues are the primary concern. For example, Web site visitors often provide extensive personal information that might leave them open to abuse by unscrupulous marketers. Moreover, both Intel and Microsoft have been accused of covert, high-tech computer chip and software invasions of customers' personal computers to obtain information for marketing purposes. Most companies are now careful to fully disclose their Internet privacy policies.[36]

Throughout the text, we present Marketing at Work exhibits that summarize the main public policy and social responsibility issues surrounding major marketing decisions. These exhibits discuss the legal issues that marketers should understand and the common ethical and societal concerns that marketers face. In Chapter 16, we discuss a broad range of societal marketing issues in greater depth.

Cause-Related Marketing. To exercise their social responsibility and build more positive images, many companies are now linking themselves to worthwhile causes. These days, every product seems to be tied to some cause. Buy a pink mixer from KitchenAid and support breast cancer research. Shop at EddieBauer.com and have a percentage of your purchase go to support your local grade school. Purchase Habitat Coffee and help Habitat for Humanity build a house for a needy family. Order the City Harvest Lunch at Le Bernardin in New York City, and the restaurant donates $5 to City Harvest, which feeds the hungry by rescuing millions of pounds of edible food thrown away each year by the city's food businesses. Pay for these purchases with the right charge card and you can support a local cultural arts group or help fight heart disease.

■ Cause-related marketing: Nike's yellow "LiveSTRONG" wristbands created a national craze and helped the Lance Armstrong Foundation raise tens of millions of dollars.

Cause-related marketing has become a primary form of corporate giving. It lets companies "do well by doing good" by linking purchases of the company's products or services with fund-raising for worthwhile causes or charitable organizations. Companies now sponsor dozens of cause-related marketing campaigns each year. Many are backed by large budgets and a full complement of marketing activities. Consider this example:

In May 2004, Nike began selling simple yellow synthetic silicon rubber bracelets—stamped with the phrase "LiveSTRONG"—at Niketown outlets around the country. The price was $1, and proceeds were given to the Lance Armstrong Foundation, the nonprofit charitable organization associated with the champion cyclist, who is also a Nike athlete and famous cancer survivor. "LiveSTRONG" is the foundation's motto; yellow echoes the color of the lead rider's jersey in the Tour de France. Nike paid for the entire first run of five million bracelets, meaning that 100 percent of the proceeds, plus another $1 million Nike threw in, went straight to the foundation.

Sales really took off when the Tour de France got under way that summer. Armstrong wore the wristband and so did his whole team. As the tour wore on, competitors and even officials started wearing them. As Armstrong cruised to his record-setting sixth consecutive Tour de France victory, celebrities started wearing them, and suddenly the bracelets were everywhere—a charitable must-have. In less than a year, the foundation had sold more than 40 million "Live-STRONG" bracelets for $1 each. On one day alone, the Foundation sold an amazing 900,000 bracelets when Armstrong appeared on *The Oprah Winfrey Show* and Winfrey challenged her viewers to break the previous single-day record of 382,000.[37]

Cause-related marketing has stirred some controversy. Critics worry that cause-related marketing is more a strategy for selling than a strategy for giving—that "cause-related" marketing is really "cause-exploitative" marketing. Thus, companies using cause-related marketing might find themselves walking a fine line between increased sales and an improved image, and facing charges of exploitation.

However, if handled well, cause-related marketing can greatly benefit both the company and the cause. The company gains an effective marketing tool while building a more positive public image. The charitable organization or cause gains greater visibility and important new sources of funding. U.S. companies now spend an estimated $1 billion a year on cause-related marketing programs, compared to only $120 million in 1990.[38]

CULTURAL ENVIRONMENT

Cultural environment
Institutions and other forces that affect society's basic values, perceptions, preferences, and behaviors.

The **cultural environment** is made up of institutions and other forces that affect a society's basic values, perceptions, preferences, and behaviors. People grow up in a particular society that shapes their basic beliefs and values. They absorb a worldview that defines their relationships with others. The following cultural characteristics can affect marketing decision making.

Persistence of Cultural Values   People in a given society hold many beliefs and values. Their core beliefs and values have a high degree of persistence. For example, most Americans believe in working, getting married, giving to charity, and being honest. These beliefs shape more specific attitudes and behaviors found in everyday life. *Core* beliefs and values are passed on from parents to children and are reinforced by schools, churches, business, and government.

Secondary beliefs and values are more open to change. Believing in marriage is a core belief; believing that people should get married early in life is a secondary belief. Marketers have some chance of changing secondary values but little chance of changing core values. For example, family-planning marketers could argue more effectively that people should get married later than that they should not get married at all.

Shifts in Secondary Cultural Values   Although core values are fairly persistent, cultural swings do take place. Consider the impact of popular music groups, movie personalities, and other celebrities on young people's hairstyling and clothing norms. Marketers want to predict cultural shifts in order to spot new opportunities or threats. Several firms offer "futures" forecasts in this connection, such as the Yankelovich Monitor, Market Facts' BrainWaves Group, and the Trends Research Institute.

The Yankelovich Monitor has tracked consumer value trends for years. At the dawn of the twenty-first century, it looked back to capture lessons from the past decade that might offer insight into the 2000s.[39] Yankelovich maintains that the "decade drivers" for the 2000s will primarily come from the baby boomers and Generation Xers. The baby boomers will be driven by four factors in the 2000's: "adventure" (fueled by a sense of youthfulness), "smarts" (fueled by a sense of empowerment and willingness to accept change), "intergenerational support" (caring for younger and older, often in nontraditional arrangements), and "retreading" (embracing early retirement with second career or phase of their work life). Gen Xers will be driven by three factors: "redefining the good life" (being highly motivated to improve their economic well-being and remain in control), "new rituals" (returning to traditional values but with a tolerant mind-set and active lifestyle), and "cutting and pasting" (balancing work, play, sleep, family, and other aspects of their lives).

The major cultural values of a society are expressed in people's views of themselves and others, as well as in their views of organizations, society, nature, and the universe.

People's Views of Themselves.   People vary in their emphasis on serving themselves versus serving others. Some people seek personal pleasure, wanting fun, change, and escape. Others seek self-realization through religion, recreation, or the avid pursuit of careers or other life goals. People use products, brands, and services as a means of self-expression, and they buy products and services that match their views of themselves.

Yankelovich Monitor recently discovered a conflicted consumer segment whose purchases are motivated by self-views of both duty and fun:[40]

Yankelovich's Monitor has identified a paradoxical consumer segment motivated equally by duty and fun. Comprising more than one-third of the population, these folks want to have their cake and rely on it, too. "Duty and Fun" consumers agree that "duty should always come before pleasure" *and* say that they "try to have as much fun as they can now and let the future take care of itself." Their split personalities indicate an internal struggle that affects everyday life and buying. To reach these conflicted consumers, marketers must give them something that makes them smile at the register, while offering sound payment options, guarantees, testimonials, and other forms of assurance. For example, PETsMART

■ People's self-views: PETsMART serves the conflicted "Duty and Fun" segment by permitting customers to bring their pets shopping, allowing duty and fun to happily coexist.

permits shoppers to bring their pets shopping, allowing duty and fun to happily coexist. And with its hybrid Prius, Toyota merges a respected company brand (duty) and leading-edge technology (fun), turning what could have been a fuddy-duddy failure into a ride for those sold on dutiful fun.

People's Views of Others.   Recently, observers have noted a shift from a "me society" to a "we society" in which more people want to be with and serve others.[41]

After years of serious "nesting"—staying close to the security and creature comforts of home and hearth—Americans are now venturing out of their homes to hang out in the real world. The nesting instinct has gone in and out of fashion before. When the first big wave hit in the early 1980s, trend watchers coined the term "cocooning" to describe the surge of boomers buying their first homes and filling them up with oversize furniture and fancy gadgets. The dot-com boom set off another round, partly fueled by cool home gizmos like plasma TVs and PlayStations. Though many expected 9/11 to send people even deeper into nesting mode, sociologists say it actually got people out looking for companionship. After being hunkered down through terror alerts and the war in Iraq, many people were naturally itching to get out. Marketers are beginning to address the shift. In Las Vegas, the Saks Fifth Avenue store is trying to ease folks back out of the house with a simulated living room, complete with sofas where shoppers can sit and mingle, or munch from bowls of candy and watch a giant TV.

More and more, people want to get out of the house and be with others. This trend suggests a greater demand for "social support" products and services that improve direct communication between people, such as health clubs and family vacations.

People's Views of Organizations.   People vary in their attitudes toward corporations, government agencies, trade unions, universities, and other organizations. By and large, people are willing to work for major organizations and expect them, in turn, to carry out society's work.

The late 1980s saw a sharp decrease in confidence in and loyalty toward America's business and political organizations and institutions. In the workplace, there has been an overall decline in organizational loyalty. During the 1990s, waves of company downsizings bred cynicism and distrust. And in this decade, corporate scandals at Enron, WorldCom, Tyco International, and other large companies have resulted in a further loss of confidence in big business. Many people today see work not as a source of satisfaction but as a required chore to earn money to enjoy their nonwork hours. This trend suggests that organizations need to find new ways to win consumer and employee confidence.

People's Views of Society.   People vary in their attitudes toward their society; patriots defend it, reformers want to change it, malcontents want to leave it. People's orientation to their society influences their consumption patterns and attitudes toward the marketplace. American patriotism has been increasing gradually for the past two decades. It surged, however, following the September 11 terrorist attacks and the Iraq war. For example, the summer following the Iraq war saw a surge of pumped-up Americans visiting U.S. historic sites, ranging from the Washington, D.C., monuments, Mount Rushmore, the Gettysburg battlefield, and the *USS Constitution* ("Old Ironsides") to Pearl Harbor and the Alamo.[42]

Marketers responded with patriotic products and promotions, offering everything from floral bouquets to clothing with patriotic themes. Although most of these marketing efforts were tasteful and well received, waving the red, white, and blue can prove tricky. Except in cases where companies tie product sales to charitable contributions, such flag-waving promotions can be viewed as attempts to cash in on the tragedy. Marketers must take care when responding to such national emotions.

People's Views of Nature. People vary in their attitudes toward the natural world. Some feel ruled by it, others feel in harmony with it, and still others seek to master it. A long-term trend has been people's growing mastery over nature through technology and the belief that nature is bountiful. More recently, however, people have recognized that nature is finite and fragile, that it can be destroyed or spoiled by human activities.

This renewed love of things natural has created a sizable "lifestyles of health and sustainability" (LOHAS) market, consumers who seek out everything from natural, organic, and nutritional products to fuel-efficient cars and alternative medicine. In the words of one such consumer:

> I am not an early adopter, a fast follower, or a mass-market stampeder. But I am a gas-conscious driver. So that's why I was standing in a Toyota dealership . . . this week, the latest person to check out a hybrid car. Who needs $40 fill-ups? After tooling around in three different hybrid car brands—Toyota, Honda and a Ford—I thought: How cool could this be? Saving gas money and doing well by the environment. Turns out there's a whole trend-watchers' classification for people who think like that: LOHAS. Lifestyles of Health and Sustainability. Buy a hybrid. Shop at places like Whole Foods. Pick up the Seventh Generation paper towels at Albertsons. No skin off our noses. Conscientious shopping, with no sacrifice or hippie stigma.[43]

Business has responded by offering more products and services catering to such interests. For example, food producers have found fast-growing markets for natural and organic foods. Sales of White Wave's Silk soymilk, for instance, jumped from $4 million in 1998 to $414 million last year. Organic products are now a $10.8 billion industry in the United States, growing at a rate of 20 percent annually. Niche marketers, such as Whole Foods Markets, have sprung up to serve this market, and traditional food chains such as Kroger and Safeway have added separate natural and organic food sections. Even pet owners are joining the movement as they become more aware of what goes into Fido's food. Almost every major pet food brand now offers several types of natural foods. [44]

■ People's views of nature: Marketers are responding to changes in people's views of the natural environment by offering more natural and organic products. White Wave's Silk soymilk has found success in the $10.5 billion organic products industry.

People's Views of the Universe. Finally, people vary in their beliefs about the origin of the universe and their place in it. Although most Americans practice religion, religious conviction and practice have been dropping off gradually through the years. Some futurists, however, have noted a renewed interest in spirituality, perhaps as a part of a broader search for a new inner purpose. People have been moving away from materialism and dog-eat-dog ambition to seek more permanent values—family, community, earth, faith—and a more certain grasp of right and wrong.

"Americans are on a spiritual journey, increasingly concerned with the meaning of life and issues of the soul and spirit," observes one expert. People "say they are increasingly looking to religion—Christianity, Judaism, Hinduism, Islam, and others—as a source of comfort in a chaotic world." This new spiritualism affects consumers in everything from the television shows they watch and the books they read to the products and services they buy. "Since consumers don't park their beliefs and values on the bench outside the marketplace," adds the expert, "they are bringing this awareness to the brands they buy. Tapping into this heightened sensitivity presents a unique marketing opportunity for brands."[45]

Slow down and cool your engine. You've now read about a large number of environmental forces. How are all of these environments *linked* with each other? With company marketing strategy?

- How are major demographic forces linked with economic changes? With major cultural trends? How are the natural and technological environments linked? Think of an example of a company that has recognized one of these links and turned it into a marketing opportunity.
- Is the marketing environment uncontrollable—something that the company can only prepare for and react to? Or can companies be proactive in changing environmental factors? Think of a good example that makes your point, then read on.

Responding to the Marketing Environment

Someone once observed, "There are three kinds of companies: those who make things happen, those who watch things happen, and those who wonder what's happened."[46] Many companies view the marketing environment as an uncontrollable element to which they must react and adapt. They passively accept the marketing environment and do not try to change it. They analyze the environmental forces and design strategies that will help the company avoid the threats and take advantage of the opportunities the environment provides.

Other companies take a *proactive* stance toward the marketing environment. Rather than simply watching and reacting, these firms take aggressive actions to affect the publics and forces in their marketing environment. Such companies hire lobbyists to influence legislation affecting their industries and stage media events to gain favorable press coverage. They run advertorials (ads expressing editorial points of view) to shape public opinion. They press lawsuits and file complaints with regulators to keep competitors in line, and they form contractual agreements to better control their distribution channels.

Often, companies can find positive ways to overcome seemingly uncontrollable environmental constraints. For example:

> Cathay Pacific Airlines . . . determined that many travelers were avoiding Hong Kong because of lengthy delays at immigration. Rather than assuming that this was a problem they could not solve, Cathay's senior staff asked the Hong Kong government how to avoid these immigration delays. After lengthy discussions, the airline agreed to make an annual grant-in-aid to the government to hire more immigration inspectors—but these reinforcements would service primarily the Cathay Pacific gates. The reduced waiting period increased customer value and thus strengthened [Cathay's competitive advantage].[47]

Marketing management cannot always control environmental forces. In many cases, it must settle for simply watching and reacting to the environment. For example, a company would have little success trying to influence geographic population shifts, the economic environment, or major cultural values. But whenever possible, smart marketing managers will take a *proactive* rather than *reactive* approach to the marketing environment.

REST STOP → REVIEWING THE CONCEPTS

In this chapter and the next two chapters, you'll examine the environments of marketing and how companies analyze these environments to better understand the marketplace and consumers. Companies must constantly watch and manage the *marketing environment* in order to seek opportunities and ward off threats. The marketing environment comprises all the actors and forces influencing the company's ability to transact business effectively with its target market.

1. Describe the environmental forces that affect the company's ability to serve its customers.

The company's *microenvironment* consists of other actors close to the company that combine to form the company's value delivery network or that affect its ability to serve its customers. It includes the company's *internal environment*—its several departments and management levels—as it influences marketing decision making. *Marketing-channel firms*—suppliers and marketing intermediaries, including resellers, physical distribution firms, marketing services agencies, and financial intermediaries—cooperate to create customer value. Five types of customer *markets* include consumer, business, reseller, government, and international markets. *Competitors* vie with the company in an effort to serve customers better. Finally, various *publics* have an actual or potential interest in, or impact on, the company's ability to meet its objectives.

The *macroenvironment* consists of larger societal forces that affect the entire microenvironment. The six forces making up the company's macroenvironment include demographic, economic, natural, technological, political, and cultural forces. These forces shape opportunities and pose threats to the company.

2. Explain how changes in the demographic and economic environments affect marketing decisions.

Demography is the study of the characteristics of human populations. Today's *demographic environment* shows a changing age structure, shifting family profiles, geographic population shifts, a better-educated and more white-collar population, and increasing diversity. The *economic environment* consists of factors that affect buying power and patterns. The economic environment is characterized by more consumer concern for value and shifting consumer spending patterns. Today's squeezed consumers are seeking greater value—just the right combination of good quality and service at a fair price. The distribution of income also is shifting. The rich have grown richer, the middle class has shrunk, and the poor have remained poor, leading to a two-tiered market. Many companies now tailor their marketing offers to two different markets—the affluent and the less affluent.

3. Identify the major trends in the firm's natural and technological environments.

The *natural environment* shows three major trends: shortages of certain raw materials, higher pollution levels, and more government intervention in natural resource management. Environmental concerns create marketing opportunities for alert companies. The marketer should watch for four major trends in the *technological environment:* the rapid pace of technological change, high R&D budgets, the concentration by companies on minor product improvements, and increased government regulation. Companies that fail to keep up with technological change will miss out on new product and marketing opportunities.

4. Explain the key changes in the political and cultural environments.

The *political environment* consists of laws, agencies, and groups that influence or limit marketing actions. The political environment has undergone three changes that affect marketing worldwide: increasing legislation regulating business, strong government agency enforcement, and greater emphasis on ethics and socially responsible actions. The *cultural environment* is made up of institutions and forces that affect a society's values, perceptions, preferences, and behaviors. The environment shows long-term trends toward a "we society," a lessening trust of institutions, increasing patriotism, greater appreciation for nature, a new spiritualism, and the search for more meaningful and enduring values.

5. Discuss how companies can react to the marketing environment.

Companies can passively accept the marketing environment as an uncontrollable element to which they must adapt, avoiding threats and taking advantage of opportunities as they arise. Or they can take a *proactive* stance, working to change the environment rather than simply reacting to it. Whenever possible, companies should try to be proactive rather than reactive.

Navigating the Key Terms

Baby boomers (69)
Cultural environment (86)
Demography (68)
Economic environment (78)
Engel's laws (79)

Generation X (70)
Generation Y (71)
Macroenvironment (65)
Marketing environment (65)
Marketing intermediaries (66)

Microenvironment (65)
Natural environment (80)
Political environment (83)
Public (67)
Technological environment (80)

Travel Log

Discussing the Issues

1. List the actors in a company's microenvironment. How might the goals of the *publics* in a company's microenvironment be opposed to one another? How would opposing goals among a company's relevant publics impact its strategy?

2. List the six primary forces shaping a company's macroenvironment. Which do you think has the largest impact on a retail clothing store? Which has the largest impact on a not-for-profit organization serving the homeless? Why?

3. The changing structure of the American family has a tremendous impact on the opportunities for, and threats to, a company. Explain how a grocery store could change its positioning to appeal to each of the following segments: married couples with children, single parents, and adults living alone.

4. Americans are becoming more concerned about the natural environment. Explain how this trend might affect a company that markets packaging for (a) candy bars, (b) tires, (c) gas-powered lawnmowers, and (d) electrical power. Suggest some effective responses to the concerns that consumers might have about these products.

5. Identify a cause-related marketing campaign. Does the link between the product and the cause make you more likely to purchase the product? Does the campaign change your opinion of the company?

6. Identify a company that you believe is taking a proactive, rather than reactive, approach to dealing with the marketing environment. What specific actions do they take to influence their environment? What benefits have resulted from those actions?

Application Questions

1. For educational institutions, the number, quality, and characteristics of its student body are heavily impacted by changes in the size and structure of the general population. How will an aging population, a growing population, a changing definition of the family, geographic shifts in population, a more white-collar workforce, and increasing ethnic and cultural diversity likely impact your school? For those trends that have a negative impact, what strategy would you recommend for mitigating the negative influence?

2. In small groups, brainstorm several new technologies emerging in today's market. What older technologies might these newer options replace? What can the marketers selling products relying on outdated technologies do to maintain their share of the market?

3. Select two of the shifts in secondary cultural values that are discussed in the text. For each value, identify a company that has benefited from the shift and one whose position has worsened. For those organizations that have not fared as well under the shift, what can they do to better adjust to this trend?

Under the Hood: Focus on Technology

The FTC recently hosted a public workshop on radio frequency identification (RFID) to discuss all of the technology's applications as well as its potential pitfalls. At the workshop, one speaker commented that RFID "promises to reform, if not revolutionize, many corners of the marketplace." As discussed in the chapter, RFID is already a part of many consumers' daily lives. And, as companies like Wal-Mart and Procter & Gamble embrace the technology, RFID is truly changing the way suppliers and retailers work together.

At the FTC workshop, Simon Langford, Manager of RFID Strategy for Wal-Mart, offered his thoughts on the benefits of RFID. Review his presentation online at www.ftc.gov/bcp/workshops/rfid/langford.pdf and answer the following questions:

1. How does RFID help strengthen Wal-Mart's relationships with its many partners?

2. What are some of the benefits for Wal-Mart? For Wal-Mart's suppliers?

3. How does RFID technology increase value and satisfaction for Wal-Mart's customers?

4. How might consumer privacy concerns impact the widespread acceptance of RFID technology?

Focus on Ethics

How many times has your family purchased a new computer in the past five years? As computers become more powerful, regular updating of computer equipment has become common. Have you ever wondered where all of the old computers and monitors go? Concerns over decreasing raw materials, increasing pollution levels, and global warming have gained momentum over the last several years. While many companies have been accused of polluting the environment, some have used society's concern over the natural environment to differentiate themselves from competitors. Dell recently initiated a program for businesses and consumers to recycle and reuse old computers, monitors, keyboards, and mice. For a fee of $15 per 50 pounds of weight, Dell sends someone to your door to pick up old components. Dell then recycles or resells the old computer equipment, sparing land-fills from the hazardous materials contained in much of today's computer equipment.

1. Assume that the price paid by the owners of the old computer equipment does not cover Dell's cost of recycling. What benefits might Dell gain from the recycling program that would justify the expense?

2. What actions might government take if concerned about the disposal of unwanted computer equipment elevated? Are Dell's proactive recycling efforts enough, in your opinion, to keep regulators at bay?

3. Might Dell's computer recycling program help to differentiate it from other computer manufacturers? How much influence would a recycling program like the one described here for Dell computer have on your decision to buy a computer from a particular company?

Videos

The American Express video case that accompanies this chapter is located in Appendix 1.

Chapter 4

➜ **AFTER READING THIS CHAPTER, YOU SHOULD BE ABLE TO**

1. explain the importance of information to the company and its understanding of the marketplace

2. define the marketing information system and discuss its parts

3. outline the steps in the marketing research process

4. explain how companies analyze and distribute marketing information

5. discuss the special issues some marketing researchers face, including public policy and ethics issues

Managing Marketing Information

Road Map Previewing the Concepts

In the last chapter, you learned about the complex and changing marketing environment. In this chapter, we'll continue our exploration of how marketers go about understanding the marketplace and consumers. We'll look at how companies develop and manage information about important marketplace elements—about customers, competitors, products, and marketing programs. We'll examine marketing information systems designed to give managers the right information, in the right form, at the right time to help them make better marketing decisions. We'll also take a close look at the marketing research process and at some special marketing research considerations. To succeed in today's marketplace, companies must know how to manage mountains of marketing information effectively.

We'll start the chapter with a story about Coach, a company long known for its classic, high-quality leather handbags and accessories. Until recently, Coach seemed to get along just fine in the mature and stable handbag industry without much consumer research. But when consumer needs and preferences shifted and sales slowed, all that changed. Motor on to see how Coach used exhaustive marketing research to give itself an extreme strategic makeover.

Coach first opened its doors in 1941 as a family-owned, leather-goods workshop. Over the next 50 years, the company developed a strong following for its classically styled, high-quality leather handbags and accessories.

In those early years, it seemed, Coach didn't need a lot of marketing research to understand its customers. For most buyers, handbags were largely functional, used for carrying keys, a wallet, and cosmetics. Women typically bought only two purses a year—one for everyday use and one for special occasions. The everyday handbag lasted a long time and styles changed infrequently. Women didn't waste much time or energy on their purse-buying decisions.

Coach offered basic handbag designs in understated colors, black and brown. The classic Coach bag's only ornamentation was a small gold latch and a small leather tag embossed with the Coach name. Over the years, with their understated styling and quality image, Coach handbags earned a reputation as classy but "traditional sturdy standbys." Conservative professionals, who liked the look, quality, and value of Coach's handbags, became the company's loyal core customers. Coach, by then a unit of Sara Lee Corporation, cruised along comfortably.

By the mid-1990s, however, Coach's world had changed dramatically and sales started to slow. As more and more women entered the workforce, they needed different types of bags to carry their work and their laptops. These increasingly influential women fueled the "mass luxury movement." They wanted the designer brands that only affluent women had been able to afford. And they wanted more stylish and colorful bags to spruce up the plain fashions of the day.

High-end designers such as Prada, Fendi, Gucci, and Chanel were responding to these trends. According to one analyst, the industry saw "a sharp uptick in demand for handbags with extra flair, such as bright colors, exotic leathers and even materials such as wool, velvet, and fur." Many of these designer bags sold for more than $1,000, some for as much as $3,000. By comparison, Coach's traditional styles began to look downright plain.

It was time for an extreme makeover. But where to start? To gain a better understanding of the new handbag buyer, Coach began with marketing research—lots of marketing research. "Coach started thinking like a consumer-products company," says the analyst, "relentlessly testing the market to see what holes it could fill."

Based on extensive marketing research, Coach overhauled its strategy. In the process, it helped engineer a shift in the way women shop for handbags.

[Coach] decided to translate the elite notion of the handbag as fashion statement into something the average American woman could afford, [dubbing] the strategy "accessible luxury." Coach [now] creates and markets new kinds of bags to fill what it calls "usage voids," activities that range from weekend getaways to dancing at nightclubs to trips to the grocery store. . . . Known for decades as a sturdy purveyor of conservative, long-lasting handbags, it has [now] successfully convinced women to buy weekend bags, evening bags, backpacks, satchels, clutches, totes, briefcases, diaper bags, coin purses, duffels, and a mini handbag that doubles as a bag-within-a-bag. . . . [Coach now] updates its collections nearly every month with new colors, fabrics, and sizes. It prices bags lower than luxury designers but high enough for women to buy as a special treat.

As a starter, consumer research revealed that even Coach's conservative customers wanted more fashion pizzazz in their handbags. So, in early 2001, the company launched the "Signature" collection, stylish and colorful bags made of leather and fabric and covered in the letter *C*. Coach designers even began to use adjectives like *sexy, fun, sophisticated, playful, grounded, luxurious,* and *quality-driven* to describe Coach's customers and the company itself.

About that same time, research revealed another "usage void." Women were carrying small Coach cosmetic cases inside their larger handbags to hold essentials—such as keys, credit cards, and even cell phones—making them easier to find. However, when crammed into larger bags, these smaller cases caused bulges, making the larger bags appear misshapen and bulky. To fill the void, Coach designed a 4-inch by 6-inch zippered bag with a looped strap, which a woman could either dangle from her wrist or clip inside a larger bag. Coach called the new product the "wristlet" and introduced it at prices as low as $38. In only the first 10 months, women snapped up more than 100,000 wristlets. By 2004, Coach was selling more than a million wristlets a year in 75 styles.

Still more research revealed additional usage voids. For example, Coach's consumer researchers learned that women were increasingly interested in non-leather bags. They also faced the problem that customers did most of their handbag shopping only during the holiday season. To fill both voids, in 2003, the company developed its "Hamptons Weekend" line, stylish fabric bags designed for summer weekend use. Unlike competitors' uninspired black nylon or basic canvas bags, the new Coach line featured an easily foldable shape, hot colors, and a durable, water-resistant material befitting a "relaxed-but-sophisticated" lifestyle. The new bags flew off the shelves at Coach's retail stores.

Now, Coach thinks that its research points to yet another market void. Researchers noticed that more women are now mixing formal clothing, stilettos, and diamonds with blue jeans and other casual clothes. This suggests an opportunity to get women to use formal accessories—including evening bags—during daylight hours. So, Coach has introduced the "Madison" collection, sleek satin or bejeweled versions of its more traditional purses. Ads for the line show casually dressed woman carrying a Madison bag in daylight, while also carrying a larger, casual tote bag.

Thus, Coach watches its customers closely, looking for trends that might suggest new market voids to fill. This year alone, Coach will spend $3 million on marketing research, interviewing 14,000 women about everything from lifestyles to purse styles to strap lengths. According to a coach executive, everything Coach does is thoroughly "girlfriend tested, down to the last stitch."

Such exhaustive marketing research has more than paid for itself. The company's sales, profits, and share prices are now soaring. Coach has achieved double-digit sales and earnings growth every period since spinning off from Sara Lee and going public in 2000. In only the past two years, sales are up 84 percent and profits have more than tripled. Since going public, Coach's stock price has jumped 940 percent. It looks like investors are going to need bigger purses.[1]

In order to produce superior customer value and satisfaction, companies need information at almost every turn. As the Coach story highlights, good products and marketing programs begin with solid information on consumer needs and wants. Companies also need an abundance of information on competitors, resellers, and other actors and forces in the marketplace.

With the recent explosion of information technologies, companies can now generate information in great quantities. In fact, today's managers often receive too much information. One study found that with all the companies offering data, and with all the information now available through supermarket scanners, large retailers typically now have the equivalent of 320 miles of bookshelves of information on their products. Wal-Mart, the largest retailer of all, has more than three-and-a-half times that much information in its data warehouse. Thus, running out of information is not a problem, but seeing through the "data smog" is. "In this oh-so-overwhelming Information age," comments one observer, "it's all too easy to be buried, burdened, and burned out by data overload.[2]

Despite this data glut, marketers frequently complain that they lack enough information of the right kind. They don't need *more* information, they need *better* information. And they need to make better *use* of the information they already have. A former CEO at Unilever once said that if Unilever only knew what it knows, it would double its profits. The meaning is clear: Many companies sit on rich information but fail to manage and use it well.[3]

■ Information overload: "In this oh-so-overwhelming Information age, it's all too easy to be buried, burdened, and burned out by data overload."

Companies must design effective marketing information systems that give managers the right information, in the right form, at the right time to help them make better marketing decisions.

A **marketing information system (MIS)** consists of people, equipment, and procedures to gather, sort, analyze, evaluate, and distribute needed, timely, and accurate information to marketing decision makers. Figure 4.1 shows that the MIS begins and ends with information users—marketing managers, internal and external partners, and others who need marketing information. First, it interacts with these information users to *assess information needs*. Next, it *develops needed information* from internal company databases, marketing intelligence activities, and marketing research. Then it helps users to analyze information to put it in the right form for making marketing decisions and managing customer relationships. Finally, the MIS *distributes* the marketing information and helps managers *use* it in their decision making.

Marketing information system (MIS)
People, equipment, and procedures to gather, sort, analyze, evaluate, and distribute needed, timely, and accurate information to marketing decision makers.

Assessing Marketing Information Needs

The marketing information system primarily serves the company's marketing and other managers. However, it may also provide information to external partners, such as suppliers, resellers, or marketing services agencies. For example, Wal-Mart gives key suppliers access to information on customer buying patterns and inventory levels. And Dell creates tailored Premium Pages for large customers, giving them access to product design, order status, and product support and service information. In designing an information system, the company must consider the needs of all of these users.

FIGURE 4.1
The Marketing Information System

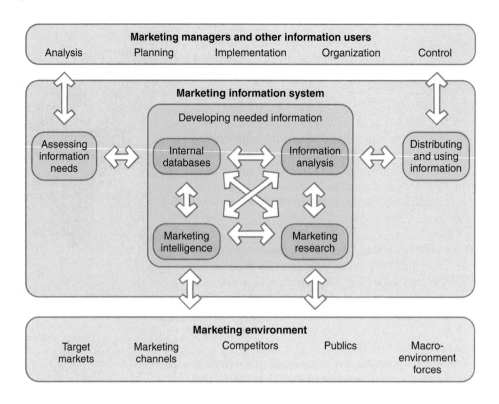

A good marketing information system balances the information users would *like* to have against what they really *need* and what is *feasible* to offer. The company begins by interviewing managers to find out what information they would like. Some managers will ask for whatever information they can get without thinking carefully about what they really need. Too much information can be as harmful as too little. Other managers may omit things they ought to know, or they may not know to ask for some types of information they should have. For example, managers might need to know that a competitor plans to introduce a new product during the coming year. Because they do not know about the new product, they do not think to ask about it. The MIS must monitor the marketing environment in order to provide decision makers with information they should have to make key marketing decisions.

Sometimes the company cannot provide the needed information, either because it is not available or because of MIS limitations. For example, a brand manager might want to know how competitors will change their advertising budgets next year and how these changes will affect industry market shares. The information on planned budgets probably is not available. Even if it is, the company's MIS may not be advanced enough to forecast resulting changes in market shares.

Finally, the costs of obtaining, processing, storing, and delivering information can mount quickly. The company must decide whether the benefits of having additional information are worth the costs of providing it, and both value and cost are often hard to assess. By itself, information has no worth; its value comes from its *use*. In many cases, additional information will do little to change or improve a manager's decision, or the costs of the information may exceed the returns from the improved decision. Marketers should not assume that additional information will always be worth obtaining. Rather, they should weigh carefully the costs of getting more information against the benefits resulting from it.

Developing Marketing Information

Marketers can obtain the needed information from *internal data, marketing intelligence,* and *marketing research*.

INTERNAL DATA

Many companies build extensive **internal databases**, electronic collections of consumer and market information obtained from data sources within the company network. Marketing managers can readily access and work with information in the database to identify marketing opportunities and problems, plan programs, and evaluate performance.

Information in the database can come from many sources. The accounting department prepares financial statements and keeps detailed records of sales, costs, and cash flows. Operations reports on production schedules, shipments, and inventories. The marketing department furnishes information on customer transactions, demographics, psychographics, and buying behavior. The customer service department keeps records of customer satisfaction or service problems. The sales force reports on reseller reactions and competitor activities, and marketing channel partners provide data on point-of-sale transactions. Harnessing such information can provide powerful competitive advantage (see Marketing at Work 4.1).

Here is an example of how one company uses its internal database to make better marketing decisions:

Pizza Hut claims to have the largest fast-food customer database in the world. The database contains detailed customer information data on 40 million U.S. households, gleaned from phone orders, online orders, and point of sale transactions at its 7,500 restaurants around the nation. The company can slice and dice the data by favorite toppings, what you ordered last, and whether you buy a salad with your cheese and pepperoni pizza. Pizza Hut also tracks in real time what commercials people are watching and responding to. It then uses all this data to enhance customer relationships. For example, it can target coupon offers to specific households based on past buying behaviors and preferences.[4]

■ Internal databases: Pizza Hut can slice and dice its extensive customer database by favorite toppings, what you ordered last, and whether you buy a salad with your cheese and pepperoni pizza, targeting coupon offers to specific households based on past buying behaviors and preferences.

Internal databases usually can be accessed more quickly and cheaply than other information sources, but they also present some problems. Because internal information was often collected for other purposes, it may be incomplete or in the wrong form for making marketing decisions. For example, sales and cost data used by the accounting department for preparing financial statements must be adapted for use in evaluating the value of specific customer segment, sales force, or channel performance. Data also ages quickly; keeping the database current requires a major effort. In addition, a large company produces mountains of information, which must be well integrated and readily accessible so that managers can find it easily and use it effectively. Managing that much data requires highly sophisticated equipment and techniques.

MARKETING INTELLIGENCE

Marketing intelligence is a systematic collection and analysis of publicly available information about competitors and developments in the marketplace. The goal of marketing intelligence is to improve strategic decision making, assess and track competitors' actions, and provide early warning of opportunities and threats.

Competitive intelligence gathering has grown dramatically as more and more companies are now busily snooping on their competitors. Techniques range from quizzing the company's own employees and benchmarking competitors' products to researching the Internet, lurking around industry trade shows, and even rooting through rivals' trash bins.

Internal databases
Electronic collections of consumer and market information obtained from data sources within the company network.

Marketing intelligence
The systematic collection and analysis of publicly available information about competitors and developments in the marketing environment.

BudNet: Making Customer Information the Lifeblood of the Organization

Every time a six-pack of Bud Light moves off the shelf at the Piggly Wiggly, Anheuser-Busch's top-secret BudNet nationwide data network knows it. The network will also likely record what the customer pays, when the beer was brewed, whether it was purchased warm or chilled, and whether the buyer could have gotten a better deal down the street. Anheuser has made a deadly accurate science out of finding out what beer lovers are buying, as well as when, where, and why. "If Anheuser-Busch loses shelf space in a store in Clarksville, Tennessee, they know it right away," says an industry consultant. "They're better at [the information] game than anyone, even Coca-Cola."

Until recently, the beer industry lagged technologically. The major breweries had little information, and they made poor use of what data they had. But Anheuser changed the rules in 1997, when Chairman August Busch III vowed to make his company a leader in mining its customers' buying patterns. The result was BudNet, an extensive, finely-tuned consumer and market data network.

Anheuser now works hand-in-hand with its distributors to amass detailed store-level data. "Wholesaler and store-level data has become the lifeblood of our organization," says a high-level Anheuser executive. Distributor sales reps scour their territories, snapping up every scrap of useful information, such as how much shelf space their retailers devote to all beer brands, which ones have the most visible displays, and which ones are on sale.

Take Dereck Gurden, a rep for one of Anheuser's central California distributors. When Gurden pulls up at one of his customers' stores—7-Eleven, Buy N Save, or one of dozens of liquor marts and restaurants—thanks to BudNet, he's loaded with useful account information. And, of course, he's hungry for more. Toting a brick-sized handheld PC, his constant companion and his window into BudNet, Gurden starts his routine. "First I'll scroll through and check the accounts receivable, make sure everything's current," he says. "Then it'll show me an inventory screen with a four-week history. I can get past sales, package placements—facts and numbers on how much of the sales they did when they had a display in a certain location."

After consulting with his customer, Gurden "walks the store, inputting what I see"—not just what he sees about his own brands, but also about competitors' products, prices, and displays,

which go into the handheld, too. A few years ago, still toting around clipboards and invoices, Gurden didn't even bother keeping track of the Coors and Miller displays in his customers' stores. Today those are among the most important data fields in his handheld. "It's no extra work to get the competitive info," he says. "You always want to walk the store." All done, Gurden jacks the handheld into his cell phone and fires off new orders to the warehouse, along with the data he's gathered. "Honestly? I think I know more about these guys' businesses than they do," he says. "At least in the beer section."

■ BudNet: Every time a six-pack of Bud Light moves off a grocery store shelf, Anheuser-Busch's nationwide BudNet data network knows it. Anheuser has made a deadly accurate science out of finding out what beer lovers are buying, as well as when, where, and why.

Gurden and several thousand reps and drivers serve as the eyes and ears of the BudNet data network through which Anheuser distributors report, in excruciating detail, on sales, shelf stocks, and displays at thousands of outlets. But amassing the data is just the first step. "It's not just collecting data," says Harry Schumacher, editor of Beer Business Daily. "It depends on brainpower. Anheuser-Busch is the smartest in figuring out how to use it." And knowing how to use it gives Anheuser Wal-Mart-like clout in its markets.

Collecting the data in a nightly nationwide sweep of its distributors' servers, Anheuser can draw a picture each morning of what brands are selling in which packages using which medley of displays, discounts, and promotions. Additional data from other sources helps to complete the picture. Today, Anheuser is the only major brewer to rely heavily on data from Information Resources, Inc., which tracks every bar-coded product swiped at checkout and performs Nielsen-style consumer surveys. Anheuser also conducts its own monthly surveys to see what beer drinkers buy and why.

Anheuser uses the data to constantly change marketing strategies, to design promotions to suit the ethnic makeup of its markets, and as early warning radar that detects where rivals might have an edge. None of the other brewers approaches Anheuser's data-mining savvy. Mining the aggregate data tells Anheuser every-

thing from what images or ideas to push in its ads to what new products to unveil—such as low-carb Michelob Ultra, Anheuser's most successful launch since Bud Light.

Crossing store-level data with U.S. Census figures on the ethnic and economic makeup of neighborhoods helps Anheuser tailor marketing campaigns with a local precision only dreamed of a few years ago. The data reveals trends by city (Tequiza may be hot in San Antonio, but Bud Light plays better in Peoria), by neighborhood (gay models appear on posters in San Francisco's Castro district, but not on those in the Mission), by holiday (the Fourth of July is a big seller in Atlanta, but St. Patrick's Day isn't), and by class (cans for blue-collar stores, bottles for white-collar). "They're drilling down to the level of the individual store," says the industry consultant. "They can pinpoint if customers are gay, Latino, 30-year-old, college-educated conservatives."

The BudNet data-mining operation is the King of Beers's little-known crown jewel. It's a primary reason that Anheuser's volume share of the $75 billion U.S. beer market stands at an astounding 50 percent, putting Miller, Molson Coors, and other brewers on ice.

Sources: Adapted from Kevin Kelleher, "66,207,896 Bottles of Beer on the Wall," Business 2.0, January–February, 2004, pp. 47–50. Adapted with permission. Also see "Anheuser-Busch Companies, Inc.," Hoover's Company Records, Austin, June 1, 2005, p. 10116.

Much intelligence can be collected from people inside the company—executives, engineers and scientists, purchasing agents, and the sales force. The company can also obtain important intelligence information from suppliers, resellers, and key customers. Or it can get good information by observing competitors and monitoring their published information. It can buy and analyze competitors' products, monitor their sales, check for new patents, and examine various types of physical evidence. For example, one company regularly checks out competitors' parking lots—full lots might indicate plenty of work and prosperity; half-full lots might suggest hard times.

Some companies have even rifled their competitors' garbage, which is legally considered abandoned property once it leaves the premises. In one garbage snatching incident, Oracle was caught rifling through rival Microsoft's dumpsters. In another case, Procter & Gamble admitted to "dumpster diving" at rival Unilever's headquarters. "P&G got its mitts on just about every iota of info there was to be had about Unilever's [hair-care] brands," notes an analyst. However, when news of the questionable tactics reached top P&G managers, they were shocked. They immediately stopped the project and voluntarily set up negotiations with Unilever to right whatever competitive wrongs had been done. Although P&G claims it broke no laws, the company reported that the dumpster raids "violated our strict guidelines regarding our business policies."[5]

■ Marketing intelligence: Procter & Gamble admitted to "dumpster diving" at rival Unilever's Helene Curtis headquarters. When P&G's top management learned of the questionable practice, it stopped the project, voluntarily informed Unilever, and set up talks to right whatever competitive wrongs had been done.

Competitors often reveal intelligence information through their annual reports, business publications, trade show exhibits, press releases, advertisements, and Web pages. The Internet is proving to be a vast new source of competitor-supplied information. Using Internet search engines, marketers can search specific competitor names, events, or trends and see what turns up. Moreover, most companies now place volumes of information on their Web sites, providing details to attract customers, partners, suppliers, investors, or franchisees. This can provide a wealth of useful information about competitors' strategies, markets, new products, facilities, and other happenings.

Something as simple as a competitor's job postings can be very revealing. For example, a few years back, while poking around on Google's company Web site, Microsoft's Bill Gates came across a help-wanted page describing all of the jobs available at Google. To his surprise, he noted that Google was looking for engineers with backgrounds that had nothing to do with its Web-search business but everything to do with Microsoft's core software businesses. Forewarned that Google might be preparing to become more than just a search engine company, Gates e-mailed a handful of Microsoft executives, saying, in effect, "We have to watch these guys. It looks like they are building something to compete with us." Notes a marketing intelligence consultant, companies "are often surprised that there's so much out there to know. They're busy with their day-to-day operations and they don't realize how much information can be obtained with a few strategic keystrokes."[6]

Intelligence seekers can also pore through any of thousands of online databases. Some are free. For example, the U.S. Security and Exchange Commission's database provides a huge stockpile of financial information on public competitors, and the U.S. Patent and Trademark Office database reveals patents competitors have filed. And for a fee, companies can subscribe to more than 3,000 online databases and information search services such as Dialog, Hoover's, DataStar, LexisNexis, Dow Jones News Retrieval, ProQuest, and Dun & Bradstreet's Online Access.

The intelligence game goes both ways. Facing determined marketing intelligence efforts by competitors, most companies are now taking steps to protect their own information. For example, Unilever has begun widespread competitive intelligence training. Employees are taught not just how to collect intelligence information, but also how to protect company information from competitors. According to a former Unilever staffer, "We were even warned that spies from competitors could be posing as drivers at the mini-cab company we used." Unilever even performs random checks on internal security. Says the former staffer, "At one [internal marketing] conference, we were set up when an actor was employed to infiltrate the group. The idea was to see who spoke to him, how much they told him, and how long it took to realize that no one knew him. He ended up being there for a long time."[7]

The growing use of marketing intelligence raises a number of ethical issues. Although most of the preceding techniques are legal, and some are considered to be shrewdly competitive, some may involve questionable ethics. Clearly, companies should take advantage of publicly available information. However, they should not stoop to snoop. With all the legitimate intelligence sources now available, a company does not have to break the law or accepted codes of ethics to get good intelligence.

Marketing Research

In addition to information about competitor and marketplace happenings, marketers often need formal studies of specific situations. For example, General Electric wants to know what appeals will be most effective in its corporate advertising campaign. Or Sony wants to know how many and what kinds of people will buy its next-generation plasma televisions. In such situations, marketing intelligence will not provide the detailed information needed. Managers will need marketing research.

Marketing research
The systematic design, collection, analysis, and reporting of data relevant to a specific marketing situation facing an organization.

Marketing research is the systematic design, collection, analysis, and reporting of data relevant to a specific marketing situation facing an organization. Companies use marketing research in a wide variety of situations. For example, marketing research can help marketers understand customer satisfaction and purchase behavior. It can help them assess market potential and market share, or to measure the effectiveness of pricing, product, distribution, and promotion activities.

Some large companies have their own research departments that work with marketing managers on marketing research projects. This is how Procter & Gamble, Kraft, Citigroup, and many other corporate giants handle marketing research. In addition, these companies—like their smaller counterparts—frequently hire outside research specialists to consult with management on specific marketing problems and conduct marketing research studies. Sometimes firms simply purchase data collected by outside firms to aid in their decision making.

The marketing research process has four steps (see Figure 4.2): defining the problem and research objectives, developing the research plan, implementing the research plan, and interpreting and reporting the findings.

DEFINING THE PROBLEM AND RESEARCH OBJECTIVES

Marketing managers and researchers must work closely together to define the problem and agree on research objectives. The manager best understands the decision for which information is needed; the researcher best understands marketing research and how to obtain the information. Defining the problem and research objectives is often the hardest step in the research process. The manager may know that something is wrong, without knowing the specific causes.

FIGURE 4.2 The Marketing Research Process

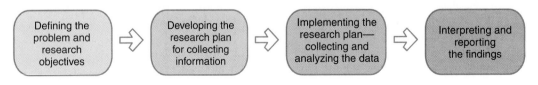

| Defining the problem and research objectives | Developing the research plan for collecting information | Implementing the research plan—collecting and analyzing the data | Interpreting and reporting the findings |

After the problem has been defined carefully, the manager and researcher must set the research objectives. A marketing research project might have one of three types of objectives. The objective of **exploratory research** is to gather preliminary information that will help define the problem and suggest hypotheses. The objective of **descriptive research** is to describe things, such as the market potential for a product or the demographics and attitudes of consumers who buy the product. The objective of **causal research** is to test hypotheses about cause-and-effect relationships. For example, would a 10 percent decrease in tuition at a private college result in an enrollment increase sufficient to offset the reduced tuition? Managers often start with exploratory research and later follow with descriptive or causal research.

The statement of the problem and research objectives guides the entire research process. The manager and researcher should put the statement in writing to be certain that they agree on the purpose and expected results of the research.

DEVELOPING THE RESEARCH PLAN

Once the research problems and objectives have been defined, researchers must determine the exact information needed, develop a plan for gathering it efficiently, and present the plan to management. The research plan outlines sources of existing data and spells out the specific research approaches, contact methods, sampling plans, and instruments that researchers will use to gather new data.

Research objectives must be translated into specific information needs. For example, suppose Campbell Soup Company decides to conduct research on how consumers would react to the introduction of new heat-and-go microwavable cups for its Franco-American Spaghetti and SpaghettiOs. Such packaging has been successful for Campbell's soups—including its Soup at Hand line of hand-held, shippable soups and its Chunky and Select soup line in microwavable bowls, dubbed "M'm! M'm! Good! To Go!" The containers would cost more but would allow consumers to heat their SpaghettiOs in a microwave oven and to eat them without using dishes. This research might call for the following specific information:

- The demographic, economic, and lifestyle characteristics of current SpaghettiOs users. (Busy working couples might find the convenience of the new packaging worth the price; families with children might want to pay less and wash the bowls.)
- Consumer-usage patterns for SpaghettiOs and related products: how much they eat, where, and when. (The new packaging might be ideal for adults eating lunch on the go, but less convenient for parents feeding lunch to several children.)
- Retailer reactions to the new packaging. (Failure to get retailer support could hurt sales of the new package.)
- Forecasts of sales of both new and current packages. (Will the new packaging create new sales or simply take sales from the current packaging? Will the package increase Campbell's profits?)

Campbell managers will need these and many other types of information to decide whether to introduce the new packaging.

The research plan should be presented in a *written proposal*. A written proposal is especially important when the research project is large and complex or when an outside firm carries it out. The proposal should cover the management problems addressed and the research objectives, the information to be obtained, and the way the results will help management decision making. The proposal also should include research costs.

To meet the manager's information needs, the research plan can call for gathering secondary data, primary data, or both. **Secondary data** consist of information that already exists somewhere, having been collected for another purpose. **Primary data** consist of information collected for the specific purpose at hand.

GATHERING SECONDARY DATA

Researchers usually start by gathering secondary data. The company's internal database provides a good starting point. However, the company can also tap a wide assortment of

Exploratory research
Marketing research to gather preliminary information that will help define problems and suggest hypotheses.

Descriptive research
Marketing research to better describe marketing problems, situations, or markets, such as the market potential for a product or the demographics and attitudes of consumers.

Causal research
Marketing research to test hypotheses about cause-and-effect relationships.

Secondary data
Information that already exists somewhere, having been collected for another purpose.

Primary data
Information collected for the specific purpose at hand.

TABLE 4.1
Selected External Information Sources

For business data:

ACNielsen Corporation (http://www.acnielsen.com) provides supermarket scanner data on sales, market share, and retail prices; data on household purchasing; and data on television audiences.

Information Resources, Inc. (http://www.infores.com) provides supermarket scanner data for tracking grocery product movement and new product purchasing data.

Arbitron (http://www.arbitron.com) provides local-market and Internet radio audience and advertising expenditure information, among other media and ad spending data.

IMS Health (http://www.ndchealth.com) tracks drug sales, monitors performance of pharmaceutical sales representatives, and offers pharmaceutical market forecasts.

Simmons Market Research Bureau (http://www.smrb.com) provides detailed analysis of consumer patterns in 400 product categories in selected markets.

Dun & Bradstreet (http://www.dunandbradstreet.com) maintains a database containing information on more than 50 million individual companies around the globe.

comScore Networks (http://www.comscore.com) provides consumer behavior information and geodemographic analysis of Internet and digital media users around the world.

Thomson Dialog (http://library.dialog.com) offers access to more than 900 databases containing publications, reports, newsletters, and directories covering dozens of industries.

LexisNexis (www.lexisnexis.com) features articles from business, consumer, and marketing publications plus tracking of firms, industries, trends, and promotion techniques.

Factiva (http://www.factiva.com) specializes in in-depth financial, historical, and operational information on public and private companies.

Hoover's, Inc. (http://www.hoovers.com) provides business descriptions, financial overviews, and news about major companies around the world.

CNN (http://www.cnn.com) reports U.S. and global news and covers the markets and news-making companies in detail.

American Demographics (http://www.demographics.com) reports on demographic trends and their significance for businesses.

For government data:

Securities and Exchange Commission Edgar database (http://www.sec.gov) provides financial data on U.S. public corporations.

Small Business Administration (http://www.sba.gov) features information and links for small business owners.

Federal Trade Commission (http://www.ftc.gov) shows regulations and decisions related to consumer protection and anti-trust laws.

Stat-USA (http://www.stat-usa.gov), a Department of Commerce site, highlights statistics on U.S. business and international trade.

U.S. Census (http://www.census.gov) provides detailed statistics and trends about the U.S. population.

U.S. Patent and Trademark Office (http://www.uspto.gov) allows searches to determine who has filed for trademarks and patents.

For Internet data:

ClickZ Stats/CyberAtlas (www.clickz.com/stats) brings together a wealth of information about the Internet and its users, from consumers to e-commerce.

Interactive Advertising Bureau (http://www.iab.net) covers statistics about advertising on the Internet.

Jupiter Research (http://www.jupiterresearch.com) monitors Web traffic and ranks the most popular sites.

external information sources, including commercial data services and government sources (see Table 4.1).

Companies can buy secondary data reports from outside suppliers. For example, Information Resources, Inc., sells supermarket scanner purchase data from a panel of 70,000 households nationally, with measures of trial and repeat purchasing, brand loyalty, and buyer demographics. The *Monitor* service by Yankelovich sells information on important social and lifestyle trends. These and other firms supply high-quality data to suit a wide variety of marketing information needs.[8]

Using commercial **online databases**, marketing researchers can conduct their own searches of secondary data sources. General database services such as Dialog, ProQuest, and LexisNexis put an incredible wealth of information at the keyboards of marketing decision makers. Beyond commercial Web sites offering information for a fee, almost every industry association, government agency, business publication, and news medium offers free information to those tenacious enough to find their Web sites. There are so many Web sites offering data that finding the right ones can become an almost overwhelming task.

Online databases
Computerized collections of information available from online commercial sources or via the Internet.

Secondary data can usually be obtained more quickly and at a lower cost than primary data. Also, secondary sources can sometimes provide data an individual company cannot collect on its own—information that either is not directly available or would be too expensive to collect. For example, it would be too expensive for Kraft Foods to conduct a continuing retail store audit to find out about the market shares, prices, and displays of competitors' brands. But it can buy the InfoScan service from Information Resources, Inc., which provides this information from thousands of scanner-equipped supermarkets in dozens of U.S. markets.

Secondary data can also present problems. The needed information may not exist—researchers can rarely obtain all the data they need from secondary sources. For example, Campbell will not find existing information about consumer reactions to new packaging that it has not yet placed on the market. Even when data can be found, they might not be very usable. The researcher must evaluate secondary information carefully to make certain it is *relevant* (fits research project needs), *accurate* (reliably collected and reported), *current* (up-to-date enough for current decisions), and *impartial* (objectively collected and reported).

■ Online database services such as Dialog put an incredible wealth of information at the keyboards of marketing decision makers. Dialog puts "information to change the world, or your corner of it," at your fingertips.

PRIMARY DATA COLLECTION

Secondary data provide a good starting point for research and often help to define research problems and objectives. In most cases, however, the company must also collect primary data. Just as researchers must carefully evaluate the quality of secondary information, they also must take great care when collecting primary data. They need to make sure that it will be relevant, accurate, current, and unbiased. Table 4.2 shows that designing a plan for primary data collection calls for a number of decisions on *research approaches, contact methods, sampling plan,* and *research instruments.*

Research Approaches   Research approaches for gathering primary data include observation, surveys, and experiments. Here, we discuss each one in turn.

Research Approaches	Contact Methods	Sampling Plan	Research Instruments
Observation	Mail	Sampling unit	Questionnaire
Survey	Telephone	Sample size	Mechanical instruments
Experiment	Personal	Sampling procedure	
	Online		

TABLE 4.2
Planning Primary Data Collection

Observational research
The gathering of primary data by observing relevant people, actions, and situations.

Observational Research.

Observational research involves gathering primary data by observing relevant people, actions, and situations. For example, a consumer packaged-goods marketer might visit supermarkets and observe shoppers as they browse the store, pick up and examine packages, and make buying decisions. Or a bank might evaluate possible new branch locations by checking traffic patterns, neighborhood conditions, and the location of competing branches. Fisher-Price even set up an observation lab in which it could observe the reactions of little tots to new toys:

> The Fisher-Price Play Lab is a sunny, toy-strewn space where, since 1961, lucky kids have tested Fisher-Price prototypes. Today three boys and three girls, all four-year-olds, speed through the front door. Two boys tug quietly, but firmly, for the wheel of a new radio-controlled race set—a brand-new offering. The girls skid to a stop near a small sub development of dollhouses. And from behind the one-way glass, toy designers study the action intently, occasionally stepping out to join the play. At the Play Lab, creation and (attempted) destruction happily coexist. Over an eight-week session with these kids, designers will test dozens of toy concepts, sending out crude models, then increasingly sophisticated revisions, to figure out what gets kids worked up into a new-toy frenzy.[9]

Observational research can obtain information that people are unwilling or unable to provide. In some cases, observation may be the only way to obtain the needed information. In contrast, some things simply cannot be observed, such as feelings, attitudes and motives, or private behavior. Long-term or infrequent behavior is also difficult to observe. Because of these limitations, researchers often use observation along with other data collection methods.

A wide range of companies now use *ethnographic research*. Ethnographic research involves sending trained observers to watch consumers in their "natural habitat":[10]

> A girl walks into a bar and says to the bartender, "Give me a Diet Coke and a clear sight line to those guys drinking Miller Lite in the corner." No joke. The "girl" is Emma Gilding, corporate ethnographer at the Ogilvy & Mather ad agency. Her assignment is to hang out in bars across the country, watching guys in their native habitat as they knock back beers with their friends. As a videographer films the action, Gilding keeps tabs on how closely the guys stand to one another. She sees that high-living is out, fist-pounding is in. She eavesdrops on stories, and observes how the mantle is passed from one speaker to another, as in a tribe around a campfire. Back at the office, a team of trained anthropologists and psychologists pored over more than 70 hours of footage from five similar nights in bars from San Diego to Philadelphia. One key insight: Miller is favored by groups of drinkers, while its main competitor, Bud Lite, is a beer that sells to individuals.

■ Observational research: Fisher-Price set up an observation lab in which it could observe the reactions of little tots to new toys.

Miller drinkers felt more comfortable expressing affection for friends than did the Bud Lite boys. The result was a hilarious series of ads that cut from a Miller Lite drinker's weird experiences in the world—getting caught in the subway taking money from a blind musician's guitar case, or hitching a ride in the desert with a deranged trucker—to shots of him regaling friends with tales over a brew. The Miller Lite ads got high marks from audiences for their entertainment value and emotional resonance. Notes Miller's brand manager, "so much other research is done in isolation of social groups. But [ethnographic research] helped us to understand the Miller Lite drinker and his friends as genuine people."

Ethnographic research often yields the kinds of intimate details that just don't emerge from traditional focus groups. To glean greater insights into buying behavior, one company even went so far as to set up an actual retail store that serves as an ethnographic lab.

Survey Research.
Survey research, the most widely used method for primary data collection, is the approach best suited for gathering *descriptive* information. A company that wants to know about people's knowledge, attitudes, preferences, or buying behavior can often find out by asking them directly.

Some firms provide marketers with a more comprehensive look at buying patterns through **single-source data systems**. These systems start with surveys of huge consumer panels—carefully selected groups of consumers who agree to participate in ongoing research. Then, they electronically monitor survey respondents' purchases and exposure to various marketing activities. Combining the survey and monitoring information gives a better understanding of the link between consumer characteristics, attitudes, and purchase behavior.

The major advantage of survey research is its flexibility—it can be used to obtain many different kinds of information in many different situations. However, survey research also presents some problems. Sometimes people are unable to answer survey questions because they cannot remember or have never thought about what they do and why. People may be unwilling to respond to unknown interviewers or about things they consider private. Respondents may answer survey questions even when they do not know the answer in order to appear smarter or more informed. Or they may try to help the interviewer by giving pleasing answers. Finally, busy people may not take the time, or they might resent the intrusion into their privacy.

Experimental Research.
Whereas observation is best suited for exploratory research and surveys for descriptive research, **experimental research** is best suited for gathering *causal* information. Experiments involve selecting matched groups of subjects, giving them different treatments, controlling unrelated factors, and checking for differences in group responses. Thus, experimental research tries to explain cause-and-effect relationships.

For example, before adding a new sandwich to its menu, McDonald's might use experiments to test the effects on sales of two different prices it might charge. It could introduce the new sandwich at one price in one city and at another price in another city. If the cities are similar, and if all other marketing efforts for the sandwich are the same, then differences in sales in the two cities could be related to the price charged.

Contact Methods
Information can be collected by mail, telephone, personal interview, or online. Table 4.3 shows the strengths and weaknesses of each of these contact methods.

Mail, Telephone, and Personal Interviewing.
Mail questionnaires can be used to collect large amounts of information at a low cost per respondent. Respondents may give more honest answers to more personal questions on a mail questionnaire than to an unknown interviewer in person or over the phone. Also, no interviewer is involved to bias the respondent's answers.

However, mail questionnaires are not very flexible—all respondents answer the same questions in a fixed order. Mail surveys usually take longer to complete, and the response rate—the number of people returning completed questionnaires—is often very low. Finally,

Survey research
The gathering of primary data by asking people questions about their knowledge, attitudes, preferences, and buying behavior.

Single-source data systems
Electronic monitoring systems that link consumers' exposure to television advertising and promotion (measured using television meters) with what they buy in stores (measured using store checkout scanners).

Experimental research
The gathering of primary data by selecting matched groups of subjects, giving them different treatments, controlling related factors, and checking for differences in group responses.

TABLE 4.3

Strengths and Weaknesses of Contact Methods

	Mail	Telephone	Personal	Online
Flexibility	Poor	Good	Excellent	Good
Quantity of data that can be collected	Good	Fair	Excellent	Good
Control of interviewer effects	Excellent	Fair	Poor	Fair
Control of sample	Fair	Excellent	Good	Excellent
Speed of data collection	Poor	Excellent	Good	Excellent
Response rate	Fair	Good	Good	Good
Cost	Good	Fair	Poor	Excellent

Source: Donald S. Tull and Del I. Hawkins, *Marketing Research: Measurement and Method,* 7th ed. (New York: Macmillan Publishing, 1993). Adapted with permission of the authors.

the researcher often has little control over the mail questionnaire sample. Even with a good mailing list, it is hard to control *who* at the mailing address fills out the questionnaire.

Telephone interviewing is one of the best methods for gathering information quickly, and it provides greater flexibility than mail questionnaires. Interviewers can explain difficult questions and, depending on the answers they receive, skip some questions or probe on others. Response rates tend to be higher than with mail questionnaires, and interviewers can ask to speak to respondents with the desired characteristics or even by name.

However, with telephone interviewing, the cost per respondent is higher than with mail questionnaires. Also, people may not want to discuss personal questions with an interviewer. The method introduces interviewer bias—the way interviewers talk, how they ask questions, and other differences may affect respondents' answers. Finally, different interviewers may interpret and record responses differently, and under time pressures some interviewers might even cheat by recording answers without asking questions.

Personal interviewing takes two forms—individual and group interviewing. *Individual interviewing* involves talking with people in their homes or offices, on the street, or in shopping malls. Such interviewing is flexible. Trained interviewers can guide interviews, explain difficult questions, and explore issues as the situation requires. They can show subjects actual products, advertisements, or packages and observe reactions and behavior. However, individual personal interviews may cost three to four times as much as telephone interviews.

Group interviewing consists of inviting 6 to 10 people to talk with a trained moderator to talk about a product, service, or organization. Participants normally are paid a small sum for attending. The moderator encourages free and easy discussion, hoping that group interactions will bring out actual feelings and thoughts. At the same time, the moderator "focuses" the discussion—hence the name **focus group interviewing**. Researchers and marketers watch the focus group discussions from behind one-way glass and comments are recorded in writing or on videotape for later study.

Focus group interviewing has become one of the major marketing research tools for gaining insight into consumer thoughts and feelings. However, focus group studies usually employ small sample sizes to keep time and costs down, and it may be hard to generalize from the results. Because interviewers have more freedom in personal interviews, the problem of interviewer bias is greater.

Today, many researchers are changing the way they conduct focus groups. Some are employing videoconferencing technology to connect marketers in distant locations with live focus group action. Using cameras and two-way sound systems, marketing executives in a far-off boardroom can look in and listen, even using remote controls to zoom in on faces and pan the focus group at will. Other researchers are changing the environments in which they conduct focus groups. To help consumers relax and to elicit more authentic responses, they are using settings that are more comfortable and more relevant to the products being researched. For example, they might conduct focus groups for cooking products in a kitchen setting, or focus groups for home furnishings in a living room setting. One research firm offers facilities that look just like anything from a living room or play room to a bar or even a courtroom.

Focus group interviewing
Personal interviewing that involves inviting 6 to 10 people to gather for a few hours with a trained interviewer to talk about a product, service, or organization. The interviewer "focuses" the group discussion on important issues.

Online Marketing Research. Advances in communication technologies have resulted in a number of high-tech contact methods. One is *computer-assisted telephone interviewing (CATI),* in which interviewers sit at computers, read questions on the screen, and type in respondents' answers. Another is *completely automated telephone surveys (CATS),* in which respondents are dialed by computer and asked prerecorded questions. They enter responses by voice or through the phone's touchpad. Other high-tech contact methods include disks-by-mail and computer-based fax surveys.

The latest technology to hit marketing research is the Internet. Increasingly, marketing researchers are collecting primary data through **online (Internet) marketing research**—*Internet surveys, experiments,* and *online focus groups.* In fact, by 2006, companies will spend an estimated 30 percent of their marketing research dollars online, making it the largest single data collection methodology.[11]

Internet research can take many forms. A company can include a questionnaire on its Web site and offer incentives for completing it. Or it can use e-mail, Web links, or Web pop-ups to invite people to answer questions and possibly win a prize. The company can sponsor a chat room and introduce questions from time to time or conduct live discussions or virtual focus groups. A company can learn about the behavior of online customers by following their *clickstreams* as they visit the Web site and move to other sites. A company can experiment with different prices, use different headlines, or offer different product features on different Web sites or at different times to learn the relative effectiveness of its offerings. It can float "trial balloons" to quickly test new product concepts.

Web research offers some real advantages over traditional surveys and focus groups. The most obvious advantages are speed and low costs. Online focus groups require some advance scheduling, but results are practically instantaneous. For example, one soft drink company conducted an online survey to test teenager opinions of new packaging ideas. The 10- to 15-minute Internet survey included dozens of questions along with 765 different images of labels and bottle shapes. Some 600 teenagers participated over a three- to four-day period. Detailed analysis from the survey was available just five days after all the responses had come in—lightning quick compared to offline efforts.[12]

Internet research is also relatively low in cost. Participants can dial in for a focus group from anywhere in the world, eliminating travel, lodging, and facility costs. For surveys, the Internet eliminates most of the postage, phone, labor, and printing costs associated with other approaches. As a result, an Internet survey may be only 10 to 20 percent as expensive as mail, telephone, or personal surveys. Moreover, sample size has little influence on costs. Once the questionnaire is set up, there's little difference in cost between 10 and 10,000 respondents on the Web.

Online surveys and focus groups are also excellent for reaching the hard-to-reach—the often-elusive teen, single, affluent, and well-educated audiences. It's also good for reaching working mothers and other people who lead busy lives. They respond in their own space and at their own convenience. The Internet also works well for bringing together people from different parts of the country, especially those in higher-income groups who can't spare the time to travel to a central site.

Using the Internet to conduct marketing research does have some drawbacks. For one, restricted Internet access can make it difficult to get a broad cross section of Americans. However, with Internet penetration now approaching 75 percent in the United States, this is less and less of a problem. However, another major problem is controlling who's in the sample. Without seeing respondents, it's difficult to know who they really are.

■ Focus group technology: Today, many researchers are employing videoconferencing and Internet technology to connect marketers with live focus group action. ActiveGroup allows researchers to view their focus groups and collaborate remotely from any location, no matter how distant. Says the company, "no traveling, no scheduling, no problems."

Online (Internet) marketing research

Collecting primary data through Internet surveys and online focus groups.

Brand manager eliminates pilot costs, becomes hero

Testing new package designs online with rotating 3-D images not only saved the client expensive tooling costs but also saved time. Now manufacturers can design today and test tomorrow. Eliminating pilot costs and shortening "time to market" are just some of the many ways that Greenfield Online quantitative research beats the old-fashioned kind.

Put our expert consultants and advanced technology to work for you.
www.greenfield.com
888.291.9997

Greenfield Online
Leading the Research Revolution

- Quantitative Studies
- Qualitative Studies
- Media Research
- Self-Directed Research
- Syndicated Studies
- Website Evaluations

HERO

■ Increasingly, companies are moving their research onto the Web. According to this Greenfield Online ad, in many ways, it "beats the old-fashioned kind."

Sample
A segment of the population selected for marketing research to represent the population as a whole.

Even when you reach the right respondents, online surveys and focus groups can lack the dynamics of more personal approaches. The online world is devoid of the eye contact, body language, and direct personal interactions found in traditional focus group research. And the Internet format—running, typed commentary and online "emoticons" (punctuation marks that express emotion, such as :-) to signify happiness)—greatly restricts respondent expressiveness. "You're missing all of the key things that make a focus group a viable method," says the executive. "You may get people online to talk to each other and play off each other, but it's very different to watch people get excited about a concept."

To overcome such sample and response problems, many online research firms use opt-in communities and respondent panels. For example, online research firm Greenfield Online provides access to more than 5 million opt-in panel members in more than 40 countries. Advances in technology—such as the integration of animation, streaming audio and video, and virtual environments—also help to overcome online sample and research dynamics limitations.

Perhaps the most explosive issue facing online researchers concerns consumer privacy. Some fear that unethical researchers will use the e-mail addresses and confidential responses gathered through surveys to sell products after the research is completed. They are concerned about the use of electronic agents (such as Spambots or Trojans) that collect personal information without the respondents' consent. Failure to address such privacy issues could result in angry, less cooperative consumers and increased government intervention. Despite these concerns, online research now accounts for 8 percent of all spending on quantitative marketing research, and most industry insiders predict healthy growth.[13]

Sampling Plan Marketing researchers usually draw conclusions about large groups of consumers by studying a small sample of the total consumer population. A **sample** is a segment of the population selected to represent the population as a whole. Ideally, the sample should be representative so that the researcher can make accurate estimates of the thoughts and behaviors of the larger population.

Designing the sample requires three decisions. First, *who* is to be surveyed (what *sampling unit*)? The answer to this question is not always obvious. For example, to study the decision-making process for a family automobile purchase, should the researcher interview the husband, wife, other family members, dealership salespeople, or all of these? The researcher must determine what information is needed and who is most likely to have it.

Second, *how many* people should be surveyed (what *sample size*)? Large samples give more reliable results than small samples. It is not necessary to sample the entire target market or even a large portion to get reliable results, however. If well chosen, samples of less than 1 percent of a population can often give good reliability.

Third, *how* should the people in the sample be *chosen* (what *sampling procedure*)? Table 4.4 describes different kinds of samples. Using *probability samples*, each population member has a known chance of being included in the sample, and researchers can calculate confidence limits for sampling error. But when probability sampling costs too much or takes too much time, marketing researchers often take *nonprobability samples*, even though their sampling error cannot be measured. These varied ways of drawing samples have different costs and time limitations as well as different accuracy and statistical properties. Which method is best depends on the needs of the research project.

Research Instruments In collecting primary data, marketing researchers have a choice of two main research instruments—the *questionnaire* and *mechanical devices*. The *questionnaire* is by far the most common instrument, whether administered in person, by phone, or online.

TABLE 4.4
Types of Samples

Probability sample:	
Simple random sample	Every member of the population has a known and equal chance of selection.
Stratified random sample	The population is divided into mutually exclusive groups (such as age groups), and random samples are drawn from each group.
Cluster (area) sample	The population is divided into mutually exclusive groups (such as blocks), and the researcher draws a sample of the groups to interview.
Nonprobability sample:	
Convenience sample	The researcher selects the easiest population members from which to obtain information.
Judgment sample	The researcher uses his or her judgment to select population members who are good prospects for accurate information.
Quota sample	The researcher finds and interviews a prescribed number of people in each of several categories.

Questionnaires are very flexible—there are many ways to ask questions. *Closed-end questions* include all the possible answers, and subjects make choices among them. Examples include multiple-choice questions and scale questions. *Open-end questions* allow respondents to answer in their own words. In a survey of airline users, Southwest might simply ask, "What is your opinion of Southwest Airlines?" Or it might ask people to complete a sentence: "When I choose an airline, the most important consideration is. . . ." These and other kinds of open-end questions often reveal more than closed-end questions because respondents are not limited in their answers. Open-end questions are especially useful in exploratory research, when the researcher is trying to find out *what* people think but not measuring *how many* people think in a certain way. Closed-end questions, on the other hand, provide answers that are easier to interpret and tabulate.

Researchers should also use care in the *wording* and *ordering* of questions. They should use simple, direct, unbiased wording. Questions should be arranged in a logical order. The first question should create interest if possible, and difficult or personal questions should be asked last so that respondents do not become defensive. A carelessly prepared questionnaire usually contains many errors (see Table 4.5).

Although questionnaires are the most common research instrument, researchers also use *mechanical instruments* to monitor consumer behavior. Nielsen Media Research attaches *people meters* to television sets in selected homes to record who watches which programs. Retailers use *checkout scanners* to record shoppers' purchases.

Other mechanical devices measure subjects' physical responses. For example, advertisers use eye cameras to study viewers' eye movements while watching ads—at what points their eyes focus first and how long they linger on any given ad component. IBM's BlueEyes human recognition technology goes even further.

TABLE 4.5
A "Questionable Questionnaire"

Suppose that a summer camp director had prepared the following questionnaire to use in interviewing the parents of prospective campers. How would you assess each question?

1. What is your income to the nearest hundred dollars? *People don't usually know their income to the nearest hundred dollars, nor do they want to reveal their income that closely. Moreover, a researcher should never open a questionnaire with such a personal question.*

2. Are you a strong or weak supporter of overnight summer camping for your children? *What do "strong" and "weak" mean?*

3. Do your children behave themselves well at a summer camp? Yes ( ) No ( ) *"Behave" is a relative term. Furthermore, are yes and no the best response options for this question? Besides, will people answer this honestly and objectively? Why ask the question in the first place?*

4. How many camps mailed or e-mailed information to you last year? This year? *Who can remember this?*

5. What are the most salient and determinant attributes in your evaluation of summer camps? *What are salient and determinant attributes? Don't use big words on me!*

6. Do you think it is right to deprive your child of the opportunity to grow into a mature person through the experience of summer camping? *A loaded question. Given the bias, how can any parent answer yes?*

■ Mechanical measures of consumer response: New technologies can record and interpret human facial reactions. In the not-too-distant future, marketers may be using machines that "know how you feel" to not just gauge customers' physical reactions, but to respond to them as well.

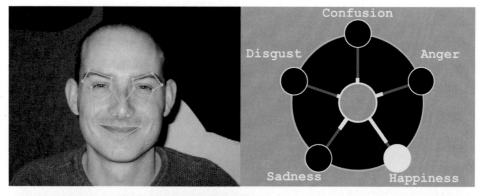

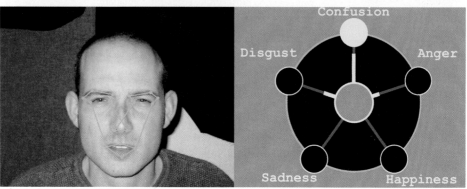

BlueEyes uses sensing technology to identify and interpret user reactions. The technology was originally created to help users to interact more easily with a computer. For example, IBM is perfecting an "emotion mouse" that will figure out computer users' emotional states by measuring pulse, temperature, movement, and galvanic skin response. Another BlueEyes technology records and interprets human facial reactions by tracking pupil, eyebrow, and mouth movement. BlueEyes offers a host of potential marketing uses. Retailers are already using the technology to study customers and their responses. And in the not-to-distant future, more than just measuring customers' physical reactions, marketers will be able to respond to them as well. An example: creating marketing machines that "know how you feel." Sensing through an emotion mouse that a Web shopper is frustrated, an Internet marketer offers a different screen display. An elderly man squints at a bank's ATM screen and the font size doubles almost instantly. A woman at a shopping center kiosk smiles at a travel ad, prompting the device to print out a travel discount coupon. Several users at another kiosk frown at a racy ad, leading a store to pull it.[14]

IMPLEMENTING THE RESEARCH PLAN

The researcher next puts the marketing research plan into action. This involves collecting, processing, and analyzing the information. Data collection can be carried out by the company's marketing research staff or by outside firms. The data collection phase of the marketing research process is generally the most expensive and the most subject to error. Researchers should watch closely to make sure that the plan is implemented correctly. They must guard against problems with contacting respondents, with respondents who refuse to cooperate or who give biased answers, and with interviewers who make mistakes or take shortcuts.

Researchers must also process and analyze the collected data to isolate important information and findings. They need to check data for accuracy and completeness and code it for analysis. The researchers then tabulate the results and compute statistical measures.

INTERPRETING AND REPORTING THE FINDINGS

The market researcher must now interpret the findings, draw conclusions, and report them to management. The researcher should not try to overwhelm managers with numbers and fancy statistical techniques. Rather, the researcher should present important findings that are useful in the major decisions faced by management.

However, interpretation should not be left only to the researchers. They are often experts in research design and statistics, but the marketing manager knows more about the problem and the decisions that must be made. The best research is meaningless if the manager blindly accepts faulty interpretations from the researcher. Similarly, managers may be biased—they might tend to accept research results that show what they expected and to reject those that they did not expect or hope for. In many cases, findings can be interpreted in different ways, and discussions between researchers and managers will help point to the best interpretations. Thus, managers and researchers must work together closely when interpreting research results, and both must share responsibility for the research process and resulting decisions.[15]

 Linking the Concepts

Whew! We've covered a lot of territory. Hold up a minute, take a breather, and see if you can apply the marketing research process you've just studied.

- What specific kinds of research can Coach use to learn more about its customers' preferences and buying behaviors? Sketch out a brief research plan for discovering Coach's next new product.
- Could you use the marketing research process to analyze your career opportunities and job possibilities? (Think of yourself as a "product" and employers as potential "customers.") What would your research plan look like?

Analyzing Marketing Information

Information gathered in internal databases and through marketing intelligence and marketing research usually requires more analysis. And managers may need help applying the information to their marketing decisions. This help may include advanced statistical analysis to learn more about the relationships within a set of data. Such analysis allows managers to go beyond means and standard deviations in the data and to answer questions about markets, marketing activities, and outcomes.

Information analysis might also involve a collection of analytical models that will help marketers make better decisions. Each model represents some real system, process, or outcome. These models can help answer the questions of *what if* and *which is best*. Marketing scientists have developed numerous models to help marketing managers make better marketing mix decisions, design sales territories and sales call plans, select sites for retail outlets, develop optimal advertising mixes, and forecast new-product sales.

CUSTOMER RELATIONSHIP MANAGEMENT (CRM)

The question of how best to analyze and use individual customer data presents special problems. Most companies are awash in information about their customers. In fact, smart companies capture information at every possible customer *touch point*. These touch points include customer purchases, sales force contacts, service and support calls, Web site visits, satisfaction surveys, credit and payment interactions, market research studies—every contact between the customer and the company.

The trouble is that this information is usually scattered widely across the organization. It is buried deep in the separate databases and records of different company departments. To overcome such problems, many companies are now turning to **customer relationship management (CRM)** to manage detailed information about individual customers and carefully manage customer touch points in order to maximize customer loyalty.

Customer relationship management (CRM)
Managing detailed information about individual customers and carefully managing customer "touch points" in order to maximize customer loyalty.

SAS SOFTWARE
FOR CUSTOMER INTELLIGENCE

THE POWER TO KNOW

how to keep your customers from
testing new waters with the competition.

OPERATIONAL EFFECTIVENESS

FRAUD PREVENTION

REGULATORY COMPLIANCE

RISK MANAGEMENT

CUSTOMER INTELLIGENCE

Your competitors are doing whatever they can to have customers walk their way. And since attrition is contagious, a targeted, personalized response to customer needs is more important than ever in the financial services industry. SAS® business intelligence and analytics software now offers the broadest and most sophisticated capabilities to generate and leverage customer intelligence. So you can recognize and counteract attrition. Create cross-sell and up-sell opportunities. Understand the true costs of campaigns. And keep a profitable, loyal customer base while driving toward growth. Learn why 98% of FORTUNE Global 500® banks and more than one-third of the world's insurers rely on SAS to increase awareness, profits and shareholder value.

go Beyond BI™ at www.sas.com/fscustomer

§sas.

■ CRM: SAS customer intelligence software helps companies to keep a profitable, loyal customer base by leveraging customer information and developing targeted, personalized responses to customer needs.

CRM first burst onto the scene in the early 2000s. Many companies rushed in, implementing overly ambitious CRM programs that produced disappointing results and many failures. More recently, however, companies are moving ahead more cautiously and implementing CRM systems that really work. A recent study by Gartner Group found that 60 percent of the businesses surveyed intend to adopt or expand their CRM usage over the next two years. By 2007, U.S. companies will spend an estimated $73.8 billion on CRM systems from companies such as Siebel Systems, Oracle, Microsoft, and SAS.[16]

CRM consists of sophisticated software and analytical tools that integrate customer information from all sources, analyze it in depth, and apply the results to build stronger customer relationships. CRM integrates everything that a company's sales, service, and marketing teams know about individual customers to provide a 360-degree view of the customer relationship.

CRM analysts develop *data warehouses* and use sophisticated *data mining* techniques to unearth the riches hidden in customer data. A data warehouse is a company-wide electronic database of finely detailed customer information that needs to be sifted through for gems. The purpose of a data warehouse is not just to gather information, but to pull it together into a central, accessible location. Then, once the data warehouse brings the data together, the company uses high-powered data mining techniques to sift through the mounds of data and dig out interesting findings about customers.

By using CRM to understand customers better, companies can provide higher levels of customer service and develop deeper customer relationships. They can use CRM to pinpoint high-value customers, target them more effectively, cross-sell the company's products, and create offers tailored to specific customer requirements. Consider the following example:

Harrah's Entertainment, the world's largest casino operator, maintains a vast customer database. More than 75 percent of Harrah's gaming revenue is tracked to a Total Rewards card. And information from every swipe of every card feeds into a data warehouse in Memphis, Tennessee. Analyzing this information gives Harrah's detailed insights into the behavior of individual customers—how often they visit, how long they stay, and how and how much they gamble and entertain. The data reveal that the best casino customers aren't the high-rollers, but rather the slot-playing, middle-aged or retired teachers, bankers, and doctors with time and discretionary income. Harrah's CRM system helps the company to focus its branding, marketing, and service development strategies on the needs of its most important customers. The insights also let Harrah's do a better job of managing day-to-day customer relationships. By the next morning, it knows which customers should be rewarded with free show tickets, dinner vouchers or room upgrades, enticing them to spend more of their gambling and entertainment dollars in Harrah's rather than in rival casinos. "It's no different from what a good retailer or grocery store does," says a Harrah's marketing executive. "We're trying to figure out which products sell, and we're trying to increase our customer loyalty."[17]

CRM benefits don't come without cost or risk, not only in collecting the original customer data but also in maintaining and mining it. The most common CRM mistake is to view CRM only as a technology and software solution. But technology alone cannot build profitable customer relationships. "CRM is not a technology solution—you can't achieve . . . improved customer relationships by simply slapping in some software," says a CRM expert. Instead, CRM is just one part of an effective overall *customer relationship management strategy.* "Focus on the *R,*" advises the expert. "Remember, a relationship is what CRM is all about."[18]

When it works, the benefits of CRM can far outweigh the costs and risks. Based on regular polls of its customers, Siebel Systems claims that customers using its CRM software report an average 16 percent increase in revenues and 21 percent increase in customer loyalty and staff efficiency. "No question that companies are getting tremendous value out of this," says a CRM consultant. "Companies [are] looking for ways to bring disparate sources of customer information together, then get it to all the customer touch points." The powerful new CRM techniques can unearth "a wealth of information to target that customer, to hit their hot button."[19]

Distributing and Using Marketing Information

Marketing information has no value until it is used to make better marketing decisions. Thus, the marketing information system must make the information readily available to the managers and others who make marketing decisions or deal with customers. In some cases, this means providing managers with regular performance reports, intelligence updates, and reports on the results of research studies.

■ Customer relationship management: Harrah's CRM system helps the company to focus its branding, marketing, and service development strategies on the needs of its most important customers. "We're trying to figure out which products sell, and we're trying to increase our customer loyalty."

But marketing managers may also need nonroutine information for special situations and on-the-spot decisions. For example, a sales manager having trouble with a large customer may want a summary of the account's sales and profitability over the past year. Or a retail store manager who has run out of a best-selling product may want to know the current inventory levels in the chain's other stores. Increasingly, therefore, information distribution involves entering information into databases and making it available in a timely, user-friendly way.

Many firms use a company *intranet* to facilitate this process. The intranet provides ready access to research information, stored reports, shared work documents, contact information for employees and other stakeholders, and more. For example, iGo, a catalog and Web retailer, integrates incoming customer service calls with up-to-date database information about customers' Web purchases and e-mail inquiries. By accessing this information on the intranet while speaking with the customer, iGo's service representatives can get a well-rounded picture of each customer's purchasing history and previous contacts with the company.

In addition, companies are increasingly allowing key customers and value-network members to access account, product, and other data on demand through *extranets.* Suppliers, customers, resellers, and select other network members may access a company's extranet to update their accounts, arrange purchases, and check orders against inventories to improve customer service. For example, one insurance firm allows its 200 independent agents access to a Web-based database of claim information covering one million customers. This allows the agents to avoid high-risk customers and to compare claim data with their own customer databases. And Wal-Mart stores around the globe use the RetailLink system, which provides suppliers with up to two years' worth of data on how their products have sold in Wal-Mart stores.

Thanks to modern technology, today's marketing managers can gain direct access to the information system at any time and from virtually any location. They can tap into the system while working at a home office, from a hotel room, or from the local Starbuck's through a wireless network—anyplace where they can turn on a laptop and link up. Such systems allow managers to get the information they need directly and quickly and to tailor it to their own needs. From just about anywhere, they can obtain information from company or outside databases, analyze it using statistical software, prepare reports and presentations, and communicate directly with others in the network.

 Linking the Concepts

Let's stop here for a bit, think back, and be certain that you've got the "big picture" concerning marketing information systems.

- What's the overall goal of an MIS? How are the individual components linked and what does each contribute? Take another look at Figure 4.1—it provides a good organizing framework for the entire chapter.
- Apply the MIS framework to Coach (as described in the chapter-opening story). What does Coach appear to be doing well? Poorly?

Other Marketing Information Considerations

This section discusses marketing information in two special contexts: marketing research in small businesses and nonprofit organizations, and international marketing research. Finally, we look at public policy and ethics issues in marketing research.

MARKETING RESEARCH IN SMALL BUSINESSES AND NONPROFIT ORGANIZATIONS

Just like larger firms, small organizations need market information. Start-up businesses need information about their industries, competitors, potential customers, and reactions to new market offers. Existing small businesses must track changes in customer needs and wants, reactions to new products, and changes in the competitive environment.

Managers of small businesses and nonprofit organizations often think that marketing research can be done only by experts in large companies with big research budgets. True, large-scale research studies are beyond the budgets of most small businesses. However, many of the marketing research techniques discussed in this chapter also can be used by smaller organizations in a less formal manner and at little or no expense. Consider how one small-business owner conducted market research on a shoestring before even opening his doors:[20]

> After a string of bad experiences with his local dry cleaner, Robert Byerley decided to open his own dry-cleaning business. But before jumping in, he conducted plenty of market research. Making a careful tour of the town, he observed a dry-cleaning establishment in practically every strip mall. How would his stand out? To find an answer, Byerley spent an entire week in the library, researching the dry-cleaning industry. From government reports and trade publications, he learned it was a $16 billion-a-year industry dominated by mom-and-pop establishments. Better Business Bureau reports showed that dry cleaners accounted for a high number of complaints. The number-one criticism: "Cleaners didn't stand behind what they did," he says. To get input from potential customers, using a marketing firm, Byerley held focus groups on the store's name, look, and brochure. He also took clothes to the 15 best cleaners in town and had focus-group members critique their work. In all, Byerley says he spent about $15,000 for the focus groups. Based on his research, he made a list of features for his new business. First on his list: His business would stand behind everything it did. Not on the list: cheap prices. Creating the perfect dry-cleaning establishment simply wasn't compatible with a discount operation.

His research complete, Byerley opened Bibbentuckers, a high-end dry cleaner positioned on high quality service and convenience. Bibbentuckers featured a bank-like drive-through area with curbside delivery. A computerized bar-code system read customer cleaning preferences and tracked clothes all the way through the cleaning process. Byerley added other differentiators, such as decorative awnings, refreshments, and TV screens. "I wanted a place people would be comfortable leaving their best clothes, a place that paired five-star service and quality with an establishment that didn't look like a dry cleaner," he says. The market research yielded results—Bibbentucker's business took off, turning a profit after only four months. Today, it's a thriving three-store operation. "Too many small-business owners have a technician's mind-set rather than a marketing mind-set," says a small-business consultant. "You have to think like Procter & Gamble. What would they do before launching a new product? They would find out who their customer is and who their competition is."

■ Small businesses need market research, too. Before opening his own dry-cleaning business, Bibbentuckers owner Robert Byerley conducted plenty of low-budget market research, including talking with prospective customers. "You have to think like Procter & Gamble."

Thus, managers of small businesses and nonprofit organizations can obtain good marketing information simply by *observing* things around them. For example, retailers can evaluate new locations by observing vehicle and pedestrian traffic. They can monitor competitor advertising by collecting ads from local media. They can evaluate their customer mix by recording how many and what kinds of customers shop in the store at different times. In addition, many small business managers routinely visit their rivals and socialize with competitors to gain insights.

Managers can conduct informal *surveys* using small convenience samples. The director of an art museum can learn what patrons think about new exhibits by conducting informal focus groups—inviting small groups to lunch and having discussions on topics of interest. Retail salespeople can talk with customers visiting the store; hospital officials can interview patients. Restaurant managers might make random phone calls during slack hours to interview consumers about where they eat out and what they think of various restaurants in the area.

Managers also can conduct their own simple *experiments*. For example, by changing the themes in regular fund-raising mailings and watching the results, a nonprofit manager can find out much about which marketing strategies work best. By varying newspaper advertisements, a store manager can learn the effects of things such as ad size and position, price coupons, and media used.

Small organizations can obtain most of the secondary data available to large businesses. In addition, many associations, local media, chambers of commerce, and government agencies provide special help to small organizations. The U.S. Small Business Administration offers dozens of free publications and a Web site (www.sbaonline.sba.gov) that give advice on topics ranging from starting, financing, and expanding a small business to ordering business cards. Other excellent Web resources for small businesses include the U.S. Census Bureau (www.census.gov) and the Bureau of Economic Analysis (www.bea.doc.gov).

The business sections at local libraries can also be a good source of information. Local newspapers often provide information on local shoppers and their buying patterns. Finally, small businesses can collect a considerable amount of information at very little cost on the Internet. They can scour competitor and customer Web sites and use Internet search engines to research specific companies and issues.

In summary, secondary data collection, observation, surveys, and experiments can all be used effectively by small organizations with small budgets. Although these informal research methods are less complex and less costly, they still must be conducted carefully. Managers must think carefully about the objectives of the research, formulate questions in advance, recognize the biases introduced by smaller samples and less skilled researchers, and conduct the research systematically.[21]

INTERNATIONAL MARKETING RESEARCH

International marketing researchers follow the same steps as domestic researchers, from defining the research problem and developing a research plan to interpreting and reporting the results. However, these researchers often face more and different problems. Whereas domestic researchers deal with fairly homogenous markets within a single country, international researchers deal with diverse markets in many different countries. These markets often vary greatly in their levels of economic development, cultures and customs, and buying patterns.

In many foreign markets, the international researcher may have a difficult time finding good secondary data. Whereas U.S. marketing researchers can obtain reliable secondary data from dozens of domestic research services, many countries have almost no research services at all. Some of the largest international research services do operate in many countries. For example, ACNielsen Corporation (owned by VNU NV, the world's largest marketing research company) has offices in more than 100 countries. And 65 percent of the revenues of the world's 25 largest marketing research firms comes from outside their home countries.[22] However, most research firms operate in only a relative handful of countries. Thus, even when secondary information is available, it usually must be obtained from many different sources on a country-by-country basis, making the information difficult to combine or compare.

Because of the scarcity of good secondary data, international researchers often must collect their own primary data. Here again, researchers face problems not found domestically. For example, they may find it difficult simply to develop good samples. U.S. researchers can use current telephone directories, census tract data, and any of several sources of socioeconomic data to construct samples. However, such information is largely lacking in many countries.

Once the sample is drawn, the U.S. researcher usually can reach most respondents easily by telephone, by mail, on the Internet, or in person. Reaching respondents is often not so easy in other parts of the world. Researchers in Mexico cannot rely on telephone, Internet, and mail data collection—most data collection is door to door and concentrated in three or four of the largest cities. In some countries, few people have phones or personal computers. For example, whereas there are 668 main telephones and 555 PCs per thousand people in the United States, there are only 117 phones and 54 PCs per thousand in Mexico. In Ghana, the numbers drop to 12 phones and 3 PCs per thousand people. In some countries, the postal system is notoriously

■ Some of the largest research services firms have large international organizations. ACNielsen has offices in more than 100 countries, here Germany and Japan.

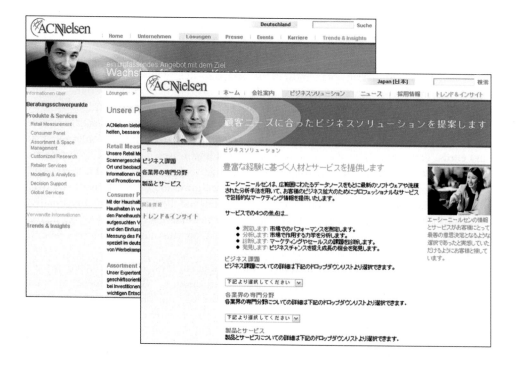

unreliable. In Brazil, for instance, an estimated 30 percent of the mail is never delivered. In many developing countries, poor roads and transportation systems make certain areas hard to reach, making personal interviews difficult and expensive.[23]

Cultural differences from country to country cause additional problems for international researchers. Language is the most obvious obstacle. For example, questionnaires must be prepared in one language and then translated into the languages of each country researched. Responses then must be translated back into the original language for analysis and interpretation. This adds to research costs and increases the risks of error.

Translating a questionnaire from one language to another is anything but easy. Many idioms, phrases, and statements mean different things in different cultures. For example, a Danish executive noted, "Check this out by having a different translator put back into English what you've translated from English. You'll get the shock of your life. I remember [an example in which] 'out of sight, out of mind' had become 'invisible things are insane.'"[24]

Consumers in different countries also vary in their attitudes toward marketing research. People in one country may be very willing to respond; in other countries, nonresponse can be a major problem. Customs in some countries may prohibit people from talking with strangers. In certain cultures, research questions often are considered too personal. For example, in many Latin American countries, people may feel embarrassed to talk with researchers about their choices of shampoo, deodorant, or other personal care products. Similarly, in most Muslim countries, mixed-gender focus groups are taboo, as is videotaping female-only focus groups.

Even when respondents are *willing* to respond, they may not be *able* to because of high functional illiteracy rates. And middle-class people in developing countries often make false claims in order to appear well-off. For example, in a study of tea consumption in India, over 70 percent of middle-income respondents claimed that they used one of several national brands. However, the researchers had good reason to doubt these results—more than 60 percent of the tea sold in India is unbranded generic tea.

Despite these problems, the recent growth of international marketing has resulted in a rapid increase in the use of international marketing research. Global companies have little choice but to conduct such research. Although the costs and problems associated with international research may be high, the costs of not doing it—in terms of missed opportunities and mistakes—might be even higher. Once recognized, many of the problems associated with international marketing research can be overcome or avoided.

PUBLIC POLICY AND ETHICS IN MARKETING RESEARCH

Most marketing research benefits both the sponsoring company and its consumers. Through marketing research, companies learn more about consumers' needs, resulting in more satisfying products and services and stronger customer relationships. However, the misuse of marketing research can also harm or annoy consumers. Two major public policy and ethics issues in marketing research are intrusions on consumer privacy and the misuse of research findings.

Intrusions on Consumer Privacy Many consumers feel positively about marketing research and believe that it serves a useful purpose. Some actually enjoy being interviewed and giving their opinions. However, others strongly resent, or even mistrust, marketing research. A few consumers fear that researchers might use sophisticated techniques to probe our deepest feelings or peek over our shoulders and then use this knowledge to manipulate our buying (see Marketing at Work 4.2). Or they worry that marketers are building huge databases full of personal information about customers. For example, consider a company called Acxiom:

> Never heard of Acxiom? Chances are it's heard of you. Once upon a time in America, a savvy local store clerk knew that you had, say, three kids, an old Ford, a pool, and a passion for golf and yellow sweaters. Today Acxiom is that store clerk. It's the world's largest processor of consumer data, collecting and messaging more than a billion records a day. Acxiom's database on 96 percent of U.S. households gives

MARKETING AT WORK   4.2
Video Mining

Stepping into a Gap store at the South Shore Shopping Plaza on a recent evening, Laura Munro became a research statistic. Twelve feet above her, a device resembling a smoke detector, mounted on the ceiling and equipped with a hidden camera, took a picture of her head and shoulders. The image was fed to a computer and shipped to a database in Chicago, where ShopperTrak, a consumer research firm, keeps count of shoppers nationwide using 40,000 cameras placed in stores and malls.

ShopperTrak is a leader in an emerging market research field called "video mining." Video miners use advanced computer software to sort through video images, plucking data of interest to marketers, without a human ever seeing the video. ShopperTrak says it doesn't take pictures of faces. The company worries that shoppers would perceive that as an invasion of privacy. But nearly all of its videotaping is done without the knowledge of

the people being taped. "I didn't even know there was a camera up there," says Ms. Munro, who popped into the mall on her way home from work to find a gift for her 12-year-old daughter.

Using such video information, ShopperTrak calculates and sells many valuable tidbits of data. For example, by comparing the number of people taped entering the store with the number of transactions, it arrives at a so-called "conversion rate"—the percentage of shoppers that buys versus the percentage that only browses. At a broader level, by combining video data gleaned from 130 retail clients and 380 malls with consumer spending data obtained from credit-card companies and banks, ShopperTrak can estimate sales and store traffic figures for the entire retail industry. Gap and other retail clients pay ShopperTrak for the store-level data. ShopperTrak sells the broader industry data to economists, bankers, and retailers.

More and more companies are now employing video miners to help them peek in on their customers. Video-tracking cameras, with lenses as small as a quarter, can provide data on everything from the density of shopping traffic in an aisle to the reactions of a shopper gazing at the latest plasma TV set. The cash register is a popular spot for cameras. But cameras can also be found in banks, fast-food outlets, and hotel lobbies (but not guest rooms).

Many companies now use video mining along with other traditional methods to help gain more rapid, accurate, and complete insights. For example, Kahn Research Group recently used video mining along with sales analysis and in-store behavioral tracking to determine what was and was not working to increase sales at Subway fast-food restaurants. Kahn's researchers hid golf ball-sized cameras in several Subway restaurants to track customers' eye movements during the

■ *Serving customers better or invading their privacy? Video miners use advanced computer software to sort through video images, plucking data of interest to marketers. Smile, you're being video mined!*

marketers a so-called real-time, 360-degree view of their customers. How? Acxiom provides a 13-digit code for every person, "so we can identify you wherever you go," says the company's demographics guru. Each person is placed into one of 70 lifestyle clusters, ranging from "Rolling Stones" and "Single City Struggles" to "Timeless Elders." Acxiom's catalog offers customers hundreds of lists, including a "pre-movers file," updated daily, of people preparing to change residences, as well as lists of people sorted by the frequency with which they use credit cards, the square footage of their homes, and their interest in the "strange and unusual." Its customers include nine of the country's top-ten credit-card issuers, as well as nearly all the major retail banks, insurers, and automakers. Acxiom may even know things about you that you don't know yourself.[25]

order process. Video analysis revealed that before and while sandwiches were being assembled, customers focused on the "sandwich artists" rather than on the menuboard or promotional displays. In particular, drinks and sides received little customer notice. The researchers suggested that Subway move drinks and sides to a point where consumers would view them after making the major sandwich decision but before reaching the cash register. The research also revealed that promotions dangling from the ceiling were often ignored—Subway now uses table tents to remind customers to buy a snack for later.

Video mining software is fast—taking only hours to complete image interpretation tasks that might have taken weeks for humans to do. For example, Kahn's computers took only a couple of days to sift through 192 hours of tape on some 1,200 shoppers. Had Kahn tried to personally interview that many people, the process would have taken much longer, and the presence of the researchers might have annoyed shoppers and affected the results. "Nobody knew they were being recorded," says Greg Kahn, of Kahn Research Group, "and our work didn't interfere with the store environment." Moreover, had people known they were being taped, he says, "I know many of the shoppers would have stuck their hands in front of the camera lens and refused to be recorded."

Video mining proponents say their research cameras are less invasive than security cameras, because their subjects aren't scrutinized as closely as security suspects. The images are studied only by the software and not by people, they say, and the videos are destroyed when the research is done. And marketers use the information to give their customers improved prod-

ucts and better service. "A driving force behind this technology is the fact that businesses want to be better prepared to serve their customers," says one marketing professor.

Still, the eavesdropping potential of video mining can be a bit unnerving. For example, Advanced Interfaces, another shopper-monitoring firm, set up cameras in two McDonald's restaurants last year to find out which customer types would find a new salad item most appealing. The research was done without consumers' knowledge. By measuring the shapes of people's faces, Advanced's sensors were able to provide a breakdown of each salad buyer's race, gender, and age. The videos also revealed the length of time these customers spent waiting in line or looking at the menu before ordering. Looking ahead, the technology already exists for matching a photo with an individual's identity. Theoretically, retailers with customer databases built from the use of loyalty cards, store credit cards, and other in-house programs could link a transaction at a cash register with the face of a shopper appearing on the videotape. Smile, you're being video mined!

So, although video mining offers much promise for marketers and researchers, it also raises important privacy issues. People have pretty much learned to live with the approximately 29 million security cameras around the nation videotaping them in airports, government buildings, offices, schools, stores, busy intersections, and elsewhere. But few consumers are aware that they are being filmed for market research. Security is one thing, but the American public isn't likely to be as tolerant of secret market research using videotape.

Marketers appear to recognize this fact. ShopperTrak discloses its clients—the list includes, among others, Gap and its Banana Republic unit, The Limited and its Victoria's Secret chain, PaylessShoe Source; American Eagle Outfitters, and The Children's Place Retail Stores. However, several other research companies that videotape shoppers say they sign agreements with clients in which they pledge not to disclose their names. Their clients want the taping to be secret, worrying that shoppers would feel alienated or complain of privacy invasion if they knew.

They're probably right to worry. Katherine Albrecht, founder and director of Caspian, a consumer-advocacy group, says consumers have "no idea such things as video tracking are going on," and they should be informed. When she tells them about such activities, she says the response she often hears is, "Isn't this illegal, like stalking? Shouldn't there be a law against it?" Robert Bulmash, a consumer-privacy advocate, says that being in a retailer's store doesn't give a retailer "the right to treat me like a guinea pig." He says he wonders about assurances that images are destroyed, since there isn't any way to verify such claims. The pictures "could be saved somewhere in that vast digital universe and some day come back to haunt us," he says.

Sources: Portions adapted from Joseph Pereira, "Spying on the Sales Floor: 'Video Miners' Use Cameras Hidden in Stores to Analyze Who Shops, What They Like," *Wall Street Journal,* December 21, 2004, p. B1. Other information from Kelly Sitch, "'Mining' Software Studies Shoppers," *The Digital Collegian,* January 11, 2005, accessed at www.collegian.psu.edu/archive/2005/01/01-11-05tdc/01-11-05dscihealth-01.asp; and Kahn Research Group, July 2005.

Other consumers may have been taken in by previous "research surveys" that actually turned out to be attempts to sell them something. Still other consumers confuse legitimate marketing research studies with telemarketing efforts and say "no" before the interviewer can even begin. Most, however, simply resent the intrusion. They dislike mail, telephone, or Web surveys that are too long or too personal or that interrupt them at inconvenient times.

Increasing consumer resentment has become a major problem for the research industry. One recent survey found that 70 percent of Americans say that companies have too much of consumers' personal information, and 76 percent feel that their privacy has been compromised if a company uses the collected personal information to sell them products. These concerns have led to lower survey response rates in recent years.[26]

Another study found that 59 percent of consumers had refused to give information to a company because they thought it was not really needed or too personal, up from 42 percent five years earlier. "Some shoppers are unnerved by the idea of giving up any information at all," says an analyst. When asked for something as seemingly harmless as a Zip code, "one woman told me she always gives the Zip code for Guam, and another said she never surrenders any information, not even a Zip code, because 'I don't get paid to help them with market research.' "[27]

The research industry is considering several options for responding to this problem. One example is the Council for Marketing and Opinion Research's "Your Opinion Counts" and "Respondent Bill of Rights" initiatives to educate consumers about the benefits of marketing research and to distinguish it from telephone selling and database building. The industry also has considered adopting broad standards, perhaps based on The International Chamber of Commerce's International Code of Marketing and Social Research Practice. This code outlines researchers' responsibilities to respondents and to the general public. For example, it says that researchers should make their names and addresses available to participants. It also bans companies from representing activities such as database compilation or sales and promotional pitches as research.[28]

Many companies—including IBM, CitiGroup, American Express, Bank of America, DoubleClick, EarthLink, and Microsoft—have now appointed a "chief privacy officer (CPO)," whose job is to safeguard the privacy of consumers who do business with the company. The chief privacy officer for Microsoft says that his job is to come up with data policies for the company to follow, make certain that every program the company creates enhances customer privacy, and inform and educate company employees about privacy issues and concerns. Some 2,000 U.S. companies now employ such privacy chiefs and the number is expected to grow.[29]

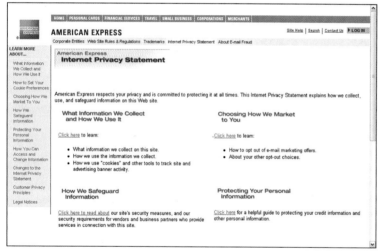

■ Consumer privacy: American Express was one of the first companies to post its privacy policies on the Web. "American Express respects your privacy and is committed to protecting it at all times."

American Express, which deals with a considerable volume of consumer information, has long taken privacy issues seriously. The company developed a set of formal privacy principles in 1991, and in 1998 it became one of the first companies to post privacy policies on its Web site. This penchant for customer privacy led American Express to introduce new services that protect consumers' privacy when they use an American Express card to buy items online. American Express views privacy as a way to gain competitive advantage—as something that leads consumers to choose one company over another.[30]

In the end, if researchers provide value in exchange for information, customers will gladly provide it. For example, Amazon.com's customers do not mind if the firm builds a database of products they buy in order to provide future product recommendations. This saves time and provides value. Similarly, BizRate users gladly complete surveys rating e-tail sites because they can view the overall ratings of others when making purchase decisions. The best approach is for researchers to ask only for the information they need, to use it responsibly to provide customer value, and to avoid sharing information without the customer's permission.

Misuse of Research Findings Research studies can be powerful persuasion tools; companies often use study results as claims in their advertising and promotion. Today, however, many research studies appear to be little more than vehicles for pitching the sponsor's products. In fact, in some cases, the research surveys appear to have been designed just to produce the intended effect. Few advertisers openly rig their research designs or blatantly misrepresent the findings; most abuses tend to be subtle "stretches." Consider the following examples:[31]

A study by Chrysler contends that Americans overwhelmingly prefer Chrysler to Toyota after test-driving both. However, the study included just 100 people in each of two tests. More importantly, none of the people surveyed owned a foreign car brand, so they appear to be favorably predisposed to U.S. brands.

A Black Flag survey asked: "A roach disk . . . poisons a roach slowly. The dying roach returns to the nest and after it dies is eaten by other roaches. In turn these roaches become poisoned and die. How effective do you think this type of product would be in killing roaches?" Not surprisingly, 79 percent said effective.

A poll sponsored by the disposable diaper industry asked: "It is estimated that disposable diapers account for less than 2 percent of the trash in today's landfills. In contrast, beverage containers, third-class mail, and yard waste are estimated to account for about 21 percent of the trash in landfills. Given this, in your opinion, would it be fair to ban disposable diapers?" Again, not surprisingly, 84 percent said no.

Thus, subtle manipulations of the study's sample or the choice or wording of questions can greatly affect the conclusions reached.

In others cases, so-called independent research studies are actually paid for by companies with an interest in the outcome. Small changes in study assumptions or in how results are interpreted can subtly affect the direction of the results. For example, at least four widely quoted studies compare the environmental effects of using disposable diapers to those of using cloth diapers. The two studies sponsored by the cloth diaper industry conclude that cloth diapers are more environmentally friendly. Not surprisingly, the other two studies, sponsored by the disposable diaper industry, conclude just the opposite. Yet both appear to be correct *given* the underlying assumptions used.

Recognizing that surveys can be abused, several associations—including the American Marketing Association, Marketing Research Association, and the Council of American Survey Research Organizations (CASRO)—have developed codes of research ethics and standards of conduct. For example, the CASRO Code of Standards and Ethics for Survey Research outlines researcher responsibilities to respondents, including confidentiality, privacy, and avoidance of harassment. It also outlines major responsibilities in reporting results to clients and the public.[32] In the end, however, unethical or inappropriate actions cannot simply be regulated away. Each company must accept responsibility for policing the conduct and reporting of its own marketing research to protect consumers' best interests and its own.

REST STOP → REVIEWING THE CONCEPTS

In the previous chapter, we discussed the marketing environment. In this chapter, we've continued our exploration of how marketers go about understanding the marketplace and consumers. We've studied tools used to gather and manage information that marketing managers and others can use to assess opportunities in the marketplace and the impact of a firm's marketing efforts. After this brief pause for rest and reflection, we'll head out again in the next chapter to take a closer look at the object of all of this activity—consumers and their buying behavior.

In today's complex and rapidly changing marketplace, marketing managers need more and better information to make effective and timely decisions. This greater need for information has been matched by the explosion of information technologies for supplying information. Using today's new technologies, companies can now obtain great quantities of information, sometimes even too much. Yet marketers often complain that they lack enough of the *right* kind of information or have an excess of the *wrong* kind. In response, many companies are now studying their managers' information needs and designing information systems to help managers develop and manage market and customer information.

1. Explain the importance of information to the company and its understanding of the marketplace.

The marketing process starts with a complete understanding of the marketplace and consumer needs and wants. Thus, the company needs sound information in order to produce superior value and satisfaction for customers. The company also requires information on competitors, resellers, and other actors and forces in the marketplace. Increasingly, marketers are viewing information not only as an input for making better decisions but also as an important strategic asset and marketing tool.

2. Define the marketing information system and discuss its parts.

The marketing information system (MIS) consists of people, equipment, and procedures to gather, sort, analyze, evaluate, and distribute needed, timely, and accurate information to marketing decision makers. A well-designed information system begins and ends with users.

The MIS first *assesses information needs*. The MIS primarily serves the company's marketing and other managers, but it may also provide information to external partners. Then, the MIS *develops information* from internal databases, marketing intelligence activities, and marketing research. *Internal databases* provide information on the company's own operations and departments. Such data can be obtained quickly and cheaply but often needs to be adapted for marketing decisions. *Marketing intelligence* activities supply everyday information about developments in the external marketing environment. *Market research* consists of collecting information relevant to a specific marketing problem faced by the company. Lastly, the MIS *distributes information* gathered from these sources to the right managers, in the right form, and at the right time.

3. Outline the steps in the marketing research process.

The first step in the marketing research process involves *defining the problem and setting the research objectives,* which may be exploratory, descriptive, or causal research. The second step consists of *developing a research plan* for collecting data from primary and secondary sources. The third step calls for *implementing the marketing research plan* by gathering, processing, and analyzing the information. The fourth step consists of *interpreting and reporting the findings.* Additional information analysis helps marketing managers apply the information and provides them with sophisticated statistical procedures and models from which to develop more rigorous findings.

Both *internal* and *external* secondary data sources often provide information more quickly and at a lower cost than primary data sources, and they can sometimes yield information that a company cannot collect by itself. However, needed information might not exist in secondary sources. Researchers must also evaluate secondary information to ensure that it is *relevant, accurate, current,* and *impartial.* Primary research must also be evaluated for these features. Each primary data collection method—*observational, survey,* and *experimental*—has its own advantages and disadvantages. Each of the various primary research contact methods—mail, telephone, personal interview, and online—also has its own advantages and drawbacks. Similarly, each contact method has its pluses and minuses.

4. Explain how companies analyze and distribute marketing information.

Information gathered in internal databases and through marketing intelligence and marketing research usually requires more analysis. This may include advanced statistical analysis or the application of analytical models that will help marketers make better decisions. To analyze individual customer data, many companies have now acquired or developed special software and analysis techniques—called *customer relationship management (CRM)*—that integrate, analyze, and apply the mountains of individual customer data contained in their databases.

Marketing information has no value until it is used to make better marketing decisions. Thus, the marketing information system must make the information available to the managers and others who make marketing decisions or deal with customers. In some cases, this means providing regular reports and updates; in other cases it means making nonroutine information available for special situations and on-the-spot decisions. Many firms use company intranets and extranets to facilitate this process. Thanks to modern technology, today's marketing managers can gain direct access to the information system at any time and from virtually any location.

5. Discuss the special issues some marketing researchers face, including public policy and ethics issues.

Some marketers face special marketing research situations, such as those conducting research in small business, nonprofit, or international situations. Marketing research can be conducted effectively by small businesses and nonprofit organizations with limited budgets. International marketing researchers follow the same steps as domestic researchers but often face more and different problems. All organizations need to respond responsibly to major public policy and ethical issues surrounding marketing research, including issues of intrusions on consumer privacy and misuse of research findings.

Navigating the Key Terms

Causal research (103)
Customer relationship management (CRM) (113)
Descriptive research (103)
Experimental research (107)
Exploratory research (103)
Focus group interviewing (108)

Internal databases (99)
Marketing information system (MIS) (97)
Marketing intelligence (99)
Marketing research (102)
Observational research (106)
Online databases (105)
Online (Internet) marketing research (109)

Primary data (103)
Sample (110)
Secondary data (103)
Single-source data systems (107)
Survey research (107)

Travel Log

Discussing the Issues

1. Distinguish between internal databases, marketing intelligence, and marketing research as methods for developing marketing information. How do these sources work together to meet an organization's information needs?

2. List three ways to collect primary data. For each, list a product or service for which that method is well suited.

3. What advantages do secondary data have over primary data? What advantages do primary data have over secondary data? Why is secondary data typically the starting point for marketing researchers?

4. List several touch points for a consumer interacting with John Deere. What kind of information might John Deere collect at each of these opportunities for use with CRM software?

5. Small businesses face budget constraints that can limit the type and scope of research conducted. In a small group, brainstorm what a small furniture retailer might be able to do to gain competitor and consumer information on a limited budget.

6. Discuss some of the unique challenges U.S. researchers may encounter in conducting research in other countries. How might these obstacles be overcome?

Application Questions

1. How might observational research be used to understand a consumer's decision process in selecting a greeting card? What other information that is not observable might you want to know about consumer's greeting card choices, and how would you get it?

2. More than 7 million people have discontinued their regular home phone line, opting instead to use a cellular phone to place all of their calls. Assume you work for Bell South. Which method for primary data collection would you use to discern why consumers are making this choice? Why? If, in addition to your earlier choice, you were to conduct a telephone interview, what questions would you ask of those who have already switched? What would you ask consumers still using land lines?

3. Assume you work for Barnes & Noble and serve on a committee making decisions about an upcoming customer satisfaction questionnaire. In a small group, assign each student to one of the following contact methods: mail, telephone, personal, and online. Debate the pros and cons of the different contact methods, and then have the group vote for one of the four methods.

Under the Hood: Focus on Technology

SAP is the leading enterprise software company claiming the majority of FORTUNE 500 companies among its clients. Its products are used to manage sales and distribution, production, inventory, and accounting, among other things. One of its products is a customer relationship management module that is designed to help companies manage the vast amounts of data associated with individual customers. Visit the SAP Web site (http://www.sap.com) and read about the customer relationship management tools under the "solutions" link.

1. Based on information available at the SAP Web site, describe some of the capabilities of CRM.

2. If you were creating a customer database to use individual customer data for CRM in a hotel chain, what type of information would you capture about the customer?

3. How would you collect information about the hotel customer, and how could a marketing manager use it to improve the relationship with that customer.

Focus on Ethics

Although gathering information is essential for marketers trying to create relevant products and services that meet changing consumer needs, doing so can sometimes threaten consumer privacy. The advent of spyware, software that tracks activity on individual computers without the user's knowledge, is certainly alarming. And the increasing use of observational research concerns many consumer advocates. In response, many consumers refuse to participate in even legitimate marketing research.

1. How can marketers gather essential information while respecting the privacy rights of consumers?

2. How have you responded in the past when asked to participate in a survey on the phone or Internet? Did you participate? Why or why not? Was privacy a concern?

3. Is it the responsibility of researchers to safeguard the privacy of consumers or does that responsibility rest with consumers themselves?

Videos

The Wild Planet video case that accompanies this chapter is located in Appendix 1.

➡ AFTER STUDYING THIS CHAPTER, YOU SHOULD BE ABLE TO

1. understand the consumer market and the major factors that influence consumer buyer behavior

2. identify and discuss the stages in the buyer decision process

3. describe the adoption and diffusion process for new products

4. define the business market and identify the major factors that influence business buyer behavior

5. list and define the steps in the business buying decision process

Consumer and Business Buyer Behavior

Road Map Previewing the Concepts

In the previous chapter, you studied how marketers obtain, analyze, and use information to understand the marketplace and to assess marketing programs. In this chapter, you'll continue your marketing journey with a closer look at the most important element of the marketplace—customers. The aim of marketing is to affect how customers think about, and behave toward, the organization and its marketing offers. To affect the *whats*, *whens*, and *hows* of buying behavior, marketers must first understand the *whys*. We look first at *final consumer* buying influences and processes and then at the buying behavior of *business customers*. You'll see that understanding buying behavior is an essential but very difficult task.

Our first point of interest: Harley-Davidson, maker of the nation's top-selling heavyweight motorcycles. Who rides these big Harley "Hogs"? What moves them to tattoo their bodies with the Harley emblem, abandon home and hearth for the open road, and flock to Harley rallies by the hundreds of thousands? *You* might be surprised, but Harley-Davidson knows *very* well.

Few brands engender such intense loyalty as that found in the hearts of Harley-Davidson owners. Harley buyers are granite-like in their devotion to the brand. "You don't see people tattooing Yamaha on their bodies," observes the publisher of *American Iron,* an industry publication. And according to another industry insider, "For a lot of people, it's not that they want a motorcycle; it's that they want a Harley—the brand is that strong."

Each year, in early March, more than 500,000 Harley bikers rumble through the streets of Daytona Beach, Florida, to attend Harley-Davidson's Bike Week celebration. Bikers from across the nation lounge on their low-slung Harleys, swap biker tales, and sport T-shirts proclaiming "I'd rather push a Harley than drive a Honda."

Riding such intense emotions, Harley-Davidson has rumbled its way to the top of the heavyweight motorcycle market. Harley's "Hogs" capture 23 percent of all U.S. bike sales and 50 percent of the heavyweight segment. For several years running, sales have outstripped supply, with customer waiting lists of up to two years for popular models and street prices running well above suggested list prices. During just the past 6 years, Harley sales have more than doubled, and earnings have tripled. By 2005, the company had experienced 19 straight years of record sales and income.

Harley-Davidson's marketers spend a great deal of time thinking about customers and their buying behavior. They want to know who their customers are, what they think and how they feel, and why they buy a Harley Fat Boy Softail rather than a Yamaha or a Kawasaki or a big Honda American Classic. What is it that makes Harley buyers so fiercely loyal? These are difficult questions; even Harley owners themselves don't know exactly what motivates their buying. But Harley management puts top priority on understanding customers and what makes them tick.

Who rides a Harley? You might be surprised. It's no longer the Hell's Angels crowd—the burly, black-leather-jacketed rebels and biker chicks who once made up Harley's core clientele. Motorcycles are attracting a new breed of riders—older, more affluent, and better educated. Harley now appeals more to "rubbies" (rich urban bikers) than to rebels. "While the outlaw bad-boy biker image is what we might typically associate with Harley riders," says an analyst, "they're just as likely to be CEOs and investment bankers." The average Harley customer is a 46-year-old husband with a median household income of $78,300. More than 10 percent of Harley purchases today are made by women.

Harley-Davidson makes good bikes, and to keep up with its shifting market, the company has upgraded its showrooms and sales approaches. But Harley customers are buying a lot more than just a quality bike and a smooth sales pitch. To gain a better understanding of customers' deeper motivations, Harley-Davidson conducted focus groups in which it invited bikers to make cut-and-paste collages of pictures that expressed their feelings about Harley-Davidsons. (Can't you just see a bunch of hard-core bikers doing this?) It then mailed out 16,000 surveys containing a typical battery of psychological, sociological, and demographic questions as well as subjective questions such as "Is Harley more typified by a brown bear or a lion?"

The research revealed seven core customer types: adventure-loving traditionalists, sensitive pragmatists, stylish status seekers, laid-back campers, classy capitalists, cool-headed loners, and cocky misfits. However, all owners appreciated their Harleys for the same basic reasons. "It didn't matter if you were the guy who swept the floors of the factory or if you were the CEO at that factory, the attraction to Harley was very similar," says a Harley executive. "Independence, freedom, and power were the universal Harley appeals."

It's much more than a machine," says the analyst. "It is part of their own self expression and lifestyle." Another analyst suggests that owning a Harley makes you "the toughest, baddest guy on the block. Never mind that [you're] a dentist or an accountant. You [feel] wicked astride all that power." Your Harley renews your spirits and announces your independence. As the Harley Web site's home page announces, "Thumbing the starter of a Harley-Davidson does a lot more than fire the engine. It fires the imagination." Adds a Harley dealer: "We sell a dream here." The classic look, the throaty sound, the very idea of a Harley—all contribute to its mystique. Owning this "American legend" makes you a part of something bigger, a member of the Harley family.

Such strong emotions and motivations are captured in a classic Harley-Davidson advertisement. The ad shows a close-up of an arm, the bicep adorned with a Harley-Davidson tattoo. The headline asks, "When was the last time you felt this strongly about anything?" The ad copy outlines the problem and suggests a solution: "Wake up in the morning and life picks up where it left off. . . . What once seemed exciting has now become part of the numbing routine. It all begins to feel the same. Except when you've got a Harley-Davidson. Something strikes a nerve. The heartfelt thunder rises up, refusing to become part of the background. Suddenly things are different. Clearer. More real. As they should have been all along. Riding a Harley changes you from within. The effect is permanent. Maybe it's time you started feeling this strongly. Things are different on a Harley."[1]

The Harley-Davidson example shows that many different factors affect consumer buying behavior. Buying behavior is never simple, yet understanding it is the essential task of marketing management. First we explore the dynamics of the consumer market and consumer buyer behavior. We then examine business markets and the business buying process.

Consumer Markets and Consumer Buyer Behavior

Consumer buyer behavior
The buying behavior of final consumers—individuals and households who buy goods and services for personal consumption.

Consumer market
All the individuals and households who buy or acquire goods and services for personal consumption.

Consumer buyer behavior refers to the buying behavior of final consumers—individuals and households who buy goods and services for personal consumption. All of these final consumers combine to make up the **consumer market**. The American consumer market consists of more than 296 million people who consume many trillions of dollars' worth of goods and services each year, making it one of the most attractive consumer markets in the world. The world consumer market consists of more than 6.4 *billion* people.[2]

Consumers around the world vary tremendously in age, income, education level, and tastes. They also buy an incredible variety of goods and services. How these diverse consumers connect with each other and with other elements of the world around them impacts their choices among various products, services, and companies. Here we examine the fascinating array of factors that affect consumer behavior.

MODEL OF CONSUMER BEHAVIOR

Consumers make many buying decisions every day. Most large companies research consumer buying decisions in great detail to answer questions about what consumers buy, where they buy, how and how much they buy, when they buy, and why they buy. Marketers can study actual consumer purchases to find out what they buy, where, and how much. But learning about the *whys* of consumer buying behavior is not so easy—the answers are often locked deep within the consumer's head.

Penetrating the dark recesses of the consumer's mind is no easy task. Often, consumers themselves don't know exactly what influences their purchases. "Ninety-five percent of the thought, emotion, and learning [that drive our purchases] occur in the unconscious mind—that is, without our awareness," notes one consumer behavior expert.[3]

The central question for marketers is: How do consumers respond to various marketing efforts the company might use? The starting point is the stimulus-response model of buyer behavior shown in Figure 5.1. This figure shows that marketing and other stimuli enter the consumer's "black box" and produce certain responses. Marketers must figure out what is in the buyer's black box.

Marketing stimuli consist of the Four Ps: product, price, place, and promotion. Other stimuli include major forces and events in the buyer's environment: economic, technological, political, and cultural. All these inputs enter the buyer's black box, where they are turned into a set of observable buyer responses: product choice, brand choice, dealer choice, purchase timing, and purchase amount.

The marketer wants to understand how the stimuli are changed into responses inside the consumer's black box, which has two parts. First, the buyer's characteristics influence how he or she perceives and reacts to the stimuli. Second, the buyer's decision process itself affects the buyer's behavior. We look first at buyer characteristics as they affect buying behavior and then discuss the buyer decision process.

CHARACTERISTICS AFFECTING CONSUMER BEHAVIOR

Consumer purchases are influenced strongly by cultural, social, personal, and psychological characteristics, shown in Figure 5.2. For the most part, marketers cannot control such factors, but they must take them into account.

Cultural Factors   Cultural factors exert a broad and deep influence on consumer behavior. The marketer needs to understand the role played by the buyer's *culture, subculture,* and *social class.*

Culture
The set of basic values, perceptions, wants, and behaviors learned by a member of society from family and other important institutions.

Culture. **Culture** is the most basic cause of a person's wants and behavior. Human behavior is largely learned. Growing up in a society, a child learns basic values, perceptions, wants, and behaviors from the family and other important institutions. A child in the United

FIGURE 5.1 Model of Buyer Behavior

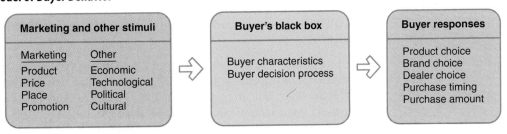

FIGURE 5.2 Factors Influencing Consumer Behavior

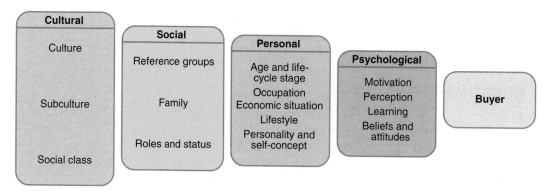

States normally learns or is exposed to the following values: achievement and success, activity and involvement, efficiency and practicality, progress, material comfort, individualism, freedom, humanitarianism, youthfulness, and fitness and health. Every group or society has a culture, and cultural influences on buying behavior may vary greatly from country to country. Failure to adjust to these differences can result in ineffective marketing or embarrassing mistakes.

Marketers are always trying to spot *cultural shifts* in order to discover new products that might be wanted. For example, the cultural shift toward greater concern about health and fitness has created a huge industry for health and fitness services, exercise equipment and clothing, more-natural foods, and a variety of diets. The shift toward informality has resulted in more demand for casual clothing and simpler home furnishings.

Subculture
A group of people with shared value systems based on common life experiences and situations.

Subculture. Each culture contains smaller **subcultures**, or groups of people with shared value systems based on common life experiences and situations. Subcultures include nationalities, religions, racial groups, and geographic regions. Many subcultures make up important market segments, and marketers often design products and marketing programs tailored to their needs. Examples of four such important subculture groups include Hispanic, African-American, Asian, and mature consumers.

The U.S. *Hispanic market*—Americans of Cuban, Mexican, Central American, South American, and Puerto Rican descent—consists of almost 42 million consumers. It's the fastest growing U.S. subsegment—one in every two new Americans since 2000 is Hispanic. By 2050, this group will almost triple in size, making up close to a quarter of the total U.S. population. Hispanic purchasing power, currently at more than $686 billion annually, is expected to increase 44 percent by 2009.[4]

Hispanic consumers tend to buy more branded, higher-quality products—generics don't sell well to this group. They tend to make shopping a family affair, and children have a big say in what brands they buy. Perhaps more important, Hispanics are brand loyal, and they favor companies who show special interest in them.

Most major marketers now produce products tailored to the Hispanic market and promote them using Spanish-language ads and media. For example, Procter & Gamble, one of the nation's leading multicultural marketers, spent almost $170 million last year on Hispanic print and television advertising for major brands such as Pantene, Tide, Crest, and Pampers.[5] It creates special Hispanic versions of some of its products. For instance, its Pantene Extra Liso (extra straight) line of hair care products is specially formulated with Hispanic women in mind.

But P&G's Hispanic marketing efforts run much deeper. Consider the following example:[6]

Julieta Parilla, a new mother living in a predominantly Hispanic working-class suburb of Los Angeles, is a die-hard Pampers fan. She first heard about pampers from her sister. But strong marketing from Procter & Gamble has turned the 21-year-old single mother into a very loyal customer. Julieta recalls a Pampers television ad she liked, broadcast in both English and Spanish, showing a smiling baby crawling in the diapers. The nurses at the medical center where she had her baby, Fatima, gave her free samples of Pampers as she checked out, along with other P&G brands like Crest and Tide. At a local health clinic, Julieta picked up a copy of *Avanzando con Tu Familia* (Helping Your Family Move Ahead), a P&G-published, *Martha Stewart Living*-type magazine for recent Hispanic immigrants that reaches a million homes across the country. Besides coupons for P&G products, the magazine provides recipes, exercise tips, and lifestyle advice. Julieta especially liked a story on how to clean her newborn, and she has been impressed by P&G's support for the Hispanic Scholarship Fund.

Over the past five years, such targeted marketing efforts have helped P&G to increase Pampers' share of the Hispanic market by 25 percent. More broadly, six of the twelve brands managed by P&G's ethnic-marketing division are now ranked number-one among Hispanics in their categories, and five others rank second.

With annual buying power of $723 million and growing, the nation's 39 million *African-American* consumers also attract much marketing attention. The U.S. black population is growing in affluence and sophistication. Although more price conscious than other segments, blacks are also strongly motivated by quality and selection. Brands are important. So is shopping—black consumers seem to enjoy shopping more than other groups, even for something as mundane as groceries. Black consumers are also the most fashion-conscious of the ethnic groups.[7]

In recent years, many companies have developed special products and services, appeals, and marketing programs to reach African-American consumers. For example, Hallmark launched its Afrocentric brand, Mahogany, with only 16 cards in 1987. Today the brand features more than 800 cards designed to celebrate African-American culture, heritage, and traditions.[8] St. Joseph Aspirin, focusing on unique African-American health issues, runs print ads noting that their aspirin comes in the dosage recommended by the Association of Black Cardiologists for daily heart therapy.

Financial services provider JP Morgan Chase makes a special effort to target African-American consumers with home financing products and services. Rather than the standard approach of touting low interest rates, Chase stresses the benefits of home ownership. It sponsors and participates in hundreds of conferences for minority professional groups, such as the National Association of Real Estate Brokers, the Urban League, 100 Black Men, and local gatherings of community leaders and politicians.[9]

A wide variety of magazines, television channels, and other media now target African-American consumers. Marketers are also reaching out to the African-American virtual community. Per capita, black consumers spend twice as much as white consumers for online services. African Americans are increasingly turning to Web sites such as BlackPlanet.com, an African-American community site with more than 15 million registered users. BlackPlanet.com's mission is to enable members to "cultivate meaningful personal and professional relationships, stay informed about the world, and gain access to goods and services that allow members to do more in life." Other popular sites include BET.com and BlackVoices.com.[10]

Asian Americans are the most affluent U.S. demographic segment. They now number more than 12.5 million and wield more than $363 billion in annual spending power. Chinese

■ Pantene: Procter & Gamble spends heavily on Hispanic print and television advertising for major brands such as Pantene. It also creates special Hispanic versions of some of its products, like Pantene Extra Liso (extra straight) hair care products specially formulated with Hispanic women in mind.

■ Targeting Asian-American consumers: Wal-Mart print ads feature actual Asian-American shoppers speaking in their native languages about why they shop at Wal-Mart. In this Chinese-language ad, a family recounts how its weekly Wal-Mart shopping trip is a family bonding experience.

Social class
Relatively permanent and ordered divisions in a society whose members share similar values, interests, and behaviors.

Americans constitute the largest group, followed by Filipinos, Japanese Americans, Asian Indians, and Korean Americans. The U.S. Asian-American population is expected to more than double by 2050, when it will make up more than 9 percent of the U.S. population.[11]

Asian consumers may be the most tech savvy segment—over 70 percent of Asians go online every day and 34 percent, the highest out of all ethnic groups, get their daily news online. As a group, Asian consumers shop frequently and are the most brand-conscious of all the ethnic groups. They can be fiercely brand loyal.[12]

Because of the segment's rapidly growing buying power, many firms are now targeting the Asian-American market. For example, consider Wal-Mart. Today, in one Seattle store, where the Asian-American population represents over 13 percent of the population, Wal-Mart stocks a large selection of CDs and videos from Asian artists, Asian-favored health and beauty products, and children's learning videos that feature multiple language tracks. The giant retailer recently launched an Asian-language television, radio, and print advertising blitz in markets with high concentrations of Asian Americans, such as Los Angeles, San Francisco, San Diego, and Houston. The ads feature actual Asian-American shoppers speaking in their native languages about why they shop at Wal-Mart. In a Chinese ad, a family recounts how its weekly Wal-Mart shopping trip is a family bonding experience.[13]

As the U.S. population ages, *mature consumers* are becoming a very attractive market. Now 75 million strong, the population of U.S. seniors will more than double in the next 25 years. The 65-and-over crowd alone numbers 36 million, more than 12 percent of the population. Mature consumers are better off financially than are younger consumer groups. Because mature consumers have more time and money, they are an ideal market for exotic travel, restaurants, high-tech home entertainment products, leisure goods and services, designer furniture and fashions, financial services, and health care services.[14]

Their desire to look as young as they feel also makes more-mature consumers good candidates for cosmetics and personal care products, health foods, fitness products, and other items that combat the effects of aging. The best strategy is to appeal to their active, multidimensional lives. For example, Kellogg aired a TV spot for All-Bran cereal in which individuals ranging in age from 53 to 81 are featured playing ice hockey, water skiing, running hurdles, and playing baseball, all to the tune of "Wild Thing." A Pepsi ad features a young man in the middle of a mosh pit at a rock concert who turns around to see his father rocking out nearby. And an Aetna commercial portrays a senior who, after retiring from a career as a lawyer, fulfills a lifelong dream of becoming an archeologist.[15]

Social Class. Almost every society has some form of social class structure. **Social classes** are society's relatively permanent and ordered divisions whose members share similar values, interests, and behaviors. Social scientists have identified the seven American social classes shown in Figure 5.3.

Social class is not determined by a single factor, such as income, but is measured as a combination of occupation, income, education, wealth, and other variables. In some social systems, members of different classes are reared for certain roles and cannot change their social positions. In the United States, however, the lines between social classes are not fixed and rigid; people can move to a higher social class or drop into a lower one. Marketers are interested in social class because people within a given social class tend to exhibit similar buying behavior. Social classes show distinct product and brand preferences in areas such as clothing, home furnishings, leisure activity, and automobiles.

Social Factors A consumer's behavior also is influenced by social factors, such as the consumer's *small groups*, *family*, and *social roles* and *status*.

FIGURE 5.3
The Major American Social Classes

Wealth → **Education** → **Occupation** → **Income**

Upper Class
Upper Uppers (1 percent): The social elite who live on inherited wealth. They give large sums to charity, own more than one home, and send their children to the finest schools.

Lower Uppers (2 percent): Americans who have earned high income or wealth through exceptional ability. They are active in social and civic affairs and buy expensive homes, educations, and cars.

Middle Class
Upper Middles (12 percent): Professionals, independent businesspersons, and corporate managers who possess neither family status nor unusual wealth. They believe in education, are joiners and highly civic minded, and want the "better things in life."

Middle Class (32 percent): Average-pay white- and blue-collar workers who live on "the better side of town." They buy popular products to keep up with trends. Better living means owning a nice home in a nice neighborhood with good schools.

Working Class
Working Class (38 percent): Those who lead a "working-class lifestyle," whatever their income, school background, or job. They depend heavily on relatives for economic and emotional support, for advice on purchases, and for assistance in times of trouble.

Lower Class
Upper Lowers (9 percent): The working poor. Although their living standard is just above poverty, they strive toward a higher class. However, they often lack education and are poorly paid for unskilled work.

Lower Lowers (7 percent): Visibly poor, often poorly educated unskilled laborers. They are often out of work and some depend on public assistance. They tend to live a day-to-day existence.

Groups. A person's behavior is influenced by many small **groups**. Groups that have a direct influence and to which a person belongs are called membership groups. In contrast, reference groups serve as direct (face-to-face) or indirect points of comparison or reference in forming a person's attitudes or behavior. People often are influenced by reference groups to which they do not belong. For example, an aspirational group is one to which the individual wishes to belong, as when a young girl soccer player hopes to someday emulate Mia Hamm and play on the U.S. women's Olympic soccer team.

Marketers try to identify the reference groups of their target markets. Reference groups expose a person to new behaviors and lifestyles, influence the person's attitudes and self-concept, and create pressures to conform that may affect the person's product and brand choices. The importance of group influence varies across products and brands. It tends to be strongest when the product is visible to others whom the buyer respects.

Manufacturers of products and brands subjected to strong group influence must figure out how to reach **opinion leaders**—people within a reference group who, because of special skills, knowledge, personality, or other characteristics, exert influence on others. Some experts call this 10 percent of Americans *the influentials* or *leading adopters*. These consumers "drive trends, influence mass opinion, and, most importantly, sell a great many products," says one expert. They often use their big circle of acquaintances to "spread their knowledge on what's good and what's bad."[16]

Many marketers try to identify opinion leaders for their products and direct marketing efforts toward them. They use *buzz marketing* by enlisting or even creating opinion leaders

Group
Two or more people who interact to accomplish individual or mutual goals.

Opinion leader
Person within a reference group who, because of special skills, knowledge, personality, or other characteristics, exerts influence on others.

■ Aspirational groups: Awestruck young soccer hopefuls catch a glimpse of retired soccer great Mia Hamm at a book signing.

to spread the word about their brands. For example, one New York marketing firm, Big Fat Promotions, enlists bar "leaners" to talk casually with tavern patrons about merits of certain liquors, mothers to chat up new laundry products at their kids' little-league games, and commuters to play with new PDAs during the ride home.[17]

BzzAgent, a Boston marketing firm, takes a different approach to creating opinion leaders:

> BzzAgent has assembled a nationwide volunteer army of 85,000 natural-born buzzers, and they will channel their chatter toward products and services they deem authentically worth talking about. "Our goal is to find a way to capture honest word of mouth," says David Baiter, BzzAgent's founder, "and to build a network that will turn passionate customers into brand evangelists." Once a client signs on, BzzAgent searches its database for "agents" matching the demographic and psychographic profile of target customers of the product or service. Selected volunteers receive a sample product and a training manual for buzz-creating strategies. These volunteers aren't just mall rats on cell phones. Some 65 percent are over 25, 60 percent are women, and two are FORTUNE 500 CEOs. They've buzzed products as diverse as Estée Lauder facial masks, Lee jeans, Rock Bottom Restaurants, and The March of Dimes. In Alabama, BzzAgent ArnoldGinger123 buttonholed her probation officer to chat up a tush-flattering new brand of jeans. In Illinois, BzzAgent GeminiDreams spent a family Christmas party extolling the features of Monster.com's new networking site. And, in an especially moving final tribute in New Jersey, BzzAgent Karnj buzzed her grandpa into the great beyond with a round of Anheuser World Select beer at the old gent's wake. The service's appeal is its authenticity. "What I like is that BzzAgents aren't scripted," says Steve Cook, vice president of worldwide strategic marketing at Coca-Cola. "[The company tells its agents] 'Here's the information; if you believe in it, say whatever you think.' It's . . . genuine."[18]

Family. Family members can strongly influence buyer behavior. The family is the most important consumer buying organization in society, and it has been researched extensively. Marketers are interested in the roles and influence of the husband, wife, and children on the purchase of different products and services.

Husband-wife involvement varies widely by product category and by stage in the buying process. Buying roles change with evolving consumer lifestyles. In the United States, the wife traditionally has been the main purchasing agent for the family in the areas of food, household products, and clothing. But with 70 percent of women holding jobs outside the home and the willingness of husbands to do more of the family's purchasing, all this is changing. Whereas women make up just 40 percent of drivers, they now influence more than 80 percent of car-buying decisions. Men now account for about 40 percent of all food-shopping dollars. In all, women now make almost 85 percent of all purchases, spending $6 trillion each year.[19]

Such changes suggest that marketers in industries that have sold their products to only men or only women are now courting the opposite sex. For example, consider Barbara K Enterprises:

> Just like a man can't slip comfortably into a leather pump, it's no surprise that many women feel awkward using home-repair tools designed for men. Enter Barbara Kavovit, CEO of Barbara K Enterprises. A self-made woman, Barbara entered the home improvement business by starting her own construction company, passing out fliers and going door-to-door in Westchester County, New York. Seven years later,

she created a lifestyle brand that offers innovative, women-friendly home repair and improvement products. On a mission to "inspire women to become more self-reliant and confident in their own abilities," and to help them overcome the fear factor of do-it-yourself home repair, Barbara K has developed a strong market niche. More than 70 percent of female homeowners do minor home repairs themselves, and 37 percent say they would rather work on a home improvement project than cook or shop. For these women, Barbara K Enterprises has created a line of high-quality tools and accessories, from hammers and cordless drills to putty knives and pliers. The tools are shaped for smaller hands, have spring-assisted grips, are guaranteed for life, and come in stylish blue and black designs—not pink! Last year, the company sold more than $5 million worth of tools and tool kits emblazoned with the Barbara K name, at stores such as Target, Ace Hardware, and Bed Bath & Beyond.[20]

Children may also have a strong influence on family buying decisions. For example, children as young as age six may influence the family car purchase decision. Recognizing this fact, Toyota launched a new kid-focused ad campaign for its Sienna minivan. Whereas most other minivan ads have focused on soccer moms, the Sienna ads showed kids expressing what they want out of a minivan. In one spot, for example, engineers in Sienna's design center anxiously awaited what looked to be a shakedown by company big shots. Instead, in rushed three little girls on bicycles who began demanding certain features and offering other advice. "I want a hundred cup holders," said one. "Is 14 all right?" asked the engineer. The ad concluded: "It has everything kids want and everything you need."[21]

I spy the ultimate family vehicle.

TOYOTA SIENNA

■ Family buying influences: Toyota launched a kid-focused ad campaign for its Sienna minivan. Says its Web site, "I spy the ultimate family vehicle."

Roles and Status. A person belongs to many groups—family, clubs, organizations. The person's position in each group can be defined in terms of both role and status. A role consists of the activities people are expected to perform according to the persons around them. Each role carries a status reflecting the general esteem given to it by society.

People usually choose products appropriate to their roles and status. Consider the various roles a working mother plays. In her company, she plays the role of a brand manager; in her family, she plays the role of wife and mother; at her favorite sporting events, she plays the role of avid fan. As a brand manager, she will buy the kind of clothing that reflects her role and status in her company.

Personal Factors   A buyer's decisions also are influenced by personal characteristics such as the buyer's *age and life-cycle stage, occupation, economic situation, lifestyle,* and *personality and self-concept.*

Age and Life-Cycle Stage.   People change the goods and services they buy over their lifetimes. Tastes in food, clothes, furniture, and recreation are often age related. Buying is also shaped by the stage of the family life cycle—the stages through which families might pass as they mature over time. Marketers often define their target markets in terms of life-cycle stage and develop appropriate products and marketing plans for each stage.

Traditional family life-cycle stages include young singles and married couples with children. Today, however, marketers are increasingly catering to a growing number of alternative, nontraditional stages such as unmarried couples, singles marrying later in life, childless couples, same-sex couples, single parents, extended parents (those with young adult children returning home), and others.

Sony recently overhauled its marketing approach in order to target products and services to consumers based on their life stages. It created a new unit called the Consumer Segment Marketing Division, which has identified seven life-stage segments. They include, among others, Gen Y (under 25), Young Professionals/DINKs (double income no kids, 25 to 34), Families (35 to 54), and Zoomers (55 and over). A recent Sony ad aimed at Zoomers, people who have just retired or are close to doing so, shows a man living his dream by going into outer space. The ad deals not just with going into retirement, but with the psychological life-stage changes that go with it. "The goal is to get closer to consumers," says a Sony segment marketing executive.[22]

■ Occupation: Carhartt makes rugged, durable, no nonsense work clothes—what it calls "original equipment for the American worker."

Lifestyle
A person's pattern of living as expressed in his or her activities, interests, and opinions.

Occupation. A person's occupation affects the goods and services bought. Blue-collar workers tend to buy more rugged work clothes, whereas executives buy more business suits. Marketers try to identify the occupational groups that have an above-average interest in their products and services. A company can even specialize in making products needed by a given occupational group.

For example, Carhartt makes rugged, durable, no nonsense work clothes—what it calls "original equipment for the American worker. From coats to jackets, bibs to overalls . . . if the apparel carries the name Carhartt, the performance will be legendary." Its Web site carries real-life testimonials of hard-working Carhartt customers. One electrician, battling the cold in Canada's arctic region, reports wearing Carhartt's lined Arctic bib overalls, Arctic jacket, and other clothing for more than two years without a single "popped button, ripped pocket seam, or stuck zipper." And an animal trainer in California says of his favorite pair of Carhartt jeans: "Not only did they keep me warm but they stood up to one playful lion and her very sharp claws."[23]

Economic Situation. A person's economic situation will affect product choice. Marketers of income-sensitive goods watch trends in personal income, savings, and interest rates. If economic indicators point to a recession, marketers can take steps to redesign, reposition, and reprice their products closely. Some marketers target consumers who have lots of money and resources, charging prices to match. For example, Rolex positions its luxury watches as "a tribute to elegance, an object of passion, a symbol for all time." Other marketers target consumers with more modest means. Timex makes more affordable watches that "take a licking and keep on ticking."

Lifestyle. People coming from the same subculture, social class, and occupation may have quite different lifestyles. **Lifestyle** is a person's pattern of living as expressed in his or her psychographics. It involves measuring consumers' major AIO dimensions—activities (work, hobbies, shopping, sports, social events), interests (food, fashion, family, recreation), and opinions (about themselves, social issues, business, products). Lifestyle captures something more than the person's social class or personality. It profiles a person's whole pattern of acting and interacting in the world.

Several research firms have developed lifestyle classifications. The most widely used is the SRI Consulting's *Values and Lifestyles (VALS)* typology. VALS classifies people according to how they spend their time and money. It divides consumers into eight groups based on two major dimensions: primary motivation and resources. *Primary motivations* include ideals, achievement, and self-expression. According to SRI Consulting, consumers who are primarily motivated by ideals are guided by knowledge and principles. Consumers who are primarily motivated by *achievement* look for products and services that demonstrate success to their peers. Consumers who are primarily motivated by *self-expression* desire social or physical activity, variety, and risk.

Consumers within each orientation are further classified into those with *high resources* and those with *low resources,* depending on whether they have high or low levels of income, education, health, self-confidence, energy, and other factors. Consumers with either very high or very low levels of resources are classified without regard to their primary motivations (Innovators, Survivors). Innovators are people with so many resources that they exhibit all three primary motivations in varying degrees. In contrast, Survivors are people with so few resources that they do not show a strong primary motivation. They must focus on meeting needs rather than fulfilling desires.

Iron City beer, a well-known brand in Pittsburgh, used VALS to update its image and improve sales. Iron City was losing sales—its aging core users were drinking less beer, and younger men weren't buying the brand. VALS research showed that one VALS segment, male Experiencers, drink the most beer, followed by Strivers. Men in these segments perceived Iron City drinkers as blue-collar steelworkers stopping off at the local bar. However, they saw themselves as more modern, hardworking, and fun loving. They strongly rejected the outmoded, heavy-industry image of Pittsburgh. Based on this research, Iron City created ads linking its beer to the new self-image of target consumers. The ads mingled images of the old Pittsburgh with those of the new, dynamic city and scenes of young Experiencers and Strivers having fun and working hard. Within just one month of the start of the campaign, Iron City sales shot up by 26 percent.[24]

Lifestyle segmentation can also be used to understand how consumers use the Internet, computers, and other technology. Forrester developed its "Technographics" scheme, which segments consumers according to motivation, desire, and ability to invest in technology. The framework splits people into 10 categories, such as:[25]

- *Fast Forwards:* The biggest spenders on computer technology. Fast Forwards are career focused, time-strapped, driven, and top users of technology.
- *New Age Nurturers:* Also big spenders, however, they are focused on technology for home uses, such as a family education and entertainment.
- *Mouse Potatoes:* Consumers who are dedicated to interactive entertainment and willing to spend for the latest in "technotainment."
- *Techno-Strivers:* Consumers who are up-and-coming believers in technology for career advancement.
- *Traditionalists:* Small-town folks, suspicious of technology beyond the basics.

Delta Airlines used Technographics to better target online ticket sales. It created marketing campaigns for time-strapped Fast Forwards and New Age Nurturers, and eliminated Technology Pessimists (those skeptical of technology) from its list of targets. When used carefully, the lifestyle concept can help marketers understand changing consumer values and how they affect buying behavior.

Personality
The unique psychological characteristics that lead to relatively consistent and lasting responses to one's own environment.

Personality and Self-Concept. Each person's distinct personality influences his or her buying behavior. **Personality** refers to the unique psychological characteristics that lead to relatively consistent and lasting responses to one's own environment. Personality is usually described in terms of traits such as self-confidence, dominance, sociability, autonomy, defensiveness, adaptability, and aggressiveness. Personality can be useful in analyzing consumer behavior for certain product or brand choices. For example, coffee marketers have discovered that heavy coffee drinkers tend to be high on sociability. Thus, to attract customers, Starbucks and other coffeehouses create environments in which people can relax and socialize over a cup of steaming coffee.

The idea is that brands also have personalities, and that consumers are likely to choose brands with personalities that match their own. A *brand personality* is the

■ Brand personality: Well-known brands tend to be strongly associated with one or more traits. Mountain Dew is associated with extreme "excitement."

specific mix of human traits that may be attributed to a particular brand. One researcher identified five brand personality traits:[26]

1. **Sincerity** (down-to-earth, honest, wholesome, and cheerful)
2. **Excitement** (daring, spirited, imaginative, and up-to-date)
3. **Competence** (reliable, intelligent, and successful)
4. **Sophistication** (upper class and charming)
5. **Ruggedness** (outdoorsy and tough)

The researcher found that a number of well-known brands tended to be strongly associated with one particular trait: Levi's with "ruggedness," MTV with "excitement," CNN with "competence," and Campbell's with "sincerity." Hence, these brands will attract persons who are high on the same personality traits.

Many marketers use a concept related to personality—a person's *self-concept* (also called *self-image*). The basic self-concept premise is that people's possessions contribute to and reflect their identities; that is, "we are what we have." Thus, in order to understand consumer behavior, the marketer must first understand the relationship between consumer self-concept and possessions.

Psychological Factors   A person's buying choices are further influenced by four major psychological factors: *motivation, perception, learning,* and *beliefs* and *attitudes.*

Motivation.   A person has many needs at any given time. Some are biological, arising from states of tension such as hunger, thirst, or discomfort. Others are psychological, arising from the need for recognition, esteem, or belonging. A need becomes a motive when it is aroused to a sufficient level of intensity. A **motive** (or drive) is a need that is sufficiently pressing to direct the person to seek satisfaction. Psychologists have developed theories of human motivation. Two of the most popular—the theories of Sigmund Freud and Abraham Maslow—have quite different meanings for consumer analysis and marketing.

Sigmund Freud assumed that people are largely unconscious about the real psychological forces shaping their behavior. He saw the person as growing up and repressing many urges. These urges are never eliminated or under perfect control; they emerge in dreams, in slips of the tongue, in neurotic and obsessive behavior, or ultimately in psychoses.

Freud's theory suggests that a person's buying decisions are affected by subconscious motives that even the buyer may not fully understand. Thus, an aging baby boomer who buys a sporty BMW 330Ci convertible might explain that he simply likes the feel of the wind in his thinning hair. At a deeper level, he may be trying to impress others with his success. At a still deeper level, he may be buying the car to feel young and independent again.

The term *motivation research* refers to qualitative research designed to probe consumers' hidden, subconscious motivations. Consumers often don't know or can't describe just why they act as they do. Thus, motivation researchers use a variety of probing techniques to uncover underlying emotions and attitudes toward brands and buying situations. These sometimes bizarre techniques range from sentence completion, word association, and inkblot or cartoon interpretation tests, to having consumers form daydreams and fantasies about brands or buying situations. One writer offers the following tongue-in-cheek summary of a motivation research session:[27]

Good morning, ladies and gentlemen. We've called you here today for a little consumer research. Now, lie down on the couch, toss your inhibitions out the window, and let's try a little free association. First, think about brands as if they were your *friends.* Imagine you could talk to your

Motive (drive)
A need that is sufficiently pressing to direct the person to seek satisfaction of the need.

■ Motivation—an aging baby boomer who buys a sporty convertible might explain that he simply likes the feel of the wind in his thinning hair. At a deeper level, he may be buying the car to feel young and independent again.

TV dinner. What would he say? And what would you say to him? . . . Now, think of your shampoo as an animal. Go on, don't be shy. Would it be a panda or a lion? A snake or a wooly worm? For our final exercise, let's all sit up and pull out our magic markers. Draw a picture of a typical cake-mix user. Would she wear an apron or a negligee? A business suit or a can-can dress?

Such projective techniques seem pretty goofy, and some marketers dismiss such motivation research as mumbo jumbo. But many marketers routinely use such touchy-feely approaches to dig deeply into consumer psyches and develop better marketing strategies.

Many companies employ teams of psychologists, anthropologists, and other social scientists to carry out motivation research. One ad agency routinely conducts one-on-one, therapy-like interviews to delve into the inner workings of consumers. Another company asks consumers to describe their favorite brands as animals or cars (say, Cadillacs versus Chevrolets) in order to assess the prestige associated with various brands. Still others rely on hypnosis, dream therapy, or soft lights and mood music to plumb the murky depths of consumer psyches.

Abraham Maslow sought to explain why people are driven by particular needs at particular times. Why does one person spend much time and energy on personal safety and another on gaining the esteem of others? Maslow's answer is that human needs are arranged in a hierarchy, as shown in Figure 5.4, from the most pressing at the bottom to the least pressing at the top.[28] They include *physiological* needs, *safety* needs, *social* needs, *esteem* needs, and *self-actualization* needs.

A person tries to satisfy the most important need first. When that need is satisfied, it will stop being a motivator and the person will then try to satisfy the next most important need. For example, starving people (physiological need) will not take an interest in the latest happenings in the art world (self-actualization needs), nor in how they are seen or esteemed by others (social or esteem needs), nor even in whether they are breathing clean air (safety needs). But as each important need is satisfied, the next most important need will come into play.

Perception. A motivated person is ready to act. How the person acts is influenced by his or her own perception of the situation. All of us learn by the flow of information through our five senses: sight, hearing, smell, touch, and taste. However, each of us receives, organizes, and interprets this sensory information in an individual way. **Perception** is the process by which people select, organize, and interpret information to form a meaningful picture of the world.

People can form different perceptions of the same stimulus because of three perceptual processes: selective attention, selective distortion, and selective retention. People are exposed to a great amount of stimuli every day. For example, one analyst estimates that

Perception
The process by which people select, organize, and interpret information to form a meaningful picture of the world.

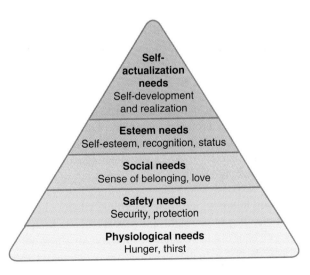

FIGURE 5.4
Maslow's Hierarchy of Needs

Self-actualization needs
Self-development and realization

Esteem needs
Self-esteem, recognition, status

Social needs
Sense of belonging, love

Safety needs
Security, protection

Physiological needs
Hunger, thirst

people are exposed to about 5,000 ads every day.[29] It is impossible for a person to pay attention to all these stimuli. *Selective attention*—the tendency for people to screen out most of the information to which they are exposed—means that marketers have to work especially hard to attract the consumer's attention.

Even noticed stimuli do not always come across in the intended way. Each person fits incoming information into an existing mind-set. *Selective distortion* describes the tendency of people to interpret information in a way that will support what they already believe. For example, if you distrust a company, you might perceive even honest ads from the company as questionable. Selective distortion means that marketers must try to understand the mind-sets of consumers and how these will affect interpretations of advertising and sales information.

■ Selective perception: It's impossible for people to pay attention to the thousands of ads they're exposed to every day, so they screen most of them out.

People also will forget much of what they learn. They tend to retain information that supports their attitudes and beliefs. Because of *selective retention*, consumers are likely to remember good points made about a brand they favor and to forget good points made about competing brands. Because of selective exposure, distortion, and retention, marketers have to work hard to get their messages through. This fact explains why marketers use so much drama and repetition in sending messages to their market.

Interestingly, although most marketers worry about whether their offers will be perceived at all, some consumers worry that they will be affected by marketing messages without even knowing it—through *subliminal advertising*. In 1957, a researcher announced that he had flashed the phrases "Eat popcorn" and "Drink Coca-Cola" on a screen in a New Jersey movie theater every five seconds for 1/300th of a second. He reported that although viewers did not consciously recognize these messages, they absorbed them subconsciously and bought 58 percent more popcorn and 18 percent more Coke. Suddenly advertisers and consumer-protection groups became intensely interested in subliminal perception. People voiced fears of being brainwashed, and California and Canada declared the practice illegal. Although the researcher later admitted to making up the data, the issue has not died. Some consumers still fear that they are being manipulated by subliminal messages.

Numerous studies by psychologists and consumer researchers have found no link between subliminal messages and consumer behavior. It appears that subliminal advertising simply doesn't have the power attributed to it by its critics. Most advertisers scoff at the notion of an industry conspiracy to manipulate consumers through "invisible" messages. Says one industry insider: "[Some consumers believe we are] wizards who can manipulate them at will. Ha! Snort! Oh my sides! As we know, just between us, most of [us] have difficulty getting a 2 percent increase in sales with the help of $50 million in media and extremely liminal images of sex, money, power, and other [motivators] of human emotion. The very idea of [us] as puppeteers, cruelly pulling the strings of consumer marionettes, is almost too much to bear."[30]

Learning
Changes in an individual's behavior arising from experience.

Learning. When people act, they learn. **Learning** describes changes in an individual's behavior arising from experience. Learning theorists say that most human behavior is learned. Learning occurs through the interplay of drives, stimuli, cues, responses, and reinforcement.

A *drive* is a strong internal stimulus that calls for action. A drive becomes a motive when it is directed toward a particular *stimulus object*. For example, a person's drive for self-actualization might motivate him or her to look into buying a digital camera. The consumer's response to the idea of buying a camera is conditioned by the surrounding cues. *Cues* are minor stimuli that determine when, where, and how the person responds. For example, the person might spot several camera brands in a shop window, hear of a special sale price, or discuss cameras with a friend. These are all cues that might influence a consumer's *response* to his or her interest in buying the product.

Suppose the consumer buys a Nikon digital camera. If the experience is rewarding, the consumer will probably use the camera more and more, and his or her response will be *reinforced*. Then, the next time the consumer shops for a camera, or for binoculars or some similar product, the probability is greater that he or she will buy a Nikon product. The practical significance of learning theory for marketers is that they can build up demand for a product by associating it with strong drives, using motivating cues, and providing positive reinforcement.

Beliefs and Attitudes. Through doing and learning, people acquire beliefs and attitudes. These, in turn, influence their buying behavior. A belief is a descriptive thought that a person has about something. Beliefs may be based on real knowledge, opinion, or faith, and may or may not carry an emotional charge. Marketers are interested in the beliefs that people formulate about specific products and services, because these beliefs make up product and brand images that affect buying behavior. If some of the beliefs are wrong and prevent purchase, the marketer will want to launch a campaign to correct them.

People have attitudes regarding religion, politics, clothes, music, food, and almost everything else. *Attitude* describes a person's relatively consistent evaluations, feelings, and tendencies toward an object or idea. Attitudes put people into a frame of mind of liking or disliking things, of moving toward or away from them. Our digital camera buyer may hold attitudes such as "Buy the best," "The Japanese make the best electronics products in the world," and "Creativity and self-expression are among the most important things in life." If so, the Nikon camera would fit well into the consumer's existing attitudes.

Attitudes are difficult to change. A person's attitudes fit into a pattern, and to change one attitude may require difficult adjustments in many others. Thus, a company should usually try to fit its products into existing attitudes rather than attempt to change attitudes. Of course, there are exceptions in which the cost of trying to change attitudes may pay off handsomely:

By 1994, milk consumption had been in decline for 20 years. The general perception was that milk was unhealthy, outdated, just for kids, or good only with cookies and cake. To counter these notions, the National Fluid Milk Processors Education Program (MilkPEP) began an ad campaign featuring milk be-mustached celebrities and the tag line Got Milk? The campaign has not only been wildly popular, it has been successful as well—not only did it stop the decline, milk consumption actually increased. The campaign is still running. Although initially the target market was women in their twenties, the campaign has been expanded to other target markets and has gained cult status with teens, much to their parents' delight. Teens collect the print ads featuring celebrities ranging from music stars Kelly Clarkson and Nelly, to actors such as Jessica Alba and Lindsay Lohan, to sports idols such as Jeff Gordon, Tracy McGrady, and Venus and Serena Williams. Building on this popularity with teens, the industry set up a Web site (www.whymilk.com) where young folks can make their own mustache, check out the latest Got Milk? ads, or get facts about "everything you ever need to know about milk." The industry also promotes milk to them through grass roots marketing efforts. It recently launched a traveling promotion event searching for

Great for dunking.

My friends told me, "T-Mac, you're gonna be big some day." Must've been the milk. About 15% of your height is added as a teen and the calcium and vitamin D can help. Will drinking a cool glass of milk make you the hottest scorer in town? Hey, it couldn't hurt.

got milk?

■ Attitudes are difficult to change, but the National Fluid Milk Processor's wildly popular milk moustache campaign succeeded in changing attitudes toward milk.

the best teen bands and dancers. The best band will receive a recording contract, and the most talented dancer will spend next summer at the MTV Beach House. Teens can also enter a contest to sport a milk mustache in *Rolling Stone* magazine alongside a famous musician, and then follow the celebrity for a day as a roadie.[31]

We can now appreciate the many forces acting on consumer behavior. The consumer's choice results from the complex interplay of cultural, social, personal, and psychological factors.

THE BUYER DECISION PROCESS

Now that we have looked at the influences that affect buyers, we are ready to look at how consumers make buying decisions. Figure 5.5 shows that the buyer decision process consists of five stages: *need recognition, information search, evaluation of alternatives, purchase decision,* and *postpurchase behavior.* Clearly, the buying process starts long before the actual purchase and continues long after. Marketers need to focus on the entire buying process rather than on just the purchase decision.[32]

The figure suggests that consumers pass through all five stages with every purchase. But in more routine purchases, consumers often skip or reverse some of these stages. A woman buying her regular brand of toothpaste would recognize the need and go right to the purchase decision, skipping information search and evaluation. However, we use the model in Figure 5.5 because it shows all the considerations that arise when a consumer faces a new and complex purchase situation.

Need Recognition The buying process starts with *need recognition*—the buyer recognizes a problem or need. The need can be triggered by *internal stimuli* when one of the person's normal needs—hunger, thirst, sex—rises to a level high enough to become a drive. A need can also be triggered by *external stimuli*. For example, an advertisement or a discussion with a friend might get you thinking about buying a new car. At this stage, the marketer should research consumers to find out what kinds of needs or problems arise, what brought them about, and how they led the consumer to this particular product.

Information Search An interested consumer may or may not search for more information. If the consumer's drive is strong and a satisfying product is near at hand, the consumer is likely to buy it then. If not, the consumer may store the need in memory or undertake an *information search* related to the need. For example, once you've decided you need a new car, at the least, you will probably pay more attention to car ads, cars owned by friends, and car conversations. Or you may actively look for reading material, phone friends, and gather information in other ways. The amount of searching you do will depend on the strength of your drive, the amount of information you start with, the ease of obtaining more information, the value you place on additional information, and the satisfaction you get from searching.

Consumers can obtain information from any of several sources. These include *personal sources* (family, friends, neighbors, acquaintances), *commercial sources* (advertising, salespeople, Web sites dealers, packaging, displays,), *public sources* (mass media, consumer-rating organizations, Internet searches), and *experiential sources*

Need recognition can be triggered by advertising. This inventive ad from Pepsi alerts consumers to the benefits of "0 calories. 0 carbs."

FIGURE 5.5 Buyer Decision Process

(handling, examining, using the product). The relative influence of these information sources varies with the product and the buyer. Generally, the consumer receives the most information about a product from commercial sources—those controlled by the marketer. The most effective sources, however, tend to be personal. Commercial sources normally *inform* the buyer, but personal sources *legitimize* or *evaluate* products for the buyer. As one marketer states, "It's rare that an advertising campaign can be as effective as a neighbor leaning over the fence and saying, 'This is a wonderful product.'"[33]

As more information is obtained, the consumer's awareness and knowledge of the available brands and features increases. In your car information search, you may learn about the several brands available. The information might also help you to drop certain brands from consideration. A company must design its marketing mix to make prospects aware of and knowledgeable about its brand. It should carefully identify consumers' sources of information and the importance of each source.

Evaluation of Alternatives   We have seen how the consumer uses information to arrive at a set of final brand choices. How does the consumer choose among the alternative brands? The marketer needs to know about *alternative evaluation*—that is, how the consumer processes information to arrive at brand choices. Unfortunately, consumers do not use a simple and single evaluation process in all buying situations. Instead, several evaluation processes are at work.

The consumer arrives at attitudes toward different brands through some evaluation procedure. How consumers go about evaluating purchase alternatives depends on the individual consumer and the specific buying situation. In some cases, consumers use careful calculations and logical thinking. At other times, the same consumers do little or no evaluating; instead they buy on impulse and rely on intuition. Sometimes consumers make buying decisions on their own; sometimes they turn to friends, consumer guides, or salespeople for buying advice.

Suppose you've narrowed your car choices to three brands. And suppose that you are primarily interested in four attributes—styling, operating economy, warranty, and price. By this time, you've probably formed beliefs about how each brand rates on each attribute. Clearly, if one car rated best on all the attributes, we could predict that you would choose it. However, the brands will no doubt vary in appeal. You might base your buying decision on only one attribute, and your choice would be easy to predict. If you wanted styling above everything else, you would buy the car that you think has the best styling. But most buyers consider several attributes, each with different importance. If we knew the importance that you assigned to each of the four attributes, we could predict your car choice more reliably.

Marketers should study buyers to find out how they actually evaluate brand alternatives. If they know what evaluative processes go on, marketers can take steps to influence the buyer's decision.

Purchase Decision   In the evaluation stage, the consumer ranks brands and forms purchase intentions. Generally, the consumer's *purchase decision* will be to buy the most preferred brand, but two factors can come between the purchase *intention* and the purchase *decision*. The first factor is the *attitudes of others*. If someone important to you thinks that you should buy the lowest-priced car, then the chances of your buying a more expensive car are reduced.

The second factor is *unexpected situational factors*. The consumer may form a purchase intention based on factors such as expected income, expected price, and expected product benefits. However, unexpected events may change the purchase intention. For example, the economy might take a turn for the worse, a close competitor might drop its price, or a friend might report being disappointed in your preferred car. Thus, preferences and even purchase intentions do not always result in actual purchase choice.

MARKETING AT WORK $\boxed{5.1}$

Lexus: Delighting Customers to Keep Them Coming Back

Close your eyes for a minute and picture a typical car dealership. Not impressed? Talk to a friend who owns a Lexus, and you'll no doubt get a very different picture. The typical Lexus dealership is . . . well, anything but typical.

In Plano, Texas, Lexus customers waiting for their cars to be serviced can lounge on an overstuffed sofa, watch a big-screen TV, surf the Internet, and sip lattes in the beverage area. The dealership is considering adding a manicure area. "We try to make it like a den would be in your own home," says the dealership's president.

In California, another Lexus dealer bought a $50,000 putting machine so customers can brush up on their golf while waiting for an oil change. Across the country, a dealer in Raleigh, North Carolina, provides a fully-furnished business center for busy executives, complete with a fax machine and wireless Internet access. Less ambitious customers can relax at a café table in the nearby lounge, chatting over a cup of fresh-brewed Starbucks coffee and a plate of still-warm chocolate chip cookies.

Why all the special amenities? Lexus knows that good marketing doesn't stop with making the sale. Keeping customers happy *after* the

sale is the key to building lasting relationships. Dealers across the country have a common goal: to delight customers and keep them coming back. Lexus believes that if you "delight the customer, and continue to delight the customer, you will have a customer for life." And Lexus understands just how valuable a customer can be—it estimates that the average lifetime value of a Lexus customer is $600,000.

Despite the amenities, few Lexus customers spend much time hanging around the dealership. Lexus knows that the best dealership visit is the one that you don't have to make at all. So it builds customer-pleasing cars to start with—high-quality cars that need little servicing. In its "Lexus Covenant," the company vows that it will make "the finest cars ever built." In 2005, J.D. Power once again rated Lexus as the top brand for initial quality. The Lexus SC 430 model set the record for the fewest quality problems ever reported.

Still, when a car does need to be serviced, Lexus goes out of its way to make it easy and painless. Most dealers will even pick up the car, and then return it when the maintenance is finished. And the car comes back spotless,

thanks to a complimentary cleaning to remove bugs and road grime from the exterior and smudges from the leather interior. You might even be surprised to find that they've touched up a door ding to help restore the car to its fresh-from-the-factory luster. "My wife will never buy another car except a Lexus," says one satisfied Lexus owner. "They come to our house, pick up the car, do an oil change, [spiff it up] and bring it back. She's sold for life."

And when a customer does bring a car in, Lexus repairs it right the first time, on time. Dealers know that their well-heeled customers have money, "but what they don't have is time." So dealers like Mike Sullivan of California are testing a system that uses three technicians instead of one for 35,000-mile service checkups. The new system will cut a customer's wait in half. "I'm not in the car business," says one dealer. "I'm in the service business."

Beyond pampering customers with outstanding service, Lexus also creates special experiences that foster long-lasting relationships. Lexus Australia, for example, rewards loyal customers with VIP packages to the theater. It gives them an opportunity to buy the

Postpurchase Behavior   The marketer's job does not end when the product is bought. After purchasing the product, the consumer will be satisfied or dissatisfied and will engage in *postpurchase behavior* of interest to the marketer. What determines whether the buyer is satisfied or dissatisfied with a purchase? The answer lies in the relationship between the *consumer's expectations* and the product's *perceived performance*. If the product falls short of expectations, the consumer is disappointed; if it meets expectations, the consumer is satisfied; if it exceeds expectations, the consumer is delighted.

The larger the gap between expectations and performance, the greater the consumer's dissatisfaction. This suggests that sellers should promise only what their brands can deliver so that buyers are satisfied. Some sellers might even understate product performance levels to boost later consumer satisfaction. For example, Boeing's salespeople tend to be conservative when they estimate the potential benefits of their aircraft. They almost always underestimate fuel efficiency—they promise a 5 percent savings that turns out to be 8 percent. Customers are delighted with better-than-expected performance; they buy again and tell other potential customers that Boeing lives up to its promises.

Cognitive dissonance
Buyer discomfort caused by postpurchase conflict.

Almost all major purchases result in **cognitive dissonance**, or discomfort caused by postpurchase conflict. After the purchase, consumers are satisfied with the benefits of the chosen brand and are glad to avoid the drawbacks of the brands not bought. However,

best seats at the Sydney Opera House. During intermission, customers can visit the exclusive Inner Circle VIP lounge and sip a complimentary glass of Domaine Chandon while opening their VIP gift pack of exclusive commemorative merchandise from the show.

According to its Web site, from the very start, Lexus set out to "revolutionize the automotive experience with a passionate commitment to the finest products, supported by dealers who create the most satisfying owner-

Lexus Covenant

Lexus will enter the most competitive, prestigious automobile race in the world. Over 50 years of Toyota automobile experience has culminated in the creation of Lexus cars. They will be the finest cars ever built.

Lexus will win the race because Lexus will do it right from the start. Lexus will have the finest dealer network in the industry. Lexus will treat each customer as we would a guest in our home.

If you think you can't you won't . . .
If you think you can, you will! We can, we will.

■ *Customer delight: The Lexus Covenant—Lexus pledges to create the most satisfying ownership experience the world has ever seen.*

ship experience the world has ever seen. We vow to value the customer as an important individual. To do things right the first time. And to always exceed expectations."

At Lexus, exceeding customer expectations sometimes means fulfilling even seemingly outrageous customer requests. Dave Wilson, owner of several Lexus dealerships in Southern California, tells of an angry letter he received from a Lexus owner who spent $374 to repair her car at his dealership. She'd owned four prior Lexus vehicles without a single problem. She said in her letter that she resented paying to fix her current one. Turns out, she thought they were maintenance free—as in get in and drive . . . and drive and drive. "She didn't think she had to do anything to her Lexus," says Wilson. "She had 60,000 miles on it, and never had the oil changed." Wilson sent back her $374.

By all accounts, Lexus has lived up to its ambitious customer-satisfaction promise. It has created what appear to be the world's most satisfied car owners. Lexus regularly tops not just the J.D. Power quality ratings, but also its customer-satisfaction ratings, and not just in the United States, but worldwide. In 2004, in the United Kingdom, Lexus achieved the highest J.D. Power customer-satisfaction score ever in the rating's 11-year history. Customer satisfaction translates into sales and customer loyalty. Last year, for the fifth straight year, Lexus was this nation's number-one selling luxury car. And once a Lexus customer, always a Lexus customer—Lexus retains 84 percent of customers who've gone to the dealership for service.

Sources: "Toyota Earns 10 Awards in the J.D. Power and Associates Initial Quality Study—Lexus Has Top-Ranked Vehicle for Five Years in a Row," press release, May 18, 2005, accessed at www.lexus.com/about/press_releases/index.html; Jean Halliday, "Dealers Improve Waiting Areas to Boost Loyalty," *Automotive News*, March 22, 2004, p. 38; Steve Finlay, "At Least She Put Fuel in It," *Ward's Dealer Business*, August 1, 2003; "Lexus Roars for Loyal Customers," *B&T Magazine*, November 27, 2003; "Keeping the Customer Satisfied," *The Derry Journal*, April 30, 2004; "Servco Lexus Customers Get a Sneak Peak at the All-New GX 470," *Servco Pacific*, April 2004; Mark Rechtin, "Lexus: Growth Won't Hurt Brand's Cachet," *Automotive News*, April 19, 2004, p. 49; Mark Rechtin, "Lexus Strives to Remain Top-Selling Brand," *Automotive News*, January 24, 2005, p. 8; Jeremy W. Peters, "Lexus Tops Owners Survey for Fifth Year," *New York Times*, May 19, 2005, p. C10; and "Lexus Covenant," accessed at www.lexus.com/about/corporate/covenant.html, August 2005.

every purchase involves compromise. Consumers feel uneasy about acquiring the drawbacks of the chosen brand and about losing the benefits of the brands not purchased. Thus, consumers feel at least some postpurchase dissonance for every purchase.[34]

Why is it so important to satisfy the customer? Customer satisfaction is a key to building profitable relationships with consumers—to keeping and growing consumers and reaping their customer lifetime value. Satisfied customers buy a product again, talk favorably to others about the product, pay less attention to competing brands and advertising, and buy other products from the company. Many marketers go beyond merely *meeting* the expectations of customers—they aim to *delight* the customer (see Marketing at Work 5.1).

A dissatisfied consumer responds differently. Bad word of mouth often travels farther and faster than good word of mouth. It can quickly damage consumer attitudes about a company and its products. But companies cannot simply rely on dissatisfied customers to volunteer their complaints when they are dissatisfied. Most unhappy customers never tell the company about their problem. Therefore, a company should measure customer satisfaction regularly. It should set up systems that *encourage* customers to complain. In this way, the company can learn how well it is doing and how it can improve.

But what should companies do about dissatisfied customers? At a minimum, most companies offer toll-free numbers and Web sites to handle complaints and inquiries. For example, over the past two decades, the Gerber help line (1-800-4-GERBER) has received more than five million calls. Help line staffers, most of them mothers or grandmothers themselves, handle customer concerns and provide baby care advice 24 hours a day, 365 days a year to more than 2,400 callers a day. Customers can also log onto the Gerber Web site and enter a phone number, and a staffer will call them.

By studying the overall buyer decision, marketers may be able to find ways to help consumers move through it. For example, if consumers are not buying a new product because they do not perceive a need for it, marketing might launch advertising messages that trigger the need and show how the product solves customers' problems. If customers know about the product but are not buying because they hold unfavorable attitudes toward it, the marketer must find ways either to change the product or change consumer perceptions.

THE BUYER DECISION PROCESS FOR NEW PRODUCTS

We have looked at the stages buyers go through in trying to satisfy a need. Buyers may pass quickly or slowly through these stages, and some of the stages may even be reversed. Much depends on the nature of the buyer, the product, and the buying situation.

We now look at how buyers approach the purchase of new products. A **new product** is a good, service, or idea that is perceived by some potential customers as new. It may have been around for a while, but our interest is in how consumers learn about products for the first time and make decisions on whether to adopt them. We define the **adoption process** as "the mental process through which an individual passes from first learning about an innovation to final adoption," and *adoption* as the decision by an individual to become a regular user of the product.[35]

New product
A good, service, or idea that is perceived by some potential customers as new.

Adoption process
The mental process through which an individual passes from first hearing about an innovation to final adoption.

Stages in the Adoption Process   Consumers go through five stages in the process of adopting a new product:

- *Awareness:* The consumer becomes aware of the new product, but lacks information about it.
- *Interest:* The consumer seeks information about the new product.
- *Evaluation:* The consumer considers whether trying the new product makes sense.
- *Trial:* The consumer tries the new product on a small scale to improve his or her estimate of its value.
- *Adoption:* The consumer decides to make full and regular use of the new product.

This model suggests that the new-product marketer should think about how to help consumers move through these stages. A manufacturer of HDTVs (high-density televisions) may discover that many consumers in the interest stage do not move to the trial stage because of uncertainty and the large investment. If these same consumers were willing to use HDTVs on a trial basis for a small fee, the manufacturer could consider offering a trial-use plan with an option to buy.

Individual Differences in Innovativeness   People differ greatly in their readiness to try new products. In each product area, there are "consumption pioneers" and early adopters. Other individuals adopt new products much later. People can be classified into the adopter categories shown in Figure 5.6. After a slow start, an increasing number of people adopt the new product. The number of adopters reaches a peak and then drops off as fewer nonadopters remain. Inno-

■ The adoption process: This ad encourages trial by offering a coupon.

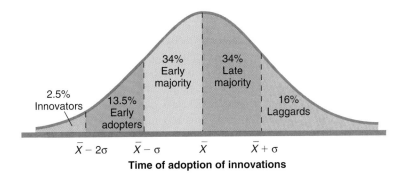

FIGURE 5.6
Adopter Categorization on the Basis of Relative Time of Adoption of Innovations

Source: Reprinted with the permission of The Free Press, a Division of Simon & Schuster, from *Diffusion of Innovations,* Fifth Edition, by Everett M. Rogers. Copyright © 2003 by The Free Press.

vators are defined as the first 2.5 percent of the buyers to adopt a new idea (those beyond two standard deviations from mean adoption time); the early adopters are the next 13.5 percent (between one and two standard deviations); and so forth.

The five adopter groups have differing values. *Innovators* are venturesome—they try new ideas at some risk. *Early adopters* are guided by respect—they are opinion leaders in their communities and adopt new ideas early but carefully. The *early majority* are deliberate—although they rarely are leaders, they adopt new ideas before the average person. The *late majority* are skeptical—they adopt an innovation only after a majority of people have tried it. Finally, *laggards* are tradition bound—they are suspicious of changes and adopt the innovation only when it has become something of a tradition itself.

This adopter classification suggests that an innovating firm should research the characteristics of innovators and early adopters and should direct marketing efforts toward them. In general, innovators tend to be relatively younger, better educated, and higher in income than later adopters and nonadopters. They are more receptive to unfamiliar things, rely more on their own values and judgment, and are more willing to take risks. They are less brand loyal and more likely to take advantage of special promotions such as discounts, coupons, and samples.

Influence of Product Characteristics on Rate of Adoption

The characteristics of the new product affect its rate of adoption. Some products catch on almost overnight (iPod), whereas others take a long time to gain acceptance (HDTV). Five characteristics are especially important in influencing an innovation's rate of adoption. For example, consider the characteristics of HDTV in relation to the rate of adoption:

- *Relative advantage:* The degree to which the innovation appears superior to existing products. The greater the perceived relative advantage of using HDTV—say, in picture quality and ease of viewing—the sooner HDTVs will be adopted.
- *Compatibility:* The degree to which the innovation fits the values and experiences of potential consumers. HDTV, for example, is highly compatible with the lifestyles found in upper middle-class homes. However, it is not very compatible with the programming and broadcasting systems currently available to consumers.
- *Complexity:* The degree to which the innovation is difficult to understand or use. HDTVs are not very complex and, therefore, once more programming is available and prices come down, will take less time to penetrate U.S. homes than more complex innovations.
- *Divisibility:* The degree to which the innovation may be tried on a limited basis. HDTVs are still very expensive. To the extent that people can lease them with an option to buy, their rate of adoption will increase.
- *Communicability:* The degree to which the results of using the innovation can be observed or described to others. Because HDTV lends itself to demonstration and description, its use will spread faster among consumers.

Other characteristics influence the rate of adoption, such as initial and ongoing costs, risk and uncertainty, and social approval. The new-product marketer has to research all these factors when developing the new product and its marketing program.

CONSUMER BEHAVIOR ACROSS INTERNATIONAL BORDERS

Understanding consumer behavior is difficult enough for companies marketing within the borders of a single country. For companies operating in many countries, however, understanding and serving the needs of consumers can be daunting. Although consumers in different countries may have some things in common, their values, attitudes, and behaviors often vary greatly. International marketers must understand such differences and adjust their products and marketing programs accordingly.

Sometimes the differences are obvious. For example, in the United States, where most people eat cereal regularly for breakfast, Kellogg focuses its marketing on persuading consumers to select a Kellogg brand rather than a competitor's brand. In France, however, where most people prefer croissants and coffee or no breakfast at all, Kellogg advertising simply attempts to convince people that they should eat cereal for breakfast. Its packaging includes step-by-step instructions on how to prepare cereal. In India, where many consumers eat heavy, fried breakfasts and many consumers skip the meal altogether, Kellogg's advertising attempts to convince buyers to switch to a lighter, more nutritious breakfast diet.

Often, differences across international markets are more subtle. They may result from physical differences in consumers and their environments. For example, Remington makes smaller electric shavers to fit the smaller hands of Japanese consumers. Other differences result from varying customs. In Japan, for example, where humility and deference are considered great virtues, pushy, hard-hitting sales approaches are considered offensive. Failing to understand such differences in customs and behaviors from one country to another can spell disaster for a marketer's international products and programs.

Marketers must decide on the degree to which they will adapt their products and marketing programs to meet the unique cultures and needs of consumers in various markets. On the one hand, they want to standardize their offerings in order to simplify operations and take advantage of cost economies. On the other hand, adapting marketing efforts within each country results in products and programs that better satisfy the needs of local consumers. The question of whether to adapt or standardize the marketing mix across international markets has created a lively debate in recent years.

 Linking the Concepts

Here's a good place to pull over and apply the concepts you've examined in the first part of this chapter.

- Think about a specific major purchase you've made recently. What buying process did you follow? What major factors influenced your decision?
- Pick a company that we've discussed in a previous chapter—Nike, NASCAR, Disney, Best Buy, Coach, Jones Soda, Lexus, or another. How does the company you chose use its understanding of customers and their buying behavior to build better customer relationships?
- Think about a company like Intel, which sells its products to computer makers and other businesses rather than to final consumers. How would Intel's marketing to business customers differ from Starbucks's marketing to final consumers? The second part of the chapter deals with this issue.

Business Markets and Business Buyer Behavior

In one way or another, most large companies sell to other organizations. Companies such as DuPont, Boeing, IBM, Caterpillar, and countless other firms, sell *most* of their products to other businesses. Even large consumer-products companies, which make products used by final consumers, must first sell their products to other businesses. For example, General Mills makes many familiar consumer brands—Big G cereals (Cheerios, Wheaties, Total, Golden Grahams); baking products (Pillsbury, Betty Crocker, Gold Medal flour), snacks

(Nature Valley, Chex Mix, Pop Secret); Yoplait Yogurt; and others. But to sell these products to consumers, General Mills must first sell them to the wholesalers and retailers that serve the consumer market.

Business buyer behavior refers to the buying behavior of the organizations that buy goods and services for use in the production of other products and services that are sold, rented, or supplied to others. It also includes the behavior of retailing and wholesaling firms that acquire goods to resell or rent them to others at a profit. In the *business buying process,* business buyers determine which products and services their organizations need to purchase, and then find, evaluate, and choose among alternative suppliers and brands. *Business-to-business (B-to-B) marketers* must do their best to understand business markets and business buyer behavior.

Business buyer behavior
The buying behavior of the organizations that buy goods and services for use in the production of other products and services or for the purpose of reselling or renting them to others at a profit.

BUSINESS MARKETS

The business market is *huge.* In fact, business markets involve far more dollars and items than do consumer markets. For example, think about the large number of business transactions involved in the production and sale of a single set of Goodyear tires. Various suppliers sell Goodyear the rubber, steel, equipment, and other goods that it needs to produce the tires. Goodyear then sells the finished tires to retailers, who, in turn, sell them to consumers. Thus, many sets of *business* purchases were made for only one set of *consumer* purchases. In addition, Goodyear sells tires as original equipment to manufacturers who install them on new vehicles, and as replacement tires to companies that maintain their own fleets of company cars, trucks, buses, or other vehicles.

Characteristics of Business Markets   In some ways, business markets are similar to consumer markets. Both involve people who assume buying roles and make purchase decisions to satisfy needs. However, business markets differ in many ways from consumer markets. The main differences are in *market structure and demand,* the *nature of the buying unit,* and the *types of decisions and the decision process* involved.

Market Structure and Demand   The business marketer normally deals with *far fewer but far larger buyers* than the consumer marketer does. Even in large business markets, a few buyers often account for most of the purchasing. For example, when Goodyear sells replacement tires to final consumers, its potential market includes the owners of the millions of cars currently in use in the United States and around the world. But Goodyear's fate in the business market depends on getting orders from one of only a handful of large automakers. Similarly, Black & Decker sells its power tools and outdoor equipment to tens of millions of consumers worldwide. However, it must sell these products through three huge retail customers—Home Depot, Lowe's, and Wal-Mart—which combined account for more than half its sales.

Derived demand
Business demand that ultimately comes from (derives from) the demand for consumer goods.

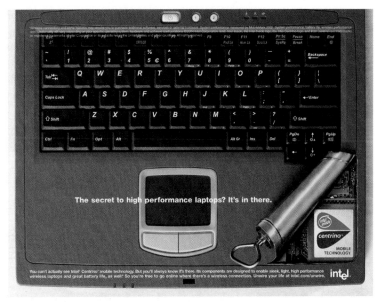

Business markets are also *more geographically concentrated.* More than half the nation's business buyers are concentrated in eight states: California, New York, Ohio, Illinois, Michigan, Texas, Pennsylvania, and New Jersey. Further, business demand is **derived demand**—it ultimately derives from the demand for consumer goods. Hewlett-Packard and Dell buy Intel microprocessor chips because consumers buy personal computers. If consumer demand for PCs drops, so will the demand for computer chips.

Therefore, B-to-B marketers sometimes promote their products directly to final consumers to increase business demand. For example, Intel's long-running "Intel Inside" advertising campaign sells personal computer buyers on the virtues of Intel microprocessors. The

■ Derived demand: Intel's long-running "Intel Inside" logo advertising campaign boosts demand for Intel chips and for the PC's containing them. "The secret to high performance laptops? It's in there."

increased demand for Intel chips boosts demand for the PCs containing them, and both Intel and its business partners win.

Similarly, INVISTA promotes Teflon directly to final consumers as a key branded ingredient in Stain-repellent, wrinkle-free fabrics and leathers. You see Teflon Fabric Protector hang tags on clothing lines such as Levi's Dockers, Donna Karan's menswear, and Ralph Lauren denim.[36] By making Teflon familiar and attractive to final buyers, INVISTA also makes the products containing it more attractive.

Nature of the Buying Unit   Compared with consumer purchases, a business purchase usually involves *more decision participants* and a *more professional purchasing effort*. Often, business buying is done by trained purchasing agents who spend their working lives learning how to buy better. The more complex the purchase, the more likely it is that several people will participate in the decision-making process. Buying committees made up of technical experts and top management are common in the buying of major goods.

Beyond this, many companies are now upgrading their purchasing functions to "supply management" or "supplier development" functions. B-to-B marketers now face a new breed of higher-level, better-trained supply managers. These supply managers sometimes seem to know more about the supplier company than it knows about itself. Therefore, business marketers must have well-trained marketers and salespeople to deal with these well-trained buyers.

Types of Decisions and the Decision Process   Business buyers usually face *more complex* buying decisions than do consumer buyers. Purchases often involve large sums of money, complex technical and economic considerations, and interactions among many people at many levels of the buyer's organization. Because the purchases are more complex, business buyers may take longer to make their decisions. The business buying process also tends to be *more formalized* than the consumer buying process. Large business purchases usually call for detailed product specifications, written purchase orders, careful supplier searches, and formal approval.

Finally, in the business buying process, buyer and seller are often much *more dependent* on each other. Consumer marketers are often at a distance from their customers. In contrast, B-to-B marketers may roll up their sleeves and work closely with their customers during all stages of the buying process—from helping customers define problems, to finding solutions, to supporting after-sale operation. They often customize their offerings to individual customer needs.

BUSINESS BUYER BEHAVIOR

At the most basic level, marketers want to know how business buyers will respond to various marketing stimuli. Figure 5.7 shows a model of business buyer behavior. In this model, marketing and other stimuli affect the buying organization and produce certain buyer responses. As with consumer buying, the marketing stimuli for business buying consist of the Four Ps: product, price, place, and promotion. Other stimuli include major forces in the environment: economic, technological, political, cultural, and competitive. These stimuli enter the organization and are turned into buyer responses: product or service choice; supplier choice; order quantities; and delivery, service, and payment terms. In

FIGURE 5.7
A Model of Business Buyer Behavior

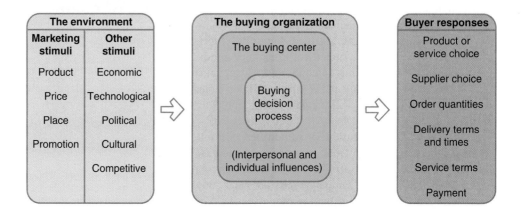

order to design good marketing mix strategies, the marketer must understand what happens within the organization to turn stimuli into purchase responses.

Within the organization, buying activity consists of two major parts: the buying center, made up of all the people involved in the buying decision, and the buying decision process. The model shows that the buying center and the buying decision process are influenced by internal organizational, interpersonal, and individual factors as well as by external environmental factors.

The model in Figure 5.7 suggests four questions about business buyer behavior: What buying decisions do business buyers make? Who participates in the buying process? What are the major influences on buyers? How do business buyers make their buying decisions?

Major Types of Buying Situations   There are three major types of buying situations.[37] At one extreme is the *straight rebuy,* which is a fairly routine decision. At the other extreme is the *new task,* which may call for thorough research. In the middle is the *modified rebuy,* which requires some research.

In a **straight rebuy**, the buyer reorders something without any modifications. It is usually handled on a routine basis by the purchasing department. Based on past buying satisfaction, the buyer simply chooses from the various suppliers on its list. "In" suppliers try to maintain product and service quality. They often propose automatic reordering systems so that the purchasing agent will save reordering time. "Out" suppliers try to offer something new or exploit dissatisfaction so that the buyer will consider them.

In a **modified rebuy**, the buyer wants to modify product specifications, prices, terms, or suppliers. The modified rebuy usually involves more decision participants than does the straight rebuy. The in suppliers may become nervous and feel pressured to put their best foot forward to protect an account. Out suppliers may see the modified rebuy situation as an opportunity to make a better offer and gain new business.

A company buying a product or service for the first time faces a **new-task situation**. In such cases, the greater the cost or risk, the larger the number of decision participants and the greater their efforts to collect information will be. The new-task situation is the marketer's greatest opportunity and challenge. The marketer not only tries to reach as many key buying influences as possible but also provides help and information.

The buyer makes the fewest decisions in the straight rebuy and the most in the new-task decision. In the new-task situation, the buyer must decide on product specifications, suppliers, price limits, payment terms, order quantities, delivery times, and service terms. The order of these decisions varies with each situation, and different decision participants influence each choice.

Many business buyers prefer to buy a packaged solution to a problem from a single seller. Instead of buying and putting all the components together, the buyer may ask sellers to supply the components *and* assemble the package or system. The sale often goes to the firm that provides the most complete system meeting the customer's needs. Thus, **systems selling** is often a key business marketing strategy for winning and holding accounts. For example, ChemStation provides a complete solution for its customers' industrial cleaning problems:

ChemStation sells industrial cleaning chemicals to a wide range of business customers, ranging from car washes to the U.S. Air Force. Whether a customer is washing down a fleet or

■ ChemStation does more than simply supply its customers with cleaning chemicals. "Our customers . . . think of us as more of a partner than a supplier."

Straight rebuy
A business buying situation in which the buyer routinely reorders something without any modifications.

Modified rebuy
A business buying situation in which the buyer wants to modify product specifications, prices, terms, or suppliers.

New-task situation
A business buying situation in which the buyer purchases a product or service for the first time.

Systems selling
Buying a packaged solution to a problem from a single seller, thus avoiding all the separate decisions involved in a complex buying situation.

a factory, a store or a restaurant, a distillery or an Army base, ChemStation comes up with the right cleaning solution every time. It supplies thousands of products in hundreds of industries. But ChemStation does more than just sell chemicals. First, ChemStation works closely with each individual customer to concoct a soap formula specially designed for that customer. It has brewed special formulas for cleaning hands, feathers, eggs, mufflers, flutes, perfume vats, cosmetic eye makeup containers, yacht-making molds, concrete trucks, ocean-going trawlers, and about anything else you can imagine. Next, ChemStation delivers the custom-made mixture to a tank installed at the customer's site. Finally, it maintains the tank by monitoring usage and automatically refilling the tank when supplies run low. Thus, ChemStation sells an entire system for dealing with the customer's special cleaning problems. The company's motto: "Our system is your solution!" Partnering with an individual customer to find a full solution creates a lasting relationship that helps ChemStation to lock out the competition. As noted in a recent issue of *Insights,* ChemStation's customer newsletter, "Our customers . . . oftentimes think of us as more of a partner than a supplier."[38]

Participants in the Business Buying Process Who does the buying of the trillions of dollars' worth of goods and services needed by business organizations? The decision-making unit of a buying organization is called its **buying center**: all the individuals and units that participate in the business decision-making process. The buying center includes all members of the organization who play a role in the purchase decision process. This group includes the actual users of the product or service, those who make the buying decision, those who influence the buying decision, those who do the actual buying, and those who control buying information.

Buying center

All the individuals and units that participate in the business buying decision process.

The buying center is not a fixed and formally identified unit within the buying organization. It is a set of buying roles assumed by different people for different purchases. Within the organization, the size and makeup of the buying center will vary for different products and for different buying situations. For some routine purchases, one person—say a purchasing agent—may assume all the buying center roles and serve as the only person involved in the buying decision. For more complex purchases, the buying center may include 20 or 30 people from different levels and departments in the organization.

The buying center concept presents a major marketing challenge. The business marketer must learn who participates in the decision, each participant's relative influence, and what evaluation criteria each decision participant uses. For example, the medical products and services group of Cardinal Health sells disposable surgical gowns to hospitals. It identifies the hospital personnel involved in this buying decision as the vice president of purchasing, the operating room administrator, and the surgeons. Each participant plays a different role. The vice president of purchasing analyzes whether the hospital should buy disposable gowns or reusable gowns. If analysis favors disposable gowns, then the operating room administrator compares competing products and prices and makes a choice. This administrator considers the gown's absorbency, antiseptic quality, design, and cost, and normally buys the brand that meets requirements at the lowest cost. Finally, surgeons affect the decision later by reporting their satisfaction or dissatisfaction with the brand.

The buying center usually includes some obvious participants who are involved formally in the buying decision. For example, the decision to buy a corporate jet will probably involve the company's CEO, chief pilot, a purchasing agent, some legal staff, a member of top management, and others formally charged with the buying decision. It may also involve less obvious, informal participants, some of

■ Buying Center: Cardinal Health deals with a wide range of buying influences, from purchasing executives and hospital administrators to the surgeons who actually use its products.

whom may actually make or strongly affect the buying decision. Sometimes, even the people in the buying center are not aware of all the buying participants. For example, the decision about which corporate jet to buy may actually be made by a corporate board member who has an interest in flying and who knows a lot about airplanes. This board member may work behind the scenes to sway the decision. Many business buying decisions result from the complex interactions of ever-changing buying center participants.

Major Influences on Business Buyers   Business buyers are subject to many influences when they make their buying decisions. Some marketers assume that the major influences are economic. They think buyers will favor the supplier who offers the lowest price or the best product or the most service. They concentrate on offering strong economic benefits to buyers. However, business buyers actually respond to both economic and personal factors. Far from being cold, calculating, and impersonal, business buyers are human and social as well. They react to both reason and emotion.

Today, most B-to-B marketers recognize that emotion plays an important role in business buying decisions. For example, you might expect that an advertisement promoting large trucks to corporate fleet buyers would stress objective technical, performance, and economic factors. However, a recent ad for Volvo heavy-duty trucks shows two drivers arm-wrestling and claims, "It solves all your fleet problems. Except who gets to drive." It turns out that, in the face of an industry-wide driver shortage, the type of truck a fleet provides can help it to attract qualified drivers. The Volvo ad stresses the raw beauty of the truck and its comfort and roominess, features that make it more appealing to drivers. The ad concludes that Volvo trucks are "built to make fleets more profitable and drivers a lot more possessive."

■ Emotions play an important role in business buying: This Volvo truck ad mentions objective factors, such as efficiency and ease of maintenance. But it stresses more emotional factors such as the raw beauty of the truck and its comfort and roominess, features that make "drivers a lot more possessive."

Figure 5.8 lists various groups of influences on business buyers—environmental, organizational, interpersonal, and individual. *Environmental factors* play a major role. For example, buyer behavior can be heavily influenced by factors in the current and expected economic environment, such as the level of primary demand, the economic outlook, and the cost of money. Another environmental factor is shortages in key materials. Many companies now are more willing to buy and hold larger inventories of scarce materials to ensure adequate supply. Business buyers also are affected by technological, political, and competitive developments in the environment. Finally, culture and customs can strongly influence business buyer reactions to the marketer's behavior and strategies, especially in the international marketing environment (see Marketing at Work 5.2).

FIGURE 5.8   Major Influences on Business Buyer Behavior

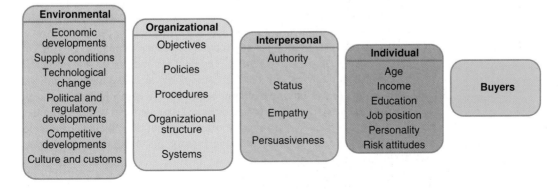

MARKETING AT WORK   5.2

International Marketing Manners: When in Rome, Do as the Romans Do

Picture this: Consolidated Amalgamation, Inc., thinks it's time that the rest of the world enjoyed the same fine products it has offered American consumers for two generations. It dispatches Vice President Harry E. Slicksmile to Europe, Africa, and Asia to explore the territory. Mr. Slicksmile stops first in London, where he makes short work of some bankers—he rings them up on the phone. He handles Parisians with similar ease: After securing a table at La Tour d'Argent, he greets his luncheon guest, the director of an industrial engineering firm, with the words, "Just call me Harry, Jacques."

In Germany, Mr. Slicksmile is a powerhouse. Whisking through a lavish, state-of-the-art marketing presentation, complete with flip charts and audiovisuals, he shows 'em that this Georgia boy *knows* how to make a buck. Heading on to Milan, Harry strikes up a conversation with the Japanese businessman sitting next to him on the plane. He flips his card onto the guy's tray and, when the two say good-bye, shakes hands warmly and clasps the man's right arm. Later, for his appointment with the owner of an Italian packaging design firm, our hero wears his comfy corduroy sport coat, khaki pants, and Topsiders. Everybody knows Italians are zany and laid back.

Mr. Slicksmile next swings through Saudi Arabia, where he coolly presents a potential client with a multimillion-dollar proposal in a classy pigskin binder. His final stop is Beijing, China, where he talks business over lunch with a group of Chinese executives. After completing the meal, he drops his chopsticks into his bowl of rice and presents each guest with an elegant Tiffany's clock as a reminder of his visit.

A great tour, sure to generate a pile of orders, right? Wrong. Six months later, Consolidated Amalgamation has nothing to show for the trip but a stack of bills. Abroad, they weren't wild about Harry.

This hypothetical case has been exaggerated for emphasis. Americans are seldom such dolts. But experts say success in international business has a lot to do with knowing the territory and its people. By learning English and extending themselves in other ways, the world's business leaders have met Americans more than halfway. In contrast, Americans too often do little except assume that others will march to their music. "We want things to be 'American' when we travel. Fast. Convenient. Easy. So we become 'ugly Americans' by demanding that others change," says one American world trade expert. "I think more business would be done if we tried harder."

Poor Harry tried, all right, but in all the wrong ways. The British do not, as a rule, make deals over the phone as much as Americans do. It's not so much a "cultural" difference as a difference in approach. A proper Frenchman neither likes instant familiarity—questions about family, church, or alma mater—nor refers to strangers by their first names. "That poor fellow, Jacques, probably wouldn't show anything, but he'd recoil. He'd *not* be pleased," explains an expert on French business practices. "It's considered poor taste," he continues. "Even after months of business dealings, I'd wait for him or her to make the invitation [to use first names]. . . . You are always right, in Europe, to say 'Mister.' "

Harry's flashy presentation would likely have been a flop with the Germans, who dislike overstatement and showiness. According to one German expert, however, German businessmen have become accustomed to dealing with Americans. Although differences in body language and customs remain, the past 20 years have softened them. "I hugged an American woman at a business meeting last night," he said. "That would be normal in France, but [older] Germans still have difficulty [with the custom]." He says that calling secretaries by their first names

---

Business buyer behavior is also influenced strongly by *organizational factors*. Each buying organization has its own objectives, policies, procedures, structure, and systems, and the business marketer must understand these factors well. Questions such as these arise: How many people are involved in the buying decision? Who are they? What are their evaluative criteria? What are the company's policies and limits on its buyers?

The buying center usually includes many participants who influence each other, so *interpersonal factors* also influence the business buying process. However, it is often difficult to assess such interpersonal factors and group dynamics. Buying center participants do not wear tags that label them as "key decision maker" or "not influential." Nor do buying center participants with the highest rank always have the most influence. Participants may influence the buying decision because they control rewards and punishments, are well liked, have special expertise, or have a special relationship with other important participants. Interpersonal factors are often very subtle. Whenever possible, business marketers must try to understand these factors and design strategies that take them into account.

■ *American companies must help their managers understand international customers and customs. For example, Japanese people revere the business card as an extension of self—they do not hand it out to people, they present it.*

When Harry Slicksmile grabbed his new Japanese acquaintance by the arm, the executive probably considered him disrespectful and presumptuous. Japan, like many Asian countries, is a "no-contact culture" in which even shaking hands is a strange experience. Harry made matters worse by tossing his business card. Japanese people revere the business card as an extension of self and as an indicator of rank. They do not *hand* it to people, they *present* it—with both hands. In addition, the Japanese are sticklers about rank. Unlike Americans, they don't heap praise on subordinates in a room; they will praise only the highest-ranking official present.

Hapless Harry also goofed when he assumed that Italians are like Hollywood's stereotypes of them. The flair for design and style that has characterized Italian culture for centuries is embodied in the businesspeople of Milan and Rome. They dress beautifully and admire flair, but they blanch at garishness or impropriety in others' attire. To the Saudi Arabians, the pigskin binder would have been considered vile. An American salesman who really did present such a binder was unceremoniously tossed out and his company was blacklisted from working with Saudi businesses. In China, Harry's casually dropping his chopsticks could have been misinterpreted as an act of aggression. Stabbing chopsticks

into a bowl of rice and leaving them signifies death to the Chinese. The clocks Harry offered as gifts might have confirmed such dark intentions. To "give a clock" in Chinese sounds the same as "seeing someone off to his end."

Thus, to compete successfully in global markets, or even to deal effectively with international firms in their home markets, companies must help their managers to understand the needs, customs, and cultures of international business buyers. "When doing business in a foreign country and a foreign culture—particularly a non-Western culture—assume nothing," advises an international business specialist. "Take nothing for granted. Turn every stone. Ask every question. Dig into every detail. Because cultures really are different, and those differences can have a major impact." So the old advice is still good advice: When in Rome, do as the Romans do.

Sources: Portions adapted from Susan Harte, "When in Rome, You Should Learn to Do What the Romans Do," *The Atlanta Journal-Constitution,* January 22, 1990, pp. D1, D6. Additional examples can be found in David A. Ricks, *Blunders in International Business Around the World* (Malden, Mass.: Blackwell Publishing, 2000); Terri Morrison, Wayne A. Conway, and Joseph J. Douress, *Dun & Bradstreet's Guide to Doing Business* (Upper Saddle River, N.J.: Prentice Hall, 2000); James K. Sebenius, "The Hidden Challenge of Cross-Border Negotiatons," *Harvard Business Review,* March 2002, pp. 76–85; Ross Thompson, "Lost in Translation," *Medical Marketing and Media,* March 2005, p. 82; and information accessed at www.executiveplanet.com, December 2005.

would still be considered rude: "They have a right to be called by the surname. You'd certainly ask—and get—permission first." In Germany, people address each other formally and correctly—someone with two doctorates (which is fairly common) must be referred to as "Herr Doktor Doktor."

Finally, business buyers are influenced by *individual factors*. Each participant in the business buying decision process brings in personal motives, perceptions, and preferences. These individual factors are affected by personal characteristics such as age, income, education, professional identification, personality, and attitudes toward risk. Also, buyers have different buying styles. Some may be technical types who make in-depth analyses of competitive proposals before choosing a supplier. Other buyers may be intuitive negotiators who are adept at pitting the sellers against one another for the best deal.

The Business Buying Process   Figure 5.9 lists the eight stages of the business buying process.[39] Buyers who face a new-task buying situation usually go through all stages of the buying process. Buyers making modified or straight rebuys may skip some of the stages. We will examine these steps for the typical new-task buying situation.

Problem Recognition.   The buying process begins when someone in the company recognizes a problem or need that can be met by acquiring a specific product or service.

FIGURE 5.9 Stages of the Business Buying Process

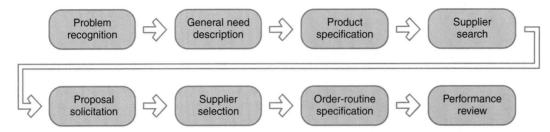

Problem recognition can result from internal or external stimuli. Internally, the company may decide to launch a new product that requires new production equipment and materials. Or a machine may break down and need new parts. Perhaps a purchasing manager is unhappy with a current supplier's product quality, service, or prices. Externally, the buyer may get some new ideas at a trade show, see an ad, or receive a call from a salesperson who offers a better product or a lower price. In fact, in their advertising, business marketers often alert customers to potential problems and then show how their products provide solutions.

General Need Description. Having recognized a need, the buyer next prepares a *general need description* that describes the characteristics and quantity of the needed item. For standard items, this process presents few problems. For complex items, however, the buyer may have to work with others—engineers, users, consultants—to define the item. The team may want to rank the importance of reliability, durability, price, and other attributes desired in the item. In this phase, the alert business marketer can help the buyers define their needs and provide information about the value of different product characteristics.

Value analysis

An approach to cost reduction in which components are studied carefully to determine if they can be redesigned, standardized, or made by less costly methods of production.

Product Specification. The buying organization next develops the item's technical *production specifications,* often with the help of a value analysis engineering team. **Value analysis** is an approach to cost reduction in which components are studied carefully to determine if they can be redesigned, standardized, or made by less costly methods of production. The team decides on the best product characteristics and specifies them accordingly. Sellers, too, can use value analysis as a tool to help secure a new account. By showing buyers a better way to make an object, outside sellers can turn straight rebuy situations into new-task situations that give them a chance to obtain new business.

Supplier Search. The buyer now conducts a *supplier search* to find the best vendors. The buyer can compile a small list of qualified suppliers by reviewing trade directories, doing a computer search, or phoning other companies for recommendations. Today, more companies are turning to the Internet to find suppliers. For marketers, this has leveled the playing field—the Internet gives smaller suppliers many of the same advantages as larger competitors.

The newer the buying task, and the more complex and costly the item, the greater the amount of time the buyer will spend searching for suppliers. The supplier's task is to get listed in major directories and build a good reputation in the marketplace. Salespeople should watch for companies in the process of searching for suppliers and make certain that their firm is considered.

Proposal Solicitation. In the *proposal solicitation* stage of the business buying process, the buyer invites qualified suppliers to submit proposals. In response, some suppliers will send only a catalog or a salesperson. However, when the item is complex or expensive, the buyer will usually require detailed written proposals or formal presentations from each potential supplier.

Business marketers must be skilled in researching, writing, and presenting proposals in response to buyer proposal solicitations. Proposals should be marketing documents, not just technical documents. Presentations should inspire confidence and should make the marketer's company stand out from the competition.

Supplier Selection. The members of the buying center now review the proposals and se-lect a supplier or suppliers. During *supplier selection,* the buying center often will draw up a list of the desired supplier attributes and their relative importance. In one survey, pur-chasing executives listed the following attributes as most important in influencing the rela-tionship between supplier and customer: quality products and services, on-time delivery, ethical corporate behavior, honest communication, and competitive prices. Other important factors include repair and servicing capabilities, technical aid and advice, geographic loca-tion, performance history, and reputation. The members of the buying center will rate sup-pliers against these attributes and identify the best suppliers.

Buyers may attempt to negotiate with preferred suppliers for better prices and terms before making the final selections. In the end, they may select a single supplier or a few suppliers. Many buyers prefer multiple sources of supplies to avoid being totally dependent on one supplier and to allow comparisons of prices and performance of several suppliers over time. Today's supplier development managers want to develop a full network of supplier-partners that can help the company bring more value to its customers.

Order-Routine Specification. The buyer now prepares an *order-routine specification.* It includes the final order with the chosen supplier or suppliers and lists items such as tech-nical specifications, quantity needed, expected time of delivery, return policies, and war-ranties. In the case of maintenance, repair, and operating items, buyers may use blanket contracts rather than periodic purchase orders. A blanket contract creates a long-term rela-tionship in which the supplier promises to resupply the buyer as needed at agreed prices for a set time period.

Many large buyers now practice *vendor-managed inventory,* in which they turn over ordering and inventory responsibilities to their suppliers. Under such systems, buyers share sales and inventory information directly with key suppliers. The suppliers then mon-itor inventories and replenish stock automatically as needed.

Performance Review. In this stage, the buyer reviews supplier performance. The buyer may contact users and ask them to rate their satisfaction. The *performance review* may lead the buyer to continue, modify, or drop the arrangement. The seller's job is to moni-tor the same factors used by the buyer to make sure that the seller is giving the expected satisfaction.

The eight-stage buying-process model provides a simple view of the business buying as it might occur in a new-task buying situation. The actual process is usually much more complex. In the modified rebuy or straight rebuy situation, some of these stages would be compressed or bypassed. Each organization buys in its own way, and each buying situation has unique requirements.

Different buying center participants may be involved at different stages of the process. Although certain buying-process steps usually do occur, buyers do not always follow them in the same order, and they may add other steps. Often, buyers will repeat certain stages of the process. Finally, a customer relationship might involve many different types of pur-chases ongoing at a given time, all in different stages of the buying process. The seller must manage the total customer relationship, not just individual purchases.

E-Procurement: Buying Electronically and on the Internet

During the past few years, advances in information technology have changed the face of the business-to-business marketing process. Electronic and online purchasing, often called *e-procurement,* have grown rapidly.

Companies can do e-procurement in any of several ways. They can set up their own *company buying sites.* For example, General Electric operates a company trading site on which it posts its buying needs and invites bids, negotiates terms, and places orders. Or the company can create extranet links with key suppliers. For instance, they can create direct procurement accounts with suppliers like Dell or Office Depot through which company buyers can purchase equipment, materials, and supplies.

■ To help customers who wish to purchase online, HP's Web site consists of some 1,500 site areas and 1 million pages. It provides product overviews, detailed technical information, purchasing solutions, e-newsletters, live chats with sales reps, online classes, and real-time customer support.

B-to-B marketers can help customers who wish to purchase online by creating well designed, easy-to-use Web sites. For example, *BtoB* magazine regularly rates Hewlett-Packard's B-to-B Web site among very best.

The HP site consists of some 1,500 site areas and 1 million pages. It integrates an enormous amount of product and company information, putting it within only a few mouse clicks of a customers' computer. IT buying-decision makers can enter the site, click directly into their customer segment—large enterprise business; small or medium business; or government, health, or educational institution—and quickly find product overviews, detailed technical information, and purchasing solutions. The site lets customers create customized catalogs for frequently purchased products, set up automatic approval routing for orders, and conduct end-to-end transaction processing. To build deeper, more personalized online relationships with customers, HP.com features flash demos that show how to use the site, e-newsletters, live chats with sales reps, online classes, and real-time customer support. The site has really paid off. Roughly 55 percent of the company's total sales now come from the Web site.[40]

E-procurement gives buyers access to new suppliers, lowers purchasing costs, and hastens order processing and delivery. In turn, business marketers can connect with customers online to share marketing information, sell products and services, provide customer support services, and maintain ongoing customer relationships.

So far, most of the products bought online are MRO materials—maintenance, repair, and operations. For instance, Los Angeles County purchases everything from chickens to lightbulbs over the Internet. National Semiconductor has automated almost all of the company's 3,500 monthly requisitions to buy materials ranging from the sterile booties worn in its fabrication plants to state-of-the-art software. General Electric, one of the world's biggest purchasers, plans to be buying *all* of its general operating and industrial supplies online within the next few years.

The actual dollar amount spent on these types of MRO materials pales in comparison to the amount spent for items such as airplane parts, computer systems, and steel tubing. Yet, MRO materials make up 80 percent of all business orders and the transaction costs for order processing are high. Thus, companies have much to gain by streamlining the MRO buying process on the Web.

Business-to-business e-procurement yields many benefits. First, it shaves transaction costs and results in more efficient purchasing for both buyers and suppliers. A Web-powered purchasing program eliminates the paperwork associated with traditional requisition and ordering procedures. One recent study found that e-procurement cuts down requisition-to-order costs by an average of 58 percent.[41]

E-procurement reduces the time between order and delivery. Time savings are particularly dramatic for companies with many overseas suppliers. Adaptec, a leading supplier of computer storage, used an extranet to tie all of its Taiwanese chip suppliers together in a kind of virtual family. Now messages from Adaptec flow in seconds from its headquarters to its Asian partners, and Adaptec has reduced the time between the order and delivery of its chips from as long as 16 weeks to just 55 days—the same turnaround time for companies that build their own chips.

Finally, beyond the cost and time savings, e-procurement frees purchasing people to focus on more-strategic issues. For many purchasing professionals, going online means reducing drudgery and paperwork and spending more time managing inventory and working creatively with suppliers. "That is the key," says the HP executive. "You can now focus people on value-added activities. Procurement professionals can now find different sources and work with suppliers to reduce costs and to develop new products."[42]

The rapidly expanding use of e-purchasing, however, also presents some problems. For example, at the same time that the Web makes it possible for suppliers and customers to share business data and even collaborate on product design, it can also erode decades-old customer-supplier relationships. Many firms are using the Web to search for better suppliers.

E-purchasing can also create potential security disasters. Although e-mail and home banking transactions can be protected through basic encryption, the secure environment that businesses need to carry out confidential interactions is often still lacking. Companies are spending millions for research on defensive strategies to keep hackers at bay. Cisco Systems, for example, specifies the types of routers, firewalls, and security procedures that its partners must use to safeguard extranet connections. In fact, the company goes even further—it sends its own security engineers to examine a partner's defenses and holds the partner liable for any security breach that originates from its computer.

REST STOP → REVIEWING THE CONCEPTS

This chapter is the last of three chapters that address understanding the marketplace and consumers. Here, we've looked closely at consumers and their buying behavior. The American consumer market consists of more than 295 million people who consume many trillions of dollars' worth of goods and services each year. The business market involves far more dollars and items than the consumer market. Final consumers and business buyers vary greatly in their characteristics and circumstances. Understanding *consumer* and *business buyer behavior* is one of the biggest challenges marketers face.

1. Describe the consumer market and the major factors that influence consumer buyer behavior.

The *consumer market* consists of all the individuals and households who buy or acquire goods and services for personal consumption. A simple stimulus-response model of consumer behavior suggests that marketing stimuli and other major forces enter the consumer's "black box." This black box has two parts: buyer characteristics and the buyer's decision process. Once in the black box, the inputs result in observable buyer responses, such as product choice, brand choice, dealer choice, purchase timing, and purchase amount.

Consumer buyer behavior is influenced by four key sets of buyer characteristics: cultural, social, personal, and psychological. Understanding these factors can help marketers to identify interested buyers and to shape products and appeals to serve consumer needs better. *Culture* is the most basic determinant of a person's wants and behavior. People in different cultural, subcultural, and social class groups have different product and brand preferences. *Social factors*—such as small group and family influences—strongly affect product

and brand choices, as do *personal characteristics,* such as age, life-cycle stage, occupation, economic circumstances, lifestyle, and personality. Finally, consumer buying behavior is influenced by four major sets of *psychological factors*—motivation, perception, learning, and beliefs and attitudes. Each of these factors provides a different perspective for understanding the workings of the buyer's black box.

2. Identify and discuss the stages in the buyer decision process.

When making a purchase, the buyer goes through a decision process consisting of need recognition, information search, evaluation of alternatives, purchase decision, and postpurchase behavior. During *need recognition,* the consumer recognizes a problem or need that could be satisfied by a product or service. Once the need is recognized, the consumer moves into the *information search* stage. With information in hand, the consumer proceeds to *alternative evaluation* and assesses brands in the choice set. From there, the consumer makes a *purchase decision* and actually buys the product. In the final stage of the buyer decision process, *postpurchase behavior,* the consumer takes action based on satisfaction or dissatisfaction. The marketer's job is to understand the buyer's behavior at each stage and the influences that are operating.

3. Describe the adoption and diffusion process for new products.

The product *adoption process* is comprised of five stages: awareness, interest, evaluation, trial, and adoption. New-product marketers must think about how to help consumers move through these stages. With regard to the *diffusion process* for new products, consumers respond at different rates, depending on consumer and product characteristics. Consumers may be innovators, early adopters, early majority, late majority, or laggards. Each group may require different marketing approaches. Marketers often try to bring their new products to the attention of potential early adopters, especially those who are opinion leaders.

4. Define the business market and identify the major factors that influence business buyer behavior.

The *business market* comprises all organizations that buy goods and services for use in the production of other products and services or for the purpose of reselling or renting them to others at a profit. As compared to consumer markets, business markets usually have fewer, larger buyers who are more geographically concentrated. Business demand is derived demand, and the business buying decision usually involves more, and more professional, buyers.

Business buyers make decisions that vary with the three types of *buying situations:* straight rebuys, modified rebuys, and new tasks. The decision-making unit of a buying organization—the *buying center*—can consist of many different persons playing many different roles. The business marketer needs to know the following: Who are the major buying center participants? In what decisions do they exercise influence and to what degree? What evaluation criteria does each decision participant use? The business marketer also needs to understand the major environ-mental, organizational, interpersonal, and individual influences on the buying process.

5. List and define the steps in the business buying decision process.

The *business buying decision process* itself can be quite involved, with eight basic stages: problem recognition, general need description, product specification, supplier search, proposal solicitation, supplier selection, order-routine specification, and performance review. Buyers who face a new-task buying situation usually go through all stages of the buying process. Buyers making modified or straight rebuys may skip some of the stages. Companies must manage the overall customer relationship, which often includes many different buying decisions in various stages of the buying decision process.

Recent advances in information technology have given birth to "e-purchasing," by which business buyers are purchasing all kinds of products and services electronically, either through electronic data interchange links (EDI) or on the Internet. Such cyberbuying gives buyers access to new suppliers, lowers purchasing costs, and hastens order processing and delivery. However, it can also erode customer-supplier relationships and create potential security problems. Still, business marketers are increasingly connecting with customers online to share marketing information, sell products and services, provide customer support services, and maintain ongoing customer relationships.

Navigating the Key Terms

Adoption process (146)	Group (133)	Perception (139)
Business buyer behavior (149)	Learning (140)	Personality (137)
Buying center (152)	Lifestyle (136)	Social class (132)
Cognitive dissonance (144)	Modified rebuy (151)	Straight rebuy (151)
Consumer buyer behavior (128)	Motive (or drive) (138)	Subculture (130)
Consumer market (128)	New product (146)	Systems selling (151)
Culture (129)	New-task situation (151)	Value analysis (156)
Derived demand (149)	Opinion leader (133)	

Travel Log

Discussing the Issues

1. Describe how subculture and social class can influence a consumer's choice of an automobile. Which of these two influences is likely to have the largest influence? Select three personal factors from those discussed in the chapter. How might each of these factors influence the same decision?

2. Name and describe an opinion leader, either in the public eye or someone you know personally. How has that person affected your decisions to buy products or services?

3. Think about a new type of product you have recently purchased. Discuss how you proceeded through the five stages of the product adoption process. Did you skip any stages? Were any of the stages in a different order from that presented in the text? How could the manufacturer have managed the decision process to build a stronger relationship with you?

4. How might a marketer influence a consumer's information search through each of the four sources discussed in the chapter? Which source do you think

marketers should focus on to build long-term relationships with customers?

5. Discuss how business buyer behavior is different from consumer buyer behavior. What does this mean for a company attempting to sell goods to other organizations?

6. List and explain three benefits and three drawbacks of e-procurement.

Application Questions

1. Go to SRI Consulting's Web site (www.sric-bi.com/VALS/presurvey.shtml) and complete the VALS survey online. How accurately are you described by your primary and secondary VALS types? Do you think you will be in a different VALS category in 5 to 10 years?

How could a realtor use your VALS classification to build a stronger relationship with you and to sell or rent you a home?

2. Review the five adopter categories discussed in the chapter. How might Apple position its video iPod differently to appeal to consumers in each of the five adopter categories? Which group do you think would be the most interested? Which group might be the most profitable?

3. Suppose that you own a small business that provides PC repair services to local businesses. In addition to the basic fix-it services you now provide, you are thinking about offering new services. Applying the "systems-selling" concept, what additional services could you offer that would make a complete package or systems solution for your customers?

Under the Hood: Focus on Technology

This chapter discusses consumer and business buyer behavior—how they are similar and how they differ. Although these similarities and differences may be noticeable throughout the marketplace, they are, perhaps, most noticeable on the Web. Visit and investigate the corporate Web sites for Dow Chemical (www.dow.com) and for Kellogg's (www.kelloggs.com).

1. How are the Web sites different? How are they similar? What types of information are presented on both Web sites?

2. Who is each Web site designed for?

3. Is it clear which buyers each targets? How well does each Web site communicate with its intended audience? Which Web site most appeals to you?

Focus on Ethics

For many marketers, winning over opinion leaders—people within a reference group who exert influence on others—is the key to creating buzz about their products. According to a recent study, "one American in ten tells the other nine how to vote, where to eat, and what to buy. They are *the influentials*. They drive trends, influence mass opinion and, most importantly, sell a great many products." As discussed in the chapter, some marketers leave nothing to chance. They employ opinion leaders to tout the benefits of their products by chatting with consumers at bars, ballgames, and laundromats across the country.*

1. Is it ethical for marketers to *create* opinion leaders by paying them to act as impartial consumers? How might doing so impact the relationships a company builds with its customers?

2. Would you consider working for BzzAgent? Does their approach differ from that of firms like Big Fat Promotions? Is the approach more or less ethical?

*See Edward Keller and Jonathan Berry, *The Influentials* (New York: The Free Press, 2003); and information found at www.amazon.com, July 2005.

Videos

The Eaton video case that accompanies this chapter is located in Appendix 1.

AFTER STUDYING THIS CHAPTER, YOU SHOULD BE ABLE TO

1. define the three steps of target marketing: market segmentation, target marketing, and market positioning

2. list and discuss the major bases for segmenting consumer and business markets

3. explain how companies identify attractive market segments and choose a target marketing strategy

4. discuss how companies position their products for maximum competitive advantage in the marketplace

Segmentation, Targeting, and Positioning: Building the Right Relationships with the Right Customers

Road Map Previewing the Concepts

So far, you've learned what marketing is and about the importance of understanding consumers and the marketplace environment. With that as background, you're now ready to delve deeper into marketing strategy and tactics. This chapter looks further into key marketing strategy decisions— how to divide up markets into meaningful customer groups (market segmentation), choose which customer groups to serve (target marketing), and create market offerings that best serve targeted customers (positioning). Then, the chapters that follow explore the tactical marketing tools—the Four Ps—by which marketers bring these strategies to life.

As an opening example of segmentation, targeting, and position at work, let's look first at Procter & Gamble, one of the world's premier consumer goods companies. Some 99 percent of all U.S. households use at least one of P&G's more than 300 brands, and the typical household regularly buys and uses from one to two *dozen* P&G brands. But why does this superb marketer compete with itself on supermarket shelves by marketing seven different brands of laundry detergent? The P&G story provides a great example of how smart marketers use segmentation, targeting, and positioning.

Procter & Gamble (P&G) sells six brands of laundry detergent in the United States (Tide, Cheer, Gain, Era, Dreft, and Ivory Snow). It also sells six brands of bath soap (Ivory, Safeguard, Camay, Olay, Zest, and Old Spice); nine brands of shampoo (Pantene, Head & Shoulders, Aussie, Herbal Essences, Daily Defense, Infusium 23, Pert Plus, Physique, and Vidal Sassoon); four brands of dishwashing detergent (Dawn, Ivory, Joy, and Cascade); three brands each of tissues and towels (Charmin, Bounty, and Puffs), and deodorant (Secret, Sure, and Old Spice); and two brands each of fabric softener (Downy and Bounce), cosmetics (Cover Girl and Max Factor), skin care potions (Olay and Noxzema), and disposable diapers (Pampers and Luvs). Moreover, P&G has many additional brands in each category for different international markets. For example, it sells 16 different laundry product brands in Latin America and 19 in Europe, the Middle East, and Africa. (See Procter & Gamble's Web site at www.pg.com for a full glimpse of the company's impressive lineup of familiar brands.)

These P&G brands compete with one another on the same supermarket shelves. But why would P&G introduce several brands in one category instead of concentrating its resources on a single leading brand? The answer lies in the fact that different people want different *mixes of benefits* from the products they buy. Take laundry detergents as an example. People use laundry detergents to get their clothes clean. But they also want other things from their detergents—such as economy, strength or mildness, bleaching power, fabric softening, fresh smell, and lots of suds or only a few. We all want *some* of every one of these benefits from our detergent, but we may have different *priorities* for each benefit. To some people, cleaning and bleaching power are most important; to others, fabric softening matters most; still others want a mild, fresh-scented detergent. Thus, there are groups—or segments—of laundry detergent buyers, and each segment seeks a special combination of benefits.

Procter & Gamble has identified at least six important laundry detergent segments, along with numerous subsegments, and has developed a different brand designed to meet the special needs of each. The six brands are positioned for different segments as follows:

- *Tide* provides "fabric cleaning and care at its best." It's the all-purpose family detergent that "helps keep everyday laundry looking clean and new."
- *Cheer* is the "color expert." It helps protect against fading, color transfer, and fabric wear, with or without bleach. *Cheer Free* is "dermatologist tested . . . contains no irritating perfume or dye."
- *Gain*, originally P&G's "enzyme" detergent, was repositioned as the detergent that gives you "great cleaning power and the smell that says clean." It "cleans and freshens like sunshine."
- *Era* is the detergent that "provides powerful stain removal and pretreating for physically active families." It contains advanced enzymes to fight a family's tough stains and helps get the whole wash clean. *Era Max* has three types of active enzymes to help fight many stains that active families encounter.
- *Ivory Snow* is "Ninety-nine and forty-four one hundredths percent pure." It provides "mild cleansing benefits for a pure and simple clean."
- *Dreft* is specially formulated "To help clean tough baby and toddler stains." It "rinses thoroughly, leaving all baby laundry feeling soft and comfortable against delicate skin."

Within each segment, Procter & Gamble has identified even *narrower* niches. For example, you can buy regular Tide (in powder or liquid form) or any of several formulations:

- *Tide Powder* helps keep everyday laundry clean and new. It comes in regular and special scents: *Tide Mountain Spring* "the scent of crisp mountain air and fresh wildflowers"; *Tide Clean Breeze* (the fresh scent of laundry line-dried in a clean breeze); *Tide Tropical Clean* (a fresh tropical scent); and *Tide Free* "has no scent at all—leaves out the dyes or perfumes."
- *Tide Liquid* combines all the great stain-fighting qualities you've come to expect in Tide powder with the pretreating ease of a liquid detergent. Available in regular and mountain spring, clean breeze, tropical clean, and free scents.
- *Tide with Bleach* helps to "clean even the dirtiest laundry." Keeps "your family's whites white and colors bright." Available in regular, clean breeze, or mountain spring scents.
- *Tide Liquid with Bleach Alternative* is the "smart alternative to chlorine bleach." It uses active enzymes in pretreating and washing to break down and remove the toughest stains while whitening whites.
- *Tide Rapid Action Tabs* offer portable cleaning power for a convenient way to get your clothes Tide clean.
- *Tide with a Touch of Downy* provides "outstanding Tide clean with a touch of Downy softness and freshness." Available in April fresh, clean breeze, and soft ocean mist scents.
- *Tide Coldwater* is specially formulated to help reduce your energy bills by delivering outstanding cleaning, even on the toughest stains, in cold water. Available in both liquid and powder formulas and in two new cool scents—fresh scent and glacier.

By segmenting the market and having several detergent brands, P&G has an attractive offering for consumers in all important preference groups. As a result, P&G is really cleaning up in the more than $4 billion U.S. laundry detergent market. Tide, by itself, captures 34 percent and 24 percent market shares in the powder and liquid detergent markets, respectively. All P&G brands combined take a whopping 75 percent market share in powder laundry detergent and 55 percent market share in liquids—more than three times that of nearest rival Unilever and much more than any single brand could obtain by itself.[1]

Companies today recognize that they cannot appeal to all buyers in the marketplace, or at least not to all buyers in the same way. Buyers are too numerous, too widely scattered, and too varied in their needs and buying practices. Moreover, the companies themselves vary widely in their abilities to serve different segments of the market. Instead, a company must identify the parts of the market that it can serve best and most profitably. It needs to design strategies to build the *right* relationships with the *right* customers.

Thus, most companies are being choosier about the customers with whom they wish to build relationships. Most have moved away from mass marketing and toward *market segmentation and targeting*—identifying market segments, selecting one or more of them, and developing products and marketing programs tailored to each. Instead of scattering their marketing efforts (the "shotgun" approach), firms are focusing on the buyers who have greater interest in the values they create best (the "rifle" approach).

Figure 6.1 shows the three major steps in target marketing. The first is **market segmentation**—dividing a market into smaller groups of buyers with distinct needs, characteristics, or behaviors who might require separate products or marketing mixes. The company identifies different ways to segment the market and develops profiles of the resulting market segments. The second step is **target marketing**—evaluating each market segment's attractiveness and selecting one or more of the market segments to enter. The third step is **market positioning**—setting the competitive positioning for the product and creating a detailed marketing mix. We discuss each of these steps in turn.

Market Segmentation

Markets consist of buyers, and buyers differ in one or more ways. They may differ in their wants, resources, locations, buying attitudes, and buying practices. Through market segmentation, companies divide large, heterogeneous markets into smaller segments that can be reached more efficiently and effectively with products and services that match their unique needs. In this section, we discuss four important segmentation topics: segmenting consumer markets, segmenting business markets, segmenting international markets, and requirements for effective segmentation.

SEGMENTING CONSUMER MARKETS

There is no single way to segment a market. A marketer has to try different segmentation variables, alone and in combination, to find the best way to view the market structure. Table 6.1 outlines the major variables that might be used in segmenting consumer markets. Here we look at the major *geographic*, *demographic*, *psychographic*, and *behavioral* variables.

Geographic Segmentation **Geographic segmentation** calls for dividing the market into different geographical units such as nations, regions, states, counties, cities, or even neighborhoods. A company may decide to operate in one or a few geographical areas, or to operate in all areas but pay attention to geographical differences in needs and wants.

Many companies today are localizing their products, advertising, promotion, and sales efforts to fit the needs of individual regions, cities, and even neighborhoods. For example, Campbell sells Cajun gumbo soup in Louisiana and Mississippi and makes its nacho cheese soup spicier in Texas and California. Starbucks offers more desserts and larger, more comfortable coffee shops in the South, where customers tend to arrive later in the day and stay longer. And Parker Brothers offers localized versions of its popular Monopoly game for several major cities, including Chicago, New York, San Diego, and Las Vegas. The Las Vegas version features a black board with The Strip (rather than Boardwalk), hotel casinos, red Vegas dice, and custom pewter tokens including blackjack cards, a wedding chapel, and a roulette wheel.

Other companies are seeking to cultivate as-yet untapped geographic territory. For example, many large companies are fleeing the fiercely competitive major cities and

Market segmentation
Dividing a market into distinct groups with distinct needs, characteristics, or behaviors who might require separate products or marketing mixes.

Target marketing
The process of evaluating each market segment's attractiveness and selecting one or more segments to enter.

Market positioning
Arranging for a product to occupy a clear, distinctive, and desirable place relative to competing products in the minds of target consumers.

Geographic segmentation
Dividing a market into different geographical units such as nations, states, regions, counties, cities, or neighborhoods.

Market segmentation	Target marketing	Market positioning
Identify bases for segmenting the market	Develop measure of segment attractiveness	Develop positioning for target segments
Develop segment profiles	Select target segments	Develop a marketing mix for each segment

FIGURE 6.1
Steps in Market Segmentation, Targeting, and Positioning

TABLE 6.1

Major Segmentation Variables for Consumer Markets

Geographic	
World region or country	North America, Western Europe, Middle East, Pacific Rim, China, India, Canada, Mexico
Country region	Pacific, Mountain, West North Central, West South Central, East North Central, East South Central, South Atlantic, Middle Atlantic, New England
City or metro size	Under 5,000; 5,000–20,000; 20,000–50,000; 50,000–100,000; 100,000–250,000; 250,000–500,000; 500,000–1,000,000; 1,000,000–4,000,000; over 4,000,000
Density	Urban, suburban, rural
Climate	Northern, southern
Demographic	
Age	Under 6, 6–11, 12–19, 20–34, 35–49, 50–64, 65+
Gender	Male, female
Family size	1–2, 3–4, 5+
Family life-cycle	Young, single; young, married, no children; young, married with children; older, married with children; older, married, no children under 18; older, single; other
Income	Under $10,000; $10,000–$20,000; $20,000–$30,000; $30,000–$50,000; $50,000–$100,000; $100,000 and over
Occupation	Professional and technical; managers, officials, and proprietors; clerical; sales; craftspeople; supervisors; operatives; farmers; retired; students; homemakers; unemployed
Education	Grade school or less; some high school; high school graduate; some college; college graduate
Religion	Catholic, Protestant, Jewish, Muslim, Hindu, other
Race	Asian, Hispanic, Black, White
Generation	Baby boomer, Generation X, Generation Y
Nationality	North American, South American, British, French, German, Italian, Japanese
Psychographic	
Social class	Lower lowers, upper lowers, working class, middle class, upper middles, lower uppers, upper uppers
Lifestyle	Achievers, strivers, survivors
Personality	Compulsive, gregarious, authoritarian, ambitious
Behavioral	
Occasions	Regular occasion; special occasion
Benefits	Quality, service, economy, convenience, speed
User status	Nonuser, ex-user, potential user, first-time user, regular user
User rates	Light user, medium user, heavy user
Loyalty status	None, medium, strong, absolute
Readiness stage	Unaware, aware, informed, interested, desirous, intending to buy
Attitude toward product	Enthusiastic, positive, indifferent, negative, hostile

suburbs to set up shop in small-town America. Consider Applebee's, the nation's largest casual-dining chain:

> Applebee's is now making sure that even far-flung suburbs and small towns can have a neighborhood bar and grill. It's extending into rural counties of 50,000 people or fewer, breaking down the misconception that rural Americans aren't interested in anything that can't be bought at Wal-Mart (or its restaurant equivalent). How's the strategy working? Just check out the dozen or more parties lined up on a typical Friday night outside the Applebee's in Hays, Kansas, a small town of 21,000 people located in an area known as "the middle of nowhere" between Denver and Kansas City. Although sales in such smaller communities average 10 percent less than at a

suburban Applebee's, that's offset by cheaper real estate and less-complicated zoning laws. And there is no real casual-dining competition in Hays. No Chili's. No Houlihan's. Not even a Bennigan's. "If you want to take someone out on a date," says one young diner, "you're not going to take them to the Golden Corral," an all-you-can-eat family restaurant next door. That's a telling statement, given that the young man is a management trainee at the Golden Corral. So far, Applebee's has opened some 150 small-town restaurants. Considering that there are about 2,200 counties in the United States with populations under 50,000, it has a lot more room to grow.[2]

In contrast, other retailers are developing new store concepts that will give them access to higher-density urban areas. For example, Home Depot is introducing neighborhood stores that look a lot like its traditional stores but at about two-thirds the size. It is placing these stores in high-density markets, such as Manhattan, where full-size stores are impractical. Similarly, Wal-Mart is opening small, supermarket-style Neighborhood Market grocery stores to complement its supercenters.[3]

Demographic Segmentation   **Demographic segmentation** divides the market into groups based on variables such as age, gender, family size, family life cycle, income, occupation, education, religion, race, generation, and nationality. Demographic factors are the most popular bases for segmenting customer groups. One reason is that consumer needs, wants, and usage rates often vary closely with demographic variables. Another is that demographic variables are easier to measure than most other types of variables. Even when market segments are first defined using other bases, such as benefits sought or behavior, their demographic characteristics must be known in order to assess the size of the target market and to reach it efficiently.

Age and Life-Cycle Stage.   Consumer needs and wants change with age. Some companies use **age and life-cycle segmentation**, offering different products or using different marketing approaches for different age and life-cycle groups. For example, for kids, P&G sells Crest SpinBrushes featuring favorite children's characters. For adults, it sells more serious models, promising "a dentist-clean feeling twice a day." And Gap has branched out to target people at different ages and life stages. In addition to its standard line of clothing, the retailer now offers babyGap, GapKids, GapBody, and GapMaternity.

Marketers must be careful to guard against stereotypes when using age and life-cycle segmentation. For example, although some 70-year-olds require wheelchairs, others play tennis. Similarly, whereas some 40-year-old couples are sending their children off to college, others are just beginning new families. Thus, age is often a poor predictor of a person's life

Demographic segmentation
Dividing the market into groups based on demographic variables such as age, sex, family size, family life cycle, income, occupation, education, religion, race, and nationality.

Age and life-cycle segmentation
Dividing a market into different age and life-cycle groups.

■ Age and life-cycle segmentation: For kids, P&G sells Crest SpinBrushes featuring favorite children's characters. For adults, it sells more serious models, promising "a dentist-clean feeling twice a day."

cycle, health, work or family status, needs, and buying power. Companies marketing to mature consumers usually employ positive images and appeals. For example, ads for Olay ProVital—designed to improve the elasticity and appearance of the "maturing skin" of women over 50—feature attractive older spokeswomen and uplifting messages.

Gender segmentation

Dividing a market into different groups based on gender.

Gender. **Gender segmentation** has long been used in clothing, cosmetics, toiletries, and magazines. For example, Procter & Gamble was among the first with Secret, a brand specially formulated for a woman's chemistry, packaged and advertised to reinforce the female image. More recently, other marketers have noticed opportunities for targeting women. Citibank launched Women & Co., a financial program created around the distinct financial needs of women. Leatherman, which has traditionally targeted its multipurpose combination tool to men, now makes Leatherman Juice for women, hip and stylish tools offered in five vibrant colors.

Nike has recently stepped up its efforts to capture the women's sports apparel market. It wasn't until 2000 that Nike made women's shoes using molds made from women's feet, rather than simply using a small man's foot mold. Since then, however, Nike has changed its approach to women. It has overhauled its women's apparel line—called NikeWomen—to create better fitting, more colorful, more fashionable workout clothes for women. Its revamped NikeWomen.com Web site now features the apparel, along with workout trend highlights. And Nike is opening NikeWomen stores in several major cities.[4]

A growing number of Web sites also target women, such as iVillage, Oxygen, Lifetime, and WE. For example, iVillage (www.iVillage.com), the leading women's online community, offers "real solutions for real women" and entreats visitors to "join our community of smart, compassionate, real women." Various iVillage channels cover topics ranging from babies, food, fitness, pets, and relationships to careers, finance, and travel.[5]

Income segmentation

Dividing a market into different income groups.

Income. **Income segmentation** has long been used by the marketers of products and services such as automobiles, boats, clothing, cosmetics, financial services, and travel. Many companies target affluent consumers with luxury goods and convenience services. Stores such as Neiman Marcus pitch everything from expensive jewelry and fine fashions to glazed Australian apricots priced at $20 a pound. And credit-card companies offer elite credit cards dripping with perks (see Marketing at Work 6.1).

To cater to its very best customers, Neiman Marcus created its InCircle Rewards program:

InCircle members, who must spend $3,000 a year using their Neiman Marcus credit cards to be eligible, earn points with each purchase—one point for each dollar charged. They then cash in points for anything from tea for two at the Plaza Athénée in New York City (5,000 points) or a Sony Network Walkman (15,000 points) to three nights in a premier room at the Lake Austin Spa Resort

■ Gender segmentation: Nike has recently stepped up its efforts to capture the women's sports apparel market by overhauling its women's apparel lines, revamping the NikeWomen.com Web site, and opening NikeWomen stores in several major cities.

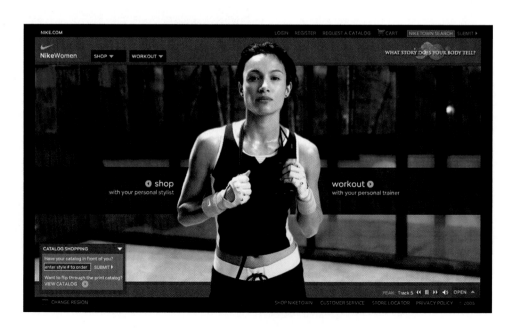

in Texas, including gourmet meals, monogrammed robes, and a spa treatment for each guest (50,000 points). For 500,000 points, InCircle members can get a $12,500 Neiman Marcus gift card and for 1.5 million points, a six night journey on a hotel barge in the French countryside, which holds up to six passengers. One of the top prizes (for 5 million points!) is a top-of-the-line Sony Home Theater, which includes a Qualia 004 projector, audio-video controls for multiple rooms, keypads in the walls, and a wireless remote to control the lights.[6]

However, not all companies that use income segmentation target the affluent. For example, many retailers—such as the Dollar General, Family Dollar, and Dollar Tree store chains—successfully target low- and middle-income groups. More than half the sales in such stores come from shoppers with family incomes under $25,000. By comparison, the typical Wal-Mart shopper has an income over $40,000. When Family Dollar real-estate experts scout locations for new stores, they look for lower-middle-class neighborhoods where people wear less expensive shoes and drive old cars that drip a lot of oil.

With their low-income strategies, the dollar stores are now the fastest growing retailers in the nation. They have been so successful that giant discounters such as Wal-Mart and Target are now taking notice. Wal-Mart is testing "Pennies-n-Cents" sections in 20 Supercenters, and Target is trying out "The 1 Spot" in 125 of its stores. "They are a major threat," says a retailing expert, "so much so that Wal-Mart will eventually have to buy one of these chains or start one."[7]

Psychographic Segmentation   **Psychographic segmentation** divides buyers into different groups based on social class, lifestyle, or personality characteristics. People in the same demographic group can have very different psychographic makeups.

In Chapter 5, we discussed how the products people buy reflect their *lifestyles*. As a result, marketers often segment their markets by consumer lifestyles. For example, consider home furnishings retailer Pottery Barn:[8]

Psychographic segmentation
Dividing a market into different groups based on social class, lifestyle, or personality characteristics.

Shortly after Hadley MacLean got married, she and her husband, Doug, agreed that their old bed had to go. It was a mattress and box spring on a cheap metal frame, a relic of Doug's Harvard days. But Hadley never anticipated how tough it would be to find a new bed. "We couldn't find anything we liked, even though we were willing to spend the money," says Hadley, a 31-year-old marketing director. It turned out to be much more than just finding a piece of furniture at the right price. It was a matter of emotion: They needed a bed that meshed with their lifestyle—with who they are and where they are going. The couple finally ended up at the Pottery Barn on Boston's upscale Newbury Street, where Doug fell in love with a mahogany sleigh bed that Hadley had spotted in the store's catalog. The couple was so pleased with how great it looked in their Dutch Colonial home that they hurried back to the store for a set of end tables. And then they bought a quilt. And a mirror for the living room. And some stools for the dining room. "We got kind of addicted," Hadley confesses. Thus, Pottery Barn sells more than just home furnishings. It sells all that its customers aspire to be. It offers idyllic scenes of the perfect childhood at Pottery Barn Kids; trendy fashion-forward self-expression at PB Teens; and an upscale yet casual, family- and friend-focused lifestyle—affluent but sensibly so—at its flagship Pottery Barn stores.

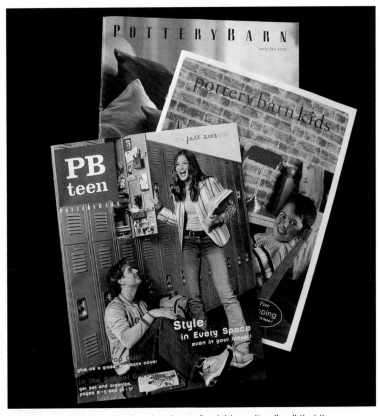

■ Pottery Barn sells more than just home furnishings; it sells all that its customers aspire to be. It offers idyllic scenes of the perfect childhood at Pottery Barn Kids; trendy, fashion-forward self-expression at PB Teen; and an upscale yet casual, family- and friend-focused lifestyle at its flagship Pottery Barn stores.

MARKETING AT WORK 6.1
Marketing Upscale: Coddling the Well-Heeled

Some companies go to extremes to coddle big spenders. From department stores like Nordstrom, to carmakers like Lexus and BMW, to hotels like Ritz-Carlton and Four Seasons, such companies give their well-heeled customers exactly what they need—and even more.

For example, concierge services are no longer the sole province of five-star hotels and fancy credit cards. They are starting to show up at airlines, retailers, and even electronic-goods makers. Sony Electronics, for instance, offers a service for its wealthiest customers, called Cierge, that provides a free personal shopper and early access to new gadgets, as well as "white-glove" help with the installation. (Translation: They will send someone over to set up the new gear.)

And then there's British Airways' "At Your Service" program—available to a hand-picked few of the airline's gold-level elite customers. There's almost nothing that the service won't do for members—tracking down hard-to-get Wimbledon tickets, for example, or running errands around town, sitting in a member's home to wait for the plumber or cable guy, or even planning your wedding, right down to the cake.

But when it comes to stalking the well-to-do, perhaps nowhere is the competition greater than in the credit-card industry. To rise above the credit-card clutter and to attract high-end card holders, the major credit-card companies have created a new top tier of superpremium cards—Visa's Signature card, MasterCard's World card, American Express's super-elite Centurion card. Affluent customers are extremely profitable. While premium cards represent only 1.5 percent of the consumer credit cards issued by Visa, MasterCard, and American Express, they account for 20 percent of the spending. And well-to-do cardholders tend to default a lot less, too.

The World MasterCard program targets what it calls the "mass affluent" and reaches 15 million wealthy households. Visa's Signature card zeros in on "new affluent" house-holds, those with incomes exceeding $125,000. Its 7 million cardholders account for 3 percent of Visa's consumer credit cards but 18 percent of Visa sales. Both cards feature a pack of special privileges. For its Signature card, Visa adver-

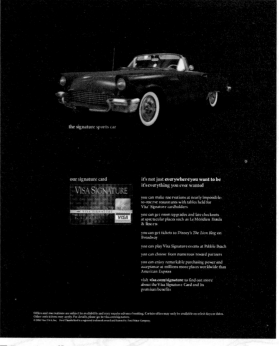

■ *Targeting affluent consumers: Visa's Signature card zeros in on the "new affluent." It offers no preset spending limit, 24-hour concierge services, and loads of "upgrades, perks, and discounts....It's not just everywhere you want to be, it's everything you ever wanted."*

tises, "It's not just everywhere you want to be, it's everything you ever wanted." In addition to the basics, such as no preset spending limit

---

Marketers also have used *personality* variables to segment markets. For example, marketing for Honda motor scooters *appears* to target hip and trendy 22-year-olds. But it is *actually* aimed at a much broader personality group. One old ad, for example, showed a delighted child bouncing up and down on his bed while the announcer says, "You've been trying to get there all your life." The ad reminded viewers of the euphoric feelings they got when they broke away from authority and did things their parents told them not to do. Thus, Honda is appealing to the rebellious, independent kid in all of us. In fact, 22 percent of scooter riders are retirees. "The older buyers are buying them for kicks," says one senior. "They never had the opportunity to do this as kids."[9]

Behavioral Segmentation **Behavioral segmentation** divides buyers into groups based on their knowledge, attitudes, uses, or responses to a product. Many marketers believe that behavior variables are the best starting point for building market segments.

Occasions. Buyers can be grouped according to occasions when they get the idea to buy, actually make their purchase, or use the purchased item. **Occasion segmentation** can help

Behavioral segmentation
Dividing a market into groups based on consumer knowledge, attitude, use, or response to a product.

Occasion segmentation
Dividing the market into groups according to occasions when buyers get the idea to buy, actually make their purchase, or use the purchased item.

and 24-hour concierge services, Visa promises "upgrades, perks, and discounts" at major airlines, restaurants, and hotels, and special treatment at partners like the Ritz-Carlton, men's fashion designer Ermenegildo Zegna, watchmaker Audemars Piguet.

But when it comes to premium cards, the American Express Centurion card is the "elite of the elite" for luxury card carriers. This mysterious, much-coveted black credit card is issued by invitation only, to customers who *spend* more than $150,000 a year on other AmEx cards and meet other not-so-clear requirements. Then, the select few who do receive the card pay a $2,500 annual fee just for the privilege of carrying it.

But the Centurion card comes dripping with perks and prestige. The elusive plastic, with its elegant matte finish, is coveted by big spenders. "A black card is plastic bling-bling," says an industry observer, "a way for celebrities, athletes, and major business people to express their status."

A real T-shirt-and-jeans kind of guy, Peter H. Shankman certainly doesn't look like a high roller, but American Express knows better. After he was snubbed by salesmen at a Giorgio Armani boutique on Fifth Avenue in New York recently, the 31-year-old publicist saw "an unbelievable attitude reversal" at the cash register when he whipped out his black AmEx Centurion Card. In June, a RadioShack cashier refused the card, thinking it was a

fake. " 'Trust me,' I said. 'Run the card,' "recalls the chief executive of Geek Factory, a public-relations and marketing firm. "I could buy a Learjet with this thing."

An exaggeration, perhaps. But AmEx's little black card is decidedly the "It" card for big spenders. Some would-be customers go to absurd lengths to get what they see as a must-have status symbol. Hopefuls have written poems to plead their cases. Others say they'll pay the fee but swear not to use the card—they want it just for show. "Every week I get phone calls or letters, often from prominent people, asking me for the card," says AmEx's head of consumer cards, Alfred F. Kelly Jr. Who, he won't say. In fact, AmEx deliberately builds an air of mystery around the sleek card, keeping hush-hush such details as the number of cards in circulation. Analysts say AmEx earns back many times what it spends on perks for black-card customers in both marketing buzz and fees.

Basic services on the Centurion card include a personal travel counselor and concierge, available 24/7. Beyond that, almost anything goes. Feel like shopping at Bergdorf Goodman or Saks Fifth Avenue at midnight? No problem. Traveling abroad in first class? Take a pal—the extra ticket is free. The royal treatment often requires elaborate planning. One AmEx concierge arranged a bachelor party for 25, which involved a four-day trip that included 11 penthouse suites, travel by private

jet, and a meet-and-greet with an owner of the Sacramento Kings basketball team. The tab was more than $300,000.

How did Shankman earn his card? All the travel and entertainment charges he racks up hosting his clients prompted AmEx to send it to him. It arrived in December, along with a 43-page manual. Recently, Shankman sought reservations for Spice Market, an often-overbooked restaurant in Manhattan, to impress a friend. He called his concierge. "Half an hour later it was done," says Shankman. Membership does have its privileges.

So, how many people actually have a Centurion card? "About the same number of people who can afford a Mercedes Maybach," says Desiree Fish, a spokeswoman for American Express, referring to a luxury car that can list for more than $300,000. The best guess is that only about 5,000 people worldwide have a Centurion card in their back pocket.

Sources: American Express example adapted from Mara Der Hovanesian, "This Black Card Gives You Carte Blanche," *BusinessWeek,* August 9, 2004, p. 54. Quotes and other information from David Carr, "No Name, but Plenty of Bling-Bling for Show," *New York Times,* September 13, 2004, p. C11; Eleena de Lisser, "How to Get an Airline to Wait for Your Plumber—In Battle for Biggest Spenders, British Airways, Sony Roll Out Hotel-Style 'Concierge' Service," *Wall Street Journal,* July 2, 2002, p. D1; James Tenser, "Cards Play Their Luxury Hand Right," *Advertising Age,* September 13, 2004, pp. S13–S14; Eric Dash, "New Spots for the Credit Card Companies Show Fierce Competition for the High-End Consumer," *New York Times,* May 11, 2005, p. C8; and www.visa.com and www.mastercard.com, June 2005.

firms build up product usage. For example, eggs are most often consumed at breakfast. But the American Egg Board, with its "incredible, edible egg" theme, promotes eating eggs at all times of the day. Its Web site offers basic egg facts and lots of recipes for egg appetizers, snacks, main dishes, and desserts.

Some holidays, such as Mother's Day and Father's Day, were originally promoted partly to increase the sale of candy, flowers, cards, and other gifts. And many marketers prepare special offers and ads for holiday occasions. For example, Altoids offers a special "Love Tin," the "curiously strong valentine." ConAgra Foods runs special Thanksgiving and Christmas ads for Reddi-wip during November and December, months that account for 30 percent of all whipped cream sales. Butterball, on the other hand, advertises "Happy Thanksgrilling" during the summer to increase the demand for Turkeys on non-Thanksgiving occasions.

Kodak, Konica, Fuji, and other camera makers use occasion segmentation in designing and marketing their single-use cameras. By mixing lenses, film speeds, and accessories, they have developed special disposable cameras for about any picture-taking occasion, from underwater photography to taking baby pictures. The Kodak Water & Sport

■ Occasion segmentation: Altoids created a special "Love Tin"—a "curiously strong valentine."

single-use camera is water resistant to 50 feet deep and features a shock-proof frame, a sunscreen and scratch resistant lens, and 800 speed film. "It survives where your regular camera won't!" claims Kodak.[10]

Benefits Sought. A powerful form of segmentation is to group buyers according to the different *benefits* that they seek from the product. **Benefit segmentation** requires finding the major benefits people look for in the product class, the kinds of people who look for each benefit, and the major brands that deliver each benefit. For example, our chapter-opening example pointed out that Procter & Gamble has identified several different laundry detergent segments. Each segment seeks a unique combination of benefits, from cleaning and bleaching to economy, fabric softening, fresh smell, strength or mildness, and lots of suds or only a few.

Benefit segmentation
Dividing the market into groups according to the different benefits that consumers seek from the product.

Champion athletic wear segments its markets according to benefits that different consumers seek from their activewear. For example, "Fit and Polish" consumers seek a balance between function and style—they exercise for results but want to look good doing it. "Serious Sports Competitors" exercise heavily and live in and love their activewear—they seek performance and function. By contrast, "Value-Seeking Moms" have low sports interest and low activewear involvement—they buy for the family and seek durability and value. Thus, each segment seeks a different mix of benefits. Champion must target the benefit segment or segments that it can serve best and most profitably using appeals that match each segment's benefit preferences.

User Status. Markets can be segmented into nonusers, ex-users, potential users, first-time users, and regular users of a product. For example, blood banks cannot rely only on regular donors. They must also recruit new first-time donors and remind ex-donors—each will require different marketing appeals. Included in the potential user group are consumers facing life-stage changes—such as newlyweds and new parents—who can be turned into heavy users. For example, P&G acquires the names of parents-to-be and showers them with product samples and ads for its Pampers and other baby products in order to capture a share of their future purchases. It invites them to visit Pampers.com and join MyPampers.com, giving them access to expert parenting advice, an e-mail newspaper, and coupons and special offers.

Usage Rate. Markets can also be segmented into light, medium, and heavy product users. Heavy users are often a small percentage of the market but account for a high percentage of total consumption. For example, in the fast-food industry, heavy users make up only 20 percent of patrons but eat up about 60 percent of all the food served. A single heavy user, typically a single male in his 20s or 30s who doesn't know how to cook, might spend as much as $40 in a day at fast-food restaurants and visit them more than 20 times a month. Despite claims by some consumers that the fast-food chains are damaging their health, these heavy users are extremely loyal. "They insist they don't need saving," says one analyst, "protesting that they are far from the clueless fatties anti-fast-food activists make them out to be." Even the heaviest users "would have to be stupid not to know that you can't eat only burgers and fries and not exercise," he says.[11]

Interestingly, although fast-food companies such as Burger King, McDonald's, and KFC depend a lot on heavy users and do all they can to keep them satisfied with every visit, these companies often target light users with their ads and promotions. The heavy users will visit the restaurants regardless. The company's marketing dollars are more often spent trying to convince light users that they want a burger in the first place.

Loyalty Status. A market can also be segmented by consumer loyalty. Consumers can be loyal to brands (Tide), stores (Wal-Mart), and companies (Ford). Buyers can be divided into groups according to their degree of loyalty. Some consumers are completely loyal—they buy one brand all the time. For example, Apple has a small but almost cult-like following of loyal users:[12]

It's the "Cult of the Mac," and it's populated by "macolytes." Urbandictionary.com defines a *macolyte* as "One who is fanatically devoted to Apple products, especially the Macintosh computer. Also known as a Mac Zealot." (Sample usage: "He's a macolyte; don't even *think* of mentioning Microsoft within earshot.") How about Anna Zisa, a graphic designer from Milan who doesn't really like tattoos but stenciled an Apple tat on her behind. "It just felt like the most me thing to have," says Zisa. "I like computers. The apple looks good and sexy. All the comments I have heard have been positive, even from Linux and Windows users." And then there's Taylor Barcroft, who has spent the last 11 years traveling the country in an RV on a mission to be the Mac cult's ultimate "multimedia historical videographer." He goes to every Macworld Expo, huge trade shows centered on the Mac, as well as all kinds of other tech shows—and videotapes anything and everything Apple. He's accumulated more than 3,000 hours of footage. And he's never been paid a dime to do any of this, living off an inheritance. Barcroft owns 17 Macs. Such fanatically loyal users helped keep Apple afloat during the lean years, and they are now at the forefront of Apple's burgeoning iPod-iTunes empire.

■ Consumer loyalty: "Macolytes"—fanatically loyal Apple users—helped keep Apple afloat during the lean years, and they are now at the forefront of Apple's burgeoning iPod and iTunes empire.

Other consumers are somewhat loyal—they are loyal to two or three brands of a given product or favor one brand while sometimes buying others. Still other buyers show no loyalty to any brand. They either want something different each time they buy or they buy whatever's on sale.

A company can learn a lot by analyzing loyalty patterns in its market. It should start by studying its own loyal customers. For example, by studying "macolytes," Apple can better pinpoint its target market and develop marketing appeals. By studying its less loyal buyers, the company can detect which brands are most competitive with its own. By looking at customers who are shifting away from its brand, the company can learn about its marketing weaknesses.

Using Multiple Segmentation Bases Marketers rarely limit their segmentation analysis to only one or a few variables. Rather, they are increasingly using multiple segmentation bases in an effort to identify smaller, better-defined target groups. Thus, a bank may not only identify a group of wealthy retired adults but also, within that group, distinguish several segments based on their current income, assets, savings and risk preferences, housing, and lifestyles.

One good example of multivariable segmentation is "geodemographic" segmentation. Several business information services—such as Claritas Inc., Experian, Acxiom, and MapInfo—have arisen to help marketing planners link U.S. Census and consumer transaction data with consumer lifestyle patterns to better segment their markets down to Zip codes, neighborhoods, and even households.

One of the leading lifestyle segmentation systems is PRIZM NE® (New Evolution) system by Claritas. The PRIZM NE system classifies every American household based on a host of demographic factors—such as age, educational level, income, occupation, family composition, ethnicity, and housing—and behavioral and lifestyle factors—such as purchases, free time activities, and media preferences. Using PRIZM NE, marketers can use where you live to paint a surprisingly precise picture of who you are and what you might buy:

> You're a 23-year-old first generation college graduate, working as a marketing assistant in a small publishing company. Starting on the bottom rung of the job ladder, you make just enough money to chip in your half of the rent for a no-frills, walk-up apartment you share downtown with an old college friend. You drive a 1-year-old Kia Spectra and spend your Friday nights socializing at the local nightclubs. Instead of cooking, you'd much rather order pizza from Papa John's and eat a few slices as you watch a re-run of Mad TV on Comedy Central. You spend most Sunday afternoons doing laundry at the local Laundromat, while you drink your usual large cup of coffee from the café down the block and reading a recent issue of *Rolling Stone*. You're living out your own, individual version of the good life. You're unique—not some demographic cliché. Right? Wrong. You're a prime example of the PRIZM NE's "City Startups" segment. If you consume, you can't hide from Claritas.[13]

Choose Wisely.

#18
Kids & Cul-de-Sacs

#21
Gray Power

Choose Claritas.
Solve your marketing challenges with segmentation solutions from Claritas. Our industry-standard segmentation systems, PRIZM® NE, P$YCLE® and ConneXions™ help you know your audience so you can tailor your marketing programs to them. Depth of knowledge gives you leverage for reaching and retaining your most profitable customers and prospects.

And, through our special analytics company, Integras, you can create a segmentation system that is specific to your company—the ultimate in precision marketing!

Choose wisely and call us today!

1-800-234-5973

www.claritas.com

CLARITAS
Adding
Intelligence
to Information

■ Using Claritas' PRIZM NE system, marketers can paint a surprisingly precise picture of who you are and what you might buy. PRIZM NE segments carry such exotic names as "Kids & Cul-de-Sacs," "Gray Power," "Blue Blood Estates," "Shotguns & Pickups," and "Bright Lites L'il City."

PRIZM NE classifies U.S. households into 66 unique segments, organized into 14 different social groups. PRIZM NE segments carry such colorful names as "Kids & Cul-de-Sacs," "Gray Power," "Blue Blood Estates," "Mayberry-ville," "Shotguns & Pickups," "Old Glories," "Multi-Culti Mosaic," "Big City Blues," and "Bright Lites L'il City." "Those image-triggered nicknames save a lot of time and geeky technical research terms explaining what you mean," says one marketer. "It's the names that bring the clusters to life," says another.[14]

Regardless of what you call the categories, such systems can help marketers to segment people and locations into marketable groups of like-minded consumers. Each segment exhibits unique characteristics and buying behavior. For example, "Blue Blood Estates" neighborhoods, part of the Elite Suburbs social group, are suburban areas populated by elite, super-rich families. People in this segment are more likely to take a golf vacation, watch major league soccer, eat at fast-food restaurants picked by kids, and read *Fortune*. In contrast, the "Shotguns & Pickups" segment, part of the Middle America social group, is populated by rural blue-collar workers and families. People in this segment are more likely to go hunting, buy hard rock music, drive a GMC Sierra 2500, watch the Daytona 500 on TV, and read *Field & Stream*.

Such segmentation provides a powerful tool for marketers of all kinds. For example, the Bonati Institute, an advanced arthroscopic spinal surgery facility, used PRIZM NE to help target prospective clients. The Institute wanted to know what its potential clients were like, where they lived, and how to reach them. Claritas began by sorting 5,000 previous Bonati Institute patients into PRIZM NE segments and ranking the segments according to their demographic, lifestyle, and media behaviors. It found that the best target groups were middle-income consumers who were not aware of their orthopedic-related choices. Armed with this information, the Institute devised a precisely-targeted direct mail campaign to inform the best potential clients about a seminar series on spinal surgery technology. The results were immediate: Seminar attendance increased 20 percent, producing a substantial increase in scheduled surgeries.[15]

SEGMENTING BUSINESS MARKETS

Consumer and business marketers use many of the same variables to segment their markets. Business buyers can be segmented geographically, demographically (industry, company size), or by benefits sought, user status, usage rate, and loyalty status. Yet, business marketers also use some additional variables, such as customer *operating characteristics*, *purchasing approaches*, *situational factors*, and *personal characteristics*. By going after segments instead of the whole market, companies can deliver just the right value proposition to each segment served and capture more value in return.

Almost every company serves at least some business markets. For example, you probably know American Express as a company that offers personal credit cards to consumers. But American Express also targets businesses in three segments— merchants, corporations, and small businesses. It has developed distinct marketing programs for each segment. In the merchants segment, American Express focuses on convincing new merchants to accept the card and on managing relationships with those that already do. For larger corporate customers, the company offers a corporate card program, which includes extensive employee expense and travel management services. It also offers this segment a wide range of asset management, retirement planning, financial education services. Finally, for small business customers, American Express has created the OPEN: Small Business Network, "the one place that's all about small business." Small business cardholders can access the network for everything from account and expense management software to expert small-business management advice and connecting with other small business owners to share ideas and get recommendations.[16]

Many companies set up separate systems for dealing with larger or multiple-location customers. For example, Steelcase, a major producer of office furniture, first segments customers into 10 industries, including banking, insurance, and electronics. Next, company salespeople work with independent Steelcase dealers to handle smaller, local, or regional Steelcase customers in each segment. But many national, multiple-location customers, such as Exxon/Mobile or IBM, have special needs that may reach beyond the scope of individual dealers. So Steelcase uses national accounts managers to help its dealer networks handle its national accounts.

Within a given target industry and customer size, the company can segment by purchase approaches and criteria. As in consumer segmentation, many marketers believe that *buying behavior* and *benefits* provide the best basis for segmenting business markets.[17]

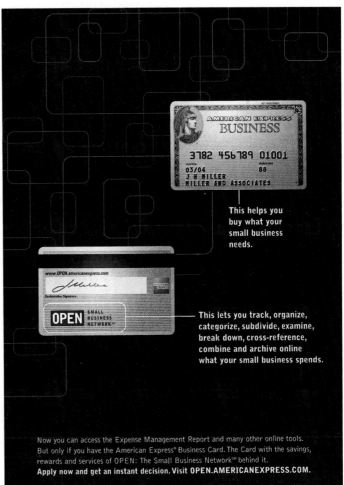

This helps you buy what your small business needs.

This lets you track, organize, categorize, subdivide, examine, break down, cross-reference, combine and archive online what your small business spends.

Now you can access the Expense Management Report and many other online tools. But only if you have the American Express® Business Card. The Card with the savings, rewards and services of OPEN: The Small Business Network℠ behind it. **Apply now and get an instant decision. Visit OPEN.AMERICANEXPRESS.COM.**

■ Segmenting business markets: For small business customers, American Express has created the OPEN: Small Business Network, "the one place that's all about small business."

SEGMENTING INTERNATIONAL MARKETS

Few companies have either the resources or the will to operate in all, or even most, of the countries that dot the globe. Although some large companies, such as Coca-Cola or Sony, sell products in more than 200 countries, most international firms focus on a smaller set. Operating in many countries presents new challenges. Different countries, even those that are close together, can vary greatly in their economic, cultural, and political makeup. Thus, just as they do within their domestic markets, international firms need to group their world markets into segments with distinct buying needs and behaviors.

Companies can segment international markets using one or a combination of several variables. They can segment by *geographic location*, grouping countries by regions such as Western Europe, the Pacific Rim, the Middle East, or Africa. Geographic segmentation assumes that nations close to one another will have many common traits and behaviors. Although this is often the case, there are many exceptions. For example, although the United States and Canada have much in common, both differ culturally and economically from neighboring Mexico. Even within a region, consumers can differ widely. For example, some U.S. marketers lump all Central and South American countries together. However, the Dominican Republic is no more like Brazil than Italy is like Sweden. Many Central and South Americans don't even speak Spanish, including 140 million Portuguese-speaking Brazilians and the millions in other countries who speak a variety of Indian dialects.

World markets can also be segmented on the basis of *economic factors*. For example, countries might be grouped by population income levels or by their overall level of economic development. A company's economic structure shapes its population's product and service needs and, therefore, the marketing opportunities it offers. Countries can be segmented by *political and legal factors* such as the type and stability of government, receptivity to foreign firms, monetary regulations, and the amount of bureaucracy. Such factors can play a crucial role in a company's choice of which countries to enter and how. *Cultural factors* can also be used, grouping markets according to common languages, religions, values and attitudes, customs, and behavioral patterns.

Segmenting international markets based on geographic, economic, political, cultural, and other factors assumes that segments should consist of clusters of countries. However, many companies use a different approach called **intermarket segmentation**. They form segments of consumers who have similar needs and buying behavior even though they are located in different countries. For example, Mercedes-Benz targets the world's well-to-do, regardless of their country.

MTV targets the world's teenagers. The world's 1.2 billion teens have a lot in common: They study, shop, and sleep. They are exposed to many of the same major issues: love, crime, homelessness, ecology, and working parents. In many ways, they have more in common with each other than with their parents. "Last year I was in seventeen different countries," says one expert, "and it's pretty difficult to find anything that is different, other than language, among a teenager in Japan, a teenager in the UK, and a teenager in China." Says another, "Global teens in Buenos Aires, Beijing, and Bangalore swing to

Intermarket segmentation
Forming segments of consumers who have similar needs and buying behavior even though they are located in different countries.

■ Intermarket segmentation: Teens show surprising similarity no matter where in the world they live. For instance, these two teens could live almost anywhere. Thus, many companies target teenagers with worldwide marketing campaigns.

the beat of MTV while sipping Coke." MTV bridges the gap between cultures, appealing to what teens around the world have in common. Sony, Reebok, Nike, and many other firms also actively target global teens. For example, Sprite's "Image is nothing—obey your thirst" theme appeals to teens the world over.[18]

REQUIREMENTS FOR EFFECTIVE SEGMENTATION

Clearly, there are many ways to segment a market, but not all segmentations are effective. For example, buyers of table salt could be divided into blond and brunette customers. But hair color obviously does not affect the purchase of salt. Furthermore, if all salt buyers bought the same amount of salt each month, believed that all salt is the same, and wanted to pay the same price, the company would not benefit from segmenting this market.

To be useful, market segments must be

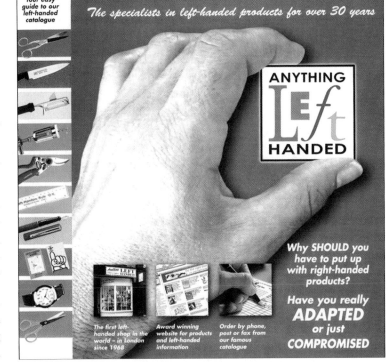

- *Measurable:* The size, purchasing power, and profiles of the segments can be measured. Certain segmentation variables are difficult to measure. For example, there are 32.5 million left-handed people in the United States—almost equaling the entire population of Canada. Yet few products are targeted toward this left-handed segment. The major problem may be that the segment is hard to identify and measure. There are no data on the demographics of lefties, and the U.S. Census Bureau does not keep track of left-handedness in its surveys. Private data companies keep reams of statistics on other demographic segments but not on left-handers.

■ The "Leftie" segment can be hard to identify and measure. As a result, few companies tailor their offers to left-handers. However, some nichers such as Anything Left-Handed in the United Kingdom target this segment.

- *Accessible:* The market segments can be effectively reached and served. Suppose a fragrance company finds that heavy users of its brand are single men and women who stay out late and socialize a lot. Unless this group lives or shops at certain places and is exposed to certain media, its members will be difficult to reach.
- *Substantial:* The market segments are large or profitable enough to serve. A segment should be the largest possible homogenous group worth pursuing with a tailored marketing program. It would not pay, for example, for an automobile manufacturer to develop cars especially for people whose height is greater than seven feet.
- *Differentiable:* The segments are conceptually distinguishable and respond differently to different marketing mix elements and programs. If married and unmarried women respond similarly to a sale on perfume, they do not constitute separate segments.
- *Actionable:* Effective programs can be designed for attracting and serving the segments. For example, although one small airline identified seven market segments, its staff was too small to develop separate marketing programs for each segment.

 Linking the Concepts

Slow down a bit and smell the roses. How do the companies you do business with employ the segmentation concepts you're reading about here?

- Can you identify specific companies, other than the examples already discussed, that practice the different types of segmentation just discussed?
- Using the segmentation bases you've just read about, segment the U.S. footwear market. Describe each of the major segments and subsegments. Keep these segments in mind as you read the next section on target marketing.

Target Marketing

Market segmentation reveals the firm's market segment opportunities. The firm now has to evaluate the various segments and decide how many and which segments it can serve best. We now look at how companies evaluate and select target segments.

EVALUATING MARKET SEGMENTS

In evaluating different market segments, a firm must look at three factors: segment size and growth, segment structural attractiveness, and company objectives and resources. The company must first collect and analyze data on current segment sales, growth rates, and expected profitability for various segments. It will be interested in segments that have the right size and growth characteristics. But "right size and growth" is a relative matter. The largest, fastest-growing segments are not always the most attractive ones for every company. Smaller companies may lack the skills and resources needed to serve the larger segments. Or they may find these segments too competitive. Such companies may target segments that are smaller and less attractive, in an absolute sense, but that are potentially more profitable for them.

The company also needs to examine major structural factors that affect long-run segment attractiveness.[19] For example, a segment is less attractive if it already contains many strong and aggressive *competitors*. The existence of many actual or potential *substitute products* may limit prices and the profits that can be earned in a segment. The relative *power of buyers* also affects segment attractiveness. Buyers with strong bargaining power relative to sellers will try to force prices down, demand more services, and set competitors against one another—all at the expense of seller profitability. Finally, a segment may be less attractive if it contains *powerful suppliers* who can control prices or reduce the quality or quantity of ordered goods and services.

Even if a segment has the right size and growth and is structurally attractive, the company must consider its own objectives and resources. Some attractive segments can be dismissed quickly because they do not mesh with the company's long-run objectives. Or the company may lack the skills and resources needed to succeed in an attractive segment. The company should enter only segments in which it can offer superior value and gain advantages over competitors.

SELECTING TARGET MARKET SEGMENTS

After evaluating different segments, the company must now decide which and how many segments it will target. A **target market** consists of a set of buyers who share common needs or characteristics that the company decides to serve.

Because buyers have unique needs and wants, a seller could potentially view each buyer as a separate target market. Ideally, then, a seller might design a separate marketing program for each buyer. However, although some companies do attempt to serve buyers individually, most face larger numbers of smaller buyers and do not find individual targeting worthwhile. Instead, they look for broader segments of buyers. More generally, target marketing can be carried out at several different levels. Figure 6.2 shows that companies can target very broadly (undifferentiated marketing), very narrowly (micromarketing), or somewhere in between (differentiated or concentrated marketing).

Target market
A set of buyers sharing common needs or characteristics that the company decides to serve.

FIGURE 6.2 Target Marketing Strategies

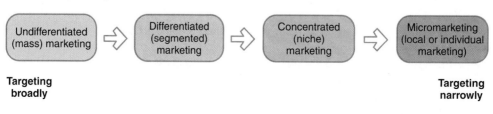

Undifferentiated (mass) marketing ⇒ Differentiated (segmented) marketing ⇒ Concentrated (niche) marketing ⇒ Micromarketing (local or individual marketing)

Targeting broadly   Targeting narrowly

Undifferentiated Marketing   Using an **undifferentiated marketing (or mass marketing)** strategy, a firm might decide to ignore market segment differences and target the whole market with one offer. This mass-marketing strategy focuses on what is *common* in the needs of consumers rather than on what is *different*. The company designs a product and a marketing program that will appeal to the largest number of buyers.

As noted earlier in the chapter, most modern marketers have strong doubts about this strategy. Difficulties arise in developing a product or brand that will satisfy all consumers. Moreover, mass marketers often have trouble competing with more focused firms that do a better job of satisfying the needs of specific segments and niches.

Differentiated Marketing   Using a **differentiated marketing (or segmented marketing)** strategy, a firm decides to target several market segments and designs separate offers for each. General Motors tries to produce a car for every "purse, purpose, and personality." Gap Inc. has created four different retail store formats—Gap, Banana Republic, Old Navy, and Forth & Towne to serve the varied needs of different fashion segments. And Estée Lauder offers hundreds of different products aimed at carefully defined segments:

> Estée Lauder is an expert in creating differentiated brands that serve the tastes of different market segments. Five of the top ten, best-selling prestige perfumes in the United States belong to Estée Lauder. So do eight of the top ten prestige makeup brands. There's the original Estée Lauder brand, with it's gold and blue packaging, which appeals to older, 50+ baby boomers. Then there's Clinique, the company's most popular brand, perfect for the middle-aged mom with no time to waste and for younger women attracted to its classic free gift offers. For young, fashion-forward consumers, there's M.A.C., which provides makeup for clients like Pamela Anderson and Marilyn Manson. For the young and trendy, there's the Stila line, containing lots of shimmer and uniquely packaged in clever containers. And, for the New Age type, there's upscale Aveda, with its salon, makeup, and lifestyle products, based on the art and science of Earthy origins and pure flower and plant essences, celebrating the connection between Mother Nature and human nature.[20]

By offering product and marketing variations to segments, companies hope for higher sales and a stronger position within each market segment. Developing a stronger position within several segments creates more total sales than undifferentiated marketing across all segments. Estée Lauder's combined brands give it a much greater market share than any single brand could. The Estée Lauder and Clinique brands alone reap a combined 40 percent share of the prestige cosmetics market.

But differentiated marketing also increases the costs of doing business. A firm usually finds it more expensive to develop and produce, say, 10 units of 10 different products than

■ Differentiated marekting: Estée Lauder offers hundreds of different products aimed at carefully defined segments, from its original Estée Lauder brand appealing to age 50+ baby boomers to Aveda, with earthy origins that appeal to younger new age types.

100 units of one product. Developing separate marketing plans for the separate segments requires extra marketing research, forecasting, sales analysis, promotion planning, and channel management. And trying to reach different market segments with different advertising increases promotion costs. Thus, the company must weigh increased sales against increased costs when deciding on a differentiated marketing strategy.

Concentrated (niche) marketing
A market-coverage strategy in which a firm goes after a large share of one or a few segments or niches.

Concentrated Marketing
A third market-coverage strategy, **concentrated marketing (or niche marketing)**, is especially appealing when company resources are limited. Instead of going after a small share of a large market, the firm goes after a large share of one or a few smaller segments or niches. For example, Oshkosh Truck is the world's largest producer of airport rescue trucks and front-loading concrete mixers. Tetra sells 80 percent of the world's tropical fish food, and Steiner Optical captures 80 percent of the world's military binoculars market.

Through concentrated marketing, the firm achieves a strong market position because of its greater knowledge of consumer needs in the niches it serves and the special reputation it acquires. It can market more *effectively* by fine-tuning its products, prices, and programs to the needs of carefully defined segments. It can also market more *efficiently*, targeting its products or services, channels, and communications programs toward only consumers that it can serve best and most profitably.

Whereas segments are fairly large and normally attract several competitors, niches are smaller and may attract only one or a few competitors. Niching offers smaller companies an opportunity to compete by focusing their limited resources on serving niches that may be unimportant to, or overlooked by, larger competitors. Consider Apple Computer. Although it once enjoyed a better than 13 percent market share, Apple is now a market nicher, capturing less than 3 percent of the U.S. desktop computer market and less than 5 percent in portables. Rather than competing head-on with other PC makers as they slash prices and focus on volume, Apple invests in research and development, making it the industry trendsetter. For example, when the company introduced iTunes, it captured more than 70 percent of the music download market. Such innovation has created a loyal base of consumers who are willing to pay more for Apple's cutting-edge products.[21]

Many companies start as nichers to get a foothold against larger, more resourceful competitors, then grow into broader competitors. For example, Southwest Airlines began by serving intrastate, no-frills commuters in Texas but is now one of the nation's largest airlines. In contrast, as markets change, some mega-marketers develop niche markets to create sales growth. For example, in recent years, Pepsi has introduced several niche products, such as Sierra Mist, Pepsi Edge, Mountain Dew Code Red, and Mountain Dew LiveWire. Initially, these brands combined accounted for barely 5 percent of Pepsi's overall soft-drink sales. However, Sierra Mist has now blossomed into Pepsi's fastest-growing beverage brand, and Code Red and LiveWire have revitalized the Mountain Dew brand. Says Pepsi-Cola North America's chief marketing officer, "The era of the mass brand has been over for a long time."[22]

Today, the low cost of setting up shop on the Internet makes it even more profitable to serve seemingly minuscule niches. Small businesses, in particular, are realizing riches from serving small niches on the Web. Here is a "Webpreneur" who achieved astonishing results:

Sixty-two-year-old British artist Jacquie Lawson taught herself to use a computer only a few years ago. Last year, her online business had sales of $1.7 million. What does she sell? Online cards. Lawson occupies a coveted niche in the electronic world: a profitable, subscription-based

■ Small businesses, in particular, are realizing riches from serving small niches on the Web. "Webpreneur" Jacquie Lawson operates a profitable, subscription-based Web site where she sells her highly stylized e-cards without a bit of advertising.

Web site (www.jacquielawson.com) where she sells her highly stylized e-cards without a bit of advertising. While the giants—Hallmark and American Greetings—offer hundreds of e-cards for every occasion, Lawson offers only about 50 in total, the majority of which she intricately designed herself. Revenue comes solely from 300,000 members—81 percent from the United States—who pay $8 a year. Lawson's success with a business model that has stumped many media giants speaks to both the Internet's egalitarian nature and her own stubborn belief that doing it her way is the right way. With a renewal rate of 70 percent and more new members subscribing every day, sales will reach an estimated $5 million next year.[23]

Concentrated marketing can be highly profitable. At the same time, it involves higher-than-normal risks. Companies that rely on one or a few segments for all of their business will suffer greatly if the segment turns sour. Or larger competitors may decide to enter the same segment with greater resources. For these reasons, many companies prefer to diversify in several market segments.

Micromarketing   Differentiated and concentrated marketers tailor their offers and marketing programs to meet the needs of various market segments and niches. At the same time, however, they do not customize their offers to each individual customer. **Micromarketing** is the practice of tailoring products and marketing programs to suit the tastes of specific individuals and locations. Rather than seeing a customer in every individual, micromarketers see the individual in every customer. Micromarketing includes *local marketing* and *individual marketing*.

Micromarketing
The practice of tailoring products and marketing programs to the needs and wants of specific individuals and local customer groups—includes *local marketing* and *individual marketing*.

Local Marketing.   **Local marketing** involves tailoring brands and promotions to the needs and wants of local customer groups—cities, neighborhoods, and even specific stores. Citibank provides different mixes of banking services in each of its branches, depending on neighborhood demographics. Kraft helps supermarket chains identify the specific cheese assortments and shelf positioning that will optimize cheese sales in low-income, middle-income, and high-income stores and in different ethnic communities.

Local marketing
Tailoring brands and promotions to the needs and wants of local customer groups—cities, neighborhoods, and even specific stores.

Local marketing has some drawbacks. It can drive up manufacturing and marketing costs by reducing economies of scale. It can also create logistics problems as companies try to meet the varied requirements of different regional and local markets. Further, a brand's overall image might be diluted if the product and message vary too much in different localities.

Still, as companies face increasingly fragmented markets, and as new supporting technologies develop, the advantages of local marketing often outweigh the drawbacks. Local marketing helps a company to market more effectively in the face of pronounced regional and local differences in demographics and lifestyles. It also meets the needs of the company's first-line customers—retailers—who prefer more fine-tuned product assortments for their neighborhoods.

Individual Marketing.   In the extreme, micromarketing becomes **individual marketing**—tailoring products and marketing programs to the needs and preferences of individual customers. Individual marketing has also been labeled *one-to-one marketing*, *mass customization,* and *markets-of-one marketing*.

Individual marketing
Tailoring products and marketing programs to the needs and preferences of individual customers—also labeled "markets-of-one marketing," "customized marketing," and "one-to-one marketing."

The widespread use of mass marketing has obscured the fact that for centuries consumers were served as individuals: The tailor custom-made the suit, the cobbler designed shoes for the individual, the cabinetmaker made furniture to order. Today, however, new technologies are permitting many companies to return to customized marketing. More powerful computers, detailed databases, robotic production and flexible manufacturing, and interactive communication media such as e-mail and the Internet—all have combined to foster "mass customization." *Mass customization* is the process through which firms interact one-to-one with masses of customers to design products and services tailor-made to individual needs.[24]

Dell creates custom-configured computers and Ford lets buyers "build a vehicle" from a palette of options. Hockey-stick maker Branches Hockey lets customers choose from more than two-dozen options—including stick length, blade patterns, and blade curve—and turns out a customized stick in five days. Visitors to Nike's NikeID Web site can personalize their

■ Individual marketing: At Target's "Target to a T" Web site, customers can personalize selected clothing items to "create a clothing look that's all you."

sneakers by choosing from hundreds of colors and putting an embroidered word or phrase on the tongue. And at Target's "Target to a T" Web site, customers can personalize selected clothing items to "create a clothing look that's all you." The Target to a T Web site proclaims: "You'll experience the perfect fit—for your personality, your lifestyle, your wardrobe, your body—without setting foot in a dressing room."

Companies selling all kinds of products—from computers, candy, clothing, and golf clubs to fire trucks—are customizing their offerings to the needs of individual buyers. Consider this example:

> Looking to sweeten up a party or special celebration? Try the Customized M&M's section at the M&M's Brand Store site, where you can special order the tasty little candies in whatever combination of colors suits your fancy. The site lets you pick from a palette of 21 colors and order in 8-ounce or 5-pound customized bags. Mix up a patriotic combo of red, white, and blue M&Ms for the chocolate lovers at your Fourth of July celebration. Or special order a blend of your school colors for the next tailgate party. Send customized promotional tins or gift bags featuring your company colors to special customers. You can even print your very own M&Ms with personalized messages tailored to a special occasion. How about "boo" on your Halloween M&Ms, or "HO HO HO" at Christmas? Want to see your name on a batch of aqua-green M&Ms? No problem. Customized M&Ms are a bit costly—nearly three times the cost of regular M&Ms. But business is booming, with sales doubling every year.[25]

Consumer goods marketers aren't the only ones going one-to-one. Business-to-business marketers are also finding new ways to customize their offerings. For example, John Deere manufactures seeding equipment that can be configured in more than two million versions to individual customer specifications. The seeders are produced one at a time, in any sequence, on a single production line.

Mass customization provides a way to stand out against competitors. Consider Oshkosh Truck:

> Oshkosh Truck specializes in making heavy-duty fire, airport-rescue, cement, garbage, snow-removal, ambulance, and military vehicles. According to one account, "Whether you need to plow your way through Sahara sands or Buffalo snow, Oshkosh has your vehicle, by gosh." Oshkosh has grown rapidly and profitably over the past decade. What's its secret? Mass customization—the ability to personalize its products and services to the needs of individual customers. For example, when firefighters order a truck from Oshkosh, it's an event. They travel to the plant to watch the vehicle, which may cost as much as $800,000, take shape. The firefighters can choose from 19,000 options. A stripped-down fire truck costs $130,000, but 75 percent of Oshkosh's customers order lots of extras, like hideaway stairs, ladders, special doors, compartments, and firefighting foam systems for those difficult-to-extinguish fires. Some bring along paint chips so they can customize the color of their fleet. Others are content just to admire the vehicles, down to the water tanks and hideaway ladders. "Some chiefs even bring their wives; we encourage it," says the president of Oshkosh's firefighting unit, Pierce Manufacturing. "Buying a fire truck is a very personal thing." Indeed, Pierce customers are in town so often

that the Holiday Inn renamed its lounge the Hook and Ladder. Through such customization and personalization, Oshkosh has gained a big edge over its languishing larger rivals.[26]

Unlike mass production, which eliminates the need for human interaction, one-to-one has made relationships with customers more important than ever. Just as mass production was the marketing principle of the last century, mass customization is becoming a marketing principle for the twenty-first century. The world appears to be coming full circle—from the good old days when customers were treated as individuals, to mass marketing when nobody knew your name, and back again.

The move toward individual marketing mirrors the trend in consumer *self-marketing*. Increasingly, individual customers are taking more responsibility for determining which products and brands to buy. Consider two business buyers with two different purchasing styles. The first sees several salespeople, each trying to persuade him to buy his or her product. The second sees no salespeople but rather logs on to the Internet. She searches for information on available products; interacts electronically with various suppliers, users, and product analysts; and then makes up her own mind about the best offer. The second purchasing agent has taken more responsibility for the buying process, and the marketer has had less influence over her buying decision.

As the trend toward more interactive dialogue and less advertising monologue continues, self-marketing will grow in importance. As more buyers look up consumer reports, join Internet product discussion forums, and place orders via phone or online, marketers will have to influence the buying process in new ways. They will need to involve customers more in all phases of the product development and buying processes, increasing opportunities for buyers to practice self-marketing.

Choosing a Target Marketing Strategy Companies need to consider many factors when choosing a target-marketing strategy. Which strategy is best depends on *company resources*. When the firm's resources are limited, concentrated marketing makes the most sense. The best strategy also depends on the degree of *product variability*. Undifferentiated marketing is more suited for uniform products such as grapefruit or steel. Products that can vary in design, such as cameras and automobiles, are more suited to differentiation or concentration. The *product's life-cycle stage* also must be considered. When a firm introduces a new product, it may be practical to launch only one version, and undifferentiated marketing or concentrated marketing may make the most sense. In the mature stage of the product life cycle, however, differentiated marketing begins to make more sense.

Another factor is *market variability*. If most buyers have the same tastes, buy the same amounts, and react the same way to marketing efforts, undifferentiated marketing is appropriate. Finally, *competitors' marketing strategies* are important. When competitors use differentiated or concentrated marketing, undifferentiated marketing can be suicidal. Conversely, when competitors use undifferentiated marketing, a firm can gain an advantage by using differentiated or concentrated marketing.

SOCIALLY RESPONSIBLE TARGET MARKETING

Smart targeting helps companies to be more efficient and effective by focusing on the segments that they can satisfy best and most profitably. Targeting also benefits consumers—companies reach specific groups of consumers with offers carefully tailored to satisfy their needs. However, target marketing sometimes generates controversy and concern. The biggest issues usually involve the targeting of vulnerable or disadvantaged consumers with controversial or potentially harmful products.

For example, over the years, the cereal industry has been heavily criticized for its marketing efforts directed toward children. Children make up almost half of the $6 billion U.S. cereal market. Critics worry that premium offers and high-powered advertising appeals presented through the mouths of lovable animated characters will overwhelm children's defenses. The marketers of toys and other children's products have been similarly battered, often with good justification.

Other problems arise when the marketing of adult products spills over into the kid segment—intentionally or unintentionally. For example, the Federal Trade Commission (FTC) and citizen action groups have accused tobacco companies of targeting underage smokers. And a recent FTC study found that 80 percent of R-rated movies and 70 percent of video games with a mature rating were targeted to children under 17. Some critics have even called for a complete ban on advertising to children.[27] To encourage responsible advertising, the Children's Advertising Review Unit, the advertising industry's self-regulatory agency, has published extensive children's advertising guidelines that recognize the special needs of child audiences.

Cigarette, beer, and fast-food marketers have also generated much controversy in recent years by their attempts to target inner-city minority consumers. For example, McDonald's and other chains have drawn criticism for pitching their high-fat, salt-laden fare to low-income, urban residents who are much more likely than are suburbanites to be heavy consumers. Similarly, R.J. Reynolds took heavy flak in the early 1990s when it announced plans to market Uptown, a menthol cigarette targeted toward low-income blacks. It quickly dropped the brand in the face of a loud public outcry and heavy pressure from black leaders.

The meteoric growth of the Internet and other carefully targeted direct media has raised fresh concerns about potential targeting abuses. The Internet allows increasing refinement of audiences and, in turn, more precise targeting. This might help makers of questionable products or deceptive advertisers to more readily victimize the most vulnerable audiences. Unscrupulous marketers can now send tailor-made deceptive messages directly to the computers of millions of unsuspecting consumers. For example, the FBI's Internet Fraud Complaint Center Web site alone received more than 207,000 complaints last year, an increase of more than 66 percent over the previous year.[28]

Not all attempts to target children, minorities, or other special segments draw such criticism. In fact, most provide benefits to targeted consumers. For example, Colgate makes a large selection of toothbrushes and toothpaste flavors and packages for children—from Colgate Barbie, Blues Clues, and SpongeBob SquarePants Sparkling Bubble Fruit toothpastes to Colgate LEGO BIONICLE and Bratz character toothbrushes. Such products help make tooth brushing more fun and get children to brush longer and more often. American Girl appropriately targets minority consumers with African-American, Mexican, and American-Indian versions of its highly acclaimed dolls and books. And Nacara Cosmetiques markets a multiethnic cosmetics line for "ethnic women who have a thirst for the exotic." The line is specially formulated to complement the darker skin tones of African-American women and dark-skinned women of Latin-American, Indian, and Caribbean origins.

■ Most target marketing benefits both the marketer and the consumer. Nacara Cosmetiques markets cosmetics for "ethnic women who have a thirst for the exotic."

Thus, in target marketing, the issue is not really *who* is targeted but rather *how* and for *what*. Controversies arise when marketers attempt to profit at the expense of targeted segments—when they unfairly target vulnerable segments or target them with questionable products or tactics. Socially responsible marketing calls for segmentation and targeting that serve not just the interests of the company but also the interests of those targeted.

Linking the Concepts

Time to coast for a bit and take stock.

■ At the last speed bump, you segmented the U.S. footwear market. Refer to Figure 6.2 and select two companies that serve this market. Describe their segmentation and targeting strategies. Can you come up with one that targets many different segments versus another that focuses on only one or a few segments?

■ How does each company you chose differentiate its market offering and image? Has each done a good job of establishing this differentiation in the minds of targeted consumers? The final section in this chapter deals with such positioning issues.

Positioning for Competitive Advantage

Beyond deciding which segments of the market it will target, the company must decide what positions it wants to occupy in those segments. A **product's position** is the way the product is *defined by consumers* on important attributes—the place the product occupies in consumers' minds relative to competing products. "Products are created in the factory, but brands are created in the mind," says a positioning expert.[29]

Product position

The way the product is defined by consumers on important attributes—the place the product occupies in consumers' minds relative to competing products.

Tide is positioned as a powerful, all-purpose family detergent; Ivory Snow is positioned as the gentle detergent for fine washables and baby clothes. At Subway restaurants, you "Eat Fresh"; at Olive Garden, "When You're Here, You're Family"; and at Applebee's you're "Eatin' Good in the Neighborhood." In the automobile market, the Toyota Echo and Ford Focus are positioned on economy, Mercedes and Cadillac on luxury, and Porsche and BMW on performance. Volvo positions powerfully on safety. And Toyota positions its fuel-efficient, hybrid Prius as a high-tech solution to the energy shortage. "How far will you go to save the planet?" it asks.

Consumers are overloaded with information about products and services. They cannot reevaluate products every time they make a buying decision. To simplify the buying process, consumers organize products, services, and companies into categories and "position" them in their minds. A product's position is the complex set of perceptions, impressions, and feelings that consumers have for the product compared with competing products.

Consumers position products with or without the help of marketers. But marketers do not want to leave their products' positions to chance. They must *plan* positions that will give their products the greatest advantage in selected target markets, and they must design marketing mixes to create these planned positions.

POSITIONING MAPS

In planning their positioning strategies, marketers often prepare *perceptual positioning maps,* which show consumer perceptions of their brands versus competing products on important buying dimensions. Figure 6.3 shows a positioning map for the U.S. large luxury sport utility vehicle market.[30] The position of each circle on the map indicates the

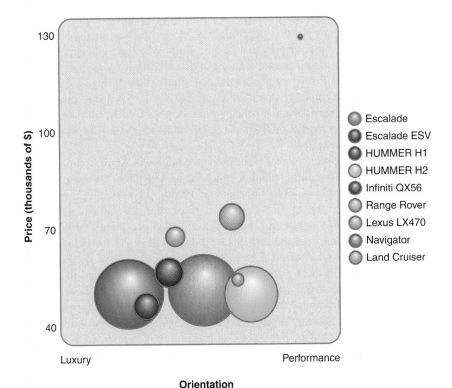

FIGURE 6.3
Positioning Map: Large Luxury SUVs

brand's perceived positioning on two dimensions—price and orientation (luxury versus performance). The size of each circle indicates the brand's relative market share. Thus, customers view the market-leading Cadillac Escalade as a moderately-priced large luxury SUV with a balance of luxury and performance.

The original HUMMER H1 is positioned as a very high performance SUV with a price tag to match. HUMMER targets the current H1 Alpha toward a small segment of well-off, rugged individualists. According to the H1 Web site, "The H1 was built around one central philosophy: function—the most functional off-road vehicle ever made available to the civilian market. The H1 Alpha not only sets you apart, but truly sets you free."

By contrast, although also oriented toward performance, the HUMMER H2 is positioned as a more luxury-oriented and more reasonably priced luxury SUV. The H2 is targeted toward a larger segment of urban and suburban professionals. "In a world where SUVs have begun to look like their owners, complete with love handles and mushy seats, the H2 proves that there is still one out there that can drop and give you 20," says the H2 Web site. The H2 "strikes a perfect balance between interior comfort, on-the-road capability, and off-road capability."

CHOOSING A POSITIONING STRATEGY

Some firms find it easy to choose their positioning strategy. For example, a firm well known for quality in certain segments will go for this position in a new segment if there are enough buyers seeking quality. But in many cases, two or more firms will go after the same position. Then, each will have to find other ways to set itself apart. Each firm must differentiate its offer by building a unique bundle of benefits that appeals to a substantial group within the segment.

The positioning task consists of three steps: identifying a set of possible competitive advantages upon which to build a position, choosing the right competitive advantages, and selecting an overall positioning strategy. The company must then effectively communicate and deliver the chosen position to the market.

Identifying Possible Competitive Advantages   To build profitable relationships with target customers, marketers must understand customer needs better than competitors do and deliver more value. To the extent that a company can position itself as providing superior value, it gains **competitive advantage**. But solid positions cannot be built on empty promises. If a company positions its product as *offering* the best quality and service, it must then *deliver* the promised quality and service. Thus, positioning begins with actually *differentiating* the company's market offering so that it will give consumers superior value.

To find points of differentiation, marketers must think through the customer's entire experience with the company's product or service. An alert company can find ways to differentiate itself at every customer contact point. In what specific ways can a company differentiate itself or its market offer? It can differentiate along the lines of *product, services, channels, people,* or *image.*

Product differentiation takes place along a continuum. At one extreme we find physical products that allow little variation: chicken, steel, aspirin. Yet even here some meaningful differentiation is possible. For example, Perdue claims that its branded chickens are better—fresher and more tender—and gets a 10 percent price premium based on this differentiation. At the other extreme are products that can be highly differentiated, such as automobiles, clothing, and furniture. Such products can be differentiated on features, performance, or style and design. Thus, Volvo provides new and better safety features; Whirlpool designs its dishwasher to run more quietly; Bose positions its speakers on their striking design and sound characteristics. Similarly, companies can differentiate their products on such attributes as consistency, durability, reliability, or repairability.

Beyond differentiating its physical product, a firm can also differentiate the services that accompany the product. Some companies gain *services differentiation* through speedy, convenient, or careful delivery. For example, Commerce Bank has positioned itself as "the most convenient bank in America"—it remains open seven days a week, including evenings, and you can get a debit card while you wait. Installation service can also differ-

Competitive advantage
An advantage over competitors gained by offering consumers greater value, either through lower prices or by providing more benefits that justify higher prices.

entiate one company from another, as can repair services. Many an automobile buyer will gladly pay a little more and travel a little farther to buy a car from a dealer that provides top-notch repair services.

Some companies gain service differentiation by providing customer training service or consulting services—data, information systems, and advising services that buyers need. McKesson Corporation, a major drug wholesaler, consults with its 12,000 independent pharmacists to help them set up accounting, inventory, and computerized ordering systems. By helping its customers compete better, McKesson gains greater customer loyalty and sales.

Firms that practice *channel differentiation* gain competitive advantage through the way they design their channel's coverage, expertise, and performance. Amazon.com, Dell, and Avon set themselves apart with their high-quality direct channels. Caterpillar's success in the construction-equipment industry is based on superior channels. Its dealers worldwide are renowned for their first-rate service.

Companies can gain a strong competitive advantage through *people differentiation*—hiring and training better people than their competitors do. Disney people are known to be friendly and upbeat. And Singapore Airlines enjoys an excellent reputation, largely because of the grace of its flight attendants. People differentiation requires that a company select its customer-contact people carefully and train them well. For example, Disney trains its theme-park employees thoroughly to ensure that they are competent, courteous, and friendly—from the hotel check-in agents, to the monorail drivers, to the ride attendants, to the people who sweep Main Street USA. Each employee is carefully trained to understand customers and to "make people happy."

Even when competing offers look the same, buyers may perceive a difference based on company or brand *image differentiation*. A company or brand image should convey the product's distinctive benefits and positioning. Developing a strong and distinctive image calls for creativity and hard work. A company cannot develop an image in the public's mind overnight using only a few advertisements. If Ritz-Carlton means quality, this image must be supported by everything the company says and does.

Symbols—such as the McDonald's golden arches, the Prudential rock, the Nike swoosh, or Google's colorful logo—can provide strong company or brand recognition and image differentiation. The company might build a brand around a famous person, as Nike did with its Air Jordan basketball shoes and Tiger Woods golfing products. Some companies even become associated with colors, such as IBM (blue) or UPS (brown). The chosen symbols, characters, and other image elements must be communicated through advertising that conveys the company's or brand's personality.

Choosing the Right Competitive Advantages Suppose a company is fortunate enough to discover several potential competitive advantages. It now must choose the ones on which it will build its positioning strategy. It must decide *how many* differences to promote and *which ones*.

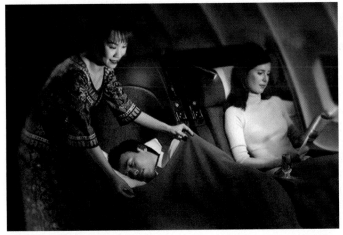

■ People differentiation: Singapore Airlines enjoys an excellent reputation, largely because of the grace of its flight attendants.

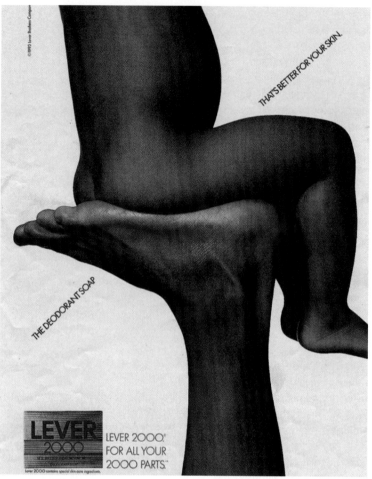

■ Unilever positioned its best-selling Lever 2000 soap on three benefits in one: cleansing, deodorizing, and moisturizing benefits. It's good "for all your 2000 parts."

How Many Differences to Promote? Many marketers think that companies should aggressively promote only one benefit to the target market. Ad man Rosser Reeves, for example, said a company should develop a *unique selling proposition* (USP) for each brand and stick to it. Each brand should pick an attribute and tout itself as "number one" on that attribute. Buyers tend to remember number one better, especially in an overcommunicated society. Thus, Crest toothpaste consistently promotes its anticavity protection and Wal-Mart promotes low prices.

Other marketers think that companies should position themselves on more than one differentiator. This may be necessary if two or more firms are claiming to be the best on the same attribute. Today, in a time when the mass market is fragmenting into many small segments, companies are trying to broaden their positioning strategies to appeal to more segments. For example, Unilever introduced the first three-in-one bar soap—Lever 2000—offering cleansing, deodorizing, *and* moisturizing benefits. Clearly, many buyers want all three benefits. The challenge was to convince them that one brand can deliver all three. Judging from Lever 2000's outstanding success, Unilever easily met the challenge. However, as companies increase the number of claims for their brands, they risk disbelief and a loss of clear positioning.

Which Differences to Promote? Not all brand differences are meaningful or worthwhile; not every difference makes a good differentiator. Each difference has the potential to create company costs as well as customer benefits. A difference is worth establishing to the extent that it satisfies the following criteria:

- *Important:* The difference delivers a highly valued benefit to target buyers.
- *Distinctive:* Competitors do not offer the difference, or the company can offer it in a more distinctive way.
- *Superior:* The difference is superior to other ways that customers might obtain the same benefit.
- *Communicable:* The difference is communicable and visible to buyers.
- *Preemptive:* Competitors cannot easily copy the difference.
- *Affordable:* Buyers can afford to pay for the difference.
- *Profitable:* The company can introduce the difference profitably.

Many companies have introduced differentiations that failed one or more of these tests. When the Westin Stamford hotel in Singapore advertised that it is the world's tallest hotel, it was a distinction that was not important to most tourists—in fact, it turned many off. Polaroid's Polarvision, which produced instantly-developed home movies, bombed too. Although Polarvision was distinctive and even preemptive, it was inferior to another way of capturing motion, namely, camcorders. Thus, choosing competitive advantages upon which to position a product or service can be difficult, yet such choices may be crucial to success.

Selecting an Overall Positioning Strategy The full positioning of a brand is called the brand's **value proposition**—the full mix of benefits upon which the brand is positioned. It is the answer to the customer's question "Why should I buy your brand?" Volvo's value proposition hinges on safety but also includes reliability, roominess, and styling, all for a price that is higher than average but seems fair for this mix of benefits.

Figure 6.4 shows possible value propositions upon which a company might position its products. In the figure, the five green cells represent winning value propositions—

Value proposition
The full positioning of a brand—the full mix of benefits upon which it is positioned.

FIGURE 6.4
Possible Value Propositions

Price

	More	The same	Less
More	More for more	More for the same	More for less
The same			The same for less
Less			Less for much less

Benefits

positioning that gives the company competitive advantage. The red cells, however, represent losing value propositions. The center yellow cell represents, at best, a marginal proposition. In the following sections, we discuss the five winning value propositions upon which companies can position their products: more for more, more for the same, the same for less, less for much less, and more for less.

More for More. "More-for-more" positioning involves providing the most upscale product or service and charging a higher price to cover the higher costs. Ritz-Carlton Hotels, Mont Blanc writing instruments, BMW automobiles—each claims superior quality, craftsmanship, durability, performance, or style and charges a price to match. Not only is the market offering high in quality, it also gives prestige to the buyer. It symbolizes status and a loftier lifestyle. Often, the price difference exceeds the actual increment in quality.

Sellers offering "only the best" can be found in every product and service category, from hotels, restaurants, food, and fashion to cars and household appliances. Consumers are sometimes surprised, even delighted, when a new competitor enters a category with an unusually high-priced brand. Starbucks coffee entered as a very expensive brand in a largely commodity category. Dyson came in as a premium vacuum cleaner with a price to match, touting "No clogged bags, no clogged filters, and no loss of suction means only one thing. It's a Dyson."

In general, companies should be on the lookout for opportunities to introduce a "more-for-more" brand in any underdeveloped product or service category. Yet "more-for-more" brands can be vulnerable. They often invite imitators who claim the same quality but at a lower price. Luxury goods that sell well during good times may be at risk during economic downturns when buyers become more cautious in their spending.

More for the Same. Companies can attack a competitor's more-for-more positioning by introducing a brand offering comparable quality but at a lower price. For example, Toyota introduced its Lexus line with a "more-for-the-same" value proposition versus Mercedes and BMW. Its headline read: "Perhaps the first time in history that trading a $72,000 car for a $36,000 car could be considered trading up." It communicated the high quality of its new Lexus through rave reviews in car magazines and through a widely distributed videotape showing side-by-side comparisons of Lexus and Mercedes automobiles. It

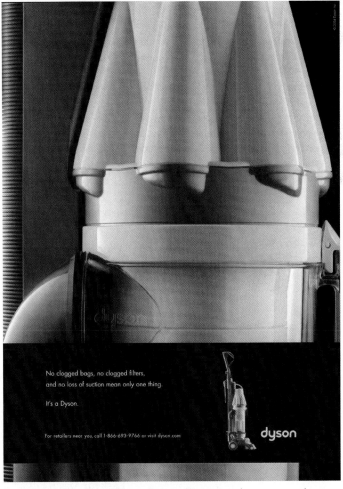

No clogged bags, no clogged filters, and no loss of suction mean only one thing.

It's a Dyson.

For retailers near you, call 1-866-693-9766 or visit dyson.com

dyson

■ "More-for-more" positioning: Dyson offers a premium vacuum cleaner with a price to match. "No clogged bags. No clogged filters, and no loss of suction mean only one thing. It's a Dyson."

MARKETING AT WORK   6.2
Southwest's Value Proposition: "Less for Much Less"

In an industry beset by hard times, Southwest Airlines soars above its competition. In the wake of a global economic slump and the effects of increased terrorism, most airlines have suffered huge losses in recent years. Some major airlines have even declared bankruptcy, and others threaten to follow suit. Yet even in these bleak times, Southwest has yet to suffer a loss in a single quarter. Amazingly, Southwest has experienced 32 straight years of profits. What's the secret? Southwest is the most strongly and clearly positioned airline in the world. It offers a classic "less-for-much-less" value proposition.

From the start, Southwest has positioned itself firmly as *the* no-frills, low-price airline. Southwest's passengers have learned to fly without the amenities. For example, the airline provides no meals—just peanuts. It also offers no first-class section, only three-across seating in all of its planes. There's no in-flight entertainment, either, and there's no such thing as a reserved seat on a Southwest flight. Passengers are assigned to boarding groups when checking in and herded onto the plane in groups of 45. "Southwest will get you and your luggage where you're going," comments an industry analyst, "but we don't call their planes cattle cars for nothing."

Why, then, do so many passengers love Southwest? Perhaps most importantly, Southwest excels at the basics of getting passengers where they want to go on time. Every year, Southwest ranks among the industry's leaders in on-time performance, baggage handling, and customer service. All this makes Southwest passengers a satisfied bunch. In 13 of the past 14 years, Southwest has ranked number one in fewest customer complaints in the U.S. Department of Transportation's Air Travel Consumer Report. And for at least the last eleven years, it has rated number-one in the airline industry in customer satisfaction on the American Customer Satisfaction Index.

Beyond the basics, however, there are two key elements to Southwest's strong positioning. The analyst sums up Southwest's positioning this way: "It is not luxurious, . . . but it's cheap and it's fun." Southwest is a model of efficiency and low-cost operations. As a result, its prices are shockingly low. When it enters a new market, Southwest proclaims: "Southwest is coming to town, and airline prices are coming down." Its average one-way fare is just $91.15. In fact, prices are so low that when Southwest enters a market, it actually increases total air traffic by attracting customers who might otherwise travel by car or bus. For example, when Southwest began its Louisville-Chicago flight at a one-way rate of $49 versus competitors' $250, total weekly air passenger traffic between the two cities increased from 8,000 to 26,000.

No frills and low prices, however, don't mean drudgery. To lighten things up, Southwest adds another key positioning ingredient—lots of good, clean fun. With its happy-go-lucky Chairman and co-founder, Herb Kelleher, leading the charge, Southwest refuses to take itself seriously. Cheerful employees go out of their way to amuse, surprise, or somehow entertain passengers. According to one account:

Southwest employees are apt to dress as leprechauns on St. Patrick's Day, rabbits on Easter, and almost anything on Halloween. I have heard flight attendants sing the safety lecture as country music, blues, and rap; I have heard them compare the pilot to Rocky Raccoon and insist that passengers introduce themselves to one another, then hug, then kiss, then propose marriage.

Kelleher himself has been known to dress up as Elvis Presley to greet passengers.

During delays at the gate, ticket agents will award prizes to the passenger with the largest hole in his or her sock. Flight attendants have

published surveys showing that Lexus dealers were providing customers with better sales and service experiences than were Mercedes dealerships. Many Mercedes owners switched to Lexus, and the Lexus repurchase rate has been 60 percent, twice the industry average.

The Same for Less. Offering "the same for less" can be a powerful value proposition—everyone likes a good deal. For example, Dell offers equivalent quality computers at a lower "price for performance." Discount stores such as Wal-Mart and "category killers" such as Best Buy, Circuit City, and Sportmart also use this positioning. They don't claim to offer different or better products. Instead, they offer many of the same brands as department stores and specialty stores but at deep discounts based on superior purchasing power and lower-cost operations. Other companies develop imitative but lower-priced brands in an effort to lure customers away from the market leader. For example, AMD makes less expensive versions of Intel's market-leading microprocessor chips.

Less for Much Less. A market almost always exists for products that offer less and, therefore, cost less. Few people need, want, or can afford "the very best" in everything they buy. In many cases, consumers will gladly settle for less than optimal performance or give up

■ *Southwest offers a classic "less for much less" value proposition, with lots of zany fun. It all starts at the top with company Cofounder and Chairman Herb Kelleher.*

screaming, grab the mask, and pull it over your face. If you have small children traveling with you, secure your mask before assisting with theirs. If you are traveling with two small children, decide now which one you love more."

Even the company's headquarters reflect the airline's sense of humor.

Pay a visit to Southwest's headquarters just off Love Field in Dallas, and you'll probably think you've wandered onto the set of Pee-Wee's Playhouse. The walls are festooned with more than ten thousand picture frames—no exaggeration—containing photos of employees' pets, of Herb dressed like Elvis or in drag, of stewardesses in miniskirts, and of Southwest planes gnawing on competitors' aircraft. Then there are the teddy bears, and jars of pickled hot peppers, and pink flamingos. There is . . . lots of chuckling and nary a necktie to be seen.

As a result of its strong positioning, Southwest has grown to become one of the nation's largest carriers. The company has successfully beaten off determined challenges from

several major competitors who have tried to copy its winning formula, including AirTran Airways, JetBlue, and Delta's Song Airlines. Southwest now makes more than 3,000 flights a day, serving 61 cities in 31 states. Through good times and bad, Southwest has been the *only* airline to consistently turn a profit. Last year, the U.S. airline industry lost an estimated $5.5 billion; Southwest *made* $313 million, more than all other U.S. airlines combined.

Simple, clear positioning has made Southwest *Fortune* magazine's most admired airline for the past nine years running. And last year, Southwest was *Fortune's* number-five most admired company overall. Southwest not only promises an appealing value proposition, it delivers on the promise. It's not ritzy, but it gets you where you want to go, when you want to get there. You get low, low prices and lots of good fun. Just the ticket when you need a good lift!

Sources: Quotes and other information from Molly Ivins, "From Texas, with Love and Peanuts," *New York Times*, March 14, 1999, p. 11; Wendy Zellner, "Southwest: After Kelleher, More Blue Skies," *BusinessWeek*, April 2, 2001, p. 45; Ron Suskind, "Humor Has Returned After 9/11 Hiatus," *Wall Street Journal*, January 13, 2003, p. A1; Melanie Trottman and Susan Carey, "Big Airlines Post Weak Fourth-Quarter Results," *Wall Street Journal*, January 20, 2005, p. A6; Bill McGee, "DOT Grades Airline Industry in Consumer Travel Reports," *USA Today*, March 8, 2005, accessed at www.usatoday.com; and *Southwest Airlines Fact Sheet*, June 9, 2005, accessed at www.southwest.com.

been known to hide in overhead luggage bins and then pop out when passengers start filing on board. Veteran Southwest fliers have learned to listen up to announcements over the intercom. On a recent flight, the pilot suggested, "Flight attendants will please prepare their hair for departure." Safety instructions from the flight attendant included the advice: "In the unlikely event of a sudden loss of cabin pressure, oxygen masks will descend from the ceiling. Stop

some of the bells and whistles in exchange for a lower price. For example, many travelers seeking lodgings prefer not to pay for what they consider unnecessary extras, such as a pool, attached restaurant, or mints on the pillow. Hotel chains such as Ramada Limited suspend some of these amenities and charge less accordingly.

"Less-for-much-less" positioning involves meeting consumers' lower performance or quality requirements at a much lower price. For example, Family Dollar and Dollar General stores offer more affordable goods at very low prices. Sam's Club and Costco warehouse stores offer less merchandise selection and consistency, and much lower levels of service; as a result, they charge rock-bottom prices. Southwest Airlines, the nation's most profitable air carrier, also practices less-for-much-less positioning. It charges incredibly low prices by not serving food, not assigning seats, and not using travel agents (see Marketing at Work 6.2).

More for Less. Of course, the winning value proposition would be to offer "more for less." Many companies claim to do this. And, in the short run, some companies can actually achieve such lofty positions. For example, when it first opened for business, Home Depot had arguably the best product selection, the best service, *and* the lowest prices compared to local hardware stores and other home improvement chains.

Yet in the long run, companies will find it very difficult to sustain such best-of-both positioning. Offering more usually costs more, making it difficult to deliver on the "for-less" promise. Companies that try to deliver both may lose out to more focused competitors. For example, facing determined competition from Lowe's stores, Home Depot must now decide whether it wants to compete primarily on superior service or on lower prices.

All said, each brand must adopt a positioning strategy designed to serve the needs and wants of its target markets. "More for more" will draw one target market, "less for much less" will draw another, and so on. Thus, in any market, there is usually room for many different companies, each successfully occupying different positions.

The important thing is that each company must develop its own winning positioning strategy, one that makes it special to its target consumers. Offering only "the same for the same" provides no competitive advantage, leaving the firm in the middle of the pack. Companies offering one of the three losing value propositions—"the same for more," "less for more," and "less for the same"—will inevitably fail. Customers soon realize that they've been underserved, tell others, and abandon the brand.

Developing a Positioning Statement Company and brand positioning should be summed up in a **positioning statement**. The statement should follow the form: *To (target segment and need) our (brand) is (concept) that (point-of-difference)*.[31] For example: "*To busy, mobile professionals who need to always be in the loop, BlackBerry is a wireless connectivity solution that allows you to stay connected to data, people, and resources while on the go, easily and reliably—more so than competing technologies.*" Sometimes a positioning statement is more detailed:

> To young, active soft-drink consumers who have little time for sleep, Mountain Dew is the soft drink that gives you more energy than any other brand because it has the highest level of caffeine. With Mountain Dew, you can stay alert and keep going even when you haven't been able to get a good night's sleep.

Note that positioning first states the product's membership in a category (Mountain Dew is a soft drink) and then shows its point-of-difference from other members of the category (has more caffeine). Placing a brand in a specific category suggests similarities that it might share with other products in the category. But the case for the brand's superiority is made on its points of difference.

Sometimes marketers put a brand in a surprisingly different category before indicating the points of difference. DiGiorno is a frozen pizza whose crust rises when the pizza is heated. But instead of putting it in the frozen pizza category, the marketers positioned it in the delivered pizza category. Their ad shows party guests asking which pizza delivery service the host used. But, says the host, "It's not delivery, its DiGiorno!" This helped highlight DiGiorno's fresh quality and superior taste over the normal frozen pizza.

COMMUNICATING AND DELIVERING THE CHOSEN POSITION

Once it has chosen a position, the company must take strong steps to deliver and communicate the desired position to target consumers. All the company's marketing mix efforts must support the positioning strategy.

Positioning the company calls for concrete action, not just talk. If the company decides to build a position on better quality and service, it must first *deliver* that position. Designing the marketing mix—product, price, place, and promotion—involves working out the tactical details of the positioning strategy. Thus, a firm that seizes a more-for-more position knows that it must produce high-quality products, charge a high price, distribute through high-quality dealers, and advertise in high-quality media. It must hire and train more service people, find retailers who have a good reputation for service, and develop sales and advertising messages that broadcast its superior service. This is the only way to build a consistent and believable more-for-more position.

Companies often find it easier to come up with a good positioning strategy than to implement it. Establishing a position or changing one usually takes a long time. In contrast, positions that have taken years to build can quickly be lost. Once a company has built the desired position, it must take care to maintain the position through consistent perfor-

---

Positioning statement

A statement that summarizes company or brand positioning—it takes this form: *To (target segment and need) our (brand) is (concept) that (point-of-difference).*

mance and communication. It must closely monitor and adapt the position over time to match changes in consumer needs and competitors' strategies. However, the company should avoid abrupt changes that might confuse consumers. Instead, a product's position should evolve gradually as it adapts to the ever-changing marketing environment.

REST STOP → REVIEWING THE CONCEPTS

It's time to stop and stretch your legs. In this chapter, you've learned about the major elements of marketing strategy: segmentation, targeting, and positioning. Marketers know that they cannot appeal to all buyers in their markets, or at least not to all buyers in the same way. Buyers are too numerous, too widely scattered, and too varied in their needs and buying practices. Therefore, most companies today practice *target marketing*—identifying market segments, selecting one or more of them, and developing products and marketing mixes tailored to each.

1. Define the three steps of target marketing: market segmentation, target marketing, and market positioning.

Market segmentation is the act of dividing a market into distinct groups of buyers with different needs, characteristics, or behaviors who might require separate products or marketing mixes. Once the groups have been identified, *target marketing* evaluates each market segment's attractiveness and selects one or more segments to serve. Target marketing involves designing strategies to build the *right relationships* with the *right customers*. *Market positioning* consists of deciding how to best serve target customers—setting the competitive positioning for the product and creating a detailed marketing plan.

2. List and discuss the major bases for segmenting consumer and business markets.

There is no single way to segment a market. Therefore, the marketer tries different variables to see which give the best segmentation opportunities. For consumer marketing, the major segmentation variables are geographic, demographic, psychographic, and behavioral. In *geographic segmentation,* the market is divided into different geographical units such as nations, regions, states, counties, cities, or neighborhoods. In *demographic segmentation,* the market is divided into groups based on demographic variables, including age, gender, family size, family life cycle, income, occupation, education, religion, race, generation, and nationality. In *psychographic segmentation,* the market is divided into different groups based on social class, lifestyle, or personality characteristics. In *behavioral segmentation,* the market is divided into groups based on consumers' knowledge, attitudes, uses, or responses to a product.

Business marketers use many of the same variables to segment their markets. But business markets also can be segmented by business consumer *demographics* (industry, company size), *operating characteristics, purchasing approaches, situational factors,* and *personal characteristics.* The effectiveness of segmentation analysis depends on finding segments that are *measurable, accessible, substantial, differentiable,* and *actionable.*

3. Explain how companies identify attractive market segments and choose a target marketing strategy.

To target the best market segments, the company first evaluates each segment's size and growth characteristics, structural attractiveness, and compatibility with company objectives and resources. It then chooses one of four target marketing strategies—ranging from very broad to very narrow targeting. The seller can ignore segment differences and target broadly using *undifferentiated* (or *mass*) *marketing.* This involves mass-producing, mass-distributing, and mass-promoting the same product in about the same way to all consumers. Or the seller can adopt *differentiated marketing*—developing different market offers for several segments. *Concentrated marketing* (or *niche marketing*) involves focusing on only one or a few market segments. Finally, *micromarketing* is the practice of tailoring products and marketing programs to suit the tastes of specific individuals and locations. Micromarketing includes *local marketing* and *individual marketing.* Which targeting strategy is best depends on company resources, product variability, product life-cycle stage, market variability, and competitive marketing strategies.

4. Discuss how companies position their products for maximum competitive advantage in the marketplace.

Once a company has decided which segments to enter, it must decide on its *market positioning* strategy—on which positions to occupy in its chosen segments. The positioning task consists of three steps: identifying a set of possible competitive advantages upon which to build a position, choosing the right competitive advantages, and selecting an overall positioning strategy. The brand's full positioning is called its *value proposition*—the full mix of benefits upon which the brand is positioned. In general, companies can choose from one of five winning value propositions upon which to position their products: more for more, more for the same, the same for less, less for much less, or more for less. Company and brand positioning are summarized in positioning statements that state the target segment and need, positioning concept, and specific points of difference. The company must then effectively communicate and deliver the chosen position to the market.

Navigating the Key Terms

Age and life-cycle segmentation (167)
Behavioral segmentation (170)
Benefit segmentation (172)
Competitive advantage (186)
Concentrated (niche) marketing (180)
Demographic segmentation (167)
Differentiated (segmented)
   marketing (179)
Gender segmentation (168)

Geographic segmentation (165)
Income segmentation (168)
Individual marketing (181)
Intermarket segmentation (176)
Local marketing (181)
Market positioning (165)
Market segmentation (165)
Micromarketing (181)
Occasion segmentation (170)

Positioning statement (192)
Product position (185)
Psychographic segmentation (169)
Target market (178)
Target marketing (165)
Undifferentiated (or mass) marketing (179)
Value proposition (188)

Travel Log

Discussing the Issues

1. List a product or service example for each of the four major groups of segmentation variables in Table 6.1. Then discuss an example that employs multiple variables.

2. Need help with your financial planning? Intuit's Quicken (financial planning) and TurboTax (income-tax preparation) software have ensured the company's success in the rapidly growing financial planning and services market. Assume that the company wants to expand. Which of the target marketing strategies in Figure 6.2 would you suggest? Explain how your strategy helps Intuit overcome competitive challenges from other financial software makers, such as Microsoft.

3. Discuss how Mountain Dew has differentiated itself from other soft drink brands on the basis of product, services, channels, people, and image differentiation.

4. Socially responsible marketing calls for segmentation and targeting that serve not just the interests of the company but also the interests of those targeted. Do these goals conflict? Provide an example of a company that takes a socially responsible approach to segmentation and targeting. How does the company balance the interests of both the company and the consumer?

5. McDonald's has long been an innovator in fast food. To avoid the flat growth that has recently plagued the fast-food industry, McDonald's plans to experiment with waiter-service diners, McDonuts, Internet access for patrons, and SPAM breakfast platters. Use Figure 6.4 to discuss the value propositions McDonald's would be addressing with each of these innovations. Write a positioning statement for one of the new ventures.

6. Review Figure 6.4. Give examples of a hotel chain that falls into each of the five value propositions. What does each hotel do on the benefits dimension to offer more, the same, or less than competitors?

Application Questions

1. For years, auto makers have segmented markets to position themselves and their various offerings. If you could drive any car, which one would it be? Consider your favorite make and model—BMW, VW, Porsche, Mustang, Prius. How is the make positioned? How is your specific model positioned? How are other models from the same maker positioned differently? Draw a picture of the "typical" consumer you think the maker of your favorite model is targeting. Are you a member of the intended target market? What additional models could the car maker offer to target additional segments?

2. Visit the "You Are Where You Live" Web site (www.clusterbigip1.claritas.com/MyBestSegments/Default.jsp?ID=20) operated by Claritas, which demonstrates the PRIZM NE system in action. Enter in your hometown zip code and review the results. Do you identify with a cluster associated with your hometown? Do your parents fit into a cluster? Now enter the zip code for your college town. How do the results differ from that of your home town? Based on these segments, identify some products or services that might be well suited to the population in your home town. Name a few products that might fare better in your college town. Why?

3. In a small group, select a product or service that you believe could be better positioned in the market. Detail a plan for repositioning the product. Explain why you think the new positioning will be more successful.

Under the Hood: Focus on Technology

If you have ever made a purchase at Amazon.com, you've probably experienced the company's version of segmentation and targeting. To help customers navigate the overwhelming number of books, CDs, toys, and other merchandise that the site offers, Amazon.com relies on sophisticated software that builds a personalized Web site for each customer. Every time you log on, the software tracks your searches and purchases and then builds targeted recommendations for your next visit. The goal? Says Jeff Bezos, "We want Amazon.com to be the right store for you as an individual. If we have 40 million customers, we should have 40 million stores."

1. Log on to Amazon.com (www.amazon.com) and click on the "Your Store" tab to begin personalizing your own page. Create a personal profile. Then check out "The Page You Made." How accurate are Amazon.com's recommendations?

2. Would you consider making a purchase based on these recommendations?

3. Is it really possible for Amazon.com to effectively segment its millions of consumers into "markets of one"?

Focus on Ethics

How many credit cards do you have in your wallet? If you're like the typical student, you probably have one or two. Extending credit to students can be risky. Students are nearly three times as likely as older adults to be at least 90 days delinquent on their credit-card payments, and they are more likely to incur late fees. Yet companies like Capital One and MBNA aggressively target students. They hope to build long-term relationships with people who are likely to need auto loans, home mortgages, and other financial services in the future.

But many critics argue that creditors are looking for more than just long-term relationships. Concerned parents point out that one-fifth of college students hold four or more credit cards, leaving the average undergraduate with $2,169 in credit-card debt. And according to a recent Georgetown University study, nearly 20 percent of college students carry balances on their cards exceeding $10,000.

Such numbers have led activist groups and some federal law makers to propose legislation to curb credit-card marketers' access to students. And roughly 15 percent of colleges no longer allow credit-card marketers to set up tables offering free T-shirts, mugs, and other incentives on campus. In response, credit-card issuers now provide targeted educational materials designed to help students manage their money and argue that having credit helps students learn about financial responsibility.*

1. What do you think? Does targeting undergraduates with credit-card offers foster financial responsibility or prey on vulnerable students?

2. How effective are companies like Capital One in targeting students? How many credit cards do you have? What persuaded you to sign up for those cards?

*For more information, "Undergraduate Students and Credit Cards in 2004: An Analysis of Usage Rates and Trends by Nellie Mae," May 2005, accessed online at www.nelliemae.com; and information accessed online at www.bankrate.com.

Videos

The Procter & Gamble video case that accompanies this chapter is located in Appendix 1 at the back of the book.

The Taste
of Paradise

Chapter 7

AFTER READING THIS CHAPTER, YOU SHOULD BE ABLE TO

1. define *product* and the major classifications of products and services

2. describe the decisions companies make regarding their individual products and services, product lines, and product mixes

3. discuss branding strategy—the decisions companies make in building and managing their brands

4. identify the four characteristics that affect the marketing of a service and the additional marketing considerations that services require

5. discuss two additional product issues: socially responsible product decisions and international product and services marketing

Product, Services, and Branding Strategy

Road Map Previewing the Concepts

Now that you've had a good look at marketing strategy, we'll take a deeper look at the marketing mix—the tactical tools that marketers use to implement their strategies. In this and the next chapter, we'll study how companies develop and manage products and brands. Then, in the chapters that follow, we'll look at pricing, distribution, and marketing communication tools. The product is usually the first and most basic marketing consideration. We'll start with a seemingly simple question: What *is* a product? As it turns out, however, the answer is not so simple.

First stop on this leg of the journey: a cool drink of water. Remember that seemingly simple question—what is a product? Well, what is water? That's right, *water?* As it turns out, to a FIJI Water customer, water is more than just a liquid you draw out of the tap to wash down a sandwich or to quench your thirst after a work-out. FIJI Water is "The Taste of Paradise!"

The best things in life are free. That's what the old song says. *The flowers in spring, the robins that sing, the sunbeams that shine, they're yours, they're mine!* The air that we breathe, the water we drink . . . oops, not so fast. The water we drink? Free? Consider the following account:

> At Jean-Georges, a celebrated Manhattan restaurant known for its artful cuisine and fine wines, a waiter lifts a tall silver decanter and fills three goblets from the bottle cradled within. Its contents must be precious: Chef Jean-Georges Vongerichten even uses this beverage as an ingredient in broths and sorbets. A rare vintage, perhaps? Try again. It's FIJI Natural Artesian Water, the latest bottled water brand to elevate the world's simplest drink to celebrity status. Today, at all of his restaurants, Mr. Vongerichten exclusively pours FIJI, which looks and sounds almost as exotic as the French dishes on his menu.

> FIJI water may be one of the best things in life, but it's certainly not free. A quick check of the Jean-Georges menu shows that FIJI sells there for $10 a bottle. $10! Shop around, perhaps at a lesser restaurant, and you might find a bottle at the bargain price of $2.75. And you thought gas was expensive. Why would anyone pay those kinds of prices for water, something they could get for free out of the tap?

> Well, it turns out the FIJI water is very, very good water. Drawn from an underground source on Viti Levu, the main island of the South Pacific country of Fiji, it has an ultra-clean taste and contains not a hint of impurities or pollutants. But when you drink FIJI Water, you're getting a lot more than just pure,

good-tasting water. According to the company, you're getting "The Taste of Paradise!"

Rainfall in a Fijian forest is a symphony of sound in a theater of green. Somewhere overhead, raindrops strike palm fronds that move with the wind, clicking and tapping like hundreds of castanets. Around you is a glimpse of Eden: giant leaves large enough to lie on, ferns like trees, bamboo and grasses taller than a man. And the rain, formed in clouds above the blue Pacific, dances down through the forest canopy and seeps into the rich volcanic soil, wending its way to the aquifer far below the forest floor. Water, like wine, gets its taste from the terrain that forms it. FIJI Water comes from a virgin ecosystem deep in the South Pacific, from tropical rain filtered for hundreds of years through volcanic stone. This natural artesian water is known for its signature soft, smooth taste and well-balanced mineral content including a high level of silica, a youth-preserving anti-oxidant. You can taste the purity in every sip. It's the Taste of Paradise!

Everything about FIJI Water contributes to this "Taste of Paradise" brand experience—from its name, packaging, and label to the places that sell and serve it, to the celebrities that drink and endorse it. The name was a natural—FIJI Natural Artesian Water evokes visions of unspoiled natural beauty and purity. The unique square bottle and colorful labeling also set the brand apart. The clear plastic front label presents the FIJI name, with pictures of tropical plants and flowers at the sides. Looking through the front label to the inside of the back label, you see a picture of a cascading waterfall. In combination, the front and back labels create a striking 3-D picture that emphasizes FIJI Water's clarity and purity. "The bottle appears to have a magic in it," says a company official.

Skillful marketing has also helped to build the brand's ultra-chic image. Initial ads played up FIJI's exotic origins—raindrops falling into Fiji's pristine tropical forests and filtering through layers of volcanic rock. "We're sure you'll agree, it was worth the 450-year wait," said the ads. To boost the brand's status, the company sent samples to movie stars, athletes, and other celebrities, and it pursued product placements in films and TV shows. For example, in the movie *Dodgeball*, Lance Armstrong, the six-time Tour de France winner, sat at a bar while drinking FIJI water. And Drew Barrymore clutched a bottle of FIJI in *50 First Dates*. Such efforts have given FIJI top billing as what one observer calls "the bottled water of the stars."

At the same time, the company convinced luxury hotels and restaurants of the merits of FIJI Water, urging that superb food and atmosphere needed to be paired with water of the same quality. It trained restaurant wait staff to educate consumers on the brand's taste and purity. The company even convinced chefs at leading restaurants to use FIJI Water as a *cooking ingredient* in their kitchens. "Great chefs spend all their time carefully choosing ingredients and crafting a wine list, then they use a water that doesn't complement the taste of either," notes FIJI's chief executive. Finally, to make FIJI Water's plastic bottles more table worthy, the company came up with its own distinctive silver serving sleeve, custom-made to fit FIJI's square bottle. That silver sleeve tells everyone in a restaurant that the customer who ordered FIJI water appreciates the best and can afford it.

So not all waters are created equal. When you need something to quench your thirst after a good workout, gulping a glass of water from the tap might do the trick. But for special occasions, you may want something more—something that tastes really good, or that makes you feel special, or that tells others something about who you are. On such occasions, the FIJI brand promises a special experience—much like a fine wine with a gourmet meal. When FIJI sells water, it sells more than just the tangible liquid. It sells purity and great taste, good health, refinement, status, and exclusivity.

But, still, could any water be worth $10 a bottle, or even $2.75? Apparently so! Despite an increasingly crowded bottled-water market—more than 120 bottled waters were introduced in 2004 alone—FIJI is scrambling to keep up with surging demand. In a year when primary competitor Evian's U.S. sales volume decreased 23 percent, FIJI's sales shot up 61 percent. Last year, the company added a new bottling line that tripled its capacity. Thus, more people are buying into FIJI's "The Taste of Paradise" brand promise, despite the high price—or maybe because of it.[1]

Clearly, water is more than just water when FIJI sells it. This chapter begins with a deceptively simple question: *What is a product?* After answering this question, we look at ways to classify products in consumer and business markets. Then we discuss the important decisions that marketers make regarding individual products, product lines, and product mixes. Next, we look into the critically important issue of how marketers build and manage brands. Finally, we examine the characteristics and marketing requirements of a special form of product—services.

What Is a Product?

We define a **product** as anything that can be offered to a market for attention, acquisition, use, or consumption that might satisfy a want or need. Products include more than just tangible goods. Broadly defined, products include physical objects, services, events, persons, places, organizations, ideas, or mixes of these entities. Throughout this text, we use the term *product* broadly to include any or all of these entities. Thus, an Apple iPod, a Toyota Camry, and a Caffé Mocha at Starbucks are products. But so are a European vacation, Fidelity online investment services, and advice from your family doctor.

Because of their importance in the world economy, we give special attention to services. **Services** are a form of product that consists of activities, benefits, or satisfactions offered for sale that are essentially intangible and do not result in the ownership of anything. Examples are banking, hotel, airline, retail, tax preparation, and home-repair services. We will look at services more closely later in this chapter.

Product
Anything that can be offered to a market for attention, acquisition, use, or consumption that might satisfy a want or need.

Service
Any activity or benefit that one party can offer to another that is essentially intangible and does not result in the ownership of anything.

PRODUCTS, SERVICES, AND EXPERIENCES

Product is a key element in the overall *market offering*. Marketing-mix planning begins with formulating an offering that brings value to target customers. This offering becomes the basis upon which the company builds profitable relationships with customers.

A company's market offering often includes both tangible goods and services. Each component can be a minor or a major part of the total offer. At one extreme, the offer may consist of a *pure tangible good*, such as soap, toothpaste, or salt—no services accompany the product. At the other extreme are *pure services*, for which the offer consists primarily of a service. Examples include a doctor's exam or financial services. Between these two extremes, however, many goods-and-services combinations are possible.

Today, as products and services become more commoditized, many companies are moving to a new level in creating value for their customers. To differentiate their offers, beyond simply making products and delivering services, they are creating and managing customer *experiences* with their products or company.

Experiences have always been important in the entertainment industry—Disney has long manufactured memories through its movies and theme parks. Today, however, all kinds of firms are recasting their traditional goods and services to create experiences. For example, Starbucks's patrons are paying for more than just coffee. The company treats customers to poetry on its wallpaper, apron-clad performers behind espresso machines, and a warm but modern interior ambience that leaves them feeling more affluent and fulfilled. And American Girl, Inc., does more than just make and sell high-end dolls. It now takes additional steps to create special experiences between the dolls and the girls who adore them.[2]

To extend its reach and to put more smiles on the faces of the girls who adore their American Girl dolls, the company has opened American Girl Places in Chicago and New York. Inside a Place—please don't call it a store—are a series of wonderfully engaging experiences for girls, mothers, and grandmothers (not to mention the occasional male who's either dragged into the Place or who loves his daughter very much). There's a theater with a live play centered on the doll collection; there's a Café for a grown-up dining experience; there's a salon to style a doll's hair; and a doll hospital to fix one up as

■ Marketing experiences: American Girl, Inc., does more than just make and sell high-end dolls. It now takes additional steps to create special experiences between the dolls and the girls who adore them.

good as new. Before, during, and after all these experiences, shopping does go on—and the purchases become memorabilia for the experiences visitors have. Moreover, these same visitors buy more from the catalog, frequent the Web site to purchase items more often, and tell their friends about their American Girl Place experience. Much more than a store that sells dolls, says the company, "It's the place where imaginations soar—from boutiques to special events, from the Café to the Theater and beyond."

Companies that market experiences realize that customers are really buying much more than just products and services. They are buying what those offers will *do* for them.

LEVELS OF PRODUCT AND SERVICES

Product planners need to think about products and services on three levels (see Figure 7.1). Each level adds more customer value. The most basic level is the *core benefit*, which addresses the question *What is the buyer really buying?* When designing products, marketers must first define the core, problem-solving benefits or services that consumers seek. A woman buying lipstick buys more than lip color. Charles Revson of Revlon saw this early: "In the factory, we make cosmetics; in the store, we sell hope." And young parents buying a Sony Handycam are buying more than a digital camcorder. They are buying a convenient, high-quality way to capture important moments and memories.

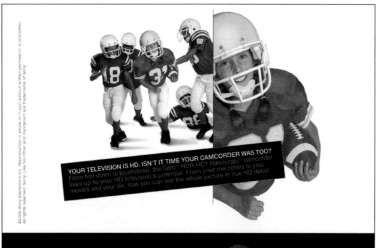

At the second level, product planners must turn the core benefit into an *actual product*. They need to develop product and service features, design, a quality level, a brand name, and packaging. For example, the Sony camcorder is an actual product. Its name, parts, styling, features, packaging, and other attributes have all been combined carefully to deliver the core benefit of capturing memories.

Finally, product planners must build an *augmented product* around the core benefit and actual product by offering additional consumer services and benefits. Sony must offer more than just a camcorder. It must provide consumers with a complete solution to their picture-taking problems. Thus, when consumers buy a Sony camcorder, Sony and its dealers also might give buyers a warranty on parts and workmanship, instructions on how to use the camcorder, quick repair services when needed, and a toll-free telephone number to call if they have problems or questions.

Consumers see products as complex bundles of benefits that satisfy their needs. When developing products, marketers first must identify the *core* consumer needs the product will satisfy. They must then design the *actual* product and find ways to *augment* it in order to create the bundle of benefits that will provide the most satisfying customer experience.

■ Core, actual, and augmented product: Consumers perceive a Sony Handycam as a complex bundle of intangible features and services that deliver a core benefit—a convenient high-quality way to capture important moments.

PRODUCT AND SERVICE CLASSIFICATIONS

Products and services fall into two broad classes based on the types of consumers that use them—*consumer products* and *industrial products*. Broadly defined, products also include other marketable entities such as experiences, organizations, persons, places, and ideas.

Consumer product
Product bought by final consumer for personal consumption.

Consumer Products   **Consumer products** are products and services bought by final consumers for personal consumption. Marketers usually classify these products and ser-

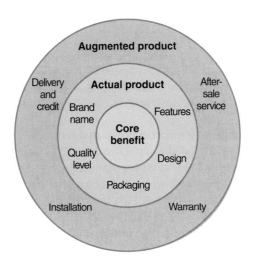

FIGURE 7.1
Three Levels of Product

vices further based on how consumers go about buying them. Consumer products include *convenience products, shopping products, specialty products*, and *unsought products*. These products differ in the ways consumers buy them and, therefore, in how they are marketed (see Table 7.1).

Convenience products are consumer products and services that the customer usually buys frequently, immediately, and with a minimum of comparison and buying effort. Examples include soap, candy, newspapers, and fast food. Convenience products are usually low priced, and marketers place them in many locations to make them readily available when customers need them.

Shopping products are less frequently purchased consumer products and services that customers compare carefully on suitability, quality, price, and style. When buying shopping products and services, consumers spend much time and effort in gathering information and making comparisons. Examples include furniture, clothing, used cars, major appliances, and hotel and airline services. Shopping products marketers usually distribute their products through fewer outlets but provide deeper sales support to help customers in their comparison efforts.

Specialty products are consumer products and services with unique characteristics or brand identification for which a significant group of buyers is willing to make a special purchase effort. Examples include specific brands and types of cars, high-priced photographic equipment, designer clothes, and the services of medical or legal specialists. A Lamborghini automobile, for example, is a specialty product because buyers are usually willing to travel great distances to buy one. Buyers normally do not compare specialty products. They invest only the time needed to reach dealers carrying the wanted products.

Convenience product
Consumer product that the customer usually buys frequently, immediately, and with a minimum of comparison and buying effort.

Shopping product
Consumer good that the customer, in the process of selection and purchase, characteristically compares on such bases as suitability, quality, price, and style.

Specialty product
Consumer product with unique characteristics or brand identification for which a significant group of buyers is willing to make a special purchase effort.

TABLE 7.1 Marketing Considerations for Consumer Productions

Marketing Considerations	Type of Consumer Product			
	Convenience	**Shopping**	**Specialty**	**Unsought**
Customer buying behavior	Frequent purchase, little planning, little comparison or shopping effort, low customer involvement	Less frequent purchase, much planning and shopping effort, comparison of brands on price, quality, style	Strong brand preference and loyalty, special purchase effort, little comparison of brands, low price sensitivity	Little product awareness, knowledge (or, if aware, little or even negative interest)
Price	Low Price	Higher price	High price	Varies
Distribution	Widespread distribution, convenient locations	Selective distribution in fewer outlets	Exclusive distribution in only one or a few outlets per market area	Varies
Promotion	Mass promotion by the producer	Advertising and personal selling by both producer and resellers	More carefully targeted promotion by both producer and resellers	Aggressive advertising and personal selling by producer and resellers
Examples	Toothpaste, magazines, laundry detergent	Major appliances, televisions, furniture, clothing	Luxury goods, such as Rolex watches or fine crystal	Life insurance, Red Cross blood donations

Unsought product
Consumer product that the consumer either does not know about or knows about but does not normally think of buying.

Unsought products are consumer products that the consumer either does not know about or knows about but does not normally think of buying. Most major new innovations are unsought until the consumer becomes aware of them through advertising. Classic examples of known but unsought products and services are life insurance, preplanned funeral services, and blood donations to the Red Cross. By their very nature, unsought products require a lot of advertising, personal selling, and other marketing efforts.

Industrial product
Product bought by individuals and organizations for further processing or for use in conducting a business.

Industrial Products
Industrial products are those purchased for further processing or for use in conducting a business. Thus, the distinction between a consumer product and an industrial product is based on the *purpose* for which the product is bought. If a consumer buys a lawn mower for use around the home, the lawn mower is a consumer product. If the same consumer buys the same lawn mower for use in a landscaping business, the lawn mower is an industrial product.

The three groups of industrial products and services include materials and parts, capital items, and supplies and services. *Materials and parts* include raw materials and manufactured materials and parts. Raw materials consist of farm products (wheat, cotton, livestock, fruits, vegetables) and natural products (fish, lumber, crude petroleum, iron ore). Manufactured materials and parts consist of component materials (iron, yarn, cement, wires) and component parts (small motors, tires, castings). Most manufactured materials and parts are sold directly to industrial users. Price and service are the major marketing factors; branding and advertising tend to be less important.

Capital items are industrial products that aid in the buyer's production or operations, including installations and accessory equipment. Installations consist of major purchases such as buildings (factories, offices) and fixed equipment (generators, drill presses, large computer systems, elevators). Accessory equipment includes portable factory equipment and tools (hand tools, lift trucks) and office equipment (computers, fax machines, desks). They have a shorter life than installations and simply aid in the production process.

The final group of business products is *supplies and services*. Supplies include operating supplies (lubricants, coal, paper, pencils) and repair and maintenance items (paint, nails, brooms). Supplies are the convenience products of the industrial field because they are usually purchased with a minimum of effort or comparison. Business services include maintenance and repair services (window cleaning, computer repair) and business advisory services (legal, management consulting, advertising). Such services are usually supplied under contract.

Organizations, Persons, Places, and Ideas
In addition to tangible products and services, in recent years marketers have broadened the concept of a product to include other market offerings—organizations, persons, places, and ideas.

Organizations often carry out activities to "sell" the organization itself. *Organization marketing* consists of activities undertaken to create, maintain, or change the attitudes and behavior of target consumers toward an organization. Both profit and not-for-profit organizations practice organization marketing. Business firms sponsor public relations or corporate advertising campaigns to polish their images. *Corporate image advertising* is a major tool companies use to market themselves to various publics. For example, BASF ads say "We don't make a lot of the products you buy, we make a lot of the products you buy better." And General Electric stands for "imagination at work." Similarly, not-for-profit organizations, such as churches, colleges, charities, museums, and performing arts groups, market their organizations in order to raise funds and attract members or patrons.

People can also be thought of as products. *Person marketing* consists of activities undertaken to create, maintain, or change attitudes or behavior toward particular people. People ranging from presidents, entertainers, and sports figures to professionals such as doctors, lawyers, and architects use person marketing to build their reputations and increase business. Businesses, charities, sports teams, and other organizations also use person marketing. Creating or associating with well-known personalities often helps these organizations achieve their goals better. That's why more than a dozen different companies—including Nike, Apple, Tag Heuer, Buick, American Express, Wheaties, and Accenture—combine to pay more than $70 million a year to link themselves with golf superstar Tiger Woods.[3]

The skillful use of person marketing can turn a person's name into a powerhouse brand. Michael Jordan has his own brand of Nike shoes and apparel, a chain of namesake restaurants, car dealerships, a brand of cologne, and more. The brand power of Oprah Winfrey's name has made her a billionaire: Oprah-branded products include her television show, TV and feature movies, *O, The Oprah Magazine*, Oprah's Angel Network, Oprah's Boutiques online shop, and Oprah's Book Club. And businessman Donald Trump has slapped his well-known name on everything from sky-scrapers and casinos to bottled water, magazines, and real-ity TV programs:

■ People as brands: Businessman Donald Trump has put his well-known name on everything from skyscrapers and casinos to bottled water, magazines, and reality TV programs.

> Donald Trump has made and lost fortunes as a real-estate developer. But Trump's genius is in brand building, and he is the brand. Thanks to tireless self-promotion, "The Donald" has estab-lished the Trump brand as a symbol of quality, luxury, and success. What's the value of the Trump brand? Plenty. In residential real estate in particular, Trump's name commands a premium. "I put my name on a building and I get $5,000 a square foot," says Trump. "That's twice what the guy gets across the street. I put my name on a golf course, Trump National in Briarcliff Manor, and I get $300,000 per member. Other guys only get $25,000. If I didn't put my name on it, I'd get nothing." Based on this real-estate success, Trump's name now adorns everything from mag-azines and bottled water (Trump Ice) to a cologne (Trump: The Fragrance), and reality TV shows (*The Apprentice*). Trump does commercials for Verizon, was host of *Saturday Night Live*, and recently unveiled Trump Visa, which rewards cardholders with casino discounts. "He's like P.T. Barnum on steroids," says a friend. "What's his greatest asset? It's his name. He's a skillful mar-keting person, and what he markets is his name."[4]

Place marketing involves activities undertaken to cre-ate, maintain, or change attitudes or behavior toward particular places. Cities, states, regions, and even entire nations compete to attract tourists, new residents, conventions, and company offices and factories. Texas advertises "It's Like a Whole Other Country" and New York state shouts, "I Love New York!" Michigan says "Great Lakes, Great Times" to attract tourists, "Great Lakes, Great Jobs" to attract residents, and "Great Lakes, Great Location" to attract businesses. The Iceland Tourist Board invites visitors to Iceland by advertising that it has "Discoveries the Entire Year." Icelandair, the only airline that serves the island, partners with the tourist board to sell world travelers on the wonders of Iceland—everything from geother-mal spas and glacier tours to midnight golf and clubbing.[5]

Ideas can also be marketed. In one sense, all marketing is the marketing of an idea, whether it is the general idea of brushing your teeth or the specific idea that Crest tooth-pastes "create smiles every day." Here, however, we narrow our focus to the marketing of *social ideas*. This area has been called **social marketing**, defined by the Social Marketing Institute as the use of commercial marketing concepts and tools in programs designed to influence individuals' behavior to improve their well-being and that of society.[6]

Social marketing
The design, implementation, and control of programs seeking to increase the acceptability of a social idea, cause, or practice among a target group.

MARKETING AT WORK 7.1

The Advertising Council: Advertising for the Common Good

When it comes to creating positive social change through advertising, no organization grabs the headlines like the Advertising Council. Consider these familiar phrases: "Friends Don't Let Friends Drive Drunk," "Only You Can Prevent Wildfires," "Take a Bite Out of Crime," "A Mind Is a Terrible Thing to Waste," and "I Am an American." Or how about these familiar characters: Smokey Bear, Rosie the Riveter, the Crash Test Dummies, and McGruff the Crime Dog. These are only a fraction of the phrases and icons created by Ad Council public service campaigns over the years.

The Ad Council was formed in 1942, at a time when people were especially cynical about advertising and all the money spent on it, to show the good that advertising can do. The Ad Council's mission is "to identify a select number of significant public issues and stimulate action on those issues through communications programs that make a measurable difference in our society." To that end, the Ad Council works to connect ad agencies (who donate their time), sponsors (who donate their money), and media (who donate their advertising time and space) with worthy nonprofit organizations and governmental agencies that need a promotional voice.

Through this joint volunteer effort, the Ad Council has created thousands of public service campaigns on issues such as improving the quality of life for children, preventive health, education, community well-being, environmental preservation, crime awareness and prevention, and strengthening families. These campaigns have produced more than just catchy slogans—they've created positive and lasting social change as well. Ad Council campaigns have achieved significant results on a wide range of issues:

Environment: Launched in 1944, Smokey Bear has been urging children and adults not to play with matches, not to leave a campfire unattended, and to keep a bucket of water and a shovel nearby. Since the campaign began, the number of forest acres lost to fires annually has decreased from 22 million to 8.4 million.

Education: The Ad Council teamed with Young & Rubicam advertising agency to create the campaign message, "A Mind Is a Terrible Thing to Waste." Now in its thirtieth year, the campaign has helped raise more than $2.2 billion for the United Negro College Fund and helped more than 300,000 minority students graduate college.

Emergency preparedness: The Ad Council joined with the U.S. Department of Homeland Security to sponsor new public service advertisements that encourage American parents to develop a family communications plan for potential terrorist attacks and other emergencies. For the past two years, this campaign has received by far the largest share of the Ad Council's donated time and space. As a result, the proportion of parents who stock emergency supplies and create family communications plans has increased significantly. The Ready.gov Web site received more than 18 million unique visitors within the first 10 months of the launch of the campaign.

Health: In the 1940s, Ad Council campaigns urged Americans to get vaccinated against polio—not an easy sell at the time because the vaccination involved three sets of unpleasant shots. Today, polio is virtually unheard-of in this country. Today, working with the U.S. Department of Health and Human Services, the Ad Council has launched campaigns on a number of current health issues, such as obesity prevention, disease prevention, and infant and child nutrition.

Crime awareness and prevention: In 1978, working with the National Crime Prevention Council and the ad firm Saatchi & Saatchi, the Ad Council helped give birth to McGruff the Crime Dog. Since then, McGruff the Crime Dog has taught both children and adults valuable crime awareness and crime prevention lessons, encouraging all of us to "Take a Bite Out of Crime." The familiar bloodhound in a trench coat has become a popular icon. A 2000 study showed that 92 percent of American children recognize the character and believe he offers advice that helps them stay safe. In 1989 and 1990, McGruff the Crime

Social marketing programs include public health campaigns to reduce smoking, alcoholism, drug abuse, and overeating. Other social marketing efforts include environmental campaigns to promote wilderness protection, clean air, and conservation. Still others address issues such as family planning, human rights, and racial equality. The Ad Council of America has developed dozens of social advertising campaigns, involving issues ranging from preventive health, education, and personal safety to environmental preservation (see Marketing at Work 7.1).

But social marketing involves much more than just advertising—the Social Marketing Institute (SMI) encourages the use of a broad range of marketing tools. "Social marketing goes well beyond the promotional '*P*' of the marketing mix to include every other element to achieve its social change objectives," says the SMI's executive director.[7]

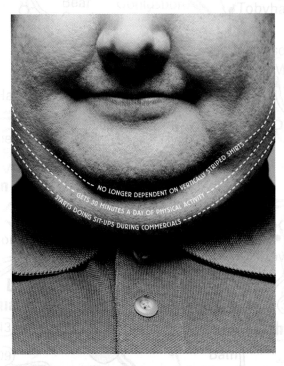

■ *The Ad Council has created thousands of public service campaigns that have created positive and lasting social change. Its Small Step obesity prevention campaign encourages families to live healthier lifestyles by making small dietary and physical changes.*

Dog's popularity was surpassed only by that of Mickey Mouse.

Seat Belt Safety: When Vince & Larry, the Crash Test Dummies, first flew through a windshield on network TV in 1985, seat-belt usage was at 21 percent, and most states did not mandate seat-belt usage by law. Since then, most states have adopted seat-belt laws, and safety-belt usage has increased from 21 percent to 73 percent, saving an estimated 85,000 lives.

Drunk Driving: Since the Ad Council began its drunk-driving prevention campaign, the old saying "One more for the road" has been replaced with "Friends Don't Let Friends Drive Drunk." Some 68 percent of Americans say they have personally stopped someone from driving drunk.

Social Issues: More than 6,000 children were paired with a mentor in just the first 18 months of the Ad Council's mentoring campaign. And public awareness about child abuse has increased from just 10 percent in the mid-1970s to more than 90 percent today. According to the CEO of Prevent Child Abuse America, "When we first started our child-abuse prevention campaign, the public's understanding of the issue was very low. But our partnership with the Ad Council has brought child abuse and neglect out into the open."

The Ad Council has drawn widespread support for its social marketing mission. Some 28,000 media outlets have contributed free ad space and time, and hundreds of socially-conscious corporations, foundations, and individuals have provided crucial operating funds. Made up largely of donations, the Ad Council's annual operating budget totals more than $35 million. And last year, the Ad Council received more than $1.7 billion in donated time and space.

Big ad agencies willingly donate their creative energies to create Ad Council campaigns. And the campaigns often turn out to be some of their very best work. For example, ad agency Marstellar's "People Start Pollution, People Can Stop It" campaign on behalf of Keep America Beautiful rates as one of the most memorable campaigns in history. The campaign ranked fiftieth on Advertising Age's list of top-100 ad campaigns of the century. And Foote, Cone & Belding's Smokey Bear and "Only you can prevent forest fires" campaign ranked twenty-sixth on the Advertising Age's top-100 list.

The Ad Council has proven that advertising can be used to do good, and its success has spawned other social marketing efforts. Nonprofit groups such as Partnership for a Drug-Free America have followed suit with additional public service announcements. And TV networks now routinely use their stars to promote worthy causes (such as NBC's "The More You Know. . . ." series). "The Ad Council was a model that proved it could work," says former Ad Council president Ruth Wooden. Advertising no longer just pushes products—it improves, and even saves, human lives.

Sources: See Bob Garfield, "Inspiration and Urge-to-Serve Mark the Best of the Ad Council," *Advertising Age,* April 29, 2002, pp. c2–c20; MEDIA WEEK Special Advertising Section, June 10, 2002; Ira Teinowitz, "Ad Council Seeks Partners for $50 Million Initiative," *Advertising Age,* March 1, 2004, p. 2; and Nat Ives, "In the Struggle for Time and Space, Public Service Spots Are Finding New Ways to Hold Their Own," *New York Times,* May 13, 2005, p. C6. Portions adapted from "The Advertising Council," accessed at www.adcouncil.org/about, August 2005.

Product and Service Decisions

Marketers make product and services decisions at three levels: individual product decisions, product line decisions, and product mix decisions. We discuss each in turn.

INDIVIDUAL PRODUCT AND SERVICE DECISIONS

Figure 7.2 shows the important decisions in the development and marketing of individual products and services. We will focus on decisions about *product attributes*, *branding*, *packaging*, *labeling*, and *product support services*.

FIGURE 7.2 Individual Product Decisions

Product and Service Attributes   Developing a product or service involves defining the benefits that it will offer. These benefits are communicated and delivered by product attributes such as *quality*, *features*, and *style and design*.

Product quality

The ability of a product to perform its functions; it includes the product's overall durability, reliability, precision, ease of operation and repair, and other valued attributes.

Product Quality.   **Product quality** is one of the marketer's major positioning tools. Quality has a direct impact on product or service performance; thus, it is closely linked to customer value and satisfaction. In the narrowest sense, quality can be defined as "freedom from defects." But most customer-centered companies go beyond this narrow definition. Instead, they define quality in terms of creating customer value and satisfaction. The American Society for Quality defines quality as the characteristics of a product or service that bear on its ability to satisfy stated or implied customer needs. Similarly, Siemens defines quality this way: "Quality is when our customers come back and our products don't."[8]

Total quality management (TQM) is an approach in which all the company's people are involved in constantly improving the quality of products, services, and business processes. Companies large and small have credited TQM with greatly improving their market shares and profits. Over the years, however, many companies have encountered problems in implementing TQM. Some companies viewed TQM as a magic cure-all and created token total quality programs that applied quality principles only superficially. Still others became obsessed with narrowly defined TQM principles and lost sight of broader concerns for customer value and satisfaction. As a result, many such programs failed, causing a backlash against TQM.

When applied in the context of creating customer satisfaction, however, *total quality* principles remain a requirement for success. Although many firms don't use the TQM label anymore, for most top companies customer-driven quality has become a way of doing business. Today, companies are taking a "return on quality" approach, viewing quality as an investment and holding quality efforts accountable for bottom-line results.[9]

Product quality has two dimensions—level and consistency. In developing a product, the marketer must first choose a *quality level* that will support the product's positioning. Here, product quality means *performance quality*—the ability of a product to perform its functions. For example, a Rolls-Royce provides higher performance quality than a Chevrolet: It has a smoother ride, provides more "creature comforts," and lasts longer. Companies rarely try to offer the highest possible performance quality level—few customers want or can afford the high levels of quality offered in products such as a Rolls-Royce automobile, a Viking range, or a Rolex watch. Instead, companies choose a quality level that matches target market needs and the quality levels of competing products.

Beyond quality level, high quality also can mean high levels of quality consistency. Here, product quality means *conformance quality*—freedom from defects and *consistency* in delivering a targeted level of performance. All companies should strive for high levels of conformance quality. In this sense, a Chevrolet can have just as much quality as a Rolls-Royce. Although a Chevy doesn't perform as well as a Rolls-Royce, it can as consistently deliver the quality that customers pay for and expect.

Many companies today have turned customer-driven quality into a potent strategic weapon. They have created customer satisfaction and value by consistently and profitably meeting customers' needs and preferences for quality.

Product Features.   A product can be offered with varying features. A stripped-down model, one without any extras, is the starting point. The company can create higher-level models by adding more features. Features are a competitive tool for differentiating the company's product from competitors' products. Being the first producer to introduce a needed and valued new feature is one of the most effective ways to compete.

How can a company identify new features and decide which ones to add to its product? The company should periodically survey buyers who have used the product and ask these questions: How do you like the product? Which specific features of the product do you like most? Which features could we add to improve the product? The answers provide the company with a rich list of feature ideas. The company can then assess each feature's *value* to customers versus its *cost* to the company. Features that customers value little in relation to costs should be dropped; those that customers value highly in relation to costs should be added.

Product Style and Design. Another way to add customer value is through distinctive *product style and design*. Design is a larger concept than style. *Style* simply describes the appearance of a product. Styles can be eye-catching or yawn-producing. A sensational style may grab attention and produce pleasing aesthetics, but it does not necessarily make the product *perform* better. Unlike style, *design* is more than skin deep—it goes to the very heart of a product. Good design contributes to a product's usefulness as well as to its looks.

Good design begins with a deep understanding of customer needs. More than simply creating product or service attributes, it involves shaping the customer's product-use *experience*. Consider the design process behind Procter & Gamble's Swiffer CarpetFlick.

P&G's amazingly successful Swiffer was really cleaning up. The innovative home-cleaning gadget was capturing a 75 percent share of the quick-clean market, and P&G's products were cleaning more hardwood, tile, and linoleum floors than anyone's. The problem? Some 75 percent of U.S. floors are carpeted. The answer: P&G needed to find a way to "Swiffer" a carpet. With the help of award-winning design firm IDEO, P&G set out to design a solution. But IDEO didn't start in its labs with R&D-like scientific research. Instead, it started with consumer research. IDEO designers and engineers went into people's homes, snapping photos, asking questions about how folks cleaned their carpets, and soaking up customer cleaning experiences. There was a young mother who complained that the noise of the vacuum scared her child, but she had time to vacuum only when he was asleep. There was an older woman with a busted knee who relied on two vacuums—a heavy one for once a week cleaning when she took painkillers for her knee, and one she could easily lift for spot cleaning. Most consumers found vacuum cleaners bulky, noisy, and hard to use; carpet sweepers were more convenient but not very effective. "These people were crying out for better solutions," says one designer.

With this deep understanding of customer needs, IDEO's designers began what they call a "deep dive." For the next 10 months, the design team immersed itself in an intensive development effort, attacking countless messy carpet squares—sucking, scraping, stamping, sticking, and trying anything else they could come up with to clean carpet. The result was a revolutionary new carpet sweeping system, the Swiffer Carpet-Flick, which flicks dirt, crumbs, and other small bits off the carpet and traps them onto a disposable adhesive cartridge. The CarpetFlick design certainly *looks* good—it is sleek, stylish, and very

■ Good design begins with a deep understanding of customer needs. P&G's Swiffer CarpetFlick looks good, but it *works* even better than it looks.

"Swifferesque." But it *works* even better than it looks. It's quiet, convenient, and effective—just the thing for "quick carpet clean-ups between vacuuming."[10]

Thus, product designers should think less about product attributes and technical specifications and more about how customers will use and benefit from the product. IDEO has used this same customer-experience design approach to develop award-winning designs for everything from high-tech consumer electronics products and retail store layouts to the Ultimate Dilbert Office Cubicle, a modular cubicle that allows each worker to select the components and create a space based on his or her tastes and lifestyle.

Just as good design can improve customer value, cut costs, and create strong competitive advantage, poor design can result in lost sales and embarrassment.

■ Poor product design can be costly and embarrassing, as Kryptonite learned when bloggers revealed that most of the locks it had been making for the past 30 years could be picked with a Bic pen.

When you're a bike-lock maker whose slogan is "Tough World, Tough Locks," it doesn't get much tougher than finding out that most of the locks you've been making for the last 30 years can be picked with a Bic pen. That, sadly, is what happened to Ingersoll-Rand subsidiary Kryptonite, after bloggers began posting videos showing just how easy it was to pop open the company's ubiquitous U-shaped locks. Kryptonite reacted quickly, agreeing to exchange old locks for new Bic-proof ones. But the damage was already done. The news spread quickly through cycling chat rooms and blogs, and within weeks the company was sued for alleged product defects. The design mistake damaged Kryptonite's pocketbook as well as its reputation. Exchanging the locks cost the company an estimated $10 million. In the meantime, many dealers receive no shipments of new locks, costing Kryptonite as much as an additional $6 million in sales.[11]

Brand

A name, term, sign, symbol, or design, or a combination of these, intended to identify the goods or services of one seller or group of sellers and to differentiate them from those of competitors.

Branding Perhaps the most distinctive skill of professional marketers is their ability to build and manage brands. A **brand** is a name, term, sign, symbol, or design, or a combination of these, that identifies the maker or seller of a product or service. Consumers view a brand as an important part of a product, and branding can add value to a product. For example, most consumers would perceive a bottle of White Linen perfume as a high-quality, expensive product. But the same perfume in an unmarked bottle would likely be viewed as lower in quality, even if the fragrance was identical.

Branding has become so strong that today hardly anything goes unbranded. Salt is packaged in branded containers, common nuts and bolts are packaged with a distributor's label, and automobile parts—spark plugs, tires, filters—bear brand names that differ from those of the automakers. Even fruits, vegetables, and poultry are branded—Sunkist oranges, Dole pineapples, Chiquita bananas, Fresh Express salad greens, and Perdue chickens.

Branding helps buyers in many ways. Brand names help consumers identify products that might benefit them. Brands also say something about product quality and consistency—buyers who always buy the same brand know that they will get the same features, benefits, and quality each time they buy. Branding also gives the seller several advantages. The brand name becomes the basis on which a whole story can be built about a product's special qualities. The seller's brand name and trademark provide legal protection for unique product features that otherwise might be copied by competitors. And branding helps the seller to segment markets. For example, General Mills can offer Cheerios, Wheaties, Chex, Total, Kix, Golden Grahams, Trix, and many other cereal brands, not just one general product for all consumers.

Building and managing brands is perhaps the marketer's most important task. We will discuss branding strategy in more detail later in the chapter.

Packaging   **Packaging** involves designing and producing the container or wrapper for a product. The package includes a product's primary container (the tube holding Colgate Total toothpaste). It may also include a secondary package that is thrown away when the product is about to be used (the cardboard box containing the tube of Colgate). Finally, it can include a shipping package necessary to store, identify, and ship the product (a corrugated box carrying six dozen tubes of Colgate). Labeling, printed information appearing on or with the package, is also part of packaging.

Packaging
The activities of designing and producing the container or wrapper for a product.

Traditionally, the primary function of the package was to contain and protect the product. In recent times, however, numerous factors have made packaging an important marketing tool. Increased competition and clutter on retail store shelves means that packages must now perform many sales tasks—from attracting attention, to describing the product, to making the sale.

Companies are realizing the power of good packaging to create instant consumer recognition of the company or brand. For example, in an average supermarket, which stocks 15,000 to 17,000 items, the typical shopper passes by some 300 items per minute, and more than 60 percent of all purchases are made on impulse. In this highly competitive environment, the package may be the seller's last chance to influence buyers. "Not long ago, the package was merely the product's receptacle, and the brand message was elsewhere—usually on TV," says a packaging expert. But changes in the marketplace environment are now "making the package itself an increasingly important selling medium."[12]

Innovative packaging can give a company an advantage over competitors. Sometimes even seemingly small packaging improvements can make a big difference. For example, Dutch Boy came up with a long overdue innovation—paint in plastic Twist & Pour containers with twist-off caps and pour spouts. More than 50 percent of Dutch Boy's customers are now buying the plastic containers, and new stores, like Wal-Mart and Sears, are carrying it. It recently followed up with another innovation—the Ready to Roll paint container with a built-in roller tray. The container is easy to open and close, easier to transport, and neater and easier to use than previous alternatives.

Similarly, pet-product maker Hartz Mountain recently introduced a packaging improvement that should make it a leading candidate for the "Why didn't someone think of that before?" award:

Innovative packaging: Dutch Boy came up with a long overdue innovation—paint in plastic containers with twist-off caps. It created a paint can that's easy to carry, doesn't take a screwdriver to pry open, doesn't dribble when pouring, and doesn't take a hammer to bang closed.

Hartz began packaging its bird and small-animal food lines—food for little critters such as rabbits, guinea pigs, hamsters, ferrets, parakeets, cockatiels, and parrots—in standup slider-zipper bags that open and close easily. The new packaging makes life a lot simpler for pet owners. The bags make it easy to keep pet food fresh, and opening the slider to a greater or lesser extent lets users create different spout sizes for easy pouring into irregularly sized animal food trays. The new packaging also benefits Hartz. Unlike many pet food bags that lie flat on store shelves, the standup pouches are highly visible, providing an effective platform for brand messaging. And at home, consumers are more likely to leave the pet food in its packaging rather than storing it in plastic containers. This means that the Hartz brand messaging stays in front of a consumer longer. Hartz has already seen significant sales increases resulting from this innovative new packaging.[13]

In contrast, poorly designed packages can cause headaches for consumers and lost sales for the company. In recent years, product safety has also become a major packaging concern. We have all learned to deal with hard-to-open "childproof" packaging. And after the rash of product tampering scares during the 1980s, most drug producers and food makers now put their products in tamper-resistant packages. In making packaging decisions, the company also must heed growing environmental concerns. Fortunately, many companies have gone "green" by reducing their packaging and using environmentally responsible packaging materials.

Labeling   Labels may range from simple tags attached to products to complex graphics that are part of the package. They perform several functions. At the very least, the label *identifies* the product or brand, such as the name Sunkist stamped on oranges. The label might also *describe* several things about the product—who made it, where it was made, when it was made, its contents, how it is to be used, and how to use it safely. Finally, the label might help to *promote* the product and support its positioning.

For example, in the never-ending search for ways to stand out, the apparel industry seems to be rediscovering the promotional value of the product label.

■ Innovative labeling can help to promote a product.

Some clothing labels send strong messages. A "booklet tag" hanging from a workout garment might reinforce the brand's positioning, describing in detail how the garment is used by certain high-profile athletes or what types of special materials are used in its construction. Other brasher statements include pocket flashers and "lenticular tags," which generate 3-D or animation effects. At the other extreme, tagless heat-transfer labels are replacing sewn-in woven labels, promising ultimate comfort. Even low-key labels are using more brilliant colors or elaborate graphics, beautifying the product and reinforcing the brand message. Rich treatments on labels add pizzazz to luxury items; futuristic tags support emerging technical, man-made fabrications; tags adorned with playful characters evoke a sense of fun for kids' garments. "The product label is a key cog in branding strategy," says a labeling expert. "The look, feel, or even smell of the label—if done creatively—can complement a brand."[14]

Along with the positives, labeling also raises concerns. There has been a long history of legal concerns about packaging and labels. The Federal Trade Commission Act of 1914 held that false, misleading, or deceptive labels or packages constitute unfair competition. Labels can mislead customers, fail to describe important ingredients, or fail to include needed safety warnings. As a result, several federal and state laws regulate labeling. The most prominent is the Fair Packaging and Labeling Act of 1966, which set mandatory labeling requirements, encouraged voluntary industry packaging standards, and allowed federal agencies to set packaging regulations in specific industries.

Labeling has been affected in recent times by *unit pricing* (stating the price per unit of standard measure), *open dating* (stating the expected shelf life of the product), and *nutritional labeling* (stating the nutritional values in the product). The Nutritional Labeling and Educational Act of 1990 requires sellers to provide detailed nutritional information on food products, and recent sweeping actions by the Food and Drug Administration regulate the use of health-related terms such as *low-fat*, *light*, and *high-fiber*. Sellers must ensure that their labels contain all the required information.

Product Support Services   Customer service is another element of product strategy. A company's offer usually includes some support services, which can be a minor or a major part of the total offering. Later in the chapter, we will discuss services as products themselves. Here, we discuss services that augment actual products.

The first step is to survey customers periodically to assess the value of current services and to obtain ideas for new ones. For example, Cadillac holds regular focus group interviews with owners and carefully watches complaints that come into its dealerships. From this careful monitoring, Cadillac has learned that buyers are very upset by repairs that are not done correctly the first time.

Once the company has assessed the value of various support services to customers, it must next assess the costs of providing these services. It can then develop a package of services that will both delight customers and yield profits to the company. Based on its consumer interviews, Cadillac has set up a system directly linking each dealership with a group of 10 engineers who can help walk mechanics through difficult repairs. Such actions helped Cadillac jump, in one year, from fourteenth to seventh in independent rankings of service. For the past several years, Cadillac has rated at or near the top of its industry on the American Customer Satisfaction Index.[15]

Many companies are now using a sophisticated mix of phone, e-mail, fax, Internet, and interactive voice and data technologies to provide support services that were not possible before. Consider the following example:

Some online merchants are watching where you surf, then opening a chat window on your screen to ask—just as they would in the store—if you have questions about the goods they see you eyeing. For example, at the Scion Web site, clicking on the Scion Chat button puts you in real-time touch with someone who can answer your questions or help you to design your personalized Scion. Last year, Hewlett-Packard began sending pop-up chat boxes to visitors who were shopping on HP.com's pages for digital-photography products. If a shopper loiters a few minutes over some gear, up pops a photo of an attractive woman with the words, "Hello, Need Information? An HP live chat representative is standing by to assist you." Click on "Go" and type a question, and a live sales agent responds immediately. SunTrust Banks, which has been inviting customers to chat about loan and bank products for about two years, is taking proactive chat one step further by experimenting with cobrowsing. This feature essentially lets chat agents take control of a customer's computer screen, opening Web pages directly on their browser to help them find what they're looking for. In the future, "call cams" will even let customers see an agent on their screen and talk directly through voice-over-Web capabilities.[16]

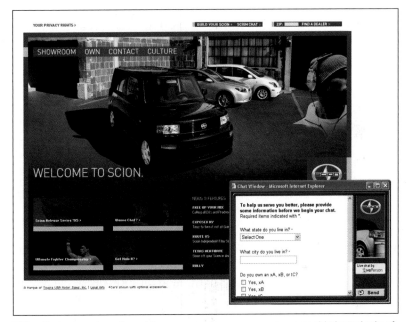

■ Product support services: Many companies are now using a sophisticated mix of interactive technologies to provide support services that were not possible before. For example, at the Scion Web site, clicking the Scion Chat button puts you in real-time touch with someone who can answer your questions or help you to design your own personalized Scion.

PRODUCT LINE DECISIONS

Beyond decisions about individual products and services, product strategy also calls for building a product line. A **product line** is a group of products that are closely related because they function in a similar manner, are sold to the same customer groups, are marketed through the same types of outlets, or fall within given price ranges. For example, Nike produces several lines of athletic shoes and apparel, Nokia produces several lines of telecommunications products, and Charles Schwab produces several lines of financial services.

The major product line decision involves *product line length*—the number of items in the product line. The line is too short if the manager can increase profits by adding items; the line is too long if the manager can increase profits by dropping items. The company should manage its product lines carefully. Product lines tend to lengthen over time, and most companies

Product line
A group of products that are closely related because they function in a similar manner, are sold to the same customer groups, are marketed through the same types of outlets, or fall within given price ranges.

eventually need to prune unnecessary or unprofitable items from their lines to increase overall profitability. Managers need to conduct a periodic *product-line analysis* to assess each product item's sales and profits and to understand how each item contributes to the line's performance.

Product line length is influenced by company objectives and resources. For example, one objective might be to allow for upselling. Thus BMW wants to move customers up from its 3-series models to 5- and 7-series models. Another objective might be to allow cross-selling: Hewlett-Packard sells printers as well as cartridges. Still another objective might be to protect against economic swings: Gap Inc. runs several clothing-store chains (Gap, Old Navy, Banana Republic, Forth & Towne) covering different price points.

A company can lengthen its product line in two ways: by *line stretching* or by *line filling*. *Product line stretching* occurs when a company lengthens its product line beyond its current range. The company can stretch its line downward, upward, or both ways.

Companies located at the upper end of the market can stretch their lines *downward*. A company may stretch downward to plug a market hole that otherwise would attract a new competitor or to respond to a competitor's attack on the upper end. Or it may add low-end products because it finds faster growth taking place in the low-end segments. DaimlerChrysler stretched its Mercedes line downward for all these reasons. Facing a slow-growth luxury car market and attacks by Japanese automakers on its high-end positioning, it successfully introduced its Mercedes C-Class cars. These models sell in the $30,000 range without harming the firm's ability to sell other Mercedes at much higher prices.

Companies at the lower end of a market can stretch their product lines *upward*. Sometimes, companies stretch upward in order to add prestige to their current products. Or they may be attracted by a faster growth rate or higher margins at the higher end. For example, each of the leading Japanese auto companies introduced an upmarket automobile: Toyota launched Lexus; Nissan launched Infinity; and Honda launched Acura. They used entirely new names rather than their own names.

Companies in the middle range of the market may decide to stretch their lines in *both directions*. Marriott did this with its hotel product line. Along with regular Marriott hotels, it has added new branded hotel lines to serve both the upper and lower ends of the market. Renaissance aims to attract and please top executives; Marriott, upper and middle managers; Courtyard, salespeople and other "road warriors"; and Fairfield Inn, vacationers and business travelers on a tight travel budget. ExecuStay by Marriott provides temporary housing for those relocating or away on long-term assignments of 30 days or longer. Marriott's Residence Inn provides a relaxed, residential atmosphere—a home away from home for people who travel for a living. Marriott TownePlace Suites provide a comfortable atmosphere at a moderate price for extended-stay travelers. And Marriott SpringHill

■ Product line stretching: Marriott offers a full line of hotel brands, each aimed at a different target market.

Suites has 25 percent more space than an average hotel room—offering a separate living and work space for business travelers.[17] The major risk with this strategy is that some travelers will trade down after finding that the lower-price hotels in the Marriott chain give them pretty much everything they want. However, Marriott would rather capture its customers who move downward than lose them to competitors.

An alternative to product line stretching is *product line filling*—adding more items within the present range of the line. There are several reasons for product line filling: reaching for extra profits, satisfying dealers, using excess capacity, being the leading full-line company, and plugging holes to keep out competitors. Sony filled its Walkman line by adding solar-powered and waterproof Walkmans, ultralight models for exercisers in a variety of formats, such as mini disk, cassette, radio, CD, and hard disk. However, line filling is overdone if it results in cannibalization and customer confusion. The company should ensure that new items are noticeably different from existing ones.

PRODUCT MIX DECISIONS

An organization with several product lines has a product mix. A **product mix (or product portfolio)** consists of all the product lines and items that a particular seller offers for sale. Avon's product mix consists of five major product lines: beauty products, wellness products, jewelry and accessories, gifts, and "inspirational" products (inspiring gifts, books, music, and home accents). Each product line consists of several sublines. For example, the beauty line breaks down into makeup, skin care, bath and beauty, fragrance, salon and spa, and outdoor protection products. Each line and subline has many individual items. Altogether, Avon's product mix includes 1,300 items. In contrast, 3M markets more than 60,000 products, a typical Wal-Mart stocks 100,000 to 120,000 items, and General Electric manufactures as many as 250,000 items.

> **Product mix (or product portfolio)**
> The set of all product lines and items that a particular seller offers for sale.

A company's product mix has four important dimensions: width, length, depth, and consistency. Product mix *width* refers to the number of different product lines the company carries. For example, Colgate markets a fairly wide product mix, consisting of dozens of brands that you can "trust to care for yourself, your home, and the ones you love." This product mix is organized into five major product lines: oral care, personal care, household care, fabric care, and pet nutrition.

Product mix *length* refers to the total number of items the company carries within its product lines. Colgate typically carries many brands within each line. For example, its personal-care line includes Softsoap liquid soaps and body washes, Irish Spring bar soaps, Speed Stick and Crystal Clean deodorants, and Skin Bracer, Afta, and Colgate toiletries and shaving products.

Product line *depth* refers to the number of versions offered of each product in the line. Colgate toothpastes come in 11 varieties, ranging from Colgate Total, Colgate Tartar Control, Colgate 2in1, and Colgate Cavity Protection to Colgate Sensitive, Colgate Fresh Confidence, Colgate Max Fresh, Colgate Simply White, Colgate Sparkling White, Colgate Kids Toothpastes, and Colgate Baking Soda & Peroxide. Then, each variety comes in its own special forms and formulations. For example, you can buy Colgate Total in regular, mint fresh stripe, whitening paste and gel, advanced fresh gel, or 2in1 liquid gel versions.[18] (Talk about niche marketing! Remember our Chapter 6 discussion?)

Finally, the *consistency* of the product mix refers to how closely related the various product lines are in end use, production requirements, distribution channels, or some other way. Colgate's product lines are consistent insofar as they are consumer products that go through the same distribution channels. The lines are less consistent insofar as they perform different functions for buyers.

These product mix dimensions provide the handles for defining the company's product strategy. The company can increase its business in four ways. It can add new product lines, widening its product mix. In this way, its new lines build on the company's reputation in its other lines. The company can lengthen its existing product lines to become a more full-line company. Or it can add more versions of each product and thus deepen its product mix. Finally, the company can pursue more product line consistency—or less—depending on whether it wants to have a strong reputation in a single field or in several fields.

Linking the Concepts

Slow down for a minute. To get a better sense of how large and complex a company's product offering can become, investigate Procter & Gamble's product mix.

- Using P&G's Web site (www.pg.com), its annual report, or other sources, develop a list of all the company's product lines and individual products. What surprises you about this list of products?
- Is P&G's product mix consistent? What overall strategy or logic appears to have guided the development of this product mix?

Branding Strategy: Building Strong Brands

Some analysts see brands as *the* major enduring asset of a company, outlasting the company's specific products and facilities. John Stewart, cofounder of Quaker Oats, once said, "If this business were split up, I would give you the land and bricks and mortar, and I would keep the brands and trademarks, and I would fare better than you." A former CEO of McDonald's agrees: "If every asset we own, every building, and every piece of equipment were destroyed in a terrible natural disaster, we would be able to borrow all the money to replace it very quickly because of the value of our brand. . . . The brand is more valuable than the totality of all these assets."[19]

Thus, brands are powerful assets that must be carefully developed and managed. In this section, we examine the key strategies for building and managing brands.

BRAND EQUITY

Brands are more than just names and symbols. Brands represent consumers' perceptions and feelings about a product and its performance—everything that the product or service *means* to consumers. In the final analysis, brands exist in the minds of consumers.

Brand equity
The positive differential effect that knowing the brand name has on customer response to the product or service.

The real value of a strong brand is its power to capture consumer preference and loyalty. Brands vary in the amount of power and value they have in the marketplace. Some brands—such as Coca-Cola, Tide, Nike, Harley-Davidson, Disney, and others—become larger-than-life icons that maintain their power in the market for years, even generations. These brands win in the marketplace not simply because they deliver unique benefits or reliable service. Rather, they succeed because they forge deep connections with customers.

A powerful brand has high *brand equity*. **Brand equity** is the positive differential effect that knowing the brand name has on customer response to the product or service. One measure of a brand's equity is the extent to which customers are willing to pay more for the brand. One study found that 72 percent of customers would pay a 20 percent premium for their brand of choice relative to the closest competing brand; 40 percent said they would pay a 50 percent premium.[20] Tide and Heinz lovers are willing to pay a 100 percent premium. Loyal Coke drinkers will pay a 50 percent premium and Volvo users a 40 percent premium.

A brand with strong brand equity is a very valuable asset. *Brand valuation* is the process of estimating the total financial value of a brand. Measuring such value is difficult. However, according to one estimate, the brand value of Coca-Cola is almost $67 billion, Microsoft is $61 billion, and IBM is $53 billion. Other brands rating among the world's most valuable include General Electric, Intel, Nokia, Disney, McDonald's, Toyota, Marlboro, and Mercedes.[21]

■ A strong brand is a valuable asset. How many familiar brands and brand symbols can you find in this picture?

FIGURE 7.3 Major Brand Strategy Decisions

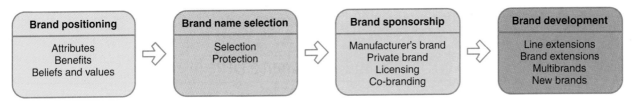

Brand positioning		Brand name selection		Brand sponsorship		Brand development
Attributes Benefits Beliefs and values	⇨	Selection Protection	⇨	Manufacturer's brand Private brand Licensing Co-branding	⇨	Line extensions Brand extensions Multibrands New brands

High brand equity provides a company with many competitive advantages. A powerful brand enjoys a high level of consumer brand awareness and loyalty. Because consumers expect stores to carry the brand, the company has more leverage in bargaining with resellers. Because the brand name carries high credibility, the company can more easily launch line and brand extensions, as when Coca-Cola used its well-known brand to introduce Diet Coke and Vanilla Coke, and when P&G introduced Crest Whitestrips and Crest Spinbrush toothbrushes. A powerful brand offers the company some defense against fierce price competition.

Above all, a powerful brand forms the basis for building strong and profitable customer relationships. Therefore, the fundamental asset underlying brand equity is *customer equity*—the value of the customer relationships that the brand creates. A powerful brand is important, but what it really represents is a profitable set of loyal customers. The proper focus of marketing is building customer equity, with brand management serving as a major marketing tool.[22]

BUILDING STRONG BRANDS

Branding poses challenging decisions to the marketer. Figure 7.3 shows that the major brand strategy decisions involve brand positioning, brand name selection, brand sponsorship, and brand development.

Brand Positioning Marketers need to position their brands clearly in target customers' minds. They can position brands at any of three levels.[23] At the lowest level, they can position the brand on *product attributes.* Thus, marketers of Crest toothpaste can talk about the product's innovative ingredients and good taste. However, attributes are the least desirable level for brand positioning. Competitors can easily copy attributes. More important, customers are not interested in attributes as such; they are interested in what the attributes will do for them.

A brand can be better positioned by associating its name with a desirable *benefit.* Thus, Crest marketers can go beyond the brand's ingredients and talk about the resulting cavity prevention or teeth-whitening benefits. Some successful brands positioned on benefits are Volvo (safety), Hallmark (caring), Harley-Davidson (adventure), FedEx (guaranteed on-time delivery), Nike (performance), and Lexus (quality).

The strongest brands go beyond attribute or benefit positioning. They are positioned on strong *beliefs and values.* These brands pack an emotional wallop. Thus, Crest's marketers can talk not just about ingredients and cavity-prevention benefits, but about how these give customers "healthy, beautiful smiles for life."[24] Successful brands engage customers on a deep, emotional level. Brands such

■ Brand positioning: The strongest brands go beyond attribute or benefit positioning. Godiva engages customers on a deeper level, touching universal emotions.

MARKETING AT WORK   7.2

Naming Brands: Part Science, Part Art, and More Than a Little Instinct

Every company wants a name that's "sticky"—one that stands out from the crowd, a catchy handle that will remain fresh and memorable over time. But the issue of stickiness turns out to be kind of, well, sticky. Such names are hard to find, especially because naming trends change—often decade by decade. While the giddy 1990s were all about quirky names (Yahoo, Google, Fogdog) or trademark-proof monikers concocted from scratch (Novartis, Aventis, Lycos), tastes have shifted amid the uncertainties of the new millennium.

Today's style is to build corporate identity around words that have real meaning, to name things in the spirit of what they actually are. The new names are all about purity, clarity, and organicism. For example, names like Silk (soy milk), Method (home products), Blackboard (school software), and Smartwater (beverages) are simple and make intuitive sense. "There's a trend toward meaning in words. When it comes down to evocative words versus straightforward names, straightforward will win in testing every time," says an executive from a New York branding firm.

Embracing real words over fake ones hardly comes as a surprise, of course. But why has it taken so long for this idea to catch on? In part, the wave of meaningless names during the 1990s can be traced to a spike in trademark applications that resulted from the surge in dot-com start-ups. In 1985, 64,677 applications were filed. Ten years later that number had almost tripled, before peaking at 375,428 in 2000. As the pool of registered trademarks has grown, so has the challenge of finding an available name. In that context, choosing a whimsical or made-up name was a simple way to sidestep the crowd. There was also some method to this madness: A company with a new and different word can supply whatever associations it chooses and expand into any business it wants.

But the problem with all these meaningless names became clear as the number of companies adopting them grew. As more and more Accentures and Covisints dotted the landscape, it became harder for consumers to keep track of the differences between them. Change came after the economic boom went bust and the number of trademark applications declined. Coming up with unique names is still difficult, but the pressure to come up with something—anything—that a company can call its own has subsided.

Hence, the return to grace of real, natural-sounding names. Of course, there's really nothing all that novel about using natural-sounding brand names. Apple Computer did it more than 25 years ago, as did Simple Shoes in 1991. So where did JetBlue come from?

Traditionally, Airlines have borne names that either refer to the carrier's geographic roots (American, Northwest, Southwest) or evoke the idea of global reach (United, or the now defunct Pan American and Trans World Airlines). But as a new airline with plans to offer budget travelers a stylish and unique way to fly, JetBlue decided to take a different approach. "We didn't want to jump on the made-up-word bandwagon," recalls JetBlue's VP for corporate communications. "We wanted to use a real word, but we didn't want it to sound like an airline."

Working first with its New York ad agency and then with branding consultancy Landor Associates, the airline came up with early naming candidates such as Fresh Air, Taxi, Egg, and It. But the name Blue—with its simple evocation of clear skies and serenity—emerged a finalist. After trademark lawyers pointed out that it would be impossible to protect the name Blue without a distinctive qualifier, TrueBlue emerged. But that name was already held by a car-rental agency. Eventually, JetBlue was born. The name worked, and when JetBlue inaugurated service in 2000, so did the branding model. The new airline's success spawned a naming trend among other discount carriers, including Delta's Song and United's Ted.

as Starbucks, Victoria's Secret, and Godiva rely less on a product's tangible attributes and more on creating surprise, passion, and excitement surrounding a brand.

When positioning a brand, the marketer should establish a mission for the brand and a vision of what the brand must be and do. A brand is the company's promise to deliver a specific set of features, benefits, services, and experiences consistently to the buyers. The brand promise must be simple and honest. Motel 6, for example, offers clean rooms, low prices, and good service but does not promise expensive furniture or large bathrooms. In contrast, The Ritz-Carlton offers luxurious rooms and a truly memorable experience but does not promise low prices.

Brand Name Selection   A good name can add greatly to a product's success. However, finding the best brand name is a difficult task. It begins with a careful review of the product and its benefits, the target market, and proposed marketing strategies. After that, naming a brand becomes part science, part art, and a measure of instinct (see Marketing at Work 7.2).

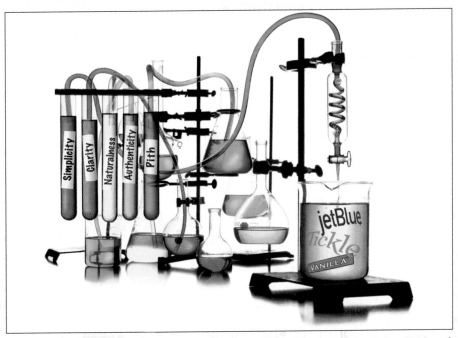

■ *Naming brands: There's some science to it, and some basic rules to be heeded, but there's also a big dose of art and more than a little instinct.*

Song and Ted? Simple and easy to remember. But what do those words have to do with the airline industry? Nothing—and that's partly the point. "It's effective to use ordinary words out of context," says consultant Laura Ries, coauthor of *The 22 Immutable Laws of Branding.* It also works to use names "that are suggestive of the category. These are names like Blockbuster, Curves, Amazon, Palm, and

Subway. Assuming the words are simple, your brand name will be easy to say, spell, and remember." Likewise, firms are also waking up to the idea that some organic names are fun to say—and that makes them easier to spread by word of mouth. In an age where everything can be found by way of Google, simple names do double duty as easy-to-remember keywords.

That's what happened to Aliph, a start-up that recently launched its first product—a device built from military-grade technology that allows people talking on cell phones to be heard over background noise. No one can remember Aliph, of course. But the product's name, Jawbone, refers to both the idiomatic expression for talking and the fact that the device works by actually monitoring jawbone and cheek vibrations. "We knew we would have to be different in every way—from the design of the device to our name," says Aliph's VP for product development. The name turned out to be a handy way for customers to find the product. Aliph was able to buy the jawbone.com domain, and now when people type "jawbone"—a common noun—into Google, the company's site comes up first in the results. Indeed, the search engine might be the best indicator of how sticky a name really is.

So, it's clear that finding just the right brand name is hard work. There's certainly some science to it, and some basic rules that need to be heeded. But there's also a big dose of art, and more than a little instinct. Try it yourself. Pick a product and see if you can come up with a better name for it. How about Moonshot? Tickle? Vanilla? Treehugger? Simplicity? Sorry. Google them and you'll find that they're already taken.

Source: Adapted from Alex Frankel, "The New Science of Naming," *Business 2.0,* December 2004, pp. 53–55. © 2004 Time Inc. All rights reserved.

Desirable qualities for a brand name include the following: (1) It should suggest something about the product's benefits and qualities. Examples: Beautyrest, Craftsman, Curves, Merry Maids, OFF! bug spray. (2) It should be easy to pronounce, recognize, and remember. Short names help. Examples: Tide, Silk, JetBlue. But longer ones are sometimes effective. Examples: "Love My Carpet" carpet cleaner, "I Can't Believe It's Not Butter" margarine. (3) The brand name should be distinctive. Examples: Lexus, Kodak, Oracle. (4) It should be extendable: Amazon.com began as an online bookseller but chose a name that would allow expansion into other categories. (5) The name should translate easily into foreign languages. Before spending $100 million to change its name to Exxon, Standard Oil of New Jersey tested several names in 54 languages in more than 150 foreign markets. It found that the name Enco referred to a stalled engine when pronounced in Japanese. (6) It should be capable of registration and legal protection. A brand name cannot be registered if it infringes on existing brand names.

Once chosen, the brand name must be protected. Many firms try to build a brand name that will eventually become identified with the product category. Brand names such as

Kleenex, Levi's, Jell-O, BAND-AID, Scotch Tape, Formica, Ziploc, and Fiberglas have succeeded in this way. However, their very success may threaten the company's rights to the name. Many originally protected brand names—such as cellophane, aspirin, nylon, kerosene, linoleum, yo-yo, trampoline, escalator, thermos, and shredded wheat—are now generic names that any seller can use. To protect their brands, marketers present them carefully using the word "brand" and the registered trademark symbol, as in "BAND-AID® Brand Adhesive Bandages."

Brand Sponsorship   A manufacturer has four sponsorship options. The product may be launched as a *manufacturer's brand* (or national brand), as when Kellogg and IBM sell their output under their own manufacturer's brand names. Or the manufacturer may sell to resellers who give it a *private brand* (also called a *store brand* or *distributor brand*). Although most manufacturers create their own brand names, others market *licensed brands*. Finally, two companies can join forces and *cobrand* a product.

Manufacturer's Brands Versus Private Brands.   Manufacturers' brands have long dominated the retail scene. In recent times, however, an increasing number of retailers and wholesalers have created their own **private brands (or store brands)**. And in many industries, these private brands are giving manufacturers' brands a real run for their money:

> Melanie Turner has forgotten her shopping list, but the 42-year-old pension consultant doesn't seem to mind. Entering her local Costco store, Turner knows right where she's going. In the dish detergent section, her hand goes past Procter & Gamble's Cascade to grab two 96-ounce bottles of Kirkland Signature, the in-store brand that Costco has plastered on everything from cashews to cross-trainer sneakers. Trolling for some fresh fish for dinner, she hauls in a 2 1/2-pound package of tilapia—it, too, emblazoned with the bold red, white, and black Kirkland logo. Then it's off to the paper aisle, where she picks up mammoth packs of Kirkland dinner napkins, Kirkland toilet paper, and . . . wait, where are the Kirkland paper towels? Her eyes scan the store's maze of hulking pallets—no sign of them—before coming to rest on a 12-pack of P&G's Bounty. A moment of decision. "I'll wait on this," she says finally.
>
> And there, in microcosm, is why Melanie Turner scares the pants off P&G, Unilever, Kraft, and just about every consumer goods company out there. Her shopping cart is headed for the checkout aisle, and there's hardly a national brand in it. . . . A subtle tectonic shift has been reshaping the world of brands. Retailers—once the lowly peddlers of brands that were made and marketed by big, important manufacturers—are now behaving like full-fledged marketers.[25]
>
> It seems that almost every retailer now carries its own store brands. Wal-Mart offers Sam's Choice beverages and food products, Spring Valley nutritional products, and White Cloud brand toilet tissue, diapers, detergent, and fabric softener. Its Ol' Roy dog food (named for Sam Walton's Irish setter), has now passed Nestlé's venerable Purina as the world's best-selling dog chow. More than half the products at your local Target are private brands, and grocery giant Kroger markets some 7,500 items under its own three brands—Private Selection, Kroger Brand, and F.M.V. (For Maximum Value). At the other end of the spectrum, upscale retailer Saks Fifth Avenue carries its own clothing line, which features $100 men's ties, $200 halter-tops, and $250 cotton dress shirts.
>
> In U.S. supermarkets, taken as a single brand, private-label products are the number-one, -two, or -three brand in over 40 percent of all grocery product categories. In all, they capture more than a 20 percent share of sales in U.S.

Private brand (or store brand)
A brand created and owned by a reseller of a product or service.

■ An increasing number of retailers have created their own store brands. Costco's Kirkland brand adorns everything from baby wipes to barbeques.

supermarkets, drug chains, and mass-merchandise stores, and this share is growing annually. Private-label apparel, such as Gap and The Limited, Arizona Jeans (JCPenney), and Liz Lange (Target), captures a 36 percent share of all U.S. apparel sales.[26]

In the so-called *battle of the brands* between manufacturers' and private brands, retailers have many advantages. They control what products they stock, where they go on the shelf, what prices they charge, and which ones they will feature in local circulars. Most retailers also charge manufacturers *slotting fees*—payments from the manufacturers before the retailers will accept new products and find "slots" for them on their shelves. Slotting fees, which generate over $9 billion for the placement of new products alone, have recently received much scrutiny from the Federal Trade Commission and state legislatures, which worry that they might dampen competition by restricting retail shelf access for smaller manufacturers who can't afford the fees.[27]

Private brands can be hard to establish and costly to stock and promote. However, they also yield higher profit margins for the reseller. And they give resellers exclusive products that cannot be bought from competitors, resulting in greater store traffic and loyalty. Retailers price their store brands lower than comparable manufacturers' brands, thereby appealing to budget-conscious shoppers, especially in difficult economic times. And most shoppers believe that store brands are often made by one of the larger manufacturers anyway.

To fend off private brands, leading brand marketers will have to invest in R&D to bring out new brands, new features, and continuous quality improvements. They must design strong advertising programs to maintain high awareness and preference. They must find ways to "partner" with major distributors in a search for distribution economies and improved joint performance.

Licensing. Most manufacturers take years and spend millions to create their own brand names. However, some companies license names or symbols previously created by other manufacturers, names of well-known celebrities, or characters from popular movies and books. For a fee, any of these can provide an instant and proven brand name.

Apparel and accessories sellers pay large royalties to adorn their products—from blouses to ties, and linens to luggage—with the names or initials of well-known fashion innovators such as Calvin Klein, Tommy Hilfiger, Gucci, or Armani. Sellers of children's products attach an almost endless list of character names to clothing, toys, school supplies, linens, dolls, lunch boxes, cereals, and other items. Licensed character names range from classics such as *Sesame Street*, Disney, Peanuts, Winnie the Pooh, the Muppets, Scooby Doo, and Dr. Seuss characters to the more recent Dora the Explorer, Powerpuff Girls, Rugrats, Blue's Clues, and Harry Potter characters. And currently a number of top-selling retail toys are products based on television shows and movies such as *Hulk Hands,* the *Spider-Man Triple Action Web Blaster,* and *Dora's Talking Dollhouse.*

Name and character licensing has grown rapidly in recent years. Annual retail sales of licensed products in the United States and Canada have grown from only $4 billion in 1977 to $55 billion in 1987 and more than $105 billion today. Licensing can be a highly profitable business for many companies. For example, Warner Brothers has turned *Looney Tunes* characters into one of the world's most sought-after licenses. More than 225 licensees generate $6 billion in annual retail sales of products sporting Bugs Bunny, Daffy Duck, Foghorn Leghorn, or one of more than 100 other *Looney Tunes* characters. Similarly, Nickelodeon has developed a stable full of hugely popular characters—such as Dora the Explorer, the Rugrats clan, and SpongeBob SquarePants. Products sporting these characters generate more than $5 billion in annual retail sales. "When it comes to licensing its brands for consumer products, Nickelodeon has proved that it has the Midas touch," states a brand licensing expert.[28]

The fastest-growing licensing category is corporate brand licensing, as more for-profit and not-for-profit organizations are licensing their names to generate additional revenues and brand recognition. Coca-Cola, for example, has some 320 licensees in 57 countries producing more than 10,000 products, ranging from baby clothes and boxer shorts to earrings, a Coca-Cola Barbie doll, and even a fishing lure shaped like a tiny coke can. Each year, licensees sold more than $1 billion worth of licensed Coca-Cola products.[29]

■ Licensing: Warner Brothers has turned Looney Tunes characters into one of the world's most sought after licenses.

Cobranding
The practice of using the established brand names of two different companies on the same product.

Cobranding. Although companies have been **cobranding** products for many years, there has been a recent resurgence in cobranded products. Last year alone, 524 new cobranded products were introduced. Cobranding occurs when two established brand names of different companies are used on the same product. For example, Bravo! Foods (which markets Slammers dairy brands) cobranded with MasterFoods (which markets M&Ms, Snickers, Skittles, Mars, Twix, Starburst, and many other familiar candy brands) to create Starburst Slammers, 3 Musketeers Slammers, and Milky Way Slammers. Ford and Eddie Bauer cobranded a sport utility vehicle—the Ford Explorer, Eddie Bauer edition. General Electric worked with Culligan to develop its Water by Culligan Profile Performance refrigerator with a built-in Culligan water filtration system. In most cobranding situations, one company licenses another company's well-known brand to use in combination with its own.[30]

Cobranding offers many advantages. Because each brand dominates in a different category, the combined brands create broader consumer appeal and greater brand equity. Cobranding also allows a company to expand its existing brand into a category it might otherwise have difficulty entering alone. For example, consider the cobranding efforts of SunTrust Banks and Wal-Mart, through which SunTrust is setting up in-store branches cobranded as "Wal-Mart Money Center by SunTrust." The arrangement gives SunTrust a presence in Wal-Mart's massive supercenters. In return, it gives Wal-Mart a foothold in financial services and lets it serve its customers better by offering check cashing, money transfers, money orders, and other services.[31]

Cobranding also has limitations. Such relationships usually involve complex legal contracts and licenses. Cobranding partners must carefully coordinate their advertising, sales promotion, and other marketing efforts. Finally, when cobranding, each partner must trust the other will take good care of its brand. For example, consider the marriage between Kmart and the Martha Stewart Everyday housewares brand. When Kmart declared bankruptcy, it cast a shadow on Martha Stewart. In turn, when Martha Stewart was convicted and jailed for illegal financial dealings, it created negative associations for Kmart. As one Nabisco manager puts it, "Giving away your brand is a lot like giving away your child—you want to make sure everything is perfect."[32]

Brand Development A company has four choices when it comes to developing brands (see Figure 7.4). It can introduce *line extensions* (existing brand names extended to new

Product Category

Existing   New

FIGURE 7.4
Brand Development Strategies

forms, sizes, and flavors of an existing product category), *brand extensions* (existing brand names extended to new product categories), *multibrands* (new brand names introduced in the same product category), or *new brands* (new brand names in new product categories).

Line Extensions.   **Line extensions** occur when a company introduces additional items in a given product category under the same brand name, such as new flavors, forms, colors, ingredients, or package sizes. Thus, Yoplait introduced several line extensions, including new yogurt flavors, a low-carb yogurt, and a yogurt with added cholesterol reducers. And Morton Salt has expanded its line to include regular iodized salt plus Morton Course Kosher Salt, Morton Lite Salt (low in sodium), Morton Popcorn Salt, and Morton Nature's Season seasoning blend. The vast majority of all new-product activity consists of line extensions.

A company might introduce line extensions as a low-cost, low-risk way to introduce new products. Or it might want to meet consumer desires for variety, to use excess capacity, or simply to command more shelf space from resellers. However, line extensions involve some risks. An overextended brand name might lose its specific meaning, or heavily extended brands can cause consumer confusion or frustration.

> Want a Coke? Not so easy. Pick from more than 16 varieties. In zero-calorie versions alone, Coke comes in three subbrands—Diet Coke, Diet Coke with Splenda, and Coca-Cola Zero. Throw in the flavored and free versions—Diet Vanilla Coke, Diet Cherry Coke, Diet Coke with Lemon, Diet Coke with Lime, and Caffeine-Free Diet Coke—and you reach a dizzying eight diets from Coke. And that doesn't count "mid-calorie" Coca-Cola C2. Each subbrand has its own hype—Diet Coke lets you "live your life," while Coke Zero gives you "real Coca-Cola taste and zero calories." And Coca-Cola C2 has "1/2 the carbs, 1/2 the calories, all the great taste." But it's unlikely that many consumers fully appreciate the differences. Instead, the glut of extensions will likely cause what one expert calls "profusion confusion." Laments one cola consumer, "How many versions of Diet Coke do they need?"[33]

Another risk is that sales of an extension may come at the expense of other items in the line. For example, the original Nabisco Fig Newtons cookies have now morphed into a full line of Newtons Fruit Chewy Cookies, including Strawberry Shortcake Newtons, Cherries'n Cheesecake Newtons, and Apple Newtons. Although all are doing well, the original Fig Newton brand now seems like just another flavor. A line extension works best when it takes sales away from competing brands, not when it "cannibalizes" the company's other items.

Brand Extensions.   A **brand extension** involves the use of a successful brand name to launch new or modified products in a new category. For example, Kimberly-Clark extended its market-leading Huggies brand from disposable diapers to a full line of toiletries for tots, from shampoos, lotions, and diaper-rash ointments to baby wash, disposable washcloths, and disposable changing pads. Victorinox extended its venerable Swiss Army brand from multi-tool knives to products ranging from cutlery and ballpoint pens to watches, luggage, and apparel. And Brinks leveraged its strong reputation in commercial security to launch Brinks Home Security Systems.

A brand extension gives a new product instant recognition and faster acceptance. It also saves the high advertising costs usually required to build a new brand name. At the same time, a brand extension strategy involves some risk. Brand extensions such as Bic pantyhose, Heinz

Line extension

Using a successful brand name to introduce additional items in a given product category under the same brand name, such as new flavors, forms, colors, added ingredients, or package sizes.

Brand extension

Using a successful brand name to launch a new or modified product in a new category.

■ Brand extensions: Brinks leveraged its strong reputation in commercial security to launch Brinks Home Security systems.

pet food, LifeSavers gum, and Clorox laundry detergent met early deaths. The extension may confuse the image of the main brand. And if a brand extension fails, it may harm consumer attitudes toward the other products carrying the same brand name. Further, a brand name may not be appropriate to a particular new product, even if it is well made and satisfying—would you consider buying Texaco milk or Alpo chili? Companies that are tempted to transfer a brand name must research how well the brand's associations fit the new product.[34]

Multibrands. Companies often introduce additional brands in the same category. Thus, P&G markets many different brands in each of its product categories. *Multibranding* offers a way to establish different features and appeal to different buying motives. It also allows a company to lock up more reseller shelf space.

A major drawback of multibranding is that each brand might obtain only a small market share, and none may be very profitable. The company may end up spreading its resources over many brands instead of building a few brands to a highly profitable level. These companies should reduce the number of brands they sell in a given category and set up tighter screening procedures for new brands.

New Brands. A company might believe that the power of its existing brand name is waning and a new brand name is needed. Or a company may create a new brand name when it enters a new product category for which none of the company's current brand names is appropriate. For example, Delta created the Song brand to differentiate its new low-cost shuttle airline from its regular airline. Toyota created the separate Scion brand, targeted toward GenY consumers. Japan's Matsushita uses separate names for its different families of consumer electronics products: Panasonic, Technics, National, and Quasar.

As with multibranding, offering too many new brands can result in a company spreading its resources too thin. And in some industries, such as consumer packaged goods, consumers and retailers have become concerned that there are already too many brands, with too few differences between them. Thus, P&G, Frito-Lay, and other large consumer-product marketers are now pursuing *megabrand* strategies—weeding out weaker brands and focusing their marketing dollars only on brands that can achieve the number-one or number-two market share positions in their categories.

MANAGING BRANDS

Companies must manage their brands carefully. First, the brand's positioning must be continuously communicated to consumers. Major brand marketers often spend huge amounts on advertising to create brand awareness and to build preference and loyalty. For example, Verizon spends $730 million annually to promote its brand. McDonald's spends more than $317 million.[35]

Such advertising campaigns can help to create name recognition, brand knowledge, and maybe even some brand preference. However, the fact is that brands are not maintained by advertising but by the *brand experience*. Today, customers come to know a brand through a wide range of contacts and touch points. These include advertising, but also personal experience with the brand, word of mouth, personal interactions with company people, company Web pages, and many others. The company must put as much care into managing these touch points as it does into producing its ads. "A brand is a living entity," says former Disney Chief Executive Michael Eisner, "and it is enriched or undermined cumulatively over time, the product of a thousand small gestures."[36]

The brand's positioning will not take hold fully unless everyone in the company lives the brand. Therefore, the company needs to train its people to be customer-centered. Even better, the company should carry on internal brand building to help employees understand and be enthusiastic about the brand promise. Many companies go even further by training and encouraging their distributors and dealers to serve their customers well.

All of this suggests that managing a company's brand assets can no longer be left only to brand managers. Brand managers do not have enough power or scope to do all the things necessary to build and enhance their brands. Moreover, brand managers often pursue short-term results, whereas managing brands as assets calls for longer-term strategy. Thus, some companies are now setting up brand asset management teams to manage their major brands. Canada Dry and Colgate-Palmolive have appointed *brand-equity managers* to maintain and protect their brands' images, associations, and quality, and to prevent short-term actions by overeager brand managers from hurting the brand.

Finally, companies need to periodically audit their brands' strengths and weaknesses.[37] They should ask: Does our brand excel at delivering benefits that consumers truly value? Is the brand properly positioned? Do all of our consumer touch points support the brand's positioning? Do the brand's managers understand what the brand means to consumers? Does the brand receive proper, sustained support? The brand audit may turn up brands that need more support, brands that need to be dropped, or brands that must be rebranded or repositioned because of changing customer preferences or new competitors.

Services Marketing

Services have grown dramatically in recent years. Services now account for 72.5 percent of U.S. gross domestic product and nearly 60 percent of personal consumption expenditures. And the service industry is growing. Between 2002 and 2012, an estimated 96 percent of all new jobs generated in the United States will be in service industries. Services are growing even faster in the world economy, making up 20 percent of the value of all international trade.[38]

Service industries vary greatly. *Governments* offer services through courts, employment services, hospitals, military services, police and fire departments, postal service, and schools. *Private, not-for-profit organizations* offer services through museums, charities, churches, colleges, foundations, and hospitals. A large number of *business organizations* offer services—airlines, banks, hotels, insurance companies, consulting firms, medical and legal practices, entertainment companies, real-estate firms, retailers, and others.

NATURE AND CHARACTERISTICS OF A SERVICE

A company must consider four special service characteristics when designing marketing programs: *intangibility*, *inseparability*, *variability*, and *perishability* (see Figure 7.5).

Service intangibility means that services cannot be seen, tasted, felt, heard, or smelled before they are bought. For example, people undergoing cosmetic surgery cannot see the result before the purchase. Airline passengers have nothing but a ticket and the promise that they and their luggage will arrive safely at the intended destination, hopefully at the same time. To reduce uncertainty, buyers look for "signals" of service quality. They draw

Service intangibility
A major characteristic of services—they cannot be seen, tasted, felt, heard, or smelled before they are bought.

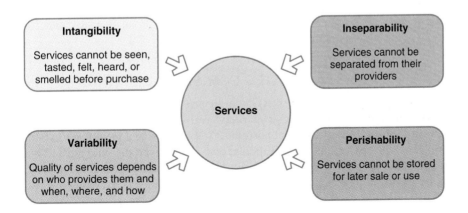

FIGURE 7.5
Four Service Characteristics

conclusions about quality from the place, people, price, equipment, and communications that they can see.

Therefore, the service provider's task is to make the service tangible in one or more ways and to send the right signals about quality. One analyst calls this *evidence management,* in which the service organization presents its customers with organized, honest evidence of its capabilities. The Mayo Clinic practices good evidence management:[39]

> When it comes to hospitals, it's very hard for the average patient to judge the quality of the "product." You can't try it on, you can't return it if you don't like it, and you need an advanced degree to understand it. And so, when we're considering a medical facility, most of us unconsciously turn detective, looking for evidence of competence, caring, and integrity. The Mayo Clinic doesn't leave that evidence to chance. By carefully managing a set of visual and experiential clues, Mayo offers patients and their families concrete evidence of its strengths and values. For example, staff at the clinic are trained to act in a way that clearly signals its patient-first focus. "My doctor calls me at home to check on how I am doing," marvels one patient. "She wants to work with what is best for my schedule." Mayo's physical facilities also send the right signals. They've been carefully designed to relieve stress, offer a place of refuge, create positive distractions, convey caring and respect, signal competence, accommodate families, and make it easy to find your way around. The result? Exceptionally positive word-of-mouth and abiding customer loyalty, which have allowed Mayo Clinic to build what is arguably the most powerful brand in health care—with very little advertising.

Physical goods are produced, then stored, later sold, and still later consumed. In contrast, services are first sold, then produced and consumed at the same time. **Service inseparability** means that services cannot be separated from their providers, whether the providers are people or machines. If a service employee provides the service, then the employee becomes a part of the service. Because the customer is also present as the service is produced, *provider-customer interaction* is a special feature of services marketing. Both the provider and the customer affect the service outcome.

Service variability means that the quality of services depends on who provides them as well as when, where, and how they are provided. For example, some hotels—say, Marriott—have reputations for providing better service than others. Still, within a given Marriott hotel, one registration-desk employee may be cheerful and efficient, whereas another standing just a few feet away may be unpleasant and slow. Even the quality of a single Marriott employee's service varies according to his or her energy and frame of mind at the time of each customer encounter.

Service perishability means that services cannot be stored for later sale or use. Some doctors charge patients for missed appointments because the service value existed only at that point and disappeared when the patient did not show up. The perishability of services is not a problem when demand is steady. However, when demand fluctuates, service firms often have difficult problems. For example, because of rush-hour demand, public transportation companies have to own much more equipment than they would if demand were even throughout the day. Thus, service firms often design strategies for producing a better match between demand and supply. Hotels and resorts charge lower prices in the off-season to attract more guests. And restaurants hire part-time employees to serve during peak periods.

Service inseparability
A major characteristic of services—they are produced and consumed at the same time and cannot be separated from their providers, whether the providers are people or machines.

Service variability
A major characteristic of services—their quality may vary greatly, depending on who provides them and when, where, and how.

Service perishability
A major characteristic of services—they cannot be stored for later sale or use.

MARKETING STRATEGIES FOR SERVICE FIRMS

Just like manufacturing businesses, good service firms use marketing to position themselves strongly in chosen target markets. Wal-Mart promises "Always Low Prices, Always." The Ritz-Carlton Hotel positions itself as offering a memorable experience that "enlivens the senses, instills well-being, and fulfills even the unexpressed wishes and needs of our guests." At the Mayo Clinic, "the needs of the patient come first." These and other service firms establish their positions through traditional marketing mix activities.

However, because services differ from tangible products, they often require additional marketing approaches. In a product business, products are fairly standardized and can sit on shelves waiting for customers. But in a service business, the customer and front-line service employee *interact* to create the service. Thus, service providers must interact effectively with customers to create superior value during service encounters. Effective interaction, in turn, depends on the skills of front-line service employees and on the support processes backing these employees.

The Service-Profit Chain   Successful service companies focus their attention on *both* their customers and their employees. They understand the **service-profit chain**, which links service firm profits with employee and customer satisfaction. This chain consists of five links:[40]

Service-profit chain
The chain that links service firm profits with employee and customer satisfaction.

1. *Internal service quality:* superior employee selection and training, a quality work environment, and strong support for those dealing with customers, which results in. . . .
2. *Satisfied and productive service employees:* more satisfied, loyal, and hardworking employees, which results in. . . .
3. *Greater service value:* more effective and efficient customer value creation and service delivery, which results in. . . .
4. *Satisfied and loyal customers:* satisfied customers who remain loyal, repeat purchase, and refer other customers, which results in. . . .
5. *Healthy service profits and growth:* superior service firm performance.

Therefore, reaching service profits and growth goals begins with taking care of those who take care of customers (see Marketing at Work 7.3). In fact, Starbucks CEO Howard Schultz goes so far as to say that "customers always come in second—employees matter more." The idea is that happy employees will unleash their enthusiasm on customers, creating even greater customer satisfaction. "If the battle cry of the company [is] to exceed the expectations of our customers," says Schultz, "then as managers, we [must] first exceed the expectations of our people."[41] Consider Wegmans, a 67-store grocery chain in New York.

Wegmans customers have zeal for the store that borders on obsession. Says one regular, "Going there isn't just shopping, it's an event." Last, year, Wegmans received more than 7,000 letters from around the country, about half of them asking Wegmans to come to their town. The secret? Wegmans knows that happy, satisfied employees produce happy, satisfied customers. So Wegmans takes care of its employees. It pays higher salaries, shells out money for employee college scholarships, covers 100 percent of health insurance premiums for employees making less than $55,000 a year, and invests heavily in employee training. In fact, last year Wegmans topped *FORTUNE* magazine's

■ The service-profit chain: Happy employees make for happy customers. "The biggest reason Wegmans is a shopping experience like no other is that it is an employer like no other."

MARKETING AT WORK   7.3

The Ritz-Carlton: Taking Care of Those Who Take Care of Customers

The Ritz-Carlton, a chain of luxury hotels renowned for outstanding service, caters to the top 5 percent of corporate and leisure travelers. The company's Credo sets lofty customer service goals: "The Ritz-Carlton Hotel is a place where the genuine care and comfort of our guests is our highest mission. . . . The Ritz-Carlton experience enlivens the senses, instills well-being, and fulfills even the unexpressed wishes and needs of our guests."

The Credo is more than just words on paper—Ritz-Carlton delivers on its promises. In surveys of departing guests, some 95 percent report that they've had a truly memorable experience. In fact, at Ritz-Carlton, exceptional service encounters have become almost commonplace. Take the experiences of Nancy and Harvey Heffner of Manhattan, who stayed at The Ritz-Carlton Naples, in Naples, Florida (recently rated the best hotel in the United States and fourth best in the world, by *Travel & Leisure* magazine). As reported in the *New York Times*:

"The hotel is elegant and beautiful," Mrs. Heffner said, "but more important is the beauty expressed by the staff. They can't do enough to please you." When the couple's son became sick last year in Naples, the hotel staff brought him hot tea with honey at all hours of the night, she said. When Mr. Heffner had to fly home on business for a day and his return flight was delayed, a driver for the hotel waited in the lobby most of the night.

Or how about this account: "An administrative assistant at The Ritz-Carlton, Philadelphia overheard a guest lamenting that he'd forgotten to pack a pair of formal shoes and would have to wear hiking boots to an important meeting. Early the next morning, she delivered to the awestruck man a new pair in his size and favorite color."

Such personal, high-quality service has also made The Ritz-Carlton a favorite among conventioneers. For six straight years, the luxury hotel came out on top in *Business Travel News's* "Top U.S. Hotel Chain Survey of Business Travel Buyers." "They not only treat us like kings when we hold our top-level meetings in their hotels, but we just never get any complaints," comments one convention planner. Says another, who had recently held a meeting at The Ritz-Carlton at Half Moon Bay, "The . . . first-rate catering and service-oriented convention services staff [and] The Ritz-Carlton's ambiance and beauty—the elegant, Grand Dame-style lodge, nestled on a bluff between two championship golf courses overlooking the Pacific Ocean—makes a day's work there seem anything but."

Since its incorporation in 1983, Ritz-Carlton has received virtually every major award that the hospitality industry bestows. In addition, in 1992, it became the first hotel company ever to win the prestigious Malcolm Baldrige National Quality Award, which it won a *second* time in 1999. More importantly, service quality has resulted in high customer retention. More than 90 percent of Ritz-Carlton customers return. And despite its hefty room rates, the chain enjoys a 70 percent occupancy rate, almost nine points above the industry average.

Most of the responsibility for keeping guests satisfied falls to Ritz-Carlton's customer-contact employees. Thus, the hotel chain takes great care in finding just the right personnel. The Ritz-Carlton goes to great lengths to "rigorously—even fanatically—select and train employees, instill pride, and compensate generously," says an industry insider. "We don't hire or recruit, we select," says The Ritz-Carlton's director of human resources. "We want only people who care about people," notes the company's vice president of quality. Once selected, employees are given intensive training in the art of coddling customers. New employees attend a two-day orientation, in which top management drums into them the "20 Ritz-Carlton Basics." Basic number one: "The Credo will be known, owned, and energized by all employees."

Employees are taught to do everything they can never to lose a guest. "There's no negotiating at Ritz-Carlton when it comes to solving customer problems," says the quality executive. Staff learn that *anyone* who receives a customer complaint *owns* that complaint until it's resolved (Ritz-Carlton Basic number eight). They are trained to drop whatever they're doing to help a customer—no matter what they're doing or what their department. The Ritz-Carlton employees are empowered to handle problems on the spot, without consulting higher-ups. Each employee can spend up to $2,000 to redress a guest grievance. And each is allowed to break from his or her routine for as long as needed

---

best-companies-to-work-for list. "The biggest reason Wegmans is a shopping experience like no other is that it is an employer like no other," says a Wegmans watcher.[42]

Thus, service marketing requires more than just traditional external marketing using the Four Ps. Figure 7.6 shows that service marketing also requires *internal marketing* and *interactive marketing*. **Internal marketing** means that the service firm must effectively train and motivate its customer-contact employees and supporting service people to work as a *team* to provide customer satisfaction. Marketers must get everyone

Internal marketing
Marketing by a service firm to train and effectively motivate its customer-contact employees and all the supporting service people to work as a team to provide customer satisfaction.

THE RITZ-CARLTON®

CREDO

The Ritz-Carlton Hotel is a place where the genuine care and comfort of our guests is our highest mission.

We pledge to provide the finest personal service and facilities for our guests who will always enjoy a warm, relaxed yet refined ambience.

The Ritz-Carlton experience enlivens the senses, instills well-being, and fulfills even the unexpressed wishes and needs of our guests.

THREE STEPS OF SERVICE

1
A warm and sincere greeting. Use the guest name, if and when possible.

2
Anticipation and compliance with guest needs.

3
Fond farewell. Give them a warm good-bye and use their name, if and when possible.

THE EMPLOYEE PROMISE

At The Ritz-Carlton, our Ladies and Gentlemen are the most important resource in our service commitment to our guests.

By applying the principles of trust, honesty, respect, integrity and commitment, we nurture and maximize talent to the benefit of each individual and the company.

The Ritz-Carlton fosters a work environment where diversity is valued, quality of life is enhanced, individual aspirations are fulfilled, and The Ritz-Carlton mystique is strengthened.

"We Are Ladies and Gentlemen Serving Ladies and Gentlemen"

■ *The Credo and Employee Promise: Ritz-Carlton knows that to take care of customers, you must first take care of those who take care of customers.*

to make a guest happy. Thus, while competitors are still reading guest comment cards to learn about customer problems, The Ritz-Carlton has already resolved them.

The Ritz-Carlton instills a sense of pride in its employees. "You serve," they are told, "but you are not servants." The company motto states, "We are ladies and gentlemen serving ladies and gentlemen." Employees understand their role in Ritz-Carlton's success. "We might not be able to afford a hotel like this," says employee Tammy Patton, "but we can make it so people who can afford it will want to keep coming here." As the general manager of The Ritz-Carlton Naples puts it, "When you invite guests to your house, you want everything to be perfect."

The Ritz-Carlton recognizes and rewards employees who perform feats of outstanding

service. Under its 5-Star Awards program, outstanding performers are nominated by peers and managers, and winners receive plaques at dinners celebrating their achievements. For on-the-spot recognition, managers award Gold Standard Coupons, redeemable for items in the gift shop and free weekend stays at the hotel. Ritz-Carlton further motivates its employees with events such as Super Sports Day, an employee talent show, luncheons celebrating employment anniversaries and birthdays, a family picnic, and special themes in employee dining rooms. As a result, Ritz-Carlton's employees appear to be just as satisfied as its customers. Employee turnover is less than 25 percent a year, compared with 44 percent at other luxury hotels.

The Ritz-Carlton's success is based on a simple philosophy: To take care of customers, you

must first take care of those who take care of customers. Satisfied employees deliver high service value, which then creates satisfied customers. Satisfied customers, in turn, create sales and profits for the company.

Sources: Quotes and other information from Duff McDonald, "Roll Out the Blue Carpet," *Business 2.0,* May 2004, pp. 53–54; Marshall Krantz, "Buyers Say Four Seasons Is Most Luxurious," *Meeting News,* May 9, 2005, pp. 1–3; Edwin McDowell, "Ritz-Carlton's Keys to Good Service," *New York Times,* March 31, 1993, p. D1; "The Ritz-Carlton, Half Moon Bay," *Successful Meetings,* November 2001, p. 40; Terry R. Bacon and David G. Pugh, "Ritz-Carlton and EMC: The Gold Standards in Operational Behavior," *Journal of Organizational Excellence,* Spring 2004, pp. 61–77; Bruce Serlen, "Ritz-Carlton Retains Hold on Corporate Deluxe Buyers," *Business Travel News,* February 7, 2005, pp. 15–17; and The Ritz-Carlton Web site at www.ritzcarlton.com, August 2005.

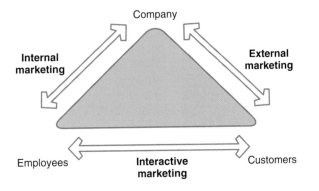

FIGURE 7.6
Three Types of Service Marketing

in the organization to be customer-centered. In fact, internal marketing must *precede* external marketing. For example, Ritz-Carlton orients its employees carefully, instills in them a sense of pride, and motivates them by recognizing and rewarding outstanding service deeds.

Interactive marketing
Marketing by a service firm that recognizes that perceived service quality depends heavily on the quality of buyer-seller interaction.

Interactive marketing means that service quality depends heavily on the quality of the buyer-seller interaction during the service encounter. In product marketing, product quality often depends little on how the product is obtained. But in services marketing, service quality depends on both the service deliverer and the quality of the delivery. Service marketers, therefore, have to master interactive marketing skills. Thus, Ritz-Carlton selects only "people who care about people" and instructs them carefully in the fine art of interacting with customers to satisfy their every need.

In today's marketplace, companies must know how to deliver interactions that are not only "high-touch" but also "high-tech." For example, customers can log on to the Charles Schwab Web site and access account information, investment research, real-time quotes, after-hours trading, and the Schwab learning center. They can also participate in live online events and chat online with customer service representatives. Customers seeking more personal interactions can contact service reps by phone or visit a local Schwab branch office. Thus, Schwab has mastered interactive marketing at all three levels—calls, clicks, *and* visits.

Today, as competition and costs increase, and as productivity and quality decrease, more service marketing sophistication is needed. Service companies face three major marketing tasks: They want to increase their *service differentiation, service quality,* and *service productivity.*

Managing Service Differentiation In these days of intense price competition, service marketers often complain about the difficulty of differentiating their services from those of competitors. To the extent that customers view the services of different providers as similar, they care less about the provider than the price.

The solution to price competition is to develop a differentiated offer, delivery, and image. The *offer* can include innovative features that set one company's offer apart from competitors' offers. Some hotels offer car-rental, banking, and business-center services in their lobbies and high-speed Internet connections in their rooms. Airlines differentiate their offers though frequent-flyer award programs and special services. For example, Qantas offers personal entertainment screens at every seat and "Skybeds" for international business class flyers. Lufthansa provides wireless Internet access and real-time surfing to every seat—it makes "an airplane feel like a cyber café." And British Airways offers spa services at its Arrivals Lounge at Heathrow airport. Says one ad: "You can step off the plane and straight into a shower, a robe, even a Molton Brown facial—all while your suit is being pressed."

Service companies can differentiate their service *delivery* by having more able and reliable customer-contact people, by developing a superior physical environment in which the service product is delivered, or by designing a superior delivery process. For example, many grocery chains now offer online shopping and home delivery as a better way to shop than having to drive, park, wait in line, and tote groceries home.

Finally, service companies also can work on differentiating their *images* through symbols and branding. The Harris Bank of Chicago adopted the lion as its symbol on its sta-

■ Services differentiation: British Airways offers spa services: "You can step off the plane and straight into a shower, a robe, even a Molton Brown facial—all while your suit is being pressed."

tionery, in its advertising, and even as stuffed animals offered to new depositors. The well-known Harris lion confers an image of strength on the bank. Other well-known service symbols include Merrill Lynch's bull, MGM's lion, McDonald's Golden Arches, and Allstate's "good hands."

Managing Service Quality One of the major ways a service firm can differentiate itself is by delivering consistently higher quality than its competitors do. Like manufacturers before them, most service industries have now joined the customer-driven quality movement. And like product marketers, service providers need to identify what target customers expect concerning service quality.

Unfortunately, service quality is harder to define and judge than is product quality. For instance, it is harder to agree on the quality of a haircut than on the quality of a hair dryer. Customer retention is perhaps the best measure of quality—a service firm's ability to hang onto its customers depends on how consistently it delivers value to them.[43]

Top service companies set high service-quality standards. They watch service performance closely, both their own and that of competitors. They do not settle for merely good service; they aim for 100 percent defect-free service. A 98-percent performance standard may sound good, but using this standard, 310,000 UPS packages would be lost each day, 10 words would be misspelled on each printed page, 225,000 prescriptions would be misfilled daily, and drinking water would be unsafe 7 days a year.[44]

Unlike product manufacturers who can adjust their machinery and inputs until everything is perfect, service quality will always vary, depending on the interactions between employees and customers. As hard as they try, even the best companies will have an occasional late delivery, burned steak, or grumpy employee. However, good *service recovery* can turn angry customers into loyal ones. In fact, good recovery can win more customer purchasing and loyalty than if things had gone well in the first place. Therefore, companies should take steps not only to provide good service every time but also to recover from service mistakes when they do occur.

The first step is to *empower* front-line service employees—to give them the authority, responsibility, and incentives they need to recognize, care about, and tend to customer needs. At Marriott, for example, well-trained employees are given the authority to do whatever it takes, on the spot, to keep guests happy. They are also expected to help management ferret out the cause of guests' problems and to inform managers of ways to improve overall hotel service and guests' comfort.

Managing Service Productivity With their costs rising rapidly, service firms are under great pressure to increase service productivity. They can do so in several ways. They can train current employees better or hire new ones who will work harder or more skillfully. Or they can increase the quantity of their service by giving up some quality. The provider can "industrialize the service" by adding equipment and standardizing production, as in McDonald's assembly-line approach to fast-food retailing. Finally, the service provider can harness the power of technology. Although we often think of technology's power to save time and costs in manufacturing companies, it also has great—and often untapped—potential to make service workers more productive.

However, companies must avoid pushing productivity so hard that doing so reduces quality. Attempts to industrialize a service or to cut costs can make a service company more efficient in the short run. But they can also reduce its longer-run ability to innovate, maintain service quality, or respond to consumer needs and desires. In short, they can take the "service" out of service.

Additional Product Considerations

Here, we discuss two additional product policy considerations: social responsibility in product decisions and issues of international product and service marketing.

PRODUCT DECISIONS AND SOCIAL RESPONSIBILITY

Product decisions have attracted much public attention. Marketers should consider carefully public policy issues and regulations involving acquiring or dropping products, patent protection, product quality and safety, and product warranties.

Regarding new products, the government may prevent companies from adding products through acquisitions if the effect threatens to lessen competition. Companies dropping products must be aware that they have legal obligations, written or implied, to their suppliers, dealers, and customers who have a stake in the dropped product. Companies must also obey U.S. patent laws when developing new products. A company cannot make its product illegally similar to another company's established product.

Manufacturers must comply with specific laws regarding product quality and safety. The Federal Food, Drug, and Cosmetic Act protects consumers from unsafe and adulterated food, drugs, and cosmetics. Various acts provide for the inspection of sanitary conditions in the meat- and poultry-processing industries. Safety legislation has been passed to regulate fabrics, chemical substances, automobiles, toys, and drugs and poisons. The Consumer Product Safety Act of 1972 established a Consumer Product Safety Commission, which has the authority to ban or seize potentially harmful products and set severe penalties for violation of the law.

If consumers have been injured by a product that has been designed defectively, they can sue manufacturers or dealers. Product liability suits are now occurring in federal and state courts at the rate of almost 110,000 per year. While manufacturers are found at fault in only 6 percent of all product liability cases, when they are found guilty, the median jury award is $6 million and individual awards can run into the tens or even hundreds of millions of dollars. For example, a jury recently ordered Ford to pay nearly $369 million to a woman paralyzed in a rollover accident involving a Ford Explorer.[45]

This phenomenon has resulted in huge increases in product liability insurance premiums, causing big problems in some industries. Some companies pass these higher rates along to consumers by raising prices. Others are forced to discontinue high-risk product lines. Some companies are now appointing "product stewards," whose job is to protect consumers from harm and the company from liability by proactively ferreting out potential product problems.

Many manufacturers offer written product warranties to convince customers of their products' quality. To protect consumers, Congress passed the Magnuson-Moss Warranty Act in 1975. The act requires that full warranties meet certain minimum standards, including repair "within a reasonable time and without charge" or a replacement or full refund if the product does not work "after a reasonable number of attempts" at repair. Otherwise, the company must make it clear that it is offering only a limited warranty. The law has led several manufacturers to switch from full to limited warranties and others to drop warranties altogether.

INTERNATIONAL PRODUCT AND SERVICE MARKETING

International product and service marketers face special challenges. First, they must figure out what products and services to introduce and in which countries. Then, they must decide how much to standardize or adapt their products and services for world markets.

On the one hand, companies would like to standardize their offerings. Standardization helps a company to develop a consistent worldwide image. It also lowers the product design, manufacturing, and marketing costs of offering a large variety of products. On the other hand, markets and consumers around the world differ widely. Companies must usually respond to these differences by adapting their product offerings. Something as simple as an electrical outlet can create big product problems:

> Those who have traveled across Europe know the frustration of electrical plugs, different voltages, and other annoyances of international travel. . . . Philips, the electrical appliance manufacturer, has to produce 12 kinds of irons to serve just its European market. The problem is that Europe does not have a universal [electrical] standard. The ends of irons bristle with different plugs for different countries. Some

have three prongs, others two; prongs protrude straight or angled, round or rectangular, fat, thin, and sometimes sheathed. There are circular plug faces, squares, pentagons, and hexagons. Some are perforated and some are notched. One French plug has a niche like a keyhole. Looking for a fix? One online travel service sells an elaborate 10-piece adapter plug set for international travelers for $65.00.[46]

Packaging also presents new challenges for international marketers. Packaging issues can be subtle. For example, names, labels, and colors may not translate easily from one country to another. A firm using yellow flowers in its logo might fare well in the United States but meet with disaster in Mexico, where a yellow flower symbolizes death or disrespect. Similarly, although Nature's Gift might be an appealing name for gourmet mushrooms in America, it would be deadly in Germany, where *gift* means poison. Packaging may also have to be tailored to meet the physical characteristics of consumers in various parts of the world. For instance, soft drinks are sold in smaller cans in Japan to fit the smaller Japanese hand better. Thus, although product and package standardization can produce benefits, companies must usually adapt their offerings to the unique needs of specific international markets.

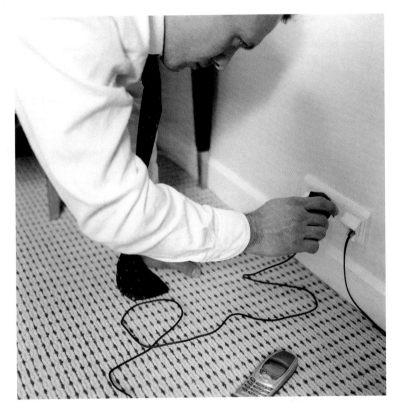

■ Companies must usually adapt their product offerings to differences in international markets. Something as simple as an electric outlet can create big product problems.

Service marketers also face special challenges when going global. Some service industries have a long history of international operations. For example, the commercial banking industry was one of the first to grow internationally. Banks had to provide global services in order to meet the foreign exchange and credit needs of their home country clients wanting to sell overseas. In recent years, many banks have become truly global. Germany's Deutsche Bank, for example, serves more than 12 million customers in 74 countries. For its clients around the world who wish to grow globally, Deutsche Bank can raise money not only in Frankfurt but also in Zurich, London, Paris, and Tokyo.[47]

Professional and business services industries such as accounting, management consulting, and advertising have only recently globalized. The international growth of these firms followed the globalization of the client companies they serve. For example, as their clients began to employ worldwide marketing and advertising strategies, advertising agencies responded by globalizing their own operations. McCann-Erickson Worldwide, a large U.S. advertising agency, operates in more than 130 countries. It serves international clients such as Coca-Cola, General Motors, ExxonMobil, Microsoft, MasterCard, Johnson & Johnson, and Unilever in markets ranging from the United States and Canada to Korea and Kazakhstan. Moreover, McCann-Erickson is one company in the Interpublic Group of Companies, an immense, worldwide network of advertising and marketing services companies.[48]

Retailers are among the latest service businesses to go global. As their home markets become saturated, American retailers such as Wal-Mart, Toys "R" Us, Office Depot, and Saks Fifth Avenue are expanding into faster-growing markets abroad. For example, every year since 1995, Wal-Mart has entered a new country; its international division's sales grew more than 16 percent last year, skyrocketing to more than $47.5 billion. Foreign retailers are making similar moves. Asian shoppers can now buy American products in French-owned Carrefour stores. Carrefour, the world's second-largest retailer behind Wal-Mart, now operates more than 11,000 stores in 31 countries. It is the leading retailer in Europe, Brazil, and Argentina and the largest foreign retailer in China.[49]

■ Retailers are among the latest service businesses to go global. Here, Asian shoppers buy American products in a Dutch-owned Makro store in Kuala Lumpur.

The trend toward growth of global service companies will continue, especially in banking, airlines, telecommunications, and professional services. Today service firms are no longer simply following their manufacturing customers. Instead, they are taking the lead in international expansion.

REST STOP → REVIEWING THE CONCEPTS

Time to kick back and reflect on the key concepts in this first marketing mix chapter on products and services. A product is more than a simple set of tangible features. In fact, many marketing offers consist of combinations of both tangible goods and services, ranging from *pure tangible goods* at one extreme to *pure services* at the other. Each product or service offered to customers can be viewed on three levels. The *core product* consists of the core problem-solving benefits that consumers seek when they buy a product. The *actual product* exists around the core and includes the quality level, features, design, brand name, and packaging. The *augmented product* is the actual product plus the various services and benefits offered with it, such as warranty, free delivery, installation, and maintenance.

1. Define *product* and the major classifications of products and services.

Broadly defined, a *product* is anything that can be offered to a market for attention, acquisition, use, or consumption that might satisfy a want or need. Products include physical objects but also services, events, persons, places, organizations, ideas, or mixes of these entities. *Services* are products that consist of activities, benefits, or satisfactions offered for sale that are essentially intangible, such as banking, hotel, tax preparation, and home-repair services.

Products and services fall into two broad classes based on the types of consumers that use them. *Consumer products*—those bought by final consumers—are usually classified according to consumer shopping habits (convenience products, shopping products, specialty products, and unsought products). *Industrial products*—purchased for further processing or for use in conducting a business—include materials and parts, capital items, and supplies and services. Other marketable entities—such as organizations, persons, places, and ideas—can also be thought of as products.

2. Describe the decisions companies make regarding their individual products and services, product lines, and product mixes.

Individual product decisions involve product attributes, branding, packaging, labeling, and product support services. *Product attribute* decisions involve product quality, features, and style and design. *Branding* decisions include selecting a brand name and developing a brand strategy. *Packaging* provides many key benefits, such as protection, economy, convenience, and promotion. Package decisions often include designing *labels,* which identify, describe, and possibly promote the product. Companies also develop *product support services* that enhance customer service and satisfaction and safeguard against competitors.

Most companies produce a product line rather than a single product. A *product line* is a group of products that are related in function, customer-purchase needs, or distribution channels. *Line stretching* involves extending a line downward, upward, or in both directions to occupy a gap that might otherwise be filled by a competitor. In contrast, *line filling* involves adding items within the present range of the line. All product lines and items offered to customers by a particular seller make up the *product mix*. The mix can be described by four dimensions: width, length, depth, and consistency. These dimensions are the tools for developing the company's product strategy.

3. Discuss branding strategy—the decisions companies make in building and managing their brands.

Some analysts see brands as *the* major enduring asset of a company. Brands are more than just names and symbols—they embody everything that the product or service *means* to consumers. *Brand equity* is the positive differential effect that knowing the brand name has on customer response to the product or service. A brand with strong brand equity is a very valuable asset.

In building brands, companies need to make decisions about brand positioning, brand name selection, brand sponsorship, and brand development. The most powerful *brand positioning* builds around strong consumer beliefs and values. *Brand name selection* involves finding the best brand name based on a careful review of product benefits, the target market, and proposed marketing strategies. A manufacturer has four *brand sponsorship* options: it can launch a *manufacturer's brand* (or national brand), sell to resellers who use a *private brand*, market *licensed brands*, or join forces with another company to *cobrand* a product. A company also has four choices when it comes to developing brands. It can introduce *line extensions, brand extensions, multibrands,* or *new brands.*

Companies must build and manage their brands carefully. The brand's positioning must be continuously communicated to consumers. Advertising can help. However, brands are not maintained by advertising but by the *brand experience.* Customers come to know a brand through a wide range of contacts and interactions. The company must put as much care into managing these touch points as it does into producing its ads.

Thus, managing a company's brand assets can no longer be left only to brand managers. Some companies are now setting up brand asset management teams to manage their major brands. Finally, companies must periodically audit their brands' strengths and weaknesses. In some cases, brands may need to be repositioned because of changing customer preferences or new competitors. Other cases may call for completely *rebranding* a product, service, or company.

4. Identify the four characteristics that affect the marketing of a service and the additional marketing considerations that services require.

Services are characterized by four key characteristics: they are *intangible, inseparable, variable,* and *perishable.* Each characteristic poses problems and marketing requirements. Marketers work to find ways to make the service more tangible, to increase the productivity of providers who are inseparable from their products, to standardize the quality in the face of variability, and to improve demand movements and supply capacities in the face of service perishability.

Good service companies focus attention on *both* customers and employees. They understand the *service-profit chain,* which links service firm profits with employee and customer satisfaction. Services marketing strategy calls not only for external marketing but also for *internal marketing* to motivate employees, and *interactive marketing* to create service delivery skills among service providers. To succeed, service marketers must create *competitive differentiation,* offer high *service quality,* and find ways to increase *service productivity.*

5. Discuss two additional product issues: socially responsible product decisions and international product and services marketing.

Marketers must consider two additional product issues. The first is *social responsibility.* This includes public policy issues and regulations involving acquiring or dropping products, patent protection, product quality and safety, and product warranties. The second involves the special challenges facing international product and service marketers. International marketers must decide how much to standardize or adapt their offerings for world markets.

Navigating the Key Terms

Brand (208)
Brand equity (214)
Brand extension (221)
Cobranding (220)
Consumer product (200)
Convenience product (201)
Industrial product (202)
Interactive marketing (228)
Internal marketing (226)

Line extension (221)
Packaging (209)
Private brand (or store brand) (218)
Product (199)
Product line (211)
Product mix (or product portfolio) (213)
Product quality (206)
Service (199)
Service inseparability (224)

Service intangibility (223)
Service perishability (224)
Service-profit chain (225)
Service variability (224)
Shopping product (201)
Social marketing (203)
Specialty product (201)
Unsought product (202)

Travel Log

Discussing the Issues

1. List and explain the core, actual, and augmented products for educational experiences that universities offer. How are these products different, if at all, from those offered by junior colleges?

2. List and summarize the characteristics of the four types of consumer products. Provide an example of each.

3. Visit a grocery store and look at the packages for competing products in two or three different product categories. Which packages are the best? Why? Do any of the packages add value to the product? Do any of the packages help build relationships with prospective or current customers?

4. Visit the Kraft Foods company Web site (www.kraft.com/brands/index.html) and examine its list of different brands. Evaluate the company's product mix on the dimensions of width, length, depth, and consistency.

5. Define *brand equity*. Name three firms that you feel have high brand equity. How does each company's brand equity compare to that of its competitors?

6. How are the services offered by a dry-cleaning company different from those offered by an auto-parts store in terms of intangibility, inseparability, variability, and perishability?

Application Questions

1. Consider the following brand extensions and evaluate how well the brand's associations fit the new product: Kodak extending into batteries, Winnebago extending into tents, Fisher-Price extending into children's eyeglass frames, Harley-Davidson extending into cigarettes, and Dunkin' Donuts extending into cereal. Which of the proposed brand extensions is likely to have the most success? The least?

2. Using the six desirable qualities that a good brand name should possess, create a brand name for a personal care product that has the following positioning statement: "Intended for X-Games sports participants and enthusiasts, _____ is a deodorant that combines effective odor protection with an enduring and seductive fragrance that will enhance your romantic fortunes."

3. How can a movie theater manage the intangibility, inseparability, variability, and perishability of its services? Give specific examples to illustrate your thoughts. How could the movie theater use internal and interactive marketing to enhance its service-profit chain?

Under the Hood: Focus on Technology

When you buy a gallon of milk, how often do you check the expiration date printed on the side of the carton? Ever wonder how accurate that date really is? According to Milco, a dairy company, the product expiration date may not always accurately predict its freshness. Shipping and storage conditions can dramatically alter a product's freshness. To address these difficulties and ease consumer concerns, Milco recently developed a packaging innovation: the Fresh-Check Indicator. By comparing two colored rings on the product package, a consumer can discern if the product has expired, is about to expire, or is still fresh. Says Milco's marketing manager, "when shopping for perishable items like fresh juices and dairy, consumers run the risk of buying expired or inconsumable goods. The Fresh-Check Indicator means customers no longer need to make that gamble."*

1. Would the Fresh-Check Indicator on a gallon of milk change your impression of a brand you otherwise overlooked?

2. How does packaging technology influence brand perception? How might the Fresh-Check Indicator change consumers' impressions of a brand of milk?

*Robbie Greenfield, "Fresh Innovation Leads Milco's Dairy Comeback," July 14, 2005, accessed at www.itp.net.

Focus on Ethics

Companies have an interest in protecting their brand names whether they are in the physical world or the cyberworld. The term *cybersquatting* has been used to refer to an individual registering a domain name that is identical to or confusingly similar to a distinctive, famous trademark. Cybersquatters typically obtain a domain name in hopes of using the similar Web address to bring traffic to their own Web site or to sell the domain name back to the company for a substantial profit. Cybersquatting was made illegal in the United States by the 2000 Anticybersquatting Consumer Protection Act, which subjects individuals who register a domain name in "bad faith" to fines of up to $100,000 per domain name. Under the law, Google recently won a case against a Russian man who registered four domain names: googkle.com, ghoogle.com, gfoogle.com and gooigle.com.*

1. Why should companies care about cybersquatters? What impact does cybersquatting have on brand names and brand equity?

2. Some people feel that domain names should be on a "first come, first served" basis with no company or individual having a claim on unregistered domain names. Do you agree?

3. How does protecting a brand name in cyberspace compare with trademark protection?

*See Keith Regan, "Arbitrators Back Google in Fight Against Typo Squatter," July 11, 2005, accessed at www.ecommercetimes.com.

Videos

The Swiss Army video case that accompanies this chapter is located in Appendix 1 at the back of the book.

➡️ **AFTER STUDYING THIS CHAPTER, YOU SHOULD BE ABLE TO**

1. explain how companies find and develop new-product ideas

2. list and define the steps in the new-product development process

3. describe the stages of the product life cycle

4. describe how marketing strategies change during the product's life cycle

New-Product Development and Product Life-Cycle Strategies

Road Map Previewing the Concepts

In the previous chapter, you learned how marketers manage individual brands and entire product mixes. In this chapter, we'll look into two additional product topics: developing new products and managing products through their life cycles. New products are the lifeblood of an organization. However, new-product development is risky, and many new products fail. So, the first part of this chapter lays out a process for finding and growing successful new products. Once introduced, marketers want their products to enjoy a long and happy life. In the second part of the chapter, you'll see that every product passes through several life-cycle stages and that each stage poses new challenges requiring different marketing strategies and tactics.

For openers, consider Apple Computer. An early new-product innovator, Apple got off to a fast and impressive start. But only a decade later, as its creative fires cooled, Apple found itself on the brink of extinction. That set the stage for one of the most remarkable turnarounds in corporate history. Read on to see how Apple's cofounder, Steve Jobs, used lots of innovation and creative new products to first start the company and then to remake it again 20 years later.

From the very start, the tale of Apple Computer is a tale of dazzling creativity and customer-driven innovation. Under the leadership of its cofounder and creative genius, Steve Jobs, Apple's very first personal computers, introduced in the late 1970s, stood apart because of their user-friendly look and feel. The company's Macintosh computer, unveiled in 1984, and its LazerWriter printers, blazed new trails in desktop computing and publishing, making Apple an early industry leader in both innovation and market share.

But then things took an ugly turn for Apple. In 1985, after tumultuous struggles with the new president he'd hired only a year earlier, Steve Jobs left Apple. With Jobs gone, Apple's creative fires cooled. By the late 1980s, the company's fortunes dwindled as a new wave of PC machines, sporting Intel chips and Microsoft software, swept the market. By the mid- to late-1990s, Apple's sales had plunged to $5 billion, 50 percent off previous highs. And its once-commanding share of the personal-computer market had dropped to a tiny 2 percent. Even the most ardent Apple fans—the "macolytes"—wavered, and the company's days seemed numbered.

Yet by 2005, Apple had engineered a remarkable turnaround. With expected sales of $13 billion, Apple was coming off a year in which revenues rose 33 percent and profits quadrupled. Its stock price was at an all-time high. "To say Apple Computer is hot just doesn't do the company justice," said one analyst. "Apple is smoking, searing, blisteringly hot, not to mention hip, with a side order of funky. . . . Gadget geeks around the world have crowned Apple the keeper of all things cool."

What caused this breathtaking turnaround? Apple rediscovered the magic that had made the company so successful in the first place: customer-driven creativity and new-product innovation. The remarkable makeover began with the return of Steve Jobs in 1997. Since leaving Apple, Jobs had started a new computer company, NeXT. He'd then bought out Pixar Animation Studios, turning it into an entertainment-industry powerhouse. Jobs returned to Apple determined to breathe new creative life and customer focus into the company he'd co-founded 20 years earlier.

Jobs's first task was to revitalize Apple's computer business. For starters, in 1998, Apple launched the iMac personal computer, which featured a sleek, egg-shaped monitor and hard drive, all in one unit, in a futuristic translucent turquoise casing. With its one-button Internet access, this machine was designed specifically for cruising the Internet (hence the "i" in "iMac"). The dramatic iMac won raves for design and lured buyers in droves. Within a year, it had sold more than a million units.

Jobs next unleashed Mac OS X, a ground-breaking new Apple operating system that one observer called "the equivalent of a cross between a Porsche and an Abram's tank." OS X served as the launching pad for a new generation of Apple computers and software products. Consider iLife, a bundle of programs that comes with every new Mac. It includes applications such as iMovie (for video editing), iDVD (for recording movies, digital-photo slide shows, and music onto TV-playable DVDs), iPhoto (for managing and touching up digital pictures), GarageBand (for making and mixing your own music), and iWork (for making presentations and newsletters).

The iMac and Mac OS X put Apple back on the map in personal computing. But Jobs knew that Apple, still a nicher claiming less than a 5 percent market share, would never catch up in computers with dominant competitors like Dell and HP. Real growth and stardom would require even more creative thinking. And it just doesn't get much more creative than iPod and iTunes, innovations that would utterly change the way people acquire and listen to music.

A music buff himself, Jobs noticed that kids by the millions were using computers and CD writers to download digital songs from illegal online services like Napster, and then burning their own music CDs. He moved quickly to make CD burners standard equipment on all Macs. Then, to help users download music and manage their music databases, Apple's programmers created state-of-the-art jukebox software called iTunes.

Even before iTunes hit the streets, according to Apple watcher Brent Schendler, Jobs "recognized that although storing and playing music on your computer was pretty cool, wouldn't it be even cooler if there was a portable, Walkman-type player that could hold all your digital music so that you could listen to it anywhere?" Less than nine months later, Apple introduced the sleek and sexy iPod, a tiny computer with an amazing capacity to store digital music and an easy-to-use interface for managing and playing it. In another 18 months, the Apple iTunes Music Store opened on the Web, enabling consumers to legally download CDs and individual songs.

The results were stunning. The iPod now ranks as one of the greatest consumer electronics hits of all time. By January of 2005, Apple had sold 10 million iPods (compared with sales of about 3 million Sony Walkmans in a comparable period), and consumers are snapping up additional iPods at a rate of 40 per minute. Some 300 million songs have been downloaded from the iTunes Music Store, with an additional 9.6 million songs downloaded each week. "We had hoped to sell a million songs in the first six months, but we did that in the first six days," notes an Apple spokesman. Both iPod and the iTunes Music Store are capturing more than 65 percent shares of their respective markets.

Apple's success is attracting a horde of large, resourceful competitors. To stay ahead, the company must keep its eye on the consumer and continue to innovate. So, Apple isn't standing still. It recently introduced a line of new, easy-to-use wireless gadgets that link home and business computers, stereos, and other devices. Its .Mac (pronounced dot-Mac) online subscription service has signed up more than 600,000 members. Apple has even opened 100 or more chic and gleaming Apple Stores. And observers see a host of new products just over the horizon: a wireless iPod; a vPod (an iPod that plays video), iHome (a magical device that powers all your digital home entertainment devices), an iPhone (a combination iPod and cell phone), and iPod on Wheels (a digital hub that integrates your iPod with your car's entertainment system). Last year, in a Boston Consulting Group survey of senior executives worldwide, Apple headed the list of top 20 innovative companies in the world, gaining twice as many votes as number-two 3M.

Thus, almost overnight, it seems, Steve Jobs has transformed Apple from a failing niche computer maker to a major force in consumer electronics, digital music, and who knows what else in the future. And he's done it through innovation—by helping those around him to "Think Different" (Apple's motto) in their quest to bring value to customers. *Time* magazine sums it up this way:

> [Steve Jobs]'s recipe for success? He's a marketing and creative genius with a rare ability to get inside the imaginations of consumers and understand what will captivate them. He is obsessed with the Apple user's experience. . . . For every product his companies have released, it's clear that someone actually asked, How can we "think different" about this? . . . Whether it's the original Macintosh, the iMac, the iPod, the flat-panel monitor, even the Apple operating system, most of the company's products over the past three decades have had designs that are three steps ahead of the competition. . . . Jobs has a drive and vision that renews itself, again and again. It leaves you waiting for his next move.[1]

As the Apple story suggests, a company has to be good at developing and managing new products. Every product seems to go through a life cycle—it is born, goes through several phases, and eventually dies as newer products come along that better serve consumer needs. This product life cycle presents two major challenges: First, because all products eventually decline, a firm must be good at developing new products to replace aging ones (the challenge of *new-product development*). Second, the firm must be good at adapting its marketing strategies in the face of changing tastes, technologies, and competition as products pass through life-cycle stages (the challenge of *product life-cycle strategies*). We first look at the problem of finding and developing new products and then at the problem of managing them successfully over their life cycles.

New-Product Development Strategy

Given the rapid changes in consumer tastes, technology, and competition, companies must develop a steady stream of new products and services. A firm can obtain new products in two ways. One is through *acquisition*—by buying a whole company, a patent, or a license to produce someone else's product. The other is through **new-product development** in the company's own research-and-development department. By *new products* we mean original products, product improvements, product modifications, and new brands that the firm develops through its own research-and-development efforts. In this chapter, we concentrate on new-product development.

New-product development
The development of original products, product improvements, product modifications, and new brands through the firm's own R&D efforts.

Innovation can be very risky. RCA lost $580 million on its SelectaVision videodisc player; Texas Instruments lost a staggering $660 million before withdrawing from the home computer business; and WebTV lost $725 million before it was shut down. Even these amounts pale in comparison to the failure of the $5 billion Iridium global satellite-based wireless telephone system. Other costly product failures from sophisticated companies include New Coke (Coca-Cola Company), Eagle Snacks (Anheuser-Busch), Zap Mail electronic mail (FedEx), Polarvision instant movies (Polaroid), Premier "smokeless" cigarettes (R.J. Reynolds), and Arch Deluxe sandwiches (McDonald's).[2]

New products continue to face tough odds. Studies indicate that more than 90 percent of all new consumer products fail within two years. Last year alone, a staggering 34,000 new consumer food, beverage, and beauty products were launched. But less than 2 percent of those products were considered successful. New industrial products appear to fare better but still face failure rates as high as 30 percent.[3]

Why do so many new products fail? There are several reasons. Although an idea may be good, the company may overestimate market size. The actual product may be poorly designed. Or maybe it might be incorrectly positioned, priced too high, or poorly advertised. A high-level executive might push a favorite idea despite poor marketing research findings. Sometimes the costs of product development are higher than expected, and sometimes competitors fight back harder than expected. However, the reasons behind some new-product failures seem pretty obvious. Try the following on for size:[4]

Strolling the aisles at Robert McMath's New Product Showcase and Learning Center is like finding yourself in some nightmare version of a supermarket. There's Gerber food for adults (pureed sweet-and-sour pork and chicken Madeira), Hot Scoop microwaveable ice cream sundaes, Premier smokeless cigarettes, and Miller Clear Beer. How about Richard Simmons Dijon Vinaigrette Salad

■ Visiting the New Product Showcase and Learning Center is like finding yourself in some nightmare version of a supermarket. Each product failure represents squandered dollars and hopes.

Spray? Most of the 73,500 products on display were abject flops. Behind each of them are squandered dollars and hopes.

McMath, the genial curator of this Smithsonian of consumerism, gets lots of laughs when he asks his favorite question, "What were they thinking?" Some companies failed because they attached trusted brand names to something totally out of character. For example, when you hear the name Ben-Gay, you immediately think of the way Ben-Gay cream sears and stimulates your skin. Can you imagine swallowing Ben-Gay aspirin? Or how would you feel about quaffing a can of Exxon fruit punch or Kodak quencher? Other misbegotten attempts to stretch a good name include Cracker Jack cereal, Smucker's premium ketchup, and Fruit of the Loom laundry detergent. Looking back, what *were* they thinking? You can tell that some innovative products were doomed as soon as you hear their names: Toaster Eggs. Cucumber antiperspirant spray. Health-Sea sea sausage. Look of Buttermilk shampoo. Dr. Care Aerosol Toothpaste (many parents questioned the wisdom of arming their kids with something like this!) Really, what were they thinking?

So companies face a problem—they must develop new products, but the odds weigh heavily against success. In all, to create successful new products, a company must understand its consumers, markets, and competitors and develop products that deliver superior value to customers. It must carry out strong new-product planning and set up a systematic *new-product development process* for finding and growing new products. Figure 8.1 shows the eight major steps in this process.

IDEA GENERATION

Idea generation
The systematic search for new-product ideas.

New-product development starts with **idea generation**—the systematic search for new-product ideas. A company typically has to generate many ideas in order to find a few good ones. According to one management consultant, on average, companies "will run through 3,000 ideas before they hit a winner." For instance, one brainstorming session for Prudential Insurance Company came up with 1,500 ideas and only 12 were considered even usable.[5]

Major sources of new-product ideas include internal sources and external sources such as customers, competitors, distributors and suppliers, and others.

Internal Idea Sources   Using *internal sources,* the company can find new ideas through formal research and development. It can pick the brains of its executives, scientists, engineers, manufacturing staff, and salespeople. Some companies have developed successful "intrapreneurial" programs that encourage employees to think up and develop new-product ideas. For example, 3M's well-known "15 percent rule" allows employees to spend 15 percent of their time "bootlegging"—working on projects of personal interest, whether or not those projects

FIGURE 8.1

Major Stages in New-Product Development

directly benefit the company. Similarly, Texas Instruments's IDEA program provides funds for employees who pursue their own ideas. Among the successful new products to come out of the IDEA program was TI's Speak 'n' Spell, the first children's toy to contain a microchip. Many other speaking toys followed, ultimately generating several hundred million dollars for TI.

External Idea Sources   Good new-product ideas also come from watching and listening to *customers*. The company can analyze customer questions and complaints to find new products that better solve consumer problems. Company engineers or salespeople can meet with and work alongside customers to get suggestions and ideas. The company can conduct surveys, hold focus groups, observe customers in natural settings, or invite customers in to learn about their needs and wants.

LEGO did just that when it invited 250 LEGO train-set enthusiasts to visit its New York office to assess new designs. "We pooh-poohed them all," says one LEGO fan, an Intel engineer from Portland. But the group gave LEGO lots of new ideas, and the company put them to good use. "We literally produced what they told us to produce," says a LEGO executive. The result was the "Santa Fe Super Chief" set. Thanks to "word-of-mouse" endorsements from the 250 enthusiasts, LEGO sold out the first 10,000 units in less than two weeks with no additional marketing.[6]

Consumers often create new products and uses on their own, and companies can benefit by putting them on the market. For example, for years customers were spreading the word that Skin-So-Soft bath oil and moisturizer was also a terrific bug repellent. Whereas some consumers were content simply to bathe in water scented with the fragrant oil, others carried it in their backpacks to mosquito-infested campsites or kept a bottle on the deck of their beach houses. Avon turned the idea into a complete line of Skin-So-Soft Bug Guard products, including Bug Guard Mosquito Repellant Moisturizing Towelettes and Bug Guard Plus, a combination moisturizer, insect repellent, and sunscreen.[7]

■ Product ideas from customers: Advice from 250 train-set enthusiasts resulted in the LEGO Santa Fe Super Chief set, a blockbuster new product that sold out in less than two weeks.

Finally, some companies even give customers the tools and resources to design their own products. Notes one expert, "Not only is the customer king, now he is market-research head, R&D chief, and product-development manager, too."[8] For example, computer games maker Electronic Arts (EA) noticed that its customers were making new content for existing games and posting it online for others to use freely. It began shipping basic game-development tools with its games, and feeding customer innovations to its designers to use in creating new games. "The fan community has had a tremendous influence on game design," says an EA executive, "and the games are better as a result."[9]

Companies must be careful not to rely too heavily on customer input when developing new products. For some products, especially highly technical ones, customers may not know what they need. "Merely giving people what they want isn't always enough," says one innovation management consultant. "People want to be surprised; they want something that's better than they imagined, something that stretches them in what they like."[10]

Competitors are another good source of new-product ideas. Companies watch competitors' ads to get clues about their new products. They buy competing new products, take them apart to see how they work, analyze their sales, and decide whether they should bring out a new product of their own. *Distributors and suppliers* can also contribute many good new-product ideas. Resellers are close to the market and can pass along information about consumer problems and new-product possibilities. Suppliers can tell the company about new concepts, techniques, and materials that can be used to develop new products.

Many companies are now *outsourcing* some of their new-product innovation to outside developers. Companies like Dell, Motorola, and Philips sometimes buy complete designs for digital devices from Asian developers, and then market them under their own brand names.[11] Other idea sources include trade magazines, shows, and seminars; government agencies;

new-product consultants; advertising agencies; marketing research firms; university and commercial laboratories; and inventors.

The search for new-product ideas should be systematic rather than haphazard. Otherwise, few new ideas will surface, and many good ideas will sputter and die. To avoid these problems, a company can install an *idea management system* that directs the flow of new ideas to a central point, where they can be collected, reviewed, and evaluated. It can appoint a respected senior person to be the company's idea manager. It can set up a toll-free number or Web site and encourage all company stakeholders—employees, suppliers, distributors, dealers—to submit new ideas. It can assign a cross-functional idea-management committee to evaluate proposed new-product ideas and create recognition programs to reward those who contribute the best ideas.[12]

The idea-manager approach yields two favorable outcomes. First, it helps create an innovation-oriented company culture. It shows that top management supports, encourages, and rewards innovation. Second, it will yield a larger number of ideas, among which will be found some especially good ones. As the system matures, ideas will flow more freely. No longer will good ideas wither for the lack of a sounding board or a senior product advocate.

IDEA SCREENING

The purpose of idea generation is to create a large number of ideas. The purpose of the succeeding stages is to *reduce* that number. The first idea-reducing stage is **idea screening**, which helps spot good ideas and drop poor ones as soon as possible. Product development costs rise greatly in later stages, so the company wants to go ahead only with the product ideas that will turn into profitable products.

Many companies require their executives to write up new-product ideas on a standard form that can be reviewed by a new-product committee. The write-up describes the product, the target market, and the competition. It makes some rough estimates of market size, product price, development time and costs, manufacturing costs, and rate of return. The committee then evaluates the idea against a set of general criteria.

For example, at Kao Company, the large Japanese consumer-products company, the new-product committee asks questions such as these: Is the product truly useful to consumers and society? Is it good for our particular company? Does it mesh well with the company's objectives and strategies? Do we have the people, skills, and resources to make it succeed? Does it deliver more value to customers than do competing products? Is it easy to advertise and distribute? Many companies have well-designed systems for rating and screening new-product ideas.

CONCEPT DEVELOPMENT AND TESTING

An attractive idea must be developed into a **product concept**. It is important to distinguish between a product idea, a product concept, and a product image. A *product idea* is an idea for a possible product that the company can see itself offering to the market. A *product concept* is a detailed version of the idea stated in meaningful consumer terms. A *product image* is the way consumers perceive an actual or potential product.

Concept Development   After more than 10 years of development, DaimlerChrysler is getting ready to commercialize its experimental fuel-cell-powered electric car. This car's nonpolluting fuel-cell system runs directly on hydrogen, which powers the fuel cell with only water as a by-product. It is highly fuel efficient and gives the new car an environmental advantage over even today's superefficient gasoline-electric hybrid cars.

DaimlerChrysler is currently testing more than 100 "F-Cell" cars under varying weather conditions, traffic situations, and driving styles in different locations worldwide. Based on the tiny Mercedes A-Class, the car accelerates quickly, reaches speeds of 85 miles per hour, and has a 250-mile driving range, giving it a huge edge over battery-powered electric cars that travel only about 80 miles before needing 3 to 12 hours of recharging. Fuel cell systems are also being tested in busses, trucks, and other vehicles.[13]

Now DaimlerChrysler's task is to develop this new product into alternative product concepts, find out how attractive each concept is to customers, and choose the best one. It might create the following product concepts for the fuel-cell electric car:

Concept 1 A moderately priced subcompact designed as a second family car to be used around town. The car is ideal for running errands and visiting friends.

Concept 2 A medium-cost sporty compact appealing to young people.

Concept 3 An inexpensive subcompact "green" car appealing to environmentally conscious people who want practical, low-polluting transportation.

Concept 4 A high-end SUV appealing to those who love the space SUVs provide but lament the poor gas mileage.

■ DaimlerChrysler's task to develop its fuel-cell-powered F-Cell car into alternative product concepts, find out how attractive each concept is to customers, and choose the best one.

Concept Testing   **Concept testing** calls for testing new-product concepts with groups of target consumers. The concepts may be presented to consumers symbolically or physically. Here, in words, is concept 3:

> An efficient, peppy, fun-to-drive, fuel-cell-powered electric subcompact car that seats four. This hydrogen-powered high-tech wonder provides practical and reliable transportation with virtually no pollution. It goes up to 85 miles per hour and, unlike battery-powered electric cars, it never needs recharging. It's priced, fully equipped, at $25,000.

Concept testing
Testing new-product concepts with a group of target consumers to find out if the concepts have strong consumer appeal.

For some concept tests, a word or picture description might be sufficient. However, a more concrete and physical presentation of the concept will increase the reliability of the concept test. After being exposed to the concept, consumers then may be asked to react to it by answering questions such as those in Table 8.1.

The answers to such questions will help the company decide which concept has the strongest appeal. For example, the last question asks about the consumer's intention to buy. Suppose 10 percent of consumers say they "definitely" would buy, and another 5 percent say "probably." The company could project these figures to the full population in this target group to estimate sales volume. Even then, the estimate is uncertain because people do not always carry out their stated intentions.

Many firms routinely test new-product concepts with consumers before attempting to turn them into actual new products. For example, AcuPOLL, a global brand-building research company, tests thousands of new product concepts every year. In past polls, M&M Mini's, "teeny-tiny" M&Ms sold in a tube container, received a rare A+ concept rating, meaning that consumers thought it was an outstanding concept that they would try

TABLE 8.1

Questions for Fuel-Cell-Powered, Electric Car Concept Test

1. Do you understand the concept of a fuel-cell-powered electric car?

2. Do you believe the claims about the car's performance?

3. What are the major benefits of the fuel-cell-powered electric car compared with a conventional car?

4. What are its advantages compared with a battery-powered electric car?

5. What improvements in the car's features would you suggest?

6. For what uses would you prefer a fuel-cell-powered electric car to a conventional car?

7. What would be a reasonable price to charge for the car?

8. Who would be involved in your decision to buy such a car? Who would drive it?

9. Would you buy such a car (definitely, probably, probably not, definitely not)?

Food,
moisture,
and
lots of
places
to hide.
No wonder
a billion germs
call your sponge
home.

Don't spread germs. Kill them.

■ AcuPOLL tests thousands of new-product concepts every year. Its polls correctly predicted that CLOROX® Wipes would be a big hit with consumers.

Marketing strategy development
Designing an initial marketing strategy for a new product based on the product concept.

and buy. Other products such as Glad Stand & Zip Bags, Clorox Wipes, the Mead Inteli-Gear learning system, and Elmer's 3D Paint Pens were also big hits.

Other product concepts didn't fare so well. Consumers didn't think much of Excedrin Tension Headache Cooling Pads. Nor did they care for Nubrush Anti-Bacterial Toothbrush Spray disinfectant, from Applied Microdontics, which received an F. Most consumers don't think they have a problem with "infected" toothbrushes. Another concept that fared poorly was Chef Williams 5 Minute Marinade, which comes with a syringe customers use to inject the marinade into meats. Some consumers found the thought of injecting something into meat a bit repulsive, and "it's just so politically incorrect to have this syringe on there," comments an AcuPOLL executive.[14]

MARKETING STRATEGY DEVELOPMENT

Suppose DaimlerChrysler finds that concept 3 for the fuel-cell-powered electric car tests best. The next step is **marketing strategy** development, designing an initial marketing strategy for introducing this car to the market.

The *marketing strategy statement* consists of three parts. The first part describes the target market; the planned product positioning; and the sales, market share, and profit goals for the first few years. Thus:

> The target market is younger, well-educated, moderate-to-high-income individuals, couples, or small families seeking practical, environmentally responsible transportation. The car will be positioned as more fun to drive and less polluting than today's internal combustion engine or hybrid cars. It is also less restricting than battery-powered electric cars, which must be recharged regularly. The company will aim to sell 100,000 cars in the first year, at a loss of not more than $15 million. In the second year, the company will aim for sales of 120,000 cars and a profit of $25 million.

The second part of the marketing strategy statement outlines the product's planned price, distribution, and marketing budget for the first year:

> The fuel-cell-powered electric car will be offered in three colors—red, white, and blue—and will have optional air-conditioning and power-drive features. It will sell at a retail price of $25,000—with 15 percent off the list price to dealers. Dealers who sell more than 10 cars per month will get an additional discount of 5 percent on each car sold that month. An advertising budget of $50 million will be split 50-50 between a national media campaign and local advertising. Advertising will emphasize the car's fun spirit and low emissions. During the first year, $100,000 will be spent on marketing research to find out who is buying the car and their satisfaction levels.

The third part of the marketing strategy statement describes the planned long-run sales, profit goals, and marketing mix strategy:

> DaimlerChrysler intends to capture a 3 percent long-run share of the total auto market and realize an after-tax return on investment of 15 percent. To achieve this, product quality will start high and be improved over time. Price will be raised in the second and third years if competition permits. The total advertising budget will be raised each year by about 10 percent. Marketing research will be reduced to $60,000 per year after the first year.

BUSINESS ANALYSIS

Once management has decided on its product concept and marketing strategy, it can evaluate the business attractiveness of the proposal. **Business analysis** involves a review of the sales, costs, and profit projections for a new product to find out whether they satisfy the company's objectives. If they do, the product can move to the product development stage.

To estimate sales, the company might look at the sales history of similar products and conduct surveys of market opinion. It can then estimate minimum and maximum sales to assess the range of risk. After preparing the sales forecast, management can estimate the expected costs and profits for the product, including marketing, R&D, operations, accounting, and finance costs. The company then uses the sales and costs figures to analyze the new product's financial attractiveness.

PRODUCT DEVELOPMENT

So far, for many new-product concepts, the product may have existed only as a word description, a drawing, or perhaps a crude mock-up. If the product concept passes the business test, it moves into **product development**. Here, R&D or engineering develops the product concept into a physical product. The product development step, however, now calls for a large jump in investment. It will show whether the product idea can be turned into a workable product.

The R&D department will develop and test one or more physical versions of the product concept. R&D hopes to design a prototype that will satisfy and excite consumers and that can be produced quickly and at budgeted costs. Developing a successful prototype can take days, weeks, months, or even years.

Often, products undergo rigorous tests to make sure that they perform safely and effectively, or that consumers will find value in them. Here are some examples of such product tests:[15]

Thunk. Thunk. Thunk. Behind a locked door in the basement of Louis Vuitton's elegant Paris headquarters, a mechanical arm hoists a brown-and-tan handbag a half-meter off the floor—then drops it. The bag, loaded with an 8-pound weight, will be lifted and dropped, over and over again, for four days. This is Vuitton's test laboratory, a high-tech torture chamber for its fabled luxury goods. Another piece of lab equipment bombards handbags with ultraviolet rays to test resistance to fading. Still another tests zippers by tugging them open and shutting them 5,000 times. There's even a mechanized mannequin hand, with a Vuitton charm bracelet around its wrist, being shaken vigorously to make sure none of the charms falls off.

At Gillette, almost everyone gets involved in new-product testing. Every working day at Gillette, 200 volunteers from various departments come to work unshaven, troop to the second floor of the company's gritty South Boston plant, and enter small booths with a sink and mirror. There they take instructions from technicians on the other side of a small window as to which razor, shaving cream, or aftershave to use. The volunteers evaluate razors for sharpness of blade, smoothness of glide, and ease of handling. In a nearby shower room, women perform the same ritual on their legs, underarms, and what the company delicately refers to as the "bikini area." "We bleed so you'll get a good shave at home," says one Gillette employee.

■ Product testing: Gillette uses employee-volunteers to test new shaving products—"We bleed so you'll get a good shave at home," says a Gillette employee.

The admissions brochure for Lenoir-Rhyne College in Hickory, North Carolina, extols the school's learned faculty and small class sizes. There is no mention, however, of perhaps one of the coolest aspects of attending the college: the chance to help advance hosiery technology—and to score some free socks in the process. Lenoir-Rhyne's 1,492 students enjoy this unusual perk because of the school's proximity to Newton, NC, the heart of the hosiery industry's answer to Silicon Valley. Companies like Moretz Sports consider the college's fields and courts a vital step in the series tests they put their socks through. For instance, when Moretz develops a new line of socks, it sends prototypes to students, who are instructed to wear them out. After answering a series of questions about comfort and durability, students send the socks back for analysis.

A new-product must have the required functional features and also convey the intended psychological characteristics. The fuel-cell electric car, for example, should strike consumers as being well built, comfortable, and safe. Management must learn what makes consumers decide that a car is well built. To some consumers, this means that the car has "solid-sounding" doors. To others, it means that the car is able to withstand heavy impact in crash tests. Consumer tests are conducted in which consumers test-drive the car and rate its attributes.

TEST MARKETING

Test marketing
The stage of new-product development in which the product and marketing program are tested in more realistic market settings.

If the product passes functional and consumer tests, the next step is **test marketing**, the stage at which the product and marketing program are introduced into more realistic market settings. Test marketing gives the marketer experience with marketing the product before going to the great expense of full introduction. It lets the company test the product and its entire marketing program—positioning strategy, advertising, distribution, pricing, branding and packaging, and budget levels.

The amount of test marketing needed varies with each new product. Test marketing costs can be high, and it takes time that may allow competitors to gain advantages. When the costs of developing and introducing the product are low, or when management is already confident about the new product, the company may do little or no test marketing. In fact, test marketing by consumer-goods firms has been declining in recent years. Companies often do not test-market simple line extensions or copies of successful competitor products.

However, when introducing a new product requires a big investment, or when management is not sure of the product or marketing program, a company may do a lot of test marketing. For instance, Frito-Lay did 18 months of testing in three markets on at least five formulations before introducing its Baked Lays line of low-fat snacks. Pepsi quietly tested Manzanita Sol and Mirinda fruit-flavored soft drinks, its number-two and number-three brands in Mexico, in Dallas, and in a few other cities before rolling out the two beverages in the U.S. market. And Nokia test-marketed its new N-Gage cell phone/ mobile game player extensively in London before introducing it worldwide.[16]

Although test-marketing costs can be high, they are often small when compared with the costs of making a major mistake. For example, Nabisco's launch of one new product without testing had disastrous—and soggy—results: [17]

■ Test marketing: Pepsi quietly tested Manzanita Sol and Mirinda fruit-flavored soft drinks, its number-two and number-three brands in Mexico, in Dallas and a few other cities before rolling out the two beverages in the U.S. market.

Nabisco hit a marketing home run with its Teddy Grahams, teddy-bear-shaped graham crackers in several different flavors. So, the company decided to extend Teddy Grahams into a new area. It introduced chocolate, cinnamon, and honey versions of Breakfast Bears Graham Cereal. When the product came out, however, consumers didn't like the taste enough, so the product developers went back to the kitchen and modified the formula. But they didn't test it. The result was a disaster. Although the cereal may have tasted better, it no longer stayed crunchy in milk, as the advertising on the box promised. Instead, it left a gooey mess of graham mush on the bottom of cereal bowls. Supermarket managers soon refused to restock the cereal, and Nabisco executives decided it was too late to reformulate the product again. So a promising new product was killed through haste to get it to market.

Still, test marketing doesn't guarantee success. For example, Procter & Gamble tested its Fit produce rinse heavily for five years and Olay cosmetics for three years. Although market tests suggested the products would be successful, P&G had to pull the plug on both shortly after their introductions.[18]

COMMERCIALIZATION

Test marketing gives management the information needed to make a final decision about whether to launch the new product. If the company goes ahead with **commercialization**—introducing the new product into the market—it will face high costs. The company may have to build or rent a manufacturing facility. And it may have to spend, in the case of a new consumer-packaged good, between $10 million and $200 million for advertising, sales promotion, and other marketing efforts in the first year.

The company launching a new product must first decide on introduction *timing*. If DaimlerChrysler's new fuel-cell electric car will eat into the sales of the company's other cars, its introduction may be delayed. If the car can be improved further, or if the economy is down, the company may wait until the following year to launch it. However, if competitors are ready to introduce their own fuel-cell models, DaimlerChrysler may push to introduce the car sooner.

Next, the company must decide *where* to launch the new product—in a single location, a region, the national market, or the international market. Few companies have the confidence, capital, and capacity to launch new products into full national or international distribution. They will develop a planned *market rollout* over time. In particular, small companies may enter attractive cities or regions one at a time. Larger companies, however, may quickly introduce new models into several regions or into the full national market.

Companies with international distribution systems may introduce new products through global rollouts. Procter & Gamble did this with its SpinBrush low-priced, battery-powered toothbrush. In a swift and successful global assault—its fastest global rollout ever—P&G quickly introduced the new product into 35 countries. Such rapid worldwide expansion overwhelmed rival Colgate's Actibrush brand. Within a year of its introduction, SpinBrush was outselling Actibrush by a margin of two to one.[19]

ORGANIZING FOR NEW-PRODUCT DEVELOPMENT

Many companies organize their new-product development process into the orderly sequence of steps shown in Figure 8.1, starting with idea generation and ending with commercialization. Under this **sequential product development** approach, one company department works individually to complete its stage of the process before passing the new product along to the next department and stage. This orderly, step-by-step process can help bring control to complex and risky projects. But it also can be dangerously slow. In fast-changing, highly competitive markets, such slow-but-sure product development can result in product failures, lost sales and profits, and crumbling market positions.

In order to get their new products to market quicker, many companies are adopting a faster, team-oriented approach called **simultaneous product development** (or team-based or collaborative product development). Under this approach, company departments work closely together through cross-functional teams, overlapping the steps in the product

Commercialization
Introducing a new product into the market.

Sequential product development
A new-product development approach in which one company department works to complete its stage of the process before passing the new product along to the next department and stage.

Simultaneous (or team-based) product development
An approach to developing new products in which various company departments work closely together, overlapping the steps in the product-development process to save time and increase effectiveness.

development process to save time and increase effectiveness. Instead of passing the new product from department to department, the company assembles a team of people from various departments that stays with the new product from start to finish. Such teams usually include people from the marketing, finance, design, manufacturing, and legal departments, and even supplier and customer companies.

Top management gives the product-development team general strategic direction but no clear-cut product idea or work plan. It challenges the team with stiff and seemingly contradictory goals—"turn out carefully planned and superior new products, but do it quickly"—and then gives the team whatever freedom and resources it needs to meet the challenge. In the sequential process, a bottleneck at one phase can seriously slow the entire project. In the simultaneous approach, if one functional area hits snags, it works to resolve them while the team moves on.

The Allen-Bradley division of Rockwell Automation, a maker of industrial controls, realized tremendous benefits by using simultaneous development. Under its old sequential approach, the company's marketing department handed off a new-product idea to designers, who worked in isolation to prepare concepts that they then passed along to product engineers. The engineers, also working by themselves, developed expensive prototypes and handed them off to manufacturing, which tried to find a way to build the new product. Finally, after many years and dozens of costly design compromises and delays, marketing was asked to sell the new product, which it often found to be too high priced or sadly out of date. Now, all of Allen-Bradley's departments work together to develop new products. The results have been astonishing. For example, the company recently developed a new electrical control in just two years; under the old system, it would have taken six years.

The simultaneous team-based approach does have some limitations. Superfast product development can be riskier and more costly than the slower, more orderly sequential approach. Moreover, it often creates increased organizational tension and confusion. And the company must take care that rushing a product to market doesn't adversely affect its quality—the objective is not only to create products faster, but to create them *better* and faster.

Despite these drawbacks, in rapidly changing industries facing increasingly shorter product life cycles, the rewards of fast and flexible product development far exceed the risks. Companies that get new and improved products to the market faster than competitors often gain a big competitive edge. They can respond more quickly to emerging consumer tastes and charge higher prices for more advanced designs. As one auto industry executive states, "What we want to do is get the new car approved, built, and in the consumer's hands in the shortest time possible. . . . Whoever gets there first gets all the marbles." [20]

Thus, new-product success requires more than simply thinking up a few good ideas, turning them into products, and finding customers for them. It requires a systematic approach for finding new ways to create valued customer experiences, from generating and screening new-product ideas to creating and rolling out want-satisfying products to customers.

More than this, successful new-product development requires a total-company commitment. At companies known for their new-product prowess—such as 3M, Intel, and Nokia—the entire culture encourages, supports, and rewards innovation (see Marketing at Work 8.1). Consider 3M, a company long known for innovation:

You see the headline in every 3M ad: "Innovation Working for You." But at 3M, innovation isn't just an advertising pitch. Throughout its

1 The world wants thinner electronics.

2 We're getting it all on tape.

3M has pioneered a whole new technology: Microflex Circuits – the world's leading mass-produced electronic circuits on tape. They're thinner, smaller, highly reliable, and allow for more connections than rigid circuit boards. They'll go anywhere a designer can dream up: phones, pagers, laptops and printers. We expand the possibilities because we make the leap *from need to...*

3M *Innovation*

For more information, call 1-800-3M-HELPS, or Internet: http://www.mmm.com

■ Innovation: At 3M, new products don't just happen. The company's entire culture encourages, supports, and rewards innovation.

MARKETING AT WORK | 8.1

"Renewal" at Nokia: A Culture of Continuous Innovation

As workers quietly eat lunch in the cafeteria at Nokia House, a slide projector flips from pictures of summer cottages in Rauhalahti to snapshots of someone's favorite Finnish hound. Taken with camera phones by some of the 1,500 employees who work at Nokia's headquarters in Finland, the pictures are part of an internal corporate competition that rewards staff creativity.

These photographs won't ever grace the cover of *National Geographic*. But they do illustrate Nokia's sharpest insight: Creativity and innovative new products don't begin and end on an R&D lab bench. A long list of Nokia's innovative firsts came from the most unlikely of places. For example, the first user-changeable handset cover? Nokia engineer Aulis Perttula invented it after watching some of his colleagues customize their phones with car paint. Predictive text? Stephen Williams, a junior Nokia applications designer, suggested it after seeing disabled people make good use of it on their PCs.

Such firsts are why the 137-year-old Scandinavian giant, with annual sales of nearly $40 billion across 130 countries, has been way out in front for most of the mobile-phone industry's short history. Nokia sells five phones every second. Its global market share, 33 percent, is more than twice that of its largest rival Motorola. But Nokia isn't just the world's *biggest* mobile-phone company. It's also the most *innovative*. In an industry that's all about exciting new products, Nokia has created a culture where innovation is built into the way the company operates. Nokia even has a watchword for its culture of continuous innovation—*renewal*.

When it comes to new products, Nokia has its foot on the accelerator. It has almost tripled the launch of new products in the last four years. Why? Because peddling the same old goods to the same old customers simply doesn't work in this fast-changing, fiercely competitive business. Nokia has to keep churning out a steady stream of good new products. That means that the company's real business isn't phones, it's innovation.

At Nokia, innovation isn't an accident—it goes to the company's very core. Nokia is a company that refuses to grow big, grow old, or grow slow. Its new-product development philosophy is simple: Small, nimble, creative units are much more likely to bubble up new ideas.

So Nokia has organized itself into autonomous units, which are then backed with cost-effective central services. "Big companies lose sensitivity," says a senior Nokia executive. "People need to feel that they can make a difference. And they need to have the power to make their ideas happen. [By allowing teams the space they need to dig deeper into their area of interest] we've created a small-company soul inside a big-company body."

The end goal is innovation, and Nokia creates new products at a head-spinning pace. In part, that's a result of the extraordinary intellectual and technical resources that Nokia invests in new-product development. The company boasts an annual R&D budget of $3 billion, and 40 percent of its 52,000 employees are involved in R&D. Most Nokia business units have at least three R&D sites.

But just as important is the emphasis that Nokia puts on continuous development. "It's a combination of putting people in the right environment to generate ideas and giving them the power to make those ideas happen," says the executive. Nokia makes a healthy habit of giving its people fresh challenges in completely new areas. Job rotation is routine, even for senior managers. Lawyers have become country managers. Network engineers have moved into handset design. The goal is to bring new thinking to familiar problems.

Beyond its prolific internal new-product development activity, Nokia mines outside sources as well. For example, to find fresh outside thinking, Nokia has set up Insight & Foresight teams that seek out new technologies, new business models, and promising entrepreneurs beyond Nokia's walls. Innovent, its U.S. team, goes a step further. It identifies early-stage entrepreneurs, buys options on their work, and introduces them to people at Nokia headquarters.

To stay atop the heap in the mobile communications industry, Nokia will need a con-

■ *In an industry that's all about exciting new products, Nokia has created a culture in which continuous innovation is built into the very way the company operates. Nokia calls it renewal.*

stant flow on innovative new products that serve the needs, preferences, and lifestyles of its customers. Even seemingly small blips in the flow of innovations can hurt, as when Nokia's failure to cash in on popular "clam shell" phone designs last year cost the company market share. But the Finnish company has been practicing renewal for a lifetime: In its history, it has gone from manufacturing paper to making rubber boots, then raincoats, then hunting rifles, and then consumer electronics, until finally betting the farm on mobile phones. It's all part of an ongoing emphasis on renewal.

Sources: Portions adapted from Ian Wylie, "Calling for a Renewable Future," *Fast Company,* May 2003, pp. 46–48. Also see Brad Smith, "Nokia: From Banks of Remote River Comes Innovation," *Wireless Week,* March 22, 2004, p. 26; Andy Reinhardt, "Can Nokia Get the Wow Back?" *BusinessWeek,* May 31, 2004, pp. 48–50; Mike Hughlett, "Motorola Is Back in Second Place," *Knight Ridder Tribune Business News,* February 3, 2005, p. 1; Norman P. Aquino, "Nokia Eyes Dominant Presence in Smart Phone Market," *Business World,* May 3, 2005, p. 1; and information from www.nokiausa.com, August 2005.

history, 3M has been one of America's most innovative companies. The company markets more than 50,000 products, ranging from sandpaper, adhesives, and hundreds of sticky tapes to contact lenses, heart-lung machines, and futuristic synthetic ligaments. Each year 3M invests $1.1 billion in research and launches more than 200 new products. But these new products don't just happen. 3M works hard to create an entrepreneurial culture that fosters innovation. For more than a century, 3M's culture has encouraged employees to take risks and try new ideas. 3M knows that it must try thousands of new-product ideas to hit one big jackpot. Trying out lots of new ideas often means making mistakes, but 3M accepts blunders and dead ends as a normal part of creativity and innovation.

In fact, "blunders" have turned into some of 3M's most successful products. Old-timers at 3M love to tell the story about 3M scientist Spencer Silver. Silver started out to develop a superstrong adhesive; instead he came up with one that didn't stick very well at all. He sent the apparently useless substance on to other 3M researchers to see whether they could find something to do with it. Nothing happened for several years. Then Arthur Fry, another 3M scientist, had a problem—and an idea. As a choir member in a local church, Mr. Fry was having trouble marking places in his hymnal—the little scraps of paper he used kept falling out. He tried dabbing some of Mr. Silver's weak glue on one of the scraps. It stuck nicely and later peeled off without damaging the hymnal. Thus were born 3M's Post-It Notes, a product that is now one of the top selling office supply products in the world.[21]

 Linking the Concepts

Take a break. Think about new products and how companies find and develop them.

- Suppose that you're on a panel to nominate the "best new products of the year." What products would you nominate and why? See what you can learn about the new-product development process for one of these products.
- Applying the new-product development process you've just studied, develop an idea for an innovative new snack-food product and sketch out a brief plan for bringing it to market. Loosen up and have some fun with this.

Product Life-Cycle Strategies

After launching the new product, management wants the product to enjoy a long and happy life. Although it does not expect the product to sell forever, the company wants to earn a decent profit to cover all the effort and risk that went into launching it. Management is aware that each product will have a life cycle, although its exact shape and length is not known in advance.

Product life cycle (PLC)
The course of a product's sales and profits over its lifetime. It involves five distinct stages: product development, introduction, growth, maturity, and decline.

Figure 8.2 shows a typical **product life cycle (PLC)**, the course that a product's sales and profits take over its lifetime. The product life cycle has five distinct stages:

1. *Product development* begins when the company finds and develops a new-product idea. During product development, sales are zero and the company's investment costs mount.
2. *Introduction* is a period of slow sales growth as the product is introduced in the market. Profits are nonexistent in this stage because of the heavy expenses of product introduction.
3. *Growth* is a period of rapid market acceptance and increasing profits.
4. *Maturity* is a period of slowdown in sales growth because the product has achieved acceptance by most potential buyers. Profits level off or decline because of increased marketing outlays to defend the product against competition.
5. *Decline* is the period when sales fall off and profits drop.

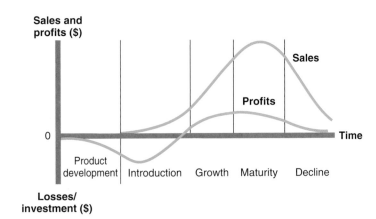

FIGURE 8.2
Sales and Profits over the Product's Life from Inception to Decline

Not all products follow this product life cycle. Some products are introduced and die quickly; others stay in the mature stage for a long, long time. Some enter the decline stage and are then cycled back into the growth stage through strong promotion or repositioning. As one analyst notes, "well-managed, a brand could live forever. American Express, Budweiser, Coca-Cola, Gillette, Western Union, Wells-Fargo, and TABASCO, for instance, are still going strong in their respective categories after 100+ years. Even if a brand dies, it can rise again, though perhaps in more limited distribution. Take Pabst Blue Ribbon and Pan Am Airlines [now Pan Am Clipper Connection]."[22]

The PLC concept can describe a *product class* (gasoline-powered automobiles), a *product form* (SUVs), or a *brand* (the Ford Explorer). The PLC concept applies differently in each case. Product classes have the longest life cycles—the sales of many product classes stay in the mature stage for a long time. Product forms, in contrast, tend to have the standard PLC shape. Product forms such as "dial telephones" and "cassette tapes" passed through a regular history of introduction, rapid growth, maturity, and decline.

A specific brand's life cycle can change quickly because of changing competitive attacks and responses. For example, although laundry soaps (product class) and powdered detergents (product form) have enjoyed fairly long life cycles, the life cycles of specific brands have tended to be much shorter. Today's leading brands of powdered laundry soap are Tide and Cheer; the leading brands 75 years ago were Fels Naptha, Octagon, and Kirkman.[23]

The PLC concept also can be applied to what are known as styles, fashions, and fads. Their special life cycles are shown in Figure 8.3. A **style** is a basic and distinctive mode of expression. For example, styles appear in homes (colonial, ranch, transitional), clothing (formal, casual), and art (realist, surrealist, abstract). Once a style is invented, it may last for generations, passing in and out of vogue. A style has a cycle showing several periods of renewed interest. A **fashion** is a currently accepted or popular style in a given field. For example, the more formal "business attire" look of corporate dress of the 1980s and early 1990s gave way to the "business casual" look of today. Fashions tend to grow slowly, remain popular for a while, and then decline slowly.

Fads are temporary periods of unusually high sales driven by consumer enthusiasm and immediate product or brand popularity.[24] A fad may be part of an otherwise normal lifecycle, as in the case of recent surges in the sales of scooters and yo-yos. Or the fad may comprise a brand's or product's entire lifecycle. "Pet rocks" are a classic example. Upon hearing his friends complain about how expensive it was to care for their dogs, advertising

■ Product life cycle: Some products die quickly: others stay in the mature stage for a long, long time. TABASCO Sauce is "over 130 years old and yet still able to totally whup your butt!"

Style
A basic and distinctive mode of expression.

Fashion
A currently accepted or popular style in a given field.

Fads
A fashion that enters quickly, is adopted with great zeal, peaks early, and declines very quickly.

FIGURE 8.3
Styles, Fashions, and Fads

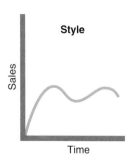

Style

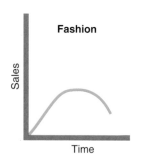

Fashion

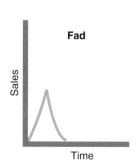

Fad

■ Fads: Pet rocks, introduced one October, had sunk like a stone by the next February.

copywriter Gary Dahl joked about his pet rock. He soon wrote a spoof of a dog-training manual for it, titled "The Care and Training of Your Pet Rock." Soon Dahl was selling some 1.5 million ordinary beach pebbles at $4 a pop. Yet the fad, which broke one October, had sunk like a stone by the next February. Dahl's advice to those who want to succeed with a fad: "Enjoy it while it lasts." Other examples of such fads include the Rubik's Cube, lava lamps, and dating and diet fads.[25]

The PLC concept can be applied by marketers as a useful framework for describing how products and markets work. And when used carefully, the PLC concept can help in developing good marketing strategies for different stages of the product life cycle. But using the PLC concept for forecasting product performance or for developing marketing strategies presents some practical problems. For example, managers may have trouble identifying which stage of the PLC the product is in or pinpointing when the product moves into the next stage. They may also find it hard to determine the factors that affect the product's movement through the stages. In practice, it is difficult to forecast the sales level at each PLC stage, the length of each stage, and the shape of the PLC curve. Using the PLC concept to develop marketing strategy also can be difficult because strategy is both a cause and a result of the product's life cycle. The product's current PLC position suggests the best marketing strategies, and the resulting marketing strategies affect product performance in later life-cycle stages.

Moreover, marketers should not blindly push products through the traditional stages of the product life cycle. "As marketers instinctively embrace the old life-cycle paradigm, they needlessly consign their products to following the curve into maturity and decline," notes one marketing professor. Instead, marketers often defy the "rules" of the life cycle and position their products in unexpected ways. By doing this, "companies can rescue products foundering in the maturity phase of their life cycles and return them to the growth phase. And they can catapult new products forward into the growth phase, leapfrogging obstacles that could slow consumers' acceptance."[26]

We looked at the product-development stage of the product life cycle in the first part of the chapter. We now look at strategies for each of the other life-cycle stages.

INTRODUCTION STAGE

Introduction stage
The product life-cycle stage in which the new product is first distributed and made available for purchase.

The **introduction stage** starts when the new product is first launched. Introduction takes time, and sales growth is apt to be slow. Well-known products such as instant coffee and frozen foods lingered for many years before they entered a stage of rapid growth.

In this stage, as compared to other stages, profits are negative or low because of the low sales and high distribution and promotion expenses. Much money is needed to attract distributors and build their inventories. Promotion spending is relatively high to inform consumers of the new product and get them to try it. Because the market is not generally ready for product refinements at this stage, the company and its few competitors produce basic versions of the product. These firms focus their selling on those buyers who are the most ready to buy.

A company, especially the *market pioneer,* must choose a launch strategy that is consistent with the intended product positioning. It should realize that the initial strategy is just the first step in a grander marketing plan for the product's entire life cycle. If the pioneer chooses its launch strategy to make a "killing," it may be sacrificing long-run revenue for the sake of short-run gain. As the pioneer moves through later stages of the life cycle, it will have to continuously formulate new pricing, promotion, and other marketing strategies. It has the best chance of building and retaining market leadership if it plays its cards correctly from the start.

GROWTH STAGE

If the new product satisfies the market, it will enter a **growth stage**, in which sales will start climbing quickly. The early adopters will continue to buy, and later buyers will start following their lead, especially if they hear favorable word of mouth. Attracted by the opportunities for profit, new competitors will enter the market. They will introduce new product features, and the market will expand. The increase in competitors leads to an increase in the number of distribution outlets, and sales jump just to build reseller inventories. Prices remain where they are or fall only slightly. Companies keep their promotion spending at the same or a slightly higher level. Educating the market remains a goal, but now the company must also meet the competition.

Profits increase during the growth stage, as promotion costs are spread over a large volume and as unit manufacturing costs fall. The firm uses several strategies to sustain rapid market growth as long as possible. It improves product quality and adds new product features and models. It enters new market segments and new distribution channels. It shifts some advertising from building product awareness to building product conviction and purchase, and it lowers prices at the right time to attract more buyers.

In the growth stage, the firm faces a trade-off between high market share and high current profit. By spending a lot of money on product improvement, promotion, and distribution, the company can capture a dominant position. In doing so, however, it gives up maximum current profit, which it hopes to make up in the next stage.

MATURITY STAGE

At some point, a product's sales growth will slow down, and the product will enter a **maturity stage**. This maturity stage normally lasts longer than the previous stages, and it poses strong challenges to marketing management. Most products are in the maturity stage of the life cycle. Therefore, most of marketing management deals with the mature product.

The slowdown in sales growth results in many producers with many products to sell. In turn, this overcapacity leads to greater competition. Competitors begin marking down prices, increasing their advertising and sales promotions, and upping their R&D budgets to find better versions of the product. These steps lead to a drop in profit. Some of the weaker competitors start dropping out, and the industry eventually contains only well-established competitors.

Although many products in the mature stage appear to remain unchanged for long periods, most successful ones are actually evolving to meet changing consumer needs. Product managers should do more than simply ride along with or defend their mature products—a good offense is the best defense. They should consider modifying the market, product, and marketing mix.

Growth stage
The product life-cycle stage in which a product's sales start climbing quickly.

Maturity stage
The stage in the product life cycle in which sales growth slows or levels off.

In *modifying the market*, the company tries to increase the consumption of the current product. It may look for new users and new market segments, as when John Deere targeted the retiring baby-boomer market with the Gator, a vehicle traditionally used on a farm. For this new market, Deere has repositioned the Gator, promising that it can "take you from a do-it-yourselfer to a do-it-a-lot-easier."

The manager may also look for ways to increase usage among present customers. Amazon.com does this by sending permission-based e-mails to regular customers, letting them know when their favorite authors or performers publish new books or CDs. The WD-40 Company has shown a real knack for expanding the market by finding new uses for its popular substance.

In 2000, the company launched a search to uncover 2,000 unique uses for WD-40. After receiving 300,000 individual submissions, it narrowed the list to the best 2,000 and posted it on the company's Web site. Some consumers suggest simple and practical uses. One teacher uses WD-40 to clean old chalkboards in her classroom. "Amazingly, the boards started coming to life again," she reports. "Not only were they restored, but years of masking and Scotch tape residue came off as well." Others, however, report some pretty unusual applications. One man uses WD-40 to polish his glass eye; another uses it to remove a prosthetic leg. And did you hear about the nude burglary suspect who had wedged himself in a vent at a cafe in Denver? The fire department extracted him with a large dose of WD-40. Or how about the Mississippi naval officer who used WD-40 to repel an angry bear? Then there's the college student who wrote to say that a friend's nightly amorous activities in the next room were causing everyone in his dorm to lose sleep—he solved the problem by treating the squeaky bedsprings with WD-40.[27]

Nip dirt and rust in the bud. For clean, smooth operation and perennial protection from the elements, spray your hand tools with WD-40® before and after each use.

wd40.com

■ The WD-40 Company's knack for finding new uses has made this popular substance one of the truly essential survival items in most American homes.

The company might also try *modifying the product*—changing characteristics such as quality, features, or style to attract new users and to inspire more usage. It might improve the product's quality and performance—its durability, reliability, speed, taste. It can improve the product's styling and attractiveness. Thus, car manufacturers restyle their cars to attract buyers who want a new look. The makers of consumer food and household products introduce new flavors, colors, ingredients, or packages to revitalize consumer buying. Or the company might add new features that expand the product's usefulness, safety, or convenience. For example, Sony keeps adding new styles and features to its Walkman and Discman lines, and Volvo adds new safety features to its cars.

Finally, the company can try *modifying the marketing mix*—improving sales by changing one or more marketing mix elements. It can cut prices to attract new users and competitors' customers. It can launch a better advertising campaign or use aggressive sales promotions—trade deals, cents-off, premiums, and contests. In addition to pricing and promotion, the company can also move into larger market channels, using mass merchandisers, if these channels are growing. Finally, the company can offer new or improved services to buyers.

Linking the Concepts

Pause for a moment and think about some products that have been around for a long time.

■ Ask a grandparent or someone else who shaved back then to compare a 1940s or 1950s Gillette razor to the most current model. Is Gillette's latest razor really a new product or just a "retread" of the previous version? What do you conclude about product life cycles?
■ Crayola Crayons have been a household staple for more than 100 years. But the brand remains vital. Sixty-five percent of all American children aged two to seven pick up a crayon at least once a day and color for an average of 28 minutes. Nearly 80 percent of the time, they pick up a Crayola crayon. How has the Binney & Smith division of Hallmark protected the Crayola brand from old age and decline (check out www.crayola.com and www.binney-smith.com)?

DECLINE STAGE

The sales of most product forms and brands eventually dip. The decline may be slow, as in the case of oatmeal cereal, or rapid, as in the cases of cassette and VHS tapes. Sales may plunge to zero, or they may drop to a low level where they continue for many years. This is the **decline stage**.

Sales decline for many reasons, including technological advances, shifts in consumer tastes, and increased competition. As sales and profits decline, some firms withdraw from the market. Those remaining may prune their product offerings. They may drop smaller market segments and marginal trade channels, or they may cut the promotion budget and reduce their prices further.

Carrying a weak product can be very costly to a firm, and not just in profit terms. There are many hidden costs. A weak product may take up too much of management's time. It often requires frequent price and inventory adjustments. It requires advertising and sales-force attention that might be better used to make "healthy" products more profitable. A product's failing reputation can cause customer concerns about the company and its other products. The biggest cost may well lie in the future. Keeping weak products delays the search for replacements, creates a lopsided product mix, hurts current profits, and weakens the company's foothold on the future.

For these reasons, companies need to pay more attention to their aging products. The firm's first task is to identify those products in the decline stage by regularly reviewing sales, market shares, costs, and profit trends. Then, management must decide whether to maintain, harvest, or drop each of these declining products.

Management may decide to *maintain* its brand without change in the hope that competitors will leave the industry. For example, Procter & Gamble made good profits by remaining in the declining liquid soap business as others withdrew. Or management may decide to reposition or reinvigorate the brand in hopes of moving it back into the growth stage of the product life cycle. Procter & Gamble has done this with several brands, including Mr. Clean and Old Spice (see Marketing at Work 8.2).

Management may decide to *harvest* the product, which means reducing various costs (plant and equipment, maintenance, R&D, advertising, sales force) and hoping that sales hold up. If successful, harvesting will increase the company's profits in the short run. Or management may decide to *drop* the product from the line. It can sell it to another firm or simply liquidate it at salvage value. In recent years, Procter & Gamble has sold off a number of lesser or declining brands such as Crisco and Jif peanut butter. If the company plans to find a buyer, it will not want to run down the product through harvesting.

Table 8.2 summarizes the key characteristics of each stage of the product life cycle. The table also lists the marketing objectives and strategies for each stage.[28]

Decline stage
The product life-cycle stage in which a product's sales decline.

MARKETING AT WORK 8.2

Procter & Gamble: Working at Both Ends of the Product Life Cycle

Not so long ago, P&G was a slumbering giant. Mired in mature markets with megabrands like Tide, Crest, Pampers, and Pantene, growth had slowed and earnings languished. But no longer. Now, thanks to a potent mixture of renewed creativity and marketing muscle, P&G is once again on the move. In the past five years, P&G's stock price has doubled and its earnings have increased an average of 17 percent a year.

The key to this success has been a renewed knack for innovation and a string of successful new products. "From its Swiffer mop to battery-powered Crest SpinBrush toothbrushes and Whitestrip tooth whiteners," says one observer, "P&G has simply done a better job than rivals of coming up with new products that consumers crave."

But it's not just *new* products—P&G has been working at both ends of the product life cycle. Along with creating innovative new products, P&G has become adept at turning yesterday's faded favorites into today's hot new products. Here are two examples.

Mr. Clean

Mr. Clean's share of the all-purpose, household-cleaner market had plunged more than 45 percent in just 10 years. But rather than abandon the 46-year-old iconic brand, P&G chose to modify and extend it. First, it reformulated the core

Mr. Clean all-purpose liquid cleaner, adding antibacterial properties and several new scents. Then came some real creativity, P&G extended the brand to include several revolutionary new products.

The first was Mr. Clean Magic Eraser, a soft, disposable self-cleaning pad that acts like an eraser to lift away tough dirt, including difficult scuff and crayon marks. The Magic Eraser was soon followed by products such as the Mr. Clean AutoDry Carwash system, which gives your car a spot-free clean and shine with no need to hand dry, and the Mr. Clean MagicReach bathroom cleaner, which helps ease the tough job of cleaning those hard to reach bathroom spots.

As for the marketing muscle, P&G backed the new-product launches with millions of dollars in marketing support. It spent $75 million on marketing the first version of the AutoDry Carwash alone. Now, after a decade of playing the 98-pound weakling, Mr. Clean is muscling its way back to a market-leading position.

Old Spice

When P&G acquired Old Spice in 1990, the brand was largely a has-been. It consisted mainly of a highly fragrant aftershave, marketed to a rapidly graying customer base through ads featuring a whistling sailor with a girl in every port. Old Spice deodorant ranked a dismal tenth in market share. But in a surprisingly short time, P&G has transformed a small stagnating brand into a men's personal-care powerhouse. Old Spice is now the top-selling deodorant and antiperspirant among teen guys. And it's not just teenagers. Old Spice has also inched by Gillette Right Guard to become the nation's leading deodorant and antiperspirant for men, with 20 percent of the $1 billion market.

To get there, P&G pulled off one of the hardest tricks in marketing: reviving a familiar brand. To shed the image of "your father's aftershave," and to appeal to younger buyers, P&G refo-

cused on performance, launching Old Spice High Endurance deodorant in 1994. It ditched the sailor ads and targeted guys 18 to 34. The deodorant business grew steadily, but P&G still wasn't drawing in men 25 to 45, who still remembered Old Spice as a relic from Dad's era.

So P&G skipped a generation and aimed Old Spice at first-time deodorant users. It started handing out samples of High Endurance to fifth-grade health classes, covering 90 percent of the nation's schools. In 2000, P&G launched Old Spice Red Zone, a sub-brand that offered even more protection than High Endurance. Sales took off, and by 2001, Old Spice was edging out Right Guard as the top teen brand.

To reach teen boys, who spend less time watching TV, P&G's marketing for Old Spice has gone well beyond the 30-second TV commercial to include lots of grassroots marketing. P&G hands out Old Spice samples at skateboarding events and gets the product into locker rooms by sponsoring a contest for high-school football player of the year. Old Spice has even partnered with Always to assemble puberty-education packages for fifth-grade classrooms, entitled "Always Changing: About You—Puberty and Stuff." The package comes complete with reading material, a video, and Old Spice product samples for boys.

P&G now has that Old Spice sailor whistling a whole new tune. The once old and stodgy is young again, and hot. Beyond deodorant, P&G sees Old Spice as a beachhead into other products. It has already launched Old Spice body sprays and body washes and has licensed sales of razors and shaving cream. It even thinks it can revive aftershave and cologne sales. "If you'd told me five years ago that Old Spice would be No. 1, I would have said you were dead wrong," says a divisional merchandise manager at Walgreens, the largest U.S. drugstore chain. But "it's now cool where it wouldn't have been cool [then]."

Sources: Examples adapted from portions of Robert Berner, "Extreme Makeover," *BusinessWeek,* November 1, 2004, pp. 105–106; and Jack Neff, "Mr. Clean Gets $50 Million Push," *Advertising Age,* August 18, 2003, pp. 3, 32; with quotes and other information from Robert Berner, "P&G Has Rivals in a Wringer," *BusinessWeek,* October 4, 2004, p. 74; Todd Wasserman, "Mr. Clean Auto Dry Gets an Overhaul," *Brandweek,* February 28, 2005, p. 17; Marek Fuchs, "Sex Ed, Provided by Old Spice," *New York Times,* May 29, 2005, p. 14; Sarah Ellison, "Focus Group—P&G Chief's Turnaround Recipe," *Wall Street Journal,* June 1, 2005, p. A1; and information accessed at www.homemadesimple.com/mrclean, August 2005.

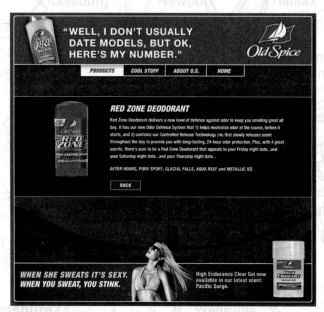

■ *Working at both ends of the product life cycle: Along with creating innovative new products, P&G has become adept at turning yesterday's faded favorites into today's hot new products. For example, it made the once old and stodgy Old Spice brand young again, and hot.*

TABLE 8.2
Summary of Product Life-Cycle Characteristics, Objectives, and Strategies

Characteristics	Introduction	Growth	Maturity	Decline
Sales	Low sales	Rapidly rising sales	Peak sales	Declining sales
Costs	High cost per customer	Average cost per customer	Low cost per customer	Low cost per customer
Profits	Negative	Rising profits	High profits	Declining profits
Customers	Innovators	Early adopters	Middle majority	Laggards
Competitors	Few	Growing number	Stable number beginning to decline	Declining number
Marketing Objectives				
	Create product awareness and trial	Maximize market share	Maximize profit while defending market share	Reduce expenditure and milk the brand
Strategies				
Product	Offer a basic product	Offer product extensions, service, warranty	Diversify brand and models	Phase out weak items
Price	Use cost-plus	Price to penetrate market	Price to match or beat competitors	Cut price
Distribution	Build selective distribution	Build intensive distribution	Build more intensive distribution	Go selective: phase out unprofitable outlets
Advertising	Build product awareness among early adopters and dealers	Build awareness and interest in the mass market	Stress brand differences and benefits	Reduce to level needed to retain hard-core loyals
Sales Promotion	Use heavy sales promotion to entice trial	Reduce to take advantage of heavy consumer demand	Increase to encourage brand switching	Reduce to minimal level

Source: Philip Kotler and Kevin Lane Keller, *Marketing Management*, 12th ed. (Upper Saddle River, N.J.: Prentice Hall, 2006), p. 332.

REST STOP → REVIEWING THE CONCEPTS

A company's current products face limited life spans and must be replaced by newer products. But new products can fail—the risks of innovation are as great as the rewards. The key to successful innovation lies in a total-company effort, strong planning, and a systematic *new-product development* process.

1. Explain how companies find and develop new-product ideas.

Companies find and develop new-product ideas from a variety of sources. Many new-product ideas stem from *internal sources*. Companies conduct formal research and development, pick the brains of their employees, and brainstorm at executive meetings. Other ideas come from *external sources*. By conducting surveys and focus groups and analyzing *customer* questions and complaints, companies can generate new-product ideas that will meet specific consumer needs. Companies track *competitors'* offerings and inspect new products, dismantling them, analyzing their performance, and deciding whether to introduce a similar or improved product. *Distributors and suppliers* are close to the market and can pass along information about consumer problems and new-product possibilities.

2. List and define the steps in the new-product development process.

The new-product development process consists of eight sequential stages. The process starts with *idea generation*. Next comes *idea screening*, which reduces the number of ideas based on the company's own criteria. Ideas that pass the screening stage continue through *product-concept development*, in which a detailed version of the new-product idea is stated in meaningful consumer terms. In the next stage, *concept testing*, new-product concepts are tested with a group of target consumers to determine whether the concepts have strong consumer appeal. Strong concepts proceed to *marketing-strategy development*, in which an initial marketing strategy for the new product is developed from the product concept. In the *business-analysis* stage, a review of the sales, costs, and profit projections for a new product is conducted to determine whether the new product is likely to satisfy the company's objectives. With positive results here, the ideas become more concrete through *product development* and *test marketing* and finally are launched during *commercialization*.

3. Describe the stages of the product life cycle.

Each product has a *life cycle* marked by a changing set of problems and opportunities. The sales of the typical product follow an S-shaped curve made up of five stages. The cycle begins with the *product-development stage* when the company finds and develops a new-product idea. The *introduction stage* is marked by slow growth and low profits as the product is distributed to the market. If successful, the product enters a *growth stage*, which offers rapid sales growth and increasing profits. Next comes a *maturity stage* when sales growth slows down and profits stabilize. Finally, the product enters a *decline stage* in which sales and profits dwindle. The company's task during this stage is to recognize the decline and to decide whether it should maintain, harvest, or drop the product.

4. Describe how marketing strategies change during the product's life cycle.

In the *introduction stage,* the company must choose a launch strategy consistent with its intended product positioning. Much money is needed to attract distributors and build their inventories and to inform consumers of the new product and achieve trial. In the *growth stage,* companies continue to educate potential consumers and distributors. In addition, the company works to stay ahead of the competition and sustain rapid market growth by improving product quality, adding new product features and models, entering new market segments and distribution channels, shifting advertising from building product awareness to building product conviction and purchase, and lowering prices at the right time to attract new buyers. In the *maturity stage,* companies continue to invest in maturing products and consider modifying the market, the product, and the marketing mix. When *modifying the market,* the company attempts to increase the consumption of the current product. When *modifying the product,* the company changes some of the product's characteristics—such as quality, features, or style—to attract new users or inspire more usage. When *modifying the marketing mix,* the company works to improve sales by changing one or more of the marketing-mix elements. Once the company recognizes that a product has entered the *decline stage*, management must decide whether to *maintain* the brand without change, hoping that competitors will drop out of the market; *harvest* the product, reducing costs and trying to maintain sales; or *drop* the product, selling it to another firm or liquidating it at salvage value.

Navigating the Key Terms

Travel Log

Discussing the Issues

1. Why do so many new products fail? What lessons can marketing managers learn from this to apply to the new-product development process?

2. Describe the major internal and external sources of new-product ideas. Which source do you think provides the best ideas? Which source delivers the most ideas?

3. What major factors should a company consider when it proceeds with the commercialization of a new product? Which factor do you believe is most important?

4. Compare sequential product development and simultaneous product development. What are the advantages and disadvantages of each approach?

5. Briefly describe the five stages of the product life cycle. Identify one product class, form, or brand that is in each stage.

6. Explain the difference between maintaining, harvesting, and dropping a brand in the decline stage. Why might a company select one of these strategies over the other?

Application Questions

1. In a small group, brainstorm ideas for a new product. Develop three different product concepts for one of the new-product ideas your group has generated.

2. Select the product concept from the previous question that you believe is the most viable. Develop a marketing-strategy statement for the new product based on that concept.

3. Identify a product that has been successfully modified to meet changing consumer needs and, as a result, has avoided the decline stage. Did the company modify the market, the product, or the marketing mix? How?

Under the Hood: Focus on Technology

Sometimes the most difficult part of new-product development is generating new ideas that solve old problems. Companies have tried everything from costly retreats to customer feedback hoping to develop ideas that are good enough to weather the product development process. Always on the lookout for fresh ways to create innovative ideas, some marketers have turned to idea-generating software. Creativity Unleashed Limited offers "Imagination Engineering" software, designed to spur creativity by thinking about problems in new ways. But can software really inspire creativity? The company's Web site reassures clients, saying "If it seems strange that something as mechanical as software can improve creativity, don't worry. It's not the software that's creative, it's you. All the software does is stimulate the bits that other stimulants can't reach."

1. Can software really help marketers generate successful new product ideas? Does such software have inherent limitations?

2. Visit Creativity Unleashed's Web site at www.cul.co.uk/software/imeng.htm and download the Imagination Engineering software. Returning, once again, to the new-product idea from Application Question 1, use the software to develop other ideas that solve the same problem. How well does the software work? Did you find it easy to use?

Focus on Ethics

In many cases, getting a new product to market before the competition is the key to rapidly building market share and establishing brand awareness. But rushing through the stages of product development to achieve commercialization has both its benefits and its drawbacks. Employees feeling pressure to make deadlines and beat the competition to market may neglect consumer needs or overlook important safety concerns. Balancing safety, quality, and speed is often difficult in an environment of rapid change and fierce competition.

1. What can a company do to ensure that all the necessary product-development steps are adequately followed under the pressure of being first to market? What controls might be put in place?

2. Discuss the potential negative consequences of rushing a new product to market. How can marketers balance these concerns with the need to innovate?

Videos

The eGO video case that accompanies this chapter is located in Appendix 1 at the back of the book.

→ **AFTER STUDYING THIS CHAPTER, YOU SHOULD BE ABLE TO**

1. discuss the importance of understanding customer value perceptions and company costs when setting prices

2. identify and define the other important internal and external factors affecting a firm's pricing decisions

3. describe the major strategies for pricing imitative and new products

4. explain how companies find a set of prices that maximizes the profits from the total product mix

5. discuss how companies adjust their prices to take into account different types of customers and situations

6. discuss key issues related to initiating and responding to price changes

Pricing: Understanding and Capturing Customer Value

Road Map Previewing the Concepts

We continue our marketing journey with a look at a second major marketing mix tool—pricing. Firms successful at creating customer value with the other marketing mix activities must capture this value in the prices they earn. According to one pricing expert, pricing involves "harvesting your profit potential."[1] If effective product development, promotion, and distribution sow the seeds of business success, effective pricing is the harvest. Yet, despite its importance, many firms do not handle pricing well. In this chapter, we begin with the question, What is a price? Next, we look at customer value perceptions, costs, and other factors that marketers must consider when setting prices. Finally, we examine pricing strategies for new-product pricing, product mix pricing, price adjustments, and dealing with price changes.

Pricing decisions can make or break a company. For openers, consider Toys "R" Us, whose low-cost, everyday-low-price strategy years ago helped it to sweep aside smaller competitors and become the nation's largest toy seller. But what goes around comes around. Read on to see how once-dominant Toys "R" Us is now fighting for survival in the toy market against an even more ruthless low-price competitor. (Can you guess which one?)

Finding the right pricing strategy and implementing it well can be critical to a company's success—even to its survival. Perhaps no company knows this better than giant toy retailer Toys "R" Us. More than three decades ago, Toys "R" Us taught smaller, independent toy retailers and department-store chains in its industry a hard pricing lesson, driving many of them to extinction. In recent years, however, Toys "R" Us has gotten a bitter taste of its own pricing medicine in return.

In the late 1970s, Toys "R" Us emerged as a toy retailing "category killer," offering consumers a vast selection of toys at everyday low prices. The then prevalent smaller toy stores, and toy sections of larger department stores, soon fell by the wayside because they couldn't match Toys "R" Us's selection, convenience, and low prices. Throughout the 1980s and early-1990s, Toys "R" Us grew explosively to become the nation's largest toy retailer, grabbing as much as a 25 percent share of the U.S. toy market.

However, in the 1990s, Toys "R" Us's heady success seemed to vanish almost overnight with the emergence of—you guessed it—Wal-Mart as a toy retailing force. Wal-Mart offered toy buyers an even more compelling value proposition. Like Toys "R" Us, it offered good toy selection and convenience. But on prices, it did Toys "R" Us one better. Wal-Mart offered not just *everyday-low* prices on toys, it offered *rock-bottom* prices.

Says one analyst, "With its mammoth stores, diverse array of products, and super-efficient supply chain, Wal-Mart can provide consumers good quality, high levels of choice and convenience, and [incredibly low] prices." What's more, he continues, "because it is a mass retailer with a broad, diverse inventory, Wal-Mart can afford to use toys as a loss-leader, losing money on toy purchases to lure in customers who then purchase higher margin goods. Focused retailers such as Toys "R" Us just don't have that luxury." In 1998, Wal-Mart pushed Toys "R" Us aside to become the country's largest toy seller.

Toys "R" Us fought back by trying to match Wal-Mart's super-low prices, but with disastrous results. Consider this *BusinessWeek* account of the 2003 Christmas season:

> He sings, he dances, he shakes it all about. For thousands of toddlers, Hokey Pokey Elmo was one of the great things about Christmas 2003. But for Toys "R" Us, Elmo was the fuzzy red embodiment of all that went wrong: He was just too cheap. Last October, two months before the heart of the holiday rush, Wal-Mart Stores surprised all of its competition by dropping Elmo's price from $25 to $19.50, a full $4.50 below what many retailers had paid for it. Within days, Toys "R" Us dropped its price to $19.99. The price war dominoed all the way down the toy aisle. "Our choice was short-term profit versus long-term market share; we chose to protect market share," says [former] CEO John Eyler, who thinks all stores could have sold out of the popular doll at $29.99.
>
> That's profit Toys "R" Us couldn't afford to lose. The holiday season [its third disappointing one in a row] resulted in a 5 percent drop in sales at Toys "R" Us stores open at least a year. Net income for the year fell 27 percent. Wal-Mart, on the other hand, [was] all smiles. . . . CEO Lee Scott called 2003 "an excellent toy season" and toys "a very profitable category with a very strong gross margin." Clearly, Toys "R" Us has little hope of competing on price with Wal-Mart. "I wouldn't want to play that game," says [an industry expert].

By early 2005, Wal-Mart held a 25 percent share of the toy market; Toys "R" Us's share had fallen to 15 percent. Later that year, new ownership took Toys "R" Us private. Despite rumors that the once dominant toy retailer would exit the toy business altogether and focus on its growing and profitable Babies "R" Us unit, the new owners vowed to remain a player in the toy industry.

However, Toys "R" Us will likely develop a dramatically new game plan. For starters, management is closing stores to cut costs and refocusing its marketing strategy. For example, the chain appears to be stepping back from cut-throat price wars that it simply can't win. Instead, it's emphasizing top-selling products and higher-margin exclusive items, such as special Bratz or Barbie dolls sold only at its stores. And in an effort to differentiate itself from the likes of Wal-Mart and Target, Toys "R" Us is making a big push to improve store atmospheres, shopper experiences, and customer service.

Still, Toys "R" Us faces an uphill battle in its efforts to win back the now price-sensitive toy buyers it helped to create decades ago. Consider this example.

> Aurore Boone of Alpharetta, Georgia, was recently at her local Wal-Mart checking out kids' bikes. She shops at Toys "R" Us to see what's on the shelves, but of the roughly $500 she and her husband Mark spend on toys a year, more than half goes to Wal-Mart, the rest to stores such as Target. It's cheaper, and she can do her other shopping there, too.

It isn't a matter of whether Toys "R" Us can *sell* toys—with more than $11 billion in sales, the company remains one of the world's largest retailers. It's a matter of whether Toys "R" Us can sell toys *profitably*. And to do that, it will have to find the right customer value and pricing formulas. As *BusinessWeek* concludes: "It's a harsh new world for Toys 'R' Us, which, as the industry's original 800-pound gorilla, wiped out legions of small toy stores in the '60s and '70s with its cut-price, no-frills, big-box outlets. Now, having taught consumers that toys should be cheap, the chain is finding that they learned the lesson all too well."[2]

Companies today face a fierce and fast-changing pricing environment. Increasing customer price-consciousness has put many companies in a "pricing vise." "Thank the Wal-Mart phenomenon," says one analyst. "These days, we're all cheapskates in search of a spend-less strategy."[3] In response, it seems that almost every company is looking for ways to slash prices, and that is hurting their profits.

Yet, cutting prices is often not the best answer. Reducing prices unnecessarily can lead to lost profits and damaging price wars. It can signal to customers that the price is more important than the customer value a brand delivers. Instead, companies should sell value, not price. They should persuade customers that paying a higher price for the company's brand is justified by the greater value they gain. The challenge is to find the price that will let the company make a fair profit by harvesting the customer value it creates. "Give people something of value," says Ronald Shaich, CEO of Panera Bread Company, "and they'll happily pay for it."[4]

What Is Price?

In the narrowest sense, **price** is the amount of money charged for a product or service. More broadly, price is the sum of all the values that customers give up in order to gain the benefits of having or using a product or service. Historically, price has been the major factor affecting buyer choice. In recent decades, nonprice factors have gained increasing importance. However, price still remains one of the most important elements determining a firm's market share and profitability.

Price is the only element in the marketing mix that produces revenue; all other elements represent costs. Price is also one of the most flexible elements of the marketing mix. Unlike product features and channel commitments, prices can be changed quickly. At the same time, pricing is the number-one problem facing many marketing executives, and many companies do not handle pricing well. One frequent problem is that companies are too quick to reduce prices in order to get a sale rather than convincing buyers that their product's greater value is worth a higher price. Other common mistakes include pricing that is too cost oriented rather than customer-value oriented, and pricing that does not take the rest of the marketing mix into account.

Some managers view pricing as a big headache, preferring instead to focus on the other marketing mix elements. However, smart managers treat pricing as a key strategic tool for creating and capturing customer value. Prices have a direct impact on a firm's bottom line. According to one expert, "a 1 percent price improvement generates a 12.5 percent profit improvement for most organizations."[5] More importantly, as part of a company's overall value proposition, price plays a key role in creating customer value and building customer relationships. "Instead of running away from pricing," says the expert, "savvy marketers are embracing it."

Price
The amount of money charged for a product or service, or the sum of all the values that customers give up in order to gain the benefits of having or using a product or service.

Factors to Consider when Setting Prices

The price the company charges will fall somewhere between one that is too high to produce any demand and one that is too low to produce a profit. Figure 9.1 summarizes the major considerations in setting price. Customer perceptions of the product's value set the ceiling for prices. If customers perceive that the price is greater than the product's value, they will not buy the product. Product costs set the floor for prices. If the company prices the product below its costs, company profits will suffer. In setting its price between these two extremes, the company must consider a number of other internal factors, including its overall marketing strategy and mix, the nature of the market and demand, competitors' strategies and prices, and a number of other internal and external factors.

FIGURE 9.1
Factors Affecting Price Decisions

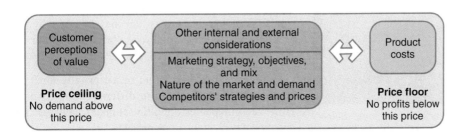

CUSTOMER PERCEPTIONS OF VALUE

In the end, the customer will decide whether a product's price is right. Pricing decisions, like other marketing mix decisions, must start with customer value. When customers buy a product, they exchange something of value (the price) in order to get something of value (the benefits of having or using the product). Effective, customer-oriented pricing involves understanding how much value consumers place on the benefits they receive from the product and setting a price that captures this value.

Value-based pricing

Setting price based on buyers' perceptions of value rather than on the seller's cost.

Value-Based Pricing   Good pricing begins with a complete understanding of the value that a product or service creates for customers. **Value-based pricing** uses buyers' perceptions of value, not the seller's cost, as the key to pricing. Value-based pricing means that the marketer cannot design a product and marketing program and then set the price. Price is considered along with the other marketing mix variables *before* the marketing program is set.

Figure 9.2 compares value-based pricing with cost-based pricing. Cost-based pricing is product driven. The company designs what it considers to be a good product, totals the costs of making the product, and sets a price that covers costs plus a target profit. Marketing must then convince buyers that the product's value at that price justifies its purchase. If the price turns out to be too high, the company must settle for lower markups or lower sales, both resulting in disappointing profits.

Value-based pricing reverses this process. The company sets its target price based on customer perceptions of the product value. The targeted value and price then drive decisions about product design and what costs can be incurred. As a result, pricing begins with analyzing consumer needs and value perceptions, and price is set to match consumers' perceived value.

It's important to remember that "good value" is not the same as "low price." For example, top-of-the-line Montblanc pens sell for several hundred dollars or more—a less expensive pen might write as well, but some consumers place great value on the intangibles they receive from a "fine writing instrument." Similarly, some car buyers consider the luxurious Bentley Continental GT automobile a real value, even at an eye-popping price of $150,000:

> Stay with me here, because I'm about to [tell you why] a certain automobile costing $150,000 is not actually expensive, but is in fact a tremendous value. Every Bentley GT is built by hand, an Old World bit of automaking requiring 160 hours per vehicle. Craftsmen spend 18 hours simply stitching the perfectly joined leather of the GT's steering wheel, almost as long as it takes to assemble an entire VW Golf. The results are impressive: Dash and doors are mirrored with walnut veneer, floor pedals are carved from aluminum, window and seat toggles are cut from actual metal rather than plastic, and every air vent is perfectly chromed. . . . The sum of all this is a fitted cabin that approximates that of a $300,000 vehicle, matched to an engine the equal of a $200,000 automobile, within a car that has brilliantly incorporated . . . technological sophistication. As I said, the GT is a bargain. [Just ask anyone on the lengthy waiting list.] The waiting time to bring home your very own GT is currently half a year.[6]

A company using value-based pricing must find out what value buyers assign to different competitive offers. However, companies often find it hard to measure the value customers will attach to its product. For example, calculating the cost of ingredients in a meal at a fancy restaurant is rela-

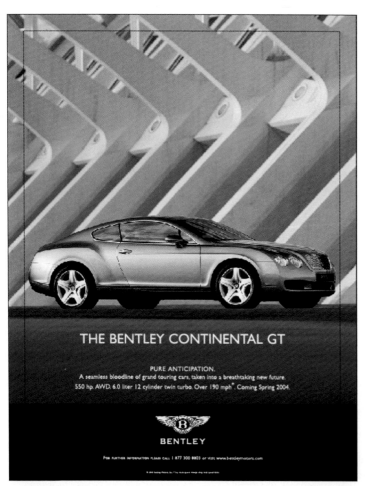

THE BENTLEY CONTINENTAL GT

PURE ANTICIPATION.
A seamless bloodline of grand touring cars, taken into a breathtaking new future.
550 hp. AWD. 6.0 liter 12 cylinder twin turbo. Over 190 mph*. Coming Spring 2004.

BENTLEY

FOR FURTHER INFORMATION PLEASE CALL 1 877 300 8803 or visit www.bentleymotors.com

■ Value-based pricing: "Good value" is not the same as "low price." Some car buyers consider the luxurious Bentley Continental GT automobile a real value, even at an eye-popping price of $150,000.

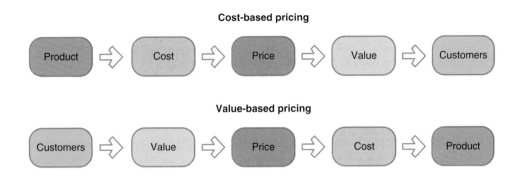

Cost-based pricing

Product ⇒ Cost ⇒ Price ⇒ Value ⇒ Customers

Value-based pricing

Customers ⇒ Value ⇒ Price ⇒ Cost ⇒ Product

FIGURE 9.2
Value-Based Pricing Versus Cost-Based Pricing

Source: Thomas T. Nagle and Reed K. Holden, *The Strategy and Tactics of Pricing*, 3rd ed. (Upper Saddle River, NJ: Prentice Hall, 2002), p. 4. Reproduced by permission of Pearson Education, Inc., Upper Saddle River, New Jersey.

tively easy. But assigning a value to other satisfactions such as taste, environment, relaxation, conversation, and status is very hard. And these values will vary both for different consumers and different situations.

Still, consumers will use these perceived values to evaluate a product's price, so the company must work to measure them. Sometimes, companies ask consumers how much they would pay for a basic product and for each benefit added to the offer. Or a company might conduct experiments to test the perceived value of different product offers. According to an old Russian proverb, there are two fools in every market—one who asks too much and one who asks too little. If the seller charges more than the buyers' perceived value, the company's sales will suffer. If the seller charges less, its products sell very well. But they produce less revenue than they would if they were priced at the level of perceived value.

We now examine two types of value-based pricing: *good-value pricing* and *value-added pricing*.

Good-Value Pricing.   During the past decade, marketers have noted a fundamental shift in consumer attitudes toward price and quality. Many companies have changed their pricing approaches to bring them into line with changing economic conditions and consumer price perceptions. More and more, marketers have adopted **good-value pricing** strategies— offering just the right combination of quality and good service at a fair price.

In many cases, this has involved introducing less-expensive versions of established, brand-name products. Fast-food restaurants such as Taco Bell and McDonald's offer "value menus." Armani offers the less-expensive, more casual Armani Exchange fashion line. Procter & Gamble created Charmin Basic—it is "slightly less 'squeezably soft' but it's a lot less pricey than P&G's other toilet paper."[7] In other cases, good-value pricing has involved redesigning existing brands to offer more quality for a given price or the same quality for less.

An important type of good-value pricing at the retail level is *everyday low pricing (EDLP)*. EDLP involves charging a constant, everyday low price with few or no temporary price discounts. In contrast, *high-low pricing* involves charging higher prices on an everyday basis but running frequent promotions to lower prices temporarily on selected items. In recent years, high-low pricing has given way to EDLP in retail settings ranging from Saturn car dealerships to Giant Eagle supermarkets to upscale department stores such as Nordstrom.

The king of EDLP is Wal-Mart, which practically defined the concept. Except for a few sale items every month, Wal-Mart promises everyday low prices on everything it sells. In contrast, Kmart's recent attempts to match Wal-Mart's EDLP strategy failed. To offer everyday low prices, a company must first have everyday low costs. However, because Kmart's costs are much higher than Wal-Mart's, it could not make money at the lower prices and quickly abandoned the attempt.[8]

Value-Added Pricing.   In many B-to-B marketing situations, the challenge is to build the company's *pricing power*—its power to escape price competition and to justify higher prices and margins without losing market share. To do this, many companies adopt *value-added* strategies. Rather than cutting prices to match competitors, they attach value-added features and services to differentiate their offers and thus support higher prices.

Good-value pricing
Offering just the right combination of quality and good service at a fair price.

Value-added pricing
Attaching value-added features and services to differentiate a marketing offer and support higher prices, rather than cutting prices to match competitors.

When a company finds its major competitors offering a similar product at a lower price, the natural tendency is to try to match or beat that price. Although the idea of undercutting competitor's prices and watching customers flock in is tempting, there are dangers. Price-cutting can lead to price wars that erode the profit margins of all competitors in an industry. Or worse, discounting a product can cheapen it in the minds of customers. This greatly reduces the seller's power to maintain profitable prices in the long term.

So, how can a company keep its pricing power when a competitor undercuts its price? Often, the best strategy is not to price below the competitor, but rather to price above and convince customers that the product is worth it. The company should ask, "What is the value of the product to the customer?" then stand up for what the product is worth. In this way, the company shifts the focus from price to value. "Even in today's economic environment, it's not about price," says a pricing expert. "It's about keeping customers loyal by providing service they can't find anywhere else."[9] Caterpillar is a master at value-added marketing:

> Caterpillar charges premium prices for its heavy-construction and mining equipment by convincing customers that its products and service justify every additional cent—or, rather, the extra tens of thousands of dollars. Caterpillar typically reaps a 20 to 30 percent price premium over competitors—that can amount to an extra $200,000 or more on one of those huge yellow, million-dollar dump trucks. When a large potential customer says, "I can get it for less from a competitor," rather than discounting the price, the Caterpillar dealer explains that, even at the higher price, Caterpillar offers the best value. Caterpillar equipment is designed with modular componentry that can be removed and repaired quickly, minimizing machine downtime. Caterpillar dealers carry an extensive parts inventory and guarantee delivery within 48 hours anywhere in the world, again minimizing downtime. Caterpillar's products are designed to be rebuilt, providing a "second life" that competitors cannot match. As a result, Caterpillar used-equipment prices are often 20 percent to 30 percent higher. In all, the dealer explains, even at the higher initial price, Caterpillar equipment delivers the lowest total cost per cubic yard of earth moved, ton of coal uncovered, or mile of road graded over the life of the product—guaranteed! Most customers seem to agree with Caterpillar's value proposition—the company dominates its markets with a more than 40 percent worldwide market share.

■ Value added: Caterpillar offers its dealers a wide range of value-added services—from guaranteed parts delivery to investment management advice and equipment training. Such added value supports a higher price.

COMPANY AND PRODUCT COSTS

Whereas customer-value perceptions set the price ceiling, costs set the floor for the price that the company can charge. The company wants to charge a price that both covers all its costs for producing, distributing, and selling the product and delivers a fair rate of return for its effort and risk. A company's costs may be an important element in its pricing strategy. Many companies, such as Southwest Airlines, Wal-Mart, and Union Carbide, work to become the "low-cost producers" in their industries. Companies with lower costs can set lower prices that result in greater sales and profits.

Fixed costs
Costs that do not vary with production or sales level.

Variable costs
Costs that vary directly with the level of production.

Types of Costs   A company's costs take two forms, fixed and variable. **Fixed costs** (also known as **overhead**) are costs that do not vary with production or sales level. For example, a company must pay each month's bills for rent, heat, interest, and executive salaries, whatever the company's output. **Variable costs** vary directly with the level of production. Each personal computer produced by Hewlett-Packard involves a cost of computer chips, wires, plastic, packaging, and other inputs. These costs tend to be the same for each unit produced.

They are called variable because their total varies with the number of units produced. **Total costs** are the sum of the fixed and variable costs for any given level of production. Management wants to charge a price that will at least cover the total production costs at a given level of production.

Total costs
The sum of the fixed and variable costs for any given level of production.

The company must watch its costs carefully. If it costs the company more than competitors to produce and sell its product, the company will have to charge a higher price or make less profit, putting it at a competitive disadvantage.

Cost-Based Pricing   The simplest pricing method is **cost-plus pricing**—adding a standard markup to the cost of the product. For example, an appliance retailer might pay a manufacturer $20 for a toaster and mark it up to sell at $30, a 50 percent markup on cost. The retailer's gross margin is $10. If the store's operating costs amount to $8 per toaster sold, the retailer's profit margin will be $2.

Cost-plus pricing
Adding a standard markup to the cost of the product.

The manufacturer that made the toaster probably used cost-plus pricing. If the manufacturer's standard cost of producing the toaster was $16, it might have added a 25 percent markup, setting the price to the retailers at $20. Similarly, construction companies submit job bids by estimating the total project cost and adding a standard markup for profit. Lawyers, accountants, architects, and other professionals typically price by adding a standard markup to their costs. Some sellers tell their customers they will charge cost plus a specified markup; for example, aerospace companies price this way to the government.

Does using standard markups to set prices make sense? Generally, no. Any pricing method that ignores customer value and competitor prices is not likely to lead to the best price. Still, markup pricing remains popular for many reasons. First, sellers are more certain about costs than about customer-value perceptions and demand. By tying the price to cost, sellers simplify pricing—they do not have to make frequent adjustments as demand changes. Second, when all firms in the industry use this pricing method, prices tend to be similar and price competition is thus minimized. Third, many people feel that cost-plus pricing is fairer to both buyers and sellers. Sellers earn a fair return on their investment but do not take advantage of buyers when buyers' demand becomes great.

Another cost-oriented pricing approach is **break-even pricing**, or a variation called **target profit pricing**. The firm tries to determine the price at which it will break even or make the target profit it is seeking. Target pricing uses the concept of a *break-even chart*, which shows the total cost and total revenue expected at different sales volume levels. Figure 9.3 shows a break-even chart for the toaster manufacturer discussed here. Fixed costs are $6 million regardless of sales volume, and variable costs are $5 per unit. Variable costs are added to fixed costs to form total costs, which rise with volume. The slope of the total revenue curve reflects the price. Here, the price is $15 (for example, the company's revenue is $12 million on 800,000 units, or $15 per unit).

Break-even pricing (target profit pricing)
Setting price to break even on the costs of making and marketing a product; or setting price to make a target profit.

At the $15 price, the company must sell at least 600,000 units to *break even*—that is, at this level, total revenues will equal total costs of $9 million. If the company wants a target profit of $2 million, it must sell at least 800,000 units to obtain the $12 million of total

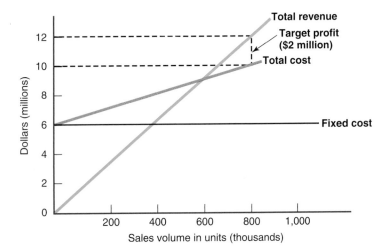

FIGURE 9.3
Break-Even Chart for Determining Price

revenue needed to cover the costs of $10 million plus the $2 million of target profits. In contrast, if the company charges a higher price, say $20, it will not need to sell as many units to break even or to achieve its target profit. In fact, the higher the price, the lower the company's break-even point will be.

The major problem with this analysis, however, is that it fails to consider customer value and the relationship between price and demand. As the *price* increases, *demand* decreases, and the market may not buy even the lower volume needed to break even at the higher price. For example, suppose the company calculates that given its current fixed and variable costs, it must charge a price of $30 for the product in order to earn its desired target profit. But marketing research shows that few consumers will pay more than $25. In this case, the company will have to trim its costs in order to lower the break-even point so that it can charge the lower price consumers expect.

Thus, although break-even analysis and target profit pricing can help the company to determine minimum prices needed to cover expected costs and profits, they do not take the price-demand relationship into account. When using this method, the company must also consider the impact of price on sales volume needed to realize target profits and the likelihood that the needed volume will be achieved at each possible price.

OTHER INTERNAL AND EXTERNAL CONSIDERATIONS AFFECTING PRICE DECISIONS

Customer perceptions of value set the upper limit for prices, and costs set the lower limit. However, in setting prices within these limits, the company must consider a number of other internal and external factors. Internal factors affecting pricing include the company's overall marketing strategy, objectives, and marketing mix, as well as other organizational considerations. External factors include the nature of the market and demand, competitors' strategies and prices, and other environmental factors.

Overall Marketing Strategy, Objectives, and Mix   Price is only one element of the company's broader marketing strategy. Thus, before setting price, the company must decide on its overall marketing strategy for the product or service. If the company has selected its target market and positioning carefully, then its marketing mix strategy, including price, will be fairly straightforward. For example, when Toyota developed its Lexus brands to compete with European luxury-performance cars in the higher-income segment, this required charging a high price. In contrast, when it introduced its "energetic but economical" Echo model, a car with "a sticker price that can really help you pursue your dreams," this positioning required charging a low price. Thus, pricing strategy is largely determined by decisions on market positioning.

General pricing objectives might include survival, current profit maximization, market share leadership, or customer retention and relationship building. At a more specific level, a company can set prices to attract new customers or to profitably retain existing ones. It can set prices low to prevent competition from entering the market or set prices at competitors' levels to stabilize the market. It can price to keep the loyalty and support of resellers or to avoid government intervention. Prices can be reduced temporarily to create excitement for a brand. Or one product may be priced to help the sales of other products in the company's line. Thus, pricing may play an important role in helping to accomplish the company's objectives at many levels.

Price is only one of the marketing mix tools that a company uses to achieve its marketing objectives. Price decisions must be coordinated with product design, distribution, and promotion decisions to form a consistent and effective marketing program. Decisions made for other marketing mix variables may affect pricing decisions. For example, a decision to position the product on high-performance quality will mean that the seller must charge a higher price to cover higher costs. And producers whose resellers are expected to support and promote their products may have to build larger reseller margins into their prices.

Companies often position their products on price and then tailor other marketing mix decisions to the prices they want to charge. Here, price is a crucial product-positioning factor that defines the product's market, competition, and design. Many firms support such price-positioning strategies with a technique called **target costing**, a potent strategic

Target costing
Pricing that starts with an ideal selling price, then targets costs that will ensure that the price is met.

weapon. Target costing reverses the usual process of first designing a new product, determining its cost, and then asking, "Can we sell it for that?" Instead, it starts with an ideal selling price based on customer-value considerations, and then targets costs that will ensure that the price is met.

P&G used target costing to price and develop its highly successful Crest SpinBrush electric toothbrush:

> P&G usually prices its goods at a premium. But with Crest SpinBrush, P&G reversed its usual thinking. It started with an attractive, low market price, and then found a way to make a profit at that price. SpinBrush's inventors first came up with the idea of a low-priced electric toothbrush while walking through their local Wal-Mart, where they saw Sonicare, Interplak, and other electric toothbrushes priced at more than $50. These pricy brushes held only a fraction of the overall toothbrush market. A less expensive electric toothbrush, the designers reasoned, would have huge potential. They decided on a target price of just $5, batteries included—only $1 more than the most expensive manual brushes—and set out to design a brush they could sell at that price. Every design element was carefully considered with the targeted price in mind. To meet the low price, P&G passed on the usual lavish new-product launch campaign. Instead, to give SpinBrush more point-of-sale impact, it relied on "Try Me" packaging that allowed consumers to turn the brush on in stores. Target-cost pricing has made Crest SpinBrush one of P&G's most successful new products ever. It has now become the nation's best-selling toothbrush, manual or electric, with a more than 40 percent share of the electric toothbrush market."[10]

Other companies deemphasize price and use other marketing mix tools to create *nonprice* positions. Often, the best strategy is not to charge the lowest price, but rather to differentiate the marketing offer to make it worth a higher price. For example, Sony builds more value into its consumer electronics products and charges a higher price than many competitors. Customers recognize Sony's higher quality and are willing to pay more to get it. Some marketers even *feature* high prices as part of their positioning. For example, Porsche proudly advertises its Boxster as "starting at $43,800" and its Cayenne as "starting at $56,300." And Steinway offers "the finest pianos in the world," with a price to match. Steinway's grand pianos can cost as much as $165,000 (see Marketing at Work 9.1).

Thus, marketers must consider the total marketing strategy and mix when setting prices. If the product is positioned on nonprice factors, then decisions about quality, promotion, and distribution will strongly affect price. If price is a crucial positioning factor, then price will strongly affect decisions made about the other marketing mix elements. But even when featuring price, marketers need to remember that customers rarely buy on price alone. Instead, they seek products that give them the best value in terms of benefits received for the price paid.

Organizational Considerations Management must decide who within the organization should set prices. Companies handle pricing in a variety of ways. In small companies, prices are often set by top management rather than by the marketing or sales departments. In large companies, pricing is typically handled by divisional or product-line managers. In industrial markets, salespeople may be allowed to negotiate with customers within certain price ranges. Even so, top management sets the

Imagining what it might be like is a poor substitute for knowing.

A more responsive throttle resonates in the open air. A re-sculpted body flexes pure roadster muscle. And the suspension you ride on feels like it's hard-wired into your senses. The new 240-hp Boxster. The roadster, reinvented. It's one thing to read about it. It's quite another to experience it firsthand. Porsche. There is no substitute.

The new Boxster. Starting at $43,800.

■ Positioning on high price: Porsche proudly advertises its Boxster as "starting at $43,800."

MARKETING AT WORK   9.1

Steinway: Price Is Nothing; The Steinway Experience Is Everything

A Steinway piano—any Steinway piano—costs a lot. A Steinway grand piano typically runs anywhere from $40,000 to $165,000. The most popular model sells for around $72,000. But Steinway buyers aren't looking for bargains. In fact, it seems, the higher the prices, the better. High prices confirm that a Steinway is the very best that money can buy—the epitome of handcrafted perfection. As important, the Steinway name is steeped in tradition. It evokes images of classical concert stages, sophisticated dinner parties, and the celebrities and performers who've owned and played Steinway pianos across more than 150 years. When it comes to Steinway, price is nothing, the Steinway experience is everything.

To be sure, Steinway & Sons makes very high-quality pianos. With 115 patents to its credit, Steinway & Sons has done more than any other manufacturer to advance the art of piano building. Steinway pioneered the development of a one-piece piano rim produced out of 17 laminations of veneer. It invented a process for bending a single 22-foot long strip of these laminated sheets inside a massive piano-shaped vise. It's this strong frame that produces Steinway's distinctive clear tones. Steinway & Sons has continued perfecting this design, and today a Steinway piano's 243 tempered, hard-steel strings exert 35 tons of pressure—enough force to implode a three-bedroom house if the strings were strung between attic and cellar.

In addition to cutting-edge technology, Steinway & Sons uses only the finest materials to construct each piano. Rock maple, spruce, birch, poplar, and four other species of wood each play a crucial, functional role in the physical and acoustical beauty of a Steinway. The expansive wooden soundboard, which turns the string vibrations into sound, is made from select Alaskan Sitka spruce—one grade higher than aircraft grade. Through delicate handcraftsmanship, Steinway transforms these select materials into pianos of incomparable sound quality. From start to finish, it takes 450 skilled workers more than a year to handcraft and assemble a Steinway piano from its 12,000 component parts. Thus, Steinway is anything but mass market. Each year, Steinway's factories in Astoria, New York, and Hamburg, Germany, craft approximately 5,000 pianos. (By comparison, Yamaha produces 100,000 pianos per year.)

Steinway's precision quality alone would command top dollar, but Steinway buyers get much more than just a well-made piano. They also get the Steinway mystique. Owning or playing a Steinway puts you in some very good company. At least 98 percent of piano soloists with the world's major symphony orchestras prefer playing on a Steinway. More than 90 percent of the world's concert pianists, some 1,300 in all, bear the title of Steinway Artist—an elite club of Steinway-owning professional musicians. Steinway customers include composers and professional musicians (from Van Cliburn to Billy Joel), upscale customers (from Lamar Alexander to Paula Zahn), and heads of state (the 25,000th Steinway was sold to Czar Alexander of Russia and Piano No. 300,000 graces the East Room of the White House, replacing Piano No. 100,000 which is now in the Smithsonian).

But Steinways aren't just for world-class pianists and the wealthy. Ninety-nine percent of all Steinway buyers are amateurs who perform only in their dens. "We see a lot of corporate executives and physicians buying Steinway grands," says a Steinway marketer. "But it is not unusual at all for a middle-income person to come in and buy a grand." The high prices don't appear to stop even the most cash-poor enthusiasts. Steinway offers a finance plan that lets them pay for their grand piano over a 12-year period.

Performers of all kinds sing Steinway's praises. "Steinway is the only piano on which the pianist can do everything he wants. And everything he dreams," declares premier pianist and

---

pricing objectives and policies, and it often approves the prices proposed by lower-level management or salespeople.

In industries in which pricing is a key factor (airlines, aerospace, steel, railroads, oil companies), companies often have pricing departments to set the best prices or to help others in setting them. These departments report to the marketing department or top management. Others who have an influence on pricing include sales managers, production managers, finance managers, and accountants.

The Market and Demand

As noted earlier, good pricing starts with an understanding of how customers' perceptions of value affect the prices they are willing to pay. Both consumer and industrial buyers balance the price of a product or service against the benefits of owning it. Thus, before setting prices, the marketer must understand the relationship between price and demand for its product. In this section, we take a deeper look at the price-demand relationship and how it varies for different types of markets. We then discuss methods for analyzing the price-demand relationship.

■ *A Steinway piano costs a lot, but buyers aren't looking for bargains. When it comes to a Steinway, price is nothing, the Steinway experience is everything.*

conductor Vladimir Ashkenazy. At the other end of the performing spectrum, contemporary singer-songwriter Randy Newman puts it this way: "I have owned and played a Steinway all my life. It's the best Beethoven piano. The best Chopin piano. And the best Ray Charles piano. I like it, too." Whereas some people want a Porsche in the garage, others prefer a Steinway in the living room—both cost about the same, and both make a statement about their owners.

Even in the worst of times, Steinway & Sons has held true to its tradition and image—and to its premium prices. Although the company is no longer owned by the Steinway family, its current owners still prize and protect the brand's exclusivity. When they bought the troubled company in 1984, new management was burdened with 900 pianos of excess inventory. But rather than slashing prices to make a quick profit at the risk of tarnishing the brand, managers restored the company's health by holding the line on prices and renewing its commitment to quality. Through such actions, Steinway has retained its cult-like following and continues to dominate its market. Despite its very high prices—or more likely because of them—Steinway enjoys a 95 percent market share in concert halls.

So, you won't find any weekend sales on Steinway pianos. Charging significantly higher prices continues to be a cornerstone of the company's "much more for much more" value proposition. And high prices have been good for Steinway & Sons. While the company accounts for only 3 percent of all U.S. pianos sold each year, it captures 25 percent of the industry's sales dollars and close to 35 percent of the profits.

To customers, whatever a Steinway costs, it's a small price to pay for the experience of owning one. Just ask the collector who recently commissioned a nine-foot re-creation of the famous Steinway Alma-Tadema piano built in 1887. The price for his dream Steinway? An eye-popping $675,000! Classical pianist Krystian Zimerman sums up his Steinway experience this way: "My friendship with the Steinway piano is one of the most important and beautiful things in my life." Who can put a price on such feelings?

Sources: Rosemary Barnes, "The Price of Perfection: Steinway Piano Commands a Premier Price," *Knight Ridder Tribune Business News,* February 26, 2005, p. 1; Andy Serwer, "Happy Birthday Steinway," *FORTUNE,* March 17, 2003, p. 94; "Books and Arts: Making the Sound of Music; Piano Manufacturers," *Economist,* June 7, 2003, p. 102; Brian T. Majeski, "The Steinway Story," *Music Trades,* September 2003, p. 18; "The Most Famous Name in Music," *Music Trades,* September 2003, pp. 118–130; Stephan Wilkinson, "High-Strung. Powerful. Very Pricey," *Popular Science,* March 1, 2003, p. 32; "Steinway Musical Instruments, Inc.," *Hoover's Company Capsules,* Austin, March 15, 2004, p. 48052; Michael Z. Wise, "Piano Versus Piano," *New York Times,* May 9, 2004; and quotes and information found at www.steinway.com, August 2005.

Pricing in Different Types of Markets. The seller's pricing freedom varies with different types of markets. Economists recognize four types of markets, each presenting a different pricing challenge.

Under *pure competition,* the market consists of many buyers and sellers trading in a uniform commodity such as wheat, copper, or financial securities. No single buyer or seller has much effect on the going market price. A seller cannot charge more than the going price because buyers can obtain as much as they need at the going price. Nor would sellers charge less than the market price, because they can sell all they want at this price. If price and profits rise, new sellers can easily enter the market. In a purely competitive market, marketing research, product development, pricing, advertising, and sales promotion play little or no role. Thus, sellers in these markets do not spend much time on marketing strategy.

Under *monopolistic competition,* the market consists of many buyers and sellers who trade over a range of prices rather than a single market price. A range of prices occurs because sellers can differentiate their offers to buyers. Either the physical product can be

■ Monopolistic competition: Moen sets its products apart through strong branding and advertising, reducing the impact of price.

varied in quality, features, or style, or the accompanying services can be varied. Buyers see differences in sellers' products and will pay different prices for them. Sellers try to develop differentiated offers for different customer segments and, in addition to price, freely use branding, advertising, and personal selling to set their offers apart. Thus, Moen differentiates its faucets and other fixtures through strong branding and advertising, reducing the impact of price. Because there are many competitors in such markets, each firm is less affected by competitors' pricing strategies than in oligopolistic markets.

Under *oligopolistic competition*, the market consists of a few sellers who are highly sensitive to each other's pricing and marketing strategies. The product can be uniform (steel, aluminum) or nonuniform (cars, computers). There are few sellers because it is difficult for new sellers to enter the market. Each seller is alert to competitors' strategies and moves. If a steel company slashes its price by 10 percent, buyers will quickly switch to this supplier. The other steelmakers must respond by lowering their prices or increasing their services.

In a *pure monopoly*, the market consists of one seller. The seller may be a government monopoly (the U.S. Postal Service), a private regulated monopoly (a power company), or a private nonregulated monopoly (DuPont when it introduced nylon). Pricing is handled differently in each case. In a regulated monopoly, the government permits the company to set rates that will yield a "fair return." Nonregulated monopolies are free to price at what the market will bear. However, they do not always charge the full price for a number of reasons: a desire not to attract competition, a desire to penetrate the market faster with a low price, or a fear of government regulation.

Analyzing the Price-Demand Relationship. Each price the company might charge will lead to a different level of demand. The relationship between the price charged and the resulting demand level is shown in the **demand curve** in Figure 9.4. The demand curve shows the number of units the market will buy in a given time period at different prices that might be charged. In the normal case, demand and price are inversely related; that is, the higher the price, the lower the demand. Thus, the company would sell less if it raised its price from P_1 to P_2. In short, consumers with limited budgets probably will buy less of something if its price is too high.

In the case of prestige goods, the demand curve sometimes slopes upward. Consumers think that higher prices mean more quality. For example, Gibson Guitar Corporation recently toyed with the idea of lowering its prices to compete more effectively with Japanese rivals such as Yamaha and Ibanez. To its surprise, Gibson found that its instruments didn't sell as well at lower prices. "We had an inverse [price-demand relationship]," noted Gibson's chief

Demand curve

A curve that shows the number of units the market will buy in a given time period, at different prices that might be charged.

FIGURE 9.4
Demand Curve

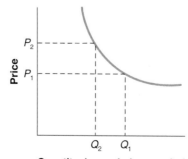

Quantity demanded per period

executive. "The more we charged, the more product we sold." At a time when other guitar manufacturers have chosen to build their instruments more quickly, cheaply, and in greater numbers, Gibson still promises guitars that "are made one-at-a-time, by hand. No shortcuts. No substitutions." It turns out that low prices simply aren't consistent with "Gibson's century-old tradition of creating investment-quality instruments that represent the highest standards of imaginative design and masterful craftsmanship."[11] Still, if the company charges too high a price, the level of demand will be lower.

Most companies try to measure their demand curves by estimating demand at different prices. The type of market makes a difference. In a monopoly, the demand curve shows the total market demand resulting from different prices. If the company faces competition, its demand at different prices will depend on whether competitors' prices stay constant or change with the company's own prices.

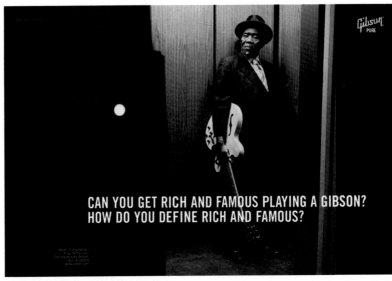

CAN YOU GET RICH AND FAMOUS PLAYING A GIBSON?
HOW DO YOU DEFINE RICH AND FAMOUS?

■ The demand curve sometimes slopes upward: Gibson was surprised to learn that its high-quality instruments didn't sell as well at lower prices.

Price Elasticity of Demand. Marketers also need to know **price elasticity**—how responsive demand will be to a change in price. If demand hardly changes with a small change in price, we say demand is *inelastic*. If demand changes greatly, we say the demand is *elastic*.

If demand is elastic rather than inelastic, sellers will consider lowering their prices. A lower price will produce more total revenue. This practice makes sense as long as the extra costs of producing and selling more do not exceed the extra revenue. At the same time, most firms want to avoid pricing that turns their products into commodities. In recent years, forces such as deregulation and the instant price comparisons afforded by the Internet and other technologies have increased consumer price sensitivity, turning products ranging from telephones and computers to new automobiles into commodities in some consumers' eyes.

Marketers need to work harder than ever to differentiate their offerings when a dozen competitors are selling virtually the same product at a comparable or lower price. More than ever, companies need to understand the price sensitivity of their customers and prospects and the trade-offs people are willing to make between price and product characteristics. In the words of Marketing Consultant Kevin Clancy, those who target only the price sensitive are "leaving money on the table."

Price elasticity
A measure of the sensitivity of demand to changes in price.

Competitors' Strategies and Prices

In setting its prices, the company must also consider competitors' costs, prices, and market offerings. Consumers will base their judgments of a product's value on the prices that competitors charge for similar products. A consumer who is considering the purchase of a Sony digital camera will evaluate Sony's customer value and price against the value and prices of comparable products made by Nikon, Kodak, Canon, and others.

In addition, the company's pricing strategy may affect the nature of the competition it faces. If Sony follows a high-price, high-margin strategy, it may attract competition. A low-price, low-margin strategy, however, may stop competitors or drive them out of the market. Sony needs to benchmark its costs and value against competitors' costs and value. It can then use these benchmarks as a starting point for its own pricing.

In assessing competitors' pricing strategies, the company should ask several questions. First, how does the company's market offering compare with competitors' offerings in terms of customer value? If consumers perceive that the company's product or service provides greater value, the company can charge a higher price. If consumers perceive less value relative to competing products, the company must either charge a lower price or change customer perceptions to justify a higher price.

Next, how strong are current competitors and what are their current pricing strategies? If the company faces a host of smaller competitors charging high prices relative to the value they deliver, it might charge lower prices to drive weaker competitors out of the market. If the market is dominated by larger, low-price competitors, the company may decide to target unserved market niches with value-added products at higher prices. For example, your local independent bookstore isn't likely to win a price war against Amazon.com or Barnes & Noble. It would be wiser to add special customer services and personal touches that justify higher prices and margins.

Finally, the company should ask, How does the competitive landscape influence customer price sensitivity?[12] For example, customers will be more price sensitive if they see few differences between competing products. They will buy whichever product costs the least. The more information customers have about competing products and prices before buying, the more price sensitive they will be. Easy product comparisons help customers to assess the value of different options and to decide what prices they are willing to pay. Finally, customers will be more price sensitive if they can switch easily from one product alternative to another.

What principle should guide decisions about what price to charge relative to those of competitors? The answer is simple in concept but often difficult in practice: No matter what price you charge—high, low, or in between—be certain to give customers superior value for that price.

Other External Factors   When setting prices, the company also must consider a number of other factors in its external environment. *Economic conditions* can have a strong impact on the firm's pricing strategies. Economic factors such as boom or recession, inflation, and interest rates affect pricing decisions because they affect both consumer perceptions of the product's price and value and the costs of producing a product. The company must also consider what impact its prices will have on other parties in its environment. How will *resellers* react to various prices? The company should set prices that give resellers a fair profit, encourage their support, and help them to sell the product effectively. The *government* is another important external influence on pricing decisions. Finally, *social concerns* may have to be taken into account. In setting prices, a company's short-term sales, market share, and profit goals may have to be tempered by broader societal considerations. We will examine public policy issues in pricing later in the chapter.

 Linking the Concepts

The concept of customer value is critical to good pricing and to successful marketing in general. Slow down for a minute and be certain that you appreciate what value really means.

- In an earlier example, one car critic called the Bentley Continental GT a great value at $150,000—"a six-figure steal" in his words. Does this fit with your idea of value?
- Pick two competing brands from a familiar product category (watches, perfume, consumer electronics, restaurants)—one low priced and the other high priced. Which, if either, offers the greatest value?
- Does *value* mean the same thing as *low price*? How do these concepts differ?

We've now seen that pricing decisions are subject to an incredibly complex array of customer, company, competitive, and environmental forces. To make things even more complex, a company sets not a single price but rather a *pricing structure* that covers different items in its line. This pricing structure changes over time as products move through their life cycles. The company adjusts product prices to reflect changes in costs and demand and to account for variations in buyers and situations. As the competitive environment changes, the company considers when to initiate price changes and when to respond to them.

We now examine the major dynamic pricing strategies available to marketers. In turn, we look at *new-product pricing strategies* for products in the introductory stage of the product life cycle, *product mix pricing strategies* for related products in the product mix, *price-adjustment strategies* that account for customer differences and changing situations, and strategies for initiating and responding to *price changes*.

New-Product Pricing Strategies

Pricing strategies usually change as the product passes through its life cycle. The introductory stage is especially challenging. Companies bringing out a new product face the challenge of setting prices for the first time. They can choose between two broad strategies: *market-skimming pricing* and *market-penetration pricing*.

Market-skimming pricing
Setting a high price for a new product to skim maximum revenues layer by layer from the segments willing to pay the high price; the company makes fewer but more profitable sales.

MARKET-SKIMMING PRICING

Many companies that invent new products set high initial prices to "skim" revenues layer by layer from the market. Sony frequently uses this strategy, called **market-skimming pricing**. When Sony introduced the world's first high-definition television (HDTV) to the Japanese market in 1990, the high-tech sets cost $43,000. These televisions were purchased only by customers who could afford to pay a high price for the new technology. Sony rapidly reduced the price over the next several years to attract new buyers. By 1993 a 28-inch HDTV cost a Japanese buyer just over $6,000. In 2001, a Japanese consumer could buy a 40-inch HDTV for about $2,000, a price that many more customers could afford. An entry-level HDTV set now sells for less than $1,000 in the United States, and prices continue to fall. In this way, Sony skimmed the maximum amount of revenue from the various segments of the market.[13]

Market skimming makes sense only under certain conditions. First, the product's quality and image must support its higher price, and enough buyers must want the product at that price. Second, the costs of producing a smaller volume cannot be so high that they cancel the advantage of charging more. Finally, competitors should not be able to enter the market easily and undercut the high price.

MARKET-PENETRATION PRICING

Rather than setting a high initial price to skim off small but profitable market segments, some companies use **market-penetration pricing**. They set a low initial price in order to *penetrate* the market quickly and deeply—to attract a large number of buyers quickly and win a large market share. The high sales volume results in falling costs, allowing the company to cut its price even further. For example, Wal-Mart and other discount retailers use penetration pricing. And Dell used penetration pricing to enter the personal computer market, selling high-quality computer products through lower-cost direct channels. Its sales soared when IBM, Apple, and other competitors selling through retail stores could not match its prices.

■ Market-skimming pricing: Sony priced its early HDTVs high, then reduced prices gradually over the years to attract new buyers.

Market-penetration pricing
Setting a low price for a new product in order to attract a large number of buyers and a large market share.

Several conditions must be met for this low-price strategy to work. First, the market must be highly price sensitive so that a low price produces more market growth. Second, production and distribution costs must fall as sales volume increases. Finally, the low price must help keep out the competition, and the penetration pricer must maintain its low-price position—otherwise, the price advantage may be only temporary. For example, Dell faced difficult times when IBM and other competitors established their own direct distribution channels. However, through its dedication to low production and distribution costs, Dell has retained its price advantage and established itself as the industry's number-one personal computer maker.

Product Mix Pricing Strategies

The strategy for setting a product's price often has to be changed when the product is part of a product mix. In this case, the firm looks for a set of prices that maximizes the profits on the total product mix. Pricing is difficult because the various products have related demand and costs and face different degrees of competition. We now take a closer look at the five product mix pricing situations summarized in Table 9.1: *product line pricing, optional-product pricing, captive-product pricing, by-product pricing,* and *product bundle pricing.*

PRODUCT LINE PRICING

Product line pricing
Setting the price steps between various products in a product line based on cost differences between the products, customer evaluations of different features, and competitors' prices.

Companies usually develop product lines rather than single products. For example, Snapper makes many different lawn mowers, ranging from simple walk-behind versions starting at $349.00, to elaborate "Yard Cruisers" and lawn tractors priced at $2,200 or more. Each successive lawn mower in the line offers more features. Sony offers not just one type of television, but several lines of televisions, each containing many models. It offers everything from Trinitrons starting at $179 to its top-of-the-line plasma WEGA flat-panel sets priced as high as $20,000. And Gramophone makes a complete line of high-quality sound systems, ranging in price from $5,000 to $120,000. In **product line pricing**, management must decide on the price steps to set between the various products in a line.

The price steps should take into account cost differences between the products in the line, customer evaluations of their different features, and competitors' prices. In many industries, sellers use well-established *price points* for the products in their line. Thus, men's clothing stores might carry men's suits at three price levels: $185, $325, and $495. The customer will probably associate low-, average-, and high-quality suits with the three price points. Even if the three prices are raised a little, men normally will buy suits at their own preferred price points. The seller's task is to establish perceived quality differences that support the price differences.

■ Product line pricing. Gramophone sells a complete line of high quality sound systems, ranging in price from $5,000 to $120,000.

OPTIONAL-PRODUCT PRICING

Optional-product pricing
The pricing of optional or accessory products along with a main product.

Many companies use **optional-product pricing** —offering to sell optional or accessory products along with their main product. For example, a car buyer may choose to order power windows and a CD changer. Refrigerators come with optional ice makers.

Pricing these options is a sticky problem. Automobile companies have to decide which items to include in the base price and which to offer as options. Until recent years, GM's normal pricing strategy was to advertise a stripped-down model at a base price to pull people into showrooms and then to devote most of the showroom space to showing option-loaded cars at

TABLE 9.1
Product Mix Pricing Strategies

Strategy	Description
Product line pricing	Setting price steps between product line items
Optional-product pricing	Pricing optional or accessory products sold with the main product
Captive-product pricing	Pricing products that must be used with the main product
By-product pricing	Pricing low-value by-products to get rid of them
Product bundle pricing	Pricing bundles of products sold together

higher prices. The economy model was stripped of so many comforts and conveniences that most buyers rejected it. Then, GM and other U.S. automakers followed the example of the Japanese and German automakers and included in the sticker price many useful items previously sold only as options. Most advertised prices today represent a well-equipped car.

CAPTIVE-PRODUCT PRICING

Companies that make products that must be used along with a main product are using **captive-product pricing**. Examples of captive products are razor blades, video games, and printer cartridges. Producers of the main products (razors, video game consoles, and printers) often price them low and set high markups on the supplies. Thus, Gillette sells low-priced razors but makes money on the replacement cartridges. HP makes very low margins on its printers but very high margins on printer cartridges and other supplies. Sony and other video game makers sell game consoles at low prices and obtain the majority of their profits from the video games. Last year alone, total industry sales of consoles were $2.4 billion, compared with total games sales of nearly $10 billion.[14]

Captive-product pricing
Setting a price for products that must be used along with a main product, such as blades for a razor and film for a camera.

In the case of services, this strategy is called *two-part pricing*. The price of the service is broken into a *fixed fee* plus a *variable usage rate*. Thus, amusement parks charge admission plus fees for food, midway attractions, and rides over a minimum. Theaters charge admission, then generate additional revenues from concessions. And cell phone companies charge a flat rate for a basic calling plan, then charge for minutes over what the plan allows. The service firm must decide how much to charge for the basic service and how much for the variable usage. The fixed amount should be low enough to induce usage of the service; profit can be made on the variable fees.

■ Captive-product pricing: HP makes very low margins on its printers but very high margins on printer cartridges and other supplies.

BY-PRODUCT PRICING

In producing processed meats, petroleum products, chemicals, and other products, there are often by-products. If the by-products have no value and if getting rid of them is costly, this will affect the pricing of the main product. Using **by-product pricing**, the manufacturer will seek a market for these by-products and should accept any price that covers more than the cost of storing and delivering them.

By-products can even turn out to be profitable. For example, papermaker MeadWestvaco has turned what was once considered chemical waste into profit-making products.

By-product pricing
Setting a price for by-products in order to make the main product's price more competitive.

> MeadWestvaco created a separate company, Asphalt Innovations, which creates useful chemicals entirely from the by-products of MeadWestvaco's wood-processing activities. In fact, Asphalt Innovations has grown to become the world's biggest supplier of specialty chemicals for the paving industry. Using the salvaged chemicals, paving companies can pave roads at a lower temperature, create longer-lasting roads, and more easily recycle road materials when roads need to be replaced. What's more, salvaging the by-product chemicals eliminates the costs and environmental hazards once associated with disposing of them.[15]

Sometimes, companies don't realize how valuable their by-products are. For example, most zoos don't realize that one of their by-products—their occupants' manure—can be an excellent source of additional revenue. But the Zoo Doo Compost Company has helped many zoos understand the costs and opportunities involved with these by-products. Zoo Doo

WOODLAND PARK ZOO DOO™

Woodland Park Zoo Doo™ is a rich, sweet-smelling compost made from the manure and bedding materials (straw, sawdust, etc.) from the zoo's herbivorous (plant-eating) animals.

It's not just compost . . . it's a movement.

www.zoo.org

SEATTLE

■ By-products can be profitable: Woodland Park Zoo in Seattle sponsors annual Fecal Fests, selling processed manure by the trash can and truck load to lucky lottery winners. "It's not just compost . . . it's a movement."

licenses its name to zoos and receives royalties on manure sales. So far, novelty sales have been the largest segment, with tiny containers of Zoo Doo (and even "Love, Love Me Doo" valentines) available in 160 zoo stores and 700 additional retail outlets. You can also buy Zoo Doo products online ("the easiest way to buy our crap," says Zoo Doo) or even send a friend (or perhaps a foe) a free Poopy Greeting via e-mail. Other zoos sell their by-products on their own. For example, the Woodland Park Zoo in Seattle sponsors annual Fecal Fests, selling processed manure by the trash can and truckload to lucky lottery winners. In all, the zoo creates 1 million pounds of compost each year, saving $60,000 a year in disposal costs.[16]

PRODUCT BUNDLE PRICING

Product bundle pricing
Combining several products and offering the bundle at a reduced price.

Using **product bundle pricing**, sellers often combine several of their products and offer the bundle at a reduced price. For example, fast-food restaurants bundle a burger, fries, and a soft drink at a combo price. Theaters and sports teams sell season tickets at less than the cost of single tickets. Resorts sell specially priced vacation packages that include airfare, accommodations, meals, and entertainment. And computer makers include attractive software packages with their personal computers. Price bundling can promote the sales of products consumers might not otherwise buy, but the combined price must be low enough to get them to buy the bundle.[17]

Price-Adjustment Strategies

Companies usually adjust their basic prices to account for various customer differences and changing situations. Here we examine the seven price adjustment strategies summarized in Table 9.2: *discount and allowance pricing, segmented pricing, psychological pricing, promotional pricing, geographical pricing, dynamic pricing,* and *international pricing*.

DISCOUNT AND ALLOWANCE PRICING

Most companies adjust their basic price to reward customers for certain responses, such as early payment of bills, volume purchases, and off-season buying. These price adjustments—called *discounts* and *allowances*—can take many forms.

Discount
A straight reduction in price on purchases during a stated period of time.

The many forms of **discounts** include a *cash discount*, a price reduction to buyers who pay their bills promptly. A typical example is "2/10, net 30," which means that although payment is due within 30 days, the buyer can deduct 2 percent if the bill is paid within 10 days. A *quantity discount* is a price reduction to buyers who buy large vol-

TABLE 9.2
Price Adjustment Strategies

Strategy	Description
Discount and allowance pricing	Reducing prices to reward customer responses such as paying early or promoting the product
Segmented pricing	Adjusting prices to allow for differences in customers, products, or locations
Psychological pricing	Adjusting prices for psychological effect
Promotional pricing	Temporarily reducing prices to increase short-run sales
Geographical pricing	Adjusting prices to account for the geographic location of customers
Dynamic pricing	Adjusting prices continually to meet the characteristics and needs of individual customers and situations
International pricing	Adjusting prices for international markets

umes. Such discounts provide an incentive to the customer to buy more from one given seller, rather than from many different sources.

A *functional discount* (also called a *trade discount*) is offered by the seller to trade-channel members who perform certain functions, such as selling, storing, and record keeping. A *seasonal discount* is a price reduction to buyers who buy merchandise or services out of season. For example, lawn and garden equipment manufacturers offer seasonal discounts to retailers during the fall and winter months to encourage early ordering in anticipation of the heavy spring and summer selling seasons. Seasonal discounts allow the seller to keep production steady during an entire year.

Allowances are another type of reduction from the list price. For example, *trade-in allowances* are price reductions given for turning in an old item when buying a new one. Trade-in allowances are most common in the automobile industry but are also given for other durable goods. *Promotional allowances* are payments or price reductions to reward dealers for participating in advertising and sales support programs.

Allowance

Promotional money paid by manufacturers to retailers in return for an agreement to feature the manufacturer's products in some way.

SEGMENTED PRICING

Companies will often adjust their basic prices to allow for differences in customers, products, and locations. In **segmented pricing**, the company sells a product or service at two or more prices, even though the difference in prices is not based on differences in costs.

Segmented pricing takes several forms. Under *customer-segment* pricing, different customers pay different prices for the same product or service. Museums, for example, may charge a lower admission for students and senior citizens. Under *product-form pricing*, different versions of the product are priced differently but not according to differences in their costs. For instance, the most expensive Cuisinart coffee maker is priced at $149.99, which is $20 more than the price of the next most expensive Cuisinart coffee maker. The top model contains an internal grinder, yet this extra feature costs only a few more dollars to make.

Segmented pricing

Selling a product or service at two or more prices, where the difference in prices is not based on differences in costs.

Using *location pricing*, a company charges different prices for different locations, even though the cost of offering each location is the same. For instance, theaters vary their seat prices because of audience preferences for certain locations, and state universities charge higher tuition for out-of-state students. Finally, using *time pricing*, a firm varies its price by the season, the month, the day, and even the hour. Some public utilities vary their prices to commercial users by time of day and weekend versus weekday. Resorts give weekend and seasonal discounts.

Segmented pricing goes by many names. Robert Cross, a longtime consultant to the airlines, calls it *revenue management*. According to Cross, the practice ensures that "companies will sell the right product to the right consumer at the right time for the right price." Airlines, hotels, and restaurants call it *yield management* and practice it religiously. The airlines, for example, routinely set prices hour-by-hour—even minute-by-minute—depending on seat availability, demand, and competitor price changes.

Continental Airlines launches more than 3,000 flights every day. Each flight has between 10 and 20 prices. Continental starts booking flights 330 days in advance, and every flying day is different from every other flying day. As a result, at any given moment, Continental may have nearly 7 million prices in the market. It's a daunting marketing task—all of those prices need to be managed, all of the time. For Continental, setting prices is a complex process of balancing demand and customer satisfaction against company profitability.[18]

The airlines know full well that we are puzzled by the frantic pricing and repricing that they do—puzzled, that is, when we aren't infuriated. "I do not set the prices," says Jim Compton, senior vice president of pricing and revenue management at Continental Airlines. "The market sets prices." That's point one. Point two: "I have a really perishable product. It's gone when the door of the plane closes. An empty seat is lost revenue." The most valuable airline seat is the one that somebody must have an hour before takeoff and is willing to pay almost any price for. An airline seat gets more profitable with time—right up to the moment it goes from being worth $1,000 one-way to being worth $0.

■ Segmented pricing: At any given moment, Continental may have nearly 7 million prices in the market. All of those prices need to be managed, all of the time.

Here's how Compton and his colleagues think about this: You want to sell every seat on the plane, except that you also want to have a handful left at the very end, for your most profitable (not to mention most grateful) customers. The airlines could easily sell out every seat, every flight, every day. They'd price 'em pretty low, book 'em up, and wait for takeoff. But that would mean there'd never be any seats available two or three weeks before a flight took off. How exasperated would customers be to call and find no seats three days out? When you understand that dilemma, all of a sudden, airline prices don't seem so exploitive. Although all of the seats on that New York–Miami flight are going to the same place, they aren't the same product. You pay less when you commit to a ticket four weeks in advance; Continental assumes a risk for holding a seat until the end—and wants to be paid a lot to balance the times when saving that last seat for you means that the seat flies empty.

For segmented pricing to be an effective strategy, certain conditions must exist. The market must be segmentable, and the segments must show different degrees of demand. The costs of segmenting and watching the market cannot exceed the extra revenue obtained from the price difference. Of course, the segmented pricing must also be legal. Most importantly, segmented prices should reflect real differences in customers' perceived value. Otherwise, in the long run, the practice will lead to customer resentment and ill will.

PSYCHOLOGICAL PRICING

Price says something about the product. For example, many consumers use price to judge quality. A $100 bottle of perfume may contain only $3 worth of scent, but some people are willing to pay the $100 because this price indicates something special.

Psychological pricing

A pricing approach that considers the psychology of prices and not simply the economics; the price is used to say something about the product.

In using **psychological pricing**, sellers consider the psychology of prices and not simply the economics. For example, consumers usually perceive higher-priced products as having higher quality. When they can judge the quality of a product by examining it or by calling on past experience with it, they use price less to judge quality. But when they cannot judge quality because they lack the information or skill, price becomes an important quality signal:

Some years ago, Heublein produced Smirnoff, then America's leading vodka brand. Smirnoff was attacked by another brand, Wolfschmidt, which claimed to have the same quality as Smirnoff but was priced at one dollar less per bottle. To hold on to market share, Heublein considered either lowering Smirnoff's price by one dollar or holding Smirnoff's price but increasing advertising and promotion expenditures. Either strategy would lead to lower profits, and it seemed that Heublein faced a no-win situation. At this point, however, Heublein's marketers thought of a third strategy. They *raised* the price of Smirnoff by one dollar! Heublein then introduced a new brand, Relska, to compete with Wolfschmidt. Moreover, it introduced yet another brand, Popov, priced even *lower* than Wolfschmidt. This clever strategy positioned Smirnoff as the elite brand and Wolfschmidt as an ordinary brand, producing a large increase in Heublein's overall profits. The irony is that Heublein's three brands were pretty much the same in taste and manufacturing costs. Heublein knew that a product's price signals its quality. Using price as a signal, Heublein sold roughly the same product at three different quality positions.

■ Psychological pricing: What do the prices marked on this tag suggest about the product and buying solution

Another aspect of psychological pricing is **reference prices**—prices that buyers carry in their minds and refer to when looking at a given product. The reference price might be formed by noting current prices, remembering past prices, or assessing the buying situation. Sellers can influence or use these consumers' reference prices when setting price. For example, a company could display its product next to more expensive ones in order to imply that it belongs in the same class. Department stores often sell women's clothing in separate departments differentiated by price: Clothing found in the more expensive department is assumed to be of better quality.

For most purchases, consumers don't have all the skill or information they need to figure out whether they are paying a good price. They don't have the time, ability, or inclination to research different brands or stores, compare prices, and get the best deals. Instead, they may rely on certain cues that signal whether a price is high or low. For example, the fact that a product is sold in a prestigious department store might signal that it's worth a higher price.

Interestingly, such pricing cues are often provided by sellers. A retailer might show a high manufacturer's suggested price next to the marked price, indicating that the product was originally priced much higher. Or the retailer might sell a selection of familiar products for which consumers have accurate price knowledge at very low prices, suggesting that the store's prices on other, less familiar products are low as well. The use of such pricing cues has become a common marketing practice (see Marketing at Work 9.2).

Even small differences in price can signal product differences. Consider a stereo priced at $300 compared to one priced at $299.95. The actual price difference is only 5 cents, but the psychological difference can be much greater. For example, some consumers will see the $299.95 as a price in the $200 range rather than the $300 range. The $299.95 will more likely be seen as a bargain price, whereas the $300 price suggests more quality. Some psychologists argue that each digit has symbolic and visual qualities that should be considered in pricing. Thus, 8 is round and even and creates a soothing effect, whereas 7 is angular and creates a jarring effect.

Reference prices
Prices that buyers carry in their minds and refer to when they look at a given product.

PROMOTIONAL PRICING

With **promotional pricing**, companies will temporarily price their products below list price and sometimes even below cost to create buying excitement and urgency. Promotional pricing takes several forms. Supermarkets and department stores will price a few products as *loss leaders* to attract customers to the store in the hope that they will buy other items at normal markups. For example, supermarkets often sell disposable diapers at less than cost in order to attract family buyers who make larger average purchases per trip. Sellers will also use *special-event pricing* in certain seasons to draw more customers. Thus, linens are promotionally priced every January to attract weary Christmas shoppers back into stores.

Manufacturers sometimes offer *cash rebates* to consumers who buy the product from dealers within a specified time; the manufacturer sends the rebate directly to the customer. Rebates have been popular with automakers and producers of durable goods and small appliances, but they are also used with consumer packaged goods. Some

Promotional pricing
Temporarily pricing products below the list price, and sometimes even below cost, to increase short-run sales.

MARKETING AT WORK   9.2

Quick, What's a Good Price for. . . ? We'll Give You a Cue.

It's Saturday morning and you stop by your local supermarket to pick up a few items for tonight's backyard barbeque. Cruising the aisles, you're bombarded with price signs, all suggesting that you just can't beat this store's deals. A 10-pound bag of Kingsford Charcoal Briquets goes for only $3.99 with your frequent shopper card ($4.39 without the card). Cans of Van Camp's Pork & Beans are 4 for $1.00 (4 for $2.16 without the card). An aisle display hawks big bags of Utz potato chips at an "everyday low price" of just $1.99. And a sign atop a huge mass of Coke 12-packs advertises 2 for $7.

These sure look like good prices, but *are* they? If you're like most shoppers, you don't really know. In a recent *Harvard Business Review* article, two pricing researchers conclude, "for most of the items they buy, consumers don't have an accurate sense of what the price should be." In fact, customers often don't even know what prices they're actually paying. In one recent study, researchers asked supermarket shoppers the price of an item just as they were putting it into their shopping carts. Less than half the shoppers gave the right answer.

To know for sure if you're paying the best price, you'd have to compare the marked price to past prices, prices of competing brands, and prices in other stores. For most purchases, consumers just don't bother. Instead, they rely on a most unlikely source. "Remarkably, . . . they rely on the retailer to tell them if they're getting a good price," say the researchers. "In subtle and not-so-subtle ways, retailers send signals [or pricing cues] to customers, telling them whether a given price is relatively high or low." In their article, the researchers outline the following common retailer pricing cues.

- *Sale Signs* The most straightforward retail pricing cue is a sale sign. It might take any of several familiar forms: "Sale!" "Reduced!" "New low price!" "Price after rebate!" or "Now 2 for only. . .!" Such signs can be very effective in signaling low prices to consumers and increasing sales for the retailer. The researchers' studies in retail stores and mail-order catalogs reveal that using the word "sale" beside a price (even without actually varying the price) can increase demand by more than 50 percent.

  While sales signs can be effective, overuse or misuse can damage both the seller's credibility and its sales. Unfortunately, some retailers don't always use such signs truthfully. Still, consumers trust sale signs. Why? "Because they are accurate most of the time," say the researchers. "And besides, customers are not that easily fooled." They quickly become suspicious when sale signs are used improperly.

- *Prices Ending in 9* Just like a sale sign, a 9 at the end of a price often signals a bargain. You see such prices everywhere. For example, browse the Web sites of discounters such as Target, Best Buy, or PETsMART: It's almost impossible to find even one price that *doesn't* end in 9 (really, try it!). "In fact, this pricing tactic is so common," say the researchers, "you'd think customers would ignore it. Think again. Response to this pricing cue is remarkable." Normally, you'd expect that demand for an item will fall as the price goes up. Yet in one study involving women's clothing, raising the price of a

dress from $34 to $39 *increased* demand by a third. By comparison, raising the price from $34 to $44 yielded no difference in demand.

  But are prices ending in *9* accurate as pricing cues? "The answer varies," the researchers report. "Some retailers do reserve prices that end in 9 for their discounted items. For instance, J. Crew and Ralph Lauren generally use 00-cent endings on regularly priced merchandise and 99-cent endings on discounted items. Comparisons of prices at major department stores reveal that this is common, particularly for apparel. But at some stores, prices that end in *9* are a miscue—they are used on all products regardless of whether the items are discounted."

- *Signpost Pricing (or Loss-Leader Pricing)* Unlike sale signs or prices that end in *9*, signpost pricing is used on frequently purchased products about which consumers tend to have accurate price knowledge. For example, you probably know a good price on a 12-pack of Coke when you see one. New parents usually know how much they should expect to pay for disposable diapers. Research suggests that customers use the prices of such "signpost" items to gauge a store's overall prices. If a store has a good price on Coke or Pampers or Tide, they reason, it probably also has good prices on other items.

  Retailers have long known the importance of signpost pricing, often called "loss-leader pricing." They offer selected signpost items at or below cost to pull customers into the store, hoping to make money on the shopper's other purchases.

manufacturers offer *low-interest financing*, *longer warranties*, or *free maintenance* to reduce the consumer's "price." This practice has become a favorite of the auto industry. Or, the seller may simply offer *discounts* from normal prices to increase sales and reduce inventories.

Promotional pricing, however, can have adverse effects. Used too frequently and copied by competitors, price promotions can create "deal-prone" customers who wait until brands go on sale before buying them. Or, constantly reduced prices can erode a brand's

For instance, Best Buy often sells recently released DVDs at several dollars below wholesale price. Customers get a really good deal. And although Best Buy loses money on every DVD sold, the low DVD prices increase store traffic and purchases of higher-margin complementary products, such as DVD players.

■ *Pricing-Matching Guarantees* Another widely used retail pricing cue is price matching, whereby stores promise to meet or beat any competitor's price. Best Buy, for example, says "we'll meet or beat any local competitor's price, guaranteed!" If you find a better price within 30 days on something you bought at Best Buy, the retailer will refund the difference plus 10 percent. Tweeter, a New England consumer-electronics retailer, even offers a self-enforced price-matching policy. When Tweeter finds a competitor advertising a lower advertised price, it mails a check for the difference to any customers who paid a higher price at Tweeter in the previous 30 days.

Evidence suggests that customers perceive that stores offering price-matching guarantees have overall lower prices than competing stores, especially in markets where they perceive price comparisons to be relatively easy. But are such perceptions accurate? "The evidence is mixed," say the researchers. Consumers can usually be confident that they'll pay the lowest price on eligible items. However, some manufacturers make it hard to take advantage of price-matching policies by introducing "branded variants"—slightly different versions of products with different model numbers for different retailers. "When Tweeter introduced its highly effective automatic price-matching policy," the

■ *Pricing cues such as sales signs and prices ending in 9 can be effective in signaling low prices to consumers and increasing sales for the retailer.*

researchers note, "only 6 percent of its transactions were actually eligible for refunds." At a broader level, some pricing experts argue that price-matching policies are not really targeted at customers. Rather, they may serve as a warning to competitors: "If you cut your prices, we will, too." If this is true, price-matching policies might actually reduce price competition, leading to higher overall prices.

Used properly, pricing cues can help consumers. Careful buyers really can take advantage of signals such as sale signs, 9-endings, loss leaders, and price guarantees to locate good deals. Used improperly, however, these pricing cues can mislead consumers, tarnishing a brand and damaging customer relationships.

The researchers conclude: "Customers need price information, just as they need products.

They look to retailers to provide both. Retailers must manage pricing cues in the same way that they manage quality. . . . No retailer . . . interested in [building profitable long-term relationships with customers] would purposely offer a defective product. Similarly, no retailer who [values customers] would deceive them with inaccurate pricing cues. By reliably signaling which prices are low, companies can retain customers' trust—and [build more solid relationships]."

Sources: Quotes and other information from Eric Anderson and Duncan Simester, "Mind Your Pricing Cues," *Harvard Business Review,* September 2003, pp. 96–103. Also see Joydeep Srivastava and Nicholas Lurie, "Price-Matching Guarantees as Signals of Low Store Prices: Survey and Experimental Evidence," *Journal of Retailing* 2004; and Michael J. Barone, Kenneth C. Manning, and Paul W. Minard, "Consumer Response to Retailers' Use of Partially Comparative Pricing," *Journal of Marketing,* July 2004, pp. 37–47.

value in the eyes of customers. Marketers sometimes use price promotions as a quick fix instead of sweating through the difficult process of developing effective longer-term strategies for building their brands. In fact, one observer notes that price promotions can be downright addicting to both the company and the customer: "Price promotions are the brand equivalent of heroin: easy to get into but hard to get out of. Once the brand and its customers are addicted to the short-term high of a price cut it is hard to wean them away to real brand building. . . . But continue and the brand dies by 1,000 cuts."[19]

■ Promotional pricing: Companies offer promotional prices to create buying excitement and urgency.

The frequent use of promotional pricing can also lead to industry price wars. Such price wars usually play into the hands of only one or a few competitors—those with the most efficient operations. For example, until recently, the computer industry avoided price wars. Computer companies, including IBM, HP, and Gateway, showed strong profits as their new technologies were snapped up by eager consumers. When the market cooled, however, many competitors began to unload PCs at discounted prices. In response, Dell, the industry's undisputed low-cost leader, started a brutal price war that only it could win. The result was nothing short of a rout. IBM has since sold off its PC unit, and HP continues to struggle for profitability, with PC profit margins averaging just 1 percent compared to Dell's 6 percent. Dell has emerged atop the worldwide PC industry.[20]

The point is that promotional pricing can be an effective means of generating sales for some companies in certain circumstances. But it can be damaging for other companies if taken as a steady diet.

Linking the Concepts

Here's a good place to take a brief break. Think about some of the companies and industries you deal with that are "addicted" to promotional pricing.

■ Many industries have created "deal-prone" consumers through the heavy use of promotional pricing—fast food, automobiles, airlines, tires, furniture, and others. Pick a company in one of these industries and suggest ways that it might deal with this problem.

■ How does the concept of value relate to promotional pricing? Does promotional pricing add to or detract from customer value?

GEOGRAPHICAL PRICING

A company also must decide how to price its products for customers located in different parts of the country or world. Should the company risk losing the business of more distant customers by charging them higher prices to cover the higher shipping costs? Or should the company charge all customers the same prices regardless of location? We will look at five **geographical pricing** strategies for the following hypothetical situation:

Geographical pricing
Setting price based on the buyer's geographic location.

The Peerless Paper Company is located in Atlanta, Georgia, and sells paper products to customers all over the United States. The cost of freight is high and affects the companies from whom customers buy their paper. Peerless wants to establish a geographical pricing policy. It is trying to determine how to price a $100 order to three specific customers: Customer A (Atlanta), Customer B (Bloomington, Indiana), and Customer C (Compton, California).

One option is for Peerless to ask each customer to pay the shipping cost from the Atlanta factory to the customer's location. All three customers would pay the same factory price of $100, with Customer A paying, say, $10 for shipping; Customer B, $15; and Customer C, $25. Called *FOB-origin pricing,* this practice means that the goods are placed *free on board* (hence, *FOB*) a carrier. At that point the title and responsibility pass to the customer, who pays the freight from the factory to the destination. Because each customer picks up its own cost, supporters of FOB pricing feel that this is the fairest way to assess freight charges. The disadvantage, however, is that Peerless will be a high-cost firm to distant customers.

Uniformed-delivered pricing is the opposite of FOB pricing. Here, the company charges the same price plus freight to all customers, regardless of their location. The freight charge is set at the average freight cost. Suppose this is $15. Uniform-delivered pricing, therefore, results in a higher charge to the Atlanta customer (who pays $15 freight instead of $10) and a lower charge to the Compton customer (who pays $15 instead of $25). Although the Atlanta customer would prefer to buy paper from another local paper company that uses FOB-origin pricing, Peerless has a better chance of winning over the California customer. Other advantages of uniform-delivered pricing are that it is fairly easy to administer and it lets the firm advertise its price nationally.

Zone pricing falls between FOB-origin pricing and uniform-delivered pricing. The company sets up two or more zones. All customers within a given zone pay a single total price; the more distant the zone, the higher the price. For example, Peerless might set up an East Zone and charge $10 freight to all customers in this zone, a Midwest Zone in which it charges $15, and a West Zone in which it charges $25. In this way, the customers within a given price zone receive no price advantage from the company. For example, customers in Atlanta and Boston pay the same total price to Peerless. The complaint, however, is that the Atlanta customer is paying part of the Boston customer's freight cost.

Using *basing-point pricing,* the seller selects a given city as a "basing point" and charges all customers the freight cost from that city to the customer location, regardless of the city from which the goods are actually shipped. For example, Peerless might set Chicago as the basing point and charge all customers $100 plus the freight from Chicago to their locations. This means that an Atlanta customer pays the freight cost from Chicago to Atlanta, even though the goods may be shipped from Atlanta. If all sellers used the same basing-point city, delivered prices would be the same for all customers and price competition would be eliminated. Industries such as sugar, cement, steel, and automobiles used basing-point pricing for years, but this method has become less popular today. Some companies set up multiple basing points to create more flexibility: They quote freight charges from the basing-point city nearest to the customer.

Finally, the seller who is anxious to do business with a certain customer or geographical area might use *freight-absorption pricing.* Using this strategy, the seller absorbs all or part of the actual freight charges in order to get the desired business. The seller might reason that if it can get more business, its average costs will fall and more than compensate for its extra freight cost. Freight-absorption pricing is used for market penetration and to hold on to increasingly competitive markets.

DYNAMIC PRICING

Throughout most of history, prices were set by negotiation between buyers and sellers. *Fixed-price* policies—setting one price for all buyers—is a relatively modern idea that arose with the development of large-scale retailing at the end of the nineteenth century. Today, most prices are set this way. However, some companies are now reversing the fixed-pricing trend. They are using **dynamic pricing**—adjusting prices continually to meet the characteristics and needs of individual customers and situations.

For example, think about how the Internet has affected pricing. From the mostly fixed pricing practices of the past century, the Web seems now to be taking us back—into a new age of fluid pricing. "Potentially, [the Internet] could push aside sticker prices and usher in

Dynamic pricing
Adjusting prices continually to meet the characteristics and needs of individual customers and situations.

an era of dynamic pricing," says one writer, "in which a wide range of goods would be priced according to what the market will bear—instantly, constantly."[21]

Dynamic pricing offers many advantages for marketers. For example, Internet sellers such as Amazon.com can mine their databases to gauge a specific shopper's desires, measure his or her means, instantaneously tailor products to fit that shopper's behavior, and price products accordingly. Catalog retailers such as L.L.Bean or Spiegel can change prices on the fly according to changes in demand or costs, changing prices for specific items on a day-by-day or even hour-by-hour basis. Online music retailer MusicRebellion.com lets consumer demand set the price for downloaded songs. Each song is initially available for download at $.10. As demand increases, however, prices may increase to $1 per song or more.[22]

Many direct marketers monitor inventories, costs, and demand at any given moment and adjust prices instantly. For example, Dell uses dynamic pricing to achieve real-time balancing of supply and demand for computer components. Author Thomas Friedman describes Dell's dynamic pricing system this way:[23]

> [Dell's] supply chain symphony—from my order over the phone to production to delivery to my house—is one of the wonders of the flat world. . . . Demand shaping goes on constantly. . . . It works like this: At 10 AM Austin time, Dell discovers that so many customers have ordered notebooks with 40-gigabyte hard drives since the morning that its supply chain will run short in two hours. That signal is automatically relayed to Dell's marketing department and to Dell.com and to all the Dell phone operators taking orders. If you happen to call to place your Dell order at 10:30 AM, the Dell representative will say to you, "Tom, it's your lucky Day! For the next hour we are offering 60-gigabyte hard drives with the notebook you want—for only $10 more than the 40-gig drive. And if you act now, Dell will throw in a carrying case along with your purchase, because we so value you as a customer." In an hour or two, using such promotions, Dell can reshape the demand for any part of any notebook or desktop to correspond with the projected supply in its global supply chain. Today memory might be on sale, tomorrow it might be CD-ROMs.

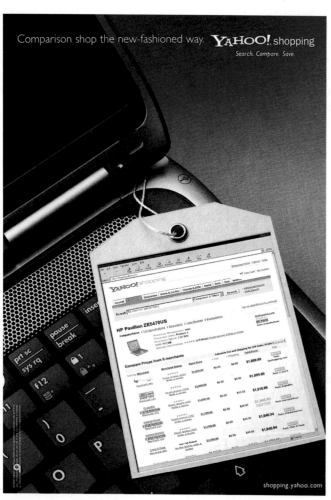

■ Buyers benefit from the Web and dynamic pricing. Sites like Yahoo! Shopping give instant product and price comparisons from thousands of vendors, arming customers with price information they need to get the lowest prices.

Buyers also benefit from the Web and dynamic pricing. A wealth of Web sites—such as Froogle.com, Yahoo! Shopping, BizRate.com, NexTag.com, epinion.com, PriceGrabber.com, mysimon.com, and PriceScan.com—give instant product and price comparisons from thousands of vendors. Yahoo! Shopping, for instance, lets shoppers browse by category or search for specific products and brands. It then searches the Web and reports back links to sellers offering the best prices. In addition to simply finding the vendor with the best price, customers armed with price information can often negotiate lower prices.

Buyers can also negotiate prices at online auction sites and exchanges. Suddenly the centuries-old art of haggling is back in vogue. Want to sell that antique pickle jar that's been collecting dust for generations? Post it on eBay, the world's biggest online flea market. Want to purchase vintage baseball cards at a bargain price? Go to HeavyHitter.com. Want to name your own price for a hotel room or rental car? Visit Priceline.com or another reverse auction site.

INTERNATIONAL PRICING

Companies that market their products internationally must decide what prices to charge in the different countries in which they operate. In some cases, a company can set a uniform worldwide price. For example, Boeing sells its jetliners at about the same price everywhere, whether in the United States, Europe, or a third-world country. However, most companies adjust their prices to reflect local market conditions and cost considerations.

The price that a company should charge in a specific country depends on many factors, including economic conditions, competitive situations, laws and regulations, and development of the wholesaling and retailing system. Consumer perceptions and preferences also may vary from country to country, calling for different prices. Or the company may have different marketing objectives in various world markets, which require changes in pricing strategy. For example, Samsung might introduce a new product into mature markets in highly developed countries with the goal of quickly gaining mass-market share—this would call for a penetration-pricing strategy. In contrast, it might enter a less developed market by targeting smaller, less price-sensitive segments; in this case, market-skimming pricing makes sense.

Costs play an important role in setting international prices. Travelers abroad are often surprised to find that goods that are relatively inexpensive at home may carry outrageously higher price tags in other countries. A pair of Levi's selling for $30 in the United States might go for $63 in Tokyo and $88 in Paris. A McDonald's Big Mac selling for a modest $2.90 here might cost $6.00 in Reykjavik, Iceland, and an Oral-B toothbrush selling for $2.49 at home may cost $10 in China. Conversely, a Gucci handbag going for only $140 in Milan, Italy, might fetch $240 in the United States. In some cases, such *price escalation* may result from differences in selling strategies or market conditions. In most instances, however, it is simply a result of the higher costs of selling in another country—the additional costs of product modifications, shipping and insurance, import tariffs and taxes, exchange-rate fluctuations, and physical distribution.

For example, Campbell Soup Company found that distribution in the United Kingdom cost 30 percent more than in the United States. U.S. retailers typically purchase soup in large quantities—48-can cases of a single soup by the dozens, hundreds, or carloads. In contrast, English grocers purchase soup in small quantities—typically in 24-can cases of *assorted* soups. Each case must be hand-packed for shipment. To handle these small orders, Campbell had to add a costly extra wholesale level to its European channel. The smaller orders also mean that English retailers order two or three times as often as their U.S. counterparts, bumping up billing and order costs. These and other factors caused Campbell Soup Company to charge much higher prices for its soups in the United Kingdom.[24]

Thus, international pricing presents some special problems and complexities. We discuss international pricing issues in more detail in Chapter 15.

Price Changes

After developing their pricing structures and strategies, companies often face situations in which they must initiate price changes or respond to price changes by competitors.

INITIATING PRICE CHANGES

In some cases, the company may find it desirable to initiate either a price cut or a price increase. In both cases, it must anticipate possible buyer and competitor reactions.

Initiating Price Cuts   Several situations may lead a firm to consider cutting its price. One such circumstance is excess capacity. Another is falling market share in the face of strong price competition. In such cases, the firm may aggressively cut prices to boost sales and share. But as the airline, fast-food, and other industries have learned in recent years, cutting prices in an industry loaded with excess capacity may lead to price wars as competitors try to hold on to market share.

A company may also cut prices in a drive to dominate the market through lower costs. Either the company starts with lower costs than its competitors, or it cuts prices in the hope of gaining market share that will further cut costs through larger volume. Bausch & Lomb used an aggressive low-cost, low-price strategy to become an early leader in the competitive soft contact lens market. And Dell used this strategy in the personal computer market.

Initiating Price Increases

A successful price increase can greatly increase profits. For example, if the company's profit margin is 3 percent of sales, a 1 percent price increase will increase profits by 33 percent if sales volume is unaffected. A major factor in price increases is cost inflation. Rising costs squeeze profit margins and lead companies to pass cost increases along to customers. Another factor leading to price increases is overdemand: When a company cannot supply all that its customers need, it may raise its prices, ration products to customers, or both.

When raising prices, the company must avoid being perceived as a price gouger. Customers have long memories, and they will eventually turn away from companies or even whole industries that they perceive as charging excessive prices. There are some techniques for avoiding this problem. One is to maintain a sense of fairness surrounding any price increase. Price increases should be supported by company communications telling customers why prices are being raised. Making low-visibility price moves first is also a good technique: some examples include dropping discounts, increasing minimum-order sizes, and curtailing production of low-margin products. The company sales force should help business customers find ways to economize.

Wherever possible, the company should consider ways to meet higher costs or demand without raising prices. For example, it can consider more cost-effective ways to produce or distribute its products. It can shrink the product or substitute less expensive ingredients instead of raising the price, as candy-bar manufacturers often do. Or it can "unbundle" its market offering, removing features, packaging, or services and separately pricing elements that were formerly part of the offer. IBM, for example, now offers training and consulting as separately priced services.

Buyer Reactions to Price Changes

Customers do not always interpret price changes in a straightforward way. They may view a price *cut* in several ways. For example, what would you think if Joy perfume, "the costliest fragrance in the world," were to cut its price in half? Or what if Sony suddenly cut its personal computer prices drastically? You might think that the computers are about to be replaced by newer models or that they have some fault and are not selling well. You might think that Sony is abandoning the computer business and may not stay in this business long enough to supply future parts. You might believe that quality has been reduced. Or you might think that the price will come down even further, and that it will pay to wait and see.

Similarly, a price *increase*, which would normally lower sales, may have some positive meanings for buyers. What would you think if Sony *raised* the price of its latest personal computer model? On the one hand, you might think that the item is very "hot" and may be unobtainable unless you buy it soon. Or you might think that the computer is an unusually good performer. On the other hand, you might think that Sony is greedy and charging what the traffic will bear.

Competitor Reactions to Price Changes

A firm considering a price change has to worry about the reactions of its competitors as well as those of its customers. Competitors are most likely to react when the number of

TEN PERFECTLY RATIONAL REASONS FOR WEARING THE COSTLIEST FRAGRANCE IN THE WORLD.

1. "JOY ADDS LENGTH TO MY LEGS, WIT TO MY CONVERSATION AND A BETTER ACCENT TO MY FRENCH."

2. "A SINGLE WHIFF OF JOY TURNS A RICH MAN INTO A GENEROUS MAN."

3. "JOY IS THAT RARE BOUQUET OF 10,400 JASMINE FLOWERS AND 28 DOZEN ROSES THAT NEVER NEEDS WATERING AND NEVER DIES."

4. "A DAB OF JOY ON MY CHECK WRITING WRIST HELPS THE ZEROS FLOW WITH EASE."

5. "MY 76 YEAR OLD GRANDMOTHER WEARS JOY, AND SHE'S LIVING WITH HER 28 YEAR OLD FENCING INSTRUCTOR."

6. "MY ANTIDOTE FOR BAD DAYS IS A SPLASH OF JOY AND A GLASS OF CHAMPAGNE. ON WORSE DAYS, I DOUBLE THE RECIPE."

7. "MONEY CAN'T BUY HAPPINESS, BUT IT CAN FILL THE CUPBOARDS WITH JOY."

8. "JOY BODY CREAM MAKES ME FEEL LIKE A MILLION WITHOUT SPENDING A MINT."

9. "A SPLASH OF JOY BEFORE COFFEE AND CORNFLAKES PUTS THE GLAMOUR BACK INTO BREAKFAST."

10. "I WEAR DIAMONDS BEFORE FIVE, BLACK BEFORE DARK AND JOY EAU DE TOILETTE BEFORE EVERYTHING."

The most precious flowers on earth are just a few of the things that make JOY the costliest fragrance in the world.

■ Buyer reactions to price changes: What would you think if the price of Joy was suddenly cut in half?

firms involved is small, when the product is uniform, and when the buyers are well informed about products and prices.

How can the firm anticipate the likely reactions of its competitors? The problem is complex because, like the customer, the competitor can interpret a company price cut in many ways. It might think the company is trying to grab a larger market share, or that it's doing poorly and trying to boost its sales. Or it might think that the company wants the whole industry to cut prices to increase total demand.

The company must guess each competitor's likely reaction. If all competitors behave alike, this amounts to analyzing only a typical competitor. In contrast, if the competitors do not behave alike—perhaps because of differences in size, market shares, or policies—then separate analyses are necessary. However, if some competitors will match the price change, there is good reason to expect that the rest will also match it.

RESPONDING TO PRICE CHANGES

Here we reverse the question and ask how a firm should respond to a price change by a competitor. The firm needs to consider several issues: Why did the competitor change the price? Is the price change temporary or permanent? What will happen to the company's market share and profits if it does not respond? Are other competitors going to respond? Besides these issues, the company must also consider its own situation and strategy and possible customer reactions to price changes.

Figure 9.5 shows the ways a company might assess and respond to a competitor's price cut. Suppose the company learns that a competitor has cut its price and decides that this price cut is likely to harm company sales and profits. It might simply decide to hold its current price and profit margin. The company might believe that it will not lose too much market share, or that it would lose too much profit if it reduced its own price. Or it might decide that it should wait and respond when it has more information on the effects of the competitor's price change. However, waiting too long to act might let the competitor get stronger and more confident as its sales increase.

If the company decides that effective action can and should be taken, it might make any of four responses. First, it could *reduce its price* to match the competitor's price. It may decide that the market is price sensitive and that it would lose too much market share to the lower-priced competitor. Cutting the price will reduce the company's profits in the short run. Some companies might also reduce their product quality, services, and marketing communications to retain profit margins, but this will ultimately hurt long-run market share. The company should try to maintain its quality as it cuts prices.

Alternatively, the company might maintain its price but *raise the perceived value* of its offer. It could improve its communications, stressing the relative value of its product over that

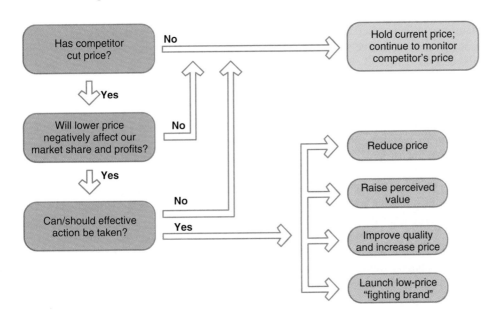

FIGURE 9.5

Assessing and Responding to Competitor Price Changes

The epitome of common sense.

Softest Ever!

Scott Tissue

1000 Sheets

UNSCENTED
BATHROOM TISSUE

*1000 sheets that last and last. Plus being our softest ever.
And not to get too highfalutin, but we think you'll find
that adds up to an uncommon value as well.*

Common Sense on a Roll.

■ Fighting brands: Kimberly-Clark offers its value-priced Scott brand as "the Bounty killer." It scores well on customer satisfaction but sells for a lower price than P&G's Bounty.

of the lower-price competitor. The firm may find it cheaper to maintain price and spend money to improve its perceived value than to cut price and operate at a lower margin. Or, the company might *improve quality and increase price*, moving its brand into a higher price-value position. The higher quality creates greater customer value which justifies the higher price. In turn, the higher price preserves the company's higher margins.

Finally, the company might *launch a low-price "fighting brand"*—adding a lower-price item to the line or creating a separate lower-price brand. This is necessary if the particular market segment being lost is price sensitive and will not respond to arguments of higher quality. Thus, when challenged on price by Southwest Airlines and JetBlue, Delta created low-fare Song airlines and United created Ted. To counter store brands and other low-price entrants, P&G turned a number of its brands into fighting brands, including Luvs disposable diapers, Joy dishwashing detergent, and Camay beauty soap. In turn, P&G-competitor Kimberly-Clark positions its value-priced Scott Towels brand as "the Bounty killer." It advertises Scott Towels as "Common Sense on a Roll." The brand scores well on customer satisfaction measures but sells for a lower price than P&G's Bounty brand. Scott Towels provide ample quantity and reliable quality and performance in every roll," says the company, "without the costly, unnecessary extras."[25]

Public Policy and Pricing

Price competition is a core element of our free-market economy. In setting prices, companies are not usually free to charge whatever prices they wish. Many federal, state, and even local laws govern the rules of fair play in pricing. In addition, companies must consider broader societal pricing concerns. The most important pieces of legislation affecting pricing are the Sherman, Clayton, and Robinson-Patman acts, initially adopted to curb the formation of monopolies and to regulate business practices that might unfairly restrain trade. Because these federal statutes can be applied only to interstate commerce, some states have adopted similar provisions for companies that operate locally.

Figure 9.6 shows the major public policy issues in pricing. These include potentially damaging pricing practices within a given level of the channel (price-fixing and predatory pricing) and across levels of the channel (retail price maintenance, discriminatory pricing, and deceptive pricing).[26]

PRICING WITHIN CHANNEL LEVELS

Federal legislation on *price-fixing* states that sellers must set prices without talking to competitors. Otherwise, price collusion is suspected. Price-fixing is illegal per se—that is, the government does not accept any excuses for price-fixing. Companies found guilty of such practices can receive heavy fines. For example, when the U.S. Justice Department found that Archer Daniels Midland Company and three of its competitors had met regularly in the early 1990s to illegally fix prices, the four companies paid more than $100 million to settle the charges. ADM paid an additional $400 million to settle related lawsuits brought by Coca-Cola, PepsiCo, and other customers who claimed they were damaged by the price-fixing.[27] Recently, governments at the state and national levels have been aggressively enforcing price-fixing regulations in industries ranging from gasoline, insurance, and credit cards to concrete and CDs.

Sellers are also prohibited from using *predatory pricing*—selling below cost with the intention of punishing a competitor or gaining higher long-run profits by putting competitors

FIGURE 9.6 Public Policy Issues in Pricing

Source: Adapted with permission from Dhruv Grewel and Larry D. Compeau, "Pricing and Public Policy: A Research Agenda and Overview of Special Issue," *Journal of Public Policy and Marketing,* Spring 1999, pp. 3–10, Figure 1.

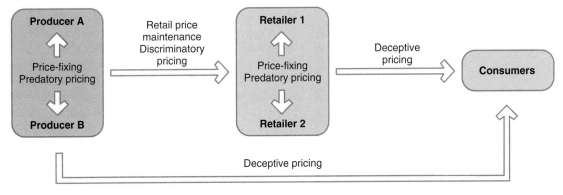

out of business. This protects small sellers from larger ones who might sell items below cost temporarily or in a specific locale to drive them out of business. The biggest problem is determining just what constitutes predatory-pricing behavior. Selling below cost to sell off excess inventory is not considered predatory; selling below cost to drive out competitors is. Thus, the same action may or may not be predatory depending on intent, and intent can be very difficult to determine or prove.

In recent years, several large and powerful companies have been accused of predatory pricing. For example, Wal-Mart has been sued by dozens of small competitors charging that it lowered prices in their specific areas to drive them out of business. In fact, the State of New York passed a bill requiring companies to price gas at or above 98 percent of cost to "address the more extreme cases of predatory pricing by big-box stores" like Wal-Mart. Yet, in North Dakota, the same gas pricing proposal was rejected because state representatives did not view the practice as predatory pricing.[28]

PRICING ACROSS CHANNEL LEVELS

The Robinson-Patman Act seeks to prevent unfair *price discrimination* by ensuring that sellers offer the same price terms to customers at a given level of trade. For example, every retailer is entitled to the same price terms from a given manufacturer, whether the retailer is Sears or your local bicycle shop. However, price discrimination is allowed if the seller can prove that its costs are different when selling to different retailers—for example, that it costs less per unit to sell a large volume of bicycles to Sears than to sell a few bicycles to the local dealer.

The seller can also discriminate in its pricing if the seller manufactures different qualities of the same product for different retailers. The seller has to prove that these differences are proportional. Price differentials may also be used to "match competition" in "good faith," provided the price discrimination is temporary, localized, and defensive rather than offensive.

Laws also prohibit *retail price maintenance*—a manufacturer cannot require dealers to charge a specified retail price for its product. Although the seller can propose a manufacturer's *suggested* retail price to dealers, it cannot refuse to sell to a dealer who takes independent pricing action, nor can it punish the dealer by shipping late or denying advertising allowances. For example, the Florida attorney general's office investigated Nike for allegedly fixing the retail price of its shoes and clothing. It was concerned that Nike might be withholding items from retailers who were not selling its most expensive shoes—like the Air Jordan and Shox lines—at prices the company considered suitable.[29]

Deceptive pricing occurs when a seller states prices or price savings that mislead consumers or are not actually available to consumers. This might involve bogus reference or comparison prices, as when a retailer sets artificially high "regular" prices then announces "sale" prices close to its previous everyday prices. For example, Overstock.com recently came under scrutiny for inaccurately listing manufacturer's suggested retail prices, often quoting them higher than the actual price. Such comparison pricing is widespread.

■ Deceptive pricing concerns: The widespread use of checkout scanners has led to increasing complaints of retailers overcharging their customers.

Comparison pricing claims are legal if they are truthful. However, the FTC's *Guides Against Deceptive Pricing* warns sellers not to advertise a price reduction unless it is a saving from the usual retail price, not to advertise "factory" or "wholesale" prices unless such prices are what they are claimed to be, and not to advertise comparable value prices on imperfect goods.[30]

Other deceptive pricing issues include *scanner fraud* and price confusion. The widespread use of scanner-based computer checkouts has led to increasing complaints of retailers overcharging their customers. Most of these overcharges result from poor management—from a failure to enter current or sale prices into the system. Other cases, however, involve intentional overcharges. *Price confusion* results when firms employ pricing methods that make it difficult for consumers to understand just what price they are really paying. For example, consumers are sometimes misled regarding the real price of a home mortgage or car leasing agreement. In other cases, important pricing details may be buried in the "fine print."

Many federal and state statutes regulate against deceptive pricing practices. For example, the Automobile Information Disclosure Act requires automakers to attach a statement to new-car windows stating the manufacturer's suggested retail price, the prices of optional equipment, and the dealer's transportation charges. However, reputable sellers go beyond what is required by law. Treating customers fairly and making certain that they fully understand prices and pricing terms is an important part of building strong and lasting customer relationships.

REST STOP → REVIEWING THE CONCEPTS

Before you put pricing in the rearview mirror, let's review the important concepts. *Price* can be defined as the sum of all the values that customers give up in order to gain the benefits of having or using a product or service. Pricing decisions are subject to an incredibly complex array of company, environmental, and competitive forces.

1. Discuss the importance of understanding customer value perceptions and company costs when setting prices.

Good pricing begins with a complete understanding of the value that a product or service creates for customers and setting a price that captures that value. The price the company charges will fall somewhere between one that is too high to produce any demand and one that is too low to produce a profit.

Customer perceptions of the product's value set the ceiling for prices. If customers perceive that the price is greater than the product's value, they will not buy the product. At the other extreme, company and product costs set the floor for prices. If the company prices the product below its costs, its profits will suffer.

Costs are an important consideration in setting prices. However, cost-based pricing is product driven. The company designs what it considers to be a good product and sets a price that covers costs plus a target profit. If the price turns out to be too high, the company must settle for lower markups or lower sales, both resulting in disappointing profits. Value-based pricing reverses this process. The company sets its target price based on customer perceptions of the product value. The targeted value and price then drive decisions about product design and what costs can be incurred. As a result, pricing begins with analyzing customer needs and value perceptions, and price is set to match customers' perceived value.

2. Identify and define the other important external and internal factors affecting a firm's pricing decisions.

Other *internal* factors that influence pricing decisions include the company's overall marketing strategy, objectives, mix, and organization for pricing. Price is only one element of the company's broader marketing strategy. If the company has selected its target market and positioning carefully, then its marketing mix strategy, including price, will be fairly straightforward. Some companies position their products on price and then tailor other marketing mix decisions to the prices they want to charge. Other companies deemphasize price and use other marketing mix tools to create *nonprice* positions.

Common pricing objectives might include survival, current profit maximization, market share leadership, or customer retention and relationship building. Price decisions must be coordinated with product design, distribution, and promotion decisions to form a consistent and effective marketing program. Finally, in order to coordinate pricing goals and decisions, management must decide who within the organization is responsible for setting price.

Other *external* pricing considerations include the nature of the market and demand, competitors' strategies and prices, and environmental factors such as the economy, reseller needs, and government actions. The seller's pricing freedom varies with different types of markets. Ultimately, the customer decides whether the company has set the right price. The customer weighs the price against the perceived values of using the product—if the price exceeds the sum of the values, consumers will not buy. So the company must understand concepts like demand curves (the price-demand relationship) and price elasticity (consumer sensitivity to prices). Consumers also compare a product's price to the prices of competitors' products. A company, therefore, must learn the customer value and prices of competitors' offers.

3. Describe the major strategies for pricing imitative and new products.

Pricing is a dynamic process. Companies design a *pricing structure* that covers all their products. They change this structure over time and adjust it to account for different customers and situations. Pricing strategies usually change as a product passes through its life cycle. In pricing innovative new products, it can follow a *skimming policy* by initially setting high prices to "skim" the maximum amount of revenue from various segments of the market. Or it can use *penetration pricing* by setting a low initial price to penetrate the market deeply and win a large market share.

4. Explain how companies find a set of prices that maximizes the profits from the total product mix.

When the product is part of a product mix, the firm searches for a set of prices that will maximize the profits from the total mix. In *product line pricing*, the company decides on price steps for the entire set of products it offers. In addition, the company must set prices for *optional products* (optional or accessory products included with the main product), *captive products* (products that are required for use of the main product), *by-products* (waste or residual products produced when

making the main product), and *product bundles* (combinations of products at a reduced price).

5. Discuss how companies adjust their prices to take into account different types of customers and situations.

Companies apply a variety of *price-adjustment strategies* to account for differences in consumer segments and situations. One is *discount and allowance pricing*, whereby the company establishes cash, quantity, functional, or seasonal discounts, or varying types of allowances. A second strategy is *segmented pricing*, whereby the company sells a product at two or more prices to accommodate different customers, product forms, locations, or times. Sometimes companies consider more than economics in their pricing decisions, using *psychological pricing* to better communicate a product's intended position. In *promotional pricing*, a company offers discounts or temporarily sells a product below list price as a special event, sometimes even selling below cost as a loss leader. Another approach is *geographical pricing*, whereby the company decides how to price to near and distant customers. *Dynamic pricing* involves adjusting prices continually to meet the characteristics and needs of individual customers and situations. Finally, *international pricing* means that the company adjusts its price to meet conditions and expectations in different world markets.

6. Discuss the key issues related to initiating and responding to price changes.

When a firm considers initiating a *price change*, it must consider customers' and competitors' reactions. There are different implications to *initiating price cuts* and *initiating price increases*. Buyer reactions to price changes are influenced by the meaning customers see in the price change. Competitors' reactions flow from a set reaction policy or a fresh analysis of each situation.

There are also many factors to consider in responding to a competitor's price changes. The company that faces a price change initiated by a competitor must try to understand the competitor's intent as well as the likely duration and impact of the change. If a swift reaction is desirable, the firm should preplan its reactions to different possible price actions by competitors. When facing a competitor's price change, the company might sit tight, reduce its own price, raise perceived value, improve quality and raise price, or launch a fighting brand.

Companies are not usually free to charge whatever prices they wish. Many federal, state, and even local laws govern the rules of fair play in pricing. The major public policy issues in pricing include potentially damaging pricing practices within a given level of the channel (price-fixing and predatory pricing) and across levels of the channel (retail price maintenance, discriminatory pricing, and deceptive pricing).

Navigating the Key Terms

Allowance (279)

Break-even pricing (target profit pricing) (267)

By-product pricing (277)

Captive-product pricing (277)

Cost-plus pricing (267)

Demand curve (272)

Discount (278)

Dynamic pricing (285)

Fixed costs (266)

Geographical pricing (284)

Good-value pricing (265)

Market-penetration pricing (275)

Market-skimming pricing (275)

Optional-product pricing (276)

Price (263)

Price elasticity (273)

Product bundle pricing (278)

Product line pricing (276)

Promotional pricing (281)

Psychological pricing (280)

Reference prices (281)

Segmented pricing (279)

Target costing (268)

Total costs (267)

Value-added pricing (265)

Value-based pricing (264)

Variable costs (266)

Travel Log

Discussing the Issues

1. Many companies have a difficult time with pricing. What mistakes do companies make when setting prices?

2. Explain the differences between value-based pricing and cost-based pricing. Under what conditions might a company favor one approach over the others?

3. Your major competitor has just cut its prices by 20 percent on all products. How should you react? What information do you need before you consider a response?

4. Review the geographical pricing strategies of FOB-origin pricing, uniform-delivered pricing, zone pricing, basing-point pricing, and freight absorption pricing. What factors influence the choice of a geographical pricing strategy?

5. Psychological pricing is a pricing-adjustment strategy often used by retailers. Explain this pricing strategy. How do reference prices affect psychological pricing decisions?

6. What difficulties might an international company encounter by setting uniform, worldwide prices for a commodity product?

Application Questions

1. "Give people something of value," says Ronald Shaich, CEO of Panera Bread Company, "and they'll happily pay for it." Do you agree? List three compact cars in different price ranges. How does each create customer value? How does the price correlate with that value? How do nonprice factors affect the cars' perceived values and actual costs?

2. Your company is about to launch a new brand of paper towels. The new towels are more absorbent and durable than current paper towels on the market. Your boss wants you to consider both market-skimming pricing and market-penetration pricing strategies. What factors should you consider in making your decision? Which strategy would you recommend?

3. How do price decisions affect the other three Ps? Select a product that you regularly buy. How does price impact your purchase decision for this product? How does it impact your perception of the brand? Does the company's pricing strategy help build a long-term relationship with you by creating value? Why or why not?

Under the Hood: Focus on Technology

Simply put, technology has changed the reality of pricing. With nearly 125 million personal computers and 180 million cell phone users in the United States, consumers have more access to information than ever before. Car buyers can obtain invoice prices and average sales prices in their communities from Web sites such as Wards.com. Sites like Streetprices.com, Nextag.com, and PriceScan.com allow consumers to quickly comparison shop for specific products at dozens of retailers, online and off. And consumers have instant access to pricing information almost anywhere they go. Buyers can even use their cell phones to compare prices right in the store. Within seconds of sending a text message with the 12-digit UPC code of an item to Google, a shopper can have a list of the best prices available from a host of retailers provided by Google's Froogle shopping

service. The result? For some manufacturers, the pressure to compete on the basis of price is almost insurmountable.*

1. Chances are good that you've used a price comparison Web site or Google's Froogle shopping service in making a purchase. How did the site impact your purchase decision? Did you select the retailer offering the lowest price? Why or why not?

2. How can marketers use cell phones and the Internet to their advantage when setting prices? How does consumers' ready access to pricing information impact marketers' pricing decisions?

* See Wendy Widman, "Web Search Hits the Streets," August 3, 2005, accessed at www.forbes.com.

Focus on Ethics

For movie theaters, restaurants, and even many airlines, segmented pricing is a central part of pricing strategies. Early bird specials, children's meals, and matinee prices all attract customers who might otherwise spend their dollars elsewhere. Consumers are usually pleased to benefit from such discounts and don't mind paying more for an evening showing of the latest movie. But for the pharmaceutical industry, segmented pricing has become a hotly contested issue. Rather than offering price breaks to certain income or age groups, the pharmaceutical industry has long offered different prices to consumers according to where in the world they live, often based on deals brokered with government agencies. Says one U.S. Congresswoman, "Americans pay the highest prescription-drug prices in the world—30 percent to 300 percent higher than abroad. Just across the border in Canada, for example, patients pay 50 percent to 80 percent less for the same brand-name drugs." Drug companies argue that research and development for a new, potentially life-saving drug, is expensive and that consumers that can afford to pay more should pay more.*

1. Is it ethical for pharmaceutical companies to segment markets and offer different prices based on government contracts? Is it ethical to alter prices based on the customer's ability to pay? What do you believe would be the most ethical pricing choice for drug companies to make?

2. How do the segment pricing strategies of pharmaceutical companies affect customer perceptions of value?

*See Anne M. Northup, "Importation and Prescription Prices," *Washington Times*, July 6, 2005, accessed at www.washingtontimes.com.

Videos

The Song video case that accompanies this chapter is located in Appendix 1 at the back of the book.

Marketing Channels and Supply Chain Management

Road Map Previewing the Concepts

We now arrive at the third marketing mix tool—distribution. Firms rarely work alone in creating value for customers and building profitable customer relationships. Instead, most are only a single link in a larger supply chain and distribution channel. As such, an individual firm's success depends not only on how well *it* performs but also on how well its *entire distribution channel* competes with competitors' channels. To be good at customer relationship management, a company must also be good at partner relationship management. The first part of this chapter explores the nature of distribution channels and the marketer's channel design and management decisions. We then examine physical distribution—or logistics—an area that is growing dramatically in importance and sophistication. In the next chapter, we'll look more closely at two major channel intermediaries—retailers and wholesalers.

While your engine's warming up, we'll take a close look at Caterpillar. You might think that Caterpillar's success, and its ability to charge premium prices, rests on the quality of the heavy construction and mining equipment that it produces. But Caterpillar sees things differently. The company's dominance, it claims, results from its unparalleled distribution and customer support system—from the strong and caring partnerships that it has built with independent Caterpillar dealers. Read on and see why.

For more than seven decades, Caterpillar has dominated the world's markets for heavy construction, mining, and logging equipment. Its familiar yellow tractors, crawlers, loaders, bulldozers, and trucks are a common sight at any construction area. Caterpillar sells more than 300 products in nearly 200 countries, generating sales of more than $30 billion annually. Last year, sales grew 33 percent; profits shot up 85 percent. It captures some 30 percent of the worldwide construction-equipment business, more than double that of number-two Komatsu. Its share of the North American market is more than twice that of competitors Komatsu and Deere combined.

Many factors contribute to Caterpillar's enduring success—high-quality products, flexible and efficient manufacturing, and a steady stream of innovative new products. Yet these are not the most important reasons for Caterpillar's dominance. Instead, Caterpillar credits its focus on customers and its corps of 200 outstanding independent dealers worldwide, who do a superb job of taking care of every customer need. According to former Caterpillar CEO Donald Fites:

After the product leaves our door, the dealers take over. They are the ones on the front line. They're the ones who live with the product for its lifetime. They're the ones customers see. . . . They're out there making sure that when a machine is delivered, it's in the condition it's supposed to be in. They're out there training a customer's operators. They service a product frequently throughout its life, carefully monitoring a machine's health and scheduling repairs to prevent costly downtime. The customer . . . knows that there is a [$30-billion-plus] company called Caterpillar. But the dealers create the image of a company that doesn't just stand *behind* its products but *with* its products, anywhere in the world. Our dealers are the reason that our motto—Buy the Iron, Get the Company—is not an empty slogan.

"Buy the Iron, Get the Company"—that's a powerful value proposition. It means that when you buy Cat equipment, you become a member of the Caterpillar family. Caterpillar and its dealers work in close harmony to find better ways to bring value to customers. Dealers play a vital role in almost every aspect of Caterpillar's operations, from product design and delivery, to product service and support, to market intelligence and customer feedback.

In the heavy-equipment industry, in which equipment downtime can mean big losses, Caterpillar's exceptional service gives it a huge advantage in winning and keeping customers. Consider Freeport-McMoRan, a Cat customer that operates one of the world's largest copper and gold mines, 24 hours a day, 365 days a year. High in the mountains of Indonesia, the mine is accessible only by aerial cableway or helicopter. Freeport-McMoRan relies on more than 500 pieces of Caterpillar mining and construction equipment—worth several hundred million dollars—including loaders, tractors, and mammoth 240-ton, 2,000-plus-horsepower trucks. Many of these machines cost well over $1 million apiece. When equipment breaks down, Freeport-McMoRan loses money fast. Freeport-McMoRan gladly pays a premium price for machines and service it can count on. It knows that it can count on Caterpillar and its outstanding distribution network for superb support.

The close working relationship between Caterpillar and its dealers comes down to more than just formal contracts and business agreements. The powerful partnership rests on a handful of basic principles and practices:

- *Dealer profitability:* Caterpillar's rule: "Share the gain as well as the pain." When times are good, Caterpillar shares the bounty with its dealers rather than trying to grab all the riches for itself. When times are bad, Caterpillar protects its dealers. In the mid-1980s, facing a depressed global construction-equipment market and cutthroat competition, Caterpillar sheltered its dealers by absorbing much of the economic damage. It lost almost $1 billion dollars in just three years but didn't lose a single dealer. In contrast, competitors' dealers struggled and many failed. As a result, Caterpillar emerged with its distribution system intact and its competitive position stronger than ever.

- *Extraordinary dealer support:* Nowhere is this support more apparent than in the company's parts delivery system, the fastest and most reliable in the industry. Caterpillar maintains 36 distribution centers and 1,500 service facilities around the world, which stock 320,000 different parts and ship 84,000 items per day, every day of the year. In turn, dealers have made huge investments in inventory, warehouses, fleets of trucks, service bays, diagnostic and service equipment, and information technology. Together, Caterpillar and its dealers guarantee parts delivery within 48 hours anywhere in the world. The company ships 80 percent of parts orders immediately and 99 percent on the same day the order is received. In contrast, it's not unusual for competitors' customers to wait four or five days for a part.

- *Communications:* Caterpillar communicates with its dealers—fully, frequently, and honestly. According to Fites, "There are no secrets between us and our dealers. We have the financial statements and key operating data of every dealer in the world. . . . In addition, virtually all Caterpillar and dealer employees have real-time access to continually updated databases of service information, sales trends and forecasts, customer satisfaction surveys, and other critical data."

- *Dealer performance:* Caterpillar does all it can to ensure that its dealerships are run well. It closely monitors each dealership's sales, market position, service capability, financial situation, and other performance measures. It genuinely wants each dealer to succeed, and when it sees a problem, it jumps in to help. As a result, Caterpillar dealerships, many of which are family businesses, tend to be stable and profitable.

- *Personal relationships:* In addition to more formal business ties, Cat forms close personal ties with its dealers in a kind of family relationship. One Caterpillar executive relates the following example: "When I see Chappy Chapman, a retired executive vice-president . . . , out on the golf course, he always asks about particular dealers or about their children, who may be running the business now. And every time I see those dealers, they inquire, 'How's Chappy?' That's the sort of relationship we have. . . . I consider the majority of dealers personal friends."

Thus, Caterpillar's superb distribution system serves as a major source of competitive advantage. The system is built on a firm base of mutual trust and shared dreams. Caterpillar and its dealers feel a deep pride in what they are accomplishing together. As Fites puts it, "There's a camaraderie among our dealers around the world that really makes it more than just a financial arrangement. They feel that what they're doing is good for the world because they are part of an organization that makes, sells, and tends to the machines that make the world work."[1]

Most firms cannot bring value to customers by themselves. Instead, they must work closely with other firms in a larger value delivery network.

Supply Chains and the Value Delivery Network

Producing a product or service and making it available to buyers requires building relationships not just with customers, but also with key suppliers and resellers in the company's *supply chain.* This supply chain consists of "upstream" and "downstream" partners. Upstream from the company is the set of firms that supply the raw materials, components, parts, information, finances, and expertise needed to create a product or service. Marketers, however, have traditionally focused on the "downstream" side of the supply chain—on the *marketing channels* or *distribution channels* that look forward toward the customer. Downstream marketing channel partners, such as wholesalers and retailers, form a vital connection between the firm and its customers.

Both upstream and downstream partners may also be part of other firms' supply chains. But it is the unique design of each company's supply chain that enables it to deliver superior value to customers. An individual firm's success depends not only on how well *it* performs, but also on how well its entire supply chain and marketing channel competes with competitors' channels.

The term *supply chain* may be too limited—it takes a *make-and-sell* view of the business. It suggests that raw materials, productive inputs, and factory capacity should serve as the starting point for market planning. A better term would be *demand chain* because it suggests a *sense-and-respond* view of the market. Under this view, planning starts with the needs of target customers, to which the company responds by organizing a chain of resources and activities with the goal of creating customer value.

Even a demand-chain view of a business may be too limited, because it takes a step-by-step, linear view of purchase-production-consumption activities. With the advent of the Internet and other technologies, however, companies are forming more numerous and complex relationships with other firms. For example, Ford manages numerous supply chains. It also sponsors or transacts on many B-to-B Web sites and online purchasing exchanges as needs arise. Like Ford, most large companies today are engaged in building and managing a continuously evolving *value delivery network.*

As defined in Chapter 2, a **value delivery network** is made up of the company, suppliers, distributors, and ultimately customers who "partner" with each other to improve the performance of the entire system. For example, Palm, Inc., the leading manufacturer of handheld devices, manages a whole community of suppliers and assemblers of semiconductor components, plastic cases, LCD displays, and accessories. Its network also includes offline and online resellers, and tens of thousands of complementors who have created thousands of applications for the Palm operating system. All of these diverse partners must work effectively together to bring superior value to Palm's customers.

This chapter focuses on marketing channels—on the downstream side of the value delivery network. However, it is important to remember that this is only part of the full value network. To bring value to customers, companies need upstream supplier partners just as they need downstream channel partners. Increasingly, marketers are participating in and influencing their

■ Value delivery network: Palm, Inc., manages a whole community of suppliers, assemblers, resellers, and complementors who must work effectively together to make life easier for Palm's customers.

company's upstream activities as well as its downstream activities. More than marketing channel managers, they are becoming full value-network managers.

The chapter examines four major questions concerning marketing channels: What is the nature of marketing channels and why are they important? How do channel firms interact and organize to do the work of the channel? What problems do companies face in designing and managing their channels? What role do physical distribution and supply chain management play in attracting and satisfying customers? In Chapter 11, we will look at marketing channel issues from the viewpoint of retailers and wholesalers.

The Nature and Importance of Marketing Channels

Marketing channel (distribution channel)
A set of interdependent organizations that help make a product or service available for use or consumption by the consumer or business user.

Few producers sell their goods directly to the final users. Instead, most use intermediaries to bring their products to market. They try to forge a **marketing channel** (or **distribution channel**)—a set of interdependent organizations that help make a product or service available for use or consumption by the consumer or business user.

A company's channel decisions directly affect every other marketing decision. Pricing depends on whether the company works with national discount chains, uses high-quality specialty stores, or sells directly to consumers via the Web. The firm's sales force and communications decisions depend on how much persuasion, training, motivation, and support its channel partners need. Whether a company develops or acquires certain new products may depend on how well those products fit the capabilities of its channel members.

Companies often pay too little attention to their distribution channels, sometimes with damaging results. In contrast, many companies have used imaginative distribution systems to *gain* a competitive advantage. FedEx's creative and imposing distribution system made

■ Innovative marketing channels: Calyx & Corolla sells fresh flowers and plants direct to consumers by phone and from its Web site, cutting a week or more off the time it takes flowers to reach consumers through conventional retail channels.

it a leader in express delivery. Dell revolutionized its industry by selling personal computers directly to consumers rather than through retail stores. Amazon.com pioneered the sales of books and a wide range of other goods via the Internet. And Calyx & Corolla led the way in selling fresh flowers and plants direct to consumers by phone and from its Web site, cutting a week or more off the time it takes flowers to reach consumers through conventional retail channels.

Distribution channel decisions often involve long-term commitments to other firms. For example, companies such as Ford, IBM, or McDonald's can easily change their advertising, pricing, or promotion programs. They can scrap old products and introduce new ones as market tastes demand. But when they set up distribution channels through contracts with franchisees, independent dealers, or large retailers, they cannot readily replace these channels with company-owned stores or Web sites if conditions change. Therefore, management must design its channels carefully, with an eye on tomorrow's likely selling environment as well as today's.

HOW CHANNEL MEMBERS ADD VALUE

Why do producers give some of the selling job to channel partners? After all, doing so means giving up some control over how and to whom they sell their products. Producers use intermediaries because they create greater efficiency in making goods available to target markets. Through their contacts, experience, specialization, and scale of operation, intermediaries usually offer the firm more than it can achieve on its own.

Figure 10.1 shows how using intermediaries can provide economies. Figure 10.1A shows three manufacturers, each using direct marketing to reach three customers. This system requires nine different contacts. Figure 10.1B shows the three manufacturers working through one distributor, which contacts the three customers. This system requires only six contacts. In this way, intermediaries reduce the amount of work that must be done by both producers and consumers.

From the economic system's point of view, the role of marketing intermediaries is to transform the assortments of products made by producers into the assortments wanted by consumers. Producers make narrow assortments of products in large quantities, but consumers want broad assortments of products in small quantities. Marketing channel members buy large quantities from many producers and break them down into the smaller quantities and broader assortments wanted by consumers.

FIGURE 10.1 How a Distributor Reduces the Number of Channel Transactions

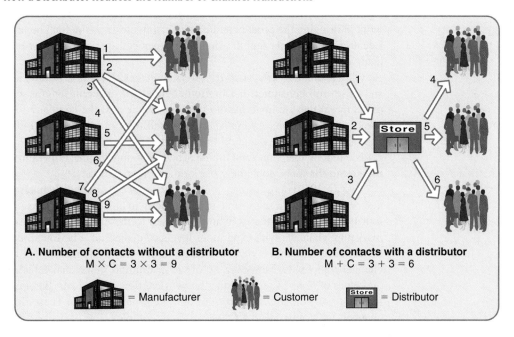

A. Number of contacts without a distributor
$$M \times C = 3 \times 3 = 9$$

B. Number of contacts with a distributor
$$M + C = 3 + 3 = 6$$

= Manufacturer   = Customer   = Distributor

For example, Unilever makes millions of bars of Lever 2000 hand soap each day, but you want to buy only a few bars at a time. So big food, drug, and discount retailers, such as Kroger, Walgreens, and Wal-Mart, buy Lever 2000 by the truckload and stock it on their store's shelves. In turn, you can buy a single bar of Lever 2000, along with a shopping cart full of small quantities of toothpaste, shampoo, and other related products as you need them. Thus, intermediaries play an important role in matching supply and demand.

In making products and services available to consumers, channel members add value by bridging the major time, place, and possession gaps that separate goods and services from those who would use them. Members of the marketing channel perform many key functions. Some help to complete transactions:

- *Information:* Gathering and distributing marketing research and intelligence information about actors and forces in the marketing environment needed for planning and aiding exchange.
- *Promotion:* Developing and spreading persuasive communications about an offer.
- *Contact:* Finding and communicating with prospective buyers.
- *Matching:* Shaping and fitting the offer to the buyer's needs, including activities such as manufacturing, grading, assembling, and packaging.
- *Negotiation:* Reaching an agreement on price and other terms of the offer so that ownership or possession can be transferred.

Others help to fulfill the completed transactions:

- *Physical distribution:* Transporting and storing goods.
- *Financing:* Acquiring and using funds to cover the costs of the channel work.
- *Risk taking:* Assuming the risks of carrying out the channel work.

The question is not *whether* these functions need to be performed—they must be—but rather *who* will perform them. To the extent that the manufacturer performs these functions, its costs go up and its prices have to be higher. When some of these functions are shifted to intermediaries, the producer's costs and prices may be lower, but the intermediaries must charge more to cover the costs of their work. In dividing the work of the channel, the various functions should be assigned to the channel members who can add the most value for the cost.

NUMBER OF CHANNEL LEVELS

Channel level
A layer of intermediaries that performs some work in bringing the product and its ownership closer to the final buyer.

Direct marketing channel
A marketing channel that has no intermediary levels.

Indirect marketing channel
Channel containing one or more intermediary levels.

Companies can design their distribution channels to make products and services available to customers in different ways. Each layer of marketing intermediaries that performs some work in bringing the product and its ownership closer to the final buyer is a **channel level**. Because the producer and the final consumer both perform some work, they are part of every channel.

The *number of intermediary levels* indicates the *length* of a channel. Figure 10.2A shows several consumer distribution channels of different lengths. Channel 1, called a **direct marketing channel**, has no intermediary levels; the company sells directly to consumers. For example, Avon and Amway sell their products door-to-door, through home and office sales parties, and on the Web; 1-800-Flowers sells flowers, gifts, and greeting cards direct by telephone and online. The remaining channels in Figure 10.2A are **indirect marketing channels**, containing one or more intermediaries.

Figure 10.2B shows some common business distribution channels. The business marketer can use its own sales force to sell directly to business customers. Or it can sell to various types of intermediaries, who in turn sell to these customers. Consumer and business marketing channels with even more levels can sometimes be found, but less often. From the producer's point of view, a greater number of levels means less control and greater channel complexity. Moreover, all of the institutions in the channel are connected by several types of *flows*. These include the *physical flow* of products, the *flow of ownership*, the *payment flow*, the *information flow*, and the *promotion flow*. These flows can make even channels with only one or a few levels very complex.

FIGURE 10.2 Consumer and Business Marketing Channels

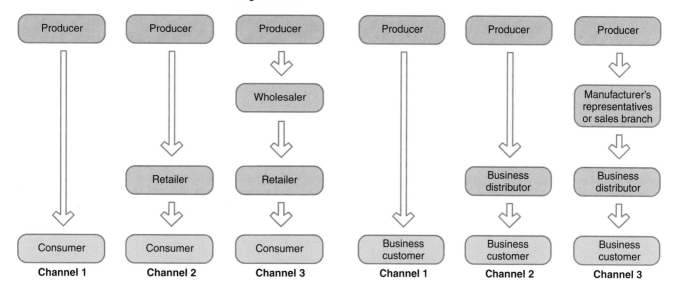

A. Customer marketing channels   B. Business marketing channels

Channel Behavior and Organization

Distribution channels are more than simple collections of firms tied together by various flows. They are complex behavioral systems in which people and companies interact to accomplish individual, company, and channel goals. Some channel systems consist only of informal interactions among loosely organized firms. Others consist of formal interactions guided by strong organizational structures. Moreover, channel systems do not stand still— new types of intermediaries emerge and whole new channel systems evolve. Here we look at channel behavior and at how members organize to do the work of the channel.

CHANNEL BEHAVIOR

A marketing channel consists of firms that have partnered for their common good. Each channel member depends on the others. For example, a Ford dealer depends on Ford to design cars that meet consumer needs. In turn, Ford depends on the dealer to attract consumers, persuade them to buy Ford cars, and service cars after the sale. Each Ford dealer also depends on other dealers to provide good sales and service that will uphold the brand's reputation. In fact, the success of individual Ford dealers depends on how well the entire Ford marketing channel competes with the channels of other auto manufacturers.

Each channel member plays a specialized role in the channel. For example, Sony's role is to produce consumer electronics products that consumers will like and to create demand through national advertising. Best Buy's role is to display these Sony products in convenient locations, to answer buyers' questions, and to complete sales. The channel will be most effective when each member assumes the tasks it can do best.

Ideally, because the success of individual channel members depends on overall channel success, all channel firms should work together smoothly. They should understand and accept their roles, coordinate their activities, and cooperate to attain overall channel goals. However, individual channel members rarely take such a broad view. Cooperating to achieve overall channel goals sometimes means giving up individual company goals. Although channel members depend on one another, they often act alone in their own short-run best interests. They often disagree on who should do what and for what rewards. Such disagreements over goals, roles, and rewards generate **channel conflict**.

Horizontal conflict occurs among firms at the same level of the channel. For instance, some Ford dealers in Chicago might complain the other dealers in the city steal sales from

Channel conflict
Disagreement among marketing channel members on goals and roles—who should do what and for what rewards.

them by pricing too low or by advertising outside their assigned territories. Or Holiday Inn franchisees might complain about other Holiday Inn operators overcharging guests or giving poor service, hurting the overall Holiday Inn image.

Vertical conflict, conflicts between different levels of the same channel, is even more common. For example, office furniture maker Herman Miller created conflict with its dealers when it opened an online store—www.hmstore.com—and began selling its products directly to customers. Although Herman Miller believed that the Web site was reaching only smaller customers who weren't being served by current channels, dealers complained loudly. As a result, the company closed down its online sales operations.

Similarly, Goodyear created hard feelings and conflict with its premier independent-dealer channel when it began selling through mass-merchant retailers:[2]

> For more than 60 years, Goodyear sold replacement tires exclusively through its premier network of 5,300 independent Goodyear dealers. In mid-1992, however, Goodyear jolted its dealers by agreeing to sell its tires through Sears Auto Centers. Similar pacts soon followed with Wal-Mart and Sam's club, pitting dealers against the nation's most potent retailers. Goodyear claimed that the change was essential. Value-minded tire buyers were increasingly buying from cheaper, multibrand discount outlets and department stores. By selling exclusively through its dealer network, Goodyear simply wasn't putting its tires where many consumers were going to buy them. Unfortunately, as Goodyear expanded into the new channels, it took few steps to protect its prized exclusive-dealer network.
>
> Since the shift, Goodyear's relations with its dealers have steadily deteriorated. Dealers complain not just about competition from mega-retailers but also about shoddy treatment and unfair pricing from Goodyear. For example, to sell more tires, Goodyear until recently offered bulk discounts to its biggest retailers and wholesalers. "The result was pricing insanity," notes one observer. "Some smaller dealers were paying more for tires than what Sears charged at retail." As a result, some of Goodyear's best dealers have defected to competitors, and many others now carry and push competing brands. Says one former dealer, "After someone punches you in the face a few times, you say, 'Enough is enough.'" Goodyear's replacement tire sales—which make up 70 percent of the company's revenues—have gone flat.
>
> Patching Goodyear's dealer relations, damaged over many years, will take time. "We still have a long way to go on this," admits Goodyear's VP for replacement tire sales. "We lost sight of the fact that it's in our interest that our dealers succeed." Larry Hauck, owner of Wells Tire of Alton, Illinois, would agree. An exclusive Goodyear dealer for 35 years until the late 1990s, he's the kind of once-loyal dealer that the company says it wants to woo back. Recently, though, Goodyear kicked him out of its dealer network. The reason? He wasn't buying enough tires. Says Hauck, "I just don't understand why they would cut the legs out from under people who have been loyal to them all these years."

■ Channel conflict: Goodyear's conflicts with its independent dealers have caused hard feelings and flattened the company's replacement tire sales.

Some conflict in the channel takes the form of healthy competition. Such competition can be good for the channel—without it, the channel could become passive and noninnovative. But severe or prolonged conflict, as in the case of Goodyear, can disrupt channel effectiveness and cause lasting harm to channel relationships. Companies should manage channel conflict to keep it from getting out of hand.

VERTICAL MARKETING SYSTEMS

For the channel as a whole to perform well, each channel member's role must be specified and channel conflict must be managed. The channel will perform better if it includes a firm, agency, or mechanism that provides leadership and has the power to assign roles and manage conflict.

Historically, *conventional distribution channels* have lacked such leadership and power, often resulting in damaging conflict and poor performance. One of the biggest channel developments over the years has been the emergence of *vertical marketing systems* that provide channel leadership. Figure 10.3 contrasts the two types of channel arrangements.

A **conventional distribution channel** consists of one or more independent producers, wholesalers, and retailers. Each is a separate business seeking to maximize its own profits, perhaps even at the expense of the system as a whole. No channel member has much control over the other members, and no formal means exists for assigning roles and resolving channel conflict.

In contrast, a **vertical marketing system (VMS)** consists of producers, wholesalers, and retailers acting as a unified system. One channel member owns the others, has contracts with them, or wields so much power that they must all cooperate. The VMS can be dominated by the producer, wholesaler, or retailer.

We look now at three major types of VMSs: *corporate, contractual,* and *administered.* Each uses a different means for setting up leadership and power in the channel.

Corporate VMS   A **corporate VMS** integrates successive stages of production and distribution under single ownership. Coordination and conflict management are attained through regular organizational channels. For example, grocery giant Kroger owns and operates 42 factories that crank out more than 4,300 of the food and drink items found on its store shelves. Giant Food Stores operates an ice-cube processing facility, a soft-drink bottling operation, its own dairy, an ice cream plant, and a bakery that supplies Giant stores with everything from bagels to birthday cakes. And little-known Italian eyewear maker Luxottica produces many famous eyewear brands—including Ray-Ban, Vogue, Anne Klein, Ferragamo, and Bulgari. It then sells these brands through two of the world's largest optical chains, LensCrafters and Sunglass Hut, which it also owns.[3]

Controlling the entire distribution chain has turned Spanish clothing chain Zara into the world's fastest-growing fashion retailer.

The secret to Zara's success is its control over almost every aspect of the supply chain, from design and production to its own worldwide distribution network. Zara

Conventional distribution channel
A channel consisting of one or more independent producers, wholesalers, and retailers, each a separate business seeking to maximize its own profits even at the expense of profits for the system as a whole.

Vertical marketing system (VMS)
A distribution channel structure in which producers, wholesalers, and retailers act as a unified system. One channel member owns the others, has contracts with them, or has so much power that they all cooperate.

Corporate VMS
A vertical marketing system that combines successive stages of production and distribution under single ownership—channel leadership is established through common ownership.

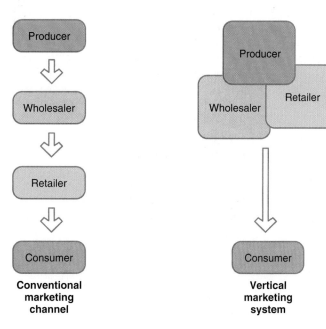

FIGURE 10.3

Comparison of Conventional Distribution Channel with Vertical Marketing System

makes 40 percent of its own fabrics and produces more than half of its own clothes, rather than relying on a hodgepodge of slow-moving suppliers. New styles take shape in Zara's own design centers, supported by real-time sales data. New designs feed into Zara manufacturing centers, which ship finished products directly to 741 Zara stores in 54 countries, saving time, eliminating the need for warehouses, and keeping inventories low. Effective vertical integration makes Zara faster, more flexible, and more efficient than international competitors such as Gap, Benetton, and Sweden's H&M. Its finely tuned distribution systems makes Zara seem more like Dell or Wal-Mart than Gucci or Louis Vuitton. Zara can make a new line from start to finish in less than 15 days, so a look seen on MTV can be in Zara stores within a month, versus an industry average of nine months. And Zara's low costs let it offer midmarket chic at downmarket prices. The company's stylish but affordable offerings have attracted a cult following, and the company's sales have more than doubled to $4.9 billion in the past six years.[4]

Contractual VMS

A vertical marketing system in which independent firms at different levels of production and distribution join together through contracts to obtain more economies or sales impact than they could achieve alone.

Franchise organization

A contractual vertical marketing system in which a channel member, called a franchisor, links several stages in the production-distribution process.

Contractual VMS   A **contractual VMS** consists of independent firms at different levels of production and distribution who join together through contracts to obtain more economies or sales impact than each could achieve alone. Coordination and conflict management are attained through contractual agreements among channel members.

The **franchise organization** is the most common type of contractual relationship—a channel member called a *franchisor* links several stages in the production-distribution process. In the United States alone, an estimated 760,000 franchise outlets account for more than $1.5 trillion in annual sales. Industry analysts estimate that a new franchise outlet opens somewhere in the United States every eight minutes and that about one out of every twelve retail business outlets is a franchised business.[5] Almost every kind of business has been franchised—from motels and fast-food restaurants to dental centers and dating services, from wedding consultants and maid services to fitness centers and funeral homes.

There are three types of franchises. The first type is the *manufacturer-sponsored retailer franchise system*—for example, Ford and its network of independent franchised dealers. The second type is the *manufacturer-sponsored wholesaler franchise system*—Coca-Cola licenses bottlers (wholesalers) in various markets who buy Coca-Cola syrup concentrate and then bottle and sell the finished product to retailers in local markets. The

■ Contractual VMS: In the United States, an estimated 2,000 franchised companies with over 760,000 franchise outlets account for more than $1.5 trillion in annual sales.

third type is the *service-firm-sponsored retailer franchise system*—examples are found in the auto-rental business (Hertz, Avis), the fast-food service business (McDonald's, Burger King), and the hotel/motel business (Holiday Inn, Ramada Inn).

The fact that most consumers cannot tell the difference between contractual and corporate VMSs shows how successfully the contractual organizations compete with corporate chains. Chapter 11 presents a fuller discussion of the various contractual VMSs.

Administered VMS   In an **administered VMS**, leadership is assumed not through common ownership or contractual ties but through the size and power of one or a few dominant channel members. Manufacturers of a top brand can obtain strong trade cooperation and support from resellers. For example, General Electric, Procter & Gamble, and Kraft can command unusual cooperation from resellers regarding displays, shelf space, promotions, and price policies. Large retailers such as Wal-Mart, Home Depot, and Barnes & Noble can exert strong influence on the manufacturers that supply the products they sell.

HORIZONTAL MARKETING SYSTEMS

Another channel development is the **horizontal marketing system**, in which two or more companies at one level join together to follow a new marketing opportunity. By working together, companies can combine their financial, production, or marketing resources to accomplish more than any one company could alone.

Companies might join forces with competitors or noncompetitors. They might work with each other on a temporary or permanent basis, or they may create a separate company. For example, the Lamar Savings Bank of Texas arranged to locate its savings offices and automated teller machines in Safeway stores. Lamar gained quicker market entry at a low cost, and Safeway was able to offer in-store banking convenience to its customers. Similarly, McDonald's now places "express" versions of its restaurants in Wal-Mart stores. McDonald's benefits from Wal-Mart's heavy store traffic, while Wal-Mart keeps hungry shoppers from having to go elsewhere to eat.

Such channel arrangements also work well globally. For example, because of its excellent coverage of international markets, Nestlé jointly sells General Mills's cereal brands in 80 countries outside North America. Similarly, Coca-Cola and Nestlé formed a joint venture, Beverage Partners Worldwide, to market ready-to-drink coffees, teas, and flavored milks in more than 40 countries worldwide. Coke provides worldwide experience in marketing and distributing beverages, and Nestlé contributes two established brand names—Nescafé and Nestea.[6]

MULTICHANNEL DISTRIBUTION SYSTEMS

In the past, many companies used a single channel to sell to a single market or market segment. Today, with the proliferation of customer segments and channel possibilities, more and more companies have adopted **multichannel distribution systems**—often called *hybrid marketing channels*. Such multichannel marketing occurs when a single firm sets up two or more marketing channels to reach one or more customer segments. The use of multichannel systems has increased greatly in recent years.

Administered VMS
A vertical marketing system that coordinates successive stages of production and distribution, not through common ownership or contractual ties, but through the size and power of one of the parties.

Horizontal marketing system
A channel arrangement in which two or more companies at one level join together to follow a new marketing opportunity.

Multichannel distribution system
A distribution system in which a single firm sets up two or more marketing channels to reach one or more customer segments.

The perfect handful for your little handful.

Made from four healthy whole grains-corn, oats, rice and wheat-Cheerios are the perfect choice for growing families. Small and round, they make ideal finger food for toddlers too. **There's a whole lot of good in those little 'o's.**

■ Horizontal marketing systems: Nestle jointly sells General Mills cereal brands in markets outside North America.

FIGURE 10.4
Hybrid Marketing Channel

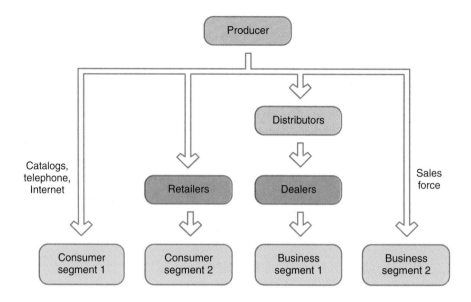

Figure 10.4 shows a hybrid channel. In the figure, the producer sells directly to consumer segment 1 using direct-mail catalogs, telemarketing, and the Internet and reaches consumer segment 2 through retailers. It sells indirectly to business segment 1 through distributors and dealers and to business segment 2 through its own sales force.

These days, almost every large company and many small ones distribute through multiple channels. Fidelity Investments reaches customers by telephone, over the Internet, and through its branch offices. It invites its customer to "call, click, or visit" Fidelity. Staples markets through its traditional retail outlets, a direct-response Internet site, virtual malls, and 30,000 links on affiliated sites.

Hewlett-Packard uses multiple channels to serve dozens of segments and niches, ranging from large corporate and institutional buyers to small businesses to home office buyers. The HP sales force sells the company's information technology equipment and services to large and mid-size business customers. HP also sells through a network of distributors and value-added resellers, which sell HP computers, systems, and services to a variety of special business segments. Home office buyers can buy HP personal computers and printers from specialty computer stores or any of several large retailers. And both business and home office buyers can buy directly from HP by phone or online from the company's Web site (www.hp.com).

Multichannel distribution systems offer many advantages to companies facing large and complex markets. With each new channel, the company expands its sales and market coverage and gains opportunities to tailor its products and services to the specific needs of diverse customer segments. But such multichannel systems are harder to control, and they generate conflict as more channels compete for customers and sales. For example, when HP began selling directly to customers through its own Web site, many of its retail dealers cried "unfair competition." Many salespeople felt that they were being undercut by the new "inside channels."

CHANGING CHANNEL ORGANIZATION

Disintermediation
The cutting out of marketing channel intermediaries by product or service producers, or the displacement of traditional resellers by radical new types of intermediaries.

Changes in technology and the explosive growth of direct and online marketing are having a profound impact on the nature and design of marketing channels. One major trend is toward **disintermediation**—a big term with a clear message and important consequences. Disintermediation occurs when product or service producers cut out intermediaries and go directly to final buyers, or when radically new types of channel intermediaries displace traditional ones.

Thus, in many industries, traditional intermediaries are dropping by the wayside. For example, companies such as Dell and American Airlines sell directly to final buyers, cutting retailers from their marketing channels altogether. In other cases, new forms of resellers are displacing traditional intermediaries. For example, e-commerce is growing rapidly, taking business from traditional brick-and-mortar retailers. Consumers can buy flowers from Calyx & Corolla (calyxandcorolla.com); clothes from L.L.Bean (llbean.com) or Gap (gap.com); and books, videos, toys, jewelry, consumer electronics, and almost anything else from Amazon.com; all without ever stepping into a traditional retail store. And online music download services such as iTunes and Musicmatch are threatening the very existence of traditional music-store retailers (see Marketing at Work 10.1).

Disintermediation presents problems and opportunities for both producers and intermediaries. To avoid being swept aside, traditional intermediaries must find new ways to add value in the supply chain. To remain competitive, product and service producers must develop new channel opportunities, such as Internet and other direct channels. However, developing these new channels often brings them into direct competition with their established channels, resulting in conflict.

To ease this problem, companies often look for ways to make going direct a plus for the entire channel. For example, Black & Decker knows that many customers would prefer to buy its power tools and outdoor power equipment online. But selling directly through its Web site would create conflicts with important and powerful retail partners, such as Home Depot, Lowe's, Target, Wal-Mart, and Amazon.com. So, while Black & Decker's Web site provides detailed information about the company's products, you can't buy a Black & Decker cordless drill, laser level, leaf blower, or anything else there. Instead, the Black & Decker site refers you to resellers' Web sites and stores. Thus, Black & Decker's direct marketing helps both the company and its channel partners.

■ Avoiding disintermediation problems: Black & Decker's Web site provides detailed information, but you can't buy any of the company's products there. Instead, Black & Decker refers you to resellers' Web sites and stores.

MARKETING AT WORK | 10.1

Disintermediation: The Music Industry Dances to a New iTune

Buying music can be a pretty frustrating experience. Perhaps you can identify with the following scenario:

You whistle a happy tune as you stroll into Tower Records to do a little music shopping. But when you pick up *The Essential Bruce Springsteen*, your temperature starts to rise. You should be ecstatic at the discovery of 12 new releases by the Boss, but instead you're furious: You can't buy them unless you shell out $25.99 for the entire three-CD set that includes 30 "career-spanning classics" that you already own from his other hit records. You shove Bruce back into his display case and pick up *The Ragpicker's Dream* by Mark Knopfler. It has one funny, tender tune that you love, called "Devil Baby"—but what about those other 16 songs? It'll cost you $23.99 to find out. Suddenly, everything seems like a crapshoot. Why do they keep insisting that you buy an entire CD when you can just go online and get only the tunes you really want from *iTunes* or Musicmatch for 99 cents each? Fed up, you walk away without buying anything.

Experiences like these, coupled with revolutionary changes in the way music is being distributed and purchased, have thrown the music industry into turmoil. Today, online music download services, such as Musicmatch.com, MusicNow.com, BuyMusic.com, and Apple's iTunes.com, offer an attractive alternative to buying over-priced standard CDs from the limited assortments of traditional music retailers.

Instead, you can go online, choose from hundreds of thousands of individual tracks, digitally download one or a dozen in any of several formats, burn them onto a CD or dump them into your iPod, and listen to them wherever and whenever you please.

It seems like everyone is getting into the music download business these days. Coffee chain Starbucks opened an in-store music service—Hear Music—letting customers burn downloaded tracks onto CDs while sipping their lattes. Mobile-phone makers are now unveiling music-playing phones that can hold thousands of downloaded songs. And fearsome competitors like Microsoft, Yahoo!, and Sony have launched their own online music stores.

These new distribution options are great for consumers. But the new channel forms

■ *Disintermediation: Online music download services, such as Apple's iTunes.com, are threatening to make traditional CD sellers obsolete.*

 Linking the Concepts

Stop here for a moment and apply the distribution channel concepts we've discussed so far.

■ Compare the Caterpillar and Goodyear channels. Draw a diagram that shows the types of intermediaries in each channel. What kind of channel system does each company use?
■ What are the roles and responsibilities of the members in each channel? How well do these channel members work together toward overall channel success?

Channel Design Decisions

We now look at several channel decisions manufacturers face. In designing marketing channels, manufacturers struggle between what is ideal and what is practical. A new firm

threaten the very existence of traditional music retailers. There's even a fancy word to describe this phenomenon—*disintermediation*. Strictly speaking, disintermediation means the elimination of a layer of intermediaries from a marketing channel—skipping a step between the source of a product or service and its consumers. For example, when Dell began selling personal computers directly to consumers, it eliminated—or disintermediated—retailers from the traditional PC distribution channel.

More broadly, disintermediation includes not only the elimination of channel levels through direct marketing but also the displacement of traditional resellers by radically new types of intermediaries. For example, only a few decades ago, most recorded music was sold through independent music retailers or small chains. Many of these smaller retailers were later disintermediated by large specialty music superstores, such as Tower Records, Virgin Records, and Musicland. The superstores, in turn, have faced growing competition from broad-line discount retailers such as Wal-Mart and Best Buy. In fact, Wal-Mart is currently the world's number-one CD seller.

Now, the surge of new online music sellers is threatening to make traditional CD sellers obsolete. "Tower Records and the other music-store chains are in a dizzying tailspin," comments one industry expert. Retail CD sales have dropped nearly 20 percent since 1999—the year Napster (the original music download site) was launched. Last year, number-one music retailer Tower Records declared bankruptcy and number-two Musicland shuttered 260 of its 1,230 stores. Smaller chains like

National Record Mart have disappeared altogether. Things will likely get worse before they get better. One retail consultant predicts that half of today's music stores will be out of business within five years and that, eventually, "CDs, DVDs, and other forms of physical media will become obsolete."

How are the traditional retailers responding to the disintermediation threat? Some are following the "if you can't beat them, join them" principle by creating their own downloading services. For example, Best Buy partnered with Napster to offer music downloads, as did Virgin Records. Wal-Mart offers in-store and online downloads at a bargain rate of only 88 cents a song. And Tower Records emerged from bankruptcy this year announcing that it also would open online and in-store music download services.

Music stores do still have several advantages over their online counterparts. The stores have a larger base of existing customers, and a physical store provides a shopping experience for customers that's difficult to duplicate online. Retailers can morph their stores into comfortable, sociable gathering spots where people hang out, chat with friends, listen to music, go to album signings, and perhaps attend a live performance.

But the traditional store retailers also face daunting economics. Store rents are rising while CD prices are falling. And running stores generates considerable inventory and store operating costs. New online entrants face none of those traditional distribution costs. Whereas store retailers can physically stock only a limited number of in-print titles, the music down-

load sites can provide millions of selections and offer out-of-print songs.

What's more crippling is that music stores are stuck selling pre-compiled CDs at high album prices, while music download sites let customers buy only the songs they want at low per-song rates. Finally, the old retailing model of selling CDs like they were LP vinyl records doesn't work so well anymore. That was fine in an era when people had one stereo in the living room and maybe one in the kids' room. But now consumers want music in a variety of formats that they can play anywhere, anytime: on boomboxes, Walkmans, car stereos, computers, and MP3 players like Apple's iPod, which can store thousands of songs in a nifty credit-card-sized device.

Thus, disintermediation is a big word but the meaning is clear. Disintermediation occurs only when a new channel form succeeds in serving customers better than the old channels. Marketers who continually seek new ways to create real value for customers have little to fear. However, those who fall behind in adding value risk being swept aside. Will today's music-store retailers survive? Stay iTuned.

Sources: Opening extract adapted from Paul Keegan, "Is the Music Store Over?" *Business 2.0,* March 2004, pp. 114–118. Other quotes and information from Lorin Cipolla, "Music's on the Menu." *Promo,* May 1, 2004; Sarah E. Lockyer, "Full Steam Ahead," *Nation's Restaurant News,* May 3, 2004, p. 4; Peter Lewis, "Drop a Quarter in the Internet," *FORTUNE,* March 22, 2004, p. 56; Erik Gruenwedel, "Tower Records Spins Profits, Suitors," *Video Store Magazine,* December 5–December 11, 2004, p. 8; Mike Hughlett, "More Companies Enter Musical Phone Field," *Knight Ridder Tribune Business News,* June 16, 2005, p. 1; and "How to Get Your Music Mobile," *Music Week,* June 25, 2005, p. S11.

with limited capital usually starts by selling in a limited market area. Deciding on the best channels might not be a problem: The problem might simply be how to convince one or a few good intermediaries to handle the line.

If successful, the new firm can branch out to new markets through the existing intermediaries. In smaller markets, the firm might sell directly to retailers; in larger markets, it might sell through distributors. In one part of the country, it might grant exclusive franchises; in another, it might sell through all available outlets. Then, it might add a Web store that sells directly to hard-to-reach customers. In this way, channel systems often evolve to meet market opportunities and conditions.

For maximum effectiveness, however, channel analysis and decision making should be more purposeful. Designing a channel system calls for analyzing consumer needs, setting channel objectives, identifying major channel alternatives, and evaluating them.

ANALYZING CONSUMER NEEDS

As noted previously, marketing channels are part of the overall *customer value delivery network*. Each channel member adds value for the customer. Thus, designing the marketing channel starts with finding out what target consumers want from the channel. Do consumers want to buy from nearby locations or are they willing to travel to more distant centralized locations? Would they rather buy in person, over the phone, through the mail, or via the Internet? Do they value breadth of assortment or do they prefer specialization? Do consumers want many add-on services (delivery, credit, repairs, installation), or will they obtain these elsewhere? The faster the delivery, the greater the assortment provided, and the more add-on services supplied, the greater the channel's service level.

Providing the fastest delivery, greatest assortment, and most services may not be possible or practical. The company and its channel members may not have the resources or skills needed to provide all the desired services. Also, providing higher levels of service results in higher costs for the channel and higher prices for consumers. The company must balance consumer needs not only against the feasibility and costs of meeting these needs but also against customer price preferences. The success of discount retailing shows that consumers will often accept lower service levels in exchange for lower prices.

SETTING CHANNEL OBJECTIVES

Companies should state their marketing channel objectives in terms of targeted levels of customer service. Usually, a company can identify several segments wanting different levels of service. The company should decide which segments to serve and the best channels to use in each case. In each segment, the company wants to minimize the total channel cost of meeting customer service requirements.

The company's channel objectives are also influenced by the nature of the company, its products, its marketing intermediaries, its competitors, and the environment. For example, the company's size and financial situation determine which marketing functions it can handle itself and which it must give to intermediaries. Companies selling perishable products may require more direct marketing to avoid delays and too much handling.

In some cases, a company may want to compete in or near the same outlets that carry competitors' products. In other cases, producers may avoid the channels used by competitors. Mary Kay Cosmetics, for example, sells direct to consumers through its corps of more than 1 million independent beauty consultants in 34 markets worldwide rather than going head-to-head with other cosmetics makers for scarce positions in retail stores. And GEICO markets auto insurance directly to consumers via the telephone and Web rather than through agents.

Finally, environmental factors such as economic conditions and legal constraints may affect channel objectives and design. For example, in a depressed economy, producers want to distribute their goods in the most economical way, using shorter channels and dropping unneeded services that add to the final price of the goods.

IDENTIFYING MAJOR ALTERNATIVES

When the company has defined its channel objectives, it should next identify its major channel alternatives in terms of *types* of intermediaries, the *number* of intermediaries, and the *responsibilities* of each channel member.

Types of Intermediaries A firm should identify the types of channel members available to carry out its channel work. For example, suppose a manufacturer of test equipment has developed an audio device that detects poor mechanical connections in machines with moving parts. Company executives think this product would have a market in all industries in which electric, combustion, or steam engines are made or used. The company's current sales force is small, and the problem is how best to reach these different industries. The following channel alternatives might emerge:

■ Channel objectives: GEICO markets auto insurance via the telephone and Web for those looking to save money and do business directly with the company. "Take your pick," says this ad. "Call or click."

Company sales force: Expand the company's direct sales force. Assign outside salespeople to territories and have them contact all prospects in the area, or develop separate company sales forces for different industries. Or, add an inside telesales operation in which telephone salespeople handle small or midsize companies.

Manufacturer's agency: Hire manufacturer's agents—independent firms whose sales forces handle related products from many companies—in different regions or industries to sell the new test equipment.

Industrial distributors: Find distributors in the different regions or industries who will buy and carry the new line. Give them exclusive distribution, good margins, product training, and promotional support.

Number of Marketing Intermediaries   Companies must also determine the number of channel members to use at each level. Three strategies are available: intensive distribution, exclusive distribution, and selective distribution. Producers of convenience products and common raw materials typically seek **intensive distribution**—a strategy in which they stock their products in as many outlets as possible. These products must be available where and when consumers want them. For example, toothpaste, candy, and other similar items are sold in millions of outlets to provide maximum brand exposure and consumer convenience. Kraft, Coca-Cola, Kimberly-Clark, and other consumer goods companies distribute their products in this way.

By contrast, some producers purposely limit the number of intermediaries handling their products. The extreme form of this practice is **exclusive distribution**, in which the

Intensive distribution
Stocking the product in as many outlets as possible.

Exclusive distribution
Giving a limited number of dealers the exclusive right to distribute the company's products in their territories.

■ Exclusive distribution: Luxury car makers such as Bentley sell exclusively through a limited number of retailers. Such limited distribution enhances the car's image and generates stronger retailer support.

Selective distribution
The use of more than one, but fewer than all, of the intermediaries who are willing to carry the company's products.

producer gives only a limited number of dealers the exclusive right to distribute its products in their territories. Exclusive distribution is often found in the distribution of luxury automobiles and prestige women's clothing. For example, Bentley dealers are few and far between—even large cities, such as Houston, may have only one dealer. By granting exclusive distribution, Bentley gains stronger distributor selling support and more control over dealer prices, promotion, credit, and services. Exclusive distribution also enhances the car's image and allows for higher markups.

Between intensive and exclusive distribution lies **selective distribution**—the use of more than one, but fewer than all, of the intermediaries who are willing to carry a company's products. Most television, furniture, and home appliance brands are distributed in this manner. For example, KitchenAid, Maytag, Whirlpool, and General Electric sell their major appliances through dealer networks and selected large retailers. By using selective distribution, they can develop good working relationships with selected channel members and expect a better-than-average selling effort. Selective distribution gives producers good market coverage with more control and less cost than does intensive distribution.

Responsibilities of Channel Members   The producer and intermediaries need to agree on the terms and responsibilities of each channel member. They should agree on price policies, conditions of sale, territorial rights, and specific services to be performed by each party. The producer should establish a list price and a fair set of discounts for intermediaries. It must define each channel member's territory, and it should be careful about where it places new resellers.

Mutual services and duties need to be spelled out carefully, especially in franchise and exclusive distribution channels. For example, McDonald's provides franchisees with promotional support, a record-keeping system, training at Hamburger University, and general management assistance. In turn, franchisees must meet company standards for physical facilities, cooperate with new promotion programs, provide requested information, and buy specified food products.

EVALUATING THE MAJOR ALTERNATIVES

Suppose a company has identified several channel alternatives and wants to select the one that will best satisfy its long-run objectives. Each alternative should be evaluated against economic, control, and adaptive criteria.

Using *economic criteria*, a company compares the likely sales, costs, and profitability of different channel alternatives. What will be the investment required by each channel alternative, and what returns will result? The company must also consider *control issues*. Using intermediaries usually means giving them some control over the marketing of the product, and some intermediaries take more control than others. Other things being equal, the company prefers to keep as much control as possible. Finally, the company must apply *adaptive criteria*. Channels often involve long-term commitments, yet the company wants to keep the channel flexible so that it can adapt to environmental changes. Thus, to be considered, a channel involving long-term commitments should be greatly superior on economic and control grounds.

DESIGNING INTERNATIONAL DISTRIBUTION CHANNELS

International marketers face many additional complexities in designing their channels. Each country has its own unique distribution system that has evolved over time and changes very slowly. These channel systems can vary widely from country to country. Thus, global marketers must usually adapt their channel strategies to the existing structures within each country.

In some markets, the distribution system is complex and hard to penetrate, consisting of many layers and large numbers of intermediaries. Consider Japan:

The Japanese distribution system stems from the early seventeenth century when cottage industries and a [quickly growing] urban population spawned a merchant class. . . . Despite Japan's economic achievements, the distribution system has remained remarkably faithful to its antique pattern. . . . [It] encompasses a wide range of wholesalers and other agents, brokers, and retailers, differing more in number than in function from their American counterparts. There are myriad tiny retail shops. An even greater number of whole-salers supplies goods to them, layered tier upon tier, many more than most U.S. executives would think necessary. For example, soap may move through three wholesalers plus a sales company after it leaves the manufacturer before it ever reaches the retail outlet. A steak goes from rancher to consumers in a process that often involves a dozen middle agents. . . . The distribution network . . . reflects the traditionally close ties among many Japanese companies . . . [and places] much greater emphasis on personal relationships with users. . . . Although [these channels appear] inefficient and cumbersome, they seem to serve the Japanese customer well. . . . Lacking much storage space in their small homes, most Japanese homemakers shop several times a week and prefer convenient [and more personal] neighborhood shops.[7]

■ The Japanese distribution system has remained remarkably traditional. A profusion of tiny retail shops are supplied by an even greater number of small wholesalers.

Many Western firms have had great difficulty breaking into the closely knit, tradition-bound Japanese distribution network.

At the other extreme, distribution systems in developing countries may be scattered and inefficient, or altogether lacking. For example, China and India are huge markets, each with populations over 1 billion. However, because of inadequate distribution systems, most companies can profitably access only a small portion of the population located in each country's most affluent cities. "China is a very decentralized market," notes a China trade expert. "[It's] made up of two dozen distinct markets sprawling across 2,000 cities. Each has its own culture. . . . It's like operating in an asteroid belt." China's distribution system is so fragmented that logistics costs amount to 15 percent of the nation's GDP, far higher than in most other countries. After 10 years of effort, even Wal-Mart executives admit that they have been unable to assemble an efficient supply chain in China.[8]

Thus, international marketers face a wide range of channel alternatives. Designing efficient and effective channel systems between and within various country markets poses a difficult challenge. We discuss international distribution decisions further in Chapter 15.

Channel Management Decisions

Once the company has reviewed its channel alternatives and decided on the best channel design, it must implement and manage the chosen channel. Channel management calls for selecting, managing, and motivating individual channel members and evaluating their performance over time.

SELECTING CHANNEL MEMBERS

Producers vary in their ability to attract qualified marketing intermediaries. Some producers have no trouble signing up channel members. For example, when Toyota first introduced its Lexus line in the United States, it had no trouble attracting new dealers. In fact, it had to turn down many would-be resellers.

At the other extreme are producers who have to work hard to line up enough qualified intermediaries. When Polaroid started, for example, it could not get photography stores to carry its new cameras, and it had to go to mass-merchandising outlets. Similarly, when the U.S. Time Company first tried to sell its inexpensive Timex watches through regular jewelry stores, most jewelry stores refused to carry them. The company then managed to get its watches into mass-merchandise outlets. This turned out to be a wise decision because of the rapid growth of mass merchandising.

When selecting intermediaries, the company should determine what characteristics distinguish the better ones. It will want to evaluate each channel member's years in business, other lines carried, growth and profit record, cooperativeness, and reputation. If the intermediaries are sales agents, the company will want to evaluate the number and character of other lines carried and the size and quality of the sales force. If the intermediary is a retail store that wants exclusive or selective distribution, the company will want to evaluate the store's customers, location, and future growth potential.

MANAGING AND MOTIVATING CHANNEL MEMBERS

Once selected, channel members must be continuously managed and motivated to do their best. The company must sell not only *through* the intermediaries but *to* and *with* them. Most companies see their intermediaries as first-line customers and partners. They practice strong *partner relationship management (PRM)* to forge long-term partnerships with channel members. This creates a marketing system that meets the needs of both the company *and* its marketing partners.

In managing its channels, a company must convince distributors that they can succeed better by working together as a part of a cohesive value delivery system.[9] Thus, Procter & Gamble and Wal-Mart work together to create superior value for final consumers. They jointly plan merchandising goals and strategies, inventory levels, and advertising and promotion plans. Similarly, GE Appliances has created an alternative distribution system called *CustomerNet* to coordinate, support, and motivate its dealers.

GE CustomerNet gives dealers instant online access to GE Appliances' distribution and order-processing system, 24 hours a day, seven days a week. By logging on to the GE CustomerNet Web site, dealers can obtain product specifications, photos, feature lists, and side-by-side model comparisons for hundreds of GE appliance models. They can check on product availability and prices, place orders, and review order status. They can even create custom brochures, order point-of-purchase materials, or download "advertising slicks"—professionally prepared GE appliance ads ready for insertion in local media. GE promises next-day delivery on most appliance models, so dealers need carry only display models in their stores. This greatly reduces inventory costs, making even small dealers more price competitive. GE CustomerNet also helps dealers to sell GE appliances more easily and effectively. A dealer can put a computer terminal on the showroom floor, where salespeople and

■ Creating dealer satisfaction and profitability: Using GE's CustomerNet system, dealers have instant online access to GE Appliances' distribution system, 24 hours a day, 7 days a week to check on product availability and prices, place orders, and review order status. "Simply put, it's an electronic one-stop shopping breakthrough that can help you sell."

customers together can use the system to dig through detailed product descriptions and check availability for GE's entire line of appliances. Perhaps the biggest benefit to GE Appliances, however, is that the system builds strong bonds between the company and its dealers and motivates dealers to put more push behind the company's products.[10]

Many companies are now installing integrated high-tech partner relationship management systems to coordinate their whole-channel marketing efforts. Just as they use customer relationship management (CRM) software systems to help manage relationships with important customers, companies can now use PRM and supply chain management (SCM) software to help recruit, train, organize, manage, motivate, and evaluate relationships with channel partners.

EVALUATING CHANNEL MEMBERS

The producer must regularly check channel member performance against standards such as sales quotas, average inventory levels, customer delivery time, treatment of damaged and lost goods, cooperation in company promotion and training programs, and services to the customer. The company should recognize and reward intermediaries who are performing well and adding good value for consumers. Those who are performing poorly should be assisted or, as a last resort, replaced. A company may periodically "requalify" its intermediaries and prune the weaker ones.

Finally, manufacturers need to be sensitive to their dealers. Those who treat their dealers poorly risk not only losing dealer support but also causing some legal problems. The next section describes various rights and duties pertaining to manufacturers and their channel members.

 Linking the Concepts

Time for another break. This time, compare the Caterpillar and GE Appliances channel systems.

- Diagram the Caterpillar and GE Appliances systems. How do they compare in terms of channel levels, types of intermediaries, channel member roles and responsibilities, and other characteristics. How well is each system designed?
- Assess how well Caterpillar and GE Appliances have managed and supported their channels. With what results?

Public Policy and Distribution Decisions

For the most part, companies are legally free to develop whatever channel arrangements suit them. In fact, the laws affecting channels seek to prevent the exclusionary tactics of some companies that might keep another company from using a desired channel. Most channel law deals with the mutual rights and duties of the channel members once they have formed a relationship.

Many producers and wholesalers like to develop exclusive channels for their products. When the seller allows only certain outlets to carry its products, this strategy is called *exclusive distribution*. When the seller requires that these dealers not handle competitors' products, its strategy is called *exclusive dealing*. Both parties can benefit from exclusive arrangements: The seller obtains more loyal and dependable outlets, and the dealers obtain a steady source of supply and stronger seller support. But exclusive arrangements also exclude other producers from selling to these dealers. This situation brings exclusive dealing contracts under the scope of the Clayton Act of 1914. They are legal as long as they do not substantially lessen competition or tend to create a monopoly and as long as both parties enter into the agreement voluntarily.

Exclusive dealing often includes *exclusive territorial agreements*. The producer may agree not to sell to other dealers in a given area, or the buyer may agree to sell only in its own territory. The first practice is normal under franchise systems as a way to increase dealer enthusiasm and commitment. It is also perfectly legal—a seller has no legal obligation to sell through more outlets than it wishes. The second practice, whereby the producer tries to keep a dealer from selling outside its territory, has become a major legal issue.

Producers of a strong brand sometimes sell it to dealers only if the dealers will take some or all of the rest of the line. This is called full-line forcing. Such *tying agreements* are not necessarily illegal, but they do violate the Clayton Act if they tend to lessen competition substantially. The practice may prevent consumers from freely choosing among competing suppliers of these other brands.

Finally, producers are free to select their dealers, but their right to terminate dealers is somewhat restricted. In general, sellers can drop dealers "for cause." However, they cannot drop dealers if, for example, the dealers refuse to cooperate in a doubtful legal arrangement, such as exclusive dealing or tying agreements.[11]

Marketing Logistics and Supply Chain Management

In today's global marketplace, selling a product is sometimes easier than getting it to customers. Companies must decide on the best way to store, handle, and move their products and services so that they are available to customers in the right assortments, at the right time, and in the right place. Physical distribution and logistics effectiveness has a major impact on both customer satisfaction and company costs. Here we consider the nature and importance of logistics management in the supply chain, goals of the logistics system, major logistics functions, and the need for integrated supply chain management.

NATURE AND IMPORTANCE OF MARKETING LOGISTICS

Marketing logistics (physical distribution)
The tasks involved in planning, implementing, and controlling the physical flow of materials, final goods, and related information from points of origin to points of consumption to meet customer requirements at a profit.

To some managers, marketing logistics means only trucks and warehouses. But modern logistics is much more than this. **Marketing logistics**—also called **physical distribution**—involves planning, implementing, and controlling the physical flow of goods, services, and related information from points of origin to points of consumption to meet customer requirements at a profit. In short, it involves getting the right product to the right customer in the right place at the right time.

In the past, physical distribution typically started with products at the plant and then tried to find low-cost solutions to get them to customers. However, today's marketers prefer customer-centered logistics thinking, which starts with the marketplace and works backward to the factory, or even to sources of supply. Marketing logistics involves not only *outbound distribution* (moving products from the factory to resellers and ultimately to customers) but also *inbound distribution* (moving products and materials from suppliers to the factory) and *reverse distribution* (moving broken, unwanted, or excess products returned by consumers or resellers). That is, it involves the entire **supply chain management**—managing upstream and downstream value-added flows of materials, final goods, and related information among suppliers, the company, resellers, and final consumers, as shown in Figure 10.5.

Supply chain management
Managing upstream and downstream value-added flows of materials, final goods, and related information among suppliers, the company, resellers, and final consumers.

FIGURE 10.5 Supply Chain Management

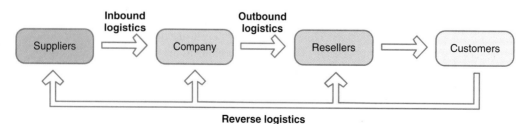

The logistics manager's task is to coordinate activities of suppliers, purchasing agents, marketers, channel members, and customers. These activities include forecasting, information systems, purchasing, production planning, order processing, inventory, warehousing, and transportation planning.

Companies today are placing greater emphasis on logistics for several reasons. First, companies can gain a powerful competitive advantage by using improved logistics to give customers better service or lower prices. Second, improved logistics can yield tremendous cost savings to both the company and its customers. As much as 20 percent of an average product's price is accounted for by shipping and transport alone. This far exceeds the cost of advertising and many other marketing costs. Last year, American companies spent more than $1 trillion—about 8.6 percent of gross domestic product—to wrap, bundle, load, unload, sort, reload, and transport goods. By itself, Ford has more than 500 million tons of finished vehicles, production parts, and aftermarket parts in transit at any given time, running up an annual logistics bill of around $4 billion.[12] Shaving off even a small fraction of these costs can mean substantial savings.

Third, the explosion in product variety has created a need for improved logistics management. For example, in 1911 the typical A&P grocery store carried only 270 items. The store manager could keep track of this inventory on about 10 pages of notebook paper stuffed in a shirt pocket. Today, the average A&P carries a bewildering stock of more than 25,000 items. A Wal-Mart Supercenter store carries more than 100,000 products, 30,000 of which are grocery products.[13] Ordering, shipping, stocking, and controlling such a variety of products presents a sizable logistics challenge.

Finally, improvements in information technology have created opportunities for major gains in distribution efficiency. Today's companies are using sophisticated supply chain management software, Web-based logistics systems, point-of-sale scanners, uniform product codes, satellite

■ The importance of logistics: At any given time, Ford has more than 500 million tons of finished vehicles, production parts, and aftermarket parts in transit, running up an annual logistics bill of around $4 billion.

tracking, and electronic transfer of order and payment data. Such technology lets them quickly and efficiently manage the flow of goods, information, and finances through the supply chain.

GOALS OF THE LOGISTICS SYSTEM

Some companies state their logistics objective as providing maximum customer service at the least cost. Unfortunately, no logistics system can *both* maximize customer service *and* minimize distribution costs. Maximum customer service implies rapid delivery, large inventories, flexible assortments, liberal returns policies, and other services—all of which raise distribution costs. In contrast, minimum distribution costs imply slower delivery, smaller inventories, and larger shipping lots—which represent a lower level of overall customer service.

The goal of marketing logistics should be to provide a *targeted* level of customer service at the least cost. A company must first research the importance of various distribution services to customers and then set desired service levels for each segment. The objective is to maximize *profits*, not sales. Therefore, the company must weigh the benefits of providing higher levels of service against the costs. Some companies offer less service than their competitors and charge a lower price. Other companies offer more service and charge higher prices to cover higher costs.

MAJOR LOGISTICS FUNCTIONS

Given a set of logistics objectives, the company is ready to design a logistics system that will minimize the cost of attaining these objectives. The major logistics functions include *warehousing, inventory management, transportation,* and *logistics information management.*

Warehousing Production and consumption cycles rarely match. So most companies must store their tangible goods while they wait to be sold. For example, Snapper, Toro, and other lawn mower manufacturers run their factories all year long and store up products for the heavy spring and summer buying seasons. The storage function overcomes differences in needed quantities and timing, ensuring that products are available when customers are ready to buy them.

A company must decide on *how many* and *what types* of warehouses it needs and *where* they will be located. The company might use either *storage warehouses* or *distribution centers*. Storage warehouses store goods for moderate to long periods. **Distribution centers** are designed to move goods rather than just store them. They are large and highly automated warehouses designed to receive goods from various plants and suppliers, take orders, fill them efficiently, and deliver goods to customers as quickly as possible.

For example, Wal-Mart operates a network of close to 100 huge U.S. distribution centers and another 57 around the globe. A single center, which might serve the daily needs of 120 Wal-Mart stores, typically contains some 1.2 million square feet of space (about 29 football fields) under a single roof. One huge center near Williamsburg, Virginia, contains more than 3 million square feet. At a typical center, laser scanners route as many as 190,000 cases of goods per day along 11 miles of conveyor belts, and the center's 1,000 workers load or unload some 500 trucks daily. Wal-Mart's Monroe, Georgia, distribution center contains a 127,000-square-foot freezer that can hold 10,000 pallets—room enough for 58 million Popsicles.[14]

Like almost everything else these days, warehousing has seen dramatic changes in technology in recent years. Older, multistoried warehouses with outdated materials-handling methods are steadily being replaced by newer, single-storied *automated warehouses* with advanced, computer-controlled materials-handling systems requiring few employees. Computers and scanners read orders and direct lift trucks, electric hoists, or robots to gather goods, move them to loading docks, and issue invoices.

Inventory Management Inventory management also affects customer satisfaction. Here, managers must maintain the delicate balance between carrying too little inventory and carrying too much. With too little stock, the firm risks not having products when customers want to buy. To remedy this, the firm may need costly emergency shipments or production. Carrying too much inventory results in higher-than-necessary inventory-carrying costs and stock obsolescence. Thus, in managing inventory, firms must balance the costs of carrying larger inventories against resulting sales and profits.

Many companies have greatly reduced their inventories and related costs through *just-in-time* logistics systems. With such systems, producers and retailers carry only small inventories of parts or merchandise, often only enough for a few days of operations. For example, Dell, a master just-in-time producer, carries just 3 to 4 days of inventory, whereas competitors might carry 40 days or even 60.[15] New stock arrives exactly when needed, rather than being stored in inventory until being used. Just-in-time systems require accurate forecasting along with fast, frequent, and flexible delivery so that new supplies will be available when needed. However, these systems result in substantial savings in inventory-carrying and handling costs.

Marketers are always looking for new ways to make inventory management more efficient. In the not-too-distant future, handling inventory might even become fully automated. For example, in Chapter 3, we discussed RFID or "smart tag" technology, by which small transmitter chips are embedded in products and packaging on everything from flowers and razors to tires. "Smart" products could make the entire supply chain—

Distribution center
A large, highly automated warehouse designed to receive goods from various plants and suppliers, take orders, fill them efficiently, and deliver goods to customers as quickly as possible.

■ Logistics technology: In the not-to-distant future, RFID or "smart tag" technology could make the entire supply chain—which accounts for nearly 75 percent of a product's cost—intelligent and automated.

which accounts for nearly 75 percent of a product's cost—intelligent and automated. Companies using RFID would know, at any time, exactly where a product is located physically within the supply chain. "Smart shelves" would not only tell them when it's time to reorder, but would also place the order automatically with their suppliers. Such exciting new information technology applications will revolutionize distribution as we know it. Many large and resourceful marketing companies, such as Procter & Gamble, IBM, Wal-Mart, and Best Buy, are investing heavily to make the full use of RFID technology a reality.[16]

Transportation   The choice of transportation carriers affects the pricing of products, delivery performance, and condition of the goods when they arrive—all of which will affect customer satisfaction. In shipping goods to its warehouses, dealers, and customers, the company can choose among five main transportation modes: truck, rail, water, pipeline, and air, along with an alternative mode for digital products: the Internet.

Trucks have increased their share of transportation steadily and now account for nearly 32 percent of total cargo ton-miles (more than 58 percent of actual tonnage).[17] Each year in the United States, trucks travel more than 600 billion miles—equal to nearly 1.3 million round trips to the moon—carrying 9.2 billion tons of freight. Trucks are highly flexible in their routing and time schedules, and they can usually offer faster service than railroads. They are efficient for short hauls of high-value merchandise. Trucking firms have added many services in recent years. For example, Roadway Express and most other major carriers now offer everything from satellite tracking and 24-hour shipment information to logistics planning software and "border ambassadors" who expedite cross-border shipping operations.

Railroads account for 28 percent of total cargo ton-miles moved. They are one of the most cost-effective modes for shipping large amounts of bulk products—coal, sand, minerals, and farm and forest products—over long distances. In recent years, railroads have increased their customer services by designing new equipment to handle special categories of goods, providing flatcars for carrying truck trailers by rail (piggyback), and providing in-transit services such as the diversion of shipped goods to other destinations en route and the processing of goods en route.

Water carriers, which account for about 16 percent of cargo ton-miles, transport large amounts of goods by ships and barges on U.S. coastal and inland waterways. Although the cost of water transportation is very low for shipping bulky, low-value, nonperishable products such as sand, coal, grain, oil, and metallic ores, water transportation is the slowest mode and may be affected by the weather. *Pipelines*, which also account for about 16 percent of cargo ton-miles, are a specialized means of shipping petroleum, natural gas, and chemicals from sources to markets. Most pipelines are used by their owners to ship their own products.

Although *air* carriers transport less than 1 percent of the nation's goods, they are an important transportation mode. Airfreight rates are much higher than rail or truck rates, but airfreight is ideal when speed is needed or distant markets have to be reached. Among the most frequently airfreighted products are perishables (fresh fish, cut flowers) and high-value, low-bulk items (technical instruments, jewelry). Companies find that airfreight also reduces inventory levels, packaging costs, and the number of warehouses needed.

WE HELP YOU
STAY ON TOP
OF YOUR
BUSINESS.

At Roadway Express, your Customer Care Team is on top of your business. This team of experts delivers a level of personal attention that's indispensable to you. You can depend on your dedicated team of knowledgeable professionals to solve your dilemmas today and take on your challenges down the road. Empowered to address your every transportation need, your local Customer Care Team stands behind you... and the transportation promises you make to your customers. Which means we have you covered, from top to bottom.

ROADWAY.COM 1-888-550-9800

ROADWAY *Express*
ROADWAY. YOUR WAY.

■ Roadway and other trucking firms have added many services in recent years—everything from satellite tracking and 24-hour shipment information to logistics planning software and "border ambassadors" who expedite cross-border shipping operations. Roadway's Customer Care Teams can help customers "solve your [transportation] challenges today and take on your challenges down the road."

The *Internet* carries digital products from producer to customer via satellite, cable modem, or telephone wire. Software firms, the media, music companies, and education all make use of the Internet to transport digital products. While these firms primarily use traditional transportation to distribute CDs, newspapers, and more, the Internet holds the potential for lower product distribution costs. Whereas planes, trucks, and trains move freight and packages, digital technology moves information bits.

Shippers also use **intermodal transportation**—combining two or more modes of transportation. *Piggyback* describes the use of rail and trucks; *fishyback*, water and trucks; *trainship*, water and rail; and *airtruck*, air and trucks. Combining modes provides advantages that no single mode can deliver. Each combination offers advantages to the shipper. For example, not only is piggyback cheaper than trucking alone but it also provides flexibility and convenience.

In choosing a transportation mode for a product, shippers must balance many considerations: speed, dependability, availability, cost, and others. Thus, if a shipper needs speed, air and truck are the prime choices. If the goal is low cost, then water or pipeline might be best.

Logistics Information Management Companies manage their supply chains through information. Channel partners often link up to share information and to make better joint logistics decisions. From a logistics perspective, information flows such as customer orders, billing, inventory levels, and even customer data are closely linked channel performance. The company wants to design a simple, accessible, fast, and accurate process for capturing, processing, and sharing channel information.

Information can be shared and managed in many ways—by mail or telephone, through salespeople, or through traditional or Internet-based *electronic data interchange (EDI)*, the computerized exchange of data between organizations. Wal-Mart, for example, maintains EDI links with almost all of its 91,000 suppliers. And in one month alone, J.C. Penney relies on EDI to share more than 5.5 million documents with its partners.[18]

In some cases, suppliers might actually be asked to generate orders and arrange deliveries for their customers. Many large retailers—such as Wal-Mart and Home Depot—work closely with major suppliers such as Procter & Gamble or Black & Decker to set up *vendor-managed inventory* (VMI) systems or *continuous inventory replenishment* systems. Using VMI, the customer shares real-time data on sales and current inventory levels with the supplier. The supplier then takes full responsibility for managing inventories and deliveries. Some retailers even go so far as to shift inventory and delivery costs to the supplier. Such systems require close cooperation between the buyer and seller.

INTEGRATED LOGISTICS MANAGEMENT

Today, more and more companies are adopting the concept of **integrated logistics management**. This concept recognizes that providing better customer service and trimming distribution costs require *teamwork*, both inside the company and among all the marketing channel organizations. Inside, the company's various departments must work closely together to maximize the company's own logistics performance. Outside, the company must integrate its logistics system with those of its suppliers and customers to maximize the performance of the entire distribution system.

Cross-Functional Teamwork Inside the Company
In most companies, responsibility for various logistics activities is assigned to many different functional units—marketing, sales, finance, operations, purchasing. Too often, each function tries to optimize its own logistics performance without regard for the activities of the other functions. However, transportation, inventory, warehousing, and order-processing activities interact, often in an inverse way. Lower inventory levels reduce inventory-carrying costs. But they may also reduce customer service and increase costs from stock outs, back orders, special production runs, and costly fast-freight shipments. Because distribution activities involve strong trade-offs, decisions by different functions must be coordinated to achieve better overall logistics performance.

Intermodal transportation
Combining two or more modes of transportation.

Integrated logistics management
The logistics concept that emphasizes teamwork, both inside the company and among all the marketing channel organizations, to maximize the performance of the entire distribution system.

The goal of integrated supply chain management is to harmonize all of the company's logistics decisions. Close working relationships among functions can be achieved in several ways. Some companies have created permanent logistics committees, made up of managers responsible for different physical distribution activities. Companies can also create supply chain manager positions that link the logistics activities of functional areas. For example, Procter & Gamble has created supply managers, who manage all of the supply chain activities for each of its product categories. Many companies have a vice president of logistics with cross-functional authority. Finally, companies can employ sophisticated, systemwide supply chain management software, now available from a wide range of suppliers.[19] The important thing is that the company must coordinate its logistics and marketing activities to create high market satisfaction at a reasonable cost.

Building Logistics Partnerships   Companies must do more than improve their own logistics. They must also work with other channel partners to improve whole-channel distribution. The members of a distribution channel are linked closely in creating customer value and building customer relationships. One company's distribution system is another company's supply system. The success of each channel member depends on the performance of the entire supply chain. For example, Wal-Mart can charge the lowest prices at retail only if its entire supply chain—consisting of thousands of merchandise suppliers, transport companies, warehouses, and service providers—operates at maximum efficiency.

Smart companies coordinate their logistics strategies and forge strong partnerships with suppliers and customers to improve customer service and reduce channel costs. Many companies have created *cross-functional, cross-company teams*. For example, Procter & Gamble has a team of more than 200 people working in Bentonville, Arkansas, home of Wal-Mart.[20] The P&Gers work jointly with their counterparts at Wal-Mart to find ways to squeeze costs out of their distribution system. Working together benefits not only P&G and Wal-Mart but also their final consumers.

Other companies partner through *shared projects*. For example, many large retailers are working closely with suppliers on in-store programs. Home Depot allows key suppliers to use its stores as a testing ground for new merchandising programs. The suppliers

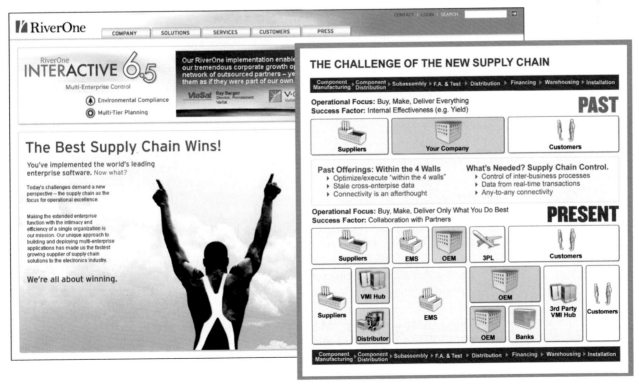

■ Supply chain management: Many companies use sophisticated, systemwide supply chain management software, such as that available from RiverOne and other software providers.

MARKETING AT WORK | 10.2

UPS: "Let Us Manage the Supply Chain; You Focus on What You Do Best"

Mention UPS, and most people envision one of those familiar brown trucks with a friendly driver, rumbling around their neighborhood dropping off parcels. That makes sense. The company's 80,000 brown-clad drivers deliver more than 3.6 billion packages each year, an average of 14.1 million a day.

For most of us, seeing a brown UPS truck evokes fond memories of past package deliveries. If you close your eyes and listen, you can probably imagine the sound of the UPS truck pulling up in front of your home. Even the company's brown color has come to mean something special to customers. "We've been referred to for years as Big Brown," says a UPS marketing executive. "People love our drivers, they love our brown trucks, they love everything we do." Thus was born UPS's current "What Can Brown Do for You?" marketing campaign.

However, you might be surprised to learn that most of UPS's revenues come not from the residential customers who receive the packages, but from the business customers who send them. And for these business customers, package delivery is just part of a much more complex logistics process that involves purchase orders, inventory, order status checks, invoices, payments, returned merchandise, and fleets of delivery vehicles. UPS knows that all these work-a-day logistical concerns can be a nightmare. Moreover, most companies don't see these activities as strate-

gic competencies that give them competitive advantage.

That's where Big Brown comes in. These are exactly the things that UPS does best. Over the years, UPS has grown to become much more than a neighborhood, small-package delivery service. It is now a $37 billion corporate giant providing a broad range of logistics solutions. "UPS is leveraging decades of experience managing its own global delivery network to serve as the traffic manager for Corporate America's sprawling distribution networks," observes an industry analyst. If it has to do with logistics, at home or abroad, UPS can probably do it better than anyone can.

UPS has the resources to handle the logistics needs of just about any size business. It employs 384,000 people, some 88,000 vehicles (package cars, vans, tractors, and motorcycles), 565 aircraft, and more than 1,000 warehouse facilities in 120 countries. UPS now moves an astounding 6 percent of the gross domestic product in the United States, linking 1.8 million sellers with 6 million buyers every day. It serves 90 percent of the world population and 99 percent of businesses in the FORTUNE 1000.

Beyond moving their packages efficiently around the world, UPS can provide the advice and technical resources needed to help business customers large and small improve their own logistics operations. UPS Consulting

■ Third party logistics: UPS's Supply Chain Solutions group can help a company shorten its supply chains and turn it into a strategic asset.

spend time at Home Depot stores watching how their product sells and how customers relate to it. They then create programs specially tailored to Home Depot and its customers. Clearly, both the supplier and the customer benefit from such partnerships. The point is that all supply chain members must work together in the cause of serving final consumers.

Third-Party Logistics
Most big companies love to make and sell their products. But many loathe the associated logistics "grunt work." They detest the bundling, loading, unloading, sorting, storing, reloading, transporting, customs-clearing, and tracking required to supply their factories and to get products out to customers. They hate it so much that a growing number of firms now outsource some or all of their logistics to **third-party logistics (3PL) providers**.

Third-party logistics (3PL) provider
An independent logistics provider that performs any or all of the functions required to get their client's product to market.

advises companies on redesigning logistics systems to align them better with business strategies. UPS Supply Chain Solutions helps customers to synchronize the flow of goods, funds, and information up and down their supply chains. UPS Logistics Technologies supplies software that improves customers' distribution efficiency, including street-level route optimization, territory planning, mobile delivery execution, real-time wireless dispatch, and GPS tracking. For example, UPS applied all these resources to help Ford overhaul its dated distribution system:

For years, the bane of most Ford dealers was the automaker's antiquated system for getting cars from factory to showroom. Cars could take as long as a month to arrive—that is, when they weren't lost along the way. And Ford was not always able to tell its dealers exactly what was coming, or even what was in inventory at the nearest rail yards. "We'd lose track of whole trainloads of cars," recalls Jerry Reynolds, owner of Prestige Ford in Garland, Texas. "It was crazy."

But three years ago, Ford handed its tortuous distribution network to an unlikely source: UPS. In a joint venture with the carmaker, UPS redesigned Ford's entire North American delivery network. Ultimately, UPS deployed a tracking system similar to the one it uses to monitor its own 14.1 million packages daily—right down to slapping bar codes on the windshields of the 4 million cars rolling out of Ford's North American plants each year and onto railcars. The result: UPS has cut the time it takes autos to arrive

at dealer lots by 40 percent, to 10 days on average. In the first year alone, that trimmed Ford's inventory carrying costs by $125 million. And the new system makes it easy for dealers to track down the models most in demand. "It was the most amazing transformation I had ever seen," marvels dealer Reynolds. "My last comment to UPS was: 'Can you get us spare parts like this?' "

UPS helped Birkenstock Footprint Sandals, Inc. (BFSI), the exclusive distributor in the United States of the Birkenstock brand, to navigate the complexities of international shipping, saving money while at the same time providing better service to Birkenstock's retailers and customers.

Thanks to UPS, BFSI has slashed the time and money it takes to get its shoes from Birkenstock factories in Germany to U.S. stores. Here's how. In Germany, Birkenstock packs the shoes in crates bar-coded with their final U.S. destination. Then, UPS takes over. It trucks the crates to Rotterdam, and then ships them across the Atlantic to New Jersey ports (instead of routing them through the Panama Canal to BFSI's California warehouses). UPS clears incoming shipments through customs and whisks them away to its nearby distribution hub. Minutes after arriving, the crates are opened, shoes are sorted, and brown trucks speed them to any of 3,000 stores. By handing over its keys to UPS, BFSI has cut the time it takes to get shoes to stores from as many as seven weeks to just three weeks. "Our spring fashion merchandise shipped 100 percent on time —and it was the first time in history I've

been able to say that," says BFSi's chief operating officer.

In all, UPS will undertake just about any logistics task for customers, anything from fixing busted electronics to answering customer phone calls to issuing corporate credit cards.

For Jockey International, UPS not only manages a warehouse but also handles Internet order fulfillment. Apparel bought on the Jockey Web site is boxed for shipping by UPS warehouse staffers and delivered by UPS drivers. And if there's a problem, calls are handled by UPS phone reps. Big Brown also handles laptop repairs for Toshiba America, installs X-ray machines in Europe for Philips Medical Systems, and dresses teddy bears for TeddyCrafters.

Thus, for most residential customers, the answer to the question "What can Brown do for you?" is pretty simple: "Deliver my package as quickly as possible." But for UPS's business customers, Big Brown can do much more than just get Grandma's holiday package there on time. It can be a strategic logistics partner, working hand-in-hand with customers to solve their complex logistics problems. UPS's new logistics pitch can be summed up this way: Let us manage the supply chain; you focus on the things that you do best.

Sources: Examples, quotes, and other information adapted from or found in Dean Foust, "Big Brown's New Bag," *BusinessWeek,* July 19, 2004, pp. 54–56; and www. pressroom.ups.com/mediakits/factsheet/0,2305,866,00.html, August 2005. Birkenstock example used with permission of Birkenstock Footprint Sandals, Inc. Also see Nabil Alghalith, "Competing with IT: The UPS Case," *Journal of American Academy of Business,* September 2005, pp. 7–16.

These "3PLs"—companies such as UPS Supply Chain Services, Ryder Systems, FedEx Logistics, Roadway Logistics Services, or Emery Global Logistics—help clients to tighten up sluggish, overstuffed supply chains, slash inventories, and get products to customers more quickly and reliably. For example, UPS's Supply Chain Services unit provides clients with a wide range of logistics services, from inventory control, warehousing, and transportation management to customer service and fulfillment (see Marketing at Work 10.2). According to a recent survey of chief logistics executives at FORTUNE 500 companies, 81 percent of these companies use third-party logistics (also called *3PL, outsourced logistics,* or *contract logistics*) services.[21]

Companies use third-party logistics providers for several reasons. First, because getting the product to market is their main focus, these providers can often do it more efficiently and at lower cost. Outsourcing typically results in a 15 percent to 30 percent cost savings. Second, outsourcing logistics frees a company to focus more intensely on its core business. Finally, integrated logistics companies understand increasingly complex logistics environments. This can be especially helpful to companies attempting to expand their global market coverage. For example, companies distributing their products across Europe face a bewildering array of environmental restrictions that affect logistics, including packaging standards, truck size and weight limits, and noise and emissions pollution controls. By outsourcing its logistics, a company can gain a complete pan-European distribution system without incurring the costs, delays, and risks associated with setting up its own system.

REST STOP → REVIEWING THE CONCEPTS

So, what have you learned about distribution channels and integrated supply chain management? Marketing channel decisions are among the most important decisions that management faces. A company's channel decisions directly affect every other marketing decision. Management must make channel decisions carefully, incorporating today's needs with tomorrow's likely selling environment. Some companies pay too little attention to their distribution channels, but others have used imaginative distribution systems to gain competitive advantage.

1. Explain why companies use marketing channels and discuss the functions these channels perform.

Most producers use intermediaries to bring their products to market. They try to forge a *marketing channel* (or *distribution channel*)—a set of interdependent organizations involved in the process of making a product or service available for use or consumption by the consumer or business user. Through their contacts, experience, specialization, and scale of operation, intermediaries usually offer the firm more than it can achieve on its own.

Marketing channels perform many key functions. Some help *complete* transactions by gathering and distributing *information* needed for planning and aiding exchange; by developing and spreading persuasive *communications* about an offer; by performing *contact* work—finding and communicating with prospective buyers; by *matching*—shaping and fitting the offer to the buyer's needs; and by entering into *negotiation* to reach an agreement on price and other terms of the offer so that ownership can be transferred. Other functions help to *fulfill* the completed transactions by offering *physical distribution*—

transporting and storing goods; *financing*—acquiring and using funds to cover the costs of the channel work; and *risk taking*—assuming the risks of carrying out the channel work.

2. Discuss how channel members interact and how they organize to perform the work of the channel.

The channel will be most effective when each member is assigned the tasks it can do best. Ideally, because the success of individual channel members depends on overall channel success, all channel firms should work together smoothly. They should understand and accept their roles, coordinate their goals and activities, and cooperate to attain overall channel goals. By cooperating, they can more effectively sense, serve, and satisfy the target market. In a large company, the formal organization structure assigns roles and provides needed leadership. But in a distribution channel made up of independent firms, leadership and power are not formally set. Traditionally, distribution channels have lacked the leadership needed to assign roles and manage conflict. In recent years, however, new types of channel organizations have appeared that provide stronger leadership and improved performance.

3. Identify the major channel alternatives open to a company.

Each firm identifies alternative ways to reach its market. Available means vary from direct selling to using one, two, three, or more intermediary *channel levels*. Marketing channels face continuous and sometimes dramatic change. Three of the most important trends are the growth of *vertical, horizontal,* and *multichannel marketing systems.* These trends affect channel cooperation, conflict, and competition. *Channel design* begins with assessing customer channel service needs and company channel objectives and constraints. The company then identifies the major channel alternatives in terms of the *types* of intermediaries, the *number* of intermediaries, and the *channel responsibilities* of each. Each channel alternative must be evaluated according to economic, control, and adaptive criteria. Channel management calls for selecting qualified intermediaries and motivating them. Individual channel members must be evaluated regularly.

4. Explain how companies select, motivate, and evaluate channel members.

Producers vary in their ability to attract qualified marketing intermediaries. Some producers have no trouble signing up channel members. Others have to work hard to line up enough qualified intermediaries. When selecting intermediaries, the company should evaluate each channel member's qualifications and select those that best fit its channel objectives. Once selected, channel members must be continuously motivated to do their best. The company must sell not only *through* the intermediaries but *to* them. It should work to forge long-term partnerships with their channel partners to create a marketing system that meets the needs of both the manufacturer *and* the partners. The company must also regularly check channel member performance against established performance standards, rewarding intermediaries who are performing well and assisting or replacing weaker ones.

5. Discuss the nature and importance of marketing logistics and integrated supply chain management.

Just as firms are giving the marketing concept increased recognition, more business firms are paying attention to *marketing logistics* (or *physical distribution*). Logistics is an area of potentially high cost savings and improved customer satisfaction. Marketing logistics addresses not only *outbound distribution* but also *inbound distribution* and *reverse distribution.* That is, it involves entire *supply chain management*— managing value-added flows between suppliers, the company, resellers, and final users. No logistics system can both maximize customer service and minimize distribution costs. Instead, the goal of logistics management is to provide a *targeted* level of service at the least cost. The major logistics functions include *order processing, warehousing, inventory management,* and *transportation.*

The *integrated supply chain management concept* recognizes that improved logistics requires teamwork in the form of close working relationships across functional areas inside the company and across various organizations in the supply chain. Companies can achieve logistics harmony among functions by creating cross-functional logistics teams, integrative supply manager positions, and senior-level logistics executives with cross-functional authority. Channel partnerships can take the form of cross-company teams, shared projects, and information sharing systems. Today, some companies are outsourcing their logistics functions to third-party logistics (3PL) providers to save costs, increase efficiency, and gain faster and more effective access to global markets.

Navigating the Key Terms

Administered VMS (307)
Channel conflict (303)
Channel level (302)
Contractual VMS (306)
Conventional distribution channel (305)
Corporate VMS (305)
Direct marketing channel (302)
Disintermediation (308)
Distribution center (320)

Exclusive distribution (313)
Franchise organization (306)
Horizontal marketing system (307)
Indirect marketing channel (302)
Integrated logistics management (322)
Intensive distribution (313)
Intermodal transportation (322)
Marketing channel (distribution channel) (300)

Marketing logistics (physical distribution) (318)
Multichannel distribution system (307)
Selective distribution (314)
Supply chain management (318)
Third-party logistics (3PL) provider (324)
Vertical marketing system (VMS) (305)

Travel Log

Discussing the Issues

1. Discuss the differences between a conventional distribution channel, a corporate VMS, a contractual VMS, and an administered VMS. Give one example of each.

2. What is a horizontal marketing system? Think of a real-world horizontal marketing system not discussed in the chapter. How does the partnership benefit the companies involved? How does it benefit the consumer?

3. Define *disintermediation*. List three industries for which changes in channel systems have resulted in disintermediation.

4. Discuss the conditions under which a manufacturer might want its distribution to be exclusive, selective, or intensive. List two products or brands that are currently distributed at each level. Do you think any of these products might be more profitable if distributed through a different number of intermediaries?

5. What is partner relationship management (PRM) and why is it important? How does PRM impact customer relationship management?

6. List and briefly describe the major logistics functions. Provide an example of a decision a logistics manager would make for each major function.

Application Questions

1. Think of a product that is a part of your daily life. Outline the likely channel members that work together to bring this product to you. What value does each member add?

2. Consider a product that you might buy at your local electronics store. How would your interest in and access to that product change if it were only sold directly from the manufacturer. What impact, positive or negative, would eliminating channel members have on the manufacturer's ability to build and maintain customer relationships?

3. Discuss the rationale behind the text's argument that "demand chain" may be a better term than "supply chain." Do you agree or disagree? How does the concept of a value delivery network fit with these two concepts?

Under the Hood: Focus on Technology

How often, when shopping online, have you wished you could pick up the phone and get an immediate answer to a question? How tall is that pool table? Is that software compatible with my operating system? Providing immediate customer service for those shopping online can be a real challenge for marketers selling direct. While customers shopping Circuit City can ask a salesperson about the features of different digital video cameras, those shopping online at Buy.com rely on product pictures and descriptions to answer their questions. To better address consumer concerns and answer questions, many online retailers offer customer service "live" through an instant messaging "chat" box. Not only can service representatives answer ques-

tions, they can guide customers through a company Web site to find just the right product.

1. Visit Lands' End online (www.landsend.com) and investigate the company's online customer service options. Does live chat appeal to you as a consumer? Does it add value to Lands' End's products?

2. Do you think live customer service differentiates Lands' End from online retailers without this feature? How does it impact the relationship Lands' End builds with its customers?

Focus on Ethics

The explosive growth of the Internet has made it easier for companies to sell directly to consumers. Although intermediaries were once essential to providing excellent customer service and creating easy access to a variety of products and services, the Internet makes it possible for a product manufacturer to sell direct while maintaining, or even improving, customer service and satisfaction. And, in many cases, to remain competitive, product and service producers must develop new channel opportunities, such as Internet and other direct channels. However, developing these new channels often brings them into direct competition with their established channel partners. For example, Sony now sells its products directly to consumers on its www.sonystyle.com Web site, putting it into competition with Sony dealers ranging from small mom-and-pop consumer electronics chains to giants like Wal-Mart and Best Buy.

1. Is it ethical for product manufacturers to compete with loyal, established channel members by selling directly to consumers?

2. What impact does channel conflict have on customer relationships?

3. How could a manufacturer sell direct while protecting the livelihood of loyal channel members?

Videos

The Hasbro video case that accompanies this chapter is located in Appendix 1 at the back of the book.

AFTER STUDYING THIS CHAPTER, YOU SHOULD BE ABLE TO

1. explain the roles of retailers and wholesalers in the distribution channel

2. describe the major types of retailers and give examples of each

3. identify the major types of wholesalers and give examples of each

4. explain the marketing decisions facing retailers and wholesalers

Retailing and Wholesaling

Road Map Previewing the Concepts

In the previous chapter, you learned the basics of distribution channel design and management. Now, we'll look deeper into the two major intermediary channel functions, retailing and wholesaling. You already know something about retailing—you're served every day by retailers of all shapes and sizes. However, you probably know much less about the hoard of wholesalers that work behind the scenes. In this chapter, we'll navigate through the characteristics of different kinds of retailers and wholesalers, the marketing decisions they make, and trends for the future.

To start the tour, we'll look at Whole Foods Market. In today's marketing world, almost every retailer, large or small, worries about competing with Wal-Mart, the world's largest retailer—the world's largest *company*. Few retailers *can* compete directly with Wal-Mart and survive. Yet, little Whole Foods is thriving in the shadow of the giant. Read on to see how.

These days, Wal-Mart sells just about everything. That means that it competes ruthlessly with almost every other retailer, no matter what the product category. Wal-Mart outsells Toys "R" Us in the toy market and sells half as many groceries as the leading groceries-only retailer, Kroger. It gives Blockbuster big headaches in DVD and video sales, and puts a big dent in Best Buy's consumer electronics business. Almost every retailer, large or small, has its hands full devising strategies by which it can compete with Wal-Mart and survive.

So, how *do* you compete with a behemoth like Wal-Mart? The best answer: You don't—at least not directly. Perhaps the worst strategy is trying to out-Wal-Mart Wal-Mart. Instead of competing head-to-head, smart competitors choose their turf carefully.

In fact, this story isn't even about Wal-Mart—we'll cover that colossus later in the chapter. Instead, this is a David-and-Goliath story about Whole Foods Market, a small, upscale grocery chain that's doing very well by carving out its own turf in the giant's shadow. Whole Foods has only 170 stores worldwide versus Wal-Mart's more than 5,000, and its annual sales total about $4 billion, compared to Wal-Mart's $285 billion.

Although it may not seem like a fair fight, Whole Foods is thriving. It succeeds through careful positioning—specifically, by positioning *away* from Wal-Mart. Rather than pursuing mass-market sales volume and razor-thin margins, Whole Foods targets a select group of upscale customers and offers them "organic, natural, and gourmet foods, all swaddled in Earth Day politics." As one analyst puts it, "While other grocers are looking over their shoulder, watching and worrying about Wal-Mart, Whole Foods is going about business as usual. The tofu is still selling; the organic eggs are fresh in the back dairy cooler; and meats are still hormone free."

331

Whole Foods' value proposition is summed up in its motto: "Whole Foods, Whole People, Whole Planet." Step into your local Whole Foods market and you'll quickly see that it's not your typical food store. In place of the sugary mass-market colas that fill whole aisles in a traditional grocery store, Whole Foods carries organic sodas and Odwalla juices. In the produce department, you'll find blue potatoes, dinner-plate-sized portabello mushrooms, taro root, and edamame (green Japanese soybeans). Natural soaps and toilet papers displace the usual national brands. Or pick up some meatless mousaka and herbal tea for your post-meditation snack. In keeping with the company's positioning, most of the store's goods carry labels proclaiming "organic," "100% natural," and "contains no additives."

The Whole Foods Web site, bathed in earth tones, reinforces the company's positioning. The site offers up recipes for healthy eating, such as "Sweet Potato Pancakes with Creamy Dill Sauce," "Baked Basmati & Currant Stuffed Trout," and "Beginner's Tips for Tofu, Tempeh, and Other Soy Foods." The site bursts at the seams with information on a wide range of health and wellness issues, from sources such as the WholeHealthMD reference library and the American Botanical Council. You'll find all you ever wanted to know about topics ranging from the potential medical uses of over 100 herbs to alternative therapies such as acupuncture, reflexology, and homeopathy.

Both online and in the flesh, a visit to Whole Foods is more than just a shopping trip, it's an experience. And the experience is anything but what you'd find at Wal-Mart. "We create store environments that are inviting, fun, unique, informal, comfortable, attractive, nurturing, and educational," the company claims. "We want our stores to become community meeting places where our customers come to join their friends and to make new ones."

By design, Whole Foods is not for everyone—the upscale retailer caters to a carefully selected segment of consumers. Whole Foods customers are affluent, liberal, educated people living in university towns like Austin, Texas, Boulder, Colorado, and Ann Arbor, Michigan. Their median annual household income exceeds the U.S. average by almost $8,000. Whole Foods customers live a health-conscious lifestyle, care about the food they eat, and worry about the environment. They tend to be social do-gooders who abhor soulless corporate greed. Whole Foods doesn't really have to compete with mass merchandisers like Wal-Mart for these customers. In fact, a Whole Foods customer is more likely to boycott the local Wal-Mart than to shop at it.

Whole Foods customers like the fact that the store's commitment to quality reaches far beyond what's on its shelves. In its "Declaration of Interdependence," the company recognizes that living up to its "Whole Foods, Whole People, Whole Planet" motto means doing more than simply selling food. It means caring about the well-being and quality of life of everyone associated with the business, from customers and employees, to suppliers, to the broader communities in which it operates.

Its concern for customers runs deep. "We go to extraordinary lengths to satisfy and delight our customers," says a company spokesperson. "We want to meet or exceed their expectations on every shopping trip." Whole Foods also cares about its employees—for the past eight years, it's been listed among FORTUNE magazine's "Top 100 Companies to Work for in America." Whole Foods cares about its suppliers. The Declaration of Interdependence states, "We view our trade partners as allies in serving our stakeholders. We treat them with respect, fairness, and integrity, and expect the same in return." To back this up, the company supports sustainable, environmentally-friendly agriculture practices, offering organically-grown foods almost exclusively.

Whole Foods also cares about its communities. It provides financial support for employees doing voluntary community service. And it invests in the local environment. One store in Berkeley, California, gets most of its electrical power from rooftop solar panels. A special electrical system and energy-conserving features make the most of the sun. Perhaps most telling of Whole Foods broad community commitment: It donates 5 percent of its after-tax profits to not-for-profit organizations.

Such commitment, along with strong targeting and positioning, have made Whole Foods one of the nation's fastest growing and most profitable food retailers. It's now the world's number-one natural food chain. Its upscale stores ring up an average of $689 in sales per square foot, almost twice that of a traditional grocer. And the chain reaps 2.9 percent profit margins, two and one-half times the grocery industry average. Whereas other grocers have faced limited sales and profit growth or even declines in the face of the withering Wal-Mart assault, Whole Foods' sales have increased by 44 percent during the past two years; profits are up by 62 percent.

So, Whole Foods can't compete directly with the Wal-Marts of the world. It can't match Wal-Mart's massive economies of scale, incredible volume purchasing power, ultra-efficient logistics, wide selection, and hard-to-beat prices. But then again, it doesn't even try. Instead, it targets customers that Wal-Mart can't serve, offering them value that Wal-Mart can't deliver. By positioning away from Wal-Mart and other mainstream grocers, Whole Foods has found its own very profitable place in the world.[1]

The Whole Foods story sets the stage for examining the fast-changing world of today's resellers. This chapter looks at *retailing* and *wholesaling*. In the first section, we look at the nature and importance of retailing, major types of store and nonstore retailers, the decisions retailers make, and the future of retailing. In the second section, we discuss these same topics as they relate to wholesalers.

Retailing

What is retailing? We all know that Wal-Mart, Home Depot, and Target are retailers, but so are Avon representatives, Amazon.com, the local Holiday Inn, and a doctor seeing patients. **Retailing** includes all the activities involved in selling products or services directly to final consumers for their personal, nonbusiness use. Many institutions—manufacturers, wholesalers, and retailers—do retailing. But most retailing is done by **retailers**: businesses whose sales come *primarily* from retailing.

Although most retailing is done in retail stores, in recent years *nonstore retailing* has been growing much faster than has store retailing. Nonstore retailing includes selling to final consumers through direct mail, catalogs, telephone, the Internet, TV home shopping shows, home and office parties, door-to-door contact, vending machines, and other direct selling approaches. We discuss such direct-marketing approaches in detail in Chapter 13. In this chapter, we focus on store retailing.

TYPES OF RETAILERS

Retail stores come in all shapes and sizes, and new retail types keep emerging. The most important types of retail stores are described in Table 11.1 and discussed in the following sections. They can be classified in terms of several characteristics, including the *amount of*

Retailing
All activities involved in selling goods or services directly to final consumers for their personal, nonbusiness use.

Retailer
Businesses whose sales come *primarily* from retailing.

TABLE 11.1
Major Store Retailer Types

Specialty Stores: Carry a narrow product line with a deep assortment, such as apparel stores, sporting-goods stores, furniture stores, florists, and bookstores. A clothing store would be a *single-line* store, a men's clothing store would be a *limited-line* store, and a men's custom-shirt store would be a *superspecialty* store. Examples: Gap, The Athlete's Foot, Williams-Sonoma.

Department Stores: Carry several product lines—typically clothing, home furnishings, and household goods—with each line operated as a separate department managed by specialist buyers or merchandisers. Examples: Sears, Macy's, Marshall Field's.

Supermarkets: A relatively large, low-cost, low-margin, high-volume, self-service operation designed to serve the consumer's total needs for grocery and household products. Examples: Kroger, Vons, A&P, Food Lion.

Convenience Stores: Relatively small stores located near residential areas, open long hours seven days a week, and carrying a limited line of high-turnover convenience products at slightly higher prices. Examples: 7-Eleven, Stop-N-Go, Circle K.

Discount Stores: These stores carry standard merchandise sold at lower prices with lower margins and higher volumes. Examples: General—Wal-Mart, Target, Kmart; Specialty—Circuit City.

Off-Price Retailers: Sell merchandise bought at less-than-regular wholesale prices and sold at less-than-retail, often leftover goods, overruns, and irregulars obtained at reduced prices from manufacturers or other retailers. These include *factory outlets* owned and operated by manufacturers (example: Mikasa); *independent off-price retailers* owned and run by entrepreneurs or by divisions of larger retail corporations (example: TJ Maxx); and *warehouse (or wholesale) clubs* selling a limited selection of brand-name groceries, appliances, clothing, and other goods at deep discounts to consumers who pay membership fees (examples: Costco, Sam's Club, BJ's Wholesale Club).

Superstores: Very large stores traditionally aimed at meeting consumers' total needs for routinely purchased food and nonfood items. Includes *category killers,* which carry a deep assortment in a particular category and have a knowledgeable staff (examples: Best Buy, PETsMART, Staples); *supercenters,* combined supermarket and discount stores (examples: Wal-Mart Supercenters, SuperTarget, Super Kmart Center, Meijer); and *hypermarkets* with up to 220,000 square feet of space combining supermarket, discount, and warehouse retailing (examples: Carrefour [France], Pyrca [Spain]).

service they offer, the breadth and depth of their *product lines*, the *relative prices* they charge, and how they are *organized*.

Amount of Service   Different products require different amounts of service, and customer-service preferences vary. Retailers may offer one of three levels of service—self service, limited service, and full service.

Self-service retailers serve customers who are willing to perform their own "locate-compare-select" process to save money. Self service is the basis of all discount operations and is typically used by sellers of convenience goods (such as supermarkets) and nationally branded, fast-moving shopping goods (such as Best Buy).

Limited-service retailers, such as Sears or JCPenney, provide more sales assistance because they carry more shopping goods about which customers need information. Their increased operating costs result in higher prices.

In *full-service retailers*, such as specialty stores and first-class department stores, salespeople assist customers in every phase of the shopping process. Full-service stores usually carry more specialty goods for which customers like to be "waited on." They provide more services resulting in much higher operating costs, which are passed along to customers as higher prices.

Product Line   Retailers also can be classified by the length and breadth of their product assortments. Some retailers, such as **specialty stores**, carry narrow product lines with deep assortments within those lines. Today, specialty stores are flourishing. The increasing use of market segmentation, market targeting, and product specialization has resulted in a greater need for stores that focus on specific products and segments.

In contrast, **department stores** carry a wide variety of product lines. In recent years, department stores have been squeezed between more focused and flexible specialty stores on the one hand, and more efficient, lower-priced discounters on the other. In response, many have added promotional pricing to meet the discount threat. Others have stepped up the use of store brands and single-brand "designer shops" to compete with specialty stores. Still others are trying mail-order, telephone, and Web selling. Service remains the key differentiating factor. Retailers such as Nordstrom, Saks, Neiman Marcus, and other high-end department stores are doing well by emphasizing high-quality service.

Supermarkets are the most frequently shopped type of retail store. Today, however, they are facing slow sales growth because of slower population growth and an increase in competition from discount food stores and supercenters on the one hand, and upscale specialty food stores on the other. Supermarkets also have been hit hard by the rapid growth of out-of-home eating. Thus, many traditional supermarkets are facing hard times.[2]

Thus, most supermarkets are making improvements to attract more customers. In the battle for "share of stomachs," many large supermarkets are moving upscale, providing improved store environments and higher quality food offerings, such as from-scratch bakeries, gourmet deli counters, and fresh seafood departments. For example, Safeway recently converted 300 of its stores to "lifestyle" formats, featuring subdued lighting, hardwood floors and display cabinets, and home departments. Others are cutting costs, establishing more efficient operations, and lowering prices in order to compete more effectively with food discounters. Finally, a few have added Web-based sales. Today, one quarter of all grocery stores sell their goods online—including Safeway, Albertsons, D'Agostino, and others—the number is slowly growing. Forrester Research estimates that online grocery buying will grow to $17.4 billion by 2008.[3]

Convenience stores are small stores that carry a limited line of high-turnover convenience goods. Some 138,000 U.S. convenience stores posted sales last year of $394.7 billion. More than two-thirds of convenience store revenues come from sales of gasoline; more than half of in-store revenues are from tobacco and beverage sales.[4]

In recent years, the convenience store industry has suffered from overcapacity as its primary market of young, blue-collar men has shrunk. As a result, many chains are redesigning their stores to attract female shoppers. They are shedding the image of a "truck stop" where men go to buy beer, cigarettes, and magazines, and instead offer fresh, prepared foods and cleaner, safer, more upscale environments. Consider this example:[5]

Specialty store
A retail store that carries a narrow product line with a deep assortment within that line.

Department store
A retail organization that carries a wide variety of product lines—typically clothing, home furnishings, and household goods; each line is operated as a separate department managed by specialist buyers or merchandisers.

Supermarket
Large, low-cost, low-margin, high-volume, self-service store that carries a wide variety of food, laundry, and household products.

Convenience store
A small store located near a residential area that is open long hours seven days a week and carries a limited line of high-turnover convenience goods.

■ Convenience store makeover: 7-Eleven is shedding its "truck stop" image and transforming its stores to offer more upscale assortments and environments.

There's something familiar about the place, with its muted orange-and-green color scheme. The aisles are wider, though, and the displays tonier. Chilling in the fridge is the house Chardonnay, not far from a glass case packed with baguettes and cream cheese croissants that come piping-hot out of the onsite oven. An aisle away is the snazzy cappuccino machine, which offers up bananas foster and pumpkin spice java. There's sushi and, of course, bouquets of fresh-cut flowers. They're right next to the Slurpee machine. Yes, this decidedly upscale little shoppe is a 7-Eleven—or it will be, once the company's team of ace technologists, trendspotters, and product developers wrap up one of the most ambitious makeovers in business history. The convenience king, most commonly known for lowbrow of popular features such as the Big Gulp and around-the-clock access to Twinkies, is moving up the food chain in search of flusher customers and fatter margins. After all, the majority of convenience-store sales come from gasoline and cigarettes—two increasingly stagnant categories. So 7-Eleven is banking on a new, inventive inventory mix that competes more with Starbucks than with Shell. The transformation seems to be working. After declaring bankruptcy in 1990, the company's fortunes turned around last year. Sales were up 12 percent; profits jumped 66 percent.

Superstores are much larger than regular supermarkets and offer a large assortment of routinely purchased food products, nonfood items, and services. Wal-Mart, Target, Kmart, Meijer, and other discount retailers offer *supercenters*, very large combination food and discount stores. Supercenters are growing in the United States at an annual rate of 25 percent, compared with a supermarket industry growth rate of only 1 percent. Wal-Mart, which opened its first supercenter in 1988, now has almost 2,000 worldwide, capturing more than 70 percent of all supercenter volume.[6]

Recent years have also seen the explosive growth of superstores that are actually giant specialty stores, the so-called **category killers**. They feature stores the size of airplane hangars that carry a very deep assortment of a particular line with a knowledgeable staff. Category killers are prevalent in a wide range of categories, including books, baby gear, toys, electronics, home improvement products, linens and towels, party goods, sporting goods, even pet supplies. Another superstore variation, a *hypermarket,* is a huge superstore,

Superstore

A store much larger than a regular supermarket that carries a large assortment of routinely purchased food products, nonfood items, and service.

Category killer

Giant specialty store that carries a very deep assortment of a particular line and is staffed by knowledgeable employees.

MARKETING AT WORK   11.1

Wal-Mart: The World's Largest Company

In 1962, Sam Walton and his brother opened the first Wal-Mart discount store in small-town Rogers, Arkansas. It was a big, flat, warehouse-like store that sold everything from apparel to automotive supplies to small appliances at very low prices. Experts gave the fledgling retailer little chance—conventional wisdom suggested that discount stores could succeed only in large cities.

Yet, from these modest beginnings, the chain exploded onto the national retailing scene. Incredibly, Wal-Mart's annual sales now exceed $288 billion—more than 1.7 times the sales of Target, Sears, JCPenney, and Costco combined—making it the world's largest company. Wal-Mart is the number-one seller in multiple categories of consumer products, including groceries, toys, CDs, and pet-care products. It sells more clothes than the Gap and Limited combined. Incredibly, Wal-Mart sells 30 percent of the disposable diapers purchased in the United States each year, 30 percent of the hair-care products, 26 percent of the toothpaste, and 20 percent of the pet food.

Wal-Mart's sales of $1.52 billion on one day in 2003 exceeded the GDPs of 26 countries. The company is now well established in larger cities and is expanding rapidly into international markets. For example, Wal-Mart is now the largest private employer in Mexico. The giant retailer has had a substantial impact on the U.S. economy. One out of every 235 men, women, and children in the United States is a Wal-Mart associate. According to one study,

Wal-Mart was responsible for some 25 percent of the nation's astonishing productivity gains during the 1990s.

What are the secrets behind this spectacular success? First and foremost, Wal-Mart is passionately dedicated to its value proposition of "Always Low Prices, *Always!*" Its mission is to "lower the world's cost of living." To deliver on this promise, it listens to and takes care of its customers, treats employees as partners, and keeps a tight rein on costs.

Wal-Mart knows its customers well and takes good care of them. As one analyst puts it, "The company gospel . . . is relatively simple: Be an agent for customers, find out what they want, and sell it to them for the lowest possible price." The company stays close to customers—for example, each top Wal-Mart executive spends at least two days a week visiting stores, talking directly with customers and getting a firsthand look at operations. Then, Wal-Mart delivers what customers want: a broad selection of carefully selected goods at unbeatable prices. Concludes Wal-Mart's current president and chief executive, "We're obsessed with delivering value to customers."

Beyond listening to and taking care of customers, Wal-Mart also takes good care of employees. It believes that, in the final accounting, the company's people are what really make it better. Wal-Mart was first to call employees "associates," a practice now widely copied by competitors. The associates work as partners, become deeply involved in operations, and share rewards for good performance.

Everyone at Wal-Mart [is] an associate—from [the CEO] . . . to a cashier named Janet at the Wal-Mart on Highway 50 in Ocoee, Florida. "We," "us," and "our" are the operative words. Wal-Mart department heads, hourly associates who look after one or more of 30-some departments ranging from sporting goods to electronics, see figures that many companies never show general managers: costs, freight charges, profit margins. The company sets a profit margin for each store, and if the store exceeds it, then the hourly associates share part of the additional profit.

Finally, Wal-Mart delivers real value by keeping a sharp eye on costs. Wal-Mart is a lean, mean, distribution machine—it has the lowest cost structure in the industry. This lets the giant retailer charge lower prices but still reap higher profits. For example, grocery prices drop an average of 10 to 15 percent in markets Wal-Mart has entered, and Wal-Mart's food prices average 20 percent less than its grocery-store rivals. Wal-Mart's lower prices attract more shoppers, producing more sales, making the company more efficient, and enabling it to lower prices even more.

Wal-Mart's low costs result in part from superior management and more sophisticated technology. Its Bentonville, Arkansas, headquarters contains a computer communications system that is second in size only to the U.S. Department of Defense, giving managers around the country instant access to sales and operating information. And its huge, fully automated distribution centers employ

perhaps as large as *six* football fields. Although hypermarkets have been very successful in Europe and other world markets, they have met with little success in the United States.

Finally, for some retailers, the product line is actually a service. Service retailers include hotels and motels, banks, airlines, colleges, hospitals, movie theaters, tennis clubs, bowling alleys, restaurants, repair services, hair salons, and dry cleaners. Service retailers in the United States are growing faster than product retailers.

Relative Prices   Retailers can also be classified according to the prices they charge (see Table 11.1). Most retailers charge regular prices and offer normal-quality goods and cus-

and they use their buying power more forcefully than anyone else in America," says the marketing vice president of a major vendor. "They talk softly, but they have piranha hearts, and if you aren't totally prepared when you go in there, you'll have your [head] handed to you."

Some critics argue that Wal-Mart squeezes its suppliers too hard, driving some out of business. Wal-Mart proponents counter, however, that it is simply acting in its customers' interests by forcing suppliers to be more efficient. "Wal-Mart is tough, but totally honest and straightforward in its dealings with vendors," says an industry consultant. "Wal-Mart has forced manufacturers to get their act together." In fact, in order to sell $288 billion worth of goods each year, Wal-Mart must first develop a network of partners to *supply* those goods. That requires skillful, supplier-relationship management.

Some observers wonder whether Wal-Mart can be so big and still retain its focus and positioning. They wonder if an ever-larger Wal-Mart can stay close to its customers and employees. The company's managers are betting on it. No matter where it operates, Wal-Mart's announced policy is to take care of customers "one store at a time." Says one top executive: "We'll be fine as long as we never lose our responsiveness to the consumer."

■ *Leading discounters, such as Wal-Mart, now dominate the retail scene. First and foremost, Wal-Mart is passionately dedicated to its value proposition of "Always Low Prices, Always!"*

Sources: Quotes and other information from Bill Saporito, "Is Wal-Mart Unstoppable?" *FORTUNE,* May 6, 1991, pp. 50–59; Carol J. Loomis, "Sam Would Be Proud," *FORTUNE,* April 17, 2001, pp. 131–144; Cait Murphy, "Introduction: Wal-Mart Rules," *FORTUNE,* April 15, 2002, pp. 94–98; Jerry Useem, "One Nation Under Wal-Mart," *FORTUNE,* March 3, 2003, pp. 65–78; Bruce Upbin, "Wall-to-Wall Wal-Mart," *Forbes,* April 12, 2004, p. 76; Sandra O'Loughlin and Barry Janoff, "Wal-Mart Keeps Smiling, and Rivals Are Not Happy," *Brandweek,* June 21, 2004, p. S62; Don Longo, "Wal-Mart on Its Way to Becoming the First Trillion Dollar Corporation," *Retail Merchandiser,* March 2005, p. 7; "100 Top Retailers," *Stores,* July 2005, accessed at www.stores.org; and Wal-Mart 2005 Annual Report, accessed at www.walmartstores.com in April 2005.

the latest technology to supply stores efficiently. Wal-Mart also spends less than competitors on advertising as a percentage of sales. Because Wal-Mart has what customers want at the prices they'll pay, its reputation has spread rapidly by word of mouth. It has not needed more advertising.

Finally, Wal-Mart keeps costs down through good old "tough buying." Whereas the company is known for the warm way it treats customers, it is equally well known for the calculated way it wrings low prices from suppliers. The following passage describes a visit to Wal-Mart's buying offices:

Don't expect a greeter and don't expect friendly.... Once you are ushered into one of the spartan, little buyers' rooms, expect a steely eye across the table and be prepared to cut your price. "They are very, very focused people,

---

tomer service. Others offer higher-quality goods and service at higher prices. The retailers that feature low prices are discount stores and "off-price" retailers.

Discount Stores. A **discount store** sells standard merchandise at lower prices by accepting lower margins and selling higher volume. The early discount stores cut expenses by offering few services and operating in warehouse-like facilities in low-rent, heavily traveled districts. Today's discounters have improved their store environments and increased their services, while at the same time keeping prices low through lean, efficient operations. Leading discounters, such as Wal-Mart, now dominate the retail scene (see Marketing at Work 11.1).

Discount store

A retail institution that sells standard merchandise at lower prices by accepting lower margins and selling at higher volume.

Off-price retailer

Retailer that buys at less-than-regular wholesale prices and sells at less than retail. Examples are factory outlets, independents, and warehouse clubs.

Independent off-price retailer

Off-price retailer that is either owned and run by entrepreneurs or is a division of a larger retail corporation.

Factory outlet

Off-price retailing operation that is owned and operated by a manufacturer and that normally carries the manufacturer's surplus, discontinued, or irregular goods.

Warehouse club

Off-price retailer that sells a limited selection of brand-name grocery items, appliances, clothing, and a hodgepodge of other goods at deep discounts to members who pay annual membership fees.

Off-Price Retailers.   As the major discount stores traded up, a new wave of **off-price retailers** moved in to fill the ultralow-price, high-volume gap. Ordinary discounters buy at regular wholesale prices and accept lower margins to keep prices down. In contrast, off-price retailers buy at less-than-regular wholesale prices and charge consumers less than retail. Off-price retailers can be found in all areas, from food, clothing, and electronics to no-frills banking and discount brokerages.

The three main types of off-price retailers are *independents, factory outlets,* and *warehouse clubs.* **Independent off-price retailers** either are owned and run by entrepreneurs or are divisions of larger retail corporations. Although many off-price operations are run by smaller independents, most large off-price retailer operations are owned by bigger retail chains. Examples include store retailers such as TJ Maxx and Marshall's, owned by TJX Companies, and Web sellers such as Overstock.com.

Factory outlets—producer-operated stores by firms such as Liz Claiborne, Carters, Levi Strauss, and others—sometimes group together in *factory outlet malls* and *value-retail centers,* where dozens of outlet stores offer prices as low as 50 percent below retail on a wide range of items. Whereas outlet malls consist primarily of manufacturers' outlets, value-retail centers combine manufacturers' outlets with off-price retail stores and department store clearance outlets, such as Nordstrom Rack, Neiman Marcus Last Call Clearance Centers, and Off 5th (Saks Fifth Avenue outlets). Factory outlet malls have become one of the hottest growth areas in retailing.

The malls now are moving upscale—and even dropping "factory" from their descriptions—narrowing the gap between factory outlet and more traditional forms of retailers. As the gap narrows, the discounts offered by outlets are getting smaller. However, a growing number of outlet malls now feature brands such as Coach, Polo, Ralph Lauren, Dolce & Gabbana, Giorgio Armani, Gucci, and Versace, causing department stores to protest to the manufacturers of these brands. Given their higher costs, the department stores have to charge more than the off-price outlets. Manufacturers counter that they send last year's merchandise and seconds to the factory outlet malls, not the new merchandise that they supply to the department stores. Still, the department stores are concerned about the growing number of shoppers willing to make weekend trips to stock up on branded merchandise at substantial savings.

Warehouse clubs   (or *wholesale clubs* or *membership warehouses*), such as Sam's Club, Costco, and BJ's, operate in huge, drafty, warehouse-like facilities and offer few frills. Customers themselves must wrestle furniture, heavy appliances, and other large items to the checkout line. Such clubs make no home deliveries and often accept no credit cards. However, they do offer ultralow prices and surprise deals on select branded merchandise.

Although they account for only about 4 percent of total U.S. retail sales, warehouse clubs have grown rapidly in recent years. These retailers appeal not just to low-income consumers seeking bargains on bare-bones products. They appeal to all kinds of customers shopping for a wide range of goods, from necessities to extravagances. Consider Costco, the nation's largest warehouse retailer:

> What Costco has come to stand for is a retail segment where high-end products meet deep-discount prices. It's the U.S.'s biggest seller of fine wines (including the likes of a Chateau Cheval-Blanc Bordeaux for $229.99 a bottle) and baster of poultry (55,000 rotisserie chickens a day). Last year it sold 45 million hot dogs at $1.50 each and 60,000 carats of diamonds at up to $100,000. It even offered a Pablo Picasso drawing at Costco.com—for only $129,999.99. Yuppies seek the latest gadgets there. Even people who don't have to pinch pennies shop at Costco.

> There was a time when only the great unwashed shopped at off-price stores. But ware-

■ Off-price retailers: Shoppers at warehouse clubs such as Costco "trade down" to private labels for things like paper towels, detergent, and vitamins. At the same time, they "trade up," getting good prices on items that make their hearts pound. Costco even offered a Pablo Picasso drawing at its Web site—for only $129,999.99.

house clubs attract a breed of urban sophisticates attuned to what one retail consultant calls the "new luxury." These shoppers shun Seiko watches for TAG Heuer; Jack Nicklaus golf clubs for Callaway; Maxwell House coffee (it goes without saying) for Starbucks. They "trade up," eagerly spending more for items that make their hearts pound and for which they don't have to pay full price. Then they "trade down" to private labels for things like paper towels, detergent, and vitamins. Catering to this fast-growing segment, Costco has exploded too. "It's the ultimate concept in trading up and trading down," says the consultant. "It's a brilliant innovation for the new luxury."[7]

Organizational Approach   Although many retail stores are independently owned, others band together under some form of corporate or contractual organization. The major types of retail organizations—*corporate chains*, *voluntary chains* and *retailer cooperatives*, *franchise organizations*, and *merchandising conglomerates*—are described in Table 11.2.

Chain stores are two or more outlets that are commonly owned and controlled. They have many advantages over independents. Their size allows them to buy in large quantities at lower prices and gain promotional economies. They can hire specialists to deal with areas such as pricing, promotion, merchandising, inventory control, and sales forecasting.

The great success of corporate chains caused many independents to band together in one of two forms of contractual associations. One is the *voluntary chain*—a wholesaler-sponsored group of independent retailers that engages in group buying and common merchandising—which we discussed in Chapter 10. Examples include Independent Grocers Alliance (IGA), Western Auto, and Do-It Best Hardware Center. The other form of contractual association is the *retailer cooperative*—a group of independent retailers that bands together to set up a jointly owned, central wholesale operation and conducts joint merchandising and promotion efforts. Examples are Associated Grocers and Ace Hardware. These organizations give independents the buying and promotion economies they need to meet the prices of corporate chains.

> **Chain stores**
> Two or more outlets that are owned and controlled in common, have central buying and merchandising, and sell similar lines of merchandise.

TABLE 11.2
Major Types of Retail Organizations

Type	Description	Examples
Corporate chain stores	Two or more outlets that are commonly owned and controlled, employ central buying and merchandising, and sell similar lines of merchandise. Corporate chains appear in all types of retailing, but they are strongest in department stores, food stores, drug stores, shoe stores, and women's clothing stores.	Sears, Safeway (grocery stores), CVS (drug stores), Williams-Sonoma (cookware and dinnerware)
Voluntary chains	Wholesaler-sponsored groups of independent retailers engaged in bulk buying and common merchandising.	Independent Grocers Alliance (IGA), Do-It Best Hardware Center, Western Auto, True Value
Retailer cooperatives	Groups of independent retailers who set up a central buying organization and conduct joint promotion efforts.	Associated Grocers (groceries), Ace (hardware)
Franchise organizations	Contractual association between a franchiser (a manufacturer, wholesaler, or service organization) and franchisees (independent businesspeople who buy the right to own and operate one or more units in the franchise system). Franchise organizations are normally based on some unique product, service, or method of doing business, or on a trade name or patent, or on goodwill that the franchiser had developed.	McDonald's, Subway, Pizza Hut, Jiffy Lube, Meineke Mufflers, 7-Eleven
Merchandising conglomerates	A free-form corporation that combines several diversified conglomerates retailing lines and forms under central ownership, along with some integration of their distribution and management functions.	Limited Brands

Franchise

A contractual association between a manufacturer, wholesaler, or service organization (a franchiser) and independent businesspeople (franchisees) who buy the right to own and operate one or more units in the franchise system.

Another form of contractual retail organization is a **franchise**. The main difference between franchise organizations and other contractual systems (voluntary chains and retail cooperatives) is that franchise systems are normally based on some unique product or service; on a method of doing business; or on the trade name, goodwill, or patent that the franchiser has developed. Franchising has been prominent in fast foods, health and fitness centers, haircutting, auto rentals, motels, travel agencies, real estate, and dozens of other product and service areas.

But franchising covers a lot more than just burger joints and fitness centers. Franchises have sprung up to meet about any need. Franchiser Mad Science Group franchisees put on science programs for schools, scout troops, and birthday parties. Mr. Handyman provides repair services for homeowners, while Merry Maids tidies up their houses.

Once considered upstarts among independent businesses, franchises now command 40 percent of all retail sales in the United States. These days, it's nearly impossible to stroll down a city block or drive on a suburban street without seeing a McDonald's, Subway, Jiffy Lube, or Holiday Inn. One of the best-known and most successful franchisers, McDonald's, now has more than 31,000 stores in 119 countries. It serves nearly 50 million customers a day and racks up more than $31 billion in annual systemwide sales. More than 70 percent of McDonald's restaurants worldwide are owned and operated by franchisees. Gaining fast is Subway Sandwiches and Salads, one of the fastest-growing franchises, with some 24,000 shops in 84 countries, including about 18,000 in the United States.[8]

Finally, *merchandising conglomerates* are corporations that combine several different retailing forms under central ownership. An example is Limited Brands, which operates The Limited (fashion-forward women's clothing), Express (trendy private-label women's and men's apparel), Victoria's Secret (glamorous lingerie and beauty products), Bath & Body Works (natural but luxurious beauty and body care products), and The White Barn Candle Company (home fragrance and décor items). Such diversified retailing, similar to a multibranding strategy, provides superior management systems and economies that benefit all the separate retail operations.

 Linking the Concepts

Slow down and think about all the different kinds of retailers you deal with regularly, many of which overlap in the products they carry.

■ Pick a familiar product: a camera, microwave oven, lawn tool, or something else. Shop for this product at two very different store types, say a discount store or category killer on the one hand, and a department store or smaller specialty store on the other. Compare the stores on product assortment, services, and prices. If you were going to buy the product, where would you buy it and why?

■ What does your shopping trip suggest about the futures of the competing store formats that you sampled?

RETAILER MARKETING DECISIONS

Retailers are always searching for new marketing strategies to attract and hold customers. In the past, retailers attracted customers with unique product assortments and more or better services. Today, retail assortments and services are looking more and more alike. National-brand manufacturers, in their drive for volume, have placed their branded goods everywhere. Such brands are found not only in department stores but also in mass-merchandise discount stores, off-price discount stores, and on the Web. Thus, it's now more difficult for any one retailer to offer exclusive merchandise.

Service differentiation among retailers has also eroded. Many department stores have trimmed their services, whereas discounters have increased theirs. Customers have become smarter and more price sensitive. They see no reason to pay more for identical brands, especially when service differences are shrinking. For all these reasons, many retailers today are rethinking their marketing strategies.

As shown in Figure 11.1, retailers face major marketing decisions about their *target market* and *positioning*, *product assortment and services*, *price*, *promotion*, and *place*.

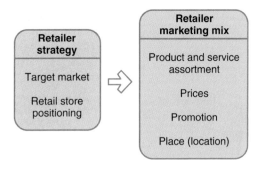

FIGURE 11.1
Retailer Marketing Decisions

Target Market and Positioning Decision   Retailers first must define their target markets and then decide how they will position themselves in these markets. Should the store focus on upscale, midscale, or downscale shoppers? Do target shoppers want variety, depth of assortment, convenience, or low prices? Until they define and profile their markets, retailers cannot make consistent decisions about product assortment, services, pricing, advertising, store décor, or any of the other decisions that must support their positions.

Too many retailers fail to define their target markets and positions clearly. They try to have "something for everyone" and end up satisfying no market well. In contrast, successful retailers define their target markets well and position themselves strongly. For example, Wal-Mart positions itself stronger on low prices. In a recent survey testing consumers on their recall of the slogans for American brands, 67 percent of consumers associated Wal-Mart with its "Always low prices. *Always*" promise. Sprite, in second place, scored just 35 percent recognition.[9]

If Wal-Mart owns the low-price position, how can other discounters hope to compete? Again, the answer is good targeting and positioning. For example, rather than facing Wal-Mart head-on, Target—or Tar-*zhay* as many fans call it—thrives by aiming at a seemingly oxymoronic "upscale discount" niche. It has become the nation's number-two discount chain by offering discount prices but rising above the discount fray with upmarket style and design and higher-grade service. Target's "expect more, pay less" positioning sets it apart and helps insulate it from Wal-Mart.

In the same way, pet-supply chain PETCO competes effectively with low-priced competitors Wal-Mart and PETsMART by positioning upscale:

> With Gen Xers postponing child rearing and baby boomers coping with empty nests, more Americans are treating pets like spoiled kids with fur. "The way people view animals in the household has changed dramatically" in recent years, says a PETCO executive, noting that 55 percent of pet canines now sleep in their owners' beds. People are now spending "more on what could be considered frivolous products," adds an industry consultant, "such as things to coddle their pets."
>
> This trend has been a boon for pets everywhere, but Sparky's not the only one wagging his tail. It's also been good for PETCO, which remade its business model to cash in on the trend. Ten years ago PETCO made most of its money selling food. Today two-thirds of its revenue comes from services like grooming and training, and from specialty goods like $7.50 beef-flavored toothpaste and $30 pheromone-emitting stress reducers. This shift to pricier offerings has helped PETCO avoid a catfight with Wal-Mart, a growing pet-supply power. Of PETCO's 10,000 offerings, only 40 overlap with Wal-Mart's. And going upscale has given PETCO higher operating margins than the more warehouse-focused PETsMART, the industry's top dog. Such smart targeting and positioning have earned PETCO more than 11 consecutive years of double-digit income growth.[10]

Product Assortment and Services Decision   Retailers must decide on three major product variables: *product assortment*, *services mix*, and *store atmosphere*.

The retailer's *product assortment* should differentiate the retailer while matching target shoppers' expectations. One strategy is to offer merchandise that no other competitor

■ Retail positioning: To avoid dog-eat-dog competition with Wal-Mart and cost-focused market leader PETsMART, PETCO has transformed itself into an emporium of luxury pet supplies.

carries, such as private brands or national brands on which it holds exclusives. For example, Saks gets exclusive rights to carry a well-known designer's labels. It also offers an exclusive home fashion line under its own Jane Seymour private brand. Another strategy is to feature blockbuster merchandising events—Bloomingdale's is known for running spectacular shows featuring goods from a certain country, such as India or China. Or the retailer can offer surprise merchandise, as when Costco offers surprise assortments of seconds, overstocks, and closeouts. Finally, the retailer can differentiate itself by offering a highly targeted product assortment—Lane Bryant carries plus-size clothing; Brookstone offers an unusual assortment of gadgets in what amounts to an adult toy store.

The *services mix* can also help set one retailer apart from another. For example, some retailers invite customers to ask questions or consult service representatives in person or via phone or keyboard. Home Depot offers a diverse mix of services to do-it-yourselfers, from "how-to" classes to a proprietary credit card.

The *store's atmosphere* is another element in the reseller's product arsenal. Every store has a physical layout that makes moving around in it either hard or easy. Each store has a "feel"; one store is cluttered, another cheerful, a third plush, a fourth somber. The retailer must design an atmosphere that suits the target market and moves customers to buy. For example, consider how Urban Outfitters sets itself apart by creating unique store environments:

> The inside of an Urban Outfitters store is a far cry from the stark, cookie-cutter interiors you'll find at Gap or Express. "Shopping here should be like a treasure hunt," says Laura O'Connor, Urban's 34-year-old general merchandising manager. O'Connor and her team give every store the feel of a boutique. Urban delivers small batches of new merchandise daily to keep things fresh. New and recycled fashions are sold alongside housewares (think beaded curtains and cocktail shakers), encouraging serious browsing and creating a thrill-of-the-hunt vibe suited to a thrift store. Visual arts teams at each store—typically four artists per location—overhaul each store's look every two weeks. The men's department at one store—this week, at least—is wallpapered with newspaper sports pages dyed

pink. That art deco jewelry? O'Connor got the idea while visiting a museum in Prague. The quick-changing assortments and décor get customers stopping in often to see what's new, while the "organized clutter" design keeps them around by selling unexpected items side by side. Urban even places Xboxes and vintage arcade games in its menswear sections so bored boyfriends won't pressure female shoppers to leave. As a result, Urban's customers stay an average of 45 minutes per visit—more than twice as long as shoppers linger in most clothing stores. That helps the company's stores generate $596 in sales per square foot each year—80 percent more than at Limited and Express. That, in turn, makes Urban Outfitters one of the best-performing clothing chains around.[11]

Other retailers practice "experiential retailing." At an REI store, consumers can try out climbing equipment on a huge wall in the store, or they can test GORE-TEX raincoats by going under a simulated rain shower. At Lifestyles Spa in Van Nuys, California, shoppers are invited to wear their bathing suits to the store and slip into water-filled Jacuzzis and hot tubs for a "test drive." Similarly, Maytag has set up "try-before-you-buy" stores in which it displays products in realistic home kitchen and laundry room settings, beckoning customers to try out products before making a choice. "Potential buyers of washers and dryers can do a load of laundry," notes an analyst. "Or if [they need] a new range, consumers can bake a sheet of cookies first. They can listen to a dishwasher to see whether it's really quiet."[12]

Increasingly, retailers are turning their stores into theaters that transport customers into unusual, exciting shopping environments. For example, outdoor goods retailer Cabela's stores are as much natural history museums for outdoor enthusiasts as they are retail outlets (see Marketing at Work 11.2). And the huge Mall of America near Minneapolis is a veritable playground that attracts as many as 42 million visitors each year. Under a single roof, it shelters more than 520 specialty stores, 50 restaurants, a seven-acre Camp Snoopy amusement park featuring 25 rides and attractions, an enormous LEGO Imagination Center, an ice-skating rink, an aquarium, a two-story miniature golf course, and Underwater Adventures, which features hundreds of marine specimens and a dolphin show.[13]

All of this confirms that retail stores are much more than simply assortments of goods. They are environments to be experienced by the people who shop in them. Store atmospheres offer a powerful tool by which retailers can differentiate their stores from those of competitors.

Price Decision A retailer's price policy must fit its target market and positioning, product and service assortment, and competition. All retailers would like to charge high markups and achieve high volume, but the two seldom go together. Most retailers seek *either* high markups on lower volume (most specialty stores) *or* low markups on higher volume (mass merchandisers and discount stores).

Thus, Bijan's boutique on Rodeo Drive in Beverly Hills sells "the most expensive menswear in the world." Its million dollar wardrobes include $375 silk ties and $19,000 ostrich-skin vests. Its "by appointment only" policy is designed to make its wealthy, high-profile clients comfortable with these prices. Says Mr. Bijan, "If a man is going to spend $400,000 on his visit, don't you think it's only fair that he have my full attention?"[14] Bijan's sells a low volume but makes hefty profits on each sale. At the other extreme, TJ Maxx sells brand-name clothing at discount prices, settling for a lower margin on each sale but selling at a much higher volume.

Retailers must also decide on the extent to which they will use sales and other price promotions. Some

■ Bijan's boutique on Rodeo Drive in Beverly Hills sells $375 silk ties and $19,000 ostrich-skin vests. It's "by appointment only" policy makes wealthy, high-profile clients comfortable with these prices.

MARKETING AT WORK   11.2

Cabela's: Creating a Sense of Wonder for People Who Hate to Shop

At first glance, outdoor products retailer Cabela's seems to break all the rules of retailing. First, it locates its stores in tiny, off-the-beaten-path locations—places like Sidney, Nebraska, Prairie du Chien, Wisconsin, Dundee, Michigan, Lehi, Utah, and Owatonna, Minnesota. Then, to make matters worse, it targets customers who hate to shop! The typical Cabela's customer is a reclusive male outdoorsman who yearns for the great outdoors, someone who detests jostling crowds and shopping.

So how do you explain Cabela's surging success? Over the past decade, Cabela's has evolved from a popular mail-order catalog business into one of the nation's hottest store retailers. Despite Cabela's often remote locations, customers are flocking to its 11 superstores to buy hunting, fishing, and outdoor gear. A typical Cabela's store draws 4.4 million customers a year—an average of 40,000 customers on a Saturday and 50,000–100,000 on a holiday weekend. Half of Cabela's customers drive 100 miles or more to get there, and many travel up to 350 miles. Schools even send busloads of kids.

In fact, Cabela's stores have become tourist destinations. Its store in Michigan is the state's largest tourist attraction, drawing more than 6 million people a year. The Minnesota store trails only the Mall of America in the number of annual visitors. And the Cabela's in Sidney, Nebraska, a town of only 6,000 people located 150 miles from the nearest city (Denver), attracts 1.2 millions visitors a year, making it

Nebraska's second-largest tourist attraction behind The Omaha Zoo.

Just what is it that attracts these hordes of otherwise reluctant shoppers to Cabela's remote stores? Part of the answer lies in all the stuff the stores sell. Cabela's huge 230,000 square foot superstores (one and one-half times larger than a typical Wal-Mart supercenter) house a vast assortment of quality merchandise at reasonable prices. Cabela's competes on price with discounters, but carries a selection that's six to ten times deeper—more than 200,000 kinds of items for hunting, fishing, boating, camping, and archery. "I'd have to go to two or three different stores to find all the brands they have at Cabela's," says Jason Gies, a 26-year-old mechanical engineer who drove 150 miles to purchase a vintage used Remington shotgun.

Cabela's also sells lines of branded clothing and gifts that appeal to customers' wives and children, making it a popular stop for the whole family. And to top things off, Cabela's offers first-class service. It staffs its departments with a generous supply of employees, all of whom must pass a 100-question test on the products they sell. For customers who stop by

during hunting trips, Cabela's even offers use of outdoor kennels and corrals to house their hunting dogs or horses while they shop. Hunters with rifles are welcomed.

But deep product assortments and good service don't explain the huge crowds that show up at Cabela's. The retailer's real magic lies in the *experiences* it creates for those who visit. "This is more than a place to go get fish-hooks," says a Cabela's spokesperson. "The Cabelas"—Nebraska brothers Dick and Jim—"wanted to create a sense of wonder." Mission accomplished! In each of its stores, Cabela's has created what amounts to a natural history theme park for outdoor enthusiasts.

Take the new store near Fort Worth, Texas, for example, Cabela's eleventh store and the largest

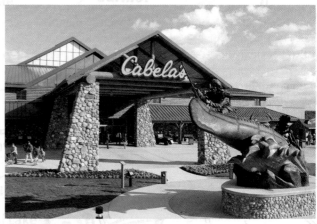

■ *Cabela's: "This is more than a place to get fishhooks …"*

retailers use no price promotions at all, competing instead on product and service quality rather than on price. For example, it's difficult to imagine Bijan's holding a two-for-the-price-of-one sale. Other retailers practice *"high-low" pricing*—charging higher prices on an everyday basis, coupled with frequent sales and other price promotions to increase store traffic, clear out unsold merchandise, create a low-price image, or attract customers who will buy other goods at full prices. Still others—such as Wal-Mart, Costco, Home Depot, and other mass retailers—practice *everyday low pricing (EDLP)*, charging constant, everyday low prices with few sales or discounts. Which strategy is best depends on the retailer's marketing strategy and the pricing approaches of its competitors.[15]

Promotion Decision   Retailers use any or all of the promotion tools—advertising, personal selling, sales promotion, public relations, and direct marketing—to reach consumers. They advertise in newspapers, magazines, radio, television, and on the Internet. Advertising may be supported by newspaper inserts and direct mail. Personal selling requires care-

■ *"…we want to create a sense of wonder."*

so far. Dominating the center of the store is Conservation Mountain, a two-story mountain replica with two waterfalls and cascading streams. The mountain is divided into four ecosystems and five bioregions: a Texas prairie, an Alaskan habitat, an Arctic icecap, an American woodlands, and an Alpine mountaintop. Each bioregion is populated by life-like, museum-quality taxidermy animals in action poses—everything from prairie dogs, deer, elk, and cari-

bou to brown bears, polar bears, musk oxen, and mountain goats.

Elsewhere in the store, Cabela's has created an African diorama, complete with African animals depicted in their natural habitats—an elephant, a rhinoceros, a Cape buffalo, and lions downing their prey. Other store attractions include a trophy deer museum and three walk-through aquariums, where visitors can view trophy-quality freshwater fish and learn to identify them. Getting hungry? Drop by the Mesquite Grill café for an elk, ostrich, or wild boar sandwich—no Big Macs here! The nearby General Store offers old-fashioned candy and snacks.

Cabela's spares no expense in developing this sportsman's paradise. A stuffed polar bear can cost up to $10,000. The Fort Worth store presents 800 such animals, right down to a Texas rattlesnake. Cabela's even created a new post—Taxidermy Purchasing Specialist—an executive who seeks out stuffed animals and mounts them in authentic scenes—two grizzly bears locked in battle, a leopard leaping for a monkey—even the droppings are real. "The muscle tone of the animal, the eyes, the posture—everything must be just right," says the executive. The taxidermy collection at Cabela's Fort Worth store is twice as large as the one at the Fort Worth Museum of Science and History.

So, if you scratch a little deeper, you find that far from breaking the rules, Cabela's is doing all

the right things. It's creating total experiences that delight the senses as well as the wallets of carefully targeted customers. Put it all together and you've got a powerful magnet for outdoorsmen and their families. Just ask one of the millions of anything-but-reluctant Cabela's customers:

"I'll do just about anything to avoid shopping," says John Brown, a small-business owner in Cheyenne, Wyoming. In 35 years of marriage, his wife says she's persuaded him to go shopping only twice. Yet one day last month he invited her to drive 100 miles with him for a day of shopping at Cabela's. "I'm like a kid in a candy store here," he said, dropping a new tackle box into his cart.

The trick . . . is appealing to the family member who is usually most reluctant to shop: Dad. One recent morning, Lara Miller was trying to round up her husband and three kids, as their morning trip to Cabela's stretched into afternoon. Mrs. Miller—normally the only family member who likes to shop—now was the one most ready to leave. "We haven't had breakfast yet," she moaned. Her husband, Darren Miller, a farmer in Jerome, Idaho, said, "I love this place."

Sources: Extracts, quotes, and other information from Heather Landy, "Plenty in Store," *Knight Ridder Tribune Business News*, May 22, 2005, p. 1; Kevin Helliker, "Hunter Gatherer: Rare Retailer Scores by Targeting Men Who Hate to Shop," *Wall Street Journal*, December 17, 2002, p. A1; Heather Landry, "Many Counting on New Cabela's to Be Quite a Draw," *Knight Ridder Tribune Business News*, May 22, 2005, p. 1; John Seward, "Outdoor Retailers Plan for Expansion," *Wall Street Journal*, June 8, 2005, p. 1; and Bud Kennedy, "Bud Kennedy Column," *Fort Worth Star-Telegram*, May 26, 2005, p. 1.

ful training of salespeople in how to greet customers, meet their needs, and handle their complaints. Sales promotions may include in-store demonstrations, displays, contests, and visiting celebrities. Public relations activities, such as press conferences and speeches, store openings, special events, newsletters, magazines, and public service activities, are always available to retailers. Most retailers have also set up Web sites, offering customers information and other features and often selling merchandise directly.

Place Decision   Retailers often point to three critical factors in retailing success: *location*, *location*, and *location*! It's very important that retailers select locations that are accessible to the target market in areas that are consistent with the retailer's positioning. Small retailers may have to settle for whatever locations they can find or afford. Large retailers, however, usually employ specialists who select locations using advanced methods.

Most stores today cluster together to increase their customer pulling power and to give consumers the convenience of one-stop shopping. *Central business districts* were the main form of retail cluster until the 1950s. Every large city and town had a central business district with department stores, specialty stores, banks, and movie theaters. When people began to move to the suburbs, however, these central business districts, with their traffic, parking, and crime problems, began to lose business. Downtown merchants opened branches in suburban shopping centers, and the decline of the central business districts continued. In recent years, many cities have joined with merchants to try to revive downtown shopping areas by building malls and providing underground parking.

Shopping center
A group of retail businesses planned, developed, owned, and managed as a unit.

A **shopping center** is a group of retail businesses planned, developed, owned, and managed as a unit. A *regional shopping center*, or *regional shopping mall*, the largest and most dramatic shopping center, contains from 40 to over 200 stores. It is like a covered mini-downtown and attracts customers from a wide area. A *community shopping center* contains between 15 and 40 retail stores. It normally contains a branch of a department store or variety store, a supermarket, specialty stores, professional offices, and sometimes a bank. Most shopping centers are *neighborhood shopping centers* or *strip malls* that generally contain between 5 and 15 stores. They are close and convenient for consumers. They usually contain a supermarket, perhaps a discount store, and several service stores—dry cleaner, self-service laundry, drugstore, video-rental outlet, barber or beauty shop, hardware store, or other stores.

A recent addition to the shopping center scene is the so-called *power center*. These huge unenclosed shopping centers consist of a long strip of retail stores, including large, freestanding anchors such as Wal-Mart, Home Depot, Costco, Best Buy, Michaels, OfficeMax, and CompUSA. Each store has its own entrance with parking directly in front for shoppers who wish to visit only one store. Power centers have increased rapidly during the past few years to challenge traditional indoor malls.

Combined, the nation's nearly 47,700 shopping centers now account for about 75 percent of U.S. retail activity (not counting cars and gasoline). The average American makes 9.5 trips to the mall over any three-month period, shopping for an average of 82 minutes per trip and spending about $83. However, many experts suggest that America is now "over-malled." During the 1990s, mall shopping space grew at about twice the rate of population growth. As a result, as many as 20 percent of America's shopping malls are either dead or dying. There "is a glut of retail space," says one insider. "There's going to have to be a shakeout."[16]

Thus, despite the recent development of many new "megamalls," such as the spectacular Mall of America, the current trend is toward value-oriented outlet malls and power centers on the one hand, and smaller "lifestyle centers" on the other. These lifestyle centers—smaller malls with upscale stores, convenient locations, and expensive atmospheres—are usually located near affluent residential neighborhoods and cater to the retail needs of consumers in their areas. "Think of lifestyle centers as part Main Street and part Fifth Avenue," comments an industry observer. "The idea is to combine the hominess and community of an old-time village square with the cachet of fashionable urban stores; the smell and feel of a neighborhood park with the brute convenience of a strip center." The future of malls "will be all about creating places to be rather than just places to buy."[17]

THE FUTURE OF RETAILING

Retailers operate in a harsh and fast-changing environment, which offers threats as well as opportunities. For example, the industry suffers from chronic overcapacity, resulting in fierce competition for customer dollars. Consumer demographics, lifestyles, and shopping patterns are changing rapidly, as are retailing technologies. To be successful, then, retailers will have to choose target segments carefully and position themselves strongly. They will have to take the following retailing developments into account as they plan and execute their competitive strategies.

New Retail Forms and Shortening Retail Life Cycles   New retail forms continue to emerge to meet new situations and consumer needs, but the life cycle of new retail forms is getting shorter. Department stores took about 100 years to reach the mature stage of the life cycle; more recent forms, such as warehouse stores, reached maturity in about

■ Shopping centers: The spectacular Mall of America contains more than 520 specialty stores, 50 restaurants, and a 7-acre indoor theme park, an Underwater World featuring hundreds of marine specimens and a dolphin show, and a two-story miniature golf course.

10 years. In such an environment, seemingly solid retail positions can crumble quickly. Of the top 10 discount retailers in 1962 (the year that Wal-Mart and Kmart began), not one still exists today.

Consider the Price Club, the original warehouse store chain. When Sol Price pioneered his first warehouse store outside San Diego in 1976, he launched a retailing revolution. Selling everything from tires and office supplies to five-pound tubs of peanut butter at super low prices, his store chain was generating $2.6 billion a year in sales within 10 years. But Price refused to expand beyond its California base. And as the industry quickly matured, Price ran headlong into wholesale clubs run by such retail giants as Wal-Mart and Kmart. (In his autobiography, Sam Walton confesses: "I guess I've stolen—I actually prefer the word 'borrowed'—as many ideas from Sol Price as from anybody else in the business.") Only 17 years later, in a stunning reversal of fortune, a faltering Price sold out to competitor Costco. Price's rapid rise and fall shows that even the most successful retailers can't sit back with a winning formula. To remain successful, they must keep adapting.[18]

Many retailing innovations are partially explained by the **wheel-of-retailing concept**.[19] According to this concept, many new types of retailing forms begin as low-margin, low-price, low-status operations. They challenge established retailers that have become "fat" by letting their costs and margins increase. The new retailers' success leads them to upgrade their facilities and offer more services. In turn, their costs increase, forcing them to increase their prices. Eventually, the new retailers become like the conventional retailers they replaced. The cycle begins again when still newer types of retailers evolve with lower costs and prices. The wheel-of-retailing concept seems to explain the initial success and later troubles of department stores, supermarkets, and discount stores, and the recent success of off-price retailers.

Wheel-of-retailing concept
A concept of retailing that states that new types of retailers usually begin as low-margin, low-price, low-status operations but later evolve into higher-priced, higher-service operations, eventually becoming like the conventional retailers they replaced.

Growth of Nonstore Retailing

Most of us still make most of our purchases the old-fashioned way: We go to the store, find what we want, wait patiently in line to plunk down our cash or credit card, and bring home the goods. However, consumers now have an array of alternatives, including mail-order, television, phone, and online shopping. Americans are increasingly avoiding the hassles and crowds at malls by doing more of their shopping by phone or computer. Although such retailing advances may threaten some traditional retailers, they offer exciting opportunities for others. Most store retailers have now developed direct retailing channels. In fact, more online retailing is conducted by "click-and-brick" retailers than by "click-only" retailers.[20]

Online retailing is the newest form of nonstore retailing. Only a few years ago, prospects for online retailing were soaring. As more and more consumers flocked to the Web, some experts even saw a day when consumers would bypass stodgy "old economy" store retailers and do almost all of their shopping via the Internet. However, the dot-com meltdown of 2000 dashed these overblown expectations. Many once-brash Web sellers crashed and burned and expectations reversed almost overnight. The experts began to predict that e-tailing was destined to be little more than a tag-on to in-store retailing.

However, today's online retailing is alive, well, and growing. With easier-to-use Web sites, improved online service, and the increasing sophistication of search technologies, online business is booming. In fact, online buying is growing at a much brisker pace than retail buying as a whole. Last year's U.S. online sales reached $145 billion, a 26 percent leap over the previous year and nearly 7 percent of all retail sales.[21]

All types of retailers now use the Web as an important marketing tool. The online sales of giant brick-and-mortar retailers, such as Sears, Wal-Mart, and Gap, are increasing rapidly. Several large click-only retailers—Amazon.com, online auction site eBay, online travel companies such as Travelocity and Expedia, and others—are now making it big on the Web. At the other extreme, hordes of niche marketers are using the Web to reach new markets and expand their sales. Today's more sophisticated search engines (Google, Yahoo!) and comparison shopping sites (Shopping.com, Buy.com, Shopzilla, and others) put almost any e-tailer within a mouse click or two's reach of millions of customers.

Still, much of the anticipated growth in online sales will go to multichannel retailers—the click-and-brick marketers who can successfully merge the virtual and physical worlds. Consider Staples, the $14.5 billion office-supply retailer. After just seven years on the Web, Staples captures annual online sales of more than $3 billion. Its online sales have averaged double-digit quarterly growth for more than four years. But it's not robbing from store sales in the process. The average yearly spending of small-business customers jumps from $600 when they shop in Staples stores to $2,800 when they shop online. As a result,

■ Online retailing: Today's e-tailing is alive, well, and growing, especially for click-and-brick competitors such as Staples. Its online sales have averaged double digit quarterly growth for more than four years. Business is also booming for click-only e-tailers, such as Travelocity.

although Staples has slowed new store openings, it plans to keep building its Web presence. It recently redesigned its site to extend its "Staples—That was easy" marketing promise to its online business. Based on two years of research, the retailer rebuilt online product pages around the way customers shop, including how they shop offline.[22]

Retail Convergence   Today's retailers are increasingly selling the same products at the same prices to the same consumers in competition with a wider variety of other retailers. For example, you can buy books at outlets ranging from independent local bookstores to discount stores such as Wal-Mart, superstores such as Barnes & Noble or Borders, or Web sites such as Amazon.com. When it comes to brand-name appliances, department stores, discount stores, home improvement stores, off-price retailers, electronics superstores, and a slew of Web sites all compete for the same customers. So if you can't find the microwave oven you want at Sears, just step across the street and find one for a better price at Lowe's or Home Depot—or order one online.

This merging of consumers, products, prices, and retailers is called *retail convergence*:[23]

> Retail convergence is the coming together of shoppers, goods, and prices. Customers of all income levels are shopping at the same stores, often for the same goods. Old distinctions such as discount store, specialty store, and department store are losing significance: The successful store must match a host of rivals on selection, service, and price. Where you go for what you want—that has created the biggest challenge facing retailers. Consider fashion. Once the exclusive of the wealthy, fashion now moves just as quickly from the runways of New York and Paris to retailers at all levels. Ralph Lauren sells in department stores and in the Marshall's at the strip mall. Designer Stephen Sprouse, fresh off designing a limited edition of Louis Vuitton handbags and luggage, has designed a summer line of clothing and other products for Target.

Such convergence means greater competition for retailers and greater difficulty in differentiating offerings. The competition between chain superstores and smaller, independently owned stores has become particularly heated. Because of their bulk-buying power and high sales volume, chains can buy at lower costs and thrive on smaller margins. The arrival of a superstore can quickly force nearby independents out of business. For example, the decision by electronics superstore Best Buy to sell CDs as loss leaders at rock-bottom prices pushed a number of specialty record store chains into bankruptcy. And Wal-Mart has been accused of destroying independents in countless small towns around the country.

Yet the news is not all bad for smaller companies. Many small, independent retailers are thriving. They are finding that sheer size and marketing muscle are often no match for the personal touch small stores can provide or the specialty niches that small stores fill for a devoted customer base.

The Rise of Megaretailers   The rise of huge mass merchandisers and specialty superstores, the formation of vertical marketing systems, and a rash of retail mergers and acquisitions have created a core of superpower megaretailers. Through their superior information systems and buying power, these giant retailers can offer better merchandise selections, good service, and strong price savings to consumers. As a result, they grow even larger by squeezing out their smaller, weaker competitors.

The megaretailers are also shifting the balance of power between retailers and producers. A relative handful of retailers now controls access to enormous numbers of consumers, giving them the upper hand in their dealings with manufacturers. For example, in the United States, Wal-Mart's revenues are more than five times those of Procter & Gamble, and Wal-Mart generates almost 20 percent of P&G's revenues. Wal-Mart can, and often does, use this power to wring concessions from P&G and other suppliers.[24]

Growing Importance of Retail Technology   Retail technologies are becoming critically important as competitive tools. Progressive retailers are using advanced information technology and software systems to produce better forecasts, control inventory costs, order electronically from suppliers, send information between stores, and even sell to customers within stores. They are adopting checkout scanning systems, online transaction processing, electronic data interchange, in-store television, and improved merchandise-handling systems.

Perhaps the most startling advances in retailing technology concern the ways in which today's retailers are connecting with customers. Many retailers now routinely use technologies such as touch-screen kiosks, customer-loyalty cards, electronic shelf labels and signs, handheld shopping assistants, smart cards, self-scanning systems, and virtual-reality displays. For example, in its new pilot store—Bloom—Southeastern grocery chain Food Lion is using technology to make shopping easier for its customers:

■ Retail technology: In its new pilot store—Bloom—Southeastern grocery chain Food Lion is using technology to make shopping easier for its customers.

Ever stood in the wine aisle at the grocery store and felt intimidated? You think that bottle of Shiraz looks pretty good, but you're not sure what it goes with. It's the sort of problem the creators of Food Lion's new concept store—Bloom—thought about, and one they will use technology to solve. The store relies on technology to enhance the shopping experience and to help customers find products, get information, and check out with greater ease. A computerized kiosk in the wine section lets you scan a bottle and get serving suggestions. The kiosk, and a second one in the meat section, lets you print recipes off the screen. Eight stations with touch screens and scanners around the store let you check an item's price or locate it on the map. To make it easier to keep track of purchases and check out, you can pick up a personal handheld scanner as you walk in the door, then scan and bag items as you shop. Checkout then is just a simple matter of paying as you leave. The personal scanners also give you a running total of the items you've selected as you shop, helping you stay within your budget and avoid surprises at the checkout. And if you drop off a prescription, the pharmacy can send a message to your scanner when your order is ready.[25]

Global Expansion of Major Retailers Retailers with unique formats and strong brand positioning are increasingly moving into other countries. Many are expanding internationally to escape mature and saturated home markets. Over the years, several giant U.S. retailers—McDonald's, Gap Inc., Toys "R" Us—have become globally prominent as a result of their great marketing prowess. Others, such as Wal-Mart, are rapidly establishing a global presence. Wal-Mart, which now operates more than 1,500 stores in nine countries abroad, sees exciting global potential. Its international division alone last year racked up sales of more than $56 billion, an increase of 18 percent over the previous year and 10 percent more than rival Target's *total* sales. Profits from international operations increased more than 20 percent last year.[26]

However, most U.S retailers are still significantly behind Europe and Asia when it comes to global expansion. Thirteen of the world's largest retailers are U.S. companies; only two of these retailers have set up stores outside of North America. Of the 17 non-U.S. retailers in the world's top 30, 13 have stores in at least ten countries. Among foreign retailers that have gone global are France's Carrefour, Germany's Metro and Aldi chains, the Netherlands' Royal Ahold, Britain's Tesco, Japan's Yaohan supermarkets, and Sweden's IKEA home furnishings stores.[27]

French discount retailer Carrefour, the world's second largest retailer after Wal-Mart, has embarked on an aggressive mission to extend its role as a leading international retailer:

The Carrefour Group has an interest in more than 11,000 stores in 31 countries in Europe, Asia, and the Americas, including 823 hypermarkets. It leads Europe in supermarkets and the world in hypermarkets. Carrefour is outpacing Wal-

Mart in several emerging markets, including South America, China, and the Pacific Rim. It's the leading retailer in Brazil and Argentina, where it operates close to 1,000 stores, compared to Wal-Mart's 160 units in those two countries. Carrefour is the largest foreign retailer in China, where it operates 240 stores versus Wal-Mart's 43. In the Pacific Rim, excluding China, Carrefour operates 118 hypermarkets in 6 countries to Wal-Mart's 16 units in South Korea alone. In short, Carrefour is forging ahead of Wal-Mart in most markets outside North America. The only question: Can the French retailer hold its lead? While no one retailer can safely claim to be in the same league with Wal-Mart as an overall retail presence, Carrefour stands a better chance than most to hold its own in global retailing.[28]

Retail Stores as "Communities" or "Hangouts" With the rise in the number of people living alone, working at home, or living in isolated and sprawling suburbs, there has been a resurgence of establishments that, regardless of the product or service they offer, also provide a place for people to get together. These places include cafés, tea shops, juice bars, bookshops, superstores, children's play spaces, and urban greenmarkets. Today's bookstores have become part bookstore, part library, part living room, and part coffee house. On an early evening at your local Barnes & Noble, you'll likely find back-pack toting high school students doing homework with friends in the coffee bar. Nearby, retirees sit in cushy chairs thumbing through travel or gardening books while parents read aloud to their children. Barnes & Noble sells more than just books, it sells comfort, relaxation, and community.

Brick-and-mortar retailers are not the only ones creating community. Others have also built virtual communities on the Internet.

■ Many retailers are expanding internationally to escape mature and saturated home markets. French discount retailer Carrefour, the world's second largest retailer after Wal-Mart, has embarked on an aggressive mission to extend its role as a leading international retailer.

Sony actively builds community among its PlayStation customers. For example, click on "Community" at the Playstation.com Web site, and you'll be invited to join The PlayStation Underground. "No matter what you're into," you're told, "you'll get more of it here, from the latest tips and tricks to the hottest releases on the horizon. Connect with PlayStation and fellow gaming enthusiasts to share your stories, opinions, and love of gaming with others who *really get it.*" The PlayStation Underground features incredibly active message boards, where game players can swap messages about specific games and other techie topics. The message boards also provide an opportunity for members to discuss a broad range of issues, from music and moods to personal tastes, no matter how trivial. Although Sony doesn't feed messages to the boards, it sees the value in having customers engaged in spirited exchanges directly on its site. "Our customers are our evangelists. They are a very vocal and loyal fan base," says a Sony spokesperson. "There are things we can learn from them."[29]

 Linking the Concepts

Time out! So-called experts have long predicted that nonstore retailing eventually will replace store retailing as our primary way to shop. What do you think?

■ Shop for a good book at the Barnes & Noble Web site (www.bn.com), taking time to browse the site and see what it has to offer. Next, shop at a nearby Barnes & Noble, Borders, or other bookstore. Compare the two shopping experiences. Where would you rather shop? On what occasions? Why?

■ A Barnes & Noble store creates an ideal "community" where people can "hang out." How does its Web site compare on this dimension?

Wholesaling

Wholesaling
All activities involved in selling goods and services to those buying for resale or business use.

Wholesaler
A firm engaged *primarily* in wholesaling activity.

Wholesaling includes all activities involved in selling goods and services to those buying for resale or business use. We call **wholesalers** those firms engaged *primarily* in wholesaling activities.

Wholesalers buy mostly from producers and sell mostly to retailers, industrial consumers, and other wholesalers. As a result, many of the nation's largest and most important wholesalers are largely unknown to final consumers. For example, you may never have heard of SuperValu, even though it's a $19.5 billion company and the nation's largest food wholesaler.

But why are wholesalers used at all? For example, why would a producer use wholesalers rather than selling directly to retailers or consumers? Simply put, wholesalers add value by performing one or more of the following channel functions:

- *Selling and promoting:* Wholesalers' sales forces help manufacturers reach many small customers at a low cost. The wholesaler has more contacts and is often more trusted by the buyer than the distant manufacturer.
- *Buying and assortment building:* Wholesalers can select items and build assortments needed by their customers, thereby saving the consumers much work.
- *Bulk-breaking:* Wholesalers save their customers money by buying in carload lots and breaking bulk (breaking large lots into small quantities).
- *Warehousing:* Wholesalers hold inventories, thereby reducing the inventory costs and risks of suppliers and customers.
- *Transportation:* Wholesalers can provide quicker delivery to buyers because they are closer than the producers.
- *Financing:* Wholesalers finance their customers by giving credit, and they finance their suppliers by ordering early and paying bills on time.
- *Risk bearing:* Wholesalers absorb risk by taking title and bearing the cost of theft, damage, spoilage, and obsolescence.
- *Market information:* Wholesalers give information to suppliers and customers about competitors, new products, and price developments.
- *Management services and advice:* Wholesalers often help retailers train their salesclerks, improve store layouts and displays, and set up accounting and inventory control systems.

TYPES OF WHOLESALERS

Merchant wholesaler
Independently owned business that takes title to the merchandise it handles.

Wholesalers fall into three major groups (see Table 11.3): *merchant wholesalers, agents and brokers,* and *manufacturers' sales branches and offices.* **Merchant wholesalers** are the largest single group of wholesalers, accounting for roughly 50 percent of all wholesaling. Merchant wholesalers include two broad types: full-service wholesalers and limited-service wholesalers. *Full-service wholesalers* provide a full set of services, whereas the various *limited-service wholesalers* offer fewer services to their suppliers and customers. The several different types of limited-service wholesalers perform varied specialized functions in the distribution channel.

Broker
A wholesaler that does not take title to goods and whose function is to bring buyers and sellers together and assist in negotiation.

Agent
A wholesaler who represents buyers or sellers on a relatively permanent basis, performs only a few functions, and does not take title to goods.

Manufacturers' sales branches and offices
Wholesaling by sellers or buyers themselves rather than through independent wholesalers.

Brokers and *agents* differ from merchant wholesalers in two ways: They do not take title to goods, and they perform only a few functions. Like merchant wholesalers, they generally specialize by product line or customer type. A **broker** brings buyers and sellers together and assists in negotiation. **Agents** represent buyers or sellers on a more permanent basis. *Manufacturers' agents* (also called manufacturers' representatives) are the most common type of agent wholesaler. The third major type of wholesaling is that done in **manufacturers' sales branches and offices** by sellers or buyers themselves rather than through independent wholesalers.

WHOLESALER MARKETING DECISIONS

Wholesalers now face growing competitive pressures, more demanding customers, new technologies, and more direct-buying programs on the part of large industrial, institutional, and

TABLE 11.3 Major Types of Wholesalers

Type	Description
Merchant wholesalers	Independently owned businesses that take title to the merchandise they handle. In different trades they are called *jobbers, distributors,* or *mill supply houses.* Include full-service wholesalers and limited-service wholesalers:
Full-service wholesalers	Provide a full line of services: carrying stock, maintaining a sales force, offering credit, making deliveries, and providing management assistance. There are two types:
Wholesale merchants	Sell primarily to retailers and provide a full range of services. *General merchandise wholesalers* carry several merchandise lines, whereas *general line wholesalers* carry one or two lines in great depth. *Specialty wholesalers* specialize in carrying only part of a line. Examples: health-food wholesalers, seafood wholesalers.
Industrial distributors	Sell to manufacturers rather than to retailers. Provide several services, such as carrying stock, offering credit, and providing delivery. May carry a broad range of merchandise, a general line, or a specialty line.
Limited-service wholesalers	Offer fewer services than full-service wholesalers. Limited-service wholesalers are of several types:
Cash-and-carry wholesalers	Carry a limited line of fast-moving goods and sell to small retailers for cash. Normally do not deliver. Example: A small fish-store retailer may drive to a cash-and-carry fish wholesaler, buy fish for cash, and bring the merchandise back to the store.
Truck wholesalers (or truck jobbers)	Perform primarily a selling and delivery function. Carry limited line of semiperishable merchandise (such as milk, bread, snack foods), which they sell for cash as they make their rounds to supermarkets, small groceries, hospitals, restaurants, factory cafeterias, and hotels.
Drop shippers	Do not carry inventory or handle the product. On receiving an order, they select a manufacturer, who ships the merchandise directly to the customer. The drop shipper assumes title and risk from the time the order is accepted to its delivery to the customer. They operate in bulk industries, such as coal, lumber, and heavy equipment.
Rack jobbers	Serve grocery and drug retailers, mostly in nonfood items. They send delivery trucks to stores, where the delivery people set up toys, paperbacks, hardware items, health and beauty aids, or other items. They price the goods, keep them fresh, set up point-of-purchase displays, and keep inventory records. Rack jobbers retain title to the goods and bill the retailers only for the goods sold to consumers.
Producers' cooperatives	Are owned by farmer members and assemble farm produce to sell in local markets. The co-op's profits are distributed to members at the end of the year. They often attempt to improve product quality and promote a co-op brand name, such as Sun Maid raisins, Sunkist oranges, or Diamond walnuts.
Mail-order wholesalers	Send catalogs to retail, industrial, and institutional customers featuring jewelry, cosmetics, specialty foods, and other small items. Maintain no outside sales force. Main customers are businesses in small outlying areas. Orders are filled and sent by mail, truck, or other transportation.
Brokers and agents	Do not take title to goods. Main function is to facilitate buying and selling, for which they earn a commission on the selling price. Generally specialize by product line or customer type.
Brokers	Chief function is bringing buyers and sellers together and assisting in negotiation. They are paid by the party who hired them and do not carry inventory, get involved in financing, or assume risk. Examples: food brokers, real estate brokers, insurance brokers, and security brokers.
Agents	Represent either buyers or sellers on a more permanent basis than brokers do. There are several types:
Manufacturers' agents	Represent two or more manufacturers of complementary lines. A formal written agreement with each manufacturer covers pricing, territories, order handling, delivery service and warranties, and commission rates. Often used in such lines as apparel, furniture, and electrical goods. Most manufacturers' agents are small businesses, with only a few skilled salespeople as employees. They are hired by small manufacturers who cannot afford their own field sales forces and by large manufacturers who use agents to open new territories or to cover territories that cannot support full-time salespeople.
Selling agents	Have contractual authority to sell a manufacturer's entire output. The manufacturer either is not interested in the selling function or feels unqualified. The selling agent serves as a sales department and has significant influence over prices, terms, and conditions of sale. Found in product areas such as textiles, industrial machinery and equipment, coal and coke, chemicals, and metals.
Purchasing agents	Generally have a long-term relationship with buyers and make purchases for them, often receiving, inspecting, warehousing, and shipping the merchandise to the buyers. They provide helpful market information to clients and help them obtain the best goods and prices available.
Commission merchants	Take physical possession of products and negotiate sales. Normally, they are not employed on a long-term basis. Used most often in agricultural marketing by farmers who do not want to sell their own output and do not belong to producers' cooperatives. The commission merchant takes a truckload of commodities to a central market, sells it for the best price, deducts a commission and expenses, and remits the balance to the producers.
Manufacturers' and retailers' branches and offices	Wholesaling operations conducted by sellers or buyers themselves rather than through independent wholesalers. Separate branches and offices can be dedicated to either sales or purchasing.
Sales branches and offices	Set up by manufacturers to improve inventory control, selling, and promotion. *Sales branches* carry inventory and are found in industries such as lumber and automotive equipment and parts. *Sales offices* do not carry inventory and are most prominent in dry-goods and notions industries.
Purchasing officers	Perform a role similar to that of brokers or agents but are part of the buyer's organization. Many retailers set up purchasing offices in major market centers such as New York and Chicago.

retail buyers. As a result, they have had to take a fresh look at the marketing strategies. As with retailers, their marketing decisions include choices of target markets, positioning, and the marketing mix—product assortments and services, price, promotion, and place (see Figure 11.2).

Target Market and Positioning Decision   Like retailers, wholesalers must define their target markets and position themselves effectively—they cannot serve everyone. They can choose a target group by size of customer (only large retailers), type of customer (convenience stores only), need for service (customers who need credit), or other factors. Within the target group, they can identify the more profitable customers, design stronger offers, and build better relationships with them. They can propose automatic reordering systems, set up management-training and advising systems, or even sponsor a voluntary chain. They can discourage less profitable customers by requiring larger orders or adding service charges to smaller ones.

Marketing Mix Decisions   Like retailers, wholesalers must decide on product assortment and services, prices, promotion, and place. The wholesaler's "product" is the assortment of *products and services* that it offers. Wholesalers are under great pressure to carry a full line and to stock enough for immediate delivery. But this practice can damage profits. Wholesalers today are cutting down on the number of lines they carry, choosing to carry only the more profitable ones. Wholesalers are also rethinking which services count most in building strong customer relationships and which should be dropped or charged for. The key is to find the mix of services most valued by their target customers.

Price is also an important wholesaler decision. Wholesalers usually mark up the cost of goods by a standard percentage—say, 20 percent. Expenses may run 17 percent of the gross margin, leaving a profit margin of 3 percent. In grocery wholesaling, the average profit margin is often less than 2 percent. Wholesalers are trying new pricing approaches. They may cut their margin on some lines in order to win important new customers. They may ask suppliers for special price breaks when they can turn them into an increase in the supplier's sales.

Although *promotion* can be critical to wholesaler success, most wholesalers are not promotion minded. Their use of trade advertising, sales promotion, personal selling, and public relations is largely scattered and unplanned. Many are behind the times in personal selling—they still see selling as a single salesperson talking to a single customer instead of as a team effort to sell, build, and service major accounts. Wholesalers also need to adopt some of the nonpersonal promotion techniques used by retailers. They need to develop an overall promotion strategy and to make greater use of supplier promotion materials and programs.

Finally, *place* is important—wholesalers must choose their locations, facilities, and Web locations carefully. Wholesalers typically locate in low-rent, low-tax areas and tend to invest little money in their buildings, equipment, and systems. As a result, their materials-handling and order-processing systems are often outdated. In recent years, however, large and progressive wholesalers are reacting to rising costs by investing in automated warehouses and online ordering systems. Orders are fed from the retailer's system directly into the wholesaler's computer, and the items are picked up by mechan-

FIGURE 11.2
Wholesaler Marketing Decisions

ical devices and automatically taken to a shipping platform where they are assembled. Most large wholesalers are using technology to carry out accounting, billing, inventory control, and forecasting. Modern wholesalers are adapting their services to the needs of target customers and finding cost-reducing methods of doing business.

TRENDS IN WHOLESALING

The wholesaling industry faces considerable challenges. The industry remains vulnerable to one of the most enduring trends of the last decade—fierce resistance to price increases and the winnowing out of suppliers who are not adding value based on cost and quality. Progressive wholesalers constantly watch for better ways to meet the changing needs of their suppliers and target customers. They recognize that, in the long run, their only reason for existence comes from adding value by increasing the efficiency and effectiveness of the entire marketing channel. For example, Grainger, the leading wholesaler of maintenance, repair, and operating (MRO) supplies, succeeds by making life easier and more efficient for the commercial and institutional buyers and sellers it serves (see Marketing at Work 11.3).

McKesson, the nation's leading wholesaler of pharmaceuticals, health and beauty care, home health care, and medical supply and equipment products, also provides an example of progressive wholesaling. To survive, McKesson has to remain more cost-effective than manufacturers' sales branches. Thus, the company has built efficient automated warehouses, established direct computer links with drug manufacturers, and set up extensive online supply management and accounts-receivable systems for customers. It offers retail pharmacists a wide range of online resources, including supply management assistance, catalog searches, real-time order tracking, and an account management system. It has also created solutions such as automated pharmaceutical dispensing machines that assist pharmacists by reducing costs and improving accuracy.

Retailers can even use the McKesson system to maintain medical profiles on their customers. McKesson's medical-surgical supply and equipment customers receive a rich assortment of online solutions and supply management tools, including an online order-management system and real-time information on products and pricing, inventory availability, and order status. According to McKesson, it adds value in the channel by providing "supply, information, and health care management products and services designed to reduce costs and improve quality across healthcare."[30]

The distinction between large retailers and large wholesalers continues to blur. Many retailers now operate formats such as wholesale clubs and hypermarkets that perform many wholesale functions. In return, many large wholesalers are setting up their own retailing operations. For example, SuperValu is the nation's largest food wholesaler, and it's also one of the country's largest food retailers. Almost half of the company's $19.5 billion in sales comes from its Bigg's, Cub Foods, Save-A-Lot, Farm Fresh, Hornbacher's, Laneco, Metro, Scott's Foods, Shop 'n Save, and Shoppers Food Warehouse stores.[31]

Wholesalers will continue to increase the services they provide to retailers—retail pricing, cooperative advertising, marketing and management information reports, accounting services, online transactions, and others. Rising costs on the one hand, and the demand for increased services on the other, will put the squeeze on wholesaler profits. Wholesalers who do not find efficient ways to deliver value to their customers will soon drop by the wayside. However, the increased use of computerized, automated, and Web-based systems will help wholesalers to contain the costs of ordering, shipping, and inventory holding, boosting their productivity.

Finally, facing slow growth in their domestic markets and such developments as the North American Free Trade Agreement, many large wholesalers are now going global. For example, in 1991, McKesson bought out its Canadian partner, Provigo. The company now receives about 3 percent of its total revenues from Canada. Its Information Solutions group operates widely throughout North America, the United Kingdom, and other European countries.

MARKETING AT WORK   11.3

Grainger: Making Life Easier and More Efficient for Both Buyers and Sellers?

Grainger may be the biggest market leader you've never heard of. It's a $5 billion business that offers more than 500,000 products and parts to more than 1.6 million customers. Its 582 North American branches, more than 15,500 employees, and innovative Web site handle more than 100,000 transactions a day. Grainger's customers include organizations ranging from factories, garages, and grocers to schools and military bases. Most American businesses are located within 20 minutes of a Grainger branch. Customers include notables such as Abbott Laboratories, General Motors, Campbell Soup Company, American Airlines, Mercedes-Benz, and the U.S. Postal Service. Grainger also operates one of the highest-volume B-to-B sites on the Web.

So, how come you've never heard of Grainger? Most likely it's because Grainger is a wholesaler. And like most wholesalers, it operates behind the scenes, selling only to other businesses. Moreover, Grainger operates in the not-so-glamorous world of maintenance, repair, and operating (MRO) supplies.

But whereas you might know little about Grainger, to its customers the company is very well known and much valued. Through its branch network, service centers, sales reps, catalog, and Web site, Grainger links customers with the supplies they need to keep their facilities running smoothly—everything from lightbulbs, cleaners, and display cases to nuts and bolts, motors, valves, power tools, and test equipment. Grainger is by far the nation's largest MRO wholesaler. Notes one industry reporter, "If industrial America is an engine, Grainger is its lubricant."

Grainger serves as an important link between thousands of MRO supplies manufacturers on one side and millions of industrial and commercial customers on the other. It operates on a simple value proposition: to make it easier and less costly for customers to find and buy MRO supplies. It starts by acting as a one-stop shop for products to maintain facilities. Most customers will tell you that Grainger sells everything—*everything*—from the ordinary to the out-of-the-ordinary. For example, it stocks thousands of lightbulbs—about every lightbulb known to mankind. If you don't believe it, go to

www.grainger.com and search *lightbulbs*! As for the not-so-ordinary:

Grainger sells 19 different models of floor-cleaning machines, has 49 catalog pages of socket wrenches, and offers nine different sizes of hydraulic service jacks, an assortment of NFL-licensed hard hats bearing team logos, and item No. 6AV22, a $36.90 dispenser rack for two 1 gallon containers of Gatorade. According to corporate legend, [Grainger] is the only place that workers on the Alaskan Pipeline have been able to find repellent to cope with arctic bears during their mating season.

Beyond making it easier for customers to find the products they need, Grainger also helps them streamline their acquisition processes. For most companies, acquiring MRO supplies is a very costly process. In fact, 40 percent of the cost of MRO supplies stems from the purchase process, including finding a supplier, negotiating the best deal, placing the order, receiving the order, and paying the invoice. Grainger constantly seeks ways to reduce the costs associated with MRO supplies acquisition, both internally and externally. Says one analyst, "Grainger will reduce your search and your process costs for items, instead of your having to order 10 things from 10 different companies, and you'll get one invoice. That's pretty powerful."

One company found that working with Grainger cut MRO requisition time by more than 60 percent; lead times went from days to hours. Its supply chain dropped from 12,000 suppliers to 560—significantly reducing expenses. Similarly, a large timber and paper-products company has come to appreciate the value of Grainger's selection and streamlined ordering process. It orders two-thirds of its supplies from Grainger's Web site at an annual acquisition cost of only $300,000. By comparison, for the remainder of its needs, this com-

■ *Grainger, the leading wholesaler of maintenance, repair, and operating (MRO) supplies, succeeds by making life easier and more efficient for the entire marketing channel.*

pany deals with more than 1,300 small distributors at an acquisition cost of $2.4 million each year—eight times the cost of dealing with Grainger for half of the volume. As a result, the company is now looking for ways to buy all of its MRO supplies from Grainger.

You might think that helping customers find what they need easily and efficiently would be enough to keep Grainger atop of the MRO mountain. But Grainger goes even further. On a broader level, it builds lasting relationships with customers by helping them find *solutions* to their overall MRO problems. Acting as consultants, Grainger sales reps help buyers with everything from improving their supply chain management to reducing inventories and streamlining warehousing operations.

Branches . . . serve as the base for Grainger territory managers who provide on-site help to big facilities. . . . [Reps can] tour a factory or an office complex or even a hotel and suggest to its managers exactly what supplies they really need to keep the place up to snuff, right down to how many gallons of carpet cleaner they'll require each week. That's how Grainger knows, for example, that one

Biltmore Hotel has 7,000 lightbulbs. . . . "Our reps can pretty much stand outside a building and get a general feel for what kinds of products the customer needs," [says Grainger's executive vice president of marketing, sales, and service].

Grainger has launched a series of programs designed to add value to its commodity business. For example, through its "Click & Sell" program, Grainger uses information collected about customers, such as industry data and purchase histories, to help sales reps find solutions for customer needs. If, for example, a customer places an order for a pump to use with caustic chemicals, the Grainger rep might also suggest gloves and safety glasses. If an item is unavailable, the database identifies alternative products to get the job done.

Grainger also offers value to customers through its links to and clout with suppliers.

Jason Eastin is facilities operations director for JRV Management, a . . . company that runs community and private sports facilities in metropolitan Detroit. He relies on Grainger in part because of its clout with factory reps. When his company was opening up its newest complex, he asked Chris Clemens, a Grainger territory manager, for help figuring out the number and kinds of fixtures that would be required. Clemens summoned a rep from Newell Rubbermaid, the household-products maker, who showed up with a laptop and a software program that churned out a reasonable supply chain within 20 minutes. Similarly, Clemens worked with a General Electric salesperson who figured out how Eastin could stretch out "relamping" his facilities to every two years, instead of annually, and cut costs significantly as well by switching to a different kind of metal-halide bulb as the primary kind of illumination for his ice arenas. "To have General Electric provide that service to me at no charge would never happen," Eastin says. "But Grainger has that buying-power structure. They open up those kinds of opportunities to me."

So now you've heard of Grainger, a wholesaler that succeeds by making life easier and more efficient for commercial and industrial buyers and sellers. Although a market leader, Grainger still captures only 4 percent of the highly fragmented U.S. market for MRO goods. That leaves a lot of room for growth. But to take advantage of the opportunities, Grainger must continue to find innovative ways to add value. "Our system makes our business partners and suppliers more efficient," says Fred Loepp, vice president of product management at Grainger, "and that benefits the entire supply chain." Says Theresa Dubiel, branch manager at Grainger's Romulus, Michigan, branch, "If we don't save [customers] time and money every time they come [to us], they won't come back."

Sources: Excerpts from Dale Buss, "The New Deal," *Sales & Marketing Management*, June 2002, pp. 25–30; and Colleen Gourley, "Redefining Distribution," *Warehousing Management*, October 2000, pp. 28–30. Also see Steve Konicki and Eileen Colkin, "Attitude Adjustment," *Informationweek*, March 25, 2002, pp. 20–22; "Grainger to Add, Relocate and Expand Branches," *Industrial Distribution*, June 2004, p. 20; "W.W. Grainger, Inc.," *Hoover's Company Profiles*, Austin, July 1, 2005, p. 11593; and the Grainger 2005 Fact Book and other information accessed at www.grainger.com, August 2005.

REST STOP → REVIEWING THE CONCEPTS

Pull in here and reflect back on this retailing and wholesaling chapter, the last of two chapters on distribution channels. In this chapter, we first looked at the nature and importance of retailing, major types of retailers, the decisions retailers make, and the future of retailing. We then examined these same topics for wholesalers. Although most retailing is conducted in retail stores, in recent years, nonstore retailing has increased rapidly. In addition, although many retail stores are independently owned, an increasing number are now banding together under some form of corporate or contractual organization. Wholesalers, too, have experienced recent environmental changes, most notably mounting competitive pressures. They have faced new sources of competition, more demanding customers, new technologies, and more direct-buying programs on the part of large industrial, institutional, and retail buyers.

1. Explain the roles of retailers and wholesalers in the distribution channel.

Retailing and wholesaling consist of many organizations bringing goods and services from the point of production to the point of use. *Retailing* includes all activities involved in selling goods or services directly to final consumers for their personal, nonbusiness use. *Wholesaling* includes all the activities involved in selling goods or services to those who are buying for the purpose of resale or for business use. Wholesalers perform many functions, including selling and promoting, buying and assortment building, bulk breaking, warehousing, transporting, financing, risk bearing, supplying market information, and providing management services and advice.

2. Describe the major types of retailers and give examples of each.

Retailers can be classified as *store retailers* and *nonstore retailers*. Although most goods and services are sold through stores, nonstore retailing has been growing much faster than has store retailing. Store retailers can be further classified by the *amount of service* they provide (self service, limited service, or full service), *product line sold* (specialty stores, department stores, supermarkets, convenience stores, superstores, and service businesses), and *relative prices* (discount stores and off-price retailers). Today, many retailers are banding together in corporate and contractual *retail organizations* (corporate chains, voluntary chains and retailer cooperatives, franchise organizations, and merchandising conglomerates).

3. Identify the major types of wholesalers and give examples of each.

Wholesalers fall into three groups. First, *merchant wholesalers* take possession of the goods. They include *full-service wholesalers* (wholesale merchants, industrial distributors) and *limited-service wholesalers* (cash-and-carry wholesalers, truck wholesalers, drop shippers, rack jobbers, producers' cooperatives, and mail-order wholesalers). Second, *brokers* and *agents* do not take possession of the goods but are paid a commission for aiding buying and selling. Finally, *manufacturers' sales branches and offices* are wholesaling operations conducted by nonwholesalers to bypass the wholesalers.

4. Explain the marketing decisions facing retailers and wholesalers.

Each retailer must make decisions about its target markets and positioning, product assortment and services, price, promotion, and place. Retailers need to choose target markets carefully and position themselves strongly. Today, wholesaling is holding its own in the economy. Progressive wholesalers are adapting their services to the needs of target customers and are seeking cost-reducing methods of doing business. Faced with slow growth in their domestic markets and developments such as the North American Free Trade Association, many large wholesalers are also now going global.

Navigating the Key Terms

Agent (352)
Broker (352)
Category killer (335)
Chain stores (339)
Convenience store (334)
Department store (334)
Discount store (337)
Factory outlet (338)

Franchise (340)
Independent off-price retailer (338)
Manufacturers' sales branches and offices (352)
Merchant wholesaler (352)
Off-price retailer (338)
Retailer (333)
Retailing (333)

Shopping center (346)
Specialty store (334)
Supermarket (334)
Superstore (335)
Warehouse club (338)
Wheel-of-retailing concept (347)
Wholesaler (352)
Wholesaling (352)

Travel Log

Discussing the Issues

1. Define both *retailing* and *wholesaling*. What are the primary differences between the two?

2. Distinguish between specialty stores, department stores, supermarkets, convenience stores, superstores, and category killers. Give one example of each.

3. Describe the target market and positioning for each of the stores you listed in the previous question. Do any of those markets overlap? If so, how does each store differentiate itself on the basis of product assortment and services?

4. The popularity of nonstore retailing is on the rise. What advantages do mail-order catalogs, television shopping networks, and the Internet offer consumers? Do you think nonstore retailing will continue to grow?

5. Define *retail convergence*. Consider your own shopping preferences. Do you frequent independently owned stores or shop primarily at larger chains? Why?

6. Describe the primary functions that wholesalers perform. How do those activities affect the relationships that companies build with consumers? How do they impact relationships with other channel partners?

Application Questions

1. The chapter opens with a discussion of Whole Foods. Have you shopped at Whole Foods? What was your impression of the store? Would you shop there again? Are you part of the chain's target market? How does the chain compete with other grocers?

2. Develop a table with the retail characteristics of amount of service, product line length and breadth, relative prices, and organizational structure as the rows of the table. Place the following retailers at the top of each column in the table: Best Buy, Sears, Sam's Club, Gap, Wal-Mart, and a local convenience store. Complete the cells in the table by describing each of the retailers on each of the

characteristics. What implications can you draw from this table?

3. Visit Grainger's Web site (www.grainger.com). Which of the channel functions discussed in the chapter does Grainger perform? How does the wholesaler create value for its customers? How does Grainger use its Web site to build customer relationships?

Under the Hood: Focus on Technology

Piggly Wiggly, a chain of grocery stores, has always focused on providing innovative, customer-centered shopping experiences. In fact, the chain was the first to allow customers to browse for their own groceries, rather than having a clerk behind a counter retrieve needed items. Continuing with that tradition, Piggly Wiggly now offers Pay By Touch, a technology that allows customers to pay for their groceries with the simple touch of a finger. After completing a two-minute registration process, customers link their unique fingerprint with payment information, including a credit card or checking account numbers, and loyalty card accounts. When checking out, customers place a finger on a small scanner located next to the register and the transaction is complete. No credit cards or loyalty card required. Within a month of adding Pay By Touch technology to its stores nationwide, nearly 20 percent of the store's noncash customers had signed on. And, according to

loyalty-card statistics, says Rich Farrell, vice president of information services at Piggly Wiggly, customers "are buying more than they used to. It must be the ease of the purchasing process. When we first purchased this technology, we were looking for a payment system that would enhance speed, convenience, and security, and this does all three."*

1. How comfortable are you with fingerprint scanning technology in a retail setting? Would you complete the registration process and use the Pay By Touch technology when checking out?

2. How might Pay By Touch, and other retail technologies, help build relationships with new consumers and grow relationships with loyal customers?

*See Andrea Orr, "Piggly Wiggly Finds the Right Touch," July, 18, 2005, accessed at www.extremenano.com.

Focus on Ethics

Large discount stores and superstores can wield enormous power and impact a community. Because of their bulk-buying power and high sales volume, national chains can buy at lower costs and thrive on smaller margins. By doing so, Wal-Mart has been accused of destroying independents in countless small towns around the country. As a result, the megaretailer has been the target of considerable criticism. Sam Walton once responded to the criticism, saying, "Of all the notions I've heard about Wal-Mart, none has ever baffled me more than this idea that we are somehow the enemy of small-town America. Nothing could be further from the truth. Wal-Mart has actually kept quite a number of small towns from becoming extinct by saving literally billions of dollars for the people who live in them, as well as by creating hundreds of thousands of jobs in our stores . . . I don't want to be too critical of small-town merchants, but the truth is that a lot of these folks just weren't doing a very good job of taking care of their customers.

Whenever we put a Wal-Mart store into a town, customers would just flock to us from the variety stores. With our low prices, we ended an era of 45 percent markups and limited selection."*

1. What is your reaction to Sam Walton's remarks? Do you agree with his perspective?

2. Does Wal-Mart have a responsibility to the small retailers it puts out of business? Why or why not?

3. Should communities be concerned about the plight of small businesses competing with Wal-Mart? What are the benefits and drawbacks of having big-box retailers in a community? What, if anything, should city governments do to protect local retailers from the threat of large retailers?

*See www.emich.edu/public/geo/557book/c313.impactwalmart.html

Videos

The Reebok video case that accompanies this chapter is located in Appendix 1 at the back of the book.

Chapter 12

Night-Night Jet Set, Night-Night

→ AFTER STUDYING THIS CHAPTER, YOU SHOULD BE ABLE TO

1. discuss the process and advantages of integrated marketing communications in communicating customer value

2. define the five promotion tools and discuss the factors that must be considered in shaping the overall promotion mix

3. describe and discuss the major decisions involved in developing an advertising program

4. explain how sales promotion campaigns are developed and implemented

5. explain how companies use public relations to communicate with their publics

Communicating Customer Value: Advertising, Sales Promotion, and Public Relations

Road Map Previewing the Concepts

We'll forge ahead now into the last of the marketing mix tools—promotion. Companies must do more than just create customer value. They must also use promotion to clearly and persuasively communicate that value. You'll find that promotion is not a single tool but rather a mix of several tools. Ideally, under the concept of *integrated marketing communications,* the company will carefully coordinate these promotion elements to deliver a clear, consistent, and compelling message about the organization and its products. We'll begin by introducing you to the various promotion mix tools. Next, we'll examine the rapidly changing communications environment and the need for integrated marketing communications. Finally, we'll look more closely at three of the promotion tools—advertising, sales promotion, and public relations. In the next chapter, we'll visit the other two promotion mix tools, personal selling and direct marketing.

To start this chapter, let's look behind the scenes at an award-winning advertising agency—Crispin Porter + Bogusky (CP+B). As it turns out, CP+B's success reflects all the current trends in the fast-changing world of modern marketing communications. As one advertising insider puts it: "CP+B is right where it's at in today's advertising." Let's take a closer look.

Inside its sparkling steel-and-granite Miami headquarters, ad agency Crispin Porter + Bogusky was unveiling pieces of the campaign for new client Virgin Atlantic Airways. At presentations like this, agency executives typically hold up TV commercial storyboards and explain why everyone is going to love this particular dancing cat or flatulent horse. This morning, however, the presenters from CP+B—led by a pregnant woman, a young dude with a flop of unruly blond curls, and a guy with Elvis sideburns—had no TV storyboards. But they sure had a lot of other stuff, and it came flying from all sides at the three Virgin clients.

There were ads designed to look like those flight safety cards found in airplane seat backs. There were samples of a newspaper comic strip called *The Jet Set*, as well as a mock-up for a lifestyle magazine titled *Jetrosexual*, a term CP+B created to describe Virgin's target audience. Both played off the Virgin campaign's theme, "Go Jet Set, Go!" There was something titled *Night-Night Jet Set, Night-Night* that resembled an illustrated children's book, though it actually contained bedtime ditties for adult business flyers—something that flight attendants would leave on pillows in Virgin's sleeping cabins.

And speaking of those flight attendants? CP+B wouldn't mind hiring a high-fashion designer to spruce up the uniforms. And how about staging "concert flights"? And wouldn't it be cool to hire celebrities to work as "guest flight attendants"? And by the way, could the pilots fly at a higher altitude so Virgin can claim it soars above the competition? And there's one more thing—well, no, actually there were 160 more, because that was how many far-flung ideas CP+B had come up with since starting work on the campaign.

Welcome to advertising as practiced by Crispin Porter + Bogusky, the agency of the moment. CP+B is as hot as South Beach on a Saturday night, and it's at the epicenter of all that's current in today's advertising world. The agency has snapped up every top advertising creative award lately while reeling in prime accounts including BMW's MINI cars, Google, IKEA furniture stores, Virgin Atlantic Airways, and recently Burger King—a $300 million-plus account.

Working with modest ad budgets, CP+B has riveted customers' attention with startling guerrilla tactics, unconventional uses of media, and holistic marketing strategies that tie together everything from product design to packaging to event marketing to stuff that can't even be categorized. "Anything and everything is an ad," preaches CP+B's 40-something creative director, Alex Bogusky. What the agency uses sparingly, however, is the traditional TV commercial. This is very close to heresy in a business that grew fat on those million-dollar 30-second spots. There's no good buzzword for what CP+B does (the term *integrated marketing communication* comes closest), but here are some appropriate adjectives: fresh, radical, street-smart, mischievous, all-over-the-lot, maybe-the-next-big-thing. In other words, it's extreme, dude.

CP+B's Coconut Grove offices are far removed from mainstream Madison Avenue. Being far away from big agencies and big media has allowed CP+B to evolve as an independent species. "They're not breathing the same air as everybody else in advertising," observes the creative director of a competing New York agency. "Instead of being surrounded by ad people, they're surrounded by artists, music people, and the whole Cuban/Latin/European/gay/South Beach culture." Alex Bogusky is a homegrown product of that culture, and he looks it. He wears loose polo shirts over athletic shoulders, with long hair coming out from under a skullcap. He has an easy smile, calls people "bud," and politely asks if you "need a pee-pee break." But beneath Bogusky's sunny demeanor, "Alex plays advertising like an extreme sport," says a former creative director. "He is fearless."

During the early 1990s, CP+B produced ads that swept local award shows. Locals still admiringly recall a Sunglass Hut billboard featuring a gigantic pair of shades and the headline "What to Wear to a Nude Beach." To promote a local homeless shelter, CP+B put ads in the darndest places: on shopping carts, trash dumpsters, park benches. The agency's

reputation grew, and in 1997 CP+B finally got hold of a project that could draw national attention—the Florida teen antismoking campaign "Truth."

Through street-level research with local teenagers, CP+B learned that conventional antismoking appeals—"This will kill you"—made rebellious kids want to smoke even more. So instead of using conventional marketing, such as slick TV commercials, CP+B used guerrilla-ambush tactics to create an "anti-brand" that kids could latch on to. Bogusky named the brand "Truth." The agency scattered the "Truth" logo across Florida on posters, leaflets, T-shirts, stickers, and other gear. It rented trucks and trains to traverse the state, staging impromptu live events and parties where "Truth" swag was disseminated. The "Truth" Web site served as information central for the whole campaign.

The "Truth" campaign worked: Between 1998 and 2002, smoking among middle and high school students in Florida declined an average of 38 percent. The American Legacy Foundation eventually took the "Truth" campaign national, complete with big-budget Super Bowl commercials. But the beauty of "Truth" was its grassroots origin—which showed that CP+B could build a popular movement around an unknown brand, using any and all available means.

"Truth" begat the celebrated BMW MINI campaign, in which CP+B created a huge buzz for the quirky, anything-but-ordinary little British-made MINI car with an anything-but-ordinary "Let's Motor" campaign. The campaign employed a rich mix of unconventional media, carefully integrated to create personality for the car and a tremendous buzz of excitement among consumers. The "Let's Motor" campaign was a smashing success, creating an almost cult-like following for the personable little car. And suddenly everyone—from IKEA and Virgin Atlantic to big old Burger King and even Coca-Cola—wanted a piece of CP+B.

How does CP+B do it? For starters, the agency swings for the fences on each new brand assignment, going beyond cute slogans to try to start a consumer movement behind the brand. "Truth" was a mobilizing idea, as were "motoring" in a MINI and joining "the jet set" on Virgin. Once a central theme is in place, the ad making begins—and this is where CP+B really turns the process upside down. Most copywriters and art directors instinctively start by sketching ideas for print ads and TV commercials. But CP+B begins with a blank slate. "What if there were no TV and no magazines—how would we make this brand famous?" Bogusky demands. The goal is to figure out the best places to reach the target audience and the most interesting vehicles to carry the message, even if those vehicles have to be invented.

This leads to another CP+B difference: the agency often sticks its nose into things unrelated to advertising. For example, the agency recently convinced Virgin Atlantic to brand its flights by giving them names, such as "The Fly Chi" for flight number 020, San Francisco to London. Similarly, it persuaded MINI to rewrite its lease agreement to match the tone of the overall MINI campaign. What does CP+B know about car leases? "Nothing," Bogusky admits, but that doesn't stop him from trying to ensure that every consumer "touch point" conveys the same message as the ad campaign. And CP+B talked previously-conservative Burger King into hosting a bawdy "Subservient Chicken" Internet microsite, in which a man in a dingy apartment wearing a chicken suit and garter belt hangs out in front of his Web cam and does almost anything you ask him to. The site has been incredibly successful, attracting more than 385 million hits so far and solidifying Burger King's "have it your way" positioning.

Although unconventional, Crispin Porter + Bogusky just keeps winning awards, including top honors at last year's International Advertising Festival and a remarkable 2005 Grand Clio for its Subservient Chicken campaign. In 2005, *Advertising Age* named CP+B its agency of the year. The industry's titans are watching CP+B closely. "They've turned guerrilla into an art form, and it's working," admits one of advertising's most revered creative stars, Dan Wieden of ad agency Wieden & Kennedy. "Did I mention I hate them?"[1]

Building good customer relationships calls for more than just developing a good product, pricing it attractively, and making it available to target customers. Companies must also *communicate* that value to customers, and what they communicate should not be left to chance. All of their communications must be planned and blended into a carefully integrated marketing communications program. Just as good communication is important in building and maintaining any kind of relationship, it is a crucial element in a company's efforts to build profitable customer relationships.

The Promotion Mix

A company's total **promotion mix**—also called its **marketing communications mix**—consists of the specific blend of advertising, sales promotion, public relations, personal selling, and direct-marketing tools that the company uses to persuasively communicate customer value and build customer relationships. Definitions of the five major promotion tools follow:[2]

Advertising: Any paid form of nonpersonal presentation and promotion of ideas, goods, or services by an identified sponsor.

Sales promotion: Short-term incentives to encourage the purchase or sale of a product or service.

Public relations: Building good relations with the company's various publics by obtaining favorable publicity, building up a good corporate image, and handling or heading off unfavorable rumors, stories, and events.

Personal selling: Personal presentation by the firm's sales force for the purpose of making sales and building customer relationships.

Direct marketing: Direct connections with carefully targeted individual consumers to both obtain an immediate response and cultivate lasting customer relationships—the use of telephone, mail, fax, e-mail, the Internet, and other tools to communicate directly with specific consumers.

Each category involves specific promotional tools used to communicate with consumers. For example, advertising includes broadcast, print, Internet, outdoor, and other forms. Sales promotion includes discounts, coupons, displays, and demonstrations. Personal selling includes sales presentations, trade shows, and incentive programs. Public relations includes press releases, sponsorships, special events, and Web pages. And direct marketing includes catalogs, telephone marketing, kiosks, the Internet, and more.

At the same time, marketing communication goes beyond these specific promotion tools. The product's design, its price, the shape and color of its package, and the stores that sell it—*all* communicate something to buyers. Thus, although the promotion mix is the company's primary communication activity, the entire marketing mix—promotion *and* product, price, and place—must be coordinated for greatest communication impact.

Promotion mix
The specific mix of advertising, personal selling, sales promotion, public relations, and direct marketing that a company uses to persuasively communicate customer value and build customer relationships.

Advertising
Any paid form of nonpersonal presentation and promotion of ideas, goods, or services by an identified sponsor.

Sales promotion
Short-term incentives to encourage the purchase or sale of a product or service.

Public relations
Building good relations with the company's various publics by obtaining favorable publicity, building up a good "corporate image," and handling or heading off unfavorable rumors, stories, and events.

Personal selling
Personal presentation by the firm's sales force for the purpose of making sales and building customer relationships.

Direct marketing
Direct connections with carefully targeted individual consumers to both obtain an immediate response and cultivate lasting customer relationships—the use of telephone, mail, fax, e-mail, the Internet, and other tools to communicate directly with specific consumers.

Integrated Marketing Communications

In past decades, marketers have perfected the art of mass marketing—selling highly standardized products to masses of customers. In the process, they have developed effective mass-media communications techniques to support these mass-marketing strategies. Large companies routinely invest millions or even billions of dollars in television, magazine, or other mass-media advertising, reaching tens of millions of customers with a single ad. Today, however, marketing managers face some new marketing communications realities.

THE NEW MARKETING COMMUNICATIONS LANDSCAPE

Two major factors are changing the face of today's marketing communications. First, as mass markets have fragmented, marketers are shifting away from mass marketing. More and more, they are developing focused marketing programs designed to build closer relationships with customers in more narrowly defined micromarkets. Second, vast improvements in information technology are speeding the movement toward segmented marketing. With today's new information technologies, marketers can amass detailed customer information and keep closer track of customer needs.

Improved information technology has also caused striking changes in the ways in which companies and customers communicate with each other. The digital age has spawned a host of new information and communication tools—from the Internet and cell phones to satellite and cable television systems and digital video recorders (DVRs). The new technologies give companies exciting new digital tools for interacting with targeted consumers. They also give consumers more control over the nature and timing of messages they choose to send and receive.

THE SHIFTING MARKETING COMMUNICATIONS MODEL

The shift toward segmented marketing and the explosive developments in information and communications technology have had a dramatic impact on marketing communications. Just as mass marketing once gave rise to a new generation of mass-media communications, the shift toward targeted marketing and the changing communications environment are giving birth to a new marketing communications model. Although television, magazines, and other mass media remain very important, their dominance is now declining.

■ The shifting marketing communications model: CP+B's Let's Motor campaign for the MINI uses a rich mix of media: conventional but clever magazine ads coupled with novel displays—here an actual MINI that looks like a children's ride ("Rides $16,850. Quarters only") and airport displays featuring oversize newspaper vending machines next to billboards proclaiming, "Makes everything else seem a little too big."

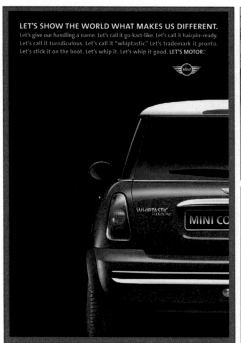

Advertisers are now adding a broad selection of more specialized and highly targeted media to reach smaller customer segments with more personalized messages. The new media range from specialty magazines and cable television channels to product placements in television programs and video games, to Internet catalogs and e-mail. In all, companies are doing less *broadcasting* and more *narrowcasting*.

Some advertising industry experts even predict a doom-and-gloom "chaos scenario," in which the old mass-media communications model will collapse entirely. They believe that marketers will increasingly abandon traditional mass media in favor of "the glitzy promise of new digital technologies—from Web sites and e-mail to cell phone content and video on demand. . . . Fragmentation, the bane of network TV and mass marketers everywhere, will become the Holy Grail, the opportunity to reach—and have a conversation with—small clusters of consumers who are consuming not what is force-fed them, but exactly what they want."[3]

As mass-media costs rise, audiences shrink, and more viewers use TiVo and other DVR systems to skip past disruptive television commercials, the skeptics predict the demise of the old mass-media mainstay—the 30-second television commercial. They point out that many large advertisers are now shifting their advertising budgets away from broadcast television in favor of more targeted, cost-effective, interactive, and engaging media. "The ad industry's plotline used to be a lot simpler: See a commercial, go to the store, buy the product," says one observer. "Now advertisers have to reach consumers in less-conventional ways—on the subway, on the street, on a cell phone, [online,] on a mug, in a skate park, in a store, on a truck."[4]

Other industry insiders, however, see a more gradual shift to the new marketing communications model. They note that broadcast television and other mass media still capture a lion's share of the promotion budgets of most major marketing firms, a fact that isn't likely to change quickly. In fact, company spending on broadcast television advertising actually increased last year. One advertising expert explains: "TV audiences remain coveted because—shrinking though they are—they represent the last vestige of mass media and marketing, or as [one executive asserts] 'the last surviving conglomeration of human beings in the living room.'"[5]

Thus, it seems likely that the new marketing communications model will consist of a gradually shifting mix of both traditional mass media and a wide array of exciting new, more targeted, more personalized media. "We need to reinvent the way we market to consumers," says A. G. Lafley, chief executive of Procter & Gamble. "Mass marketing still has an important role, [but] we need new models to initially coexist with mass marketing, and eventually to succeed it."[6]

THE NEED FOR *INTEGRATED* MARKETING COMMUNICATIONS

The shift toward a richer mix of media and communication approaches poses a problem for marketers. Consumers today are bombarded by commercial messages from a broad range of sources. But consumers don't distinguish between message sources the way marketers do. In the consumer's mind, messages from different media and promotional approaches all become part of a single message about the company. Conflicting messages from these different sources can result in confused company images, brand positions, and customer relationships.

All too often, companies fail to integrate their various communications channels. The result is a hodgepodge of communications to consumers. Mass-media advertisements say one thing, while a price promotion sends a different signal, and a product label creates still another message. Company sales literature says something altogether different, and the company's Web site seems out of sync with everything else.

The problem is that these communications often come from different parts of the company. Advertising messages are planned and implemented by the advertising department or an advertising agency. Personal selling communications are developed by sales management. Other company specialists are responsible for public relations, sales promotion events, Internet marketing, and other forms of marketing communications.

However, whereas these companies have separated their communications tools, customers won't. According to one marketing communications expert:[7]

The truth is, most [consumers] won't compartmentalize their use of the [different media]. They won't say, "Hey, I'm going off to do a bit of Web surfing. Burn my TV, throw out all my radios, cancel all my magazine subscriptions and, by the way, take out my telephone and don't deliver any mail anymore." It's not that kind of world for consumers, and it shouldn't be that kind of world for marketers either.

Integrated marketing communications (IMC)
The concept under which a company carefully integrates its many communications channels to deliver a clear, consistent, and compelling message about the organization and its products.

Today, more companies are adopting the concept of **integrated marketing communications (IMC)**. Under this concept, as illustrated in Figure 12.1, the company carefully integrates its many communications channels to deliver a clear, consistent, and compelling message about the organization and its brands.[8]

IMC calls for recognizing all contact points where the customer may encounter the company and its brands. Each *brand contact* will deliver a message, whether good, bad, or indifferent. The company wants to deliver a consistent and positive message with each contact. IMC leads to a total marketing communications strategy aimed at building strong customer relationships by showing how the company and its products can help customers solve their problems.

IMC ties together all of the company's messages and images. The company's advertising and personal selling communications have the same message, look, and feel as its e-mail promotions. And its public relations materials project the same image as its Web site.[9] For example, print and television ads for Jeep vehicles build consumer preference for the brand. But the ads also point viewers to the company's Web site, which offers lots of help and very little hype. The site helps serious car buyers build and price a model, find a dealer online, and learn more about "the Jeep life." Later, at the dealership, Jeep salespeople communicate the Jeep-life message in person while customers kick the tires and test the vehicle's ride before deciding to purchase.

In the past, no one person or department was responsible for thinking through the communication roles of the various promotion tools and coordinating the promotion mix. To help implement integrated marketing communications, some companies appoint a marketing communications director who has overall responsibility for the company's communications efforts. This helps to produce better communications consistency and greater sales impact. It places the responsibility in someone's hands—where none existed before—to unify the company's image as it is shaped by thousands of company activities.

Integrated marketing communications involves identifying the target audience and shaping a well-coordinated promotional program to elicit the desired audience response. Too often, marketing communicators focus on creating immediate brand awareness, image, or preference in the target market. But this approach to communications is too shortsighted. Today, marketers are viewing communications as helping to *manage the customer relationship over time*. Because customers differ, communications programs need to be developed for specific segments, niches, and even individuals. And, in these days of new interactive digital communications technologies, companies must ask not only, "How can we reach our customers?" but also, "How can we find ways to let our customers reach us?"

THE MOST CAPABLE WEB SITE COULD ONLY BELONG TO JEEP 4x4s.

JEEP.COM ONLY IN A Jeep

■ Today, all marketing communication tools must be carefully integrated. For example, this Jeep brand print ad points consumers to the company's Web site, where serious car buyers can build and price a model, find a dealer, and learn more about "the Jeep life."

Shaping the Overall Promotion Mix

The concept of integrated marketing communications suggests that the company must blend the promotion tools carefully into a coordinated *promotion mix*. But how does the company determine what mix of promotion tools it will use? Companies within the same

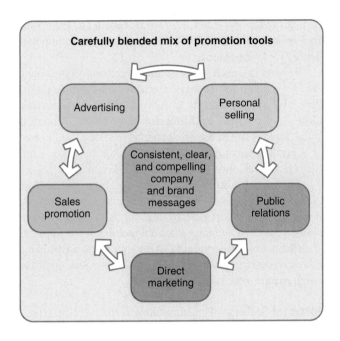

FIGURE 12.1
Integrated Marketing Communications

industry differ greatly in the design of their promotion mixes. For example, Mary Kay spends most of its promotion funds on personal selling and direct marketing, whereas Covergirl spends heavily on consumer advertising. Hewlett-Packard relies on advertising and promotion to retailers, whereas Dell uses more direct marketing. We now look at factors that influence the marketer's choice of promotion tools.

THE NATURE OF EACH PROMOTION TOOL

Each promotion tool has unique characteristics and costs. Marketers must understand these characteristics in shaping the promotion mix.

Advertising   Advertising can reach masses of geographically dispersed buyers at a low cost per exposure, and it enables the seller to repeat a message many times. For example, television advertising can reach huge audiences. An estimated 86.1 million Americans tuned in to at least part of the most recent Super Bowl, about 41 million people watched at

■ Promotion mix—Companies within the same industry may use different mixes. Mary Kay relies heavily on personal selling and direct marketing; Covergirl devotes significant resources to advertising.

least part of the last Academy Awards broadcast, and 33 million fans tuned in to watch the final episode of *Everybody Loves Raymond*. For companies that want to reach a mass audience, TV is the place to be.[10]

Beyond its reach, large-scale advertising says something positive about the seller's size, popularity, and success. Because of advertising's public nature, consumers tend to view advertised products as more legitimate. Advertising is also very expressive—it allows the company to dramatize its products through the artful use of visuals, print, sound, and color. On the one hand, advertising can be used to build up a long-term image for a product (such as Coca-Cola ads). On the other hand, advertising can trigger quick sales (as when Kohl's advertises weekend specials).

Advertising also has some shortcomings. Although it reaches many people quickly, advertising is impersonal and cannot be as directly persuasive as can company salespeople. For the most part, advertising can carry on only a one-way communication with the audience, and the audience does not feel that it has to pay attention or respond. In addition, advertising can be very costly. Although some advertising forms, such as newspaper and radio advertising, can be done on smaller budgets, other forms, such as network TV advertising, require very large budgets.

Personal Selling   Personal selling is the most effective tool at certain stages of the buying process, particularly in building up buyers' preferences, convictions, and actions. It involves personal interaction between two or more people, so each person can observe the other's needs and characteristics and make quick adjustments. Personal selling also allows all kinds of customer relationships to spring up, ranging from matter-of-fact selling relationships to personal friendships. An effective salesperson keeps the customer's interests at heart in order to build a long-term relationship. Finally, with personal selling, the buyer usually feels a greater need to listen and respond, even if the response is a polite "No thank you."

These unique qualities come at a cost, however. A sales force requires a longer-term commitment than does advertising—advertising can be turned on and off, but sales force size is harder to change. Personal selling is also the company's most expensive promotion tool, costing companies $329 on average per sales call. In some industries, the average cost of a sales call reaches $452.[11] U.S. firms spend up to three times as much on personal selling as they do on advertising.

■ With personal selling, the customer feels a greater need to listen and respond, even if the response is a polite "No thank you."

Sales Promotion   Sales promotion includes a wide assortment of tools—coupons, contests, cents-off deals, premiums, and others—all of which have many unique qualities. They attract consumer attention, offer strong incentives to purchase, and can be used to dramatize product offers and to boost sagging sales. Sales promotions invite and reward quick response—whereas advertising says, "Buy our product," sales promotion says, "Buy it now." Sales promotion effects are often short-lived, however, and often are not as effective as advertising or personal selling in building long-run brand preference and customer relationships.

Public Relations   Public relations is very believable—news stories, features, sponsorships, and events seem more real and believable to readers than ads do. Public relations can also reach many prospects who avoid salespeople and advertisements—the message gets to the buyers as "news" rather than as a sales-directed communication. And, as with advertising, public relations can dramatize a company or product. Marketers tend to under use public relations or to use it as an afterthought. Yet a well-thought-out public relations campaign used with other promotion mix elements can be very effective and economical.

Direct Marketing Although there are many forms of direct marketing—telephone marketing, direct mail, online marketing, and others—they all share four distinctive characteristics. Direct marketing is *nonpublic*: The message is normally directed to a specific person. Direct marketing is *immediate* and *customized*: Messages can be prepared very quickly and can be tailored to appeal to specific consumers. Finally, direct marketing is *interactive*: It allows a dialogue between the marketing team and the consumer, and messages can be altered depending on the consumer's response. Thus, direct marketing is well suited to highly targeted marketing efforts and to building one-to-one customer relationships.

PROMOTION-MIX STRATEGIES

Marketers can choose from two basic promotion mix strategies—*push* promotion or *pull* promotion. Figure 12.2 contrasts the two strategies. The relative emphasis on the specific promotion tools differs for push and pull strategies. A **push strategy** involves "pushing" the product through marketing channels to final consumers. The producer directs its marketing activities (primarily personal selling and trade promotion) toward channel members to induce them to carry the product and to promote it to final consumers.

Using a **pull strategy**, the producer directs its marketing activities (primarily advertising and consumer promotion) toward final consumers to induce them to buy the product. If the pull strategy is effective, consumers will then demand the product from channel members, who will in turn demand it from producers. Thus, under a pull strategy, consumer demand "pulls" the product through the channels.

Some industrial goods companies use only push strategies; some direct-marketing companies use only pull. However, most large companies use some combination of both. For example, Kraft uses mass-media advertising and consumer promotions to pull its products and a large sales force and trade promotions to push its products through the channels. In recent years, consumer goods companies have been decreasing the pull portions of their mixes in favor of more push. This has caused concern that they may be driving short-run sales at the expense of long-term brand equity.

Companies consider many factors when designing their promotion mix strategies, including *type of product/market* and the *product life-cycle stage*. For example, the importance of different promotion tools varies between consumer and business markets. Business-to-consumer (B2C) companies usually "pull" more, putting more of their funds into advertising, followed by sales promotion, personal selling, and then public relations. In contrast, business-to-business (B2B) marketers tend to "push" more, putting more of their funds into personal selling, followed by sales promotion, advertising, and public relations. In general, personal selling is used more heavily with expensive and risky goods and in markets with fewer and larger sellers.

Push strategy
A promotion strategy that calls for using the sales force and trade promotion to push the product through channels.

Pull strategy
A promotion strategy that calls for spending a lot on advertising and consumer promotion to build up consumer demand that will pull the product through channels.

FIGURE 12.2 Push Versus Pull Promotion Strategy

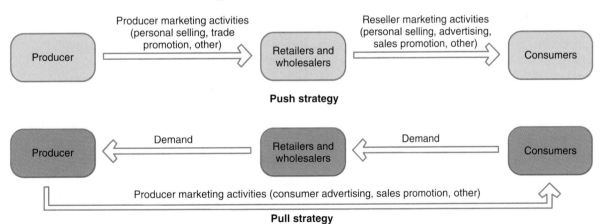

Now that we've examined the concept of integrated marketing communications and the factors that firms consider when shaping their promotion mixes, let's look more closely at the specific marketing communications tools.

 **Linking the Concepts**

Pull over here for a few minutes. Flip back through and link the parts of the chapter you've read so far.

- How do the *integrated marketing communications (IMC)* and *promotion mix* concepts relate to one another?
- How has the changing communications environment affected the ways in which companies communicate with you about their products and services? If you were in the market for a new car, where might you hear about various available models? Where would you *search* for information?

Advertising

Advertising can be traced back to the very beginnings of recorded history. The Romans painted walls to announce gladiator fights, and the Phoenicians painted pictures promoting their wares on large rocks along parade routes. Modern advertising, however, is a far cry from these early efforts. U.S. advertisers now run up an estimated annual advertising bill of more than $264 billion; worldwide ad spending exceeds an estimated $550 billion. Procter & Gamble, the world's largest advertiser, last year spent almost $4 billion on U.S. advertising and more than $5.7 billion worldwide.[12]

Although advertising is used mostly by business firms, it also is used by a wide range of not-for-profit organizations, professionals, and social agencies that advertise their causes to various target publics. In fact, the twenty-fifth largest advertising spender is a not-for-profit organization—the U.S. government. Advertising is a good way to inform and persuade, whether the purpose is to sell Coca-Cola worldwide or to get consumers in a developing nation to use birth control.

Marketing management must make four important decisions when developing an advertising program (see Figure 12.3): *setting advertising objectives, setting the advertising budget, developing advertising strategy (message decisions and media decisions), and evaluating advertising campaigns.*

SETTING ADVERTISING OBJECTIVES

The first step is to set *advertising objectives*. These objectives should be based on past decisions about the target market, positioning, and marketing mix, which define the job that advertising must do in the total marketing program.

FIGURE 12.3 Major Decisions in Advertising

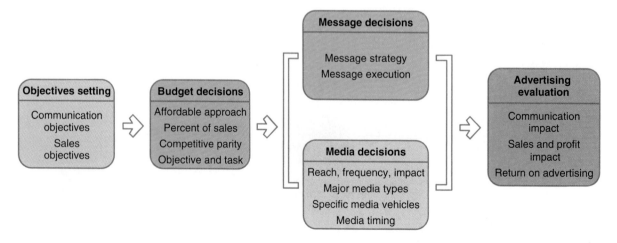

An **advertising objective** is a specific communication *task* to be accomplished with a specific *target* audience during a specific period of *time*. Advertising objectives can be classified by primary purpose—whether the aim is to *inform*, *persuade*, or *remind*. Table 12.1 lists examples of each of these objectives.

Informative advertising is used heavily when introducing a new product category. In this case, the objective is to build primary demand. Thus, early producers of DVD players first had to inform consumers of the image quality and convenience benefits of the new product. *Persuasive advertising* becomes more important as competition increases. Here, the company's objective is to build selective demand. For example, once DVD players became established, Sony began trying to persuade consumers that *its* brand offered the best quality for their money.

Some persuasive advertising has become *comparative advertising*, in which a company directly or indirectly compares its brand with one or more other brands. Comparative advertising has been used for products ranging from soft drinks, beer, and pain relievers to computers, batteries, car rentals, and credit cards. For example, in its classic comparative campaign, Avis positioned itself against market-leading Hertz by claiming, "We're number two, so we try harder."

More recently, Suave ran ads featuring a woman with beautiful hair questioning "Suave or Matrix? Can You Tell?" The ad then explains that you can't tell because Suave hair products perform just as well as Matrix products, "even though Matrix costs five times as much." Similarly, P&G ran an ad comparing its Tide with Bleach to Oxy10. In the ad, consumers spread iodine, tomato sauce, mud, and grass on a white T-shirt that was then cut in half and treated with the two detergents. All the while, "Anything You Can Do I Can Do Better" played in the background. Of course, Tide did a better job of removing stains. Advertisers should use comparative advertising with caution. All too often, such ads invite competitor responses, resulting in an advertising war that neither competitor can win.

Reminder advertising is important for mature products—it helps to maintain customer relationships and keep consumers thinking about the product. Expensive Coca-Cola television ads primarily build and maintain the Coca-Cola brand relationship rather than informing or persuading customers to buy in the short run.

SETTING THE ADVERTISING BUDGET

After determining its advertising objectives, the company next sets its *advertising budget* for each product. No matter what method is used, setting the advertising budget is no easy task. Here, we look at four common methods used to set the total budget for advertising: the *affordable method*, the *percentage-of-sales method*, the *competitive-parity method*, and the *objective-and-task method*.[13]

Advertising objective
A specific communication *task* to be accomplished with a specific *target* audience during a specific period of *time*.

TABLE 12.1
Possible Advertising Objectives

Informative Advertising

Telling the market about a new product	Describing available services
Suggesting new uses for a product	Correcting false impressions
Informing the market of a price change	Reducing consumers' fears
Explaining how the product works	Building a company image

Persuasive Advertising

Building brand preference	Persuading customer to purchase now
Encouraging switching to your brand	Persuading customer to receive a sales call
Changing customer's perception of product attributes	

Reminder Advertising

Building and maintaining the customer relationship	Reminding consumer where to buy the product
Reminding consumer that the product may be needed in the near future	Keeping it in the customer's mind during off-seasons

Affordable Method   Some companies use the **affordable method**: They set the promotion budget at the level they think the company can afford. Small businesses often use this method, reasoning that the company cannot spend more on advertising than it has. They start with total revenues, deduct operating expenses and capital outlays, and then devote some portion of the remaining funds to advertising. Unfortunately, this method of setting budgets completely ignores the effects of promotion on sales. It tends to place advertising last among spending priorities, even in situations in which advertising is critical to the firm's success. It leads to an uncertain annual promotion budget, which makes long-range market planning difficult.

Percentage-of-Sales Method   Other companies use the **percentage-of-sales method**, setting their promotion budget at a certain percentage of current or forecasted sales. Or they budget a percentage of the unit sales price. The percentage-of-sales method has advantages. It is simple to use and helps management think about the relationships between promotion spending, selling price, and profit per unit.

Despite these claimed advantages, however, the percentage-of-sales method has little to justify it. It wrongly views sales as the *cause* of promotion rather than as the *result*. It bases the ad budget on the availability of funds rather than on marketing needs and opportunities. Larger brands tend to receive more advertising, whether they need it or not. Meanwhile, smaller or failing brands receive less spending even though they may need more. Also, under the percentage-of-sales method, because the budget varies with year-to-year sales, long-range planning is difficult. Finally, the method does not provide any basis for choosing a *specific* percentage, except what has been done in the past or what competitors are doing.

Competitive-Parity Method   Still other companies use the **competitive-parity method**, setting their promotion budgets to match competitors' outlays. They monitor competitors' advertising or get industry promotion spending estimates from publications or trade associations, and then set their budgets based on the industry average.

Two arguments support this method. First, competitors' budgets represent the collective wisdom of the industry. Second, spending what competitors spend helps prevent promotion wars. Unfortunately, neither argument is valid. There are no grounds for believing that the competition has a better idea of what a company should be spending on promotion than does the company itself. Companies differ greatly, and each has its own special promotion needs. Finally, there is no evidence that budgets based on competitive parity prevent promotion wars.

Objective-and-Task Method   The most logical budget-setting method is the **objective-and-task method**, whereby the company sets its promotion budget based on what it wants to accomplish with promotion. This budgeting method entails (1) defining specific promotion objectives, (2) determining the tasks needed to achieve these objectives, (3) estimating the costs of performing these tasks, and (4) summing these costs to obtain the proposed promotion budget.

The objective-and-task method is the best method for setting advertising budgets. It forces management to spell out its assumptions about the relationship between dollars spent and promotion results. But it is also the most difficult method to use. Often, it is hard to figure out which specific tasks will achieve specific objectives. For example, suppose Sony wants 95 percent awareness for its latest camcorder model during the six-month introductory period. What specific advertising messages and media schedules should Sony use to attain this objective? How much would these messages and media schedules cost? Sony management must consider such questions, even though they are hard to answer.

DEVELOPING ADVERTISING STRATEGY

Advertising strategy consists of two major elements: creating advertising *messages* and selecting advertising *media*. In the past, companies often viewed media planning as secondary to the message-creation process. The creative department first created good advertisements, and then the media department selected the best media for carrying these advertisements to desired target audiences. This often caused friction between creatives and media planners.

Today, however, media fragmentation, soaring media costs, and more-focused target marketing strategies have promoted the importance of the media-planning function. More and more, advertisers are orchestrating a closer harmony between their messages and the media that deliver them. Among the more noteworthy ad campaigns based on tight media-creative partnerships is the pioneering campaign for Absolut vodka, made by V&S Absolut Spirits.

Since the iconic "bottle" campaign began in 1979, the Absolut team and its ad agency meet once a year with a slew of magazines to set Absolut's media schedule. The agency's creative department then creates media-specific ads. The result is a wonderful assortment of very creative ads for Absolut, tightly targeted to audiences of the media in which they appear. For example, an "Absolut Bravo" ad in playbills has roses adorning a clear bottle, while business magazines contain an "Absolut Merger" foldout. In New York-area magazines, "Absolut Manhattan" ads feature a satellite photo of Manhattan, with Central Park assuming the distinctive outline of an Absolut bottle. In London, ads show the famous entry to the Prime Minister's residence at No. 10 Downing Street with the door in the shape of an Absolut bottle. An "Absolute Primary" ad run during the political season featured the well-known bottle spattered with mud. In "Absolut Love," run in February to celebrate Valentine's Day, two Absolut bottles embrace, silhouetted by a shining heart in the background. In some cases, the creatives even develop ads for magazines not yet on the schedule, such as a clever "Absolut Centerfold" ad for *Playboy* magazine. The ad portrayed a clear, unadorned playmate bottle ("11-inch bust, 11-inch waist, 11-inch hips"). In all, Absolut has developed more than 1,500 ads for the more than two-decades-old campaign. At a time of soaring media costs and cluttered communication channels, a closer cooperation between creative and media people has paid off handsomely for Absolut. Largely as a result

■ Media planners for Absolut vodka work with creatives to design ads targeted to specific media audiences. "Absolut Bravo" appears in theater playbills. "Absolut London" shows the famous entry to the Prime Minister's residence at No. 10 Downing Street.

of its breakthrough advertising, in the United States, Absolut remains the nation's number-one imported vodka and the number-three liquor brand overall. The Absolut ads have developed a kind of cult following, and Absolut is one of only three original brands to be inducted into the American Advertising Hall of Fame.[14]

Creating the Advertising Message No matter how big the budget, advertising can succeed only if advertisements gain attention and communicate well. Good advertising messages are especially important in today's costly and cluttered advertising environment. The average number of receivable television channels per U.S. household has skyrocketed from 3 in 1950 to more than 100 today, and consumers have more than 21,000 magazines from which to choose.[15] Add the countless radio stations and a continuous barrage of catalogs, direct-mail, Internet e-mail and pop-up ads, and out-of-home media, and consumers are being bombarded with ads at home, at work, and at all points in between. One expert estimates that the average person is exposed to some 1,600 ad messages a day. Another puts the number at an eye-popping 5,000 ads a day.[16]

Breaking Through the Clutter. If all this advertising clutter bothers some consumers, it also causes big problems for advertisers. Take the situation facing network television advertisers. They pay an average of $372,000 to make a single 30-second commercial. Then, each time they show it, they regularly pay $300,000 or more for 30 seconds of advertising time during a popular prime-time program. They pay even more if it's an especially popular program such as *American Idol* ($658,000), *Survivor* ($413,000), or a mega-event such as the Super Bowl (as much as $2.6 million per 30 seconds).[17]

Then, their ads are sandwiched in with a clutter of other commercials, announcements, and network promotions, totaling more than 15 minutes of nonprogram material per prime-time hour, more than 21 minutes per daytime hour. Such clutter in television and other ad media has created an increasingly hostile advertising environment. According to one recent study, 65 percent of Americans say they are "constantly bombarded with too much" advertising and about two-thirds say that their view of advertising is "much more negative than just a few years ago."[18]

Until recently, television viewers were pretty much a captive audience for advertisers. But today's digital wizardry has given consumers a rich, new set of information and entertainment choices. With the growth in cable and satellite TV, the Internet, video on demand (VOD), and DVD rentals, today's viewers have many more options. Digital technology has also armed consumers with an arsenal of weapons for choosing what they watch or don't watch. Increasingly, consumers are choosing *not* to watch ads. They "zap" commercials by fast-forwarding through recorded programs. With the remote control, they mute the sound during a commercial or "zip" around the channels to see what else is on. A recent study found that nearly half of all television viewers now switch channels when the commercial break starts.

Adding to the problem is the rapid growth of TiVo-style DVR (digital video recorder) systems. About 8 percent of American homes now have DVR technology, and this is expected to grow to 40 percent by 2009. One ad agency executive calls DVR systems "electronic weed whackers." "In time, the number of people using them to obliterate commercials will totally erode faith in the 30-second commercial," he declares. Similarly, the number of VOD viewers is expected to quadruple during the next five years. These viewers will be able to watch programming on their own time terms, with or without commercials.[19]

Thus, advertisers can no longer force-feed the same old cookie-cutter ad messages to captive consumers through traditional media. Just to gain and hold attention, today's advertising messages must be better planned, more imaginative, more entertaining, and more rewarding to consumers. "A commercial has to cut through the clutter and seize the viewers in one to three seconds, or they're gone," says one advertising executive. "Interruption or disruption as the fundamental premise of marketing" no longer works, says another. "You have to create content that is interesting, useful, or entertaining enough to invite [consumers]."[20]

In fact, many marketers are now subscribing to a new merging of advertising and entertainment, dubbed "Madison & Vine." You've probably heard of Madison Avenue. It's the

New York City street that houses the headquarters of many of the nation's largest advertising agencies. You may also have heard of Hollywood & Vine, the intersection of Hollywood Avenue and Vine Street in Hollywood, California, long the symbolic heart of the U.S. entertainment industry. Now, Madison Avenue and Hollywood & Vine are coming together to form a new intersection—*Madison & Vine*—which represents the merging of advertising and entertainment in an effort to break through the clutter and create new avenues for reaching consumers with more engaging messages (see Marketing at Work 12.1).

Message Strategy. The first step in creating effective advertising messages is to plan a *message strategy*—to decide what general message will be communicated to consumers. The purpose of advertising is to get consumers to think about or react to the product or company in a certain way. People will react only if they believe that they will benefit from doing so. Thus, developing an effective message strategy begins with identifying customer *benefits* that can be used as advertising appeals. Ideally, advertising message strategy will follow directly from the company's broader positioning and customer value strategies.

Message strategy statements tend to be plain, straightforward outlines of benefits and positioning points that the advertiser wants to stress. The advertiser must next develop a compelling *creative concept*—or "*big idea*"—that will bring the message strategy to life in a distinctive and memorable way. At this stage, simple message ideas become great ad campaigns. Usually, a copywriter and art director will team up to generate many creative concepts, hoping that one of these concepts will turn out to be the big idea. The creative concept may emerge as a visualization, a phrase, or a combination of the two.

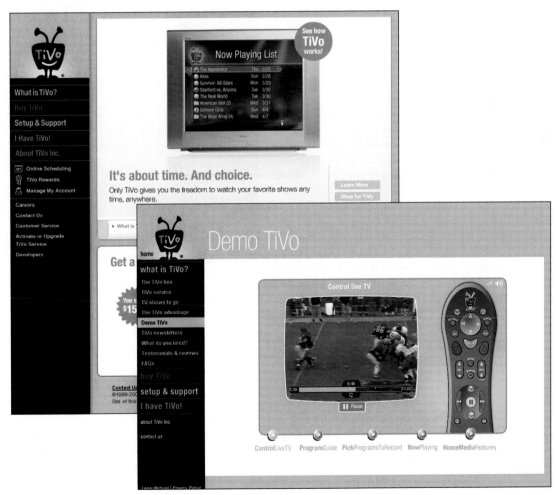

■ A new advertising challenge: The new wave of digital video recorder services, such as TiVo, have armed viewers with an arsenal of new-age zipping and zapping weapons. One ad agency executive calls TiVo an "electronic weedwhacker."

MARKETING AT WORK   12.1

Madison & Vine: The New Intersection of Advertising and Entertainment

Welcome to the ever-busier intersection of Madison & Vine, where the advertising industry meets the entertainment industry. In today's cluttered advertising environment, Madison Avenue knows that it must find new ways to engage ad-weary consumers with more-compelling messages. The answer? Entertainment! And who knows more about entertainment than the folks at Hollywood & Vine? The term *Madison & Vine* has come to represent the merging of advertising and entertainment. It takes one of two primary forms: *advertainment* or *branded entertainment.*

The aim of *advertainment* is to make ads themselves so entertaining, or so useful, that people *want* to watch them. It's advertising by invitation rather than by intrusion. There's no chance that you'd watch ads on purpose, you say? Think again. For example, the Super Bowl has become an annual advertainment showcase. Tens of millions of people tune in to the Super Bowl each year, as much to watch the entertaining ads as to see the game.

And rather than bemoaning TiVo and other DVR systems, many advertisers are now using them as a new medium for showing useful or entertaining ads that consumers actually volunteer to watch. For example, Best Buy created a TiVo showcase, which offered subscribers a chance to access two exclusive videos, win a CD, and opt in to six entertaining product vignettes. Sixty-three percent of TiVo subscribers opted in to the showcase, staying an average of 3.36 minutes. Interestingly, a recent study found that DVR users aren't necessarily skipping all the ads. According to the study, 55 percent of DVR users take their finger off the fast-forward button to

watch a commercial that is entertaining or relevant, sometimes even watching it more than once. "If advertising is really entertaining, you don't zap it," notes an industry observer. "You might even go out of your way to see it."

Beyond making their regular ads more entertaining, advertisers are also creating new advertising forms that look less like ads and more like short films or shows. For example, American Express created a series of entertaining five-minute, online-only "Webisodes" starring Jerry Seinfeld. One Webisode teamed Seinfeld with Superman. When a street thug steals Seinfeld's new DVD player, the Man of Steel leaps into action and nabs the crook, damaging Jerry's DVD player in the process. Luckily, Seinfeld bought it with his American Express card so the damage is covered. The American Express Webisodes avoid hard-sell hucksterism, relying instead on soft-sell entertainment. "We're trying to create media content where people actually opt in to watch," says an American Express marketing executive. So far, it's working. The creative and engaging Seinfeld/Superman Web ad garnered 1.1 million unique visitors in just its first two weeks.

Branded entertainment (or *brand integrations*) involves making the brand an inseparable part of some other form of entertainment. The most common form of branded entertainment is product placements—imbedding brands as props within other programming. In all,

advertisers paid an estimated $4.25 billion on product placements last year, up 23 percent from the previous year. The nature of the placement can very widely, from a brief glimpse of a Tropicana carton sitting on the kitchen table on

■ *Welcome to Madison & Vine. As this book cover suggests, in today's cluttered advertising environment, Madison Avenue must find new ways to engage ad-weary consumers with more compelling messages. The answer? Entertainment!*

The creative concept will guide the choice of specific appeals to be used in an advertising campaign. *Advertising appeals* should have three characteristics: First, they should be *meaningful*, pointing out benefits that make the product more desirable or interesting to consumers. Second, appeals must be *believable*—consumers must believe that the product or service will deliver the promised benefits.

However, the most meaningful and believable benefits may not be the best ones to feature. Appeals should also be *distinctive*—they should tell how the product is better than the competing brands. For example, the most meaningful benefit of owning a wristwatch

HBO's *The Sopranos* to having products scripted into the theme of the program.

For the right price, a brand can even play the starring role in a popular show. For example, by its second season, Donald Trump's *The Apprentice* had evolved into a lush outlet for brand integrations. Blue-chip companies like Procter & Gamble, General Motors, Staples, Unilever, and Burger King paid $1 to $4 million per episode to integrate their brands into the hit reality show. Most of these placements have been hugely successful. In one episode, *Apprentice* teams competed to promote a new variant of P&G's Crest toothpaste. An online contest held in conjunction with the show generated the heaviest single day of traffic ever for a P&G brand Web site, with more than 3 million hits. A spokesperson for P&G's oral-care group called it "The best money we've ever spent."

Perhaps no company has gotten more mileage out of such brand integrations than GM's Pontiac division. It all started with an extraordinary giveaway on a popular talk show:

When *The Oprah Winfrey Show* opened its 19th season with a "Wildest Dreams" theme, Oprah electrified the studio audience by giving every one of the 276 people in attendance a new, fully loaded Pontiac G6 sedan worth $28,400. The program also included footage of Oprah helping on the G6's production line and praising a variety of the car's features. On later shows, Oprah revisited two audience members to explore how their Pontiacs changed their lives. The Oprah giveaway set a new benchmark in the field of branded entertainment. The effort cost Pontiac about $8 million but generated an estimated $20 million in unpaid media coverage and favorable PR. "It's got talk value,

PR spin, there's an emotional connection," said a branding expert. "It is something you couldn't have paid for."

Pontiac followed quickly with another stunningly successful placement, this time on *The Apprentice*. Generally viewed as the most successful *Apprentice* brand integration yet, Pontiac used the show to announce a national early-order program for its new Solstice two-seat roadster. In a show that included photo shoots of the sleek new car and discussions of Solstice benefits, *Apprentice* teams pulled all-nighters to create Solstice promotion brochures. The result: Pontiac's Web site traffic skyrocketed 1,400 percent the night the episode aired, and some 41,000 people filled out online registration forms. When the car went on sale at 2 PM the next day, Pontiac sold 1,000 vehicles within 41 minutes and 7,100 within 10 days, selling out all the Solstices it planned to build for the year.

Originally created with TV in mind, branded entertainment has spread quickly into other sectors of the entertainment industry. It's widely used in movies—think about Ray Ban sunglasses and *Men in Black*, or Audi's sleek concept car in *I, Robot*. And when DreamWorks built the terminal for its movie *The Terminal*, along with United Airlines, more than 35 companies chipped in millions to build real stores—Brookstone, Discovery Store, Borders Books, Paul Mitchell—as well as a working food court with a Starbucks, Baskin-Robbins, Burger King, and Baja Fresh. If you look carefully, you'll also see subtle and not-so-subtle product placements in online video games, magazines, Internet sites, and even Broadway musicals. For example, the script for *Sweet Charity* was revised to fit Jose Cuervo's Gran Centenario tequila into a scene.

So, Madison & Vine is *the* new meeting place for the advertising and entertainment industries. When done right, advertainment and branded entertainment can pay big dividends. However, experts caution that Madison & Vine can also be a dangerous crossing. They worry that making ads too entertaining might detract from the seller's brand message—consumers will remember the clever ad but forget the brand or advertiser. And they note that the intersection is getting pretty congested. With all these new ad formats and product placements, Madison & Vine threatens to create even more of the very clutter that it's designed to break through.

They also worry about potential customer resentment and backlash. Some TV shows outright bristle with product placements. A heavily branded show like *American Idol* contains, on average, more than 66 product placement shots per hour. In the second quarter of 2005, the 10 prime-time TV shows with the most placements included 11,579 "brand shout-outs." At what point will consumers decide that the intersection of Madison & Vine is just too congested and take yet a different route?

Sources: Pontiac example adapted from portions of Gail Schiller, "Win, Draw for Burnett Branding," *The Hollywood Reporter,* June 1, 2005, accessed at www.hollywoodreporter.com; and Jean Halliday and Claire Atkinson, "Pontiac Gets Major Mileage Out of $8 Million 'Oprah' Deal," *Advertising Age,* September 20, 2004, p. 12. Other quotes and information from "10 Biggest Madison & Vine Deals," *Advertising Age,* December 20, 2004; Stuart Elliott, "Seinfeld and Superman Join Forces Again in Spots for American Express, This Time on the Web," *New York Times,* March 30, 2004, p. C.5; Marc Graser, "Product-Placement Spending Poised to Hit $4.25 Billion in '05," *Advertising Age,* April 4, 2005, p. 16; Jim Edwards, "Will Product Placement Get Its Own Comeuppance?" *Brandweek,* July 25–August 1, p. 13; and "Study Spots Ad-Skipping Trends," August 19, 2005, accessed at www.hollywoodreporter.com.

is that it keeps accurate time, yet few watch ads feature this benefit. Instead, based on the distinctive benefits they offer, watch advertisers might select any of a number of advertising themes. For years, Timex has been the affordable watch that "Takes a lickin' and keeps on tickin.'" In contrast, Fossil has featured style and fashion, whereas Rolex stresses luxury and status.

Message Execution.   The advertiser now has to turn the big idea into an actual ad execution that will capture the target market's attention and interest. The creative team must find the best style, tone, words, and format for executing the message. Any message can be presented in different *execution styles*, such as the following:

- *Slice of life:* This style shows one or more "typical" people using the product in a normal setting. For example, two mothers at a picnic discuss the nutritional benefits of Jif peanut butter.
- *Lifestyle:* This style shows how a product fits in with a particular lifestyle. For example, an ad for Mongoose mountain bikes shows a serious biker traversing remote and rugged but beautiful terrain and states, "There are places that are so awesome and so killer that you'd like to tell the whole world about them. But please, *don't.*"
- *Fantasy:* This style creates a fantasy around the product or its use. For instance, many ads are built around dream themes. Gap even introduced a perfume named Dream. Ads show a woman sleeping blissfully and suggests that the scent is "the stuff that clouds are made of."
- *Mood or image:* This style builds a mood or image around the product or service, such as beauty, love, or serenity. Few claims are made about the product except through suggestion. For example, ads for Singapore Airlines feature soft lighting and refined flight attendants pampering relaxed but happy customers.
- *Musical:* This style shows people or cartoon characters singing about the product. For example, one of the most famous ads in history was a Coca-Cola ad built around the song "I'd Like to Teach the World to Sing." Similarly, Oscar Mayer has long run ads showing children singing its now classic "I wish I were an Oscar Mayer wiener . . ." jingle.
- *Personality symbol:* This style creates a character that represents the product. The character might be *animated* (the Kool-Aid man, Tony the Tiger, the GEICO gecko) or *real* (the Marlboro man, Ol' Lonely the Maytag repairman, Morris the 9-Lives Cat, or the AFLAC duck).
- *Technical expertise:* This style shows the company's expertise in making the product. Thus, Maxwell House shows one of its buyers carefully selecting coffee beans, and Gallo tells about its many years of wine-making experience.
- *Scientific evidence:* This style presents survey or scientific evidence that the brand is better or better liked than one or more other brands. For years, Crest toothpaste has used scientific evidence to convince buyers that Crest is better than other brands at fighting cavities.
- *Testimonial evidence or endorsement:* This style features a highly believable or likable source endorsing the product. It could be ordinary people saying how much they like a given product or a celebrity presenting the product. For example, Gatorade ran an ad showing how Gatorade helped triathlete Chris Legh win an Ironman triathlon victory following a near fatal collapse a few years earlier due to dehydration.

The advertiser also must choose a *tone* for the ad. Procter & Gamble always uses a positive tone: Its ads say something very positive about its products. P&G usually avoids humor that might take attention away from the message. In contrast, many advertisers now use edgy humor to break through the commercial clutter. These days, it seems as though almost every company is using humor in its advertising, from consumer product firms such as Anheuser-Busch to the scholarly American Heritage Dictionary.

The advertiser must use memorable and attention-getting *words* in the ad. For example, rather than claiming simply that "a BMW is a well-engineered automobile," BMW uses more creative and higher-impact phrasing: "The ultimate driving machine." Instead of stating plainly that Hanes socks last longer than less expensive ones, Hanes suggests, "Buy cheap socks and you'll pay through the toes." It's not Häagen-Dazs is "a good-tasting luxury ice cream," it's "Our passport to indulgence: passion in a touch, perfection in a cup, summer in a spoon, one perfect moment."

Finally, *format* elements make a difference in an ad's impact as well as in its cost. A small change in ad design can make a big difference in its effect. In a print ad, the *illustration* is the first thing the reader notices—it must be strong enough to draw attention. Next, the *headline* must effectively entice the right people to read the copy. Finally, the *copy*—the main block of text in the ad—must be simple but strong and convincing. Moreover, these three elements must effectively work *together* to persuasively present customer value.

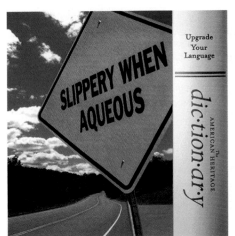  

■ Humor in advertising: These days, it seems as though almost every company is using humor in its advertising, even the scholarly American Heritage Dictionary.

Selecting Advertising Media The major steps in media selection are (1) deciding on *reach, frequency*, and *impact*; (2) choosing among major *media types*; (3) selecting specific *media vehicles*; and (4) deciding on *media timing*.

Deciding on Reach, Frequency, and Impact. To select media, the advertiser must decide on the reach and frequency needed to achieve advertising objectives. *Reach* is a measure of the *percentage* of people in the target market who are exposed to the ad campaign during a given period of time. For example, the advertiser might try to reach 70 percent of the target market during the first three months of the campaign. *Frequency* is a measure of how many *times* the average person in the target market is exposed to the message. For example, the advertiser might want an average exposure frequency of three.

The advertiser also must decide on the desired *media impact*—the *qualitative value* of a message exposure through a given medium. For example, for products that need to be demonstrated, messages on television may have more impact than messages on radio because television uses sight *and* sound. The same message in one magazine (say, *Newsweek*) may be more believable than in another (say, *The National Enquirer*). In general, the more reach, frequency, and impact the advertiser seeks, the higher the advertising budget will have to be.

Choosing Among Major Media Types. The media planner has to know the reach, frequency, and impact of each of the major media types. As summarized in Table 12.2, the major media types are newspapers, television, direct mail, radio, magazines, outdoor, and the Internet. Each medium has advantages and limitations. Media planners consider many factors when making their media choices. They want to choose media that will effectively and efficiently present the advertising message to target customers. Thus, they must consider each medium's impact, message effectiveness, and cost.

The mix of media must be reexamined regularly. For a long time, television and magazines have dominated in the media mixes of national advertisers, with other media often neglected. However, as discussed at the start of the chapter, the media mix appears to be shifting. As mass-media costs rise, audiences shrink, and exciting new digital media emerge, many advertisers are finding new ways to reach consumers. They are supplementing the traditional mass media with more specialized and highly targeted media that cost less and target more effectively.

For example, cable television and satellite television systems are booming. Such systems allow narrow programming formats such as all sports, all news, nutrition, arts, home improvement and gardening, cooking, travel, history, finance, and others that target select groups. Time Warner and other cable operators are even testing systems that will let them target specific types of ads to specific types of customers. For example, only pet owners would

TABLE 12.2
Profiles of Major Media Types

Medium	Advantages	Limitations
Newspapers	Flexibility; timeliness; good local market coverage; broad acceptability; high believability	Short life; poor reproduction quality; small pass-along audience
Television	Good mass-marketing coverage; low cost per exposure; combines sight, sound, and motion; appealing to the senses	High absolute costs; high clutter; fleeting exposure; less audience selectivity
Direct mail	High audience selectivity; flexibility; no ad competition within the same medium; allows personalization	Relatively high cost per exposure, "junk mail" image
Radio	Good local acceptance; high geographic and demographic selectivity; low cost	Audio only, fleeting exposure; low attention ("the half-heard" medium); fragmented audiences
Magazines	High geographic and demographic selectivity; credibility and prestige; high-quality reproduction; long life and good pass-along readership	Long ad purchase lead time; high cost; no guarantee of position
Outdoor	Flexibility; high repeat exposure; low cost; low message competition; good positional selectivity	Little audience selectivity; creative limitations
Internet	High selectivity; low cost; immediacy; interactive capabilities	Small, demographically skewed audience; relatively low impact; audience controls exposure

see ads from pet food companies.[21] Advertisers can take advantage of such "narrowcasting" to "rifle in" on special market segments rather than use the "shotgun" approach offered by network broadcasting. Cable and satellite television media seem to make good sense. But, increasingly, ads are popping up in far less likely places. In their efforts to find less costly and more highly targeted ways to reach consumers, advertisers have discovered a dazzling collection of "alternative media" (see Marketing at Work 12.2).

Another important trend affecting media selection is the rapid growth in the number of "media multitaskers," people who absorb more than one medium at a time:

It looks like people who aren't satisfied with "just watching TV" are in good company.

According to a recent survey, three-fourths of U.S. TV viewers read the newspaper while they watch TV, and two-thirds of them go online during their TV time. According to the study, 70 percent of media users say they, at one time or another, try to absorb two or more forms of media at once. What's more, if today's kids are any indication, media multitasking is on the rise. Nearly one-third of kids 8 to 18 say when they're doing schoolwork at home, they're often talking on the phone, surfing the Web, instant messaging, watching TV or listening to music at the same time.[22]

Media planners need to take such media interactions into account when selecting the types of media they will use.

Selecting Specific Media Vehicles.   The media planner now must choose the best *media vehicles*—specific media within each general media type. For example, television vehicles include *Scrubs* and *ABC World News Tonight*. Magazine vehicles include *Newsweek*, *People*, and *Sports Illustrated*.

Media planners must compute the cost per thousand persons reached by a vehicle. For example, if a full-page, four-color advertisement in the U.S. national edition of *Newsweek* costs $210,000 and *Newsweek*'s readership is 3.1 million people, the cost of reaching each group of 1,000 persons is about $68. The same advertisement in *BusinessWeek* may cost only $106,500 but reach only 970,000 persons—at a cost per thousand of about $110. The media planner ranks each magazine by cost per thousand and favors those magazines with the lower cost per thousand for reaching target consumers.[23] The media planner must also consider the costs of producing ads for different media. Whereas newspaper ads may cost

As consumers, we're used to ads on television, in magazines and newspapers, on the radio, and along the roadways. But these days, no matter where you go or what you do, you probably will run into some new form of advertising.

Tiny billboards attached to shopping carts, ads on shopping bags, and even advertising decals on supermarket floors urge you to buy Jell-O Pudding Pops or Pampers. Signs atop parking meters hawk everything from Jeeps to Minolta cameras to Recipe dog food. A city bus rolls by, fully wrapped for Trix cereal. You escape to the ballpark, only to find billboard-size video screens running Budweiser ads while a blimp with an electronic message board circles lazily overhead. How about a quiet trip in the country? Sorry—you find an enterprising farmer using his milk cows as four-legged billboards mounted with ads for Ben & Jerry's ice cream.

You pay to see a movie at your local theater, only to learn that the movie is full of not-so-subtle promotional plugs for Pepsi, Domino's Pizza, MasterCard, Mercedes, Ray Ban sunglasses, or any of a dozen other products. You head home for a little TV to find your favorite sitcom full of "virtual placements" of Coca-Cola, Sony, or M&M/Mars products digitally inserted into the program. You pop in the latest video game and find your action character jumping into a Jeep on the way to the skateboarding park.

At the local rail station, it's the Commuter Channel; at the airport, you're treated to the CNN Airport Network. Shortly after your plane lifts off the runway, you look out the window and spot a 500-foot-diameter crop circle carved into a farmer's field depicting Monster.com's mascot and corporate logo. As you wait to pick up your luggage, ads for Kenneth Cole luggage roll by on the baggage carousel conveyor belt.

These days, you're likely to find ads—well, anywhere. Boats cruise along public beaches flashing advertising messages for Sundown Sunscreen as sunbathers spread their towels over ads for Snapple pressed into the sand. Ad space is being sold on video cases, parking-lot tickets, golf scorecards, delivery trucks, gas pumps, ATMs, municipal garbage cans, police cars,

and church bulletins. One agency even leases space on the foreheads of college students for temporary advertising tattoos. And Goodyear recently paid Detroit Pistons guard Richard Hamilton to wear his hair in the style of the tread pattern of its latest tire. "The way he plays fits nicely with the product: confident maneuvering, handles well in all conditions," said a Goodyear spokesperson.

The following account takes a humorous look ahead at what might be in store for the future:

Tomorrow your alarm clock will buzz at 6 AM, as usual. Then the digital readout will morph into an ad for Burger King's breakfast special. Hungry for a Croissan'wich, you settle for a bagel that you plop into the toaster. The coils burn a Toastmaster brand onto the sides. Biting into your embossed bread, you pour a cup of coffee as the familiar green-and-white Starbucks logo forms on the side. Sipping the brew, you slide on your Nikes to go grab the newspaper. The pressure sensitive shoes leave a temporary trail of swooshes behind them wherever you step. Walking outside, you pick up the *Times* and gaze at your lawn, where the fertilizer you put down last month time-releases ads for Scotts Turf Builder, Toro lawn mowers, Weber grills. . . .

Even some of the current alternative media seem a bit far-fetched, and they sometimes irritate consumers who resent it all as "ad nau-seam." But for many marketers, these media can save money and provide a way to hit selected consumers where they live, shop, work, and play. "We like to call it the captive pause," says an executive of an alternative-media firm, where consumers "really have nothing else to do but either look at the person in front of them or look at some engaging content as well as 15-second commercials"—the average person waits in line about 30 minutes a day. Many spend even more time on mass transit. So, companies like Target, Snapple, Calvin Klein, and American Express are testing new technologies to reach captive consumers. Riders on Manhattan's subway system now see a series of light boxes speed by that create a moving commercial in the subway car's windows.

Of course, this may leave you wondering if there are any commercial-free havens remaining for ad-weary consumers. The back seat of a taxi, perhaps, or public elevators, or stalls in a public restroom? Forget it! Each has already been invaded by innovative marketers.

Sources: See Cara Beardi, "From Elevators to Gas Stations, Ads Multiplying," *Advertising Age,* November 13, 2000, pp. 40–42; Charles Pappas, "Ad Nauseam," *Advertising Age,* July 10, 2000, pp. 16–18; Stephanie Mehta, "Ads Invade Video Games," *FORTUNE,* May 26, 2003, p. 46; Brian Hindo, "Getting a Head," *BusinessWeek,* January 12, 2004, p. 14; Sam Jaffe, "Easy Riders," *American Demographics,* March 2004, pp. 20–23; and "Pistons' Hamilton Models Hairstyle After Goodyear Tire Tread," January 31, 2005, accessed at www.bloomberg.com.

■ *Marketers have discovered a dazzling array of "alternative media."*

very little to produce, flashy television ads may cost millions. A few years ago, Nike paid a cool $2 million to make a single ad called "The Wall."[24]

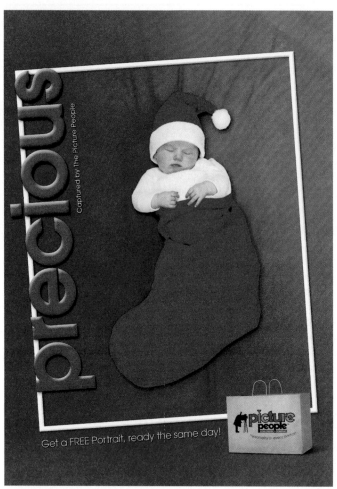

precious

Captured by The Picture People

Get a FREE Portrait, ready the same day!

picture people

■ Media timing: The Picture People, the national chain of family portrait studios, advertises more heavily before special holidays.

In selecting specific media vehicles, the media planner must balance media costs against several media-effectiveness factors. First, the planner should evaluate the media vehicle's *audience quality*. For a Huggies disposable diapers advertisement, for example, *Parenting* magazine would have a high exposure value; *Gentlemen's Quarterly* would have a low exposure value. Second, the media planner should consider *audience attention*. Readers of *Vogue*, for example, typically pay more attention to ads than do *Newsweek* readers. Third, the planner should assess the vehicle's *editorial quality*—*Time* and the *Wall Street Journal* are more believable and prestigious than *The National Enquirer*.

Deciding on Media Timing. The advertiser must also decide how to schedule the advertising over the course of a year. Suppose sales of a product peak in December and drop in March. The firm can vary its advertising to follow the seasonal pattern, to oppose the seasonal pattern, or to be the same all year. Most firms do some seasonal advertising. For example, The Picture People, the national chain of portrait studios, advertises more heavily before major holidays such as Christmas, Easter, and Valentine's Day. Some marketers do *only* seasonal advertising: For instance, Hallmark advertises its greeting cards only before major holidays.

Finally, the advertiser has to choose the pattern of the ads. *Continuity* means scheduling ads evenly within a given period. *Pulsing* means scheduling ads unevenly over a given time period. Thus, 52 ads could either be scheduled at one per week during the year or pulsed in several bursts. The idea behind pulsing is to advertise heavily for a short period to build awareness that carries over to the next advertising period. Those who favor pulsing feel that it can be used to achieve the same impact as a steady schedule but at a much lower cost. However, some media planners believe that although pulsing achieves minimal awareness, it sacrifices depth of advertising communications.

EVALUATING ADVERTISING EFFECTIVENESS AND RETURN ON ADVERTISING INVESTMENT

Advertising accountability has become a hot issue for most companies. Increasingly, top management is asking: "What return are we getting on our advertising investment?" and "How do we know that we're spending the right amount?" According to a recent survey by the Association of National Advertisers (ANA), measuring advertising's efficiency and effectiveness is the number-one issue in the minds of today's advertisers. In the survey, 61.5 percent of respondents said that it is important that they define, measure, and take action in the area of advertising accountability.[25]

Advertisers should regularly evaluate two types of advertising results: communication effects and the sales and profit effects. Measuring the *communication effects* of an ad or ad campaign tells whether the ads and media are communicating the ad message well. Individual ads can be tested before or after they are run. Before an ad is placed, the advertiser can show it to consumers, ask how they like it, and measure message recall or attitude changes resulting from it. After an ad is run, the advertiser can measure how the ad affected consumer recall or product awareness, knowledge, and preference. Pre- and post-evaluations of communication effects can be made for entire advertising campaigns as well.

Advertisers have gotten pretty good at measuring the communication effects of their ads and ad campaigns. However, *sales and profits* effects of advertising are often much harder to measure. For example, what sales and profits are produced by an ad campaign that increases brand awareness by 20 percent and brand preference by 10 percent? Sales and profits are affected by many factors besides advertising—such as product features, price, and availability.

One way to measure the sales and profit effects of advertising is to compare past sales and profits with past advertising expenditures. Another way is through experiments. For example, to test the effects of different advertising spending levels, Coca-Cola could vary the amount it spends on advertising in different market areas and measure the differences in the resulting sales and profit levels. More complex experiments could be designed to include other variables, such as differences in the ads or media used.

However, because so many factors affect advertising effectiveness, some controllable and others not, measuring the results of advertising spending remains an inexact science. For example, despite the growing importance of advertising accountability, only 19 percent of ANA study respondents were satisfied with their ability to measure return on advertising investments. When asked if they would be able to "forecast the impact on sales" of a 10 percent cut in advertising spending, 63 percent said no.

"Marketers are tracking all kinds of data and they still can't answer basic questions" about advertising accountability, says a marketing analyst, "because they don't have real models and metrics by which to make sense of it."[26] Thus, although the situation is improving as marketers seek more answers, managers often must rely on large doses of judgment along with quantitative analysis when assessing advertising performance.

OTHER ADVERTISING CONSIDERATIONS

In developing advertising strategies and programs, the company must address two additional questions. First, how will the company organize its advertising function—who will perform which advertising tasks? Second, how will the company adapt its advertising strategies and programs to the complexities of international markets?

ORGANIZING FOR ADVERTISING

Different companies organize in different ways to handle advertising. In small companies, advertising might be handled by someone in the sales department. Large companies set up advertising departments whose job it is to set the advertising budget, work with the ad agency, and handle other advertising not done by the agency. Most large companies use outside advertising agencies because they offer several advantages.

How does an **advertising agency** work? Advertising agencies were started in the mid-to-late 1800s by salespeople and brokers who worked for the media and received a commission for selling advertising space to companies. As time passed, the salespeople began to help customers prepare their ads. Eventually, they formed agencies and grew closer to the advertisers than to the media.

Advertising agency
A marketing-services firm that assists companies in planning, preparing, implementing, and evaluating all or portions of their advertising programs.

Today's agencies employ specialists who can often perform advertising tasks better than the company's own staff. Agencies also bring an outside point of view to solving the company's problems, along with lots of experience from working with different clients and situations. So, today, even companies with strong advertising departments of their own use advertising agencies.

Some ad agencies are huge—the largest U.S. agency, McCann Erickson Worldwide, has worldwide annual gross revenue of more than $1.1 billion. In recent years, many agencies have grown by gobbling up other agencies, thus creating huge agency holding companies. The largest of these agency "megagroups," Omincom Group, includes several large advertising, public relations, and promotion agencies with combined worldwide revenues of $9.75 billion.[27] Most large advertising agencies have the staff and resources to handle all phases of an advertising campaign for their clients, from creating a marketing plan to developing ad campaigns and preparing, placing, and evaluating ads.

International Advertising Decisions   International advertisers face many complexities not encountered by domestic advertisers. The most basic issue concerns the degree to which global advertising should be adapted to the unique characteristics of various country markets. Some large advertisers have attempted to support their global brands with highly standardized worldwide advertising, with campaigns that work as well in Bangkok as they do in Baltimore. For example, Jeep has created a worldwide brand image of ruggedness and reliability; Coca-Cola's Sprite brand uses standardized appeals to target the world's youth. Ads for Gillette's Venus razors are almost identical worldwide, with only minor adjustments to suit the local culture.

Standardization produces many benefits—lower advertising costs, greater global advertising coordination, and a more consistent worldwide image. But it also has drawbacks. Most importantly, it ignores the fact that country markets differ greatly in their cultures, demographics, and economic conditions. Thus, most international advertisers "think globally but act locally." They develop global advertising *strategies* that make their worldwide advertising efforts more efficient and consistent. Then they adapt their advertising *programs* to make them more responsive to consumer needs and expectations within local markets. For example, Coca-Cola has a pool of different commercials that can be used in or adapted to several different international markets. Some can be used with only minor changes—such as language—in several different countries. Local and regional managers decide which commercials work best for which markets.

Global advertisers face several special problems. For instance, advertising media costs and availability differ vastly from country to country. Countries also differ in the extent to which they regulate advertising practices. Many countries have extensive systems of laws restricting how much a company can spend on advertising, the media used, the nature of advertising claims, and other aspects of the advertising program. Such restrictions often require advertisers to adapt their campaigns from country to country.

For example, alcoholic products cannot be advertised or sold in Muslim countries. In many countries, Sweden and Norway, for example, food ads are banned from kid's TV. To play it safe, McDonald's advertises itself as a family restaurant in Sweden. Comparative ads, while acceptable and even common in the United States and Canada, are less commonly used in the United Kingdom, unacceptable in Japan, and illegal in India and Brazil.

China has restrictive censorship rules for TV and radio advertising; for example, the words *the best* are banned, as are ads that "violate social customs" or present women in "improper ways." McDonald's recently avoided government sanctions there by publicly apologizing for an ad that crossed cultural norms by showing a customer begging for a discount. Similarly, Coca-Cola's Indian subsidiary was forced to end a promotion that offered

■ Standardized worldwide advertising: Gillette's ads for its Gillette for Women Venus razors are almost identical worldwide, with only minor adjustments to suit the local culture.

prizes, such as a trip to Hollywood, because it violated India's established trade practices by encouraging customers to buy in order to "gamble."[28]

Thus, although advertisers may develop global strategies to guide their overall advertising efforts, specific advertising programs must usually be adapted to meet local cultures and customs, media characteristics, and advertising regulations.

 Linking the Concepts

Think about what goes on behind the scenes for the ads we all tend to take for granted.

■ Pick a favorite print or television ad. Why do you like it? Do you think that it's effective? Can you think of an ad that people like that may not be effective?

■ Dig a little deeper and learn about the campaign *behind* your ad. What are the campaign's objectives? What is its budget? Assess the campaign's message and media strategies. Looking beyond your own feelings about the ad, is the campaign likely to be effective?

Sales Promotion

Advertising often works closely with another promotion tool, sales promotion. *Sales promotion* consists of short-term incentives to encourage purchase or sales of a product or service. Whereas advertising offers reasons to buy a product or service, sales promotion offers reasons to buy *now*.

Examples of sales promotions are found everywhere. A freestanding insert in the Sunday newspaper contains a coupon offering $1 off Folgers coffee. An e-mail from EddieBauer.com offers free shipping on your next purchase over $100. The end-of-the-aisle display in the local supermarket tempts impulse buyers with a wall of Coke cases. An executive buys a new Sony laptop and gets a free carrying case, or a family buys a new Explorer and receives a factory rebate of $1,000. A hardware store chain receives a 10 percent discount on selected Black & Decker portable power tools if it agrees to advertise them in local newspapers. Sales promotion includes a wide variety of promotion tools designed to stimulate earlier or stronger market response.

RAPID GROWTH OF SALES PROMOTION

Sales promotion tools are used by most organizations, including manufacturers, distributors, retailers, and not-for-profit institutions. They are targeted toward final buyers (*consumer promotions*), retailers and wholesalers (*trade promotions*), business customers (*business promotions*), and members of the sales force (*sales force promotions*). Today, in the average consumer packaged-goods company, sales promotion accounts for 74 percent of all marketing expenditures.[29]

Several factors have contributed to the rapid growth of sales promotion, particularly in consumer markets. First, inside the company, product managers face greater pressures to increase their current sales, and promotion is viewed as an effective short-run sales tool. Second, externally, the company faces more competition and competing brands are less differentiated. Increasingly, competitors are using sales promotion to help differentiate their offers. Third, advertising efficiency has declined because of rising costs, media clutter, and legal restraints. Finally, consumers have become more deal oriented, and ever-larger retailers are demanding more deals from manufacturers.

The growing use of sales promotion has resulted in *promotion clutter*, similar to advertising clutter. Consumers are increasingly tuning out promotions, weakening their ability to trigger immediate purchase. Manufacturers are now searching for ways to rise above the clutter, such as offering larger coupon values or creating more dramatic point-of-purchase displays.

In developing a sales promotion program, a company must first set sales promotion objectives and then select the best tools for accomplishing these objectives.

SALES PROMOTION OBJECTIVES

Sales promotion objectives vary widely. Sellers may use *consumer promotions* to increase short-term sales or to help build long-term market share. Objectives for *trade promotions* include getting retailers to carry new items and more inventory, getting them to advertise the product and give it more shelf space, and getting them to buy ahead. For the *sales force*, objectives include getting more sales force support for current or new products or getting salespeople to sign up new accounts. Sales promotions are usually used together with advertising, personal selling, or other promotion mix tools. Consumer promotions must usually be advertised and can add excitement and pulling power to ads. Trade and sales force promotions support the firm's personal selling process.

In general, rather than creating only short-term sales or temporary brand switching, sales promotions should help to reinforce the product's position and build long-term *customer relationships*. If properly designed, every sales promotion tool has the potential to build both short-term excitement and long-term consumer relationships. Increasingly, marketers are avoiding "quick fix," price-only promotions in favor of promotions designed to build brand equity. Examples include all of the "frequency marketing programs" and loyalty clubs that have mushroomed in recent years. Most hotels, supermarkets, and airlines now offer frequent-guest/buyer/flyer programs offering rewards to regular customers. For example, Cendant, which owns hotel chains such as Ramada, Days Inn, Travelodge, Howard Johnson, and Super 8, offers a loyalty program called TripRewards, a program that targets its core market of not-so-frequent leisure travelers.

Customer-relationship building promotions: Cendant's TripRewards program makes frequent customers out of not-so-frequent leisure travelers.

In designing its TripRewards loyalty program, Cendant knew that Ramada, Days Inn, Travelodge, and the rest of its lodging family could not out-Marriott Marriott Rewards or duplicate the elite tiers of Starwood Preferred Guest. Cendant caters to more budget-minded leisure travelers who venture out on a half-dozen trips or less annually. Unlike frequent business travelers, these folks don't travel enough to take advantage of most travel loyalty programs. So Cendant put together a network of TripRewards retailers that lets members earn points with everyday purchases. TripRewards members can earn points for purchases at retailers ranging from JCPenney and Best Buy to FTD Florists and CheapTickets.com. Cendant's "It's fun to get more" ad campaign plays up the fun of getting a bonus from everyday shopping transactions. TripRewards' low redemption threshold (as low as 65,000 points for a week-long resort stay versus Marriott Rewards' 140,000) means that Cendant can win the patronage of consumers who would otherwise be decades away from earning anything in a competing program. The TripRewards program drew 2.8 million members in its first eight months, 60 percent of them first-time Cendant hotel customers. It's attracting younger and more affluent consumers with higher average room rates and longer stays—and it keeps them coming back. "They're going to be repeat business," says the manager of one Cendant hotel. "The points add up pretty quick, [and] once we get [guests] through the . . . door, they're not going back to Hilton."[30]

MAJOR SALES PROMOTION TOOLS

Many tools can be used to accomplish sales promotion objectives. Descriptions of the main consumer, trade, and business promotion tools follow.

Consumer Promotion Tools   The main *consumer promotion tools* include samples, coupons, cash refunds, price packs, premiums, advertising specialties, patronage rewards, point-of-purchase displays and demonstrations, and contests, sweepstakes, and games.

Samples are offers of a trial amount of a product. Sampling is the most effective—but most expensive—way to introduce a new product or to create new excitement for an existing one. Some samples are free; for others, the company charges a small amount to offset its cost. The sample might be delivered door-to-door, sent by mail, handed out in a store, attached to another product, or featured in an ad. Sometimes, samples are combined into sample packs, which can then be used to promote other products and services. Sampling can be a powerful promotional tool. Consider this example:

> Fisherman's Friend throat lozenges used sampling as the centerpiece of a very successful brand-building program. It began by passing out 250,000 samples of its lozenges at more than 25 fairs, sporting events, and other happenings where it was a sponsor. Each sample contained an invitation to visit the Fisherman's Friend Web site, where customers could enter a contest to win a MINI Cooper by submitting a slogan to be used in the future "Tell a Friend" (about Fisherman's Friend) ad campaign. The sampling promotion was a complete success. U.S. sales of Fisherman's Friend lozenges grew 115 percent for the year, 25 percent better than expectations. Some 5,000 people submitted a slogan for the company's new ad campaign. The winner and proud owner of a new MINI Cooper—Shirley Tucker of Pittsburgh—suggested the slogan, "Lose a Cough. Gain a Friend," which is now featured in ads and on the Web site. The successful sampling campaign continues via the company's Web site, which invites consumers to sign themselves and a friend up to receive free samples of Fisherman's Friend in the mail.[31]

Coupons are certificates that give buyers a saving when they purchase specified products. Most consumers love coupons. U.S. companies distribute 251 billion coupons a year. Seventy-seven percent of consumers clip some 3.6 billion of them, with an average face value of $1.03, for a total savings of over $3 billion.[32] Coupons can promote early trial of a new brand or stimulate sales of a mature brand. However, as a result of coupon clutter, redemption rates have been declining in recent years. Thus, most major consumer goods companies are issuing fewer coupons and targeting them more carefully.

Marketers are also cultivating new outlets for distributing coupons, such as supermarket shelf dispensers, electronic point-of-sale coupon printers, or even text-messaging systems. For example, text-message couponing is popular in Europe, India, and Japan, and it's slowly gaining popularity in the United States. At the University of South Florida, local businesses can send out text-message coupons directly to interested students' cell phones via the university's MoBull Messenger system. For instance, if a local pizza place is having a slow night, it can log in and blast out a two-for-one pizza coupon to students who have opted-in. Some companies also offer coupons on their Web sites or through online coupon services such as

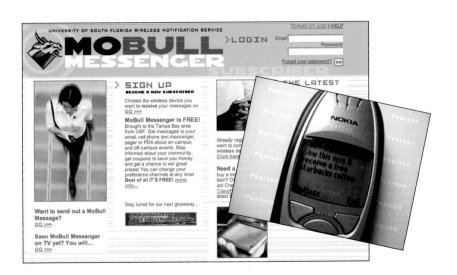

■ New forms of coupons: Text message couponing is gaining popularity. At the University of South Florida, local businesses can blast out text message coupons directly to interested students' cell phones via the university's MoBull Messenger system.

Hotcoupons.com, Valpak.com, and Mycoupons.com. Last year, as a result of sites like these, the number of coupons distributed online more than doubled.[33]

Cash refunds (or rebates) are like coupons except that the price reduction occurs after the purchase rather than at the retail outlet. The consumer sends a "proof of purchase" to the manufacturer, who then refunds part of the purchase price by mail. For example, Toro ran a clever preseason promotion on some of its snowblower models, offering a rebate if the snowfall in the buyer's market area turned out to be below average. Competitors were not able to match this offer on such short notice, and the promotion was very successful.

Price packs (also called cents-off deals) offer consumers savings off the regular price of a product. The reduced prices are marked by the producer directly on the label or package. Price packs can be single packages sold at a reduced price (such as two for the price of one), or two related products banded together (such as a toothbrush and toothpaste). Price packs are very effective—even more so than coupons—in stimulating short-term sales.

Premiums are goods offered either free or at low cost as an incentive to buy a product, ranging from toys included with kids' products to phone cards and DVDs. A premium may come inside the package (in-pack), outside the package (on-pack), or through the mail. Kellogg's galactic-gadgets promotion offered Star Wars Episode III prizes via an assortment of channels. Packages of Frosted Flakes contained a free light-up Saberspoon. Crispix buyers could mail in two UPC labels along with $6.99 and receive an R2-D2 snack bowl that beeps and whistles. And if your specially-marked package of Pop-Tarts played Darth Vader music and contained a winning game piece, you won a Darth Vader Voice Changer.

Advertising specialties, also called *promotional products*, are useful articles imprinted with an advertiser's name, logo, or message that are given as gifts to consumers. Typical items include T-shirts and other apparel, pens, coffee mugs, calendars, key rings, mouse pads, matches, tote bags, coolers, golf balls, and caps. Such items can be very effective. In a recent study, 71 percent of all consumers surveyed had received at least one promotional product in the last 12 months. Seventy-six percent of those were able to recall the advertiser's name on the promotional product they received, compared to only 53.5 percent who could recall the name of an advertiser in a print publication they had read in the past week.[34]

Patronage rewards are cash or other awards offered for the regular use of a certain company's products or services. For example, airlines offer frequent flier plans, awarding points for miles traveled that can be turned in for free airline trips. And supermarkets issue frequent shopper cards that dole out a wealth of discounts at the checkout. Baskin-Robbins offers frequent-purchase awards—for every 10 purchases, customers receive a free quart of ice cream.

Point-of-purchase (POP) promotions include displays and demonstrations that take place at the point of purchase or sale. Think of your last visit to the local Safeway, Costco, CVS, or Bed Bath & Beyond. Chances are good that you were tripping over aisle displays, promotional signs, "shelf talkers," or demonstrators offering free tastes of featured food products. Unfortunately, many retailers do not like to handle the hundreds of displays, signs, and posters they receive from manufacturers each year. Manufacturers have responded by offering better POP materials, tying them in with television or print messages, and offering to set them up.

Contests, sweepstakes, and *games* give consumers the chance to win something, such as cash, trips, or goods, by luck or through extra effort. A *contest* calls for consumers to submit an entry—a jingle, guess, suggestion—to be judged by a panel that will select the best entries. A *sweepstakes* calls for consumers to submit their names for a drawing. A *game* presents consumers with something—bingo numbers, missing letters—every time they buy, which may or may not help them win a prize. A sales contest urges dealers or the sales force to increase their efforts, with prizes going to the top performers.

Trade-Promotion Tools   Manufacturers direct more sales promotion dollars toward retailers and wholesalers (78 percent) than to consumers (22 percent).[35] Trade promotion can persuade resellers to carry a brand, give it shelf space, promote it in advertising, and push it to consumers. Shelf space is so scarce these days that manufacturers often have to offer price-offs, allowances, buy-back guarantees, or free goods to retailers and wholesalers to get products on the shelf and, once there, to keep them on it.

Manufacturers use several trade promotion tools. Many of the tools used for consumer promotions—contests, premiums, displays—can also be used as trade promotions. Or the manufacturer may offer a straight discount off the list price on each case purchased during a stated period of time (also called a *price-off*, *off-invoice*, or *off-list*). Manufacturers also may offer an allowance (usually so much off per case) in return for the retailer's agreement to feature the manufacturer's products in some way. An *advertising allowance* compensates retailers for advertising the product. A *display allowance* compensates them for using special displays.

Manufacturers may offer *free goods*, which are extra cases of merchandise, to resellers who buy a certain quantity or who feature a certain flavor or size. They may offer *push money*—cash or gifts to dealers or their sales forces to "push" the manufacturer's goods. Manufacturers may give retailers free *specialty advertising items* that carry the company's name, such as pens, pencils, calendars, paperweights, matchbooks, memo pads, and yardsticks.

Business Promotion Tools Companies spend billions of dollars each year on promotion to industrial customers. *Business promotion tools* are used to generate business leads, stimulate purchases, reward customers, and motivate salespeople. Business promotion includes many of the same tools used for consumer or trade promotions. Here, we focus on two additional major business promotion tools—conventions and trade shows, and sales contests.

Many companies and trade associations organize *conventions and trade shows* to promote their products. Firms selling to the industry show their products at the trade show. Vendors receive many benefits, such as opportunities to find new sales leads, contact customers, introduce new products, meet new customers, sell more to present customers, and educate customers with publications and audiovisual materials. Trade shows also help companies reach many prospects not reached through their sales forces. Some trade shows are huge. For example, at this year's International Consumer Electronics Show, 2,500 exhibitors attracted more than 140,000 professional visitors. Even more impressive, at the BAUMA mining and construction equipment trade show in Munich, Germany, some 2,800 exhibitors from 47 countries presented their latest product innovations to more than 416,000 attendees from 171 countries.[36]

A *sales contest* is a contest for salespeople or dealers to motivate them to increase their sales performance over a given period. Sales contests motivate and recognize good company performers, who may receive trips, cash prizes, or other gifts. Some companies award points for performance, which the receiver can turn in for any of a variety of prizes. Sales contests work best when they are tied to measurable and achievable sales objectives (such as finding new accounts, reviving old accounts, or increasing account profitability).

■ Some trade shows are huge. At this year's International Consumer Electronics Show, 2,400 exhibitors attracted more than 130,000 professional visitors.

DEVELOPING THE SALES PROMOTION PROGRAM

Beyond selecting the types of promotions to use, marketers must make several other decisions in designing the full sales promotion program. First, they must decide on the *size of the incentive*. A certain minimum incentive is necessary if the promotion is to succeed; a larger incentive will produce more sales response. The marketer also must set *conditions for participation*. Incentives might be offered to everyone or only to select groups.

Marketers must also decide how to *promote and distribute the promotion* program itself. A 50-cents-off coupon could be given out in a package, at the store, via the Internet, or in an advertisement. Each distribution method involves a different level of reach and cost. Increasingly, marketers are blending several media into a total campaign concept. The *length of the promotion* is also important. If the sales promotion period is too short, many prospects (who may not be buying during that time) will miss it. If the promotion runs too long, the deal will lose some of its "act now" force.

Evaluation is also very important. Many companies fail to evaluate their sales promotion programs, and others evaluate them only superficially. Yet marketers should work to measure the returns on their sales promotion investments, just as they should seek to assess the returns on other marketing activities. The most common evaluation method is to compare sales before, during, and after a promotion. Marketers should ask, Did the promotion attract new customers or more purchasing from current customers? Can we hold onto these new customers and purchases? Will the long-run customer relationship and sales gains from the promotion justify its costs?

Clearly, sales promotion plays an important role in the total promotion mix. To use it well, the marketer must define the sales promotion objectives, select the best tools, design the sales promotion program, implement the program, and evaluate the results. Moreover, sales promotion must be coordinated carefully with other promotion mix elements within the integrated marketing communications program.

Public Relations

Public relations (PR)

Building good relations with the company's various publics by obtaining favorable publicity, building up a good "corporate image," and handling or heading off unfavorable rumors, stories, and events.

Another major mass-promotion tool is **public relations (PR)**—building good relations with the company's various publics by obtaining favorable publicity, building up a good corporate image, and handling or heading off unfavorable rumors, stories, and events. Public relations departments may perform any or all of the following functions:[37]

- *Press relations or press agency:* Creating and placing newsworthy information in the news media to attract attention to a person, product, or service.
- *Product publicity:* Publicizing specific products.
- *Public affairs:* Building and maintaining national or local community relations.
- *Lobbying:* Building and maintaining relations with legislators and government officials to influence legislation and regulation.
- *Investor relations:* Maintaining relationships with shareholders and others in the financial community.
- *Development:* Public relations with donors or members of nonprofit organizations to gain financial or volunteer support.

Public relations is used to promote products, people, places, ideas, activities, organizations, and even nations. Companies use public relations to build good relations with consumers, investors, the media, and their communities. Trade associations have used public relations to rebuild interest in declining commodities such as eggs, apples, milk, and potatoes. The state of New York turned its image around when its "I ♥ New York!" publicity and advertising campaign took root, bringing in millions more tourists. Johnson & Johnson's masterly use of public relations played a major role in saving Tylenol from extinction after its product-tampering scare. Nations have used public relations to attract more tourists, foreign investment, and international support.

THE ROLE AND IMPACT OF PUBLIC RELATIONS

Public relations can have a strong impact on public awareness at a much lower cost than advertising can. The company does not pay for the space or time in the media. Rather, it pays for a staff to develop and circulate information and to manage events. If the company develops an interesting story, it could be picked up by several different media, having the same effect as advertising that would cost millions of dollars. And it would have more credibility than advertising.

PR results can sometimes be spectacular. Here's how publisher Scholastic, Inc., uses public relations to turn a simple new book introduction into a major international event, all on a very small budget:

Secret codes. A fiercely guarded text. Huddled masses lined up in funny hats at the witching hour. Welcome to one of the biggest literary events in history. As the clock creeps past midnight, kids worldwide rush to buy the next installment of Harry Potter. It's the fastest-shrinking book pile in history. *Harry Potter and the Half-Blood Prince,* the sixth book in the series, sold an astonishing 8.9 million copies in just the first 24 hours in the United States and Britain alone—some 370,000 per hour. How do you whip up a consumer frenzy with a miserly $1.8 million promotion budget and only a few well-placed ads? The spellbinding plots, written by Scottish welfare-mom-turned-millionaire J. K. Rowling, captivate kids everywhere. But the hidden hand of public relations plays a large role, too. Publisher Scholastic works behind the scenes with retailers to prepare contests, theme parties, and giveaways leading up to each new release. It communicates through amateur fan sites such as The Leaky Cauldron and MuggleNet.com to keep fans informed about print runs and store events. It works with the mainstream media to create a sense of celebration and excitement. NBC's *Today Show* ran an entire week of "Countdown to Harry" events leading up to the publication of the *Half-Blood Prince.* Scholastic's Web site reaches out to obsessed fans with essay contests and video clips. Scholastic heightens the tension by keeping each new book's title and book jacket under wraps almost until the last minute, even forcing booksellers to sign secrecy agreements. With all this PR hype, by the time the book hits the shelves, conditions are hot for Harry.[38]

■ Public relations results can sometimes be spectacular. Scholastic sponsored low-cost sleepovers, games, and costume contests to whip up consumer frenzy for the sixth installment of its Harry Potter series.

Despite its potential strengths, public relations is sometimes described as a marketing stepchild because of its often limited and scattered use. The PR department is usually located at corporate headquarters. Its staff is so busy dealing with various publics—stockholders, employees, legislators, the press—that PR programs to support product marketing objectives may be ignored. Marketing managers and PR practitioners do not always talk the same language. Many PR practitioners see their job as simply communicating. In contrast, marketing managers tend to be much more interested in how advertising and public relations affect brand building, sales and profits, and customer relationships.

This situation is changing, however. Although public relations still captures only a small portion of the overall marketing budgets of most firms, PR is playing an increasingly important brand-building role. Public relations can be a powerful brand-building tool. Two well-known marketing consultants even go so far as to conclude that advertising doesn't build brands, PR does. In their book *The Fall of Advertising & the Rise of PR,* the consultants proclaim that the dominance of advertising is over, and that public relations is quietly becoming the most powerful marketing communications tool.

The birth of a brand is usually accomplished with [public relations], not advertising. Our general rule is [PR] first, advertising second. [Public relations] is the nail, advertising the hammer. [PR] creates the credentials that provide the credibility for advertising. . . . Anita Roddick built the Body Shop into a major brand with no advertising at all. Instead, she traveled the world on a relentless quest for publicity. . . . Until recently Starbucks Coffee Co. didn't spend a hill of beans on advertising, either. In 10 years, the company spent less than $10 million on advertising, a trivial amount for a brand that delivers annual sales of [in the billions]. Wal-Mart Stores became the world's largest retailer . . . with very little advertising. . . . On the Internet, Amazon.com became a powerhouse brand with virtually no advertising.[39]

Although the book created much controversy, and most advertisers wouldn't agree about the "fall of advertising" part of the title, the point is a good one. Advertising and public relations should work hand in hand to build and maintain brands.

MAJOR PR TOOLS

Public relations uses several tools. One of the major tools is *news*. PR professionals find or create favorable news about the company and its products or people. Sometimes news stories occur naturally, and sometimes the PR person can suggest events or activities that would create news. *Speeches* can also create product and company publicity. Increasingly, company executives must field questions from the media or give talks at trade associations or sales meetings, and these events can either build or hurt the company's image. Another common PR tool is *special events*, ranging from news conferences, press tours, grand openings, and fireworks displays to laser shows, hot-air balloon releases, multimedia presentations, star-studded spectaculars, or educational programs designed to reach and interest target publics.

PR people also prepare *written materials* to reach and influence their target markets. These materials include annual reports, brochures, articles, and company newsletters and magazines. *Audiovisual materials*, such as films, slide-and-sound programs, and video and audio CDs, are being used increasingly as communication tools. *Corporate identity materials* can also help create a corporate identity that the public immediately recognizes. Logos, stationery, brochures, signs, business forms, business cards, buildings, uniforms, and company cars and trucks—all become marketing tools when they are attractive, distinctive, and memorable. Finally, companies can improve public goodwill by contributing money and time to *public service activities*.

As we discussed in Chapter 5, many marketers are now also designing *buzz marketing* campaigns to generate excitement and favorable word-of-mouth for their brands. Buzz marketing creates publicity by getting consumers themselves to spread information about a product or service to others in their communities. Procter & Gamble understands the importance of buzz. It created a separate marketing arm called Tremor, which has enlisted an army of buzzers to create word-of-mouth not just about P&G products, but for those of other client companies as well.

Gina Lavagna is the ideal pitch gal. After receiving a $2 minidisc for Sony's Net MD and six $10-off coupons, she rushed four of her chums to a mall near her home to show them the digital-music player, which sells for $99 and up. "I've probably told 20 people about it," she says, adding, "At least 10 are extremely interested in getting one." Her parents got her one for Christmas. Gina is a member of the huge stealth teenage marketing force—some 280,000 strong—enlisted by Tremor, a marketing arm of P&G. Their mission is to help companies spread the word about their brands among teens, who are maddeningly difficult to influence through advertising.

Tremor recruits what it calls "connectors"—teens with a wide social circle and a gift of gab. While it screens the kids it taps, it doesn't coach them beyond encouraging them to feel free to talk to friends. Tremorites deliver endorsements in school cafeterias, at sleepovers, by cell phone, and by e-mail. The kids, natural talkers, do the work without pay, not counting the coupons, product samples, and the thrill of being something of an "insider." Initially focused only on P&G brands, Tremor's forces are now being tapped to talk up just about any brand, from Sony, Coca-Cola, and Kraft to Toyota and Valvoline motor oil. Tremor's buzz marketing effort has been so successful that P&G is now building a new network that will focus on moms—a much bigger and more affluent target than teens.[40]

■ Buzz marketing: P&G's Tremor unit has enlisted an army of buzzers—teens, with a wide social circle and a gift of gab—to create word-of-mouth about brands.

MARKETING AT WORK | 12.3 |

Marketing on a Roll: Charmin's Potty Palooza

"People walk from half a mile away," says John Baker, a festival organizer. No wonder: Charmin's 27-room traveling bathroom facility, painted sky blue with white clouds and latched to the bed of an 18-wheeler, inspires awe wherever it goes. "It's like a ride at the state fair," Baker marvels. "They wait in line 10 to 15 minutes sometimes!"

Depending on your point of view, Potty Palooza represents either the epitome or the pits of experiential, mobile marketing—a marketing approach that touches consumers in places no advertising campaign would go. It's a showroom on wheels, a rolling free trial for . . . toilet paper.

"The media is fracturing, costs are rising," says Charmin's brand manager at Procter & Gamble.

"It's difficult to reach consumers these days." Unless, that is, you've got a big semi and a trailer fitted with flushing porcelain toilets, hardwood floors, and air conditioning—plus aromatherapy, skylights, changing stations, a "Little Squirts" stall for kids, and an LCD video screen in every room.

Since its debut in 2002, the Potty Palooza truck has been on the road 11 months a year, visiting 26 to 30 events annually—from the Super Bowl to the Arizona Balloon Festival. All told, Charmin's 5 million annual guests go through some 10,000 cushioned rolls. (A supply truck joins in the Potty Palooza caravan.)

As guests wait, they take part in the full branding experience. The Charmin Bear teaches the Charmin dance while smiling brand reps guide visitors to and from stalls and spruce up rooms after every use. At the Covered Bridge Festival, that can mean cleaning up after 5,000 guests a day. Says the director of the Palooza road team: "We can't budge when that thing is full. We have to empty the black water 5 to 10 times a day."

Yuck. Is it worth it? P&G claims the truck is part of one of the biggest consumer-sampling programs anywhere. And while P&G won't talk dollar returns on its mobile-marketing effort, it's getting something right. After Potty Palooza made its first appearance at the Covered Bridge Festival in 2002, 30,000 people signed a petition to keep it coming back.

Source: Adapted with permission from Lucas Conley, "On a Roll," *Fast Company*, February 2005, p. 28.

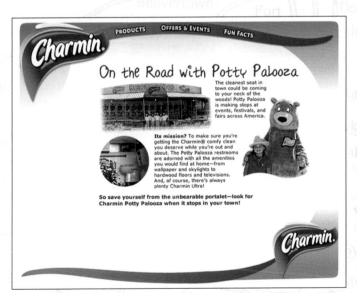

■ Mobile marketing: Charmin's "Potty Palooza" serves as a rolling showcase for—you guessed it—toilet paper.

Another recent PR development is *mobile marketing*—traveling promotional tours that bring the brand to consumers. Mobile marketing has emerged as an effective way to build one-to-one relationships with targeted consumers. These days, it seems that almost every company is putting its show on the road. For example, Home Depot recently brought do-it-yourself home-project workshops and demonstrations to 26 NASCAR racetracks. Microsoft teams with local partners to field Across America Mobile Solutions Centers, 27-foot techie dream vans that visit information-technology workers in offices around the country to demonstrate Microsoft's latest software products. And Charmin's "Potty Palooza" serves as a rolling showcase for—you guessed it—toilet paper (see Marketing at Work 12.3).[41]

A company's Web site can be a good public relations vehicle. Consumers and members of other publics can visit the site for information and entertainment. Such sites can be extremely popular. For example, Butterball's site (www.butterball.com), which features cooking and carving tips, once received 550,000 visitors in one day during Thanksgiving week. The Web site supplements the Butterball Turkey Talk-Line (1-800-BUTTERBALL)—called by some the "granddaddy of all help lines—staffed by 50 home economists and nutritionists who respond to more than 100,000 questions each November and December.[42]

Web sites can also be ideal for handling crisis situations. For example, when several bottles of Odwalla apple juice sold on the West Coast were found to contain E. coli bacteria, Odwalla initiated a massive product recall. Within only three hours, it set up a Web site laden with information about the crisis and Odwalla's response. Company staffers also combed the Internet looking for newsgroups discussing Odwalla and posted links to the site. In this age where "it's easier to disseminate information through e-mail marketing, blogs, and online chat," notes an analyst, "public relations is becoming a valuable part of doing business in a digital world."[43]

As with the other promotion tools, in considering when and how to use product public relations, management should set PR objectives, choose the PR messages and vehicles, implement the PR plan, and evaluate the results. The firm's public relations should be blended smoothly with other promotion activities within the company's overall integrated marketing communications effort.

REST STOP ➡ REVIEWING THE CONCEPTS

In this chapter, you've learned how companies use integrated marketing communications (IMC) to communicate customer value. Modern marketing calls for more than just creating customer value by developing a good product, pricing it attractively, and making it available to target customers. Companies also must clearly and persuasively *communicate* that value to current and prospective customers. To do this, they must blend five communication-mix tools, guided by a well-designed and implemented integrated marketing communications strategy.

1. Discuss the process and advantages of integrated marketing communications in communicating customer value.

Recent shifts toward targeted or one-to-one marketing, coupled with advances in information and communication technology, have had a dramatic impact on marketing communications. As marketing communicators adopt richer but more fragmented media and promotion mixes to reach their diverse markets, they risk creating a communications hodgepodge for consumers. To prevent this, more companies are adopting the concept of *integrated marketing communications (IMC)*. Guided by an overall IMC strategy, the company works out the roles that the various promotional tools will play and the

extent to which each will be used. It carefully coordinates the promotional activities and the timing of when major campaigns take place. Finally, to help implement its integrated marketing strategy, the company appoints a marketing communications director who has overall responsibility for the company's communications efforts.

2. Define the five promotion tools and discuss factors that must be considered in shaping the overall promotion mix.

A company's total *promotion mix*—also called its *marketing communications mix*—consists of the specific blend of *advertising, personal selling, sales promotion, public relations,* and *direct-marketing* tools that the company uses to persuasively communicate customer value and build customer relationships. Advertising includes any paid form of nonpersonal presentation and promotion of ideas, goods, or services by an identified sponsor. In contrast, public relations focuses on building good relations with the company's various publics by obtaining favorable unpaid publicity. Personal selling is any form of personal presentation by the firm's sales force for the purpose of making sales and building customer relationships. Firms use sales promotion to provide short-term incentives to encourage the purchase or sale of a product or service. Finally, firms seeking immediate response from targeted individual customers use nonpersonal direct-marketing tools to communicate with customers.

The company wants to create an integrated *promotion mix*. It can pursue a *push* or a *pull* promotional strategy, or a combination of the two. The best specific blend of promotion tools depends on the type of product/market and the product life-cycle stage. People at all levels of the organization must be aware of the many legal and ethical issues surrounding marketing communications.

3. Describe and discuss the major decisions involved in developing an advertising program.

Advertising—the use of paid media by a seller to inform, persuade, and remind about its products or organization—is a strong promotion tool that takes many forms and has many uses. *Advertising decision making* involves decisions about the objectives, the budget, the message, the media, and, finally, the evaluation of results. Advertisers should set clear *objectives* as to whether the advertising is supposed to inform, persuade, or remind buyers. The advertising *budget* can be based on what is affordable, on sales, on competitors' spending, or on the objectives and tasks. The *message decision* calls for planning a message strategy and executing it effectively. The *media decision* involves defining reach, frequency, and impact goals; choosing major media types; selecting media vehicles; and deciding on media timing. Message and media decisions must be closely coordinated for maximum campaign effectiveness. Finally, *evaluation* calls for evaluating the communication and sales effects of advertising before, during, and after the advertising is placed and measuring advertising return on investment.

4. Explain how sales promotion campaigns are developed and implemented.

Sales promotion covers a wide variety of short-term incentive tools—coupons, premiums, contests, buying allowances— designed to stimulate final buyers and business consumers, the trade, and the company's own sales force. Sales promotion spending has been growing faster than advertising spending in recent years. A sales promotion campaign first calls for setting sales-promotion objectives (in general, sales promotions should be *consumer relationship building*). It then calls for developing and implementing the sales promotion program by using consumer promotion tools (*samples, coupons, cash refunds* or *rebates, price packs, premiums, advertising specialties, patronage rewards*, and others); trade promotion tools (*dis-counts, allowances, free goods, push money)*; and business promotion tools (*conventions* and *trade shows, sales contests*). The sales promotion effort should be coordinated carefully with the firm's other promotion efforts.

5. Explain how companies use public relations to communicate with their publics.

Public relations involves building good relations with the company's various publics. Its functions include *press agentry, product publicity, public affairs, lobbying, investor relations,* and *development*. Public relations can have a strong impact on public awareness at a much lower cost than advertising can, and PR results can sometimes be spectacular. Despite its potential strengths, however, public relations sometimes sees only limited and scattered use. PR tools include *news, speeches, special events, buzz marketing, mobile marketing, written materials, audiovisual materials, corporate identity materials,* and *public service activities*. A company's Web site can be a good PR vehicle. In considering when and how to use product public relations, management should set PR objectives, choose the PR messages and vehicles, implement the PR plan, and evaluate the results. Public relations should be blended smoothly with other promotion activities within the company's overall integrated marketing communications effort.

Navigating the Key Terms

Travel Log

Discussing the Issues

1. Briefly describe the "new marketing communications model" as discussed in the chapter. Why is it so important for today's marketers to create *integrated* marketing communications?

2. List and briefly describe the five major promotion mix tools. Broadly speaking, what objective is each promotion tool best suited to accomplish?

3. Describe the four methods discussed in the text for setting the advertising budget. For each of the four methods, list one advantage and one drawback associated with the method. Which method is best?

4. How do media reach, frequency, and impact influence consumer brand awareness? Is one more important than the others for increasing awareness?

5. Describe two promotional offers you have received recently. Which consumer promotional tools do the offers employ? How did the offers impact your purchase decision? Was the effect on your buying behavior temporary or permanent?

6. What role does public relations play in the overall marketing communications mix? List two advantages and two disadvantages of relying on public relations to promote a brand.

Application Questions

1. As a marketing manager, create a promotion plan that uses both push and pull strategies to sell picture phones (cell phones equipped with cameras) to teenagers. Detail the objectives you hope to accomplish with each component of the plan.

2. Select a primetime television show that you watch regularly. While watching the show, pay particular attention to product placements. Make a list of each product promoted. Are you surprised by the number and types of products you found? How well integrated were the product placements? What impact will they likely have on viewer preferences and behavior?

3. Flip through your local newspaper. Are there any stories that promote a product or service? How might the impact of such public relations differ from an advertisement for that product placed in the same paper?

Under the Hood: Focus on Technology

Although it may at first seem like a simple advancement in technology, digital video recorders (DVRs) are having a profound affect on advertising and, as a result, on marketing. With a few simple steps, consumers with DVRs can record an entire season of a favorite show. Just as easily, they can pause live television or flip between different programs, keeping track of multiple channels at once. While the technology is wonderful for consumers, many marketers are not so pleased. Before the advent of VCRs and DVRs, advertisers counted on a captive audience to receive marketing messages. Not surprisingly, as viewers watch recorded programs, many now skip past commercials, hurrying to continue the main attraction. The result is an "empowered" viewing audience that is very difficult to reach with traditional commercial messages.

1. Will DVRs ultimately change the nature of advertising on broadcast television? How?

2. Beyond the strategies discussed in the chapter, what alternatives to traditional advertising might a company pursue to reach consumers under the new marketing communications model?

Focus on Ethics

Although prescription drug advertising has traditionally targeted physicians, messages aimed directly at patients have recently taken a dramatic rise. In fact, drug manufacturers have increased spending on direct-to-consumer advertising by 800 percent in the last eight years, totaling $3.2 billion in 2003. The expected result? Pharmaceutical companies argue that reaching out directly to patients educates consumers about solutions to health problems that affect quality of life. Critics argue that drug companies are padding their profits by convincing consumers to buy drugs they don't need. Such critics point out that 71 percent of family physicians feel direct-to-consumer advertising pressures them to prescribe medication they wouldn't otherwise prescribe. Regardless of the motivation, the advertising appears to be working. The number of prescription drugs purchased per person in the United States has grown by more than 50 percent in just ten years, totaling 3.4 billion separate purchases nationwide. Although that number is certainly large, spending on direct-to-consumer advertising makes up only 13 percent of the total advertising outlay by drug companies. The remainder is spent targeting physicians. Still, some suggest that direct-to-consumer advertising fuels the escalating cost of prescription drugs, which are rising at an average of 7.4 percent per year, nearly triple the average inflation rate.*

1. How do you feel about the increase in direct-to-consumer advertising for prescription drugs? Are drug companies educating consumers or persuading them to buy drugs they don't need?

2. What are some of the pros and cons for marketers advertising directly to consumers? Do you believe it is more appropriate to target physicians?

*For more information, visit the Kaiser Family Foundation at www.kff.org.

Videos

The DDB Worldwide video case that accompanies this chapter is located in Appendix 1 at the back of the book.

> **10:45 pm.** Account Manager Erin Bliss finishes Advanced Linux Volume IX.
> Meanwhile, husband Gary begins XP For Dummies.

AFTER STUDYING THIS CHAPTER, YOU SHOULD BE ABLE TO

1. discuss the role of a company's salespeople in creating value for customers and building customer relationships

2. identify and explain the six major sales force management steps

3. discuss the personal selling process, distinguishing between transaction-oriented marketing and relationship marketing

4. define *direct marketing* and discuss its benefits to customers and companies

5. identify and discuss the major forms of direct marketing

Communicating Customer Value: Personal Selling and Direct Marketing

Road Map Previewing the Concepts

In the previous chapter, you learned about communicating customer value through integrated marketing communications (IMC), and about three specific elements of the marketing communications mix—advertising, sales promotion, and publicity. In this chapter, we'll move down the road and look at the final two IMC elements—personal selling and direct marketing. Personal selling is the interpersonal arm of marketing communications, in which the sales force interacts with customers and prospects to build relationships and make sales. Direct marketing consists of direct connections with carefully targeted consumers to both obtain an immediate response and cultivate lasting customer relationships. Actually, direct marketing can be viewed as more than just a communications tool. In many ways it constitutes an overall marketing approach—a blend of communication and distribution channels all rolled into one. As you read on, remember that although this chapter examines personal selling and direct marketing as separate tools, they must be carefully integrated with other elements of the marketing promotion mix.

When someone says "salesperson," what image comes to mind? Or how about "direct marketing"? Perhaps you think about a stereotypical glad-hander who's out to lighten your wallet by selling you something you don't really need, or about a high-pressure infomercial that screams "pick up the phone!" Think again. Today, for most companies, personal selling and direct marketing play an important role in building profitable customer relationships. Consider CDW Corporation, whose customer-focused "clicks and people" direct marketing strategy has helped it grow rapidly while competitors have faltered.

CDW Corporation, a leading provider of multibrand technology products and services, is thriving. In only 21 years since Michael Krasny founded the business at his kitchen table, CDW has grown to become a high-tech heavyweight in its highly volatile and competitive industry. Even as much of the tech world has slumped, CDW has increased its sales 48 percent, to $5.7 billion annually since 2000. Profits are up more than 15 percent compared to last year, and the company now serves some 415,000 active commercial accounts, up 15 percent from last year.

How has CDW managed to grow so profitably? The company owes its success to its highly effective "clicks and people" direct marketing strategy. CDW's direct model combines good old-fashioned, high-touch personal selling with a modern, high-tech Web presence to build lasting one-to-one customer relationships. The strategy is fueled by a genuine passion for solving customer problems. Under CDW's "Circle of Service" philosophy, "everything revolves around the customer."

CDW sells a complex assortment of more than 100,000 technology products and services—computers, software, accessories, and networking products—including top name brands such as Adobe, APC, Apple, Cisco, HP, IBM, Microsoft, Sony, Symantec, Toshiba, and ViewSonic. Many of CDW's competitors chase after a relative handful of very large customers. However, while CDW serves customers of all sizes, one of the company's core customer segments is small and midsize businesses (SMBs). These smaller customers often need lots of advice and support. "Many of our clients don't have IT departments," says one CDW executive, "so they look to us for expertise."

That's where the "people" part of CDW's "clicks and people" strategy comes in. The major responsibility for building and managing customer relationships falls to CDW's sales force of nearly 2,000 account managers. Each customer is assigned an account manager, who helps the customer select the right products and technologies and keeps them running smoothly.

Account managers do more than just sell technology products and services. They work closely with customers to find solutions to their technology problems. "This is a big deal to us," says Jim Grass, CDW's senior director of sales. "We want to go beyond fulfilling the order and become the trusted adviser for them. We [want to] talk . . . about what a customer is trying to accomplish and really add value to the sale, as opposed to just sending out a box."

To become trusted advisors and effective customer-relationship builders, CDW account managers really have to know their stuff. And CDW boasts some of the most knowledgeable salespeople in the industry. Before they make a single sales call, new account managers complete a six-week orientation and then a six-month training program. CDW University's College of Sales offers intensive schooling in the science behind the company's products and in the art of consultative selling. But that's just the beginning—the training never ends. Tenured account managers receive ongoing training to enhance their relationship-selling skills. Each year, CDW's sales force completes a whopping 339,000 hours of sales-specific training. John Edwardson, chairman and CEO of CDW and former head of United Airlines, likes to point out that CDW reps get more training than some pilots.

To further support salespeople's customer problem-solving efforts, CDW has also created nine technology teams consisting of more than 120 factory trained specialists and A+ certified technicians on staff. Account managers can draw on these teams to design customer-specific solutions in technology areas such as mobility/wireless, networking, security, and storage.

Customers who want to access CDW's products and expertise without going through their account manager can do so easily at any of several CDW Web sites—the "clicks" side of CDW's "clicks and people" strategy. Better yet, CDW will create a free personalized CDW@work extranet site that reflects a given customer's pricing, order status, account history, and special considerations. The extranet site serves as a 24-hour extension of the customer's account manager. This resulted in CDW Web sales of more than $1.5 billion last year. But even here, the ever-present account managers are likely to add personal guidance. Account managers receive immediate notification of their customers' online activities. So if a blurry-eyed SMB manager makes a mistake on an emergency order placed in the middle of the night, chances are good that the account manager will find and correct the error first thing in the morning.

Beyond being knowledgeable and ever-present, CDW's account managers are energetic and passionately customer-focused. Much of the energy has been passed down from CDW founder and former CEO Michael Krasny. Selling has always been a top priority for Krasny, not surprising given that he began testing his direct marketing model by selling used personal computers out of his home through classified ads. During his 17-year reign as head of CDW, Krasny created a hard-working and dedicated sales force. One favorite Krasny tale involves a windstorm that ripped off a chunk of the CDW building's roof. Within minutes, Krasny himself was up on the roof, nailing a tarp over the hole. When startled employees inside looked up, Krasny shouted down to them to get back to selling.

However, Krasny's most important legacy is the "Circle of Service" culture that he created—a culture that focuses on taking care of customers, and on the CDW employees who serve them (he calls them "coworkers"). "Whenever he made a decision, he'd always ask two questions," says current Chairman and CEO John Edwardson: " 'What will the reaction of the coworkers be?' and 'What will the response of the customers be?' "

When someone says "salesperson," you may still think of the stereotypical "traveling salesman"—the fast-talking, ever-smiling peddler who travels his territory foisting his wares on reluctant customers. Such stereotypes, however, are sadly out of date. Today, like CDW's account managers, most professional salespeople are well-educated, well-trained men and women who work to build valued customer relationships. They succeed not by taking customers in, but by helping them out—by assessing customer needs and solving customer problems.

CDW's high-touch, high-tech clicks and people direct marketing strategy instills loyalty in what are traditionally very price-conscious SMB customers. The company wants to create customer satisfaction at every touch point. Says a former CDW marketing executive, "We're competitively priced, but what's most important is the service and the customers' relationships with their account managers. It's how we actually touch people that creates our most long-lasting [success]."[1]

In this chapter, we examine two more promotion mix tools—*personal selling* and *direct marketing*. Both involve direct connections with customers aimed at communicating customer-unique value and building profitable customer relationships.

Personal Selling

Robert Louis Stevenson once noted that "everyone lives by selling something." We are all familiar with the sales forces used by business organizations to sell products and services to customers around the world. But sales forces are also found in many other kinds of organizations. For example, colleges use recruiters to attract new students, and churches use membership committees to attract new members. Museums and fine-arts organizations use fund-raisers to contact donors and raise money. Even governments use sales forces. The U.S. Postal Service, for instance, uses a sales force to sell Express Mail and other services to corporate customers. In the first part of this chapter, we examine the role of personal selling in the organization, sales force management decisions, and the personal selling process.

THE NATURE OF PERSONAL SELLING

Selling is one of the oldest professions in the world. The people who do the selling go by many names: salespeople, sales representatives, account executives, sales consultants, sales engineers, agents, district managers, and account development reps to name just a few.

People hold many stereotypes of salespeople—including some unfavorable ones. "Salesman" may bring to mind the image of Arthur Miller's pitiable Willy Loman in *Death of a Salesman* or Meredith Willson's cigar-smoking, backslapping, joke-telling Harold Hill in *The Music Man*. Or you might think of Jim Carrey's portrayal of the pushy, psychologically unbalanced Cable Guy. These examples depict salespeople as loners, traveling their territories, trying to foist their wares on unsuspecting or unwilling buyers.

However, modern salespeople are a far cry from these unfortunate stereotypes. Today, most salespeople are well-educated, well-trained professionals who work to build and maintain long-term customer relationships. They listen to their customers, assess customer needs, and organize the company's efforts to solve customer problems. Consider Boeing, the aerospace giant competing in the rough-and-tumble worldwide commercial aircraft market. It takes more than fast talk and a warm smile to sell expensive airplanes:

Selling high-tech aircraft at $100 million or more a copy is complex and challenging. A single big sale can easily run into billions of dollars. Boeing salespeople head up an extensive team of company specialists—sales and service technicians, financial analysts, planners, engineers—all dedicated to finding ways to satisfy airline customer needs. The selling process is nerve-rackingly slow—it can take two or three years from the first sales presentation to the day the sale is announced. After getting the order, salespeople then must stay in almost constant touch to keep track of the account's equipment needs and to make certain the customer stays satisfied. Success depends on building solid, long-term relationships with customers, based on performance and trust. "When you buy an airplane, it is like getting married," says the head of Boeing's commercial airplane division. "It is a long-term relationship."[2]

■ Professional selling: It takes more than fast talk and a warm smile to sell high-tech aircraft at $100 million or more a copy. Success depends on building solid, long-term relationships with customers.

Salesperson
An individual acting for a company by performing one or more of the following activities: prospecting, communicating, servicing, and information gathering.

The term **salesperson** covers a wide range of positions. At one extreme, a salesperson might be largely an *order taker*, such as the department store salesperson standing behind the counter. At the other extreme are *order getters*, whose positions demand *creative selling* and *relationship building* for products and services ranging from appliances, industrial equipment, and airplanes to insurance and information technology services. Here, we focus on the more creative types of selling and on the process of building and managing an effective sales force.

THE ROLE OF THE SALES FORCE

Personal selling is the interpersonal arm of the promotion mix. Advertising consists largely of one-way, nonpersonal communication with target consumer groups. In contrast, personal selling involves two-way, personal communication between salespeople and individual customers—whether face-to-face, by telephone, through video or Web conferences, or by other means. Personal selling can be more effective than advertising in more complex selling situations. Salespeople can probe customers to learn more about their problems, and then adjust the marketing offer and presentation to fit the special needs of each customer.

The role of personal selling varies from company to company. Some firms have no salespeople at all—for example, companies that sell only online or through catalogs, or companies that sell through manufacturer's reps, sales agents, or brokers. In most firms, however, the sales force plays a major role. In companies that sell business products and services, such as IBM or DuPont, the company's salespeople work directly with customers. In consumer product companies such as Procter & Gamble and Nike, the sales force plays an important behind-the-scenes role. It works with wholesalers and retailers to gain their support and to help them be more effective in selling the company's products.

The sales force serves as a critical link between a company and its customers. In many cases, salespeople serve both masters—the seller and the buyer. First, they *represent the company to customers*. They find and develop new customers and communicate information about the company's products and services. They sell products by approaching customers, presenting their products, answering objections, negotiating prices and terms, and closing sales. In addition, salespeople provide customer service and carry out market research and intelligence work.

At the same time, salespeople *represent customers to the company*, acting inside the firm as "champions" of customers' interests and managing the buyer-seller relationship. Salespeople relay customer concerns about company products and actions back inside to those who can handle them. They learn about customer needs and work with other marketing and nonmarketing people in the company to develop greater customer value. The old view was that salespeople should worry about sales and the company should worry about profit. However, the current view holds that salespeople should be concerned with more than just producing *sales*—they should work with others in the company to produce *customer value* and *company profit*.

Managing the Sales Force

Sales force management
The analysis, planning, implementation, and control of sales force activities. It includes designing sales force strategy and structure and recruiting, selecting, training, supervising, compensating, and evaluating the firm's salespeople.

We define **sales force management** as the analysis, planning, implementation, and control of sales force activities. It includes designing sales force strategy and structure and recruiting, selecting, training, compensating, supervising, and evaluating the firm's salespeople. These major sales force management decisions are shown in Figure 13.1 and are discussed in the following sections.

DESIGNING SALES FORCE STRATEGY AND STRUCTURE

Marketing managers face several sales force strategy and design questions. How should salespeople and their tasks be structured? How big should the sales force be? Should sales-

FIGURE 13.1   Major Steps in Sales Force Management

people sell alone or work in teams with other people in the company? Should they sell in the field or by telephone? We address these issues below.

Sales Force Structure   A company can divide up sales responsibilities along any of several lines. The decision is simple if the company sells only one product line to one industry with customers in many locations. In that case the company would use a *territorial sales force structure*. However, if the company sells many products to many types of customers, it might need either a *product sales force structure*, a *customer sales force structure*, or a combination of the two.

Territorial Sales Force Structure.   In the **territorial sales force structure**, each salesperson is assigned to an exclusive geographic area and sells the company's full line of products or services to all customers in that territory. This organization clearly defines each salesperson's job and fixes accountability. It also increases the salesperson's desire to build local customer relationships that, in turn, improve selling effectiveness. Finally, because each salesperson travels within a limited geographic area, travel expenses are relatively small.

A territorial sales organization is often supported by many levels of sales management positions. For example, Campbell Soup uses a territorial structure in which each salesperson is responsible for selling all Campbell Soup products. Starting at the bottom of the organization, *sales merchandisers* report to *sales representatives*, who report to *retail supervisors*, who report to *directors of retail sales operations*, who report to 1 of 22 *regional sales managers*. Regional sales managers, in turn, report to 1 of 4 *general sales managers* (West, Central, South, and East), who report to a *vice president* and *general sales manager*.

Product Sales Force Structure.   Salespeople must know their products—especially when the products are numerous and complex. This need, together with the growth of product management, has led many companies to adopt a **product sales force structure**, in which the sales force sells along product lines. For example, Kodak uses different sales forces for its consumer products than for its industrial products. The consumer products sales force deals with simple products that are distributed intensively, whereas the industrial products sales force deals with complex products that require technical understanding.

The product structure can lead to problems, however, if a single large customer buys many different company products. For example, Cardinal Health, the large health care products and services company, has several product divisions, each with a separate sales force. Several Cardinal salespeople might end up calling on the same hospital on the same day. This means that they travel over the same routes and wait to see the same customer's purchasing agents. These extra costs must be compared with the benefits of better product knowledge and attention to individual products.

Customer Sales Force Structure.   More and more companies are now using a **customer sales force structure**, in which they organize the sales force along customer or industry lines. Separate sales forces may be set up for different industries, for serving current customers versus finding new ones, and for major accounts versus regular accounts. Many companies even have special sales forces set up to handle the needs of individual large customers. For example, Black & Decker has a Home Depot sales organization and a Lowe's sales organization.

Organizing the sales force around customers can help a company build closer relationships with important customers. For example, a decade ago, IBM shifted from a product-based structure to a customer-based one. Before the shift, droves of salespeople representing

Territorial sales force structure
A sales force organization that assigns each salesperson to an exclusive geographic territory in which that salesperson sells the company's full line.

Product sales force structure
A sales force organization under which salespeople specialize in selling only a portion of the company's products or lines.

Customer sales force structure
A sales force organization under which salespeople specialize in selling only to certain customers or industries.

different IBM software, hardware, and services divisions might call on a single large client, creating confusion and frustration. However, such large customers wanted a "single face," one point of contact for all of IBM's vast array of products and services.

Following the restructuring, a single IBM "client executive" works with each large customer and manages a team of IBMers who work with the customer. One client executive describes his role this way: "I am the owner of the business relationship with the client. If the client has a problem, I'm the one who pulls together software or hardware specialists or consultants." According to a sales-organization expert, "This structure puts salespeople in the position of being advisors to clients, and it also allows them to offer holistic solutions to clients' business problems."[3] Such an intense focus on customers is widely credited for IBM's dramatic turnaround in the 1990s.

Complex Sales Force Structures. When a company sells a wide variety of products to many types of customers over a broad geographic area, it often combines several types of sales force structures. Salespeople can be specialized by customer and territory, by product and territory, by product and customer, or by territory, product, and customer. No single structure is best for all companies and situations. Each company should select a sales force structure that best serves the needs of its customers and fits its overall marketing strategy.

Sales Force Size Once the company has set its structure, it is ready to consider *sales force size*. Sales forces may range in size from only a few salespeople to many tens of thousands. Some sales forces are huge—for example, Microsoft employs 23,000 U.S. salespeople, PepsiCo 36,000, and The Hartford Financial Services Group 100,000.[4] Salespeople constitute one of the company's most productive—and most expensive—assets. Therefore, increasing their number will increase both sales and costs.

Many companies use some form of *workload approach* to set sales force size. Using this approach, a company first groups accounts into different classes according to size, account status, or other factors related to the amount of effort required to maintain them. It then determines the number of salespeople needed to call on each class of accounts the desired number of times. The company might think as follows: Suppose we have 1,000 Type-A accounts and 2,000 Type-B accounts. Type-A accounts require 36 calls a year and Type-B accounts require 12 calls a year. In this case, the sales force's *workload*—the number of calls it must make per year—is 60,000 calls [(1,000 $\times$ 36) + (2,000 $\times$ 12) = 36,000 + 24,000 = 60,000]. Suppose our average salesperson can make 1,000 calls a year. Thus, the company needs 60 salespeople (60,000 $\times$ 1,000).[5]

■ Some sales forces are huge—for example, Microsoft employs 23,000 salespeople, PepsiCo 36,000, and The Hartford Financial Services Group 100,000.

Other Sales Force Strategy and Structure Issues Sales management must also decide who will be involved in the selling effort and how various sales and sales-support people will work together.

Outside and Inside Sales Forces. The company may have an **outside sales force** (or **field sales force**), an **inside sales force**, or both. Outside salespeople travel to call on customers in the field. Inside salespeople conduct business from their offices via telephone, the Internet, or visits from buyers.

Some inside salespeople provide support for the outside sales force, freeing them to spend more time selling to major accounts and finding new prospects. For example,

Outside sales force (or field sales force)
Outside salespeople who travel to call on customers in the field.

Inside sales force
Inside salespeople who conduct business from their offices via telephone, the Internet, or visits from prospective buyers.

technical sales-support people provide technical information and answers to customers' questions. *Sales assistants* provide clerical backup for outside salespeople. They call ahead and confirm appointments, follow up on deliveries, and answer customers' questions when outside salespeople cannot be reached.

Other inside salespeople do more just provide support. *Telemarketers* and *Web sellers* use the phone and Internet to find new leads and qualify prospects or to sell and service accounts directly. Telemarketing and Web selling can be very effective, less costly ways to sell to smaller, harder-to-reach customers. Depending on the complexity of the product and customer, for example, a telemarketer can make from 20 to 33 decision-maker contacts a day, compared to the average of 4 that an outside salesperson can make. And whereas an average business-to-business field sales call costs $329, a routine industrial telemarketing call costs only about $5 and a complex call about $20.[6]

For some smaller companies, telephone and Web selling may be the primary sales approaches. However, larger companies also use these tactics. For example, IBM uses phone and internet reps to pitch IBM solutions to and nurture relationships with its small and midsize (SMB) customers. IBM's roughly 1,200 inside reps now generate 30 percent of IBM's revenues from SMB clients.[7]

For many types of products and selling situations, phone or Web selling can be as effective as a personal sales call. Notes a DuPont telemarketer: "I'm more effective on the phone. [When you're in the field], if some guy's not in his office, you lose an hour. On the phone, you lose 15 seconds. . . . Through my phone calls, I'm in the field as much as the rep is." There are other advantages. "Customers can't throw things at you," quips the rep, "and you don't have to outrun dogs."[8] What's more, although they may seem impersonal, the phone and Internet can be surprisingly personal when it comes to building customer relationships:

If you're one of CDW Account Manager Ron Kelly's regular customers, you probably know that he's 35 and has a wife named Michelle, a 9-year-old son named Andrew, and a German shepherd named Bones. You know that he majored in journalism and poly sci at SIU (that's Southern Illinois University) and was supposed to attend Northwestern's law school, but instead came to work at CDW. You know that he bleeds red and black for the Chicago Blackhawks. You also know that he knows as much, if not more, about you. Kelly, an affable account manager, is a master at relationship-based selling, CDW's specialty. Customers love it. "He's my sales rep, but he's also my friend," says Todd Greenwald, director of operations for Heartland Computers, which sells barcode scanners. "Most of the time we don't even talk about price. I trust Ron."

What's particularly impressive is that, for the most part, the interaction occurs over the phone and Internet. Despite the lack of face time, CDW account managers forge close ties. One customer invited his CDW contact to his wedding. Kelly and Greenwald share Blackhawks season tickets. It's not uncommon to find customers and reps whose partnership has outlasted job changes, budget cuts, and marriages. Of course, the relationships aren't based solely on being likable. They're grounded in helping customers succeed. Account managers think like the customer and try to anticipate problems. For instance, before storms rocked Florida one summer, some account managers called or e-mailed clients there with battery and backup-storage solutions. "Instead of just sending a purchase order, we want to ask, 'Why are you buying [that product]?' " says a CDW executive. "That's how you identify customers' needs." In this way, to their customers, CDW account managers are much more than just peddlers. When asked if she thinks of her CDW rep as a salesperson anymore, one customer replied "Never. He's my business partner." And it all happens over the phone or the Web—both supposedly "arms-length" media.[9]

■ Inside sales force: Although they may seem impersonal, the phone and Internet can be surprisingly personal when it comes to building customer relationships. "He's my business partner," says one CDW customer about her account manager, who manages account relationships almost entirely by phone.

MARKETING AT WORK | 13.1

Point, Click, and Sell: Welcome to the Web-Based Sales Force

There are few rules at Fisher Scientific International's sales training sessions. The chemical company's salespeople are allowed to show up for new workshops in their pajamas. And no one flinches if they stroll in at midnight for their first class, take a dozen breaks to call clients, or invite the family cat to sleep in their laps while they take an exam. Sound unorthodox? It would be if Fisher's salespeople were trained in a regular classroom. But for the past few years, the company has been using the Internet to teach the majority of its salespeople in the privacy of their homes, cars, hotel rooms, or wherever else they bring their laptops.

To get updates on Fisher's pricing or refresh themselves on one of the company's highly technical products, all salespeople have to do is log on to the Web site and select from the lengthy index. Any time of the day or night, they can get information on a new product, take an exam, or post messages for product experts—all without ever entering a corporate classroom. Welcome to the world of the Web-based sales force.

In the past few years, sales organizations around the world have begun saving money and time by using a host of Web approaches to train reps, hold sales meetings, and even conduct live sales presentations. Fisher Scientific's reps can dial up the Web site at their leisure, and whereas newer reps might spend hours online going through each session in order, more seasoned sellers might just log on for a quick refresher on a specific product before a sales call. "It allows them to manage their time better, because they're only getting training when they need it, in the doses they need it

in," says John Pavlik, director of the company's training department. If salespeople are spending less time on training, Pavlik says, they're able to spend more time on what they do best: selling.

Training is only one of the ways sales organizations are using the Internet. Many companies are using the Web to make sales presentations and service accounts. For example, computer and communications equipment maker NEC Corporation has adopted Web-based selling as an essential marketing tool.

After launching a new server line on September 11, 2001, NEC had to rethink its

sales approach. Following the 9/11 terrorist attacks, and facing the early-decade economic slowdown, NEC began looking for ways to cut down on more difficult and costly sales force travel. According to Dick Csaplar, marketing manager for the new server line, NEC's old sales approach—traveling to customer sites to pitch NEC products—became unworkable literally overnight. Instead, NEC adopted a new Web-based sales approach. While the initial goal was to keep people off airplanes, however, Web selling has now grown into an intrinsic part of NEC's sales efforts. Web selling reduces travel time and costs. Whereas the average daily cost of

■ *Internet selling support: Sales organizations around the world are now using a host of new Web approaches to train reps, hold sales meetings, and even conduct live sales presentations.*

Both inside and outside salespeople now have a growing array of tools at their disposal for interacting with and serving customers. For example, the Internet offers explosive potential for restructuring sales forces and conducting sales operations. More companies are now using the Internet to support their personal selling efforts—not just for selling, but for everything from training salespeople to conducting sales meetings and servicing accounts (see Marketing at Work 13.1).

Team Selling. As products become more complex, and as customers grow larger and more demanding, a single salesperson simply can't handle all of a large customer's

salesperson travel is $663, an hour-long Web conference costs just $60. More importantly, Web selling lets sales reps meet with more prospective customers than ever before, creating a more efficient and effective sales organization. Csaplar estimates that he's doing 10 customer Web conferences a week, during which he and his sales team show prospects product features and benefits. Customers love it because they get a clear understanding of NEC's technology without having to host the NEC team on-site. And Csaplar was pleased to find that Web-based selling is an effective way to interact with customers and to build customer relationships. "By the time we're done with the Webcast, the customer understands the technology, the pricing, and the competition, and we understand the customer's business and needs," he says. Without Webcasts, "we'd be lost on how to communicate with the customer without spending a lot of money," says Csaplar. "I don't see us ever going back to the heavy travel thing."

The Web can be a good channel tool for selling to hard-to-reach customers. For example, the big U.S. pharmaceutical companies currently employ some 87,000 sales reps (often called "detailers") to reach roughly 600,000 practicing physicians. However, these reps are finding it harder than ever to get through to the busy doctors. "Doctors need immense amounts of medical information, but their patient loads limit their ability to see pharmaceutical reps or attend outside conferences," says an industry researcher. The answer: Increasingly, it's the Web. The pharmaceutical companies now regularly use product Web sites, e-mail marketing, and video confer-

encing to help reps deliver useful information to physicians on their home or office PCs. One study found that last year more than 200,000 physicians participated in "e-detailing"—the process of receiving drug marketing information via the Web—a 400 percent jump in only three years. Using direct-to-doctor Web conferences, companies can make live, interactive medical presentations to any physician with a PC and Web access, saving both the customer's and the rep's time.

The Internet can also be a handy way to hold sales strategy meetings. Consider Cisco Systems, which provides networking solutions for the Internet. Sales meetings used to take an enormous bite out of Cisco's travel budget. Now the company saves about $1 million per month by conducting many of those sessions on the Web. Whenever Cisco introduces a new product, it holds a Web meeting to update salespeople, in groups of 100 or more, on the product's marketing and sales strategy.

Usually led by the product manager or a vice president of sales, the meetings typically begin with a 10-minute slide presentation that spells out the planned strategy. Then, salespeople spend the next 50 or so minutes asking questions via teleconference. The meeting's leader can direct attendees' browsers to competitors' Web sites or ask them to vote on certain issues by using the software's instant polling feature. "Our salespeople are actually meeting more online then they ever were face-to-face," says Mike Mitchell, Cisco's distance learning manager, adding that some salespeople who used to meet with other reps and managers only a few times a quarter are meeting online nearly every day. "That's very empowering for the sales force because they're able to make suggestions at every step of the way

about where we're going with our sales and marketing strategies."

Thus, Web-based technologies can produce big organizational benefits for sales forces. They help conserve salespeople's valuable time, save travel dollars, and give salespeople a new vehicle for selling and servicing accounts. But the technologies also have some drawbacks. For starters, they're not cheap. And such systems can intimidate low-tech salespeople or clients. "As simple as it is, if your salespeople or clients aren't comfortable using the Web, you're wasting your money," says one marketing communications manager. Also, Web tools are susceptible to server crashes and other network difficulties, not a happy event when you're in the midst of an important sales meeting or presentation.

For these reasons, some high-tech experts recommend that sales executives use Web technologies for training, sales meetings, and preliminary client sales presentations, but resort to old-fashioned, face-to-face meetings when the time draws near to close the deal. "When push comes to shove, if you've got an account worth closing, you're still going to get on that plane and see the client in person," says sales consultant Sloane. "Your client is going to want to look you in the eye before buying anything from you, and that's still one thing you just can't do online."

Sources: Portions adapted from Tom Kontzer, "Web Conferencing Embraced," *Information Week,* May 26, 2003, pp. 68–70; Melinda Ligos, "Point, Click, and Sell," *Sales & Marketing Management,* May 1999, pp. 51–55; and Rich Thomaselli, "Pharma Replacing Reps," *Advertising Age,* January 2005, p. 50. Also see Julia Chang, "No Instructor Required," *Sales & Marketing Management,* May 2003, p. 26; Daniel Tynan, "Next Best Thing to Being There," *Sales & Marketing Management,* April 2004, p. 22; and Judith Lamont, "Collaboration: Web Conferencing Spans the Distance," *KM World,* June 2005, pp. 16–18.

needs. Instead, most companies now use **team selling** to service large, complex accounts. Sales teams can unearth problems, solutions, and sales opportunities that no individual salesperson could. Such teams might include experts from any area or level of the selling firm—sales, marketing, technical and support services, R&D, engineering, operations, finance, and others. In team-selling situations, the salesperson shifts from "soloist" to "orchestrator."

In many cases, the move to team selling mirrors similar changes in customers' buying organizations. "Today, we're calling on teams of buying people, and that requires more firepower on our side," says one sales vice president. "One salesperson just can't do it all—can't

Team selling
Using teams of people from sales, marketing, engineering, finance, technical support, and even upper management to service large, complex accounts.

■ This Procter & Gamble "customer business development team" serves a major southeastern grocery retailer. It consists of a customer business development manager and five account executives (shown here), along with specialists from other functional areas.

be an expert in everything we're bringing to the customer. We have strategic account teams, led by customer business managers, who basically are our quarterbacks."[10]

Some companies, such as IBM, Xerox, and Procter & Gamble, have used teams for a long time. P&G sales reps are organized into "customer business development (CBD) teams." Each CBD team is assigned to a major P&G customer, such as Wal-Mart, Safeway, or CVS Pharmacy. Teams consist of a customer business development manager, several account executives (each responsible for a specific category of P&G products), and specialists in marketing strategy, operations, information systems, logistics, and finance. This organization places the focus on serving the complete needs of each important customer. It lets P&G "grow business by working as a 'strategic partner' with our accounts, not just as a supplier. Our goal: to grow their business, which also results in growing ours."[11]

Team selling does have some pitfalls. For example, selling teams can confuse or overwhelm customers who are used to working with only one salesperson. Salespeople who are used to having customers all to themselves may have trouble learning to work with and trust others on a team. Finally, difficulties in evaluating individual contributions to the team-selling effort can create some sticky compensation issues.

RECRUITING AND SELECTING SALESPEOPLE

At the heart of any successful sales force operation is the recruitment and selection of good salespeople. The performance difference between an average salesperson and a top salesperson can be substantial. In a typical sales force, the top 30 percent of the salespeople might bring in 60 percent of the sales. Thus, careful salesperson selection can greatly increase overall sales force performance. Beyond the differences in sales performance, poor selection results in costly turnover. When a salesperson quits, the costs of finding and training a new salesperson—plus the costs of lost sales—can be very high. Also, a sales force with many new people is less productive, and turnover disrupts important customer relationships.

What sets great salespeople apart from all the rest? In an effort to profile top sales performers, Gallup Management Consulting Group, a division of the well-known Gallup polling organization, has interviewed hundreds of thousands of salespeople. Its research suggests that the best salespeople possess four key talents: intrinsic motivation, disciplined work style, the ability to close a sale, and perhaps most important, the ability to build relationships with customers.[12]

Super salespeople are motivated from within. "Different things drive different people—pride, happiness, money, you name it," says one expert. "But all great salespeople have one thing in common: an unrelenting drive to excel." Some salespeople are driven by money, a hunger for recognition, or the satisfaction of competing and winning. Others are driven by the desire to provide service and to build relationships. The best salespeople possess some of each of these motivations.

Whatever their motivations, salespeople must also have a disciplined work style. If salespeople aren't organized and focused, and if they don't work hard, they can't meet the ever-increasing demands customers make these days. Great salespeople are tenacious about laying out detailed, organized plans, then following through in a timely, disciplined way. Says one sales trainer, "Some people say it's all technique or luck. But luck happens to the best salespeople when they get up early, work late, stay up till two in the morning working on a proposal, or keep making calls when everyone is leaving at the end of the day."

Other skills mean little if a salesperson can't close the sale. So what makes for a great closer? For one thing, it takes unyielding persistence. "Great closers are like great athletes," says one sales trainer. "They're not afraid to fail, and they don't give up until they close." Great closers also have a high level of self-confidence and believe that they are doing the right thing.

Perhaps most important in today's relationship-marketing environment, top salespeople are customer problem solvers and relationship builders. They have an instinctive understanding of their customers' needs. Talk to sales executives and they'll describe top performers in these terms: Empathetic. Patient. Caring. Responsive. Good listeners. Honest. Top performers can put themselves on the buyer's side of the desk and see the world through their customers' eyes. They don't want just to be liked, they want to add value for their customers.

When recruiting, companies should analyze the sales job itself and the characteristics of its most successful salespeople to identify the traits needed by a successful salesperson in their industry. Then, it must recruit the right salespeople. The human resources department looks for applicants by getting names from current salespeople, using employment agencies, placing classified ads, searching the Web, and working through college placement services. Another source is to attract top salespeople from other companies. Proven salespeople need less training and can be immediately productive.

Recruiting will attract many applicants from whom the company must select the best. The selection procedure can vary from a single informal interview to lengthy

■ Great salespeople: The best salespeople, such as Jennifer Hansen of 3M, possess intrinsic motivation, disciplined work style, the ability to close a sale, and perhaps most important, the ability to build relationships with customers.

testing and interviewing. Many companies give formal tests to sales applicants. Tests typically measure sales aptitude, analytical and organizational skills, personality traits, and other characteristics. But test scores provide only one piece of information in a set that includes personal characteristics, references, past employment history, and interviewer reactions.

TRAINING SALESPEOPLE

New salespeople may spend anywhere from a few weeks or months to a year or more in training. Then, most companies provide continuing sales training via seminars, sales meetings, and the Web throughout the salesperson's career. In all, U.S. companies spend more than $7 billion annually on training salespeople. Although training can be expensive, it can also yield dramatic returns. For example, one recent study showed that sales training conducted by a major telecommunications firm paid for itself in 16 days and resulted in a six-month return on investment of 812 percent. Similarly, Nabisco analyzed the return on its two-day Professional Selling Program, which teaches sales reps how to plan for and make professional presentations. Although it cost about $1,000 to put each sales rep through the program, the training resulted in additional sales of more than $122,000 per rep and yielded almost $21,000 of additional profit per rep.[13]

Training programs have several goals. First, salespeople need to know about customers and how to build relationships with them. So the training program must teach them about different types of customers and their needs, buying motives, and buying habits. And it must teach them how to sell effectively and train them in the basics of the selling process. Salespeople also need to know and identify with the company, its products, and its competitors. So an effective training program teaches them about the company's objectives, organization, and chief products and markets, and about the strategies of major competitors.

Today, many companies are adding Web-based training to their sales training programs. In fact, the industry for online training reached an estimated $23.7 billion by 2006 and is expected to grow by more than 35 percent a year.[14] Such training may range from simple text-based product information to Internet-based sales exercises that build sales skills to sophisticated simulations that re-create the dynamics of real-life sales calls. Networking equipment and software maker Cisco Systems has learned that using the Internet to train salespeople offers many advantages.

Keeping a large sales force up to speed on hundreds of complex, fast-changing products can be a daunting task. Under the old training process, newly hired Cisco salespeople traveled to a central location for several five-day training sessions each year. "We used to fly people in and put them through a week of death-by-PowerPoint," says a Cisco training executive. This approach involved huge program-development and travel costs. Perhaps worse, it cost salespeople precious lost-opportunity time spent away from their customers. To address these issues, Cisco launched an internal e-learning portal through which Cisco's salespeople around the world can plan, track, develop, and measure their skills and knowledge.

The e-learning site links salespeople to tens of thousands of Web-based learning aids. Learning involves the blending of audio and video, live broadcasts of classes, and straight content. Content can be turned into an MP3 file, viewed on-screen, downloaded to the computer, even printed out in magazine form. Under the e-learning system, Cisco can conduct a single training session that reaches up to 3,000 people at once, worldwide, by broadcasting it over the company's global intranet. Live events can then be archived as video-on-demand modules for viewers who missed the live broadcast. The system also provides electronic access to Cisco experts or "e-mentors," who can respond via e-mail or phone, or meet learners in a virtual lab, connect to their screens, and walk them through exercises. The e-learning portal has improved training by giving Cisco salespeople anywhere, anytime access to a vast system of training resources. At the same time, it has cut field-training costs by 40 percent to 60 percent while boosting salesperson "face time" with customers by 40 percent.[15]

COMPENSATING SALESPEOPLE

To attract good salespeople, a company must have an appealing compensation plan. Compensation is made up of several elements—a fixed amount, a variable amount, expenses, and fringe benefits. The fixed amount, usually a salary, gives the salesperson some stable income. The variable amount, which might be commissions or bonuses based on sales performance, rewards the salesperson for greater effort and success.

Management must decide what *mix* of these compensation elements makes the most sense for each sales job. Different combinations of fixed and variable compensation give rise to four basic types of compensation plans—straight salary, straight commission, salary plus bonus, and salary plus commission. A study of sales force compensation plans showed that 70 percent of all companies surveyed use a combination of base salary and incentives. The average plan consisted of about 60 percent salary and 40 percent incentive pay.[16]

The sales force compensation plan can both motivate salespeople and direct their activities. Compensation should direct the sales force toward activities that are consistent with overall marketing objectives. Table 13.1 illustrates how a company's compensation plan should reflect its overall marketing strategy. For example, if the strategy is to grow rapidly and gain market share, the compensation plan might include a larger commission component, coupled with a new-account bonus to encourage high sales performance and new-account development. In contrast, if the goal is to maximize current account profitability, the compensation plan might contain a larger base-salary component with additional incentives for current account sales or customer satisfaction.

In fact, more companies are moving away from high commission plans that may drive salespeople to make short-term grabs for business. They worry that a salesperson who is pushing too hard to close a deal may ruin the customer relationship. Instead, companies are designing compensation plans that reward salespeople for building customer relationships and growing the long-run value of each customer.

TABLE 13.1
The Relationship Between Overall Marketing Strategy and Sales Force Compensation

	Strategic Goal		
	To Gain Market Share Rapidly	**To Solidify Market Leadership**	**To Maximize Profitability**
Ideal salesperson	An independent self-starter	A competitive problem solver	A team player A relationship manager
Sales focus	Deal making Sustained high effort	Consultative selling	Account penetration
Compensation role	To capture accounts To reward high performance	To reward new and existing account sales	To manage the product mix To encourage team selling To reward account management

Source: Based on Sam T. Johnson, "Sales Compensation: In Search of a Better Solution," *Compensation & Benefits Review,* November–December 1993, pp. 53–60 .

SUPERVISING AND MOTIVATING SALESPEOPLE

New salespeople need more than a territory, compensation, and training—they need supervision and motivation. The goal of *supervision* is to help salespeople "work smart" by doing the right things in the right ways. The goal of *motivation* is to encourage salespeople to "work hard" and energetically toward sales force goals. If salespeople work smart and work hard, they will realize their full potential, to their own and the company's benefit.

Companies vary in how closely they supervise their salespeople. Many help their salespeople to identify target customers and set call norms. Some may also specify how much time the sales force should spend prospecting for new accounts and set other time-management priorities. One tool is the weekly, monthly, or annual *call plan* that shows which customers and prospects to call on and which activities to carry out. Another tool is *time-and-duty analysis.* In addition to time spent selling, the salesperson spends time traveling, waiting, taking breaks, and doing administrative chores.

Figure 13.2 shows how salespeople spend their time. On average, actual face-to-face selling time accounts for less than 30 percent of total working time! If selling time could be raised from 30 percent to 40 percent, this would be a 33 percent increase in the time spent selling. Companies always are looking for ways to save time—simplifying record keeping, finding better sales call and routing plans, supplying more and better customer information,

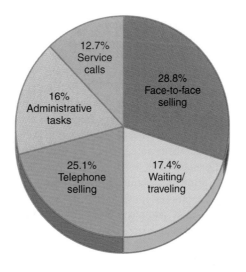

FIGURE 13.2
How Salespeople Spend Their Time

Source: Reprinted with permission of *How Salespeople Spend Their Time.* Copyright 1999 by LRP Publications, P.O. Box 24668, West Palm Beach, FL 33416-4668. All rights reserved. For more information on this or other products published by LRP Publications, please call 1-800-341-7874.

and using phones, e-mail, or video conferencing instead of traveling. Consider the changes GE made to increase its sales force's face-to-face selling time.[17]

> When Jeff Immelt became GE's new chairman, he was dismayed to find that members of the sales team were spending far more time on deskbound administrative chores than in face-to-face meetings with customers and prospects. "He said we needed to turn that around," recalls Venki Rao, an IT leader in global sales and marketing at GE Power Systems, a division focused on energy systems and products. "[We need] to spend four days a week in front of the customer and one day for all the admin stuff." GE Power's salespeople spent much of their time at their desks because they had to go to many sources for the information needed to sell multimillion-dollar turbines, turbine parts, and services to energy companies worldwide. To fix the problem, GE created a new sales portal, a kind of "one-stop shop" for just about everything they need. The sales portal connects the vast array of existing GE databases, providing everything from sales tracking and customer data to parts pricing and information on planned outages. GE also added external data, such as news feeds. "Before, you were randomly searching for things," says Bill Snook, a GE sales manager. Now, he says, "I have the sales portal as my home page, and I use it as the gateway to all the applications that I have." The sales portal has freed Snook and 2,500 other users around the globe from once time-consuming administrative tasks, greatly increasing their face time with customers.

Many firms have adopted *sales force automation systems*—computerized, digitized sales force operations that let salespeople work more effectively anytime, anywhere. Companies now routinely equip their salespeople with new-age technologies such as laptops, smart phones, wireless Web connections, Webcams for videoconferencing, and customer-contact and relationship-management software. Armed with these technologies, salespeople can more effectively and efficiently profile customers and prospects, analyze and forecast sales, schedule sales calls, make presentations, prepare sales and expense reports, and manage account relationships. The result is better time management, improved customer service, lower sales costs, and higher sales performance.[18]

■ Sales force automation: Many sales forces have gone high tech, equipping salespeople with everything from smart phones, wireless Web connections, and videoconferencing to customer-contact and relationship management software that helps them to be more effective and efficient.

Beyond directing salespeople, sales managers must also motivate them. Some salespeople will do their best without any special urging from management. To them, selling may be the most fascinating job in the world. But selling can also be frustrating. Salespeople often work alone and they must sometimes travel away from home. They may face aggressive competing salespeople and difficult customers. Therefore, salespeople often need special encouragement to do their best.

Management can boost sales force morale and performance through its organizational climate, sales quotas, and positive incentives. *Organizational climate* describes the feeling that salespeople have about their opportunities, value, and rewards for a good performance. Some companies treat salespeople as if they are not very important, and performance suffers accordingly. Other companies treat their salespeople as valued contributors and allow virtually unlimited opportunity for income and promotion. Not surprisingly, these companies enjoy higher sales force performance and less turnover.

Sales quota

A standard that states the amount a salesperson should sell and how sales should be divided among the company's products.

Many companies motivate their salespeople by setting **sales quotas**—standards stating the amount they should sell and how sales should be divided among the company's products. Compensation is often related to how well salespeople meet their quotas. Companies also use various *positive incentives* to increase sales force effort. *Sales meetings* provide social occasions, breaks from routine, chances to meet and talk with "company brass," and opportunities to air feelings and to identify with a larger group.

Companies also sponsor *sales contests* to spur the sales force to make a selling effort above what would normally be expected. Other incentives include honors, merchandise and cash awards, trips, and profit-sharing plans. In all, American companies spend some $29 billion a year on such incentives to motivate and reward sales force performance.[19]

EVALUATING SALESPEOPLE AND SALES FORCE PERFORMANCE

We have thus far described how management communicates what salespeople should be doing and how it motivates them to do it. This process requires good feedback. And good feedback means getting regular information about salespeople to evaluate their performance.

Management gets information about its salespeople in several ways. The most important source is *sales reports,* including weekly or monthly work plans and longer-term territory marketing plans. Salespeople also write up their completed activities on *call reports* and turn in *expense reports* for which they are partly or wholly repaid. The company can also monitor the sales and profit performance of the salesperson's territory. Additional information comes from personal observation, customer surveys, and talks with other salespeople.

Using various sales force reports and other information, sales management evaluates members of the sales force. It evaluates salespeople on their ability to "plan their work and work their plan." Formal evaluation forces management to develop and communicate clear standards for judging performance. It also provides salespeople with constructive feedback and motivates them to perform well.

On a broader level, management should evaluate the performance of the sales force as a whole. Is the sales force accomplishing its customer-relationship, sales, and profit objectives? Is it working well with other areas of the marketing and company organization? Are sales force costs in line with outcomes? As with other marketing activities, the company wants to measure its *return on sales investment.*[20]

■ Sales force incentives: Many companies offer cash, trips, or merchandise as incentives. Marriott suggests that companies reward outstanding sales performers by letting them "spread their wings and reenergize."

 Linking the Concepts

Take a break and reexamine your thoughts about salespeople and sales management.

■ Again, when someone says "salesperson," what image comes to mind? Have your perceptions of salespeople changed after what you've just read? How? Be specific.
■ Apply each of the steps in sales force management shown in Figure 13.1 to the chapter-opening CDW example.
■ Find and talk with someone employed in professional sales. Ask about and report on how this salesperson's company designs its sales force and recruits, selects, trains, compensates, supervises, and evaluates its salespeople. Would you like to work as a salesperson for this company?

The Personal Selling Process

We now turn from designing and managing a sales force to the actual personal selling process. The **selling process** consists of several steps that the salesperson must master. These steps focus on the goal of getting new customers and obtaining orders from them.

Selling process
The steps that the salesperson follows when selling, which include prospecting and qualifying, preapproach, approach, presentation and demonstration, handling objections, closing, and follow-up.

However, most salespeople spend much of their time maintaining existing accounts and building long-term customer *relationships*. We discuss the relationship aspect of the personal selling process in a later section.

STEPS IN THE SELLING PROCESS

As shown in Figure 13.3, the selling process consists of seven steps: prospecting and qualifying, preapproach, approach, presentation and demonstration, handling objections, closing, and follow-up.

Prospecting
The step in the selling process in which the salesperson identifies qualified potential customers.

Prospecting and Qualifying   The first step in the selling process is **prospecting**—identifying qualified potential customers. Approaching the right potential customers is crucial to selling success. As one expert puts it: "If the sales force starts chasing anyone who is breathing and seems to have a budget, you risk accumulating a roster of expensive-to-serve, hard-to-satisfy customers who never respond to whatever value proposition you have." He continues, "The solution to this isn't rocket science. [You must] train salespeople to actively scout the right prospects." Another expert concludes: "Increasing your prospecting effectiveness is the fastest single way to boost your sales."[21]

The salesperson must often approach many prospects to get just a few sales. Although the company supplies some leads, salespeople need skill in finding their own. The best source is referrals. Salespeople can ask current customers for referrals and cultivate other referral sources, such as suppliers, dealers, noncompeting salespeople, and bankers. They can also search for prospects in directories or on the Web and track down leads using the telephone and direct mail. Or they can drop in unannounced on various offices (a practice known as "cold calling").

Salespeople also need to know how to *qualify* leads—that is, how to identify the good ones and screen out the poor ones. Prospects can be qualified by looking at their financial ability, volume of business, special needs, location, and possibilities for growth.

Preapproach
The step in the selling process in which the salesperson learns as much as possible about a prospective customer before making a sales call.

Preapproach   Before calling on a prospect, the salesperson should learn as much as possible about the organization (what it needs, who is involved in the buying) and its buyers (their characteristics and buying styles). This step is known as the **preapproach**. The salesperson can consult standard industry and online sources, acquaintances, and others to learn about the company. The salesperson should set *call objectives*, which may be to qualify the prospect, to gather information, or to make an immediate sale. Another task is to decide on the best approach, which might be a personal visit, a phone call, or a letter. The best timing should be considered carefully because many prospects are busiest at certain times. Finally, the salesperson should give thought to an overall sales strategy for the account.

Approach
The step in the selling process in which the salesperson meets the customer for the first time.

Approach   During the **approach** step, the salesperson should know how to meet and greet the buyer and get the relationship off to a good start. This step involves the salesperson's appearance, opening lines, and the follow-up remarks. The opening lines should be positive to build goodwill from the beginning of the relationship. This opening might be followed by some key questions to learn more about the customer's needs or by showing a display or sample to attract the buyer's attention and curiosity. As in all stages of the selling process, listening to the customer is crucial.

FIGURE 13.3
Major Steps in Effective Selling

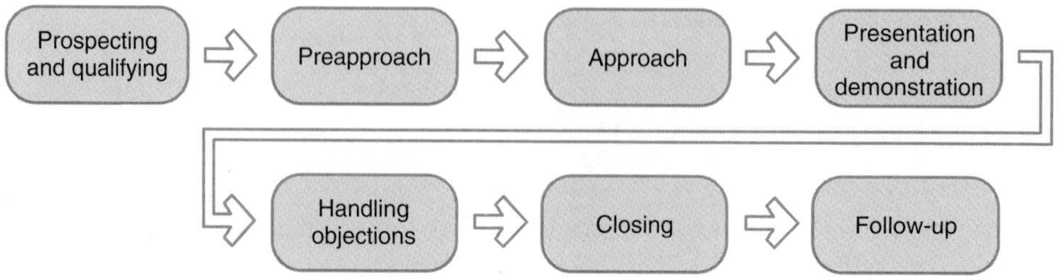

Presentation and Demonstration   During the **presentation** step of the selling process, the salesperson tells the product "story" to the buyer, presenting customer benefits and showing how the product solves the customer's problems. The problem-solver salesperson fits better with today's marketing concept than does a hard-sell salesperson or the glad-handing extrovert. Buyers today want solutions, not smiles; results, not razzle-dazzle. They want salespeople who listen to their concerns, understand their needs, and respond with the right products and services.

This *need-satisfaction approach* calls for good listening and problem-solving skills. "To me, sales is listening to customers, finding out what they want, finding out what their concerns are, and then trying to fill them," notes one experienced salesperson. "Listening is basically the foundation for success." Another salesperson suggests, "It's no longer enough to have a good relationship with a client. You have to understand their problems. You have to feel their pain." One sales manager suggests that salespeople need to put themselves in their customers' shoes: "Make yourself a customer and see firsthand how it feels," he says.[22]

The qualities that buyers *dislike most* in salespeople include being pushy, late, deceitful, and unprepared or disorganized. The qualities they *value most* include good listening, empathy, honesty, dependability, thoroughness, and follow-through. Great salespeople know how to sell, but more importantly they know how to listen and to build strong customer relationships.

Today, advanced presentation technologies allow for full multimedia presentations to only one or a few people. CDs and DVDs, online presentation technologies, and handheld and laptop computers with presentation software have replaced the flip chart. Here's an example:[23]

> Until six months ago, Credant Technologies, a firm that sells security software programs for handhelds, used standard presentation equipment—laptops and LCD projectors—to showcase its products to potential clients. That's no longer the case. Each member of the company's sales team is now equipped with Presenter-to-Go, a credit card-sized device that slips into handheld PDAs or pocket PCs to make them compatible with projectors. The $200 device reads PowerPoint, Word, and Excel files, as well as Web pages, allowing salespeople to create presentations on computers, then transfer them to a PDA. It also lets reps add notes to presentations instantaneously by transmitting handwriting on their pocket PC to the screen. And it includes a wireless remote control, so sales reps can move freely throughout the presentation room, unattached to their laptop or projector-advancing button. When Credant Regional Account Executive Tom Gore met recently with an important prospect, he wowed buying executives with a feature that enabled him to type some of their comments into his PDA. Within seconds, their comments appeared on screen. "It makes each presentation more personal and interactive," Gore says.

■ Today's advanced presentation technologies allow for full multimedia presentations to only one or a few people. Online presentation technologies and hand-held and laptop computers with presentation software have replaced the flip chart.

Handling Objections   Customers almost always have objections during the presentation or when asked to place an order. The problem can be either logical or psychological, and objections are often unspoken. In **handling objections**, the salesperson should use a positive approach, seek out hidden objections, ask the buyer to clarify any objections, take objections as opportunities to provide more information, and turn the objections into reasons for buying. Every salesperson needs training in the skills of handling objections.

Closing   After handling the prospect's objections, the salesperson now tries to close the sale. Some salespeople do not get around to **closing** or do not handle it well. They may lack confidence, feel guilty about asking for the order, or fail to recognize the right moment to close the sale. Salespeople should know how to recognize closing signals from the buyer, including physical actions, comments, and questions. For example, the customer might sit forward and nod approvingly or ask about prices and credit terms. Salespeople can use one of several closing techniques. They can ask for the order, review points of agreement, offer to help write up the order, ask whether the buyer wants this model or that one, or note that the buyer will lose out if the order is not placed now. The salesperson may offer the buyer special reasons to close, such as a lower price or an extra quantity at no charge.

Follow-Up   The last step in the selling process—**follow-up**—is necessary if the salesperson wants to ensure customer satisfaction and repeat business. Right after closing, the salesperson should complete any details on delivery time, purchase terms, and other matters. The salesperson then should schedule a follow-up call when the initial order is received, to make sure there is proper installation, instruction, and servicing. This visit would reveal any problems, assure the buyer of the salesperson's interest, and reduce any buyer concerns that might have arisen since the sale.

PERSONAL SELLING AND CUSTOMER RELATIONSHIP MANAGEMENT

The steps in the selling process as just described are *transaction oriented*—their aim is to help salespeople close a specific sale with a customer. But in most cases, the company is not simply seeking a sale: It has targeted a major customer that it would like to win and keep. The company would like to show that it has the capabilities to serve the customer over the long haul in a mutually profitable *relationship*. The sales force usually plays an important role in building and managing profitable customer relationships.

Today's large customers favor suppliers who can sell and deliver a coordinated set of products and services to many locations, and who can work closely with customer teams to improve products and processes. For these customers, the first sale is only the beginning of the relationship. Unfortunately, some companies ignore these relationship realities. They sell their products through separate sales forces, each working independently to close sales. Their technical people may not be willing to lend time to educate a customer. Their engineering, design, and manufacturing people may have the attitude that "it's our job to make good products and the salesperson's to sell them to customers." Their salespeople focus on pushing products toward customers rather than listening to customers and providing solutions.

Other companies, however, recognize that winning and keeping accounts requires more than making good products and directing the sales force to close lots of sales. It requires listening to customers, understanding their needs, and carefully coordinating the whole company's efforts to create customer value and to build lasting relationships.

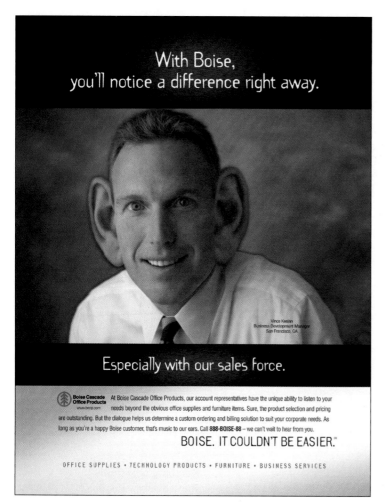

■ Building customer relationships: Smart companies listen to customers, understand their needs, and carefully coordinate the whole company's efforts toward creating customer value.

Direct Marketing

Many of the marketing and promotion tools that we've examined in previous chapters were developed in the context of *mass marketing:* targeting broad markets with standardized messages and offers distributed through intermediaries. Today, however, with the trend toward more narrowly targeted marketing, many companies are adopting *direct marketing,* either as a primary marketing approach or as a supplement to other approaches. In this section, we explore the exploding world of direct marketing.

Direct marketing consists of direct connections with carefully targeted individual consumers to both obtain an immediate response and cultivate lasting customer relationships. Direct marketers communicate directly with customers, often on a one-to-one, interactive basis. Using detailed databases, they tailor their marketing offers and communications to the needs of narrowly defined segments or even individual buyers.

Beyond brand and image building, direct marketers usually seek a direct, immediate, and measurable consumer response. For example, Dell interacts directly with customers, by telephone or through its Web site, to design built-to-order systems that meet customers' individual needs. Buyers order directly from Dell, and Dell quickly and efficiently delivers the new computers to their homes or offices.

Direct marketing
Direct communications with carefully targeted individual consumers to obtain an immediate response.

THE NEW DIRECT MARKETING MODEL

Early direct marketers—catalog companies, direct mailers, and telemarketers—gathered customer names and sold goods mainly by mail and telephone. Today, however, fired by rapid advances in database technologies and new marketing media—especially the Internet—direct marketing has undergone a dramatic transformation.

In previous chapters, we've discussed direct marketing as direct distribution—as marketing channels that contain no intermediaries. We also include direct marketing as one element of the promotion mix—as an approach for communicating directly with consumers. In actuality, direct marketing is both these things.

Most companies still use direct marketing as a supplementary channel or medium for marketing their goods. Thus, Lexus markets mostly through mass-media advertising and its high-quality dealer network but also supplements these channels with direct marketing. Its direct marketing includes promotional CDs and other materials mailed directly to prospective buyers and a Web page (www.lexus.com) that provides consumers with information about various models, competitive comparisons, financing, and dealer locations. Similarly, most department stores sell the majority of their merchandise off their store shelves but also sell through direct mail and online catalogs.

However, for many companies today, direct marketing is more than just a supplementary channel or medium. For these companies, direct marketing—especially in its most recent transformation, Internet marketing and e-commerce—constitutes a complete model for doing business. More than just another marketing channel or advertising medium, this new *direct model* is rapidly changing the way companies think about building relationships with customers.

Rather than using direct marketing and the Internet only as supplemental approaches, firms employing the direct model use it as the *only* approach. Some of these companies, such as Dell, Amazon.com, and eBay, began as only direct marketers. Other companies—such as Cisco Systems, Charles Schwab, and many others—have transformed themselves into direct marketing superstars. The company that perhaps best exemplifies this new direct marketing model is Dell (see Marketing at Work 13.2). Dell has built its entire approach to the marketplace around direct marketing.

BENEFITS AND GROWTH OF DIRECT MARKETING

Whether employed as a complete business model or as a supplement to a broader integrated marketing mix, direct marketing brings many benefits to both buyers and sellers. As a result, direct marketing is growing very rapidly.

For buyers, direct marketing is convenient, easy to use, and private. From the comfort of their homes or offices, they can browse mail catalogs or company Web sites at any time of the

MARKETING AT WORK | 13.2

Dell: Be Direct!

When 19-year-old Michael Dell began selling personal computers out of his college dorm room in 1984, competitors and industry insiders scoffed at the concept of mail-order computer marketing. Yet young Michael proved the skeptics wrong—way wrong. In little more than two decades, he has turned his dorm-room, mail-order business into the burgeoning, $49 billion Dell computer empire, recently named by *FORTUNE* magazine as America's Most Admired Company.

Dell is now the world's largest direct marketer of computer systems and the number-one PC maker worldwide. In the United States, Dell is number-one in desktop PC sales, number-one in laptops, number-one in servers, and number-two (and gaining) in printers. Over the past 10 years, despite downward-spiraling prices in the PC industry, Dell has experienced a more than 12-fold increase in sales and a 14-fold increase in profits. Last year, Dell grew twice as fast as number-two Hewlett-Packard. It has produced a 10-year average annual return to investors of 52 percent, one and a half times the average return of the next best FORTUNE 100 company.

What's the secret to Dell's stunning success? Anyone at Dell can tell you without hesitation: It's the company's radically different business model—the *direct model*. "We have a tremendously clear business model," says

Michael Dell, the company's 40-year-old founder and chairman. "There's no confusion about what the value proposition is, what the company offers, and why it's great for customers." An industry analyst agrees: "There's no better way to make, sell, and deliver PCs than

the way Dell does it, and nobody executes that model better than Dell."

Dell's direct marketing approach delivers greater customer value through an unbeatable combination of product customization, low prices, fast delivery, and award-winning

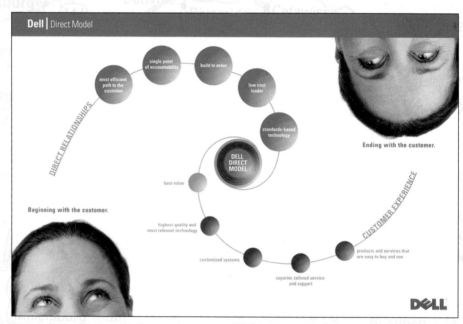

■ *The Dell Direct Model: Dell's direct marketing approach delivers greater customer value through an unbeatable combination of product customization, low prices, fast delivery, and award-winning customer service.*

day or night. Direct marketing gives buyers ready access to a wealth of products and information, at home and around the globe. Finally, direct marketing is immediate and interactive— buyers can interact with sellers by phone or on the seller's Web site to create exactly the configuration of information, products, or services they desire, then order them on the spot.

For sellers, direct marketing is a powerful tool for building customer relationships. Using database marketing, today's marketers can target small groups or individual consumers, tailor offers to individual needs, and promote these offers through personalized communications. Direct marketing can also be timed to reach prospects at just the right moment. Because of its one-to-one, interactive nature, the Internet is an especially potent direct marketing tool. Direct marketing also gives sellers access to buyers that they could not reach through other channels. For example, the Internet provides access to *global* markets that might otherwise be out of reach.

customer service. A customer can talk by phone with a Dell representative at 1-800-Buy-Dell or log onto www.dell.com on Monday morning; order a fully customized, state-of-the-art PC to suit his or her special needs; and have the machine delivered to his or her doorstep or desktop by Wednesday—all at a price that's 10 to 15 percent below competitors' prices for a comparably performing PC. Dell backs its products with high-quality service and support. As a result, Dell consistently ranks among the industry leaders in product reliability and service, and its customers are routinely among the industry's most satisfied.

Dell customers get exactly the machines they need. Michael Dell's initial idea was to serve individual buyers by letting them customize machines with the special features they wanted at low prices. However, this one-to-one approach also appeals strongly to corporate buyers, because Dell can so easily preconfigure each computer to precise requirements. Dell routinely preloads machines with a company's own software and even undertakes tedious tasks such as pasting inventory tags onto each machine so that computers can be delivered directly to a given employee's desk. As a result, more than 70 percent of Dell's sales come from large corporate, government, and educational buyers.

The direct model results in more efficient selling and lower costs, which translate into lower prices for customers. "Nobody, but nobody, makes [and markets] computer hardware more efficiently than Dell," says another analyst. "No unnecessary costs: This is an all-but-sacred mandate of the famous Dell direct business model." Because Dell builds machines to order, it carries barely any inventory—less than three day's worth by some accounts. Dealing one-to-one with customers helps the company react immediately to shifts in demand, so Dell doesn't get stuck with PCs no one wants. Finally, by selling directly, Dell has no dealers to pay. As a result, on average, Dell's costs are 12 percent lower than those of its leading PC competitor.

Dell knows that time is money, and the company is obsessed with "speed." According to one account, Dell squeezes "time out of every step in the process—from the moment an order is taken to collecting the cash. [By selling direct, manufacturing to order, and] tapping credit cards and electronic payment, Dell converts the average sale to cash in less than 24 hours." By contrast, competitors selling through dealers might take 35 days or longer.

Such blazing speed results in more satisfied customers and still lower costs. For example, customers are often delighted to find their new computers arriving within as few as 36 hours of placing an order. And because Dell doesn't order parts until an order is booked, it can take advantage of ever-falling component costs. On average, its parts are 60 days newer than those in competing machines, and, hence, 60 days farther down the price curve. This gives Dell a 6 percent profit advantage from parts costs alone.

As you might imagine, competitors are no longer scoffing at Michael Dell's vision of the future. In fact, competing and noncompeting companies alike are studying the Dell model closely. "Somehow Dell has been able to take flexibility and speed and build it into their DNA. It's almost like drinking water," says the CEO of another FORTUNE 500 company, who visited recently to absorb some of the Dell magic to apply to his own company. "I'm trying to drink as much water here as I can."

It's hard to argue with success, and Michael Dell has been very successful. By following his hunches, at the tender age of 40 he has built one of the world's hottest companies. In the process, he's become one of the world's richest men, amassing a personal fortune of more than $16 billion.

Sources: Quotes, performance statistics, and other information from Kathryn Jones, "The Dell Way," *Business 2.0,* February 2003, pp. 60–66; "The InternetWeek Interview—Michael Dell," *InternetWeek,* April 13, 1999, p. 8; Andy Serwer, "Dell Does Domination," *FORTUNE,* January 21, 2002, pp. 71–75; "Dell Computer Corporation," *Hoover's Company Profiles,* Austin, March 15, 2005, p. 13193; www.dell.com/us/en/gen/corporate/access_company_direct_model.htm, September 2005; Tom Krazit, "PC Sales Strong in 2004," *PC World,* January 19, 2005, accessed at www.pcworld.com; Jerry Useem, "America's Most Admired Companies," *FORTUNE,* March 27, 2005, pp. 67+; Andy Serwer, "The Education of Michael Dell, *FORTUNE,* March 7, 2005, pp. 73–78; and Luisa Kroll and Lea Goldman, "The World's Billionaires," *FORTUNE,* March 10, 2005, accessed at www.FORTUNE.com.

Finally, direct marketing can offer sellers a low-cost, efficient alternative for reaching their markets. For example, direct marketing has grown rapidly in B2B marketing, partly in response to the ever-increasing costs of marketing through the sales force. When personal sales calls cost $329 per contact, they should be made only when necessary and to high-potential customers and prospects. Lower cost-per-contact media—such as telemarketing, direct mail, and company Web sites—often prove more cost effective in reaching and selling to more prospects and customers.

As a result of these advantages to both buyers and sellers, direct marketing has become the fastest growing form of marketing. According to the Direct Marketing Association, direct sales to consumers and businesses in the United States last year reached $2.3 trillion, about 18 percent of the national economy. And while total U.S. sales grew 6 percent last year, direct sales grew more than 8 percent.[24]

CUSTOMER DATABASES AND DIRECT MARKETING

Customer database

An organized collection of comprehensive data about individual customers or prospects, including geographic, demographic, psychographic, and behavioral data.

Effective direct marketing begins with a good customer database. A **customer database** is an organized collection of comprehensive data about individual customers or prospects, including geographic, demographic, psychographic, and behavioral data. The database gives companies "a snapshot of how customers look and behave." A good customer database can be a potent relationship-building tool. "If there's been any change in the past decade it's the knowledge we now can have about our customers," says one expert. "Strategically, the most essential tool is our customer database. A company is no better than what it knows."[25]

Many companies confuse a customer database with a customer mailing list. A customer mailing list is simply a set of names, addresses, and telephone numbers. A customer database contains much more information. In consumer marketing, the customer database might contain a customer's demographics (age, income, family members, and birthdays), psychographics (activities, interests, and opinions), and buying behavior (buying preferences and the recency, frequency, and monetary value—RFM—of past purchases). In B2B marketing, the customer profile might contain the products and services the customer has bought; past volumes and prices; key contacts (and their ages, birthdays, hobbies, and favorite foods); competitive suppliers; status of current contracts; estimated customer spending for the next few years; and assessments of competitive strengths and weaknesses in selling and servicing the account.

Some of these databases are huge. For example, casino operator Harrah's Entertainment has built a customer database containing 30 terabytes worth of customer information, roughly three times the number of printed characters in the Library of Congress. Internet portal Yahoo! records every click made by every visitor, adding some 400 billion bytes of data per day to its database—the equivalent of 800,000 books. And Wal-Mart's database contains more than 100 terabytes of data—that's 100 trillion bytes, equivalent to 16,000 bytes for every one of the world's 6 billion people.[26]

Companies use their databases in many ways. They use databases to locate good potential customers and to generate sales leads. They can mine their databases to learn about customers in detail, and then fine-tune their market offerings and communications to the special preferences and behaviors of target segments or individuals. In all, a company's database can be an important tool for building stronger long-term customer relationships.

For example, an analysis of Harrah's database revealed that its best casino customers were not the free-spending, limousine-riding high rollers, but rather the slot-playing, middle-aged or retired teachers, bankers, and doctors with free time and discretionary income. Based on these database insights, Harrah's shapes incentives for individual customers—free casino chips, dinner vouchers, free show tickets, or room upgrades—tailored to their gambling and entertainment behavior and preferences. As a result, Harrah's has the most devoted customers in the industry.[27]

Here's another example of a company that uses its database to create strong customer relationships:

> USAA provides financial services to U.S. military personnel and their families, largely through direct marketing via the telephone and Internet. It maintains a customer database built from customer purchasing histories and from information collected directly from customers. To keep the database fresh, the organization regularly surveys its more than 5 million customers worldwide to learn such things as whether they have children (and if so, how old they are), if they have moved recently, and when they plan to retire. USAA uses the database to tailor direct marketing offers to the specific needs of individual customers. For example, if the family has college-age children, the USAA sends those children information on how to manage their credit cards. If the family has younger children, it sends booklets on things like financing a child's education. Or, for customers looking toward retirement, it sends information on estate planning. Through skillful use of its database, USAA serves each customer uniquely, resulting in high levels of customer loyalty and sales growth. The average customer household owns almost five USAA products, and the $11.3 billion company retains 97 percent of its customers.[28]

Like many other marketing tools, database marketing requires a special investment. Companies must invest in computer hardware, database software, analytical programs, communication links, and skilled personnel. The database system must be user-friendly and available to various marketing groups, including those in product and brand management, new-product development, advertising and promotion, direct mail, telemarketing, Web marketing, field sales, order fulfillment, and customer service. A well-managed database should lead to sales and customer-relationship gains that will more than cover its costs.

FORMS OF DIRECT MARKETING

The major forms of direct marketing—as shown in Figure 13.4—include personal selling, telephone marketing, direct-mail marketing, catalog marketing, direct-response television marketing, kiosk marketing, and online marketing. We examined personal selling in depth earlier in this chapter and will look closely at online marketing in Chapter 14. Here, we examine the other direct marketing forms.

Telephone Marketing   **Telephone marketing** involves using the telephone to sell directly to consumers and business customers. We're all familiar with telephone marketing directed toward consumers, but B2B marketers also use telephone marketing extensively, accounting for more than 60 percent of all telephone-marketing sales.

Marketers use *outbound* telephone marketing to sell directly to consumers and businesses. *Inbound* toll-free 800 numbers are used to receive orders from television and print ads, direct mail, or catalogs. The use of 800 numbers has taken off in recent years as more companies have begun using them, and as current users have added new features such as toll-free fax numbers. To accommodate this rapid growth, new toll-free area codes, such as 888, 877, and 866, have been added.

Properly designed and targeted telemarketing provides many benefits, including purchasing convenience and increased product and service information. However, the explosion in unsolicited outbound telephone marketing over the years annoyed many consumers, who objected to the almost daily "junk phone calls" that pull them away from the dinner table or fill the answering machine.

In 2003, U.S. lawmakers responded with a National Do-Not-Call Registry, managed by the Federal Trade Commission. The legislation bans most telemarketing calls to registered phone numbers (although people can still receive calls from nonprofit groups, politicians, and

Telephone marketing
Using the telephone to sell directly to customers.

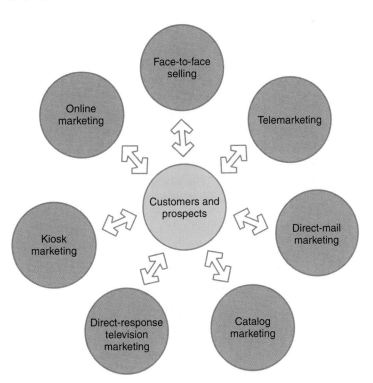

FIGURE 13.4
Forms of Direct Marketing

Careful...you might sprain a taste bud.

Don't wait another day! Call now to place an order or request a catalog. Also, go on line at **www.carolinacookie.com** to place an order, request a catalog or view our entire selection of products.

1-800-447-5797

CAROLINA COOKIE COMPANY · JUST BAKED

■ Marketers use inbound toll-free 800 numbers to receive orders from television and print ads, direct mail, or catalogs. Here, the Carolina Cookie Company urges, "Don't wait another day. Call now to place an order or request a catalog."

Direct-mail marketing
Direct marketing by sending an offer, announcement, reminder, or other item to a person at a particular address.

companies with which they have recently done business). Delighted consumers have responded enthusiastically. To date, they have registered more than 87 million phone numbers at www.donotcall.com or by calling 888-382-1222. Businesses that break do-not-call laws can be fined up to $11,000 per violation.

Do-not-call legislation has hurt the telemarketing industry, but not all that much. Two major forms of telemarketing—inbound consumer telemarketing and outbound B2B telemarketing—remain strong and growing. Telemarketing also remains a major fund-raising tool for nonprofit groups. However, many telemarketers are shifting to alternative methods for capturing new customers and sales, from direct mail, direct-response TV, and live-chat technology to sweepstakes that prompt customers to call in.

For example, ServiceMaster's TruGreen lawn-care service used to generate about 90 percent of its sales through telemarketing. It now uses more direct mail, as well as having employees go door-to-door in neighborhoods where it already has customers. The new approach appears to be working even better than the old cold-calling one. The company's sales were up last year, and less than 50 percent of sales came from telemarketing. "We were nervous, but were thrilled with what we've accomplished," says ServiceMaster's chief executive.[29]

Interestingly, do-not-call appears to be helping most direct marketers more than it's hurting them. Many of these marketers are shifting their call-center activity from making cold calls on often resentful customers to managing existing customer relationships. They are developing "opt-in" calling systems, which provide useful information and offers to customers who have invited the company to contact them by phone or by e-mail. These "sales tactics have [produced] results as good—or even better—than telemarketing," declares one analyst. "The opt-in model is proving [more] valuable for marketers [than] the old invasive one."[30]

Direct-Mail Marketing   **Direct-mail marketing** involves sending an offer, announcement, reminder, or other item to a person at a particular address. Using highly selective mailing lists, direct marketers send out millions of mail pieces each year—letters, ads, brochures, samples, video- and audiotapes, CDs, and other "salespeople with wings."

Direct mail is well suited to direct, one-to-one communication. It permits high target-market selectivity, can be personalized, is flexible, and allows easy measurement of results. Although the cost per thousand people reached is higher than with mass media such as television or magazines, the people who are reached are much better prospects. Direct mail has proved successful in promoting all kinds of products, from books, magazine subscriptions, and insurance to gift items, clothing, gourmet foods, and industrial products. Direct mail is also used heavily by charities to raise billions of dollars each year.

The direct-mail industry constantly seeks new methods and approaches. For example, CDs and DVDs are now among the fastest-growing direct-mail media. A recent study showed that including a CD or DVD in a marketing offer generates responses between 50 to 600 percent greater than traditional direct mail. For instance, last year the developer of Bald Head Island, North Carolina, mailed 10,000 CDs promoting rental properties and the resort's attractions. The CDs attracted more than 1,600 users, who checked out the CD an average 1.5 times.[31] Used in conjunction with the Internet, CDs offer an affordable way to drive traffic to Web pages personalized for a specific market segment or a specific promotion.

Until recently, all direct mail was paper based and handled by the U.S. Postal Service or delivery services such as FedEx and UPS. Recently, however, new forms of delivery have become popular, such as *fax mail, voice mail,* and *e-mail.* Fax mail and voice mail are subject to the same do-not-call restrictions as telemarketing, so their use has been limited in recent years. However, e-mail is booming as a direct marketing tool. Today's e-mail messages have moved far beyond the drab text-only messages of old. The new breed of e-mail ad uses animation, interactive links, streaming video, and personalized audio messages to reach out and grab attention.

E-mail and other new forms deliver direct mail at incredible speeds compared to the post office's "snail mail" pace. Yet, much like mail delivered through traditional channels, they may be resented as "junk mail" or spam if sent to people who have no interest in them. For this reason, smart marketers are targeting their direct mail carefully so as not waste their money and recipients' time. They are designing permission-based programs, sending e-mail ads only to those who want to receive them.

Catalog Marketing   Advances in technology, along with the move toward personalized, one-to-one marketing, have resulted in exciting changes in **catalog marketing**. *Catalog Age* magazine used to define a *catalog* as "a printed, bound piece of at least eight pages, selling multiple products, and offering a direct ordering mechanism." Today, only a few years later, this definition is sadly out of date.

With the stampede to the Internet, more catalogs are going digital. Most print catalogers have added Web-based catalogs to their marketing mixes, and a variety of new Web-only catalogers have emerged. One recent study found that consumers now make 36 percent of their catalog purchases online. However, although the Internet has provided a new avenue for catalog sales, all you have to do is check your mailbox to know that printed catalogs remain the primary medium. Research shows that print catalogs generate many of those online orders. Customers who receive print catalogs are more likely to buy online, and they spend 16 percent more than customers who did not receive catalogs.[32]

Catalog marketing
Direct marketing through print, video, or electronic catalogs that are mailed to select customers, made available in stores, or presented online.

■ Catalogs: With the stampede to the Internet, more and more catalogs are going digital. And almost every print cataloger, like L.L.Bean, has a Web-based catalog as well.

Catalog marketing has grown explosively during the past 25 years. Annual catalog sales amounted to about $143 billion last year and are expected to grow to top $175 billion by 2008.[33] Some large general-merchandise retailers—such as JCPenney and Spiegel—sell a full line of merchandise through catalogs. In recent years, these giants have been challenged by thousands of specialty catalogs that serve highly specialized market niches. According to one study, some 10,000 companies now produce 14,000 unique catalog titles in the United States.[34]

Consumers can buy just about anything from a catalog. Sharper Image catalogs hawk everything from $300 robot vacuum cleaners to $4,500 see-through kayaks. Each year Lillian Vernon sends out 23 editions of its 6 catalogs with total circulation of 102 million copies to its 20-million-person database, selling more than 6,000 different items, ranging from shoes to decorative lawn birds and monogrammed oven mitts.[35] Specialty department stores, such as Neiman Marcus, Bloomingdale's, and Saks Fifth Avenue, use catalogs to cultivate upper-middle-class markets for high-priced, often exotic, merchandise. Several major corporations have also developed or acquired catalog divisions. For example, Avon now issues 10 women's fashion catalogs along with catalogs for children's and men's clothes. The Walt Disney Company mails out over 6 million catalogs each year featuring videos, stuffed animals, and other Disney items.

Web-based catalogs present a number of benefits versus printed catalogs. They save on production, printing, and mailing costs. Whereas print-catalog space is limited, online catalogs can offer an almost unlimited amount of merchandise. Web catalogs also allow real-time merchandising: Products and features can be added or removed as needed, and prices can be adjusted instantly to match demand. Finally, online catalogs can be spiced up with interactive entertainment and promotional features, such as games, contests, and daily specials.

Along with the benefits, however, Web-based catalogs also present challenges. Whereas a print catalog is intrusive and creates its own attention, Web catalogs are passive and must be marketed. Attracting new customers is much more difficult for a Web catalog than for a print catalog. Thus, even catalogers who are sold on the Web are not likely to abandon their print catalogs.

Direct-response television marketing
Direct marketing via television, including direct-response television advertising or infomercials and home shopping channels.

Direct-Response Television Marketing   **Direct-response television marketing** takes one of two major forms. The first is direct-response advertising. Direct marketers air television spots, often 60 or 120 seconds long, which persuasively describe a product and give customers a toll-free number or Web site for ordering. Television viewers also often encounter full 30-minute or longer advertising programs, or infomercials, for a single product.

Some successful direct-response ads run for years and become classics. For example, Dial Media's ads for Ginsu knives ran for seven years and sold almost 3 million sets of knives worth more than $40 million in sales; its Armourcote cookware ads generated more than twice that much. Bowflex has grossed more than $1.3 billion in infomercial sales. And over the past 40 years, infomercial czar Ron Popeil's company, Ronco, has sold billions of dollars worth of TV-marketed gadgets, including the original Veg-O-Matic, the Pocket Fisherman, Mr. Microphone, "Hair in a Can," the Giant Food Dehydrator and Beef Jerky Machine, and the Showtime Rotisserie & BBQ.[36]

For years, infomercials have been associated with somewhat questionable pitches for juicers and other kitchen gadgets, get-rich-quick schemes, and nifty ways to stay in shape without working very hard at it. Traditionally, they have "almost been the Wild West of advertising, where people make rules for themselves as they go along," says Jack Kirby, chairman of the Electronic Retailing Association.[37] In recent years, however, a number of large companies—GTE, Johnson & Johnson, Sears, Procter & Gamble, Disney, Revlon, IBM, GM, Land Rover, Anheuser-Busch, even AARP and the U.S. Navy—have begun using infomercials to sell their wares over the phone, refer customers to retailers, send out coupons and product information, recruit members, or attract buyers to their Web sites (see Marketing at Work 13.3). An estimated 20 percent of all new infomercials now come to you courtesy of FORTUNE 1000 companies.[38] According to Kirby, it's "time to really set some standards and move forward."

Direct-response TV commercials are usually cheaper to make and the media purchase is less costly. Moreover, results are easily measured. Unlike most media campaigns, direct-response ads always include a 1-800 number or Web address, making it easier for marketers to track the impact of their pitches.

MARKETING AT WORK | 13.3

Infomercials: But Wait, There's More!

It's late at night and you can't get to sleep. So you grab the TV remote, surf channels, and chance upon a fast-talking announcer, breathlessly pitching some new must-have kitchen gadget. A grinning blonde co-announcer fawns over the gadget's every feature, and the studio audience roars its approval. After putting the gadget through its paces, the announcer asks, "How much would you expect to pay? Three hundred dollars? Two hundred? Well, think again! This amazing gadget can be yours for just four easy payments of $19.95, plus shipping and handling!" "Oooooh!" the audience screams. "But wait! There's more," declares the announcer. "If you act now, you will also receive an additional gadget, absolutely free. That's two for the price of one." With operators standing by, you don't have a minute to lose.

Sound familiar? We've all seen countless infomercials like this, hawking everything from kitchen gadgets, cleaning solutions, and fitness solutions to psychic advice and get-rich-quick schemes. Traditionally, such pitches have had a kind of fly-by-night feel about them. And in the cold light of day, such a purchase may not seem like such a good deal after all. Such is the reputation of direct-response TV advertising. Yet, behind the hype is a powerful approach to marketing that is becoming more mainstream every day.

Ron Popeil pioneered direct-response product sales. Whether you realize it or not, you've probably been exposed to dozens of Popeil's inventions over the years, and his direct marketing model has become the standard for the infomercial industry. His company, Ronco, has brought us such classics as the Veg-o-Matic, the Electric Food Dehydrator, the Showtime Rotisserie Oven, the GLH Formula Hair System, the Automatic 5-Minute Pasta and Sausage Maker, the Popeil Pocket Fisherman, the Inside the Egg Shell Electric Egg Scrambler, and the Dial-O-Matic Food Slicer.

The use of infomercials has grown explosively in recent years. Why? Because they can produce spectacular results. Although only one in sixty infomercials turns a profit, "successful pitches can generate annual sales of as much as $50 million," notes one analyst. "And

breakout hits become gold mines: Ron Popeil has sold $1 billion worth of Ronco rotisserie ovens, while the Tae-Bo Workout infomercial . . . netted $300 million in its first year. Other benefits include viewer recall that can be three times higher than for traditional 30-second spots and phenomenal brand awareness: 92 percent of consumers have heard of the Nautilus Bowflex home fitness system—about the same number of folks that recognize the Nike brand." Says the head of an infomercial advertising agency, "It's the power of the half-hour."

Moreover, the retail store revenue from a successful infomercial can be many times the actual infomercial sales. For example, more than 85 percent of George Foreman's Mean Lean Grilling Machine sales came from retail locations. Mass retailers have embraced such direct-response staples as Foreman's grill, OxiClean, and Orange Glo. Some, such as drug-chain heavyweight Walgreens, devote entire front-of-store sections to such goods. Whereas it used to take years to get retail distribution for "As seen on TV" products, many now make it to store shelves within a month of going on television.

Such infomercial success hasn't gone unnoticed among the big hitters in corporate America. Direct-response television marketing is rapidly becoming a mainstay weapon in the marketing arsenals of even the most reputable companies. Marketing heavyweights like Dell, Procter & Gamble, Disney, Time-Life, General Motors, Apple, Motorola, and Sears now use direct-response TV to peddle specific products and promotions and to draw new customers into their other direct-to-consumer channels. For example, P&G used a series of infomercials to help propel the Swiffer WetJet past rival Clorox's ReadyMop when other marketing efforts alone failed to do the trick. And P&G launched its Swiffer Dusters product with a campaign that included direct-response ads and a tie-in to the DVD release of the Jennifer Lopez film *Maid in*

■ *Ronco and Ron Popeil, with his Veg-o-Matics, food dehydrators, and electronic egg scramblers, paved the way for a host of mainstream marketers who now use direct-response ads.*

Manhattan. Consumers contacting the 1-800 number got coupons for both the new Swiffer Duster and the DVD.

Today's infomercials have evolved with the times—most now include highly professional pitches and Web sites to go along with the ever-present toll-free phone number. They also employ a new breed of spokesperson. Once a refuge for Hollywood has-beens such as Suzanne Somers, who squeezed away on her thigh master to bleary-eyed insomniacs, infomercials now are now enlisting A-list celebrities. One of the nation's largest infomercial companies, Gunthy-Renker, pays top dollar for a stable of stars to pitch its Proactiv acne treatment. It paid Sean (P. Diddy) Combs $3 million for a four-hour shoot. In four months, the Combs Proactiv infomercial ran an average of more than 10 times on each of 1,400 local TV stations. Other Proactiv ads have featured Jessica Simpson (paid $2.5 million), Vanessa Williams ($2.5 million), Alicia Keys ($3 million), and Britney Spears ($1 million). In all, the ads produced some $650 million in Proactiv sales last year.

(continued)

Interest in direct response has now expanded beyond the usual fitness, personal-care, and home-care fare. For instance, submarine-sandwich giant Quiznos has turned to late-night infomercials to sell franchises. Trailing only Subway and Starbucks in the number of franchises opened annually, Quiznos created a successful 30-minute spot in which current franchise owners discussed the benefits of owning a Quiznos restaurant and encouraged interested people to attend informational meetings at local hotels. And the Arkansas Department of Travel and Tourism has used infomercials to help promote visits to the state. The 30-minute ads show the variety of activities available in Arkansas and invites viewers to call a toll-free number or go to the state's Web site to obtain a free Arkansas Vacation Planning Kit.

So, direct-response TV ads are no longer just the province of Ron Popeil and his Veg-o-Matics, food dehydrators, and electric egg scramblers. While Popeil and his imitators paved the way, their success now has mainstream marketers tuning in to direct-response ads. In fact, last year marketers spent $24.3 billion on direct-response television advertising, reaping more than $150 billion in revenues in return. What does the future hold for the direct-response TV industry? Wait, there's more!

Sources: Thomas Mucha, "Stronger Sales in Just 28 Minutes," *Business 2.0,* June 2005, pp. 56–60; Jack Neff, "Direct Response Getting Respect," *Advertising Age,* January 20, 2003, p. 4; Nat Ives, "Infomercials Clean Up Their Pitch," *New York Times,* April 12, 2004, p. C1; Kristi Arellano, "Quiznos' Success Not Without Problems," *Knight Ridder Tribune Business News,* June 19, 2005, p. 1; Peter Latterman, "So Long Suzanne Somers," *Forbes,* July 4, 2005, p. 60; and Victor Grillo, Jr., "Calling All Brands," *Mediaweek,* July 11, 2005, p. 14.

Home shopping channels, another form of direct-response television marketing, are television programs or entire channels dedicated to selling goods and services. Some home shopping channels, such as the Quality Value Channel (QVC), Home Shopping Network (HSN), and ShopNBC, broadcast 24 hours a day. On QVC, the program's hosts offer bargain prices on products ranging from jewelry, lamps, collectible dolls, and clothing to power tools and consumer electronics—usually obtained by the home shopping channel at closeout prices. Viewers call a toll-free number to order goods from one of six QVC call centers.

With widespread distribution on cable and satellite television, the top-three shopping networks combined now reach 248 million homes worldwide, selling more than $7.5 billion of goods each year. They are now combining direct-response television marketing with online and on-land selling. For example, HSN recently launched interactive television (iTV), which allows consumers to purchase products using their remotes. And QVC, which offers more than 1,700 items each week, offers a feature called "61st Minutes," in which viewers are urged to go online immediately after a given product showcase. Once there, viewers find a Webcast continuation of the product pitch. Those who miss out on a deal on the tube or online can now visit one of six QVC outlet stores or the company's full-line store at the Mall of America.[39]

Kiosk Marketing As consumers become more comfortable with computer and digital technologies, many companies are placing information and ordering machines—called *kiosks* (in contrast to vending machines, which dispense actual products)—in stores, airports, and other locations. Kiosks are popping up everywhere these days, from self-service hotel and airline check-in devices to in-store ordering kiosks that let you order merchandise not carried in the store.

■ Kiosks: REI uses in-store kiosks that give customers access to the REI Web site and lets them purchase items that are out of stock or not available in the store.

In-store Kodak and Fujifilm kiosks let customers transfer pictures from memory sticks, mobile phones, and other digital storage devices, edit them, and make high-quality color prints. Sears home improvement kiosks in selected Kmart stores allow customers to order windows, siding, countertops, and cabinets via Sears.com. Outdoor equipment retailer REI has at least four Web-enabled kiosks in each of its 63 stores that provide customers with product information and let them place orders online. At CarMax, the used-car superstore, customers use a kiosk with a touch-screen computer to get information about its vast inventory of as many as 1,000 cars and trucks. Customers can choose a handful and print out photos, prices, features, and location on the store's lot.[40]

Business marketers also use kiosks. For example, Dow Plastics places kiosks at trade shows to collect sales leads and to provide information on its 700 products. The kiosk system reads customer data from encoded registration badges and produces technical data sheets that can be printed at the kiosk or faxed or mailed to the customer. The system has resulted in a 400 percent increase in qualified sales leads.[41]

  Linking the Concepts

Hold up a moment and think about the impact of direct marketing on your life.

- When was the last time that you *bought* something via direct marketing? What did you buy, and why did you buy it direct? When was the last time that you *rejected* a direct marketing offer? Why did you reject it? Based on these experiences, what advice would you give to direct marketers?
- For the next week, keep track of all the direct marketing offers that come your way via direct mail and catalogs, telephone, direct-response television, and the Internet. Then analyze the offers by type, source, and what you liked or disliked about each offer and the way it was delivered. Which offer best hit its target (you)? Which missed by the widest margin?

INTEGRATED DIRECT MARKETING

Too often, a company's different direct marketing efforts are not well integrated with one another or with other elements of its marketing and promotion mixes. For example, a firm's media advertising may be handled by the advertising department working with a traditional advertising agency. Meanwhile, its direct-mail and catalog business may be handled by direct marketing specialists, while its Web site is developed and operated by an outside Internet firm. Even within a given direct marketing campaign, too many companies use only a "one-shot" effort to reach and sell a prospect or a single vehicle in multiple stages to trigger purchases.

A more powerful approach is **integrated direct marketing**, which involves using carefully coordinated multiple-media, multiple-stage campaigns. Such campaigns can greatly improve response. Whereas a direct-mail piece alone might generate a 2 percent response, adding a Web site and toll-free phone number might raise the response rate by 50 percent. Then, a well-designed outbound e-mail campaign might lift response by an additional 500 percent. Suddenly, a 2 percent response has grown to 15 percent or more by adding interactive marketing channels to a regular mailing.

Integrated direct marketing
Direct marketing campaigns that use multiple vehicles and multiple stages to improve response rates and profits.

More elaborate integrated direct marketing campaigns can be used. Consider the multimedia, multistage campaign shown in Figure 13.5. Here, the paid ad creates product awareness and stimulates phone, mail, or Web inquiries. The company immediately sends direct mail or e-mail responses to those who inquire. Within a few days, the company follows up with an outbound telemarketing or e-mail seeking an order. Some prospects will order by phone or the company's Web site; others might request a face-to-face sales call. In such a campaign, the marketer seeks to improve response rates and profits by adding media and stages that contribute more to additional sales than to additional costs.

FIGURE 13.5 An Integrated Direct Marketing Campaign

PUBLIC POLICY AND ETHICAL ISSUES IN DIRECT MARKETING

Direct marketers and their customers usually enjoy mutually rewarding relationships. Occasionally, however, a darker side emerges. The aggressive and sometimes shady tactics of a few direct marketers can bother or harm consumers, giving the entire industry a black eye. Abuses range from simple excesses that irritate consumers to instances of unfair practices or even outright deception and fraud. The direct marketing industry has also faced growing concerns about invasion-of-privacy issues.

Irritation, Unfairness, Deception, and Fraud   Direct marketing excesses sometimes annoy or offend consumers. Most of us dislike direct-response TV commercials that are too loud, too long, and too insistent. Especially bothersome are dinnertime or late-night phone calls. Beyond irritating consumers, some direct marketers have been accused of taking unfair advantage of impulsive or less sophisticated buyers. TV shopping channels and program-long "infomercials" targeting television-addicted shoppers seem to be the worst culprits. They feature smooth-talking hosts, elaborately staged demonstrations, claims of drastic price reductions, "while they last" time limitations, and unequaled ease of purchase to inflame buyers who have low sales resistance.

Worse yet, so-called heat merchants design mailers and write copy intended to mislead buyers. Even well-known direct mailers have been accused of deceiving consumers. Sweepstakes promoter Publishers Clearing House recently paid $52 million to settle accusations that its high-pressure mailings confused or misled consumers, especially the elderly, into believing that they had won prizes or would win if they bought the company's magazines.[42]

Other direct marketers pretend to be conducting research surveys when they are actually asking leading questions to screen or persuade consumers. Fraudulent schemes, such as investment scams or phony collections for charity, have also multiplied in recent years. Crooked direct marketers can be hard to catch: Direct marketing customers often respond quickly, do not interact personally with the seller, and usually expect to wait for delivery. By the time buyers realize that they have been bilked, the thieves are usually somewhere else plotting new schemes.

Invasion of Privacy   Invasion of privacy is perhaps the toughest public policy issue now confronting the direct marketing industry. These days, it seems that almost every time consumers enter a sweepstakes, apply for a credit card, take out a magazine subscription, or order products by mail, telephone, or the Internet, their names are entered into some company's already bulging database. Using sophisticated computer technologies, direct marketers can use these databases to "microtarget" their selling efforts.

Consumers often benefit from such database marketing—they receive more offers that are closely matched to their interests. However, many critics worry that marketers may know *too* much about consumers' lives and that they may use this knowledge to take unfair advantage of consumers. At some point, they claim, the extensive use of databases intrudes on consumer privacy.

For example, they ask, should AT&T be allowed to sell marketers the names of customers who frequently call the 800 numbers of catalog companies? Should a company such as American Express be allowed to make data on its millions of cardholders worldwide available to merchants who accept AmEx cards? Is it right for credit bureaus to compile and sell lists of people who have recently applied for credit cards—people who are considered prime direct marketing targets because of

■ Privacy: The explosion of information technology has put sometimes frightening capabilities into the hands of almost any business. One bar owner discovered the power of information technology after he acquired a simple, inexpensive device to check IDs.

their spending behavior? Or is it right for states to sell the names and addresses of driver's license holders, along with height, weight, and gender information, allowing apparel retailers to target tall or overweight people with special clothing offers?

In their drives to build databases, companies sometimes get carried away. For example, when first introduced, Intel's Pentium III chip contained an embedded serial number that allowed the company to trace users' equipment. When privacy advocates screamed, Intel disabled the feature. Similarly, Microsoft caused substantial privacy concerns when one version of its Windows software used a "Registration Wizard" that snooped into users computers. When users went online to register, without their knowledge, Microsoft "read" the configurations of their PCs to learn about the major software products they were running. Users protested loudly and Microsoft abandoned the practice.

These days, it's not only the large companies that can access such private information. The explosion of information technology has put these capabilities into the hands of almost any business. For example, one bar owner discovered the power of information technology after he acquired a simple, inexpensive device to check IDs.

About 10,000 people a week go to The Rack, a bar in Boston. . . . One by one, they hand over their driver's licenses to a doorman, who swipes them through a sleek black machine. If a license is valid and its holder is over 21, a red light blinks and the patron is waved through. But most of the customers are not aware that it also pulls up the name, address, birth date, and other personal details from a data strip on the back of the license. Even height, eye color, and sometimes Social Security number are registered. "You swipe the license, and all of a sudden someone's whole life as we know it pops up in front of you," said Paul Barclay, the bar's owner. "It's almost voyeuristic." Mr. Barclay soon found that he could build a database of personal information, providing an intimate perspective on his clientele that can be useful in marketing. Now, for any given night or hour, he can break down his clientele by sex, age, zip code, or other characteristics. If he wanted to, he could find out how many blond women named Karen over 5 feet 2 inches came in over a weekend, or how many of his customers have the middle initial M. More practically, he can build mailing lists based on all that data—and keep track of who comes back.[43]

Such access to and use of information has caused much concern and debate among companies, consumers, and public policy makers. Consumer privacy has become a major regulatory issue.

The direct marketing industry is addressing issues of ethics and public policy. For example, in an effort to build consumer confidence in shopping direct, the Direct Marketing Association (DMA)—the largest association for businesses practicing direct, database, and interactive marketing, with more than 4,700 member companies— launched a "Privacy Promise to American Consumers." The Privacy Promise requires that all DMA members adhere to a carefully developed set of consumer-privacy rules. Members must agree to notify customers when any personal information is rented, sold, or exchanged with others. They must also honor consumer requests to "opt out" of receiving further solicitations or having their contact information transferred to other marketers. Finally, they must abide by the DMA's Preference Service by removing the names of consumers who wish not to receive mail, telephone, or e-mail offers.[44]

■ The DMA's "Privacy Promise to American Consumers" attempts to build customer confidence by requiring that all DMA members adhere to certain carefully developed customer privacy rules.

Direct marketers know that, left untended, such problems will lead to increasingly negative consumer attitudes, lower response rates, and calls for more restrictive state and federal legislation. "Privacy and customer permission have become the cornerstones of customer trust, [and] trust has become the cornerstone to a continuing relationship," says one expert. Companies must "become the custodians of customer trust and protect the privacy of their customers."[45]

Most direct marketers want the same things that consumers want: honest and well-designed marketing offers targeted only toward consumers who will appreciate and respond to them. Direct marketing is just too expensive to waste on consumers who don't want it.

REST STOP → REVIEWING THE CONCEPTS

Hit the brakes, pull over, and revisit this chapter's key concepts. The chapter is the second of two chapters covering the final marketing mix element—promotion. The previous chapter dealt with advertising, sales promotion, and public relations. This one investigates personal selling and direct marketing.

Personal selling and direct marketing are both direct tools for persuasively communicating customer value and building customer relationships. Selling is the interpersonal arm of the communications mix. To be successful in personal selling, a company must first build and then manage an effective sales force. Firms must also be good at direct marketing, the process of forming one-to-one connections with customers. Today, many companies are turning to direct marketing in an effort to reach carefully targeted customers more efficiently and to build stronger, more personal, one-to-one relationships with them.

1. Discuss the role of a company's salespeople in creating value for customers and building customer relationships.

Most companies use salespeople, and many companies assign them an important role in the marketing mix. For companies selling business products, the firm's salespeople work directly with customers. Often, the sales force is the customer's only direct contact with the company and, therefore, may be viewed by customers as representing the company itself. In contrast, for consumer product companies that sell through intermediaries, consumers usually do not meet salespeople or even know about them. The sales force works behind the scenes, dealing with wholesalers and retailers to obtain their support and helping them become effective in selling the firm's products.

As an element of the promotion mix, the sales force is very effective in achieving certain marketing objectives and carrying out such activities as prospecting, communicating, selling and servicing, and information gathering. But with

companies becoming more market oriented, a customer-focused sales force also works to produce both *customer satisfaction* and *company profit*. The sales force plays a key role in developing and managing profitable *customer relationships*.

2. Identify and explain the six major sales force management steps.

High sales force costs necessitate an effective sales management process consisting of six steps: designing sales force strategy and structure, recruiting and selecting, training, compensating, supervising, and evaluating salespeople and sales force performance.

In designing a sales force, sales management must address strategy issues such as what type of sales force structure will work best (territorial, product, customer, or complex structure); how large the sales force should be; who will be involved in the selling effort; and how its various sales and sales support people will work together (inside or outside sales forces and team selling).

To hold down the high costs of hiring the wrong people, salespeople must be recruited and selected carefully. In recruiting salespeople, a company may look to job duties and the characteristics of its most successful salespeople to suggest the traits it wants in its salespeople and then look for applicants through recommendations of current salespeople, employment agencies, classified ads, and the Internet or by contacting college students. In the selection process, the procedure can vary from a single informal interview to lengthy testing and interviewing. After the selection process is complete, training programs familiarize new salespeople not only with the art of selling but also with the company's history, its products and policies, and the characteristics of its market and competitors.

The sales force compensation system helps to reward, motivate, and direct salespeople. In compensating salespeople, companies try to have an appealing plan, usually close to the going rate for the type of sales job and needed skills. In addition to compensation, all salespeople need supervision, and many need continuous encouragement because they must make many decisions and face many frustrations. Periodically, the company must evaluate their performance to help them do a better job. In evaluating salespeople, the company relies on getting regular information gathered through sales reports, personal observations, customers' letters and complaints, customer surveys, and conversations with other salespeople.

3. Discuss the personal selling process, distinguishing between transaction-oriented marketing and relationship marketing.

The art of selling involves a seven-step *selling process*: *prospecting and qualifying*, *preapproach*, *approach*, *presentation and demonstration*, *handling objections*, *closing*, and *follow-up*. These steps help marketers close a specific sale and as such are *transaction oriented*. However, a seller's dealings with customers should be guided by the larger concept of *relationship marketing*. The company's sales force should help to orchestrate a whole-company effort to develop profitable long-term relationships with key customers based on superior customer value and satisfaction.

4. Define *direct marketing* and discuss its benefits to customers and companies.

Direct marketing consists of direct connections with carefully targeted individual consumers to both obtain an immediate response and cultivate lasting customer relationships. Using detailed databases, direct marketers tailor their offers and communications to the needs of narrowly defined segments or even individual buyers.

For buyers, direct marketing is convenient, easy to use, and private. It gives them ready access to a wealth of prod-

ucts and information, at home and around the globe. Direct marketing is also immediate and interactive, allowing buyers to create exactly the configuration of information, products, or services they desire, then order them on the spot. For sellers, direct marketing is a powerful tool for building customer relationships. Using database marketing, today's marketers can target small groups or individual consumers, tailor offers to individual needs, and promote these offers through personalized communications. It also offers them a low-cost, efficient alternative for reaching their markets. As a result of these advantages to both buyers and sellers, direct marketing has become the fastest growing form of marketing.

5. Identify and discuss the major forms of direct marketing.

The main forms of direct marketing include personal selling, telephone marketing, direct-mail marketing, catalog marketing, direct-response television marketing, kiosk marketing, and online marketing. We discuss personal selling in the first part of this chapter and will examine online marketing in detail in Chapter 14.

Telephone marketing consists of using the telephone to sell directly to consumers. Direct-mail marketing consists of the company sending an offer, announcement, reminder, or other item to a person at a specific address. Recently, new forms of "mail delivery" have become popular, such as e-mail marketing. Some marketers rely on catalog marketing, or selling through catalogs mailed to a select list of customers, or made available in stores or on the Web. Direct-response television marketing has two forms: direct-response advertising or infomercials and home shopping channels. Kiosks are information and ordering machines that direct marketers place in stores, airports, and other locations. Online marketing involves online channels and e-commerce, which electronically link consumers with sellers.

Navigating the Key Terms

Approach (414)

Catalog marketing (423)

Closing (416)

Customer database (420)

Customer sales force structure (403)

Direct-mail marketing (422)

Direct marketing (417)

Direct-response television marketing (424)

Follow-up (416)

Handling objections (415)

Inside sales force (404)

Integrated direct marketing (427)

Outside sales force (404)

Preapproach (414)

Presentation (415)

Product sales force structure (403)

Prospecting (414)

Sales force management (402)

Sales quota (412)

Salesperson (402)

Selling process (413)

Team selling (407)

Telephone marketing (421)

Territorial sales force structure (403)

Travel Log

Discussing the Issues

1. According to the chapter, salespeople serve "two masters." What does this mean? Is it a good or bad thing?

2. List and briefly describe the three sales force structures outlined in the chapter. What sales force structure does CDW employ?

3. How does the inside sales force differ from the outside sales force? How might a company benefit from having both?

4. The chapter argues that the ability to build relationships with customers is the most important part of a salesperson's key talents? Do you agree? Explain.

5. Describe how direct marketing benefits both buyers and sellers.

6. For each of the forms of direct marketing discussed in the text, identify a product or service that could be effectively marketed using that approach. Explain why each form of direct marketing is well suited to the product you have chosen.

Application Questions

1. Describe the link between personal selling and customer relationship management. How might decisions sales managers make when recruiting, training, motivating, and evaluating salespeople impact customer relationships? Apply your answers to the Procter & Gamble customer business-development sales organization described in the chapter.

2. Select a product or service with which you are familiar. Craft several "opening lines" to sell that product or service to a classmate or friend as a prospective buyer. After approaching the prospective buyer, evaluate your chosen opening lines. How effective were they at creating interest and curiosity?

3. The text notes that, surprisingly, many direct marketers are thriving in spite of new regulations such as the National Do-Not-Call Registry. In your opinion, how has such legislation hurt direct marketers? How has it helped?

Under the Hood: Focus on Technology

You have probably seen them popping up everywhere. There are kiosks at REI, in the mall, and at the airport. "The market demand for self-service [kiosk] technology touches virtually every industry including retail, hospitality, financial services, and beyond," says Greg Swistak, executive director of the Kiosks.org Association. Kiosks are offered by marketers as one more way to reach consumers directly. But these days, customers at kiosks can do much more than simply surf the Web. At the most recent Self-Service and Kiosk Show, many companies exhibited new technologies that will make kiosks more personal and more interactive. Livewire International showcased new kiosks that activate and dispense gift and travel cards. Hand Held Products now offers technology that allows direct mar-keters to target customers, creating one-to-one marketing offers. And, at the show, Kioware demonstrated a mobile kiosk, capable of offering passengers in taxicabs access to searchable maps and information on restaurants, nightlife, and hotels.*

1. Have you ever used a kiosk in a retail setting or at the airport? Describe how the kiosk impacted your customer experience?

2. How can direct marketers use kiosks, and the new technologies detailed above, to build customer relationships?

*See "Companies Display New Technology at the Self-Service and Kiosk Show," August 16, 2005, accessed at www.atmmarketplace.com.

Focus on Ethics

They come in the mail regularly, several a day for some consumers, with messages of hope and good fortune. Cover letters and authentic looking certificates shout, "You are already a winner!" Since the birth of direct marketing, sweepstakes and lotteries have helped companies deliver information to consumers about new products and marketing offers. For a sales pitch or direct marketing campaign to work, it must grab consumers' attention and build curiosity. But even for reputable and experienced marketers, walking the line between grabbing attention and acting appropriately can be tricky. Unfortunately, the widespread use of direct marketing communications has helped to disguise misleading statements as legitimate offers. As one columnist puts it, a "visit to the U.S. Postal Service Web site will provide a consumer with a list of mail-fraud schemes including: employment fraud, multilevel marketing, work-at-home, '900' telephone numbers, charity fraud, cut-rate health insurance, solicitations disguised as invoices, sweepstakes and lotteries, chain letters, free prizes and vacations, foreign lotteries by mail, government look-alike mail, prison pen pal money-order scams, and fraudulent health and medical products, to name just a few."

Unfortunately, the fraudulent solicitations work. Last year the FTC received nearly 400,000 complaints about direct-mail fraud. And the U.S. Postal Service estimates that consumers lose more than $120 million each year to international scams alone. Such experiences make consumers more suspicious of even legitimate offers that might interest them. So, direct marketers take matters of fraud and deception very seriously. On its Web site (www.dmaconsumers.org/sweepstakeshelp.html), the DMA advises U.S. citizens on their rights as consumers and offers advice on identifying fraudulent direct-mail offers.*

1. Is it possible to use sweepstakes and giveaways as a part of an ethical direct marketing campaign? What are some of the considerations marketers should make when using such promotions to sell a product?

2. Visit the DMA consumer Web site and learn more about the association's efforts to educate consumers. Do you think the direct marketing industry should monitor itself or is more government regulation required to protect consumers?

*See Susan E. Rice, "Scammers Target Most Trusting in Hopes of Stealing Easy Money," *The Chetek Alert*, July 20, 2005, accessed at www.zwire.com.

Videos

The Motorola video case that accompanies this chapter is located in Appendix 1 at the back of the book.

Chapter**14**

→ **AFTER STUDYING THIS CHAPTER, YOU SHOULD BE ABLE TO**

1. discuss how the digital age is affecting both consumers and the marketers who serve them

2. explain how companies have responded to the Internet and other powerful new technologies with e-business strategies, and how these strategies have resulted in benefits to both buyers and sellers

3. describe the four major e-marketing domains

4. discuss how companies go about conducting e-marketing to profitably deliver more value to customers

5. overview the promise and challenges that e-commerce presents for the future

Marketing in the Digital Age

Road Map Previewing the Concepts

You've come a long way on your marketing journey. You've learned that the aim of marketing is to create value *for* customers in order to capture value *from* consumers in return. So far, you've learned the fundamentals of how good marketing companies win, keep, and grow customers by understanding customer needs, designing customer-driven marketing strategies, constructing value-delivering marketing programs, and building customer and marketing partner relationships. In the final three chapters, we'll extend this concept to three special areas—marketing in the digital age, global marketing, and marketing ethics and social responsibility. Although we've visited these topics regularly in each previous chapter, because of their special importance, we will focus exclusively on them here.

In this chapter, we look into marketing in the rapidly changing digital environment. Marketing strategy and practice have undergone dramatic changes during the past decade. Major technological advances, including the explosion of the Internet, have had a major impact on buyers and the marketers who serve them. To thrive in this digital age—even to survive—marketers must rethink their strategies and adapt them to today's changing environment.

As a tune-up, let's first look at Amazon.com. In only a little more than a decade, Amazon.com has blossomed from an obscure dot-com upstart into one of the best-known names on the Internet. The only problem: This seemingly successful company has yet to convince investors that it can turn consistently good profits and returns to investors. As you read on, ask yourself: Will Amazon.com eventually achieve its goal of becoming the Wal-Mart of the Internet? Or will it learn that its Internet-only model that can never be truly profitable? Roll on and see.

Chances are, when you think of shopping on the Web, you think of Amazon.com. Amazon.com first opened its virtual doors in 1995, selling books out of founder Jeff Bezos's garage in suburban Seattle. It still sells books— *lots and lots* of books. But it now sells just about everything else as well, from music, videos, electronics, tools, housewares, apparel, and kids products to loose diamonds and Maine lobsters. "We have the Earth's Biggest Selection," declares the company's Web site.

In little more than a decade, Amazon.com has become one of the best-known names on the Web. In perfecting the art of online selling, it has also rewritten the rules of marketing. Its most ardent fans view Amazon.com as *the* model for businesses in the digital age. They predict that it will grow to become the Wal-Mart of the Internet. The skeptics aren't so certain—not everything has clicked smoothly for Amazon.com over its roller-coaster ten-year history.

Attracting customers and sales hasn't been the problem. Amazon.com's customer base has grown explosively to more than 49 million active customers in more than 220 countries. Sales have rocketed from a modest $15 million a year in 1996 to more than $6.9 billion today—an incredible 57 percent average year-over-year growth rate. So, what *is* the problem? It's summed up in what one analyst calls "a chronic Amazon sticking point: *profitability*."

Amazon.com didn't turn its first full-year profit until 2003. Doubters say that Amazon.com's Web-only model can never be truly profitable. Investors seem to share this concern. Amazon's stock price has fallen double digits percentages in each of the last two years, and it's still 70 percent off its 1999 high-water mark. What's more, say the skeptics, things will only get tougher in the years to come, as the Web pioneer faces increasing competition from a horde of other online merchants and from brick-and-mortar giants setting up their own Web stores.

No matter what your view of its future, there's little doubt that Amazon.com is an outstanding marketing company. To its core, the company is relentlessly customer driven. "The thing that drives everything is creating genuine value for customers," says founder Jeff Bezos. "If you focus on what customers want and build a relationship, they will allow you to make money." In a recent promotion in Japan, Bezos donned a delivery driver's uniform and went house to house with packages. His point: Everything at Amazon—from top to bottom—begins and ends with the customer.

Anyone at Amazon.com will tell you that the company wants to do much more than just sell books or DVDs or digital cameras. It wants to deliver a special *experience* to every customer. "The customer experience really matters," says Bezos. "We've focused on just having a better store, where it's easier to shop, where you can learn more about the products, where you have a bigger selection, and where you have the lowest prices. You combine all of that stuff together and people say, 'Hey, these guys really get it.' "

And they do get it. Most Amazon.com regulars feel a surprisingly strong relationship with the company, especially given the almost complete lack of actual human interaction. Amazon.com obsesses over making each customer's experience uniquely personal. For example, the Amazon.com Web site greets customers with their very own personalized home pages, and the site's. "We have recommendations for you" feature prepares personalized product recommendations. Amazon.com was first to use "collaborative filtering" technology, which sifts through each customer's past purchases and the purchasing patterns of customers with similar profiles to come up with personalized site content. "We want Amazon.com to be the right store for you as an individual," says Bezos. "If we have 49 million customers, we should have 49 million stores."

Visitors to Amazon.com's Web site receive a unique blend of benefits: huge selection, good value, convenience, and what Amazon vice president Jason Kilar calls "discovery." In books alone, for example, Amazon.com offers an easily searchable virtual selection of more than 3 million titles, 15 times more than in any physical bookstore. Good value comes in the form of reasonable prices, plus free delivery on orders over $25. And at Amazon.com, it's irresistibly convenient to buy. You can log on, find anything and everything you want, and order with a single mouse click, all in less time than it takes to find a parking space at the local mall.

But it's the "discovery" factor that makes the Amazon.com experience really special. Once on the Web site, you're compelled to stay for a while—looking, learning, and discovering. Amazon.com has become a kind of online community, in which customers can browse for products, research purchase alternatives, share opinions and reviews with other visitors, and chat online with authors and experts. In this way, Amazon.com does much more than just sell goods on the Web. It creates personalized customer relationships and satisfying online experiences. For two of the last three years, the American Customer Satisfaction Index gave Amazon "highest-ever" ratings in customer satisfaction for a service company, regardless of industry.

In fact, Amazon.com has become so good at managing online relationships that many traditional "brick-and-mortar" retailers are turning to Amazon for help in adding more "clicks" to their "bricks." For example, Amazon.com now partners with well-known retailers such as Target and Borders to help them run their Web interfaces. The brick-and-mortar partners handle purchasing and inventory; Amazon.com oversees the customer experience—maintaining the Web site, attracting customers, and managing customer service. Amazon.com has also formed alliances with hundreds of other retailers who sell their wares through the Amazon site. For example, Amazon's "apparel store" is more of a mall, featuring the products of partners such as Nordstrom, Macy's, JC Penney, Urban Outfitters, Eddie Bauer, and Sears-owned Lands' End. In all, 28 percent of Amazon's sales now come from independent merchants who sell through its site.

So, what do you think? Will Amazon become the Wal-Mart of the Web? Or will it end up chasing unprofitable growth with an Internet-only model that can never be truly profitable? Despite its incredible successes and recently-improving financials, until Amazon proves that it can be consistently profitable, the debate will continue. No doubt, Amazon faces some sobering challenges ahead. But whatever its fate, the Internet pioneer has forever changed the face of marketing. Amazon "set a very high bar for the [online] customer service experience," says an analyst. "I'm not sure that e-commerce would be as developed today if Amazon didn't exist."[1]

Recent technological advances have created a digital age. Widespread use of the Internet and other powerful new technologies are having a dramatic impact on marketers and buyers. In this chapter, we examine how marketing strategy and practice are changing to take advantage of today's new technologies.

The Digital Age

Much of the world's business today is carried out over digital networks that connect people and companies. **Intranets** are networks that connect people within a company to each other and to the company network. **Extranets** connect a company with its suppliers, distributors, and other outside partners. And the **Internet**, a vast public web of computer networks, connects users of all types all around the world to each other and to an amazingly large information repository.

With the creation of the World Wide Web and Web browsers in 1990s, the Internet was transformed from a mere communication tool into a certifiably revolutionary technology. The Internet continues to grow explosively. Last year, Internet penetration in the United States had reached 68 percent, with more than 202 million people now using the Internet. Some 14.6 percent of the world population—more than 938 million people worldwide—are now online. Not only are more people using the Web, they are increasingly moving faster when they get there. A recent study found that just under half of all U.S. households with Internet access now go online through high-speed broadband connections.[2]

This explosive worldwide growth in Internet usage forms the heart of the digital age. The Internet has been *the* revolutionary technology of the new millennium, empowering consumers and businesses alike. The Internet enables consumers and companies to access and share huge amounts of information with just a few mouse clicks. Recent studies have shown that more and more consumers

■ The digital age: Explosive worldwide growth has made the Internet a certifiably revolutionary technology, empowering consumers and businesses alike. Worldwide, almost a trillion people are now going online.

are accessing information on the Internet before making major life decisions. One in three consumers relies heavily on the Internet to gather information about choosing a school, buying a car, finding a job, dealing with a major illness, or making investment decisions. The average U.S. Internet user spends some 28 hours a month surfing the Web at home, plus another 76 hours a month at work.[3] As a result, to be competitive in today's new marketplace, companies must adopt Internet technology or risk being left behind.

The Internet and other digital technologies have given marketers a whole new way to reach and serve customers. The amazing success of early *click-only* companies—the so-called dot-coms such as Amazon.com, eBay, Expedia, and hundreds of others—caused existing *brick-and-mortar* manufacturers and retailers to reexamine how they served their markets. Now, almost all these traditional companies have set up their own online sales and communications channels, becoming *click-and-mortar* competitors. It's hard to find a company today that doesn't have a substantial Web presence.

Intranet
A network that connects people within a company to each other and to the company network.

Extranet
A network that connects a company with its suppliers and distributors.

Internet
A vast public web of computer networks, which connects users of all types all around the world to each other and to an amazingly large "information repository."

Marketing Strategy in the Digital Age

Conducting business in the digital age calls for a new model for marketing strategy and practice. The Internet is revolutionizing how companies create value for customers and build customer relationships. The digital age has fundamentally changed customers' notions of convenience, speed, price, product information, and service. Thus, today's marketing requires new thinking and action. Companies need to retain most of the skills and practices that have worked in the past. But they will also need to add major new competencies and practices if they hope to grow and prosper in the changing digital environment.

E-BUSINESS, E-COMMERCE, AND E-MARKETING IN THE DIGITAL AGE

E-business

The use of electronic platforms—intranets, extranets, and the Internet—to conduct a company's business.

E-business involves the use of electronic platforms—intranets, extranets, and the Internet—to conduct a company's business. Almost every company has set up a Web site to inform about and promote its products and services. Others use Web sites simply to build stronger customer relationships.

Most companies have also created intranets to help employees communicate with each other and to access information found in the company's systems. For example, some 14,000 employees regularly log on to the P&G intranet, mNet, to receive training and to research marketing news from around the world. And the Cheesecake Factory, a national restaurant chain, uses its intranet to offer training tips and help employees communicate during pre-shift meetings.[4] Companies also set up extranets with their major suppliers and distributors to enable information exchange, orders, transactions, and payments.

E-commerce

Buying and selling processes supported by electronic means, primarily the Internet.

E-commerce is more specific than e-business. E-business includes all electronics-based information exchanges within or between companies and customers. In contrast, e-commerce involves buying and selling processes supported by electronic means, primarily the Internet. *E-markets* are "market*spaces*," rather than physical market*places*. Sellers use e-markets to offer their products and services online. Buyers use them to search for information, identify what they want, and place orders using credit or other means of electronic payment.

E-marketing

The marketing side of e-commerce—company efforts to communicate about, promote, and sell products and services over the Internet.

E-commerce includes *e-marketing* and *e-purchasing* (*e-procurement*). **E-marketing** is the marketing side of e-commerce. It consists of company efforts to communicate about, promote, and sell products and services over the Internet. Thus, Amazon.com, L.L.Bean, and Dell conduct e-marketing at their Web sites. The flip side of e-marketing is e-purchasing, the buying side of e-commerce. It consists of companies purchasing goods, services, and information from online suppliers. In business-to-business buying, e-marketers and e-purchasers come together in huge e-commerce networks.

E-commerce and the Internet bring many benefits to both buyers and sellers. Let's review some of these major benefits.

■ Internet buying is easy and private. Final consumers can shop the world from home with few hassles; business buyers can learn about and obtain products and information without tying up time with salespeople.

BENEFITS TO BUYERS

Internet buying benefits both final buyers and business buyers in many ways. It can be *convenient*: Customers don't have to battle traffic, find parking spaces, and trek through stores and aisles to find and examine products. They can do comparative shopping by surfing Web sites. Web marketers never close their doors. Buying is *easy* and *private*: Customers encounter fewer buying hassles and don't have to face salespeople or open themselves up to persuasion and emotional pitches. Business buyers can learn about and buy products and services without waiting for and tying up time with salespeople.

In addition, the Internet often provides buyers with greater *product access and selection*. Unrestrained by physical boundaries, Web sellers can offer an almost unlimited selection to consumers almost anywhere in the world. Just compare the incredible selections offered by many Web merchants to the more meager assortments of their brick-and-mortar counterparts. For example, log onto Bulbs.com, "the Web's no. 1 light bulb superstore," and you'll have instant access to every imaginable kind of light bulb or lamp—incandescent bulbs, fluorescent bulbs, projection bulbs, surgical bulbs, automotive bulbs—you name it. No physical store could offer handy access to such a vast selection.

E-commerce channels also give buyers access to a wealth of comparative *information* about companies, products, and competitors. Good sites often provide more information in more useful forms than even the most solicitous salesperson can. For example, Amazon.com offers top-10 product lists, extensive product descriptions, expert and user product reviews, and recommendations based on customers' previous purchases.

Finally, online buying is *interactive* and *immediate*. Buyers often can interact with the seller's site to create exactly the configuration of information, products, or services they desire, then order or download them on the spot. Moreover, the Internet gives consumers a greater measure of control. Like nothing else before it, the Internet has empowered consumers. These days, for example, 64 percent of new car buyers bargain hunt online before visiting a dealership, arming themselves with car and cost information. This is the new reality of consumer control.[5]

BENEFITS TO SELLERS

E-commerce also yields many benefits to sellers. First, the Internet is a powerful tool for *customer relationship building*. Because of its one-to-one, interactive nature, companies can interact online with customers to learn more about specific needs and wants. In turn, online customers can ask questions and volunteer feedback. Based on this ongoing interaction, companies can increase customer value and satisfaction through product and service refinements.

The Internet and other electronic channels can also *reduce costs* and *increase speed and efficiency*. By using the Internet to link directly to suppliers, factories, distributors, and customers, businesses can cut costs and pass savings on to customers. Internet-only marketers Amazon.com avoid the expense of maintaining a store and the related costs of rent, insurance, and utilities. Because customers deal directly with sellers, online selling often results in lower costs and improved efficiencies for channel and logistics functions such as order processing, inventory handling, delivery, and trade promotion. Finally, communicating electronically often costs less than communicating on paper through the mail. For instance, a company can produce digital catalogs for much less than the cost of printing and mailing paper ones.

E-marketing can also offer greater *flexibility*. It allows marketers to make ongoing adjustments to its offers and programs, or to make immediate and timely announcements and offers. For example, Southwest Airlines' DING! application takes advantage of the flexibility and immediacy of the Web to share low-fare offers directly with customers:[6]

■ Southwest Airlines "DING!" application takes advantage of the flexibility and immediacy of the Web to share low-fare offers directly with customers.

When Jim Jacobs hears a "ding" coming from his desktop computer, he thinks about discount air fares like the $122 ticket he recently bought for a flight from Tampa to Baltimore on Southwest Airlines. Several times a day, Southwest sends Jacobs and hundreds of thousands of other computer users discounts through a new application called DING! "If I move quickly," says Jacobs, a corporate telecommunications salesman who lives in Tampa, "I can usually save a lot of money." The fare to Baltimore underbid the airline's own Web site by $36, he says. DING! lets Southwest bypass the reservations system and pass bargain fares directly to interested customers. Eventually, DING! may even allow Southwest to customize fare offers based on each customer's unique characteristics and travel preferences. For now, DING! gets a Southwest icon on the customer's desktop and lets the airline build relationships with customers by helping them to save money. Following its DING! launch in early 2005, Southwest experienced its two biggest online sales days ever. In the first four months, the program produced more than $20 million worth of fares.

Finally, the Internet is a truly *global* medium that allows buyers and sellers to click from one country to another in seconds. A Web surfer from Paris or Istanbul can access an online L.L.Bean catalog as easily as someone living in Freeport, Maine, the direct retailer's hometown. Even small e-marketers find that they have ready access to global markets.

E-Marketing Domains

The four major e-marketing domains are shown in Figure 14.1 and discussed below. They include B2C (business to consumer), B2B (business to business), C2C (consumer to consumer), and C2B (consumer to business).

B2C (BUSINESS TO CONSUMER)

B2C (business-to-consumer) e-commerce
The online selling of goods and services to final consumers.

The popular press has paid the most attention to **B2C (business-to-consumer) e-commerce**—the online selling of goods and services to final consumers. Online consumer buying continues to grow at a healthy rate. Last year, U.S. consumers spent $117 billion online and consumer spending online is expected to exceed $316 billion by 2010, accounting for 12 percent of total retail sales. Today's consumers can buy almost anything online—from clothing, kitchen gadgets, and computers and cars.[7]

Online Consumers   In its early days, the Internet was populated largely by pasty-faced computer nerds or young, techy, upscale male professionals. As the Web has matured, however, Internet demographics have changed significantly. As more and more people find their way onto the Web, the cyberspace population is becoming more mainstream and diverse. The Web now offers marketers a palette of different kinds of consumers seeking different kinds of online experiences.

These days, it seems, just about everybody is logging on. For example, the Web now reaches consumers in all age groups. Children and teens are going online more than any other age group. Whereas 66 percent of American adults now use the Internet, 87 percent of teens go online; half are online daily.[8] The "net kids" and teen segments have attracted a host of e-marketers.

At the other end of the age spectrum, consumers aged 50 and older make up almost 20 percent of the online population. And more than 22 million Americans over the age of 65 are expected to buy online by 2009. Whereas younger groups are more likely to use the Internet for entertainment and socializing, older Websters go online for more serious matters. For example, 49 percent of users ages 50 to 58 have tried online banking compared to 38 percent of those ages 18 to 27. Surfing seniors tend to be well educated and well-off. More than 75 percent have attended college and 25 percent have annual incomes exceeding $65,000. Thus, older Internet users make an attractive market for many Web businesses, ranging from florists and automotive retailers to travel sites and financial services providers.[9]

FIGURE 14.1
E-Marketing Domains

	Targeted to consumers	Targeted to businesses
Initiated by business	B2C (business to consumer)	B2B (business to business)
Initiated by consumer	C2C (consumer to consumer)	C2B (consumer to business)

■ Online consumers: As more and more people find their way onto the Web, the online population is becoming more mainstream and diverse. The Web now offers marketers a palette of different kinds of online experiences.

Internet consumers differ from traditional offline consumers in their approaches to buying and in their responses to marketing. The exchange process via the Internet has become more customer initiated and customer controlled. Traditional marketing targets a somewhat passive audience. In contrast, e-marketing targets people who actively select which Web sites they will visit and what marketing information they will receive about which products and under what conditions. Thus, the new world of e-commerce requires new marketing approaches.

B2C Web Sites   Consumers can find a Web site for buying almost anything. The Internet is most useful for products and services when the shopper seeks greater ordering convenience or lower costs. The Internet also provides great value to buyers looking for information about differences in product features and value. However, consumers find the Internet less useful when buying products that must be touched or examined in advance. Still, even here there are exceptions. For example, who would have thought that tens of thousands of people would order automobiles online each year without seeing and trying them first?

People now go online to order a wide range of goods—clothing from Gap or L.L.Bean, books or electronics from Amazon.com, furniture from Ethan Allen, major appliances from Sears, flowers from Calyx & Corolla, or even home mortgages from Quicken Loans.[10]

At Quicken Loans (www.quickenloans.com), prospective borrowers receive a high-tech, high-touch, one-stop mortgage shopping experience. At the site, customers can research a wide variety of home-financing and refinancing

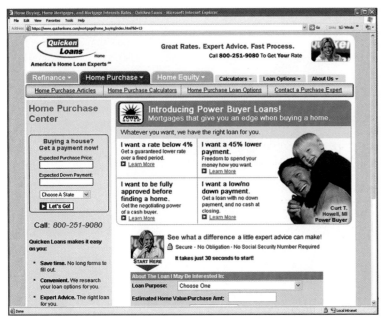

■ B2C Web sites: People now go online to order a wide range of goods and services, even home mortgages.

B2B (business-to-business) e-commerce

Using B2B trading networks, auction sites, spot exchanges, online product catalogs, barter sites, and other online resources to reach new customers, serve current customers more effectively, and obtain buying efficiencies and better prices.

Open trading exchanges

Huge e-marketspaces in which B2B buyers and sellers find each other online, share information, and complete transactions efficiently.

Private trading exchanges

B2B trading networks that link a particular seller with its own trading partners.

options, apply for a mortgage, and receive quick loan approval—all without leaving the comfort and security of their homes. The site provides useful interactive tools that help borrowers decide how much house they can afford, whether to rent or buy, whether to refinance a current mortgage, the economics of fixing up their current homes rather than moving, and much more. Customers can receive advice by phone or by chatting online with one of 2,700 mortgage experts and sign up for later e-mail rate updates. Quicken Loans closed more than $12 billion in mortgage loans last year.

B2B (BUSINESS TO BUSINESS)

Although the popular press has given the most attention to business-to-consumer (B2C) Web sites, consumer goods sales via the Web are dwarfed by **B2B (business-to-business) e-commerce**. In 2003, worldwide B2B e-commerce reached almost $4 trillion, compared with just $282 billion in 2000.[11] B2B marketers use trading networks, auction sites, spot exchanges, online product catalogs, barter sites, and other online resources to reach new customers, serve current customers more effectively, and obtain buying efficiencies and better prices.

Most major business-to-business marketers now offer product information, customer purchasing, and customer support services online. For example, corporate buyers can visit Sun Microsystems' Web site (www.sun.com), select detailed descriptions of Sun's products and solutions, request sales and service information, and interact with staff members. Some major companies conduct almost all of their business on the Web. Networking equipment and software maker Cisco Systems takes more than 80 percent of its orders over the Internet.

Some B2B e-commerce takes place in **open trading exchanges**—huge e-marketspaces in which buyers and sellers find each other online, share information, and complete transactions efficiently. For example, PlasticsNet.com, an Internet marketplace for the plastics product industry, connects more than 90,000 monthly visitors with more than 200 suppliers. However, despite the use of such open e-marketspaces, a lion's share of all B2B e-commerce is conducted through private sites. Increasingly, online sellers are setting up their own **private trading exchanges**. Open trading exchanges facilitate transactions between a wide range of online buyers and sellers. In contrast, a private trading exchange links a particular seller with its own trading partners.

Rather than simply completing transactions, private exchanges give sellers greater control over product presentation and allow them to build deeper relationships with buyers and sellers by providing value-added services. As an example, take Trane Company, a maker of air-conditioning and heating systems:

> For the past few years, Trane . . . has been red-hot with the business-to-business Internet crowd. Each of the horde of B2B [open trading] exchanges targeting the construction industry wants Trane to join. "Construction.com, MyPlant.com, MyFacility.com—we get up to five calls a week," says James A. Bierkamp, head of Trane's e-business unit. But after some consideration, Bierkamp did not see what any of those [third-party] e-marketplaces could offer that his company couldn't do itself. So Trane rolled out its own private exchange, which allows its 5,000 dealers to browse, buy equipment, schedule deliveries, and process warranties. The site lets Trane operate with greater efficiency and trim processing costs—without losing control of the presentation of its brand name or running the risks of rubbing elbows with competitors in an open exchange. "Why let another party get between us and our customers?'" asks Bierkamp.[12]

C2C (CONSUMER TO CONSUMER)

Much **C2C (consumer-to-consumer) e-commerce** and communication occurs on the Web between interested parties over a wide range of products and subjects. In some cases, the Internet provides an excellent means by which consumers can buy or exchange goods or information directly with one another. For example, eBay, Amazon.com Auctions, and other auction sites offer popular marketspaces for displaying and selling almost anything, from art and antiques, coins and stamps, and jewelry to computers and consumer electronics.

EBay's C2C online trading community of more than 150 million registered users worldwide (equal to the combined populations of France, Spain, and Britain!) transacted nearly $40 billion in trades last year, about one-quarter of all e-commerce sales for the year. On any given day, the company's Web site lists more than 16 million items up for auction in more than 45,000 categories. Such C2C sites give people access to much larger audiences than the local flea market or newspaper classifieds (which, by the way, are now also going online). Interestingly, based on its huge success in the C2C market, eBay has now attracted a large number of B2C sellers, ranging from small businesses peddling their regular wares to large businesses liquidating excess inventory at auction.[13]

In other cases, C2C involves interchanges of information through Internet forums that appeal to specific special-interest groups. Such activities may be organized for commercial or noncommercial purposes. An example is Web logs, or *blogs*, online journals where people post their thoughts, usually on a narrowly defined topic. Blogs can be about anything, from politics or baseball to haiku or car repair.

Today's blogosphere consists of more than 10 million blogs, with 40,000 new ones popping up every day. About 27 percent of American Web users now read blogs regularly.[14] Most blogs are painfully primitive, amounting to little more than personal journals that reach very few people. However, some blogs attract large audiences. "In a way," says one observer, "blogs represent everything the Web was always supposed to be: a mass medium controlled by the masses, in which getting heard depends solely on having something to say and the moxie to say it."[15]

Many marketers are now tapping into blogs as a medium for reaching carefully targeted consumers. One way is to advertise on an existing blog or to post content there. For example, Web-savvy Nike created an "Art of Speed" microsite on blog site Gawker.com. The Art of Speed showcased the work of 15 innovative filmmakers who interpreted the idea of speed. The showcase gave Nike high-quality exposure within a small audience. "Gawker is a very influential site among a community that appreciates creativity, film, and interesting projects and who are going to dig deeper and find out the back story," said Nike's communications manager. "In some circles, Gawker has more authenticity than Nike," says an online communications analyst. "That's why blogs really work for advertisers, because of the credibility of the blog."[16]

Other companies set up their own blogs. For example, Procter & Gamble launched a blog site (sparklebodyspray.com) to promote its Secret Sparkle Body Spray to tween girls (seven- to twelve-year-olds). The site features character blogs based on each of four Sparkle Body Spray Girls—Rose, Vanilla, Tropical, and Peach. Each character's writing takes on a personality similar to a real pre-teen girl. They blog about things girls are interested

C2C (consumer-to-consumer) e-commerce
Online exchanges of goods and information between final consumers.

■ Web logs: Nike created an "Art of Speed" microsite on blog site Gawker.com, giving it high-quality exposure within a small, select audience.

in, from fashion to celebrity gossip to sports. Says Secret's brand manager, "the character blog concept [allows] each visitor to create her own experience."[17]

As a marketing tool, blogs offer some advantages. They can offer a fresh, original, personal, and cheap way to reach today's fragmented audiences. However, the blogosphere is cluttered and difficult to control. "Blogs may help companies bond with consumers in exciting new ways, but they won't help them control the relationship," says a blog expert. Such Web journals remain largely a C2C medium. "If anything, blogs will continue tipping the balance of power toward the consumer," says the expert. "That isn't to suggest companies can't influence the relationship or leverage blogs to engage in a meaningful relationship, but the consumer will remain in control."

In all, C2C means that online buyers don't just consume product information—increasingly, they create it. They join Internet interest groups to share information, with the result that "word of Web" is joining "word of mouth" as an important buying influence. Word about good companies and products travels fast. Word about bad companies and products travels even faster. Many sites, including eComplaints.com, ConsumerReview.com, and BadDealings.com, have cropped up to provide consumers a forum in which to air complaints and share information about product and service experiences.

C2B (CONSUMER TO BUSINESS)

The final e-commerce domain is **C2B (consumer-to-business) e-commerce**. Thanks to the Internet, today's consumers are finding it easier to communicate with companies. Most companies now invite prospects and customers to send in suggestions and questions via company Web sites. Beyond this, rather than waiting for an invitation, consumers can search out sellers on the Web, learn about their offers, initiate purchases, and give feedback. Using the Web, consumers can even drive transactions with businesses, rather than the other way around. For example, using Priceline.com, would-be buyers bid for airline tickets, hotel rooms, rental cars, and even home mortgages, leaving the sellers to decide whether to accept their offers.

Consumers can also use Web sites such as PlanetFeedback.com to ask questions, offer suggestions, lodge complaints, ask questions, or deliver compliments to companies. The site provides letter templates for consumers to use based on their moods and reasons for contacting the company. The site then forwards the letters to the customer service manager at each company and helps to obtain a response. "About 80 percent of the companies respond to complaints, some within an hour," says a PlanetFeedback spokesperson.[18]

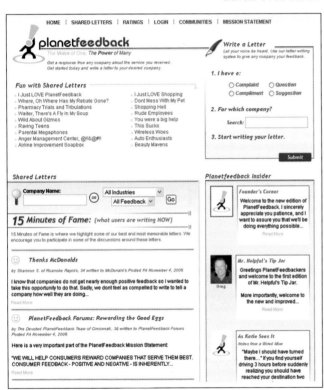

■ C2B e-commerce: Consumers can use Web sites such as PlanetFeedback.com to ask questions, offer suggestions, lodge complaints, or deliver compliments to companies.

C2B (consumer-to-business) e-commerce

Online exchanges in which consumers search out sellers, learn about their offers, and initiate purchases, sometimes even driving transaction terms.

Marketing on the Web

Companies of all types are now marketing online. In this section, we first discuss different types of e-marketers shown in Figure 14.2. Then, we examine how companies go about conducting online marketing.

CLICK-ONLY VERSUS CLICK-AND-MORTAR E-MARKETERS

The Internet gave birth to a new species of e-marketers—the *click-only* dot-coms—which operate only online without any brick-and-mortar market presence. In addition, most traditional *brick-and-mortar* companies have now added e-marketing operations, transforming themselves into *click-and-mortar* competitors.

Click-Only Companies **Click-only companies** come in many shapes and sizes. They include *e-tailers*, dot-coms that sell products and services directly to final buyers via the Internet. Examples include Amazon.com, Expedia, and Wine.com. The click-only group also includes s*earch engines* and *portals,* such as Yahoo!, Google, MSN, which began as search engines and later added services such as news, weather, stock reports, entertainment, and storefronts hoping to become the first port of entry to the Internet. *Shopping or price comparison sites,* such as Froogle.com, Yahoo! Shopping, and Bizrate.com, give instant product and price comparisons from thousands of vendors.

Internet service providers (ISPs) such as AOL and Earthlink are click-only companies that provide Internet and e-mail connections for a fee. *Transaction sites,* such as auction site eBay, take commissions for transactions conducted on their sites. Finally, various *content sites*, such as *New York Times* on the Web (www.nytimes.com), ESPN.com, and Encyclopedia Britannica Online, provide financial, news, research, and other information.

The hype surrounding such click-only Web businesses reached astronomical levels during the "dot-com gold rush" of the late 1990s, when avid investors drove dot-com stock prices to dizzying heights. However, the investing frenzy collapsed in the year 2000, and many high-flying, overvalued dot-coms came crashing back to Earth. Even some of the strongest and most attractive e-tailers—eToys.com, Pets.com, Furniture.com, Garden.com—filed for bankruptcy. Survivors such as Amazon.com and Priceline.com saw their stock values plunge.

Dot-coms failed for many reasons. Some rushed into the market without proper research or planning. Often, their primary goal was simply to launch an initial public offering (IPO) while the market was hot. Many relied too heavily on spin and hype instead of developing sound marketing strategies. They spent lavishly offline on mass marketing to attract new customers to their sites instead of building loyalty and purchasing among current customers. As one industry watcher concluded, many dot-coms failed because they "had dumb-as-dirt business models, not because the Internet lacks the power to enchant and delight customers in ways hitherto unimaginable."[19]

Now on firmer footing, many click-only dot-coms are surviving and even prospering in today's marketspace. "You needed time to heal the wounds" from the dot-com collapse of 2000, says one analyst. "Well, we've had enough time. The Internet has come back."[20] Yet, for many dot-coms, the Web is still not a highly profitable proposition. Such companies should start by rethinking how they create value for customers. How

Click-only companies
The so-called dot-coms, which operate only online without any brick-and-mortar market presence.

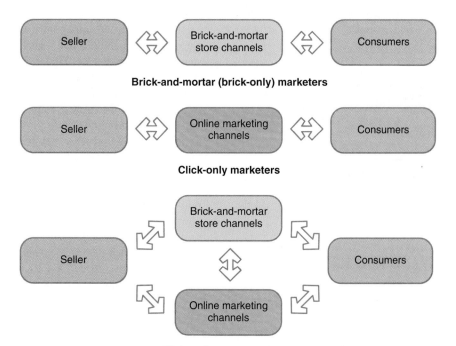

Brick-and-mortar (brick-only) marketers

Click-only marketers

Click-and-mortar marketers

FIGURE 14.2
Types of E-Marketers

can they leverage their Web-only models to compete effectively against traditional brick-and-mortar competitors on the one hand, and against the newer click-and-mortar competitors on the other?

Click-and-Mortar Companies As the Internet grew, some established companies rushed to open Web sites providing information about their companies and products. However, most resisted adding e-commerce to their sites. They worried that this would produce *channel conflict*—that by selling their products or services online they would be competing with their offline retailers and agents. For example, Hewlett Packard feared that its retailers would drop HP's computers if the company sold the same computers directly online. Merrill Lynch hesitated to introduce online stock trading fearing that its own brokers would rebel. Even store-based bookseller Barnes & Noble delayed opening its online site to challenge Amazon.com.

These companies struggled with the question of how to conduct online sales without cannibalizing the sales of their own stores, resellers, or agents. However, they soon realized that the risks of losing business to online competitors were even greater than the risks of angering channel partners. If they didn't cannibalize these sales, online competitors soon would. Thus, most established brick-and-mortar companies are now prospering as **click-and-mortar companies**.

For example, Office Depot's more than 1,000 office-supply superstores rack up annual sales of $13.5 billion in more than 23 countries. But you might be surprised to learn that Office Depot's fastest recent growth has come not from its traditional "brick-and-mortar" channels, but from the Internet.

> Whereas Office Depot's store sales have flattened lately, its online sales have soared, now accounting for almost 23 percent of total sales. Office Depot is now the third largest e-tailer in the world—behind Amazon.com and Dell. Selling on the Web lets Office Depot build deeper, more personalized relationships with customers large and small. "Contract customers"—the 80,000 or so larger businesses that have negotiated relationships with Office Depot—enjoy customized online ordering that includes company-specific product lists and pricing. For example, General Electric or Procter & Gamble can create lists of approved office products at discount prices, and then let company departments or even individuals do their own purchasing. This reduces ordering costs, cuts through the red tape, and speeds up the ordering process for customers. At the same time, it encourages companies to use Office Depot as a sole source for office supplies. Even the smallest companies find 24-hour-a-day online ordering easier and more efficient. Importantly, Office Depot's Web operations don't steal from store sales. Instead, the OfficeDepot.com site actually builds store traffic by helping customers find a local store and check stock. In return, the local store promotes the Web site through in-store kiosks. If customers don't find what they need on the shelves, they can quickly order it via the Web from the kiosk. Thus, Office Depot now offers a full range of contact points and delivery modes—online, by phone or fax, and in the store. No click-only or brick-only seller can match the call, click, or visit convenience and support afforded by Office Depot's click-and-mortar model.[21]

Most click-and-mortar marketers have found ways to resolve channel conflicts. For example, Gibson Guitars found that although

Click-and-mortar companies
Traditional brick-and-mortar companies that have added e-marketing to their operations.

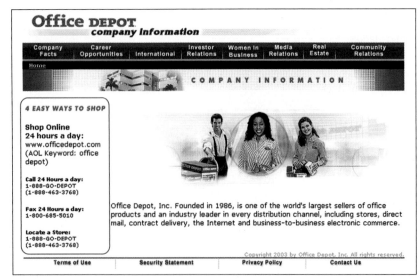

■ Click-and-mortar marketing: No click-only or brick-only seller can match the call, click, or visit convenience and support afforded by Office Depot's "4 easy ways to shop."

its dealers were outraged when it tried to sell guitars directly to consumers, the dealers didn't object to direct sales of accessories such as guitar strings and parts. Avon worried that direct online sales might cannibalize the business of its Avon ladies, who had developed close relationships with their customers. Fortunately, Avon's research showed little overlap between existing customers and potential Web customers. Avon shared this finding with the reps and then moved into online marketing. As an added bonus for the reps, Avon also offered to help them set up their own Web sites.

Despite potential channel conflict issues, many click-and-mortar companies are now having more online success than their click-only competitors. In fact, in a recent ranking of the top 50 online retail sites, only 15 were click-only retailers, while the others were multichannel retailers.[22]

What gives the click-and-mortar companies an advantage? Established companies such as Best Buy, Blockbuster, Fidelity, and Office Depot have known and trusted brand names and greater financial resources. They have large customer bases, deeper industry knowledge and experience, and good relationships with key suppliers. By combining online marketing and established brick-and-mortar operations, they can offer customers more options.

For example, consumers can choose the convenience and assortment of 24-hour-a-day online shopping, the more personal and hands-on experience of in-store shopping, or both. Customers can buy merchandise online, and then easily return unwanted goods to a nearby store. For example, those wanting to do business with Fidelity Investments can call a Fidelity agent on the phone, go online to the company's Web site, or visit the local Fidelity branch office. This lets Fidelity issue a powerful invitation in its advertising: "Call, click, or visit Fidelity Investments."

 Linking the Concepts

Pause here and cool your engine for a bit. Think about the relative advantages and disadvantages of *click-only*, *brick-and-mortar only*, and *click-and-mortar* retailers.

- Visit the Amazon.com Web site. Search for a specific book or DVD—perhaps one that's not too well known—and go through the buying process.
- Now visit www.bn.com and shop for the same book or video. Then visit a Barnes & Noble store and shop for the item there.

What advantages does Amazon.com have over Barnes & Noble? What disadvantages? How does your local independent book store, with its store-only operations, fare against these two competitors?

SETTING UP AN ONLINE MARKETING PRESENCE

Clearly all companies need to consider moving online. Companies can conduct e-marketing in any of the four ways shown in Figure 14.3: creating a Web site, placing ads and promotions online, setting up or participating in Web communities, or using e-mail.

Creating a Web Site For most companies, the first step in conducting e-marketing is to create a Web site. However, beyond simply creating a Web site, marketers must design an attractive site and find ways to get consumers to visit the site, stay around, and come back often.

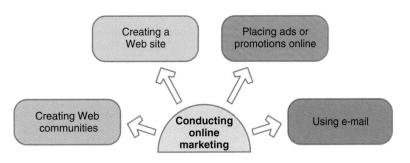

FIGURE 14.3
Setting Up for Online Marketing

Types of Web Sites. Web sites vary greatly in purpose and content. The most basic type is a **corporate Web site**. These sites are designed to build customer goodwill and to supplement other sales channels, rather than to sell the company's products directly. For example, although you can buy ice cream and other items at the gift shop on benjerry.com, the site's primary purpose is to enhance customer relationships. At the site, you can learn all about Ben & Jerry's company philosophy, products, and locations. Or you can visit the Fun Stuff area and send a free E-card to a friend, subscribe to the Chunk Mail newsletter, or while away time playing Scooper Challenge or Virtual Checkers.

Corporate Web site
A Web site designed to build customer goodwill and to supplement other sales channels, rather than to sell the company's products directly.

■ Corporate Web site: Although you can buy some ice cream at the Ben & Jerry's Web site, the site's primary purpose is to enhance customer relationships. At the site, you can learn all about the Ben & Jerry's company and do lots of "fun-related stuff."

Marketing Web site
A Web site that engages consumers in interactions that will move them closer to a direct purchase or other marketing outcome.

Corporate Web sites typically offer a rich variety of information and other features in an effort to answer customer questions, build closer customer relationships, and generate excitement about the company. They generally provide information about the company's history, its mission and philosophy, and the products and services that it offers. They might also tell about current events, company personnel, financial performance, and employment opportunities. Most corporate Web sites also provide entertainment features to attract and hold visitors. Finally, the site might also provide opportunities for customers to ask questions or make comments through e-mail before leaving the site.

Other companies create a **marketing Web site**. These sites engage consumers in an interaction that will move them closer to a direct purchase or other marketing outcome. Such sites might include a catalog, shopping tips, and promotional features such as coupons, sales events, or contests. For example, visitors to SonyStyle.com can search through dozens of categories of Sony products, review detailed features and specifications lists for specific items, read expert product reviews, and check out the latest hot deals. They can place an order for the desired Sony products online and pay by credit card, all with a few mouse clicks. Companies aggressively promote their marketing Web sites in offline print and broadcast advertising and through "banner-to-site" ads that pop up on other Web sites.

MINI USA operates a marketing Web site at www.miniusa.com. Once a potential customer clicks in, the carmaker wastes no time trying to turn the inquiry into a sale, and then into a long-term relationship. The site offers a garage full of useful information and interactive selling features, including detailed and fun descriptions of current MINI models, tools for designing your very own MINI, information on dealer locations and services, and even tools for tracking your new MINI from factory to delivery.

Before Angela DiFabio bought her MINI Cooper last September, she spent untold hours on the company's Web site, playing with dozens of possibilities before coming up with the perfect combination: A chili-pepper-red exterior, white racing stripes on the hood, and a "custom rally badge bar" on the grill. When DiFabio placed her order with her dealer, the same build-your-own tool—and all the price and product details it provided—left her feeling like she was getting a fair deal. "He even used the site to order my car," she says. While she waited for her Mini to arrive, DiFabio logged on to Mini's Web site every day, this time using its "Where's My Baby?" tracking tool to follow her car, like an expensive FedEx package, from the factory in Britain to its delivery. "To be able to check the process made the wait exciting. It definitely gave me a feeling of control in the process," says DiFabio. It's not that Mini's technology is groundbreaking. Rather, it makes an impact on the customer experience because of how it's integrated with the brand: It's fun, it's individual, it makes users feel like part of the clan. The Web site does more than just provide information or sell products or services. It keeps customers engaged, and when they're more engaged, they're usually happier, too.[23]

Designing Effective Web Sites. Creating a Web site is one thing; getting people to *visit* the site is another. The key is to create enough value and excitement to get consumers to come to the site, stick around, and come back again. Today's Web users are quick to abandon any Web site that doesn't measure up. "Whether people are online for work reasons or for personal reasons," says a Web design expert, "if a Web site doesn't meet their expectations, two-thirds say they don't return—now or ever. They'll visit you and leave and you'll never know. We call it the Internet death penalty."[24] This means that companies must constantly update their sites to keep them current, fresh, and useful. Doing so involves time and expense, but the expense is necessary if the e-marketer wishes to cut through the increasing online clutter.

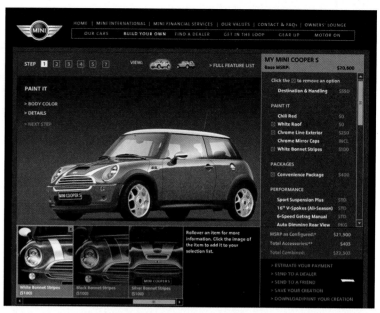

■ The MINI marketing Web site does more than just provide information or sell cars: It keeps customers engaged, from designing their very own MINI to tracking it from the factory to delivery.

In addition, many online marketers spend heavily on good old-fashioned advertising and other offline marketing avenues to attract visitors to their sites. For example, Mitsubishi recently ran a series of ads to draw visitors to its Galant Web site. The ad featured a cliffhanger of a crash-avoidance test comparing the maneuverability of a Galant GTS versus a Toyota Camry—to find out what happened, viewers had to go to the Web site. The ads attracted 1.6 million site visits.[25]

For some types of products, attracting visitors is easy. Consumers buying new cars, computers, or financial services will be open to information and marketing initiatives from sellers. Marketers of lower-involvement products, however, may face a difficult challenge in attracting Web site visitors. If you're in the market for a computer and you see a banner ad that says, "The top 10 computers under $800," you'll likely click on the banner. But what kind of ad would get you to visit a site like dentalfloss.com?

For low-interest products, the company can create a corporate Web site to answer customer questions, build goodwill and excitement, supplement selling efforts through other channels, and collect customer feedback. For example, although Wrigley's LifeSavers Candystand Web site doesn't sell candy, it does generate a great deal of consumer excitement and sales support:

The highly entertaining LifeSavers Candystand.com Web site, teeming with free videogames, endless sweepstakes, and sampling offers, has cast a fresh face on a brand that kid consumers once perceived as a stodgy adult confection. Visitors to the site—mostly children and teenagers—are not just passing through. They're clicking the mouse for an average 27-minute stay playing Super Swish, Match Maker, Stingin' Red Ants Run, Mini Golf Classic, Cool Darts, and dozens of other arcade-style games. All the while, they're soaking in a LifeSavers aura swirling with information about products. "Our philosophy is to create an exciting online experience that reflects the fun and quality associated with the Life-Savers brands," says the company's manager of new media. "For the production cost of about two television spots we have a marketing vehicle that lives 24 hours a day, seven days a week, 365 days a year."

While Candystand.com has not directly sold a single roll of candy, the buzz generated by the site makes it an ideal vehicle for offering consumers their first glimpse of a new product, usually with an offer to get free samples by mail. In addition, LifeSavers reps use the site as sales leverage to help seal distribution deals when they talk with retailers. And the site offers LifeSavers an efficient channel for gathering customer feedback. Its "What Do You Think?" feature has generated hundreds of thousands of responses since the site launched six years ago. "It's instant communication that we pass along directly to our brand people," says the manager. Comments collected from the Web site have resulted in improved packaging of one LifeSavers product and the resurrection of the abandoned flavor of another.[26]

A key challenge is designing a Web site that is attractive on first view and interesting enough to encourage repeat visits. The early text-based Web sites have largely been replaced in recent years by graphically sophisticated Web sites that provide text, sound, and animation (for examples, see www.looneytunes.com or www.nike.com). To attract new visitors and to encourage revisits, suggests one expert, e-marketers should pay close attention to the seven *C*s of effective Web site design:[27]

1. *Context:* the site's layout and design
2. *Content:* the text, pictures, sound, and video that the Web site contains
3. *Community:* the ways that the site enables user-to-user communication
4. *Customization:* the site's ability to tailor itself to different users or to allow users to personalize the site
5. *Communication:* the ways the site enables site-to-user, user-to-site, or two-way communication
6. *Connection:* the degree that the site is linked to other sites
7. *Commerce:* the site's capabilities to enable commercial transactions

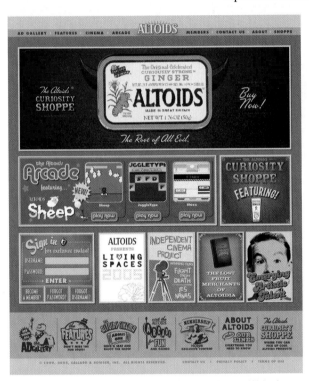

■ Effective Web sites: Applying the 7Cs of effective Web site design, is this a good site (see www.altoids.com)?

And to keep customers coming back to the site, companies need to embrace yet another "*C*"—constant change.

At the very least, a Web site should be easy to use and physically attractive. Ultimately, however, Web sites must also be *useful*. "The bottom line: People seek substance over style, usefulness over flash," says one analyst. "They want to get what they want quickly. Surfers should know almost immediately upon accessing your site why they should stick around, what's in it for them."[28] Thus, effective Web sites contain deep and useful information, interactive tools that help buyers find and evaluate products of interest, links to other related sites, changing promotional offers, and entertaining features that lend relevant excitement.

From time to time, a company needs to reassess its Web site's attractiveness and usefulness. One way is to invite the opinion of site-design experts. But a better way is to have users themselves evaluate what they like and dislike about the site. For example, women's dancewear and activewear maker Danskin asked customers for help in making its Web site more useful:

Danskin's first Web site didn't exactly set the dance world spinning on its toes. To avoid conflicts with the firm's traditional brick-and-mortar retailers, the site began with only one product line. When Danskin decided to expand the Web site two years later, it did more than just add merchandise to the previously hastily designed site. Instead, it placed a customer-satisfaction survey on its site. Random customers receive a pop-up window that gathers instant reactions from customers about what's good or bad about their online shopping experience, allowing Danskin to make midcourse corrections. Within six weeks of incorporating the customer-satisfaction surveys, Danskin learned that site navigation was one of the biggest sticking points for customers. After spending only 15 minutes making site changes, Danskin immediately began seeing online sales increase. Customer feedback led to regular additional changes. "Customers for the most part want to share their experiences and help you build a better site," says Danskin's vice president of sales operations.[29]

Placing Ads and Promotions Online   As consumers spend more and more time on the Internet, many companies are shifting more of their marketing dollars to **online advertising** to build their brands or to attract visitors to their Web sites. Last year, U.S. companies spent more than $12 billion on online advertising, up 25 percent over the previous year. Online ad spending will jump to more than $19 billion by 2010, representing some 8 percent of all ad spending, rivaling the amount spent on cable/satellite TV and radio.[30] Here, we discuss forms of online advertising and promotion and their future.

Online advertising
Advertising that appears while consumers are surfing the Web, including banners, interstitials, pop-ups, and other forms.

Forms of Online Advertising.   Online ads might appear anywhere on an Internet user's screen. The most common form of online advertising is the *banner ad*, banner-shaped ads found at the top, bottom, left, right, or center of a Web page. Banners go by many names, including *tickers* (banners that move across the screen), skyscrapers (tall, skinny banner ads at the side of a Web page), and rectangles (block ads appearing in the middle of the screen). Most banner ads contain links to the advertiser's Web site. For instance, a Web surfer looking up airline schedules or fares might encounter a flashing banner that screams, "Rent a car from Alamo and get up to 2 days free!" Clicking on the ad takes consumers to the Alamo Web site, where they can redeem the promotion.

Interstitials are online ads that appear between screen changes on a Web site, especially while a new screen is loading. For example, visit www.marketwatch.com and you'll probably see a 10-second ad for Visa, Verizon, or another sponsor before the homepage loads. *Pop-up*s are online ads that appear suddenly in a new window in front of the window being viewed. Such ads can multiply out of control, creating a major annoyance. As a result, Internet services and Web browser providers have developed applications that let users block most pop-ups. But not to worry. Many advertisers have now developed *pop-unders*, new windows that evade pop-up blockers by appearing behind the page you're viewing.

Another hot growth area for online advertising is *search-related ads* (or *contextual advertising*), in which text-based ads and links appear alongside search engine results on sites such as Google and Yahoo! (see Marketing at Work 14.1). For example, search Google for "HDTV" and you'll see inconspicuous ads for 10 or more advertisers, ranging from Circuit City, Best Buy, and Amazon.com to Dish Network and Nextag.com. Advertisers pay only if consumers click on the links. Companies will pay an estimated $1 billion on such ads by 2008.[31]

Finally, with the increase in broadband Internet access in American homes, many companies are developing exciting new *rich media* advertisements, which incorporate animation, video, sound, and interactivity. Rich media ads attract and hold consumer attention better than traditional banner ads. They employ techniques such as float, fly, and snapback—animations that jump out and sail over the Web page before retreating to their original space. But many media rich ads do more than create a little bit of jumping animation. For example, to attract would-be commodity traders to its Web site, the Chicago Board of Trade runs a small media-rich banner ad that explodes into a small site when the user's mouse rolls over it. The mouse-over site features free streaming quotes, sample research, and a virtual trading account, all of which would never fit into a traditional static ad.[32]

Other Forms of Online Promotion.   Other forms of online promotions include content sponsorships, microsites, alliances and affiliate programs, and viral advertising.

Content sponsorships are another form of Internet promotion. Many companies gain name exposure on the Internet by sponsoring special content on various Web sites, such as news or financial information or special interest topics. For example, Scotts, the lawn and garden products company, sponsors the Local Forecast section on WeatherChannel.com; and David Sunflower Seeds sponsors the ESPN Fantasy Baseball site at ESPN.com. The company pays for the sponsorship and in turn receives exclusive ad and sponsorship recognition alongside the content. Sponsorships are best placed in carefully targeted sites where they can offer relevant information or service to the audience. Similarly, e-marketers can also go online with *microsites,* limited areas on the Web managed and paid for by an external company. For example, an insurance company might create a microsite on a car-buying site, offering insurance advice for car buyers and at the same time offering good insurance deals.

MARKETING AT WORK | 14.1

"We Love You, Google Users"—and You, Too, Advertisers!

A decade ago, the early dot-com boom was rife with brash, fast-growing startups led by off-beat, young entrepreneurs offering unique work environments to attract young, talented employees. Google, the Web-search services provider, was no different. Founded in late 1998 by Sergey Brin and Larry Page, then 25 and 29 years old, Google got its start in a rented garage, complete with a washer, dryer, and hot tub.

Since then, Google has grown from 3 employees to more than 3,000. But it still offers a dot-com kind of environment. The Googleplex (the company's California head-quarters) seems more like a resort than an office complex. Youthful, healthy employees stroll along the campus's pathways amidst eco-friendly buildings or compete aggressively on the beach volleyball court in the complex's main quadrangle. Working at Google comes complete with backrubs from a company masseuse, meals from Google's resident chef, and even baking bread from scratch if the mood strikes you.

Although this start-up story mirrors that of previous dot-coms, for Google there is one big difference. Whereas other dot-coms have struggled, Google has grown at a breathtaking rate to become the world's dominant search engine. Today, nearly half of all U.S. searches are done on Google. In only the past two years, the company's revenues have grown seven-fold and profits have quadrupled. Google went public in 2004 at $85 a share; in less than a year, its stock price was nearing $300. The seven-year-old start-up now boasts a market

value of $80 billion, more than Internet super-stars eBay, Amazon.com, or Yahoo!.

What's behind this incredible success? Google's technology is an important part of the equation. The company's PageRank search technology revolutionized Internet searching. But beyond its revolutionary search engine technology, Google has triumphed by focusing heavily on simply helping users to "access, ana-lyze, organize, understand, and grapple with all the world's information." In fact, the name of the company is a play on the word *googol*, a mathematical term for a 1 followed by 100 zeros. Google chose the name to reflect its mis-

sion to organize and make accessible the immense amount of information available on the Web.

Google keeps looking for new ways to make life on the Web easy. For instance, its latest goal is to make the Internet language-independent—to make all searches to come back in the language that you enter. And the company keeps adding new services, such as a shopping-comparison site (Froogle), soft-ware to create a blog (Blogger), an e-mail ser-vice (Gmail), an instant message service (Hello), and even a map-search service with real satellite imagery (maps.google.com). The

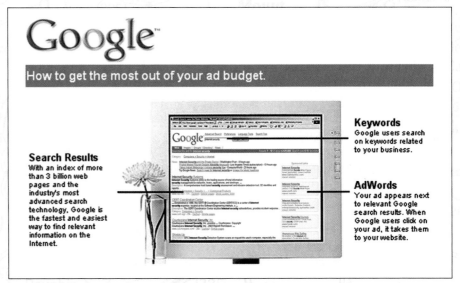

■ *With the world's largest online search audience, Google has become a very attractive advertising medium. Its highly targeted ads reach users when they are already searching for related information.*

Internet companies can also develop *alliances and affiliate programs*, in which they work with other companies, online and offline, to "promote each other." Amazon.com has more than 900,000 affiliates who post Amazon.com banners on their Web sites. And Yahoo!, whose ad revenue makes up 84 percent of its total worldwide revenue, has become a fertile ground for alliances with movie studios and TV production companies. For exam-ple, in one episode of *The Apprentice*, teams created and marketed a new flavor of Ciao Bella Ice Cream. Although Ciao Bella had previously sold its ice creams in only 18 stores in New York and San Francisco, Yahoo! convinced the manufacturer to place the new product in 760 stores around the country. An end-of-episode promotion urged viewers to

best part is that Google's extraordinary services are free to users.

But how, then, does Google make money? Some of Google's revenues come from contracts with corporate partners to provide search services for their own Internet and intranet sites. Today, more than 100 different partners rely on Google's WebSearch and SiteSearch technologies to power the search services on their Web sites. But most of Google's revenues come from advertising sales. In fact, last year Google generated more than $3 billion in ad revenues. By attracting the largest online search audience in the world, Google has made itself a very attractive advertising medium.

Google's most popular advertising program is AdWords. Here's how it works. Through constant data mining, Google determines which search terms are most popular on its various sites. It then approaches companies who sell in those categories and offers them space on search-results pages for sponsored ad messages and links. Advertisers then bid on a search term, and the highest bidder gets the highest position on the page. Then, when someone searches at a Google site for a topic related to the sponsor's product or service, a tasteful ad box appears at the top or right side of the Google results page, with a short ad message and links to the sponsor's Web site. The sponsor pays a fee for every thousand clicks on its ad.

Try it yourself. Go to the Google site (www.google.com), Google a search word or phrase, and see what advertiser messages and links appear. For example, if you search "Disneyland," you'll see ads and links at the top of the search list for Expedia and other online travel services, promising deals on hotels and resort tickets. Search "laptops" and you're greeted by ads from Dell and Toshiba and a link to www.sears.com. Side sponsor boxes link you to a half-dozen other merchants, including Gateway, USAnotebook.com, and Apple.

This "contextual advertising" on Google is subtle, not like the pop-up ads that make Web viewing on other sites like swatting flies. In fact, the ads are actually useful. Google "wants everything that appears on the page to be related to your search," says one reporter, "so a car company can't buy an ad to appear with your search for 'perfume.'" Sheryl Sandberg, one of Google's top advertising executives, loves it when people tell her that they didn't even realize that Google runs ads. "It means their advertising experience is not encroaching on their search experience," she says. "The goal is to make the ads as useful as the search results."

Whereas other forms of online advertising may produce questionable results for advertisers, advertising on Google delivers. Google's highly targeted ads reach relevant users when they are already searching for information. According to another Google advertising executive, Google is reaching the person "who is actually sticking a hand up and is interested in your product or service." Moreover, Google's matching process lets advertisers tailor their ad messages or sites closely to users' search inquiries. As a result, "click-through" rates for the typical ad on Google average 4 to 6 percent, versus less than 1 percent for traditional banner ads.

Google works hard to make advertising on its site effective. It proactively monitors ads to ensure their success, even letting advertisers know when their ads *aren't* working and suggesting that they pull ineffective ads. This approach to selling advertising space has resulted in loyalty and satisfaction among the Google clients who do stay. Online advertisers, such as Acura, Expedia, Eddie Bauer, Ernst & Young, and REI, number more than 150,000 worldwide and regularly rank Google as their top online advertising choice. This, in turn, has fueled the company's financial success.

Google has become a true cultural phenomenon, to the point that the company name is now used often as a verb—"Have you Googled yourself lately?" Google's success stems from its fervent passion to bring value to both the users who flock to its sites and the advertisers wanting to reach them. In the company's lobby in Mountain View, California, a six-foot trophy case brims with awards, including a 2000 Webby (the Internet's equivalent of an Oscar), which cofounders Brin and Page accepted wearing hockey uniforms and rollerblades. Their shared acceptance speech was simply, "We love you, Google users." They might have added, "And you, too, Google advertisers."

Sources: Quotes and other information from Betsy Cummings, "Beating the Odds," *Sales & Marketing Management*, March 2002, pp. 24–28; David Kirkpatrick, "In the Hands of Geeks, Web Advertising Actually Works," *FORTUNE*, April 14, 2003, p. 388; Michael Krauss, "Google Changes the Context of Advertising," *Marketing News*, June 1, 2004, p. 6; Melanie Warner, "What Your Company Can Learn from Google," *Business 2.0*, June 2004, pp. 100–106; Alan Deutschman, "Can Google Stay Google?" *Fast Company*, August 2005, pp 62–68; Kevin Delaney and Robert A Guth, "Yahoo, Microsoft Enhance Ad Focus," *Wall Street Journal*, August 3, 2005, p. B45; and information gathered from www.google.com, September 2005.

---

visit Yahoo!'s local online search engine to look for the store nearest them. The product sold out by 5 P.M. the next day. And thanks to Yahoo!'s registration database, it was able to provide Ciao Bella with the demographic characteristics of respondents.[33]

Finally, online marketers use **viral marketing**, the Internet version of word-of-mouth marketing. Viral marketing involves creating a Web site, e-mail message, or other marketing event that is so infectious that customers will want to pass it along to their friends. Because customers pass the message or promotion along to others, viral marketing can be very inexpensive. And when the information comes from a friend, the recipient is much more likely to open and read it. "The idea is to get your customers to do your marketing for

Viral marketing
The Internet version of word-of-mouth marketing—Web sites, e-mail messages, or other marketing events that are so infectious that customers will want to pass them along to friends.

you," notes a viral marketing expert.[34] Consider Burger King's now classic Subservient Chicken viral campaign:

■ Viral marketing: Burger King's colossally successful Subservient Chicken site gets consumers interacting with the brand and buzzing about its edgy new positioning.

> The Web site, www.subservientchicken.com, opens up on the Burger King logo, with the words "Contacting Chicken" underneath it. Then it dissolves to a living room, where the subservient chicken—someone in a giant chicken suit and a garter belt—hangs out in front of his Web cam and awaits your bidding. Type in commands, and the chicken does exactly what you ask. It will flap its wings, roll over, or jump up and down. It will also moon the viewer, dance the Electric Slide, or die. (Suggestions for lewd acts are met with a "naughty naughty" shake of the wing.) In other words, you can have your way with the chicken. Get it? Have it your way! The site promotes Burger King's TenderCrisp chicken and ties it into Burger King's successful "Have It Your Way" marketing campaign.
>
> "As viral marketing goes, subservientchicken.com is a colossal success," says an advertising expert. "There is great overlap between Web regulars and Burger King's core audience." If nothing more, the site gets consumers to interact with the brand. And it gets them buzzing about Burger King's edgy new positioning. Burger King has never advertised the site. When it was first created, the developer at CP+B, the ad agency that created the site, emailed the URL to several other CP+B people, asking them to send the link out to friends to test. From that single email, without a peep of promotion, the Subservient Chicken site ended the day with 1 *million* total hits. It received 46 million hits in only the first week following its launch, 385 million in the first nine months. Says one Burger King ad director, the award-winning site helped "sell a lot, a lot, a lot of chicken sandwiches."[35]

The Future of Online Advertising. Although online ad spending is growing rapidly, it still accounts for only a minor portion of the total advertising and marketing expenditures of most companies. It will not soon rival the major television and print media. However, online advertising serves a useful purpose, especially as a supplement to other marketing efforts. As a result, it is playing an increasingly important role in the marketing mixes of many advertisers.

Based on recent studies, the Interactive Advertising Bureau suggests that online advertising should be as much as 10 to 15 percent of the overall media mix in low-involvement product categories such as packaged goods. Kimberly-Clark found that increasing the levels of online advertising boosted the impact of the ad campaign for its Kleenex SoftPack line:[36]

> Kimberly-Clark was spending 75 percent of its SoftPack budget on TV, 23 percent on print and just 2 percent online. However, TV ads only reach about 42 percent of Kleenex's target audience. By boosting its online spending to more than 10 percent, Kimberly supplemented the light reach of TV and complemented its magazine advertising. The combination of print and online advertising helped raise brand awareness for SoftPack among its target audience from 34.7 percent to 42.7 percent; brand image from 35 percent to 41.8 percent; trial intent from 43.9 percent to 55.7 percent; and purchase intent from 24.2 to 34.0 percent. "It was surprising how impactful the lift on some of the brand [measures] were," says one Kimberly-Clark advertising executive.

Although Procter & Gamble spends only a small portion of its ad media budget online, it views the Web as an important medium. According to a P&G marketer, online marketing is "a permission-based way to offer consumers more information about a product than can be shared in a typical 30-second spot. It opens a two-way exchange where we can better educate consumers about our products."[37]

Creating or Participating in Web Communities The popularity of blogs and other Web forums has resulted in a rash of commercially sponsored Web sites called **Web communities**, which take advantage of the C2C properties of the Internet. Such sites allow members to congregate online and exchange views on issues of common interest. They are the cyberspace equivalent to a Starbucks coffeehouse, a place where everybody knows your e-mail address.

Web communities
Web sites upon which members can congregate online and exchange views on issues of common interest.

For example, iVillage.com is a Web community in which women can exchange views and obtain information, support, and solutions on families, food, fitness, relationships, relaxation, home and garden, news and issues, or just about any other topic. The site draws more than 14 million unique visitors a month, putting it in a league with magazines such as *Cosmopolitan, Glamour,* and *Vogue.* Another example is MyFamily.com, which aspires to be the largest and most active online community in the world for families. It provides free, private family Web sites upon which family members can connect online to hold family discussions, share family news, create online family photo albums, maintain a calendar of family events, share family history information, jointly build family trees, and buy gifts for family members quickly and easily.[38]

Visitors to these Internet neighborhoods develop a strong sense of community. Such communities are attractive to advertisers because they draw frequent, lengthy visits from consumers with common interests and well-defined demographics. For example, iVillage provides an ideal environment for the Web ads of companies such as Procter & Gamble, Kimberly-Clark, Nabisco, Avon, Clairol, Hallmark, and others who target women consumers. And MyFamily.com hosts The Shops@MyFamily, in which such companies as Disney, Kodak, Hallmark, Compaq, Hewlett-Packard, and Microsoft advertise and sell their family-oriented products.

■ Web communities: iVillage.com, a Web community for women, provides an ideal environment for Web ads of companies such as Procter & Gamble, Kimberly Clark, Avon, Hallmark, and others.

Web communities can be either social or work related. One successful work-related community is Agriculture Online. This site offers commodity prices, recent farm news, and chat rooms of all types. Rural surfers can visit the Electronic Coffee Shop and pick up the latest down-on-the-farm joke, join a hot discussion on controlling soybean cyst nematodes, or share best practices and barnyard common sense. Agriculture Online has been highly successful, attracting as many as 5 million hits per month. As such, it provides an excellent advertising environment for such companies as John Deere, Chevy Truck, and Farm Bureau, all of which sponsor featured areas on the site.[39]

Using E-Mail   E-mail has exploded onto the scene as an important e-marketing tool. A recent study of ad, brand, and marketing managers found that nearly half of all the B2B and B2C companies surveyed use e-mail marketing to reach consumers. Companies currently spend about $2.7 billion a year on e-mail marketing, up from just $164 million in 1999. And this spending will grow to an estimated $6.1 billion annually on e-mail marketing by 2008.[40]

To compete effectively in this ever-more-cluttered e-mail environment, marketers are designing "enriched" e-mail messages—animated, interactive, and personalized messages full of streaming audio and video. Then, they are targeting these attention-grabbers more carefully to those who want them and will act upon them. Consider Nintendo, a natural for e-mail based marketing:

> Young computer-savvy gaming fans actually look forward to Nintendo's monthly e-mail newsletter for gaming tips and for announcements of exciting new games. When the company launched its Star Fox Adventure game, it created an intensive e-mail campaign in the weeks before and after the product launch. The campaign included a variety of messages targeting potential customers. "Each message has a different look and feel, and . . . that builds excitement for Nintendo," notes an executive working on the account. The response? More than a third of all recipients opened the e-mails. And they did more than just glance at the messages: click-through rates averaged more than 10 percent. Nearly two-thirds of those opening the message watched its 30-second streaming video in its entirety. Nintendo also gathered insightful customer data from the 20 percent of people who completed an embedded survey.

MARKETING AT WORK 14.2

E-Mail Marketing: The Hot Marketing Medium? Or Pestering Millions for Profit?

E-mail is one hot marketing medium. In ever-larger numbers, e-mail ads are popping onto our computer screens and filling up our e-mailboxes. And they're no longer just the quiet, plain-text messages of old. The new breed of in-your-face e-mail ad is designed to command your attention—loaded with glitzy features such as animation, interactive links, color photos, streaming video, and personalized audio messages.

But there's a dark side to the exploding use of e-mail marketing. The biggest problem? *Spam*—the deluge of unsolicited, unwanted commercial messages that now clutter up our e-mailboxes and our lives. Various studies show that spam now accounts for an inbox-clogging 60 to 85 percent of e-mails sent daily throughout the world, up from only 7 percent in 2002. One recent study found that 75 percent of Internet users receive spam daily, receiving an average of 18.5 spam messages per day.

Despite these dismal statistics, when used properly, e-mail can be the ultimate direct marketing medium. Blue-chip marketers such as Amazon.com, Dell, L.L.Bean, Office Depot, and others use it regularly, and with great success. E-mail lets these marketers send highly-targeted, tightly-personalized, relationship-building messages to consumers who actually *want* to receive them, at a cost of only a few cents per contact. E-mail ads really can command attention and get customers to act. According to one estimate, well-designed e-mail campaigns sent to internal customer lists typically achieve 10 to 20 percent click-through rates. That's pretty good when compared with the 1 to 2 percent average response rates for traditional direct mail and the less than 1 percent response to traditional banner ads.

However, while carefully designed e-mails may be effective, and may even be welcomed by selected consumers, critics argue that most commercial e-mail messages amount to little more than annoying "junk mail" to the rest of us. Too many bulk e-mailers blast out lowest-common-denominator mailings to anyone with an e-mail address. There is no customization—no relationship building. Everyone gets the same hyperventilated messages. Moreover, too often, the spam comes from shady sources and pitches objectionable products—everything from Viagra and body-enhancement products to pornography and questionable investments. And the messages are often sent from less-than-reputable marketers. Of the 11 million spam messages studied recently by the Federal Trade Commission, 44 percent came from phony addresses.

At least in part, it's e-mail economics that are to blame for our overflowing inboxes. Sending e-mail is so easy and so inexpensive

■ *In response to the spam epidemic, Internet service providers such as AOL have created sophisticated spam filters.*

Although the company feared that the barrage of messages might create "list fatigue" and irritate customers, the campaign received very few negative responses. The unsubscribe rate was under 1 percent.[41]

As with other types of online marketing, companies must be careful that they don't cause resentment among Internet users who are already overloaded with "junk e-mail." The explosion of **spam**—unsolicited, unwanted commercial e-mail messages that clog up our e-mailboxes—has produced consumer frustration and anger. According to one research company, spam accounts for as much as 85 percent of total inbound e-mail.[42]

Spam
Unsolicited, unwanted commercial e-mail messages.

that almost anyone can afford to do it, even at paltry response rates. "In the field of direct marketing, it doesn't get much cheaper than spam," says one analyst. "One needs only a credit card (to buy lists of e-mail addresses), a computer, and an Internet connection. Otherwise, it costs nothing to send bulk e-mail, even masses of it."

For example, Data Resource Consulting, Inc., pumps out 8 million e-mails a day. That makes the company sound like a big-city, direct marketing behemoth. But in reality, it began as a home-based business run by a 44-year-old mother, Laura Betterly, in Dunedin, Florida, dubbed the Spam Queen by the *Wall Street Journal*. Betterly regularly dispatches messages to half a million or more strangers with a single click on the "send" icon. She's found she can make a profit on even very low responses. For example, if only 65 of the half million recipients respond, Betterly's company makes $40. In all, Betterly clears more than $200,000 a year in income from her small business.

The problem, of course, is that it's far easier for Betterly to hit the "send" button on an e-mail to a million and a half strangers than it is for the beleaguered recipients to hit the delete key on all those messages. One analyst calculated that the *recipient* cost of Betterly's e-mails far exceeded the $40 in revenue that it produced for her.

Assume that the average time getting rid of the junk was two seconds, and that the average recipient values his or her time at the mean wage paid in the United States, which is around $14 per hour, or $0.0039 per second. This implies a total cost, incurred by uninterested recipients, of 500,000 times 2 seconds times $.0039 per second, which gives $3,900. And such dollar calculations don't begin to account for the shear frustration of having to deal with all those many junk messages.

The impact of spam on consumers and businesses is alarming. One recent study places the average time spent at work each day deleting spam at 2.8 minutes. This loss in productivity equals $21.6 billion per year based on average U.S. wages.

In response to such costs and frustrations, Internet service providers and Web-browser producers have created sophisticated spam filters. And in 2003, Congress passed the CAN-SPAM Act (the Controlling the Assault of Non-Solicited Pornography and Marketing Act), which attempts to clean up the e-mail industry by banning deceptive subject lines, requiring a real return address, and giving consumers a way to "opt out." Such actions have helped somewhat. For example, Betterly no longer sends bulk e-mail to people with Yahoo! addresses—Yahoo!'s filter works too well, she says, so she doesn't get much response. However, most of us still get a barrage of e-mail come-ons each day.

Most legitimate e-mail marketers welcome such controls. Left unchecked, they reason, spam will make legitimate e-mail marketing less effective, or even impossible. "Long term, if the industry cannot deal with spam," says an AOL's executive, "it's going to destroy e-mail." But the industry worries that solutions such as spam filters and the CAN-SPAM Act often filter out the good e-mails with the bad, dampening the rich potential of e-mail for companies that want to use it as a valid marketing tool.

So, what's a marketer to do? Permission-based e-mail is the best solution. Companies can send e-mails only to customers who "opt in"—those who grant permission in advance. They can let consumers specify what types of messages they'd like to receive. Financial services firms such as Charles Schwab use configurable e-mail systems that let customers choose what they want to get. Others, such as Yahoo! or Amazon.com, include long lists of opt-in boxes for different categories of marketing material. Amazon.com targets opt-in customers with a limited number of helpful "we thought you'd like to know" messages based on their expressed preferences and previous purchases. Few customers object and many actually welcome such promotional messages.

Permission-based marketing ensures that e-mails are sent only to customers who want them. Still, marketers must be careful not to abuse the privilege. There's a fine line between legitimate e-mail marketing and spam. Companies that cross the line will quickly learn that "opting out" is only a click away for disgruntled consumers.

Sources: Quotes and other information from Jennifer Drumluk and Joe Tyler, "Cracking the E-Mail Marketing Code," *Association Management*, March 2005, pp. 52–56; Matt Haig, Mylene Mangalindan "Spam Queen: For Bulk E-Mailer, Pestering Millions Offers Path to Profit," *Wall Street Journal*, November 13, 2002, p. A1; Kevin G. DeMarrais, "Federal Trade Commission Says There's Just No Easy Way to Put a Lid on Spam," *Knight Ridder Tribune Business News*, June 16, 2004, p. 1; Jennifer Wolcott, "You Call It Spam, They Call It a Living," *Christian Science Monitor*, March 22, 2004, p. 12; and Nikki Swartz, "Deleting Spam Costs Business Billions," *Information Management Journal*, May–June 2005, p. 10.

E-mail marketers walk a fine line between adding value for consumers and being intrusive (see Marketing at Work 14.2).

Companies must beware of irritating consumers by sending unwanted e-mail to promote their products. Netiquette, the unwritten rules that guide Internet etiquette, suggests that marketers should ask customers for permission to e-mail marketing pitches. They should also tell recipients how to "opt in" or "opt out" of e-mail promotions at any time. This approach, known as *permission-based marketing,* has become a standard model for e-mail marketing.

The Promise and Challenges of E-Commerce

E-commerce continues to offer both great promise and many challenges for the future. We now look at both the promises of e-commerce and the "darker side" of the Web.

THE CONTINUING PROMISE OF E-COMMERCE

Its most ardent apostles still envision a time when the Internet and e-commerce will replace magazines, newspapers, and even stores as sources for information and buying. Most marketers, however, hold a more realistic view. To be sure, online marketing will become a successful business model for some companies, Internet firms such as Amazon.com, eBay, Expedia, and Google and direct-marketing companies such as Dell. Michael Dell's goal is one day "to have *all* customers conduct *all* transactions on the Internet, globally." However, for most companies, online marketing will remain just one important approach to the marketplace that works alongside other approaches in a fully integrated marketing mix.

Eventually, as companies become more adept at integrating e-commerce with their everyday strategy and tactics, the "e" will fall away from e-business or e-marketing. "The key question is not whether to deploy Internet technology—companies have no choice if they want to stay competitive—but how to deploy it," says business strategist Michael Porter. He continues: "We need to move away from the rhetoric about 'Internet industries,' 'e-business strategies,' and a 'new economy,' and see the Internet for what it is . . . a powerful set of tools that can be used, wisely or unwisely, in almost any industry and as part of almost any strategy."[43]

THE WEB'S DARKER SIDE

Along with its considerable promise, there is a "darker side" to Internet marketing. Here we examine two major sets of concerns: Internet profitability and legal and ethical issues.

Internet Profitability   One major concern is profitability, especially for B2C dot-coms. While many B2B marketers and B2C click-and-mortar retailers are marketing profitably online, surprisingly few B2C Internet-only companies are profitable. One problem is that, although expanding rapidly, online marketing still reaches only a limited marketspace. The Web audience is becoming more mainstream, but online users still tend to be somewhat more upscale, younger, and better educated than the general population.[44] This makes the Internet ideal for marketing financial services, travel services, computer hardware and software, and certain other classes of products. However, it makes online marketing less effective for selling mainstream products. Moreover, in many product categories, users still do more window browsing and product research than actual buying.

Another problem is that the Internet offers millions of Web sites and a staggering volume of information. Thus, navigating the Internet can be frustrating, confusing, and time consuming for consumers. In this chaotic and cluttered environment, many Web ads and sites go unnoticed or unopened. Even when noticed, online marketers often find it difficult to hold consumer attention. A site must capture Web surfers' attention within only a few seconds or lose them to another site. That leaves very little time for marketers to promote and sell their goods.

Finally, a great number of the click-only online retailers are small, niche marketers. With a growing number of retailers setting up shop online, the niches can become crowded and competitive. Also, consumers are more Web-savvy than ever, and new search technologies and comparison-shopping sites are emerging to help them locate the best deals. This makes the Web an even more competitive marketspace. Finally, dot-com e-tailers are facing stiffer competition from established click-and-mortar retailers entering their markets. Much of the strong recent growth in online sales comes from large companies such as Sears, L.L.Bean, Wal-Mart, Dell, and Amazon.com, established firms with recognized brands and strong customer bases. Only the most efficient and best-managed dot-coms will be able to survive profitably against such competition.

Legal and Ethical Issues   From a broader societal viewpoint, Internet marketing practices have raised a number of ethical and legal questions. In previous sections, we've touched on some of the negatives associated with the Internet, such as unwanted e-mail and the annoyance of pop-up ads. Here we examine concerns about consumer online privacy and security and other legal and ethical issues.

Online Privacy and Security.   *Online privacy* is perhaps the number one e-commerce concern. Most online marketers have become skilled at collecting and analyzing detailed consumer information. Marketers can easily track Web site visitors, and many consumers who participate in Web site activities provide extensive personal information. This may leave consumers open to information abuse if companies make unauthorized use of the information in marketing their products or exchanging databases with other companies.

Many consumers and policy makers worry that marketers have stepped over the line and are violating consumers' right to privacy. One survey found that 69 percent of Americans agree that "consumers have lost all control over how personal information is collected and used by companies." Another study found that 7 out of 10 consumers are concerned about online privacy.[45]

Many consumers also worry about *online security*. They fear that unscrupulous snoopers will eavesdrop on their online transactions or intercept their credit card numbers and make unauthorized purchases. In a recent study, six out of ten online shoppers were concerned enough about online security that they considered reducing the amount of their online holiday shopping.[46] In turn, companies doing business online fear that others will use the Internet to invade their computer systems for the purposes of commercial espionage or even sabotage. There appears to be an ongoing competition between the technology of Internet security systems and the sophistication of those seeking to break them.

In response to such online privacy and security concerns, the federal government has considered numerous legislative actions to regulate how Web operators obtain and use consumer information. Such legislation would require online service providers and commercial Web sites to get customers' permission before they disclose important personal information. In 2003, California enacted the California Online Privacy Protection Act (OPPA), under which any online business that collects personally identifiable information from California residents must take steps such as posting its privacy policy and notifying consumers about what data will be gathered and how it will be used.[47]

Of special concern are the privacy rights of children. In 1998, the Federal Trade Commission surveyed 212 Web sites directed toward children. It found that 89 percent of the sites collected personal information from children. However, 46 percent of them did not include any disclosure of their collection and use of such information. As a result, Congress passed the Children's Online Privacy Protection Act (COPPA), which requires Web site operators targeting children to post privacy policies on their sites. They must also notify parents about the information they're gathering and obtain parental consent before collecting personal information from children under age 13. Under this act, Interstate Bakeries was recently required to rework its Planet Twinkie Web site after the Children's Advertising Review Unit found that the site allowed children under 13 to submit their full name and phone number without parental consent.[48]

Many companies have responded to consumer privacy and security concerns with actions of their own. To help foster customer trust, companies such as Expedia and E-Loan have conducted voluntary audits of their privacy and security policies. Since 2000, Expedia has employed PricewaterhouseCoopers to run privacy audits of its online services. Expedia's privacy policy gives customers complete control over the use of the personal information they share with the online travel booker. Expedia also has an independent accounting firm regularly assess its Web security technology and procedures.[49]

Still others are taking a broadly, industywide approach. Founded in 1996, TRUSTe is a nonprofit, self-regulatory organization that works with a number of large corporate sponsers, including Microsoft, AT&T, and Intuit, to audit companies' privacy and security measures and help consumers navigate the Web safely. According to the company's Web site, "TRUSTe believes that an environment of mutual trust and openness will help make and keep the Internet a free, comfortable, and richly diverse community for everyone." To

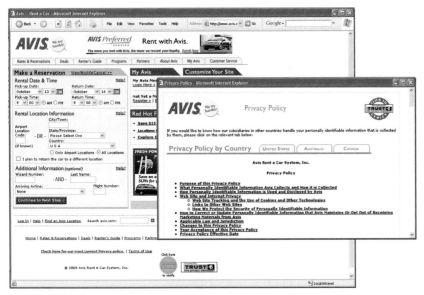

■ Tackling Internet privacy issues: The TRUSTe seal on Avis's Web page and privacy statement verify that the company's privacy policy and practices have been reviewed by TRUSTe and meet its strict program requirements.

reassure consumers, the company lends its "trustmark" stamp of approval to Web sites that meet its privacy and security standards.[50]

Still, examples of companies aggressively protecting their customers' personal information are too few and far between. And many consumers seem unwilling or unable to protect their own privacy. In a recent online consumer poll, 60 percent of respondents stated that they either did not know how to protect their personal information online or do not consistently take steps to do so, leaving them vulnerable as they use the Internet.

The costs of inaction could be great for both consumers and companies. A recent study indicated that almost 30 percent of consumers in North America who have been online and haven't made a purchase cited credit card fraud and other factors as holding them back. Another study predicts that annual online sales could be as much as 25 percent higher if consumers' concerns were adequately addressed.[51] All of this calls for strong actions by marketers to curb privacy abuses before legislators step in to do it for them.

Other Legal and Ethical Issues. Beyond issues of online privacy and security, consumers are also concerned about *Internet fraud*, including identity theft, investment fraud, and financial scams. Last year alone, the FTC received 206,000 online fraud complaints and the Federal Internet Crime Complaint Center (IC3) received almost 208,000 complaints related to Internet fraud, a whopping 330 percent increase from 2002. Such fraud cost businesses and consumers more than $68 billion last year. The IC3 reports that nearly 71 percent of reported incidents involve online auctions. Fraudulent activities are most often conducted through Web pages and e-mail, with 63.5 percent involving e-mail transactions.[52]

One common form of Internet fraud is *phishing,* a type of identity theft that uses deceptive emails and fraudulent Web sites to fool users into divulging their personal data. According to one survey, half of all Internet users have received a phishing e-mail. Although many consumers are not aware of such schemes, phishing can be extremely costly to those caught in the Net. Phishing hurts companies as well. In 2003, phishing cost banks and credit card companies $1.2 billion. Plus, phishing damages the brand identities of legitimate online marketers who have worked to build user confidence in Web and e-mail transactions. Fortunately, companies are taking action. For example, in 2004 the financial services industry set up the Identity Theft Assistance Center to help make it easier for consumers to report and resolve suspicious online activity.[53]

There are also concerns about *segmentation and discrimination* on the Internet. Some social critics and policy makers worry about the so-called *digital divide*—the gap between those who have access to the latest Internet and information technologies and those who don't. They are concerned that in this information age, not having equal access to information can be an economic and social handicap. They point out that 80 percent of American families with annual household incomes over $75,000 are online, compared with only 25 percent of the poorest U.S. families. Internationally, in most African countries, less than 1 percent of the population is online. "The ideal of the Internet was to be free," says one critic. "The reality is that not everyone can afford a computer or Internet access."[54] This leaves the poor less informed about products, services, and prices. Some people consider the digital divide to be an international crisis; others see it as an overstated nonissue.

A final Internet marketing concern is that of *access by vulnerable or unauthorized groups.* For example, marketers of adult-oriented materials have found it difficult to restrict access by minors. In a more specific example, a while back, sellers using eBay.com found themselves the victims of a 14-year-old boy who'd bid on and purchased more than $3 million worth of high-priced antiques and rare artworks on the site. eBay has a strict policy against bidding by anyone under age 18 but works largely on the honor system. Unfortunately, this honor system did little to prevent the teenager from taking a cyberspace joyride.[55]

Despite these challenges, companies large and small are quickly integrating online marketing into their marketing strategies and mixes. As it continues to grow, online marketing will prove to be a powerful tool for building customer relationships, improving sales, communicating company and product information, and delivering products and services more efficiently and effectively.

REST STOP → REVIEWING THE CONCEPTS

Recent technological advances have created a digital age. To thrive in this digital environment, marketers are adding some Internet thinking to their strategies and tactics. This chapter discusses how marketers are adapting.

1. Discuss how the digital age is affecting both consumers and the marketers who serve them.

Much of today's business operates on digital information, which flows through connected networks. Intranets, extranets, and the Internet now connect people and companies with each other and with important information. The Internet has grown explosively to become *the* technology of the new millennium, empowering consumers and businesses alike with the blessings of connectivity.

The Internet and other new technologies have changed the ways that companies reach and serve their markets. The Internet enables consumers and companies to access and share huge amounts of information with just a few mouse clicks. In turn, the Internet and other digital technologies have given marketers a whole new way to reach and serve customers. New Internet marketers and channel relationships have arisen to replace some types of traditional marketers. The new technologies are helping marketers to tailor their offers effectively to targeted customers or even to help customers customize their own marketing offers. It's hard to find a company today that doesn't have a substantial Web presence.

2. Explain how companies have responded to the Internet and other powerful new technologies with e-business strategies, and how these strategies have resulted in benefits to both buyers and sellers.

Conducting business in the digital age calls for a new model of marketing strategy and practice. Companies need to retain most of the skills and practices that have worked in the past. However, they must also add major new competencies and practices if they hope to grow and prosper in the digital environment. E-business is the use of electronic platforms to conduct a company's business. E-commerce involves buying and selling processes supported by elec-

tronic means, primarily the Internet. It includes e-marketing (the selling side of e-commerce) and e-purchasing (the buying side of e-commerce).

E-commerce benefits both buyers and sellers. For buyers, e-commerce makes buying convenient and private, provides greater product access and selection, and makes available a wealth of product and buying information. It is interactive and immediate and gives the consumer a greater measure of control over the buying process. For sellers, e-commerce is a powerful tool for building customer relationships. It also increases the sellers' speed and efficiency, helping to reduce selling costs. E-commerce also offers great flexibility and better access to global markets.

3. Describe the four major e-marketing domains.

Companies can practice e-commerce in any or all of four domains. B2C (business-to-consumer) e-marketing is initiated by businesses and targets final consumers. Despite recent setbacks following the "dot-com gold rush" of the late 1990s, B2C e-commerce continues to grow at a healthy rate. Although online consumers are still somewhat higher in income and more technology oriented than traditional buyers, the cyberspace population is becoming much more mainstream and diverse. This growing diversity opens up new e-commerce targeting opportunities for marketers. Today, consumers can buy almost anything on the Web.

B2B (business-to-business) e-commerce dwarfs B2C e-commerce. Most businesses today operate Web sites or use B2B trading networks, auction sites, spot exchanges, online product catalogs, barter sites, or other online resources to reach new customers, serve current customers more effectively, and obtain buying efficiencies and better prices. Business buyers and sellers meet in huge marketspaces—or open trading networks—to share information and complete transactions efficiently. Or, they set up private trading networks that link them with their own trading partners.

Through C2C (consumer-to-consumer) e-marketing, consumers can buy or exchange goods and information directly from or with one another. Examples include online auction sites, forums, and Weblogs (blogs). Finally, through

C2B (consumer-to-business) e-commerce, consumers are now finding it easier to search out sellers on the Web, learn about their products and services, and initiate purchases. Using the Web, customers can even drive transactions with business, rather than the other way around.

4. Discuss how companies can go about conducting e-marketing to profitably deliver more value to customers.

Companies of all types are now engaged in e-commerce. The Internet gave birth to the *click-only* dot-coms, which operate only online. In addition, many traditional brick-and-mortar companies have now added e-marketing operations, transforming themselves into *click-and-mortar* competitors. Many click-and-mortar companies are now having more online success than their click-only competitors.

Companies can conduct e-marketing in any of the four ways: creating a Web site, placing ads and promotions online, setting up or participating in Web communities, or using online e-mail. The first step typically is to set up a Web site. Beyond simply setting up a site, however, companies must make their sites engaging, easy to use, and useful in order to attract visitors, hold them, and bring them back again.

E-marketers can use various forms of online advertising to build their Internet brands or to attract visitors to their Web sites. Beyond online advertising, other forms of online promotion include content sponsorships, microsites, alliances and affiliate programs, and viral marketing, the Internet version of word-of-mouth marketing. Online marketers can also participate in Web communities, which take advantage of the C2C properties of the Web. Finally, e-mail marketing has become a hot new e-marketing tool for both B2C and B2B marketers.

5. Overview the promise and challenges that e-commerce presents for the future.

E-commerce continues to offer great promise for the future. For most companies, online marketing will become an important part of a fully integrated marketing mix. For others, it will be the major means by which they serve the market. Eventually, the "e" will fall away from e-business or e-marketing as companies become more adept at integrating e-commerce with their everyday strategy and tactics. However, e-commerce also faces many challenges. One challenge is Web profitability—surprisingly few companies, especially the Web-only dot-coms, are using the Web profitably. The other challenge concerns legal and ethical issues—issues of online privacy and security, Internet fraud, and the Digital Divide. Despite these challenges, companies large and small are quickly integrating online marketing into their marketing strategies and mixes.

Navigating the Key Terms

B2B (business-to-business) e-commerce (442)

B2C (business-to-consumer) e-commerce (440)

C2B (consumer-to-consumer) e-commerce (444)

C2C (consumer-to-consumer) e-commerce (443)

Click-and-mortar companies (446)

Click-only companies (445)

Corporate Web site (448)

E-business (438)

E-commerce (438)

E-marketing (438)

Extranet (437)

Internet (437)

Intranet (437)

Marketing Web site (448)

Online advertising (451)

Open trading exchanges (442)

Private trading exchanges (442)

Spam (456)

Viral marketing (453)

Web communities (454)

Travel Log

Discussing the Issues

1. Discuss the differences between intranets, extranets, and the Internet. What purpose does each serve for businesses?

2. How does e-commerce benefit buyers? How does it benefit sellers?

3. Define the four major e-marketing domains and provide one example of each.

4. What are the primary differences between open trading exchanges and private trading exchanges in B2B e-commerce? What are the advantages of each type of exchange?

5. Distinguish between the different forms of online advertising and promotion. What factors should a company consider in deciding between these different forms?

6. What is a blog? How are blogs different from Web communities?

Application Questions

1. Getting consumers to spend time at a company's Web site and to come back again are critical goals in Web site design. How can the seven Cs encourage revisits to a company's Web site? Are some of these factors more

important than others? Visit a Web site that you frequent and evaluate it using the seven Cs. How does it rate?

2. Browse the products and features available at Target.com. Why might a consumer choose to make a purchase through Target.com rather than going to the brick-and-mortar retail location? What benefits does the online store offer? What are some of its drawbacks? What benefits does Target.com offer over the Web sites of Internet-only retailers such as Amazon.com?

3. Web communities allow members to congregate online and exchange views on issues of common interest. Do you belong to a Web community? Why or why not? Visit iVilliage.com. What benefits does the site offer to members? What opportunities does it offer to marketers?

Under the Hood: Focus on Technology

Rich media is making a splash online. One recent survey found that click-through rates for rich media ads are five times higher than for traditional online ad formats. According to Eyeblaster, a leading provider of rich media advertising technology, "rich media ads employ graphic movement, audio, video, innovative ad formats, and interaction to cut through the clutter of common Web ads by engaging the viewer in a richer and immediately compelling experience. When branding is a goal of the campaign, rich media ads can engage consumers in an interactive brand experience by allowing them to play games, view a video stream, or expand the ad to access more information."*

1. Visit the Eyeblaster Web site and check out some of the ads the company has created (www.eyeblaster.com/ knowledge/vertical_categories.asp). Do you find the ads compelling? Did you "click-through" for more information?

2. How do the ads you viewed help marketers build brands? How do they help create and reinforce customer relationships?

*See www.eyeblaster.com for more information.

Focus on Ethics

As technology makes it easier for companies to share information about customers, consumer advocates are growing more concerned about protecting consumer privacy. Although individual consumers often say they are concerned about their privacy, very few take the time to read the privacy policies of the companies with which they build relationships. To help consumers surf the Web with confidence, TRUSTe, a nonprofit organization, is on a mission to certify and monitor privacy protection on the Internet. As a result, the company has become a leader in promoting Web site privacy policy disclosure, informed user consent, and consumer education, with nearly 1,500 Web sites displaying its seals. What does all this mean? A company that achieves the TRUSTe "trustmark" has agreed to adhere to the organization's privacy principles and to comply with TRUSTe oversight and consumer resolution. The "trustmark" assures Web users that a site will openly disclose what personal information is being gathered, where that information is going, how it will be used, and whether the user has the option to control its dissemination. TRUSTe believes it has a solution to the number-one concern of most Internet users—privacy and security.

1. Visit www.truste.com to learn more about the services TRUSTe provides. What are the advantages for an organization agreeing to self-regulate through TRUSTe? What are the disadvantages? Do the advantages outweigh the disadvantages?

2. Use the TRUSTe Search for Sealholders feature to select three of the participants and visit their Web sites. Examine the sites' privacy statements. What do the statements have in common? How do the policies help build relationships with consumers?

3. How much responsibility do marketers have in protecting the privacy of the consumers with whom they do business? How much responsibility do consumers, themselves, hold?

Videos

The iWon video case that accompanies this chapter is located in Appendix 1 at the back of the book.

→ **AFTER STUDYING THIS CHAPTER, YOU SHOULD BE ABLE TO**

1. discuss how the international trade system, economic, political-legal, and cultural environments affect a company's international marketing decisions

2. describe three key approaches to entering international markets

3. explain how companies adapt their marketing mixes for international markets

4. identify the three major forms of international marketing organizations

The Global Marketplace

Road Map Previewing the Concepts

It's time to take your marketing journey global. We've visited global topics in each previous chapter—it's difficult to find an area of marketing that doesn't contain at least some international issues. Here, however, we'll focus on special considerations that companies face when they market their brands globally. Advances in communication, transportation, and other technologies have made the world a much smaller place. Today, almost every firm, large or small, faces international marketing issues. In this chapter, we will examine six major decisions marketers make in going global.

Buckle up and let's get going! Our first stop is Coca-Cola—America's soft drink. Or *is* it just America's brand? Read on and see how finding the right balance between global standardization and local adaptation has made Coca-Cola the number-one brand worldwide.

What could be more American than Coca-Cola—right? The brand is as American as baseball and apple pie. Coke got its start in an Atlanta pharmacy in 1893, where it sold for five cents a glass. From there, the company's first president, savvy businessman Asa Candler, set out to convince America that Coca-Cola really was "the pause that refreshes." The beverage quickly became an all-American phenomenon.

But from the get-go, Coke was destined to be more than just America's soft drink. By 1900, Coca-Cola had already ventured beyond America's borders into numerous countries, including Cuba, Puerto Rico, and France. By the 1920s, Coca-Cola was slapping its logo on everything from dogsleds in Canada to the walls of bullfighting arenas in Spain. During World War II, Coca-Cola built bottling plants in Europe and Asia to supply American soldiers in the field.

Strong marketing abroad fueled Coke's popularity throughout the world. In 1971, the company ran its legendary "I'd like to buy the world a Coke" television spot, in which a crowd of children sang the song from atop a hill in Italy. More recently, Coca-Cola's increased focus on emerging markets such as China, India, and Indonesia—home to more than 2.7 billion people, almost half the world's population—has bolstered the brand's global success. Coca-Cola is now arguably the best-known and most admired brand in the world.

Coca-Cola's worldwide success results from a skillful balancing of global standardization and brand building with local adaptation. For years, the company has adhered to the mantra "Think globally, act locally." Coca-Cola spends lavishly on global Coke advertising—some $1.2 billion a year—to create a consistent overall positioning for the brand across the more than 200 countries it serves. In addition, Coke's taste and packaging are largely standardized around the world—the bottle of Coke you'd drink in New York or Philadelphia looks and tastes much the same as one you might order in Paris, Hong Kong, Moscow, Sidney, or Abu Dhabi. As one ad agency executive asserts, "There are about two products that lend themselves to global marketing—and one of them is Coca-Cola."

Although Coke's taste and positioning are fairly consistent worldwide, in other ways Coca-Cola's marketing is relentlessly local. The company carefully adapts its mix of brands and flavors, promotions, price, and distribution to local customs and preferences in each market. For example, beyond its core Coca-Cola brand, the company makes nearly 400 different beverage brands, created especially for the taste buds of local consumers. It sells a pear-flavored drink in Turkey, a berry-flavored Fanta for Germany, a honey-flavored green tea in China, Sprite with a hint of mint in Canada, and a sports drink called Aquarius in Belgium and the Netherlands.

Consistent with this local focus, within the framework of its broader global positioning, Coca-Cola adapts specific ads to individual country markets. For example, a localized Chinese New Year television ad features a dragon in a holiday parade, adorned from head to tail with red Coke cans. The spot concludes, "For many centuries, the color red has been the color for good luck and prosperity."

In India, Coca-Cola uses local promotions to aggressively cultivate a local image. It claimed official sponsorship for World Cup cricket, a favorite national sport, and used Indian cricket fans rather than actors to promote Coke products. Coca-Cola markets effectively in India to both retailers and imbibers. Observes one Coke watcher, "The company hosts massive gatherings of up to 15,000 retailers to showcase everything from the latest coolers and refrigerators, which Coke has for loan, to advertising displays. And its salespeople go house-to-house in their quest for new customers. In New Delhi alone, workers handed out more than 100,000 free bottles of Coke and Fanta last year."

Nothing better illustrates Coca-Cola's skill in balancing standardized, global brand building with local adaptation than the explosive global growth of Sprite. Sprite's advertising uniformly targets the world's young people with the tag line "Image is nothing. Thirst is everything. Obey your thirst." The campaign taps into the rebellious side of teenagers and into their need to form individual identities.

According to Sprite's director of brand marketing, "The meaning of [Sprite] and what we stand for is exactly the same globally. Teens tell us it's incredibly relevant in nearly every market we go into." However, as always, Coca-Cola tailors its message to local consumers. In China, for example, the campaign was given a softer edge: "You can't be irreverent in China, because it's not acceptable in that society. It's all about being relevant [to the specific audience]," notes the marketer. As a result of such smart targeting and powerful positioning, Sprite's worldwide sales surged 35 percent within three years of the start of the campaign, making it the world's number-four soft drink brand.

As a result of its international marketing prowess, Coca-Cola dominates the global soft drink market. About 70 percent of the company's sales and 88 percent of its profits come from abroad. In the United States Coca-Cola captures an impressive 43 percent market share versus Pepsi's 32 percent. Overseas, however, it outsells Pepsi 2.5 to 1 and boasts four of the world's five leading soft drink brands: Coca-Cola, Diet Coke, Sprite, and Fanta.

Thus, Coca-Cola is truly an all-world brand. No matter where in the world you are, you'll find Coke "within an arm's length of desire." Yet, Coca-Cola also has a very personal meaning to consumers in different parts of the globe. Coca-Cola *is* as American as baseball and apple pie. But it's also as English as Big Ben and afternoon tea, as German as bratwurst and beer, as Japanese as sumo and sushi, and as Chinese as Ping-Pong and the Great Wall. Consumers in more than 200 countries think of Coke as *their* beverage. In Spain, Coke has been used as a mixer with wine; in Italy, Coke is served with meals in place of wine or cappuccino; in China, the beverage is served at special government occasions.

Says the company's Web site, "Our local strategy enables us to listen to all the voices around the world asking for beverages that span the entire spectrum of tastes and occasions. What people want in a beverage is a reflection of who they are, where they live, how they work and play, and how they relax and recharge. Whether you're a student in the United States enjoying a refreshing Coca-Cola, a woman in Italy taking a tea break, a child in Peru asking for a juice drink, or a couple in Korea buying bottled water after a run together, we're there for you. . . . It's a special thing to have billions of friends around the world, and we never forget it."[1]

In the past, U.S. companies paid little attention to international trade. If they could pick up some extra sales through exporting, that was fine. But the big market was at home, and it teemed with opportunities. The home market was also much safer. Managers did not need to learn other languages, deal with strange and changing currencies, face political and legal uncertainties, or adapt their products to different customer needs and expectations. Today, however, the situation is much different.

Global Marketing in the Twenty-First Century

The world is shrinking rapidly with the advent of faster communication, transportation, and financial flows. Products developed in one country—Gucci purses, Sony electronics, McDonald's hamburgers, Japanese sushi, German BMWs—are finding enthusiastic acceptance in other countries. We would not be surprised to hear about a German businessman wearing an Italian suit meeting an English friend at a Japanese restaurant who later returns home to drink Russian vodka and watch *American Idol* on TV.

International trade is booming. Since 1969, the number of multinational corporations in the world has grown from 7,000 to more than 63,000. Some of these multinationals are true giants. In fact, of the largest 100 "economies" in the world, only 47 are countries. The remaining 53 are multinational corporations. ExxonMobil, the world's largest company, has annual revenues greater than the gross domestic product (GDP) of all but the world's 20 largest countries.[2]

Since 2003, world trade has been growing at 5 to 10 percent annually, while global gross domestic product has grown at only 2.5 to 4 percent annually. World trade of products and services was valued at over $10.9 trillion in 2004, which accounted for 20 percent of GDP worldwide. This trade growth is most visible in developing countries, which saw their share in world merchandise trade rise sharply to 31 percent, the highest since 1950.[3]

Many U.S. companies have long been successful at international marketing—Coca-Cola, General Electric, IBM, Colgate, Caterpillar, Ford, Boeing, McDonald's—and dozens of other American firms have made the world their market. And in the United States, names such as Sony, Toyota, BP, Nestlé, Nokia, and Prudential have become household words. Other products and services that appear to be American are in fact produced or owned by foreign companies: Bantam books, Baskin-Robbins ice cream, GE and RCA televisions, Carnation milk, Pillsbury food products, Universal Studios, and Motel 6, to name just a few. Michelin, the oh-so-French tire manufacturer, now does a third of its business in the United States and Mexico; Johnson & Johnson, the maker of quintessentially all-American products like BAND-AIDS and Johnson & Johnson's Baby Shampoo, does 42 percent of its business abroad.[4]

■ Many American companies have made the world their market.

But while global trade is growing, global competition is intensifying. Foreign firms are expanding aggressively into new international markets, and home markets are no longer as rich in opportunity. Few industries are now safe from foreign competition. If companies delay taking steps toward internationalizing, they risk being shut out of growing markets in Western and Eastern Europe, China and the Pacific Rim, Russia, and elsewhere. Firms that stay at home to play it safe not only might lose their chances to enter other markets but also risk losing their home markets. Domestic companies that never thought about foreign competitors suddenly find these competitors in their own backyards.

Ironically, although the need for companies to go abroad is greater today than in the past, so are the risks. Companies that go global may face highly unstable governments and currencies, restrictive government policies and regulations, and high trade barriers. Corruption is also an increasing problem—officials in several countries often award business not to the best bidder but to the highest briber.

A **global firm** is one that, by operating in more than one country, gains marketing, production, R&D, and financial advantages that are not available to purely domestic competitors. The global company sees the world as one market. It minimizes the importance of national boundaries and develops "transnational" brands. It raises capital, obtains materials and components, and manufactures and markets its goods wherever it can do the best job. For example, Otis Elevator gets its elevators' door systems from France, small geared parts from Spain, electronics from Germany, and special motor drives from Japan. It uses the United States only for systems integration. "Borders are so 20th century," says one global marketing expert. "Transnationals take 'stateless' to the next level."[5]

This does not mean that small- and medium-size firms must operate in a dozen countries to succeed. These firms can practice global niching. But the world is becoming smaller, and every company operating in a global industry—whether large or small—must assess and establish its place in world markets.

The rapid move toward globalization means that all companies will have to answer some basic questions: What market position should we try to establish in our country, in our economic region, and globally? Who will our global competitors be, and what are their strategies and resources? Where should we produce or source our products? What strategic alliances should we form with other firms around the world?

As shown in Figure 15.1, a company faces six major decisions in international marketing. We will discuss each decision in detail in this chapter.

Global firm
A firm that, by operating in more than one country, gains R&D, production, marketing, and financial advantages in its costs and reputation that are not available to purely domestic competitors.

Looking at the Global Marketing Environment

Before deciding whether to operate internationally, a company must understand the international marketing environment. That environment has changed a great deal in the last two decades, creating both new opportunities and new problems.

THE INTERNATIONAL TRADE SYSTEM

U.S. companies looking abroad must start by understanding the international *trade system*. When selling to another country, a firm may face restrictions on trade between nations.

FIGURE 15.1
Major International Marketing Decisions

Foreign governments may charge *tariffs*, taxes on certain imported products designed to raise revenue or to protect domestic firms. Or they may set *quotas*, limits on the amount of foreign imports that they will accept in certain product categories. The purpose of a quota is to conserve on foreign exchange and to protect local industry and employment. American firms may also face *exchange controls*, which limit the amount of foreign exchange and the exchange rate against other currencies.

The company also may face *nontariff trade barriers*, such as biases against U.S. company bids or restrictive product standards that go against American product features:

> One of the cleverest ways the Japanese have found to keep foreign manufacturers out of their domestic market is to plead "uniqueness." Japanese skin is different, the government argues, so foreign cosmetics companies must test their products in Japan before selling there. The Japanese say their stomachs are small and have room for only the *mikan*, the local tangerine, so imports of U.S. oranges are limited. Now the Japanese have come up with what may be the flakiest argument yet: Their snow is different, so ski equipment should be too.[6]

At the same time, certain forces *help* trade between nations. Examples include the General Agreement on Tariffs and Trade (GATT) and various regional free trade agreements.

The World Trade Organization and GATT   The General Agreement on Tariffs and Trade (GATT) is a 58-year-old treaty designed to promote world trade by reducing tariffs and other international trade barriers. Since the treaty's inception in 1948, member nations (currently numbering 148) have met in eight rounds of GATT negotiations to reassess trade barriers and set new rules for international trade. The first seven rounds of negotiations reduced the average worldwide tariffs on manufactured goods from 45 percent to just 5 percent.[7]

The most recently completed GATT negotiations, dubbed the Uruguay Round, dragged on for seven long years before concluding in 1993. The benefits of the Uruguay Round will be felt for many years as the accord promotes long-term, global trade growth. It reduced the world's remaining merchandise tariffs by 30 percent. The agreement also extended GATT to cover trade in agriculture and a wide range of services; and it toughened international protection of copyrights, patents, trademarks, and other intellectual property. Although the financial impact of such an agreement is difficult to measure, research suggests that cutting agriculture, manufacturing, and services trade barriers by one-third would boost the world economy by $613 billion, the equivalent of adding another Australia to the world economy.[8]

Beyond reducing trade barriers and setting global standards for trade, the Uruguay Round set up the World Trade Organization (WTO) to enforce GATT rules. In general, the WTO acts as an umbrella organization, overseeing GATT, mediating global disputes, and imposing trade sanctions. The previous GATT organization never possessed such authorities. A new round of GATT negotiations, the Doha round, began in Doha, Qatar, in late 2001 and was set to conclude in January 2005, but the discussions continue.[9]

■ The WTO and GATT: The General Agreement on Tariffs and Trade (GATT) promotes world trade by reducing tariffs and other international trade barriers. The WTO, which oversees GATT, began a new round of negotiations in Doha, Qatar, in late 2001.

Regional Free Trade Zones   Certain countries have formed *free trade zones* or **economic communities**. These are groups of nations organized to work toward common goals in the regulation of international trade. One such community is the *European Union (EU)*. Formed in 1957, the European Union set out to create a single European market by reducing barriers to the free flow of products, services, finances, and labor among member countries and developing policies on trade with nonmember nations. Today, the European

Economic community
A group of nations organized to work toward common goals in the regulation of international trade.

■ Economic communities: The European Union represents one of the world's single largest markets. Its current 25 member countries contain more than 448 million consumers and account for 20 percent of the world's exports.

Union represents one of the world's single largest markets. Its current 25 member countries contain some 458 million consumers and account for more than 20 percent of the world's exports.[10]

European unification offers tremendous trade opportunities for U.S. and other non-European firms. However, it also poses threats. As a result of increased unification, European companies have grown bigger and more competitive. Perhaps an even greater concern, however, is that lower barriers *inside* Europe will create only thicker *outside* walls. Some observers envision a "Fortress Europe" that heaps favors on firms from EU countries but hinders outsiders by imposing obstacles.

Progress toward European unification has been slow—many doubt that complete unification will ever be achieved. In recent years, 12 member nations have taken a significant step toward unification by adopting the euro as a common currency. Many other countries are expected to follow within the next few years. Widespread adoption of the euro will decrease much of the currency risk associated with doing business in Europe, making member countries with previously weak currencies more attractive markets.[11]

However, even with the adoption of the euro, it is unlikely that the EU will ever go against 2,000 years of tradition and become the "United States of Europe." A community with two dozen different languages and cultures will always have difficulty coming together and acting as a single entity. For example, efforts to forge a single European constitution appear to have failed following French and Dutch "no" votes in mid-2005. And economic disputes between member nations have stalled long-term budget negotiations. Still, although only partly successful so far, unification has made Europe a global force with which to reckon, with a combined annual GDP of more than $11.6 trillion.[12]

In 1994, the *North American Free Trade Agreement (NAFTA)* established a free trade zone among the United States, Mexico, and Canada. The agreement created a single market of 434 million people who produce and consume over $13.8 trillion worth of goods and services annually. As it is implemented over a 15-year period, NAFTA will eliminate all trade barriers and investment restrictions among the three countries. Thus far, the agreement has allowed trade between the countries to flourish. Each day the United States exchanges more than half a trillion dollars in goods and services with Canada, its largest trading partner. And in 1998, Mexico passed Japan to become America's second largest trading partner.[13]

Following the apparent success of NAFTA, in 2005 the Central American Free Trade Agreement (CAFTA), established a free trade zone between the United States and Costa Rica, the Dominican Republic, El Salvador, Guatemala, Honduras, and Nicaragua. And talks are now under way to investigate establishing a Free Trade Area of the Americas (FTAA). This mammoth free trade zone would include 34 countries stretching from the Bering Strait to Cape Horn, with a population of 800 million, a combined GDP of about $17 trillion.[14]

Other free trade areas have formed in Latin America and South America. For example, MERCOSUR links nine Latin American and South American countries and the Andean Community (CAN, for its Spanish initials) links five more. In late 2004, MERCOSUR and CAN agreed to unite, creating the South American Community of Nations (CSN), which will be modeled after the European Union. Complete integration between the two trade blocs is expected by 2007 and all tariffs between the nations are to be eliminated by 2019. With a population of more than 367 million, a combined economy of more than $2.8 trillion a year, and exports worth $181 billion, the CSN will make up the largest trading bloc after NAFTA and the European Union.[15]

Although the recent trend toward free trade zones has caused great excitement and new market opportunities, some see it as a mixed blessing. For example, in the United States, unions fear that NAFTA will lead to the further exodus of manufacturing jobs to

Mexico, where wage rates are much lower. Environmentalists worry that companies that are unwilling to play by the strict rules of the U.S. Environmental Protection Agency will relocate in Mexico, where pollution regulation has been lax.[16]

Each nation has unique features that must be understood. A nation's readiness for different products and services and its attractiveness as a market to foreign firms depend on its economic, political-legal, and cultural environments.

ECONOMIC ENVIRONMENT

The international marketer must study each country's economy. Two economic factors reflect the country's attractiveness as a market: the country's industrial structure and its income distribution.

The country's *industrial structure* shapes its product and service needs, income levels, and employment levels. The four types of industrial structures are as follows:

1. *Subsistence economies:* In a subsistence economy, the vast majority of people engage in simple agriculture. They consume most of their output and barter the rest for simple goods and services. They offer few market opportunities.
2. *Raw-material exporting economies:* These economies are rich in one or more natural resources but poor in other ways. Much of their revenue comes from exporting these resources. Examples are Chile (tin and copper), Democratic Republic of Congo (copper, cobalt, and coffee), and Saudi Arabia (oil). These countries are good markets for large equipment, tools and supplies, and trucks. If there are many foreign residents and a wealthy upper class, they are also a market for luxury goods.
3. *Industrializing economies:* In an industrializing economy, manufacturing accounts for 10 to 20 percent of the country's economy. Examples include Egypt, India, and Brazil. As manufacturing increases, the country needs more imports of raw textile materials, steel, and heavy machinery, and fewer imports of finished textiles, paper products, and automobiles. Industrialization typically creates a new rich class and a small but growing middle class, both demanding new types of imported goods.
4. *Industrial economies:* Industrial economies are major exporters of manufactured goods, services, and investment funds. They trade goods among themselves and also export them to other types of economies for raw materials and semifinished goods. The varied manufacturing activities of these industrial nations and their large middle class make them rich markets for all sorts of goods.

The second economic factor is the country's *income distribution*. Industrialized nations may have low-, medium-, and high-income households. In contrast, countries with subsistence economies may consist mostly of households with very low family incomes. Still other countries may have households with only either very low or very high incomes. However, even poor or developing economies may be attractive markets for all kinds of goods, including luxuries. For example, many luxury brand marketers are rushing to take advantage of China's rapidly developing consumer markets:[17]

> More than half of China's 1.3 billion consumers can barely afford rice, let alone luxuries. According to The World Bank, more than 400 million Chinese live on less than $2 a day. For now, only some 1 percent of China's population (about 13 million people) earns enough to even consider purchasing luxury-brand products. Yet posh brands—from Gucci and Cartier to BMW and Bentley—are descending on China in force. How can purveyors of $2,000 handbags, $20,000 watches, and $1 million limousines thrive in a developing economy? Easy, says a Cartier executive. "Remember, even medium-sized cities in China . . . have populations larger than Switzerland's. So it doesn't matter if the percentage of people in those cities who can afford our products is very small."
>
> Dazzled by the pace at which China's booming economy is minting millionaires and swelling the ranks of the middle class, luxury brands are rushing to stake out shop space, tout their wares, and lay the foundations of a market they hope will eventually include as many as 100 million conspicuous consumers. "The Chinese

■ Economic environment: Many luxury brand marketers are rushing to take advantage of China's rapidly developing consumer markets.

are a natural audience for luxury goods," notes one analyst. After decades of socialism and poverty, China's elite are suddenly "keen to show off their newfound wealth."

Europe's fashion houses are happy to assist. Giorgio Armani recently hosted a star-studded fashion show to celebrate the opening of his 12,000-square-foot flagship store on Shanghai's waterfront; Armani promises 30 stores in China before the 2008 Beijing Olympics. Gucci recently opened stores in Hangzhou and Chengdu, bringing its China total to six. And it's not just clothes. Cartier, with nine stores in China and seven on the drawing board, has seen its China sales double for the past several years. Carmakers, too, are racing in. BMW recently cut the ribbon on a new Chinese factory that has the capacity to produce 50,000 BMWs a year. Audi's sleek A6 has emerged as the car of choice for the Communist Party's senior ranks, despite its $230,000 price tag. Bentley, which sold 70 cars in China in 2003—including 19 limousines priced at more than $1 million each—boasts three dealerships in China, as does Rolls-Royce.[18]

Thus, country and regional economic environments will affect an international marketer's decisions about which global markets to enter and how.

POLITICAL-LEGAL ENVIRONMENT

Nations differ greatly in their political-legal environments. In considering whether to do business in a given country, a company should consider factors such as the country's attitudes toward international buying, government bureaucracy, political stability, and monetary regulations.

Some nations are very receptive to foreign firms; others are less accommodating. For example, India has tended to bother foreign businesses with import quotas, currency restrictions, and other limitations that make operating there a challenge. In contrast, neighboring Asian countries such as Singapore and Thailand court foreign investors and shower them with incentives and favorable operating conditions. Political stability is another issue. For example, India's government is notoriously unstable—the country has elected 10 new governments in the past 20 years—increasing the risk of doing business there. Although most international marketers still find India's huge market attractive, the unstable political situation will affect how they handle business and financial matters.[19]

Companies must also consider a country's monetary regulations. Sellers want to take their profits in a currency of value to them. Ideally, the buyer can pay in the seller's currency or in other world currencies. Short of this, sellers might accept a blocked currency—one whose removal from the country is restricted by the buyer's government—if they can buy other goods in that country that they need themselves or can sell elsewhere for a needed currency. Besides currency limits, a changing exchange rate also creates high risks for the seller.

Most international trade involves cash transactions. Yet many nations have too little hard currency to pay for their purchases from other countries. They may want to pay with other items instead of cash, which has led to a growing practice called **countertrade**. Countertrade takes several forms: *Barter* involves the direct exchange of goods or services, as when Azerbaijan imported wheat from Romania in exchange for crude oil, and Vietnam exchanged rice for Philippine fertilizer and coconuts. Another form is *compensation* (or *buyback*), whereby the seller sells a plant, equipment, or technology to another country and agrees to take payment in the resulting products. Thus, Japan's Fukusuke Corporation sold knitting machines and raw textile materials to Shanghai clothing manufacturer Chinatex in exchange for finished textiles produced on the machines. The most common form of countertrade is *counterpurchase*, in which the seller receives

Countertrade
International trade involving the direct or indirect exchange of goods for other goods instead of cash.

full payment in cash but agrees to spend some of the money in the other country. For example, Boeing sells aircraft to India and agrees to buy Indian coffee, rice, castor oil, and other goods and sell them elsewhere.[20]

Countertrade deals can be very complex. For example, a few years back, DaimlerChrysler agreed to sell 30 trucks to Romania in exchange for 150 Romanian jeeps, which it then sold to Ecuador for bananas, which were in turn sold to a German supermarket chain for German currency. Through this roundabout process, DaimlerChrysler finally obtained payment in German money.

CULTURAL ENVIRONMENT

Each country has its own folkways, norms, and taboos. When designing global marketing strategies, companies must understand how culture affects consumer reactions in each of its world markets. In turn, they must also understand how their strategies affect local cultures.

The Impact of Culture on Marketing Strategy   The seller must examine the ways consumers in different countries think about and use certain products before planning a marketing program. There are often surprises. For example, the average French man uses almost twice as many cosmetics and grooming aids as his wife. The Germans and the French eat more packaged, branded spaghetti than do Italians. Italian children like to eat chocolate bars between slices of bread as a snack. Women in Tanzania will not give their children eggs for fear of making them bald or impotent.

Companies that ignore such differences can make some very expensive and embarrassing mistakes. Here's an example:

> McDonald's and Coca-Cola managed to offend the entire Muslim world by putting the Saudi Arabian flag on their packaging. The flag's design includes a passage from the Koran (the sacred text of Islam), and Muslims feel very strongly that their Holy Writ should never be wadded up and tossed in the garbage. Nike faced a similar situation in Arab countries when Muslims objected to a stylized "Air" logo on its shoes, which resembled "Allah" in Arabic script. Nike apologized for the mistake and pulled the shoes from distribution.[21]

Business norms and behavior also vary from country to country. For example, American executives like to get right down to business and engage in fast and tough face-to-face bargaining. However, Japanese and other Asian businesspeople often find this behavior offensive. They prefer to start with polite conversation, and they rarely say no in face-to-face conversations. As another example, South Americans like to sit or stand very close to each other when they talk business—in fact, almost nose-to-nose. The American business executive tends to keep backing away as the South American moves closer. Both may end up being offended. American business executives need to be briefed on these kinds of factors before conducting business in another country.[22]

By the same token, companies that understand cultural nuances can use them to their advantage when positioning products internationally. Consider the following example:

■ Overlooking cultural differences can result in embarrassing mistakes. When Nike learned that this stylized "Air" logo resembled "Allah" in Arabic script, it apologized and pulled the shoes from the distribution.

> A television ad running these days in India shows a mother lapsing into a daydream: Her young daughter is in a beauty contest dressed as Snow White, dancing on a stage. Her flowing gown is an immaculate white. The garments of other contestants, who dance in the background, are a tad gray. Snow White, no surprise, wins the blue ribbon. The mother awakes to the laughter of her adoring family—and glances

■ Global cultural environment: By understanding cultural nuances, Whirlpool has become the leading brand in India's fast-growing market for automatic washing machines. It designed machines that keep whites whiter.

proudly at her Whirlpool White Magic washing machine. The TV spot is the product of 14 months of research by Whirlpool into the psyche of the Indian consumer. Among other things, [Whirlpool] learned that Indian homemakers prize hygiene and purity, which they associate with white. The trouble is, white garments often get discolored after frequent machine washing in local water. Besides appealing to this love of purity in its ads, Whirlpool custom-designed machines that are especially good with white fabrics. Whirlpool now is the leading brand in India's fast-growing market for fully automatic washing machines.[23]

Thus, understanding cultural traditions, preferences, and behaviors can help companies not only to avoid embarrassing mistakes but also to take advantage of cross-cultural opportunities.

The Impact of Marketing Strategy on Cultures

Whereas marketers worry about the impact of culture on their global marketing strategies, others may worry about the impact of marketing strategies on global cultures. For example, some critics argue that "globalization" really means "Americanization."

Down in the mall, between the fast-food joint and the bagel shop, a group of young people huddles in a flurry of baggy combat pants, skateboards, and slang. They size up a woman teetering past wearing DKNY, carrying *Time* magazine in one hand and a latte in the other. She brushes past a guy in a Yankees' baseball cap who is talking on his Motorola cell phone about the Martin Scorsese film he saw last night.

It's a standard American scene—only this isn't America, it's Britain. U.S. culture is so pervasive, the scene could be played out in any one of dozens of cities. Budapest or Berlin, if not Bogota or Bordeaux. Even Manila or Moscow. As the unrivaled global superpower, America exports its culture on an unprecedented scale. . . . Sometimes, U.S. ideals get transmitted—such as individual rights, freedom of speech, and respect for women—and local cultures are enriched. At other times, materialism or worse becomes the message and local traditions get crushed.[24]

Critics worry that the more people around the world are exposed to American lifestyles in the food they eat, the stores they shop, and television shows and movies they watch, the more they will lose their individual cultural identities. They contend that exposure to American values and products erodes other cultures and westernizes the world. Proponents of globalization counter that the cultural exchange goes both ways (see Marketing at Work 15.1).

MARKETING AT WORK | 15.1 |

Globalization Versus Americanization: Does Globalization Wear Mickey Mouse Ears?

Many social critics argue that large American multinationals like McDonald's, Coca-Cola, Nike, Microsoft, Disney, and MTV aren't just "globalizing" their brands, they are "Americanizing" the world's cultures. "Today, globalization often wears Mickey Mouse ears, eats big Macs, drinks Coke or Pepsi, and does its computing [with Microsoft] Windows [software]," says Thomas Friedman, in his book *The Lexus and the Olive Tree.*

The critics worry that, under such "McDomination," countries around the globe are losing their individual cultural identities. Teens in India watch MTV and ask their parents for more westernized clothes and other symbols of American pop culture and values. Grandmothers in small European villas no longer spend each morning visiting local meat, bread, and produce markets to gather the ingredients for dinner. Instead, they now shop at Wal-Mart Supercenters. Women in Saudi Arabia see American films and question their societal roles. In China, most people never drank coffee before Starbucks entered the market. Now Chinese consumers rush to Starbucks stores "because it's a symbol of a new kind of lifestyle." Similarly, in China, where McDonald's operates 80 restaurants in Beijing alone, nearly half of all children identify the chain as a domestic brand.

Such concerns, fed by international disputes over U.S. foreign policy and the Iraq war, have led to a backlash against American globalization. Well-known U.S. brands have become the targets of boycotts and protests in many international markets. As symbols of American capitalism, companies such as Coca-Cola, McDonald's, Nike, and KFC have been singled out by antiglobalization protestors in hot spots all around the world, especially when anti-American sentiment peaks. For example, almost immediately after U.S. armed forces unleashed their attack on Afghanistan following the September 11, 2001, terrorist attacks, McDonald's and KFC stores in Pakistan, India, and elsewhere around the world came under attack. In Karachi, Pakistan, thousands of pro-

testers, chanting "Death to America," mobbed the U.S. consulate. When police turned them back with barricades and tear gas, "they went for the next-best option: Colonel Sanders," said a reporter at the scene. "It didn't matter that the nearby KFC, 1 of 18 in Pakistan, was locally owned. The red, white, and blue KFC logo was justification enough." The protestors set fire to the store before police could turn them away.

Despite such images, defenders of globalization argue that concerns of "Americanization" and the potential damage to American brands are overblown. U.S. brands are doing very well internationally. In the most recent *BusinessWeek*/Interbrand survey of global brands, 12 of the top 15 brands were American-owned. And based on a recent study of 3,300 consumers in 41 countries, researchers concluded that consumers did not appear to translate anti-American sentiment into anti-brand sentiment:

What we *didn't* find was anti-American sentiment that colored judgments about U.S.-based global brands. [Instead] we found that it simply didn't matter to consumers whether the global brands they bought were American. To be sure, many people *said* they cared. A French panelist called American brands "imperialistic threats that undermine French culture." A German told us that Americans "want to impose their way on everybody." But the [talk] belied the reality. When we measured the extent to which consumers' purchase decisions were influenced by products' American roots, we discovered that the impact was negligible.

More fundamentally, most studies reveal that the cultural exchange goes both ways—America gets as well as gives cultural influence:

Hollywood dominates the global movie market—capturing 90 percent of audiences in some European markets. However, British TV is giving as much as it gets in serving up competition to U.S. shows, spawning such hits as *Who*

Wants to Be a Millionaire and *American Idol.* And while West Indian sports fans are now watching more basketball than cricket, and some Chinese young people are daubing the names of NBA superstars on their jerseys, the increasing popularity of American soccer has deep international roots. Even American childhood has increasingly been influenced by Asian and European cultural imports. Most kids know all about the Power Rangers, Tamagotchi and Pokémon, Sega and Nintendo. And J. K. Rowling's so-very-British Harry Potter books are shaping the thinking of a generation of American youngsters, not to mention the millions of American oldsters who've fallen under their spell as well. For the moment, English remains cyberspace's dominant language, and having Web access often means that Third World youth have greater exposure to American popular culture. Yet these same technologies enable Balkan students studying in the United States to hear Webcast news and music from Serbia or Bosnia. Thanks to broadband communication, foreign media producers will distribute films and television programs directly to American consumers without having to pass by U.S. gatekeepers.

American companies have also learned that to succeed abroad they must adapt to local cultural values and traditions rather than trying to force their own. McDonald's CEO notes that McDonald's is "a decentralized . . . network of locally owned stores that is very flexible and adapts very well to local conditions." This concept is echoed on the McDonald's Web site and throughout its corporate culture. The company encourages franchisees to introduce menu items that reflect local tastes, including the Maharaja Mac (made of chicken) in India, the McPork Burger with Thai Basil in Thailand, and the McTempeh Burger (made from fermented soybeans) in Indonesia. In fact, McDonald's restaurants in Bombay and Delhi feature a menu that is more than 75 percent locally developed.

(continued)

Similarly, Disneyland Paris flopped at first because it failed to take local cultural values and behaviors into account. According to a Euro Disney executive, "When we first launched, there was the belief that it was enough to be Disney. Now we realize that our guests need to be welcomed on the basis of their own culture and travel habits." That realization has made Disneyland Paris the number one tourist attraction in Europe—even more popular than the Eiffel Tower. The park now attracts more the 12.5 million visitors each year. And Disney recently introduced The Walt Disney Studios Park, a movie-themed park to accompany the revitalized Paris attraction. The new park blends Disney entertainment and attractions with the history and culture of European film. A show celebrating the history of animation features Disney characters speaking six different languages. Rides are narrated by foreign-born stars, including Jeremy Irons, Isabella Rossellini, and Nastassja Kinski, speaking in their native tongues.

So, does globalization wear Mickey Mouse ears? American culture does seem to carry more weight these days than that of other countries, making the United States the world's largest exporter of culture. But globalization is a two-way street. As one expert concludes, "If globalization has Mickey Mouse ears, it is also wearing a French beret, [talking on a Nokia cell phone, buying furniture at IKEA, driving a Toyota Camry] and listening to a Sony Walkman."

Sources: Quotes and other information from Thomas L. Friedman, *The Lexus and the Olive Tree: Understanding Globalization* (New York: Anchor Books, 2000); Douglas B. Holt, John A. Quelch, and Earl L. Taylor, "How Global Brands Compete," *Harvard Business Review,* September 2004, pp. 68–75; Elisabeth Rosenthal, "Buicks, Starbucks and Fried Chicken. Still China?" *New York Times,* February 25, 2002, p. A4; Susan Postlewaite, "U.S. Marketers Try to Head Off Boycotts," *Advertising Age,* March 31, 2003, pp. 3, 90; Paulo Prada and Bruce Orwall, "A Certain 'Je Ne Sais Quoi' at Disney's New Park—Movie-Themed Site Near Paris Is Multilingual, Serves Wine and Better Sausage Variety," *Wall Street Journal,* March 12, 2002, p. B1; Mark Rice-Oxley, "In 2,000 Years, Will the World Remember Disney or Plato?" *Christian Science Monitor,* January 15, 2004, p. 16; "Euro Disney S. C. A.," *Hoover's Company Records,* Austin, Texas, July 15, 2005, p. 90721; and Robert Berner and David Kiley, "Global Brands," *BusinessWeek,* August 1, 2005, pp. 86–94.

■ *Global marketing's impact on cultures: Concerns that "globalization" really means "Americanization" have sometimes led to a backlash against American globalization.*

Deciding Whether to Go International

Not all companies need to venture into international markets to survive. For example, most local businesses need to market well only in the local marketplace. Operating domestically is easier and safer. Managers don't need to learn another country's language and laws. They don't have to deal with unstable currencies, face political and legal uncertainties, or redesign their products to suit different customer expectations. However, companies that operate in global industries, where their strategic positions in specific markets are affected strongly by their overall global positions, must compete on a worldwide basis to succeed.

Any of several factors might draw a company into the international arena. Global competitors might attack the company's home market by offering better products or lower prices. The company might want to counterattack these competitors in their home markets to tie up their resources. Or the company's home market might be stagnant or shrinking, and foreign markets may present higher sales and profit opportunities. Or the company's customers might be expanding abroad and require international servicing.

Before going abroad, the company must weigh several risks and answer many questions about its ability to operate globally. Can the company learn to understand the preferences and buyer behavior of consumers in other countries? Can it offer competitively attractive products? Will it be able to adapt to other countries' business cultures and deal effectively with foreign nationals? Do the company's managers have the necessary international experience? Has management considered the impact of regulations and the political environments of other countries?

Because of the difficulties of entering international markets, most companies do not act until some situation or event thrusts them into the global arena. Someone—a domestic exporter, a foreign importer, a foreign government—may ask the company to sell abroad. Or the company may be saddled with overcapacity and need to find additional markets for its goods.

Deciding Which Markets to Enter

Before going abroad, the company should try to define its international *marketing objectives and policies*. It should decide what *volume* of foreign sales it wants. Most companies start small when they go abroad. Some plan to stay small, seeing international sales as a small part of their business. Other companies have bigger plans, seeing international business as equal to, or even more important than, their domestic business.

The company also needs to choose *how many* countries it wants to market in. Companies must be careful not to spread themselves too thin or to expand beyond their capabilities by operating in too many countries too soon. Next, the company needs to decide on the *types* of countries to enter. A country's attractiveness depends on the product, geographical factors, income and population, political climate, and other factors. The seller may prefer certain country groups or parts of the world. In recent years, many major new markets have emerged, offering both substantial opportunities and daunting challenges.

After listing possible international markets, the company must carefully evaluate each one. It must consider many factors. For example, Colgate's decision to enter the Chinese market seems fairly straightforward: China's huge population makes it the world's largest toothpaste market. And given that only 20 percent of China's rural dwellers now brush daily, this already huge market can grow even larger. Yet Colgate must still question whether market size *alone* is reason enough to invest heavily in China.

Colgate must ask some important questions: Will it be able to overcome cultural barriers and convince Chinese consumers to brush their teeth regularly? Does China provide for the needed production and distribution technologies? Can Colgate compete effectively with dozens of local competitors, a state-owned brand managed by Unilever, and P&G's Crest? Will the Chinese government remain stable and supportive? Colgate's current success in China suggests that it could answer yes to all of these questions. By aggressively pursuing promotional and educational programs—from massive ad campaigns to visits to local schools to sponsoring oral care research—Colgate has expanded its market share from 7 percent in 1995 to 35 percent today. Still, the company's future in China is filled with uncertainties.[25]

■ Colgate's decision to enter the huge Chinese market seems fairly straightforward. Using aggressive promotional and educational programs. Colgate has expanded its market share from 7 percent to 35 percent in less than a decade.

Possible global markets should be ranked on several factors, including market size, market growth, cost of doing business, competitive advantage, and risk level. The goal is to determine the potential of each market, using indicators such as those shown in Table 15.1. Then the marketer must decide which markets offer the greatest long-run return on investment.

TABLE 15.1
Indicators of Market Potential

Demographic characteristics	Sociocultural factors
Education	Consumer lifestyles, beliefs, and values
Population size and growth	Business norms and approaches
Population age composition	Social norms
	Languages

Geographic characteristics	Political and legal factors
Climate	National priorities
Country size	Political stability
Population density—urban, rural	Government attitudes toward global trade
Transportation structure and market accessibility	Government bureaucracy
	Monetary and trade regulations

Economic factors	
GDP size and growth	
Income distribution	
Industrial infrastructure	
Natural resources	
Financial and human resources	

Deciding How to Enter the Market

Once a company has decided to sell in a foreign country, it must determine the best mode of entry. Its choices are *exporting*, *joint venturing*, and *direct investment*. Figure 15.2 shows three market entry strategies, along with the options each one offers. As the figure shows, each succeeding strategy involves more commitment and risk, but also more control and potential profits.

EXPORTING

Exporting

Entering a foreign market by selling goods produced in the company's home country, often with little modification.

The simplest way to enter a foreign market is through **exporting**. The company may passively export its surpluses from time to time, or it may make an active commitment to expand exports to a particular market. In either case, the company produces all its goods in its home country. It may or may not modify them for the export market. Exporting involves the least change in the company's product lines, organization, investments, or mission.

Companies typically start with *indirect exporting*, working through independent international marketing intermediaries. Indirect exporting involves less investment because the firm does not require an overseas marketing organization or set of contacts. It also involves less risk. International marketing intermediaries bring know-how and services to the relationship, so the seller normally makes fewer mistakes.

Sellers may eventually move into *direct exporting*, whereby they handle their own exports. The investment and risk are somewhat greater in this strategy, but so is the potential return. A company can conduct direct exporting in several ways: It can set up a domes-

FIGURE 15.2
Market Entry Strategies

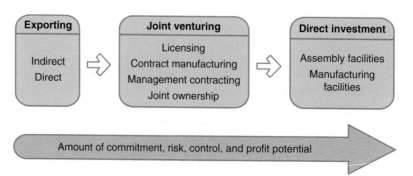

tic export department that carries out export activities. It can set up an overseas sales branch that handles sales, distribution, and perhaps promotion. The sales branch gives the seller more presence and program control in the foreign market and often serves as a display center and customer service center. The company can also send home-based salespeople abroad at certain times in order to find business. Finally, the company can do its exporting either through foreign-based distributors who buy and own the goods or through foreign-based agents who sell the goods on behalf of the company.

JOINT VENTURING

A second method of entering a foreign market is **joint venturing**—joining with foreign companies to produce or market products or services. Joint venturing differs from exporting in that the company joins with a host country partner to sell or market abroad. It differs from direct investment in that an association is formed with someone in the foreign country. There are four types of joint ventures: licensing, contract manufacturing, management contracting, and joint ownership.[26]

Licensing   **Licensing** is a simple way for a manufacturer to enter international marketing. The company enters into an agreement with a licensee in the foreign market. For a fee or royalty, the licensee buys the right to use the company's manufacturing process, trademark, patent, trade secret, or other item of value. The company thus gains entry into the market at little risk; the licensee gains production expertise or a well-known product or name without having to start from scratch.

Coca-Cola markets internationally by licensing bottlers around the world and supplying them with the syrup needed to produce the product. In Japan, Budweiser beer flows from Kirin breweries and Marlboro cigarettes roll off production lines at Japan Tobacco, Inc. Online brokerage E*TRADE has set up E*TRADE-branded Web sites under licensing agreements in several countries. And Tokyo Disneyland Resort is owned and operated by Oriental Land Company under license from The Walt Disney Company.

Licensing has potential disadvantages, however. The firm has less control over the licensee than it would over its own production facilities. Furthermore, if the licensee is very successful, the firm has given up these profits, and if and when the contract ends, it may find it has created a competitor.

Contract Manufacturing   Another option is **contract manufacturing**—the company contracts with manufacturers in the foreign market to produce its product or provide its service. Sears used this method in opening up department stores in Mexico and Spain, where it found qualified local manufacturers to produce many of the products it sells. The drawbacks of contract manufacturing are decreased control over the manufacturing process and loss of potential profits on manufacturing. The benefits are the chance to start faster, with less risk, and the later opportunity either to form a partnership with or to buy out the local manufacturer.

Management Contracting   Under **management contracting**, the domestic firm supplies management know-how to a foreign company that supplies the capital. The domestic firm exports management services rather than products. Hilton uses this arrangement in managing hotels around the world.

Joint venturing
Entering foreign markets by joining with foreign companies to produce or market a product or service.

Licensing
A method of entering a foreign market in which the company enters into an agreement with a licensee in the foreign market, offering the right to use a manufacturing process, trademark, patent, trade secret, or other item of value for a fee or royalty.

Contract manufacturing
A joint venture in which a company contracts with manufacturers in a foreign market to produce its product or provide its service.

Management contracting
A joint venture in which the domestic firm supplies the management know-how to a foreign company that supplies the capital; the domestic firm exports management services rather than products.

■ Licensing: Tokyo Disneyland Resort is owned and operated by the Oriental Land Co. Ltd. (a Japanese development company), under license from The Walt Disney Company.

Management contracting is a low-risk method of getting into a foreign market, and it yields income from the beginning. The arrangement is even more attractive if the contracting firm has an option to buy some share in the managed company later on. The arrangement is not sensible, however, if the company can put its scarce management talent to better uses or if it can make greater profits by undertaking the whole venture. Management contracting also prevents the company from setting up its own operations for a period of time.

Joint ownership

A joint venture in which a company joins investors in a foreign market to create a local business in which the company shares joint ownership and control.

Joint Ownership **Joint ownership** ventures consist of one company joining forces with foreign investors to create a local business in which they share joint ownership and control. A company may buy an interest in a local firm, or the two parties may form a new business venture. Joint ownership may be needed for economic or political reasons. The firm may lack the financial, physical, or managerial resources to undertake the venture alone. Or a foreign government may require joint ownership as a condition for entry.

KFC entered Japan through a joint ownership venture with Japanese conglomerate Mitsubishi. KFC sought a good way to enter the large but difficult Japanese fast-food market. In turn, Mitsubishi, one of Japan's largest poultry producers, understood the Japanese culture and had money to invest. Together, they helped KFC succeed in the semiclosed Japanese market. Surprisingly, with Mitsubishi's guidance, KFC developed decidedly un-Japanese positioning for its Japanese restaurants:

> When KFC first entered Japan, the Japanese were uncomfortable with the idea of fast food and franchising. They saw fast food as artificial and unhealthy. To build trust, KFC Japan created ads depicting the most authentic version of Colonel Sanders's beginnings possible. The ads featured the quintessential southern mother and highlighted the KFC philosophy—the southern hospitality, old American tradition, and authentic home cooking. With "My Old Kentucky Home" by Stephen Foster playing in the background, the commercial showed Colonel Sanders's mother making and feeding her grandchildren KFC chicken made with 11 secret spices. It conjured up scenes of good home cookin' from the American South, positioning KFC as wholesome, aristocratic food. The campaign was hugely successful—in the end, the Japanese people could not get enough of this special American chicken. Most Japanese grew to know "My Old Kentucky Home" by heart. There are now more than 1,100 KFC locations in the country.[27]

Joint ownership has certain drawbacks. The partners may disagree over investment, marketing, or other policies. Whereas many U.S. firms like to reinvest earnings for growth, local firms often prefer to take out these earnings; and whereas U.S. firms emphasize the role of marketing, local investors may rely on selling.

■ Joint ownership: KFC entered Japan through a joint ownership venture with Japanese conglomerate Mitsubishi.

DIRECT INVESTMENT

The biggest involvement in a foreign market comes through **direct investment**—the development of foreign-based assembly or manufacturing facilities. If a company has gained experience in exporting and if the foreign market is large enough, foreign production facilities offer many advantages. The firm may have lower costs in the form of cheaper labor or raw materials, foreign government investment incentives, and freight savings. The firm may improve its image in the host country because it creates jobs. Generally, a firm develops a deeper relationship with government, customers, local suppliers, and distributors, allowing it to adapt its products to the local market better. Finally, the firm keeps full control over the investment and, therefore, can develop manufacturing and marketing policies that serve its long-term international objectives.

The main disadvantage of direct investment is that the firm faces many risks, such as restricted or devalued currencies, falling markets, or government changes. In some cases, a firm has no choice but to accept these risks if it wants to operate in the host country.

Direct investment
Entering a foreign market by developing foreign-based assembly or manufacturing facilities.

 Linking the Concepts

Slow down here and think again about McDonald's global marketing issues.

- To what extent can McDonald's standardize for the Chinese market? What marketing strategy and program elements can be similar to those used in the United States and other parts of the Western world? Which ones must be adapted? Be specific.
- To what extent can McDonald's standardize its products and programs for the Canadian market? What elements can be standardized and which must be adapted?
- To what extent are McDonald's "globalization" efforts contributing to "Americanization" of countries and cultures around the world? What are the positives and negatives of such cultural developments?

Deciding on the Global Marketing Program

Companies that operate in one or more foreign markets must decide how much, if at all, to adapt their marketing strategies and programs to local conditions. At one extreme are global companies that use a **standardized marketing mix**, selling largely the same products and using the same marketing approaches worldwide. At the other extreme is an **adapted marketing mix**. In this case, the producer adjusts the marketing mix elements to each target market, bearing more costs but hoping for a larger market share and return.

The question of whether to adapt or standardize the marketing strategy and program has been much debated in recent years. On the one hand, some global marketers believe that technology is making the world a smaller place, and that consumer needs around the world are becoming more similar. This paves the way for "global brands" and standardized global marketing. Global branding and standardization, in turn, result in greater brand power and reduced costs from economies of scale.

On the other hand, the marketing concept holds that marketing programs will be more effective if tailored to the unique needs of each targeted customer group. If this concept applies within a country, it should apply even more in international markets. Despite global convergence, consumers in different countries still have widely varied cultural backgrounds. They still differ significantly in their needs and wants, spending power, product preferences, and shopping patterns. Because these differences are hard to change, most marketers adapt their products, prices, channels, and promotions to fit consumer desires in each country.

However, global standardization is not an all-or-nothing proposition but rather a matter of degree. Most international marketers suggest that companies should "think globally but act locally"—that they should seek a balance between standardization and adaptation. These

Standardized marketing mix
An international marketing strategy for using basically the same product, advertising, distribution channels, and other elements of the marketing mix in all the company's international markets.

Adapted marketing mix
An international marketing strategy for adjusting the marketing-mix elements to each international target market, bearing more costs but hoping for a larger market share and return.

marketers advocate a "glocal" strategy in which the firm standardizes certain core marketing elements and localizes others. The corporate level gives global strategic direction; local units focus on individual consumer differences across global markets. Simon Clift, head of marketing for global consumer goods giant Unilever, puts it this way: "We're trying to strike a balance between being mindlessly global and hopelessly local."[28]

McDonald's operates this way. It uses the same basic fast-food operating model in its restaurants around the world but adapts its menu to local tastes. In Korea it sells the Bulgogi Burger, a grilled pork patty on a bun with a garlicky soy sauce. In India, where cows are considered sacred, McDonald's serves McChicken, Filet-O-Fish, McVeggie (a vegetable burger), Pizza McPuffs, McAloo Tikki (a spiced-potato burger), and the Maharaja Mac—two all-chicken patties, special sauce, lettuce, cheese, pickles, onions on a sesame-seed bun. Similarly, L'Oréal markets truly global brands—including, among others, Maybelline, Garnier, Redkin, Lancombe, Helena Rubinstein, Kiehl's, Biotherm, Softsheen-Carson, Vichy, and Ralph Lauren and Giorgio Armani Parfums. But it adapts these brands to meet the cultural nuances of each local market: [29]

> How does a French company with a British CEO successfully market a Japanese version of an American lipstick in Russia? Ask L'Oréal, which sells more than $18 billion worth of cosmetics, hair-care products, and fragrances each year in 150 countries, making it the world's biggest cosmetics company. L'Oréal markets its brands globally by understanding how they appeal to cultural nuances in specific local markets. For L'Oréal, that means finding local brands, sprucing them up, positioning them for a specific target market, and exporting them to new customers all over the globe. Then, to support this effort,

■ Marketing mix adaptation: In India, McDonald's serves chicken, fish, and vegetable burgers, and the Maharaja Mac— two all-chicken patties, special sauce, lettuce, cheese, pickles, onions, on a sesame seed bun.

the company spends $4 billion annually to tailor global marketing messages to local cultures.

For example, in 1996, the company bought the stodgy American makeup producer, Maybelline. To reinvigorate and globalize the brand, it moved the unit's headquarters from Tennessee to New York City and added "New York" to the label. The resulting urban, street-smart, Big Apple image played well with the mid-price positioning of the workaday makeup brand. The makeover earned Maybelline a 20 percent market share in its category in Western Europe. The young urban positioning also hit the mark in Asia, where few women realize that the trendy "New York" Maybelline brand belongs to French cosmetics giant L'Oréal. When CEO Lindsey Owens-Jones recently addressed a UNESCO conference, nobody batted an eyelid when he described L'Oréal as "the United Nations of Beauty."

PRODUCT

Five strategies allow for adapting product and marketing communication to a global market (see Figure 15.3).[30] We first discuss the three product strategies and then turn to the two communication strategies.

Straight product extension means marketing a product in a foreign market without any change. Top management tells its marketing people, "Take the product as is and find customers for it." The first step, however, should be to find out whether foreign consumers use that product and what form they prefer.

Straight product extension has been successful in some cases and disastrous in others. Kellogg cereals, Gillette razors, Heineken beer, and Black & Decker tools are all sold successfully in about the same form around the world. But General Foods introduced its standard powdered Jell-O in the British market only to find that British consumers prefer a solid wafer or cake form. Likewise, Philips began to make a profit in Japan only after it reduced the size of its coffeemakers to fit into smaller Japanese kitchens and its shavers to fit smaller Japanese hands. Straight extension is tempting because it involves no additional product development costs, manufacturing changes, or new promotion. But it can be costly in the long run if products fail to satisfy foreign consumers.

Product adaptation involves changing the product to meet local conditions or wants. For example, Procter & Gamble's Vidal Sassoon shampoos contain a single fragrance worldwide, but the amount of scent varies by country: more in Europe but less in Japan, where subtle scents are preferred. Gerber serves Japanese baby food fare that might turn the stomachs of many Western consumers—local favorites include flounder and spinach stew, cod roe spaghetti, mugwort casserole, and sardines ground up in white radish sauce. And Finnish cell phone maker Nokia customizes its cell phones for every major market. Developers build in rudimentary voice recognition for Asia where keyboards are a problem and raise the ring volume so phones can be heard on crowded Asian streets.

Product invention consists of creating something new for a specific country's market. This strategy can take two forms. It might mean maintaining or reintroducing earlier product forms that happen to be well adapted to the needs of a given country. Volkswagen continued to produce and sell its old VW Beetle model in Mexico until just recently. Or a company might create a new product to meet a need in a given country. For example, Sony

Straight product extension
Marketing a product in a foreign market without any change.

Product adaptation
Adapting a product to meet local conditions or wants in foreign markets.

Product invention
Creating new products or services for foreign markets.

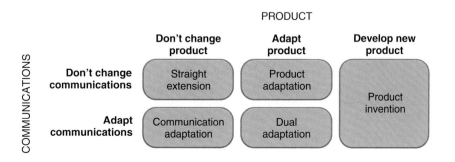

FIGURE 15.3

Five Global Product and Communications Strategies

added the "U" model to its VAIO personal computer line to meet the unique needs of Japanese consumers, even though it wouldn't have much appeal in the United States and other world markets:

> The U may be the most "Japanese" product in the entire Sony VAIO line. Dubbed a "palmtop," it is the smallest laptop in the world. Measuring less than 7 inches wide, with a 5-inch diagonal screen, it makes an ordinary laptop look sumo sized. Sony noticed that rush-hour trains to Tokyo were simply too crowded to allow many commuters to use their laptops. "The only people in Tokyo who have the luxury of a lap are the first people on the train," says Mark Hanson, a Sony vice president. The point of the U, he explains, "is to give users the experience of what I'd call a standing computer." The newest models do away with the keyboard altogether, and thus the laptop appearance. Instead, the U includes a touch screen and on-screen keyboard function, along with a separate foldable keyboard that can be attached when conditions allow. How would that translate into the U.S. market? The cultural differences are daunting. Far more Americans touch-type than do Japanese (a few Japanese characters convey a lot), and touch typists are likely to resist on-screen keyboards. And few Americans face a Tokyo-type rush-hour commute.[31]

PROMOTION

Companies can either adopt the same communication strategy they used in the home market or change it for each local market. Consider advertising messages. Some global companies use a standardized advertising theme around the world. Of course, even in highly standardized communications campaigns, some small changes might be required to adjust for language and minor cultural differences. For example, Guy Laroche uses virtually the same ads for its Drakkar Noir fragrances in Europe as in Arab countries. However, it subtly tones down the Arab versions to meet cultural differences in attitudes toward sensuality.

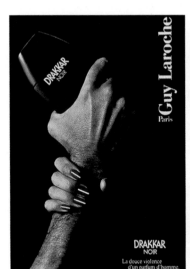 

■ Some companies standardize their advertising around the world, adapting only to meet cultural differences. Guy Larouche uses similar ads in Europe (left) and Arab countries (right), but tones down the sensuality in the Arab version—the man is clothed and the woman barely touches him.

Communication adaptation
A global communication strategy of fully adapting advertising messages to local markets.

Colors also are changed sometimes to avoid taboos in other countries. Purple is associated with death in most of Latin America, white is a mourning color in Japan, and green is associated with jungle sickness in Malaysia. Even names must be changed. Kellogg had to rename Bran Buds cereal in Sweden, where the name roughly translates as "burned farmer." And in the Americas, Mitsubishi changed the Japanese name of its Pajero SUV to Montero—it seems that *pajero* in Spanish is a slang term for sexual self-gratification. (See Marketing at Work 15.2 for more on language blunders in international marketing.)[32]

Other companies follow a strategy of **communication adaptation**, fully adapting their advertising messages to local markets. Kellogg's ads in the United States promote the taste and nutrition of Kellogg's cereals versus competitors' brands. In France, where consumers drink little milk and eat little for breakfast, Kellogg's ads must convince consumers that cereals are a tasty and healthful breakfast. In India, where many consumers eat heavy, fried breakfasts, Kellogg's advertising convinces buyers to switch to a lighter, more nutritious breakfast diet.

Similarly, Coca-Cola sells its low-calorie beverage as Diet Coke in North America, the United Kingdom, and the Middle and Far East but as Light elsewhere. According to Diet Coke's global brand manager, in Spanish-speaking countries Coke Light ads "position the soft drink as an object of desire, rather than as a way to feel good about yourself, as Diet Coke is positioned in the United States." This "desire positioning" plays off research showing that "Coca-Cola Light is seen in other parts of the world as a vibrant brand that exudes a sexy confidence."[33]

MARKETING AT WORK 15.2
Watch Your Language!

Many global companies have had difficulty crossing the language barrier, with results ranging from mild embarrassment to outright failure. Seemingly innocuous brand names and advertising phrases can take on unintended or hidden meanings when translated into other languages. Careless translations can make a marketer look downright foolish to foreign consumers.

We've all run across examples when buying products from other countries. Here's one from a firm in Taiwan attempting to instruct children on how to install a ramp on a garage for toy cars: "Before you play with, fix waiting plate by yourself as per below diagram. But after you once fixed it, you can play with as is and no necessary to fix off again." Many U.S. firms also are guilty of such atrocities when marketing abroad.

The classic language blunders involve standardized brand names that do not translate well. When Coca-Cola first marketed Coke in China in the 1920s, it developed a group of Chinese characters that, when pronounced, sounded like the product name. Unfortunately, the characters actually translated to mean "bite the wax tadpole." Now, the characters on Chinese Coke bottles translate as "happiness in the mouth."

Several U.S. carmakers have had similar problems when their brand names crashed into the language barrier. Chevy's Nova translated into Spanish as *no va*—"it doesn't go." GM changed the name to Caribe (Spanish for Caribbean) and sales increased. Buick scrambled to rename its new LaCrosse sedan the Allure in Canada after learning that the name comes too close to a Quebecois slang word for masturbation. And Rolls-Royce avoided the name Silver Mist in German markets, where *mist* means "manure." Sunbeam, however, entered the German market with its Mist Stick hair curling iron. As should have been expected, the Germans had little use for a "manure wand." A similar fate awaited Colgate when it introduced a toothpaste in France called Cue, the name of a notorious porno magazine.

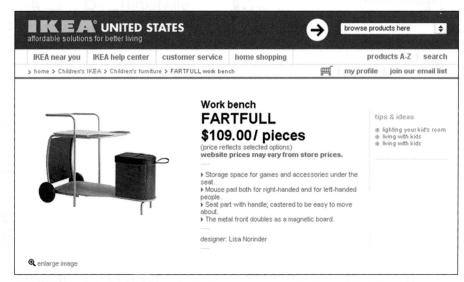

■ *Global language barriers: Some standardized brand names do not translate well globally.*

One well-intentioned firm sold its shampoo in Brazil under the name Evitol. It soon realized it was claiming to sell a "dandruff contraceptive." An American company reportedly had trouble marketing Pet milk in French-speaking areas. It seems that the word *pet* in French means, among other things, "to break wind." Similarly, IKEA marketed a children's workbench named FARTFULL (the word means "speedy" in Swedish)—it soon discontinued the product. Hunt-Wesson introduced its Big John products in Quebec as Gros Jos before learning that it means "big breasts" in French. Unlike FARTFULL, this gaffe had no apparent effect on sales.

Interbrand of London, the firm that created household names such as Prozac and Acura, recently developed a brand-name "hall of shame" list, which contains these and other foreign brand names you're never likely to see inside the local Safeway: Krapp toilet paper (Denmark), Crapsy Fruit cereal (France), Happy End toilet paper (Germany), Mukk yogurt (Italy), Zit lemonade (Germany), Poo curry powder (Argentina), and Pschitt lemonade (France).

Travelers often encounter well-intentioned advice from service firms that takes on meanings very different from those intended. The menu in one Swiss restaurant proudly stated, "Our wines leave you nothing to hope for." Signs in a Japanese hotel pronounced, "You are invited to take advantage of the chambermaid." At a laundry in Rome, it was, "Ladies, leave your clothes here and spend the afternoon having a good time." The brochure at a Tokyo car rental offered this sage advice: "When passenger of foot heave in sight, tootle the horn. Trumpet him melodiously at first, but if he still obstacles your passage, tootle him with vigor."

Advertising themes often lose—or gain—something in the translation. The Coors beer slogan "get loose with Coors" in Spanish came out as "get the runs with Coors." Coca-Cola's "Coke adds life" theme in Japanese translated into "Coke brings your ancestors back from the dead." The milk industry learned too late that its American advertising question "Got Milk?" translated in Mexico as a more provocative "Are you lactating?" In Chinese, the KFC slogan "finger-lickin' good" came out as "eat

(continued)

your fingers off." And Frank Perdue's classic line, "It takes a tough man to make a tender chicken," took on added meaning in Spanish: "It takes an aroused man to make a chicken affectionate." Even when the language is the same, word usage may differ from country to country. Thus, the British ad line for Electrolux vacuum cleaners—"Nothing sucks like an Electrolux"—would capture few customers in the United States.

So, what can a company do to avoid such mistakes? One answer is to call in the experts. Brand consultancy Lexicon Branding has been dreaming up brand names for more than 20 years, including names like Dasani, Swiffer, and Blackberry. David Placek, Lexicon's founder and president acknowledges that "coming up with catchy product names is a lot harder than

[you] might imagine, especially in this Global Age, when a word that might inspire admiration in one country can just as easily inspire red faces or unintended guffaws in another."

Lexicon maintains a global network of high-quality linguists from around the world that it calls GlobalTalk—"so we can call on them to evaluate words for language and cultural cues and miscues." Beyond screening out the bad names, the GlobalTalk network can also help find good ones. "We created the brand name Zima for Coors with help from the GlobalTalk network," says Placek. "I put out a message saying that we were looking for a name for a light alcoholic drink that would be cold, crisp, and refreshing. I got a fax in quickly from our Russian linguist saying that *zima* meant "winter" in Russian. I circled the word because I thought it

was beautiful and unusual, and the client loved it. We sent it around the world to make sure that it didn't have a negative connotation anywhere, and it didn't.

Sources: Lexicon example and quotes from "Naming Products Is No Game," *BusinessWeek Online,* April 9, 2004, accessed at www.businessweekonline.com. For the above and other examples, see David A. Ricks, "Perspectives: Translation Blunders in International Business," *Journal of Language for International Business,* vol. 7, no. 2, 1996, pp. 50–55; Ken Friedenreich, "The Lingua Too Franca," *World Trade,* April 1998, p. 98; Sam Solley, "Developing a Name to Work Worldwide," *Marketing,* December 21, 2000, p. 27; Thomas T. Sermon, "Cutting Corners in Language Risky Business," *Marketing News,* April 23, 2001, p. 9; Martin Croft, "Mind Your Language," *Marketing,* June 19, 2003, pp. 35–39; Mark Lasswell, "Lost in Translation," *Business 2.0,* August 2004, pp. 68–70; and "Lost in Translation," *Hispanic,* May 2005, p. 12.

Media also need to be adapted internationally because media availability varies from country to country. TV advertising time is very limited in Europe, for instance, ranging from four hours a day in France to none in Scandinavian countries. Advertisers must buy time months in advance, and they have little control over airtimes. Magazines also vary in effectiveness. For example, magazines are a major medium in Italy and a minor one in Austria. Newspapers are national in the United Kingdom but are only local in Spain.[34]

PRICE

Companies also face many problems in setting their international prices. For example, how might Black & Decker price its power tools globally? It could set a uniform price all around the world, but this amount would be too high a price in poor countries and not high enough in rich ones. It could charge what consumers in each country would bear, but this strategy ignores differences in the actual costs from country to country. Finally, the company could use a standard markup of its costs everywhere, but this approach might price Black & Decker out of the market in some countries where costs are high.

To deal with such issues, P&G adapts its pricing to local markets. For example, in Asia it has moved to a tiered pricing model.

When P&G first entered Asia, it used the approach that had made it so successful in the United States. It developed better products and charged slightly higher prices than competitors. It also charged nearly as much for a box of Tide or bottle of Pantene in Asia as it did in North America. But such high prices limited P&G's appeal in Asian markets, where most consumers earn just a few dollars a day. So last year P&G adopted a tiered pricing strategy to help compete against cheaper local brands while also protecting the value of its global brands. It slashed Asian production costs, streamlined distribution channels, and reshaped its product line to create more affordable prices. For example, it introduced a 320-gram bag of Tide Clean White for 23 cents compared with 33 cents for 350 grams of Tide Triple Action. Clean White doesn't offer such benefits as stain removal and fragrance, and it contains less advanced cleaning enzymes. But it costs less to make and outperforms every other brand at the lower price level. The results of P&G's new tiered pricing have been dramatic. Using the same approach for toothpaste, P&G now sells more Crest in China than in the United States. Its Olay brand is the best-selling facial cream in China and Rejoice is the best-selling shampoo.[35]

Regardless of how companies go about pricing their products, their foreign prices probably will be higher than their domestic prices for comparable products. A Gucci handbag may sell for $60 in Italy and $240 in the United States. Why? Gucci faces a *price escalation* problem. It must add the cost of transportation, tariffs, importer margin, wholesaler margin, and retailer margin to its factory price. Depending on these added costs, the product may have to sell for two to five times as much in another country to make the same profit. For example, a pair of Levi's jeans that sells for $30 in the United States typically fetches $63 in Tokyo and $88 in Paris. A computer that sells for $1,000 in New York may cost £1,000 in the United Kingdom. A Ford automobile priced at $20,000 in the United States might sell for more than $80,000 in South Korea.

Another problem involves setting a price for goods that a company ships to its foreign subsidiaries. If the company charges a foreign subsidiary too much, it may end up paying higher tariff duties even while paying lower income taxes in that country. If the company charges its subsidiary too little, it can be charged with *dumping*. Dumping occurs when a company either charges less than its costs or less than it charges in its home market. For example, the U.S. Southern Shrimp Alliance, which represents thousands of small shrimp operations in the southeast United States, recently complained that six countries (China, Thailand, Vietnam, Ecuador, India, and Brazil) have been dumping excess supplies of farmed shrimp on the U.S. market. The U.S. International Trade Commission agreed and the Commerce Department imposed duties as high as 112.81 percent on shrimp imports from the offending countries.[36] Various governments are always watching for dumping abuses, and they often force companies to set the price charged by other competitors for the same or similar products.

Recent economic and technological forces have had an impact on global pricing. For example, in the European Union, the transition to the euro is reducing the amount of price differentiation. As consumers recognize price differentiation by country, companies are being forced to harmonize prices throughout the countries that have adopted the single currency. Companies and marketers that offer the most unique or necessary products or services will be least affected by such "price transparency."

For Marie-Claude Lang, a 72-year-old retired Belgian postal worker, the euro is the best thing since bottled water—or French country sausage. Always on the prowl for bargains, Ms. Lang is now stalking the wide aisles of an Auchan hypermarket in Roncq, France, a 15-minute drive from her Wervick home.... Ms. Lang has been coming to France every other week for years to stock up on bottled water, milk, and yogurt. But the launch of the euro . . . has opened her eyes to many more products that she now sees cost less across the border. Today she sees that "saucisse de campagne," is cheaper "by about five euro cents," a savings she didn't notice when she had to calculate the difference between Belgian and French francs. At Europe's borders, the euro is turning into the coupon clipper's delight. Sure, price-conscious Europeans have long crossed into foreign territory to find everything from cheaper television sets to bargain bottles of Coca-Cola. But the new transparency is making comparisons a whole lot easier.[37]

■ International pricing: Twelve European Union countries have adopted the euro as a common currency creating "pricing transparency" and forcing companies to harmonize their prices throughout Europe.

The Internet will also make global price differences more obvious. When firms sell their wares over the Internet, customers can see how much products sell for in different countries. They might even be able to order a given product directly from the company location or dealer offering the lowest price. This will force companies toward more standardized international pricing.

DISTRIBUTION CHANNELS

Whole-channel view

Designing international channels that take into account all the necessary links in distributing the seller's products to final buyers, including the seller's headquarters organization, channels among nations, and channels within nations.

The international company must take a **whole-channel view** of the problem of distributing products to final consumers. Figure 15.4 shows the three major links between the seller and the final buyer. The first link, the *seller's headquarters organization*, supervises the channels and is part of the channel itself. The second link, *channels between nations*, moves the products to the borders of the foreign nations. The third link, *channels within nations*, moves the products from their foreign entry point to the final consumers. Some U.S. manufacturers may think their job is done once the product leaves their hands, but they would do well to pay more attention to its handling within foreign countries.

Channels of distribution within countries vary greatly from nation to nation. First, there are the large differences in the *numbers and types of intermediaries* serving each foreign market. For example, a U.S. company marketing in China must operate through a frustrating maze of state-controlled wholesalers and retailers. Chinese distributors often carry competitors' products and frequently refuse to share even basic sales and marketing information with their suppliers. Hustling for sales is an alien concept to Chinese distributors, who are used to selling all they can obtain. Working with, or getting around, this system sometimes requires much time and investment.

When Coke first entered China, for example, customers bicycled up to bottling plants to get their soft drinks. Many shopkeepers still don't have enough electricity to run soft drink coolers. Now, Coca-Cola has set up direct-distribution channels, investing heavily in refrigerators and trucks, and upgrading wiring so that more retailers can install coolers. The company has also built an army of more than 10,000 sales representatives that makes regular visits on resellers, often on foot or bicycle, to check on stocks and record sales. "Coke and its bottlers have been trying to map every supermarket, restaurant, barbershop, or market stall where a can of soda might be consumed," notes an industry observer. "Those data help Coke get closer to its customers, whether they are in large hypermarkets, Spartan noodle shops, or schools." Still, to reach the most isolated spots in the country, Coca-Cola relies on some pretty unlikely business partners—teams of delivery donkeys. "Massive advertising budgets can drum up demand," says another observer, "but if the distribution network doesn't exist properly or doesn't work, the potential of China's vast market cannot be realized."[38]

Another difference lies in the *size and character of retail units* abroad. Whereas large-scale retail chains dominate the U.S. scene, much retailing in other countries is done by many small, independent retailers. In India, millions of retailers operate tiny shops or sell in open markets. Their markups are high, but the actual price is lowered through haggling. Supermarkets could offer lower prices, but supermarkets are difficult to build and open because of many economic and cultural barriers. Incomes are low, and people prefer to shop daily for small amounts rather than weekly for large amounts. They also lack storage and refrigeration to

■ International distribution: Distribution channels vary greatly from nation to nation, as this photo from the streets of Beijing suggests.

FIGURE 15.4 Whole-Channel Concept for International Marketing

keep food for several days. Packaging is not well developed because it would add too much to the cost. These factors have kept large-scale retailing from spreading rapidly in developing countries.

Deciding on the Global Marketing Organization

Companies manage their international marketing activities in at least three different ways: Most companies first organize an export department, then create an international division, and finally become a global organization.

A firm normally gets into international marketing by simply shipping out its goods. If its international sales expand, the company organizes an *export department* with a sales manager and a few assistants. As sales increase, the export department can expand to include various marketing services so that it can actively go after business. If the firm moves into joint ventures or direct investment, the export department will no longer be adequate.

Many companies get involved in several international markets and ventures. A company may export to one country, license to another, have a joint ownership venture in a third, and own a subsidiary in a fourth. Sooner or later it will create *international divisions* or subsidiaries to handle all its international activity.

International divisions are organized in a variety of ways. An international division's corporate staff consists of marketing, manufacturing, research, finance, planning, and personnel specialists. It plans for and provides services to various operating units, which can be organized in one of three ways. They can be *geographical organizations*, with country managers who are responsible for salespeople, sales branches, distributors, and licensees in their respective countries. Or the operating units can be *world product groups*, each responsible for worldwide sales of different product groups. Finally, operating units can be *international subsidiaries*, each responsible for its own sales and profits.

Many firms have passed beyond the international division stage and become truly *global organizations*. They stop thinking of themselves as national marketers who sell abroad and start thinking of themselves as global marketers. The top corporate management and staff plan worldwide manufacturing facilities, marketing policies, financial flows, and logistical systems. The global operating units report directly to the chief executive or executive committee of the organization, not to the head of an international division. Executives are trained in worldwide operations, not just domestic *or* international. The company recruits management from many countries, buys components and supplies where they cost the least, and invests where the expected returns are greatest.

Today, major companies must become more global if they hope to compete. As foreign companies successfully invade their domestic markets, companies must move more aggressively into foreign markets. They will have to change from companies that treat their international operations as secondary, to companies that view the entire world as a single, borderless market.

REST STOP → REVIEWING THE CONCEPTS

It's time to stop and think back about the global marketing concepts you covered in this chapter. In the past, U.S. companies paid little attention to international trade. If they could pick up some extra sales through exporting, that was fine. But the big market was at home, and it teemed with opportunities. Companies today can no longer afford to pay attention only to their domestic market, regardless of its size. Many industries are global industries, and firms that operate globally achieve lower costs and higher brand awareness. At the same time, *global marketing* is risky because of variable exchange rates, unstable governments, protectionist tariffs and trade barriers, and several other factors. Given the potential gains and risks of international marketing, companies need a systematic way to make their global marketing decisions.

1. Discuss how the international trade system, economic, political-legal, and cultural environments affect a company's international marketing decisions.

A company must understand the *global marketing environment*, especially the international trade system. It must assess each foreign market's *economic*, *political-legal*, and *cultural characteristics*. The company must then decide whether it wants to go abroad and consider the potential risks and benefits. It must decide on the volume of international sales it wants, how many countries it wants to market in, and which specific markets it wants to enter. This decision calls for weighing the probable rate of return on investment against the level of risk.

2. Describe three key approaches to entering international markets.

The company must decide how to enter each chosen market—whether through *exporting*, *joint venturing*, or *direct invest-*

ment. Many companies start as exporters, move to joint ventures, and finally make a direct investment in foreign markets. In *exporting*, the company enters a foreign market by sending and selling products through international marketing intermediaries (indirect exporting) or the company's own department, branch, or sales representative or agents (direct exporting). When establishing a *joint venture*, a company enters foreign markets by joining with foreign companies to produce or market a product or service. In *licensing*, the company enters a foreign market by contracting with a licensee in the foreign market, offering the right to use a manufacturing process, trademark, patent, trade secret, or other item of value for a fee or royalty.

3. Explain how companies adapt their marketing mixes for international markets.

Companies must also decide how much their products, promotion, price, and channels should be adapted for each foreign market. At one extreme, global companies use a *standardized marketing mix* worldwide. Others use an *adapted marketing mix*, in which they adjust the marketing mix to each target market, bearing more costs but hoping for a larger market share and return.

4. Identify the three major forms of international marketing organizations.

The company must develop an effective organization for international marketing. Most firms start with an *export department* and graduate to an *international division*. A few become *global organizations*, with worldwide marketing planned and managed by the top officers of the company. Global organizations view the entire world as a single, borderless market.

Navigating the Key Terms

Adapted marketing mix (481)
Communication adaptation (484)
Contract manufacturing (479)
Countertrade (472)
Direct investment (481)
Economic community (469)

Exporting (478)
Global firm (468)
Joint ownership (480)
Joint venturing (479)
Licensing (479)
Management contracting (479)

Product adaptation (483)
Product invention (483)
Standardized marketing mix (481)
Straight product extension (483)
Whole-channel view (488)

Travel Log

Discussing the Issues

1. How do tariffs, quotas, and non-tariff trade barriers restrict international trade? Why would a government choose to restrict the import of foreign products? How do regional free trade arrangements help to encourage trade between nations?

2. What are the advantages and disadvantages of licensing, contract manufacturing, management contracting, and joint ownership?

3. Discuss the advantages and disadvantages of direct investment in a foreign market. List two foreign markets where a household appliance manufacturer would be interested in investing, and two foreign markets where it would have little interest in investing.

4. Identify the primary differences between a standardized marketing mix and an adapted marketing mix. List a category of goods or services that is well suited for each approach.

5. What are the five approaches to adapting a marketing offer for international markets?

6. Explain the difference between organizing the international marketing function as an export department, an international division, and a global organization. What drives the evolution from one organizational form to another?

Application Questions

1. Study the indicators of market potential listed in Table 15.1. Find a source of data for at least two indicators in each of the six major categories. Which of the information sources seems most and least reliable? What concerns would you have as a marketing manager evaluating market potential based on these sources?

2. Form a small group and suppose that you are members of Blockbuster's international division, headquartered in Dallas, Texas. Outline the potential cultural, political, and economic issues facing the company if it expands into Lebanon.

3. What mode of entry would you recommend for a company introducing sugar-free ice cream in Italy? What information would a company need to have before making this decision? For one of the entry modes you did not select, what would have to change for it to become the recommended choice?

Under the Hood: Focus on Technology

Communications and distribution technologies are truly making the world a smaller place. Cell phones, the Internet, and jet planes dramatically alter the way marketers reach consumers across the world. A small business anywhere in the world can open up a storefront online and receive international business overnight. Advances in distribution technology make it possible for the same small business to deliver goods around the world virtually overnight. But how do those companies navigate the regulations and cultural nuances unique to each international market? FedEx

Ship Manager allows small business managers to ship with ease. The software enables users to smoothly navigate international shipping, including customs, declarations, and licenses required as well as payment of fees, taxes, and duties.

1. Go to FedEx's Web site and learn more about FedEx Ship Manager. How might this technology help marketers reach consumers around the world?

2. What other technologies are helping marketers build relationships with consumers across the globe?

Focus on Ethics

The global marketplace exposes marketing managers to a variety of customs and traditions as companies expand internationally. The cultural and political differences between home and abroad can be difficult to navigate and fraught with ethical dilemmas. As you'll learn in the next chapter, the question arises as to whether a company must lower its ethical standards to compete effectively in countries with lower standards. For some companies, the answer is clear. "We told our people that we had the same ethical standards, same procedures, and same policies in these countries that we have in the United States, and we do," says John Hancock Chairman Stephen Brown. "We just felt that things like payoffs were wrong—and if we had to do business that way, we'd rather not do business."

1. Do you agree with John Hancock's approach to international business ethics?

2. Is it practical to apply the same standards in countries with vastly different legal and cultural environments?

3. Are there circumstances under which you believe it would be ethical to take a bribe or accept a large gift from a potential business partner?

*See John F. McGee and P. Tanganath Nayak, "Leaders' Perspectives on Business Ethics," *Prizm,* Arthur D. Little, Inc., Cambridge, Mass., first quarter 1994, pp. 71–72.

Videos

The NIVEA video case that accompanies this chapter is located in Appendix 1 at the back of the book.

Chapter**16**

→ **AFTER STUDYING THIS CHAPTER, YOU SHOULD BE ABLE TO**

1. identify the major social criticisms of marketing

2. define *consumerism* and *environmentalism* and explain how they affect marketing strategies

3. describe the principles of socially responsible marketing

4. explain the role of ethics in marketing

Marketing Ethics and Social Responsibility

Road Map Previewing the Concepts

You've almost completed your introductory marketing travels. In this final chapter, we'll focus on marketing as a social institution. First, we'll look at some common criticisms of marketing as it impacts individual consumers, other businesses, and society as a whole. Then, we'll examine consumerism, environmentalism, and other citizen and public actions to keep marketing in check. Finally, we'll see how companies themselves can benefit from proactively pursuing socially responsible and ethical practices that bring value not just to individual customers, but to society as a whole. You'll see that social responsibility and ethical actions are more than just the right thing to do; they're also good for business.

Before traveling on, let's visit the concept of social responsibility in business. Over the past several years, Nike has been a lightning rod for social responsibility criticisms. Critics have accused Nike of putting profits ahead of the interests of consumers and the broader public, both at home and abroad. You've probably read headlines alleging foreign "sweatshop" abuses and possible exploitation of inner-city consumers. Are these criticisms justified? Read on.

If you say "Nike" and "corporate social responsibility" in the same breath, most consumers will bring up the negatives. Over the past decade or more, Nike has been accused of everything from running sweatshops, using child labor, and exploiting low-income consumers to degrading the environment. However, if you look past the headlines, you might be surprised by all the socially responsible things that Nike does to make this world a better place.

Consider the Nike "sweatshop" charges. Like many other companies these days, to be more cost and price competitive, Nike outsources production to contractors in low-wage countries, such as China, Vietnam, Thailand, Indonesia, the Philippines, and Pakistan. The problem is that, through the eyes of affluent Westerners, workplace conditions in many third-world factories are truly appalling. These factories have long hours, unsafe working conditions, child labor, and substandard pay for people desperate to have any job at all. The issue became very public for Nike in 1996, when a *New York Times* editorial accused the company of running sweatshops and using child labor. Other critics quickly joined in, painting a picture of a greedy Nike, reaping profits at the expense of low-paid foreign laborers, many of them children, who were forced to work in the dismal conditions in suppliers' factories.

Nike responded that, years earlier, it had created a Code of Conduct, which demanded more socially-responsible labor practices by its contractors. What's more, according to Nike Founder and Chairman Phil Knight, Nike was actually improving the working conditions in low-wage countries. "Nike has paid, on average, double the minimum wage as defined in countries where its products are produced under contract," he claimed. Still, Nike took the charges seriously. It commissioned Andrew Young, a civil rights leader and former UN ambassador, to visit Nike factories abroad. Although Young saw room for improvement, he found none of the alleged extreme examples of abuse. Despite Nike's responses, the criticisms of its foreign manufacturing practices continued.

Nike has also received criticism at home. For example, it has been accused of wrongly targeting its most expensive shoes to low-income families, making the shoes an expensive status symbol for poor, urban street kids. Critics point to stories of youths gunned down in inner-city neighborhoods for a pair of $100 Nike sneakers. Nike isn't just selling utilitarian footwear, they claim. It's selling a hip athletic image created by a big-budget marketing campaign. The high price becomes the cost of membership in an artificial, "Just Do It" culture inhabited by the likes of Michael Jordan and LeBron James.

Although such criticisms have received most of the attention, a deeper look shows that Nike works hard at being a socially responsible global citizen. In 1998, Knight launched a radical six-point plan that raised minimum working age requirements in contract factories overseas and set targets for improving worker conditions. Nike also set up a huge corporate social responsibility department, reporting directly to Knight. In 2003, Nike began publishing a Corporate Responsibility Report (CSR). The expanded 2004 CSR report listed all of Nike's production locations, the status of its labor policies at each location, and its systematic plans for improving suppliers' employment practices. Even the skeptics have called it "a remarkable document"—the first listing of its kind for a global apparel brand.

Click on the "Responsibility" tab at the company's Web site (www.nikebiz.com), and you'll learn that Nike pursues an active agenda of good works. Nike and the Nike Foundation contributed more than $37.3 million in cash and products last year to programs that encourage youth participation in sports and that address challenges of globalization. The company's goal is to give 3 percent of annual pretax earnings to charities, nonprofit organizations, and community partners around the world. Here are just a few of the good things Nike is doing:

The NikeGo program aims to get kids more physically active, now and for the long-term. The program focuses on the belief that kids who are inspired to be active—to move, to "just GO"—become empowered to make positive life choices along the way. One of its many programs is the NikeGo Afterschool program, developed in collaboration with SPARK (Sports, Play, and Active Recreation for Kids) at San Diego State University. The program provides training, custom curricula, and equipment for after-school programs to YMCAs, local parks and recreation centers, Boys & Girls Clubs, and other organizations around the country.

Each year, Nike's Jordan Fundamentals Grant Program awards $2,500 grants to 400 teachers or professionals who design innovative learning experiences for economically disadvantaged students in grades 1 through 12. The program has already awarded more than $6 million in grants.

Nike has contributed nearly $25 million over the past five years to local charities in its home state of Oregon. For example, it recently provided grants to Portland-area high schools to help renovate running tracks using recycled athletic shoe material from Nike's Reuse-A-Shoe program.

Throughout the world, Nike works with governments, local communities, nongovernment organizations, and sports associations to actively promote kids' participation in sports through organized programs and better sports facilities. For example, Nike partnered with the United Nations High Commission for Refugees to pilot a sports program for young girls in refugee camps in Kenya. The goal is to use sports to promote girls' integration in education and to begin a process of building self-respect.

Nike also donates money for education, community development, and small business loans in the countries in which it operates. For example, Nike set up the Nike Village in Thailand, which combines progressive manufacturing with community development. This program encourages Nike contractors to set up satellite production facilities in rural areas to halt the migration into overcrowded Bangkok. The Nike Village hosts a community center, micro-loan programs, ecology and health education, and a women's advocacy group that provides business education and empowerment training.

Regarding its manufacturing practices, Nike has pledged to "make responsible sourcing a business reality that enhances workers' lives." For example, Nike's Code of Conduct is now available in 19 languages. It spells out Nike's position on child labor, forced labor, compensation, benefits, work hours, environment, safety, and health. Contractors must post the code where workers can read it and certify that they adhere to it. Today, Nike has 85 employees located in countries where Nike products are manufactured who visit suppliers' factories on a daily basis.

Nike is also committed to sustainable environmental practices. "Our [environmental] targets for products wearing the Nike name are simple and straightforward," claims Nike: "zero toxic substances, zero waste, and 100 percent recoverable product." For example, it has developed environmentally responsible products such as PVC-free footwear and a line of 100 percent organic cotton apparel. Nike's Reuse-A-Shoe program collects old shoes of any brand—some 2 million pairs a year—then grinds them up and gives them new life as athletic surfaces or in other Nike products. Through its Air to Earth program, Nike works with environmental organizations to educate students in grades 4 through 9 about conservation, reuse, and recycling.

Like most global companies, Nike isn't perfect when it comes to matters of social responsibility. But many marketing experts think that the company's corporate heart is now in the right place. "We made some mistakes," says Phil Knight. But the mistakes were not for a lack of trying to do what's right. Issues of social responsibility are seldom clear cut. Still, they are very, very important. In Knight's words:

> As a citizen of the world, Nike must Do the Right Thing. I know what makes for good performance when I see it on the running track. I know it when I read quarterly results from the finance department. I have to admit, though, I'm not sure how we measure good performance in corporate responsibility. I'm not convinced anybody [knows how]. Why not? Because there are no standards, no agreed-on definitions. . . . Until [we have such standards], we have to figure it out for ourselves. [No matter what the standards, however] the performance of Nike and every other global company in the twenty-first century will be measured as much by our impact on quality of life as it is by revenue growth and profit margins."[1]

Responsible marketers discover what consumers want and respond with market offerings that create value for buyers in order to capture value in return. The *marketing concept* is a philosophy of customer value and mutual gain. Its practice leads the economy by an invisible hand to satisfy the many and changing needs of millions of consumers.

Not all marketers follow the marketing concept, however. In fact, some companies use questionable marketing practices, and some marketing actions that seem innocent in themselves strongly affect the larger society. Consider the sale of cigarettes. On the face of it, companies should be free to sell cigarettes, and smokers should be free to buy them. But this private transaction involves larger questions of public policy. For example, the smokers are harming their health and may be shortening their own lives. Smoking places a financial burden on the smoker's family and on society at large. Other people around smokers may suffer discomfort and harm from secondhand smoke. Finally, marketing cigarettes to adults might also influence young people to begin smoking. Thus, the marketing of tobacco products has sparked substantial debate and negotiation in recent years.[2]

This chapter examines the social effects of private marketing practices. We examine several questions: What are the most frequent social criticisms of marketing? What steps have private citizens taken to curb marketing ills? What steps have legislators and government agencies taken to curb marketing ills? What steps have enlightened companies taken to carry out socially responsible and ethical marketing that creates value for both individual customers and society as a whole?

Social Criticisms of Marketing

Marketing receives much criticism. Some of this criticism is justified; much is not. Social critics claim that certain marketing practices hurt individual consumers, society as a whole, and other business firms.

MARKETING'S IMPACT ON INDIVIDUAL CONSUMERS

Consumers have many concerns about how well the American marketing system serves their interests. Surveys usually show that consumers hold mixed or even slightly unfavorable attitudes toward marketing practices. Consumer advocates, government agencies, and other critics have accused marketing of harming consumers through high prices, deceptive practices, high-pressure selling, shoddy or unsafe products, planned obsolescence, and poor service to disadvantaged consumers.

High Prices   Many critics charge that the American marketing system causes prices to be higher than they would be under more "sensible" systems. They point to three factors—*high costs of distribution*, *high advertising and promotion costs*, and *excessive markups*.

High Costs of Distribution.

A long-standing charge is that greedy intermediaries mark up prices beyond the value of their services. Critics charge that there are too many intermediaries, that intermediaries are inefficient, or that they provide unnecessary or duplicate services. As a result, distribution costs too much, and consumers pay for these excessive costs in the form of higher prices.

How do resellers answer these charges? They argue that intermediaries do work that would otherwise have to be done by manufacturers or consumers. Markups reflect services that consumers themselves want—more convenience, larger stores and assortments, more service, longer store hours, return privileges, and others. In fact, they argue, retail competition is so intense that margins are actually quite low. For example, after taxes, supermarket chains are typically left with barely 1 percent profit on their sales. If some resellers try to charge too much relative to the value they add, other resellers will step in with lower prices. Low-price stores such as Wal-Mart, Costco, and other discounters pressure their competitors to operate efficiently and keep their prices down.

High Advertising and Promotion Costs.

Modern marketing is also accused of pushing up prices to finance heavy advertising and sales promotion. For example, a few dozen tablets of a heavily promoted brand of pain reliever sell for the same price as 100 tablets of less promoted brands. Differentiated products—cosmetics, detergents, toiletries—include promotion and packaging costs that can amount to 40 percent or more of the manufacturer's price to the retailer. Critics charge that much of the packaging and promotion adds only psychological value to the product rather than functional value.

Marketers respond that advertising does add to product costs. But it also adds value by informing potential buyers of the availability and merits of a brand. Brand name products may cost more, but branding gives buyers assurances of consistent quality. Moreover, consumers can usually buy functional versions of products at lower prices. However, they *want* and are willing to pay more for products that also provide psychological benefits—that make them feel wealthy, attractive, or special. Also, heavy advertising and promotion may be necessary for a firm to match competitors' efforts—the business would lose "share of mind" if it did not match competitive spending. At the same time, companies are cost-conscious about promotion and try to spend their money wisely.

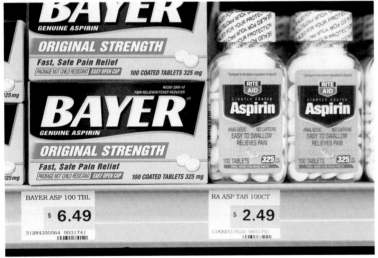

■ A heavily promoted brand of aspirin sells for much more than a virtually identical non-branded or store-branded product. Critics charge that promotion adds only psychological value to the product rather than functional value.

Excessive Markups.

Critics also charge that some companies mark up goods excessively. They point to the drug industry, where a pill costing 5 cents to make may cost the consumer $2 to buy. They point to the pricing tactics of funeral homes that prey on the confused emotions of bereaved relatives and to the high charges for auto repair and other services.

Marketers respond that most businesses try to deal fairly with consumers because they want to build customer relationships and repeat business. Most consumer abuses are unintentional. When shady marketers do take advantage of consumers, they should be reported to Better Business Bureaus and to state and federal agencies. Marketers also respond that consumers often don't understand the reasons for high markups. For example, pharmaceutical markups must cover the costs of purchasing, promoting, and distributing existing medicines plus the high research and development costs of formulating and testing new medicines.

Deceptive Practices   Marketers are sometimes accused of deceptive practices that lead consumers to believe they will get more value than they actually do. Deceptive practices fall into three groups: pricing, promotion, and packaging. *Deceptive pricing* includes practices such as falsely advertising "factory" or "wholesale" prices or a large price reduction from a phony, high retail list price. *Deceptive promotion* includes practices such as misrepresenting the product's features or performance or luring the customers to the store for a bargain that is out of stock. *Deceptive packaging* includes exaggerating package contents through subtle design, using misleading labeling, or describing size in misleading terms.

To be sure, questionable marketing practices do occur. For example, at one time or another, we've all gotten an envelope in the mail screaming something like "You have won $10,000,000!" Or a pop-up ad promises free goods or discounted prices. In recent years, sweepstakes companies have come under the gun for their deceptive communication practices. Sweepstakes promoter Publishers Clearing House recently paid heavily to settle claims that its high-pressure tactics had misled consumers into believing that they had won prizes when they hadn't. The Wisconsin Attorney General asserted that "there are older consumers who send [sweepstakes companies] checks and money orders on a weekly basis with a note that says they were very upset that the prize patrol did not come."[3]

Deceptive practices have led to legislation and other consumer protection actions. For example, in 1938 Congress reacted to such blatant deceptions as Fleischmann's Yeast's claim to straighten crooked teeth by enacting the Wheeler-Lea Act giving the FTC power to regulate "unfair or deceptive acts or practices." The FTC has published several guidelines listing deceptive practices. Despite new regulations, some critics argue that deceptive claims are still the norm.

■ Questionable marketing practices: Sweepstakes promoter Publishers Clearing House recently paid heavily to settle claims that its high-pressure tactics had misled consumers into believing that they had won prizes which they hadn't.

The toughest problem is defining what is "deceptive." For instance, an advertiser's claim that its powerful laundry detergent "makes your washing machine 10 feet tall," showing a surprised homemaker watching her appliance burst through her laundry room ceiling, isn't intended to be taken literally. Instead, the advertiser might claim, it is "puffery"—innocent exaggeration for effect. One noted marketing thinker, Theodore Levitt, once claimed that advertising puffery and alluring imagery are bound to occur—and that they may even be desirable: "There is hardly a company that would not go down in ruin if it refused to provide fluff, because nobody will buy pure functionality. . . . Worse, it denies . . . people's honest needs and values. Without distortion, embellishment, and elaboration, life would be drab, dull, anguished, and at its existential worst."[4]

However, others claim that puffery and alluring imagery can harm consumers in subtle ways, and that consumers must be protected through education:

The real danger to the public . . . comes not from outright lies—in most cases facts can ultimately be proven and mistakes corrected. But . . . advertising uses [the power of images and] emotional appeals to shift the viewer's focus away from facts. Viewers who do not take the trouble to distinguish between provable claims and pleasant but meaningless word play end up buying "the sizzle, not the steak" and often paying high. The best defense against misleading ads . . . is not tighter controls on [advertisers], but more education and more critical judgment among . . . consumers. Just as we train children to be wary of strangers offering candy, to count change at a store, and to kick the tires before buying a used car, we must make the effort to step back and judge the value of . . . advertisements, and then master the skills required to separate spin from substance.[5]

Marketers argue that most companies avoid deceptive practices because such practices harm their business in the long run. Profitable customer relationships are built upon a foundation of value and trust. If consumers do not get what they expect, they will switch to more reliable products. In addition, consumers usually protect themselves from deception. Most consumers recognize a marketer's selling intent and are careful when they buy, sometimes to the point of not believing completely true product claims.

High-Pressure Selling   Salespeople are sometimes accused of high-pressure selling that persuades people to buy goods they had no thought of buying. It is often said that insurance, real estate, and cars are *sold*, not *bought*. Salespeople are trained to deliver smooth, canned talks to entice purchase. They sell hard because sales contests promise big prizes to those who sell the most.

But in most cases, marketers have little to gain from high-pressure selling. Such tactics may work in one-time selling situations for short-term gain. However, most selling involves building long-term relationships with valued customers. High-pressure or deceptive selling can do serious damage to such relationships. For example, imagine a Procter & Gamble account manager trying to pressure a Wal-Mart buyer, or an IBM salesperson trying to browbeat a General Electric information technology manager. It simply wouldn't work.

Shoddy, Harmful, or Unsafe Products   Another criticism concerns poor product quality or function. One complaint is that, too often, products are not made well and services are not performed well. A second complaint is that many products deliver little benefit, or that they might even be harmful. For example, many critics have pointed out the dangers of today's fat-laden fast food. In fact, McDonald's recently faced a class-action lawsuit charging that its fare has contributed to the nationwide obesity epidemic:

> [Four years ago] the parody newspaper *The Onion* ran a joke article under the headline "Hershey's Ordered to Pay Obese Americans $135 Billion." The hypothesized class-action lawsuit said that Hershey "knowingly and willfully" marketed to children "rich, fatty candy bars containing chocolate and other ingredients of negligible nutritional value," while "spiking" them with "peanuts, crisped rice, and caramel to increase consumer appeal." Some joke. [In 2002] New York City attorney Sam Hirsch filed a strikingly similar suit—against McDonald's—on behalf of a class of obese and overweight children. He alleged that the fast-food chain "negligently, recklessly, carelessly and/or intentionally" markets to children food products that are "high in fat, salt, sugar, and cholesterol" while failing to warn of those ingredients' links to "obesity, diabetes, coronary heart disease, high blood pressure, strokes, elevated cholesterol intake, related cancers," and other conditions. Industry defenders decried the suit as frivolous. It is ridiculous, they claimed, to blame the fast-food industry for consumers' "own nutritional ignorance, lack of willpower, genetic predispositions, failure to exercise, or whatever else may play a role in [their] obesity." A federal judge agreed and dismissed the suit, explaining that "it is not the place of the law to protect them from their own excess." However, in 2005, the dismissal was reversed and the suit was back on the docket.[6]

Who's to blame for the nation's obesity problem? And what should responsible food companies do about it? As with most social responsibility issues, there are no easy answers. McDonald's has worked to improve its fare and make its menu and its customers healthier. It cut its "supersize" option, introduced healthier "Go Active! Adult Happy Meals, and now offers all-white-meat chicken McNuggets, low-fat "milk jugs," yogurt, fruit, and other healthier choices. However, the McDonald's menu board is still packed with some pretty less-than-healthy selections. And other fast-feeders seem to be going the other way? Hardee's, for example, recently introduced a 1,410 calorie Monster Thickburger, and Burger King launched its Enormous Omelet breakfast sandwich, packing an unapologetic 47 grams of fat. Are these companies being socially irresponsible? Or are they simply serving customers choices they want?[7] (See Marketing at Work 16.1.)

A third complaint concerns product safety. Product safety has been a problem for several reasons, including company indifference, increased product complexity, and poor quality control. For years, Consumers Union—the nonprofit testing and information organization that publishes the *Consumer Reports* magazine and Web site—has reported various hazards in tested products: electrical dangers in appliances, carbon monoxide poisoning from room heaters, injury risks from lawn mowers, and faulty automobile design, among many others. The organization's testing and other activities have helped consumers make better buying decisions and encouraged businesses to eliminate product flaws.

However, most manufacturers *want* to produce quality goods. The way a company deals with product quality and safety problems can damage or help its reputation. Companies selling poor-quality or unsafe products risk damaging conflicts with consumer groups and regulators. Moreover, unsafe products can result in product liability suits and large awards for damages. The average compensatory jury award for product liability cases from 1993 through 2002 was $700,000, but individual or class action awards frequently run into the tens of millions of dollars.[8]

More fundamentally, consumers who are unhappy with a firm's products may avoid future purchases and talk other consumers into doing the same. Thus, quality missteps can have severe consequences. Today's marketers know that customer-driven quality results in customer value and satisfaction, which, in turn, creates profitable customer relationships.

Planned Obsolescence Critics also have charged that some producers follow a program of planned obsolescence, causing their products to become obsolete before they actually should need replacement. For example, consider printer companies and their toner cartridges:

> Refilled printer cartridges offer the same or improved performance for about half the price of new ones. A number of businesses, from local shops to Office Depot and other big box stores, now offer toner cartridge refill services to businesses. You can refill most cartridges 8 to 10 times—if you can find the right parts. However, printer companies would prefer to sell their cartridges for $50 or more, rather than allow someone to refill an exhausted one for half the price. So they make it hard for refill operations by continually introducing new models and tweaking inkjet cartridges and laser toner containers. Refill parts manufacturers struggle to keep up, jockeying with the printer companies that are working to thwart refill-enabling rollers, ribbons, and other pieces. "You've got planned obsolescence," says the owner of Laser Logic, a small cartridge refilling company, as he disassembles a cartridge to inspect its drum unit, wiper blade, clips, springs, and other mechanisms for signs of wear. "It's kind of like a *Mission Impossible*: At the end of this tape, the toner cartridge will self-destruct."[9]

■ Planned obsolescence: Printer companies continually introduce new cartridge models and tweak designs. "You've got planned obsolescence," says the owner of Laser Logic, a small cartridge refilling company. "It's kind of like a *Mission Impossible*: At the end of this tape, the toner cartridge will self-destruct."

Critics charge that some producers continually change consumer concepts of acceptable styles to encourage more and earlier buying. An obvious example is constantly changing clothing fashions. Other producers are accused of holding back attractive

MARKETING AT WORK   16.1
The National Obesity Debate: Who's to Blame?

As you've no doubt heard, the United States is facing an obesity epidemic. Everyone seems to agree on the problem—as a nation, we're packing on the pounds. But still unresolved is another weighty issue: Who's to blame? Is it the fault of self-indulgent consumers who just can't say no to sticky buns, fat burgers, and other tempting treats? Or is it the fault of greedy food marketers who are cashing in on vulnerable consumers, turning us into a nation of overeaters?

The problem is a big one. Studies show that some 127 million American adults and more than 9 million children and teens are overweight or obese. According to a Rand Corporation study, the number of people in the United States who are 100 pounds or more overweight quadrupled between 1986 and 2000, from 1 adult in 200 to 1 in 50. This weight increase comes despite repeated medical studies showing that excess weight brings increased risks for heart disease, diabetes, and other maladies, even cancer.

So, here's that weighty question again. If we know that we're overweight and that it's bad for us, why do we keep putting on the pounds? Who's to blame? The answer, of course, depends on whom you ask. However, these days, lots of people are blaming food marketers. In the national obesity debate, food marketers have become a favorite target of almost everyone, from politicians, public policy makers, and the press to overweight consumers themselves. And some food marketers are looking pretty much guilty as charged.

Take Hardee's, for example. At a time when other fast-food chains such as McDonald's, Wendy's, and Subway were getting "leaner," Hardee's introduced the decadent Thickburger, featuring two-thirds of a pound of Angus beef. It followed up with the *Monster* Thickburger: two 5.7 ounce Angus beef patties, four strips of bacon, and three slices of American cheese, all nestled in a buttered sesame-seed bun slathered with mayonnaise! The Monster Thickburger weighs in at a whopping 1,410 calories and 107 grams of fat, far greater than the government's recommended fat intake for an entire day.

Surely, you say, Hardee's made a colossal blunder here. Not so! At least, not from a profit viewpoint. Sales at Hardee's 2,050 outlets have climbed 20 percent since it introduced the Thickburger line, resulting in fatter profits and a tripling of Hardee's stock price. It seems that some consumers, especially in Hardee's target market of young men aged 18 to 34, just love fat burgers. A reporter asked a 27-year-old construction worker who was downing a Monster

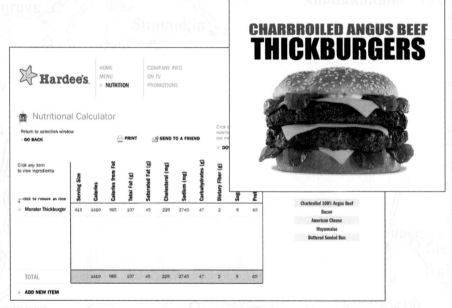

■ *The obesity debate: Is Hardee's being socially irresponsible or simply practicing good marketing by giving customers a big juicy burger that clearly pings their taste buds? Judging by the nutrition calculator at its Web site, the company certainly isn't hiding the nutritional facts.*

functional features, then introducing them later to make older models obsolete. Critics claim that this occurs in the consumer electronics and computer industries. For example, Intel and Microsoft have been accused over the years of holding back their next-generation computer chips and software until demand is exhausted for the current generation. Still other producers are accused of using materials and components that will break, wear, rust, or rot sooner than they should. One writer put it this way: "The marvels of modern technology include the development of a soda can which, when discarded, will last forever—and a . . . car, which, when properly cared for, will rust out in two or three years."[10]

Thickburger if he'd thought about its effect on his health. "I've never even thought about it," he replied, "and to be honest, I don't really care. It just tastes good."

Hardee's certainly isn't hiding the nutritional facts. Here's how it describes Thinckburgers on its Web site:

There's only one thing that can slay the hunger of a young guy on the move: the Thinkburger line at Hardee's. With nine cravable varieties, including the classic Original Thickburger and the monument to decadence, the Monster Thickburger, quick-service goes premium with 100% Angus beef and all the fixings. . . . If you want to indulge in a big, delicious, juicy burger, look no further than Hardee's.

Hardee's even offers a Nutrition Calculator on it's Web site showing the calories, fat, and other content of all its menu items.

So, should Hardee's hang its head in shame? Is it being socially irresponsible by aggressively promoting overindulgence to ill-informed or unwary consumers? Or is it simply practicing good marketing, creating more value for its customers by offering a big juicy burger that clearly pings their taste buds and letting them make their own choices? Critics claim the former; industry defenders claim the latter.

The question of blame gets even murkier when it comes to child obesity. The debate rages over the marketing of everything from fast food and soft drinks in our nation's school cafeterias to cereal, cookies, and other "not-so-good-for-you" products targeted toward kids and teens, who are seen as especially vulnerable to seductive or misleading marketing pitches. Once again, many public and private advocacy groups point the finger at food marketers. They worry that a five year old watching cute characters and fun ads for Trix sugared cereal or Oreo cookies during a Saturday morning cartoon show probably understands little about good nutrition. These critics have called on food marketers to voluntarily adopt more responsible children's marketing practices.

The food industry itself seems split on the issue. Kraft Foods appears to agree. It announced that it would no longer advertise products such as Oreos, Chips Ahoy!, and most of its Oscar Mayer Lunchables meals on programs targeted to children aged 6 to 11—programs like *SpongeBob SquarePants* and *All Grown Up*. Child advocates applauded the move. And the Grocery Manufacturers' Association seemed to follow suit, saying that it would unveil beefed-up guidelines for food advertising that targets children.

Cereal maker General Mills, however, took just the opposite tack. Rather than giving in to pressures from politicians and the press by cutting back on marketing to kids, General Mills fielded its largest-ever kids advertising effort. It proudly launched a "Choose Breakfast" TV campaign, which plays up the health benefits of eating breakfast cereal—including its Trix, Cocoa Puffs, Lucky Charms, Shrek, and other sugary cereals. To strengthen the wellness message, it's tacking 10-second trailers on to the ends of commercials promoting the importance of eating a good breakfast. The 10-second spots urge kids to visit a special Web site where they can sign a pledge to "choose a healthy breakfast and to be active each and every day."

With the "Choose Breakfast" campaign, General Mills hopes to present itself as part of the kids' health solution, not the problem. "We have a different point of view than Kraft," says General Mills' chief marketing officer. "We think that kids should be eating cereal, including pre-sweetened cereal." Critics decry the campaign: "The makers of these cereals have done a fabulous marketing job of making people think that these are healthy foods when [in fact] they are cookies," says one. However, the Children's Advertising Review Unit (CARU) of the Council of Better Business Bureaus sides with General Mills. "I think it's responsible advertising," says the CARU's director. "They're encouraging a behavior that is healthful" as opposed to not eating breakfast.

So, back to that big question: Who's to blame for our nation's obesity epidemic? Is it the marketers who promote unhealthy but irresistible fare to vulnerable consumers? Or is it the fault of consumers themselves for failing to take personal responsibility for their own health and well-being? It's a weighty decision for many food marketers. And, as is the case with most social responsibility issues, finding the answer to that question is even harder than trying to take off some of those extra pounds.

Sources: Sarah Ellison, "Kraft Limits on Kid's Ads May Cheese Off Rivals," *Wall Street Journal*, January 13, 2005, p. B3; Steven Gray, "At Fast-Food Chains, Era of the Giant Burger (Plus Bacon) Is Here," *Wall Street Journal*, January 27, 2005, p. B1; "Obesity Research Ignites Calls for Food Ad Curbs," *Marketing Week*, May 5, 2005, p. 8; John Schmeltzer, "Second Cereal Maker Announces Changes to Child Marketing Campaign," *Knight Ridder Tribune Business News*, June 23, 2005, p. 1; Janet Adamy, "General Mills Touts Sugary Cereal as Healthy Kids Breakfast," *Wall Street Journal*, June 22, 2005, p. B1; Andrew Martin, "Food Fight Begins over Children's Ads," *Knight Ridder Tribune Business News*, July 15, 2005, p. 1; and Stephanie Thompson, "General Mills Slaps Down Kraft," *Advertising Age*, June 27, 2005, pp. 1, 53.

Marketers respond that consumers *like* style changes; they get tired of the old goods and want a new look in fashion or a new design in cars. No one has to buy the new look, and if too few people like it, it will simply fail. For most technical products, customers *want* the latest innovations, even if older models still work. Companies that withhold new features run the risk that competitors will introduce the new feature first and steal the market. For example, consider personal computers. Some consumers grumble that the consumer electronics industry's constant push to produce "faster, smaller, cheaper" models means that they must continually buy new machines just to keep up. Others, however, can hardly wait for the latest model to arrive.

There was a time not so long ago when planned obsolescence was a troubling ghost in the machine. A half a century ago, consumer advocates described engineers at General Electric who intentionally shortened the life of lightbulbs and automotive engineers who proposed limiting the life spans of cars. That was then. In today's topsy-turvy world of personal computers, obsolescence is not only planned, it is extolled by marketers as a virtue. Moreover, there has been hardly a peep from consumers, who dutifully line up to buy each new generation of faster, more powerful machines, eager to embrace the promise of simpler, happier, and more productive lives. Today's computer chips are no longer designed to wear out; in fact, they will last for decades or longer. Even so, hapless consumers now rush back to the store ever more quickly, not to replace broken parts but to purchase new computers that will allow them to work faster, see more vivid colors, or play cooler games.[11]

Thus, most companies do not design their products to break down earlier, because they do not want to lose customers to other brands. Instead, they seek constant improvement to ensure that products will consistently meet or exceed customer expectations. Much of so-called planned obsolescence is the working of the competitive and technological forces in a free society—forces that lead to ever-improving goods and services.

Poor Service to Disadvantaged Consumers   Finally, the American marketing system has been accused of serving disadvantaged consumers poorly. For example, critics claim that the urban poor often have to shop in smaller stores that carry inferior goods and charge higher prices. The presence of large, national chain stores in low-income neighborhoods would help to keep prices down. However, the critics accuse major chain retailers of "redlining," drawing a red line around disadvantaged neighborhoods and avoiding placing stores there.

Similar redlining charges have been leveled at the insurance, consumer lending, banking, and health-care industries. Home and auto insurers have been accused of assigning higher premiums to people with poor credit ratings. The insurers claim that individuals with bad credit tend to make more insurance claims, and that this justifies charging them higher premiums. However, critics and consumer advocates have accused the insurers of a new form of redlining. Says one writer, "This is a new excuse for denying coverage to the poor, elderly, and minorities."[12]

More recently, consumer advocates have charged that preparers such as H&R Block and Jackson Hewitt are taking advantage of the working poor by offering them "rapid refunds" after preparing their taxes. Customers receive these rapid refunds when their taxes are prepared, rather than waiting two weeks to a month for the IRS to send the refund. The big problem is that the refunds are not free. In fact, they're "refund anticipation loans" (RALs) with fees starting around $130, which represents an APR (annual percentage rate) of 245 percent of the average, working poor person's refund. More than 10.6 million low-income families have requested rapid refunds, and tax preparers have made more than $1.4 billion in profits on them. Many states don't require loan materials to be written in a language that the average consumer can understand. Consumer advocates are pressuring state legislatures to pass such measures to avoid this injustice.[13]

Clearly, better marketing systems must be built to service disadvantaged consumers. In fact, many marketers profitably target such consumers with legitimate goods and services that create real value. In cases where marketers do not step in to fill the void, the government likely will. For example, the FTC has taken action against sellers who advertise false values, wrongfully deny services, or charge disadvantaged customers too much.

 Linking the Concepts

Hit the brakes for a moment and cool down. Few marketers *want* to abuse or anger consumers—it's simply not good business. Instead, as you know well by now, most marketers work to build long-term, profitable relationships with customers based on real value and caring. Still, some marketing abuses do occur.

- Think back over the past three months or so and list the instances in which you've suffered a marketing abuse such as those just discussed. Analyze your list: What kinds of companies were involved? Were the abuses intentional? What did the situations have in common?

- Pick one of the instances you listed and describe it in detail. How might you go about righting this wrong? Write out an action plan, and then do something to remedy the abuse. If we all took such actions when wronged, there would be far fewer wrongs to right!

MARKETING'S IMPACT ON SOCIETY AS A WHOLE

The American marketing system has been accused of adding to several "evils" in American society at large. Advertising has been a special target—so much so that the American Association of Advertising Agencies launched a campaign to defend advertising against what it felt to be common but untrue criticisms.

False Wants and Too Much Materialism   Critics have charged that the marketing system urges too much interest in material possessions. People are judged by what they *own* rather than by who they *are*. This drive for wealth and possessions hit new highs in the 1980s and 1990s, when phrases such as "greed is good" and "shop till you drop" seemed to characterize the times.

In the new millennium, many social scientists have noted a reaction against the opulence and waste of the previous decades and a return to more basic values and social commitment. However, our infatuation with material things continues.

> If you made a graph of American life since the end of World War II, every line concerning money and the things that money can buy would soar upward, a statistical monument to materialism. Inflation adjusted income per American has almost tripled. The size of the typical new house has more than doubled. A two-car garage was once a goal; now we're nearly a three-car nation. Designer everything, personal electronics, and other items that didn't even exist a half-century ago are now affordable. Although our time spent shopping has dropped in recent years to just 3 hours a week, American households currently put away only a sad 0.9 percent of their income in savings, which is about 11 percent of what it was in the 1950s. Some consumers will let nothing stand between them and their acquisitions. Recently, in a Florida Wal-Mart, post-Thanksgiving shoppers rushing to buy DVD players (on sale for $29) knocked down a woman, trampled her, and left her unconscious.[14]

THIS AD IS FULL OF LIES.

LIE #1: ADVERTISING MAKES YOU BUY THINGS YOU DON'T WANT.
Advertising is often accused of inducing people to buy things against their will. But when was the last time you returned home from the local shopping mall with a bag full of things you had absolutely no use for? The truth is, nothing short of a pointed gun can get *anybody* to spend money on something he or she doesn't want.
No matter how effective an ad is, you and millions of other American consumers make your own decisions. If you don't believe it, ask someone who knows firsthand about the limits of advertising. Like your local Edsel dealer.

LIE #2: ADVERTISING MAKES THINGS COST MORE. Since advertising costs money, it's natural to assume it costs *you* money. But the truth is that advertising often brings prices down.
Consider the electronic calculator, for example. In the late 1960s, advertising created a mass market for calculators. That meant more of them needed to be produced, which brought the price of producing each calculator down. Competition spurred by advertising brought the price down still further.
As a result, the same product that used to cost hundreds of dollars now costs as little as five dollars.

LIE #3: ADVERTISING HELPS BAD PRODUCTS SELL.
Some people worry that good advertising sometimes covers up for bad products.
But nothing can make you like a bad product. So, while advertising can help convince you to try something once, it can't make you buy it twice. If you don't like what you've bought, you won't buy it again. And if enough people feel the same way, the product dies on the shelf.
In other words, the only thing advertising can do for a bad product is help you find out it's a bad product. And you take it from there.

LIE #4: ADVERTISING IS A WASTE OF MONEY. Some people wonder why we don't just put all the money spent on advertising directly into our national economy.
The answer is, we already do.
Advertising helps products sell, which holds down prices, which helps sales even more. It creates jobs. It informs you about all the products available and helps you compare them. And it stimulates the competition that produces new and better products at reasonable prices.
If all that doesn't convince you that advertising is important to our economy, you might as well stop reading.
Because on top of everything else, advertising has paid for a large part of the magazine you're now holding. And that's the truth.

ADVERTISING.
ANOTHER WORD FOR FREEDOM OF CHOICE.
American Association of Advertising Agencies

■ The American Association of Advertising Agencies has run ads to counter common advertising criticisms.

The critics do not view this interest in material things as a natural state of mind but rather as a matter of false wants created by marketing. Businesses hire Madison Avenue to stimulate people's desires for goods, and Madison Avenue uses the mass media to create materialistic models of the good life. People work harder to earn the necessary money. Their purchases increase the output of American industry, and industry, in turn, uses Madison Avenue to stimulate more desire for the industrial output. Thus, marketing is seen as creating false wants that benefit industry more than they benefit consumers. Some critics even take their concerns to the streets.

> For the last seven years Bill Talen, also known as Reverend Billy, has taken to the streets, exhorting people to resist temptation—the temptation to shop. With the zeal of a street-corner preacher and the schmaltz of a street-corner Santa,

■ Materialism: With the zeal of a street-corner preacher and the schmaltz of a street-corner Santa. Reverend Billy—founder of the Church of Stop Shopping—will tell anyone who will listen that people are walking willingly into the hell fires of consumption.

Reverend Billy will tell anyone willing to listen that people are walking willingly into the hellfires of consumption. He believes that shoppers have almost no resistance to the media messages that encourage them, around the clock, to want things and buy them. He sees a population lost in consumption, the meaning of individual existence vanished in a fog of wanting, buying, and owning too many things. To further his message, Billy started the Church of Stop Shopping. Sporting a televangelist's pompadour, a priest's collar, and a white megaphone, Reverend Billy is often accompanied by his gospel choir when he strides into stores he considers objectionable or shows up at protests like the annual post-Thanksgiving Buy Nothing Day event on Fifth Avenue in Manhattan. When the choir, which is made up of volunteers, erupts in song, it is hard to ignore: "Stop shopping! Stop shopping! We will never shop again!"[15]

These criticisms overstate the power of business to create needs, however. People have strong defenses against advertising and other marketing tools. Marketers are most effective when they appeal to existing wants rather than when they attempt to create new ones. Furthermore, people seek information when making important purchases and often do not rely on single sources. Even minor purchases that may be affected by advertising messages lead to repeat purchases only if the product delivers the promised customer value. Finally, the high failure rate of new products shows that companies are not able to control demand.

On a deeper level, our wants and values are influenced not only by marketers but also by family, peer groups, religion, ethnic background, and education. If Americans are highly materialistic, these values arose out of basic socialization processes that go much deeper than business and mass media could produce alone.

Too Few Social Goods Business has been accused of overselling private goods at the expense of public goods. As private goods increase, they require more public services that are usually not forthcoming. For example, an increase in automobile ownership (private good) requires more highways, traffic control, parking spaces, and police services (public goods). The overselling of private goods results in "social costs." For cars, the social costs include traffic congestion, air pollution, gasoline shortages, and deaths and injuries from car accidents.

A way must be found to restore a balance between private and public goods. One option is to make producers bear the full social costs of their operations. The government could require automobile manufacturers to build cars with even more safety features, more efficient engines, and better pollution control systems. Automakers would then raise their prices to cover extra costs. If buyers found the price of some cars too high, however, the producers of these cars would disappear. Demand would then move to those producers that could support the sum of the private and social costs.

A second option is to make consumers pay the social costs. For example, many cities around the world are starting to charge "congestion tolls" in an effort to reduce traffic congestion. To unclog its streets, the city of London now levies a congestion charge of $14.50 per day per car to drive in an eight-square-mile area downtown. The charge has not only reduced traffic congestion by 18 percent, it raises money to shore up London's public transportation system. Similarly, San Diego has turned some of its HOV (high-occupancy vehicle) lanes into HOT (high-occupancy toll) lanes for drivers carrying too few passengers. Regular drivers can use the HOV lanes, but they must pay a toll ranging from $.50 off-peak to $4.00 during rush hour. If the costs of driving rise high enough, consumers will travel at nonpeak times or find alternative transportation modes.[16]

Cultural Pollution   Critics charge the marketing system with creating *cultural pollution*. Our senses are being constantly assaulted by marketing and advertising. Commercials interrupt serious programs; pages of ads obscure magazines; billboards mar beautiful scenery; spam fills our e-mailboxes. These interruptions continually pollute people's minds with messages of materialism, sex, power, or status. A recent study found that 65 percent of Americans feel constantly bombarded with too many marketing messages, and some critics call for sweeping changes.[17]

Marketers answer the charges of "commercial noise" with these arguments: First, they hope that their ads reach primarily the target audience. But because of mass-communication channels, some ads are bound to reach people who have no interest in the product and are, therefore, bored or annoyed. People who buy magazines addressed to their interests—such as *Vogue* or *FORTUNE*—rarely complain about the ads because the magazines advertise products of interest.

Second, ads make much of television and radio free to users and keep down the costs of magazines and newspapers. Many people think commercials are a small price to pay for these benefits. Finally, today's consumers have alternatives. For example, they can zip and zap TV commercials or avoid them altogether on many cable or satellite channels. Thus, to hold consumer attention, advertisers are making their ads more entertaining and informative.

Too Much Political Power   Another criticism is that business wields too much political power. "Oil," "tobacco," "auto," and "pharmaceuticals" senators support an industry's interests against the public interest. Advertisers are accused of holding too much power over the mass media, limiting media freedom to report independently and objectively. The critics ask: How can magazines afford to tell the truth about the low nutritional value of packaged foods when these magazines are being subsidized by such advertisers as General Foods, Kellogg's, Kraft, and General Mills? How can the major TV networks criticize the practices of the large auto companies when such companies invest billions of dollars a year in broadcast advertising?

American industries do promote and protect their own interests. They have a right to representation in Congress and the mass media, although their influence can become too great. Fortunately, many powerful business interests once thought to be untouchable have been tamed in the public interest. For example, Standard Oil was broken up in 1911, and the meatpacking industry was disciplined in the early 1900s after exposures by Upton Sinclair. Ralph Nader caused legislation that forced the automobile industry to build safer cars, and the Surgeon General's Report resulted in cigarette companies putting health warnings on their packages.

More recently, giants such as AT&T, R.J. Reynolds, Intel, and Microsoft have felt the impact of regulators seeking to balance the interests of big business against those of the

■ Balancing private and public goods: In response to lane-clogging traffic congestion like that above, London now levies a congestion charge. The charge has reduced congestion by 40 percent and raised money to shore up the city's public transportation system.

public. Moreover, because the media receive advertising revenues from many different advertisers, it is easier to resist the influence of one or a few of them. Too much business power tends to result in counterforces that check and offset these powerful interests.

MARKETING'S IMPACT ON OTHER BUSINESSES

Critics also charge that a company's marketing practices can harm other companies and reduce competition. Three problems are involved: acquisitions of competitors, marketing practices that create barriers to entry, and unfair, competitive marketing practices.

Critics claim that firms are harmed and competition reduced when companies expand by acquiring competitors rather than by developing their own new products. The large number of acquisitions and rapid pace of industry consolidation over the past several decades have caused concern that vigorous young competitors will be absorbed and that competition will be reduced. In virtually every major industry—retailing, entertainment, financial services, utilities, transportation, automobiles, telecommunications, health care—the number of major competitors is shrinking.

Acquisition is a complex subject. Acquisitions can sometimes be good for society. The acquiring company may gain economies of scale that lead to lower costs and lower prices. A well-managed company may take over a poorly managed company and improve its efficiency. An industry that was not very competitive might become more competitive after the acquisition. But acquisitions can also be harmful and, therefore, are closely regulated by the government.

Critics have also charged that marketing practices bar new companies from entering an industry. Large marketing companies can use patents and heavy promotion spending, and can tie up suppliers or dealers to keep out or drive out competitors. Those concerned with antitrust regulation recognize that some barriers are the natural result of the economic advantages of doing business on a large scale. Other barriers could be challenged by existing and new laws. For example, some critics have proposed a progressive tax on advertising spending to reduce the role of selling costs as a major barrier to entry.

Finally, some firms have, in fact, used unfair, competitive marketing practices with the intention of hurting or destroying other firms. They may set their prices below costs, threaten to cut off business with suppliers, or discourage the buying of a competitor's products. Various laws work to prevent such predatory competition. It is difficult, however, to prove that the intent or action was really predatory. In recent years, Wal-Mart, American Airlines, Intel, and Microsoft have all been accused of various predatory practices. Take Microsoft, for example:

> Competitors and regulators in both the United States and Europe have accused giant Microsoft of predatory "bundling" practices. That's the term used to describe Microsoft's practice of continually adding new features to Windows, the operating system installed on more than 90 percent of desktop computers. Because customers are essentially locked in to Windows, it's easy for the company to get them to use its other software—even if competitors make better products. That dampens competition, reduces choice, and could retard innovation. Since 2000, Microsoft has paid nearly $6 billion to resolve antitrust suits with other companies for damages caused by its past business practices. For example, it recently paid out more than $775 million to IBM for bullying the company in past years by withholding marketing dollars for selling machines bundled with Netscape instead of Microsoft's browser, Internet Explorer. In another action, the European Commission took dramatic steps to stop what it saw as predatory bundling by Microsoft. It ordered Microsoft to offer a version of Windows with its media-playing software stripped out. The Commission also fined Microsoft more than $600 million for using its "near monopoly" in the Windows operating system to squeeze out rivals in other types of software.[18]

Although competitors and the government charge that Microsoft's actions are predatory, the question is whether this is unfair competition or the healthy competition of a more efficient company against less efficient ones.

Citizen and Public Actions to Regulate Marketing

Because some people view business as the cause of many economic and social ills, grass-roots movements have arisen from time to time to keep business in line. The two major movements have been *consumerism* and *environmentalism*.

CONSUMERISM

American business firms have been the target of organized consumer movements on three occasions. The first consumer movement took place in the early 1900s. It was fueled by rising prices, Upton Sinclair's writings on conditions in the meat industry, and scandals in the drug industry. The second consumer movement, in the mid-1930s, was sparked by an upturn in consumer prices during the Great Depression and another drug scandal.

The third movement began in the 1960s. Consumers had become better educated, products had become more complex and potentially hazardous, and people were unhappy with American institutions. Ralph Nader appeared on the scene to force many issues, and other well-known writers accused big business of wasteful and unethical practices. President John F. Kennedy declared that consumers had the right to safety and to be informed, to choose, and to be heard. Congress investigated certain industries and proposed consumer-protection legislation. Since then, many consumer groups have been organized and several consumer laws have been passed. The consumer movement has spread internationally and has become very strong in Europe.

But what is the consumer movement? **Consumerism** is an organized movement of citizens and government agencies to improve the rights and power of buyers in relation to sellers. Traditional *sellers' rights* include:

Consumerism
An organized movement of citizens and government agencies to improve the rights and power of buyers in relation to sellers.

- The right to introduce any product in any size and style, provided it is not hazardous to personal health or safety; or, if it is, to include proper warnings and controls.
- The right to charge any price for the product, provided no discrimination exists among similar kinds of buyers.
- The right to spend any amount to promote the product, provided it is not defined as unfair competition.
- The right to use any product message, provided it is not misleading or dishonest in content or execution.
- The right to use any buying incentive programs, provided they are not unfair or misleading.

Traditional *buyers' rights* include:

- The right not to buy a product that is offered for sale.
- The right to expect the product to be safe.
- The right to expect the product to perform as claimed.

Comparing these rights, many believe that the balance of power lies on the seller's side. True, the buyer can refuse to buy. But critics feel that the buyer has too little information, education, and protection to make wise decisions when facing sophisticated sellers. Consumer advocates call for the following additional consumer rights:

- The right to be well informed about important aspects of the product.
- The right to be protected against questionable products and marketing practices.
- The right to influence products and marketing practices in ways that will improve the "quality of life."

Each proposed right has led to more specific proposals by consumerists. The right to be informed includes the right to know the true interest on a loan (truth in lending), the true cost per unit of a brand (unit pricing), the ingredients in a product (ingredient labeling), the nutritional value of foods (nutritional labeling), product freshness (open dating), and the true benefits of a product (truth in advertising). Proposals related to consumer protection

■ Consumer desire for more information led to packing labels with useful facts, from ingredients and nutrition facts to recycling and country of origin information. Jones Soda even puts customer-submitted photos on its labels.

include strengthening consumer rights in cases of business fraud, requiring greater product safety, and giving more power to government agencies. Proposals relating to quality of life include controlling the ingredients that go into certain products and packaging, reducing the level of advertising "noise," and putting consumer representatives on company boards to protect consumer interests.

Consumers have not only the *right* but also the *responsibility* to protect themselves instead of leaving this function to someone else. Consumers who believe they got a bad deal have several remedies available, including contacting the company or the media; contacting federal, state, or local agencies; and going to small-claims courts.

ENVIRONMENTALISM

Environmentalism

An organized movement of concerned citizens and government agencies to protect and improve people's living environment.

Whereas consumerists consider whether the marketing system is efficiently serving consumer wants, environmentalists are concerned with marketing's effects on the environment and with the costs of serving consumer needs and wants. **Environmentalism** is an organized movement of concerned citizens, businesses, and government agencies to protect and improve people's living environment.

Environmentalists are not against marketing and consumption; they simply want people and organizations to operate with more care for the environment. The marketing system's goal, they assert, should not be to maximize consumption, consumer choice, or consumer satisfaction, but rather to maximize life quality. And "life quality" means not only the quantity and quality of consumer goods and services, but also the quality of the environment. Environmentalists want environmental costs included in both producer and consumer decision making.

The first wave of modern environmentalism in the United States was driven by environmental groups and concerned consumers in the 1960s and 1970s. They were concerned with damage to the ecosystem caused by strip-mining, forest depletion, acid rain, loss of the atmosphere's ozone layer, toxic wastes, and litter. They also were concerned with the loss of recreational areas and with the increase in health problems caused by bad air, polluted water, and chemically treated food.

The second environmentalism wave was driven by government, which passed laws and regulations during the 1970s and 1980s governing industrial practices impacting the environment. This wave hit some industries hard. Steel companies and utilities had to invest billions of dollars in pollution control equipment and costlier fuels. The auto industry had to introduce expensive emission controls in cars. The packaging industry had to find ways to reduce litter. These industries and others have often resented and resisted environmental regulations, especially when they have been imposed too rapidly to allow companies to make proper adjustments. Many of these companies claim they have had to absorb large costs that have made them less competitive.

The first two environmentalism waves have now merged into a third and stronger wave in which companies are accepting responsibility for doing no harm to the environment. They are shifting from protest to prevention, and from regulation to responsibility. More companies are adopting policies of **environmental sustainability**—developing strategies that both sustain the environment *and* produce profits for the company (see Marketing at Work 16.2). According to one strategist, "The challenge is to develop a *sustainable global economy:* an economy that the planet is capable of supporting indefinitely. . . . [It's] an enormous challenge—and an enormous opportunity."[19]

Figure 16.1 shows a grid that companies can use to gauge their progress toward environmental sustainability. At the most basic level, a company can practice *pollution prevention*. This involves more than pollution control—cleaning up waste after it has been created. Pollution prevention means eliminating or minimizing waste before it is created. Companies emphasizing prevention have responded with "green marketing" programs—developing ecologically safer products, recyclable and biodegradable packaging, better pollution controls, and more energy-efficient operations.

For example, FedEx has been working hard at reducing greenhouse gas (GHG) emissions by designing packaging that requires less energy and creates less pollution to produce, and by developing a fleet of fuel-efficient hybrid, diesel delivery trucks, which yield a 33 percent decrease in GHG emissions. Similarly, Wal-Mart is testing environmentally friendly store designs for its supercenters. Experimental stores include everything from rubber sidewalks made with recycled tires to energy provided by wind turbines, solar panels, and recirculated water.[20]

At the next level, companies can practice *product stewardship*—minimizing not just pollution from production but all environmental impacts throughout the full product life cycle, and all the while reducing costs. Many companies are adopting *design for environment (DFE)* practices, which involve thinking ahead to design products that are easier to recover, reuse, or recycle. DFE not only helps to sustain the environment, it can be highly profitable for the company. An example is Xerox Corporation's Equipment Remanufacture and Parts Reuse Program, which converts end-of-life office equipment into new products and parts:

Xerox starts by including reuse considerations in its design process to maximize end-of-life potential of products and parts. Its machines contain fewer parts and are

Environmental sustainability
A management approach that involves developing strategies that both sustain the environment and produce profits for the company.

	Internal	External
Tomorrow	**New environmental technology** Is the environmental performance of our products limited by our existing technology base? Is there potential to realize major improvements through new technology?	**Sustainability vision** Does our corporate vision direct us toward the solution of social and environmental problems? Does our vision guide the development of new technologies, markets, products, and processes?
Today	**Pollution prevention** Where are the most significant waste and emission streams from our current operations? Can we lower costs and risks by eliminating waste at the source or by using it as useful input?	**Product stewardship** What are the implications for product design and development if we assume responsibility for a product's entire life cycle? Can we add value or lower costs while simultaneously reducing the impact of our products?

FIGURE 16.1 The Environmental Sustainability Grid

Source: Reprinted by permission of *Harvard Business Review.* From "Beyond Greening: Strategies for a Sustainable World," by Stuart L. Hart, January–February 1997, p. 74. Copyright ©1997 by the President and Fellows of Harvard College; all rights reserved.

MARKETING AT WORK | 16.2

Environmental Sustainability: Generating Profits While Helping to Save the Planet

Simply put, environmental sustainability is about generating profits while helping to save the planet. Sustainability is a crucial but difficult societal goal.

Today, almost every company is taking at least some measures to protect and preserve the environment. Sony has reduced the amount of heavy metals—such as lead, mercury, and cadmium—in its electronic products. Nike produces PVC-free shoes, recycles old sneakers, and educates young people about conservation, reuse, and recycling. Ford has helped the U.S. Bureau of Land Management move endangered wild Mustangs in the American West to safer land, and its Jaguar division operates a jaguar-preservation program that has drawn praise from top officials in Central American countries.

Wal-Mart has opened "eco-friendly" stores in which the air-conditioning systems use non-ozone-depleting refrigerant, rainwater is collected from parking lots and rooftops for landscaping, skylights supplement fluorescent lighting adjusted by photo sensors, and the electronic signs are solar powered. The giant retailer recently pledged $35 million over the next 10 years to conserve at least one acre of wildlife habitat for each acre of the company's "footprint," all the land occupied by its stores, parking lots, and distribution centers.

Some companies, however, are going even further. They are making sustainability central to their core missions. Here are some examples:

DuPont

Known during much of the twentieth century as America's worst polluter, DuPont is now transforming itself from a down-and-dirty oil-and-chemicals business into a twenty-first century, eco-friendly life sciences firm. How? For starters, DuPont is polluting less and reducing waste, emissions, and energy usage. But it's doing much more—it is recreating itself as a collection of businesses that can operate forever without depleting natural resources. To do that, it spun off businesses such as its Conoco oil and gas unit. In turn, it has invested in new businesses such as Pioneer Hi-Bred International. Pioneer Hi-Bred's seeds "produce not only food for people and livestock," notes an analyst, "but renewable materials for commercial uses—turning corn into stretch T-shirts, for example." DuPont has also introduced a bevy of new environmentally responsible products, such as Tyvek, a housing-insulation wrap that saves far more energy than is required to produce it. Other products include Super Solids, a paint that can be applied to cars without discharging toxic solvents into the air; and Solae, a nutritional soy protein formulation that goes into more than 1,000 food products. Last year, the company generated 15 percent of its revenues from renewable resources. Its goal is to achieve 25 percent by 2010.

UPS

Every day, some 70,000 boxy, brown UPS delivery trucks rumble to life across the nation. Each year they travel more than 1.3 billion miles, delivering 3.6 billion packages to almost 8 million customers. They also guzzle tens of millions of gallons of diesel fuel along the way, creating a significant environmental challenge. To meet this challenge, UPS is now turning its brown fleet "green," finding cleaner replacements for its old, smoke-belching diesels. UPS now operates some 1,700 ultra-low and 6,000 low emission vehicles throughout North America. In addition, it's working with DaimlerChrysler and the U.S. Environmental Protection Agency (EPA) to test fuel cells that run on hydrogen and other alternative fuels. UPS's goal is to reduce greenhouse gas emissions and air pollution, and to improve the renewability of the resources that it uses. UPS is also adding more modern, wide-body aircraft to its fleet, the ninth largest airline in the world, and practicing alternative landing approaches to improve efficiency and reduce environmental impact. Such actions reaffirm UPS's commitment to its consumers' well-being. UPS knows that every time one of its brown vehicles belches a malodorous cloud of black smoke, its brand is tarnished. The company's current ad campaign asks, "What can Brown do for you?" One of the answers, it

designed for easy disassembly. Parts are designed for durability over multiple product life cycles and are coded with disposition instructions. As a result, equipment returned to Xerox at end-of-life can be remanufactured reusing 70 to 90 percent by weight of old machine components, while still meeting performance standards for equipment made with all new parts. Xerox's remanufacture and reuse program creates benefits for both the environment and for the company. It prevents more than 160 million pounds of waste from entering landfills each year. And it reduces the amount of raw material and energy needed to produce new parts. Last year alone, energy savings from parts reuse totaled an estimated 1.5 million megawatt hours—enough energy to light more than 1.8 million U.S. homes for the year. Xerox estimates that its savings in raw materials, labor, and waste disposal in the first year of the program alone ranged between $300 million and $400 million. Today, 100 percent of Xerox equipment is designed with remanufacturing and reuse in mind.[21]

■ *Environmental sustainability: Dell understands that sustainability means handling its products at the ends of their useful lives. Its Dell Recycling program helps customers recycle or donate old computer equipment.*

Through this multipronged effort, Dell customers—big businesses and home buyers alike—can exchange, mail in, or drop off old computer equipment, or even have it picked up. Dell will accept any model of old computer, even competing brands. If the old machine is still useful, Dell will refurbish it and donate it to one of several charities. If the old machine is obsolete or broken beyond repair, Dell will recycle or safely dispose of component materials. Dell organizes recycling tours to educate consumers on how to recycle easily and responsibly. The first tour recovered 910 tons of old computer equipment from more than 16 cities.

Some companies have responded to consumer environmental concerns by doing only what is required to avert new regulations or to keep environmentalists quiet. Enlightened companies, however, are taking action not because someone is forcing them to, or to reap short-run profits, but because it is the right thing to do—for both the company and for the planet's environmental future.

Sources: Marc Gunther,"Tree Huggers, Soy Lovers, and Profits," *FORTUNE*, June 23, 2003, pp. 98–104;"DuPont Discusses Sustainability," *Electronic Materials Update*, April 2003, p. 1;"Social Commitment: Global Progress Report," accessed at www.dupont.com, June 2004; "Sustainability Key to UPS's Environmental Initiatives," accessed online at http://pressroom.ups.com, June 2004; UPS Sustainability Report, accessed at www. sustainability.ups.com, August 2005;"Recycling Programs at Dell," accessed at www.dell.com, August 2005; Tricia Pemberton,"Waste-not Wal-Mart: Supercenter Tests Environmentally Friendly Designs," *Knight Ridder Tribune Business News,"* July 21, 2005, p. 1; and Dale Bass,"Eco-Efforts Rely on Authenticity," *Advertising Age*, June 13, 2005, p. 32.

seems: Brown can help you breathe a littler easier about the environment.

Dell

Like many companies, Dell understands that sustainability means more than just a clean factory. It also means proper handling of its products at the ends of their useful lives. Electronics are a fast-growing portion of America's trash, with hundreds of millions of computers destined to become obsolete within just the next few years. These computers contain both toxic metals and useful, reusable materials, so Dell wants to keep them out of landfills. To accomplish this, the company set up Dell Recycling, an effort to reduce the environmental impact of old computers, monitors, keyboards, mice, and printers.

At the third level, companies look to the future and plan for *new environmental technologies*. Many organizations that have made good sustainability headway are still limited by existing technologies. To develop fully sustainable strategies, they will need to develop new technologies. Monsanto is doing this by shifting its agricultural technology base from bulk chemicals to biotechnology. By controlling plant growth and pest resistance through bioengineering, rather than through the use of pesticides or fertilizers, Monsanto hopes to fulfill its promise of environmentally sustainable agriculture. The Monsanto Pledge states the company's dedication to being capable stewards of the technologies it develops. The Pledge declares, "Monsanto is committed to providing high-quality products that benefit [both] our customers and the environment."[22]

Finally, companies can develop a *sustainability vision*, which serves as a guide to the future. It shows how the company's products and services, processes, and policies must evolve and what new technologies must be developed to get there. This vision of sustainability provides a framework for pollution control, product stewardship, and environmental technology.

Most companies today focus on the lower-left quadrant of the grid in Figure 16.1, investing most heavily in pollution prevention. Some forward-looking companies practice product stewardship and are developing new environmental technologies. Few companies have well-defined sustainability visions. Emphasizing only one or a few quadrants in the environmental sustainability grid can be shortsighted. Investing only in the bottom half of the grid puts a company in a good position today but leaves it vulnerable in the future. In contrast, a heavy emphasis on the top half suggests that a company has good environmental vision but lacks the skills needed to implement it. Thus, companies should work at developing all four dimensions of environmental sustainability.

Alcoa, the world's leading producer of aluminum is doing just that. It was one of three companies singled out last year by the *Global 100* (along with Toyota and BP) for superior sustainability excellence:

> Alcoa has distinguished itself as a leader through its sophisticated approach to identifying and managing the material sustainability risks that it faces as a company. From pollution prevention via greenhouse gas emissions reduction programs to engaging stakeholders over new environmental technology, such as controversial hydropower projects, Alcoa has the sustainability strategies in place needed to meld its profitability objectives with society's larger environmental protection goals. . . . Importantly, Alcoa's approach to sustainability is firmly rooted in the idea that sustainability programs can indeed add financial value. Perhaps the best evidence is the company's efforts to promote the use of aluminum in transportation, where aluminum—with its excellent strength-to-weight ratio—is making inroads as a material of choice that allows automakers to build low-weight, fuel-efficient vehicles that produce fewer tailpipe emissions. This kind of forward-thinking strategy of supplying the market with the products that will help solve pressing, global environmental problems shows a company that sees the future, has plotted a course, and is aligning its business accordingly. Says CEO Alain Belda, "Our values require us to think and act not only on the present challenges, but also with the legacy in mind that we leave for those who will come after us . . . as well as the commitments made by those that came before us."[23]

Environmentalism creates some special challenges for global marketers. As international trade barriers come down and global markets expand, environmental issues are having an ever-greater impact on international trade. Countries in North America, Western Europe, and other developed regions are developing strict environmental standards. In the United States, for example, more than two dozen major pieces of environmental legislation have been enacted since 1970, and recent events suggest that more regulation is on the way. A side accord to the North American Free Trade Agreement (NAFTA) set up a commission for resolving environmental matters. The European Union recently passed "end-of-life" regulations affecting automobiles and consumer electronics products. And the EU's Eco-Management and Audit Scheme provides guidelines for environmental self-regulation.[24]

However, environmental policies still vary widely from country to country. Countries such as Denmark, Germany, Japan, and the United States have fully developed environmental policies and high public expectations. But major countries such as China, India, Brazil, and Russia are in only the early stages of developing such policies. Moreover, environmental factors that motivate consumers in one country may have no impact on consumers in another. For example, PVC soft drink bottles cannot be used in Switzerland or Germany. However, they are preferred in France, which has an extensive recycling process for them. Thus, international companies have found it difficult to develop standard environmental practices that work around the world. Instead, they are creating general policies and then translating these policies into tailored programs that meet local regulations and expectations.

PUBLIC ACTIONS TO REGULATE MARKETING

Citizen concerns about marketing practices will usually lead to public attention and legislative proposals. New bills will be debated—many will be defeated, others will be modified, and a few will become workable laws.

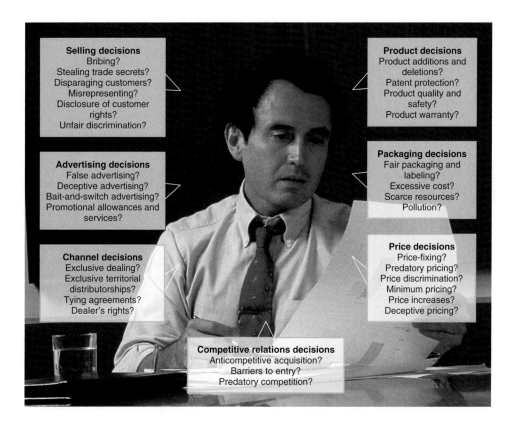

FIGURE 16.2
Major Marketing Decision Areas That May Be Called into Question Under the Law

Many of the laws that affect marketing are listed in Chapter 3. The task is to translate these laws into the language that marketing executives understand as they make decisions about competitive relations, products, price, promotion, and channels of distribution. Figure 16.2 illustrates the major legal issues facing marketing management.

Business Actions Toward Socially Responsible Marketing

At first, many companies opposed consumerism and environmentalism. They thought the criticisms were either unfair or unimportant. But by now, most companies have grown to embrace the new consumer rights, at least in principle. They might oppose certain pieces of legislation as inappropriate ways to solve specific consumer problems, but they recognize the consumer's right to information and protection. Many of these companies have responded positively to consumerism and environmentalism as a way to create greater customer value and to strengthen customer relationships.

ENLIGHTENED MARKETING

The philosophy of **enlightened marketing** holds that a company's marketing should support the best long-run performance of the marketing system. Enlightened marketing consists of five principles: *consumer-oriented marketing*, *innovative marketing*, *value marketing*, *sense-of-mission marketing*, and *societal marketing*.

Consumer-Oriented Marketing **Consumer-oriented marketing** means that the company should view and organize its marketing activities from the consumer's point of view. It should work hard to sense, serve, and satisfy the needs of a defined group of customers. Every good marketing company that we've discussed in this text has had this in common: an all-consuming passion for delivering superior value to carefully chosen customers. Only by seeing the world through its customers' eyes can the company build last-

Enlightened marketing
A marketing philosophy holding that a company's marketing should support the best long-run performance of the marketing system.

Consumer-oriented marketing
The philosophy of enlightened marketing that holds that the company should view and organize its marketing activities from the consumer's point of view.

ing and profitable customer relationships. By creating value *for* consumers, the company can capture value *from* consumers in return.

Innovative Marketing The principle of **innovative marketing** requires that the company continuously seek real product and marketing improvements. The company that overlooks new and better ways to do things will eventually lose customers to another company that has found a better way. An excellent example of an innovative marketer is Samsung Electronics:

Innovative marketing
A principle of enlightened marketing that requires that a company seek real product and marketing improvements.

Sculpted by Samsung.

Introducing the pedestal DLP™ TV that truly stands alone.
Designed to make a bold statement in any room, it uses our Cinema Smooth Light Engine™ to deliver ultra-sharp, high definition images that hover beautifully above an integrated pedestal base. So, wherever you decide to place it, it's sure to offer an experience as original as the thinking that inspired it. www.samsungusa.com/dlp

SAMSUNG

■ Innovative marketing: In less than a decade, Samsung has given its brand a cutting-edge image by unleashing a torrent of new products—not humdrum, me-too products, but innovative and stylish products, targeted to high-end users.

A decade ago, Samsung was a copycat consumer electronics brand you bought off a shipping pallet at Costco if you couldn't afford a Sony. But today, the brand holds a high-end, cutting-edge aura. In 1996, Samsung Electronics made an inspired decision. It turned its back on cheap knock-offs and set out to overtake rival Sony. The company hired a crop of fresh, young designers, who unleashed a torrent of new products—not humdrum, me-too products, but innovative and stylish products, targeted to high-end users. Samsung called them "lifestyle works of art"—from brightly colored cell phones and elegantly thin DVD players to flat-panel TV monitors that hung on walls like paintings. Every new product had to pass the "Wow!" test: If it didn't get a "Wow!" reaction during market testing, it went straight back to the design studio.

Samsung supported the innovative new products with a $400 million marketing campaign, headed by ads proclaiming that Samsung is "DigitAll" and that "everyone's invited." Samsung also changed its distribution to match its new caché. It initially abandoned low-end distributors such as Wal-Mart and Kmart, instead building strong relationships with specialty retailers such as Best Buy and Circuit City. Samsung is now one of the world's fastest growing brands. It's number one worldwide in color TVs, TFT (thin-film transistor) LCD displays, memory chips, color monitors, and DVD-VCR combos. The Samsung brand is valued at a more than $14 billion, 168 percent growth in a span of five years. "Samsung's performance continues to astound brand watchers," says one analyst. The company has become a model for others that "want to shift from being a cheap supplier to a global brand." Says a Samsung designer, "We're not el cheapo anymore."[25]

Customer-value marketing
A principle of enlightened marketing that holds that a company should put most of its resources into customer value-building marketing investments.

Customer-Value Marketing According to the principle of **customer-value marketing**, the company should put most of its resources into customer value-building marketing investments. Many things marketers do—one-shot sales promotions, minor packaging changes, direct response advertising—may raise sales in the short run but add less *value* than would actual improvements in the product's quality, features, or convenience. Enlightened marketing calls for building long-run consumer loyalty and relationships by continually improving the value consumers receive from the firm's market offering.

Sense-of-mission marketing
A principle of enlightened marketing that holds that a company should define its mission in broad social terms rather than narrow product terms.

Sense-of-Mission Marketing **Sense-of-mission marketing** means that the company should define its mission in broad *social* terms rather than narrow *product* terms. When a company defines a social mission, employees feel better about their work and have a clearer sense of direction. For example, defined in narrow product terms, the mission of Unilever's Ben & Jerry's unit might be "to sell ice cream." However, Ben & Jerry's states its mission more broadly, as one of "linked prosperity," including product, economic, and social missions (see www.benjerrys.com/our_company/our_mission). Founders Ben Cohen and Jerry

Greenfield pioneered the concept of "values-led business" or "caring capitalism." Their mission was to use business to make the world a better place:

> From its beginnings in 1978, Ben & Jerry's bought only hormone-free milk and cream and used only organic fruits and nuts to make its ice cream, which it sold in environmentally friendly containers. It went to great lengths to buy from minority and disadvantaged suppliers. From its early Rainforest Crunch to its more recent One Sweet Whirled flavors and awareness campaigns, Ben & Jerry's championed a host of social and environmental causes over the years. And from the start, Ben & Jerry's donated a whopping 7.5 percent of pretax profits to support projects that exhibited "creative problem solving and hopefulness…relating to children and families, disadvantaged groups, and the environment." By the mid-1990s, Ben & Jerry's had become the nation's number-two, superpremium ice cream brand.
>
> However, having a "double bottom line" of values and profits is no easy proposition. Through the 1990s, as competitors not shackled by their "principles before profits" missions invaded its markets, Ben & Jerry's growth and profits flattened. In 2000, after several years of less than stellar financial returns, Ben & Jerry's was acquired by giant food producer Unilever. Looking back, the company appears to have focused too much on social issues at the expense of sound business management. Cohen once commented, "There came a time when I had to admit 'I'm a businessman.' And I had a hard time mouthing those words."[26]

Such experiences taught the socially responsible business movement some hard lessons. The result is a new generation of activist entrepreneurs—not social activists with big hearts who hate capitalism, but well-trained business managers and company builders with a passion for a cause. For example, consider Honest Tea:

Honest Tea has a social mission. "We strive to live up to our name in the way we conduct our business," states the company's "Philoso-tea." "We do this in every way we can—whether we are working with growers and suppliers, answering our customer's questions, or trying to leave a lighter environmental footprint." Like Ben & Jerry's, it all starts with a socially responsible product, an "Honest Tea"—tasty, barely sweetened, and made from all-natural ingredients, many purchased from poorer communities seeking to become more self sufficient. But unlike old revolutionaries like Ben and Jerry, Honest Tea's founders are businesspeople—and proud of it—who appreciate solid business training. Cofounder Seth Goldman won a business-plan competition as a student at the Yale School of Management and later started the company with one of his professors.

Honest Tea's managers know that good deeds alone don't work. They are just as dedicated to building a viable, profitable business as to shaping a mission. "A commitment to socially responsible business cannot be used as an excuse to make poor business decisions," says Goldman. For Honest Tea, social responsibility is not about marketing and hype. It goes about its good deeds quietly. A few years ago, Honest Tea became the first (and only) company to sell a Fair Trade bottled tea—every time the company purchases the tea for its Peach Oo-la-long tea, a donation is made to the workers who pick the tea leaves. The workers invest the money in their community for a variety of

HONEST TEA®
Real Tea. Real Taste. Honest.

Real Tea.

We use only organic tea leaves. For generations, cultures around the world have enjoyed tea grown without chemical pesticides and fertilizers and we don't see any reason to include them in our recipes today.

Real Taste.

Our goal is to create a product in which the true taste of the leaves comes through. We don't pulverize, process or concentrate our tea leaves. Instead we brew the whole leaf in spring water in a way that Shen Nung would still recognize. We add just a touch of natural sweetener - enough to accentuate the tea's natural flavor, but not so much that the sweetener drowns out the tea taste.

Honest.

Tea is consumed by some of the world's wealthiest populations, yet it is produced by some of the poorest. We hope that by introducing new teas and exciting new tastes under the Honest Tea name, we can help to create greater economic opportunity in communities that are seeking to become more self-sufficient. We also try to present our teas in a culturally authentic context, using our labels to illustrate the tea's origin or story-a Crow Native American Chief, a Chinese rubbing from the Tang Dynasty, an oil painting from Guatemala or a hand-drawn sketch from Haarlem South Africa.

www.honesttea.com
800.865.4736

■ Societal marketing: Today's new activist entrepreneurs are not social activists with big hearts who hate capitalism, but well-trained business managers and company builders with a passion for a cause.

uses, including a computer lab for children in the village and a fund for families. Royalties from sales of Honest Tea's First Nation Peppermint tea go to l'tchik Herbal Tea, a small, woman-owned company on the Crow Reservation in Montana, as well as a Native American organization called Pretty Shield Foundation, which includes foster care among its activities. However, "when we first brought out our peppermint tea, our label didn't mention that we were sharing the revenues with the Crow Nation," says Goldman. "We didn't want people to think that was a gimmick."[27]

Thus, today's new activist entrepreneurs are not social activists with big hearts, but well-trained business managers and company builders with a passion for a cause.

Societal Marketing Following the principle of **societal marketing**, an enlightened company makes marketing decisions by considering consumers' wants and interests, the company's requirements, and society's long-run interests. The company is aware that neglecting consumer and societal long-run interests is a disservice to consumers and society. Alert companies view societal problems as opportunities.

A societally-oriented marketer wants to design products that are not only pleasing but also beneficial. The difference is shown in Figure 16.3. Products can be classified according to their degree of immediate consumer satisfaction and long-run consumer benefit. **Deficient products**, such as bad-tasting and ineffective medicine, have neither immediate appeal nor long-run benefits. **Pleasing products** give high immediate satisfaction but may hurt consumers in the long run. Examples include cigarettes and junk food. **Salutary products** have low appeal but may benefit consumers in the long run; for instance, seat belts and air bags. **Desirable products** give both high immediate satisfaction and high long-run benefits, such as a tasty *and* nutritious breakfast food.

Examples of desirable products abound. Philips Lighting's Earth Light compact fluorescent lightbulb provides good lighting at the same time that it gives long life and energy savings. Toyota's hybrid Prius gives both a quiet ride and fuel efficiency. Maytag's front-loading Neptune washer provides superior cleaning along with water savings and energy efficiency. And Herman Miller's office chairs are not only attractive and functional but also environmentally responsible:

> Herman Miller, one of the world's largest office furniture makers, has received numerous awards for environmentally responsible products and business practices. More than a decade ago, the company formed a Design for the Environment team responsible for infusing the company's design process with its environmental values. The team carries out "cradle-to-cradle" life cycle analyses on the company's products, including everything from how much of a product can be made from recycled materials to how much of the product itself can be recycled at the end of its useful life. For example, the team redesigned the company's chairs for the lowest possible ecological impact and high recyclability. Herman Miller's Aeron chair is constructed of 66 percent recycled materials (from pop bottles and recycled aluminum) and is 90 percent recyclable. The frames need no paint or other finish. No ozone-depleting materials are used. Chairs are shipped partially assembled, thus reducing the packaging and energy needed to ship them. Finally, materials schematics are imbedded in the bottoms of chair seats to help recycle chairs at the ends of their lives. Herman Miller chairs are truly desirable products—they've won awards for design and function *and* for environmental responsibility. And it inspired future models of environ-

---

Societal marketing
A principle of enlightened marketing that holds that a company should make marketing decisions by considering consumers' wants, the company's requirements, consumers' long-run interests, and society's long-run interests.

Deficient products
Products that have neither immediate appeal nor long-run benefits.

Pleasing products
Products that give high immediate satisfaction but may hurt consumers in the long run.

Salutary products
Products that have low appeal but may benefit consumers in the long run.

Desirable products
Products that give both high immediate satisfaction and high long-run benefits.

FIGURE 16.3
Societal Classification of Products

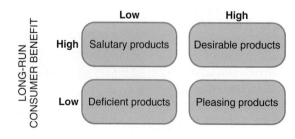

IMMEDIATE SATISFACTION

LONG-RUN CONSUMER BENEFIT

	Low	High
High	Salutary products	Desirable products
Low	Deficient products	Pleasing products

mentally friendly chairs. Most recently, Herman Miller introduced the Cella chair, which is made from 33 percent recycled materials and is 99 percent recyclable.[28]

Companies should try to turn all of their products into desirable products. The challenge posed by pleasing products is that they sell very well but may end up hurting the consumer. The product opportunity, therefore, is to add long-run benefits without reducing the product's pleasing qualities. The challenge posed by salutary products is to add some pleasing qualities so that they will become more desirable in consumers' minds.

  Linking the Concepts

Pause here, hold your place with your finger, and go way back and take another look at the Societal Marketing Concept section in Chapter 1.

- How does Figure 1.4 apply to the Enlightened Marketing section in this chapter?
- Use the five principles to assess the actions of a company that you believe exemplifies socially responsible marketing. (If you can't think of one, use Johnson & Johnson or one of the companies discussed in this chapter.)
- Use the principles of enlightened marketing to assess the actions of a company that you believe falls short of socially responsible marketing.

MARKETING ETHICS

Conscientious marketers face many moral dilemmas. The best thing to do is often unclear. Because not all managers have fine moral sensitivity, companies need to develop *corporate marketing ethics policies*—broad guidelines that everyone in the organization must follow. These policies should cover distributor relations, advertising standards, customer service, pricing, product development, and general ethical standards.

The finest guidelines cannot resolve all the difficult ethical situations the marketer faces. Table 16.1 lists some difficult ethical situations marketers could face during their careers. If marketers choose immediate sales-producing actions in all these cases, their marketing behavior might well be described as immoral or even amoral. If they refuse to go along with *any* of the actions, they might be ineffective as marketing managers and unhappy because of the constant moral tension. Managers need a set of principles that will help them figure out the moral importance of each situation and decide how far they can go in good conscience.

But *what* principle should guide companies and marketing managers on issues of ethics and social responsibility? One philosophy is that such issues are decided by the free market and legal system. Under this principle, companies and their managers are not responsible for making moral judgments. Companies can, in good conscience, do whatever the market and legal systems allow.

A second philosophy puts responsibility not on the system but in the hands of individual companies and managers. This more enlightened philosophy suggests that a company should have a "social conscience." Companies and managers should apply high standards of ethics and morality when making corporate decisions, regardless of "what the system allows." History provides an endless list of examples of company actions that were legal but highly irresponsible. Consider the following example:

> Prior to the Pure Food and Drug Act, the advertising for a diet pill promised that a person taking this pill could eat virtually anything at any time and still lose weight. Too good to be true? Actually the claim was quite true; the product lived up to its billing with frightening efficiency. It seems that the primary active ingredient in this "diet supplement" was tapeworm larvae. These larvae would develop in the intestinal tract and, of course, be well fed; the pill taker would in time, quite literally, starve to death.[29]

Each company and marketing manager must work out a philosophy of socially responsible and ethical behavior. Under the societal marketing concept, each manager must look beyond what is legal and allowed and develop standards based on personal integrity, corporate conscience, and long-run consumer welfare. A clear and responsible philosophy will help the company deal with knotty issues such as this one faced by 3M:

TABLE 16.1
Some Morally Difficult Situations in Marketing

1. You work for a cigarette company. Public policy debates over the past few years now leave no doubt in your mind that cigarette smoking and cancer are closely linked. Although your company currently runs an "if you don't smoke, don't start" promotion campaign, you believe that other company promotions might encourage young (although legal age) nonsmokers to pick up the habit. What would you do?

2. Your R&D department has changed one of your products slightly. It is not really "new and improved," but you know that putting this statement on the package and in advertising will increase sales. What would you do?

3. You have been asked to add a stripped-down model to your line that could be advertised to pull customers into the store. The product won't be very good, but salespeople will be able to switch buyers up to higher-priced units. You are asked to give the green light for the stripped-down version. What would you do?

4. You are thinking of hiring a product manager who has just left a competitor's company. She would be more than happy to tell you all the competitor's plans for the coming year. What would you do?

5. One of your top dealers in an important territory recently has had family troubles, and his sales have slipped. It looks like it will take him a while to straighten out his family trouble. Meanwhile you are losing many sales. Legally, you can terminate the dealer's franchise and replace him. What would you do?

6. You have a chance to win a big account that will mean a lot to you and your company. The purchasing agent hints that a "gift" would influence the decision. Your assistant recommends sending a fine color television set to the buyer's home. What would you do?

7. You have heard that a competitor has a new product feature that will make a big difference in sales. The competitor will demonstrate the feature in a private dealer meeting at the annual trade show. You can easily send a snooper to this meeting to learn about the new feature. What would you do?

8. You have to choose between three ad campaigns outlined by your agency. The first (a) is a soft-sell, honest, straight-information campaign. The second (b) uses sex-loaded emotional appeals and exaggerates the product's benefits. The third (c) involves a noisy, somewhat irritating commercial that is sure to gain audience attention. Pretests show that the campaigns are effective in the following order: c, b, and a. What would you do?

9. You are interviewing a capable female applicant for a job as salesperson. She is better qualified than the men just interviewed. Nevertheless, you know that some of your important customers prefer dealing with men, and you will lose some sales if you hire her. What would you do?

In late 1997, a powerful new research technique for scanning blood kept turning up the same odd result: Tiny amounts of a chemical 3M had made for nearly 40 years were showing up in blood drawn from people living all across the country. If the results held up, it meant that virtually all Americans may be carrying some minuscule amount of the chemical, called perfluorooctane sulfonate (PFOS), in their systems. Even though at the time they had yet to come up with a definitive answer as to what harm the chemical might cause, the company reached a drastic decision. In mid-2000, although under no mandate to act, 3M decided to phase out products containing PFOS and related chemicals, including its popular Scotchgard fabric protector. This was no easy decision. Since there was as yet no replacement chemical, it meant a potential loss of $500 million in annual sales. 3M's voluntary actions drew praise from regulators. "3M deserves great credit for identifying the problem and coming forward," says an EPA administrator. "It took guts," comments another government scientist. "The fact is that most companies . . . go into anger, denial, and the rest of that stuff. [We're used to seeing] decades-long arguments about whether a chemical is really toxic." For 3M, however, it wasn't all that difficult a decision—it was simply the right thing to do.[30]

As with environmentalism, the issue of ethics provides special challenges for international marketers. Business standards and practices vary a great deal from one country to the next. For example, whereas bribes and kickbacks are illegal for U.S. firms, they are standard business practice in many South American countries. One recent study found that companies from some nations were much more likely to use bribes when seeking contracts in emerging-market nations. The most flagrant bribe-paying firms were from Russia and China, with Taiwan and South Korea close behind. Other countries where corruption is common include India, Pakistan, and Bangladesh. The least corrupt were companies from Australia, Sweden, Switzerland, Austria, and Canada.[31]

The question arises as to whether a company must lower its ethical standards to compete effectively in countries with lower standards. The answer: No. Companies should make a commitment to a common set of shared standards worldwide. For example, John Hancock Mutual Life Insurance Company operates successfully in Southeast Asia, an area that by Western standards has widespread questionable business and government practices. Despite warnings from locals that Hancock would have to bend its rules to succeed, the company set out strict guidelines. "We told our people that we had the same ethical standards, same procedures, and same policies in these countries that we have in the United States, and we do," says Hancock Chairman Stephen Brown. "We just felt that things like payoffs were wrong—and if we had to do business that way, we'd rather not do business." Hancock employees feel good about the consistent levels of ethics. "There may be countries where you have to do that kind of thing," says Brown. "We haven't found that country yet, and if we do, we won't do business there."[32]

Many industrial and professional associations have suggested codes of ethics, and many companies are now adopting their own codes. For example, the American Marketing Association, an international association of marketing managers and scholars, developed the code of ethics shown in Table 16.2. Companies are also developing programs to teach managers about important ethics issues and help them find the proper responses. They hold ethics workshops and seminars and set up ethics committees. Furthermore, most major U.S. companies have appointed high-level ethics officers to champion ethics issues and to help resolve ethics problems and concerns facing employees.

TABLE 16.2 American Marketing Association Code of Ethics

Ethical Norms and Values for Marketers

Preamble

The American Marketing Association commits itself to promoting the highest standard of professional ethical norms and values for its members. Norms are established standards of conduct that are expected and maintained by society and/or professional organizations. Values represent the collective conception of what people find desirable, important and morally proper. Values serve as the criteria for evaluating the actions of others. Marketing practitioners must recognize that they not only serve their enterprises but also act as stewards of society in creating, facilitating, and executing the efficient and effective transactions that are part of the greater economy. In this role, marketers should embrace the highest ethical norms of practicing professionals and the ethical values implied by their responsibility toward stakeholders (e.g., customers, employees, investors, channel members, regulators and the host community).

General Norms

1. Marketers must do no harm. This means doing work for which they are appropriately trained or experienced so that they can actively add value to their organizations and customers. It also means adhering to all applicable laws and regulations and embodying high ethical standards in the choices they make.

2. Marketers must foster trust in the marketing system. This means that products are appropriate for their intended and promoted uses. It requires that marketing communications about goods and services are not intentionally deceptive or misleading. It suggests building relationships that provide for the equitable adjustment and/or redress of customer grievances. It implies striving for good faith and fair dealing so as to contribute toward the efficacy of the exchange process.

Marketers must embrace, communicate, and practice the fundamental ethical values that will improve consumer confidence in the integrity of the marketing exchange system. These basic values are intentionally aspirational and include honesty, responsibility, fairness, respect, openness, and citizenship.

Ethical Values

Honesty—to be truthful and forthright in our dealings with customers and stakeholders.

- We will tell the truth in all situations and at all times.
- We will offer products of value that do what we claim in our communications.
- We will stand behind our products if they fail to deliver their claimed benefits.
- We will honor our explicit and implicit commitments and promises.

Responsibility—to accept the consequences of our marketing decisions and strategies.

- We will make strenuous efforts to serve the needs of our customers.
- We will avoid using coercion with all stakeholders.
- We will acknowledge the social obligations to stakeholders that come with increased marketing and economic power.
- We will recognize our special commitments to economically vulnerable segments of the market such as children, the elderly and others who may be substantially disadvantaged.

Fairness—to try to balance justly the needs of the buyer with the interests of the seller.

- We will represent our products in a clear way in selling, advertising and other forms of communication; this includes the avoidance of false, misleading and deceptive promotion.
- We will reject manipulations and sales tactics that harm customer trust.
- We will not engage in price fixing, predatory pricing, price gouging or "bait-and-switch" tactics.
- We will not knowingly participate in material conflicts of interest.

Respect—to acknowledge the basic human dignity of all stakeholders.

- We will value individual differences even as we avoid stereotyping customers or depicting demographic groups (e.g., gender, race, sexual orientation) in a negative or dehumanizing way in our promotions.

(continued)

TABLE 16.2 Continued

- We will listen to the needs of our customers and make all reasonable efforts to monitor and improve their satisfaction on an ongoing basis.
- We will make a special effort to understand suppliers, intermediaries and distributors from other cultures.
- We will appropriately acknowledge the contributions of others, such as consultants, employees and coworkers, to our marketing endeavors.

Openness—to create transparency in our marketing operations.

- We will strive to communicate clearly with all our constituencies.
- We will accept constructive criticism from our customers and other stakeholders.
- We will explain significant product or service risks, component substitutions or other foreseeable eventualities that could affect customers or their perception of the purchase decision.
- We will fully disclose list prices and terms of financing as well as available price deals and adjustments.

Citizenship—to fulfill the economic, legal, philanthropic and societal responsibilities that serve stakeholders in a strategic manner.

- We will strive to protect the natural environment in the execution of marketing campaigns.
- We will give back to the community through volunteerism and charitable donations.
- We will work to contribute to the overall betterment of marketing and its reputation.
- We will encourage supply chain members to ensure that trade is fair for all participants, including producers in developing countries.

Implementation

Finally, we recognize that every industry sector and marketing subdiscipline (e.g., marketing research, e-commerce, direct selling, direct marketing, advertising) has its own specific ethical issues that require policies and commentary. An array of such codes can be accessed through links on the AMA Web site. We encourage all such groups to develop and/or refine their industry and discipline-specific codes of ethics to supplement these general norms and values.

Source: Reprinted with permission of the American Marketing Association.

■ Ethics programs: PricewaterhouseCoopers established a comprehensive ethics program, which begins with a code of conduct, called "The Way We Do Business," says PwC's CEO, "Ethics in everything we say and do."

PricewaterhouseCoopers (PwC) is a good example. In 1996, PwC established an ethics office and comprehensive ethics program, headed by a high-level chief ethics officer. The ethics program begins with a code of conduct, called "The Way We Do Business." PwC employees learn about the code of conduct and about how to handle thorny ethics issues in a comprehensive ethics training program, called "Navigating the Grey." The program also includes an ethics help line and regular communications at all levels. "It is obviously not enough to distribute a document," says PwC's CEO, Samuel DiPiazza. "Ethics is in everything we say and do." Last year alone, the PwC training program involved 40,000 employees, and the help line received over 1,000 calls from people asking for guidance in working through difficult ethics dilemmas.[33]

Still, written codes and ethics programs do not ensure ethical behavior. Ethics and social responsibility require a total corporate commitment. They must be a component of the overall corporate culture. According to PwC's DiPiazza, "I see ethics as a mission-critical issue . . . deeply imbedded in who we are and what we do. It's just as important as our product development cycle or our distribution system. . . . It's about creating a culture based on integrity and respect, not a culture based on dealing with the crisis of the day. . . . We ask ourselves every day, 'Are we doing the right things?' "[34]

REST STOP → REVIEWING THE CONCEPTS

Well—here you are at the end of your introductory marketing travels! In this chapter, we've closed with many important concepts involving marketing's sweeping impact on individual consumers, other businesses, and society as a whole. You learned that responsible marketers discover what consumers want and respond with the right market offerings, priced to give good value to buyers and profit to the producer. A marketing system should deliver customer value and improve the quality of consumers' lives. In working to meet consumer needs, marketers may take some actions that are not to everyone's liking or benefit. Marketing managers should be aware of the main *criticisms of marketing*.

1. Identify the major social criticisms of marketing.

Marketing's *impact on individual consumer welfare* has been criticized for its high prices, deceptive practices, high-pressure selling, shoddy or unsafe products, planned obsolescence, and poor service to disadvantaged consumers. Marketing's *impact on society* has been criticized for creating false wants and too much materialism, too few social goods, cultural pollution, and too much political power. Critics have also criticized marketing's *impact on other businesses* for harming competitors and reducing competition through acquisitions, practices that create barriers to entry, and unfair, competitive marketing practices. Some of these concerns are justified; some are not.

2. Define *consumerism* and *environmentalism* and explain how they affect marketing strategies.

Concerns about the marketing system have led to *citizen action movements*. *Consumerism* is an organized social movement intended to strengthen the rights and power of consumers relative to sellers. Alert marketers view it as an opportunity to serve consumers better by providing more consumer information, education, and protection. *Environmentalism* is an organized social movement seeking to minimize the harm done to the environment and quality of life by marketing practices. The first wave of modern environmentalism was driven by environmental groups and concerned consumers, whereas the second wave was driven by government, which passed laws and regulations governing industrial practices impacting the environment. The first two environmentalism waves are now merging into a third and stronger wave in which companies are accepting responsibility for doing no environmental harm. Companies now are adopting policies of *environmental sustainability*—developing strategies that both sustain the environment and produce profits for the company.

3. Describe the principles of socially responsible marketing.

Many companies originally opposed these social movements and laws, but most of them now recognize a need for positive consumer information, education, and protection. Some companies have followed a policy of *enlightened marketing,* which holds that a company's marketing should support the best long-run performance of the marketing system. Enlightened marketing consists of five principles: *consumer-oriented marketing, innovative marketing, customer-value marketing, sense-of-mission marketing*, and *societal marketing*.

4. Explain the role of ethics in marketing.

Increasingly, companies are responding to the need to provide company policies and guidelines to help their managers deal with questions of *marketing ethics*. Of course even the best guidelines cannot resolve all the difficult ethical decisions that individuals and firms must make. But there are some principles that marketers can choose among. One principle states that such issues should be decided by the free market and legal system. A second, and more enlightened principle, puts responsibility not in the system but in the hands of individual companies and managers. Each firm and marketing manager must work out a philosophy of socially responsible and ethical behavior. Under the societal marketing concept, managers must look beyond what is legal and allowable and develop standards based on personal integrity, corporate conscience, and long-term consumer welfare.

Because business standards and practices vary from country to country, the issue of ethics poses special challenges for international marketers. The growing consensus among today's marketers is that it is important to make a commitment to a common set of shared standards worldwide.

Navigating the Key Terms

Consumerism (507)
Consumer-oriented marketing (513)
Customer-value marketing (514)
Deficient products (516)
Desirable products (516)

Enlightened marketing (513)
Environmental sustainability (509)
Environmentalism (508)
Innovative marketing (514)

Pleasing products (516)
Salutary products (516)
Sense-of-Mission marketing (514)
Societal marketing (516)

Travel Log

Discussing the Issues

1. Which criticism of marketing mentioned in this chapter concerns you the most? Which criticism concerns you the least? Which criticism do you think is most valid?

2. Does a company's socially responsible behavior influence your buying decisions? Do irresponsible or unethical actions influence your decisions?

3. What is the difference between consumerism and environmentalism? How are they alike? Give an example of a cause that would be championed by each movement.

4. Can an organization be focused on both consumerism and environmentalism at the same time? Why or why not?

5. Distinguish between the five principles of enlightened marketing: consumer-oriented marketing, innovative marketing, value marketing, sense-of-mission marketing, and societal marketing.

6. Classify three of the products you regularly buy using Figure 16.3. How does analyzing the products this way impact your future buying decisions?

Application Questions

1. Study Figure 16.1. Select two companies, one you regard as very environmentally active and one you believe is not.

After researching the companies, rate each company in the areas of pollution prevention, product stewardship, new environmental technology, and sustainability vision. Are you surprised by any of your findings?

2. Write a corporate marketing ethics policy for a company selling mortgage services online. How would such a policy influence ethical decision making among employees in this company?

3. In small groups, consider the four issues regarding marketing's impact on society as a whole. Debate each issue and after each debate take a poll of where your group stands on the issue.

Under the Hood: Focus on Technology

Technology surges forward at an ever-quickening pace. As computers work faster, cars get better gas mileage, and televisions offer more vivid colors, consumers constantly upgrade products to reap the benefits. But critics argue that continual improvement often stems from planned obsolescence rather than from meaningful technological breakthroughs, causing products to become obsolete before they actually should need replacement. Marketers respond that much of so-called planned obsolescence is the working of the competitive and technological forces in a free society—forces that lead to ever-improving goods and services

According to Gary Coleman, a manager with Deloitte & Touche, managing product innovation and new features is a must for any successful marketer hoping to stay ahead of the competition. He argues that, "the so-so companies will wait the extra year while they perfect their product and will put all the

quality in and all the bells and whistles on. The great innovating companies will go to market with 80 percent of the design features and a facelift or upgrade strategy. It's not planned obsolescence. It's planning according to a profit cycle rather than a product cycle and it gives you speed to market. They get five to seven years out of the product instead of one big hit and rapid fall off."*

1. Do you agree with Gary Coleman's assertion that managing the release of innovations and features is a necessary part of successful marketing?

2. Is Coleman's approach ethical?

3. As a consumer, does the issue of planned obsolescence concern you?

*See Ian Porter, "Agility and Innovation the Winners," *Manufacturing Reporter*, August 16, 2005.

Focus on Ethics

We've all heard about the community outreach efforts of retailers like Ben & Jerry's and Body Shop. But, unlike the social activists of the past, today's values-led businesses are founded by well-trained business managers and company builders with a passion for a cause. The result is socially minded businesses with the know-how needed to target and connect with customers. For example, to make money and follow its values at the same time, WorldWise offers garden, home, and pet products made from recycled or organic materials. WorldWise's strategy for getting up and running, built around the concept of environmentally responsible products, illustrates double-bottom-line thinking. Company CEO Aaron Lamstein comments, "You can't be successful if you can't do both. Our whole concept was

that our products had to work as well as or better than others, look as good or finer, cost the same or less, and be better for the environment."

1. Visit the WorldWise Web site (www.worldwise.com) and learn about the company and its products. Would you be interested in these products? Are you confident in their quality and the value they offer?

2. What impact does the company's double bottom line approach (values and profits) have on your interest in its products?

3. Do you believe a company can be truly successful when focusing on a double bottom line?

Videos

The NFL video case that accompanies this chapter is located in Appendix 1 at the back of the book.

Appendix 1 Video Cases

Managing Profitable Customer Relationships

Case in Point: Harley-Davidson

Harley-Davidson's massive motorcycles epitomize rugged individualism and the freedom of the open road. The signature throaty roar of the big V-twin engine of a "hog" announces the arrival of the big machine and the attitude of its rider. Yet for all the tough reputations of the big bike's unconventional owners, the company strives to connect with its customers.

Harley-Davidson creates its own community in many ways. It sponsors dozens of events and participates in hundreds of motorcycle-related happenings each year. Cross-country tours, rallies, and just plain get-togethers let riders enjoy the road together or show off all the chrome and accessories on their bikes. Harley-Davidson's presence—reinforcing the brand, displays of the latest bikes, and sales of branded apparel—helps to strengthen the Harley-Davidson name and to cement its relationships with customers.

In 1983, Harley-Davidson created H.O.G., or Harley Owners Group, as a way to bring riders both closer together and closer to the company. The company created local chapters, sponsored rallies, created the *Hog Tales* magazine, and designed apparel for proud owners. H.O.G. members can access a wide range of services—insurance, roadside assistance, shipping, and a theft reward program that gives money to people who provide tips leading to the recovery of stolen motorcycles. H.O.G. really ties the rider to the company—only Harley-Davidson owners can be full members and the membership is tied to the VIN (Vehicle Identification Number) of each motorcycle.

With the rise of the Internet, H.O.G. moved online to Hog.com and added online games and screen savers. An online photo center lets members upload pictures of their latest road trip, share them with others, and buy prints. Harley also encourages people to send in their stories and photos—the best are published in the bimonthly *Hog Tales* magazine.

"The appearance of the riders mimics the outlaw look—a mean look, but really for our riders it's one way for them to express themselves," says Ryan Eichler, a Harley-Davidson spokesman. "If you are a doctor, then on the weekend you can become a different person. That's what makes it so romantic. You can get on the bike and be somebody else."

Riders aren't just customers of the Harley-Davidson corporation; they are also customers of Harley-Davidson's network of 1,300 dealers. H.O.G.'s 1,300 local chapters in some two dozen countries each have a sponsor in the form of a local dealership. That keeps dealers in the loop and linked to customers as well.

Pins, patches, and medallions let Harley-Davidson riders document their travels and show their pride in their machines. Pins and patches go on jackets, vests, and hats. Medallions attach directly to the bike. The company provides innumerable opportunities to obtain these symbols. For example, Harley-Davidson hosts what it calls "pinstops" at motorcycle-related events and festivals. H.O.G. members can pick up a pin or patch as a souvenir and proof of attendance. A dedicated rider can accumulate dozens of these items for his or her riding jacket. Such a jacket reads like a map of the rider's activities and keeps the rider looking to the next horizon, the next event, and the next opportunity to be part of the Harley-Davidson family.

Harley-Davidson even has a mileage program for enrolled H.O.G. members—the farther you ride, the more pins and patches you collect. The mileage awards start at 10,000 miles and progress from there to a million miles. Because the dealer checks the mileage to verify the distance, the dealer gets a chance to reconnect with customers, show them new bikes, or interest them in the latest apparel or accessories for their bike.

Although Harley-Davidson is a 100 percent American icon, the bikes have a loyal following overseas. Even the usually picky Japanese have made Harley-Davidson the leading brand in the heavy motorcycle category in Japan. H.O.G. chapters span the globe and Harley-Davidson encourages them to ride in distant lands. The Harley-Davidson "Fly and Ride" program lets H.O.G. members fly to destinations in the United States, Canada, Australia, and Europe and rent a bike from a dealer.

Harley-Davidson's carefully cultured bad-boy image has endeared it to a new breed of well-bred owners. "Getting on a motorcycle is a great release," says Eichler. "It involves all the senses—you can't be thinking about the presentation you have to give next week. It's a nice way to vent, really." The average Harley customer is a 46-year-old husband with a median household income of $78,300. Some 42 percent of Harley-Davidson buyers are loyal, repeat buyers. Given the $16,000 average cost of the machines and sales growing past 300,000 motorcycles per year, it's not hard to see that Harley-Davidson stays on the road to success by creating a strong bond with its customers.

Questions for Discussion

1. What are the key elements of Harley-Davidson's efforts to build relationships with its customers?
2. Can you think of other companies that create such strong relationships with their customers? How do they do that?
3. How else can Harley-Davidson build or deepen its relationships with its customers?

Partnering to Build Customer Relationships

Case in Point: Mayo Clinic

From its beginning in the 1880s to the present day, the Mayo Clinic has always stood for high quality health care. When the two Mayo brothers, Dr. William Mayo and Dr. Charles Mayo, joined their father's clinic, they used a horse and buggy to make house calls and help the frontier farming community of Rochester, Minnesota. But the Mayos wanted to become more than just another small doctor's office. What started as a practice on the frontier of America moved to become a leader on the frontiers of medicine. The clinic's strong reputation has led to many famous people making the trek to Minnesota, such as George Harrison of the Beatles and King Hussein of Jordan.

The Mayo Clinic pioneered many medical treatments. Cancer therapies, open-heart surgery, tuberculosis treatments, and knee-replacement and hip-replacement surgeries are just a few of the medical miracles that the clinic helped to perfect. Along with improvements in care, the Mayo Clinic started accumulating and creating medical knowledge. The clinic developed one of the first centralized medical records systems to help track patients. It published cases on patients' ailments, treatments, and outcomes to make the clinic become an important source of medical knowledge. In 1914, the clinic started the first graduate studies program for clinicians. In 1950, two doctors from the Mayo Clinic were among the winners of the Nobel Prize in Physiology or Medicine.

The Mayo Clinic not only pioneered new treatments, it also changed how medical care was organized. The clinic developed the group practice concept to expand the range of services and improve care. "It [has become] necessary to develop medicine as a cooperative science; the clinician, the specialist, and the laboratory workers uniting for the good of the patient," explained Dr. William Mayo. "Individualism in medicine can no longer exist."

The Mayo Clinic went beyond perfecting the science of medicine and the organization of medical professionals. It also perfected the human side of medicine to deepen the relationship with the customer. The Mayo brothers always believed in creating a less intimidating atmosphere than the typical sterile hospital setting. Examination rooms at the Mayo Clinic include a couch for family members; the buildings are light and airy. Sculptures, fountains, and marble stairways help the Mayo Clinic avoid the institutional feel common to many medical facilities. Instead of white coats, the Mayo Clinic's doctors wear suits as a sign of respect and professionalism. "It did not seem like a doctor's office when we went to the Mayo Clinic. There was no tension," said one patient.

BIRTH OF A HEALTHY BRAND

For many decades, the Mayo Clinic was content to do its research and help its now 600,000 patients a year. The clinic had no marketing department or advertising budget. But that didn't mean that the marketplace was unaware of the clinic. Unbeknownst to the Mayo Clinic, a brand image was forming for the clinic. Doctors learned about the cutting-edge research performed at the clinic. The Mayo Clinic's publications of cutting-edge procedures and unusual medical cases led many doctors to refer seemingly incurable patients to the Mayo Clinic.

From the clinic's earliest days, its patients and families of patients extolled the virtues of the clinic. Early in its history, the Mayo Clinic starting paying doctors a straight salary so that doctors had less incentive to push patients out the door or foist costly tests and treatments on them. Patients touted the miracles worked by the clinic. Families of ailing people discussed their hopes for a cure at the clinic. The result was that the clinic created an 84 percent market awareness overall, and a 90 percent brand awareness among those older than 45. In short, the Mayo Clinic became renowned for what it did, not for how it marketed or advertised what it did. Word of mouth among decision makers and influencers created a powerful brand with little intervention on the part of the clinic.

In the 1980s, as the fame of the clinic grew, demand for services climbed, too. The clinic grew to 10 million square feet in Rochester. To help meet the demand and help bring the clinic to the patients, the Mayo Clinic expanded geographically to new facilities in Scottsdale, Arizona, and Jacksonville, Florida. This brought the clinic to the aging retirement populations in those areas and meant that patients didn't have to come to Minnesota for treatment.

The clinic also began to realize it had created an extremely valuable brand without thinking about it. That led to a process of trying to leverage the equity in the brand. For example, the Mayo Clinic started publishing a health newsletter and a health book. Later, the Mayo Clinic launched a popular Web site called MayoClinic.com.

NURTURING THE MAYO NAME

As the value of the brand grew, the responsibilities to nurture and preserve that brand grew as well. In 1999, the Mayo Clinic formed an Office of Brand Management to help shepherd its brand. This office protects and enhances the brand of the Mayo Clinic. The office monitors the brand to track its use, connotations, and to forestall its misuse. They educate staff and news media about the brand.

The Mayo Clinic has found that a strong brand is both a blessing and a curse. The blessing is that the Mayo Clinic only has to spend 0.25% of revenues on marketing even as it continues to attract multitudes of new customers. The curse is that the Mayo Clinic's brand has nowhere to go but down. A 1996 brand equity study found that consumers had no negative associations with the Mayo Clinic's name. The Mayo Clinic knows that one bad scandal could adversely affect a century of hard work delivering the best medical services.

Although advanced, high-quality service would continue to hold the Mayo Clinic's brand in high esteem, the clinic knew it needed to begin thinking more strategically about its marketing strategy and the partners it might choose. In particular, the role of partners would be more important as other companies sought to link with the Mayo Clinic or pursue joint ventures with the famous clinic.

Every year, numerous third-party companies and organizations approach the Mayo Clinic with new opportunities. Given this onslaught, the clinic needed to think about which partners to choose, how to structure the agreements, and how to control risk to the Mayo Clinic's brand. Brand extensions might dilute the brand, and the quality of the partner is paramount because a potential scandal at a partner firm would taint the Mayo Clinic's brand.

When should the clinic partner with someone? The Mayo Clinic created a series of guidelines for evaluating potential partnerships. The Mayo Clinic's brand management guidelines emphasize four criteria. First, the Mayo Clinic wants control—it doesn't want any partner to pull the clinic's brand in the wrong direction. Second, the Mayo Clinic won't license the brand to products or services that wouldn't be successful on their own. Third, the Mayo Clinic avoids opportunities that might trivialize the brand. Fourth, the Mayo Clinic won't let its brand be shared or sold.

The Mayo Clinic's partner relationships span the gamut from sponsorship of the National Kidney Foundation to research ventures with universities to joint ventures with private companies. For example, the Mayo Clinic and the Translational Genomics Research Institute, a nonprofit Phoenix-based bioscience group, built a $25 million three-story research lab on the clinic's Scottsdale campus to foster medical research. The joint venture hopes to attract or help create new medical businesses, including suppliers.

But some collaborations go further afield, literally. The Mayo Clinic Executive Travel Response is a collaboration with NetJets, a business-jet time-share company, that will provide NetJets' owners and guests with a wide range of medical services. The venture enables NetJets' flight crews to contact the Mayo Clinic any time of the day or night, in the event of an in-flight medical problem. The Mayo Clinic even designed the emergency medical kit that goes on NetJets' planes. The services don't stop when the passenger leaves the plane. On the ground, anywhere in the world, a NetJets owner can call a special 24-hour medical resource line. The collaboration both extends the Mayo Clinic's name to NetJets' well-heeled clients and helps NetJets make its jet-setting passengers feel medically safe and secure.

Questions for Discussion

1. What is the Mayo Clinic's mission? Who are the Mayo Clinic's target customers and what is the Mayo Clinic's relationship with them? How has the Mayo Clinic positioned itself?
2. What is the Mayo Clinic's marketing mix and how might it change in the future?
3. What should the Mayo Clinic do next, strategically, with regard to its brand? How can it grow profitably?

The Marketing Environment

Case in Point: American Express

Ever wonder why American Express is called "American Express" and not "American Card" or "AmeriCard" or something like that? The reason is because when the company was founded in 1850, it was more like FedEx than a financial services company. In the 1800s, American Express handled packages, just like FedEx does today. In those days, rail was the fastest way to ship goods, and American Express owned 71,280 miles of track. As a freight forwarder, American Express discovered that one of the most important things people needed to ship was money. In particular, travelers needed a way to get and spend money in remote locations. Recognizing this as a business need started American Express on a long series of changes.

In 1882, after 32 years in the shipping business, American Express changed with the environment and introduced money orders that could be express-shipped. In 1891, the company introduced the now-famous travelers' checks in convenient denominations. People in remote locations would accept these checks on the basis of the good name of American Express as a large shipping company with some 10,000 offices.

American Express continued to monitor the environment and offered new services where it saw new opportunities. In 1958, for example, it introduced its first charge card, targeting traveling salesmen who needed a way to handle expenses on the road. From the beginning, American Express cultivated a sense of exclusivity—"Membership Has Its Privileges" was the company tagline. Advertising used actor Karl Malden's serious admonition to "Don't Leave Home Without It" and extolled the advantages of American Express.

Over the years, American Express differentiated its card offerings. In 1966, the company added the Gold card for its more affluent customers. In 1984, it added the Platinum card for an even higher level of customer. American Express then introduced a true credit card—a card that let people borrow money—in the form of the Optima card. In 1999, the invitation-only black Centurion card was introduced—offered only to people who charged $250,000 or more per year on their card and who were willing to pay the $1,000 annual membership fee. These higher-level cards bring increasing levels of privileges such as access to airport lounges and free nights at certain hotels.

For many decades, the American Express card was unlike cards such as Visa and MasterCard in that it was not a credit card, but a charge card. That is, American Express did not lend money on credit. Rather, it required customers to pay off the balance of charges every month. The flipside of this approach was that American Express cards carried no preset spending limit, a feature that was welcomed by business travelers who might need to buy a plane ticket or pay for a hotel on short notice. American Express used this fact in its marketing, showing a series of ads in which customers used credit cards for extraordinary, high-cost occasions like taking the boss and some important clients to an expensive restaurant and facing the embarrassment of a declined, over-the-limit credit card charge.

These ads highlighted American Express's no-spending-limit policy and encouraged people to use the card.

Then, changes in how people used credit cards motivated changes in how American Express marketed its cards. In the past, people only used cards for big purchases; cash and checks formed the bulk of all payments for goods and services. Over the years, however, card usage increased to the point where it now outweighs the use of cash and checks combined. People now use cards at grocery stores, gas stations, and even McDonald's. Seeing this trend, American Express wanted to be more than just a card for travel and special occasions. The company hired comedian Jerry Seinfeld to do a series of humorous ads showing Jerry using the card at the gas station, supermarket, hardware store, etc. The ads changed perceptions about American Express and boosted usage.

Over the decades, the marketing environment for American Express has changed in many ways, adding new communication channels while reducing the effectiveness of other channels. New marketing media, such as the Web and e-mail, mean new ways to reach potential card users. For example, American Express repurposed its Jerry Seinfeld ads into a series of entertaining "webisodes." At the same time, pop-up blockers, ad-blockers, and spam filters make using these new media a challenge.

Other, traditional media have also changed in ways that lower advertising effectiveness. The three major TV networks have lost market share to a rising sea of smaller cable channels. On the one hand, media fragmentation makes it harder for American Express to reach a big audience. On the other hand, cable offers the opportunity to target segments of the customer base.

Direct marketing channels have encountered their own obstacles. Households now face a flood of credit card offers in the mail, averaging six offers per month. The response rate for direct mail has dropped to only 2 percent. Telemarketing has been slowed as the Federal Trade Commission's Do-Not-Call Registry attracted more than 62 million numbers. Busy, finicky consumers are now much harder to reach.

To meet some of these challenges, American Express created new offers, such as building a new generation of card members, when it started offering cards to college students. The cards were cosigned by the parents to reduce the risk of default. American Express found that a person's first card enjoyed higher loyalty, and the "member since" date on the card served as an unbeatable, constant reminder to the consumer of how long American Express had had a relationship with them. Yet even this tactic lost its effectiveness as other credit card companies pummeled college students—and even high-schoolers—with credit card offers.

As American Express looks to the future, it sees people shipping money via information online. Instead of paper checks or plastic cards, silicon is becoming an increasing means for storing and transporting funds. To take advantage of these new technologies, and to meet the needs of a younger, tech-savvy generation, American Express introduced Blue. The new American Express Blue card targets these changes with a built-in microchip tied to a secure online account. The introductory ads in 1999 spoofed Y2K fears by announcing that Blue would be "Y3K compliant."

American Express prides itself on its number-one attribute of "knowing where consumers are going, new needs, evolving needs, and coming up with ways to satisfy the customer." A major issue for consumers is convenience: making it easier for customers to access and use the card when shopping. To do this, American Express has changed the technology in its Blue card to something it calls ExpressPay. American Express replaced the embedded microchip with gold-plated contacts including a wireless, contactless RFID solution that lets the customer simply wave the card past the reader for faster payment. American Express's ExpressPay comes in both standard credit card form and in a new key fob design. Tests of ExpressPay found that it is 63 percent faster than cash and 53 percent faster than a traditional card-swipe payment. As the future changes, so, too, will American Express.

Questions for Discussion

1. How might the six macro-environment forces affect American Express in the future?
2. What might American Express do to meet the needs of the next generation and to convince the next generation that American Express can meet those needs?
3. What services or products could American Express offer in the future?

Managing Marketing Information

Case in Point: Wild Planet

For toymaker Wild Planet, research is the key to creating a successful toy. The notion that adults can simply design toys that they would have wanted as a child does not work. "Kids have changed a lot, I think, and the biggest lesson that I have to remind myself of all the time is, you can't just take what you thought as a kid and make it true today," said Samara Tool, vice president of strategic initiatives.

Every year, toy makers must design and market new toys because the average shelf-life of a toy is only one year. Given the millions of dollars needed to develop, test, manufacture, market, and distribute a new toy, it pays to get it right.

So, how does San Francisco-based Wild Planet develop its products? Ideas come from many sources; not just designers and the marketing team, but also straight from the minds of kids. Regardless of where the idea comes from, Wild Planet is very concerned with gaining insights directly from the customer. "We do research all of the time. One of our missions in the company is to champion kids, and to do that we really value our closeness to kids. We really want to be in touch with kids," Tool said.

And they are in touch. Wild Planet talks to about 5,000 kids a year, but they don't do it through focus groups. The company feels that in order to really get a pulse on children's true thoughts, you have to keep it real. That's why they do what they call "Ethnographic Research," which is, essentially, watching kids in their natural play environments.

This means going out to visit the kids in their own homes, not bringing the kids to some sterile lab. "Throughout the years, we've found that research becomes more authentic the closer to a real environment that we're in. So in other words, kids don't typically play in focus group facilities, so even though it takes a little more time and effort, we like to meet kids in their homes. We arrange play groups where four or five people get together, we show them new toy ideas and get their feedback," said Jennifer Karsh, senior research manager.

Wild Planet also holds innovative "shop along" studies where it gives kids $30 and then trails them at the mall to see how they spend the money. "It's critical to understand how consumers interact with the products that you give them. In many cases, especially with kids, they'll do something that's completely unexpected, so it's really important to watch for what they do," explains Wild Planet's founder and CEO, Daniel Grossman.

The company's penchant for research dates back to its founding. In 1993, Daniel Grossman saw a growing need to create more imaginative kids' toys that parents could support—and that kids would also find cool. This meant understanding kids' own definition of cool and understanding the balance between imagination and interactivity for toys.

The result is that "we sell great products for kids. Some of them are toys, some of them may not look like toys, but in all cases we make sure that those products enhance their imagination, prompt them to be interactive, take them outdoors," Grossman said.

An example of one of Wild Planet's most successful toy lines is Spy Gear, a series of imaginative sleuthing toys for exploring and playing in the world around us. "We've had fantastic success with Spy Gear, which is our largest line, and it's the perfect line for our vision because it is a line that kids find very cool and parents can really endorse, because kids exploring and learning about things is one of our core developmental areas," Grossman said.

But Wild Planet is not just listening to kids. It also cares deeply about—and researches—what parents think. Parents play a major role in toy selection, so Wild Planet talks to the mothers and fathers, too. "In addition to research with kids, we do research with parents because they can share with you some of the nuances. Motivation is a lot about nuances. We can learn about what's so important to them. So, for example, if I say that Spy Gear is appealing to parents because they know kids will find it cool, and developmentally, to explore and sleuth is a good thing, that's a motivation that we can get a hold of," Karsh said.

Research helps Wild Planet understand what influences kids to buy. "Peer pressure does come into play a bit when it comes to purchasing toys, but more than peer pressure, I think, there's more of a phenomenon of "Schoolyard buzz." Every kid wants to be the first on the block to get the latest and greatest toy. So, in the case of an innovative toy, we know that if we give this to the hands of a trendsetter kid, that creates a certain buzz," Karsh said.

Buzz can be a boost to a toy, especially with so much competition. Finding the right mix of interactivity and imagination can be tricky. Throw in the differences between how girls like to play, and what toys boys are into, and you've got yourself a complicated marketing equation. Research is the answer to this complication at Wild Planet. Because girls and boys buy in very different ways, Wild Planet conducts exploratory testing with both groups.

"We had something that was called 'Spy Camera.' While this was a very popular item with boys, girls said, 'I don't want it to look so obvious.' So, where boys were perfectly happy about displaying their gadgetry, girls were a little more covert," Karsh said.

Of course, not all toys are for both boys and girls. When the company launched its "Room Gear" line, it was originally designed and marketed to both sexes. Room Gear was intended to be a line of cool toys that both boys and girls might use to decorate their room. However, after the company conducted usability testing—that is, after the product hit the market—it learned that the "Room Gear" products for boys were not a hit.

Wild Planet had tried hard to create room-oriented toys for both boys and girls. "We developed all of these different gadgets that were kind of 'techie' and kind of decorative, and we combined the two ideas. But it didn't work out because, while we realized later that while both genders wanted things for their rooms, they wanted very different things," said Kim Bratcher, PR manager for Wild Planet.

After usability testing proved that boys didn't want even the techiest of the Room Gear line, Wild Planet refocused the line on girls. The company changed the Room Gear line to female-only products and renamed it Girls Living in Style, or GLS. The new line emphasizes what the company learned from its research—girls were much more interested in decorating and accessorizing than playing with toys.

Wild Planet's research shows even deeper differences between boys and girls. Girls are abandoning the toy store at a much earlier age than boys. It's part of a growing trend of kids getting older younger. "Girls really spend more time in their rooms than boys do, and really seem to care about the decor of their rooms. For that reason, instead of trying to go down the middle line, and try to appeal to both boys and girls, we would just speak directly to girls," Karsh said.

And it appears girls are listening. Twelve-year-old Jennifer Farmer explains it best when she says, "it's very important to me to have my room decorated how I like it so when my friends come over, they go, 'Oh wow! I really like that! What is this? Where did you get it?' So that's what I like about my room."

Opinions, such as Jennifer Farmer's, really count at Wild Planet. That's why the company has what it calls a Toy Opinion Panel. "Our toy opinion panel, or TOP for short, is our research program. Our TOP database has literally thousands of families that we can call upon at any time when we need opinions on toys. Generally the way that it works is through surveys or in home groups, kids have a chance to test out the newest toy ideas and give us their feedback," said Karsh.

But the company's involvement with children doesn't end there. Perhaps the most exciting and innovative program at Wild Planet is one in which kids get to enter their own ideas for cool toys. "The Kid Inventor Challenge is an annual contest for thousands of kids to have the opportunity to submit their toy ideas to us. So, all they need to do is brainstorm the idea, draw it, label it, and they can even do a little marketing sheet on it if they want to. They send it in, and we review them. And we select the very best toys to be manufactured," Karsh said.

One hot toy that arose from the contest was "Explorer's Gloves." The gloves have a built-in set of gadgets for fun in the outdoors. "Kids are great inventors because I think they are great brainstormers. They are not fettered by a lot of constraints that adults have, about why this isn't a great idea, or maybe you're not going to like it," said Grossman.

There are other advantages to the contest as well. "A lot of kids write to us and say that because of the Kid Inventor Challenge, they want to be a toy inventor now as their profession. Kids' interests definitely change as they grow, but I know that we've definitely sparked a lot of imagination in the process," said Karsh. Imagination, and that all-important buzz, which can travel all the way to the checkout line.

"Getting a hold of kids' motivations is key in today's environment. And it's also crucial to remember that kids 25 years ago are nothing like kids today," said Grossman. "Kids now are a lot more savvy and sophisticated. They live in a world where they always have known the Internet. They know and are very comfortable with being videotaped and having their opinions asked of them, so I think they have a certain sophistication to them that we haven't seen in generations before. But at the end of the day, I think kids are kids are kids, and they love to play with cool toys," Kirsh said. With the help of research, Wild Planet can stay in synch with kids' changing definitions of what is cool.

Questions for Discussion

1. What are the different ways in which Wild Planet gains insight into customers' opinions? Are the insights gained from its market research worth the costs?
2. When conducting ethnographic research, what might Wild Planet watch for?
3. Toys represent a product in which the designers, developers, and marketers of the product are not the intended users, so these professionals don't have the benefit of relying on their own tastes and desires in creating the product. What other product categories face this issue that the creator of the product may be unlike the customer of the product?

Consumer and Business Buyer Behavior

Case in Point: Eaton

As a consumer, you might not recognize the name Eaton—but this huge industrial B2B company touches your life in many ways. If you drive, fly, or live in a building, you've probably used an Eaton product without knowing it. Eaton's engine valves and torque converters are in your automobiles; they're also in the airplane hydraulics systems of many aircraft. In your home, you'll find Eaton's products in your circuit breaker box. Overall, Eaton sells tens of thousands of different products to hundreds of major companies around the world. How does this $9.8 billion company carry out its marketing initiatives?

THE B2B MARKETING PROCESS

B2B marketing differs from selling to consumers in two important ways. First, business buyers are often very sophisticated, informed, and discriminating. The buying decision may involve millions of dollars' worth of some product and may be crucial to the customer's own product, so buyers tend to make those purchases very carefully. The buyers who are Eaton's customers have access to a tremendous amount of data. They're often engineers who are designing products like trucks, or they're operations people who are running large factories. Eaton's customers have employees whose job is to study the specifications of products, scrutinize the competing suppliers, and negotiate prices.

Second, the B2B sales process involves many layers of decision makers and influencers. Eaton's marketing effort must address the needs not only of the customer's design engineers but also the needs of buying influencers like operations people and plant managers. These managers typically don't know the specifics about an individual piece of equipment their company will be buying, but they know the value that equipment must deliver.

To market to multiple decision makers and meet their diverse needs, Eaton maps the decision makers inside customer companies and assesses the needs of every person involved. Doing this requires a deep understanding of the customer and the competition; it even involves knowing the legislation and regulations associated with critical parts like those found in aircraft or in safety equipment such as circuit breakers. The marketing effort thus becomes more like a partnership—Eaton and its customers exchange ideas about the customer's problems and discuss solutions, which Eaton can deliver to address those problems.

SELLING THROUGH MULTIPLE CHANNELS

Like many large businesses, Eaton sells its products through multiple channels. Consider, for example, a product such as Eaton's VORAD system. VORAD (or Vehicle Onboard RADar) is an early-warning system for impending vehicle collisions. The tiny radar unit mounted on the back of a vehicle, such as a truck, can alert the driver to objects behind the vehicle so the driver doesn't hit anything or anyone when backing up.

To what types of customers does Eaton sell VORAD? First, Eaton markets the system to OEMs (Original Equipment Manufacturers) like Peterbilt and Monaco Coach, who install the systems into the new models of their trucks or motor homes, respectively. To customers such as Peterbilt, installing VORAD distinguishes Peterbilt trucks from its competitors. Trucking companies are more likely to buy Peterbilt trucks because they know that Eaton's VORAD units can reduce accidents.

Second, another channel through which Eaton sells VORAD and other products is called the *aftermarket*. The aftermarket consists of networks of automotive maintenance garages, distributors, and retailers that handle parts and accessories for vehicles on the road. Because VORAD can also be retrofitted into existing RVs, Eaton's national service and installation centers are a third channel that sells VORAD systems.

In short, Eaton sells through OEMs, distributors, its own service centers, its own sales force, and the Web. As a result, an Eaton customer may interact with an Eaton salesperson on one day, a partner's salesperson on another day, and through the Web on the third day. Managing all these channels is a blend of art and science. First, Eaton must carefully balance the needs and advantages of different channel partners because there is a potential for competition among these channels. Second, to market successfully across these different channels, Eaton must deliver a consistent message that creates an Eaton brand while differentiating the message to fit each channel. Eaton must create a thread that runs through the marketing for the different channels, to establish the Eaton brand and make clear what the brand stands for. Regardless of the product sold, or the channel used, the Eaton brand emphasizes reliability, quality, and high value.

VALUE-BASED PRICING

Another aspect of B2B marketing involves pricing the product or service. Eaton uses a value-based approach to pricing, which means that Eaton looks at the value of what its product does for the customer rather than at the costs of the parts in that product. Thus, the same product could sell for different prices to different customers. For example, pricing of the VORAD system isn't based on the cost of the electronics. Rather, it is based on the value that buyers assign to the product's attributes, namely improved safety. The value of that safety can be high. Nonetheless, the value that customers put on safety varies. For trucking companies, safety has a major, measurable impact on the bottom line: if a trucking company reduces its accident rate, the company can reduce its insurance costs as well as lawsuit costs. In contrast, the same device on an RV has a lower perceived value. Prices for VORAD units are, therefore, higher for trucks than for RVs, even though the cost of the units is essentially the same.

CONSTANT INNOVATION

Value-based pricing, in Eaton's case, also means working with the customer to evolve the product. Eaton can't simply sell the same product three years in a row. The products must be constantly changing and improving. This is especially important in today's market. In the past, customers typically bought on the basis of price. Today, customers still demand good prices, but they also demand on-time delivery and good quality. At the same time, their demand for product innovation has accelerated, so Eaton needs to innovate even faster. A new product may have a lifespan of only 18 months before competition arrives.

One way that Eaton innovates is by listening to the customer and solving problems for the customer. In the early stages of VORAD, for example, the product only had a visual indicator on the driver's dashboard that indicated if an object was too close. Customers suggested that an auditory alarm would also be useful, so Eaton added that feature. Additional innovations created systems to detect objects not just behind vehicles but on the sides and in front of the vehicle as well, to help in situations like merging into traffic. When mounted on the front of the vehicle, the unit can also regulate cruise control to ensure a safe following distance and avoid rear-end collisions.

BUILDING A RELATIONSHIP

As Eaton co-innovates with its customers, it builds relationships with them. Whereas B2C sales are often anonymous (P&G does not know each and every buyer of Tide detergent), Eaton develops long-term, multi-year relationships with OEMs and after-market distribution partners. The relationship is important because people buy from people they like and trust. As Eaton points out, the true test of a relationship often lies in how a company reacts when something goes wrong. Inevitably, a mistake will be made or something won't show up on time. In such cases, customers look to see how the company will respond. Eaton turns those potential problem situations into opportunities. "When people know that you can bail them out of a particular issue they've got, that memory stays in place for a long time," says Alexander Cutler, chairman and CEO of Eaton.

Questions for Discussion

1. How might Eaton's marketing messages and discussions differ for an engineer, purchasing manager, operations manager, or CEO of an OEM?

2. What are the advantages and disadvantages of Eaton's value-based pricing approach?

3. What makes Eaton's channel management challenging? Why does the company continue to sell through multiple channels?

Building the Right Relationships with the Right Customers

Case in Point: P&G

Consider something as simple as laundry detergent—you put your dirty clothes in the washer, dump in some detergent, and press a button. It seems so simple until you visit the grocery store and are confronted by that long sprawling aisle with shelf after shelf of detergents accosting the eyes with color and assaulting the nose with scents. How many different detergents do people really need? Well, P&G has found that people need a surprising number of different laundry detergents. P&G alone accounts for many of the competing brand names you might see on the shelf, such as Cheer, Dreft, Era, Gain, Ivory, and Tide.

Why does P&G have so many brands that seem to be competing with each other? The answer is that each one of these is a distinct brand with its own image, own marketing, and own target market. For example, Dreft is a gentle detergent with no harsh chemicals that is designed to wash out completely from fabrics. Dreft is the number one choice of pediatricians and comes in a gentle pink container with a mother and baby on the label. Ivory Snow extends the Ivory soap brand's classic image of old-fashioned purity and simplicity to laundry. Era touts its advanced stain-removing enzymes that can "fight your family's tough stains." Gain is marketed for its "smell that says clean" scent. Each brand offers some unique combination of value and special features.

P&G's strategy of diverse targeted brands in each category extends around the world. Overseas, P&G sells other brands of detergents such as Daz, Ariel, Bold, Bonux, Dash, Fairy, Myth, Rindex, and Vizir alongside some of the familiar U.S. brands. The same brand can even serve different targets in different countries. Whereas Dreft is marketed for cleaning baby clothes in the United States with its claim as the pediatrician's favorite, it is marketed for gently cleaning delicate fabrics in the United Kingdom with its claim of being recommended by the International Wool Secretariat and the Cotton Council International.

P&G also targets consumers' different preferences for the form of the detergent. These options can differ by country. In the United States, P&G offers only two alternatives: powder or liquid. But in the United Kingdom, P&G offers four forms: powder, tablet, liquid, and liquitabs. Some overseas brands also target hand washing with higher sudsing action desired for non-machine washing applications. With all the combinations of brands, scents, additives, forms, and package sizes, P&G offers hundreds and hundreds of different SKUs (Stock Keeping Units) in just this one category of laundry detergent. And this doesn't even include all the supplementary fabric-care products, such as separate bleaches, fabric softeners, prewash stain fighters, or specialty products such as the Dryel home dry cleaning kit.

P&G even creates subtargets within a single brand. For example, Cheer comes in six different formulations: regular Cheer, Cheer Free & Gentle (free of dyes and perfumes), Cheer Complete (with nonbleach cleaning booster), Cheer High Efficiency Liquid (for high-efficiency washing machines), Cheer Fresh Linen (crisp fresh scent), and Cheer Dark Formula (twice the fade-protection for dark clothing). Nearly every Cheer detergent comes in either powder or liquid and in a variety of packaging styles—from petite single-wash boxes for coin laundries to mega-econobox-packaging for discounters such as Costco.

Cheer isn't the only hypersegmented anomaly in the P&G line up. Tide has some 29 different combinations of formulations, scents, additives, and liquid or powder alternatives. Marketed with an "It's Got to Be Tide" motto, this premium-brand detergent is the number-one best-selling brand in the United States. A $3 billion brand, Tide could be a FORTUNE 500 company all by itself.

Adding new segments through new product formulations is a serious task at P&G. For example, P&G realized that some consumers wanted the pleasant feel created by a fabric softener but didn't like the hassle of adding a separate product during the middle of the cycle. So P&G went to work. Combining Tide with one brand of its fabric softeners, Downy, required careful study. "We ran a test of more then 125 different concepts among thousands of consumers and this was a leading idea," said P&G spokesperson Randy Chinchilla. The winning combination was "Tide with a Touch of Downy." Even a seemingly narrow product such as Tide with a Touch of Downy comes in two forms (liquid or powder), three scents, and five sizes for a total of 30 new SKUs.

Convincing consumers that they need a 150-ounce bottle of the April Fresh scent version of the liquid form of Tide with a Touch of Downy is only half the challenge for P&G's segmentation efforts. The company must find extensions that retailers will also accept. In fact, some SKUs don't just target consumers, they target different types of retailers. A discounter such as Sam's Club is unlikely to carry the little 50-ounce bottle of Tide liquid, while a convenience store is unlikely to carry the mammoth 300-ounce bottle of that same product.

As huge as the laundry detergent aisle seems, shelf space is a critically scarce commodity and a zero-sum game. Retailers can't stock every one of the 30 SKUs of new Tide with a Touch of Downy. P&G knows that if the retailer wants to add a new product, then the retailer must take something else away. P&G hopes that the brand taken away will be a competitor's brand. Yet retailers are wary of removing products—3 percent of customers switch retailers when the store stops carrying a preferred product. Careful testing and market data help P&G convince the retailer that it will increase its sales per square foot if it adds one or more SKUs of the new product.

Laundry detergents are a microcosm—this one category is only one small part of the total consumer packaged goods space. A careful trip down any aisle of any grocery store will uncover a similar proliferation of SKUs in every category: multiple mustards, tons of toothpastes, or a plethora of disposable paper products. P&G is just one company creating brands and line extensions to cover the diverse space of consumer and retailer needs.

Questions for Discussion

1. What are some of the product dimensions that P&G targets?
2. Discuss how P&G might balance brand extensions versus cannibalism to optimize the total number of SKUs available.
3. Discuss targeting and brand extensions from the retailer's perspective.

Product, Services, and Branding Strategies

Case in Point: Swiss Army Brands

It seems appropriate that the maker of multifunction knives would build a multiproduct brand. Swiss Army Brands is the international marketing arm of Victorinox and Wenger, the two Swiss companies officially licensed by the government of Switzerland to manufacture the world-renowned Swiss Army Knives. The popularity of the "Swiss Army Knife" concept has enabled the company to expand into all manner of consumer goods: watches, luggage, apparel, and other lines.

When it was founded in 1884, the company didn't intend to become such a household name. Originally, the company was just a small family-owned cutlery company that got a Swiss Army government contract in 1891. Based on its official tie to the Swiss military, in 1897 the company registered its title as the "Original Swiss Army Knife." For nearly 50 years, the company subsisted as a local supplier to the Swiss Army. During that time, it created the now-familiar cross-and-shield emblem and named itself Victorinox after the deceased mother of the founder (Victoria) and the INOXidizable stainless steel of the knives.

World War II marked a sharp turning point in the company's fortunes. American GIs were intrigued and enamored by the multifunction pocket knives of their Swiss counterparts. GIs bartered for these fascinating gadgets, started buying them from the company for sale at local military "PX" stores, and brought them back to the United States. Soon, Victorinox had a growing export business to supplement its Swiss government contracts. Sales grew as exports surged. Currently, 90 percent of the knives leave the tiny Swiss federation to satisfy a growing global customer base.

With growth came expansion of the product mix. At first, the company only expanded the range of pocket knives to suit different applications beyond what the company offered the army. For example, a fisherman's knife might include a fish scaler and hook remover. A golfer's knife might include a tool for repairing divots or cleaning the spikes of golf shoes. A petite, discrete knife for a woman's purse might include a toothpick, tweezers, nail file, and clippers. These extensions retained the core idea of a multifunctional pocket knife even as they extended the line to other categories of customers.

In the late 1980s, the company realized that it had created a massively popular brand. The term "Swiss Army Knife" achieved widespread recognition as synonymous with high-quality, highly-useful, multifunctional objects in any category. Brand recognition stands at 92 percent. Thus, the company looked at ways to leverage its brand in new product lines.

The first brand extension beyond the trademark knives was the Swiss Army Watch, launched in 1987. The watch became one of the top watches under $500 and one of the most popular watch brands over the last decade. Initially, the company subcontracted watch manufacturing to another company. Six years after launching Swiss Army Watches, the company bought a watch manufacturing operation in Switzerland.

At Swiss Army Brands, brand extension begins with consumer research. The company believes that it is important to consider what consumers think of the brand, and what values and attributes they associate with the brand, so that any extension of the brand reflects what consumers already feel about the brand. In the 1990s, research indicated that the brand could be extended to two new product categories: travel gear and apparel.

Extending the brand allowed the company to start its own retail channel in 2001. The company opened a trendy store in New York City to highlight the brand and sell its expanding array of knives, watches, luggage, and apparel. With breadth comes enough product range to justify such store openings. A second store in Tokyo in 2005 signals the company's plans for global expansion that leverages the expanded product mix.

Yet some might wonder if Swiss Army has strayed too far. On the one hand, the watches and luggage share much in common with the namesake knives. They have the same rugged, multifunctional ethos. They come in the same no-nonsense color schemes that include stainless steel, white, black, and the Swiss flag's signature red. In short, these products exude Swiss stolidity and mechanical ingenuity. Watches are clearly a natural for a Swiss company and the association of Switzerland with travel is a natural for North American consumers.

On the other hand, Swiss Army has branched further into fashion apparel. Although some of the clothing provides a multifunctional, travel-oriented feel and muted travel-safe colors, the company's more recent designs seem to stray ever farther from that core. Polo shirts in the latest fashion-oriented colors reflect the Swiss Army brand only by the almost incidental presence of the cross-and-shield logo. Like an oversized pocket knife with too many blades and attachments, the Swiss Army brand may be becoming too bulky for its own good.

The company continues to consider various directions and has registered its trademark in connection with products such as tents, sleeping bags, canteens, office equipment, shoes, bicycles, and other products. Whether these products will ever appear under the Swiss Army cross-and-shield remains to be seen. The future of the brand is in the hands of consumers.

Questions for Discussion

1. What additional products and lines might Swiss Army Brands consider?
2. How do brand extensions affect a company such as Swiss Army Brands, in both positive and negative ways?
3. Why did Swiss Army Brands open a retail stores? How do these stores help the company build its brand?

New Product Development and Product Life-Cycle Strategies

Case in Point: eGO

Every new product starts with an idea. For computer techies Andrew Kallfelz and Jim Hamann, the idea was about a better way to run out and pick up a gallon of milk—a vehicle that would be small, environmentally friendly, and very cheap to operate. The result, two years after the initial idea, was the eGO Cycle electric scooter.

The company did far more than just dream up the product and mass produce it. "We spent two years developing the eGO Cycle," said eGO Vehicles President Andrew Kallfelz. First, they built four prototypes and took them to football games, shows, and events. Free rides helped the company gain feedback on what consumers liked and didn't like about the product.

The company also did its research into consumers' movement habits. From the U.S. Bureau of Transportation Statistics, they learned that nearly 60 percent of all automobile trips are less than five miles, and 50 percent of trips are for personal (single passenger) transportation. eGO designed the range and speed of the eGO Cycle to match these short single-person trips.

Getting a new product on the road can involve government red tape, especially when the product will be—well—on the road. After positive market tests, eGO sought approval from the Highway Transportation Safety Agency. This meant adding a headlight, taillight, and brake light. Today, the eGO Cycle is the only vehicle of its type that can be registered in every state. But making the eGO street legal wasn't the company's only regulatory concern. They also designed it with 23-inch handlebars to make it acceptable for bringing on the subway.

The company designed the machine to be cost-efficient. At $1,400, the scooter doesn't cost much compared to a car, especially considering the price of gas. With gas at $2 or even $3 a gallon, a car can be 20 to 30 times more expensive than the $.10 worth of electricity needed to recharge the eGO.

The result of the company's efforts was a two-wheel vehicle with a sleek, low-slung footboard that contains the battery and compact electric motor. Although it lacks pedals, the cycle is slimmer and trimmer than a moped. And it doesn't have the bulky, noisy engine of a moped. "[It] is the perfect product for the urban commuter, college student, or gated community resident," said Kallfelz. A small luggage rack on the back can easily hold a backpack, laptop bag, or briefcase.

The product enjoyed a great launch that included a media blitz with appearances on CNN, *Good Morning America*, and the *Today* shows. Articles in trade magazines such as *RV Market* and *Practical Horseman* provided more targeted—and more valuable—exposure. The company brought its product to upscale events where environmentally-conscious consumers could see it such as at the Newport Jazz Festival and at an Earth Day event in Fairhope, Alabama. The scooter won awards and made its way onto published holiday gift-giving lists.

As the 2003 Oprah Holiday Gift Guide said, "Unlike a moped, the eGO Cycle 2 is quiet and nonpolluting, and never runs out of gas." The bike has its own built-in charger so that the rider can plug in anywhere.

The eGO Cycle seems like a great product and is, in fact, much-loved by customers. Despite rapidly growing sales approaching 1,000 per month, the company hasn't been able to establish a solid network of dealers for the battery-based bike. The company thought that the 5,000 independent bicycle shops in the United States would be a natural outlet for the environmentally-friendly product. But bicycle shops turned up their noses at the product's lack of pedals and the sacrilegious thought of battery power.

A similar problem means that motorcycle shops don't want to carry the diminutive electric scooter. From a retail standpoint, the eGO falls in the cracks between bicycles and motorcycles. In total, only 60 dealers in the United States carry the product. This means that the company must rely on online sales and catalog sales, which hampers sales of a product that a customer might like to test-drive.

Despite these challenges, the product sells well in the places that do sell it. "Wherever we've sold one, there has been a cluster of additional sales in that area," said the company's president. The company continues to expand, adding international sales channels in more than 18 countries. This has meant upgrading some of the safety features, such as adding front and rear turn signals to satisfy European regulators.

The eGO is a well-developed product that just needs a better-developed channel. With a range of 20 to 25 miles and a top speed of 20 to 25 mph, it is perfect for short neighborhood trips, such as getting that gallon of milk, that started the founders thinking.

Questions for Discussion

1. Discuss some of the hurdles to developing and launching a new product. What sort of obstacles did eGO face?
2. Discuss what eGO might do next to continue its growth phase or reach maturity.
3. What is eGO's likely target segment(s)? What are your reasons for these suppositions?

Pricing

Case in Point: Song

Song, Delta Airlines' most recent attempt at a low-cost airline, arose from Delta's observation that the post-9/11 world didn't hurt every airline equally. Delta saw that low-price, low-cost carriers such as Southwest and JetBlue managed to eek out profits even as the major airlines lost billions.

Although Delta didn't lose any airplanes on September 11, 2001, the company faced many problems. An already slow economy combined with new-found fears of air travel created a serious slump in airline revenues. In addition, new costs—rising fuel prices, new security costs, and rising employee health care costs—cut into revenues for most airlines. The event stalled several of the big players, forcing airlines such as United and USAir into bankruptcy. But 9/11 also created opportunities for new carriers to enter the marketplace without the amount of corporate baggage that older airlines carried.

Tim Mapes, Song's former chief marketing officer, explained, "When you look at the background and the environment that we created Song out of, it was three years of the company losing a billion dollars or more. In that environment, it was easy to say, 'look, maybe we can try something radically different, how much worse can it be?'"

Out of that environment, Delta decided to try a new experiment: a separately-branded airline called Song. The pricing strategy to create this low-cost airline involved more than just simple discounting. Song implemented an upfront pricing structure that took the mystery out of trying to figure out how much your seatmate in the same row was paying for the same flight. In many traditional full-fare airlines, two people on the same flight in the same row of seats might have paid radically different prices for their seats. Airlines have multiple fares at different times for the same flight. Price ratios between the highest fare and the lowest fare might exceed 10:1. For example, a leisure-fare traveler (with three-week advance purchase, Saturday-night stay, and nonrefundable/nonchangeable tickets) might pay only $99 whereas a last-minute, walk-up, full-fare, refundable/changeable ticket for the business traveler may cost more than a thousand dollars.

This practice of charging different prices to different passengers on the same flight is known as yield management, and it is common in the travel industry. (Airlines, hotels, and rental car companies all use yield management pricing strategies.) The practice reflects the cost structure of airline operations—high fixed costs (the high cost of flying even an empty plane to a destination) mean that the marginal cost of putting another passenger into an empty seat is relatively low. Airlines would rather fill seats at low prices than let seats fly empty. At the same time, some travelers are less price-sensitive than others. A business traveler trying to secure a multi-million-dollar deal wants the convenience of flying anytime, anywhere, and is less concerned with price. In contrast, a vacation traveler might not take any flight if the price is too high. Maximizing the revenue per flight is very challenging: Selling too many vacation-fare seats in the months before the flight means the plane has no room for full-fare, last-minute business travelers; selling too few seats to vacationers means the plane flies half-empty.

Online booking allowed anyone to find the lowest fares. In addition, the post-bubble, post-9/11 recession forced people to start looking for low fares. "The market as it exists today is really defined by people who want the lowest possible price, be they business travelers or leisure travelers, so our strategy was to provide them with the lowest possible fares in a simple, transparent way," said Mapes. "We created a new strategy that said, 'Okay let's take away those thousand-dollar fares that people resent, 'cause they're not paying them anyway. Let's make the highest fare $299—that would be the businessman walk-up fare—make the lowest fare $79, and try to get a mix,'" said John Selvaggio, Song's former president.

LOW COSTS TO MATCH LOW FARES

Offering low airfares was great for attracting customers, but unless Delta also had low costs at Song, the concept wouldn't be good for business. Delta used a multipronged approach to reduce costs at its new subsidiary. "The key for us was to increase utilization of the same fixed cost asset. That's done by flying the planes more hours during the day, using gates more frequently, and driving distribution to lower cost channels like the Internet," said Mapes. First, Song removed the first-class section of a Delta plane and added more economy seats.

Second, Song looked at how to get more flights per day per airplane. Selvaggio explained this prong of Song's approach to maximizing asset utilization: "We really looked at how can we turn planes faster. By turning them faster, if you could take twenty or thirty minutes off ground time every time the airplane lands, at the end of the day that adds two hours and that gives you enough time to fly another flight." By adding more flights per day, Song got more use out of its very expensive asset without adding any gate fees or more employees.

Song also had to decide what type of plane to fly. "The only way to get our cost down was to get our unit cost down. We had to create more units. So, simply put, we could not make money on a small 737 carrying 110 people. We could get a lower breakeven load factor with a larger 199-seat airplane, but we're adding 70 percent more seats," said Selvaggio.

Labor is another big cost for airlines, so Song changed the way it scheduled flight attendants. "What we did was told the flight attendants that if you change some of the rules about how you fly, they might fly more hours in a day, but they would have to work less days per month, and get more days off in order to make the same amount of money. That was a compelling argument for most of our flight attendants," Selvaggio said. Changing some of Delta's old work rules—and, in some cases, eliminating the cost of putting workers up at hotels—further helped Song create a cost structure that enabled its low-price structure.

By changing its planes, taking out first class, adding more seats, and offering lower fares, Song operated at 23 percent to 25 percent lower operating costs than the same plane in what was a traditional Delta configuration. Through those changes, Song was able to lower Delta's costs overall.

NOT JUST ANOTHER CUT-PRICE AIRLINE

As in the retail world, airlines differentiate themselves on more than just price. For example, Southwest is like Wal-Mart with its everyday low fares and no frills. JetBlue, with its multiple TV channels of in-flight entertainment and leather seats, is more like Target—a better quality service at a lower price. Song wasn't Delta's first attempt at a low-cost airline. Delta Express was a cut-rate, no-frills operation, which was ill-received by the market due to its cramped legroom and lower level of service. Based on Delta's experience with Delta Express, Song executives knew that low fares alone wouldn't be enough. The new airline would need to have a great product unique enough to attract 70 percent more people to fill up Song's new, larger planes.

The company's research showed that women were responsible for 75 percent of leisure travel decisions. So Song went after them, targeting women by offering amenities like healthy gourmet organic food, vibrant colors, leather seats, and personal in-flight entertainment units. Song even enlisted designers Kate and Andy Spade to craft new fashionable uniforms for the flight attendants. "We created a completely different brand, created a different market segment that we attract. We are very focused on women. We call them our discount divas—those people that still like to get a good fare, appreciate good service, and are good shoppers," said Selvaggio at the time.

Some might wonder whether the extra amenities added costs not in keeping with Song's discount prices. Song took several steps to offer more without costing the airline more. For example, Song converted some traditional cost centers, like food and entertainment, into profit centers. Consider airline food—a much maligned item that seems to both add costs and create dissatisfaction. Rather than hand out free brown-bag lunches or the proverbial meager bags of peanuts, Song went for-pay and gourmet. The company hired a famous chef and transformed food into another profit center. "We took a cost of an airline that was completely unappreciated by the customer and converted it into a revenue stream. So we have no cost for food. We only sell food and make money doing it," Selvaggio said.

On its very first flight, Song sold $600 worth of gourmet organic food. Song then used the same strategy for its in-flight entertainment. Digital TV was free—but if customers wanted a pay-per-view movie, they had to order and pay for it at their seat. Upon debut, Song said that it sold 10,000 in-flight movies in one day.

Other Song amenities were actually shrewd cost-cutting or no-cost measures in disguise. "Everyone [looked] at us and [said], 'This can't be a low cost airline, they have leather seats—leather seats cost more than cloth seats.' However, they last longer. They're so much easier to clean, you wipe a spill off them, and you don't have to send it to the dry cleaner," Selvaggio said. As for their designer uniforms, according to Song, the uniforms didn't cost any more than the uniforms flight attendants wore on Delta but hated. It was all part of the Song experience: low fares but not low service or appeal. Three years after inception, Song was filling 78 percent of the seats on its flights.

In the end, however, the Song strategy was not enough to sustain both Song and its parent Delta. When Delta declared bankruptcy on September 14, 2005, it announced that it would merge Song back into Delta, thereby reducing the costs of marketing two separate airlines. Delta would use Song's airplanes for its own flights, but it would also incorporate Song's successes back into the parent airline. Delta incorporated Song's simpler fare system, adopted the new uniforms, installed new leather interiors, and improved in-flight entertainment systems. Song was a successful experiment that allowed Delta to try new services, according to Jim Whitehurst, Delta's chief operating officer, but going forward, the company is going to focus more on business travelers than leisure travelers.

Questions for Discussion

1. How did Song compete with traditional carriers like American Airlines and upstarts like JetBlue? What lessons did Delta learn from its Song experience?

2. How important are amenities in the airline business? What other factors are important to air travelers? How do customers define value?

3. What are the fixed costs and the variable costs of operating an airline route? What control did Song have over these costs?

4. How did Song's customer value and pricing formulas compare to those of the industry's low-price, no-frills leader, Southwest Airlines. What might Song have done to improve its competitiveness even further? Will incorporating Song's successes help Delta be more competitive?

Distribution Channels and Logistics Management

Case in Point: Hasbro

Hasbro is a true giant in the toy industry with such long-running favorites as GI Joe, Mr. Potato Head, Scrabble, Monopoly, the Easy-Bake Oven, and more. With $3 billion in sales and decades of successful toy lines, Hasbro is the second-largest toy maker. Yet the toy industry has consolidated on the retail channel end, and Hasbro now finds itself dwarfed by the $285 billion Wal-Mart and other massive retail chains such as Toys "R" Us and Target.

On the consumer side, the company keeps pace with the changing needs of the market, constantly modernizing its products through the years to make toys and games relevant to its consumers. "We work with one thousand new products every year and have to launch them into the market and then have to launch 80 percent of them as brand new the next year. It's high pressure but fun, in that there is big opportunity if you're right for a big win—or you know very quickly if you're wrong," said Brian Goldner, president, U.S. Toys Group for Hasbro.

RISE OF THE BIG BOX

A hot product means nothing if Hasbro can't get toys on store shelves. Retail industry consolidation means Wal-Mart, Target, and Toys "R" Us account for 60 percent of Hasbro's toy and game sales—a distribution channel that allows the company to move a lot of product in a short period of time.

These big customers demand high performance from Hasbro. "Some of the mass merchants will tell you that if you don't perform at a superior level in the field of logistics, they're not going to carry the product—even if it's a hot product because they're so focused on making sure they manage the supply chain," said CEO Al Verrecchia. Thus, Hasbro must streamline logistics—getting the right product to the right place at the right time for the right price, while ensuring that the shelves and warehouses are neither too full nor empty.

"One advantage of the mass channels is you can really focus on improving your supply chain because if you're dealing with one, two, or three major retailers that make up a significant piece of the business, then you can effect a lot of change in improving your supply chain," said Verrecchia.

Sophisticated technology such as real-time point-of-sale data, forecasting software, and supply chain optimization software helps. Hasbro gets information daily from its key customers, which tells them which products are selling. The amount and timeliness of the information is much better than it was a few years ago.

NEW CHANNELS, NEW CHALLENGES

At the same time that retail, and especially toy retailing, has consolidated to a few major chains, toy shopping has become more diversified. For instance, Hasbro's CEO cited the simple trend of kids "getting older" sooner, which means that Hasbro has to look at new channels as a way of reaching 8- to 12-year-olds—an age group referred to as the "tween" market. "If we're selling little girls' products, little girls spend a lot of time in a store like Limited 2, so we need to be there. Young boys love to go to Best Buy; we need to be there. We try to make our product not only affordable but designed in a way that it can sell in a variety of channels."

The expanding array of channels, including clothing stores, electronics stores, wholesale clubs, drug stores, grocery stores, and online retailers, increases channel conflict. "Very often, these channels don't want to compete with the mass merchants. They want to have a product differentiation. The whole purpose of what we're trying to do is make sure our product is where our customers are," said Verrecchia. "Because they want unique product, that puts a lot of pressure on the R&D folks to come up with unique packages. And sometimes, it's difficult to take GI Joe and make it so unique and different that some drug store chains and grocery store chains are willing to carry it," said Verrecchia.

Sometimes, that extra energy means bundling products together to reach a specific consumer. "Let's say we have an item like VideoNow [a toy video player unit]. So when you go to Wal-Mart and Toys "R" Us, you have the VideoNow player, and you can buy software, a carrying case, and headphones. We may go into a Best Buy with a product that includes all of those items in one pack. It's a higher-ticket item. They're not competing directly with Wal-Mart or Target, but it's the same item but packed out differently," said Verrecchia.

MORE THAN MAKING TOYS

"It's not about just making a product and selling it everywhere. Clearly, consumers across the country have options; and those options include a Wal-Mart trip, a Target trip, or a Best Buy trip, or a trip to the grocery store or a drug store. And what we do is try to help them to differentiate their offerings, so that we provide them with our product and our brands in the way that we want to market and provide them to the consumer, but also reflect the different ways of going to business," said Goldner. Being a modern-day toy maker means more than making toys. Hasbro must manage all its downstream channels and ensure that these channels get what they want and what they need because if the retailer isn't successful, then Hasbro isn't successful.

Questions for Discussion

1. Discuss why the supply chain is so important to Hasbro.
2. How should Hasbro manage competition between different channels and avoid channel conflict? What does a toy store think when a toy is on sale in a clothing store? What if the same toy is on sale in different locations for different prices?
3. If you were Hasbro, how might you differentiate toys to avoid pure price competition between Wal-Mart and Target?

Retailing and Wholesaling

Case in Point: Reebok

No brand is an island. When Reebok thinks about a new line of shoes or new ad campaign, the company also thinks about its retail channel partners.

In many ways, the retailer—not the end-consumer—is the customer for Reebok. Reebok's sales force sells to retailers, not to individual consumers. The retailers are the ones to whom Reebok ships its shoes and apparel, and retailers are the ones who pay Reebok. Finally, it's the retailers who call Reebok with questions about orders, forthcoming products, promotions, and sales forecasts. Reebok even manages its relationships with retailers using CRM software.

Yet Reebok's relationships with retailers are deeper than a simple buyer-seller relationship. These relationships are more like partnerships, in that Reebok works with retailers to craft consumer product and marketing strategies to the advantage of both. Reebok knows that to sell shoes to retailers, the retailers need to sell shoes to consumers.

Reebok doesn't just market shoes to consumers; rather, the company crafts a multiway tie between the consumer, the product line, the retailer, endorsement personalities, and the ad channel. "Our strong partnership with Reebok allows us to differentiate each of our retail brands by offering an exclusive style that is relevant to each core customer through our targeted marketing programs," said Rick Mina, president and CEO of Foot Locker. With 3,900 outlets in 17 countries, it makes sense for Reebok to work closely with Foot Locker to jointly maximize sales.

For example, Reebok created an exclusive ad for the athletic shoe line, Classic Clyp Groove, for Foot Locker subsidiary Champ Sports. The ad featured Philadelphia Eagles quarterback Donovan McNabb and ran on ESPN. A product-driven ad for Lady Foot Locker had girls literally painting the town pink and red as their pink and red Reeboks touched where they walked. Ads for Kids Foot Locker on Nickelodeon, Cartoon Network, and Fox Box highlighted Reebok Classic Lights with children catching fireflies attracted to the blinking lights of the shoes' soles. Rapper 50 Cent plugged Reebok GXTs (available only at FootLocker) on spots that ran on MTV and BET in time for back-to-school shoe sales.

Collaborations with retailers help Reebok access key consumer segments. For example, Limited Too is a specialty retailer targeting tweens—consumers that aren't children but aren't yet teenagers. In 2002, Reebok was unhappy with its low sales to tweens and Limited Too was unhappy with its athletic footwear lineup. The two got together at Reebok's headquarters to craft an unusually deep partnership.

Specifically, Limited Too would provide input during product development, use its stores for product testing, help pick colors, and enjoy exclusives on certain colors. Reebok would become the retailer's "preferred" athletic footwear brand, enjoy prime merchandise locations at the front and back of the store, and be the only athletic footwear brand on the retailer's Web site and in the promotional magazine mailed to 4 million girls.

The result was a major success for both companies. "We're going to make our strongest impact at back-to-school since we started footwear four years ago," predicted Paula Damaso, Limited Too's senior vice president and general merchandise manager. Jan Sharkansky, Reebok's vice president and women's general merchandise manager, said being in Limited Too is like "getting inside these girls' heads, reaching them where they live."

"I don't believe any other large athletic footwear company would have been as flexible with a fashion specialty store," added Damaso. That flexibility is a key competitive advantage for Reebok as it looks at other partnerships with retailers. "We will look at every opportunity if we think there is a fit," says Sharkansky. That ability to work with retailers gives Reebok a solid footing with its retailer customers as well as with end-consumers.

Questions for Discussion

1. What factors make a retailer more than just a simple customer for Reebok and encourage the creation of partnerships?
2. What advantages have Reebok's partnerships with retailers brought the company? What disadvantages do you see?
3. On August 3, 2005, Adidas announced its intention to purchase Reebok. What issues might this merger bring? Do you think Adidas will keep Reebok as a separate brand? Why or why not?

Integrated Marketing Communications: Advertising, Sales Promotions, and Public Relations

Case in Point: DDB

Think of a TV ad—a 30-second mix of glamour, wit, humor, emotion, and brand message. On the surface, a well-done ad seems like a simple act of inspired creativity. But for a client, such as JCPenney, and an ad agency, such as DDB, each ad is something far too important to be done as only an inspired brainstorm. A single 30-second ad costs half a million dollars or more to produce and that doesn't even count the millions that can be spent on TV airtime. In all, Penney spends some $368 million a year on media to drive some $18 billion in retail sales. In creating an ad campaign, a lot of hard work occurs behind the scenes and the agency must prove to clients that it is on target with the ads.

DDB Worldwide, a global communications firm, has successfully mounted advertising campaigns for mega marketers including McDonald's, ExxonMobil, Johnson & Johnson, and Volkswagen. The agency strives to offer a unique approach to targeting and communicating with its clients' consumers. As a result, DDB is one of the most decorated advertising agencies in the world.

The ad process begins with understanding the client. In the case of DDB's client, JCPenney, the retailer needed an image overhaul. But what image should it create? What image would best resonate with the consumers that might want to shop at JCPenney's 1000 department stores? To gain insight into creating this message, DDB didn't just sit in a room and wait for a bolt-out-of-the-blue creative idea to hit.

Rather, the agency sent cultural anthropologists to customers' homes. The anthropologists asked the customers to open their closets and show them their favorite clothes. The anthropologists looked at how the closets were organized and the clothes people had. The purpose of this research was to give DDB insights into the consumer so that they could create campaign that reflected who the new consumers were. The ad agency also studied the media habits of these consumers by reading what target customers read and seeing what shows they watch, the Web sites they visit, and the time they spent with each type of media.

Then, DDB had to present its findings and conclusions to JCPenney executives. To demonstrate to JCPenney that it understood the needs of new consumers, DDB created a slideshow based on the cultural anthropologists' research. The slideshow included photographs of the kinds of clothes that were in closets—and the homes and people to whom these clothes belonged. This gave the client and the agency an understanding of which customers were the kind of women who wore leopard-skin boots, for example.

The research and slideshow provided a dramatic representation of JCPenney's target customer. The customer tended to be a working mother in a middle-income family with middle-American values. These women didn't have a lot of money to spend on clothes, but when they did buy clothes, they wanted the clothes to be an expression of their individuality. Clothes were a way customers could express themselves. So JCPenney morphed itself into a source of self-expression, while retaining middle-American values.

The resulting TV commercials reflected self-expression, and they showed working mothers out on a Saturday shopping while dad stayed home with the kids.

Research and planning are just the beginning of the ad-creation process. Creating an ad involves a partnership between the ad agency and the client—sharing ideas and providing feedback on footage shot for ads under development. "When TV commercials are produced, we're on a tight schedule throughout the review, editing, and approval process," explains JCPenney's chief engineer, Scott Hamil. This collaboration presents a logistical challenge because Penney's headquarters in Texas are a thousand miles from DDB's Chicago office.

Fortunately, new technology lets DDB send video and audio over the Internet to get immediate client approvals. "Besides approvals, we use it to send rough cuts and directors' reels for review of various work styles," said Harold Smith, digital systems manager for DDB. DDB also uses high-speed data connections to connect to specialized post-production houses that work on the ads.

Finally, DDB and JCPenney must consider ad placement—matching the ad's style and demographics to the TV show and to the target demographic of the campaign. Because of the popularity of the Academy Awards with women, JCPenney often launches its spring ad campaign on the award show with its 43 million viewers.

For example, the 2004 Academy Awards included six new television ads, created by DDB Worldwide for JCPenney. These multi-facetted ads—running the gamut from intimate apparel to home furnishing—developed the theme of "For All the Sides of You" and explored the various roles women assume in their everyday lives. Three of the ads highlighted celebrity designers—a nice tie to the chic apparel worn on the red carpet before the Academy Awards.

When they overhauled the brand, JCPenney didn't know if its investment of millions of dollars would pay off, but it did: sales rose 3.5 percent. DDB's success was due to the agency understanding the target consumers and presenting messages that the target audience would value.

Questions for Discussion

1. What other kinds of marketing communications besides TV ads could JCPenney use to reach customers and build relationship with them?

2. Are the roles of the ad agency and the client fixed or flexible?

3. How might the process of creating an ad in other media differ from that used to create a TV ad?

Integrated Marketing Communications:
Personal Selling and Direct Marketing

Case in Point: Motorola

Motorola, like many companies, knows that consumers are bombarded with tons of advertisements and other communications from companies every day. This onslaught of media reaches such a level that we just tune it out. Companies and advertisers know this, too. Other companies' usual answer, however, is to send even more "ad weight" (the term for spending even more advertising dollars) to expose you to even more messages, so that hopefully you'll hear at least some of them.

Motorola, a $31 billion maker of cell phones and other electronics, took a different approach. Although the frequency of advertisements may help to get a message through, Motorola's tactic is to make sure that every communiqué it aims at a customer sends a consistent image about Motorola and its products. That's the idea behind "integrated marketing communications." If you run a TV ad and a radio spot, or a public announcement and a print ad, the essence of their messages must be the same in content and similar in execution so that the consumer starts putting two and two together. "Oh, this print ad in my magazine is advertising Motorola's new flip phone, like those posters I've seen on busses" or "Wow, the TV ad makes the phone look like fun, and there's a lot of information on the Web site about the phone's fun features."

A different form of integrated marketing communications question is, "how do you make your message consistent to customers all over the world?" The answer lies with global branding. Moto, the cute name for Motorola's global branded cell phone, is a name that will be easy to pronounce by anyone in the world, and a name that doesn't mean anything bad or weird anywhere in the world. The name is actually the slang that Taiwanese teenagers use for their cellphones. It's also a name that carries part of the Motorola name, a strong positive brand name that reminds consumers of the company's heritage. The way Motorola's advertising agency, Ogilvy & Mather, talks about it, Motorola wants to express the same core idea about the product or brand, but it wants to do so in a way that makes sense to each local market.

Ogilvy & Mather's Brand Integration Group (BIG) launched the Moto campaign in 2001. Although the main account is run from New York, local O&M offices create adaptations on the "Moto" theme. In the UK, activity includes the sponsorship of ITV1 movies, with creative featuring *My MotoMovies*—short films created by people on their mobile phones. *MotoMovies* highlight how the phones let users take video footage and create their own movies while also being able to download and play video clips, make video calls, and send video messages.

Global research supported the global branding effort. Ethnographic research in China, Europe, and South America helped the ad agency understand younger, fashion-conscious consumers around the world. Research photos of real people using cell phones inspired the campaign's use of stories of phone use and print ads. The print ads introduced a fanciful, futuristic series of Moto-phone using characters such as AlphaMoto, BuddyMoto, CandyMoto, ChattyMoto, HypnoMoto, MeetingMoto, NightMoto, and more.

In creating an integrated message, BIG even included a remake of Motorola's retail packaging and point-of-presence materials. Ethnographic research suggested that the cacophony of brand images in many retail environments leads to consumer confusion. BIG created simple, brightly-colored box packaging with Motorola's distinctive circle-M logo wrapped around the box. Stacking the square boxes creates an eye-catching, poster-like effect. Fay Tellefsen, creative director for Motorola's personal communication division said, "It was amazing. I'd walk past a store and see managers had put our boxes in the window because they just looked so bright, so artistic. The Motorola products stood out and could be immediately identified." Standing out in a crowded world is just what Motorola wants.

Discussion Questions

1. If you were to design an integrated marketing communications plan for the Moto in the United States, using billboards, the Internet, radio, and print, what features and benefits of the cell phone would you play up in each of these media? Why? What needs to be consistent across the media? What could differ?

2. Next, how would you modify your plans to promote the phone in China? In Finland (home of Nokia)? In Brazil (big youth market)?

3. Has Motorola "succeeded"? Do you consider it or its phones to be "cool"?

Marketing in the Digital Age

Case in Point: iWon

Where do you go when you want to search the Web? Do you use Google? Yahoo? What makes you choose that portal as your entrée into the World Wide Web?

The people at iWon think that they've created "portal with a difference." The core of what iWon provides is online information and entertainment. To distinguish itself, iWon offers lotteries—a chance to win as you surf. IWon offers its users a daily chance to win $10,000. It's not a one-time gimmick but an integral part of iWon's brand definition.

In exchange for this chance to win lots of cash, iWon wants your data: your demographics and psychographic profile. This data is sold to advertisers, who can then tailor ads to your particular tastes, or at least selectively post ads on your browser. The data are also sold, once you've given permission to iWon to do so. iWon sells the information to retailers who are going to try their best to entice you to buy their goods or services. In this Web-induced era of permission-based marketing, some people have no problem offering their personal information and attitudes. Others resist, however, because they are concerned about privacy and the potential for misuse of their data.

The ads which iWon sells on its Web site are critical to iWon's business: without ad dollars, iWon couldn't afford to give away $10,000 in prize money every day. More than 250 advertisers support iWon. Every company wants information about you, the consumer, for its customer relationship management databases. Big-name players like Amazon, Capital One, Dell, and Xerox are all involved.

Companies that do business with iWon get value from consumer information. What, in turn, is the value to consumers who use iWon? The chance to win prizes, of course. Daily giveaways are an incentive to attract a large group of loyal, responsive users.

But iWon also figures that it can shape its users' behaviors. If you sign onto iWon.com to check the weather this morning and

you don't win a prize, will you refuse to go back? Not likely. Look at the millions of people who buy lottery tickets every week. You don't expect to win every time. So you might go back to iWon in the evening when you're thinking about going to a movie and want to know the movie times. Did you win? Probably not. Does it deter you from making dinner reservations for the weekend at iWon.com? Nope.

Now they've got you: You've been trained by iWon.com to come to this site, get familiar with it, and keep coming back. After all, some day you might win cash, and now you've got a habit. When you want information, you go to iWon.com out of habit. And iWon loads its site with information and rewards to keep you there and keep you involved.

The company has been very successful with it strategy. Initially, the strategy got the attention of CBS, which pumped $100 million into the company. Thanks in part to the CBS connection, iWon got lots of press conferences, buzz, and media attention. Three years after its founding, iWon had doled out more than $50 million to about 300,000 users. In 2004, the company was bought by another online search engine, AskJeeves. AskJeeves continued to let iWon operate as it had in the past. In March 2005, when AskJeeves itself was acquired, according to ComScore Media Metrix, the iWon portal ranked as the No. 9 most visited Internet site.

Discussion Questions

1. Go to iWon.com. What do you think of the Web site? What about the information aspect? The entertainment aspect? Would you visit this site if there were no lottery?

2. How is this lure, offering a chance to win money, different from a retail store that offers "everyday low prices"? Is a Web site that offers money to attract visitors going to be perceived as the "cheap" site, or are the issues different because visiting every Web site is free?

3. Think about the issues of trust and privacy. What does IWon do to encourage people to trust it enough to give iWon information about themselves?

Global Marketing

Case in Point: NIVEA

Nothing can be more local than your own face and nothing can be more global than NIVEA, a worldwide brand of facial and bodycare products. A billion people in 160 countries have bought more than 11 billion containers of NIVEA creme.

Although NIVEA's cool blue on all its products seems modern, it's really timeless. NIVEA Creme was invented by Paul C. Beiersdorf, a German pharmacist, in 1911. NIVEA creme was the first affordable facial creme for the mass market. Even the packaging is timeless—since 1924, NIVEA has come in its familiar blue container. Since the invention of NIVEA creme, the company has branched out into a wide array of personal care products, such as body lotions, soaps, shampoos, make-up, baby care, men's facial and shaving products, and sunscreen. In 2004, Beiersdorf's sales of NIVEA products amounted to 2.7 billion Euros.

NIVEA's global branding for such a personal product reflects the fact that the differences between people really are only skin deep. Underneath, we all want to look good on the surface. "In the summer, women wear short dresses, shorts, skirts and tank tops, and they want to look good from head to toe," explained Catherine Lair, director of marketing, NIVEA Body, Beiersdorf.

That's why NIVEA standardizes globally on the core values in all its marketing. "NIVEA has been synonymous with skincare around the world and represents core values of human coexistence, such as care, reliability, understanding, humanity, love and harmony," said Ann-Christin Wagenmann, Beiersdorf Managing Director. These values are a part of each campaign in every country. Only one marketing strategy should be used worldwide, NIVEA believes.

Despite NIVEA's worldwide presence, a quick survey reveals that, regardless of where they live, NIVEA's customers believe that the company' products are locally manufactured and marketed. Why? Because NIVEA carefully adjusts the marketing mix to cater to local cultures and preferences. Helping people look their best requires adjustments for different beauty fashions, age groups, and ethnic groups.

For example, in 2002, Beiersdorf launched the NIVEA Body Silky Shimmer lotion to meet the trend for glamorous, jeweled-looking skin, especially in the warmer months. Yet the single-variety product didn't work equally well on all skin types—the shimmering pigments did not show up as well on darker skin as they did on fair skin. "We realized we were ignoring 50 percent of the female population in the U.S.," said Ms. Lair. So in 2004, Beiersdorf repositioned the brand with two varieties: NIVEA Body Silky Shimmer lotion for Light to Medium Skin and NIVEA Body Silky Shimmer lotion for Medium to Dark Skin.

NIVEA's global/local strategy also extends to the Web. All of NIVEA's international Web sites share a common design to ensure "consistent worldwide brand identity, emphasizing its skincare competence and strengthening customer loyalty, especially in younger target groups," says the company. Behind the scenes, a content management system and online style guide gives Beiersdorf global control of marketing-related media.

The result is consistent brand appearance and cost-efficiency. Yet the company customizes its Web sites for some 30 different countries. Language, product emphasis, and the choice of photographic models all help give NIVEA an online image suited to that country.

This localization is much more subtle than just showing ethnically-local models in NIVEA's ads or on the Web. In some countries, such as Japan, sales actually improve when Western models are used. Sometimes, the best localization highlights the foreignness of the product.

A modular site design lets NIVEA tailor the site for the products available in that country. For example, NIVEA doesn't sell NIVEA Baby Care products in its home country of Germany, so all Web elements related to that product are absent from NIVEA.de.

NIVEA also supports the ultimate in localization—one-to-one advice on an array of beauty and body-care topics. "Advice is one of NIVEA's core competencies. That's why we aim to offer the highest possible standard of advice via our international Web sites. The specifically-developed contents targeted at the various audiences of these advice modules fully meet those claims," said Dominik Dommick, who is responsible for eBrandManagement at Beiersdorf.

This combination of globalization and localization works. In a consumer survey of trusted brands in 14 different countries in Europe, NIVEA was named the #1 most trusted brand of skin care in every one of them—from fair-skinned Sweden to darker-complexioned Italy. In a broader survey of 57 countries and a wider variety of brands, NIVEA brands took 183 first-place positions. NIVEA has market-share leadership in dozens of countries. Now, NIVEA is turning its sights toward China. With a fast-growing middle class, NIVEA is enjoying 30 percent growth as newly-minted consumers turn their attention to looking good.

"Outstanding quality products to meet consumer needs at the right time and constant updating of the advertising approach—these are the essential factors in NIVEA's success, keeping the brand young, attractive, sympathetic, and familiar," said Mr. Uwe Wolfer, Board Member of Beiersdorf AG.

Discussion Questions

1. Does NIVEA offer a standardized marketing strategy and mix or an adapted marketing strategy and mix?
2. What makes it easier for some products to be both global and local?
3. How does technology affect NIVEA's ability to be both global and local?

*Marketing and Society: Social Responsibility
and Marketing Ethics*

Case in Point: NFL

When you think of the NFL, you probably think first of the Super Bowl or Monday night football. Since 1920, the league has brought professional football to fans across the country and around the world. You may also know that the league provides more than just athletic entertainment for fans. The NFL strives to have a positive impact on communities across America. In 1974, the league formed a partnership with the United Way, the $4 billion charitable organization. Today, that partnership has grown into a charitable enterprise that generates funds and services for more than 30 million people each year.

Many companies feel the need to do more than just selling products and services. "I think any good corporation in America wants to give back to its customers, and in our case our customers are our fans who attend the games and watch TV," said Joe Browne, executive vice president of communications and government affairs for the NFL. This leads the NFL to do good works on multiple levels.

For example, the NFL donates airtime to the United Way. The high popularity of the NFL on TV—more than 120 million people watch their games on television each week—means great exposure for advertisers. It also means sky-high ad rates. To help the United Way get its message out, the NFL gives free airtime to the charity.

The ultimate NFL game is the Super Bowl. It's the event of the year for TV viewership and the nearly $5 million-per-minute ad rates. This makes the Super Bowl a perfect—and generous—time to run free charity-focused ads that get results. "We ran a commercial during the Super Bowl to promote volunteerism, called 'Join the Team,' at first to build some awareness about it. The very next morning, we had thousands of calls go to NFL teams across the country, saying, 'Okay, I'm ready to join the team, what do you want me to do?'" explained Beth Colleton.

Other charitable activities include a youth football fund, scholarships for students pursuing college degrees in athletic training, and a disaster relief fund which the NFL established after 9/11 to those public servants who were killed. Some of the efforts bring the fans into the act, such as asking them to nominate the NFL teacher of the year. The NFL even tries to make some good come from the fines it levies against wayward players: the proceeds are donated to charity.

The NFL isn't a corporation in a traditional sense. Rather, it's a trade organization—an umbrella group of the 32 independently-owned football teams around the country. Thus, each team has its own community relations initiative. "Both through NFL charities and some of the national programs that come out of New York, as well as through team organizations, team charitable foundations, that almost every one of our clubs has, we give back in some way whether it is to youth and education to youth sports, because again, the fans have supported us and we think its right to support them as well," says Joe Browne.

Even the individual players play a valuable community service role. "The guys realize that they were given a gift by getting to play in the NFL, and they're doing a lot better than a lot of folks, and they believe as part of the commitment of being a player in the NFL, you give back," says Ms. Colleton.

The natural adulation of the fans means that the players are especially good role models for community service and charitable acts. This stature provides tremendous leverage for NFL's charitable activities. "If Payton Manning [of the Indianapolis Colts] can give his money and his time, it's wonderful for the people that it directly serves, but if Payton Manning can give his money and give his time and get 100 other people to do the same, that growth can really be mind-boggling," says Beth Colleton.

All of these efforts resonate with the NFL's core values. "I think the NFL stands for quality, for tradition. I definitely think it stands for integrity, and I think a lot of those things come together to stand for what I guess you'd say is Americana. I think there's nothing that captures the American energy more than the National Football League," says Ms. Colleton.

The benefit to the community and to the United Way is clear, but the NFL benefits from its charitable efforts as well. The multi-level effort helps the NFL connect to fans, bond with the community, and improve its national reputation. Good works beget good will and, for any business that depends on an emotional bond with the customer, good will is good business.

Questions for Discussion

1. Why do you think the NFL partners with the United Way? How does the United Way benefit? How does the NFL benefit?

2. Make a list of criticisms about the NFL in terms of any detrimental impact on society. Does the NFL's partnership with the United Way lessen any of those concerns?

3. Do you think it's important for companies to give back and support their communities? Explain.

Appendix 2 Marketing Plan

The Marketing Plan: An Introduction

As a marketer, you'll need a good marketing plan to provide direction and focus for your brand, product, or company. With a detailed plan, any business will be better prepared to launch a new product or build sales for existing products. Nonprofit organizations also use marketing plans to guide their fundraising and outreach efforts. Even government agencies put together marketing plans for initiatives such as building public awareness of proper nutrition and stimulating area tourism.

THE PURPOSE AND CONTENT OF A MARKETING PLAN

Unlike a business plan, which offers a broad overview of the entire organization's mission, objectives, strategy, and resource allocation, a marketing plan has a more limited scope. It serves to document how the organization's strategic objectives will be achieved through specific marketing strategies and tactics, with the customer as the starting point. It is also linked to the plans of other departments within the organization. Suppose a marketing plan calls for selling 200,000 units annually. The production department must gear up to make that many units, the finance department must have funding available to cover the expenses, the human resources department must be ready to hire and train staff, and so on. Without the appropriate level of organizational support and resources, no marketing plan can succeed.

Although the exact length and layout will vary from company to company, a marketing plan usually contains the sections described in Chapter 2. Smaller businesses may create shorter or less formal marketing plans, whereas corporations frequently require highly structured marketing plans. To guide implementation effectively, every part of the plan must be described in considerable detail. Sometimes a company will post its marketing plan on an internal Web site, which allows managers and employees in different locations to consult specific sections and collaborate on additions or changes.

THE ROLE OF RESEARCH

Marketing plans are not created in a vacuum. To develop successful strategies and action programs, marketers need up-to-date information about the environment, the competition, and the market segments to be served. Often, analysis of internal data is the starting point for assessing the current marketing situation, supplemented by marketing intelligence and research investigating the overall market, the competition, key issues, and threats and opportunities issues. As the plan is put into effect, marketers use a variety of research techniques to measure progress toward objectives and identify areas for improvement if results fall short of projections. Finally, marketing research helps marketers learn more about their customers' requirements, expectations, perceptions, and satisfaction levels. This deeper understanding provides a foundation for building competitive advantage through well-informed segmenting, targeting, and positioning decisions. Thus, the marketing plan should outline what marketing research will be conducted and how the findings will be applied.

THE ROLE OF RELATIONSHIPS

The marketing plan shows how the company will establish and maintain profitable customer relationships. In the process, however, it also shapes a number of internal and external relationships. First, it affects how marketing personnel work with each other and with other departments to deliver value and satisfy customers. Second, it affects how the company works with suppliers, distributors, and strategic alliance partners to achieve the objectives listed in the plan. Third, it influences the company's dealings with other stakeholders, including government regulators, the media, and the community at large. All of these relationships are important to the organization's success, so they should be considered when a marketing plan is being developed.

FROM MARKETING PLAN TO MARKETING ACTION

Companies generally create yearly marketing plans, although some plans cover a longer period. Marketers start planning well in advance of the implementation date to allow time for marketing research, thorough analysis, management review, and coordination between departments. Then, after each action program begins, marketers monitor ongoing results, compare them with projections, analyze any differences, and take corrective steps as needed. Some marketers also prepare contingency plans for implementation if certain conditions emerge. Because of inevitable and sometimes unpredictable environmental changes, marketers must be ready to update and adapt marketing plans at any time.

For effective implementation and control, the marketing plan should define how progress toward objectives will be measured. Managers typically use budgets, schedules, and performance standards for monitoring and evaluating results. With budgets, they can compare planned expenditures with actual expenditures for a given week, month, or other period. Schedules allow management to see when tasks were supposed to be completed—and when they were actually completed. Performance standards track the outcomes of marketing programs to see whether the company is moving forward toward its objectives. Some examples of performance standards are: market share, sales volume, product profitability, and customer satisfaction.

Sample Marketing Plan for Sonic

This section takes you inside the sample marketing plan for Sonic, a hypothetical start-up company. The company's first product is the Sonic 1000, a multimedia personal digital assistant (PDA), also known as a handheld computer. Sonic will be competing with Palm, HP, and other well-established PDA rivals in a crowded, fast-changing marketplace where enhanced cell phones and many other electronics devices have PDA functionality. The annotations explain more about what each section of the plan should contain and why.

EXECUTIVE SUMMARY

Sonic is preparing to launch a new multimedia PDA product, the Sonic 1000, in a maturing market. Despite the dominance of PDA leader Palm, we can compete because our product offers a unique combination of features at a value-added price. We are targeting specific segments in the consumer and business markets, taking advantage of opportunities indicated by higher demand for easy-to-use PDAs with expanded communications, entertainment, and storage functionality.

The primary marketing objective is to achieve first-year U.S. market share of 3 percent with unit sales of 240,000. The primary financial objectives are to achieve first-year sales revenues of $60 million, keep first-year losses to less than $10 million, and break even early in the second year.

CURRENT MARKETING SITUATION

Sonic, founded 18 months ago by two entrepreneurs with experience in the PC market, is about to enter the now mature PDA market. Multifunction cell phones and e-mail devices are increasingly popular today, intensifying competition as PDA demand flattens, industry consolidation continues, and downward pricing pressure squeezes profitability. In the peak year for PDA sales, 6.4 million units were sold in the United States; more recently, yearly PDA sales for the U.S. market totaled about 5 million units. Around the world, fewer than 10 million PDAs were sold last year, compared with 13 million multifunction cell phones. To gain market share in this dynamic environment, Sonic must carefully target specific segments with features that deliver benefits valued by each customer group.

Market Description   Sonic's market consists of consumers and business users who prefer to use a single device for communication, information storage and exchange, and entertainment on the go. Specific segments being targeted during the first year include professionals, corporations, students, entrepreneurs, and medical users. Exhibit 1 shows how the Sonic 1000 addresses the needs of targeted consumer and business segments.

PDA purchasers can choose between models based on several different operating systems, including systems from Palm, Microsoft, and Symbian, plus Linux variations. Sonic licenses a Linux-based system because it is somewhat less vulnerable to attack by hackers and viruses. With hard drives becoming commonplace in the PDA market, Sonic is equipping its first product with an ultra-fast one-gigabyte hard drive for information and entertainment storage. Technology costs are decreasing even as capabilities are increasing, which makes value-priced models more appealing to consumers and to customers with older PDAs who want to trade up to newer, high-end multifunction units.

Product Review   Our first product, the Sonic PDA 1000, offers the following standard features:

- Hands-free operation of all functions
- Digital music/video downloading and playback capabilities
- Global positioning system (GPS) for identifying locations, obtaining directions and maps
- Integrated cell phone with 100-number auto-dial capability
- Wireless Web access, e-mail, instant messaging functionality
- Organization and communication functions, including calendar, address book, memo pad, Internet browser, e-mail program, word processing and spreadsheet software, text and instant messaging programs

---

Executive summary

This section summarizes the main goals, recommendations, and points as an overview for senior managers who must read and approve the marketing plan. Generally a table of contents follows this section, for management convenience.

Current marketing situation

In this section, marketing managers discuss the overall market, identify the market segments they will target, and provide information about the company's current situation.

Market description

By describing the targeted segments in detail, marketers provide context for the marketing strategies and detailed action programs discussed later in the plan.

Benefits and product features

Exhibit 1 clarifies the benefits that product features will deliver to satisfy the needs of customers in each market segment.

Product review

The product review should summarize the main features for all of the company's products. The information may be organized by product line, by type of customer, by market, or (as here) by order of product introduction.

EXHIBIT 1

Segment Needs and Features/Benefits of Sonic PDA

Targeted Segment	Customer Need	Corresponding Feature/Benefit
Professionals (consumer market)	■ Stay in touch conveniently and securely while on the go	■ Built-in cell phone, wireless e-mail/Web access from anywhere; Linux-based operating system less vulnerable to hackers
	■ Perform many functions hands-free without carrying multiple gadgets	■ Voice-activated phone dialing, Web and IM messaging, music/video playback, file exchange; built-in camera and GPS functions add value
Students (consumer market)	■ Perform many functions hands-free without carrying multiple gadgets	■ Built-in cell phone, wireless e-mail/Web access from anywhere; hands-free note-taking; built-in camera and GPS functions add value
	■ Express style and individuality	■ Wardrobe of PDA cases in different colors, patterns, and materials
Corporate users (business market)	■ Security and adaptability for proprietary tasks	■ Customizable to fit diverse corporate tasks and networks; Linux-based operating system less vulnerable to hackers
	■ Obtain driving directions to business meetings	■ Built-in GPS allows voice-activated access to directions and maps
Entrepreneurs (business market)	■ Organize and access contacts, schedule details, and business and financial files	■ No-hands, wireless access to calendar, address book, information files for checking appointments and data, connecting with contacts
	■ Photograph products or business situations to maintain a visual record	■ Built-in camera allows fast and easy photography, stores images for later retrieval
Medical users (business market)	■ Update, access, and exchange medical records	■ No-hands, wireless recording and exchange of information to reduce paperwork and increase productivity
	■ Photograph medical situations to maintain a visual record	■ Built-in camera allows fast and easy photography, stores images for later retrieval

- Large, high-resolution color display
- Virtual keyboard for input without additional accessories
- USB connector for synchronizing data with PC
- One-gigabyte hard drive with expansion potential
- Wardrobe of PDA cases in different colors, patterns, and materials

First-year sales revenues are projected to be $60 million, based on sales of 240,000 Sonic 1000 units at a wholesale price of $250 each. During the second year, we plan to introduce the Sonic 2000 as a higher-end product with the following standard features:

- Translation capabilities to send English text as Spanish text (other languages to be offered as add-on options)
- Integrated five megapixel camera

Competitive Review   Competition from cell phone manufacturers and makers of specialized devices for text and e-mail messaging is an important factor. With non-PDA companies entering the market, current industry participants must continually add features and cut prices or focus on other electronics products. Sony recently stopped offering its Clie PDAs in the United States after suffering a dramatic drop in market share. Currently, key competitors include:

- *Palm* Palm has struggled financially, in part, because of the need to reduce prices for competitive reasons. As the best-known maker of PDAs, Palm has achieved good distribution in nearly every channel and is gaining distribution among U.S. cell phone service carriers. Its $499 LifeDrive, which includes a four-gigabyte hard drive and speedy file-transfer software, has revived interest in PDAs with advanced capabilities.

Competitive review
The purpose of a competitive review is to identify key competitors, describe their market positions, and briefly discuss their strategies.

- *HP* HP is targeting business and professional markets with its iPAQ Pocket PC devices. Many have wireless capabilities, large screen displays, longer battery life for extended use, and slots for removable memory cards. HP enjoys excellent distribution, and its products are priced from below $300 to more than $600.
- *Garmin* Garmin's iQue M5 has built-in GPS capability as well as a range of business-oriented software applications. Priced at $750, its mapping software and verbal commands eliminate the need for an automotive device. Garmin's PDA uses a Windows operating system and has other functions, including a digital voice recorder for brief memos.
- *Dell* Dell's basic Axim X30 PDA model is light, slender, and priced starting at $199. However, this entry-level model lacks wireless functionality as a standard feature, although more advanced X30 models include Wi-Fi and Bluetooth wireless capabilities. New, more powerful models are expected at regular intervals from this low-cost competitor, which markets directly to customers.
- *Research in Motion* Known for its highly popular BlackBerry wireless e-mail devices, Research in Motion now offers models that operate as a cell phone and provide e-mail, instant messaging, and Web browsing functions. The $199.99 price is very competitive, but the input keys are small.

Despite this strong competition, Sonic can carve out a definite image and gain recognition among the targeted segments. Our unique communication/entertainment/location combination with hands-free voice command operation is a critical point of differentiation for competitive advantage. Exhibit 2 shows a selection of competitive PDA products and prices.

Distribution review

In this section, marketers list the most important channels, provide an overview of each channel arrangement, and mention any new developments or trends.

Distribution Review   Sonic-branded products will be distributed through a network of retailers in the top 50 U.S. markets. Among the most important channel partners being contacted are:

- *Office supply superstores* Office Max and Staples will both carry Sonic products in stores, in catalogs, and online.
- *Computer stores* CompUSA will carry Sonic products.
- *Electronics specialty stores* Circuit City and Best Buy will carry Sonic PDAs.

EXHIBIT 2
Selected Competing Products and Pricing

Competitor	Model	Features	Price
Palm	LifeDrive	PDA functions, four-gigabyte hard drive, Wi-Fi and Bluetooth connections, digital music/video functions, memory card slot, Palm OS, no keyboard	$499
Palm	Tungsten E2	PDA functions, wireless capabilities, color screen, Bluetooth connection, Palm OS, stylish design, memory card slot, long battery life	$249
Dell	Axim X30 312 MHz	PDA functions, large color screen, Microsoft OS, very light and slim, no wireless capabilities	$199
Research in Motion	BlackBerry 7100t	PDA and cell phone functions in phone-style design, Web browsing and IM functions, small keys, Bluetooth connection, very light	$199.99
Siemens	SX66	PDA and cell phone functions, slide-out keyboard, Pocket PC system, Wi-Fi and Bluetooth connections, larger than many smart phones	$499.99

- *Online retailers* Amazon.com will carry Sonic PDAs and, for a promotional fee, will give Sonic prominent placement on its home page during the introduction.

Although distribution will initially be restricted to the United States, we plan to expand into Canada and beyond, according to demand. We will emphasize trade sales promotion in the first year.

STRENGTHS, WEAKNESSES, OPPORTUNITIES, AND THREAT ANALYSIS

Sonic has several powerful strengths on which to build, but our major weakness is lack of brand awareness and image. The major opportunity is demand for multimedia PDAs that deliver a number of valued benefits, eliminating the need for customers to carry more than one device. We also face the threat of ever-higher competition from consumer electronics manufacturers, as well as downward pricing pressure. Exhibit 3 summarizes Sonic's main strengths, weaknesses, opportunities, and threats.

Strengths   Sonic can build on three important strengths:

1. *Innovative product* The Sonic 1000 combines a variety of features that would otherwise require customers to carry multiple devices; these include cell phone and wireless e-mail functionality, GPS capability, and digital video/music storage and playback—all with hands-free operation.
2. *Security* Our PDA uses a Linux-based operating system that is less vulnerable to hackers and other security threats that can result in stolen or corrupted data.
3. *Pricing* Our product is priced lower than competing multifunction models—none of which offer the same bundle of features—which gives us an edge with price-conscious customers.

Weaknesses   By waiting to enter the PDA market until considerable consolidation of competitors has occurred, Sonic has learned from the successes and mistakes of others. Nonetheless, we have two main weaknesses:

1. *Lack of brand awareness* Sonic has not yet established a brand or image in the marketplace, whereas Palm and others have strong brand recognition. We will address this area with promotion.
2. *Heavier weight* The Sonic 1000 is slightly heavier than most competing models because it incorporates multiple features and a sizable hard drive. To counteract this weakness, we will emphasize our unique combination of features and our value-added pricing, two compelling competitive strengths.

Strengths
Strengths are internal capabilities that can help the company reach its objectives.

Weaknesses
Weaknesses are internal elements that may interfere with the company's ability to achieve its objectives.

EXHIBIT 3
Sonic's Strengths, Weaknesses, Opportunities, and Threats

Strengths	Weaknesses
■ Innovative combination of functions operated hands-free in one portable device	■ Lack of brand awareness and image
■ Value pricing	■ Heavier than most competing models
■ Security due to Linux-based operating system	

Opportunities	Threats
■ Increased demand for multimedia models with diverse functions and benefits	■ Intense competition
■ Lower technology costs	■ Downward pricing pressure
	■ Compressed product life

Opportunities

Opportunities are external elements that the company may be able to exploit to its advantage.

Opportunities   Sonic can take advantage of two major market opportunities:

1. *Increasing demand for multimedia models with multiple functions* The market for multimedia, multifunction devices is growing much faster than the market for single-use devices. Customers are now accustomed to seeing users with PDAs in work and educational settings, which is boosting primary demand. Also, customers who bought entry-level models are replacing older models with more advanced models.
2. *Lower technology costs* Better technology is now available at a lower cost than ever before. Thus, Sonic can incorporate technically advanced features at a value-added price that allows for reasonable profits.

Threats

Threats are current or emerging external elements that may possibly challenge the company's performance.

Threats   We face three main threats at the introduction of the Sonic 1000:

1. *Increased competition* More companies are entering the U.S. PDA market with models that offer some but not all of the features and benefits provided by Sonic's PDA. Therefore, Sonic's marketing communications must stress our clear differentiation and value-added pricing.
2. *Downward pressure on pricing* Increased competition and market-share strategies are pushing PDA prices down. Still, our objective of seeking a 10 percent profit on second-year sales of the original model is realistic, given the lower margins in the PDA market.
3. *Compressed product life cycle* PDAs have reached the maturity stage of their life cycle more quickly than earlier technology products. We have contingency plans to keep sales growing by adding new features, targeting additional segments, and adjusting prices.

OBJECTIVES AND ISSUES

We have set aggressive but achievable objectives for the first and second years of market entry.

Objectives and issues

The company's objectives should be defined in specific terms so management can measure progress and, if needed, take corrective action to stay on track. This section describes any major issues that might affect the company's marketing strategy and implementation.

First-Year Objectives   During the Sonic 1000's initial year on the market, we are aiming for a 3 percent share of the U.S. PDA market through unit sales volume of 240,000.

Second-Year Objectives   Our second-year objectives are to achieve a 6 percent share based on sales of two models and to achieve break-even early in this period.

Issues   In relation to the product launch, our major issue is the ability to establish a well-regarded brand name linked to a meaningful positioning. We will have to invest heavily in marketing to create a memorable and distinctive brand image projecting innovation, quality, and value. We also must measure awareness and response so we can adjust our marketing efforts as necessary.

MARKETING STRATEGY

Sonic's marketing strategy is based on a positioning of product differentiation. Our primary consumer target is middle- to upper-income professionals who need one portable device to coordinate their busy schedules, communicate with family and colleagues, get driving directions, and be entertained on the go. Our secondary consumer target is high school, college, and graduate students who want a multimedia device. This segment can be described demographically by age (16 to 30) and education status.

Our primary business target is mid- to large-sized corporations that want to help their managers and employees stay in touch and input or access critical data when out of the office. This segment consists of companies with more than $25 million in annual sales and more than 100 employees. A secondary business target is entrepreneurs and small-business owners. We are also targeting medical users who want to reduce paperwork and update or access patients' medical records.

Positioning

A positioning built on meaningful differences, supported by appropriate strategy and implementation, can help the company build competitive advantage.

Positioning   Using product differentiation, we are positioning the Sonic PDA as the most versatile, convenient, value-added model for personal and professional use. The marketing strategy will focus on the hand-free operation of multiple communication, entertainment, and information capabilities differentiating the Sonic 1000.

Product Strategy   The Sonic 1000, including all the features described in the earlier "Product Review" section, will be sold with a one-year warranty. We will introduce a more compact, powerful high-end model (the Sonic 2000) during the following year. Building the Sonic brand is an integral part of our product strategy. The brand and logo (Sonic's distinctive yellow thunderbolt) will be displayed on the product and its packaging, and reinforced by its prominence in the introductory marketing campaign.

Pricing Strategy   The Sonic 1000 will be introduced at $250 wholesale/$350 estimated retail price per unit. We expect to lower the price of this first model when we expand the product line by launching the Sonic 2000, to be priced at $350 wholesale per unit. These prices reflect a strategy of (1) attracting desirable channel partners and (2) taking share from Palm and other established competitors.

Distribution Strategy   Our channel strategy is to use selective distribution, marketing Sonic PDAs through well-known stores and online retailers. During the first year, we will add channel partners until we have coverage in all major U.S. markets and the product is included in the major electronics catalogs and Web sites. We will also investigate distribution through cell-phone outlets maintained by major carriers such as Cingular Wireless. In support of our channel partners, Sonic will provide demonstration products, detailed specification handouts, and full-color photos and displays featuring the product. We will also arrange special trade terms for retailers that place volume orders.

Marketing Communications Strategy   By integrating all messages in all media, we will reinforce the brand name and the main points of product differentiation. Research about media consumption patterns will help our advertising agency choose appropriate media and timing to reach prospects before and during product introduction. Thereafter, advertising will appear on a pulsing basis to maintain brand awareness and communicate various differentiation messages. The agency will also coordinate public relations efforts to build the Sonic brand and support the differentiation message. To attract customer attention and encourage purchasing, we will offer as a limited-time premium a leather carry-case. To attract, retain, and motivate channel partners for a push strategy, we will use trade sales promotions and personal selling. Until the Sonic brand has been established, our communications will encourage purchases through channel partners rather than from our Web site.

Marketing Research   Using research, we are identifying the specific features and benefits that our target market segments value. Feedback from market tests, surveys, and focus groups will help us develop the Sonic 2000. We are also measuring and analyzing customers' attitudes toward competing brands and products. Brand awareness research will help us determine the effectiveness and efficiency of our messages and media. Finally, we will use customer satisfaction studies to gauge market reaction.

Marketing Organization   Sonic's chief marketing officer, Jane Melody, holds overall responsibility for all of the company's marketing activities. Exhibit 4 shows the structure of the eight-person marketing organization. Sonic has hired Worldwide Marketing to handle national sales campaigns, trade and consumer sales promotions, and public relations efforts.

ACTION PROGRAMS

The Sonic 1000 will be introduced in February. Following are summaries of the action programs we will use during the first six months of next year to achieve our stated objectives.

January   We will initiate a $200,000 trade sales promotion campaign to educate dealers and generate excitement for the product launch in February. We will exhibit at the major consumer electronics trade shows, Webcast the product launch, and provide samples to

Marketing mix
These sections summarize the broad logic that will guide decisions made about the marketing tools to be used in the period covered by the plan.

Marketing research
Management should explain in this section how marketing research will be used to support development, implementation, and evaluation of strategies and action programs.

Marketing organization
The marketing department may be organized by function, as in this sample, by geography, by product, or by customer (or some combination).

Action programs
Action programs should be coordinated with the resources and activities of other departments, including production, finance, purchasing, etc.

EXHIBIT 4
Sonic's Marketing Organization

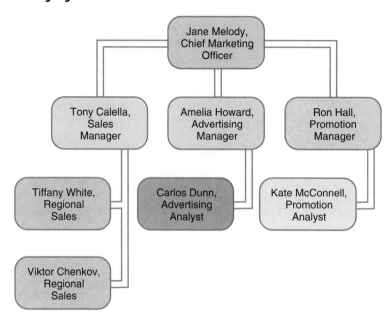

selected product reviewers, opinion leaders, and celebrities as part of our public relations strategy. Our training staff will work with sales personnel at major retail chains to explain the Sonic 1000's features, benefits, and competitive advantages.

February   We will start an integrated print/radio/Internet campaign targeting professionals and consumers. The campaign will show how many functions the Sonic PDA can perform and emphasize the convenience of a single, powerful handheld device. This multimedia campaign will be supported by point-of-sale signage as well as online-only specials.

March   As the multimedia advertising campaign continues, we will add consumer sales promotion tactics such as giving away leather carry-cases as a premium. We will also distribute new point-of-purchase displays to support our retailers.

April   We will hold a trade sales contest offering prizes for the salesperson and retail organization that sells the most Sonic PDAs during the four-week period.

May   We plan to roll out a new national advertising campaign this month. The radio ads will feature celebrity voices telling their Sonic PDAs to perform functions such as initiating a phone call, sending an e-mail, playing a song or video, and so on. The print ads will show these celebrities holding their Sonic PDAs.

June   Our radio campaign will add a new voice-over tag line promoting the Sonic 1000 as a graduation gift. We will also exhibit at the semiannual electronics trade show and provide channel partners with new competitive comparison handouts as a sales aid. In addition, we will tally and analyze the results of customer satisfaction surveys for use in future promotions and to provide feedback for product and marketing activities.

BUDGETS

Budgets
Budgets serve two main purposes: to project profitability and to help managers plan for expenditures, scheduling, and operations related to each action program.

Total first-year sales revenue for the Sonic 1000 is projected at $60 million, with an average wholesale price of $250 per unit and variable cost per unit of $150 for unit sales volume of 240,000. We anticipate a first-year loss of up to $10 million on the Sonic 1000 model. Break-even calculations indicate that the Sonic 1000 will become profitable after the sales volume exceeds 267,500, early in the product's second year. Our break-even analysis of Sonic's first PDA product assumes per-unit wholesale revenue of $250 per unit, variable cost of $150 per unit, and estimated first-year fixed costs of $26,750,000. Based on these assumptions, the break-even calculation is:

$$\frac{\$26,750,000}{\$250 - \$150} = 267,500 \text{ units}$$

CONTROLS

We are planning tight control measures to closely monitor quality and customer service satisfaction. This will enable us to react very quickly in correcting any problems that may occur. Other early warning signals that will be monitored for signs of deviation from the plan include monthly sales (by segment and channel) and monthly expenses. Given the PDA market's volatility, we are developing contingency plans to address fast-moving environmental changes such as new technology and new competition.

Controls

Controls help management assess results after the plan is implemented, identify any problems or performance variations, and initiate corrective action.

Marketing Plan Tools

Prentice Hall offers two valuable resources to assist you in developing a marketing plan:

- *The Marketing Plan Handbook* by Marian Burk Wood explains the process of creating a marketing plan, complete with checklists, real-world examples, and information about useful Web sites.
- *Marketing Plan Pro* software is an award-winning package that includes sample marketing plans, step-by-step guides, help wizards, and customizable charts for documenting a marketing plan.

Sources: Background information and market data adapted from Sascha Segan, "A New Driving Force in PDAs," *PC Magazine,* July 2005, p. 40; Sascha Segan, "Wi-Fi Phone Gets You Connected," *PC Magazine,* June 7, 2005, p. 58; Pui-Wing Tam, "The Hand-Helds Strike Back," *Wall Street Journal,* May 18, 2005, pp. D1, D6; "Writing Handhelds," *BusinessWeek,* June 6, 2005, p. 48; "Our Top PDAs and Phones," *PC Magazine,* June 28, 2005, p. 45; Mike Musgrove, "Sony Pulling Handheld from U.S. Market," *Washington Post,* June 2, 2004, p. E1; and Michael V. Copeland, Om Malik, and Rafe Needleman, "The Next Big Thing," *Business 2.0,* July 2003, pp. 62–69.

Appendix 3 Marketing Math

One aspect of marketing not discussed within the text is marketing math. The calculation of sales, costs, and certain ratios is important for many marketing decisions. This appendix describes three major areas of marketing math: the *operating statement, analytic ratios,* and *markups and markdowns*.

Operating Statement

The operating statement and the balance sheet are the two main financial statements used by companies. The **balance sheet** shows the assets, liabilities, and net worth of a company at a given time. The **operating statement** (also called **profit-and-loss statement** or **income statement**) is the more important of the two for marketing information. It shows company sales, cost of goods sold, and expenses during a specified time period. By comparing the operating statement from one time period to the next, the firm can spot favorable or unfavorable trends and take appropriate action.

Table 1 shows the 2005 operating statement for Dale Parsons Men's Wear, a specialty store in the Midwest. This statement is for a retailer; the operating statement for a manufacturer would be somewhat different. Specifically, the section on purchases within the "cost of goods sold" area would be replaced by "cost of goods manufactured."

Balance sheet
A financial statement that shows assets, liabilities, and net worth of a company at a given time.

Operating statement
A financial statement that shows company sales, cost of goods sold, and expenses during a specified time period.

TABLE 1
Operation Statement: Dale Parsons Men's Wear Year Ending December 31, 2005

Gross Sales			$325,000
Less: Sales returns and allowances			25,000
Net sales			$300,000
Cost of goods sold			
Beginning inventory, January 1, at cost		$ 60,000	
Gross purchases	$165,000		
Less: Purchase discounts	15,000		
Net Purchases	$150,000		
Plus: Freight-in	10,000		
Net cost of delivered purchases		$160,000	
Cost of goods available for sale		$220,000	
Less: Ending inventory, December 31, at cost		45,000	
Cost of goods sold			$175,000
Gross margin			$125,000
Expenses			
Selling expenses			
Sales, salaries, and commissions	$ 40,000		
Advertising	5,000		
Delivery	5,000		
Total selling expenses		$ 50,000	
Administrative expenses			
Office salaries	$ 20,000		
Office supplies	5,000		
Miscellaneous (outside consultant)	5,000		
Total administrative expenses		$ 30,000	
General expenses			
Rent	$ 10,000		
Heat, light, telephone	5,000		
Miscellaneous (insurance, depreciation)	5,000		
Total general expenses		$ 20,000	
Total expenses			$100,000
Net profit			$ 25,000

The outline of the operating statement follows a logical series of steps to arrive at the firm's $25,000 net profit figure:

Net sales	$300,000
Cost of goods sold	−175,000
Gross margin	$125,000
Expenses	−100,000
Net profit	$ 25,000

The first part details the amount that Parsons received for the goods sold during the year. The sales figures consist of three items: *gross sales*, *returns and allowances*, and *net sales*. **Gross sales** is the total amount charged to customers during the year for merchandise purchased in Parsons's store. As expected, some customers returned merchandise because of damage or a change of mind. If the customer gets a full refund or full credit on another purchase, we call this a *return*. Or the customer may decide to keep the item if Parsons will reduce the price. This is called an *allowance*. By subtracting returns and allowances from gross sales, we arrive at net sales—what Parsons earned in revenue from a year of selling merchandise:

Gross sales	$325,000
Returns and allowances	−25,000
Net sales	$300,000

The second major part of the operating statement calculates the amount of sales revenue Dale Parsons retains after paying the costs of the merchandise. We start with the inventory in the store at the beginning of the year. During the year, Parsons bought $165,000 worth of suits, slacks, shirts, ties, jeans, and other goods. Suppliers gave the store discounts totaling $15,000, so that net purchases were $150,000. Because the store is located away from regular shipping routes, Parsons had to pay an additional $10,000 to get the products delivered, giving the firm a net cost of $160,000. Adding the beginning inventory, the cost of goods available for sale amounted to $220,000. The $45,000 ending inventory of clothes in the store on December 31 is then subtracted to come up with the $175,000 **cost of goods sold**. Here again we have followed a logical series of steps to figure out the cost of goods sold:

Amount Parsons started with	
(beginning inventory)	$ 60,000
Net amount purchased	+150,000
Any added costs to obtain these purchases	+10,000
Total cost of goods Parsons had	
available for sale during year	$220,000
Amount Parsons had left over	
(ending inventory)	−45,000
Cost of goods actually sold	$175,000

The difference between what Parsons paid for the merchandise ($175,000) and what he sold it for ($300,000) is called the **gross margin** ($125,000).

In order to show the profit Parsons "cleared" at the end of the year, we must subtract from the gross margin the *expenses* incurred while doing business. *Selling expenses* included two sales employees, local newspaper and radio advertising, and the cost of delivering merchandise to customers after alterations. Selling expenses totaled $50,000 for the year. *Administrative expenses* included the salary for an office manager, office supplies such as stationery and business cards, and miscellaneous expenses including an administrative audit conducted by an outside consultant. Administrative expenses totaled $30,000 in 2004. Finally, the general expenses of rent, utilities, insurance, and depreciation came to $20,000. Total expenses were, therefore, $100,000 for the year. By subtracting expenses ($100,000) from the gross margin ($125,000), we arrive at the net profit of $25,000 for Parsons during 2005.

Analytic Ratios

The operating statement provides the figures needed to compute some crucial ratios. Typically these ratios are called **operating ratios**—the ratio of selected operating state-

Gross sales
The total amount that a company charges during a given period of time for merchandise.

Cost of goods sold
The net cost to the company of goods sold.

Gross margin
The difference between net sales and cost of goods sold.

Operating ratios
The ratios of selected operating statement items to net sales that allow marketers to compare the firm's performance in one year with that in previous years (or with industry standards and competitors in the same year).

ment items to net sales. They let marketers compare the firm's performance in one year to that in previous years (or with industry standards and competitors in the same year). The most commonly used operating ratios are the *gross margin percentage*, the *net profit percentage*, the *operating expense percentage*, and the *returns and allowances percentage*.

Ratio		Formula	Computation from Table 1
Gross margin percentage	=	$\dfrac{\text{gross margin}}{\text{net sales}}$	$= \dfrac{\$125,000}{\$300,000} = 42\%$
Net profit percentage	=	$\dfrac{\text{net profit}}{\text{net sales}}$	$= \dfrac{\$25,000}{\$300,000} = 8\%$
Operating expense percentage	=	$\dfrac{\text{total expenses}}{\text{net sales}}$	$= \dfrac{\$100,000}{\$300,000} = 33\%$
Returns and allowances percentage	=	$\dfrac{\text{returns and allowances}}{\text{net sales}}$	$= \dfrac{\$25,000}{\$300,000} = 8\%$

Another useful ratio is the *stockturn rate* (also called *inventory turnover rate*). The stockturn rate is the number of times an inventory turns over or is sold during a specified time period (often one year). It may be computed on a cost, selling price, or units basis. Thus the formula can be:

$$\text{Stockturn rate} = \frac{\text{cost of goods sold}}{\text{average inventory at cost}}$$

or

$$\text{Stockturn rate} = \frac{\text{selling price of goods sold}}{\text{average selling price of inventory}}$$

or

$$\text{Stockturn rate} = \frac{\text{sales in units}}{\text{average inventory in units}}$$

We will use the first formula to calculate the stockturn rate for Dale Parsons Men's Wear:

$$\frac{\$175,000}{(\$60,000 + \$45,000)/2} = \frac{\$175,000}{\$52,500} = 3.3$$

That is, Parsons's inventory turned over 3.3 times in 2005. Normally, the higher the stockturn rate, the higher the management efficiency and company profitability.

Return on investment (ROI) is frequently used to measure managerial effectiveness. It uses figures from the firm's operating statement and balance sheet. A commonly used formula for computing ROI is:

$$\text{ROI} = \frac{\text{net profit}}{\text{sales}} \times \frac{\text{sales}}{\text{investment}}$$

Return on investment (ROI)
A common measure of managerial effectiveness—the ratio of net profit to investment.

You may have two questions about this formula: Why use a two-step process when ROI could be computed simply as net profit divided by investment? And what exactly is *investment?*

To answer these questions, let's look at how each component of the formula can affect the ROI. Suppose Dale Parsons Men's Wear has a total investment of $150,000. Then ROI can be computed as follows:

$$\text{ROI} = \frac{\$25,000 \text{ (net profit)}}{\$300,000 \text{ (sales)}} \times \frac{\$300,000 \text{ (sales)}}{\$150,000 \text{ (investment)}}$$
$$= 8.3\% \times 2 = 16.6\%$$

Now suppose that Parsons had worked to increase his share of market. He could have had the same ROI if his sales had doubled while dollar profit and investment stayed the same (accepting a lower profit ratio to get higher turnover and market share):

$$\text{ROI} = \frac{\$25,000 \text{ (net profit)}}{\$600,000 \text{ (sales)}} \times \frac{\$600,000 \text{ (sales)}}{\$150,000 \text{ (investment)}}$$

$$= 4.16\% \times 4 = 16.6\%$$

Parsons might have increased his ROI by increasing net profit through more cost cutting and more efficient marketing:

$$\text{ROI} = \frac{\$50,000 \text{ (net profit)}}{\$300,000 \text{ (sales)}} \times \frac{\$300,000 \text{ (sales)}}{\$150,000 \text{ (investment)}}$$

$$= 16.6\% \times 2 = 33.2\%$$

Another way to increase ROI is to find some way to get the same levels of sales and profits while decreasing investment (perhaps by cutting the size of Parsons's average inventory):

$$\text{ROI} = \frac{\$25,000 \text{ (net profit)}}{\$300,000 \text{ (sales)}} \times \frac{\$300,000 \text{ (sales)}}{\$75,000 \text{ (investment)}}$$

$$= 8.3\% \times 4 = 33.2\%$$

What is *investment* in the ROI formula? *Investment* is often defined as the total assets of the firm. But many analysts now use other measures of return to assess performance. These measures include *return on net assets (RONA), return on stockholders' equity (ROE), or return on assets managed (ROAM)*. Because investment is measured at a point in time, we usually compute ROI as the average investment between two time periods (say, January 1 and December 31 of the same year). We can also compute ROI as an "internal rate of return" by using discounted cash flow analysis (see any finance textbook for more on this technique). The objective in using any of these measures is to determine how well the company has been using its resources. As inflation, competitive pressures, and cost of capital increase, such measures become increasingly important indicators of marketing and company performance.

Markups and Markdowns

Markup

The percentage of the cost or price of a product added to the cost in order to arrive at the selling price.

Markdown

A percentage reduction from the original selling price.

Retailers and wholesalers must understand the concepts of **markups** and **markdowns**. They must make a profit to stay in business, and the markup percentage affects profits. Markups and markdowns are expressed as percentages.

There are two different ways to compute markups—on *cost* or on *selling price:*

$$\text{Markup percentage on cost} = \frac{\text{dollar markup}}{\text{cost}}$$

$$\text{Markup percentage on selling price} = \frac{\text{dollar markup}}{\text{selling price}}$$

Dale Parsons must decide which formula to use. If Parsons bought shirts for $15 and wanted to mark them up $10 to a price of $25, his markup percentage on cost would be $10/$15 = 67.7%. If Parsons based markup on selling price, the percentage would be $10/$25 = 40%. In figuring markup percentage, most retailers use the selling price rather than the cost.

Suppose Parsons knew his cost ($12) and desired markup on price (25%) for a man's tie, and wanted to compute the selling price. The formula is:

$$\text{Selling price} = \frac{\text{cost}}{1 - \text{markup}}$$

$$\text{Selling price} = \frac{\$12}{.75} = \$16$$

As a product moves through the channel of distribution, each channel member adds a markup before selling the product to the next member. This "markup chain" is shown for a suit purchased by a Parsons customer for $200:

		$ Amount	% of Selling Price
Manufacturer	Cost	$108	90%
	Markup	12	10
	Selling price	120	100
Wholesaler	Cost	120	80
	Markup	30	20
	Selling price	150	100
Retailer	Cost	150	75
	Markup	50	25
	Selling price	200	100

The retailer whose markup is 25 percent does not necessarily enjoy more profit than a manufacturer whose markup is 10 percent. Profit also depends on how many items with that profit margin can be sold (stockturn rate) and on operating efficiency (expenses).

Sometimes a retailer wants to convert markups based on selling price to markups based on cost, and vice versa. The formulas are:

$$\text{Markup percentage on selling price} = \frac{\text{markup percentage on cost}}{100\% + \text{markup percentage on selling cost}}$$

$$\text{Markup percentage on cost} = \frac{\text{markup percentage on selling price}}{100\% - \text{markup percentage on selling price}}$$

Suppose Parsons found that his competitor was using a markup of 30 percent based on cost and wanted to know what this would be as a percentage of selling price. The calculation would be:

$$\frac{30\%}{100\% + 30\%} = \frac{30\%}{130\%} = 23\%$$

Because Parsons was using a 25 percent markup on the selling price for suits, he felt that his markup was suitable compared with that of the competitor.

Near the end of the summer Parsons still had an inventory of summer slacks in stock. Therefore, he decided to use a *markdown,* a reduction from the original selling price. Before the summer he had purchased 20 pairs at $10 each, and he had since sold 10 pairs at $20 each. He marked down the other pairs to $15 and sold 5 pairs. We compute his *markdown ratio* as follows:

$$\text{Markdown percentage} = \frac{\text{dollar markdown}}{\text{total net sales in dollars}}$$

The dollar markdown is $25 (5 pairs at $5 each) and total net sales are $275 (10 pairs at $20 + 5 pairs at $15). The ratio, then, is $25/$275 = 9%.

Larger retailers usually compute markdown ratios for each department rather than for individual items. The ratios provide a measure of relative marketing performance for each department and can be calculated and compared over time. Markdown ratios can also be used to compare the performance of different buyers and salespeople in a store's various departments.

Key Terms

Balance sheet (MM1)
Cost of goods sold (MM2)
Gross margin (MM2)
Gross sales (MM2)

Markdown (MM4)
Markup (MM4)
Operating ratios (MM2)

Operating statement (or profit-and-loss statement or income statement) (MM1)
Return on investment (ROI) (MM3)

Appendix 4 Careers in Marketing

Now that you have completed this course in marketing, you have a good idea of what the field entails. You may have decided you want to pursue a marketing career because it offers many challenges, stimulating problems, the opportunity to work with people, and excellent advancement opportunities. But you still may not know which part of marketing best suits you—marketing is a very broad field offering a wide variety of career options. This appendix helps you discover what types of marketing jobs best match your special skills and interests, shows you how to conduct the kind of job search that will get you the position you want in the company of your choice, describes marketing career paths open to you, and suggests other information resources.

Marketing Careers Today

The field of marketing is booming in the twenty-first century, with nearly a third of all Americans now employed in marketing-related positions. Marketing salaries may vary by company, position, and region, and salary figures change constantly. In general, entry-level marketing salaries usually are only slightly below those for engineering and chemistry but equal or exceed starting salaries in economics, finance, accounting, general business, and the liberal arts. Moreover, if you succeed in an entry-level marketing position, it's likely that you will be promoted quickly to higher levels of responsibility and salary. In addition, because of the consumer and product knowledge you will gain in these jobs, marketing positions provide excellent training for the highest levels in an organization.

OVERALL MARKETING FACTS AND TRENDS

In conducting your job search, consider the following facts and trends that are changing the world of marketing.

Technology Technology is changing the way marketers work. For example, price coding allows instantaneous retail inventorying. Software for marketing training, forecasting, and other functions is changing the ways we market. And the Internet is creating new jobs and new recruiting rules. Consider the explosive growth in new media marketing. Whereas advertising firms have traditionally recruited "generalists" in account management, "generalist" has now taken on a whole new meaning—advertising account executives must now have both broad and specialized knowledge.

Diversity The number of women and minorities in marketing continues to rise. Traditionally, women were mainly in retailing. However, women and minorities have now moved fully into all industries. They also are rising rapidly into marketing management. For example, women now outnumber men by nearly two to one as advertising account executives. As marketing becomes more global, the need for diversity in marketing positions will continue to increase, opening new opportunities.

Global Companies such as Coca-Cola, McDonald's, IBM, MTV, and P&G have become multinational, with offices and manufacturing operations in hundreds of countries. Indeed, such companies often make more profit from sales outside the United States than from within. And it's not just the big companies that are involved in international marketing. Organizations of all sizes have moved into the global arena. Many new marketing opportunities and careers will be directly linked to the expanding global marketplace. The globalization of business also means that you will need more cultural, language, and people skills in the marketing world of the twenty-first century.

Not-for-profit organizations Increasingly, colleges, arts organizations, libraries, hospitals, and other not-for-profit organizations are recognizing the need for effectively marketing their "products" and services to various publics. This awareness has led to new marketing positions—with these organizations hiring their own marketing directors and marketing vice presidents or using outside marketing specialists.

Looking for a Job in Today's Marketing World

To choose and find the right job, you will need to apply the marketing skills you've learned in this course, especially marketing analysis and planning. Follow these nine steps for marketing yourself: (1) Conduct a self-assessment and seek career counseling; (2) examine job descriptions; (3) develop job search objectives; (4) explore the job market and assess opportunities; (5) develop search strategies; (6) prepare a résumé; (7) write a cover letter and assemble supporting documents; (8) interview for jobs; and (9) follow up.

CONDUCT A SELF-ASSESSMENT AND SEEK CAREER COUNSELING

If you're having difficulty deciding what kind of marketing position is the best fit for you, start out by doing some self-testing or get some career counseling. Self-assessments require that you honestly and thoroughly evaluate your interests, strengths, and weaknesses. What do you do well (your best and favorite skills) and not so well? What are your favorite interests? What are your career goals? What makes you stand out from other job seekers?

The answers to such questions may suggest which marketing careers you should seek or avoid. For help in making an effective self-assessment, look at the following books in your local bookstore: Susan Johnston, *The Career Adventure: Your Guide to Personal Assessment, Career Exploration, and*

Decision Making, 4th ed. (Upper Saddle River, N.J.: Prentice Hall, 2006) and Richard Bolles, *What Color Is Your Parachute?* (Berkeley, Calif.: Ten Speed Press, 2005). Many Web sites also offer self-assessment tools, such as the Keirsey Temperament Theory and the Temperament Sorter, a free but broad assessment available at AdvisorTeam.com. For a more specific evaluation, CareerLeader.com offers a complete online business career self-assessment program designed by the Directors of MBA Career Development at Harvard Business School. You can use this program for a fee.

For help in finding a career counselor to guide you in making a career assessment, Richard Bolles's, *What Color Is Your Parachute?* contains a useful state-by-state sampling. CareerLeader.com also offers personal career counseling. (Some counselors can help you in your actual job search, too.) You can also consult the career counseling, testing, and placement services at your college or university.

EXAMINE JOB DESCRIPTIONS

After you have identified your skills, interests, and desires, you need to see which marketing positions are the best match for them. Two U.S. Department of Labor publications (available in your local library or online)—the *Occupation Outlook Handbook* (www.bls.gov/oco) and the *Dictionary of Occupational Titles* (www.occupationalinfo.org)—describe the duties involved in various occupations, the specific training and education needed, the availability of jobs in each field, possibilities for advancement, and probable earnings.

Your initial career shopping list should be broad and flexible. Look for different ways to achieve your objectives. For example, if you want a career in marketing management, consider the public as well as the private sector, and local and regional as well as national and international firms. Be open initially to exploring many options, then focus on specific industries and jobs, listing your basic goals as a way to guide your choices. Your list might include "a job in a start-up company, near a big city on the West Coast, doing new product planning, with a computer software firm."

EXPLORE THE JOB MARKET AND ASSESS OPPORTUNITIES

At this stage, you need to look at the market and see what positions are actually available. You do not have to do this alone. Any of the following may assist you.

Career Development Centers   Your college's career development center is an excellent place to start. Besides checking with your career development center on specific job openings, check the current edition of the National Association of Colleges and Employers *Job Outlook* (www.jobweb.com). It contains a national forecast of hiring intentions of employers as they relate to new college graduates. More college career development centers are also going online. For example, the Web site of the undergraduate career services of Indiana University's Kelley School of Business, has a list of career links (http://ucso.indiana.edu/cgi-bin/students/careerResources) that can help to focus your job search.

In addition, find out everything you can about the companies that interest you by consulting business magazines, Web sites, annual reports, business reference books, faculty, career counselors, and others. Try to analyze the industry's and the company's future growth and profit potential, advancement opportunities, salary levels, entry positions, travel time, and other factors of significance to you.

Job Fairs   Career development centers often work with corporate recruiters to organize on-campus job fairs. You might also use the Internet to check on upcoming career fairs in your region. For example, visit JobWeb's College Career Fairs page at www.jobweb.com/employ/fairs/public_fairs.asp.

Networking and the Yellow Pages   Networking, or asking for job leads from friends, family, people in your community, and career centers, is one of the best ways to find a marketing job. A recent study estimated that 60.7 percent of jobs are found through networking. The idea is to spread your net wide, contacting anybody and everybody.

The phone book's yellow pages are another effective way to job search. Check out employers in your field of interest in whatever region you want to work, then call and ask if they are hiring for the position of your choice.

Cooperative Education and Internships   According to the National Association of Colleges and Employers 2004 Experimental Education Survey, employers on average give full-time employment offers to about 58 percent of students who have had internships with their companies. They give offers to more than 67 percent of the students that participate in co-ops with their organizations. Many company Internet sites have separate internship areas. For example, check out WetFeet (www.wetfeet.internshipprograms.com), Monster TRAK.com, CampusCareerCenter.com (www.campuscareercenter.com/students/intern.asp), InternJobs.com, and Intern Abroad.com. If you know of a company for which you wish to work, go to that company's corporate Web site, enter the human resources area, and check for internships. If none are listed, try e-mailing the human resources department, asking if internships are offered.

The Internet   A constantly increasing number of sites on the Internet deal with job hunting. You can also use the Internet to make contacts with people who can help you gain information on companies and research companies that interest you. The Riley Guide offers a great introduction to what jobs are available (www.rileyguide.com). Other helpful sites are Employment Opportunities for People with Disabilities (www.dol.gov/odep/joblinks/joblinks.htm) and HireDiversity (www.hirediversity.com), which contains information on opportunities for African Americans, Hispanic Americans, Asian Americans, and Native Americans.

Most companies have their own Web sites upon which they post job listings. This may be helpful if you have a specific and fairly limited number of companies that you are keeping your eye on for job opportunities. But if this is not the case, remember that to find out what interesting marketing jobs the companies themselves are posting, you may have to visit hundreds of corporate sites.

DEVELOP SEARCH STRATEGIES

Once you've decided which companies you are interested in, you need to contact them. One of the best ways is through on-campus interviews. But not every company you are interested in will visit your school. In such instances, you can write (this includes e-mail) or phone the company directly or ask marketing professors or school alumni for contacts.

PREPARE RÉSUMÉS

A résumé is a concise yet comprehensive written summary of your qualifications, including your academic, personal, and professional achievements, that showcases why you are the best candidate for the job. Since an employer will spend an average of 15 to 20 seconds reviewing your résumé, you want to be sure that you prepare a good one.

In preparing your résumé, remember that all information on it must be accurate and complete. Résumés typically begin with the applicant's full name, telephone and fax numbers, and traditional mail and e-mail addresses. A simple and direct statement of career objectives generally appears next, followed by work history and academic data (including awards and internships), and then by personal activities and experiences applicable to the job sought. The résumé sometimes ends with a list of references the employer may contact (at other times, references may be listed separately). If your work or internship experience is limited, nonexistent, or irrelevant, then it is a good idea to emphasize your academic and nonacademic achievements, showing skills related to those required for excellent job performance.

There are three types of résumés. Reverse *chronological* résumés, which emphasize career growth, are organized in reverse chronological order, starting with your most recent job. They focus on job titles within organizations, describing the responsibilities required for each job. *Functional* résumés focus less on job titles and work history and more on assets and achievements. This format works best if your job history is scanty or discontinuous. *Mixed,* or *combination,* résumés take from each of the other two formats. First, the skills used for a specific job are listed, then the job title is stated. This format works best for applicants whose past jobs are in other fields or seemingly unrelated to the position.

Your local bookstore or library has many books that can assist you in developing your résumé. Popular guides are Brenda Greene, *Get the Interview Every Time: FORTUNE 500 Hiring Professionals' Tips for Writing Winning Résumés and Cover Letters* (Chicago: Dearborn Trade, 2004) and Arthur Rosenberg and David Hizer, *The Résumé Handbook* (Cincinnati: Adams Media Corporation, 2003). Computer software programs, such as *RésuméMaker Career Edition,* provide hundreds of sample résumés and ready-to-use phrases while guiding you through the résumé preparation process. America's

Career InfoNet (www.acinet.org/acinet/resume/resume_intro.asp) offers a step-by-step résumé tutorial, and Monster (www.resume.monster.com) offers résumé advice and writing services.

ELECTRONIC RÉSUMÉS

Use of the Internet as a tool in the job search process is increasing, so it's a good idea to have your résumé ready for the online environment. You can forward an electronic résumé to networking contacts or recruiting professionals through e-mail. You can also post it in online databases with the hope that employers and recruiters will find it.

Successful electronic résumés require a different strategy than paper résumés. For instance, when companies search résumé banks, they search for key words and industry buzz words that describe a skill or core work required for each job, so nouns are much more important than verbs. Two good resources for preparing electronic résumés are Susan Ireland's Electronic Resume Guide (http://susanireland.com/eresumeguide) and The Riley Guide (www.rileyguide.com/eresume.html).

After you have written your electronic résumé, you need to post it. The following sites may be good locations to start: Monster.com (www.monster.com) and Yahoo! Hotjobs (www.hotjobs.yahoo.com). However, be careful when posting your résumé on various sites. In this era of identity theft, you need to select sites with care so as to protect your privacy. Limit access to your personal contact information and don't use sites that offer to "blast" your résumé into cyberspace.

Résumé Tips

- Communicate your worth to potential employers in a concrete manner, citing examples whenever possible.
- Be concise and direct.
- Use active verbs to show you are a doer.
- Do not skimp on quality or use gimmicks. Spare no expense in presenting a professional résumé.
- Have someone critique your work. A single typo can eliminate you from being considered.
- Customize your résumé for specific employers. Emphasize your strengths as they pertain to your targeted job.
- Keep your résumé compact, usually one page.
- Format the text to be attractive, professional, and readable. Times New Roman is often the font of choice. Avoid too much "design" or gimmicky flourishes.

WRITE COVER LETTER, FOLLOW UP, AND ASSEMBLE SUPPORTING DOCUMENTS

Cover Letter   You should include a cover letter informing the employer that a résumé is enclosed. But a cover letter does more than this. It also serves to summarize in one or two paragraphs the contents of the résumé and explains why you think you are the right person for the position. The goal is to persuade the employer to look at the more detailed résumé. A typical cover letter is organized as follows: (1) the name and position of the person you are contacting; (2) a statement identifying the position you are applying for, how you heard of the vacancy, and the reasons for your interest; (3) a summary of your qualifications for the job; (4) a description of what follow-ups you intend to make, such as phoning in two weeks to see if the résumé has been received; and (5) an expression of gratitude for the opportunity of being a candidate for the job. America's Career InfoNet (www.acinet.org/acinet/resume/resume_intro. asp) offers a step-by-step tutorial on how to create a cover letter, and Susan Ireland's Web site contains more than 50 cover letter samples (http://susanireland.com/coverletterindex.htm).

Follow Up   So once you send your cover letter and résumé to perspective employers via the method they prefer—e-mail, their Web site, fax, or regular mail—it's often a good idea to follow up. In today's market, job seekers can't afford to wait for interviews to find them. A quality résumé and an attractive cover letter are crucial, but a proper follow-up may be the key to landing an interview. However, before you engage your potential employer, be sure to research the company. Knowing about the company and understanding its place in the industry will help you shine. When you place a call, send an e-mail, or mail a letter to a company contact, be sure to restate your interest in the position, check on the status of your résumé, and ask the employer about any questions they may have.

Letters of Recommendation   Letters of recommendation are written references by professors, former and current employers, and others that testify to your character, skills, and abilities. Some companies may request letters of recommendation, to be submitted either with the résumé or at the interview. Even if letters of recommendation aren't requested, it's a good idea to bring them with you to the interview. A good reference letter tells why you would be an excellent candidate for the position. In choosing someone to write a letter of recommendation, be confident that the person will give you a good reference. In addition, do not assume the person knows everything about you or the position you are seeking. Rather, provide the person with your résumé and other relevant data. As a courtesy, allow the reference writer at least a month to complete the letter and enclose a stamped, addressed envelope with your materials.

In the packet containing your résumé, cover letter, and letters of recommendation, you may also want to attach other relevant documents that support your candidacy, such as academic transcripts, graphics, portfolios, and writing samples.

INTERVIEW FOR JOBS

As the old saying goes, "The résumé gets you the interview; the interview gets you the job." The job interview offers you an opportunity to gather more information about the organization, while at the same time allowing the organization to gather more information about you. You'll want to present your best self. The interview process consists of three parts: before the interview, the interview itself, and after the interview. If you successfully pass through these stages, you will be called back for the follow-up interview.

Before the Interview   In preparing for your interview, do the following:

1. Understand that interviewers have diverse styles, including the "chitchat," let's-get-to-know-each-other style; the interrogation style of question after question; and the tough-probing "why, why, why" style, among others. So be ready for anything.
2. With a friend, practice being interviewed and then ask for a critique. Or, videotape yourself in a practice interview so that you can critique your own performance. Your college placement service may also offer "mock" interviews to help you.
3. Prepare at least five good questions whose answers are not easily found in the company literature, such as "What is the future direction of the firm?" "How does the firm differentiate itself from competitors?" "Do you have a new-media division?"
4. Anticipate possible interview questions, such as "Why do you want to work for this company?" or "Why should we hire you?" Prepare solid answers before the interview. Have a clear idea of why you are interested in joining the company and the industry to which it belongs. (See Susan Ireland's site for additional interview questions (http://susanireland. com/interviewwork.html.)
5. Avoid back-to-back interviews—they can be exhausting and it is unpredictable how long they will last.
6. Prepare relevant documents that support your candidacy, such as academic transcripts, letters of recommendation, graphics, portfolios, and writing samples. Bring multiple copies with you to the interview.
7. Dress conservatively and professionally. Be neat and clean.
8. Arrive 10 minutes early to collect your thoughts and review the major points you intend to cover. Check your name on the interview schedule, noting the name of the interviewer and the room number. Be courteous and polite to office staff.
9. Approach the interview enthusiastically. Let your personality shine through.

During the Interview   During the interview, do the following:

1. Shake hands firmly in greeting the interviewer. Introduce yourself, using the same form of address the interviewer uses. Focus on creating a good initial impression.
2. Keep your poise. Relax, smile when appropriate, be upbeat throughout.
3. Maintain eye contact, good posture, and speak distinctly. Don't clasp your hands or fiddle with jewelry, hair, or clothing. Sit comfortably in your chair. Do not smoke, even if asked.
4. Along with the copies of relevant documents that support your candidacy, carry extra copies of your résumé with you.
5. Have your story down pat. Present your selling points. Answer questions directly. Avoid one-word or too-wordy answers.
6. Let the interviewer take the initiative but don't be passive. Find an opportunity to direct the conversation to things about yourself that you want the interviewer to hear.

7. To end on a high note, make your most important point or ask your most pertinent question during the last part of the interview.
8. Don't hesitate to "close." You might say, "I'm very interested in the position, and I have enjoyed this interview."
9. Obtain the interviewer's business card or address and phone number so that you can follow up later.

A tip for acing the interview: Before you open your mouth, find out *what it's like* to be a brand manager, sales representative, market researcher, advertising account executive, or other position for which you're interviewing.

After the Interview   After the interview, do the following:

1. After leaving the interview, record the key points that arose. Be sure to note who is to follow up and when a decision can be expected.
2. Analyze the interview objectively, including the questions asked, the answers to them, your overall interview presentation, and the interviewer's responses to specific points.
3. Immediately send a thank-you letter, mentioning any additional items and your willingness to supply further information.
4. If you do not hear within the specified time, write or call the interviewer to determine your status.

FOLLOW-UP INTERVIEW

If your first interview takes place off-site, such as at your college or at a job fair, and if you are successful with that initial interview, you will be invited to visit the organization. The in-company interview will probably run from several hours to an entire day. The organization will examine your interest, maturity, enthusiasm, assertiveness, logic, and company and functional knowledge. You should ask questions about issues of importance to you. Find out about the working environment, job role, responsibilities, opportunity for advancement, current industrial issues, and the company's personality. The company wants to discover if you are the right person for the job, whereas you want to find out if it is the right job for you. The key is to determine if the right fit exists between you and the company.

Marketing Jobs

This section describes some of the key marketing positions.

ADVERTISING

Advertising is one of today's hottest fields in marketing. In fact, *Money* magazine lists a position in advertising as among the 50 best jobs in America.

Job Descriptions   Key advertising positions include copywriter, art director, production manager, account executive, and media planner/buyer.

- *Copywriters* write advertising copy and help find the concepts behind the written words and visual images of advertisements.

- *Art directors,* the other part of the creative team, help translate the copywriters' ideas into dramatic visuals called "layouts." Agency artists develop print layouts, package designs, television layouts (called "storyboards"), corporate logotypes, trademarks, and symbols.
- *Production managers* are responsible for physically creating ads, in-house or by contracting through outside production houses.
- *Account development executives* research and understand clients' markets and customers and help develop marketing and advertising strategies to impact them.
- *Account executives* serve as liaisons between clients and agencies. They coordinate the planning, creation, production, and implementation of an advertising campaign for the account.
- *Media planners (or buyers)* determine the best mix of television, radio, newspaper, magazine, and other media for the advertising campaign.

Skills Needed, Career Paths, and Typical Salaries

Work in advertising requires strong people skills in order to interact closely with an often difficult and demanding client base. In addition, advertising attracts people with high skills in planning, problem solving, creativity, communication, initiative, leadership, and presentation. Advertising involves working under high levels of stress and pressure created by unrelenting deadlines. Advertisers frequently have to work long hours to meet deadlines for a presentation. But work achievements are very apparent, with the results of creative strategies observed by thousands or even millions of people.

Because they are so sought after, positions in advertising sometimes require an MBA. But there are many jobs open for business, graphics arts, and liberal arts undergraduates. Advertising positions often serve as gateways to higher-level management. Moreover, with large advertising agencies opening offices all over the world, there is the possibility of eventually working on global campaigns.

Starting advertising salaries are relatively low compared to some other marketing jobs because of strong competition for entry-level advertising jobs. You may even want to consider working for free to break in. Compensation will increase quickly as you move into account executive or other management positions. For more facts and figures, see the Web pages of *Advertising Age,* a key ad industry publication (www.adage.com, click on the Job Bank button), and the American Association of Advertising Agencies (www.aaaa.org).

BRAND AND PRODUCT MANAGEMENT

Brand and product managers plan, direct, and control business and marketing efforts for their products. They are involved with research and development, packaging, manufacturing, sales and distribution, advertising, promotion, market research, and business analysis and forecasting.

Job Descriptions   A company's brand management team consists of people in several positions.

- *Brand managers* guide the development of marketing strategies for a specific brand.
- *Assistant brand managers* are responsible for certain strategic components of the brand.
- *Product managers* oversee several brands within a product line or product group.
- *Product category managers* direct multiple product lines in the product category.
- *Market analysts* research the market and provide important strategic information to the project managers.
- *Project directors* are responsible for collecting market information on a marketing or product project.
- *Research directors* oversee the planning, gathering, and analyzing of all organizational research.

Skills Needed, Career Paths, and Typical Salaries

Brand and product management requires high problem-solving, analytical, presentation, communication, and leadership skills, as well as the ability to work well in a team. Product management requires long hours and involves the high pressure of running large projects. In consumer goods companies, the newcomer—who usually needs an MBA—joins a brand team as an assistant and learns the ropes by doing numerical analyses and watching senior brand people. This person eventually heads the team and later moves on to manage a larger brand, then several brands. Many industrial goods companies also have product managers. Product management is one of the best training grounds for future corporate officers. Product management also offers good opportunities to move into international marketing. Product managers command relatively high salaries. Because this job category encourages or requires a master's degree, starting pay tends to be higher than in other marketing categories such as advertising or retailing.

SALES, SALES MANAGEMENT

Sales and sales management opportunities exist in a wide range of profit and nonprofit organizations and in product and service organizations, including financial, insurance, consulting, and government organizations.

Job Descriptions

Key jobs include consumer sales, industrial sales, national account manager, service support, sales trainers, sales management, and teleseller.

- *Consumer* sales involves selling consumer products and services through retailers.
- *Industrial sales* includes selling products and services to other businesses.
- *National account managers (NAM)* oversee a few very large accounts.
- *Service support* personnel support salespeople during and after the sale of a product.
- *Sales trainers* train new hires and provide refresher training for all sales personnel.
- *Sales management* includes a sequence of positions ranging from district manager to vice president of sales.

- The *teleseller* (not to be confused with the home consumer telemarketer) offers service and support to field salespeople.

Salespeople enjoy active professional lives, working outside the office and interacting with others. They manage their own time and activities. Competition for top jobs can be intense. Every sales job is different, but some positions involve extensive travel, long workdays, and working under pressure, which can negatively impact personal life. You can also expect to be transferred more than once between company headquarters and regional offices.

Skills Needed, Career Paths, and Typical Salaries

Selling is a people profession in which you will work with people every day, all day long. Besides people skills, sales professionals need sales and communication skills. Most sales positions also require high problem-solving, analytical, presentation, and leadership ability as well as creativity and initiative. Teamwork skills are increasingly important.

Career paths lead from salesperson to district, regional, and higher levels of sales management and, in many cases, to the top management of the firm. Today, most entry-level sales management positions require a college degree. Increasingly, people seeking selling jobs are acquiring sales experience in an internship capacity or from a part-time job before graduating. Although there is a high turnover rate (one in four people leave their jobs in a year), sales positions are great springboards to leadership positions, with more CEOs starting in sales than in any other entry-level position. Possibly this explains why competition for top sales jobs is intense.

Starting base salaries in sales may be moderate, but compensation is often supplemented by significant commission, bonus, or other incentive plans. In addition, many sales jobs include a company car or car allowance. Successful salespeople are among most companies' highest paid employees.

OTHER MARKETING JOBS

Retailing Retailing provides an early opportunity to assume marketing responsibilities. Key jobs include store manager, regional manager, buyer, department manager, and salesperson.

Store managers direct the management and operation of an individual store. *Regional managers* manage groups of stores across several states and report performance to headquarters. *Buyers* select and buy the merchandise that the store carries. The *department manager* acts as store manager of a department, such as clothing, but on the department level. The *salesperson* sells merchandise to retail customers. Retailing can involve relocation, but generally there is little travel, unless you are a buyer. Retailing requires high people and sales skills because retailers are constantly in contact with customers. Enthusiasm, willingness, and communication skills are very helpful for retailers, too.

Retailers work long hours, but their daily activities are often more structured than some types of marketing positions. Starting salaries in retailing tend to be low, but pay increases as you move into management or some retailing specialty job.

Marketing Research Marketing researchers interact with managers to define problems and identify the information needed to resolve them. They design research projects, prepare questionnaires and samples, analyze data, prepare reports, and present their findings and recommendations to management. They must understand statistics, consumer behavior, psychology, and sociology. A master's degree helps. Career opportunities exist with manufacturers, retailers, some wholesalers, trade and industry associations, marketing research firms, advertising agencies, and governmental and private nonprofit agencies.

New-Product Planning People interested in new-product planning can find opportunities in many types of organizations. They usually need a good background in marketing, marketing research, and sales forecasting; they need organizational skills to motivate and coordinate others; and they may need a technical background. Usually, these people work first in other marketing positions before joining the new-product department.

Marketing Logistics (Physical Distribution) Marketing logistics, or physical distribution, is a large and dynamic field, with many career opportunities. Major transportation carriers, manufacturers, wholesalers, and retailers all employ logistics specialists. Increasingly, marketing teams include logistics specialists, and marketing managers' career paths include marketing logistics assignments. Coursework in quantitative methods, finance, accounting, and marketing will provide you with the necessary skills for entering the field.

Public Relations Most organizations have a public relations staff to anticipate problems with various publics, handle complaints, deal with media, and build the corporate image. People interested in public relations should be able to speak and write clearly and persuasively, and they should have a background in journalism, communications, or the liberal arts. The challenges in this job are highly varied and very people oriented.

Nonprofit Services The key jobs in nonprofits include marketing director, director of development, event coordinator, publication specialist, and intern-volunteers. The *marketing director* is in charge of all marketing activities for the organization. The *director of development* organizes, manages, and directs the fund-raising campaigns that keep a nonprofit in existence. An *event coordinator* directs all aspects of fund-raising events, from initial planning through implementation. The *publication specialist* oversees publications designed to promote awareness of the organization. Although typically an unpaid position, the *intern-volunteer* performs various marketing functions, and this work can be an important step to gaining a full-time position. The nonprofit sector is typically not for someone who is money driven. Rather, most nonprofits look for people with a strong sense of community spirit and the desire to help others. So starting pay is usually lower than in other marketing fields. However, the bigger the nonprofit, the better your chance of rapidly increasing your income when moving into upper management.

Other Resources

Professional marketing associations and organizations are another source of information about careers. Marketers belong to many such societies. You may want to contact some of the following in your job search:

American Advertising Federation, 1101 Vermont Avenue, NW, Suite 500, Washington, DC 20005. (202) 898-0089 (www.aaf.org)

American Marketing Association, 311 South Wacker Drive, Suite 5800, Chicago, IL 60606. (800) AMA-1150 (www.ama.org)

Market Research Association, 2189 Silas Deane Highway, Suite 5, Rocky Hill, CT 06067. (860) 257-4008 (www.mra-net. org)

National Association of Sales Professionals, 11000 North 130th Place, Scottsdale, AZ 85259. (480) 951-4311 (www.nasp.com)

National Management Association, 2210 Arbor Boulevard, Dayton, OH 45439. (937) 294-0421 (www.nma1.org)

National Retail Federation, 325 Seventh Street NW, Suite 1100, Washington, DC 20004. (800) NRF-HOW2 (www.nrf.com)

Product Development and Management Association, 15000 Commerce Parkway, Suite C, Mount Laurel, NJ 08054 (800) 232-5241 (www.pdma.org)

Public Relations Society of America, 33 Maiden Lane, Eleventh Floor, New York, NY 10038. (212) 460-1400 (www.prsa.org)

Sales and Marketing Executives International, PO Box 1390, Sumas, WA 98295-1390. (312) 893-0751 (www.smei.org)

The Association of Women in Communications, 780 Ritchie Highway, Suite 28-S, Severna Park, MD 21146. (410) 544-7442 (www.womcom.org)

Women Executives in Public Relations, FDR Station, PO Box 7657, New York, NY 10150-7657. (212) 859-7375 (www.wepr.org)

Glossary

Adapted marketing mix   An international marketing strategy for adjusting the marketing-mix elements to each international target market, bearing more costs but hoping for a larger market share and return.

Administered VMS   A vertical marketing system that coordinates successive stages of production and distribution, not through common ownership or contractual ties, but through the size and power of one of the parties.

Adoption process   The mental process through which an individual passes from first hearing about an innovation to final adoption.

Advertising   Any paid form of nonpersonal presentation and promotion of ideas, goods, or services by an identified sponsor.

Advertising agency   A marketing-services firm that assists companies in planning, preparing, implementing, and evaluating all or portions of their advertising programs.

Advertising objective   A specific communication task to be accomplished with a specific target audience during a specific period of time.

Affordable method   Setting the promotion budget at the level management thinks the company can afford.

Age and life-cycle segmentation   Dividing a market into different age and life-cycle groups.

Agent   A wholesaler who represents buyers or sellers on a relatively permanent basis, performs only a few functions, and does not take title to goods.

Allowance   Promotional money paid by manufacturers to retailers in return for an agreement to feature the manufacturer's products in some way.

Approach   The step in the selling process in which the salesperson meets the customer for the first time.

B2B (business-to-business) e-commerce   Using B2B trading networks, auction sites, spot exchanges, online product catalogs, barter sites, and other online resources to reach new customers, serve current customers more effectively, and obtain buying efficiencies and better prices.

B2C (business-to-consumer) e-commerce   The online selling of goods and services to final consumers.

Baby boomers   The 78 million people born during the baby boom following World War II and lasting until the early 1960s.

Behavioral segmentation   Dividing a market into groups based on consumer knowledge, attitude, use, or response to a product.

Benefit segmentation   Dividing the market into groups according to the different benefits that consumers seek from the product.

Brand   A name, term, sign, symbol, or design, or a combination of these, intended to identify the goods or services of one seller or group of sellers and to differentiate them from those of competitors.

Brand equity   The positive differential effect that knowing the brand name has on customer response to the product or service.

Brand extension   Using a successful brand name to launch a new or modified product in a new category.

Break-even pricing (target profit pricing)   Setting price to break even on the costs of making and marketing a product; or setting price to make a target profit.

Broker   A wholesaler that does not take title to goods and whose function is to bring buyers and sellers together and assist in negotiation.

Business analysis   A review of the sales, costs, and profit projections for a new product to find out whether these factors satisfy the company's objectives.

Business buyer behavior   The buying behavior of the organizations that buy goods and services for use in the production of other products and services or for the purpose of reselling or renting them to others at a profit.

Business portfolio   The collection of businesses and products that make up the company.

Buying center   All the individuals and units that participate in the business buying decision process.

By-product pricing   Setting a price for by-products in order to make the main product's price more competitive.

C2B (consumer-to-business) e-commerce   Online exchanges in which consumers search out sellers, learn about their offers, and initiate purchases, sometimes even driving transaction terms.

C2C (consumer-to-consumer) e-commerce   Online exchanges of goods and information between final consumers.

Captive-product pricing   Setting a price for products that must be used along with a main product, such as blades for a razor and film for a camera.

Catalog marketing   Direct marketing through print, video, or electronic catalogs that are mailed to select customers, made available in stores, or presented online.

Category killer   Giant specialty store that carries a very deep assortment of a particular line and is staffed by knowledgeable employees.

Causal research   Marketing research to test hypotheses about cause-and-effect relationships.

Chain stores   Two or more outlets that are owned and controlled in common, have central buying and merchandising, and sell similar lines of merchandise.

Channel conflict   Disagreement among marketing channel members on goals and roles—who should do what and for what rewards.

Channel level   A layer of intermediaries that performs some work in bringing the product and its ownership closer to the final buyer.

Click-and-mortar companies   Traditional brick-and-mortar companies that have added e-marketing to their operations.

Click-only companies   The so-called dot-coms, which operate only online without any brick-and-mortar market presence.

Closing   The step in the selling process in which the salesperson asks the customer for an order.

Cobranding   The practice of using the established brand names of two different companies on the same product.

Cognitive dissonance   Buyer discomfort caused by postpurchase conflict.

Commercialization   Introducing a new product into the market.

Communication adaptation   A global communication strategy of fully adapting advertising messages to local markets.

Competitive advantage   An advantage over competitors gained by offering consumers greater value, either through lower prices or by providing more benefits that justify higher prices.

Competitive-parity method Setting the promotion budget to match competitors' outlays.

Concentrated (niche) marketing A market-coverage strategy in which a firm goes after a large share of one or a few segments or niches.

Concept testing Testing new-product concepts with a group of target consumers to find out if the concepts have strong consumer appeal.

Consumer buyer behavior The buying behavior of final consumers—individuals and households who buy goods and services for personal consumption.

Consumer market All the individuals and households who buy or acquire goods and services for personal consumption.

Consumer product Product bought by final consumer for personal consumption.

Consumerism An organized movement of citizens and government agencies to improve the rights and power of buyers in relation to sellers.

Consumer-oriented marketing The philosophy of enlightened marketing that holds that the company should view and organize its marketing activities from the consumer's point of view.

Contract manufacturing A joint venture in which a company contracts with manufacturers in a foreign market to produce its product or provide its service.

Contractual VMS A vertical marketing system in which independent firms at different levels of production and distribution join together through contracts to obtain more economies or sales impact than they could achieve alone.

Convenience product Consumer product that the customer usually buys frequently, immediately, and with a minimum of comparison and buying effort.

Convenience store A small store located near a residential area that is open long hours seven days a week and carries a limited line of high-turnover convenience goods.

Conventional distribution channel A channel consisting of one or more independent producers, wholesalers, and retailers, each a separate business seeking to maximize its own profits even at the expense of profits for the system as a whole.

Corporate VMS A vertical marketing system that combines successive stages of production and distribution under single ownership—channel leadership is established through common ownership.

Corporate Web site A Web site designed to build customer goodwill and to supplement other sales channels, rather than to sell the company's products directly.

Cost-plus pricing Adding a standard markup to the cost of the product.

Countertrade International trade involving the direct or indirect exchange of goods for other goods instead of cash.

Cultural environment Institutions and other forces that affect society's basic values, perceptions, preferences, and behaviors.

Culture The set of basic values, perceptions, wants, and behaviors learned by a member of society from family and other important institutions.

Customer database An organized collection of comprehensive data about individual customers or prospects, including geographic, demographic, psychographic, and behavioral data.

Customer equity The total combined customer lifetime values of all of the company's customers.

Customer lifetime value The value of the entire stream of purchases that the customer would make over a lifetime of patronage.

Customer perceived value The customer's evaluation of the difference between all the benefits and all the costs of a marketing offer relative to those of competing offers.

Customer relationship management (CRM) Managing detailed information about individual customers and carefully managing customer "touch points" in order to maximize customer loyalty.

Customer relationship management The overall process of building and maintaining profitable customer relationships by delivering superior customer value and satisfaction.

Customer sales force structure A sales force organization under which salespeople specialize in selling only to certain customers or industries.

Customer satisfaction The extent to which a product's perceived performance matches a buyer's expectations.

Customer value marketing A principle of enlightened marketing that holds that a company should put most of its resources into customer value-building marketing investments.

Decline stage The product life-cycle stage in which a product's sales decline.

Deficient products Products that have neither immediate appeal nor long-run benefits.

Demand curve A curve that shows the number of units the market will buy in a given time period, at different prices that might be charged.

Demands Human wants that are backed by buying power.

Demographic segmentation Dividing the market into groups based on demographic variables such as age, sex, family size, family life cycle, income, occupation, education, religion, race, and nationality.

Demography The study of human populations in terms of size, density, location, age, gender, race, occupation, and other statistics.

Department store A retail organization that carries a wide variety of product lines—typically clothing, home furnishings, and household goods; each line is operated as a separate department managed by specialist buyers or merchandisers.

Derived demand Business demand that ultimately comes from (derives from) the demand for consumer goods.

Descriptive research Marketing research to better describe marketing problems, situations, or markets, such as the market potential for a product or the demographics and attitudes of consumers.

Desirable products Products that give both high immediate satisfaction and high long-run benefits.

Differentiated (segmented) marketing A market-coverage strategy in which a firm decides to target several market segments and designs separate offers for each.

Direct investment Entering a foreign market by developing foreign-based assembly or manufacturing facilities.

Direct marketing Direct connections with carefully targeted individual consumers to both obtain an immediate response and cultivate lasting customer relationships—the use of telephone, mail, fax, e-mail, the Internet, and other tools to communicate directly with specific consumers.

Direct marketing channel A marketing channel that has no intermediary levels.

Direct-mail marketing Direct marketing by sending an offer, announcement, reminder, or other item to a person at a particular address.

Direct-response television marketing Direct marketing via television, including direct-response television advertising or infomercials and home shopping channels.

Discount   A straight reduction in price on purchases during a stated period of time.

Discount store   A retail institution that sells standard merchandise at lower prices by accepting lower margins and selling at higher volume.

Disintermediation   The cutting out of marketing channel intermediaries by product or service producers, or the displacement of traditional resellers by radical new types of intermediaries.

Distribution center   A large, highly automated warehouse designed to receive goods from various plants and suppliers, take orders, fill them efficiently, and deliver goods to customers as quickly as possible.

Diversification   A strategy for company growth through starting up or acquiring businesses outside the company's current products and markets.

Downsizing   Reducing the business portfolio by eliminating products or business units that are not profitable or that no longer fit the company's overall strategy.

Dynamic pricing   Adjusting prices continually to meet the characteristics and needs of individual customers and situations.

E-business   The use of electronic platforms—intranets, extranets, and the Internet—to conduct a company's business.

E-commerce   Buying and selling processes supported by electronic means, primarily the Internet.

Economic community   A group of nations organized to work toward common goals in the regulation of international trade.

Economic environment   Factors that affect consumer buying power and spending patterns.

E-marketing   The marketing side of e-commerce—company efforts to communicate about, promote, and sell products and services over the Internet.

Engel's laws   Differences noted over a century ago by Ernst Engel in how people shift their spending across food, housing, transportation, health care, and other goods and services categories as family income rises.

Enlightened marketing   A marketing philosophy holding that a company's marketing should support the best long-run performance of the marketing system.

Environmental sustainability   A management approach that involves developing strategies that both sustain the environment and produce profits for the company.

Environmentalism   An organized movement of concerned citizens and government agencies to protect and improve people's living environment.

Exchange   The act of obtaining a desired object from someone by offering something in return.

Exclusive distribution   Giving a limited number of dealers the exclusive right to distribute the company's products in their territories.

Experimental research   The gathering of primary data by selecting matched groups of subjects, giving them different treatments, controlling related factors, and checking for differences in group responses.

Exploratory research   Marketing research to gather preliminary information that will help define problems and suggest hypotheses.

Exporting   Entering a foreign market by selling goods produced in the company's home country, often with little modification.

Extranet   A network that connects a company with its suppliers and distributors.

Factory outlet   Off-price retailing operation that is owned and operated by a manufacturer and that normally carries the manufacturer's surplus, discontinued, or irregular goods.

Fad   A fashion that enters quickly, is adopted with great zeal, peaks early, and declines very quickly.

Fashion   A currently accepted or popular style in a given field.

Fixed costs   Costs that do not vary with production or sales level.

Focus group interviewing   Personal interviewing that involves inviting 6 to 10 people to gather for a few hours with a trained interviewer to talk about a product, service, or organization. The interviewer "focuses" the group discussion on important issues.

Follow-up   The last step in the selling process in which the salesperson follows up after the sale to ensure customer satisfaction and repeat business.

Franchise   A contractual association between a manufacturer, wholesaler, or service organization (a franchiser) and independent businesspeople (franchisees) who buy the right to own and operate one or more units in the franchise system.

Franchise organization   A contractual vertical marketing system in which a channel member, called a franchisor, links several stages in the production-distribution process.

Gender segmentation   Dividing a market into different groups based on gender.

Generation X   The 49 million people born between 1965 and 1976 in the "birth dearth" following the baby boom.

Generation Y   The 72 million children of the baby boomers, born between 1977 and 1994.

Geographic segmentation   Dividing a market into different geographical units such as nations, states, regions, counties, cities, or neighborhoods.

Geographical pricing   Setting price based on the buyer's geographic location.

Global firm   A firm that, by operating in more than one country, gains R&D, production, marketing, and financial advantages in its costs and reputation that are not available to purely domestic competitors.

Good-value pricing   Offering just the right combination of quality and good service at a fair price.

Group   Two or more people who interact to accomplish individual or mutual goals.

Growth-share matrix   A portfolio-planning method that evaluates a company's strategic business units in terms of their market growth rate and relative market share. SBUs are classified as stars, cash cows, question marks, or dogs.

Growth stage   The product life-cycle stage in which a product's sales start climbing quickly.

Handling objections   The step in the selling process in which the salesperson seeks out, clarifies, and overcomes customer objections to buying.

Horizontal marketing system   A channel arrangement in which two or more companies at one level join together to follow a new marketing opportunity.

Idea generation   The systematic search for new-product ideas.

Idea screening   Screening new-product ideas in order to spot good ideas and drop poor ones as soon as possible.

Income segmentation   Dividing a market into different income groups.

Independent off-price retailer   Off-price retailer that is either owned and run by entrepreneurs or is a division of a larger retail corporation.

Indirect marketing channel   Channel containing one or more intermediary levels.

Individual marketing   Tailoring products and marketing programs to the needs and preferences of individual customers—also labeled "markets-of-one marketing," "customized marketing," and "one-to-one marketing."

Industrial product   Product bought by individuals and organizations for further processing or for use in conducting a business.

Innovative marketing   A principle of enlightened marketing that requires that a company seek real product and marketing improvements.

Inside sales force   Inside salespeople who conduct business from their offices via telephone, the Internet, or visits from prospective buyers.

Integrated direct marketing   Direct marketing campaigns that use multiple vehicles and multiple stages to improve response rates and profits.

Integrated logistics management   The logistics concept that emphasizes teamwork, both inside the company and among all the marketing channel organizations, to maximize the performance of the entire distribution system.

Integrated marketing communications (IMC)   The concept under which a company carefully integrates its many communications channels to deliver a clear, consistent, and compelling message about the organization and its products.

Intensive distribution   Stocking the product in as many outlets as possible.

Interactive marketing   Marketing by a service firm that recognizes that perceived service quality depends heavily on the quality of buyer-seller interaction.

Intermarket segmentation   Forming segments of consumers who have similar needs and buying behavior even though they are located in different countries.

Intermodal transportation   Combining two or more modes of transportation.

Internal databases   Electronic collections of consumer and market information obtained from data sources within the company network.

Internal marketing   Marketing by a service firm to train and effectively motivate its customer-contact employees and all the supporting service people to work as a team to provide customer satisfaction.

Internet   A vast public web of computer networks, which connects users of all types all around the world to each other and to an amazingly large "information repository."

Intranet   A network that connects people within a company to each other and to the company network.

Introduction stage   The product life-cycle stage in which the new product is first distributed and made available for purchase.

Joint ownership   A joint venture in which a company joins investors in a foreign market to create a local business in which the company shares joint ownership and control.

Joint venturing   Entering foreign markets by joining with foreign companies to produce or market a product or service.

Learning   Changes in an individual's behavior arising from experience.

Licensing   A method of entering a foreign market in which the company enters into an agreement with a licensee in the foreign market, offering the right to use a manufacturing process, trademark, patent, trade secret, or other item of value for a fee or royalty.

Lifestyle   A person's pattern of living as expressed in his or her activities, interests, and opinions.

Line extension   Using a successful brand name to introduce additional items in a given product category under the same brand name, such as new flavors, forms, colors, added ingredients, or package sizes.

Local marketing   Tailoring brands and promotions to the needs and wants of local customer groups—cities, neighborhoods, and even specific stores.

Macroenvironment   The larger societal forces that affect the microenvironment—demographic, economic, natural, technological, political, and cultural forces.

Management contracting   A joint venture in which the domestic firm supplies the management know-how to a foreign company that supplies the capital; the domestic firm exports management services rather than products.

Manufacturers' sales branches and offices   Wholesaling by sellers or buyers themselves rather than through independent wholesalers.

Market   The set of all actual and potential buyers of a product or service.

Market development   A strategy for company growth by identifying and developing new market segments for current company products.

Market offering   Some combination of products, services, information, or experiences offered to a market to satisfy a need or want.

Market penetration   A strategy for company growth by increasing sales of current products to current market segments without changing the product.

Market-penetration pricing   Setting a low price for a new product in order to attract a large number of buyers and a large market share.

Market positioning   Arranging for a product to occupy a clear, distinctive, and desirable place relative to competing products in the minds of target consumers.

Market segment   A group of consumers who respond in a similar way to a given set of marketing efforts.

Market segmentation   Dividing a market into distinct groups with distinct needs, characteristics, or behaviors who might require separate products or marketing mixes.

Market-skimming pricing   Setting a high price for a new product to skim maximum revenues layer by layer from the segments willing to pay the high price; the company makes fewer but more profitable sales.

Marketing   The process by which companies create value for customers and build strong customer relationships in order to capture value from customers in return.

Marketing audit   A comprehensive, systematic, independent, and periodic examination of a company's environment, objectives, strategies, and activities to determine problem areas and opportunities and to recommend a plan of action to improve the company's marketing performance.

Marketing channel (distribution channel)   A set of interdependent organizations that help make a product or service available for use or consumption by the consumer or business user.

Marketing concept   The marketing management philosophy that holds that achieving organizational goals depends on knowing the needs and wants of target markets and delivering the desired satisfactions better than competitors do.

Marketing control   The process of measuring and evaluating the results of marketing strategies and plans, and taking corrective action to ensure that objectives are achieved.

Marketing environment   The actors and forces outside marketing that affect marketing management's ability to build and maintain successful relationships with target customers.

Marketing implementation   The process that turns marketing strategies and plans into marketing actions in order to accomplish strategic marketing objectives.

Marketing information system (MIS)   People, equipment, and procedures to gather, sort, analyze, evaluate, and distribute needed, timely, and accurate information to marketing decision makers.

Marketing intelligence The systematic collection and analysis of publicly available information about competitors and developments in the marketing environment.

Marketing intermediaries Firms that help the company to promote, sell, and distribute its goods to final buyers; they include resellers, physical distribution firms, marketing service agencies, and financial intermediaries.

Marketing logistics (physical distribution) The tasks involved in planning, implementing, and controlling the physical flow of materials, final goods, and related information from points of origin to points of consumption to meet customer requirements at a profit.

Marketing management The art and science of choosing target markets and building profitable relationships with them.

Marketing mix The set of controllable tactical marketing tools—product, price, place, and promotion—that the firm blends to produce the response it wants in the target market.

Marketing myopia The mistake of paying more attention to the specific products a company offers than to the benefits and experiences produced by these products.

Marketing research The systematic design, collection, analysis, and reporting of data relevant to a specific marketing situation facing an organization.

Marketing strategy The marketing logic by which the business unit hopes to achieve its marketing objectives.

Marketing strategy development Designing an initial marketing strategy for a new product based on the product concept.

Marketing supply chain management Managing upstream and downstream value-added flows of materials, final goods, and related information among suppliers, the company, resellers, and final consumers.

Marketing Web site A Web site that engages consumers in interactions that will move them closer to a direct purchase or other marketing outcome.

Maturity stage The stage in the product life cycle in which sales growth slows or levels off.

Merchant wholesaler Independently owned business that takes title to the merchandise it handles.

Microenvironment The actors close to the company that affect its ability to serve its customers—the company, suppliers, marketing intermediaries, customer markets, competitors, and publics.

Micromarketing The practice of tailoring products and marketing programs to the needs and wants of specific individuals and local customer groups—includes local marketing and individual marketing.

Mission statement A statement of the organization's purpose—what it wants to accomplish in the larger environment.

Modified rebuy A business buying situation in which the buyer wants to modify product specifications, prices, terms, or suppliers.

Motive (drive) A need that is sufficiently pressing to direct the person to seek satisfaction of the need.

Multichannel distribution system A distribution system in which a single firm sets up two or more marketing channels to reach one or more customer segments.

Natural environment Natural resources that are needed as inputs by marketers or that are affected by marketing activities.

Needs States of felt deprivation.

New product A good, service, or idea that is perceived by some potential customers as new.

New-product development The development of original products, product improvements, product modifications, and new brands through the firm's own R&D efforts.

New-task situation A business buying situation in which the buyer purchases a product or service for the first time.

Objective-and-task method Developing the promotion budget by (1) defining specific objectives, (2) determining the tasks that must be performed to achieve these objectives, and (3) estimating the costs of performing these tasks. The sum of these costs is the proposed promotion budget.

Observational research The gathering of primary data by observing relevant people, actions, and situations.

Occasion segmentation Dividing the market into groups according to occasions when buyers get the idea to buy, actually make their purchase, or use the purchased item.

Off-price retailer Retailer that buys at less-than-regular wholesale prices and sells at less than retail. Examples are factory outlets, independents, and warehouse clubs.

Online advertising Advertising that appears while consumers are surfing the Web, including banners, interstitials, pop-ups, and other forms.

Online databases Computerized collections of information available from online commercial sources or via the Internet.

Online (Internet) marketing research Collecting primary data through Internet surveys and online focus groups.

Open trading exchanges Huge e-marketspaces in which B2B buyers and sellers find each other online, share information, and complete transactions efficiently.

Opinion leader Person within a reference group who, because of special skills, knowledge, personality, or other characteristics, exerts influence on others.

Optional-product pricing The pricing of optional or accessory products along with a main product.

Outside sales force (or field sales force) Outside salespeople who travel to call on customers in the field.

Packaging The activities of designing and producing the container or wrapper for a product.

Partner relationship management Working closely with partners in other company departments and outside the company to jointly bring greater value to customers.

Percentage-of-sales method Setting the promotion budget at a certain percentage of current or forecasted sales or as a percentage of the unit sales price.

Perception The process by which people select, organize, and interpret information to form a meaningful picture of the world.

Personal selling Personal presentation by the firm's sales force for the purpose of making sales and building customer relationships.

Personality The unique psychological characteristics that lead to relatively consistent and lasting responses to one's own environment.

Pleasing products Products that give high immediate satisfaction but may hurt consumers in the long run.

Political environment Laws, government agencies, and pressure groups that influence and limit various organizations and individuals in a given society.

Portfolio analysis The process by which management evaluates the products and businesses making up the company.

Positioning statement A statement that summarizes company or brand positioning—it takes this form: To (target segment and need) our (brand) is (concept) that (point-of-difference).

Preapproach The step in the selling process in which the salesperson learns as much as possible about a prospective customer before making a sales call.

Presentation The step in the selling process in which the salesperson tells the product "story" to the buyer, highlighting customer benefits.

Price The amount of money charged for a product or service, or the sum of all the values that customers give up in order to gain the benefits of having or using a product or service.

Price elasticity A measure of the sensitivity of demand to changes in price.

Primary data Information collected for the specific purpose at hand.

Private brand (or store brand) A brand created and owned by a reseller of a product or service.

Private trading exchanges B2B trading networks that link a particular seller with its own trading partners.

Product Anything that can be offered to a market for attention, acquisition, use, or consumption that might satisfy a want or need.

Product adaptation Adapting a product to meet local conditions or wants in foreign markets.

Product bundle pricing Combining several products and offering the bundle at a reduced price.

Product concept A detailed version of the new-product idea stated in meaningful consumer terms.

Product concept The idea that consumers will favor products that offer the most quality, performance, and features and that the organization should devote its energy to making continuous product improvements.

Product development A strategy for company growth by offering modified or new products to current market segments.

Product development Developing the product concept into a physical product in order to ensure that the product idea can be turned into a workable product.

Product invention Creating new products or services for foreign markets.

Product life cycle The course of a product's sales and profits over its lifetime. It involves five distinct stages: product development, introduction, growth, maturity, and decline.

Product line A group of products that are closely related because they function in a similar manner, are sold to the same customer groups, are marketed through the same types of outlets, or fall within given price ranges.

Product line pricing Setting the price steps between various products in a product line based on cost differences between the products, customer evaluations of different features, and competitors' prices.

Product mix (or product portfolio) The set of all product lines and items that a particular seller offers for sale.

Product position The way the product is defined by consumers on important attributes—the place the product occupies in consumers' minds relative to competing products.

Product quality The ability of a product to perform its functions; it includes the product's overall durability, reliability, precision, ease of operation and repair, and other valued attributes.

Product sales force structure A sales force organization under which salespeople specialize in selling only a portion of the company's products or lines.

Product/market expansion grid A portfolio-planning tool for identifying company growth opportunities through market penetration, market development, product development, or diversification.

Production concept The idea that consumers will favor products that are available and highly affordable and that the organization should therefore focus on improving production and distribution efficiency.

Promotion mix (or marketing communications mix) The specific mix of advertising, personal selling, sales promotion, public relations, and direct marketing that a company uses to persuasively communicate customer value and build customer relationships.

Promotional pricing Temporarily pricing products below the list price, and sometimes even below cost, to increase short-run sales.

Prospecting The step in the selling process in which the salesperson identifies qualified potential customers.

Psychographic segmentation Dividing a market into different groups based on social class, lifestyle, or personality characteristics.

Psychological pricing A pricing approach that considers the psychology of prices and not simply the economics; the price is used to say something about the product.

Public Any group that has an actual or potential interest in, or impact on, an organization's ability to achieve its objectives.

Public relations (PR) Building good relations with the company's various publics by obtaining favorable publicity, building up a good "corporate image," and handling or heading off unfavorable rumors, stories, and events.

Public relations Building good relations with the company's various publics by obtaining favorable publicity, building up a good "corporate image," and handling or heading off unfavorable rumors, stories, and events.

Pull strategy A promotion strategy that calls for spending a lot on advertising and consumer promotion to build up consumer demand that will pull the product through channels.

Push strategy A promotion strategy that calls for using the sales force and trade promotion to push the product through channels.

Reference prices Prices that buyers carry in their minds and refer to when they look at a given product.

Retailer Business whose sales come primarily from retailing.

Retailing All activities involved in selling goods or services directly to final consumers for their personal, nonbusiness use.

Return on marketing (or marketing ROI) The net return from a marketing investment divided by the costs of the marketing investment.

Sales force management The analysis, planning, implementation, and control of sales force activities. It includes designing sales force strategy and structure and recruiting, selecting, training, supervising, compensating, and evaluating the firm's salespeople.

Sales promotion Short-term incentives to encourage the purchase or sale of a product or service.

Sales quota A standard that states the amount a salesperson should sell and how sales should be divided among the company's products.

Salesperson An individual acting for a company by performing one or more of the following activities: prospecting, communicating, servicing, and information gathering.

Salutary products Products that have low appeal but may benefit consumers in the long run.

Sample A segment of the population selected for marketing research to represent the population as a whole.

Secondary data Information that already exists somewhere, having been collected for another purpose.

Segmented pricing Selling a product or service at two or more prices, where the difference in prices is not based on differences in costs.

Selective distribution The use of more than one, but fewer than all, of the intermediaries who are willing to carry the company's products.

Selling concept The idea that consumers will not buy enough of the firm's products unless it undertakes a large-scale selling and promotion effort.

Selling process The steps that the salesperson follows when selling, which include prospecting and qualifying, preapproach, approach, presentation and demonstration, handling objections, closing, and follow-up.

Sense-of-mission marketing A principle of enlightened marketing that holds that a company should define its mission in broad social terms rather than narrow product terms.

Sequential product development A new-product development approach in which one company department works to complete its stage of the process before passing the new product along to the next department and stage.

Service Any activity or benefit that one party can offer to another that is essentially intangible and does not result in the ownership of anything.

Service inseparability A major characteristic of services—they are produced and consumed at the same time and cannot be separated from their providers, whether the providers are people or machines.

Service intangibility A major characteristic of services—they cannot be seen, tasted, felt, heard, or smelled before they are bought.

Service perishability A major characteristic of services—they cannot be stored for later sale or use.

Service-profit chain The chain that links service firm profits with employee and customer satisfaction.

Service variability A major characteristic of services—their quality may vary greatly, depending on who provides them and when, where, and how.

Share of customer The portion of the customer's purchasing that a company gets in its product categories.

Shopping center A group of retail businesses planned, developed, owned, and managed as a unit.

Shopping product Consumer good that the customer, in the process of selection and purchase, characteristically compares on such bases as suitability, quality, price, and style.

Simultaneous (or team-based) product development An approach to developing new products in which various company departments work closely together, overlapping the steps in the product-development process to save time and increase effectiveness.

Single-source data systems Electronic monitoring systems that link consumers' exposure to television advertising and promotion (measured using television meters) with what they buy in stores (measured using store checkout scanners).

Social class Relatively permanent and ordered divisions in a society whose members share similar values, interests, and behaviors.

Social marketing The design, implementation, and control of programs seeking to increase the acceptability of a social idea, cause, or practice among a target group.

Societal marketing concept A principle of enlightened marketing that holds that a company should make good marketing decisions by considering consumers' wants, the company's requirements, consumers' long-run interests, and society's long run interests.

Spam Unsolicited, unwanted commercial e-mail messages.

Specialty product Consumer product with unique characteristics or brand identification for which a significant group of buyers is willing to make a special purchase effort.

Specialty store A retail store that carries a narrow product line with a deep assortment within that line.

Standardized marketing mix An international marketing strategy for using basically the same product, advertising, distribution channels, and other elements of the marketing mix in all the company's international markets.

Straight product extension Marketing a product in a foreign market without any change.

Straight rebuy A business buying situation in which the buyer routinely reorders something without any modifications.

Strategic planning The process of developing and maintaining a strategic fit between the organization's goals and capabilities and its changing marketing opportunities. It involves defining a clear company mission, setting supporting objectives, designing a sound business portfolio, and coordinating functional strategies.

Style A basic and distinctive mode of expression.

Subculture A group of people with shared value systems based on common life experiences and situations.

Supermarket Large, low-cost, low-margin, high-volume, self-service store that carries a wide variety of food, laundry, and household products.

Superstore A store much larger than a regular supermarket that carries a large assortment of routinely purchased food and nonfood items and offers services such as dry cleaning, post offices, photo finishing, check cashing, bill paying, lunch counters, car care, and pet care.

Survey research The gathering of primary data by asking people questions about their knowledge, attitudes, preferences, and buying behavior.

SWOT analysis An overall evaluation of the company's strengths (S), weaknesses (W), opportunities (O), and threats (T).

Systems selling Buying a packaged solution to a problem from a single seller, thus avoiding all the separate decisions involved in a complex buying situation.

Target costing Pricing that starts with an ideal selling price, then targets costs that will ensure that the price is met.

Target market A set of buyers sharing common needs or characteristics that the company decides to serve.

Target marketing The process of evaluating each market segment's attractiveness and selecting one or more segments to enter.

Team selling Using teams of people from sales, marketing, engineering, finance, technical support, and even upper management to service large, complex accounts.

Technological environment Forces that create new technologies, creating new product and market opportunities.

Telephone marketing Using the telephone to sell directly to customers.

Territorial sales force structure A sales force organization that assigns each salesperson to an exclusive geographic territory in which that salesperson sells the company's full line.

Test marketing The stage of new-product development in which the product and marketing program are tested in more realistic market settings.

Third-party logistics (3PL) provider An independent logistics provider that performs any or all of the functions required to get their client's product to market.

Total costs   The sum of the fixed and variable costs for any given level of production.

Undifferentiated (mass) marketing   A market-coverage strategy in which a firm decides to ignore market segment differences and go after the whole market with one offer.

Unsought product   Consumer product that the consumer either does not know about or knows about but does not normally think of buying.

Value-added pricing   Attaching value-added features and services to differentiate a marketing offer and support higher prices, rather than cutting prices to match competitors.

Value analysis   An approach to cost reduction in which components are studied carefully to determine if they can be redesigned, standardized, or made by less costly methods of production.

Value-based pricing   Setting price based on buyers' perceptions of value rather than on the seller's cost.

Value chain   The series of departments that carry out value-creating activities to design, produce, market, deliver, and support a firm's products.

Value-delivery network   The network made up of the company, suppliers, distributors, and ultimately customers who "partner" with each other to improve the performance of the entire system.

Value proposition   The full positioning of a brand—the full mix of benefits upon which it is positioned.

Variable costs   Costs that vary directly with the level of production.

Vertical marketing system (VMS)   A distribution channel structure in which producers, wholesalers, and retailers act as a unified system. One channel member owns the others, has contracts with them, or has so much power that they all cooperate.

Viral marketing   The Internet version of word-of-mouth marketing—Web sites, e-mail messages, or other marketing events that are so infectious that customers will want to pass them along to friends.

Wants   The form human needs take as shaped by culture and individual personality.

Warehouse club   Off-price retailer that sells a limited selection of brand-name grocery items, appliances, clothing, and a hodgepodge of other goods at deep discounts to members who pay annual membership fees.

Web communities   Web sites upon which members can congregate online and exchange views on issues of common interest.

Wheel-of-retailing concept   A concept of retailing that states that new types of retailers usually begin as low-margin, low-price, low-status operations but later evolve into higher-priced, higher-service operations, eventually becoming like the conventional retailers they replaced.

Whole-channel view   Designing international channels that take into account all the necessary links in distributing the seller's products to final buyers, including the seller's headquarters organization, channels among nations, and channels within nations.

Wholesaler   A firm engaged primarily in wholesaling activity.

Wholesaling   All activities involved in selling goods and services to those buying for resale or business use.

References

Chapter 1

1. Quotes and other information from Paul Farriss, "NASCAR Rides the Fast Track," *Marketing,* April 11, 2005, pp. 11–12; Jonathon Wegner, "NASCAR Sponsorship Can Be Expensive, but Rewards for Companies Could Be Great," *Knight Ridder Tribune Business News,* November 21, 2004, p. 1; Mark Woods, "Readers Try to Explain Why Racin' Rocks," *Florida Times-Union,* February 16, 2003, p. C1; Peter Spiegel, "Heir Gordon," *Forbes,* December 14, 1998, pp. 42–46; Tony Kontzer, "Backseat Drivers—NASCAR Puts You in the Race," *InformationWeek,* March 25, 2002, p. 83; Tom Lowry, "The Prince of NASCAR," *BusinessWeek,* February 23, 2004, pp. 91–98; "Record Viewing Audience Once Again Proves Daytona 500 Is Motorsports' Premier Event," Daytona International Speedway.com, February 22, 2005, accessed at www.daytonainternationalspeedway.com/news/news.jsp?news_id=707, March 2, 2005; Paul Owens, "Office Depot to Sponsor NASCAR," *Knight Ridder Tribune Business News,* January 28, 2005, p. 1; and www.NASCAR.com, December 2005.

2. The American Marketing Association offers this definition: "Marketing is an organizational function and a set of processes for creating, communicating, and delivering value to customers and for managing customer relationships in ways that benefit the organization and its stakeholders." Accessed at www.marketingpower.com/mg-dictionary-view1862.php?, September 2005. Also see Lisa M. Keefe, "What Is the Meaning of 'Marketing,'" *Marketing News,* September 15, 2004, pp. 17–18; and Chekitan S. Dev and Don E. Schultz, "A Customer-Focused Approach Can Bring the Current Marketing Mix into the 21st Century," *Marketing Management,* January–February 2005, pp. 18–24.

3. Jeffrey Pfeffer, "A Field Day for Executives," *Business 2.0,* December 2004, p. 88; and Scott Kirsner, "Leaders You Need to Know," *Fast Company,* February 2005, pp. 68–72.

4. See Theodore Levitt's classic article, "Marketing Myopia," *Harvard Business Review,* July–August 1960, pp. 45–56. For more recent discussions, see James R. Stock, "Marketing Myopia Revisited: Lessons for Logistics," *International Journal of Physical Distribution & Logistics Management,* vol. 2, issue 1/2, 2002, pp. 12–21; and Yves Doz, Jose Santos, and Peter J. Williamson, "Marketing Myopia Revisited: Why Every Company Needs to Learn from the World," *Ivey Business Journal,* January–February 2004, p. 1.

5. See Erika Rasmusson, "Marketing More Than a Product," *Sales & Marketing Management,* February 2000, p. 99; and Lawrence A. Crosby and Sheree L. Johnson, "Managing Experiences," *Marketing Management,* January–February 2005, pp. 12–14.

6. See David Lewis, "Southwest Staff Go Nuts (for Customers!)," *Sales & Marketing Institute,* May 2005, accessed at www.salesmarketing.org.nz/ article623.html. For more on market orientation and firm performance, see Ahmet H. Kirca, Satish Jayachandran, and William O. Bearden, "Marketing Orientation: A Meta-Analytic Review and Assessment of Its Antecedents and Impact on Performance," *Journal of Marketing,* April 2005, pp. 24–41.

7. See "America's Most Fattening Burger," *Time,* January 3, 2005, p. 186; and "For the Health-Unconscious, Era of Mammoth Burger Is Here," *Wall Street Journal,* January 27, 2005, p. B.1.

8. See "Leaders of the Most Admired," *FORTUNE,* January 29, 1990, pp. 40–54; Alex Taylor III, "Can J&J Keep the Magic Going?" *FORTUNE,* May 27, 2002, pp. 117–121; Allan Weisberg, "Prescribing Learning and Business Success," *Chief Learning Officer,* December 2004, pp. 38–42; Larry Edwards, et. al., "75 Years of Ideas," *Advertising Age,* February 14, 2005, p. 14; and www.jnj.com/our_company/our_credo/index.htm, January 2006.

9. "The 2004 Total Value Awards: Incentives Don't Correlate to Value Says Strategic Vision," *Strategic Vision,* October 4, 2004, accessed at www.strategicvision.com, February 2005; Chad Lawhorn, "Gas Costs Steer Study into Hybrids," *Knight Ridder Tribune Business News,* April 29, 2005, p. 1; and Ronald D. White, "Car Buyers Think Hard and Long Distance About Mileage," *Los Angeles Times,* April 30, 2005, p. C.1.

10. Catherine Arnold, "Satisfaction's the Name of the Game," *Marketing News,* October 15, 2004, pp. 39, 45; Eugene W. Anderson, Claes Fornell, and Sanal K. Mazvancheryl, "Customer Satisfaction and Shareholder Value," *Journal of Marketing,* October 2004, pp. 172–185; and Christian Homburg, Nicole Koschate, and Wayne D. Hoyer, "Do Satisfied Customers Really Pay More? A Study Between Customer Satisfaction and Willingness to Pay," *Journal of Marketing,* April 2005, pp. 84–96.

11. Information about the Harley Owners Group accessed at www.hog.com, November 2005.

12. See https://supply.mckesson.com/portal/index.jsp?pageID=aboutsmo.

13. Adapted from information found in Elizabeth Esfahani, "How to Get Tough with Bad Customers," *Business 2.0,* October 2004, p. 52. Also see Amey Stone, "Bare Bones, Plump Profits," *BusinessWeek,* March 14, 2005, p. 88.

14. See Renee Houston Zemansky and Jeff Weiner, "Just Hang On to What You Got," *Selling Power,* March 2002, pp. 60–64; Marc R. Okrant, "How to Convert '3's and '4's into '5's," *Marketing News,* October 14, 2002, pp. 14, 17; and Andrew Grossman, "When Bigger Isn't Better," *Catalog Age,* February 2005, pp. 0–1.

15. Philip Kotler and Kevin Lane Keller, *Marketing Management,* 12th ed. (Upper Saddle River, N.J.: Prentice Hall, 2006), p. 27.

16. See Robert D. Hof, "Netflix 1, Wal-Mart 0," *BusinessWeek Online,* May 20, 2005, accessed at www.businessweek.com/technology/content/may2005/tc20050520_3983_tc024.htm; and Mike Duff, "Older and Wiser—and Gaining Ground," *DSN Retailing Today,* June 13, 2005, pp. 52–55.

17. Thor Valdmanis, "Alliances Gain Favor over Risky Mergers," *USA Today,* February 4, 1999, p. 3B. Also see Matthew Schifrin, "Partner or Perish," *Forbes,* May 21, 2001, pp. 26–28; and Kim T. Gordon, "Strong Partnerships Build Marketing Muscle," *CRN,* February 10, 2003, p. 14A.

18. For more discussion of customer loyalty, see Fred Reichheld and Christine Detrick, "Loyalty: A Prescription for Cutting Costs," *Marketing Management,* September–October, 2003, pp. 24–25; Jacquelyn S. Thomas, Robert C. Blattberg, and Edward J. Fox, "Recapturing Lost Customers," *Journal of Marketing Research,* February 2004, pp. 31–45; and Clara Agustin and Jagdip Singh, "Curvilinear Effects of Consumer Loyalty Determinants in Relational Exchanges," *Journal of Marketing Research,* February 2005, pp. 96–108.

19. "Stew Leonard's," *Hoover's Company Records,* May 1, 2005, p. 104226; and www.stew-leonards.com/html/about.cfm, December 2005.

20. For an interesting discussion on assessing and using customer lifetime value, see Charlotte H. Mason, "Tuscan Lifestyles: Assessing Customer Lifetime Value," *Journal of Interactive Marketing,* Autumn 2003, pp. 54–60; Rajkumar Venkatesan and V Kumar, "A Customer Lifetime

Value Framework for Customer Selection and Resource Allocation Strategy," *Journal of marketing,* October 2004, pp. 106–125; and Guy du Torcy, "Customer Lifetime Value," *Financial World,* January 2005, p. 52.

21. Erin Stout, "Keep Them Coming Back for More," *Sales and Marketing Management*, February 2002, pp. 51–52; and Fiona Haley, "Fast Talk," *Fast Company,* December 2003, p. 57. Also see Arthur Hughes, "Customer Retention: Integrating Lifetime Value into Marketing Strategies," June 21, 2005, accessed at www.dbmarketing.com/articles/Art112.htm.

22. Don Peppers and Martha Rogers, "Customers Don't Grow on Trees," *Fast Company,* July 2005, pp. 25-26.

23. See Roland T. Rust, Valerie A. Zeithaml, and Katherine A. Lemon, *Driving Customer Equity* (New York: Free Press 2000); Robert C. Blattberg, Gary Getz, Jacquelyn S. Thomas, *Customer Equity* (Boston: Harvard Business School Press, 2001); Roland T. Rust, Katherine N. Lemon, and Valarie A. Zeithaml, "Return on Marketing: Using Customer Equity to Focus Marketing Strategy," *Journal of Marketing*, January 2004, pp. 109–127; James D. Lenskold, "Customer-Centered Marketing ROI," *Marketing Management,* January–February 2004, pp. 26–32; and Rust, Zeithaml, and Lemon, "Customer-Centered Brand Management," *Harvard Business Review*, September 2004, p. 110.

24. This example is adapted from information in Roland T. Rust, Katherine N. Lemon, and Valarie A. Zeithaml, "Where Should the Next Marketing Dollar Go?" *Marketing Management*, September–October 2001, pp. 24–28. Also see David Welch and David Kiley, "Can Caddy's Driver Make GM Cool?" *BusinessWeek,* September 20, 2004, pp. 105–106; John K. Teahen Jr., and "Cadillac Kid: 'Gotta Compete,'" *Knight Ridder Tribune Business News,* May 7, 2005, p. 1.

25. Ravi Dhar and Rashi Glazer, "Hedging Customers," *Harvard Business Review,* May 2003, pp. 86–92.

26. Werner Relnartz and Vishesh Kumar, "The Mismanagement of Customer Loyalty," *Harvard Business Review,* July 2002, pp. 86–94. For more on customer equity management, see Sunil Gupta, Donald R. Lehman, and Jennifer Ames Stuart, "Valuing Customers," *Journal of Marketing Research,* February 2004, pp. 7–18; Michael D. Johnson and Fred Selnes, "Customer Portfolio Management: Toward a Dynamic Theory of Exchange Relationships," *Journal of Marketing,* April 2004, pp. 1–17; Sunil Gupta and Donald R. Lehman, *Managing Customers as Investments* (Philadelphia: Wharton School Publishing, 2005); and Roland T. Rust, Katherine N. Lemon, and Das Narayandas, *Customer Equity Management* (Upper Saddle River, N.J.: Prentice Hall, 2005).

27. "Population Explosion!" *ClickZ Stats,* March 16, 2005, accessed at www.clickz.com/stats/sectors/geographics/article.php/151151.

28. Steve Hamm, "E-Biz: Down but Hardly Out," *BusinessWeek,* March 26, 2001, pp. 126–130; "B2B E-Commerce Headed for Trillions," March 6, 2002, accessed online at cyberatlas.internet.com; and Mullaney, "E-biz Surprise," pp. 60–68.

29. Anver Versi, "MTV Rolls Out African Channel," *African Business,* January 2005, pp. 58–59; and Emmanuel Legrand, "Music Makes the World Go Round," *Billboard,* April 30, 2005, p. 32.

30. Quotes and information found at www.patagonia.com/enviro/main_enviro_action.shtml, December 2005.

31. Example adapted from Alison Stein Wellner, "Oh Come All Ye Faithful," *American Demographics,* June 2001, pp. 52–55. Other information is from www.marblechurch.com, January 2006.

32. For other examples, and for a good review of nonprofit marketing, see Philip Kotler and Alan R. Andreasen, *Strategic Marketing for Nonprofit Organizations,* 6th ed. (Upper Saddle River, N.J.: Prentice Hall, 2003); Philip Kotler and Karen Fox, *Strategic Marketing for Educational Institutions* (Upper Saddle River, N.J.: Prentice Hall, 1995); Norman Shawchuck, Philip Kotler, Bruce Wren, and Gustave Rath, *Marketing for Congregations: Choosing to Serve People More Effectively* (Nashville, TN: Abingdon Press, 1993); Philip Kotler, John Bowen, and James Makens, *Marketing for Hospitality and Tourism,* 3rd ed. (Upper Saddle River, N.J.: Prentice Hall, 2003); and "The Nonprofit Marketing Landscape," special section, *Journal of Business Research,* June 2005, pp. 797–862.

33. Craig Endicott, "100 Leading National Advertisers," *Advertising Age,* June 28, 2004, p. S1. For more on social marketing, see Philip Kotler, Ned Roberto, and Nancy R. Lee, *Social Marketing: Improving the Quality of Life,* 2nd ed. (Upper Saddle River, N.J.: Prentice Hall, 2002).

Chapter 2

1. Quotes and other information from Stanley Holmes, "The New Nike," *BusinessWeek,* September 20, 2004, pp. 78–86; "Nike, Inc.," *Hoover's Company Records,* May 15, 2005, p. 14254; Daniel Roth, "Can Nike Still Do It Without Phil Knight?" *FORTUNE,* April 4, 2005, pp. 59–68; and www.nikebiz.com, August 2005.

2. For a more detailed discussion of corporate- and business-level strategic planning as they apply to marketing, see Philip Kotler and Kevin Lane Keller, *Marketing Management,* 12th ed. (Upper Saddle River, N.J.: Prentice Hall, 2006), Chapter 2.

3. See Forest David and Fred David, "It's Time to Redraft Your Mission Statement," *The Journal of Business Strategy,* January–February 2003, pp. 11–15; "Crafting Mission Statements," *Association Management,* January 2004, p. 23; and Charles N. Toftoy and Joydeep Chartterjee, "Mission Statements and the Small Business," *Business Strategy Review,* Autumn 2004, pp. 41–44 .

4. Monsanto Company Pledge Report, accessed at http://monsanto.com/monsanto/layout/our_pledge/default.asp, January 2006.

5. The following discussion is based in part on information found at www.bcg.com/this_is_bcg/mission/growth_share_matrix.jsp, December 2005. For more on strategic planning, see Dennis Rheault, "Freshening Up Strategic Planning: More then Fill-in-the-Blanks," *The Journal of Business Strategy,* Vol. 24, Iss. 6, 2004, pp. 33–37; Anthony Lavia, "Strategic Planning in Times of Turmoil," *Business Communications Review,* March 2004, pp. 56–60; Rita Gunther McGrath and Ian C. MacMillan. "Market Busting," *Harvard Business Review,* March 2005, pp. 80–89.

6. H. Igor Ansoff, "Strategies for Diversification," *Harvard Business Review,* September–October 1957, pp. 113–124. Also see Kevin Lane Keller, *Strategic Brand Management,* 2nd edition (Upper Saddle River, N.J.: Prentice Hall, 2003), pp. 576–578; and Kotler and Keller, *Marketing Management,* pp. 47–48.

7. Quotes and information in the Starbucks examples and in the growth discussion that follows are from Monica Soto Ouchi, "Starbucks Ratchets Up Growth Forecast," *Knight Ridder Tribune News,* October 15, 2004, p. 1; Stanley Holmes, "First the Music, Then the Coffee," *BusinessWeek,* November 22, 2004, p. 66; Barbara Clements, *Knight Ridder Tribune News,* April 28, 2005, p. 1; and Patricia Sellers, "Starbucks: The Next Generation," *FORTUNE,* April 4, 2005, p. 30.

8. Nirmalya Kumar, "Kill a Brand, Keep a Customer," *Harvard Business Review,* December 2003, pp. 87–95.

9. Michael E. Porter, *Competitive Advantage: Creating and Sustaining Superior Performance* (New York: Free Press, 1985); and Michel E. Porter, "What Is Strategy?" *Harvard Business Review,* November–December 1996, pp. 61–78. Also see Kim B. Clark, et al., *Harvard Business School on Managing the Value Chain* (Boston: Harvard Business School Press, 2000); "Buyer Value and the Value Chain," *Business Owner,* September–October 2003, p. 1; and "The Value Chain," accessed at www.quickmba.com/strategy/value-chain, January 2006.

10. Kotler, *Kotler on Marketing* (New York: The Free Press, 1999), pp. 20–22. Also see Philip Kotler, *Marketing Insights from A to Z* (Hoboken, N.J.: Wiley, 2003), pp. 102–107.

11. *McDonald's Corporation Investor Fact Sheet,* January 2004, accessed at http://www.mcdonalds.com/corp/invest/pub/2004_fact_sheet.html; "McDonald's Corporation," *Hoover's Company Records,* May 1, 2005, pp. 135–45; and "McDonald's Fetes 50th Birthday, Opens Aniversary Restaurant," *Knight Ridder Tribune Business News,* April 15, 2005, p. 1.

12. Quotes and other information from Jeffery K. Liker and Thomas Y. Choi, "Building Deep Supplier Relationships," *Harvard Business Review,* December 2004, pp. 104–113; and Lindsey Chappell, "Toyota Aims to Satisfy Its Suppliers," *Automotive News,* February 21, 2005, p. 10.

13. Jack Trout, "Branding Can't Exist Without Positioning," *Advertising Age,* March 14, 2005, p. 28.

14. "100 Leading National Advertisers," *Advertising Age's Special Report: Profiles Supplement,* June 27, 2005, p. 6; and Ford Motor Company 2004 Annual report, accessed at http://www.ford.com, August 1, 2005.

15. The four Ps classification was first suggested by E. Jerome McCarthy, *Basic Marketing: A Managerial Approach* (Homewood, Ill: Irwin, 1960). For the 4Cs, other proposed classifications, and more discussion, see Robert Lauterborn, "New Marketing Litany: 4P's Passé; C-Words Take Over," *Advertising Age,* October 1, 1990, p. 26; Elliott Ettenberg, "Goodbye 4Ps, Hello 4Rs," *Marketing Magazine,* April 14, 2003, p. 8; Michael R. Hyman, "Revising the Structural Framework for Marketing Management," *Journal of Business Research,* September 2004, p. 923; and Don E. Schultz, "New Definition of Marketing Reinforces Idea of Integration," *Marketing News,* January 15, 2005, p. 8.

16. Brian Dumaine, "Why Great Companies Last," *FORTUNE,* January 16, 1995, p. 129. Also see James C. Collins and Jerry I. Porras, *Built to Last: Successful Habits of Visionary Companies* (New York: HarperBusiness, 1995); Jeff Rosenthal and Mary Ann Masarech, "High-Performance Cultures: How Values Can Drive Vision," *Journal of Organizational Excellence,* Spring 2003, pp. 3–18; and Jeffrey S. Klein, "Corporate Cultures: Why Values Matter," *Folio,* December 2004, p. 23.

17. For more on brand and product management, see Kevin Lane Keller, *Strategic Brand Management,* 2nd ed. (Upper Saddle River, N.J.: Prentice Hall, 2003).

18. For details, see Kotler and Keller, *Marketing Management,* pp. 719–725. Also see Neil A. Morgan, Bruce H. Clark, and Rich Gooner, "Marketing Productivity, Marketing Audits, and Systems for Marketing Performance Assessment: Integrating Multiple Perspectives," *Journal of Marketing,* May 2002, pp. 363–375.

19. Diane Brady, "Making Marketing Measure Up," *BusinessWeek,* December 13, 2004, pp. 112–113; and "Kotler Readies World for One-on-One," *Point,* June 2005, p. 3.

20. Mark McMaster, "ROI: More Vital than Ever," *Sales & Marketing Management,* January 2002, pp. 51–52. Also see Paul Hyde, Ed Landry, and Andrew Tipping, "Are CMOs Irrelevant?" Association of National Advertisers/Booz, Allen, Hamilton white paper, p. 4, accessed at www.ana.net/mrc/ANABoozwhitepaper, June 2005.

21. Matthew Creamer, "Shops Push Affinity, Referrals Over Sales," *Advertising Age,* June 20, 2005, p. S4.

22. For a full discussion of this model and details on customer-centered measures of return on marketing, see Roland T. Rust, Katherine N. Lemon, and Valarie A. Zeithaml, "Return on Marketing: Using Customer Equity to Focus Marketing Strategy," *Journal of Marketing,* January 2004, pp. 109–127; and Roland T. Rust, Katherine N. Lemon, and Das Narayandas, *Customer Equity Management* (Upper Saddle River, N.J.: Prentice Hall, 2005).

23. James D. Lenskold, "Marketing ROI: Playing to Win," *Marketing Management,* May–June 2002, pp. 30–36. Also see Lenskold, *Marketing ROI: The Path to Campaign, Customer, and Corporate Profitability* (New York: McGraw-Hill, 2003); and Rishad Tobaccowala, "The High Cost of Arrogance and the Need to Focus on Outputs," *Point,* May 2005, p. 6.

Chapter 3

1. John O'Connor, "Golden Arches Still Standing After 50 Years," *Knight Ridder Tribune Business News,* April 19, 2005, p. 1; Kate MacArthur, "Big Mac's Back," *Advertising Age,* December 13, 2004, pp. S1–S6; Shirley Leung, "McDonald's Makeover," *Wall Street Journal,* January 28, 2004, p. B1; Sherri Day, "After Years at Top, McDonald's Strives To Regain Ground," *New York Times,* March 3, 2003, p. A.1; Amy Garber, "Bistro Gourmet at McDonald's," *Nation's Restaurant News,* January 31, 2005, pp. 34-35; Michael V. Copeland, "Ronald Gets Back in Shape," *Business 2.0,* January/February 2005, pp. 46–47; Kate MacArthur, "McD's '05 Strategy Hinges on Balance," *Advertising Age,* January 10, 2005, p. 6; "It's What I Eat and What I Do . . . I'm Lovin' It: McDonalds's Launches New Worldwide Balanced, Active, Lifestyles Public Awareness Campaign," press release, March 8, 2005, accessed at http://www.mcdepk.com/globalbalancedlifestyles/media.html; and financial information accessed at www.mcdonalds.com/corp/invest. html, July 2005.

2. See Sarah Lorge, "The Coke Advantage," *Sales & Marketing Management,* December 1998, p. 17; and Chad Terhune "Coke Wins a 10-Year Contract From Subway, Ousting PepsiCo," *Wall Street Journal,* November 28, 2003, p. B.3.

3. World POPClock, U.S. Census Bureau, accessed online at www.census.gov, January 2006. This Web site provides continuously updated projections of the U.S. and world populations.

4. Adapted from Frederik Balfour, "Educating the 'Little Emperors': There's a Big Market for Products That Help China's Coddled Kids Get Ahead," *BusinessWeek,* November 10, 2003, p. 22. Also see Clay Chandler, "Little Emperors," *FORTUNE,* October 4, 2004, pp. 138–150.

5. See "China's Golden Oldies," *The Economist,* February 26, 2005, p. 74.

6. Alison Stein Wellner, "The Next 25 Years," *American Demographics,* April 2003, pp. 23–27; and U.S. Census Bureau projections and POPClock Projection, U.S. Census Bureau, accessed at www.census.gov, January 2006.

7. Kristin Davis, "Oldies But Goodies," *U.S. News & World Report,* March 14, 2005, pp. 45–38.

8. Linda S. Morris, "Home Is Where Your RV Is," *Knight Ridder Tribune Business News,* February 20, 2005, p. 1. Also see Carol Park, "Resorts Scramble to Corral Latest Generation of Luxury Recreational Vehicles," *Knight Ridder Business Tribune News,* September 13, 2004, p. 1; and Alina Tugend, "RV's Find a New Fan Base: The Baby Boomers," *New York Times,* January 16, 2005.

9. "Mixed Success: One Who Targeted Gen X and Succeeded—Sort Of," *Journal of Financial Planning,* February 2004, p. 15. Also see Neil Leslie, "Farther Along on the X Axis," *American Demographics,* May 2004, pp. 21–24.

10. See "Overlooked and Under X-Plointed," *American Demographics,* May 2004, p. 48; and Howard Schneider, "Grunge Marketing," *Mortgage Banking,* November 2004, p. 106.

11. Mike Brandt, "Young Customers: Who, What, and Y," *ABA Bank Marketing,* March 25, 2005, pp. 37–42; and information from www.wamu.com, August 2005.

12. See "TRU Projects Teens Will Spend $169 Billion in 2004," press release, Teenage Research Unlimited, December 1, 2004, accessed at http://www.teenresearch.com.

13. Tobi Elkin, "Gen Y Quizzed about On-Demand," *Advertising Age,* February 14, 2003, p. 37. Also see Rebecca Gardyn, "Born to Be Wired," *American Demographics,* April 2003, pp. 14–15; Noah Rubin Brier, "Coming of Age," *American Demographics*, November 2004, pp. 16–20; and Michael A. Belch, Kathleen A. Krentler, and Laura A. Willis-Flurry, "Teen Internet Mavens: Influence in Family Decision Making," *Journal of Business Research,* May 2005, pp. 569–575.

14. Gregg Bennett and Tony Lachowtz, "Marketing to Lifestyles: Action Sports and Generation Y," *Sports Marketing Quarterly*, 2004, pp. 239–243.

15. See "Automakers Mix It up to Chase Young Buyers," *Automotive News,* April 26, 2004, p. 28B; and Elusive Gen Y Demand Edgier Marketing," *Automotive News,* April 25, 2005, p. 28B.

16. Jason Fields, "America's Families and Living Arrangements: 2003," U.S. Census Bureau, November 2004, accessed at www.census.gov/population/www/socdemo/hh-fam.html.

17. Renee E. Spraggins, "We the People: Women and Men in the United States," U.S. Census Bureau, January 2005, accessed online at www.census.gov/prod/2005pubs/censr-20.pdf, March 2005.

18. See U.S. Census Bureau, "'Stay-at-Home' Parents Top 5 Million," Census Bureau Reports," November 30, 2004, accessed at www.census.gov/PressRelease/www/releases/archives/families_households/003118.html; and Sula Kim, "More Dads Staying at Home," March 16, 2005, accessed at www.tell-my-mom.com/athome-dads/ in_the_news.htm.

19. "Mary Beth Schweigert, "These Dinners Are a Dream Come True for Harried Cooks," *Knight Ridder Tribune,* February 23, 2005, p. 1.

20. U.S. Census Bureau, "Geographical Mobility," March 2004, accessed online at www.census.gov/prod/2004pubs/p20-549.pdf; and Jim Taylor, "Manifest Destiny," *American Demographics,* September 2004, pp. 29–34; and Bradley Johnson, "Population Migrates South and West," *American Demographics,* April 4, 2005, p. 41.

21. See U.S. Census Bureau, www.census.gov/population/www/estimates/aboutmetro.html, June 2005; "Redefining Where We Live: New Concepts and Definitions of Statistical Areas," *Industrial Relations,* January 2004, pp. 293–294; and "Sales Ablaze in 'Micropolitan' Areas," *Casual Living,* February 2005, pp. 70–74.

22. See "FedEx Rebrands Kinko's," FedEx Press Release, April 27, 2004, accessed at http://fedex.com/us/about/news/update/officeprint.html; Sean Wood, "FedEx Kinko's Plans Keep Multiplying," *Knight Ridder Tribune Business News,* February 14, 2005, p. 1; and information found at www.fedexkinkos.com, July 2005.

23. Nicole Stoops, "Educational Attainment in the United States: 2003," U.S. Census Bureau, June 2004, accessed online at www.census.gov/population/www/socdemo/educ-attn.html.

24. See U.S. Bureau of Labor Statistics, "Labor Force, Employment, and Earnings," p. 416, accessed at http://landview.census.gov/prod/2001pubs/statab/sec13.pdf, June 2004; and U.S. Department of Labor, *Occupational Outlook Handbook,* June 29, 2004, accessed at www.bls.gov/emp/home.htm.

25. See Sabrina Jones, "Hispanics Surpass Blacks as Growth Market for Ads," *Washington Post,* January 5, 2004, p. E.01; Brian Grow, "Hispanic Nation," *BusinessWeek,* March 15, 2004, pp. 59–70; and U.S. Census Bureau reports accessed online at www.census.gov, January 2006.

26. Adapted from William F. Gloede, "The Art of Cultural Correctness," *American Demographics,* November 2004, pp. 27–33.

27. Information accessed at www.rivendellmarketing.com/ngng/ngng_profiles_set.html, June 2005.

28. Ellen Florian, "Queer Eye Makes Over the Economy," *FORTUNE,* February 9, 2004, p. 38. Also see Gillian K. Oakenfull and Timothy B. Greenlee, "Queer Eye for a Gay Guy: Using Market-Specific Symbols in Advertising to Attract Gay Consumers Without Alienating the Mainstream," *Psychology and Marketing,* May 2005, pp. 421+.

29. For these and other examples, see John Fetto, "In Broad Daylight," *American Demographics*, February 2001, pp. 16, 20; Sandra Yin, "Coming Out in Print," *American Demographics,* February 2003, pp. 18–21; Todd Wasserman, "IBM Targets Gay Business Owners," *Adweek,* October 6, 2003, p. 8; Jennifer Gilbert, "Small but Mighty," *Sales & Marketing Management,* January 2004, pp. 30–35; Deborah Vence, "Pride Power," *Marketing News,* September 1, 2004, pp. 1, 13; and Robyn Taylor Parets, "Marketing to Gay Community Can Pay Dividends to Hotels," *Hotel and Motel Management,* March 7, 2005, pp. 6–7; and information from www.306.ibm.com/employment/us/diverse/50/exectask.shtml, July 2005.

30. Information accessed at Volkswagen's Web site (www.vw.com) and www.vsarts.org/programs/vw, June 2004.

31. See Alison Stein Wellner, "The Money in the Middle," *American Demographics,* April 2000, pp. 56–64; and Wellner, "The Wealth Effect," *American Demographics*, January 2003, p. 35.

32. "How Levi Strauss Rekindled the Allure of Brand America," *World Trade,* March 2005, p. 28; and Levi Strauss Press Releases, accessed at www.levistrauss.com on March 18, 2005.

33. Information from "Pollution Prevention Pays," accessed at http://solutions.3m.com/wps/portal/_l/en_US/_s.155/113842/_s.155/115848, June 2005; and "Sustainability Key to UPS's Environmental Initiatives," accessed at www.pressroom.ups.com/mediakits/factsheet/0,2305,1140,00.html, June 2005. For more discussion, see the "Environmentalism" section in Chapter 16.

34. Ann Bednarz, "IBM Has Some Tall RFID Plans," *Network World,* May 2, 2005, pp. 17–18; Jack Neff, "P&G Products to Wear Wire," *Advertising Age,* December 15, 2004, pp. 1, 32; Tom Van Riper, "Retailers Eye RFID Technology to Make Shopping Easier," *Knight Ridder Tribune Business News,* May 23, 2005, p. 1; and information accessed online at www.autoidlabs.org, December 2005.

35. See "U.S. R&D Spending to Rise by 3.6%, Forecast Predicts," *Aerospace Daily & Defense Report,* January 12, 2005, p. 6.

36. For more on online privacy, see Eric Goldman, "The Internet Privacy Fallacy," *Computer and Internet Lawyer,* January 2003, p. 20; "The Spies in Your Computer," *New York Times,* February 18, 2004, p. A18; Amir M. Hormozi, "Cookies and Privacy," *Information Systems Security,* January–February 2005, pp. 51–60; and Alan R. Peslak, "Internet Privacy Policies: A Review and Survey of the FORTUNE 50," *Information Resources Management Journal,* January–March 2005, pp. 29+.

37. Adapted from Rob Walker, "Yellow Fever," *New York Times Magazine,* August 29, 2004, p. 23; with information from Zan Dubin Scott, "Style & Culture; On Wrist Watch; Ribbons, Make Way for Rubber," *Los Angeles Times,* March 20, 2005, p. E.25.

38. "The Growth of Cause Marketing," accessed at www.causemarketingforum.com/page.asp?ID=188, June 2005.

39. For more on Yankelovich Monitor, see www.yankelovich.com/y-monitor.asp.

40. Adapted from Becky Ebenkamp, "Fun/Duty Now, for the Future," *Brandweek,* January 5, 2004, p. 16.

41. Portions of this example are adapted from information in Eileen Daspin, "The End of Nesting," *Wall Street Journal,* May 16, 2003, p. W1. Also see "The Cocoon Cracks Open," *Brandweek,* April 28, 2003, pp. 32–36;

and Dan Lippe, "Gimme Shelter," *Advertising Age,* special report, April 5, 2004, pp. S1–S8.

42. See Paula Szuchman, "Stars, Stripes . . . and Lines," *Wall Street Journal,* May 23, 2003, p. W1.

43. L. A. Chung, "New Greetings of Hybrid Fans: Aloha, LOHAS," *The Mercury News,* April 29, 2005, accessed at www.mercurynews.com/mld/mercurynews/news/columnists/la_chung/11520890.htm.

44. See "Annual Organic Sales in the U.S. Reach 10.8 Billion," *In Business,* September–October 2004, p. 8; Christina Cheddar Berk, "Silk Soy Milk Looks to Strengthen Healthy Image with national Ads," *Wall Street Journal,* April 21, 2004, p. 1; "Latest Organic News," The O'Mama Report, accessed at www.theorganicreport.com, June 2005; and Doug Desjardins, "Latest Natural-Food Trend Going to the Dogs," *DSN Retailing Today,* March 14, 2005, p. 26.

45. Quotes from Myra Stark, "Celestial Season," *Brandweek,* November 16, 1998, pp. 25–26; and Becky Ebankamp, "The Young and Righteous," *Brandweek,* April 5, 2004, p. 18.

46. See Philip Kotler, *Kotler on Marketing* (New York: Free Press, 1999), p. 3; and Kotler, *Marketing Insights from A to Z* (Hoboken, N.J.: John Wiley & Sons, 2003), pp. 23–24.

47. Howard E. Butz Jr. and Leonard D. Goodstein, "Measuring Customer Value: Gaining the Strategic Advantage," *Organizational Dynamics,* Winter 1996, pp. 66–67.

Chapter 4

1. Quotes and extracts from Ellen Byron, "Case by Case: How Coach Won a Rich Purse by Inventing New Uses for Bags," *Wall Street Journal,* November 17, 2004, p. A1. Other information from Pallavi Gogoi, "I Am Woman, Hear Me Shop," *BusinessWeek Online,* February 14, 2005; Pallavi Gogoi, "How a Woman Spends Her Money," *BusinessWeek Online,* February 14, 2005; Lauren Foster, "How Coach Pulled into Luxury's Fast Lane," *Financial Times (London, England),* June 30, 2004, p. 12; and Vicki M. Young, "Coach's Green Spring: Profits Shoot Up 53% in First Quarter," *WWD,* April 27, 2005, p. 89.

2. See Leslie Langnau, "Drowning in Data," *Material Handling Management,* December 2003, p. 22; Rick Mullin, "Dealing with Information Overload," *Chemical and Engineering News,* March 22, 2004, p. 19; and Evan Schuman, "At Wal-Mart, World's Largest Retail Data Warehouse Gets Larger," *eWeek,* October 13, 2004, accessed at www.eweek.com; and Daniel Lyons, "Too Much Information," *Forbes,* December 13, 2004, pp. 110–115.

3. See Philip Kotler, *Marketing Insights from A to Z* (Hoboken, N.J.: John Wiley & Sons, 2003), pp. 80–82.

4. Jennifer Brown, "Pizza Hut Delivers Hot Results Using Data Warehousing," *Computing Canada,* October 17, 2003, p. 24; and "Pizza Hut, Inc.," *Hoover's Company Records,* May 15, 2005, p. 89521.

5. Andy Serwer, "P&G's Covert Operation," *FORTUNE,* September 17, 2001, pp. 42–44. Also see Andrew Crane, "In the Company of Spies: When Competitive Intelligence Gathering Becomes Industrial Espionage," *Business Horizons,* May–June 2005, pp. 233+.

6. Fred Vogelstein and Peter Lewis, "Search and Destroy," *FORTUNE,* May 2, 2005.

7. James Curtis, "Behind Enemy Lines," *Marketing,* May 21, 2001, pp. 28–29. Also see Brian Caufield, "Know Your Enemy," *Business 2.0,* June 2004, p. 89; ad Michael Fielding, "Damage Control: Firms Must Plan for Counterintelligence," *Marketing News,* September 15, 2004, pp. 19–20.

8. For more on research firms that supply marketing information, see Jack Honomichl, "Honomichl 50," special section, *Marketing News,* June 15, 2004, pp. H1–H55. Other information from www.infores.com/public/global/ content/consumernetwork/householdpanel.htm and www.yankelovich.com/monitor_new.asp, July 2005.

9. Example adapted from Douglas McGray, "Babes in R&D Toyland," *Fast Company,* December 2002, p. 46.

10. Adapted from Linda Tischler, "Every Move You Make," *Fast Company,* April 2004, pp. 73–75.

11. Online Research: The Time Has Come," Greenfield Online white paper, accessed at www.greenfieldcentral.com/rcwhitepapers.htm, June 2005. Also see Kate Maddox, "Market Research Charges Online," *B to B,* April 4, 2005, p. 28.

12. This and other examples and quotes in this section, unless otherwise noted, are from "Market Trends: Online Research Growing," accessed at www.greenfieldcentral.com/research_solutions/rsrch_solns_main.htm, June 2003; Noah Shachtman, "Web Enhanced Market Research," *Advertising Age,* June 18, 2001, p. T18; "Cybersurveys Come of Age," *Marketing Research,* Spring 2003, pp. 32–37; Richard Lee, "Stamford, Conn.-Based Market Research Firm Able to Reach Millions," *Knight Ridder Tribune Business News,* May 6, 2004. p. 1. Also see Catherine Arnold, "Not Done Net," *Marketing News,* April 2004, p. 17; and Richard Kottler, "Eight Tips Offer Best Practices for Online MR," *Marketing News,* April 1, 2005, pp. 24–25.

13. For more on Internet privacy, see James R. Hagerty and Dennis K. Berman, "Caught in the Net: New Battleground Over Web Privacy," *Wall Street Journal,* August 27, 2004, p. A1; "The Spies in Your Computer," *Wall Street Journal,* February 18, 2004, p. A18; Susan Llewelyn Leach, "Privacy Lost with the Touch of a Keystroke?" Christian Science Monitor, November 10, 2004, p. 15; and Alan R. Peslak, "Internet Privacy Policies," *Information Resources Management Journal,* January–March 2005, pp. 29+.

14. See Gary H. Anthes, "Smile, You're on Candid Computer," *Computerworld,* December 3, 2001, p. 50; Claire Tristram, "Behind BlueEyes," *Technology Review,* May 2001, p. 32; and "Creating Computers That Know How You Feel," accessed at www.almaden.ibm.com/cs/BlueEyes/index.html, January 2006.

15. For a good discussion, see Deborah L. Vence, "Better! Faster! Cheaper! Pick Any Three. That's Not a Joke," *Marketing News,* February 1, 2004, pp. 1, 31–32.

16. David Harding, David Chiefetz, Scott DeAngelo, and Elizabeth Ziegler, "CRM's Silver Lining," *Marketing Management,* March–April 2004, pp. 27–32; and Ellen Neuborne, "A Second Act of CRM," *Inc.,* March 2005, p. 40.

17. Adapted from information in Daniel Lyons, "Too Much Information," *Forbes,* December 13, 2004, pp. 110–115. Also see Phil Bligh and Doug Turk, "Cashing in on Customer Loyalty," *Customer Relationship Management,* June 2004, p. 48–51; and Suzette Parmley, "When Its Customers Return, A Casino Always Wins Big," *Knight Ridder Business Tribune News,* April 15, 2005, p. 1.

18. Michael Krauss, "At Many Firms, Technology Obscures CRM," *Marketing News,* March 18, 2002, p. 5. Also see Darrell K. Rigby and Dianne Ledingham, "CRM Done Right," *Harvard Business Review,* November 2004, pp. 129; and Barton Goldenberg, "Let's Keep to the High Road," *CRM Magazine,* March 2005, p. 22.

19. See Robert McLuhan, "How to Reap the Benefits of CRM," *Marketing,* May 24, 2001, p. 35; Stewart Deck, "Data Mining," *Computerworld,* March 29, 1999, p. 76; Jason Compton, "CRM Gets Real," *Customer Relationship Management,* May 2004, pp. 11–12; and Ellen Neuborne, "A Second Act of CRM," *Inc.,* March 2005, p. 40.

20. Adapted from information in Ann Zimmerman, "Small Business; Do the Research," *Wall Street Journal,* May 9, 2005, p. R3.

21. For some good advice on conducting market research in a small business, see "Marketing Research . . . Basics 101," accessed at www.onlinewbc.gov/docs/market/mkt_res_basics.html, June 2005; and "Researching Your Market," U.S. Small Business Administration, accessed at www.sba.gov/library/pubs/mt-8.doc, September 2005.

22. Jack Honomichl, "Despite Acquisitions, Firms' Revenue Dips," *Marketing News,* August 13, 2004, pp. H3–H27; and the ACNielsen International Research Web site, accessed at www.acnielsen.com/services/ir/, September 2005.

23. Phone, PC, and other country media stats are from www.nationmaster.com, July 2005.

24. Subhash C. Jain, *International Marketing Management*, 3rd edition (Boston: PWS-Kent, 1990), p. 338. Also see Debra L. Vence, "Leave It to the Experts," *Marketing News,* April 28, 2003, p. 37.

25. Adapted from Richard Behar, "Never Heard of Acxiom? Chances Are It's Heard of You," *FORTUNE,* February 23, 2004, pp. 140–148. Also see D. Murali, "You're Being Watched," *Businessline,* May 16, 2005, p. 1.

26. See "Too Much Information?" *Marketing Management,* January–February 2004, p. 4.

27. Margaret Webb Pressler, "Too Personal to Tell?" *Washington Post,* April 18, 2004, p. F05.

28. "ICC/ESOMAR International Code of Marketing and Social Research Practice," accessed at www.iccwbo.org/home/menu_advert_marketing.asp, June 2005. Also see "Respondent Bill of Rights," accessed at www.cmor.org/what_is_research_rights.htm, July 2005.

29. Catherine Siskos, "In the Service of Guarding Secrets," *Kiplinger's Personal Finance,* February 2003, p. 26; John Schwartz, "Chief Privacy Officers Forge Evolving Corporate Roles," *New York Times,* February 12, 2001, p. C1; Steve Ulfelder, "CPOs: Hot or Not?" *Computerworld,* March 15, 2004, p. 40; and Bob Evans, "Protecting Consumer Data Is Good Business," *InformationWeek,* May 9, 2005, p. 82.

30. Schwartz, "Chief Privacy Officers Forge Evolving Corporate Roles," p. C1.

31. Cynthia Crossen, "Studies Galore Support Products and Positions, but Are They Reliable?" *Wall Street Journal,* November 14, 1991, pp. A1, A9. Also see Allan J. Kimmel, "Deception in Marketing Research and Practice: An Introduction," *Psychology and Marketing,* July 2001, pp. 657–661; and Alvin C. Burns and Ronald F. Bush, *Marketing Research* (Upper Saddle River, N.J.: Prentice Hall, 2005), pp. 63–75.

32. Information accessed at www.casro.org/codeofstandards.cfm#intro, September 2005.

Chapter 5

1. Quotes and other information from Greg Schneider, "Rebels with Disposable Income; Aging Baby Boomers Line Up to Buy High-end Versions of Youthful Indulgences," *Washington Post,* April 27, 2003, p. F1; Ian P. Murphy, "Aided by Research, Harley Goes Whole Hog," *Marketing News,* December 2, 1996, pp. 16, 17; Ted Bolton, "Tattooed Call Letters: The Ultimate Test of Brand Loyalty," accessed online at www.boltonresearch.com, April 2003; Jay Palmer, "Vroom at the Top," *Barron's,* March 29, 2004, pp. 17–18; Chris Woodyard, "Motorcycle Sales Rev Up to Top 1 Million," *USA Today,* January 20, 2005; Rick Barrett, "Harley-Davidson Revs Up Profits," *Knight Ridder Tribune Business News,* January 21, 2005, p. 1; and the Harley-Davidson Web site at www.Harley-Davidson.com, September 2005.

2. World POPClock, U.S. Census Bureau, www.census.gov, July 2005. This Web site provides continuously updated projections of the U.S. and world populations.

3. Brad Weiners, "Getting Inside—Way Inside—Your Customer's Head," *Business 2.0,* April 2003, pp. 54–55.

4. Statistics from Hispanic Fact Pack, supplement to *Advertising Age,* 2004, p. 37; Deborah L. Vance, "Companies Target Lifestyle Segments of Hispanics," *Marketing News,* March 15, 2005, pp. 13–14; Jon Kamman, "1 in 2 New Americans Since 2000 Is Hispanic," *The Arizona Republican,* June 9, 2005, accessed at www.azcentral.com; and U.S. Census Bureau reports accessed online at www.census.gov, January 2006.

5. Deborah L. Vence, "Get a Little Closer: Interest, Competition Grow in Multicultural Market," *Marketing News,* January 15, 2005, pp. 17, 29.

6. Example adapted from Sean Gregory, "Diapers for Fatima," *Time,* January 18, 2005, accessed at www.time.com. Also see www.pg.com/company/who_we_are/diversity/multi/hispanic.jhtml.

7. Louise Witt, "Color Code Red," *American Demographics*, February 2004, pp. 23–25; Vence, "Companies Target Lifestyle Segments," p. 13; and Sonia Alleyne, "Diversity Leader," *Black Enterprise*, March 2005, p. 54.

8. "Facts About Mahogany," accessed at http://pressroom.hallmark.com/mahogany_cards_facts.html, January 2006.

9. See Mike Beirne, "Has This GROUP Been Left BEHIND?" *Brandweek*, March 14, 2005, pp. 33–36.

10. See Steve Jarvis, "Ethnic Sites Draw New Ad Wave," *Marketing News,* August 5, 2002; pp. 4, 6; information accessed at www.BlackPlanet.com, July 2005; and a list of the most popular African-American Web sites at www.blackwebportal.com/web, January 2006.

11. See Vence, "Companies Target Lifestyle Segments," p. 13; and U.S. Census Bureau reports accessed at www.census.gov, September 2005.

12. Jeffrey M. Humphreys, "The Multicultural Economy 2004," *Georgia Business and Economic Conditions*, The Selig Center for Economic Growth, third quarter 2004; Christopher Reynolds, "Far East Moves West," *American Demographics*, October 2004, p. 56; and Mike Troy, "Wal-Mart Unveils Asian Ad Campaign," *DSN Retailing Today,* April 11, 2005, pp. 5–6.

13. Rong-Gong Lin II, "Wal-Mart Pursues Asian Americans," *Los Angeles Times,* April 2, 2005, p. C.

14. See Peter Francese, "Older and Wealthier," *American Demographics*, November 2002, pp. 40–41; Alison Stein Wellner, "The Next 25 Years," *American Demographics*, April 2003, pp. 24–27; and information accessed at http://www.census.gov, April 2005.

15. See D. Allen Kerr, "Where There's Gray, There's Green," *Marketing News,* May 25, 1998, p. 2; Laura Petrecca, "Savvy, Aging Boomers Buy into Pharma Mantra," *Advertising Age*, July 8, 2002, pp. S8–S9; Peter Francese, "Consumers Today," *American Demographics,* April 2003, pp. 28–29; and Robin Goldwyn Blumenthal, "Gray Is Good," *Barron's,* March 22, 2004, p. 37.

16. See Edward Keller and Jonathan Berry, *The Influentials* (New York: The Free Press, 2003); John Battelle, "The Net of Influence," *Business 2.0,* March 2004, p. 70; "Alicia Clegg, "Following the Leaders," *Marketing Week,* September 30, 2004, pp. 47–49; Ronald E. Goldsmith, "The Influentials," *Journal of Product & Brand Management,* 2005, pp. 371–372; and Matthew Creamer, "Study: Go Traditional to Influence Influencers," *Advertising Age,* March 7, 2005, p. 8.

17. Daniel Eisenberg and Laura Bradford, "It's an Ad, Ad, Ad, Ad World," *Time,* September 2, 2002, pp. 38–41; and information accessed at www.bigfatpromo.com/about.asp, July 2005. Also see Thomas Mucha, "Psst. Have You Heard About the Word-of-Mouth Industry?" *Business 2.0,* April 7, 2005, accessed at www.business2.com/b2/web/articles/-0,17863,1046202,00.html.

18. Example adapted from Linda Tischler, "What's the Buzz?" *Fast Company*, May 2004, p. 76. Also see Naomi Kooker, "What's the Buzz," *Boston Business Journal*, October 29, 2004, p. 36; and Hiawatha Bray, "Bill Would Curb Use of Kids in Internet Marketing," *Boston Globe*, April 28, 2005, accessed at www.boston.com.

19. See Sharon Goldman Edry, "No Longer Just Fun and Games," *American Demographics*, May 2001, pp. 36–38; Hillary Chura, "Marketing Messages for Women Fall Short," *Advertising Age*, September 23, 2002, pp. 4, 14–15; and Pallavi Gogoi, "I Am Woman, Hear Me Shop," *BusinessWeek Online*, February 14, 2005, accessed at www.bwonline.com.

20. See Johneen Manning, "Female Em-POWER-Ing Tools, Handywomen Rejoice!" www.GFKA.com, November 2003; Allen P. Roberts Jr., "Barbara K: How I Did It: With Great Power Tools Comes Great Responsibility," *Inc.*, May 2005, pp. 112–114; and information accessed at www.barbarak.com, November 2005.

21. Example drawn from Karl Greenberg, "The Kids Stay in the Future," *Brandweek*, March 31, 2003.

22. Tobi Elkin, "Sony Marketing Aims at Lifestyle Segments," *Advertising Age*, March 18, 2002, pp. 3, 72; and Kenneth Hein, "When Is Enough Enough?" *Brandweek*, December 2, 2002, pp. 26–28.

23. Quotes and examples from http://usa.carhartt.com/rugged/tales.cgi?routine=show, September 2005.

24. See Rebecca Piirto, "Measuring Minds in the 1990s," *American Demographics*, December 1990, pp. 35–39; and Rebecca Piirto, "VALS the Second Time," *American Demographics*, July 1991, p. 6. VALS information and examples accessed at www.sric-bi.com?VALS/types.shtml and www.sric-bi.com/VALS/projects.shtml, August 2005.

25. Information accessed at www.forrester.com/Data/ConsumerTechno, July 2005; and Colin Chung, "Quantitative Research Approach to Understanding How Consumers Adopt Technology-related Products and Services," accessed at www.onetooneinteractive.com/advisor_chung.html, July 2005.

26. Jennifer Aaker, "Dimensions of Measuring Brand Personality," *Journal of Marketing Research*, August 1997, pp. 347–356. Also see Aaker, "The Malleable Self: The Role of Self Expression in Persuasion," *Journal of Marketing Research*, May 1999, pp. 45–57; and Audrey Azoulay and Jean-Noel Kapferer, "Do Brand Personality Scales Really Measure Brand Personality?" *Journal of Brand Management*, November 2003, p. 143.

27. Annetta Miller and Dody Tsiantar, "Psyching Out Consumers," *Newsweek*, February 27, 1989, pp. 46–47. Also see Alison Stein Wellner, "Research on a Shoestring," *American Demographics*, April 2001, pp. 38–39; and Leon G. Schiffman and Leslie L. Kanuk, *Consumer Behavior*, 8th ed. (Upper Saddle River, N.J.: 2004), Chapter 4.

28. See Abraham. H. Maslow, "A Theory of Human Motivation," *Psychological Review*, 50 (1943), pp. 370–396. Also see Maslow, *Motivation and Personality*, 3rd ed. (New York: HarperCollins Publishers, 1987); and Barbara Marx Hubbard, "Seeking Our Future Potentials," *The Futurist*, May 1998, pp. 29–32.

29. Charles Pappas, "Ad Nauseam," *Advertising Age*, July 10, 2000, pp. 16–18.

30. Bob Garfield, "'Subliminal' Seduction and Other Urban Myths," *Advertising Age*, September 18, 2000, pp. 4, 105. Also see "We Have Ways of Making You Think," *Marketing Week*, September 25, 2003, p. 14; and Si Cantwell, "Common Sense; Scrutiny Helps Catch Catchy Ads," *Wilmington Star-News*, April 1, 2004, p. 1B.

31. Rebecca Flass, "'Got Milk?' Takes a Serious Look Inside the Body," *Adweek*, January 27, 2003, p. 5; Katie Koppenhoefer, "MilkPEP Ads Make Big Impact with Hispanics," press release, International Dairy Foods Association, March 3, 2003, accessed at www.idfa.org/news/gotmilk/ 2003/miklpepads.cfm; Jeff Manning and Kevin Lane Keller, "Got Advertising That Works?" *Marketing Management*, January–February 2004, pp. 16–20; and information from www.whymilk.com, September 2005.

32. For a deeper discussion of the buyer decision process, see Philip Kotler and Kevin Lane Keller, *Marketing Management*, 12th ed. (Upper Saddle River, N.J.: 2006), pp. 191–203.

33. Duglas Pruden and Terry G. Vavra, ""Controlling the Grapevine," *Marketing Management*, July–August 2004, pp. 25–30.

34. See Leon Festinger, *A Theory of Cognitive Dissonance* (Stanford, CA: Stanford University Press, 1957); Schiffman and Kanuk, *Consumer Behavior*, pp. 219–220; Patti Williams and Jennifer L. Aaker, "Can Mixed Emotions Peacefully Coexist?" March 2002, pp. 636–649; Adam Ferrier, "Young Are Not Marketing Savvy; They're Suckers," *B&T Weekly*, October 22, 2004, p. 13; and "Cognitive Dissonance and the Stability of Service Quality Perceptions," *The Journal of Services Marketing*, 2004, pp. 433+.

35. The following discussion draws from the work of Everett M. Rogers. See his *Diffusion of Innovations*, 5th ed. (New York: Free Press, 2003). Also see Eric Waarts, Yvonne M. van Everdingen, and Jos van Hillegersberg, "The Dynamics of Factors Affecting the Adoption of Innovations," *Journal of Product Innovation Management*, November 2002, pp. 412–423; Chaun-Fong Shih and Alladi Venkatesh, "Beyond Adoption: Development and Application of a Use-Diffusion Model," *Journal of Marketing*, January 2004, pp. 59–72; and Richard R. Nelson, Alexander Peterhansl, and Bhaven Sampat, "Why and How Innovations Get Adopted: A Tale of Four Models," *Industrial and Corporate Change*, October 2004, pp. 679–699.

36. See Kate Macarthur, "Teflon Togs Get $40 Million Ad Push," *Advertising Age*, April 8, 2002, p. 3; "Neat Pants for Sloppy People," *Consumer Reports: Publisher's Edition Including Supplemental Guides*, May 2003, p. 10; "Sales Makes the Wearables World Go 'Round," *Wearables Business*, April 24, 2004, p. 22; and Rosamaria Mancini, *HFN*, May 16, 2005, p. 17.

37. Patrick J. Robinson, Charles W. Faris, and Yoram Wind, *Industrial Buying Behavior and Creative Marketing* (Boston: Allyn & Bacon, 1967). Also see James C. Anderson and James A. Narus, *Business Market Management*, 2nd ed. (Upper Saddle River, N.J.: 2004), Chapter 3.

38. See "BJ's Knows . . . Our System Is Their Solution," *Insights*, March 2002, p. 1; "Soap, Detergent Maker to Open Its First Franchise in Port of Stockton, California," *Knight Ridder Tribune Business News*, September 9, 2003, p. 1; and information accessed online at www.chemstation.com, December 2005.

39. Robinson, Faris, and Wind, *Industrial Buying Behavior*, p. 14.

40. Kate Maddox, "#1 Hewlett-Packard Co.: www.hp.com," *BtoB*, August 11, 2003, p. 1; and "Great Web Sites: www.hp.com; *BtoB Online*, September 13, 2004, accessed at www.btobonline.com/article.cms?articleId=21878.

41. Demir Barlas, "E-Procurement: Steady Value," *Line56.com*, January 4, 2005, accessed at www.line56.com.

42. Michael A. Verespej, "E-Procurement Explosion," *Industry Week*, March 2002, pp. 25-28.

Chapter 6

1. See Veronica MacDonald, "Soaps and Detergents: Going the World Over to Clean," *Chemical Week*, January 26, 2005, pp. 21–23; and information accessed at www.pg.com and www.tide.com, January 2006.

2. Based on information found in Steven Gray, "How Applebee's Is Making It Big in Small Towns," *Wall Street Journal,* August 2, 2004, B1; and Applebee's International, Inc., *Hoover's Company Records,* Austin, June 1, 2005, p. 13585.

3. See "Customer Experience and 'Small-Marts,'" January 28, 2005, accessed at http://learned.typepad.com/learned_on_women/2005/01/customer_experi.html; Tim Craig, "Home Depot 'Lite' Gets It Right," *DSN Retailing Today,* May 19, 2003, p. 6; Marianne Rohrlich, "Manhattanites Will Soon Find Depots Close to Home," *New York Times,* April 15, 2004, p. F10; and Doug Desjardins, "Smaller Format Rolls Dice with Multiple Openings in Vegas," *DSN Retailing Today,* February 28, 2005, p. 46.

4. See Fara Warner, "Nike Changes Strategy on Women's Apparel," *New York Times,* May 16, 2005, accessed at www.nytimes.com.

5. Information accessed at www.ivillage.com and www.oxygen.com, July 2005.

6. Information accessed at www.neimanmarcus.com/store/sitelets/incircle/index.jhtml, July, 2005.

7. Debbie Howell, "Another Day, Another Dollar," *Chain Store Age,* Spring 2005, pp. 8–10; Robert Berner, "Out-Discounting the Discounter," *BusinessWeek,* May 10, 2004, pp. 78–79; and "Family Dollar Stores, Inc.," *Hoover's Company Records,* June 1, 2005, p. 129730; and Ann Zimmerman, "The Almighty Dollar Store," *Wall Street Journal: The Classroom Edition,* March 2005, accessed at www.wsjclassroomedition.com/archive/05mar/econ_dollarstore.htm.

8. Portions adapted from Linda Tischler, "How Pottery Barn Wins with Style," *Fast Company,* June 2003, pp. 106–113; with information from www.potterybarn.com; www.potterybarnkids.com, and www.pbteen.com, July 2005.

9. See Maureen Wallenfang, "Appleton, Wis,—Area Dealers See Increase in Moped Sales," *Knight Ridder Tribune Business News,* August 15, 2004, p. 1; and Honda's Web site at www.powersports.honda.com/scooters, July 2005.

10. Information from www.kodak.com, July 2005.

11. See Jennifer Ordonez, "Fast-Food Lovers, Unite!" *Newsweek,* May 24, 2004, p. 56.

12. Portions adapted from Alan T. Saracevic, "Author Plumbs Bottomless Depth of Mac Worship," December 12, 2004, accessed at www.sfgate.com. Definition from http://www.urbandictionary.com/define.php?term=Macolyte&r=d, August 2005.

13. Based on PRIZM cluster information accessed at www.claritas.com, January 2006.

14. John Fetto, American Neighborhoods' First Page," *American Demographics,* July–August 2003, p. 34.

15. Example from http://www.clusterbigip1.claritas.com/claritas/Default.jsp?main=2, accessed April 2005.

16. Information from http://home.americanexpress.com/home/mt_personal. shtml, August, 2005.

17. For more on segmenting business markets, see Turan Senguder, "An Evaluation of Consumer and Business Segmentation Approaches," *Journal of the Academy of Business,* March 2003, pp. 618–624; and James C. Anderson and James A. Narus, *Business Market Management,* 2nd ed. (Upper Saddle River, N.J.: Prentice Hall, 2004), pp. 45–52.

18. See Arundhati Parmar, "Global Youth United," *Marketing News,* October 28, 2002, pp. 1, 49; "Teen Spirit," *Global Cosmetic Industry,* March 2004, p. 23; Johnnie L. Roberts, "World Tour," *Newsweek,* June 6, 2005, pp. 34–36; and the MTV Worldwide Web site, www.mtv.com/mtvinternational.

19. See Michael Porter, *Competitive Advantage* (New York: Free Press, 1985), pp. 4–8, 234–236. For more recent discussions, see Stanley Slater and Eric Olson, "A Fresh Look at Industry and Market Analysis," *Business Horizons,* January–February 2002, pp. 15–22; Kenneth Sawka and Bill Fiora, "The Four Analytical Techniques Every Analyst Must Know: Porter's Five Forces Analysis," *Competitive Intelligence Magazine,* May–June 2003, p. 57; and Philip Kotler and Kevin Lane Keller, *Marketing Management,* 12th ed. (Upper Saddle River, N.J.: 2006), pp. 342–343.

20. Nina Munk, "Why Women Find Lauder Mesmerizing," *FORTUNE,* May 25, 1998, pp. 97–106; Christine Bittar, "New Faces, Same Name," *Brandweek,* March 11, 2002, pp. 28–34; Robin Givhan, "Estee Lauder, Sending a Message in a Bottle," *Washington Post,* April 26, 2004, p. C.01; and information accessed at www.elcompanies.com, www.stila.com, and www.macmakeup.com, July 2005.

21. Peter Burrows, "How to Milk an Apple," *BusinessWeek,* February, 3, 2003, p. 44; and Josh Quittner, "Steve Jobs," *Time,* April 26, 2004, p. 75; and Jim Dalrymple, "Apple Desktop Market Share on the Rise: Will the Mac Mini, iPod Help?" *Macworld,* March 20, 2005, accessed at www.macworld.com/news/2005/03/20/marketshare/index.php.

22. See Gerry Khermouch, "Call it the Pepsi Blue Generation," *BusinessWeek,* February 3, 2003, p. 96; Kathleen Sampey, "Sweet on Sierra Mist," *Adweek,* February 2, 2004, p. 20; and Nat Ives, "Mountain Dew Double-Dose for Times Square Passers-By," *New York Times,* April 8, 2004, p. C9.

23. Gwendolyn Bounds, "How an Artist Fell into a Profitable Online Card Business," *Wall Street Journal,* December 21, 2004, p. B1.

24. For a good discussion of mass customization and relationship building, see Don Peppers and Martha Rogers, *Managing Customers Relationships: A Strategic Framework* (Hoboken, N.J.: John Wiley & Sons, 2004), Chapter 10.

25. See Faith Keenan, "A Mass Market of One," *BusinessWeek,* December 2, 2002, pp. 68–72; and information accessed at http://shop.mms.com/customized/index.asp?UID=, August 2005.

26. Adapted from information found in Mark Tatge, "Red Bodies, Black Ink," *Forbes,* September 18, 2000, p. 114; "Oshkosh Truck Corporation," *Hoover's Company Profiles,* Austin, June 1, 2005, p. 14345; and information accessed at www.oshkoshtruckcorporation.com, November 2005.

27. Sony A. Grier, "The Federal Trade Commission's Report on the Marketing of Violent Entertainment to Youths: Developing Policy-Tuned Research," *Journal of Public Policy and Marketing,* Spring 2001, pp. 123–132; Deborah L. Vence, "Marketing to Minors Still Under Careful Watch," *Marketing News,* March 31, 2003, pp. 5–6; Susan Linn, *Consuming Kids: The Hostile Takeover of Childhood* (New York: The New Press, 2004); and Suzy Bashford, "Time to Take More Responsibility?" *Marketing,* May 11, 2005, pp. 32–36.

28. See Michelle Singletary, "Don't Get Baited by These Scams," *Washington Post,* February 5, 2004, p. 1; and information at the FBI's Internet Fraud Complaint Center Web site, www. ifccfbi.gov, July 2005.

29. Jack Trout, "Branding Can't Exist Without Positioning," *Advertising Age,* March 14, 2005, p. 28.

30. Adapted from a positioning map prepared by students Brian May, Josh Payne, Meredith Schakel, and Bryana Sterns, University of North Carolina, April 2003. SUV sales data furnished by www.WardsAuto.com, June 2005. Price data from www.edmunds.com, June 2005.

31. See Bobby J. Calder and Steven J. Reagan, "Brand Design," in Dawn Iacobucci, ed. *Kellogg on Marketing* (New York: John Wiley & Sons, 2001) p. 61. The Mountain Dew example is from Alice M. Tybout and

Brian Sternthal, "Brand Positioning," in Iacobucci, ed., *Kellogg on Marketing*, p. 54.

Chapter 7

1. Extracts adapted from Betsy McKay and Cynthia Cho, "Water Works: How FIJI Brand Got Hip to Sip," *Wall Street Journal*, August 16, 2004, p. B1; and information found at www.fijiwater.com, July 2005. Also see Kate Macarthur, "Drink Your Fruits, Veggies: Water's the New Fitness Fad," *Advertising Age*, January 3, 2005, p. 4.

2. Adapted from an example in B. Joeseph Pine II and James H. Gilmore, "Trade in Ads for Experiences," *Advertising Age*, September 27, 2004, p. 36; with information from www.americangirlplace.com, July 2005.

3. See "The Celebrity 100," *Forbes*, accessed at www.forbes.com, June 2005; Siddhartha Finch "Tiger Woods Signs Long-term Deal with Apple Computer as Mac OS X 'Tiger' Spokesperson," *Mac Daily News*, April 1, 2005, accessed at www.macdailynews.com; and www.tigerwoods.com, accessed March 2005.

4. See Daniel Roth, "The Trophy Life," *FORTUNE*, April 19, 2004, p. 70; Donald Trump, *Trump: The Art of the Comeback* (New York: Random House, 1997); Adam Lashinsky, "For Trump, Fame Is Easier Than FORTUNE," *FORTUNE*, February 23, 2004, p. 38; Daniel Roth, "The Trophy Life," *FORTUNE*, April 19, 2004, pp. 70–84; Ryan Underwood, "Bring on the Clown," *Fast Company*, January 2005, p. 28; and "New Trump Products on the Market," *Knight Ridder Tribune Business News*, February 26, 2005, p. 1.

5. For more on marketing places, see Philip Kotler, Donald Haider, and Irving J. Rein, *Marketing Places* (New York: Free Press, 2002). Examples information found in Steve Dougherty, "In a Cold Country, the Nights Are Hot," *New York Times*, December 19, 2004, sect. 5, p. 1; and at www.TravelTex.com, www.michigan.org, and www.iloveny.state.ny.us, January 2006.

6. Accessed online at www.social-marketing.org/aboutus.html, January 2006.

7. See Alan R. Andreasen, Rob Gould, and Karen Gutierrez, "Social Marketing Has a New Champion," *Marketing News*, February 7, 2000, p. 38. Also see Philip Kotler, Ned Roberto, and Nancy Lee, *Social Marketing: Improving the Quality of Life*, 2nd ed. (Thousand Oaks, Calif.: Sage Publications, 2002); and www.social-marketing.org, August 2005.

8. Quotes and definitions from Philip Kotler, *Kotler on Marketing* (New York: Free Press, 1999), p. 17; and www.asq.org, December 2005.

9. See Roland T. Rust, Anthony J. Zahorik, and Timothy L. Keiningham, "Return on Quality (ROQ): Making Service Quality Financially Accountable," *Journal of Marketing*, April 1995, pp. 58–70; Roland T. Rust, Christine Moorman, and Peter R. Dickson, "Getting Return on Quality: Revenue Expansion, Cost Reduction, or Both?" *Journal of Marketing*, October 2002, pp. 7–24; and Roland T. Rust, Katherine N. Lemon, and Valarie A. Zeithaml, "Return on Marketing: Using Customer Equity to Focus Marketing Strategy," *Journal of Marketing*, January 2004, p. 109.

10. Example adapted from Bruce Nussbaum, "The Power of Design," *BusinessWeek*, May 17, 2004, pp. 86–94.

11. Based on Adam Horowitz, et. al., "101 Dumbest Moments in Business," *Business 2.0*, January–February 2005, p. 104; and Ben DeLaney, "Kryptonite on Level Ground Six Months After U-Lock Publicity Crisis," *Bicycle Retailer and Industry News*, April 1, 2005, p. 25.

12. See Kate Fitzgerald, "Packaging Is the Capper," *Advertising Age*, May 5, 2003, p. 22.

13. Based on "Hartz's Zippered Bags: Perched for Success," *Packaging Digest*, March 2005, p. 44.

14. Based on Thomas J. Ryan, "Labels Grow Up," *Apparel*, February 2005, pp. 26–29.

15. Bro Uttal, "Companies That Serve You Best," *FORTUNE*, December 7, 1987, p. 116; and American Customer Satisfaction Index ratings accessed at www.theacsi.org, July 2005.

16. Example adapted from Michelle Higgins, "Pop-Up Sales Clerks: Web Sites Try the Hard Sell," *Wall Street Journal*, April 15, 2004, p. D1.

17. Information accessed online at www.marriott.com, December 2005.

18. Information about Colgate's product lines accessed at www.colgate.com/app/Colgate/US/Corp/Products.cvsp, August 2005.

19. See "McAtlas Shrugged," *Foreign Policy*, May–June 2001, pp. 26–37; and Philip Kotler and Kevin Lane Keller, *Marketing Management*, 12th ed. (Upper Saddle River, N.J.: Prentice Hall, 2006), pp. 290–291.

20. David C. Bello and Morris. B. Holbrook, "Does an Absence of Brand Equity Generalize Across Product Classes?" *Journal of Business Research*, October 1995, p. 125; and Scott Davis, *Brand Asset Management: Driving Profitable Growth Through Your Brands* (San Francisco: Jossey-Bass, 2000). Also see Kevin Lane Keller, *Building, Measuring, and Managing Brand Equity*, 2nd ed. (Upper Saddle River, N.J.: Prentice Hall, 2003), Chapter 2; and Kusum Ailawadi, Donald R. Lehman, and Scott A. Neslin, "Revenue Premium as an Outcome Measure of Brand Equity," *Journal of Marketing*, October 2003, pp. 1–17.

21. "The 100 Top Brands," *BusinessWeek*, August 1, 2005, pp. 90–94.

22. See Roland Rust, Katherine Lemon, and Valarie Zeithaml "Return on Marketing: Using Customer Equity to Focus Marketing Strategy," *Journal of Marketing*, January 2004, p. 109.

23. See Scott Davis, *Brand Asset Management*, 2nd ed. (San Francisco: Jossey-Bass, 2002). For more on brand positioning, see Philip Kotler and Kevin Lane Keller, *Marketing Management*, 12th ed. (Upper Saddle River, N.J.: Prentice Hall, 2006), Chapter 10.

24. See Jack Neff, "P&G Bets $100 Million on Crest Brand Plan," *Advertising Age*, March 22, 2004, pp. 5, 33; and http://crest.com/home/index.jsp, August 2005.

25. Example adapted from Matthew Boyle, "Brand Killers," *FORTUNE*, August 11, 2003, pp. 89–100.

26. See Sue Stock, "Grocer's Expand Private-Label Marketing Share," *Knight Ridder Tribune Business News*, May 26, 2005, p. 1; Sandra Yin, "Shelf Life," *American Demographics*, March 2004, p. 16; and Debbie Howell, "Dollars Add Up with Name-brand, Private-label Mix," *DNS Retailing*, March 14, 2005, p. 13.

27. William Wilkie, "Marketing Research and Public Policy: The Case of Slotting Fees," *Journal of Public Policy and Marketing*, Fall 2002, pp. 275–189; Margaret Webb Pressler, "Shelf Game; When Stores Force Makers to Pay Them Fees, You Lose," *Washington Post*, January 18, 2004, p. F5; and Dania Akkad, "Grocery Stores' Game of Slots," *Knight Ridder Tribune Business News*, March 14, 2005, p. 1.

28. Jay Sherman, "Nick Puts Muscle Behind everGirl," *TelevisionWeek*, January 5, 2004, p. 3; and Stephanie Kang, "Can Foam Feet and 'Darth Tater' Restore Movie-toy Sales?" *Wall Street Journal*, March 14, 2005, p. B1.

29. See Laura Petrecca, "Corporate Brands Put Licensing in the Spotlight," *Advertising Age*, June 14, 1999, p. 1; and Bob Vavra, "The Game of the Name," *Supermarket Business*, March 15, 2001, pp. 45–46; Jim Cioletti, "Making the Brand: Behind the Badge," *Beverage World*, December 15, 2004, pp. 36–37.

30. Laura Liebeck, "Two Tastes Can Be Better Than One," *Retail Merchandiser*, February 2005, p. 20.

31. Wendy Zellner, "Your New Banker?" *BusinessWeek*, February 7, 2005, pp. 28–31.

32. Gabrielle Solomon, "Co-Branding Alliances: Arranged Marriages Made by Marketers," *FORTUNE*, October 12, 1998, p. 188; "Martha Stewart, Kmart Continue Partnership," *Gourmet News*, June 2004, p. 14; and Bradford McKee, "Move Over, Martha Stewart," *New York Times*, February 17, 2005, p. F8.

33. Based on information from Kate McArthur, "Cannibalization a Risk as Coke Diet Brand Tally Grows to Sever," *Advertising Age*, March 28, 2005, pp. 3, 123; and "Coca-Cola Zero Pops into Stores Today," *Atlanta Business Chronicle*, June 13, 2005, accessed at http://atlanta.bizjournals.com/atlanta/stories/2005/06/13/daily7.html.

34. For more on the use of line and brand extensions and consumer attitudes toward them, see Subramanian Balachander and Sanjoy Ghose, "Reciprocal Spillover Effects: A Strategic Benefit of Brand Extensions," *Journal of Marketing*, January 2003, pp. 4–13; Eva Martinez and Leslie de Chernatony, "The Effect of Brand Extension Strategies Upon Brand Image," *Journal of Consumer Marketing*, 2004, p. 39; and Devon DeiVecchio and Danile Smith, "Brand-Extension Price Premiums: The Effect of Perceived Fit and Extension Product Category Risk," *Journal of Academy of Marketing Science*, Spring 2005, pp. 184–192.

35. "Top 200 Megabrands," accessed at www.adage.com, June 2005.

36. Stephen Cole, "Value of the Brand," *CA Magazine*, May 2005, pp. 39–40.

37. See Kevin Lane Keller, "The Brand Report Card," *Harvard Business Review*, January 2000, pp. 147–157; Keller, *Strategic Brand Management*, pp. 766–767; and David A. Aaker, "Even Brands Need Spring Cleaning," *Brandweek*, March 8, 2004, pp. 36–40.

38. See CIA, *The World Factbook*, accessed at www.cia.gov/cia/publications/factbook/geos/us.html, July 2005; *International Trade Statistics 2004*, World Trade Organization, p. 23, accessed at http://www.wto.org, July 2005; and information from the Bureau of Labor Statistics, www.bls.gov, accessed April 2005.

39. Adapted from information in Leonard Berry and Neeli Bendapudi, "Clueing in Customers," *Harvard Business Review*, February 2003, pp. 100–106 and information accessed at www.mayoclinic.org, August 2005.

40. See James L. Heskett, W. Earl Sasser Jr., and Leonard A. Schlesinger, *The Service Profit Chain: How Leading Companies Link Profit and Growth to Loyalty, Satisfaction, and Value* (New York: Free Press, 1997); Heskett, Sasser, and Schlesinger, *The Value Profit Chain: Treat Employees Like Customers and Customers Like Employees* (New York: Free Press, 2003); and Garry A. Gelade and Stephen Young, "Test of the Service Profit Chain Model in the Retail Banking Sector," *Journal of Occupational and Organizational Psychology*, March 2005, pp. 1–22.

41. Jeremy B. Dann, "How to Find a Hit as Big as Starbucks," *Business 2.0*, May 2004, pp. 66–68.

42. Based on Matthew Boyle, "The Wegmans Way," *FORTUNE*, January 24, 2005, pp. 62–68.

43. For discussions of service quality, see Valerie A. Zeithaml, A. Parasuraman, and Leonard L. Berry, *Delivering Quality Service: Balancing Customer Perceptions and Expectations* (New York: The Free Press, 1990); Valerie A. Zeithaml, Leonard L. Berry, and A. Parasuraman, "The Behavioral Consequences of Service Quality," *Journal of Marketing*, April 1996, pp. 31–46; Y. H. Hung, M. L. Huang, and K. S. Chen, "Service Quality Evaluation by Service Quality Performance Matrix," *Total Quality Management & Business Excellence*, January 2003, pp. 79–89; and Bo Edvardsson, "Service Quality: Beyond Cognitive Assessment," *Managing Service Quality*, vol. 2, no. 2, pp. 127–131.

44. See "UPS 4th Quarter Shows 10% Revenue Gain," accessed at http://pressroom.ups.com, April 2005.

45. See "Jury Awards in Product Liability Cases Increasing in Recent Years," *Chemical Market Reporter*, February 12, 2001, p. 5; Carrie Coolidge, "The Last Rung," *Forbes*, January 12, 2004, p. 52; "Ford Motor Co.: Jury Orders Auto Maker to Pay $369 in Explorer Case," *Wall Street Journal*, June 4, 2004, p. 1; and Lanny R. Berke, "Design for Safety," *Machine Design*, February 17, 2005, pp. 48–49.

46. See Philip Cateora, *International Marketing*, 8th ed. (Homewood, Ill.: Irwin, 1993), p. 270; David Fairlamb, "One Currency—But 15 Economies," *BusinessWeek*, December 31, 2001, p. 59; and www.walkabouttravelgear.com/elect.htm, December 2005.

47. Information accessed online at www.deutsche-bank.com, July 2005.

48. Information accessed online at www.interpublic.com and www.mccann.com, July 2005.

49. See "Wal-Mart International Operations," accessed at www.walmartstores.com, July 2005; "2005 Global Powers of Retailing," *Stores*, January 2005, accessed at www.stores.org; and information accessed at www.carrefour.com/english/groupecarrefour/profil.jsp, July 2005.

Chapter 8

1. Quotes and other information in this Apple story from Terry Semel, "Steve Jobs: Perpetual Innovation Machine," *Time*, April 18, 2005, p. 78; Steve Maich, "Nowhere to Go But Down," *Maclean's*, May 9, 2005, p. 32; Brent Schlender, "How Big Can Apple Get," *FORTUNE*, February 21, 2005, pp. 67–76; Jim Dalrymple, "Apple's Uphill Climb," *Macworld*, June 2005, p. 16; and Paul Sloan and Paul Kaihla, "What's Next for Apple," *Business 2.0*, April 2005; Peter Burrows and Andrew Park, "Apple's Bold Swim Downstream," *BusinessWeek*, January 24, 2005, p. 32; and Bruce Nussbaum, Get Creative!" *BusinessWeek*, August 1, 2005, pp. 61–70.

2. For these and other examples, see Simon Romero, "Once Proudly Carried, and Now Mere Carrion," *New York Times*, November 22, 2001, p. G5; Kelly Carroll, "Satellite Telephony: Not for the Consumer," *Telephony*," March 4, 2002, p. 17; and Eric Almquist, Martin Kon, and Wolfgang Bock, "The Science of Demand," *Marketing Management*, March–April 2004, pp. 20–26.

3. See Alison Stein Wellner, "The New Science of Focus Groups," *American Demographics*. March 2003, p. 30; Kevin J. Clancy and Peter C. Krieg, "Surviving Innovation," *Marketing Management*, March–April 2003, pp. 14–20; "Market Research: So What's the Big Idea?" *Marketing Week*, March 11, 2004, p. 37; and Deborah Ball, et al., "Just What You Need!" *Wall Street Journal*, October 28, 2004, p. B1.

4. Information and examples from Gary Slack, "Innovations and Idiocities," *Beverage World*, November 15, 1998, p. 122; Robert M. McMath and Thom Forbes, *What Were They Thinking? Money-Saving, Time-Saving, Face-Saving Marketing Lessons You Can Learn from Products That Flopped* (New York: Times Business, 1999), various pages; Melissa Master, "Spectacular Failures," *Across the Board*, March–April 2001, p. 24; and www.newproductworks.com/npw_difference/ product_collection.html, August 2005.

5. Joel Berg, "Product Development Look for Children's Insight," *Central Penn Business*, October 15, 2004, p. 3.

6. Based on quotes and information from Robert D. Hof, "The Power of Us," *BusinessWeek*, June 20, 2005, pp. 74–82.

7. Information accessed online at www.avon.com, August 2005.

8. "Business: The Rise of the Creative Consumer; the Future of Innovation," *The Economist*, March 12, 2005, p. 75.

9. Ibid., p. 75.

10. Robert Gray, "Not Invented Here," *Marketing,* May 6, 2004, pp. 34–37.

11. For examples, see Pete Engardio and Bruce Einhorn, "Outsourcing Innovation," *BusinessWeek,* March 21, 2005, pp. 84–94.

12. See Philip Kotler, *Kotler on Marketing* (New York, NY: The Free Press, 1999), pp. 43-44; and Judy Lamont, "Idea Management: Everyone's an Innovator, *KM World,* November–December 2004, pp. 14–16.

13. See "DaimlerChrysler Presents California with Three F-Cell Fuel Cell Vehicles," *Fuel Cell Today,* June 1, 2005, accessed at www.fuelcelltoday.com; and Steven Ashley, "On the Road to Fuel-Cell Cars," *Scientific American,* March 1, 2005, p. 62.

14. Becky Ebenkamp, "It's Like Cheers and Jeers, Only for Brands," *Brankweek,* March 19, 2001; Ebenkamp, "The Focus Group Has Spoken," *Brandweek,* April 23, 2001, p. 24; and information furnished by Mark Sneider, General Manager, AcuPoll, October 2004.

15. Examples adapted from those found in Emily Nelson, "Focus Groupies: P&G Keeps Cincinnati Busy with All Its Studies—While Her Sons Test Old Spice, Linda Geil Gets Swabbed," *Wall Street Journal,* January 24, 2002, p. A1; Carol Matlack, "The Vuitton Machine," *BusinessWeek,* March 22, 2004, pp. 98–102; and Brendan Koerner, "For Every Sport, A Super Sock," *New York Times,* March 27, 2005, p. 3.2.

16. Judann Pollack, "Baked Lays," *Advertising Age,* June 24, 1996, p. S2; Dean Takahashi, "Nokia's N-Gage Shakes Up the Gaming Market," *Electronic Business,* April 1, 2003, p. 28; and Karen Robinson-Jacobs, "PepsiCo to Market Fruit Flavored Soft Drink, *Knight Ridder Tribune Business News*, March 26, 2005, p. 1

17. This and other examples can be found in Robert McMath, "To Test or Not to Test," *Advertising Age,* June 1998, p. 64; and "Skipping Research a Major Error," *Marketing News,* March 4, 2002, p. 50. For more on test marketing, see Philip Kotler and Kevin Lane Keller, *Marketing Management,* 12th edition (Upper Saddle River, N.J.: Prentice Hall, 2006), pp. 653–655.

18. Jack Neff, "Is Testing the Answer?" *Advertising Age,* July 9, 2001, p. 13; and Dale Buss, "P&G's Rise," *Potentials,* January 2003, pp. 26–30.

19. See Jack Neff, "New SpinBrush Line Backed by $30 Million," *Advertising Age,* September 9, 2002, p. 36; and Jenn Abelson, "Firms Likely to Shed Some Products," *Knight Ridder Tribune Business News,* June 22, 1005, p.1.

20. For a review of research on new-product development, see Rajesh Sethi, "New Product Quality and Product Development Teams," *Journal of Marketing,* April 2000, pp. 1–14; Sandra Valle and Lucia Avella, "Cross-Functionality and Leadership of the New Product Development Teams," *European Journal of Innovation Management,* 2003, pp. 32–47; Z. Ayag, "An Integrated Approach to Evaluating Conceptual Design Alternatives in a New Product Development Environment," *International Journal of Production Research*, February 15, 2005, pp 27–37; and Ken Kono, "Planning Makes Perfect," *Marketing Management,* April 2005, pp. 31–35. For an interesting view of an alternative new product development process, see Bruce Nussbaum, "The Power of Design," *BusinessWeek,* May 17, 2004, pp. 86–94.

21. See Michael Arndt, "3M: A Lab for Growth," *BusinessWeek,* January 21, 2002, pp. 50–51; Tim Studt, "3M—Where Innovation Rules," *R&D,* April 2003, pp. 20–24; Tim Stevens, "3M Reinvents Its Innovation Process," *Research Technology Management,* March–April 2004, p. 3; Michael Arndt and Diane Brady, "3M's Rising Star," *BusinessWeek,* April 12, 2004, pp. 62+; and "A Century of Innovation," accessed at www.3m.com/about3m/innovation/index.jhtml, January 2006.

22. Kevin Clancy and Peter Krieg, "Product Life Cycle: A Dangerous Idea", *Brandweek*, March 1, 2004, p. 26.

23. Laurie Freeman, "Study: Leading Brands Aren't Always Enduring," *Advertising Age,* February 28, 2000, p. 26. Also see, Veronica MacDonald, "Soaps and Detergents: Going the World Over to Clean," *Chemical Week,* January 6, 2005, pp. 21–24.

24. This definition is based on one found in Bryan Lilly and Tammy R. Nelson, "Fads: Segmenting the Fad-Buyer Market," *Journal of Consumer Marketing,* vol. 20, no. 3, 2003, pp. 252–265.

25. See "Scooter Fad Fades, as Warehouses Fill and Profits Fall," *Wall Street Journal,* June 14, 2001, p. B4; Katya Kazakina, "Toy Story: Yo-Yos Make a Big Splash," *Wall Street Journal,* April 11, 2003, p. W-10; and Robert Johnson, "A Fad's Father Seeks a Sequel," *New York Times,* May 30, 2004, p. 3.2.

26. Youngme Moon, "Break Free from the Product Life Cycle," *Harvard Business Review,* May 2005, pp. 87–94.

27. These and other uses found in "Always Another Use," www.wd40.com/Brands/wd40.cfm, July 2005.

28. For a more comprehensive discussion of marketing strategies over the course of the product life cycle, see Philip Kotler and Kevin Lane Keller, *Marketing Management*, 12th ed. (Upper Saddle River, N.J.: Prentice Hall, 2006), pp. 321–335.

Chapter 9

1. Thomas T. Nagle and Reed K. Holden, *The Strategy and Tactics of Pricing,* 4th ed. (Upper Saddle River, N.J.: Prentice Hall, 2005), Chapter 1.

2. Extracts and quotes from Nanette Byrnes, "Toys 'R' Us: Beaten at Its Own Game, *BusinessWeek,* March 29, 2004, pp. 89–90. Additional information from "Toys 'R' Us, Inc.," *Hoovers Company Records,"* Austin, July 15, 2005, p. 11495; Clayton M. Christensen and Scott D. Anthony, "Toys 'R' History," *Wall Street Journal,* August 31, 2004, p. B4; and Joan Verdon, "Toys 'R' Us Closes Deal to Go Private," *Knight Ridder Tribune Business News,* July 22, 2005, p. 1.

3. George Mannes, "The Urge to Unbundle," *Fast Company,* February 27, 2005, pp. 23–24.

4. Linda Tischler, "The Price is Right," *Fast Company*, November 2003, pp. 83–91.

5. Paul S. Hunt, "Seizing the Fourth P," *Marketing Management,* May–June 2005, pp. 40–44.

6. John Tayman, "The Six-Figure Steal," *Business 2.0,* June 2005, pp. 148–150.

7. See Claudia H. Deutsch, "Name Brands Exbrace Some Less-Well-Off Kinfolk," *New York Times,* June 24, 2005, p. C7.

8. See "Hi-Lo Versus EDLP: We Want Both!" *Retail World,* August 18, 2003, p. 30; Laura Heller, "EDLP Has Only Scratched the Surface," *DSN Retailing Today,* January 26, 2004, pp. 35–36; Lucia Moses, "Giant Eagle Latest to Go EDLP Route," *Supermarket News,* November 8, 2004, p. 1; and Supermarkets Take New Tack in Battle Against EDLP," *DSN Retailing Today,* May 23, 2005, pp. 7–8.

9. Erin Stout, "Keep Them Coming Back for More," *Sales & Marketing Management,* February 2002, pp. 51–52. Also see Andreas Hinterhuber, "Towards Value-Based Pricing—An Integrative Framework for Decision Making," *Industrial Marketing Management,* November 2004, pp. 765+; and Helen Atkinson, "Adding New Value," *Traffic World,* March 28, 2005, pp. 18–22.

10. See Robert Berner, "Why P&G's Smile Is So Bright," *BusinessWeek,* August 12, 2002, pp. 58–60; Jack Neff, "Power Brushes a Hit at Every Level," *Advertising Age,* May 26, 2003, p. 10; Matt Phillips, "Sales of Toothbrushes Decline as Consumers Look to Electric Models," *Knight*

Ridder Tribune Business News, November 12, 2004, p. 1; Robert Brenner and William C. Symonds, "Welcome to Procter & Gadget," *BusinessWeek,* February 7, 2005, p. 76; and information accessed at www.spinbrush.com, September 2005.

11. Joshua Rosenbaum, "Guitar Maker Looks for a New Key," *Wall Street Journal,* February 11, 1998, p. B1; and information accessed online at www.gibson.com, August 2005.

12. See Robert J. Dolan, "Pricing: A Value-Based Approach," *Harvard Business School Publishing,* 9-500-071, November 3, 2003.

13. See Philip Kotler and Kevin Lane Keller, *Marketing Management,* 12th ed. (Upper Saddle River, N.J.: Prentice Hall, 2006), p. 438; Cliff Edwards, "HDTV: High-Anxiety Television," *BusinessWeek,* June 10, 2002, pp. 142–146; Eric Taub, "HDTV's Acceptance Picks Up Pace as Prices Drop and Networks Sign On," *New York Times,* March 31, 2003, p. C1; and Stephen H. Wildstrom, "Buying the Right HDTV," *BusinessWeek,* February 2, 2004, p. 22.

14. Doug Desjardins, "Handhelds Offer Hope After Flat Year," *DSN Retailing Today,* February 7, 2005, p. 20.

15. Michael Buettner, "Charleston, S.C.-Based Asphalt Innovations Turns Waste into Helpful Product," *Knight Ridder Tribune Business News,* October 18, 2004, p. 1.

16. Susan Krafft, "Love, Love Me Doo," *American Demographics,* June 1994, pp. 15–16; "That Zoo Doo that You Do So Well," accessed at www.csis.org/states/expzoodoo,html, March 2004; "Time Again for Zoo's Annual Spring Fecal Fest!" Woodland Park Zoo Press Release, February 27, 2004, accessed at www.zoo.org; and "Woodland Park Zoo Doo," accessed at http://zoo.org/zoo_info/special/zoodoo.htm, October 2005.

17. See Nagle and Holdenolden, *The Strategy and Tactics of Pricing,* pp. 244–247; Stefan Stremersch and Gerard J. Tellis, "Strategic Bundling of Products and Prices: A New Synthesis for Marketing," *Journal of Marketing Research,* January 2002, pp. 55–72; and Chris Janiszewski and Marcus Cunha, Jr., "The Influence of Price Discount Framing on the Evaluation of a Product Bundle," *Journal of Marketing Research,* March 2004, pp. 534–546.

18. Example adapted from Charles Fishman, "Which Price Is Right?" *Fast Company,* March 2003, pp. 92–96. Additional data from "Continental Airlines Reports March 2005 Operational Performance," Continental Financial and Traffic Releases, www.continental.com/company/investor/news.asp, accessed April 2005. Also see Robert G. Cross, *Revenue Management: Hard-Core Tactics for Market Domination* (New York: Broadway Books, 1998); Edward Wong, "Airline Economics: Fasten Your Seat Belt," *New York Times,* December 9, 2003, p. G6; Lynn DeLain and Edward O'Meara, "Building a Business Case for Revenue Management," *Journal of Revenue Management and Pricing Management,* January 2004, pp. 338–353; and Dimitris Bertsimas and Sanne de Boer, "Dynamic Pricing and Inventory Control for Multiple Products," *Journal of Pricing Management,* January 2005, pp. 303–319.

19. Tim Ambler, "Kicking Price Promotion Habit Is Like Getting Off Heroin—Hard," *Marketing,* May 27, 1999, p. 24. Also see Robert Gray, "Driving Sales at Any Price?" *Marketing,* April 11, 2002, p. 24; Lauren Kellere Johnson, "Dueling Pricing Strategies," *MIT Sloan Management Review,* Spring 2003, pp. 10–11; and Peter R. Darke and Cindy M. Y. Chung, "Effects of Pricing and Promotion on Consumer Perceptions: It Depends on How Your Frame It," *Journal of Retailing,* 2005, pp. 35–47.

20. See "Dell, the Conqueror," *BusinessWeek,* September 24, 2001, pp. 92–102; Andy Serwer, "Dell Does Domination," *FORTUNE,* January 21, 2002, pp. 70–75; and Pui–Wing Tam, "H-P Gains Applause as It Cedes PC Market Share to Dell, *Wall Street Journal,* January 18, 2005, p. C1.

21. Robert D. Hof, "Going, Going, Gone," *BusinessWeek,* April 12, 1999, pp. 30–32. Also see Philip Kotler and Kevin Lane Keller, *Marketing Management,* 12th ed. (Upper Saddle River, N.J.: Prentice Hall, 2006) pp. 432–433.

22. "MusicRebellion: Dynamic Pricing for Music Starts with 10-Cent Tunes," *Wall Street Journal,* January 9, 2004; "MusicRebellion, Inc." *Hoover's Company Capsules,* Austin, July 15, 2005, p. 132322; and www.musicrebellion.com, accessed December 2005.

23. Thomas L. Friedman, *The World Is Flat: A Brief History of the Twenty-First Century* (New York: Farrar, Straus and Giroux, 2005), pp. 417–418.

24. Philip R. Cateora, *International Marketing,* 7th ed. (Homewood, Ill.: Irwin, 1990), p. 540. Also see Barbara Stottinger, "Strategic Export Pricing: A Long and Winding Road," *Journal of International Marketing,* 2001, pp. 40–63; and Warren J. Keegan, *Global Marketing Management* (Upper Saddle River, N.J.: Prentice Hall, 2002), Chapter 12.

25. Jack Neff, "Kimberly-Clark Loses 'Bounty Killer,'" *Advertising Age,* April 2, 2001, p. 34; and information accessed at www.scottbrand.com/products/towels, September 2005.

26. For discussions of these issues, see Dhruv Grewel and Larry D. Compeau, "Pricing and Public Policy: A Research Agenda and Overview of Special Issue," *Journal of Public Policy and Marketing,* Spring 1999, pp. 3–10; and Michael V. Marn, Eric V. Roegner, and Craig C. Zawada, *The Price Advantage* (Hoboken, N.J.: John Wiley & Sons, 2004), Appendix 2.

27. Kurt Eichenwald, "Archer Daniels Settles Suit Accusing It of Price Fixing," *New York Times,* June 18, 2004.

28. "Predatory-pricing Law Passed by New York Governor," *National Petroleum News,* December 2003, p. 7; and Brenden Timpe, "House Rejects Bill to Protect Gas Stations from Wal-Mart Style Competition," *Knight Ridder Tribune Business News,* March 26, 2005, p. 1.

29. See "Nike's Pricing Practices Under Investigation in Florida," *New York Times,* February 19, 2003, p. C4.

30. "FTC Guides Against Deceptive Pricing," accessed at www.ftc.gov/bcp/guides/decptprc.htm, January 2006.

Chapter 10

1. Quotes and other information from Donald V. Fites, "Make Your Dealers Your Partners," *Harvard Business Review,* March–April 1996, pp. 84–95; Sandra Ward, "The Cat Comes Back," *Barron's,* February 25, 2002, pp. 21–24; Mark Tatge, "Caterpillar Reports 26% Jump in Net Despite Weak Sales," *Wall Street Journal,* April 19, 2000; Shirley A. Lazo, "The Cat's Meow," *Barron's,* June 14, 2004, p. 35; *Hoover's Company Capsules,* June 1, 2005, pp. 103–104; and information accessed at www.caterpillar.com, July 2005.

2. Portions of this example adapted from Kevin Kelleher, "Giving Dealers a Raw Deal," *Business 2.0,* December 2004, pp. 82–84.

3. Matthew Boyle, "Brand Killers," *FORTUNE,* August 11, 2003, pp. 89–100; and information accessed at www.giantfood.com and www.luxottica.com/english/profilo_aziendale/index_keyfacts.html, August 2005.

4. Miguel Helft, "Fashion Fast Forward," *Business 2.0,* May 2002, p. 60; John Tagliabue, "A Rival to Gap That Operates Like Dell," *New York Times,* May 30, 2003, p. W-1; Susan Reda, "Retail's Great Race," *Stores,* March 2004, p. 36; Kasra Ferdows, Michael A. Lewsi, and Jose A D Machuca, "Rapid-Fire Fulfillment," *Harvard Business Review,* November 2004, pp. 104–110; and www.inditex.com; August 2005.

5. See Ilan Alon, "The Use of Franchising by U.S.-Based Retailers," *Journal of Small Business Management,* April 2001, pp. 111–122; John

Reynolds, "Economics 101: How Franchising Makes Music for the U.S. Economy," *Franchising World,* May 2004, pp. 37–40; Stacy Perman, "Extending the Front Lines of Franchising," *BusinessWeek Online,* April 12, 2005, accessed at www.bwonline.com; and "Answers to the 21 Most Commonly Asked Questions About Franchising," accessed online at the International Franchise Association Web Site: www.franchise.org/content.asp?contentid=379, July 2005.

6. Information accessed at www.mind-advertising.com/ch/nestea_ch.htm and www.nestle.com/Our_Brands/Breakfast_Cereals/Overview/Breakfast+Cereals.htm, January 2006.

7. See Subhash C. Jain, *International Marketing Management,* 3rd ed. (Boston: PWS-Kent Publishing, 1990), pp. 489–491. Also see Warren J. Keegan, *Global Marketing Management* (Upper Saddle River, N.J.: Prentice Hall, 2002), pp. 403–404.

8. Quotes and information from Normandy Madden, "Two Chinas," *Advertising Age,* August 16, 2004, pp. 1, 22; Dana James, "Dark Clouds Should Part for International Marketers," *Marketing News,* January 7, 2002, pp. 9, 13; Russell Flannery, "Red Tape," *Forbes,* March 3, 2003, pp. 97–100; and Russell Flannery, "China: The Slow Boat," *Forbes,* April 12, 2004, p. 76.

9. For more on channel relationships, see "Supply Chain Challenges," *Harvard Business Review,* July 2003, pp. 65–73; James C. Anderson and James A. Narus, *Business Market Management,* 2nd ed. (Upper Saddle River, N.J.: Prentice Hall, 2004), chap. 9; Jeffery K. Liker and Thomas Y. Choi, "Building Deep Supplier Relationships," *Harvard Business Review,* December 2004, pp. 104–113; and David Hannon, "Supplier Relationships Key to Future Success," *Purchasing,* June 2, 2005, pp. 25–29.

10. Mitch Betts, "GE Appliance Park Still an IT Innovator," *Computerworld,* January 29, 2001, pp. 20–21; and "What Is GE CustomerNet?" accessed online at www.geappliances.com/buildwithge/index_cnet.htm, August 2005.

11. For a full discussion of laws affecting marketing channels, see Coughlin, Anderson, Stern, and El-Ansary, *Marketing Channels,* chap. 12.

12. Martin Piszczalksi, "Logistics: A Difference Between Winning and Losing," *Automotive Manufacturing & Production,* May 2001, pp. 16–18; Neil Shister, "Redesigned Supply Chain Positions Ford for Global Competition," *World Trade,* May 2005, pp. 20–26; and Alan Field, "Record Logistics Spending," *Journal of Commerce Online,* June 27, 2005, accessed at www.joc.com.

13. Shlomo Maital, "The Last Frontier of Cost Reduction," *Across the Board,* February 1994, pp. 51–52; "Wal-Mart to Expand Supercenters to California," *BusinessJournal,* May 15, 2002, accessed online at http://sanjose.bizjournals.com; and information accessed online at www.walmart.com, August 2005.

14. Gail Braccidiferro, "One Town's Rejection Is Another's 'Let's Do Business,' " *New York Times,* June 15, 2003, p. 2; Christopher Dinsmore, "Wal-Mart to Add 1 Million Square Feet to Virginia Import Distribution Center," *Knight Ridder Tribune Business News,* May 29, 2004, p. 1; *Hoover's Company Capsules,* April 29, 2005, p. 11600; and Dan Scheraga, "Wal-Mart's Muscle," *Chain Store Age,* June 2005, pp. 64–65.

15. "Adding a Day to Dell," *Traffic World,* February 21, 2005, p. 1; and William Hoffman, "Dell Ramps Up RFID," *Traffic World,* April 18, 2005, p. 1.

16. See Ann Bednarz, "IBM Has Some Tall RFID Plans," *Network World,* May 2, 2005, pp. 17–18; "RFID: From Potential to Reality," *Frozen Food Age,* April 2005, p. 40; Jack Neff, "P&G Products to Wear Wire," *Advertising Age,* December 15, 2004, pp. 1, 32; Tom Van Riper, "Retailers Eye RFID Technology to Make Shopping Easier," *Knight Ridder Tribune Business News,* May 23, 2005, p. 1; John S.

McClenahen, "Wal-Mart's Big Gamble," *Industry Week,* April 2005, pp. 42–46; and information accessed online at www.autoidlabs.org, January 2006.

17. Transportation percentages and other figures in this section are from Bureau of Transportation Statistics, "Freight Shipments in America," April 2004, accessed at www.bts.gov/publications/freight_shipments_in_america/; and Bureau of Transportation Statistics, "Pocket Guide to Transportation 2005," January 2005, accessed at www.bts.gov/publications/pocket_guide_to_transportation/2005/.

18. Carol Sliwa, "EDI: Alive and Well After All These Years," *Computerworld,* June 14, 2004, p. 1; Ann Bednarz, "Internet EDI: Blending Old and New," *Network World,* Febraury 23, 2004, pp. 29–31; and Scott Bury, "Piggly Wiggly's Doing It," *Manufacturing Business Technology,* February 2005, p. 42.

19. See Martin Grossman, "The Role of Trust and Collaboration in the Internet-Enabled Supply Chain," *Journal of American Academy of Business,* September 2004, p. 391; and "Supply Chain Management Systems," *Logistics Today,* January 25, 2005, pp. 30–32.

20. Michael Barbaro, "Upscale Tastes Invade Wal-Mart's Hometown," *Washington Post,* June 27, 2005, p. A1.

21. See "Add Value to Your Supply Chain—Hire a 3PL," *Materials Management and Distribution,* January–February 2004, p. A3; and Paul Stastny, "Outsourcing Global Supply Chain Management," *Canadian Transpotation Logistics,* March 2005, pp. 32–34.

Chapter 11

1. Based on quotes and information from Samantha Thompson Smith, "Grocer's Success Seems Entirely Natural," *News & Observer,* May 21, 2004, p. D1; "Whole Foods Pushing for Organic Profit Growth," *Money Digest,* February 2003, p. 14; "Whole Foods Market, Inc.," *Hoover's Company Capsules,* June 15, 2005, p. 10952; "Script for Conference Call on 4Q04 Press Release," June 30, 2005, accessed at www.wholefoodsmarket.com/investor/script_Q404.html; Marianne Wilson, "Retail as Theater, Naturally," *Chain Store Age,* May 25, 2005, p. 182; and www.wholefoods.com, October 2005.

2. See "Traditional Grocers Face Uncertain Times," *Corporate Finance Weekly,"* March 7, 2005, p. 1; and David Merrefield, "Supermarket Revitalization Efforts Cast Long Shadows," *Supermarket News,* June 27, 2005, p. 10.

3. See Sonia Reyes, "Online Grocers: Ready to Deliver?" *Brandweek,* May 3, 2004, p. 26; Phil Lempert, "Talking 'Bout an Evolution," *Progressive Grocer,* April 15, 2005, p. 20; Debbie Howell, "Supermarkets Take New Tack in Battle Against EDLP," *DSN Retailing Today,* May 23, 2005, p. 7; and "Supermarkets," *Chain Store Age,* June 2005, pp. 18–21.

4. "Convenience Store Industry Sales Hit New Highs in 2004," April 12, 2005, accessed online at http://cstorescentral.com.

5. Adapted from Elizabeth Esfahani, "7-Eleven Gets Sophisticated," *Business 2.0,* January–February 2005, pp. 93–100.

6. Patricia Callahan and Ann Zimmerman, "Price War in Aisle 3—Wal-Mart Tops Grocery List with Supercenter Format," *Wall Street Journal,* May 27, 2003, p. B-1; Mike Troy, "What Setback? Supercenters Proliferate," *DSN Retailing Today,* May 17, 2004, p. 1; Elliot Zwiebach, "Wal-Mart's Next Weapon," *Supermarket News,* March 7, 2005, p. 14; and Wal-Mart 2005 Annual Report, accessed at www.walmartstores. com.

7. Adapted from John Helyar, "The Only Company Wal-Mart Fears," *FORTUNE,* November 24, 2003, pp. 158–166. Also see Tiffany Meyers, "Marketers Learn Luxury Isn't Simply for the Very Wealthy," *Advertising Age,* September 13, 2004, pp. S2, S10; and Susan Reda,

"Filling My Cart at Costco," *Stores*, February 2005, p. 8; and Costco Wholesale Corporation, *Hoover's Company Records*, Austin, June 15, 2005, p. 17060.

8. See David Stires, "Fallen Arches," *FORTUNE*, April 29, 2002, pp. 74–76; Anne Field, "Your Ticket to a New Career," *BusinessWeek*, May 12, 2003, pp. 100–101; "Quick Franchise, Franchising, Facts and Statistics," accessed at www.azfranchises.com/franchisefacts.htm, August 2005; "McDonald's Reports May Global Comparable Sales," June 8, 2005, accessed at http://money.cnn.com; and information accessed at www.subway.com and www.mcdonalds.com/corp.html, October 2005.

9. "Who Said That?" *Marketing Management*, January–February 2005, p. 4.

10. Portions adapted from Bridget Finn, "For PETCO, Success Is a Bitch," *Business 2.0*, November 2003, p. 54. Also see PETCO Animal Supplies, Inc., *Hoover's Company Records*, Austin, June 15, 2005, p. 17256; and Frank Green, "Event Brief of Q1 2005 PETCO Animal Supplies Earning Conference Call," *Fair Disclosure Wire*, May 25, 2005.

11. Adapted from Susanna Hamner, "Lessons from a Retail Rebel," *Business 2.0*, June 2005, pp. 62–64.

12. See Lorrie Grant, "Maytag Stores Let Shoppers Try Before They Buy," *USA Today*, June 7, 2004, p. 7B; and Candice Choi, "More Retailers Letting Customers Try Out Big-Ticket Items Before They Buy," *Knight Ridder Tribune Business News*, October 30, 2004, p. 1.

13. Information drawn from "The History of Mall of America," accessed online at www.mallofamerica.com, December 2005.

14. Andrea Bermudez, "Bijan Dresses the Wealthy for Success," *Apparel News.Net*, December 1–7, 2000, accessed online at www. apparelnews.net/Archieve/120100/News/newsfeat.htm; Mimi Avins, "FASHION; More is More; Over-the-top Isn't High Enough for Bijan, Whose Boutique Embraces Excess," *Los Angeles Times*, January 5, 2003, p. E.1; and information accessed at www.bijan.com/boutique, October 2005.

15. For a good discussion of retail pricing and promotion strategies, see Kathleen Seiders and Glenn B. Voss, "From Price to Purchase," *Marketing Management*, November–December 2005, pp. 38–43.

16. James Morrow, "X–IT Plans," *American Demographics*, May 2004, pp. 34–38; Paul Lukas, "Our Malls, Ourselves," *FORTUNE*, October 18, 2004, pp. 243–256; and information accessed on the International Council of Shopping Centers Web site, www.icsc.org, October 2005.

17. Dean Starkman, "The Mall, Without the Haul—'Lifestyle Centers' Slip Quietly into Upscale Areas, Mixing Cachet and 'Curb Appeal,' " *Wall Street Journal*, July 25, 2001, p. B1; "To Mall or Not to Mall?" *Buildings*, June 2004, p. 99; and Arlyn Tobian Gajilan, "Wolves in Shops' Clothing," *FORTUNE Small Business*, February 2005, pp. 17–18; and information accessed on the International Council of Shopping Centers Web site, www.icsc.org, October 2005.

18. See Amy Barrett, "A Retailing Pacesetter Pulls Up Lame," *BusinessWeek*, July 12, 1993, pp. 122–123; and John Helyar, "The Only Company Wal-Mart Fears," *FORTUNE*, November 24, 2003, pp. 158–166; Heather Todd, "Club Stores Pack 'Em In," *Beverage World*, April 15, 2005, pp. 44–45.

19. See Malcolm P. McNair and Eleanor G. May, "The Next Revolution of the Retailing Wheel," *Harvard Business Review*, September–October 1978, pp. 81–91; Stephen Brown, "The Wheel of Retailing: Past and Future," *Journal of Retailing*, Summer 1990, pp. 143–147; Stephen Brown, "Variations on a Marketing Enigma: The Wheel of Retailing Theory," *Journal of Marketing Management*, vol. 7, no. 2, 1991, pp. 131–155; Jennifer Negley, "Retrenching, Reinventing, and Remaining Relevant," *Discount Store News*, April 5, 1999, p. 11; and Don E. Schultz, Another Turn of the Wheel," *Marketing Management*,

March–April 2002, pp. 8–9; and Carol Krol, "Staples Preps Easier E–Commerce Site," *B to B*, March 14, 2005, pp. 3–4.

20. See Sungwook Min and Mary Wolfinbarger, "Market Share, Profit Margin, and Marketing Efficiency of Early Movers, Bricks and Clicks, and Specialists in E-Commerce," *Journal of Business Research*, August 2005, pp. 1030+.

21. Timothy J. Mullaney and Robert D. Hof, "E–Tailing Finally Hits Its Stride," *BusinessWeek*, December 20, 2004, pp. 36–37; "Online Retail Sales, Profitability Continue to Climb," May 24, 2005, accessed at www.shop.org/press/05/052405.asp; and Carol Krol, "Staples Preps Easier E-Commerce Site," *B to B*, March 14, 2005, pp. 3–4.

22. Richard Karpinski, "Web Delivers Big Results for Staples," *B to B*, November 11, 2002, p. 14; and Joseph Pereira, "Staples Posts Strong Earnings on High-Margin Internet Sales," *Wall Street Journal*, March 5, 2004, p. A13.

23. Excerpt adapted from Alice Z. Cuneo, "What's in Store?" *Advertising Age*, February 25, 2002, pp. 1, 30–31. Also see Robert Berner, "Dark Days in White Goods for Sears," *BusinessWeek*, March 10, 2003, pp. 78–79.

24. See "The FORTUNE 500," *FORTUNE*, April 18, 2005, p. F1.

25. Adapted from information found in Christina Rexrode, "Concept Store in Bloom," *Herald-Sun*, June 6, 2004, pp. F1, F3; "Food Lion Opens First Bloom Concept Store," press release, May 25, 2004, accessed at www.foodlion.com/news.asp?parm=323; Sally Praskey, "Marketecnics 2005," *Canadian Grocer*, May 2005, pp. 51–54; and Richard Shulman, "Applied Science," *Progressive Grocer*, April 1, 2005, pp. 22–24.

26. "Wal-Mart International Operations," July 2005, accessed online at www.walmartstores.com.

27. See "Top 250 Global Retailers," *Stores*, January 2005, accessed at www.stores.com.

28. See Dexter Roberts, Wendy Zellner, and Carol Matlack, "Let the Retail Wars Begin," *BusinessWeek*, January 17, 2005, pp. 44–45; "Carrefour: At the Intersection of Global," *DSN Retailing Today*, September 18, 2000, p. 16; "Top 250 Global Retailers," *Stores*, January 2005, accessed at www.stores.com; and information from www.walmartstores.com and www.carrefour.com, accessed September 2005.

29. See Kathleen Cholewka, "Standing Out Online: the Five Best E-Marketing Campaigns," *Sales & Marketing Management*, January 2001, pp. 51–58; and information from www.playstation.com, July 2005.

30. "McKesson: Raising Expectations," *Modern Materials Handling*, February 2004, p. 53; and information from "About the Company" and "Supply Management Online," accessed online at www.mckesson.com, October 2005.

31. Facts accessed at www.supervalu.com, September 2005; and from "SuperValu, Inc.," *Hoover's Company Capsules*, Austin, July 15, 2005, p. 11419.

Chapter 12

1. Portions adapted from Warren Berger, "Dare-Devils," *Business 2.0*, April 2004, p. 110. Also see Matthew Creamer, "Agency of the Year," *Advertising Age*, January 10, 2005, pp. S1–S2; Mae Anderson, "CP+B, Burger King Win Grand Clio," May 24, 2005, accessed at www.adweek.com; Ryan Underwood, "Ruling the Roost," *Fast Company*, April 2005, pp. 70–77; and Brian Steinberg, "Ad Agency Focuses on Creating Content You Can't Do Without," *Wall Street Journal*, July 13, 2005, p. 1.

2. The first four of these definitions are adapted from Peter D. Bennett, *The AMA Dictionary of Marketing Terms*, 2nd ed. (New York: McGraw-

Hill, 2004). Other definitions can be found at www. marketingpower.com/live/mg–dictionary.php?, January 15, 2006.

3. Bob Garfield, "The Chaos Scenario," *Advertising Age,* April 4, 2005, pp. 1, 57+; and "Readers Respond to 'Chaos Scenario,'" *Advertising Age,* April 18, 2005, pp. 1+.

4. Linda Tischler, "Blowing Out Advertising's Walls," *Fast Company,* June 2005, pp. 63–64.

5. Garfield, "The Chaos Scenario," p. 57.

6. Jack Neff, "P&G Chief: We Need New Model Now," *Advertising Age,* November 15, 2004, pp. 1, 53.

7. Don E. Schultz, "New Media, Old Problem: Keep Marcom Integrated," *Marketing News,* March 29, 1999, p. 11. Also see Claire Atkinson, "Integration Still a Pipe Dream for Many," *Advertising Age,* March 10, 2003, pp. 1, 47; and "Too Soon to Create a Hierarchy of Online Advertising," *New Media Age,* February 3, 2005, p. 14.

8. See, Chapter 3 and Chapter 4. Also see Don E. Schultz and Philip J. Kitchen, *Communication Globally: An Integrated Marketing Approach* (New York: McGraw-Hill, 2000); and Don E. Schultz and Heidi Schultz, *IMC: The Next Generation* (New York: McGraw-Hill, 2004).

9. For more on integrated marketing communications, see Don E. Schultz, Stanley I. Tannenbaum, and Robert F. Lauterborn, *Integrated Marketing Communications* (Chicago, Ill.: NTC, 1992); Don E. Schultz and Philip J. Kitchen, *Communication Globally: An Integrated Marketing Approach* (New York: McGraw-Hill, 2000); Prasad A. Naik and Kalyan Raman, "Understanding the Impact of Synergy in Multimedia Communications," *Journal of Marketing Research,* November 2003, pp. 375–388; and Don E. Schultz and Heidi Schultz, *IMC: The Next Generation* (New York: McGraw-Hill, 2004).

10. See "Super Bowl Audience Falls from Last Year," *Wall Street Journal,* February 8, 2005, p. 1; Krysten Crawford, "Oscar Ratings Sink with Rock," February 28, 2005, accessed at www.money.cnn.com; and Lisa de Moraes, "Wrapping Up the Season with Some Big Numbers," *Washington Post,* May 25, 2005, p. C7.

11. "Evaluating the Cost of Sales Calls in Business-to-Business Markets," *Cahners Business Information,* Cahners Research, January 2002; and Roy Chitwood, "Making the Most out of Each Outside Sales Call," February 4, 2005, accessed at http://seattle.bizjournals.com/seattle/stories/2005/02/07/smallb3.html.

12. For information on U.S. and international advertising spending, see "Special Report: 100 Leading Advertisers Supplement," *Advertising Age,* June 27, 2005, pp. 4, 6; "Top 100 Global Marketers," *Advertising Age,* November 8, 2004, p. 32; and "Ad Spend to Rise Further in 2005," BBC News, accessed at http://bbc.co.uk/1/hi/business/4073257.stm.

13. For more on advertising budgets, see George E. Belch and Michael A. Belch, *Advertising and Promotion: An Integrated Marketing Communications Perspective,* 6th ed. (New York: McGraw-Hill, 2004), pp. 211–232.

14. Information from Gary Levin, "'Meddling' in Creative More Welcome," *Advertising Age,* April 9, 1990, pp. S4, S8; "Absolut Vodka Turns 25 Tomorrow," press release, April 19, 2004, accessed at www.absolut.com; the Q&A section at www.absolut.com, August 2004; Matthew Miller, "Absolut Chaos," *Forbes,* December 13, 2004, p. 84; and Stuart Elliott, "Vodka Goes Beyond Plain Vanilla," *New York Times,* June 16, 2005, p. C6.

15. "500 Channels with Nothing On? Nah—No Channels at All," July 2, 2004, accessed at www.corante.com/importance/archives/004736.html; and "Number of Magazines by Category," accessed at www.magazine.org/editorial/editorial_trends_and_magazine_handbook/1145.cfm, August 2005.

16. Charles Pappas, "Ad Nauseam," *Advertising Age,* July 10, 2000, pp. 16–18; and Mark Ritson, "Marketers Need to Find a Way to Control the Contagion of Clutter," *Marketing,* March 6, 2003, p. 16.

17. See Claire Atkinson, "'Idol' Takes Prize for Priciest Spots," *TelevisionWeek,* October 4, 2004, p. 18; Abbey Klaassen, "Super Bowl Chatter: ABC's Asking Price is $2.6M for 30-Second Spot," *Advertising Age,* April 18, 2005, p. 39; and Christopher Lawton, "Gravity of the Situation: Cadbury Goes Weightless With Diet 7-Up," *Wall Street Journal,* May 25, 2005, p. B3.

18. Paul Holmes, "Programs That Demonstrate the Value of Public Relations," *Advertising Age,* January 24, 2005, pp. C12–C16.

19. Wayne Friedman, "PVR Users Skip Most Ads: Study," *Advertising Age,* July 1, 2002, pp. 4, 46; Daren Fonda, "Prime-Time Peddling," *Time,* May 30, 2005, pp. 50–52; Kevin Downey, "Fast-Forwarding Through Fears of TiVo," June 30, 2005, accessed at http://www.medialifemagazine.com; and Allison Fass, "Advertising on Demand," *Forbes,* July 25, 2005, p. 72.

20. Edward A. Robinson, "Frogs, Bears, and Orgasms: Think Zany If You Want to Reach Today's Consumers," *FORTUNE,* June 9, 1997, pp. 153–156. Also see Tobi Elkin, "Courting Craftier Consumers," July 1, 2002, p. 28; Devin Leonard, "Nightmare on Madison Avenue," *FORTUNE,* June 28, 2004, pp. 93–108; and Theresa Howard, "'Viral' Advertising Spreads Through Marketing Plans," *USA Today,* June 6, 2005, accessed at www.usatoday.com/money/advertising/2005–06–22–viral–usat_x.htm.

21. See David Kiley, "Cable's Big Bet on Hyper-Targeting," *BusinessWeek,* July 4, 2005, pp. 58–59.

22. Adapted from information found in "Multi–Taskers," *Journal of Marketing Management,* May–June 2004, p. 6; and "Kids Today: Media Multitaskers," March 9, 2005, accessed at www.cbsnews.com/stories/2005/03/09/tech/main678999.shtml.

23. *Newsweek* and *BusinessWeek* cost and circulation data accessed online at http://mediakit.businessweek.com and www.newsweekmediakit.com, August 2005.

24. See Marty Bernstein, "Why TV Commercials Are So Costly," *Automotive News,* May 10, 2004, p. 30H.

25. Stuart Elliot, "How Effective Is This Ad, in Real Numbers? Beats Me," *New York Times,* July 20, 2005, p. C8.

26. Elliot, "How Effective Is This Ad, in Real Numbers? Beats Me," p. C8. Also see, Dan Lippe, "Media Scorecard: How ROI Adds Up," *Advertising Age,* June 20, 2005, p. S6.

27. Information on advertising agency revenues from "Advertising Age's Special Agency Report," *Advertising Age,* May 2, 2005.

28. See Alexandra Jardine and Laurel Wentz, "It's a Fat World After All," *Advertising Age,* March 7, 2005, p. 3; George E. Belch and Michael A. Belch, *Advertising and Promotion* (New York: McGraw-Hill/Irwin, 2004), pp. 666–668; and Jonathan Cheng, "China Demands Concrete Proof of Ads," *Wall Street Journal,* July 8, 2005, p. B1.

29. "Rusty Relations," *Convenience Store News,* August 3, 2005, accessed at www.csnews.com.

30. Adapted from Mike Beirne, "Scoring Points, Having Fun," *Brandweek,* October 18, 2004, pp. 18–19.

31. "Casting the Net Wider," *Candy Industry,* February 2005, p. 24; Damian J. Troise, "Fisherman's Friend Coughs Up MINI Cooper for Slogan Contest Winner," *Knight Ridder Tribune Business News,* February 25, 2005, p. 1; and www.fishermansfriendusa.com, accessed May 2005.

32. See "Do Coupons Make Cents?" *Incentive,* May 2003, p. 19; Catherine Arnold, "No Coup Online," *Marketing News,* May 26, 2003, p. 3;

Natalie Schwartz, "Clipping Path," *Promo Magazine*, April 1, 2004; Noreen O'Leary, "Dealing with Coupons," *Adweek*, February 21, 2005, p. 29; and Dahleen Glanton, "Coupon Clippers Clean Up with 'Free Money'," *Knight Ridder Tribune Business News*, May 8, 2005, p. 1.

33. See Lucia Moses, "Coupons Make Move Online," *Editor & Publisher*, February 24, 2003, p. 10; and Leo Jakobson, "Coupons on the Go," *Incentive*, February 2005, p. 16.

34. See "Promotional Products—Impact, Exposure, and Influence" at Promotional Products Association International Web site, www.ppai.org, May 2005.

35. "Rusty Relations," *Convenience Store News*, August 3, 2005, accessed at www.csnews.com.

36. See "Nearly Half a Million Attend Bauma Trade Show," *Pit & Quarry*, May 2004, p. 16; and information found at the Consumer Electronics Association Web site, www.cesweb.org/press/default_flash.asp, August 2005.

37. Adapted from Scott Cutlip, Allen Center, and Glen Broom, *Effective Public Relations*, 9th ed. (Upper Saddle River, N.J.: Prentice Hall, 2006), Chapter 1.

38. Adapted from information found in Diane Brady, "Wizard of Marketing," *BusinessWeek*, July 24, 2000, pp. 84–87; Mira Serrill-Robins, "Harry Potter and the Cyberpirates," *BusinessWeek*, August 1, 2005, p. 9; and Keith O'Brien, "Publisher Puts Fans First for New Harry Potter Release," *PRWeek*, July 18, 2005, p. 3.

39. Al Ries and Laura Ries, "First Do Some Publicity," *Advertising Age*, February 8, 1999, p. 42. Also see Al Ries and Laura Ries, *The Fall of Advertising and the Rise of PR* (New York: HarperBusiness, 2002). For points and counterpoints, see O. Burtch Drake, "'Fall' of Advertising? I Differ," *Advertising Age*, January 13, 2003, p. 23; Robert E. Brown, "Book Review: The Fall of Advertising & the Rise of PR," *Public Relations Review*, March 2003, pp. 91–93; and Mark Cheshire, "Roundtable Discussion—Making & Moving the Message," *Daily Record*, January 30, 2004, p. 1.

40. Adapted from portions of Melanie Wells, "Kid Nabbing," *Forbes*, February 2, 2004, pp. 84–88. Also see Samar Farah, "Making Waves," *CMO Magazine*, July 2005.

41. See Kate Fitzgerald, "Marketing on the Move," *Advertising Age*, March 18, 2002, p. 59; Jeff St. John, "Microsoft Sends Mobile Marketing Van to Kennewick, Wash., Area," *Knight Ridder Tribune Business News*, April 28, 2004, p. 1; and Lucas Conley, "On a Roll," *Fast Company*, February 2005, p. 28.

42. See "Butterball Turkey Talk-Line Fact Sheet," accessed at www.butterball.com/en/files/PDF/Fact_Sheet_sheet.PDF, August 2005.

43. Paul Holmes, "Senior Marketers Are Sharply Divided About the Role of PR in the Overall Mix," *Advertising Age*, January 24, 2005, pp. C1–C2.

Chapter 13

1. Quotes and other information from Jeff O'Heir, "Michael Krasny—IT Sales Innovator." *Computer Reseller News*, November 18, 2002; Ed Lawler, "Integrated Campaign Winner: CDW Computer Centers," *B to B*, December 9, 2002, p. 20; "CDW Chooses Richardson to Strengthen Customer Focus," *Business Wire*, July 23, 2003, p. 5397; Mark Del Franco, Paul Miller, and Margery Weinstein, "Smooth Sailing in Choppy Waters," *Catalog Age*, March 2004, pp. 42–46; Scott Campbell, "CDW Snags Companywide Cisco Premier Status," *CRN*, April 12, 2004, p. 12; Chuck Salter, "The Soft Sell," *Fast Company*, January 2005, pp. 72–73; and www.cdw.com, October 2005.

2. Quote from Laurence Zuckerman, "Selling Airplanes with a Smile," *New York Times*, February 17, 2002, p. 32. Also see See Bill Kelley,

"How to Sell Airplanes, Boeing-Style," *Sales & Marketing Management*, December 9, 1985, pp. 32–34; J. Lynn Lunsford, "Boeing Beats Out Airbus to Sell Virgin Blue $3 Billion in Jets," *Wall Street Journal*, January 16, 2003, p. B6; Joann Muller, "7 Digital 7," *Forbes*, June 21, 2004, p. 117; and "China's Appetite for 737 Shows No Sign of Slowing," *Knight Ridder Tribune Business News*, May 11, 2005, p. 1.

3. Quotes and other information from Geoffrey Brewer, "Love the Ones You're With," *Sales & Marketing Management*, February 1997, pp. 38–45; and Erin Stout, "Blue Skies Ahead?" *Sales & Marketing Management*, March 2003, pp. 25–29.

4. "Selling Power 500," accessed at www.sellingpower.com/sp500/index.asp, May 2005.

5. For more on this and other methods for determining sales force size, see Douglas J. Dalrymple, William L. Cron, and Thomas E. DeCarlo, *Sales Management*, 8th ed. (New York: John Wiley & Sons, 2004), pp. 112–116.

6. "Evaluating the Cost of Sales Calls in Business-to-Business Markets," *Cahners Business Information*, Cahners Research, January 2002; "How Many Personal Sales Calls Does It Take to Close a Sale?" accessed at www.cahnerscarr.com/5425d.htm, August 2004; and Roy Chitwood, "Making the Most Out of Each Outside Sales Call," February 4, 2005, accessed at http://seattle.bizjournals.com/seattle/stories/2005/02/07/smallb3.html.

7. Adapted from Geoffrey Brewer, "Lou Gerstner Has His Hands Full," *Sales & Marketing Management*, May 8, 1998, pp. 36–41. Also see Michelle Cioci, "Marketing to Small Businesses," *Sales & Marketing Management*, December 2000, pp. 94–100.

8. See Martin Everett, "Selling by Telephone," *Sales & Marketing Management*, December 1993, pp. 75–79. Also see Terry Arnold, "Telemarketing Strategy," *Target Marketing*, January 2002, pp. 47–48.

9. Adapted from Chuck Salter, "The Soft Sell," *Fast Company*, January 2005, pp. 72–73.

10. William F. Kendy, "No More Lone Rangers," *Selling Power*, April 2004, pp. 70–74. Also see Jon Bacot, "Team Selling: A Winning Approach," *Paperboard Packaging*, April 2005, pp. 44–50.

11. "Customer Business Development," accessed at www.pg.com/jobs/jobs_us/work_we_offer/advisor_overview.jhtml?sl=jobs_advisor_business_development, October 2005.

12. Quotes and other information in this section on super salespeople are from Geoffrey Brewer, "Mind Reading: What Drives Top Salespeople to Greatness?" *Sales & Marketing Management*, May 1994, pp. 82–88; Andy Cohen, "The Traits of Great Sales Forces," *Sales & Marketing Management*, October 2000, pp. 67–72; Julia Chang, "Born to Sell?" *Sales & Marketing Management*, July 2003, pp. 34–38; Henry Canaday, "Recruiting the Right Stuff," *Selling Power*, April 2004, pp. 94–96; and Tom Andel, "How to Cultivate Sales Talent," *Official Board Markets*, April 23, 2005, pp. 14–16.

13. Robert Klein, "Nabisco Sales Soar After Sales Training," *Marketing News*, January 6, 1997, p. 23; and Geoffrey James, "The Return of Sales Training," *Selling Power*, May 2004, pp. 86–91.

14. "Major Growth Forecast for Multi-Billion Dollar Online Training Market," *eMediaWire*, January 26, 2005, accessed at www.emediawire.com.

15. See "SMM's Best of Sales and Marketing: Best Trained Sales Force—Cisco Systems," *Sales & Marketing Magazine*, September 2001, pp. 28–29; "Cisco Systems Canada Wins 2002 National Award for Learning Technologies in the Workplace," May 8, 2002, accessed at http://newsroom.cisco.com/dlls/corp_050802.html; and "E–Learning: Field Training—How Cisco Spends Less Time in the Classroom and More Time with Customers," accessed at http://business.cisco.com, August 2003.

16. See *Dartnell's 30th Sales Force Compensation Survey,* Dartnell Corporation, August 1999; and Christine Galea "2005 Compensation Survey," *Sales & Marketing Management*, May 2005, pp. 24–29.

17. See Gary H. Anthes, "Portal Powers GE Sales," *Computerworld,* June 2, 2003, pp. 31–32. Also see Betsy Cummings, "Increasing Face Time," *Sales & Marketing Management,* January 2004, p. 12.

18. For extensive discussions of sales force automation, see the May 2005 issue of *Industrial Marketing Management,* which is devoted to the subject.

19. Kathy Bergen, "Loosening the Stranglehold on Employee Incentives," *Knight Ridder Tribune Business News*, December 25, 2004, p. 1.

20. For more on return on sales investment, see Tim Lukes and Jennifer Stanley, "Bring Science to Sales," *Marketing Management,* September–October 2004, pp. 36–41.

21. Quotes from Bob Donath, "Delivering Value Starts with Proper Prospecting," *Marketing News,* November 10, 1997, p. 5; and Bill Brooks, "Power-Packed Prospecting Pointers," *Agency Sales,* March 2004, p. 37.

22. Quotes from Dana Ray, "Are You Listening?" *Selling Power,* October 2004, pp. 24–27; Erin Stout, "Throwing the Right Pitch," *Sales & Marketing Management,* April 2001, pp. 61–63; Andy Cohen, "Customers Know Best," *Sales & Marketing Management,* January 2003, p. 10; and William F. Kennedy, "How to Be a Good Listener," *Selling Power,* April 2004, pp. 41–44.

23. Adapted from Betsy Cummings, "On the Cutting Edge," *Sales & Marketing Management,* June 3, 2003, pp. 39–43.

24. For these and other direct marketing statistics in this section, see "Economic Impact: U.S. Direct Marketing Today," along with a wealth of other information, accessed at www.the-dma.org, December 2005.

25. Alicia Orr Suman, "Ideas You Can Take to the Bank! 10 Big Things All Direct Marketers Should Be Doing Now," *Target Marketing,* February 2003, pp. 31–33; and Mary Ann Kleinfelter, "Know Your Customer," *Target Marketing,* January 2005, pp. 28–31.

26. Dana Blakenhorn, "Marketers Hone Targeting," *Advertising Age,* June 18, 2001, p. T16; Thomas H. Davenport, "How Do They Know Their Customers So Well?" *MIT Sloan Management Review,* Winter 2001, pp. 63–73; and Daniel Lyons, "Too Much Information," *Forbes,* December 13, 2004, p. 110.

27. Daniel Lyons, "Too Much Information," *Forbes,* December 13, 2004, pp. 110–115; Shawn Thelen, Sandra Mottner, and Barry Berman, "On the Trail of Marketing Gold," *Business Horizons,* November–December 2004, pp. 25–32; and Suzette Parmley, "When Its Customers Return, A Casino Always Wins Big," *Knight Ridder Tribune Business News,* April 15, 2005, p. 1.

28. Geoffrey Brewer, "The Customer Stops Here," *Sales & Marketing Management,* March 1998, pp. 31–36; Andy Patrizio, "Home-Grown CRM," *Insurance & Technology,* February 2001, pp. 49–50; "USAA," *Hoover's Company Capsules,* July 15, 2005, pp. 405–08; and information from www.usaa.com, September 2005.

29. Ira Teinowitz, "'Do Not Call' Does Not Hurt Direct Marketing," *Advertising Age,* April 11, 2005, pp. 3, 95.

30. Teinowitz, "'Do Not Call' Does Not Hurt Direct Marketing," p. 3.

31. David Ranii, "Compact Discs, DVDs Get More Use as Promotional Tool," *Knight Ridder Tribune Business News,* May 5, 2004, p. 1.

32. Jim Emerson, "Print and the Internet Go Hand-in-Hand," *Printing News,* June 20, 2005, p. 2; and "Abacus Report: Web Sales Soon to Overtake Catalog Sales," August 3, 2005, accessed at http://multichannelmerchant. com/news/Abacus-trend-report-080305.

33. "Live from ACC: Catalog Sales Growth Outpaces Employment Growth," *Catalog Age*, June 2 2003, accessed online at http:// catalogagemag.com/ar/marketing_live_acc_catalog; "US Catalogue Sales to Top $175bn," *Precision Marketing,* May 14, 2004, p. 9; and "The DMA Co-Underwrites Email Authentication Implementation Summit 2005," *PR Newswire,* May 11, 2005, accessed at http://biz.yahoo.com/prnews/050511/nyw182.html?.v=6.

34. "Catalog Study Now Available," *Business Forms, Labels, and Systems,* June 20, 2001, p. 24; Richard S. Hodgson, "It's Still the Catalog Age," *Catalog Age,* June 2001, p. 156; and Sherry Chiger, "It's Raining Catalogs," *Catalog Age,* June 2004, p. 12.

35. See "About Lillian Vernon," accessed at www.lillianvernon.com, August 2005; and "Lillian Vernon Corporation," *Hoover's Company Capsules,* Austin, May 11, 2005, p. 12111.

36. Ron Donoho, "One-Man Show," *Sales & Marketing Management,* June 2001, pp. 36–42; and information accessed at www.ronco.com, March 2004; and Brian Steinberg, "Read This Now!; But Wait! There's More! The Infomercial King Explains," *Wall Street Journal,* March 9, 2005, p. 1.

37. Nat Ives, "Infomercials Clean Up Their Pitch," *New York Times,* April 12, 2004, p. C1.

38. Thomas Mucha, "Stronger Sales in Just 28 Minutes," *Business 2.0,* June 2005, pp. 56–60.

39. See Eugene Gilligan, "The Show Must Go On," *Journal of Commerce,* April 12, 2004, p. 1; Barbara Moss, "Must See SHOPNBC," *Modern Jeweler,* April 2005, pp. 84–84; and Nicole Urso, "HSN Viewers Shop with Their Remotes," *Response,* May 2005, p. 8.

40. Shayn Ferriolo, "The Key to Kiosks," *Catalog Age,* June 2003, pp. 103–108; Charlotte Goddard, "Mobile Offers Kiosks a New Role," *Revolution,* January 2004, p. 21; Gary Alden, "Kiosks: Self-Serving Devices for Boosting Store Sales," *Dealerscope,* October 2004, p. 74; and Becky Yerak, "Kenmore, Craftsman Brands Start Showing Up at Kmart," *Knight Ridder Tribune Business News,* April 26, 2005, p. 1.

41. "Interactive: Ad Age Names Finalists," *Advertising Age,* February 27, 1995, pp. 12–14.

42. "Sweepstakes Groups Settles with States," *New York Times,* June 27, 2001, p. A14; and "PCH Reaches $34 Million Sweepstakes Settlement with 26 States," *Direct Marketing,* September 2001, p. 6.

43. Jennifer Lee, "Welcome to the Database Lounge," *New York Times*, March 21, 2002, p. G1.

44. Information on the DMA Privacy Promise obtained at www. the-dma.org/privacy/privacypromise.shtml, November 2005.

45. Debbie A. Connon, "The Ethics of Database Marketing," *Information Management Journal,* May–June 2002, pp. 42–44.

Chapter 14

1. Information and quotes from Monica Soto Ouchi, "Amazon at 10: Will It Keep Clicking?" *Knight Ridder Tribune Business News,* July 10, 2005, p. 1; Michael West, "Amazon.com Pursues Customer Satisfaction," *Chain Store Age,* July 2005, p. 44A; Gary Rivlin, "A Retail Revolution Turns 10," *New York Times,* July 10, 2005, p. 3.1; "Amazon.com, Inc." *Hoover's Company Records,* July 15, 2005, p. 51493; Mylene Mangalindan, "Outside Merchants Boost Amazon," *Wall Street Journal,* July 27, 2005, p. A3; and information accessed at www.amazon.com, September 2005.

2. See "Top Ten Countries in the World with the Highest Internet Penetration Rates," Internet World Stats, July 31, 2005, accessed at www.internetworldstats/top10.htm; and Enid Burns, "Broadband Population Growth Continues," ClickZ Stats, June 2, 2005, accessed at clickz.com.

3. "United States: Average Web Usage," Nielsen/NetRatings, April 2005, accessed at www.nielsen-netratings.com.

4. Jack Neff, "Using Tech Tools to Speed Marketing," *Advertising Age,* October 28, 2002, p. 14; and Amy Spector, "Cheesecake Factory Staff, Execs Raise the Bar on Service Together," *Nation's Restaurant News,* May 24, 2004, p. 32.

5. Dena Levitz, "Many Auto Shoppers Consult Internet for Information Before Making Purchase," *Knight Ridder Tribune Business News,* November 26, 2004, p. 1.

6. Portions adapted from Christopher Elliott, "Your Very Own Personal Air Fare," *New York Times,* August 9, 2005, p. C5. Also see Matthew Creamer, "Southwest Rings $20 Million in Fares with Killer App," *Advertising Age,* July 11, 2005, p. 8.

7. See Patti Freeman Evans, "Market Forecast: Retail Spending Online," Jupiter Research, January 8, 2004, accessed at www.jup.com; and Carrie A, Johnson, "US eCommerce Overview: 2004 to 2010," August 2, 2004, accessed at www.forrester.com/Research/Document/Excerpt/ 0,7211,34576,00.html; and "Online Holiday Spending Surges Beyond Expectations, Driving E-Commerce to Record Annual Sales of $117 Billion," comScore Networks, January 10, 2005, accessed at www.comscore.com.

8. See Michelle Quinn, "More Teens Using the Internet," *Knight Ridder Tribune Business News,* July 28, 2005, p. 1.

9. See Rob McGann, "Online Banking Increased 47 Percent Since 2002," ClickZ Stats, February 9, 2005, accessed at http://www.clickz.com; and Kenin McKenna, "Selling to Seniors on the Internet," *LIMRA's MarketFacts Quarterly,* Spring 2005, pp. 28–29.

10. Information for this example accessed at http://quickenloans.quicken.com, August 2005.

11. See Steve Hamm, "E-Biz: Down but Hardly Out," *BusinessWeek,* March 26, 2001, pp. 126–130; "B2B E-Commerce Headed for Trillions," March 6, 2002, accessed at www.clickz.com/stats/sectors/b2b/article.php/986661; and Timothy Mullaney, "The E-Biz Surprise," *BusinessWeek,* May 12, 2003, pp. 60–68.

12. Darnell Little, "Let's Keep This Exchange to Ourselves," *BusinessWeek,* December 4, 2000, p. 48. Also see Eric Young, "Web Marketplaces That Really Work," *FORTUNE/CNET Tech Review,* Winter 2002, pp. 78–86.

13. "Leaders: Anniversary Lessons From eBay," *The Economist,* June 11, 2005, p. 9; Erick Schonfeld, "Corporate America's New Outlet Mall," *Business 2.0,* April 2004, pp. 43–45; and facts from eBay annual reports and other information accessed at www.ebay.com, September 2005.

14. Stephen Baker and Heather Green, "Blogs Will Change Your Business," *BusinessWeek,* May 2, 2005, pp. 57–67.

15. Lev Grossman, "Meet Joe Blog," *Time,* June 21, 2004, p. 65.

16. Chris Oser, "Nike Assays Blog as Marketing Tool," *Advertising Age,* June 14, 2004, p. 26.

17. "The Secret Is Out: Secret Sparkle Body Spray Launches New Website," May 16, 2005, accessed at www.imc2.com; and Jack Neff, "Strong Enough for a Man But Made for a Tween," *Advertising Age,* April 25, 2005, p. 26.

18. Michelle Slatalla, "Toll-Free Apology Soothes Savage Beast," *New York Times,* February 12, 2004, p. G4; and information from www.planet-feedback.com/consumer, August 2004.

19. Gary Hamel, "Is This All You Can Build with the Net? Think Bigger," *FORTUNE,* April 30, 2001, pp. 134–138.

20. Raymond Hennessey, "IPO Outlook: Internet Returns as Active Sector," *Wall Street Journal,* November 8, 2004.

21. "Mass Merchants/Department Stores: Winning by Leveraging More of What the Web can Do," *Internet Retailer,* December 2004, accessed at www.internetretailer.com; and information from www.officedepot.com, August 2005.

22. "Best of the Web—The Top 50 Retailing Sites," *Internet Retailer,* December 2004, accessed at www.internetretailer.com.

23. Adapted from Jena McGregor, "High-Tech Achiever: MINI USA," *Fast Company,* October 2004, p. 86, with information from www.miniusa.com, August 2005.

24. Sharon Gaudin, "The Site of No Return," May 28, 2002, accessed at www.graphics-art.com/Site%20of%20no%20return.htm.

25. Marty Bernstein, "Mitsubishi Super Bowl Ad Lures Viewer to Internet," *Automotive News,* March 29, 2004, p. 56B.

26. Don Peppers and Martha Rogers, "Opening the Door to Consumers," *Sales & Marketing Management,* October 1998, pp. 22–29; Mike Beirne, "Marketers of the Next Generation: Silvio Bonvini," *Brandweek,* November 8, 1999, p. 64; Bob Tedeschi, "Consumer Products Companies Use Web Sites to Strengthen Ties with Consumers," *New York Times,* August 25, 2003, p. C.6; and information from www.candystand.com, August 2005.

27. Jeffrey F. Rayport and Bernard J. Jaworski, *e-Commerce* (New York: McGraw-Hill, 2001), p. 116. Also see Goutam Chakraborty, "What Do Customers Consider Important in B2B Websites?" Journal of Advertising, March 2003, p. 50; and David Sparrow, "Get 'Em to Bite," *Catalog Age,* April 1, 2003, pp. 35–36.

28. Reid Goldsborough, "Creating Web Sites for Web Surfers," *Black Issues in Higher Education,* June 17, 2004, p. 120.

29. Todd R. Weiss, "Apparel Maker Gets Instant Feedback with Online Survey Tool," *Computerworld,* September 13, 2004, pp. 31–32.

30. See Wendy Davis, "Jupiter Research: Internet Ad Spend to Reach $18.9 Billion by 2010," August 9, 2005, accessed at http://publications.mediapost.com; and "Forrester: Online Spending to Increase to $14.7 Billion in '05," *Boston Business Journal,* May 3, 2005, accessed at http:/boston.bizjournals.com.

31. Mike Shields, "Google Faces New Rivals," August 22, 2005, accessed at www.mediaweek.com.

32. Elliis Booker, "Vivid 'Experiences' as the New Frontier," *B to B,* March 14, 2005, p. 14; and Karen J Bannan, "Rich Media Demands Attention," *B to B,* March 14, 2005, pp. 24–25.

33. Kris Oser, "Video in Demand," *Advertising Age,* April 4, 2005, pp. S1–S5.

34. Pete Snyder, "Wanted: Standards for Viral Marketing," *Brandweek,* June 28, 2004, p. 21.

35. Adapted from information found in Bob Garfield, "War & Peace and Subservient Chicken," April 26, 2004, accessed at www.adage.com; Gregg Cebrzynski, "Burger King Says It's OK to Have Your Way with the Chicken," *Nation's Restaurant News,* May 10, 2004, p. 16; and Ryan Underwood, "Ruling the Roost," *Fast Company,* April 2005, pp. 70–78.

36. Tobi Elkin, "Net Advantages," *Advertising Age,* February 10, 2003, p. 29.

37. Jack Neff, "Taking Package Goods to the Net," *Advertising Age,* July 11, 2005, pp. S1–S3.

38. Information from "iVillage Wins More Users than Rival," *New Media Age,* March 11, 2004, p. P.3; James Hibberd, "Web Spawns Reunion Show," *TelevisionWeek,* April 5, 2004, p. 3; the iVillage Top-Line Metrics section of www.ivillage.com, October 2005; and www.MyFamily.com, September 2005.

39. See Thane Peterson, "E-I-E-I-E-Farming," *BusinessWeek,* May 1, 2000, p. 202; "Survival of the Fittest," *Agri Marketing*, March 2002, pp. 18–24; "Agriculture Online? Let's Talk Among Ourselves," *MIN's B2B*, May 9, 2005, p. 1; and www.agriculture.com, September 2005.

40. Juliana Deeks, "Online Advertising and E-mail Marketing through 2008," Jupiter Media, February 12, 2004, accessed at www. jup.com; and Kris Oser, "Marketings, ISPs Tackle 'Phishing' Expeditions," *Advertising Age*, March 28, 2005, p. 121.

41. Heidi Anderson, "Nintendo Case Study: Rules Are Made to Be Broken," *E-Mail Marketing Case Studie*s, March 6, 2003, accessed online at www.clickz.com.

42. Enid Burns. "The Deadly Duo: Spam and Viruses," April 2005, ClickZ Stats, May 11, 2005, accessed at www.clickz.com.

43. Michael Porter, "Strategy and the Internet," *Harvard Business Review,* March 2001, pp. 614–678.

44. Rob McGann, "Most Active Web Users Are Young, Affluent," ClickZ Stats, January 6, 2005, accessed at www.clickz.com.

45. See Peter Han and Angus Maclaurin, "Do Consumers Really Care About Online Privacy?" *Marketing Management*, January–February 2002, pp. 35–38; Eric Goldman, "The Internet Privacy Fallacy." *Computer and Internet Lawyer,* January 2003, p. 20; and Nancy Wong, "Getting Pragmatic about Privacy," *American Demographics*, June 2003, pp. 14–15.

46. Rob McCann, "Concerns over Online Threats This Holiday Season," ClickZ Stats, November 24, 2004, accessed at www.clickz.com on June 8, 2005.

47. See Jaikumar Vijayan, "First Online Data Privacy Law Looms in California," *Computerworld,* June 28, 2004, p. 12; and "Does Your Privacy Policy Comply with the California Online Privacy Protection Act?" *Banking and Financial Services Policy Report*, January 2005, p. 7.

48. See Jennifer DiSabatino, "FTC OKs Self-Regulation to Protect Children's Privacy," *Computerworld,* February 12, 2001, p. 32; Laurie Flynn, "New Efforts Are being Made to Keep Online Merchants from Collecting Personal Information from Children," *New York Times,* May 12, 2003, p. C4; and Ann Mack, "Marketers Challenged On Youth Safeguards," *Adweek*, June 14, 2004, p. 12.

49. Information on Expedia accessed at www.expedia.com/daily/press/releases on June 8, 2005.

50. Information on TRUSTe accessed at www.truste.com, September 2005.

51. See "Seventy Percent of US Consumers Worry About Online Privacy, But Few Take Protective Action, Reports Jupiter Media Metrix," Jupiter Media Metrix press release, June 3, 2002, accessed online at www.jmm.com; Rob McCann, "Concerns Over Online Threats This Holiday Season," ClickZ Stats, November 24, 2004, accessed at www.clickz.com; and Desiree J. Hanford, "Fraud Fears Slow Online Shopping," *Wall Street Journal*, April 13, 2005, p. 1.

52. See National White Collar Crime Center "IC3 2004 Internet Fraud—Crime Report," 2005, accessed at www.ifccfbi.gov on June 8, 2005; and Federal Trade Commission, "National and State Trends in Fraud & Identity Theft," February 1, 2005, accessed at www.ftc.gov.

53. Kris Oser, "Marketings, ISPs Tackle 'Phishing' Expeditions," *Advertising Age*, March 28, 2005, p. 121; Helen Loveless, "Net Fraud Becomes Stealthier," *Knight Ridder Tribune Business News*, May 1, 2005, p. 1; Jason Stein, "Phishers Target Customers of Smaller Banks," *Knight Ridder Tribune Business News,* May 10, 2005, p. 1; and Marshall Lager, "Fear and Loathing in the Database," *Customer Relationship Management*, June 2005, pp. 13–14.

54. Facts from Mark Warschauer, "Demystifying the Digital Divide," *Scientic American,* August 2003, p. 42. Quote from Richard J. Dalton Jr., "New York Libraries Try to Close Minorities' Digital Divide,"

Knight Ridder Tribune Business News, July 4, 2004, p. 1. Also see Patricia Hewitt, "Taking the Lead in Global Digital Excellence," *Computer Weekly,* May 3, 2005, p. 16; Laxmi Devi, "Digital Divide: Can It Be Bridged?" *Knight Ridder Tribune Service*, May 20, 2005, p. 1; Paul Lamb, "Digital Divide Has Not Disappeared," CNET News.com, June 3, 2005, accessed at www.news.com.com.

55. "114-Year-Old Bids over $3M for Items in eBay Auctions," *USA Today,* April 30, 1999, p. 10B.

Chapter 15

1. Hillary Chura and Richard Linnett, "Coca-Cola Readies Global Assault," *Advertising Age*, April 2, 2001, pp. 1, 34; Ken Hein, "Soft Drinks," *Mediaweek*, April 21, 2003, p. SR29; "Sprite Shows Off Hint of Mint up North," *Packaging Digest,* May 2003, p. 4; Julie Creswell and Julie Schlosser, "Has Coke Lost Its Fizz?" *FORTUNE,* November 10, 2003, pp. 215–217; Chad Terhune, "Market Shares Drop at Coca-Cola, PepsiCo," *Wall Street Journal*, March 7, 2005, p. B6; *Advertising Age's Fact Pack 2005,* February 2005, p. 18; and "Our Company" and annual reports accessed at www.coca-cola.com, October 2005.

2. George Melloan, "Feeling the Muscles of the Multinationals," *Wall Street Journal,* January 6, 2004, p. A19.

3. *Global Economic Prospects, 2005,* World Bank, accessed at www.worldbank.org, June 17, 2005; CIA, *The World Factbook*, accessed at www.cia.gov, June 2005; and "Developing Countries' Goods Trade Share Surges to 50-Year Peak," World Trade Organization, April 14, 2005, accessed at www.wto.org, June 18, 2005.

4. See "Compagnie Générale des Établissements Michelin," *Hoover's Company Records*, Austin, July 15, 2005, p. 41240; and "Johnson & Johnson," *Hoover's Company Records*, Austin, July 15, 2005, p. 10824.

5. Steve Hamm, "Borders Are So 20th Century," *BusinessWeek,* September 22, 2003, pp. 68–73.

6. "The Unique Japanese," *FORTUNE,* November 24, 1986, p. 8. Also see James D. Southwick, "Addressing Market Access Barriers in Japan Through the WTO," *Law and Policy in International Business,* Spring 2000, pp. 923–976; and U.S. Commercial Service, *Country Commercial Guide Japan, FY 2005,* Chapter 5, accessed at www.buyusa.gov, June 18, 2005.

7. "What Is the WTO?" accessed at www.wto.org/english/thewto_e/whatis_e/whatis_e.htm, October 2005.

8. See *WTO Annual Report 2004,* accessed at www.wto.org; and World Trade Organization, "10 Benefits of the WTO Trading System," accessed at www.wto.org, October, 2005.

9. Keith Bradsher, "W.T.O. Talks Moving Slowly, Chief Says," *New York Times*, June 14, 2005, p. C6.

10. "The European Union at a Glance," accessed online at http://europa.eu.int, January 2006.

11. "Overviews of European Union Activities: Economic and Monetary Affairs," accessed at http://europa.eu.int/pol/emu/overview_en.htm, January 2006.

12. See "World Watch," *Wall Street Journal*, May 20, 1999, p. A12; and "European Union's Heated Budget Negotiations Collapse," *New York Times,* June 18, 2005, p. A3.

13. Fay Hansen, "World Trade Update," *Business Finance,* March 2002, pp. 9–11; Daniel T. Griswold, "NAFTA at 10" *World Trade,* March 2003, p. 10; Kenneth G. Weigel, Kelley Mullaney, "Importance of U.S.-Canada Trade Relationships Highlighted at Houston Partnership," January 14, 2004, accessed at www.partnershipforgrowth.org; and Michael O'Boyle, "Nafta's Birthday Party," *Business Mexico,* February 2004, pp. 28–34.

14. See Angela Greiling Keane, "Counting on CAFTA," *Traffic World,* August 8, 2005, p. 1; Gilberto Meza, "Is the FTAA Floundering," *Business Mexico,* February 2005, pp. 46–48; Peter Robson, "Integrating the Americas: FTAA and Beyond," *Journal of Common Market Studies,*" June 2005, p. 430; "Rank Order GDP," *The World Factbook,* accessed at www.cia.gov, June 18, 2005, and "Foreign Trade Statistics," accessed at www.census.gov, June 18, 2005.

15. Richard Lapper, "South American Unity Still a Distant Dream," *Financial Times,* December 9, 2004, accessed at www.news.ft.com; and Mary Turck, "South American Community of Nations," Resource Center of the Americas.org, accessed at www.americas.org, October, 2005.

16. See Geri Smith and Cristina Lindblad, "Mexico: Was NAFTA Worth It?" *BusinessWeek,* December 22, 2003, pp. 66–72; Victoria Hirschberg, "Study Shows Negative Effects of Free Trade Agreement," *Knight Ridder Tribune Service,* August 17, 2004, p. 1; Sandy Smith-Nonini, "The Children of NAFTA: Labor Wars on the U.S./Mexico Border," *Standpoint,* Fall 2005, p. 3.

17. Adapted from information found in Clay Chandler, "China Deluxe," *FORTUNE,* July 26, 2004, pp. 148–156. Also see "Selling to China's Rich and Not So Rich," *Strategic Directions,* June 2005, pp. 5–8; and Lisa Movius, "Luxury's China Puzzle," *WWD,* June 15, 2005, p. 1.

18. See David Woodruff, "Ready to Shop Until They Drop," *BusinessWeek,* June 22, 1998, pp. 104–108; and James MacAonghus, "Online Impact of a Growing Europe," *New Media Age,* February 12, 2004, p. 15.

19. See Om Malik, "The New Land of Opportunity," *Business 2.0,* July 2004, pp. 72–79.

20. Ricky Griffin and Michael Pustay, *International Business,* 4th ed. (Upper Saddle River, N.J.: Prentice Hall, 2005), pp. 522–523.

21. Rebecca Piirto Heath, "Think Globally," *Marketing Tools,* October 1996, pp. 49–54; and "The Power of Writing," *National Geographic,* August 1999, pp. 128–129.

22. For other examples and discussion, see www.executiveplanet.com, December 2005; *Dun & Bradstreet's Guide to Doing Business Around the World* (Upper Saddle River, N.J.: Prentice Hall, 2000); Ellen Neuborne, "Bridging the Culture Gap," *Sales & Marketing Management,* July 2003, p. 22; Richard Pooley, "When Cultures Collide," *Management Services,* Spring 2005, pp. 28–31; and Helen Deresky, *International Management,* 5th ed. (Upper Saddle River, N.J.: Prentice Hall, 2006).

23. Pete Engardio, Manjeet Kripalani, and Alysha Webb, "Smart Globalization," *BusinessWeek,* August 27, 2001, pp. 132–136.

24. Adapted from Mark Rice-Oxley, "In 2,000 Years, Will the World Remember Disney or Plato?" *Christian Science Monitor,* January 15, 2004, p. 16.

25. See Jack Neff, "Submerged," *Advertising Age,* March 4, 2002, p. 14; and Ann Chen and Vijay Vishwanath, "Expanding in China," *Harvard Business Review,* March 2005, pp. 19–21.

26. For a good discussion of joint venturing, see James Bamford, David Ernst, and David G. Fubini, "Launching a World-Class Joint Venture," *Harvard Business Review,* February 2004, pp. 91–100.

27. See Cynthia Kemper, "KFC Tradition Sold Japan on Chicken," *Denver Post,* June 7, 1998, p. J4; Milford Prewitt, "Chains Look for Links Overseas," *Nation's Restaurant News,* February 18, 2002, pp. 1, 6; and Yum Brands, Inc., restaurant count, accessed at www.yum.com, June 21, 2005.

28. For good discussions, see Laura Mazur, "Globalization Is Still Tethered to Local Variations," *Marketing,* January 22, 2004, p. 18; Johny K. Johansson and Ilkka A. Ronkainen, "The Brand Challenge: Are Global Brands the Right Choice for Your Company?" *Marketing Management,* March–April 2004; Douglas B. Holt, John A. Quelch, and Earl L. Taylor, "How Global Brands Compete," *Harvard Business Review,* September 2004, pp. 68–75; and Boris Sustar and Rozana Sustar, "Managing Marketing Standardization in a Global Context," *Journal of American Academy of Business,* September 2005, pp. 302–310.

29. Quotes and other information from Richard Tomlinson, "L'Oréal's Global Makeover," *FORTUNE,* September 30, 2002, p. 141; Gail Edmondson, "The Beauty of Global Branding," *BusinessWeek,* June 28, 1999, pp.70–75; Jeremy Joesephs, "O-J's Powers of Seduction Hard to Resist," March 25, 2003, accessed at www.jeremyjoesephs.com; "Consumer Products Brief: L'Oréal," *Wall Street Journal,* February 23, 2004, p. 1; Vito J. Racanelli, "Touching Up," February 16, 2004, pp. 18–19; Ross Tucker, "L'Oréal Global Sales Rise," *WWD,* February 18, 2005, and information accessed at www.loreal.com, September 2005.

30. Warren J. Keegan, *Global Marketing Management,* 7th ed. (Upper Saddle River, N.J.: Prentice Hall, 2002), pp. 346–351. Also see Philip Kotler and Kevin Lane Keller, *Marketing Management,* 12th ed. (Upper Saddle River, N.J.: 2006), pp. 677–684.

31. Douglas McGray, "Translating Sony into English," *Fast Company,* January 2003, p. 38; Jeffrey Selingo, "Newer, Smaller, Faster, and Not in Stores Now," *New York Times,* May 8, 2003, p. G.5; and Jon L. Jacobi, "CNET Editor's Take: Sony VAIO VGN-U50," October 13, 2004, accessed at www.cnet.com.

32. See "Naming Products Is No Game," *BusinessWeek Online,* April 9, 2004, accessed at www.businessweek.com; and Ross Thomson, "Lost in Translation," *Medical Marketing and Media,* March 2005, p. 82.

33. Kate MacArthur, "Coca-Cola Light Employs Local Edge," *Advertising Age,* August 21, 2000, pp. 18–19; and "Case Studies: Coke Light Hottest Guy," Advantage Marketing, MSN India, accessed at http://advantage.msn.co.in, March 15, 2004.

34. See Alicia Clegg, "One Ad One World?" *Marketing Week,* June 20, 2002, pp. 51–52; and George E. Belch and Michael A. Belch, *Advertising and Promotion: An Integrated Marketing Communications Perspective,* 6th ed. (New York: McGraw-Hill, 2004), pp. 666–668.

35. Adapted from Normandy Madden and Jack Neff, "P&G Adapts Attitude Toward Local Markets," *Advertising Age,* February 23, 2004, p. 28; and information found in "P&G Hits No. 1 in China," *SPC Asia,* November 2004, p. 3.

36. Michael Schroeder, "The Economy: Shrimp Imports to U.S. May Face Antidumping Levy," *Wall Street Journal,* February 18, 2004, p. A.2; and Woranuj Maneerungsee, "Shrimpers Suspect Rivals of Foul Play," *Knight Ridder Tribune Business News,* April 28, 2005, p. 1.

37. Sarah Ellison, "Revealing Price Disparities, the Euro Aids Bargain-Hunters," *Wall Street Journal,* January 30, 2002, p. A15.

38. See Patrick Powers, "Distribution in China: The End of the Beginning," *China Business Review,* July–August, 2001, pp. 8–12; Drake Weisert, "Coca-Cola in China: Quenching the Thirst of a Billion," *The China Business Review,* July–August 2001, pp. 52–55; Gabriel Kahn, "Coke Works Harder at Being the Real Thing in Hinterland," *Wall Street Journal,* November 26, 2002, p. B1; Leslie Chang, Chad Terhune, and Betsy McKay, "A Global Journal Report; Rural Thing—Coke's Big Gamble in Asia," *Wall Street Journal,* August 11, 2004, p. A1; and Jo Bowman, "Target: Managing Channels," October 22, 2004, p. S8.

Chapter 16

1. Quotes and other information for this Nike story from Rebecca De Winter, "The Anti-Sweatshop Movement," *Ethics & International Affairs,* October 2001, pp. 99–117; Richard Locke, "The Promise and Perils of Globalization: The Case of Nike," *Management: Inventing and*

Delivering Its Future, 2003; Ann M. Peterson, "Nike Boosts Indians' Health, Its Reputation," *Marketing News,* June 1, 2004, p. 10; Mark Rison, "Nike Shows Way to Return from the Wilderness," *Marketing,* April 20, 2005, p. 21; Nike's *Corporate Responsibility Report,* April 2005, accessed at www.nike.com/nikebiz/nikebiz.jhtml?page=29& item=fy04; and www.nikebiz.com, September 2005.

2. See Winnie Hu, "The Smoking Ban: Clean Air, Murky Economics," *New York Times,* December 28, 2003, p. 11; "Smoking Bans Have Their Place, but Outside Isn't One of Them," *Washington Post,* February 5, 2004, p. T-04; and "EU Regulations: EU-Wide Ban on Tobacco Ads Imminent," *EIU ViewsWire,* July 8, 2005.

3. James Heckman, "Don't Shoot the Messenger: More and More Often, Marketing Is the Regulators' Target," *Marketing News,* May 24, 1999, pp. 1, 9; "Business Brief—Publishers Clearing House: Payment of $34 Million Set to Settle with 26 States," *Wall Street Journal,* June 27, 2001, p. B8; "'You're a Guaranteed Winner': Composing 'You' in a Consumer Culture," Helen Rothschild Ewald and Roberta Vann, *Journal of Business Communication,* April 2003, pp. 98–128; and "Publishers Clearing House," *Hoover's Company Capsules,* March 15, 2005, accessed at http://proquest.umi.com.

4. Theodore Levitt, "The Morality (?) of Advertising," *Harvard Business Review,* July–August 1970, pp. 84–92. For counterpoints, see Heckman, "Don't Shoot the Messenger," pp. 1, 9.

5. Lane Jennings, "Hype, Spin, Puffery, and Lies: Should We Be Scared?" *The Futurist,* January–February 2004, p. 16. For recent examples of deceptive advertising, see "Tropicana Settles Complaint by FTC over Misleading Ads," *Wall Street Journal,* June 3, 2005, p. B4; and Monty Phan, "City Sues Wireless Firms," July 22, 2005, accessed at www.newsday.com.

6. Roger Parloff, "Is Fat the Next Tobacco?" *FORTUNE,* February 3, 2003, pp. 51–54; "'Big Food' Get the Obesity Message," *New York Times,* July 10, 2003, p. A22; Carl Hulse, "Vote in House Offers Shield in Obesity Suits," *New York Times,* March 11, 2004, p. A1; and Amy Garber, "Twice-Tossed McD Obesity Suit Back on Docket," *Nation's Restaurant News,* February 7, 2005, pp. 1+.

7. "McDonald's to Cut 'Super Size' Option," *Advertising Age,* March 8, 2004, p. 13; Dave Carpenter, "Hold the Fries, Take a Walk," *News & Observer,* April 16, 2004, p. D1; Michael V. Copeland, "Ronald Gets Back in Shape," *Business 2.0,* January–February 2005, pp. 46–47; David P. Callet and Cheryl A. Falvey, "Is Restaurant Food the New Tobacco?" *Restaurant Hospitality,* May 2005, pp. 94–96; and Kate McArthur, "BK Offers Fat to the Land," *Advertising Age,* April 4, 2005, pp. 1, 60.

8. Gary Bagin, "Products Liability Verdict—Study Releases," press release, Jury Verdict Research, January 15, 2004, accessed at www.juryverdictresearch.com.

9. Adapted from information found in Mark Fagan, "Copy Competition Heats Up," *Knight Ridder Tribune Business News,* May 4, 2005, p. 1.

10. Cliff Edwards, "Where Have All the Edsels Gone?" *Greensboro News Record,* May 24, 1999, p. B6. Also see Joel Dreyfuss, "Planned Obsolescence Is Alive and Well," *FORTUNE,* February 15, 1999, p. 192; Atsuo Utaka, "Planned Obsolescence and Marketing Strategy," *Managerial and Decision Economics,* December 2000, pp. 339–344; and Tim Cooper, "Inadequate Life? Evidence of Consumer Attitudes to Product Obsolescence," *Journal of Consumer Policy,* December 2004, pp. 421–448.

11. Adapted from John Markoff, "Is Planned Obsolescence Obsolete?" *New York Times,* February 17, 2002, p. 46. Also see Kevin McKean, "Planned Obsolescence," *InfoWorld,* September 29, 2003, pp. 38–46.

12. See Brian Grow and Pallavi Gogoi, "A New Way to Squeeze the Weak?" *BusinessWeek,* January 28, 2002, p. 92; Todd Cooper, "Redlining Rears Its Ugly Head," *USBanker,* August 2003, p. 64; Marc Lifsher, "Allstate Settles over Use of Credit Scores," *Los Angeles Times,* March 2, 2004, p. C.1; and Judith Burns, "Study Finds Links in Credit Scores, Insurance Claims," *Wall Street Journal,* February 28, 2005, p. D3.

13. "Increasing Incomes and Reducing the Rapid Refund Rip-Off," A report from the ACORN Financial Justice Center, September 2004, pp. 3–4; and Candice Heckman, "Poor Often Fall Victim to Fee on Tax Refund Loans," *Seattle Post-Intelligencer,* February 21, 2005, p. B1.

14. Information from "Shop 'til They Drop?" *Christian Science Monitor,* December 1, 2003, p. 8; Gregg Easterbrook, "The Real Truth About Money," *Time,* January 17, 2005, pp. 32–35; Bradley Johnson, "Day in the Life: How Consumers Divvy Up All the Time They Have," *Advertising Age,* May 2, 2005; and Rich Miller, "Too Much Money," *BusinessWeek,* July 11, 2005, pp. 59–66.

15. Portions adapted from Constance L. Hays, "Preaching to Save Shoppers from 'Evil' of Consumerism," *New York Times,* January 1, 2003, p. C1. Also see Jo Littler, "Beyond the Boycott," *Cultural Studies,* March 2005, pp. 227–252; and www.revbilly.com, accessed July 2005.

16. See Michael Cabanatuan, "Toll Lanes Could Help Drivers Buy Time," *San Francisco Chronicle,* December 28, 2004, accessed at www.sfgate.com; and "London Mayor Increases Traffic Toll, Angers Drivers, Retailers," July 3, 2005, accessed at www.bloomberg.com.

17. "Marketing Under Fire," *Marketing Management,* July–August 2004, p. 5.

18. Adapted from information found in Steve Hamm, "Microsoft's Future," *BusinessWeek,* January 19, 1998, pp. 58–68; Dan Carney and Mike France, "The Microsoft Case: Tying It All Together," *BusinessWeek,* December 3, 2001, pp. 68–69; Paul Meller and Matt Richtel, "Europeans Rule Against Microsoft; Appeal Is Promised," *New York Times,* March 25, 2004, p. C1; and Brier Dudley, "Microsoft Pays IBM to Settle Suit," *Knight Ridder Tribune Business News,* July 2, 2005, p. 1.

19. Stuart L. Hart, "Beyond Greening: Strategies for a Sustainable World," *Harvard Business Review,* January–February 1997, pp. 66–76. Also see Subhabrata Bobby Banerjee, Easwar S. Iyer, and Rajiv K. Kashyap, "Corporate Environmentalism: Antecedents and Influence of Industry Type," *Harvard Business Review,* April 2003, pp. 106–122; Christopher Laszlo, *The Sustainable Company: How to Create Lasting Value Through Social and Environmental Performance* (Washington, D.C.: Island Press, 2003); Volkert Beekman, "Sustainable Development and Future Generations," *Journal of Agriculture and Environmental Ethics,* vol. 17, no. 1, 2004, p. 3; and Bill Hopwood, Mary Mellor, and Geoff O'Brien, "Sustainable Development: Mapping Different Approaches," *Sustainable Development,* February 2005, pp. 38+.

20. "FedEx Pushes Envelope for Environmentally Conscious Management," *Global Environmental Change Report,* March 2005, pp. 10–11; and Tricia Pemberton, "Waste-Not Wal-Mart: Supercenter Test Environmentally Friendly Designs," *Knight Ridder Tribune Business News,* July 21, 2005, p. 1.

21. Information from "Xerox Equipment Remanufacture and Parts Reuse," accessed at www.xerox.com, August 2004; and "Environment, Health, and Safety Progress Report" accessed at www.xerox.com, July 2005.

22. Accessed at www.monsanto.com/monsanto/layout/our_pledge/default.asp, September 2005.

23. Adapted from "The Top 3 in 2005," *Global 100,* accessed at www.global100.org, July 2005. For further information on Alcoa's sustainability program see Alcoa's Sustainability Report, accessed at www.alcoa.com.

24. See "EMAS: What's New?" accessed at http://europa.eu.int/comm/environment/emas, August 2005; "Special Report: Free Trade on Trial—

Ten Years of NAFTA," *Economist,* January 3, 2004, p. 13; and Daniel J. Tschopp, "Corporate Social Responsibility: A Comparison Between the United States and Europe," *Corporate Social-Responsibility and Environmental Management*, March 2005, pp. 55–59.

25. Information and quotes from Andy Milligan, "Samsung Points the Way for Asian Firms in Global Brand Race," *Media,* August 8, 2003, p. 8; Katherine Chen, Michael Jakielski, Nadia Luhr, and Joseph Mayer-Salman, "DigitAll," student paper at the University of North Carolina at Chapel Hill, Spring 2003; Gerry Khermouch, "The Best Global Brands," *BusinessWeek,* August 5, 2002, p. 92; Leslie P. Norton, "Value Brand," *Barron's,* September 22, 2003, p. 19; and Samsung Electronics Co. Ltd., *Hoover's Company Capsules,* Austin, March 15, 2004; "Cult Brands," *BusinessWeek Online,* August 2, 2004, accessed at www.businessweek.com; and Samsung annual reports and other information accessed at www.samsung.com, October 2005.

26. Information from Mike Hoffman, "Ben Cohen: Ben & Jerry's Homemade, Established in 1978," *Inc,* April 30, 2001, p. 68; and the Ben & Jerry's Web site at www.benjerrys.com and www.bodyshop.com, September 2005.

27. Quotes and other information from Thea Singer, "Can Business Still Save the World?" *Inc,* April 30, 2001, pp. 58–71, and www.honesttea. com, September, 2005.

28. Jacquelyn A. Ottman, "Green marketing: Wake Up to the Truth About Green Consuming," *In Business,* May–June 2002, p. 31; Marc Gunther, "Son of Aeron," *FORTUNE,* May 12, 2003, p. 134; and information accessed online at www.HermanMiller.com, October 2005.

29. Dan R. Dalton and Richard A. Cosier, "The Four Faces of Social Responsibility," *Business Horizons,* May–June 1982, pp. 19–27.

30. Joseph Webber, "3M's Big Cleanup," *BusinessWeek,* June 5, 2000, pp. 96–98. Also see Kara Sissell, "3M Defends Timing of Scotchgard Phase out," *Chemical Week,* April 11, 2001, p. 33; Peck Hwee Sim, "Ausimont Targets Former Scotchgard Markets," *Chemical Week,* August 7, 2002, p. 32; Jennifer Lee, "E.P.A. Orders Companies to Examine Effect of Chemicals," *New York Times,* April 15, 2003, p. F2; and Kara Sissell, "Swedish Officials Propose Global Ban on PFOS," *Chemical Week,* June 22, 2005, p. 35,

31. See "Transparency International Bribe Payers Index" and "Transparency International Corruption Perception Index," accessed at transparency.org, August 2005; David Barboza, "Wave of Corruption Tarnishes China's Extraordinary Growth," *New York Times,* March 22, 2005, p. C1; and Vladimir Kvint, "The Scary Business of Russia," *Forbes,* May 23, 2005, p. 42.

32. John F. McGee and P. Tanganath Nayak, "Leaders' Perspectives on Business Ethics," *Prizm,* Arthur D. Little, Inc., Cambridge, Mass., first quarter 1994, pp. 71–72. Also see Adrian Henriques, "Good Decision—Bad Business?" *International Journal of Management & Decision Making*, 2005, p. 273; and Augustine Nwabuzor, "Corruption and Development: New Initiatives in Economic Openness and Strengthened Rule of Law," *Journal of Business Ethics,* June 2005, pp. 121+.

33. See Samuel A. DiPiazza, Jr., "Ethics in Action," *Executive Excellence,* January 2002, pp. 15–16; Samuel A. DiPiazza, Jr., "It's All Down to Personal Values," accessed online at www.pwcglobal.com, August 2003; and "Code of Conduct: The Way We Do Business," accessed at www.pwcglobal.com/gx/eng/ins-sol/spec-int/ethics/index.html, June 2005.

34. DiPiazza, "Ethics in Action," p. 15.

Credits

Chapter 9

264 Courtesy of Bentley Motors. **266** Reprinted courtesy of Caterpillar, Inc. **269** Porsche, Boxster and the Porsche Crest are registered trademarks and the distinctive shapes of PORSCHE automobiles are trade dress of Dr. Ing. h.c. F. Porsche AG. Used with permission of Porsche Cars North America, Inc. **271** © 2005 Steinway & Sons. All rights reserved. **272** © 2004 Moen Incorporated. All rights reserved. **273** Used with permission of Gibson Guitar. All rights reserved. **275** Courtesy of Sony Electronics Inc. **276** Courtesy of Gramophone. All rights reserved. **278** Courtesy of Woodland Park Zoo. **286** Reproduced with permission of Yahoo! Inc. © 2005 by Yahoo! Inc. YAHOO! and the YAHOO! logo are trademarks of Yahoo! Inc. **288** Courtesy of JoyPerfume **290** Courtesy of Kimberly Clark.

Chapter 10

296 Reprinted courtesy of Caterpillar, Inc. **299** © Palm, Inc. All rights reserved. **300** Courtesy of Calyx & Corolla. **304** Photographer: Joe Heiner **307** Used with permission of Cereal Partners UK. **309** © 2005 Black & Decker, Inc. All rights reserved. **313** © 2005 GEICO. All rights reserved. **316** © 2004 General Electric Company. All rights reserved. **321** © 2005 Roadway Express, Inc. All rights reserved. **323** © 2005 RiverOne Inc. All rights reserved. **324** Copyright © 1994–2004 United Parcel Service of America, Inc. All rights reserved. Photo © Michale Prince/CORBIS

Chapter 11

330 Used with permission of Whole Foods Market IP, L.P. **335** © 2005, 7-Eleven, Inc. All Rights Reserved. **345** © 2005 Cabela's Incorporate. All Rights Reserved. **348** © 1996–2005 Travelocity.com LP. All rights reserved. Travelocity, The Roaming Gnome and Stars Design are service marks and trademarks of Travelocity.com LP. **348** © 2005 Staples, Inc. All rights reserved. Used with permission. **350** © 2005 Food Lion, LLC. All rights reserved.

Chapter 12

360 © Copyright 2005 Virgin Atlantic Airways Ltd. All rights reserved. Courtesy of Crispin Porter + Bogusky. **364** © 2005 BMW of North America, LLC. All rights reserved. **366** © DaimlerChrysler Corporation. All rights reserved. **367** Courtesy of Mary Kay, Inc. All rights reserved. **367** Courtesy of Procter & Gamble Company. All rights reserved. **373** Under permission by V&S Vin & Spirit AB (publ). ABSOLUT COUNTRY OF SWEDEN VODKA & LOGO, ABSOLUT, ABSOLUT BOTTLE DESIGN AND ABSOLUT CALLIGRAPHY ARE TRADEMARKS OWNED BY V&S VIN & SPIRIT AB (publ). © 2005 V&S VIN & SPIRIT AB (publ). **375** Used with permission of TiVo Inc. TiVo and the TiVo Logo are registered trademarks of TiVo Inc. Home Media Option and TiVo Series2 (logo and text) are trademarks of TiVo Inc. All rights reserved. **376** Cover image of Madison & Vine, by Scott Donaton. © 2004 The McGraw-Hill Companies. Used with permission. **379** © Houghton Mifflin Company and Mullen. All rights reserved. **382** © 2004 The Picture People Inc. All rights reserved. **384** Used with permission of Gillette. All rights reserved. **386** © 2005 Cendant Corporation. All rights reserved. **387** Courtesy of University of South Florida Wireless Notification Service. **392** Courtesy of The Procter & Gamble Company. All rights reserved. **393** Courtesy of The Procter & Gamble Company. All rights reserved.

Chapter 13

398 © 2005 CDW Corporation. All rights reserved. Used with permission. **405** © 2005 CDW Corporation. All rights reserved. Used with permission. **409** Used with permission of Jennifer Hansen. Photographer: Linda Ford. **413** Courtesy of Marriott International, Inc. All rights reserved. **416** © Copyright 1999-2004 Boise Cascade Corporation. All Rights Reserved. **418** Used with permission of Dell Inc. All rights reserved. **422** Used with permission of the Carolina Cookie Company. All rights reserved. **423** © 2005 L.L.Bean, Inc. L.L.Bean® is a registered trademark of L.L.Bean, Inc. **429** Used with permission of the Direct Marketing Association. All rights reserved.

Chapter 14

439 Used with permission of Southwest Airlines. **442** Courtesy of Quicken Loans. All rights reserved. **443** Screenshot courtesy of Nike and Gawker Media. Published at http://www.gawker.com/artofspeed/.NIKE and the Swoosh Design logo are trademarks of Nike, Inc. and its affiliates. Used by permission. **444** Courtesy of Peter Blackshaw. All rights reserved. **446** Used with permission of Office Depot. All rights reserved. **448** These materials have been reproduced with the permission of Ben & Jerry's Homemade Holdings Inc. Copyright © Ben & Jerry's Homemade Inc. All rights reserved. **449** © 2005 BMW of North America, LLC. All rights reserved. **450** © 2005 Callard & Bowser, Inc. All rights reserved. **452** © 2005 Google. All rights reserved. **454** ™ & © 2005 Burger King Brands, Inc. (USA only). ™ & © 2005 Burger King Corporation (outside USA). All rights reserved. **455** © 1995–2005 iVillage Inc. All Rights Reserved. Tide ad courtesy of Procter & Gamble Company. All rights reserved. **456** The AOL logo is a registered trademark of America Online, Inc. AOL content and website "look and feel" © 2005 America Online, Inc. Used with permission. **460** ©2005 Avis Rent A Car System, Inc., a Cendant Care Rental Group. All rights reserved.

Chapter 15

470 Courtesy of the European Commission Audiovisual Library **474** Courtesy of Whirlpool of India, LTD. All rights reserved. **482** Used with permission from McDonald's Corporation. **484** (Both) © Prestige & Collections **485** © Inter IKEA Systems B.V. 1999–2005. All rights reserved.

Chapter 16

492 Used with permission of Nike. All rights reserved. **499** Reprinted with permission of Lawrence Journal-World. **500** © 2005 Hardees Food System. All rights reserved. **503** Courtesy of the American Association of Advertising Agencies. **508** © Jones Soda Seattle. All rights reserved. **511** © Dell Inc. All rights reserved. **514** © 2005 Samsung Electronics America. All rights reserved. **515** Courtesy of Honest Tea. All rights reserved. **520** Reprinted with permission of PricewaterhouseCoopers LLP. © 2003 PWC. All rights reserved.

Index